LAROUSSE

PRATIQUE

LAROUSSE
PRATIQUE

THE PRACTICAL A-Z COOKBOOK
WITH
INGREDIENTS, TECHNIQUES AND RECIPES

CONTRIBUTING EDITOR
LEWIS ESSON

PAUL HAMLYN

Published by Reed Consumer Books,
a division of Reed International Books Limited,
Michelin House, 81 Fulham Road, London SW3 6RB,
from the French language edition
Larousse de la Cuisine published by Larousse S.A.

Paul Hamlyn is an imprint of Reed Consumer Books.

A catalogue record for this book is available from the British Library.

ISBN 0 600 57195 5

Produced by Mandarin Offset – printed in Hong Kong

Contributing editor Lewis Esson
Art direction Bobbie Colgate-Stone
Layout William Mason
Photography Larousse S.A.
Step by Step photography: Studiaphot
Full pages and special pages: Corinne Ryman and Pierre Cabannes
Pages 53, 341, 353, 377, 399, 409, 471: Daniel Czap and Patrice Dard
Pages 231, 559, 582, 605: J.-C. Billings and P. Asset
Additional photography Page 37: Melvin Grey
Pages 262, 372: Paul Kemp
Page 144: Vernon Morgan
Illustrations Chantal Beaumont
Translation Susanna Noel
Americanization Norma MacMillan

CONTENTS

NOTES AND ABBREVIATIONS

When preparing any of the recipes in this book, use only one set of measurements, either metric, imperial or American, as they are not interchangeable.

The following abbreviations have been used. Plurals do not change endings when abbreviated. Cups are not abbreviated.

kg *for* kilo
g *for* gram
cm *for* centimetre
mm *for* millimetre
m *for* metre
cl *for* centilitre
dl *for* decilitre
ml *for* millilitre
l *for* litre

lb *for* pound
oz *for* ounce
in *for* inch
ft *for* foot
pt *for* pint
qt *for* quart
fl oz *for* fluid ounces

tbsp *for* tablespoon
tsp *for* teaspoon

Spoon measures are level unless otherwise stated.

For the best results:
Read through the recipes before beginning.
Assemble all the ingredients and utensils.
Measure carefully.

PREFACE

For over half a century Larousse Gastronomique has been a source of inspiration to cooks of every level of experience, providing an unsurpassed body of reference on all aspects of food and cooking. Now, its creators have produced Larousse Pratique, the perfect companion volume and a practical cookbook in easy-to-use A-Z encyclopedia form.

Larousse Pratique is a completely new book about the ingredients, techniques and recipes of contemporary cooking. It contains a wealth of information about the foods we eat, from abalone to yogurt, and the herbs, spices and flavourings we use with them, from allspice to zest. Nutritional values and calorie counts are included, as well as invaluable hints on selecting, storing, preparing and using ingredients.

All the important techniques of cooking, from the simple – acidulation, baking blind and blanching, for example – to the more complicated, like barding and carving, are described simply and clearly, and many of them are also shown in informative step-by-step photographs. Alphabetical listings beside the entries provide a comprehensive cross-reference system, quickly leading the reader to related subjects.

Over 750 recipes, all with preparation and cooking times and many with variations, use the ingredients and illustrate the techniques in both innovative and traditional ways. Great classic recipes such as Coq au vin, Duck a l'orange and Sauce espagnole are ranged alongside those which demonstrate contemporary ideas for combining sometimes surprisingly different foods: sliced yams and tomatoes baked with white wine, or crab-stuffed grapefruit, for example. Modern thinking on healthy eating is well represented in low-fat, high-fibre recipes. Practical, basic recipes accompany entries on particular aspects of cooking, like baking, jam and sauce.

A series of recipes have been specially written for use with a microwave oven. These recipes, which together cover all aspects of microwave cooking, have been specially highlighted throughout the book: just look for the grey tint behind the recipe title, which has been printed in a heavy type.

Larousse Pratique describes many special techniques of preparation, cooking and presentation in easy-to-follow details, making use, where appropriate, of modern kitchen aids like mixers, blenders and food processors. Excellent step-by-step photographic sequences accompany many entries. With their help, procedures such as folding in whisked egg whites, slicing julienne vegetables, boning chicken and carving a duck are described and illustrated so clearly that even the most inexperienced cook will be able to tackle them with confidence.

In all, Larousse Pratique contains over 400 superb, full-colour illustrations, showing foods and ingredients as well as finished dishes and cooking techniques.

This is an immensely practical book, providing the perfect introduction to cooking for beginners, offering clear instructions on all the basic techniques and explaining the methods to developing more advanced skills. At the same time, it offers inspiration and challenge to more experienced cooks, with many exotic ingredients, comprehensive entries and a broad selection of recipes.

A

see also:
shellfish

ABALONE OR ORMER

Ormeau, oreille de mer

Several related species of marine gastropod mollusc are found feeding on algae in warmer coastal waters in many parts of the world.

Recognizable by their highly decorative shells pierced with a row of holes, they consist almost entirely of a large muscular foot. This is creamy white and is the part that is eaten.

Ormers are still found around the Channel Islands, where the name developed from the islanders' corruption of the French *oreille de mer*, or 'sea ears'. Those found in the Mediterranean tend to be slightly smaller.

The abalone of the Californian and Mexican Pacific coasts are larger and have a much finer flavour, particularly the red abalone and the black abalone, which is a special favourite with Mexicans. The abalone found in the seas off Australia are known as 'mutton fish' and the Japanese call their local variety *awabi*.

If they are large, they are usually first sliced into escalopes and, in order to make the very tough muscle edible, they have to be beaten well before being served raw or cooked very quickly. The Chinese dry much of their abalone, which is known as *pao yu*, and it requires many days' soaking before use. Most of the Oriental and Pacific catch is canned.

The French usually sauté their abalone very quickly in butter with garlic, or fry them like veal escalopes (cutlets). In California raw, sliced abalone sometimes marinated first, is popular in salads.

Low in calories, abalone is rich in many minerals, especially iron.

ORMEAUX À LA CASSEROLE

Abalone casserole

Serves 4
Preparation 30 minutes
Cooking 12–15 minutes

METRIC/IMPERIAL	AMERICAN
4–8 abalone	4–8 abalone
75 ml/5 tbsp vinegar	5 tbsp vinegar
85 g/3 oz butter	6 tbsp butter
3 garlic cloves, finely chopped	3 garlic cloves, finely chopped
4 shallots, finely chopped	4 shallots, finely chopped
115 g/¼ lb mushrooms, sliced	¼ lb mushrooms, sliced
2 tbsp finely chopped flat-leaved parsley	2 tbsp finely chopped flat-leaf parsley
100 ml/3½ fl oz crème fraîche or whipping cream	½ cup crème fraîche or whipping cream
flour, for dusting	flour, for dusting
salt and pepper	salt and pepper

Shell the abalone, trim away the dark guts and rinse the remaining flesh in the vinegar. If they are very large, cut them into slices.

Pat them dry, fold them in a clean cloth and pound them with a wooden kitchen mallet for about 10 minutes. Prick them all over with a fork and then dust them lightly with flour.

Melt the butter in a large, flameproof casserole over a moderate heat and sauté the garlic and shallots in it for about 2 minutes. Add the mushrooms and the parsley and stir to mix well.

Lower the heat, place the abalone on top of the mixture in the casserole, cover and cook gently for 8 minutes, turning the abalone over halfway through.

Add the crème fraîche or cream, season to taste and stir gently to mix well. Cover again and leave to cook for a further 2 minutes.

Serve very hot, straight from the casserole.
To drink: good bottled dry (hard) cider.

ACIDULATION

The technique of turning a mixture slightly acid, usually by adding vinegar or lemon juice or the juice of unripe fruit, is used whenever a tart, piquant or slightly sour flavour is required, or when there is a need to prevent oxidization, as in the preparation of avocados, apples, artichokes, or any fruit or vegetable which tends to discolour on contact with air. Acid mixtures also aid the process of coagulation, hence the addition of vinegar to the water for poaching eggs, etc.

AÏOLI OR AILLOLI

see also:
bourride
garlic
mayonnaise

A Provençal sauce similar to mayonnaise, with an egg yolk-and-oil base but with added garlic, it is served with cold poached fish, fish soups, eggs, salads, snails or cold meats.

The Provençal special-occasion dish *grand aïoli* is a banquet consisting of poached salt cod, hard-boiled eggs, boiled beef and mutton and stewed vegetables, and snails or squid as a garnish, with the sauce poured over all.

SAUCE AÏOLI

Garlic mayonnaise

Serves 8
Preparation 10 minutes

METRIC/IMPERIAL	AMERICAN
8 garlic cloves	8 garlic cloves
2 egg yolks	2 egg yolks
500 ml/16 fl oz olive oil	2 cups olive oil
juice of ½ lemon	juice of ½ lemon
salt and pepper	salt and pepper

Peel the garlic cloves and place them in a mortar. Pound them to a purée with a pestle. Add the egg yolks and seasoning to taste and mix to blend well.

Add the oil in a thin stream while continuing to blend, as if making mayonnaise. To promote the emulsion of the oil and egg yolks, add 2 or 3 teaspoons of warm water at regular intervals during the operation.

Finish the sauce with lemon juice and seasoning to taste.

see also:
beer
brandy, etc
cider
deglazing
liqueur
marinade
spirits
wine

ALCOHOL

Alcohols are a family of organic compounds, of which the ethyl alcohols are those we normally drink. Alcoholic beverages are mainly distilled from fermented fruit, cereals and grains or roots. Fruit, such as grapes, pears, apples, berries and stone fruit (such as cherries), can be used to make wine, cider and perries, as well as the wide range of marcs, *eaux-de-vie* and other white alcohols which form the base for Cognac, Armagnac, Calvados, Kirsch, plum brandy, mirabelle, raspberry brandy, etc. Cereals and grains, such as barley, wheat and corn, yield beer, whisky, gin, vodka and aquavit. Potatoes are used to make schnapps, and a number of more exotic plants like sugar cane and agave are used to make drinks such as rum and tequila and other local liquors.

An important part of gastronomic pleasure for many people, alcohol is drunk as an aperitif (sherries or cocktails), to accompany and complement the various dishes of a meal (wines and champagnes), or at the end of the meal as an aid to digestion (liqueurs, ports and brandies).

Alcohol is believed to have a social benefit in enhancing conviviality, as it releases inhibitions by depressing certain behavioural controls in the brain. When taken in moderation, this can be a positive effect. It should, however, be noted that each gram of alcohol contains 7 calories. Continual excessive intake of alcohol is very damaging to the body, usually producing obesity as well as high levels of dangerous toxins in the bloodstream and internal organs, and can result in permanent damage to the liver, nervous system and the brain. It should also be noted that alcohol deprives the body of its vital vitamin B supplies.

COOKING WITH ALCOHOL

Most forms of alcohol find culinary use, both in simple country cooking and in *haute cuisine*. Alcohol is used in three principal ways by cooks: as a preservative, to tenderize and cure, and as a flavouring.

Brandies, fortified wines, wines, spirits and vermouths are all often used to give depth of flavour to stocks, sauces and dressings. This is commonly achieved in the early stages of cooking by deglazing the pan in which the first flavouring ingredients are cooked. Beers and ciders are more commonly used in dishes which involve long, slow cooking, such as casseroles.

It is advisable to cook savoury dishes sufficiently after the addition of alcohol to drive off the alcohol itself, leaving only the flavouring elements. Otherwise the taste may be overpowering and the food indigestible.

The choice of flavouring alcohol is often a matter of matching the main constituents of the beverage with the ingredients of a dish or a popular accompaniment to that dish: cider and Calvados with apples and pork, Grand Marnier with oranges and duck, etc.

The powerful sweet flavours of liqueurs are a popular way of adding strength of flavour to desserts, such as soufflés and ice creams.

Literally the most flamboyant use of alcohol is in the process of flaming dishes at the table.

ALIGOT

see also:
cheese
potato

This speciality from the Auvergne region of France is made with puréed mashed potatoes, garlic and any mild, semi-soft cheese such as Cantal or Tomme, although the latter must not be fully ripe. The ingredients are warmed together until the cheese begins to run and whisked thoroughly with a fork to blend the cheese and the potatoes. The dish has reached the correct state when the mixture is smooth and uniformly elastic – in fact, waiters can stretch it several feet from the serving dish!

It is normally served as a hot first course, after offering a vin mousseux, St-Péray, for example, as an aperitif.

ALIGOT DU CANTAL

Aligot with Cantal cheese

Serves 4
Preparation 20 minutes
Cooking 25 minutes

METRIC/IMPERIAL	*AMERICAN*
700 g/1⅔ lb potatoes	*1⅔ lb potatoes*
300 g/10 oz Cantal cheese	*10 oz Cantal cheese*
85 g/3 oz butter	*6 tbsp butter*

150 ml/¼ pt crème fraîche or whipping cream
1 garlic clove, finely chopped
salt

⅔ cup crème fraîche or whipping cream
1 garlic clove, finely chopped
salt

Boil the potatoes in their skins for 25 minutes, then drain them. Leave to cool. Slice the cheese extremely thinly (do not grate it).

Put the butter, crème fraîche or cream and garlic in a heavy-bottomed casserole dish and stir over a gentle heat. Season lightly with salt.

Peel the cooled potatoes and mash them with a fork. Add the potato purée to the casserole, beating with a wooden spoon. Add the cheese, continuing to beat vigorously, lifting with the spoon to incorporate the cheese into the purée. When the mixture is smooth and elastic, serve at once. Do not overcook, otherwise it may curdle and become hard and lumpy.

ALLSPICE

Piment de la Jamaïque

see also: spices

The unripe berries of a tree which grows in the Caribbean and Central America, allspice has a strong aroma and flavour, not unlike a mixture of nutmeg, cinnamon and cloves – hence its name. A popular misunderstanding is that it is, in fact, a blend of these other spices.

Used whole and ground, allspice is a popular addition to sausages and cured meats such as salt beef, stuffings, marinades and pickles. In the Middle East it is usually added to pilafs.

A little ground allspice is very useful when only the barest hint of clove flavour is required, say with apples and pears. It is also a traditional ingredient in Christmas pudding.

ALMOND

Amande

Probably one of the most gastronomically important nuts, the almond comes from the kernel of an inedibly sour fruit related to the apricot. Originating in the eastern Mediterranean, it is now grown and used all over the world. The principal areas of cultivation and export are Spain, Italy and California.

see also: almond paste, blancmange, cakes and gâteaux, frangipane, macaroon, marzipan, nougat, nuts, petit four, praline

There are two varieties of almond: sweet almonds, which are large, oily and flat; and bitter almonds which are smaller, drier and harder and are grown mainly in Sardinia, Sicily and North Africa.

Sweet almonds are those used more commonly in cooking, baking and confectionery. They are usually sold shelled and blanched, whole, halved, slivered or ground. It is wise to avoid ground almonds (grind your own in a coffee or nut grinder) as they quickly become stale and are easily adulterated. Slivered almonds have a tendency to dry out and become rancid quickly. Do not store almonds for too long and always keep them in a tightly sealed container in a cool dark place.

Almonds are a popular accompaniment to fish, as in trout with almonds. They are also used in rich stuffings and salads. The Chinese frequently use them with pork and poultry, while the cooking of India and the Middle East favours them in pilafs and couscous. Catalan cooking makes great use of toasted almonds, pounded to a paste called *picada* with garlic and saffron and served with chicken and seafood. However, it is in the making of desserts, cakes and sweetmeats that sweet almonds excel in most cuisines, notably in marzipan, as well as in delights as diverse as blancmange or almond

fresh almonds

dried almonds

slivered almonds

milk, the English Bakewell tart or Italian *panforte*.

Bitter almonds contain an enzyme which creates deadly prussic acid (cyanide) on contact with water which is driven off by roasting. Their sale for consumption is actually prohibited in several countries, including the United States. The essence of the crushed roast kernels is used in jam making, baking and confectionery, including Italian *amaretti* and macaroons, as well as in the making of liqueurs like ratafia. Buy only the highest quality almond essence (extract) as inferior products will spoil the flavour of the finished dish, or make sparing use of an almond-flavoured liqueur instead.

To toast almonds in a microwave oven cook for 3 minutes on High, stirring 2 or 3 times.

Like most nuts, almonds are rich in protein, fibre and minerals, but high in calories; 100 g/3$\frac{1}{2}$ oz contains 600 calories.

TRUITES AUX AMANDES

Trout with almonds

Serves 4
Preparation 3 minutes
Cooking 8 minutes

METRIC/IMPERIAL	*AMERICAN*
4 whole trout, each weighing about 200 g/7 oz, gutted	*4 whole trout, each weighing about 7 oz, drawn*
2 lemons	*2 lemons*
45 g/1$\frac{1}{2}$ oz butter, diced	*3 tbsp butter, diced*
55 g/2 oz flaked almonds	*$\frac{1}{2}$ cup slivered almonds*
salt and pepper	*salt and pepper*

Wash the trout inside and out and pat them dry. Season the insides with salt and pepper. Juice one lemon and slice the other.

Place the butter pieces on a large oval dish and melt in the microwave on High for 1 minute. Add the almonds, stirring to coat them with butter. Microwave on High for 1 minute.

Arrange the trout on the dish, alternating heads and tails. Coat them with the butter and almonds and sprinkle with lemon juice. Cover with microwave-safe film and pierce the film in 2 or 3 places with a sharp knife. Microwave on High for 6 minutes. In microwave ovens which do not have a turntable, rotate the dish once half-way through cooking.

Remove the dish from the oven and arrange the trout on a warmed serving dish. Pour the cooking juices and almonds over them, garnish with lemon slices and serve.
To drink: Vouvray.

AMANDIN

Almond cake

Serves 8
Preparation 20 minutes
Cooking 50 minutes

METRIC/IMPERIAL	*AMERICAN*
4 eggs, separated	*4 eggs, separated*
250 g/8$\frac{1}{2}$ oz caster sugar	*1$\frac{1}{4}$ cups superfine sugar*
200 g/7 oz ground almonds	*2$\frac{1}{3}$ cups ground almonds*
200 ml/7 fl oz orange juice	*1 cup orange juice*
1 tbsp grated zest from an organic orange	*1 tbsp grated zest from an organic orange*
2 tbsp orange marmalade, warmed	*2 tbsp orange marmalade, warmed*
55 g/2 oz whole blanched almonds, crushed	*$\frac{1}{3}$ cup blanched whole almonds, crushed*
butter, for greasing	*butter, for greasing*

Preheat the oven to 180C/350F/gas 4. Beat the egg yolks with the sugar for 10 minutes. Add the ground almonds, orange juice and grated orange zest. Beat the egg whites to firm peaks and fold them into the mixture.

Butter a circle of parchment or greaseproof paper 24 cm/9$\frac{1}{2}$ in in diameter and place it on the bottom of a round cake pan of the same size. Pour the almond mixture into the pan and bake in the oven for 30 minutes, then increase the temperature of the oven to 200C/400F/gas 6 and bake for a further 20 minutes.

Remove the cake from the oven and leave to cool. Unmould and brush with the warmed orange marmalade. Sprinkle the crushed almonds on top.

Truites aux amandes (Trout with almonds)

ALMOND PASTE

Pâte d'amandes

see also: almond; cakes and gâteaux; marzipan; petit four

A mixture of ground sweet almonds and sugar which is extensively used in pâtisserie and confectionery, classic almond paste differs from marzipan in that it is entirely uncooked.

It is often sold ready-made in slabs or cylinders and in cans for cake-decorating or making sweets or for stuffing dried fruit. It may be coloured with food dyes.

Almond paste has a high calorie content; 100 g/$3\frac{1}{2}$ oz contains 500 calories. Obviously it should be consumed sparingly.

PÂTE D'AMANDE CRUE

Uncooked almond paste

To cover a 20 cm/8 in diameter cake
Preparation 10 minutes

METRIC/IMPERIAL	AMERICAN
150 g/$5\frac{1}{2}$ oz icing sugar	$1\frac{1}{4}$ cups confectioners' sugar
100 g/$3\frac{1}{2}$ oz caster sugar	$\frac{1}{2}$ cup granulated sugar
170 g/6 oz ground almonds	2 cups ground almonds
$\frac{1}{2}$ tsp almond or vanilla essence	$\frac{1}{2}$ tsp almond or vanilla extract
1 tsp lemon juice	1 tsp lemon juice
1 egg	1 egg

Sift the sugars and ground almonds together into a bowl.

Stir the mixture with a wooden spatula, adding the almond or vanilla essence (extract) and lemon juice.

Beat the egg and add it to the mixture. It should now have a fairly firm consistency which can still be kneaded with ease.

Continue to beat the mixture with a spatula until it is completely smooth, then roll or knead it out to the desired thickness.

Use for icing a Genoese sponge or Savoy sponge cake. Coloured and flavoured with a few drops of food colouring and coffee or vanilla essence (extract), it may also be cut into decorations for petits fours, especially those made from walnut or chocolate.

Note: for an even richer almond paste, add an extra egg yolk.

AMINO ACID

see also: proteins

There are twenty amino acids, which are the building blocks for all proteins. The human body can synthesize most of the amino acids according to its needs, but there are eight so-called 'essential' amino acids, isoleucine, leucine, lysine, methionine, phenylalanine, threonine, tryptophan and valine, which the body cannot produce for itself and must therefore be provided by the diet – lack of any one prevents the body from making its own proteins.

The best sources of protein include meat, milk, eggs, fish, rice, potatoes and dried beans, peas and lentils. Animal proteins have a better balance of amino acids than vegetable proteins; eggs have almost the perfect mixture.

ANCHOVY

Anchois

see also: condiment; fish; pizza; salad; tapenade

Numerous related species of small fish all over the world go by this name, but the best flavoured anchovy is found on the Mediterranean and southern European coasts. It is usually 8–15 cm/3–6 in long with a bigger mouth than the sardine, which it closely resembles.

Fresh anchovies should be treated like sardines – grilled whole and served with lemon juice or marinated. The tastiest anchovies are said to come from Collioure on the southwest coast of France.

Most anchovies are canned – whole or filleted – in oil, or preserved in brine or oil in jars; the latter must be kept refrigerated. They are a common ingredient in dishes from the South of France such as *salade niçoise* and *tapenade*. Their most common use nowadays is probably on pizzas.

Some anchovies are available salted in jars, the usual treatment for many centuries. Salted anchovies were once a common flavouring for meats, and anchovy essence and paste were popular condiments. It is usually necessary to remove the salt by careful rinsing before use.

Anchovy paste (minimum 90% anchovy), anchovy cream (75% anchovy) and anchovy butter (75% anchovy) are still popular for flavourings and savouries, such as anchovy toast. All these preparations should be kept in the refrigerator.

OEUFS DURS FARCIS AUX ANCHOIS

Anchovy-stuffed eggs

Serves 4
Preparation 15 minutes (mayonnaise 10 minutes)
Cooking 10 minutes

METRIC/IMPERIAL	AMERICAN
6 eggs	6 eggs
6 salted anchovy fillets, drained and desalted	6 salted anchovy fillets, drained and desalted
2 tbsp thick mayonnaise	2 tbsp thick mayonnaise
12 anchovy fillets in oil	12 anchovy fillets in oil
12 stoned black olives	12 pitted black olives

Hard boil the eggs, plunge them in cold water and peel. Halve them lengthwise. Carefully remove the yolks and refrigerate the whites.

Blend the desalted anchovies in a food processor, then add the mashed egg yolks and mayonnaise. Fill the chilled egg whites with this purée. Drain the anchovies in oil and pat dry on paper towels. Place a black olive and an anchovy fillet on each half egg. Serve chilled. *To drink: Côtes-de-Provence rosé.*

ANCHOÏADE

Anchovy and garlic purée

Serves 4
Preparation 25 minutes
Cooking 5 minutes

METRIC/IMPERIAL	AMERICAN
125 g/4½ oz anchovy fillets in oil	4½ oz anchovy fillets in oil
125 g/4½ oz salted anchovies	4½ oz salted anchovies
3 garlic cloves	3 garlic cloves
1 dried fig	1 dried fig
1 tbsp olive oil	1 tbsp olive oil
1 tsp vinegar	1 tsp vinegar
1 tsp grated lemon zest	1 tsp grated lemon zest
4–6 thick slices of country bread, to serve	4–6 thick slices of country bread, to serve

Drain all the anchovies and sponge the salted ones to remove some of the salt. Peel the garlic cloves and cut the fig into small pieces.

Preheat a hot grill (broiler). Pound all these ingredients with the oil, vinegar and lemon rind in a pestle with a mortar (or blend in a food processor) until the mixture is smooth.

To serve: spread the paste on the slices of bread, making sure the purée covers the whole slice. Then grill (broil) under high heat until lightly browned and serve at once, with a tomato salad or a salad of cos (romaine) lettuce and chopped hard boiled eggs.

ANGELICA

Angélique

A plant native to Northern Europe which is nowadays virtually impossible to buy fresh, but the aromatic green stems are sold crystallized (candied) for use in baking. Angelica is also used in the manufacture of Chartreuse.

see also:
cakes and gâteaux
liqueur

ANISEED

Anis

Aniseed is the seed of a plant which has been used as a flavouring for centuries. Nowadays it is primarily used in the making of alcoholic drinks such as pastis and anisette, which have a penetrating aroma even in small quantities. The flavour works well with all seafood and it is still used to flavour bread, cakes and soufflés and in the making of sweets.

see also:
cakes and gâteaux
dill
spirits
star anise

PETITS BISCUITS À L'ANIS

Sweet aniseed cookies

Makes about 24
Preparation 30 minutes, 24 hours ahead
Cooking 20 minutes

METRIC/IMPERIAL	AMERICAN
4 eggs	4 eggs
250 g/8½ oz caster sugar	1¼ cups sugar
1 tbsp aniseed	1 tbsp aniseed
250 g/8½ oz flour, sifted	1¾ cups flour, sifted
oil, for greasing	oil, for greasing

Break the eggs into a bowl. Add the sugar a little at a time, beating constantly. Beat the mixture for 10 minutes until pale and frothy. If not beating with an electric mixer, place the bowl over a pan of simmering water.

Add the aniseed, then gradually beat in the sifted flour.

Oil a baking sheet and sprinkle it with a little flour. Using a small spoon, place 24 small heaps of the aniseed dough set at regular intervals on the baking sheet. Flatten them slightly and leave them to stand in a dry place overnight.

The following day, heat the oven to 180C/350F/gas 4. Turn the aniseed cookies over, then bake them for 20 minutes.

These keep well in an airtight tin. Serve them with tea or as an accompaniment to fruit salad.

APPLE

Pomme

see also:
brandy, etc
charlotte
chutney
cider
drying
fritter
fruit
jams, etc
turnover

The fruit of the world's most widely cultivated fruit tree is the most important fruit grown in temperate climates. As apples can keep for months, in the past they were also often the only fresh fruit available.

There are reputed to be several thousand distinct varieties of apple in Britain and more in America. Nowadays, disappointingly few of the more gastronomically important varieties are being cultivated in any quantity.

The principal types grown in Britain include the small, round, greenish-yellow Cox's Orange Pippin, which is crisp, firm and sweet with a hint of acidity, the larger yellow Golden Delicious, a popular variety throughout the world, which is very sweet and tender, and the large, tart, green Bramley, usually reserved for cooking. The medium to large Granny Smiths have a green skin and a very crisp flesh. Russets, such as Egremont and Laxton's Superb, easily identified by the dull brown patches on their skin, not to be confused with bruising or discoloration, are soft, sweet and juicy but have sufficient texture and acidity to cook well.

The most popular eating apple in America is the Red Delicious, which is larger and longer than the Golden Delicious and has a very shiny skin, although its flesh is very tender and will not stand up to cooking. The smaller red McIntosh, which is widely available, is a good all-purpose apple. Another supermarket apple, the large, flattish Rome Beauty, which is golden yellow and streaked with red, is much used for cooking as it has a refreshingly tart flavour. Apple varieties sold more locally include the crisp Empire – a McIntosh hybrid – and the Greening, the traditional apple used in pies.

The French Reine des Reinettes and their Canadian counterparts have a yellow skin streaked with red and are delicious as an eating apple or in cooking.

Apples will continue to ripen off the tree. A good way of identifying fruit at its peak is to flick it with a finger close to the stalk: if the resulting sound is dull, the fruit is ripe. Apples are available all year round, but the tastier eating varieties are at their best from late summer to early spring.

Buy only firm fruit and avoid any which are wrinkled, bruised or otherwise blemished. Store them in a cool, well-ventilated place a little apart in single layers with their stalks down. Uncooked apples do not freeze well, but apple slices dry easily. If they are not to be peeled, always wash apples thoroughly in warm soapy water, rinse them well and pat them dry before use. Once peeled and sliced, apples will discolour very rapidly, so sprinkle them liberally with lemon juice to prevent this happening.

As well as being an excellent dessert course in themselves and the perfect accompaniment to a good cheese, apples are popular in charlottes, compotes, pies and tarts, often in combination with berry fruit. The firmer-fleshed varieties such as the Reinettes are best in tarts as they keep their texture better on cooking and their slight acidic bite enhances the flavour. Firm sweet apples also make good fritters and turnovers. Sourer 'cooking' apples, like the Bramley and Gravenstein, are more usually stewed with added sugar or made into apple sauce. Apples are also commonly used in jams and preserves as they are rich in pectin, and apple 'butters', 'cheeses', 'pastes', 'leathers' and chutneys are a common use for windfall crops in the country.

The sweet crunch of raw apples makes them a popular ingredient in fruit and savoury salads, as in the American classic Waldorf salad with celery and walnuts in mayonnaise. Their slight acidity also makes them a common accompaniment, sauce or stuffing to dishes incorporating fatty foods such as pork, black pudding or blood sausage and herring.

Possibly the most popular use for apples throughout the world is in apple pie, usually flavoured with cinnamon and often served with thick cream or ice cream. However, Austrian *Apfelstrudel*, a confection of sliced apples with raisins, lemon juice and butter between layers of strudel pastry, has become an international favourite.

Apples are used to make cider and, hence, cider vinegar, as well as Calvados and applejack, and thus combine well with any of these liquids in cooking.

Apples are rich in vitamins and minerals, especially iron and potassium, and each 100 g/ $3\frac{1}{2}$ oz produces 52 calories.

1 Granny Smith, 2 Royal Gala, 3 Jubilee, 4 Boskoop, 5 Empire, 6 Starking, 7 Spartan, 8 Reine des Reinettes, 9 Golden Delicious, 10 Red Delicious, 11 Canada, 12 Cox's Orange Pippin

POMMES BONNE FEMME

Baked apples

Serves 4
Preparation 10 minutes
Cooking $1\frac{1}{2}$ hours

METRIC/IMPERIAL	AMERICAN
4 firm strong-flavoured apples	4 firm strong-flavored apples
1 tsp ground cinnamon	1 tsp ground cinnamon
45 g/$1\frac{1}{2}$ oz caster sugar	$\frac{1}{4}$ cup superfine sugar
55 g/2 oz butter	4 tbsp butter

Preheat the oven to 200C/400F/gas 6. Wash the apples but do not peel them. Core them with an apple-corer and cut through the skin right around their middles.

Mix the cinnamon, sugar and two-thirds of the butter and spoon into the centres of the apples. Use the remaining butter to grease a baking dish and arrange the apples in it. Add 3–4 tablespoons of water. Bake for $1\frac{1}{2}$ hours and serve straight from the baking dish.

Try placing each apple on a slice of buttered brioche and serve with well-chilled whipped cream; or put a little redcurrant jelly or a few slivered almonds on top of each apple.

POMMES AUX FIGUES

Baked apples stuffed with figs

Serves 4
Preparation 15 minutes
Cooking 9 minutes

METRIC/IMPERIAL	AMERICAN
4 large firm-fleshed apples	4 large firm-fleshed apples
6 dried figs, chopped	6 dried figs, chopped
75 g/3 oz ground almonds	1 cup ground almonds
3 tbsp honey	3 tbsp honey
25 g/$\frac{3}{4}$ oz vanilla sugar	2 tbsp vanilla-flavored sugar
45 g/$1\frac{1}{2}$ oz butter, cut into small pieces	3 tbsp butter, cut into small pieces
3 tbsp quince jelly	3 tbsp quince jelly
8 walnuts, to decorate	8 walnuts, to decorate

Wash the apples but do not peel them. Cut off the top of each apple about 2 cm/$\frac{3}{4}$ in down from the stalk. Remove the core with an apple corer and enlarge the resulting cavity slightly.

In a bowl mix the figs, ground almonds, honey, vanilla sugar and butter. Cover with microwave-safe film and microwave on High for 3 minutes. Fill the apple cavities with this cooked mixture. Arrange them in a dish and add 3 tablespoons of water. Cover and microwave on High for 6 minutes.

Remove the dish from the oven and pour the cooking juices into a bowl. Add the quince jelly and stir with a spoon until it is mixed in. Arrange the stuffed apples on a serving dish, pour the sauce over them and decorate with walnuts. Serve at once.

SALADE DE NOVEMBRE

Apple, chestnut and celery salad

Serves 4
Preparation 20 minutes
Cooking 30 minutes

METRIC/IMPERIAL	AMERICAN
225 g/$\frac{1}{2}$ lb fresh chestnuts	$\frac{1}{2}$ lb fresh chestnuts
4 crisp apples	4 crisp apples
juice of $\frac{1}{2}$ lemon	juice of $\frac{1}{2}$ lemon
4 tbsp walnut oil	4 tbsp walnut oil
2 tbsp cider vinegar	2 tbsp cider vinegar
3 stalks of celery, trimmed and cut into small pieces	3 sticks of celery, trimmed and cut into small pieces
3 tbsp chopped fresh chives	3 tbsp chopped fresh chives
salt and pepper	salt and pepper

Make an incision just under the skin around the middles of the chestnuts. Bring a large saucepan of water to the boil. Add the chestnuts and cook them for 5 minutes. Drain them, remove the skins, then cook the chestnuts for 30 minutes in a pan of water which has been seasoned with salt and pepper.

Peel and core the apples. Sprinkle with lemon juice. Make a vinaigrette with the walnut oil, vinegar and salt and pepper to taste.

Pommes bonne femme (Baked apples)

In a salad bowl mix the well-drained warm chestnuts, apples and celery. Pour the vinaigrette over them and stir. Sprinkle with the chives and serve with hot braised ham.

TARTE AUX POMMES FLAMBÉES

Whisky-flamed apple tart

Serves 6
Preparation 30 minutes
Cooking 35 minutes

METRIC/IMPERIAL	*AMERICAN*
200 g/7 oz flour	*1½ cups flour*
170 g/6 oz butter	*¾ cup (1½ sticks) butter*
150 g/5½ oz soft brown sugar	*1 cup brown sugar*
1 kg/2¼ lb Reinettes or other firm-fleshed apples	*2¼ lb Reinettes or other firm-fleshed apples*
2 tsp ground cinnamon	*2 tsp ground cinnamon*
150 ml/¼ pt whisky	*⅔ cup Scotch whisky*
salt	*salt*

Preheat the oven to 250C/475F/gas 9. Make some pastry with the flour, 100 g/3½ oz/1 stick of the butter, ½ teaspoon of salt, 1 tablespoon of sugar and about 60 ml/4 tbsp of water. Use to line a 26 cm/10½ in flan ring placed on a baking sheet. Prick the pastry base with a fork.

Put a layer of dried beans in parchment or greaseproof paper on the pastry and bake it blind for 20 minutes, or until cooked and lightly golden.

Peel and core the apples. Quarter them and then cut each quarter in half lengthwise. Brown these apple portions in the rest of the butter in a frying pan over a moderate heat for 5 minutes, making sure they do not become mushy.

Add all but 2 tablespoons of the remaining sugar, 1 teaspoon of cinnamon, 60 ml/4 tbsp of water and 30 ml/2 tbsp of whisky. Cover and cook gently for 10 minutes. Put this mixture into the pastry case. Sprinkle with the reserved sugar and cinnamon.

Warm the remaining whisky, pour it over the apples and set it alight. Serve as soon as the flames die down.

APRICOT

Abricot

see also:
compote
fruit
jams, etc

Fresh apricots are a delicate, round, summer fruit with a colour which varies from pale yellow tones to rich orange. The colour is no indication of flavour, but the deeper the colour the higher the concentration of carotene and vitamin A. The skin is velvety and the flesh aromatic, but with little juice. The skin is difficult to peel without blanching the fruit first, but it is tasty and nutritious. The stone or pit comes away from the flesh easily and its inner kernel is edible and may be used to add flavour to jams, etc.

In France, the first apricots of the year arrive in mid-March from the Mediterranean countries. Apricots from the Rhône valley, Provence and Languedoc-Roussillon reach the markets between mid-June and late July. Apricots prefer moderate climates; cultivation outside Europe occurs principally in parts of the Middle East, California, China, Japan, South Africa and Australia.

One quarter of the fruit produced is canned, either in its own syrup or with sugar added, already peeled and with the stones removed. Use canned apricots in fruit salad or compotes, hot or cold, or to decorate sweet dishes. Try them in chicken salad or to garnish braised ham.

The fresh fruit loses flavour rapidly and is best appreciated at room temperature rather than chilled. Since apricots do not ripen much after being picked, buy only perfectly ripe fruit for eating. Test by rolling the fruit gently between the palms: it should feel soft. Apricots do not travel well and tend to become fibrous and tasteless with long keeping. Such fruit, and apricots which are not quite ripe, may be used in cooking to make compotes or jam, or stewed with sugar and vanilla.

For use in puddings or gâteaux, apricots are generally peeled. Blanch them briefly in boiling water, then pat dry. The skin is then easily removed with a pointed knife.

The celebrated Austrian *Marillenknödeln* are whole peeled apricots stuffed with sugar, sealed in a thin dumpling pastry, poached and finished off with a glaze of butter, sugar and cinnamon. Apricots are also delicious poached in a heavy syrup and these may be preserved in brandy.

As apricot flesh is mealy and does not turn into a mush on cooking, apricots are a favourite fruit for tarts and pies because they do not spoil the pastry. They also make excellent jam and, pickled in vinegar with cloves, a delicious relish for use with hot and cold ham and pork dishes. As evidenced by Middle Eastern cooking, fresh apricots also work well cooked in combination with meat, particularly lamb and pork.

Rich in carotene, apricots are good for the skin and each 100 g/$3\frac{1}{2}$ oz contains 44 calories.

DRIED APRICOTS

Coming mostly from California or Australia, dried apricots are generally large, pale in colour and often sticky to the touch. Those from Turkey have by far the best flavour – with a hint of muscatel – and are more expensive. They are usually a dark orange in colour. The process of drying concentrates the sugar in the fruit, so dried apricots have a higher calorie content than fresh.

Dried apricots make a good stuffing for fatty meats and poultry such as pork and duck. They can also be used like fresh apricots, mainly in stews and compotes or as garnish for stews and roasts, after being soaked in warm water for 2 hours.

It is relatively easy to dry apricots at home: split and stone them and cut the halves in two, if large; place in a single layer on a rack in a cool oven, or in full sun, until they turn dark orange.

SAUCE À L'ABRICOT

Apricot sauce

Serves 4
Preparation 10 minutes
Cooking 5 minutes

METRIC/IMPERIAL	AMERICAN
400 g/14 oz ripe apricots	14 oz ripe apricots
250 g/$8\frac{1}{2}$ oz caster sugar	$1\frac{1}{4}$ cups superfine sugar
150 ml/$\frac{1}{4}$ pt warm water	$\frac{2}{3}$ cup warm water
2 tbsp Kirsch or apricot brandy	2 tbsp Kirsch or apricot brandy

Halve the apricots and remove the stones. Purée the apricot flesh in a food processor.

In a bowl, dissolve the sugar in the warm water. Pour this syrup and the apricot purée into a heavy-bottomed saucepan. Bring this mixture to the boil and cook for 5 minutes, stirring constantly with a wooden spoon, until the sauce is thick enough to coat the back of the spoon. Remove the pan from the heat and pass the mixture through a sieve. Add the Kirsch and mix well.

Serve hot or warm with a rice ring, ice cream or any cream pudding.

ABRICOTINE AUX FRAMBOISES

Apricot Bavarian cream with raspberries

Serves 6
Preparation 20 minutes (3 hours ahead)
Chilling 3 hours

METRIC/IMPERIAL	AMERICAN
1 kg/$2\frac{1}{4}$ lb apricots	$2\frac{1}{4}$ lb apricots
2 gelatine leaves or $\frac{1}{2}$ sachet (8 g/$\frac{1}{4}$ oz) powdered gelatine	1 envelope powdered unflavored gelatine
250 g/$8\frac{1}{2}$ oz caster sugar	$1\frac{1}{4}$ cups superfine sugar
100 ml/$3\frac{1}{2}$ fl oz crème fraîche or whipping cream, chilled	$\frac{1}{2}$ cup crème fraîche or whipping cream, chilled
150 g/$5\frac{1}{2}$ oz raspberries	$1\frac{1}{2}$ cups raspberries

Bring a large pan of water to the boil and blanch the apricots for 2 minutes. Drain, cut in half, peel and remove the stones.

Soak the gelatine leaves in a little cold water for 15 minutes, then drain and dissolve in 2 tablespoons of hot water. If using powdered gelatine, dissolve it in 2 tablespoons hot water.

Purée the peeled apricots, add the sugar and mix well. Blend in the gelatine. Whip the crème fraîche or cream until it is just beginning to thicken. Fold it gently into the mixture.

Line the bottom of a 15 cm/6 in charlotte or bavarois mould with parchment or greaseproof paper. Pour the mixture into the mould and chill in the refrigerator for 3 hours until firm.

Just before serving, plunge the mould into warm water for 20 seconds, pat it dry and invert it over a serving platter to unmould the apricot cream. Remove the lining paper and garnish with the fresh raspberries.

This dessert may also be served with a raspberry coulis or purée: in a food processor, blend 200 g/7 oz/1 pt fresh or thawed frozen raspberries for 2 or 3 minutes with 100 g/3½ oz/½ cup caster (superfine) sugar until smooth.

COMPOTE D'ABRICOTS SECS AUX FIGUES

Compote of dried apricots with figs

Serves 4
Preparation 3 minutes
Cooking 11 minutes
Standing 20 minutes

METRIC/IMPERIAL	*AMERICAN*
115 g/4 oz dried figs	*4 oz dried figs*
300 g/10 oz dried apricots	*10 oz dried apricots*
1 tbsp seedless raisins or sultanas	*1 tbsp dark or golden raisins*
1 cinnamon stick, broken into pieces	*1 cinnamon stick, broken into pieces*
1 small glass (100 ml/3½ fl oz) red wine	*½ cup red wine*
1 tbsp liquid honey	*1 tbsp liquid honey*
chopped walnuts or flaked almonds, to garnish	*chopped walnuts or slivered almonds, to garnish*

Remove the stalks from the figs and arrange the apricots, raisins and figs in a deep platter. Sprinkle over the cinnamon and pour in the red wine mixed with 150 ml/¼ pt/⅔ cup of cold water.

Cover and microwave on High for 10 minutes, stirring twice during cooking. Leave to stand for 20 minutes.

Remove the cinnamon stick and add the honey. Stir well and reheat for 1 minute on High just before serving, garnished with chopped walnuts or slivered almonds.

Serve chilled crème fraîche, whipping cream or *fromage frais* separately as an accompaniment, if wished.

Note: if making this recipe for children, substitute grape juice for the wine.

ARROWROOT

see also: glazing sauce

A powdery white starch extracted from the roots of tropical plants, arrowroot has several uses.

Its fine grains make it very digestible, hence its role as an invalid food, and when mixed with liquid it produces a clear, smooth consistency. This, combined with its almost total lack of flavour, makes it a popular thickening agent in fine sauces and glazes.

ARTICHOKE OR GLOBE ARTICHOKE

Artichaut

see also: acidulation cardoon crosne Jerusalem artichoke sauce vegetables vinaigrette

The globe artichoke is the edible young flower bud of a plant of the thistle family from the Mediterranean region, which is related to the cardoon.

There are two main types: the large Breton artichoke, which is green with a barely visible purple heart, and the small purple artichokes or *petits violets* of Provence. When young and very small these are known as *poivrades* and may be eaten raw. In the larger varieties, the heart (the base or *fond* of the bud and the top of the stalk) and the fleshy bases of the leaf-like scales are eaten; some *poivrades* may be eaten in their entirety. The large artichokes are at their best in summer, the purple in spring and autumn.

Artichokes should be bought while they still

have tightly packed leaves and have no dark discoloration. They keep well standing in water like flowers. They oxidize quickly, so do not store them near eggs as they will spoil. For the same reason, do not keep cooked artichokes for longer than a day.

Before cooking, break off the stem and tough outer leaves. The tips of the leaves can also be trimmed, using a stainless steel knife, and the inedible hairy choke in the centre can be removed at this stage, or after cooking. The artichoke should then be rubbed generously with a cut lemon to prevent discoloration and cooked for 15–25 minutes, depending on size, in boiling salted water acidulated with lemon juice or vinegar in a non-oxidizing pan. A little flour or bicarbonate of soda will also help them to keep their colour. The artichoke is cooked when the outer leaves come away easily.

Whole globe artichokes are normally served with a vinaigrette dressing in which the leaves may be dipped. Trimmed of their choke they are also good baked with Mornay sauce or filled with creamed mushrooms and sprinkled with Parmesan cheese.

Artichoke hearts are sold in cans and jars, as well as frozen, and are an excellent way of giving a touch of luxury to a salad. They may also be sautéed in butter and lemon juice and served as an appetizer or vegetable accompaniment, or used as an omelette filling.

Artichokes are low in calories, with 40 calories per 100 g/3½ oz, and are a good source of iron and potassium.

ARTICHAUTS À LA VINAIGRETTE

Artichokes vinaigrette

Serves 6
Preparation 10 minutes
Cooking about 30 minutes

METRIC/IMPERIAL	AMERICAN
6 large artichokes	6 large globe artichokes
1 lemon, halved	1 lemon, halved
4–5 tbsp white wine vinegar	4–5 tbsp white wine vinegar
150 ml/¼ pt olive oil	⅔ cup olive oil
1 tsp strong Dijon mustard	1 tsp strong Dijon mustard
2 tbsp chopped fresh chives	2 tbsp chopped fresh chives
salt and pepper	salt and pepper

Wash the artichokes and break off the stems, taking with them the fibres from the heart. With a sharp, stainless steel knife, trim off the

globe artichoke

purple Provençal artichokes

top third of each leaf. Rub the cut parts of the trimmed artichokes all over with lemon.

Put the artichokes in a large, non-oxidizing pan containing boiling salted water to cover, along with the juice of the lemon. Cover (a folded cloth on top of the artichokes also helps ensure even cooking) and simmer for 15–25 minutes. They are ready when one of the large leaves at the outside base pulls away easily.

To make the vinaigrette, dissolve several pinches of salt in the vinegar. Whisk in the oil, mustard, chopped chives and pepper to taste.

Drain the cooked artichokes and leave them to cool upside down. When cool, detach the heart and carefully remove the choke with a spoon. Serve with the vinaigrette on the side.

Other suggestions for dressings are *mousseline*, lemon mayonnaise or *rémoulade*.

To cook artichokes in a pressure-cooker: allow 10–12 minutes from the time the valve begins to hiss.

BROUILLADE DE PETITS VIOLETS

Ratatouille of purple artichokes

Serves 6
Preparation 20 minutes
Cooking about 1 hour

METRIC/IMPERIAL	AMERICAN
30 small purple artichokes	*30 small purple globe artichokes*
1 lemon	*1 lemon*
225 g/½ lb lean rashers of smoked bacon	*½ lb sliced bacon*
4 unripe tomatoes, quartered	*4 unripe tomatoes, quartered*
2 ripe tomatoes, quartered	*2 ripe tomatoes, quartered*
2 garlic cloves, finely chopped	*2 garlic cloves, finely chopped*
2 small white onions, finely chopped	*2 small white onions, finely chopped*
5 tbsp olive oil	*5 tbsp olive oil*
½ tsp dried thyme	*½ tsp dried thyme*
bay leaf	*bay leaf*
10 fresh basil leaves	*10 fresh basil leaves*
salt and pepper	*salt and pepper*

Trim the leaves of each artichoke. Remove the choke with a grapefruit spoon. Sprinkle the artichokes all over with lemon juice.

Place the bacon in a sauté pan and dry fry for 5 minutes on each side. Remove the bacon and sauté the tomatoes and garlic in the bacon fat until soft. Season with salt and pepper and set aside with the bacon. Add the artichokes and onions to the pan, sprinkle with oil and sauté until browned. Add the thyme and a little crumbled bay leaf. Continue to cook over a low heat for 10 minutes. Return the tomatoes and bacon to the pan, cover and simmer for 20 minutes.

Snip the basil with scissors and add it to the mixture. Adjust the seasoning, if necessary, and cook gently for a further 10 minutes.

Serve either very hot with grilled (or broiled) lamb, fillet (tenderloin) of veal, or tournedos (filet mignons), or chilled as a first course with a vinaigrette of olive oil, lemon juice, garlic and chopped fresh tarragon.

To drink: a Bandol or rosé.

ARUGULA

see Rocket

ASPARAGUS

Asperge

see also:
hollandaise
mayonnaise
sauce
vegetables
vinaigrette

A member of the lily family, asparagus is cultivated extensively throughout Europe and the United States for its delicious young stems.

There are three main types: white, which is grown covered with earth except for the tips, and is tender but slight in flavour; purple, which is harvested as it reaches a height of only a few centimetres and is full of flavour; and the more common green asparagus, which is harvested at a height of about 15 cm/6 in and is considered to have the best taste of all.

When buying asparagus, choose firm, crisp spears which weigh heavy in the hand; the cut ends should be clean and white. A yellow tinge indicates that the vegetable is old and might be fibrous. Do not buy long spears: length may add to the weight but does not always increase the proportion that is edible. In the case of green asparagus, the pale part and the darker green part should be equal in length.

Asparagus does not take well to heat or a dry atmosphere; buy it just before it is needed for cooking. The fresher it is, the more tender and tasty it will be. Any tough outer skin of asparagus stems should be peeled off and the woody bases of the stems removed before cooking. Small green asparagus generally does not need any peeling. White asparagus freezes well for up to a year, wrapped tightly in foil, and it can be cooked straight from frozen. Early, thin and misshapen crops are sold cheaply as 'sprue' and make good soups, sauces and soufflés. When serving asparagus as an appetizer, allow 225 g/8 oz per person.

Asparagus is usually boiled or steamed, or it can be cooked standing in water so that the harder parts of the stem cook in the water while the more delicate stem and tips are gently steamed. Horizontal and upright asparagus kettles are made to accommodate the vegetable and cook them in these ways.

The cooked asparagus is usually served as a first course: hot, dressed with melted butter (and possibly a little lemon juice), or sauces such as hollandaise or maltaise; or warm, dressed with a vinaigrette or mayonnaise. In Europe it is usual to eat the spears with the fingers and to provide finger bowls.

Canned asparagus tends generally to be rather flavourless. Drain it and use in soup with herbs, in soufflés or in mixed salads. Small canned 'cocktail' asparagus tips are good for canapés.

Asparagus is a very healthy vegetable, being rich in fibre and vitamins A, B and C, and low in calories; 100 g/3½ oz contains 26 calories.

ASPERGES AU NATUREL

Plain boiled asparagus

Serves 6
Preparation 20 minutes
Cooking 20–25 minutes

METRIC/IMPERIAL	AMERICAN
1.5 kg/3½ lb fresh asparagus	3½ lb fresh asparagus
salt and pepper	salt and pepper

If necessary, place each asparagus spear flat on a chopping board and peel off the fibrous outer layer, working from the tip to the base. Cut off the tough ends. Wash the asparagus in plenty of water but do not leave it to soak. Tie the spears into bunches of 6 to 10.

Bring a large pan of water to the boil, adding about ½ tablespoon of salt per litre/1¾ pints/1 quart of water. Place the bunches of asparagus in it and allow 5–10 minutes of fast boiling, depending on their thickness and freshness: they are done when they can be easily pierced

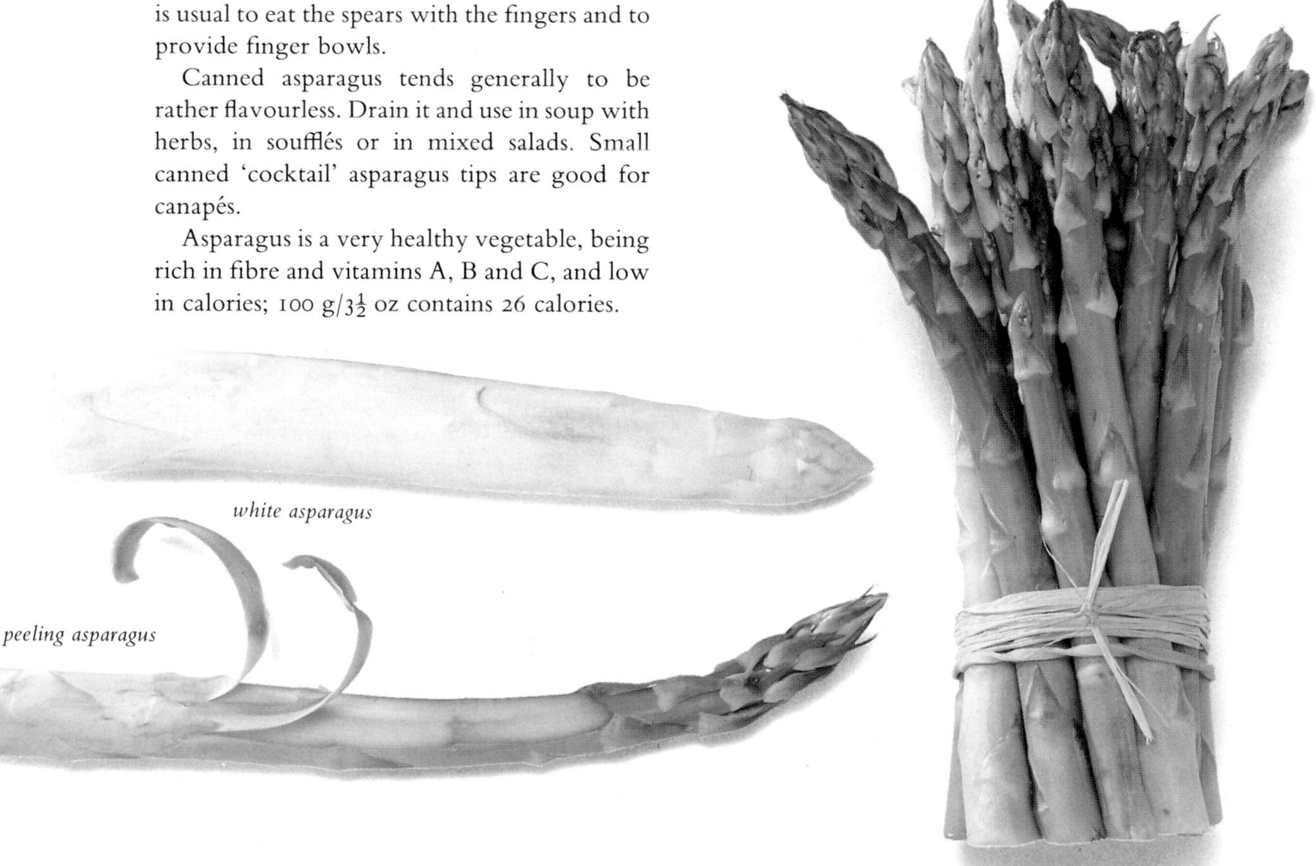

white asparagus

peeling asparagus

with the tip of a sharp knife. Take care not to overcook them. Remove from the water and drain.

Remove the string and arrange the asparagus on a folded napkin in a serving dish, or on the rack of an asparagus server.

If serving hot, cover them with a napkin dampened with the cooking liquid until ready to serve. A little melted butter, some black pepper and possibly a squeeze or two of lemon juice are the only dressings required. The Italians add a little freshly grated Parmesan.

Alternatively serve warm or cold with mayonnaise – try flavouring it with a little orange juice – or a vinaigrette dressing.
Note: if steaming the asparagus, allow 10–20 minutes.

DARNES DE SAUMON AUX ASPERGES

Salmon with asparagus

Serves 4
Preparation 20 minutes
Cooking 20 minutes, at least 2 hours in advance

METRIC/IMPERIAL	AMERICAN
100 ml/3½ fl oz white wine	½ cup white wine
bouquet garni	bouquet garni
4 thick salmon steaks, each weighing about 150 g/5½ oz	4 thick salmon steaks, each weighing about 5½ oz
12 green asparagus spears	12 green asparagus spears
150 ml/¼ pt crème fraîche or sour cream	⅔ cup crème fraîche or sour cream
2 lemons	2 lemons
24 shelled cooked prawns	24 peeled cooked shrimp
bunch of dill	bunch of dill
salt and pepper	salt and pepper

Pour 1 litre/1¾ pints/1 quart of water and the white wine into a pan. Add the bouquet garni and season with salt and pepper. Bring to the boil. Put the salmon steaks into the liquid and poach gently for 10 minutes. Remove from the heat and leave to cool in the cooking liquid.

Prepare and cook the asparagus in boiling salted water as above, drain it and cut off the tips plus a little of each stem. Set aside. Purée the remaining stems in a food processor with the crème fraîche or cream and lemon juice and seasoning to taste.

Place the drained salmon steaks on individual plates and garnish each one with 3 asparagus tips and 6 prawns (shrimp). Sprinkle with snipped dill and add a few lemon slices. Spoon the asparagus sauce over each plate and serve.
To drink: Pouilly-Fumé.

SALADE ARGENTEUIL

Asparagus and potato salad

Serves 4
Preparation 20 minutes
Cooking 5–15 minutes

METRIC/IMPERIAL	AMERICAN
2 potatoes	2 potatoes
1 tbsp white wine	1 tbsp white wine
450 g/1 lb thin green asparagus spears	1 lb thin green asparagus spears
4 tbsp olive oil	4 tbsp olive oil
juice of 1 lemon	juice of 1 lemon
2 tbsp snipped fresh tarragon	2 tbsp snipped fresh tarragon
salt and pepper	salt and pepper
lettuce leaves, to garnish	lettuce leaves, to garnish

Wash and peel the potatoes. Cook them in a pressure-cooker for 5 minutes or boil until just tender. Drain and slice them. Pour the white wine over the potato slices. Set aside to cool.

Peel and trim the asparagus spears, then slice them diagonally into 6–7 cm/2½ in pieces, keeping the tips whole. Cook them in 300 ml/½ pt/1¼ cups boiling salted water for 5 minutes. Drain them, put them in a bowl and pour 1 tablespoon of oil over them.

Make a dressing with the remaining oil, the lemon juice and tarragon. Season to taste.

Line a salad bowl with the lettuce leaves. Arrange the potatoes, asparagus pieces and tips in alternating rows on top of the lettuce. Pour the vinaigrette over the salad and serve.

ASPIC

see also:
buffet
clarification
gelatine
stock

A clear, light, savoury jelly used in the moulding and presentation of cold foods. The type of aspic jelly used varies with the food in question and is normally made with a related clarified stock. Aspic powder, which needs only dissolving in water, can be used instead; or a substitute can be made from gelatine and commercially prepared stock or stock (bouillon) cubes. The jelly can be flavoured with port, Madeira, Marsala or sherry.

Cold cooked food, such as chicken, fish, shellfish, vegetables, foie gras, etc, is presented by setting it in a moulded and decorated aspic jelly. This can be done either in individual ramekins or in charlotte or savarin moulds. The food is served unmoulded as part of a buffet or as a cold first course. Aspic is also often cut into fine dice to use as a garnish for cold meats.

ASPIC DE LÉGUMES AUX CREVETTES

Vegetables and seafood in aspic

Serves 6–8
Preparation 30 minutes
Cooking about 12 minutes, 24 hours ahead

METRIC/IMPERIAL

450 g/1 lb new carrots, finely sliced
whites of 4–5 small leeks, finely sliced
550 g/$1\frac{1}{4}$ lb fresh green asparagus
1 l/$1\frac{3}{4}$ pt liquid aspic jelly (made from 2 sachets aspic powder and 1 l/$1\frac{3}{4}$ pt water, or 2 sachets unflavoured gelatine powder and 1 l/$1\frac{3}{4}$ pt good vegetable, fish or seafood stock)
300 g/10 oz shelled cooked prawns
salt
flat-leaved parsley, to garnish

AMERICAN

1 lb new carrots, finely sliced
whites of 4–5 small leeks, finely sliced
$1\frac{1}{4}$ lb fresh green asparagus
1 quart liquid aspic jelly, made from 3 envelopes powdered unflavored gelatine and 1 quart vegetable or fish stock
10 oz (3–4 cups) peeled cooked shrimp
salt
flat-leaf parsley, to garnish

Cook the carrots for 8 minutes in boiling salted water. Lift them from the cooking liquid and refresh them under cold running water. Cook the leeks in the same water for 3–4 minutes, remove and refresh in the same way. Trim and peel the asparagus spears and cut them into 3–4 cm/$1\frac{1}{2}$ in pieces. Boil them for 3 minutes in the same water. Drain them and refresh as before. Leave all the vegetables to cool.

Pour a thin layer of the aspic jelly into a 15 cm/6 in charlotte mould. Arrange a few parsley leaves on the layer of aspic as garnish, then arrange a layer of carrot slices on top. Pour a little of the aspic over them, then add a layer of leeks, then the prawns (shrimp) and finally the asparagus, pouring a little aspic over each layer. Cover with the remainder of the aspic.

Refrigerate overnight. Unmould on a round serving dish and serve with a herb mayonnaise. *To drink: Riesling.*

AUBERGINE OR EGGPLANT

see also:
acidulation
ratatouille

A member of the tomato family, aubergine (eggplant) is cultivated in many warm climates, especially in the South of France, Spain and Italy. These vegetables are at their best from May to November, but are available all year round. The smaller varieties are pale in colour and this, together with their shape, gave rise to the name eggplant; larger varieties tend to be deep purple to black and oval or cylindrical in shape. The latter is preferable for slicing.

The flesh discolours quickly so it is wise to use a stainless steel knife to peel and slice them and to acidulate the flesh quickly with lemon juice after cutting. Whether they are to be stewed, baked or sautéed, or served raw in salads, it is sometimes necessary to remove much of their water content and bitterness by sprinkling the peeled and sliced flesh with salt, mixing well and then leaving to drain for 30 minutes before rinsing and patting dry.

If eaten on their own as a main dish, allow 200–300 g/7–10 oz unpeeled weight per person. Aubergines marry well with tomatoes, garlic, courgettes (zucchini) and onions. They are popular in the cooking of the Mediterranean countries, especially in southern France for ratatouille, in Italy, where they are baked with Parmesan cheese, and in Greece for moussaka, as well as in the Middle East.

To bake aubergines, prick them all over and place them in a hot oven until soft, then cut them in half and remove the skin to serve.

Aubergines are low in calories (100 g/3½ oz = 29 calories) and rich in fibre and minerals. They do, however, absorb a great deal of oil during the cooking process, which can make the calorie count of a finished dish very high. Use the minimum of good olive oil when frying or brush with oil and grill (broil). Baking adds no extra calories.

CAVIAR D'AUBERGINES

Aubergine or eggplant spread

Serves 4
Preparation 20 minutes
Cooking 8 minutes, 24 hours ahead

METRIC/IMPERIAL	AMERICAN
2 aubergines	2 eggplants
2 tbsp sesame seeds	2 tbsp sesame seeds
juice of ½ lemon	juice of ½ lemon
100 ml/3½ fl oz olive oil	½ cup olive oil
1 garlic clove, peeled and crushed	1 garlic clove, peeled and minced
ground coriander, to taste	ground coriander, to taste
salt and pepper	salt and pepper
chopped hard-boiled egg, to garnish	chopped hard-boiled egg, to garnish

Wash and dry the aubergines (eggplants) and remove the stalks. Wrap them in paper towels and microwave on High for 5 minutes, turning them once. Leave to stand for 5 minutes.

Spread the sesame seeds out on a plate. Microwave them for 3 minutes, shaking the plate once.

Unwrap the aubergines (eggplants) and cut them in half. Scoop out the flesh, mix with the lemon juice and mash it thoroughly or purée it in a food processor. Trickle the oil into the purée, as if making mayonnaise, until it has all been incorporated. Add the garlic, sesame seeds and coriander to taste and season with salt and pepper. Chill in the refrigerator and serve as a dip with crudités or cold on toast, garnished with chopped, hard-boiled egg.

GRATIN D'AUBERGINES À LA TOMATE

Baked aubergines or eggplants in tomato sauce

Serves 6
Preparation 30 minutes
Cooking 40 minutes

METRIC/IMPERIAL	AMERICAN
5 medium aubergines	5 medium eggplants
3 tbsp olive oil	3 tbsp olive oil
1 kg/2¼ lb tomatoes, peeled and diced	2¼ lb tomatoes, peeled and diced
2 garlic cloves, chopped	2 garlic cloves, chopped
pinch of dried thyme	pinch of dried thyme
1 bay leaf	1 bay leaf
100 g/3½ oz grated Gruyère	½ cup grated Gruyère cheese
2 tbsp chopped flat-leaved parsley	2 tbsp chopped flat-leaf parsley
salt and pepper	salt and pepper

Preheat the oven to 220C/425F/gas 7. Peel the aubergines (eggplants) and cut in thick slices. Sprinkle them with salt and leave for 30 minutes to drain.

Rinse the slices and dry them on paper towels. Heat the oil in a frying pan over a moderate heat and fry the slices for 2½ minutes on each side, then remove them with a slotted spoon and put aside to keep warm. Cook the tomatoes and garlic in the same pan until soft, adding salt and pepper. Add the thyme and bay leaf and simmer for 20 minutes.

Pour half the tomato mixture into a baking dish. Add the aubergine (eggplant) slices and sprinkle with half of the cheese.

Pour over the remainder of the tomato mixture, then the remainder of the grated cheese and the parsley. Bake for 15 minutes and serve piping hot with Creole rice to accompany grilled (or broiled) sausages.

AUBERGINES SOUFFLÉS

Aubergine or eggplant soufflés

Serves 4
Preparation 30 minutes
Cooking 40–45 minutes

METRIC/IMPERIAL	AMERICAN
4 large firm aubergines	4 large firm eggplants
1 tbsp oil	1 tbsp oil
30 g/1 oz butter	2 tbsp butter
1 onion, finely chopped	1 onion, finely chopped
30 g/1 oz flour	3 tbsp flour
200 ml/7 fl oz milk	1 cup milk
2 eggs, separated	2 eggs, separated
2 tbsp freshly grated Parmesan	2 tbsp freshly grated Parmesan cheese
salt and pepper	salt and pepper

Preheat the oven to 200C/400F/gas 6. Wipe the aubergines (eggplants) and cut them in half lengthwise. Bake them for 10–15 minutes, then remove them and scoop out the flesh and reserve, leaving a layer about 6 mm/¼ in thick in the shells. Grease a baking dish with the oil and place the aubergine (eggplant) shells in it. Reduce the oven temperature to 180C/350F/gas 4.

Melt the butter in a large pan, then add the chopped onion and cook for 2 minutes. Add the flour and cook for a further 2 minutes, stirring constantly. Gradually add the milk, then cook for a further 10 minutes, stirring frequently. Add the aubergine (eggplant) flesh and the egg yolks. Season with salt and pepper.

Beat the egg whites to firm peaks and fold them gently into the mixture. Fill the aubergine (eggplant) shells with the mixture and sprinkle with Parmesan. Bake for 15 minutes and serve immediately.

AVOCADO OR AVOCADO PEAR

Avocat

see also:
acidulation
vinaigrette

The pear-shaped or round fruit of a tree which is a member of the laurel family, avocados are grown in many semi-tropical locations, including California and Florida, Central America and Israel. The skin varies in colour from pale green to almost black and also in density, the Ettinger variety having a thin, smooth green skin and the Hass having a thicker, more woody skin. Avocados may vary in size from the small, hardy Mexican variety developed from the wild *aguacate* to the particularly large fruit cultivated in the West Indies. The creamy green flesh when ripe has a smooth, buttery texture and a nutty flavour. Many new species have been cross-bred, including a tiny stoneless 'cornichon' or 'cocktail' avocado.

Avocados drop from the tree before they are ripe, and many are still far from ripe when they reach the shops. To test for ripeness, do not press the fruit between finger and thumb as is often suggested as this will damage the fruit; instead roll it between the palms of the hands. The flesh should yield slightly to the touch. If the skin is coarse and grainy, shake the fruit gently; if ripe, the stone should detach itself slightly from the flesh and can be heard moving. If an avocado is not quite ripe, wrap it in newspaper or a brown paper bag and keep in a warm place for a few days. Ripe avocados can be stored at the bottom of the refrigerator for 1 or 2 days.

Avocado flesh oxidizes rapidly, so cut and peel the fruit with stainless-steel knives and sprinkle cut or peeled flesh generously with lemon juice to avoid discoloration. Avocados are usually served raw sliced in salads or halved lengthwise and dressed with oil and seasonings or vinaigrette, or stuffed with seafood.

Avocados are popular in many parts of the world. They are known as 'poor man's breakfast' in the West Indies, and they form an integral part of Israeli cuisine. Perhaps their most celebrated use is puréed with chilli and other spices in the ancient Mexican dish of guacamole.

Rich in fats, avocados provide 200 calories per 100 g/$3\frac{1}{2}$ oz; with this in mind, add mayonnaise or creamy sauces sparingly. They also have the highest protein content of any fruit, are rich in vitamins A and B and contain a substance which promotes healthy skin.

AVOCATS FARCIS AU CRABE

Avocados stuffed with crab meat

Serves 4
Preparation 20 minutes, mayonnaise 10 minutes
Chilling 30 minutes

METRIC/IMPERIAL	AMERICAN
2 ripe avocados	2 ripe avocados
juice of 1 lemon	juice of 1 lemon
1 small can of crab meat, drained	1 small can of crab meat, drained
2 tbsp cooked rice	2 tbsp cooked rice
3 tbsp mayonnaise	3 tbsp mayonnaise
1 tsp tomato ketchup	1 tsp tomato ketchup
1 tsp Cognac	1 tsp Cognac

Cut the avocados in half and remove the stones. Scoop out the flesh with a small teaspoon, taking care not to damage the skins. Sprinkle the flesh with lemon juice as you go.

Mix the crab meat with the rice, adding the mayonnaise, ketchup and Cognac.

Add the scoops of avocado to the mixture and mix carefully. Fill the avocado halves with it and chill for at least 30 minutes before serving.

This dish may be garnished with prawns or shrimp, slices of lime, or a teaspoon of salmon caviar or lumpfish roe.

AVOCATS AUX FRUITS

Avocado and fruit salad

Serves 4
Preparation 20 minutes
Chilling 45 minutes

METRIC/IMPERIAL	AMERICAN
1 banana	1 banana
juice of 1 lemon	juice of 1 lemon
1 orange	1 orange
1 pear	1 pear
sugar or artificial sweetener	sugar or artificial sweetener
2 ripe avocados	2 ripe avocados

Avocats farcis au crabe (Avocados stuffed with crab meat)

Peel the banana, slice it and sprinkle the slices with lemon juice. Peel the orange whole, then slice it across thinly. Peel and finely slice the pear and sprinkle the slices with lemon juice.

Combine the fruit in a bowl and sprinkle with sugar or powdered sweetener to taste. Chill for 30 minutes.

Cut each avocado in half. Remove the stone and sprinkle the flesh with lemon juice. Fill the hollow in each avocado half with the drained fruit mixture. Pour the fruit syrup over and chill for another 15 minutes before serving.

If artificial sweetener is used, this dessert is only 150 calories per serving.

SALADE À L'AVOCAT

Avocado salad

Serves 6
Preparation 20 minutes

METRIC/IMPERIAL	AMERICAN
3 ripe avocados	3 ripe avocados
juice of 1 lemon	juice of 1 lemon
1 lettuce heart	1 lettuce heart
2 tbsp good-quality wine vinegar	2 tbsp good-quality wine vinegar
1 tbsp whisky	1 tbsp Scotch whisky
7 tbsp hazelnut oil	7 tbsp hazelnut oil
3 tomatoes, peeled and diced	3 tomatoes, peeled and diced
salt	salt
pinch of cayenne pepper	pinch of cayenne

Cut the avocados in half and remove the skin and stones. Dice the flesh and sprinkle with lemon juice. Separate the lettuce leaves.

Make a vinaigrette with the vinegar, whisky and oil. Whisk for several minutes, then season with salt and cayenne pepper to taste.

Combine the avocado, tomatoes and lettuce leaves in a salad bowl and pour the vinaigrette over them. Stir carefully and serve at room temperature.

SAUCE MEXICAINE À L'AVOCAT

Guacamole (Mexican avocado sauce)

Serves 4
Preparation 10 minutes

METRIC/IMPERIAL	AMERICAN
2 ripe avocados	2 ripe avocados
juice of 1 lime	juice of 1 lime
4 firm ripe tomatoes	4 firm ripe tomatoes
1 small red chilli pepper	1 small red chili pepper
1 shallot, finely sliced	1 shallot, finely sliced
2 tbsp finely chopped coriander leaves	2 tbsp finely chopped cilantro
150 ml/$\frac{1}{4}$ pt crème fraîche or sour cream	$\frac{2}{3}$ cup crème fraîche or sour cream
salt and pepper	salt and pepper

Cut the avocados in half, extract the stone and scoop out the flesh. Sprinkle the flesh with the lime juice.

Remove the stalk and seeds from the chilli and chop it coarsely.

Put the avocado flesh together with the lime juice, tomatoes, shallot, coriander (cilantro) and chilli in a food processor. Season with salt and pepper to taste. Blend for several seconds until the ingredients are well mixed but not too smooth.

Add the crème fraîche or cream to the purée. Taste and adjust the seasoning.

Serve with tacos or tortilla chips or an assortment of raw vegetable crudités, or use to stuff cooked mushrooms or artichoke bottoms. Alternatively, spread it on slices of cooked ham or use it as a filling for crêpes.

Note: to keep the sauce from discolouring, place the avocado stone on top of it, pour a little more lemon or lime juice over the surface and cover tightly until required.

B

see also: yeast

BABA

Babas are cakes made from yeast-leavened dough, either in the form of a large ring, known as a savarin, or as individual small cakes baked in small ring or taller, slant-sided moulds. For the smaller cakes, raisins which have been soaked in rum or Kirsch are often added to the dough.

Once baked, the cakes are steeped in a syrup flavoured with rum or Kirsch, or have several coats of it poured over them, until they are well saturated. The drier the babas, the more syrup they will absorb.

They may be decorated with crystallized (candied) fruit, such as glacé cherries and small slices of angelica cut in the shapes of leaves.

Once baked and steeped in syrup, babas may be kept for up to 24 hours, wrapped in foil. Cooked babas may be made up to 2 weeks in advance and frozen.

PÂTE À BABA

Baba dough

Makes 8 babas
Preparation 30 minutes
Standing ¾–1 hour

METRIC/IMPERIAL	*AMERICAN*
15 g/½ oz baker's yeast	*½ oz compressed fresh yeast*
125 g/4½ oz butter, cut into small pieces	*9 tbsp butter, cut into small pieces*
225 g/8 oz flour	*1⅔ cups flour*
salt	*salt*
3 eggs, beaten	*3 eggs, beaten*
25 g/¾ oz caster sugar	*2 tbsp superfine sugar*
75 g/2½ oz raisins	*½ cup raisins*
100 ml/3½ fl oz rum	*½ cup rum*

Mix the yeast with 1 tablespoon of warm water and let it stand for 10 minutes. Let the butter stand at room temperature to soften it and, if necessary, knead it with the palm of the hand (1, see overleaf).

Sift the flour and salt together into a bowl and make a well in the centre of it. Pour the beaten eggs into the well and add the sugar followed by the yeast mixture. Using the hands, mix all the ingredients together to make a smooth dough.

With lightly floured fingertips, knead the

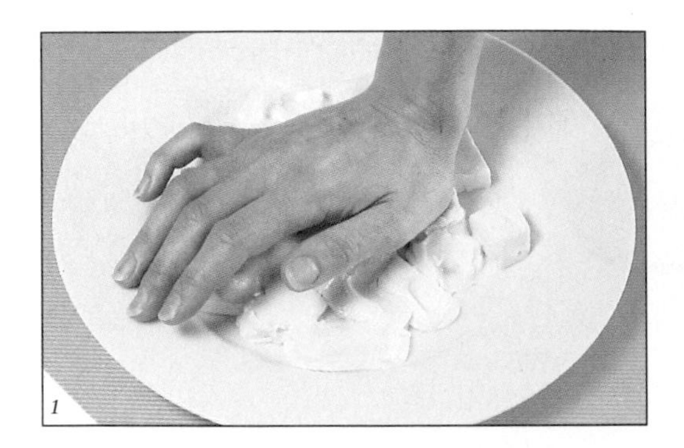

1

2

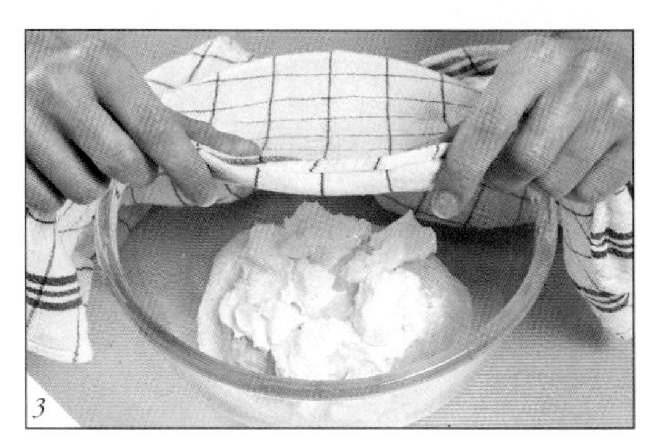

3

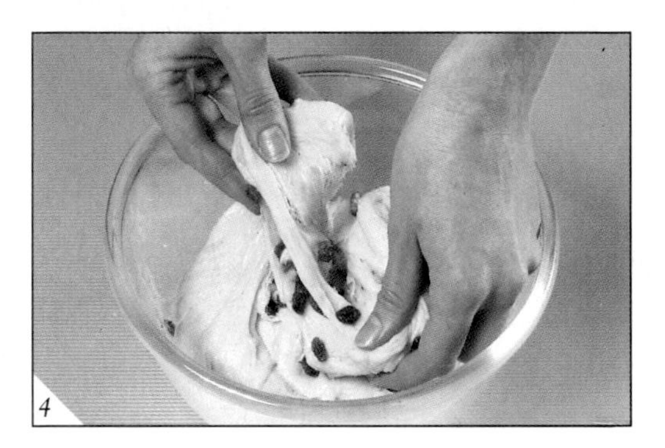

4

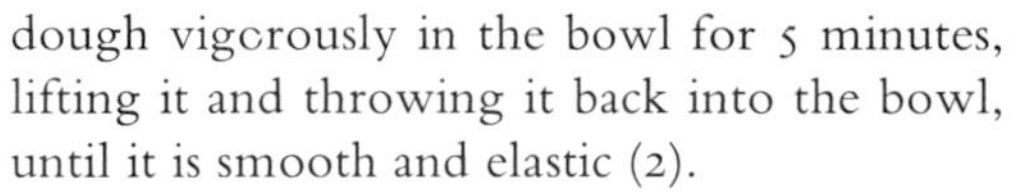

dough vigorously in the bowl for 5 minutes, lifting it and throwing it back into the bowl, until it is smooth and elastic (2).

Dot the surface of the dough with the pieces of softened butter, then cover the bowl with a damp cloth (3). Leave it to rise in a warm place for 45 minutes to 1 hour: at the end of this time the dough should have doubled in volume.

Meanwhile, soak the raisins in the rum, adding a little warm water to cover if necessary. When the dough is ready, drain the plumped-up raisins in a strainer. Knead the dough to mix in the butter until the mixture is smooth. Add the raisins and knead again to incorporate them well into the dough (4). The dough is now ready to be placed in baba moulds and cooked.

Alternatively, the softened butter and drained raisins may be kneaded in before the rising process and the dough left to rise in well-greased moulds.

PETITS BABAS AU RHUM

Rum babas

Makes 8 babas
Preparation 30 minutes, 1 hour ahead
Standing time and making syrup 1 hour
Cooking 20 minutes

METRIC/IMPERIAL	AMERICAN
Baba dough (see above)	*Baba dough (see above)*
25 g/¾ oz butter	*1½ tbsp butter*
8 glacé cherries	*8 candied cherries*
24 small candied angelica leaves	*24 small candied angelica leaves*
FOR THE RUM SYRUP:	FOR THE RUM SYRUP:
250 g/8½ oz sugar	*1¼ cups sugar*
500 ml/16 fl oz water	*2 cups water*
1 tbsp rum	*1 tbsp rum*

Prepare the baba dough, using the alternative method described (kneading in the butter and raisins before leaving the dough to rise).

Melt the butter over gentle heat and use it to grease 8 small baba or dariole moulds.

Fill each mould half full with the dough,

then leave to rise for about 1 hour, until about doubled in volume.

Meanwhile make the rum syrup: put the sugar and water in a heavy-bottomed pan, and stir over a gentle heat until all the sugar has dissolved. Then bring to the boil and continue to boil rapidly for 2–3 minutes until the syrup is clear. Flavour the syrup with the rum.

Preheat the oven to 200C/400F/gas 6.

When the dough has risen, place the moulds in the oven and bake them for 15–20 minutes until well risen and golden brown.

Remove the babas from the oven, turn them out on a wire rack and let them cool.

Bring the syrup to the boil and pour it over each baba. (Put a tray under the babas to catch excess syrup.) Repeat this process several times, reheating the syrup to boiling each time, until all the babas are well saturated.

Decorate the babas with the cherries and angelica leaves.

BACON

see also:
barding
ham
pork

The cured meat of the pig, bacon is generally sold in slices and may be either smoked or unsmoked.

In Britain slices from the belly region are known as STREAKY BACON as they are layered with fat; MIDDLE-CUT BACON is cut from the rib region and is less fatty; BACK BACON comes from the top of the animal and has a much higher meat content.

BACK BACON is also commonly rolled and sold as a piece for boiling or roasting, as is GAMMON (called HAM in America), the well-flavoured cured pork from the rump region.

AMERICAN BACON, the cured meat from the belly of the hog, has particularly soft fat which renders more readily and allows the bacon to become especially crisp.

Bacon slices are usually cooked under the grill (broiler) or fried – they are best dry fried as their fat content is so high they are soon cooking in their own fat – and commonly accompany fried or scrambled eggs for breakfast, or liver or sausages for a hearty meal.

Bacon is a useful flavouring in many dishes, such as casseroles and stews, and slices of fatty bacon are often used to bard dry poultry, such as small game birds and turkey breasts, during roasting. Pieces of chopped or crumbled crisply fried bacon make a delicious ingredient in a fresh leafy salad, particularly with spinach.

Different forms of bacon are produced in other countries: German *speck* is often eaten raw as a snack, and Italian *panchetta* and *guanciale* are common ingredients in pasta sauces.

As well as having a very high fat and salt content, bacon is very high in calories.

FOIE DE VEAU AU BACON

Calves' liver and bacon

Serves 4
Preparation 5 minutes
Cooking 5 minutes

METRIC/IMPERIAL	*AMERICAN*
4 slices of calves' liver	*4 slices of calves' liver*
flour	*flour*
8 thin slices of middle-cut bacon	*8 slices of bacon*
8 slices of lemon	*8 slices of lemon*
1 tbsp white wine vinegar or lemon juice	*1 tbsp white wine vinegar or lemon juice*
salt and pepper	*salt and pepper*

Season the slices of liver with salt and pepper and dust them lightly with flour.

Dry fry the bacon in a frying pan until just brown and crisp. Remove the bacon slices from the pan and drain them on paper towels.

In the bacon fat in the pan, cook the slices of liver briskly over a high heat for 1–2 minutes on each side, depending on size and thickness and how well cooked the liver is to be. It is unwise to overcook liver, as it quickly becomes very tough.

Arrange the cooked liver on a warmed serving dish and garnish it with the bacon and the slices of lemon.

Pour off excess fat from the frying pan, then add the vinegar or lemon juice to the pan and stir with a wooden spoon over a high heat for about a minute to deglaze the pan. Pour the cooking juices over the liver and serve.

To drink: red wine, such as Saumur-Champigny.

see also:
baking
creams and custards
pâté
sauce
terrine

BAIN-MARIE

A term used to describe a variety of utensils filled with hot water and used either to keep sauces and soups warm or to facilitate long, slow cooking, particularly in the oven, for dishes such as custards, pâtés and terrines). Because the food to be cooked is not in direct contact with the source of heat, this is a particularly gentle method. There are specially made utensils for the purpose, but a baking pan or gratin dish half-filled with boiling water will normally serve as well.

see also:
bain-marie
baking blind
baking pan
baking powder
baking sheet
bread
cakes and gâteaux
creams and custards
pastry
pâté
roasting
soufflé
terrine

BAKING

The term baking generally applies to any form of cooking which takes place in the oven. Unlike roasting, which is normally done at fairly high temperatures to produce an effect similar to that of more traditional open-fire and spit-roasting, baking usually takes place at more moderate or even fairly low oven temperatures.

The secret of good baking, especially in the making of cakes, pastries and soufflés, is usually the steady application of heat. Items to be baked, such as whole hams or other pieces of meat or poultry or pâtés, are often sealed in covered containers to help in this process and keep the moisture in.

Delicate items such as eggs and custards are usually baked in a bain-marie or bath of hot water, which protects them even further from the effects of over-heating.

OEUFS EN COCOTTE À LA CRÈME

Baked eggs in cream

Serves 4
Preparation 5 minutes
Cooking 3–5 minutes

METRIC/IMPERIAL	AMERICAN
30 g/1 oz butter	*2 tbsp butter*
4 tbsp crème fraîche or whipping cream	*4 tbsp crème fraîche or whipping cream*
4 eggs	*4 eggs*
salt and pepper	*salt and pepper*

Preheat the oven to 220C/425F/gas 7 and use the butter to grease 4 ramekins or small ovenproof porcelain moulds.

Divide half the cream among the 4 moulds, then break an egg into each. Season with salt and pepper and cover with the remaining cream.

Put the ramekins into a deep ovenproof dish and pour boiling water into it to reach half-way up the sides of the moulds.

Bake in the hot oven for 3–5 minutes, according to how well cooked the eggs are to be. Take the ramekins out of the bain-marie, wipe them dry and put them on a serving plate. Serve with buttered toast for breakfast, as a snack or as a simple first course.

Note: try adding 2 tablespoons of grated cheese, a little tomato sauce or some chopped ham or mushrooms to the cream.

JAMBON GLACÉ

Baked ham

Serves 8
Preparation 15 minutes, 6 hours ahead
Cooking 1¾ hours

METRIC/IMPERIAL	AMERICAN
1.8 kg/4 lb piece ready-to-cook boneless ham	*4 lb ready-to-cook boneless ham*
6 black peppercorns	*6 black peppercorns*
1 or 2 bay leaves	*1 or 2 bay leaves*
whole cloves	*whole cloves*
2 tbsp white wine or cider vinegar	*2 tbsp white wine or cider vinegar*
1 tbsp clear honey	*1 tbsp clear honey*
½ tsp mustard powder	*½ tsp dry mustard*
100 g/3½ oz light brown sugar	*½ cup packed light brown sugar*
watercress or parsley, to garnish	*watercress or parsley, to garnish*

Put the ham in a large pan with cold water to cover. Add the peppercorns and bay leaves, bring to the boil and simmer very gently for about 1¼ hours. Drain the ham and leave until it is cool enough to handle.

Preheat the oven to 220C/425F/gas 7. Strip off the skin and score the fat in two sets of close parallels to form a lattice pattern of diamond shapes. Stud the ham with the cloves, inserting one into each of the scoring intersections.

Heat the vinegar, honey and mustard in a pan and brush this mixture liberally over the fat. Immediately sprinkle the ham generously with the sugar and press it well into the fat.

Put in a roasting pan and bake uncovered in the oven for about 30 minutes until the glaze has caramelized and is golden brown.

Note: some ready-to-cook hams may still require soaking in cold water for several hours before cooking; ask the butcher or read the label carefully.

BAKING BLIND

see also:
barquette
flan
pastry
pie
tart

A term used to describe the practice of baking pastry cases empty before any filling is added. The base of the case is initially weighted down to prevent it from rising and distorting the shape of the pastry container.

This process is usually necessary when a creamy, or very liquid, mixture is to be poured into the pastry case, for example with a quiche, as this would keep the pastry base too moist and prevent it from cooking at the same rate as the rest of the pie or tart.

The procedure is also used when the pie or tart filling does not require any cooking, or is too delicate to be cooked at temperatures sufficiently high to cook the pastry.

Line a well-chilled pastry case with parchment or greaseproof paper and weight it down with a layer of dried beans, rice or special baking weights. Bake in a preheated moderately hot oven (200C/400F/gas 6) for 15–20 minutes until the sides of the pastry are crisp and set. Remove from the oven and carefully lift off the paper along with its contents. The beans or rice may be cooled and stored for re-use.

The procedure is also used when the pie or tart filling does not require any cooking, or is too delicate to be cooked at temperatures sufficiently high to cook the pastry.

BAKING PAN OR ROASTING PAN

see also:
bain-marie
baking
roasting

This kitchen essential, usually made from aluminium or another light alloy, is used to cook food in the oven. Normally rectangular with high sides, it may be used open for roasting or covered for baking. The open versions usually come with a wire rack insert which keeps food clear of the juices in the bottom of the pan.

If possible, it is wise to have pans of assorted sizes to match the food being cooked, otherwise the pan gets too crowded or cooking juices are spread too thinly and may be scorched.

BAKING POWDER

see also:
bread
brioche
cakes and gâteaux
pastry
yeast

A proprietary mixture of acid and alkali powders, usually a combination of bicarbonate of soda (baking soda) and cream of tartar, often with a little added flour or starch to improve keeping qualities, it is sold in small cans or sachets for use as a raising (leavening) agent in domestic cooking, particularly in cakes. The

Using oven gloves or a cloth, lift off the tart ring and return the pastry case to the oven. Continue baking for 5 minutes to crisp and brown the base. If using a loose-bottomed tart pan, place on a small inverted bowl and the outer ring will drop. Return the pastry case to the oven on the bottom of the tart pan and continue baking as above.

chemicals, when exposed to moisture and heated, give off carbon dioxide which aerates and lightens the mixture.

Generally, the richer the mixture the less baking powder is required. It is wise to use exactly the amount required in a recipe, as a slight variation can have significant effects.

see also:
baking
cookies, etc
flan
tart

BAKING SHEET

A large, flat, rectangular metal sheet, often with a slightly raised edge or lip along one side or all around for easier handling, it is used to bake small items such as biscuits, cookies or scones. It may also be called a cookie sheet. Baking sheets are sometimes used in combination with flan rings and frames for cooking tarts and flans.

It is wise to buy a baking sheet just large enough to fit the oven, leaving a 2.5 cm/1 in space around the sides to facilitate the circulation of air. Those made of heavy-gauge metal do not warp at high temperatures and also conduct the heat evenly.

see also:
boning
chicken
galantine
turkey

BALLOTTINE

This dish is usually made from a boned bird stuffed with a rich mixture, wrapped in its own skin, tied with string, then cooked in stock. It may be served hot or cold, coated with aspic.

Ballottines can also be made using stuffed meat or whole fish. These are usually wrapped in muslin or cheesecloth before cooking to retain their shape.

BALLOTTINE DE DINDE

Boned stuffed turkey

Serves 8
Preparation 1½ hours
Cooking about 2 hours, 24 hours ahead

METRIC/IMPERIAL	AMERICAN
1 small turkey, weighing about 2 kg/4½ lb	*1 small turkey, weighing about 4½ lb*
2 leeks, thinly sliced	*2 leeks, thinly sliced*
1 carrot, coarsely chopped	*1 carrot, coarsely chopped*
225 g/8 oz cooked ham	*8 oz cooked ham*
200 g/7 oz pork belly fat	*7 oz pork fatback*
225 g/8 oz lean boneless veal	*8 oz lean boneless veal*
200 g/7 oz pork sausage meat	*7 oz pork sausage meat*
1 truffle	*1 truffle*
450 g/1 lb calves' liver, cut into 2 or 3 slices	*1 lb calves' liver, cut into 2 or 3 slices*
300 g/10 oz fresh foie gras, sliced	*10 oz fresh foie gras, sliced*
coarse salt	*coarse salt*
20 whole black peppercorns	*20 whole black peppercorns*

Ask the butcher to bone the turkey without damaging the skin, and ask for the giblets.

Put the giblets in a large pan with the chopped leeks, carrot, 1½ tablespoons coarse salt and the peppercorns. Add 2.5 l/4 pt/2½ qt of water, bring to the boil and simmer for 1½ hours, then leave to cool.

Meanwhile, chop together the ham, pork fat, veal and sausage meat. Clean and peel the truffle and add the truffle peelings to the above mixture. Season with salt and pepper.

Place the boned turkey on a board, skin side down. Spread the stuffing mixture on it, then place the slices of calves' liver on top of that, followed by the slices of foie gras and the truffle cut into very thin strips.

Roll up the turkey skin, pulling gently on the edges to make the ends meet, and sew it up tightly. Wrap it in a cloth to make a neat, evenly shaped package and tie it tightly with string. Weigh the ballottine in order to calculate the cooking time.

Place it in a large saucepan and pour the strained stock over it. Add a little water, if necessary, to cover. Bring slowly to the boil and then simmer gently, allowing 20 minutes' cooking time per 450 g/1 lb. Drain the ballottine and leave it to cool.

Chill the ballottine in the refrigerator without unwrapping it. Do not untie the cloth until it is quite cold. Then remove the string, unwrap it and cut it into slices to serve.

To drink: a good red wine, such as Châteauneuf-du-Pape.

BAMBOO SHOOT

Pousse de bambou

The tender, edible shoots of an oriental plant of the grass family, bamboo shoots are usually only available in the West dried, pickled or canned in either brine or vinegar.

Dried shoots require lengthy soaking and cooking, but the canned variety is ready for use after being rinsed in cold water and drained.

Bamboo shoots are best boiled, braised, sautéed or treated like raw vegetables, and they work well in stews. Their crisp texture and slightly tart flavour make them a good accompaniment to chicken, pork or oily fish.

SALADE AUX POUSSES DE BAMBOU

Bamboo shoot and smoked chicken salad

Serves 4
Preparation 30 minutes
Cooking 5 minutes

METRIC/IMPERIAL	*AMERICAN*
85 g/3 oz dried black mushrooms	*3 oz dried black mushrooms*
1 can (800 g/1¾ lb) bamboo shoots in brine, drained	*1 can (1¾ lb) bamboo shoots in brine, drained*
300–400 g/10–14 oz smoked chicken breasts (about 2), cut into thin strips	*10–14 oz smoked chicken breast, cut into thin strips*
3 tbsp sesame oil	*3 tbsp oriental sesame oil*
1 tbsp sherry vinegar	*1 tbsp sherry vinegar*
½ lemon	*½ lemon*
115 g/4 oz shelled cooked prawns	*4 oz peeled cooked shrimp*
salt and pepper	*salt and pepper*

Soak the black mushrooms for 20 minutes in warm water. Put the bamboo shoots in a pan, cover them with water and bring it to the boil. Boil for 5 minutes, then drain the bamboo shoots and refresh them in cold water.

Make a vinaigrette with the sesame oil, sherry vinegar and lemon juice and season with salt and pepper.

Drain the mushrooms and pat them dry on paper towels. Combine the chicken, prawns (shrimp), mushrooms and bamboo shoots in a salad bowl. Pour the dressing over them and mix gently until the ingredients are all well coated. Serve at room temperature.

To drink: Chinese beer.

BANANA

Banane

see also: fruit

This tropical fruit grows in clusters on a tree-like shrub in many frost-free climates and is available throughout the year. The principal centres of production are in Africa and in Central America and the Caribbean, where bananas were first taken by Portuguese settlers who had brought them from West Africa.

The tasty, creamy-white flesh is protected by a thick skin which is very easy to peel off. There are several different types of banana. The small, pink-skinned variety is popular in India and other growing areas; the longer and thinner yellow type is the one most commonly exported to temperate climates. The green-skinned PLANTAIN banana, which has a tougher pinkish flesh, is cooked like a vegetable.

Bananas will continue to ripen off the tree, although those ripened in the sun are far tastier. Choose fruit which are uniform in size and without blemishes. They should feel heavy in the hand. If they are to be kept for three or more days, select fruit which is still slightly green. The best quality bananas often have some black spots.

Bananas should never be kept in the refrigerator as the flesh begins to deteriorate at temperatures below 5C/41F, and the skin discolours very rapidly. Once peeled, banana flesh oxidizes very quickly and should be sprinkled with lemon juice to prevent discoloration.

A popular snack and breakfast fruit, sweet bananas are also a common ingredient in many sweet dishes, particularly with ice cream and cream. They may be baked in their skins or sliced and grilled (broiled), sautéed or fried in batter.

Plantains, which are always cooked before being eaten, may be mashed, fried, or used in stews. They may also be boiled in their skins for 30 minutes. Sweet bananas which are slightly

under-ripe can also be served as vegetables.

Dried bananas, available whole as 'fig' bananas, or sliced in packets, may be used to complement winter salads.

Banana leaves find good use in tropical cuisine. Many Caribbean dishes involve wrapping food in them before cooking; this keeps the food moist and the leaves also impart their own subtle flavour to the finished dish. For open-air and special-occasion cooking, and in poorer regions, banana leaves also often serve as plates.

Bananas have a very high food value, are full of vitamins, especially A, B6, C and K, as well as minerals, particularly potassium. They are very high in energy, 91 calories per 100 g/3½ oz, mainly because they have one of the highest sugar contents of all fruit. Dried bananas are even more concentrated and are thus a popular snack for athletes.

BANANES ANTILLAISES

Caribbean flamed bananas

Serves 6
Preparation 10 minutes
Cooking 20 minutes

METRIC/IMPERIAL	AMERICAN
6 bananas	6 bananas
55 g/2 oz raisins	⅓ cup raisins
55 g/2 oz caster sugar	¼ cup superfine sugar
1 sachet (7.5 g/1¾ tsp) of vanilla-flavoured sugar	1¾ tsp vanilla-flavored sugar
55 g/2 oz butter	4 tbsp butter
juice of 2 oranges	juice of 2 oranges
100 ml/3½ fl oz rum	½ cup rum

Preheat the oven to 230C/450F/gas 8.

Peel the bananas, rinse the raisins, and mix together the two sugars.

Put a serving dish to warm in the hot oven. Heat the butter in a frying pan and fry the bananas over a low to moderate heat for 4–5 minutes on each side until golden.

Add the sugar, orange juice and raisins to the pan. Bring to the boil, then add half the rum and simmer for a further 5 minutes.

Put the contents of the frying pan into the heated serving dish. Heat the remaining rum in a ladle, pour the hot rum over the contents of the serving dish and flame it. Serve at once.

POULET AUX BANANES

Chicken with plantain bananas

Serves 4
Preparation 15 minutes
Cooking 40 minutes

METRIC/IMPERIAL	AMERICAN
1 bay leaf	1 bay leaf
5–6 fresh sage leaves	5–6 fresh sage leaves
1 large onion, sliced	1 large onion, sliced
1 chicken, 1.5 kg/3½ lb dressed weight, cut into pieces	1 chicken, 3½ lb dressed and drawn weight, cut into pieces
3 tomatoes, peeled and diced	3 tomatoes, peeled and diced
2 cloves	2 cloves
½ tsp ground nutmeg	½ tsp ground nutmeg
½ tsp cayenne pepper	½ tsp cayenne pepper
6 plantain bananas	6 plantains
1 tsp cornflour	1 tsp cornstarch
juice of ½ lime	juice of ½ lime
groundnut oil, for frying	peanut oil, for frying
salt and pepper	salt and pepper

Pour 1.5 l/2½ pt/1½ qt of water into a large pan and add the bay and sage leaves and the onion. Bring to the boil.

Put the chicken pieces into the stock, bring to the boil again and simmer for 10 minutes. Season with salt and pepper.

Heat a little oil in a frying pan. Drain the chicken pieces, reserving the stock, dry them on paper towels and brown them in the frying pan.

Put the browned chicken pieces in a flameproof casserole dish and add the tomatoes, 200 ml/7 fl oz/1 cup of the reserved stock, the cloves and several pinches of nutmeg and cayenne pepper. Cover, bring to the boil and then simmer gently for 15 minutes.

Peel the plantain bananas and slice them thickly. Add these to the casserole and cook for a further 15 minutes. Mix the cornflour (cornstarch) with the lime juice and add this mixture to the casserole, stirring it until well mixed and slightly thickened. Serve hot, with Creole rice.

To drink: a light sparkling white wine, such as Saumar Mousseux.

BARBECUING

see also:
butter
grilling
kebab
sauce

A means of cooking food by grilling it over hot charcoal, barbecuing traditionally takes place out of doors.

Various types of barbecue grills have developed. The most common simply consists of a wire grill to hold the food just over the burning charcoal. Others have a dome top to enclose the food completely and thus facilitate the cooking of large pieces of meat and whole birds. They also keep the food very moist and succulent. Some more elaborate devices incorporate electric starters and spit rôtisseries. Nowadays gas flame barbecues are also widely available.

For good results it is important to ensure that the coals are hot enough before cooking begins; they should be grey edged with gently glowing centres. All the food should be evenly set out over the coals.

A hinged grill basket is convenient for cooking small items as they can all be turned at once.

To prevent drying out during cooking, it is advisable to moisten most foods with olive oil or butter before cooking, and delicate items like fish and some vegetables are best cooked wrapped in foil. Barbecued meat and poultry is often marinated or coated with a thick sauce first to give a protective crust. All the sauces used with grilled (broiled) food also work well with barbecued food.

BARDING

see also:
bacon
game
larding
pork
poultry
roasting

This practice protects roasts of meat or poultry, or even occasionally fish, from drying out in the heat of the oven during roasting by placing thin slices of pork belly fat or back fat or fatty bacon over them. Fatty meats, such as pork and lamb, are rarely barded. Care must be taken, when cooking an item with delicate flavours, to ensure that the taste of the barding fat does not mask or overpower it.

The bards are usually tied with string around roasts, paupiettes and tournedos (filet mignons). These should be removed before serving, although game birds are normally served with the bards left on.

Having served their purpose, bards should be left on the side of the plate by those concerned with a healthy diet.

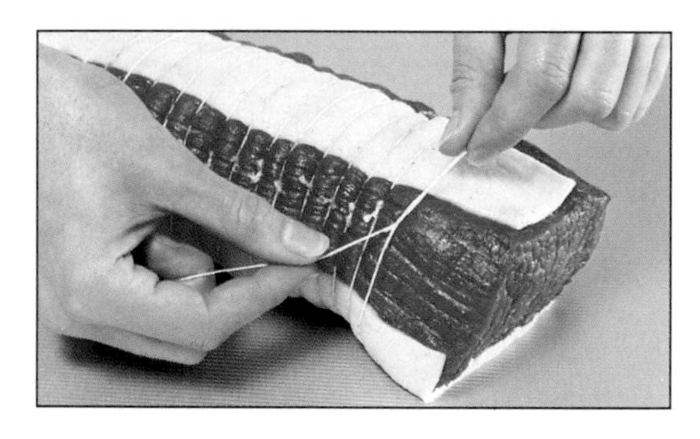

Use long strips of fat to partially wrap large roasts, and tie at regular intervals.

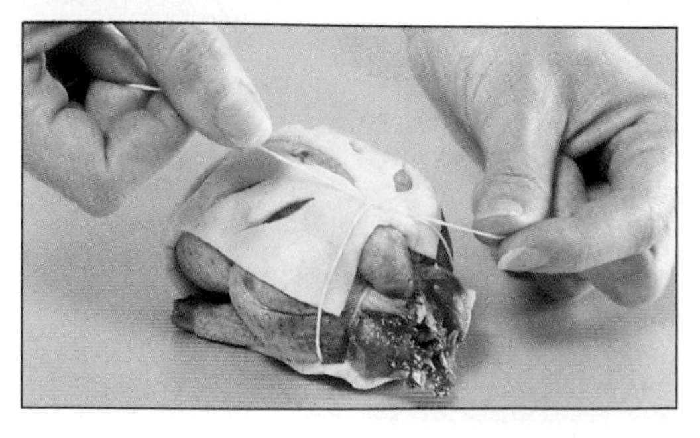

For larger poultry cover only the breast meat, but small birds need to be wrapped.

BARLEY

Orge

see also:
cereal

A cereal grain which was one of man's earliest staples, barley has little gluten so it cannot be leavened like wheat flour. It is now used principally in the manufacture of beer and whisky and as an animal foodstuff.

The main culinary use of barley is as PEARL BARLEY, which is the grain after it has been milled to remove the husk. It is common in stews and soups, especially classic Scotch broth, and its fine flavour combines well with cream.

Barley water with added sugar and lemon juice is a summer drink still popular in Britain.

Pearl barley contains 360 calories per 100 g/3½ oz uncooked weight.

CRÈME D'ORGE

Cream of barley soup

Serves 5
Preparation 10 minutes, soaking time 1 hour
Cooking 1½ hours

METRIC/IMPERIAL	*AMERICAN*
300 g/10 oz pearl barley	*1½ cups pearl barley*
2 stalks of celery, trimmed and thinly sliced	*2 sticks of celery, trimmed and thinly sliced*
1 l/1¾ pt chicken stock	*1 qt chicken stock*
100 ml/3½ fl oz milk	*½ cup milk*
200 ml/7 fl oz whipping cream	*1 cup whipping cream*
½ tsp celery salt	*½ tsp celery salt*
white pepper	*white pepper*

Rinse the pearl barley and put it into a bowl. Pour 1 l/1¾ pt/1 qt of warm water over it and leave it to soak for 1 hour.

Pour the chicken stock into a saucepan and

add the celery. Drain the barley and add it. Bring to the boil and then simmer gently, covered, for $1\frac{1}{4}$ hours.

Pour the contents of the saucepan through a fine sieve into a clean pan, rubbing as much of the solids through the sieve as possible. Add the milk to the pan and stir to mix. Set the pan over a low heat and add the cream.

Heat gently, stirring constantly. Add the celery salt and several pinches of pepper to taste. Serve very hot.

BARQUETTE

see also:
baking blind
canapé
pastry

Small, boat-shaped tarts made of shortcrust (pie) pastry, or occasionally puff pastry, baked blind in specially shaped moulds, barquettes may be filled with a variety of sweet or savoury ingredients.

Barquette cases can be prepared ahead of time, kept in a dry place and filled at the last moment to retain their crispness.

BARQUETTES AUX CREVETTES

Shrimp or prawn barquettes

Makes 12
Preparation 20 minutes, pastry 30 minutes
Cooking 10 minutes

METRIC/IMPERIAL	AMERICAN
200 g/7 oz shortcrust pastry	7 oz basic pie pastry
1 large avocado	1 large avocado
juice of $\frac{1}{2}$ lemon	juice of $\frac{1}{2}$ lemon
6 tbsp mayonnaise	6 tbsp mayonnaise
24 shelled cooked prawns	24 peeled cooked shrimp
cayenne pepper	cayenne pepper
salt and pepper	salt and pepper

Preheat the oven to 180C/350F/gas 4.

Roll out the pastry to a thickness of 6 mm/$\frac{1}{4}$ in and use to line 12 barquette moulds, each about 10 cm/4 in long. Prick the bottoms of the pastry cases with a fork and bake them blind for 10 minutes.

Remove the cooked barquette cases from the oven, take them out of the moulds and leave them to cool on a wire rack.

Meanwhile, cut the avocado in half. Remove the flesh and mash it with a fork, or purée it in a food processor, with the lemon juice. Season with salt, pepper and cayenne to taste. Add the mayonnaise and mix well.

Fill the barquette cases with this mixture and smooth the surface. Place the prawns (shrimp) on top. Serve well chilled.

Note: instead of the avocado purée, try using a purée of fresh mushrooms seasoned with lemon juice and chopped chives.

BARQUETTES AUX MARRONS

Chestnut cream barquettes

Makes 12
Preparation 15 minutes, pastry 30 minutes
Cooking 10 minutes

METRIC/IMPERIAL	AMERICAN
12 barquette cases (see left)	12 barquette cases (see left)
175 g/$6\frac{1}{2}$ oz canned chestnut cream (sweetened chestnut purée)	$6\frac{1}{2}$ oz canned chestnut cream (crème de marrons)
3 tbsp chopped marrons glacés	3 tbsp chopped candied chestnuts (marrons glacés)
24 crystallized violets	24 crystallized violets
whipped cream, to decorate (optional)	whipped cream, to decorate (optional)

Fill the cooked and cooled barquette cases with the chestnut cream and smooth the surface.

Sprinkle the chopped *marrons glacés* on the top and garnish with crystallized violets.

Decorate with rosettes of stiffly whipped cream, if desired.

BASIL

Basilic

see also:
herbs
pasta
sauce

There are several varieties of this highly aromatic plant with white flowers and deep green leaves, the most common being sweet basil. The leaves vary considerably in size, from very tiny to the size of the palm of the hand. Generally speaking, the smaller the leaf the better the flavour. The plant is distinguished by its slightly spicy, pungent aroma and flavour.

Originally from India, basil has been grown and used in Mediterranean countries for many hundreds of years. Much of it is grown there under glass in very humid conditions – particularly in Italy – where this produces the most tender and aromatic leaves.

Basil has long been regarded as the perfect accompaniment to tomatoes and other vegetable fruits. It is much favoured by the Italians in sauces to accompany fresh pasta, particularly with pine kernels (pine nuts) in the classic Ligurian *pesto* sauce. The famous French *soupe au pistou* also derives most of its character from a last-minute addition of a mixture of oil, garlic and basil pounded together.

Basil is at its best when used fresh, although there are good dried varieties (but the flavour is very different) and the leaves freeze well. Basil leaves are often also preserved in olive oil which may then be used to impart a wonderful flavour to salad dressings. It is an easy herb to grow indoors, and many fine food stores and supermarkets now sell small pots of the growing herb. Snip leaves from the top of the stem.

large leaf basil

red or purple basil

small leaf basil

PESTO AU BASILIC

Basil pesto sauce

Serves 4
Preparation 20 minutes

METRIC/IMPERIAL	AMERICAN
225 g/8 oz sprigs of fresh basil, preferably small-leaved	8 oz (about 4 cups) sprigs of fresh basil, preferably small-leaved
1 tbsp grated Pecorino	1 tbsp grated Romano cheese
2 tbsp grated Parmesan	2 tbsp grated Parmesan cheese
2 large garlic cloves, finely chopped	2 large garlic cloves, minced
100 ml/3½ fl oz olive oil	½ cup olive oil
1 tbsp crushed pine kernels	1 tbsp crushed pine nuts
salt and pepper	salt and pepper

Carefully detach the basil leaves from their stems, tear them coarsely and then crush them in a mortar or blend them briefly in a food processor. Put the basil in a bowl. Add the grated cheeses and garlic and mix well.

Add the oil to the contents of the bowl in a thin stream, whisking constantly until it has all been incorporated. Season lightly with salt and pepper.

Add the pine kernels (pine nuts) to the mixture and blend once more in the food processor until the sauce is smooth and creamy.

Serve as a topping to vegetable soup or as a sauce for fresh or dried pasta.

Notes: a small piece of butter mixed in with the pine kernels (pine nuts) will give the sauce an extra smooth creaminess.

Pesto freezes very successfully and will keep for several months.

see also:
fish

BASS

Bar

There are many freshwater species of bass, particularly in the USA, but the sea bass are the most gastronomically important.

These marine fish are found in the Mediterranean and in the Atlantic. The BLACK SEA BASS of the American northeast coast and the STRIPED BASS or ROCKFISH of both Atlantic seaboards – which can weigh anything from 10 kg/22 lb to 50 kg/110 lb – are both important, as is the SPECKLED BASS fished off the North African coast.

However, the prize specimen for taste and texture is the COMMON BASS fished in the Mediterranean and the European Atlantic coast as far north as the English Channel. Referred to by Provençal fishermen as *loup* or wolf because of its ferocity when caught, it is a voracious predator and can vary in length from 35–80 cm/14–32 in. Its flesh has a fine subtle flavour, and is dense and compact with few bones.

Common bass is relatively rare and correspondingly expensive. It is at its most plentiful in the months from January to May and in September and October.

Bass is a lean fish (3% fat) and is best poached, baked, braised or grilled (broiled). Smaller specimens may be fried. Allow 300 g/10½ oz of bass per person: to serve 4 people, select a fish at least 1 kg/2¼ lb in weight.

The fish should be cleaned through the gills and gutted via a small incision in the belly. It is best not to remove the scales if the fish is to be poached or baked as they keep the fragile flesh succulent and prevent it from disintegrating during cooking. Scale the fish if frying or grilling (broiling), but do so gently to avoid tearing the skin. Bass is also sold as steaks or fillets.

In France a favourite means of cooking bass is by barbecuing them whole, with some fennel leaves and other aromatic herbs sprinkled on the charcoal.

Steamed bass contains 127 calories per 100 g/3½ oz.

TRANCHES DE BAR À LA NORMANDE

Normandy-style bass steaks (with cider)

Serves 4
Preparation 20 minutes
Cooking about 25 minutes

METRIC/IMPERIAL	AMERICAN
1 carrot, finely sliced	*1 carrot, finely sliced*
1 onion, finely sliced	*1 onion, finely sliced*
1 stalk of celery, finely chopped	*1 stick of celery, finely chopped*
bouquet garni	*bouquet garni*
4 thick bass steaks	*4 thick bass steaks*
200 ml/7 fl oz fish stock	*1 cup fish stock*
200 ml/7 fl oz dry cider	*1 cup hard cider*
100 ml/3½ fl oz crème fraîche or whipping cream	*½ cup crème fraîche or whipping cream*
1 tsp lemon juice	*1 tsp lemon juice*
25 g/¾ oz slightly salted butter	*1½ tbsp lightly salted butter*
1 tbsp flour	*1 tbsp flour*
salt and pepper	*salt and pepper*

Mix the chopped vegetables together and put them in a layer on the bottom of a large pan along with the bouquet garni. Place the bass on top and then pour the fish stock and cider over the fish. Season with salt and pepper to taste.

Put the pan, uncovered, over a moderate heat until it just reaches boiling point, then cover and simmer very gently for approximately 20 minutes. Drain the bass steaks, put them on a warmed serving plate and keep warm.

Strain the cooking juices into a small saucepan. Bring them to the boil over a high heat and continue to boil until they are reduced by about half. Stir in the cream, add the lemon juice and continue to cook, stirring, until the sauce thickens.

Beat the butter and flour together in a bowl, then add this mixture to the sauce in small amounts, whisking constantly.

When the sauce is smooth, adjust the seasoning to taste and pour it over the steaks of bass to serve.

BAR GRILLÉ À LA COMPOTE DE TOMATES

Grilled bass with tomatoes

Serves 4
Preparation 20 minutes
Cooking about 30 minutes

METRIC/IMPERIAL	AMERICAN
1 whole bass, weighing about 1 kg/2¼ lb, cleaned and gutted but with the scales intact	1 whole bass, weighing about 2¼ lb, drawn but with the scales intact
3 tbsp olive oil	3 tbsp olive oil
1 kg/2¼ lb tomatoes, peeled and quartered	2¼ lb tomatoes, peeled and quartered
1 tbsp fennel seeds	1 tbsp fennel seeds
dried fennel (optional)	dried fennel (optional)
salt and pepper	salt and pepper

Make a few shallow incisions just through the skin on each side of the fish. Prepare the barbecue coals if using, or preheat the grill (broiler).

Brush the fish all over with oil, then season with salt and pepper. Place it in a double-faced grilling holder (fish grill), if barbecuing.

Heat the oil in a sauté pan, add the fennel seeds and stir over a medium heat.

Add the tomatoes and cook, uncovered, for 30 minutes over a moderate heat. Season with salt and pepper.

About 20 minutes before serving, start to cook the bass, turning it over half-way through cooking. It is cooked when the scales and skin come away easily. If barbecuing, throw a handful of dried fennel leaves on the barbecue coals before cooking.

Serve the bass with the tomato compote as an accompaniment.

BAR POCHÉ CHAUD

Hot poached bass

Serves 6
Preparation 15 minutes
Cooking 12–15 minutes

METRIC/IMPERIAL	AMERICAN
2 whole bass, each weighing about 800 g/1¾ lb, cleaned and gutted but with the scales intact	2 whole bass, each weighing about 1¾ lb, drawn but with the scales intact
bouquet garni	bouquet garni
bunch of parsley, to garnish	bunch of parsley, to garnish
salt	salt

Fill a fish kettle or large oval pan with cold water. Add 10 g/¼ oz/2 tsp of salt per 1 l/1¾ pt/1 qt of water and the bouquet garni.

Put the fish into the water, cover the pan, place it over a moderate heat and bring to the boil. As soon as the water boils, reduce the heat and poach the fish gently for 8–10 minutes.

Drain the bass and put them on a rack over a serving dish. Garnish the fish with sprigs of parsley and serve melted lemon butter or hollandaise sauce as accompaniments, along with plain boiled potatoes and braised fennel.

Bar grillé à la compote de tomates (Grilled bass with tomatoes)

BASTING

The practice of regularly moistening the surface of food with its own cooking juices and/or added butter, oil or marinade during cooking – usually roasting, grilling (broiling) or barbecuing – prevents the surface and exposed parts of the meat, poultry or fish from drying out. It also aids browning and adds flavour.

see also: baking, baking pan, grilling, roasting

BAVARIAN CREAM

Bavarois

This chilled, moulded dessert made from egg custard is stiffened with gelatine and often mixed with a fruit purée or other flavourings, such as vanilla, coffee or praline. It should be prepared well ahead, preferably the day before,

see also: creams and custards

and left in the refrigerator until ready to serve.

Some very striking *bavarois* are made of multiple layers, usually starting and finishing with a layer of the basic Bavarian cream with layers of set fruit purées, or Bavarian cream and fruit purée mixtures, in between.

BAVAROIS AU CASSIS

Blackcurrant Bavarian cream

Serves 8
Preparation 30 minutes, 24 hours ahead
Cooking 5–10 minutes

METRIC/IMPERIAL	*AMERICAN*
700 g/$1\frac{2}{3}$ lb blackcurrants	*$5\frac{1}{2}$ cups blackcurrants*
5 gelatine leaves or $2\frac{1}{2}$ tsp unflavoured gelatine powder	*5 gelatine leaves or $2\frac{1}{2}$ tsp powdered unflavored gelatine*
250 g/$8\frac{1}{2}$ oz caster sugar	*$1\frac{1}{4}$ cups superfine sugar*
500 ml/16 fl oz crème fraîche or double cream	*2 cups crème fraîche or whipping cream*
55 g/2 oz icing sugar	*$\frac{1}{2}$ cup confectioners' sugar*
15 g/$\frac{1}{2}$ oz butter	*1 tbsp butter*

Purée the blackcurrants using a food mill or food processor. There should be about 200 ml/7 fl oz/1 cup of fruit purée.

Soften the gelatine leaves in a bowl of cold water, or if using powdered gelatine, soften in just 2 tablespoons of water. Put the caster (superfine) sugar into a saucepan with 100 ml/$3\frac{1}{2}$ fl oz/$\frac{1}{2}$ cup of water. Bring to the boil and remove from the heat.

Add to the pan the blackcurrant purée and the softened leaves of gelatine one by one (or the softened powdered gelatine), stirring constantly. When the gelatine has completely dissolved, strain the mixture through a fine sieve to eliminate any remaining tiny specks of incompletely dissolved gelatine.

Leave to cool completely. Add the cream and icing (confectioners') sugar and mix well.

Use the butter to grease a *moule à manqué* or deep cake pan and then line it with parchment or greaseproof paper. Pour the mixture into the lined pan and chill it for 24 hours.

To turn out the bavarois, plunge the mould into hot water for 30 seconds, dry it and invert it on a round dish.

Note: this dish may also be made with any kind of soft red fruit.

To make a low-fat bavarois, use fromage blanc or thick, low-fat yogurt instead of cream, and artificial sweetener instead of sugar.

BAY

see also:
bouquet garni
court-bouillon
marinade
sauce
stock

The dark, pointed leaves of this small Mediterranean evergreen shrub are one of the most widely used culinary flavourings. Bay leaves, either fresh or dried, are always included in a bouquet garni and are a basic in most stocks and sauces, court-bouillons and stews and a wide range of other dishes.

The leaves are always discarded before serving. One leaf (sometimes even just part of a leaf) is enough to flavour a dish for 4–6 people. The dried leaves do lose almost all their flavour with time, so replenish stocks regularly.

Bay is a variety of laurel. It should not, however, be confused with the cherry laurel, the leaves of which are poisonous, or the rose laurel, which is the common ornamental shrub.

bay leaf

BEAN

Haricot

In its general sense, the term bean is applied both to the elongated vegetable pods containing edible seeds which are kidney-shaped, as distinct from round peas, and to the bean seeds themselves. In each case there are several different varieties, distinguished principally by their size and colour.

BEAN PODS

see also:
beansprout
cassoulet
chili con carne
legume
pea
pulses
vegetables

In essence, there are two main types of edible bean pod: the BROAD BEAN or FAVA BEAN and the GREEN BEAN. In turn there are two main types of green bean: the HARICOT, also called FRENCH, SNAP, STRING or BOBBY BEAN, and the RUNNER BEAN.

The BROAD BEAN or FAVA BEAN was the only bean available in Europe until the introduction of the green bean from the Americas. It is fatter and more pea-like than the any of the green beans and paler green in colour. Mostly cultivated for the seeds, the pod is much tougher than that of the green bean and only palatable when very young. Even then, they are usually cut into slices before being cooked.

The HARICOT BEAN family includes the most common FRENCH BEAN or STRING BEAN (*haricot vert*), which is very thin and long and usually deep green, although there are varieties which vary in colour from the yellow WAX BEANS to the particularly tasty *violets*, which are green speckled with purple. DWARF FRENCH BEANS (*haricot filet*) are much thinner and do not need stringing. They are relatively expensive, but have an especially good flavour. The larger SNAP BEANS are either green or yellow (*haricot beurre*) and are distinguished by their superior juiciness.

RUNNER BEANS are flatter – and generally larger – than either broad or green beans, with a distinctly different, rougher texture to their skins. Any inedibly tough strings must be removed before cooking.

Of the many other beans not included in these groups, the pale LIMA BEAN or BUTTER BEAN is probably the most significant. Native to the Americas, the lima is available fresh or dried, and it is mainly the seeds that are eaten; the young pods can be eaten but rarely are.

All these edible pods are usually prepared and cooked in roughly the same way. Choose only firm and crisp pods with a good colour and regular shape. When broken in two, beads of moisture should form at the break. Green beans should be used as quickly as possible after purchase as they lose their freshness rapidly.

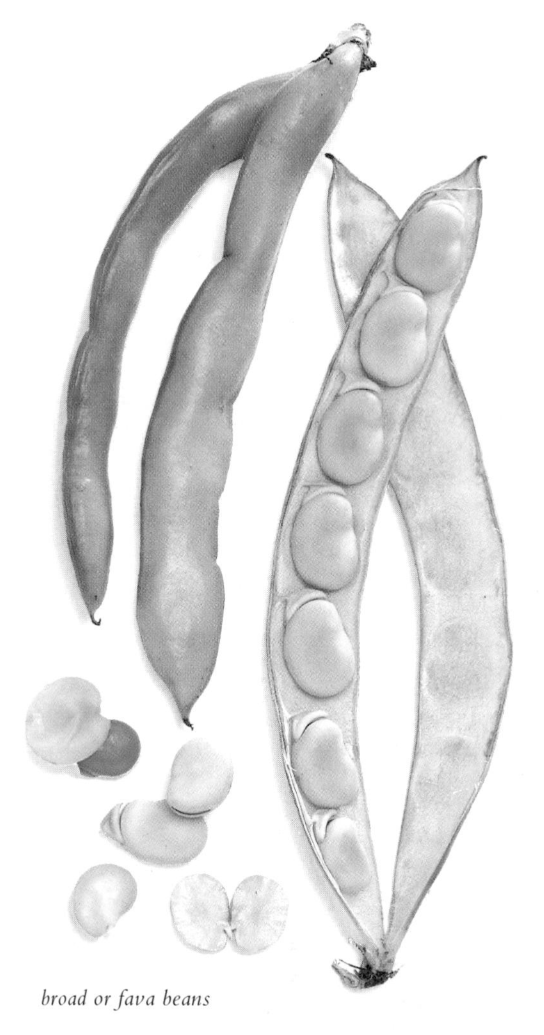

broad or fava beans

dwarf French bean

wax bean

French or string bean

purple bean

They are all usually topped and tailed and any strings removed; if uncertain, pull a top or tail off to see if any strings come with it. They are then plunged in boiling salted water and cooked until just tender. It is a good idea to refresh them quickly in cold water after cooking to keep their colour. Older beans may need to have their outer skins peeled after cooking.

Broad beans are delicious with butter and chopped parsley or summer savory. Green beans are usually served simply dressed with a little butter; but the French often serve them in cream or tomato sauces, or with sautéed chopped onion or shallot, chopped herbs, or chopped fried ham or bacon.

Green beans are rich in vitamins and easily digested. They are among the least calorific of vegetables; 100 g/3½ oz contains 40 calories.

BEAN SEEDS

Most edible bean seeds are sold fresh, but are more commonly available dried. The seeds of the broad or fava bean pods are simply known, confusingly, as BROAD BEANS or FAVA BEANS. The terms HARICOT BEANS or KIDNEY BEANS are used for most of the wide range of the seeds of green bean pods. In the USA they are also known as WHITE BEANS.

Fresh BROAD BEANS or FAVA BEANS are particularly popular in Spain, where they are stewed with sausages, black pudding (blood sausage), cured meats and plenty of garlic to make the robust Asturian dish *fabada*. The dried beans are still used in Egypt, as they have been since the times of the Pharaohs, to make *falafel*, little deep-fried patties of soaked and pounded beans flavoured with garlic and herbs.

Within the haricot bean family, which is now probably the most popular in Europe and America, there are several distinct types.

The pale green FLAGEOLETS have probably the best flavour, with a delicate texture and a low starch content. They are sold fresh only in

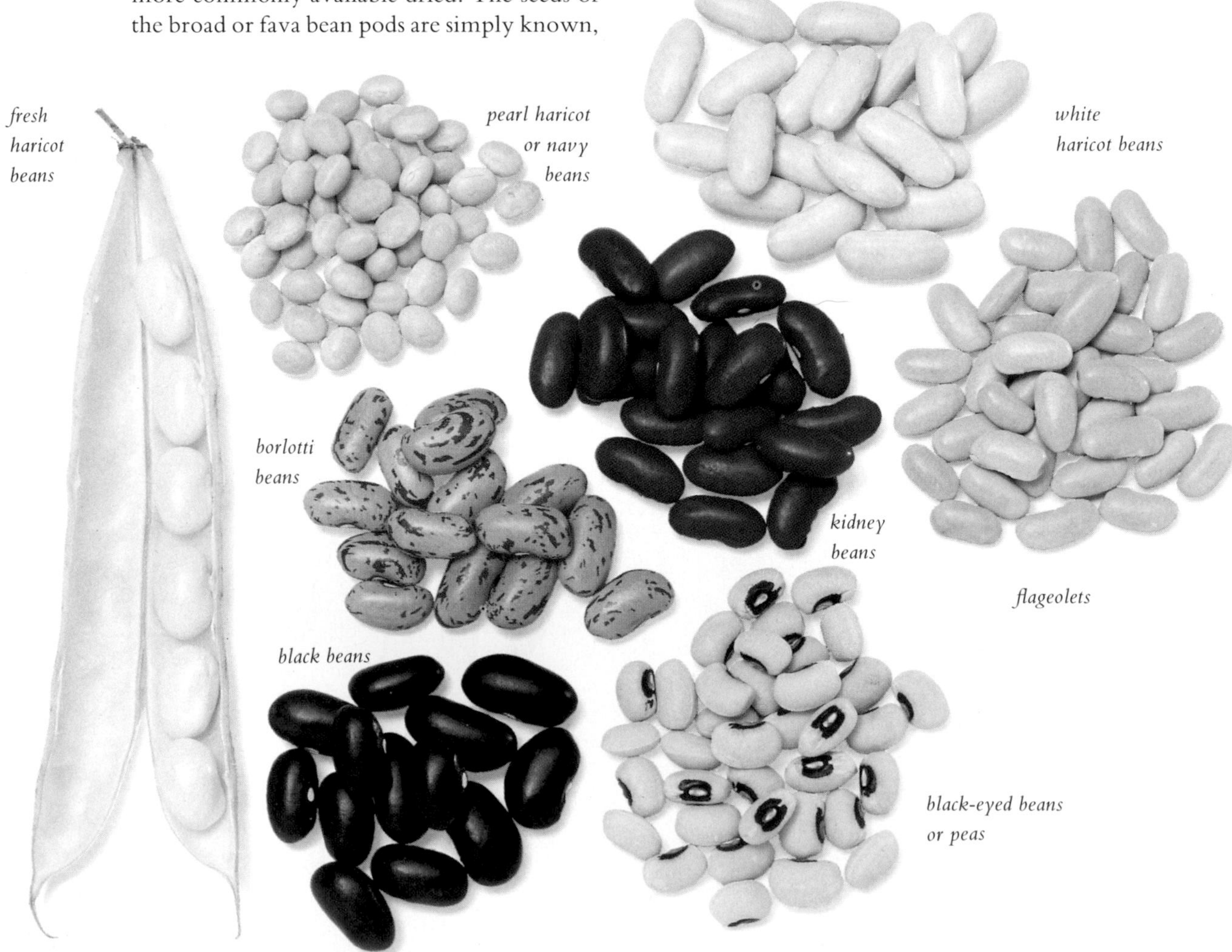

fresh haricot beans

pearl haricot or navy beans

white haricot beans

borlotti beans

kidney beans

flageolets

black beans

black-eyed beans or peas

the autumn and are more commonly sold frozen, canned or dried. Frozen and canned flageolets usually do not need any soaking before cooking. Flageolets are the classic French garnish for roast leg of lamb (*gigot d'agneau*) and the French also cook them in cream sauce as an accompaniment to fish.

Other larger WHITE HARICOT BEANS include *cocos*, *lingots* and *soissons*. They keep very well and are commonly used in casseroles and stews. The *soissons* are particularly prized in the making of the classic French *cassoulet*. The PEARL HARICOT, or NAVY BEAN, is smaller and more pea-like in appearance and is popular in the United States, especially for making the traditional American dish of Boston baked beans. It is a type of pearl haricot, known as the PEA BEAN, which is most commonly canned as 'baked beans'.

Varieties of the haricot proliferate in other countries. The very pale and slightly fatter Italian *cannellini* beans have a fluffy texture and are best known for their use with tuna fish in the dish *tonno e fagioli* and as an accompaniment to meat dishes. The Italians also have the very popular mottled red *borlotti* bean which cooks to a thick creamy purée and is often mixed with rice and pasta. The Spanish and South Americans have a very similar bean called the *pinto*. The sweet red KIDNEY BEAN is a staple of Mexican and Tex-Mex cooking, best known in *chili con carne* and pounded to a paste as *frijoles refritos* or 'refried beans', which are a common accompaniment to most meals as well as a filling for *tacos* and *tamales*. The BLACK BEAN or TURTLE BEAN is small and shiny and is also much used in Central and South America and the southern states of the USA. Its flavour works well with ham and pork and has a particular affinity with cumin. Black beans are perhaps best known cooked with a ham bone to make a very thick, dark-coloured soup.

The LIMA BEAN seed is also known as the BUTTER BEAN or MADAGASCAR BEAN and is perhaps one of the tastiest of beans. It is popular in salads and often served cold dressed with a vinaigrette as an hors d'oeuvre.

Traditionally, recipes for dried beans usually require soaking for anything from 2 hours to overnight before being used in cooking. It was once thought that long soaking promoted digestibility and reduced the tendency of dried beans to cause flatulence. However, long soaking is now thought to encourage germination and also the growth of potentially harmful micro-organisms. The best way to prepare beans for cooking is to blanch them in boiling water for 2 or 3 minutes and then soak them in fresh cold water for 2 or 3 hours at the most. Blanching halts germination and kills any bacteria. A pinch of bicarbonate of soda (baking soda) in the soaking water also helps soften the skins of older beans. Many dried beans can be successfully cooked without pre-soaking if they are immersed in cold water which is brought to the boil slowly and they are then cooked gently for at least 3 hours. Kidney and lima beans must be boiled for at least 5 minutes, to destroy natural toxins, before further cooking. Never add salt to dried beans until they have been completely cooked, or they remain hard.

Beans are a significant source of vegetable protein and are rich in minerals, vitamins and fibre. Cooked beans contain 120 calories per 100 g/$3\frac{1}{2}$ oz.

HARICOTS VERTS À LA TOMATE

Green beans with tomatoes

Serves 4
Preparation 15 minutes
Cooking about 35 minutes

METRIC/IMPERIAL	*AMERICAN*
2 tbsp olive oil	*2 tbsp olive oil*
6 small white onions, halved	*6 small white onions, halved*
4 firm medium-sized tomatoes, peeled, halved and deseeded	*4 firm medium-sized tomatoes, peeled, halved and seeded*
800 g/$1\frac{3}{4}$ lb French beans, trimmed and cut in half	*$1\frac{3}{4}$ lb green beans, trimmed and cut in half*
sprig of thyme	*sprig of thyme*
2 garlic cloves	*2 garlic cloves*
salt and pepper	*salt and pepper*

Heat the oil in a flameproof casserole over a moderate heat and brown the onions in it lightly, stirring all the time. Add the tomatoes and cook for a further 3 minutes.

Add the beans, thyme and garlic. Season with salt and pepper and mix well. Cover and simmer very gently for 30 minutes, without adding any liquid (the tomato juices provide quite enough moisture to cook the beans and will flavour them at the same time).

Serve straight from the casserole as an accompaniment to roast lamb or kebabs.

ÉTUVÉE DE LÉGUMES AUX HARICOTS BLANCS

Vegetable stew with green and white beans

Serves 6
Preparation 30 minutes
Cooking about 50 minutes

METRIC/IMPERIAL	AMERICAN
4 lettuce hearts	4 lettuce hearts
2 carrots	2 carrots
2 turnips	2 turnips
3 potatoes	3 potatoes
100 g/3½ oz butter	1 stick butter
225 g/½ lb French beans, trimmed	½ lb green beans, trimmed
200 g/7 oz shelled, large, fresh white haricot beans	1½ cups shelled, fresh white beans
200 g/7 oz shelled, fresh green peas	1⅓ cups shelled, fresh green peas
salt and pepper	salt and pepper

Preheat the oven to 180C/350F/gas 4.

Wash the lettuce hearts, pat them dry and cut them in halves or quarters. Peel the carrots, turnips and potatoes and cut them in cubes or rounds.

Use half the butter to grease a flameproof casserole. Add half the lettuce and half of each of the other vegetables. Dot the surface with half the remaining butter. Fill the casserole with the remaining vegetables, combining them well.

Dot the top with the rest of the butter and add 3 tablespoons of water. Season with salt and pepper. Cover the casserole and cook over a moderate heat for 10–12 minutes, then cook it in the oven for 40 minutes. Serve very hot.

HARICOTS ROUGES AUX LARDONS

Red kidney beans with bacon

Serves 6
Preparation 20 minutes, soaking time 2 hours
Cooking about 2 hours

METRIC/IMPERIAL	AMERICAN
450 g/1 lb dried red kidney beans	1 lb (2½ cups) dried red kidney beans
700 ml/1¼ pt red wine	3 cups red wine
1 onion	1 onion
2 cloves	2 cloves
2 garlic cloves	2 garlic cloves
2 stalks of celery, trimmed and cut into large chunks	2 sticks of celery, trimmed and cut into large chunks
bouquet garni	bouquet garni
300 g/10 oz thickly sliced, smoked streaky bacon, cut into pieces	10 oz Canadian bacon, cut into pieces
15 g/½ oz butter	1 tbsp butter
salt and pepper	salt and pepper

Put the beans into a stewpot, cover with a large amount of cold water and leave them for 2 hours to soak.

Drain the beans and discard the water. Return the beans to the stewpot and add the red wine and enough cold water to cover the beans completely. Bring slowly to the boil, skim, then season with salt and pepper. Add the onion, peeled and studded with the cloves, the garlic, celery and bouquet garni. Place the pieces of bacon in the middle of the beans. Cover and simmer very gently for about 2 hours.

Drain the beans, discard the bouquet garni, onion and celery, and set the bacon on one side. Put the beans into a warmed serving dish, or earthenware casserole dish, with about 2 tablespoons of the cooking liquid. Keep hot.

Cut the bacon into small strips and fry in the butter over a moderate heat until crisp. Add them to the beans, mix well and serve.

Etuvée de légumes aux haricots blancs (Vegetable stew with green and white beans)

see also:
bean

BEANSPROUT

The practice of sprouting a wide variety of bean and pea seeds has long been a means of providing an easily stored supply of vegetables.

The sprout of the MUNG BEAN is also a staple of Chinese cooking, usually stir-fried with other vegetables or cooked rice, and it is the beansprout now most commonly commercially produced in most parts of the world.

The beansprout has recently found great favour among health-food enthusiasts, who often eat them raw in salads. However, beansprouts do contain a substance which inhibits the body's ability to digest protein, so they should be steamed for at least 3 minutes before being consumed in any quantity.

see also:
bone marrow
bourguignon
braising
carbonade
carpaccio
châteaubriand
daube
fillet
fondue
gravy
grilling
heart
kebab
meatball
offal
oxtail
roasting
steak
tartare
tongue
tournedos
veal

BEEF

Boeuf

The term applies to the meat of all types of adult domesticated ox: cow, bull, heifer (young adult female who has not yet calved) and bullock (young castrated male). Heifers and bullocks are usually slaughtered for their meat between the ages of 24 and 40 months. The meat of the bullock is generally held to be the tastiest of beef.

Among the best types of beef cattle, reared specifically for meat production, are the *Limousin* and *Charolais* in France and Scotland's Aberdeen Angus. Most beef, however, comes from older dairy cattle and cows which have reached the end of their calving careers.

Good quality beef is bright red and shiny, with a firm, springy consistency and sweet smell. It has a network of white fat or slightly yellowish fat, if grass-fed. When a lot of such fat is present in the muscle, the meat is known as *persillé* or marbled. This gives the meat extra flavour, but leaner beef is considered to be healthier to eat.

In order for beef to become tender, and for its full flavour to develop, it must be well hung for a period varying from a few days to 2 or 3 weeks. With ageing, its colour deepens to a rich plum and it loses moisture. Nowadays, however, very little commercially produced beef has been hung for more than a week, principally because the process adds so much more to the price. Good butchers and restaurants will often complete the hanging process themselves.

BRITISH CUTS OF BEEF

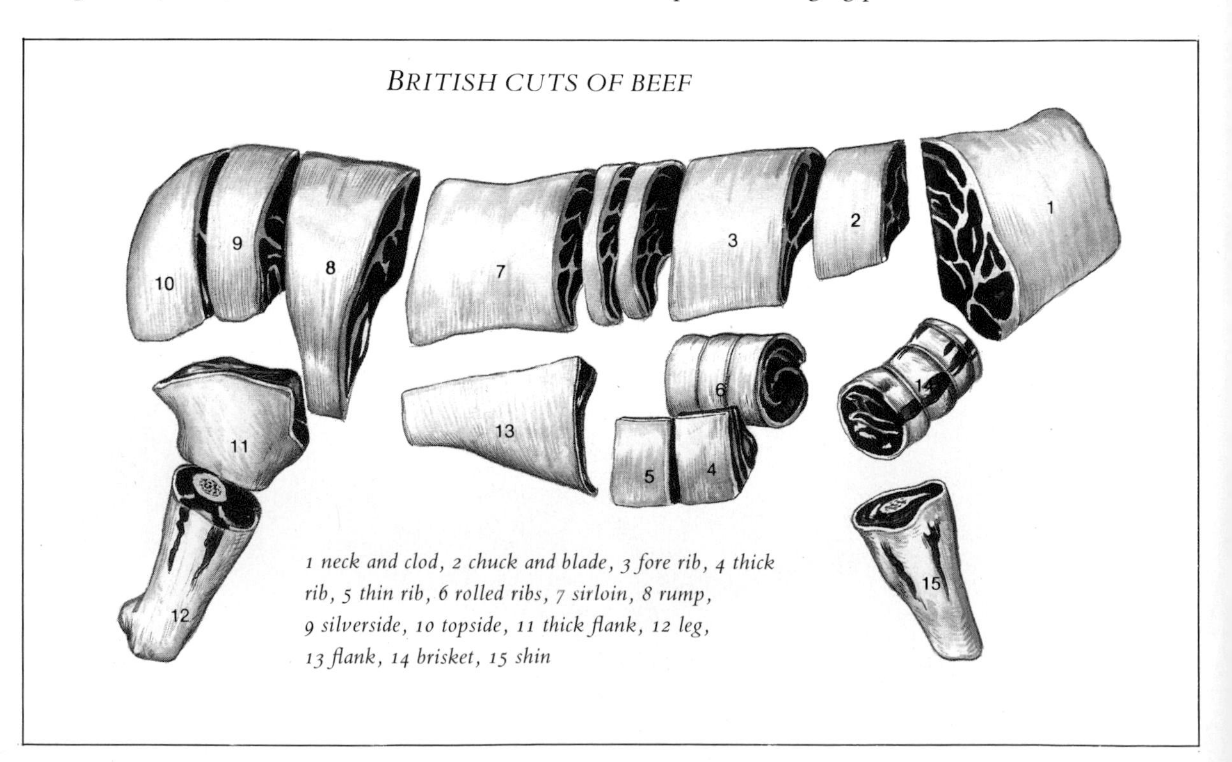

1 neck and clod, 2 chuck and blade, 3 fore rib, 4 thick rib, 5 thin rib, 6 rolled ribs, 7 sirloin, 8 rump, 9 silverside, 10 topside, 11 thick flank, 12 leg, 13 flank, 14 brisket, 15 shin

to obtain the superior flavour they require.

There are two main types of beef cuts. The more expensive, so-called 'noble', cuts such as steaks, chateaubriands and other cuts from the fillet (tenderloin) and forequarters of the animal, are tender and require only quick cooking, while the less expensive cuts, mainly from the hindquarters, are tougher and benefit from long slow cooking.

Although boiled, braised and casseroled beef is always popular, by far the favourite means of cooking large pieces of beef is roasting. The meat is normally very simply prepared, only perhaps barded with fat or bacon to keep it moist, and with no added vegetables or herbs as flavourings. So-called 'luxury' roasts, from the fillet (tenderloin) and rump (sirloin), are normally served quite rare and are lightly cooked for about 12–15 minutes per 450 g/1 lb at 190C/375F/gas 5. Less tender cuts, such as topside (top round), silverside (bottom round) and flank, need 15–25 minutes per 450 g/1 lb, depending on how well done they are to be. Large cuts from the rib are treated to longer slower roasting, from 20–30 minutes per 450 g/1 lb, but smaller rib roasts are better cooked more quickly. For best results seal the beef in the hottest possible oven for the first 20 minutes, or brown it all over in a large frying pan before roasting.

Matured beef freezes well, but avoid freezing pieces that are too large; it is better to freeze two pieces of 1.5 kg/3½ lb each than a single large one weighing 3 kg/6½ lb. Beef for freezing should not be barded beforehand, as frozen bards turn rancid very quickly.

The fat content of most commercially produced beef is considerably lower than it was until only a few years ago, for instance, 12–20% for entrecôte (sirloin steak) and rib; 5–10% for rump, fillet (filet mignon) and other steaks. Given the fact that beef loses some of its fat during cooking, it is a very healthy food if eaten in moderation. A reasonable amount would be 100–150 g/3½–5½ oz per serving without any rich sauces.

In addition, the high quality of beef protein and the fact that it is a major source of iron make it very nutritious. The calorie content of beef averaged out over all the cuts is 120–130 calories per 100 g/3½ oz, and it also averages 20% protein and 5% fat.

AMERICAN CUTS OF BEEF

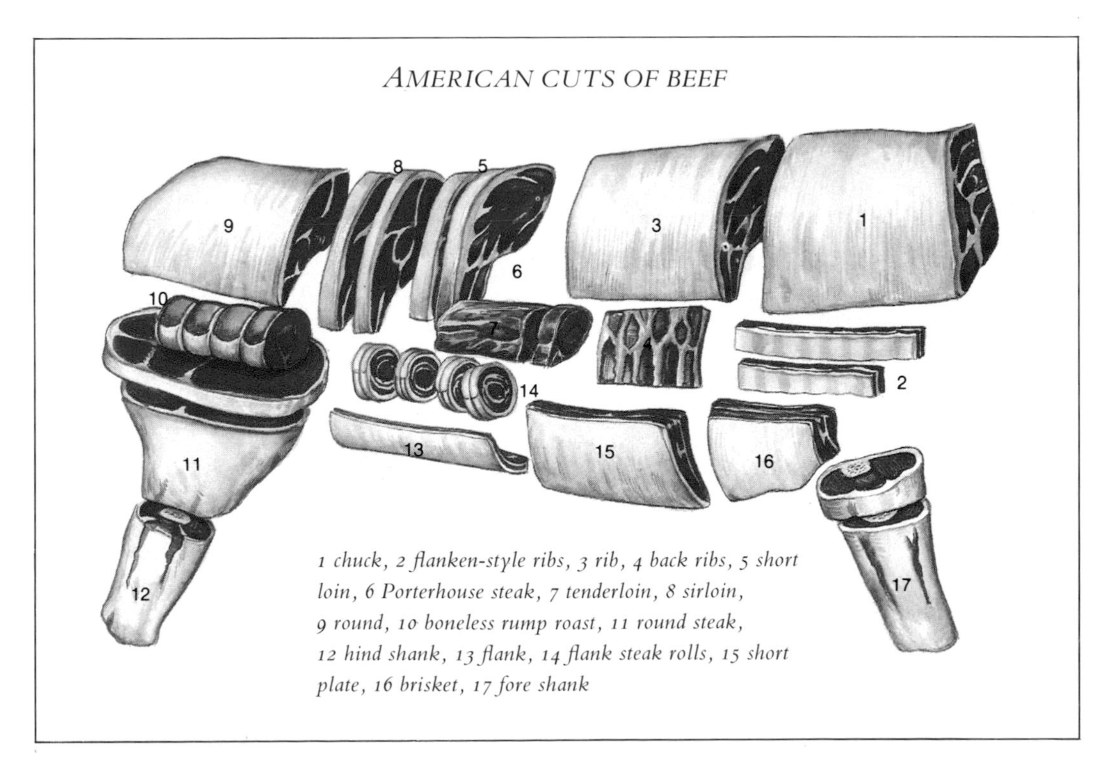

1 chuck, 2 flanken-style ribs, 3 rib, 4 back ribs, 5 short loin, 6 Porterhouse steak, 7 tenderloin, 8 sirloin, 9 round, 10 boneless rump roast, 11 round steak, 12 hind shank, 13 flank, 14 flank steak rolls, 15 short plate, 16 brisket, 17 fore shank

CARVING A SMALL RIB ROAST

Place the roast bone side toward you and separate the meat from the edge of the bone.

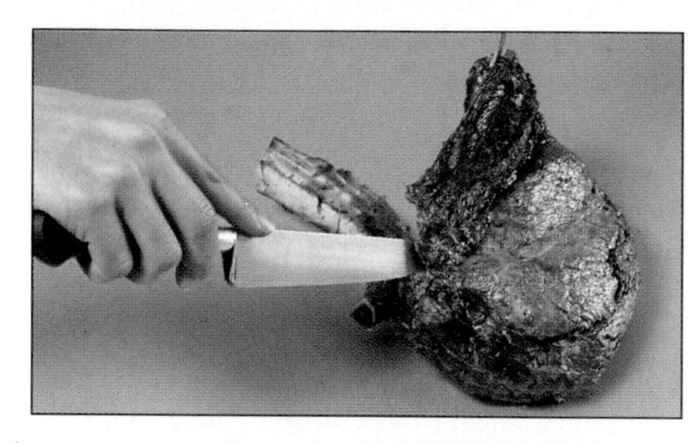

Completely detatch the meat from the bone following the contours of the ribs.

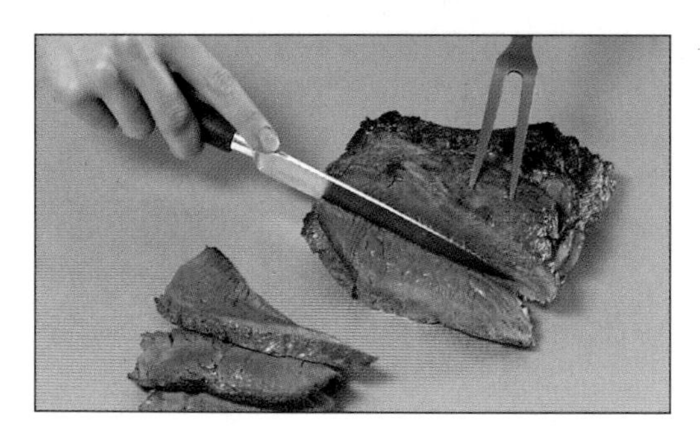

Carve the boneless meat in fairly thick slices like a steak.

CÔTE DE BOEUF À L'OS

Roast rib of beef

Serves 4
Preparation 5 minutes
Cooking about 30–40 minutes

METRIC/IMPERIAL	*AMERICAN*
1 best rib of beef, weighing about 1 kg/ $2\frac{1}{4}$ lb, chined and trimmed	*1 standing rib roast, weighing about $2\frac{1}{4}$ lb, chined and trimmed*
oil, for brushing	*oil, for brushing*
salt and pepper	*salt and pepper*

Preheat the oven to 240C/475F/gas 9. Brush the meat all over with oil. Place the meat in the roasting pan balanced on the two ends of the bone, fat side upwards, so that as the fat melts it will seep down to flavour the meat.

Put the roast into the hot oven to seal the meat. Immediately lower the heat to 210C/ 410F/gas 7 to give the interior of the meat a chance to cook through and cook for 15–18 minutes per 450 g/1 lb for medium rare beef.

Cover the meat with foil and allow it to rest in a warm place, or in the switched-off oven, for at least 10 minutes.

Serve on a wooden board, seasoned with salt and pepper and accompanied by a herb butter or barbecue sauce and French fried potatoes.
To drink: a good red Bordeaux.

BOEUF AUX OLIVES

Beef with olives

Serves 6
Preparation 20 minutes
Cooking about $2\frac{3}{4}$ hours

METRIC/IMPERIAL	*AMERICAN*
115 g/4 oz thick-sliced streaky bacon, cut into small strips	*4 oz country-style bacon, cut into small strips*
1.35 kg/3 lb piece of beef neck or chuck	*3 lb beef chuck pot-roast*
2 carrots, peeled and finely sliced	*2 carrots, peeled and finely sliced*
	3 shallots

3 shallots	*12 baby onions*
12 baby onions	*1 garlic clove*
1 garlic clove	*bouquet garni*
bouquet garni	*1$\frac{1}{2}$ cups red wine*
300 ml/$\frac{1}{2}$ pt red wine	*1$\frac{1}{2}$ cups black olives, pitted*
250 g/8$\frac{1}{2}$ oz black olives, stoned	*salt and pepper*
salt and pepper	

Put the bacon in a flameproof casserole over a gentle heat and cook it without letting it brown. Remove the bacon from the pot, put in the piece of beef and increase the heat slightly. Turn the meat to brown it lightly on all sides.

Stir in the carrots, shallots and onions, adding salt and pepper to taste. Cover and simmer for 15 minutes. Add the garlic, bouquet garni and bacon. Moisten with the wine, cover the casserole and simmer for 1$\frac{1}{2}$ hours. Add the olives and cook for a further 40 minutes.

Remove the bouquet garni before serving the meat sliced, with the remaining pan contents as a garnish and sauce.

BOEUF STROGANOFF

Beef Stroganoff

Serves 4
Preparation 20 minutes
Cooking about 25 minutes

METRIC/IMPERIAL	*AMERICAN*
2 onions, finely chopped	*2 onions, finely chopped*
225 g/$\frac{1}{2}$ lb white button mushrooms, wiped and sliced	*$\frac{1}{2}$ lb white button mushrooms, wiped and sliced*
30 g/1 oz butter	*2 tbsp butter*
1 tbsp tomato purée	*1 tbsp tomato paste*
1 tbsp Dijon mustard	*1 tbsp Dijon mustard*
100 ml/3$\frac{1}{2}$ fl oz white wine	*$\frac{1}{2}$ cup white wine*
550 g/1$\frac{1}{4}$ lb beef fillet, cut into 8 mm/$\frac{1}{3}$ in thick slices	*1$\frac{1}{4}$ lb beef tenderloin, cut into $\frac{1}{3}$ in thick slices*
3 tbsp sunflower oil	*3 tbsp sunflower oil*
200 ml/7 fl oz sour cream	*1 cup sour cream*
1 tsp paprika	*1 tsp paprika*
salt and pepper	*salt and pepper*

Melt the butter in a saucepan over a low heat and add the mushrooms and onions. Cook for 12 minutes, stirring. Combine the tomato purée (paste), mustard and white wine in a bowl. Add this mixture to the saucepan and stir well. Leave to cook over a low heat.

Cut the slices of beef into 5–6 cm/2–2$\frac{1}{4}$ in long strips. Heat the oil in a sauté pan and add the strips of meat. Sauté them briskly over a moderate to high heat for 2–3 minutes until well browned, then add salt and pepper.

Add the mushroom mixture to the sauté pan. Stir well, then add the cream and paprika. Heat gently for 2–3 minutes, adjust the seasoning if necessary and serve immediately in a deep warmed dish, accompanied by noodles or rice.

MARMITE DE BOEUF

Casseroled beef and vegetables

Serves 6
Preparation 20 minutes, 24 hours ahead
Cooking about 3$\frac{1}{4}$ hours

METRIC/IMPERIAL	*AMERICAN*
1.35 kg/3 lb beef rump, trimmed and cut into small pieces	*3 lb boneless beef rump or top round, trimmed and cut into small pieces*
4 carrots, peeled and cut into thick slices	*4 carrots, peeled and cut into thick slices*
3 shallots, sliced	*3 shallots, sliced*
2 large onions, sliced	*2 large onions, sliced*
bouquet garni	*bouquet garni*
500 ml/16 fl oz dry white wine	*2 cups dry white wine*
3 tbsp Cognac	*3 tbsp Cognac*
3 tbsp oil	*3 tbsp oil*
1 calves' foot, halved	*1 calves' foot, halved*
3 tomatoes, quartered	*3 tomatoes, quartered*
20 baby onions	*20 baby onions*
225 g/$\frac{1}{2}$ lb white button mushrooms, wiped and sliced	*$\frac{1}{2}$ lb white button mushrooms, wiped and sliced*
salt and pepper	*salt and pepper*

In a large bowl, mix the beef, carrots, shallots, sliced onions, bouquet garni, white wine, Cognac and oil. Leave to marinate for 24 hours, turning the pieces of meat 2 or 3 times.

Put the calves' foot pieces in a large flameproof casserole. Add the meat along with the marinade and the tomatoes. Season with salt and pepper. Bring to the boil, then cover, lower the heat and simmer gently for 2 hours.

Add the baby onions and mushrooms to the pot and cook for a further 1 hour.

OISEAUX SANS TÊTE

Beef olives

Serves 4
Preparation 20 minutes
Cooking 30 minutes

METRIC/IMPERIAL	*AMERICAN*
4 thin slices of trimmed beef rump or flank, each weighing about 85–115 g/3–4 oz	*4 thin slices of trimmed beef rump or flank, each weighing about 3–4 oz*
2 tsp Dijon mustard	*2 tsp Dijon mustard*
8 thin slices of smoked bacon	*8 thin slices of smoked bacon*
4 baby onions, thinly sliced	*4 baby onions, finely sliced*
4 gherkins, thinly sliced	*4 pickled cucumbers, finely sliced*
25 g/¾ oz butter	*1½ tbsp butter*
1 tbsp oil	*1 tbsp oil*
whites of 2 leeks, thinly sliced	*whites of 2 leeks, finely sliced*
200 ml/7 fl oz beef stock	*1 cup beef stock*
2 tbsp crème fraîche or whipping cream	*2 tbsp crème fraîche or whipping cream*
salt and pepper	*salt and pepper*

Using a kitchen mallet or rolling pin, pound the meat to flatten it and season with salt and pepper. Spread each slice with mustard and arrange 2 slices of bacon on top of each one.

Sprinkle the onions and gherkins (pickled cucumbers) over the bacon, roll up the beef olives and tie them securely with string.

Heat the butter and oil in a flameproof casserole over a moderate heat and cook the leeks for 2 minutes, stirring.

Add the beef olives and let them brown, turning them several times. Pour the stock over, cover and simmer for 30 minutes.

Drain the beef olives, remove their strings and put them into a warmed serving dish.

Add the cream to the casserole and deglaze the pan juices, stirring with a wooden spoon. Adjust the seasoning and coat the beef olives with the sauce (the leeks should by this time be reduced to a compote).

To drink: brown ale or lager (light beer).

BEER

Bière

see also:
alcohol
carbonade
cider

This alcoholic beverage is made from malted cereals, principally ground barley, and flavoured with hops. Cereal-derived beverages of this sort were mankind's earliest alcoholic refreshment, and beer and ALE, the old term for a beer made without hops, but nowadays used more or less synonymously with beer, were the most common drink throughout northern Europe in the days before the advent of tea and coffee.

Different types of beer are commonly distinguished from one another by their colour, which ranges from pale blond to a deep reddish brown verging on black. However, the different types are determined principally by the fermentation process involved. Low fermentation, which takes place at less than 12C/54F for a period of about 7 days, is the most popular and produces the majority of LAGERS (light beers), BITTERS and MALTED BITTERS, which include German and Alsatian beers. High fermentation, at around 18–25C/64–77F for 2 or 3 days, produces the heavier, fruitier and more strongly flavoured brown and red beers, such as Belgian beers and certain of the British and Irish beers and STOUTS.

Draught beer is generally better than canned, but only if it has a high turnover; beer that sits too long in the cask begins to oxidize. Bottled beer keeps for about 6 months, whether refrigerated, ideally at 10C/50F, or not.

Lagers are drunk cold at 10C/50F. The deeper the colour of the beer, the warmer it is served; certain of the brown ales are properly drunk *chambré*, as high as 14–15C/57–59F.

Beer was often one of the few flavouring agents present in many simple country kitchens and has thus become part of the traditional cuisine of countries such as Belgium and Ireland, where it is often used in soups and stews, principally with beef, lamb, game and strongly flavoured fish such as pike. It is also used in the making of batters – a dash of beer in the batter is said to be the secret to perfect deep fried fish, cakes and breads.

Although it is rich in vitamin B complex, beer is also high in calories: a 300 ml/½ pt glass of beer contains 12–16 g of alcohol and about 145 calories.

FILETS DE SOLES À LA BIÈRE

Sole fillets in beer

Serves 4
Preparation 35 minutes
Cooking 20 minutes

METRIC/IMPERIAL	AMERICAN
4 soles, filleted	4 soles, filleted
75 g/2½ oz butter	5 tbsp butter
5 shallots, finely chopped	5 shallots, finely chopped
500 ml/16 fl oz bitter	2 cups beer
25 g/¾ oz flour	3 tbsp flour
1 egg yolk	1 egg yolk
2 tbsp crème fraîche or sour cream	2 tbsp crème fraîche or sour cream
salt and pepper	salt and pepper

Preheat the oven to 180C/350F/gas 4.

Flatten the sole fillets and fold them in half. Melt half the butter in a saucepan, add the shallots and cook them gently until they are translucent.

Transfer the shallots to a baking dish. Spread them out over the bottom and place the folded sole fillets on top. Pour the beer over the fish, season with salt and pepper and leave them to marinate for 30 minutes.

Cook the fish in the oven for 10 minutes. Grease a serving dish with a little of the remaining butter, place the sole fillets in it and keep it hot.

Put the cooking juices in a saucepan and boil to reduce by about half.

Meanwhile, beat the remaining butter with the flour. Add it bit by bit to the reduced sauce, whisking vigorously over a high heat.

Remove the pan from the heat and add the egg yolk. Mix thoroughly, then add the cream and whisk until well blended. Coat the sole fillets with the sauce and serve at once.

To drink: a good beer, preferably that used in cooking.

LAPIN À LA BIÈRE

Rabbit in beer

Serves 6
Preparation 40 minutes, marinating 1 hour
Cooking 1–2 hours

METRIC/IMPERIAL	AMERICAN
1 rabbit, dressed weight 1.5 kg/3½ lb, cut into pieces	1 rabbit, dressed and drawn weight 3½ lb, cut in pieces
3 onions, sliced	3 onions, sliced
bay leaf	bay leaf
sprig of thyme	sprig of thyme
1 tsp coarsely ground black pepper	1 tsp coarsely ground black pepper
150 ml/¼ pt white wine vinegar	⅔ cup white wine vinegar
2 tbsp strong mustard	2 tbsp strong Dijon mustard
55 g/2 oz butter	4 tbsp butter
juice of 1 lemon	juice of 1 lemon
500 ml/16 fl oz beer, preferably bitter	2 cups beer
1 tsp caster sugar	1 tsp superfine sugar
10 prunes, soaked in warm water	10 prunes, soaked in warm water
2 tsp cornflour	2 tsp cornstarch
flour, for dusting	flour, for dusting
salt and pepper	salt and pepper

Place the rabbit portions in a dish. Add one of the sliced onions along with the bay leaf, thyme, ground black pepper and vinegar. Add just enough water to cover the pieces of rabbit and leave to marinate for 1 hour.

Drain the rabbit portions, reserving the marinade, and pat them dry on paper towels. Spread them with the mustard, season them with salt and pepper and coat them with flour. Melt the butter in a large frying pan and brown the rabbit over a high heat, turning the pieces frequently. When they are golden brown put them in a flameproof casserole.

Strain the marinade and pour 100 ml/3½ fl oz/½ cup over the rabbit. Add the remaining onion slices, lemon juice, beer and sugar and stir well.

Bring to the boil, then lower the heat, cover and cook gently for 1 hour. Add the drained prunes and cook for a further 30 minutes.

Put the rabbit and prunes in a deep, warmed serving dish. Mix the cornflour (cornstarch) with 1 tablespoon of water and add this mixture to the contents of the casserole. Cook over a high heat, stirring until the sauce is smooth.

Taste and adjust the seasonings, if necessary. Pour the sauce over the rabbit and serve at once, accompanied by fresh pasta.

To drink: bitter or lager (light beer).

see also: vegetables

BEETROOT OR BEET

Betterave

Beet is a term used to describe any one of several species of root vegetable related to spinach. The SUGAR BEET is not used in cooking, but is a major source of sugar. The RED BEET OR BEETROOT is the most gastronomically important beet and is a staple in many of the cuisines of Eastern Europe.

Finely grated raw beetroot makes a delicious *crudité* and is used in hors d'oeuvres and mixed salads. In Europe nowadays, most beetroot is sold already cooked or pickled in vinegar.

When cooking beetroot at home, handle carefully to avoid damaging the skin and prevent 'bleeding'. Twist off the tops rather than slicing them. Either bake beetroot wrapped in foil in the oven or boil for at least 2 hours (add a dash of vinegar to the water to retain the colour). Rub off the skins while the beets are still warm.

Hot cooked beetroot is best simply dressed with a little butter and lemon juice, and is a common garnish for game. Cold, it works well with sharp fruit, such as apples or sour grapes, and is delicious with sour cream or a sweet-and-sour red fruit sauce.

Beetroot is high in vitamins, some minerals, and sugar (almost twice that of most vegetables); 100 g/3½ oz contains 44 calories. As beets are high in oxalic acid they are not recommended as a regular part of the diet for people suffering from cystitis or those who are prone to bladder stones.

SOUPE FROIDE ROUGE

Chilled beetroot soup

Serves 4
Preparation 20 minutes, 2 hours ahead
Cooking 10 minutes

METRIC/IMPERIAL	*AMERICAN*
300 ml/½ pt good vegetable or chicken stock	*1½ cups good vegetable or chicken stock*
1 tbsp oil	*1 tbsp oil*
1 small onion, chopped	*1 small onion, chopped*
2 stalks of celery, cut into pieces	*2 sticks of celery, cut into pieces*
1 carrot, chopped	*1 carrot, chopped*
300 g/10 oz cooked beetroot, diced	*2 cups diced cooked beets*
pinch of ground cumin	*pinch of ground cumin*
200 g/7 oz fresh tomato sauce	*1 cup fresh tomato sauce*
juice of 1 lemon	*juice of 1 lemon*
150 ml/¼ pt natural yogurt, chilled	*½ cup unflavored yogurt, chilled*
salt and pepper	*salt and pepper*
chopped chives, to garnish	*chopped chives, to garnish*

Put the stock to heat gently in a small saucepan.

Heat the oil on High for 1 minute in a large deep dish. Add the onion, celery and carrot. Cook on High for 7 minutes, stirring once halfway through.

Add the beetroot, cumin and tomato sauce, pour the hot stock over the mixture and cook, covered, on High for 2 minutes.

Blend the contents of the dish in a food processor, then add the lemon juice and salt and pepper to taste.

Chill in the coldest part of the refrigerator for at least 1½ hours. Just before serving, swirl in the yogurt and sprinkle with chives to garnish.

BETTERAVES RAPÉES AUX NOISETTES

Grated beetroot with hazelnuts

Serves 2
Preparation 10 minutes

METRIC/IMPERIAL	AMERICAN
1 tbsp white wine vinegar	*1 tbsp white wine vinegar*
1 tbsp hazelnut oil	*1 tbsp hazelnut oil*
1 raw beetroot, peeled and finely grated	*1 raw beet, peeled and finely grated*
20 hazelnuts, coarsely chopped	*20 shelled hazelnuts (filberts), coarsely chopped*
snipped fresh chervil, to garnish	*snipped fresh chervil, to garnish*
salt and pepper	*salt and pepper*

Put the vinegar in a bowl with several pinches of salt and stir until the salt is dissolved. Add the hazelnut oil and whisk with a fork along with pepper to taste.

Put the grated beetroot in a deep dish and pour the vinaigrette over it. Add the hazelnuts and mix thoroughly. Garnish with the snipped chervil and serve.

BELGIAN ENDIVE

see Chicory

BILBERRY OR BLUEBERRY

Myrtille

see also: fruit jams, etc sorbet

The BILBERRY, BLAEBERRY OT WHORTLEBERRY is a small, late summer to autumn berry, blue with a variable purplish tinge, which comes from a plant in the heather family. It is native to many parts of northern Europe, particularly the Alpine regions. The berries have a very strong, slightly acid flavour.

The closely related American BLUEBERRY has similar qualities, but is larger and has thus become more commercially important.

Bilberries and blueberries are ideal for tarts, sorbets and compotes. Their main use is in jams and jellies, owing to their high pectin content. In America, blueberry muffins are a great breakfast treat.

Bilberries and blueberries are rich in vitamin C, but low in calories; 100 g/3½ oz contains 15 calories. They freeze well and can thus be an important part of a healthy diet in winter.

CONFITURE DE MYRTILLES

Bilberry or blueberry jam

Makes about 2 kg/4½ lb
Preparation 15 minutes
Cooking about 30 minutes

METRIC/IMPERIAL	AMERICAN
1 kg/2¼ lb bilberries or blueberries	*2¼ lb (3½ pt) blueberries*
1 kg/2¼ lb sugar cubes	*2¼ lb sugar cubes*

Pick over the berries and rinse them carefully. Place in a large pan over a low heat. Cook, uncovered, for 20 minutes, stirring from time to time, until they are soft but not mushy.

Meanwhile, put the sugar cubes into a heavy-bottomed saucepan along with about 400 ml/14 fl oz/1¾ cups of water. Dissolve the sugar over a low heat, then gently bring the liquid up to the boil. Do not stir after the mixture boils. Continue to cook gently until it becomes a golden caramel.

Pour this caramel over the hot berries and stir over low heat for 8–10 minutes.

Put into clean jars, allow to cool, and seal as described for jams.

TARTE AUX MYRTILLES

Bilberry or blueberry tart

Serves 6
Preparation 15 minutes, resting 30 minutes
Cooking 35 minutes, 15 minutes ahead

METRIC/IMPERIAL	AMERICAN
100 g/3½ oz butter, softened	1 stick butter, softened
200 g/7 oz flour	1½ cups flour
125 g/4½ oz caster sugar	10 tbsp superfine sugar
2 eggs + 1 egg yolk	2 eggs + 1 egg yolk
salt	salt
2 tbsp breadcrumbs	2 tbsp breadcrumbs
450 g/1 lb bilberries or blueberries	1 lb (about 3½ cups) blueberries
100 ml/3½ fl oz crème fraîche or whipping cream	½ cup crème fraîche or whipping cream
icing sugar, to dust	confectioners' sugar, to dust

Lightly butter a loose-bottomed tart pan.

Put the flour into a bowl. Add the remaining butter in small pieces and mix it in with the fingertips. Make a well in the centre and add 25 g/¾ oz/2 tbsp of the caster (superfine) sugar, the egg yolk, a pinch of salt and 2 tablespoons of water. Mix with the fingertips for 2–3 minutes, then form the pastry into a smooth ball and chill it for 30 minutes.

Preheat the oven to 190C/375F/gas 5. Roll out the chilled pastry to about 3 mm/⅛ in thick and use it to line the pan. Prick the bottom of the pastry case with a fork and sprinkle over the breadcrumbs; these will absorb the fruit juices and prevent the pastry from becoming soggy.

Pick clean the berries, rinse them and pat them dry, then put them into the pastry case. Bake in the oven for 20 minutes. Meanwhile, whisk together the cream, the rest of the caster (superfine) sugar and the whole eggs.

Remove the tart from the oven and reduce the heat to 180C/350F/gas 4. Carefully pour the cream and egg mixture over the fruit. Return the tart to the oven for a further 15 minutes.

Remove the tart from the oven and sprinkle it all over with icing (confectioners') sugar. Stand for 15 minutes, unmould and serve.

BISCUIT

see Cookies, crackers and biscuits

BISQUE

see also:
crayfish
langoustine
shellfish
soup

A highly seasoned shellfish purée, usually flavoured with white wine, Cognac and cream, it serves as the basis for a creamy soup. Crab, crayfish, lobster, langoustine or spiny lobster are all suitable.

The soup is usually garnished with the diced meat of the main ingredient.

BISQUE DE LANGOUSTINES

Langoustine or Dublin Bay prawn bisque

Serves 4
Preparation 30 minutes
Cooking about 35 minutes

METRIC/IMPERIAL	AMERICAN
125 g/4½ oz butter	9 tbsp butter
1 onion, finely chopped	1 onion, finely chopped
1 carrot, finely chopped	1 carrot, finely chopped
1 stalk of celery, trimmed and finely sliced	1 stick of celery, trimmed and finely sliced
pinch of thyme	pinch of thyme
½ bay leaf	½ bay leaf
8 live langoustines or Dublin Bay prawns	8 live langoustines or Dublin Bay prawns
30ml/2 tbsp Cognac	2 tbsp Cognac
200 ml/7 fl oz dry white wine	1 cup dry white wine
1 l/1¾ pt fish stock (or highly seasoned court-bouillon)	1 qt fish stock (or highly seasoned court-bouillon)
2 tbsp rice	2 tbsp rice
150 ml/¼ pt crème fraîche or whipping cream	⅔ cup crème fraîche or whipping cream
cayenne pepper	cayenne pepper
salt and pepper	salt and pepper

Melt one third of the butter in a saucepan. Add the vegetables, thyme and bay leaf. Cook gently, stirring, until the vegetables are soft. Add the shellfish to the pan and cook for 3

Tarte aux myrtilles (Bilberry or blueberry tart)

minutes over a high heat. Pour the Cognac over them and flame them. When the flames have died down, add the white wine and cook over a very gentle heat for 8–10 minutes. Using a slotted spoon, remove the langoustines from the pan.

Pour the fish stock or court-bouillon into the pan, bring to the boil and sprinkle in the rice. Lower the heat and cook for 20 minutes.

Meanwhile, shell the langoustines, keeping the heads if you wish for stock, and remove all the meat from the claws and the interiors of the bodies as well as the tails. Cut the meat from the tails into small dice. Blend the rest of the meat with the remaining butter in a food processor and set aside.

Blend the contents of the saucepan in the food processor and return this soup to a clean saucepan. Place over a low heat to warm it through.

Add the cream to the bisque and then add the langoustine butter in small pieces, whisking constantly to blend well. Season to taste with salt, pepper and cayenne pepper.

To serve, divide the tail meat among 4 hot, deep soup plates and pour the bisque over it.

see also:
fruit
jams, etc
raspberry tart

BLACKBERRY OR BRAMBLE

Mûre

The reddish-black fruit of the wild bramble and its cultivated cousin, the blackberry, is larger and darker than that of the raspberry, which belongs to the same family. There are literally hundreds of varieties of blackberry and, outside Europe, there is much confusion between types of blackberry and raspberry. Other related berries include the loganberry, boysenberry, veitchberry and dewberry, which are used in the same way as the blackberry.

Wild blackberries, picked from the hedgerow in September and October, have a very pronounced flavour. The cultivated berries tend to be slightly lacking in flavour, and they are used mainly for jams, jellies and syrups and for tarts and sorbets.

Like other small soft red fruits, blackberries freeze well. They are high in fibre and vitamins C and E; 100 g/3½ oz contains 57 calories.

TARTELETTES AUX MÛRES

Blackberry tartlets

Makes 6 tartlets
Preparation 20 minutes, standing 2 hours
Cooking 25–30 minutes

METRIC/IMPERIAL	*AMERICAN*
200 g/7 oz flour	*1½ cups flour*
150 g/5½ oz caster sugar	*¾ cup superfine sugar*
1 egg, beaten	*1 egg, beaten*
125 g/4½ oz butter, softened	*9 tbsp butter, softened*
800 g/1¾ lb blackberries, hulled	*1¾ lb (3 pt) blackberries, hulled*
salt	*salt*

Put the flour into a bowl and make a well in the centre of it. Add 55 g/2 oz/4½ tbsp of the sugar, a pinch of salt and the beaten egg. Knead the mixture with the fingertips, then add 100 g/3½ oz/1 stick of the butter. Continue to work the dough until it is smooth, then form it into a ball and let it stand for 2 hours.

Grease 6 tartlet moulds with the remaining butter and preheat the oven to 200C/400F/gas 6.

Roll out the pastry to about 3 mm/⅛ in thick and use it to line the 6 tartlet moulds.

Prick the pastry bases with a fork and sprinkle them with some of the remaining sugar. Fill the tartlet cases with the blackberries, packing them closely together. Sprinkle again with more sugar.

Bake the tartlets for 20–25 minutes, until the pastry is golden brown. When they are cooked, remove them from the oven and turn them out carefully on a wire rack. They may be served warm or cold.

see also:
bavarian cream
fruit
jams, etc
liqueur
redcurrant

BLACKCURRANT

Cassis

This fruit, related to the redcurrant, is mainly available in its principal areas of cultivation, in France the Côte d'Or, Lorraine and Val-de-Loire, although it can be found elsewhere. It does preserve and freeze well. The *noir de Bourgogne* variety, with small, black, shiny fruit, has excellent flavour. Some varieties, such as Wellington XXX yield bountifully.

Seldom eaten raw as it is too tart, the blackcurrant is principally used in the making of jams and jellies, *bavarois*, sorbets, soufflés and tarts.

A large part of the French harvest goes into the making of *cassis* liqueur. This is used to make the refreshing summer aperitif *kir*, a few drops of *cassis* topped up with white wine.

Blackcurrants are rich in vitamin C and low in calories, 100 g/3½ oz contains 28 calories, but usually require sweetening.

SORBET AU CASSIS

Blackcurrant sorbet

Serves 6
Preparation 15 minutes
Chilling about 3 hours

METRIC/IMPERIAL	AMERICAN
250 g/8½ oz granulated sugar	1¼ cups granulated sugar
400 ml/14 fl oz fresh blackcurrant juice	1¾ cups fresh blackcurrant juice
juice of 1 lemon	juice of 1 lemon
2 egg whites	2 egg whites
2 tbsp caster sugar	2 tbsp superfine sugar

Put the granulated sugar in a pan with 400 ml/14 fl oz/1¾ cups of water. Heat it for 5 minutes until it comes to the boil and all the sugar has dissolved. Skim off any froth that forms.

Add the blackcurrant and lemon juices and bring back to the boil. Strain the syrup through a sieve and leave it to cool. Pour the mixture into ice trays and freeze it for about 1 hour.

Whisk the egg whites to stiff peaks. Pour the sorbet, which will be half-frozen, into a chilled bowl and quickly incorporate the egg whites and caster (superfine) sugar. Mix thoroughly and return the mixture to the ice trays, then freeze until the sorbet has reached the desired consistency or beat the nearly frozen sorbet in a food processor until creamy, then freeze again. Repeat the process for a smoother texture.

Note: this operation is easier using a sorbetière (ice cream machine).

LIQUEUR DE CASSIS

Cassis liqueur

Makes about 1.5 l/2½ pt/1½ qt
Preparation 30 minutes, 1 month ahead

METRIC/IMPERIAL	AMERICAN
1 kg/2¼ lb blackcurrants	2¼ lb (about 4 pt) blackcurrants
1 l/1¾ pt eau-de-vie	1 qt eau-de-vie
1 clove	1 clove
1½ sticks of cinnamon	1½ sticks of cinnamon
10–12 green blackcurrant leaves	10–12 green blackcurrant leaves
800 g/1¾ lb sugar	4 cups sugar

Remove any stems from the blackcurrants, rinse the fruit and pat dry, then mash them roughly with a fork.

Mix the *eau-de-vie*, the clove, the cinnamon sticks and the blackcurrant leaves together in a bowl. Add the blackcurrants and the sugar. Mix well and pour into a large jar. Seal the jar tightly. Put the jar in a warm place, in the sun if possible, and let it stand for 1 month.

After this time, pour the mixture through a clean cloth into a large bowl, squeezing the cloth to express all the liquid. Filter the liquid and bottle it. If it is too strong, add a little sugar dissolved in cold water: 250 g/8½ oz/1¼ cups sugar to 200 ml/7 fl oz/1 cup of water.

Firmly corked and stored in a cool place, the liqueur will keep for several years.

see also:
charcuterie
pork
sausage

BLACK PUDDING OR BLOOD SAUSAGE

Boudin noir

The essential ingredients of this very dark-coloured sausage are seasoned pigs' blood and fat, encased in the pig's intestine. Some black puddings are made with ox or sheep's blood, but these are much coarser.

In Britain and the USA black pudding tends to have a high cereal filler content, usually barley, oatmeal or flour, and little seasoning, so it tends to have a fairly undistinguished flavour. In France, however, the forcemeat usually contains little cereal and is often augmented with cream, herbs, garlic, brandy, vegetables such as raw onions and spinach, fruit or nuts (mainly apples, prunes, raisins or chestnuts) so some spectacular delicacies result.

Black pudding is usually sold by length, or in pre-packed portions, and is usually cut into slices to be grilled or fried and then served piping hot. The traditional accompaniments in France are mashed potatoes and sautéed apples.

Boudin antillais, also black but very highly spiced, is generally poached whole in water.

Black pudding is an excellent source of iron, but it does have a very high fat content.

BOUDIN NOIR ET POMMES EN L'AIR

Black pudding or blood sausage with apples

Serves 4
Preparation 10 minutes
Cooking about 20 minutes

METRIC/IMPERIAL	*AMERICAN*
800 g/1¾ lb firm-fleshed dessert apples	*1¾ lb firm-fleshed apples*
juice of 1 lemon	*juice of 1 lemon*
100 g/3½ oz butter	*1 stick butter*
4 small whole black puddings	*4 small whole blood sausages or 4 thick slices*
salt and pepper	*salt and pepper*

Peel and slice the apples and sprinkle them with the lemon juice. Heat half the butter in a frying pan and cook the apple slices over a moderate heat, turning them frequently, until they are glazed and golden brown.

Melt the rest of the butter in a second frying pan and cook the black puddings (blood sausages), turning them often, until they are crisp on all sides. Cook them over a high heat for the first minute or two to seal them, but make sure that the skins do not burst.

Transfer the black puddings to the pan containing the apples and season them with salt and pepper. Mix together and heat them for 1 minute, then serve immediately while still piping hot.

BLANCHING

see also:
bean
brain
cabbage
creams and custards
deep frying
freezing
pastry
potato
refreshing
spinach
sweetbread

Three main types of culinary operation are covered by this term. The principal form of blanching denotes the brief cooking of raw foods in boiling water. This is done for several reasons: to remove impurities and lighten colour, as with brains and sweetbreads, where the blanching removes any residual blood after soaking; to remove excess salt, usually with cured products, such as hams and bacon or salt fish; to ease peeling, as with tomatoes, peaches or some nuts; to remove bitterness; to set colour; to pre-cook before some other means of cooking, such as potatoes for frying or roasting.

Depending on the purpose of the blanching and the food in question, the water may be plain, salted, or have a little vinegar added to it. The food is either brought to the boil in the water or plunged briefly into water that is already boiling.

Blanched foods, green vegetables in particular, are often immediately refreshed in cold water to arrest the cooking process.

Second, the term blanching is often used to denote the first stage of two-stage cooking: as in the deep frying of potatoes, where the first stage at a lower temperature softens the potatoes, and the later frying at a higher temperature browns them.

Third, blanching is the expression used in the making of custard creams and doughs to denote the process of vigorously blending egg yolks and sugar until they increase in volume and become light and fluffy.

see also:
almond
gelatine
jelly

BLANCMANGE OR ALMOND MILK

Blanc-manger

A cold mould of sweetened crushed almonds, now usually set with gelatine, which is said to be one of civilization's oldest desserts. The cuisines of those countries in which almonds are plentiful, such as Spain, have used almond milk or cream, sweetened with honey, as a refreshing drink or as a sweet course for centuries.

Blancmange is also often used as a base for other cold desserts and sundaes, dressed with fruit, cream or ice cream.

BLANC-MANGER AUX FRAISES

Blancmange or almond milk with strawberries

Serves 4
Preparation 20 minutes, chilling 1 hour
Cooking 2–3 minutes

METRIC/IMPERIAL	AMERICAN
2 gelatine leaves or 1 tsp gelatine powder	2 gelatine leaves or 1 tsp powdered, unflavored gelatine
200 ml/7 fl oz skimmed milk	1 cup skim milk
few drops of bitter almond essence	few drops of bitter almond extract
550 g/1¼ lb strawberries, hulled	1¼ lb (2 pt) strawberries, hulled
sugar or powdered artificial sweetener to taste	sugar or powdered artificial sweetener to taste

Soak the gelatine leaves in a little cold water for 15 minutes, then squeeze dry. Alternatively, if using powdered gelatine, soften it in 1 tablespoon of water.

Bring the milk to the boil. Remove it from the heat and add a few drops of almond essence (extract) and the gelatine. Mix well until the gelatine is completely dissolved, then pour into a deep dish. Chill until the mixture sets.

Meanwhile, purée one third of the strawberries in a food processor, adding sugar or powdered sweetener to taste. Mix well and chill. Slice the remaining strawberries.

When the blancmange is set firmly, cut it into squares and pile these on 4 plates. Top the blancmange pieces with the sliced strawberries and coat the whole thing with the well-chilled purée. Serve at once.

Note: using artificial sweetener, this dish contains only 60 calories per portion.

BLANQUETTE

see also:
fricassée
liaison
ragoût
stewing

A stew made with white meat, such as veal, lamb or chicken, or any firm white fish, such as monkfish, sea bream or brill, cooked in a white stock or in water with aromatic flavourings. The dish is usually thickened by the addition of a binding mixture of cream and egg yolk.

Blanquettes may be made well in advance, but the binding mixture should be added only at the last minute.

BLANQUETTE DE LOTTE

Monkfish stew

Serves 6
Preparation 20 minutes
Cooking 25 minutes

METRIC/IMPERIAL	AMERICAN
45 g/1½ oz butter	3 tbsp butter
1.5 kg/3½ lb monkfish fillets, cut into 2.5 cm/1 in cubes	3½ lb monkfish fillet, cut into 1 in cubes
200 ml/7 fl oz white wine	1 cup white wine
225 g/½ lb baby onions	½ lb baby onions
1 carrot, sliced	1 carrot, sliced
225 g/½ lb white button mushrooms, sliced	½ lb white button mushrooms, sliced
whites of 2 leeks, sliced	whites of 2 leeks, sliced
bouquet garni	bouquet garni
2 egg yolks	2 egg yolks
150 ml/¼ pt crème fraîche or whipping cream	⅔ cup crème fraîche or whipping cream
juice of 1 lemon	juice of 1 lemon
salt and pepper	salt and pepper

Heat the butter in a flameproof casserole over a gentle heat. Seal the monkfish pieces in the butter without allowing them to brown. Moisten the fish with the white wine and add just enough water to cover it. Add the baby onions, carrot, mushrooms, leeks and bouquet garni. Simmer gently for 15 minutes.

Using a slotted spoon, remove and discard the bouquet garni and transfer the monkfish and vegetables to a warmed, deep serving dish.

In a bowl beat the egg yolks with the cream and lemon juice. Slowly add this mixture to the casserole, whisking constantly until the sauce is smooth. Heat without letting it boil. Pour over the vegetables and fish and serve at once.

To drink: a good white wine, such as a Sancerre.

BLANQUETTE DE VEAU

White veal stew

Serves 4
Preparation 20 minutes
Cooking about 1½ hours

METRIC/IMPERIAL	AMERICAN
1 onion	1 onion
1 clove	1 clove
30 g/1 oz butter	2 tbsp butter
1 tbsp oil	1 tbsp oil
1.35 kg/3 lb boneless veal shoulder, breast or flank, cut into large cubes	3 lb boneless veal shoulder or breast, cut into large cubes
2 tbsp flour	2 tbsp flour
2 carrots, sliced	2 carrots, sliced
1 leek, trimmed and sliced	1 leek, trimmed and sliced
bouquet garni	bouquet garni
2 egg yolks	2 egg yolks
150 ml/¼ pt crème fraîche or whipping cream	⅔ cup crème fraîche or whipping cream
juice of ½ lemon	juice of ½ lemon
salt and pepper	salt and pepper

Stud the peeled onion with the clove.

Heat the butter and oil over a low heat in a large, flameproof casserole and seal the pieces of meat very gently without allowing them to brown. Season with salt and pepper.

Blanquette de veau (White veal stew)

Sprinkle with the flour, stir well and cook for 2 minutes. Add just enough hot water to cover the meat.

Add the carrots, leek, the onion studded with the clove and the bouquet garni. Cover and simmer gently for 1¼ hours.

Remove the pieces of meat, put them in a warmed deep serving dish and keep warm. Strain the cooking liquid and return it to the rinsed-out casserole. Reduce the liquid over a high heat for 5 minutes .

Mix the egg yolks with the cream and lemon juice in a bowl. Season with salt and pepper. Add this mixture to the cooking liquid and heat gently, whisking constantly, without letting it boil. Pour this sauce over the meat, stir and serve.

Notes: plain boiled rice or potato is the classic accompaniment to a blanquette. The vegetables which were cooked with the meat may also be drained and added to the contents of the serving dish before the sauce is poured over.

Try cooking the meat in an equal-parts mixture of water and white wine; 170 g/6 oz chopped button mushrooms may also be added to the sauce.

BLOOD SAUSAGE

see Black pudding

BLUEBERRY

see Bilberry

BOILING

see also:
egg
pasta
poaching
simmering
sugar

Boiling is a term properly reserved for fast cooking. It applies to cooking at very high temperatures, as in cooked sugars, or where the rapid agitation of the water keeps items separate as with pasta, or in the quick cooking of green vegetables to retain their colour.

The term boiling is, however, often used where actually gentle poaching at a simmer is required. The classic boiled egg is, in fact, simply an egg which has been poached in its shell and boiled beef is normally simmered.

POULE AU POT

Boiled chicken

Serves 8
Preparation 35 minutes
Cooking about 2 hours

METRIC/IMPERIAL	AMERICAN
1 boiling fowl (preferably a hen), dressed weight about 2 kg/4½ lb, giblets retained	1 chicken (preferably a stewing chicken), dressed and drawn weight about 4½ lb, giblets retained
100 g/3½ oz ham, chopped	⅔ cup chopped cooked ham
2 shallots, chopped	2 shallots, chopped
2 slices of white bread	2 slices of white bread
150 ml/¼ pt milk	⅔ cup milk
1 egg, beaten	1 egg, beaten
2 calves' feet, cut in pieces	2 calves' feet, cut in pieces
800 g/1¾ lb celery hearts	1¾ lb celery hearts
6 carrots	6 carrots
3 turnips	3 turnips
whites of 4 leeks	whites of 4 leeks
2 onions	2 onions
1 clove	1 clove
bouquet garni	bouquet garni
salt and pepper	salt and pepper

Season the inside of the chicken with salt and pepper. Chop the liver, heart and gizzard.

Soak the bread in the milk, then squeeze it out. Combine the bread with the chopped giblets, ham, shallots and egg. Season with salt and pepper. Use this mixture to stuff the chicken, then sew it up and truss it. Place in a large stewpot with the calves' feet. Cover with cold water and bring slowly to the boil.

Scrub or peel all the vegetables and cut into chunks. Stud one of the onions with the clove.

When the stock is boiling, skim it, add the vegetables and bouquet garni and season with salt and pepper. Bring back to the boil, lower the heat and cook gently for about 1½ hours.

Skim off as much fat as possible from the stock. Serve the stock as a soup, followed by the meat, accompanied by gherkins (pickled cucumbers), mustard and coarse salt.

BOEUF À LA FICELLE

Boiled beef fillet tied with string

Serves 6
Preparation 20 minutes
Cooking 30–40 minutes

METRIC/IMPERIAL	AMERICAN
1 kg/2¼ lb beef fillet, trimmed, rolled and tied with string	2¼ lb beef tenderloin roast, trimmed, rolled and tied with string
bouquet garni	bouquet garni
1 onion	1 onion
1 clove	1 clove
225 g/½ lb carrots, coarsely chopped	½ lb carrots, coarsely chopped
whites of 3 leeks	whites of 3 leeks
4 stalks of celery, cut into large pieces	4 sticks of celery, cut into large pieces
1 tbsp coarse salt	1 tbsp coarse salt
10 black peppercorns	10 black peppercorns

Attach a piece of string to the string at either end of the piece of beef.

Pour 2 l/3½ pt/2 qt of water into a large stewpot with handles and add the bouquet garni, the onion peeled and studded with the clove, the carrots, leeks, celery, coarse salt and peppercorns. Bring to a good rolling boil. Put the piece of beef into the boiling liquid, using the loops of string to attach it to the handles of the stewpot. Make sure it is not held too tautly.

Bring it back to a rolling boil then reduce the heat and let it simmer for 20–30 minutes. The meat must be totally immersed in the cooking liquid.

At the end of the cooking time, use the pieces of string attached to the handles to take the beef out of the hot water. Place it on a dish, remove the string and slice the meat; the slices should still be pink in the middle. Drain the vegetables, discarding the bouquet garni and clove and reserving the stock. Arrange the vegetables around the slices of meat as a garnish.

Serve, accompanied by pickled cucumbers and onions, beetroot, mustard and coarse salt. Strain and skim the stock and serve it as a soup garnished with croutons and grated Gruyère.
To drink: a soft, fruity red wine, such as Chinon.

see also:
beef
sauce

BONE MARROW

Moelle animale

A soft, fatty substance found in the cavities within the long bones of mammals, generally it is beef marrow from the knuckle (shin) that is used in cooking. Many regard bone marrow as a great delicacy, and marrow on toast was a tea-time favourite in Victorian England.

Bone marrow is used to enrich many dishes, such as risotto, and a good French *pot-au-feu* traditionally contains several chunks of bone marrow cooked along with the meat, to give depth of flavour as well as providing a tasty accompaniment.

Bone marrow can be bought fresh or frozen. It is usually poached in salted water and cut into pieces before use. It may be spread on canapés or used to stuff vegetables, such as cardoons or artichoke hearts. Bone marrow sauce is a traditional *haute cuisine* accompaniment to red meats and grilled fish.

Bone marrow has a very high fat content: 100 g/3½ oz contains 610 calories.

CROÛTONS À LA MOELLE

Croutons with bone marrow

Serves 2
Preparation 5 minutes
Cooking 7–10 minutes

METRIC/IMPERIAL	AMERICAN
2 pieces of marrow bone, each about 4 cm/1½ in long	2 pieces of beef shin bone, each about 1½ in long
200 ml/7 fl oz good beef stock or water	1 cup good beef stock or water
4 small, thin slices of bread	4 small, thin slices of bread
coarse salt	coarse salt

Put the pieces of beef bone into a saucepan and pour the beef stock or water over them. Add a good sprinkling of salt if using water and bring to the boil, then lower the heat and simmer for 5 minutes. Toast the slices of bread.

Drain the pieces of bone and arrange them on very hot plates, with the toast and coarse salt on the side.

To eat the marrow, use a small spoon to extract it from the bones, spread it on the toast and season it with a pinch of coarse salt.

Notes: marrow congeals very quickly, so serve promptly. If using frozen bone marrow, cook it as described earlier for 7–8 minutes.

BONING

see also:
ballottine
beef
chicken
lamb
pork

The removal of bones from meat, poultry, game and fish may be necessary or advisable in the preparation of certain dishes. It should be done using a specialist boning knife and with great care to avoid damaging the meat or piercing the skin of a bird or fish.

When boning at home, always use a very sharp boning knife or a suitably sturdy and pointed paring knife, and make especially sure that the tip is sharp as this is the part which does most of the work.

When you ask your butcher or fishmonger to bone a purchase for you, do make sure they also supply the bones for use in stocks or sauces.

BOUILLABAISSE

see also:
bourride
fish
rouille
soup

This Mediterranean fish soup is most commonly associated with the region around Marseilles. Essentially a fisherman's dish to make use of catch they could not sell, it relies on the use of a wide variety of shellfish and fish, boiled rapidly on the bone with olive oil, spices and flavourings.

Scorpion fish (*rascasse*), sea bass, eels, wrasse and *girelles*, a local species of rockfish, are an indispensable part of authentic bouillabaisse. However, there are many different recipes for the dish, and up to 40 fish associated with it. Although they should all strictly speaking be Mediterranean fish, any good combination of white fish, such as monkfish, John Dory, red mullet, whiting, red snapper, perch, haddock, porgy and flounder, and rich-flavoured fish such as moray or conger eel, mackerel or striped bass will give good results. Small crab are often added to the Provençal version, but the addition of other shellfish, such as lobster, has been popularized by city chefs.

The Marseilles bouillabaisse gets its unique flavour from the addition of tomatoes, fennel and saffron. Other versions include flavourings such as orange peel, aniseed or Pernod and white wine.

The soup is cooked at a rapid boil to ensure that the olive oil emulsifies in the broth, thus thickening and flavouring it. It is therefore essential that a good olive oil with a full flavour and good colour is used.

Traditionally, bouillabaisse is served over slices of warmed or toasted French bread which have been rubbed with garlic or spread with spicy *rouille* sauce. Sometimes a dollop of the sauce is floated on top.

Provided the accompanying *rouille* is eaten sparingly, bouillabaisse makes a nourishing, well-balanced, low-calorie meal.

BOUILLABAISSE MARSEILLAISE

Marseilles fish soup

Serves 6
Preparation 30 minutes
Cooking about 40 minutes

METRIC/IMPERIAL	AMERICAN
2 kg/4½ lb assorted fish (see p. 71), preferably on the bone	4½ lb assorted fish (see p. 71), preferably on the bone
3 garlic cloves	3 garlic cloves
2 onions	2 onions
2 leeks, trimmed and very finely chopped	2 leeks, trimmed and very finely chopped
3 stalks of celery, trimmed and very finely chopped	3 sticks of celery, trimmed and very finely chopped
150 ml/¼ pt good olive oil	⅔ cup good olive oil
1 fennel bulb, chopped	1 fennel bulb, chopped
3 tomatoes, peeled and cut into pieces	3 tomatoes, peeled and cut into pieces
bouquet garni	bouquet garni
few saffron threads	few saffron threads
10 small crabs, brushed and cleaned	10 small crabs, scrubbed
1 French loaf (baguette), to serve	1 French loaf (baguette), to serve
salt and pepper	salt and pepper
FOR THE ROUILLE:	FOR THE ROUILLE:
1 slice of white bread	1 slice of white bread
3 garlic cloves	3 garlic cloves
1 red chilli pepper, chopped	1 red chili pepper, chopped
1 egg yolk	1 egg yolk
200 ml/7 fl oz olive oil	1 cup olive oil
cayenne pepper	cayenne pepper

Clean and scale the fish and remove their heads. Cut the fish into pieces.

Chop 1 of the garlic cloves and 1 of the onions very finely and brown them with the leeks and the celery in 100 ml/3½ fl oz/½ cup of the oil in a large, heavy-based saucepan over a moderate heat. Season them with salt and pepper, add the fish heads and trimmings and just enough water to cover, and boil for 20 minutes.

Strain the stock, pressing to extract as much liquid from the solids as possible. Discard the solids.

Chop the remaining onion and garlic cloves and lightly brown them with the fennel in the remaining oil in a large stewpot over a moderate heat.

Pour the strained fish stock over them and add the tomatoes, bouquet garni and saffron. Add the fish, except the more delicate ones such as John Dory and whiting, and the crabs.

Boil over a high heat for 8 minutes, then add the reserved fish. Cook for a further 5–6 minutes, again at a good rolling boil.

Meanwhile, make the *rouille*: moisten the white bread with a little of the soup and then press it to squeeze out excess moisture. Pound the bread in a mortar with the garlic cloves and the chopped chilli. Add the egg yolk and then the olive oil in a thin stream, as if making mayonnaise. Season to taste with salt and cayenne pepper.

Cut the French bread into slices and warm in a low oven. Place the fish and crabs in a large warmed serving dish, discarding the bouquet garni. Pour the broth into a soup tureen. Serve the *rouille* and the warmed French bread slices separately as accompaniments.

Bouillabaisse marseillaise (Marseilles fish soup)

BOUILLON

see Stock

see also: herbs

BOUQUET GARNI

A selection of aromatic fresh or dried herbs, bouquets garnis are tied together or wrapped in muslin or cheesecloth or stout permeable paper so that they may easily be removed at the end of cooking. An essential item in most dishes involving long, slow simmering, the most usual constituents are 2 or 3 parsley sprigs, 1 sprig of thyme and 1 or 2 bay leaves.

A wide variety of other herbs (such as basil, chervil, lemon thyme, marjoram, rosemary, savory, sage and tarragon), spices (including cinnamon, cloves and mace) and other aromatics (such as celery, chilli peppers, leeks and orange zest) may be added, depending on the ingredients of the dish and the required flavour.

Ready-made bouquet garni loses its flavour rapidly and should be used within a matter of weeks. Always remember to remove a bouquet garni from any dish before serving or puréeing.

see also: beef marinade ragoût wine

BOURGUIGNON OR BOURGUIGNONNE (À LA)

The term is used to describe a wide variety of dishes which are cooked in red wine and normally garnished with chopped bacon, baby onions and button mushrooms. Items as diverse as poached eggs, poultry, calves' liver, fish and vegetables are given this treatment, but by far the most celebrated dish of this kind uses beef in *boeuf bourguignon*.

The long, slow cooking involved in the preparation of this famous stew makes the most of the more economical cuts of beef. To heighten the flavour of the dish, marinate the meat for several hours in the red wine in which it is to be cooked, along with some herbs.

It is a good idea to make double the quantity required, as beef bourguignon is one of those useful dishes which taste even better when they are reheated.

Boeuf bourguignon is not as rich as it is reputed to be. It contains only 180 calories per 100 g/3½ oz, of which 29% is protein and only 7% fat, and it is very nutritious.

BOEUF BOURGUIGNON

Beef burgundy

Serves 4
Preparation 15 minutes
Cooking 2¼ hours

METRIC/IMPERIAL	*AMERICAN*
45 g/1½ oz butter	*3 tbsp butter*
1 tbsp oil	*1 tbsp oil*
140 g/5 oz streaky bacon, cut into strips	*5 oz sliced bacon, cut into strips*
2 large onions, sliced	*2 large onions, sliced*
1 kg/2¼ lb stewing steak (chuck or rump), cut in pieces	*2¼ lb beef for stew (chuck or rump), cut in pieces*
1 bottle (750 ml/27 fl oz) of red Burgundy	*1 bottle (75 cl) of red Burgundy*
bouquet garni	*bouquet garni*
1 carrot, sliced	*1 carrot, sliced*
1 garlic clove	*1 garlic clove*
225 g/½ lb white button mushrooms, sliced	*½ lb white button mushrooms, sliced*
1 tbsp tomato purée	*1 tbsp tomato paste*
salt and pepper	*salt and pepper*

Heat half the butter with the oil in a flameproof casserole over a moderate heat and brown the bacon and onions in it. When they are golden brown, remove them from the pan.

Put the pieces of meat in the same casserole and brown them, then return the bacon and onions to the pan. Season with pepper and add the wine, the bouquet garni, carrot and the peeled garlic clove. Cover, lower the heat and simmer very gently for 2 hours.

Brown the mushroom slices in the remaining butter. About 15 minutes before the end of cooking, add them to the casserole along with the tomato purée (paste). Stir thoroughly.

Remove the bouquet garni and serve the dish from the casserole. Steamed potatoes dressed with chopped parsley are the classic accompaniment to this dish.

To drink: a good red Burgundy, such as Nuits Saint Georges.

Boeuf bourguignon (Beef burgundy)

BOURRIDE

see also:
aïoli
bouillabaisse
fish
soup

A Provençal fish soup which is like a light-coloured version of bouillabaisse, but made with very simple flavourings, including fish stock, garlic, onions and herbs.

An authentic bourride is made only with monkfish, but versions exist which use a wide variety of mixtures of local fish, such as whiting, sea bass, sea bream, John Dory, conger eel and grey and red mullet.

At the end of cooking, the soup is thickened with an *aïoli*. The dish may be poured over slices of dried bread and accompanied by more *aïoli*, or the fish is sometimes served separately with a vegetable accompaniment.

BOURRIDE

Provençal fish soup

Serves 6
Preparation 15 minutes
Cooking about 30 minutes

METRIC/IMPERIAL	*AMERICAN*
200 ml/7 fl oz dry white wine	*1 cup dry white wine*
1 onion, chopped	*1 onion, chopped*
3 lemon slices	*3 lemon slices*
piece of dried orange peel	*piece of dried orange peel*
sprig of thyme	*sprig of thyme*
bay leaf	*bay leaf*
1 tsp fennel seeds	*1 tsp fennel seeds*
1 garlic clove	*1 garlic clove*
1.5 kg/3½ lb white fish (such as monkfish, bass, turbot, hake), sliced or cut in pieces	*3½ lb white fish (such as monkfish, bass, turbot, hake), sliced or cut in pieces*
3 egg yolks	*3 egg yolks*
2 tbsp crème fraîche or whipping cream	*2 tbsp crème fraîche or whipping cream*
salt and pepper	*salt and pepper*
FOR THE AÏOLI:	*FOR THE AÏOLI:*
4 garlic cloves	*4 garlic cloves*
2 egg yolks	*2 egg yolks*
200 ml/7 fl oz olive oil	*1 cup olive oil*

Pour 1 l/$1\frac{3}{4}$ pt/1 qt of water into a stewpot along with the wine. Add the onion, lemon slices, orange peel, thyme, bay leaf, fennel seeds and garlic clove, crushed with the side of a knife. Bring to the boil. Add the pieces of fish, season with salt and pepper and cook on a low rolling boil for 12–15 minutes.

Drain the pieces of fish and set aside in a warmed, deep serving dish, adding 1 tablespoon of the stock. Strain the rest of the stock.

Make the *aïoli*: peel and pound the garlic cloves in a mortar. Mix in the egg yolks and then the olive oil in a steady stream, as if making mayonnaise. Season with salt and pepper.

Return the stock to the pan, place over a gentle heat and gradually add half the *aïoli*, whisking. Add the 3 remaining egg yolks, stirring continuously and taking care not to let the mixture boil. Add the cream and whisk until the soup is thick and creamy.

Serve the soup in a large tureen along with the fish, with the remaining *aïoli* served separately. Boiled potatoes make a good accompaniment for this soup.

BRAIN

Cervelle

see also:
blanching
lamb
offal
pork
veal

A white offal (variety meat) which is obtained from most meat-producing animals. Brains are rich in vitamins and minerals with a delicate flavour and creamy texture when cooked.

Calves' and lambs' brains are the best flavoured and thus find the most culinary use, but they are also the most expensive. Allow 1 calves' brain for 2 people and cook for about 10 minutes; allow 1 of the pink-tinged lambs' brains per person, and cook for only 5 minutes.

Ox brains are the most economical and have the firmest consistency; allow 1 brain for 4 people and cook for about 20 minutes. Pigs' brains are very similar to ox brains, but are rarely used; allow 1 brain per person and cook for 5 minutes.

Like all offal, brains must be used while still very fresh. They must be well prepared before cooking to eliminate residual blood. They are first washed under cold running water, carefully taking off any easily removed outer skin and membrane. They are then left to soak for at least 1 hour (up to 4 hours for ox brains) in cold or tepid acidulated water. The remaining outer skin and membranes are then snipped or rubbed off (for all but the very delicate lamb's brains) and the brains rinsed again under cold running water. Finally, they may be blanched briefly in salted water before being gently poached in court-bouillon prior to any further cooking.

Brains contain half the protein of most other meat and have a very high cholesterol content.

CERVELLES MEUNIÈRE

Fried brains

Serves 4
Preparation 15 minutes, plus soaking
Cooking 20 minutes

METRIC/IMPERIAL	AMERICAN
2 calves' brains	2 calves' brains
2 tbsp vinegar	2 tbsp vinegar
juice of 1 lemon + 1 lemon, sliced	juice of 1 lemon + 1 lemon, sliced
bouquet garni	bouquet garni
flour, for dusting	flour, for dusting
45 g/1½ oz butter	3 tbsp butter
1 tbsp oil	1 tbsp oil
bunch of flat-leaved parsley, chopped	bunch of flat-leaf parsley, chopped
salt and white pepper	salt and white pepper

Rinse, soak and trim the brains as described above, adding the vinegar to the soaking water.

Rinse the brains again and then put them in a saucepan with water to cover, along with the lemon juice, a little salt and the bouquet garni. Bring to the boil, lower the heat and poach them gently for 12 minutes.

Drain the brains and pat them dry with paper towels. Leave them to cool and then cut them across in even, diagonal slices. Dust the slices with flour. Heat the butter and oil in a frying pan over a moderate heat. Add the brains and brown them gently on both sides.

Drain them and arrange them on a warmed serving plate. Surround them with the lemon slices and sprinkle with the chopped parsley.

To drink: a good dry or semi-sweet white wine, such as Muscadet or Tokay d'Alsace.

CERVELLES D'AGNEAU POULETTE

Lambs' brains in white sauce

Serves 4
Preparation 15 minutes, plus soaking
Cooking about 25 minutes

METRIC/IMPERIAL	AMERICAN
4 frozen lambs' brains, defrosted	4 frozen lambs' brains, defrosted
1.1 l/2 pt fresh court-bouillon or vegetable stock	5 cups court-bouillon or vegetable stock
55 g/2 oz butter	4 tbsp butter
45 g/1½ oz flour	¼ cup flour
500 ml/16 fl oz chicken stock	2 cups chicken stock
2 egg yolks	2 egg yolks
juice of 1 lemon	juice of 1 lemon
salt and pepper	salt and pepper
snipped chives, to garnish	snipped chives, to garnish

Bring the court-bouillon or vegetable stock to the boil in a saucepan and then put in the brains, adding a little more boiling water to cover, if necessary. Simmer gently for about 5 minutes. Drain the cooked brains and cut each in half.

Melt the butter in a saucepan. Add the flour and stir it into the butter over a low heat.

Heat the chicken stock in a separate pan and then pour it over the flour and butter mixture. Cook for 15 minutes without letting it boil, stirring continuously.

In a bowl, mix the egg yolks and lemon juice with 3 tablespoons of the hot sauce, then pour the mixture into the sauce and stir over a gentle heat.

Reheat the brains gently in the sauce. Pour into a warmed, deep serving dish and garnish with the snipped chives before serving.

see also:
daube
larding
marinade
mirepoix

BRAISING

This term is used to describe the cooking of food in its own juices, or with very little liquid, such as water, stock, wine, lemon juice or a marinade, over a gentle heat for a long period of time in a closed container.

Items which suit braising include the tougher cuts of meat, older and larger poultry, and certain vegetables, including cabbage, chicory (Belgian endive), artichoke and lettuce. Certain firm-fleshed fish, such as monkfish, carp or salmon, may be braised in covered containers in the oven rather than over direct heat.

Food to be braised is often marinated beforehand. Meat is usually barded with fat or bacon and normally quickly browned before cooking, to seal it and give it a more attractive appearance. Meat and poultry are normally set on a *mirepoix*, a bed of finely cubed vegetables, which produces cooking liquid and adds flavour, as well as protecting the food from the direct heat and preventing it from boiling or frying in the cooking liquid. Vegetables normally produce enough liquid of their own, or are left wet after preparation or, at most, need a few spoonfuls of added stock.

Good braising is an art and can produce delicious results. The process can take up to 5 or 6 hours, with continual additions of heated basting liquid to prevent drying out.

BRAISE DE BOEUF

Braised beef

Serves 6
Preparation 10 minutes
Cooking about 1¾ hours

METRIC/IMPERIAL	AMERICAN
1 tbsp margarine	*1 tbsp margarine*
1.5 kg/3½ lb beef top rump, lean chuck or silverside, larded and rolled	*3½ lb boneless beef rump roast or chuck eye roast, larded and tied*
200 ml/7 fl oz white wine	*1 cup white wine*
juice of 1 lemon	*juice of 1 lemon*
3 onions, chopped	*3 onions, chopped*
1 garlic clove	*1 garlic clove*
bouquet garni	*bouquet garni*
225 g/½ lb thickly sliced streaky bacon, cut into strips	*½ lb thick-sliced bacon, cut into strips*
salt and pepper	*salt and pepper*

Heat the margarine in a large, flameproof casserole (use one large enough to ensure that the liquid does not cover the meat) over a moderate heat and brown the meat in it on all sides. Take care not to let the fat burn.

Moisten with the wine, lemon juice and 100 ml/3½ fl oz/½ cup water. Add the onions, garlic, bouquet garni and salt and pepper.

Simmer gently for 1½ hours.

About 10 minutes before serving, brown the bacon in a frying pan without fat until crisp.

Remove the beef from the casserole, take off the string and slice the meat. Skim the fat from the cooking liquid and pour it over the slices of beef. Garnish with the crisply fried bacon.

To drink: red Bordeaux, such as Médoc.

ENDIVES BRAISÉES

Braised chicory or Belgian endive

Serves 4
Preparation 10 minutes
Cooking 30 minutes

METRIC/IMPERIAL	AMERICAN
8–10 large firm heads of chicory	*8–10 large firm Belgian endives*
75 g/2½ oz butter	*5 tbsp butter*
1 tbsp oil	*1 tbsp oil*
juice of ½ lemon	*juice of ½ lemon*
caster sugar	*superfine sugar*
salt and pepper	*salt and pepper*
oil, for frying	*oil, for frying*

If necessary, rinse the chicory (Belgian endives) quickly but do not let them soak. Dry them, cut off the base and remove the bitter core of each.

Heat 15 g/½ oz/1 tbsp of the butter with the oil in a flameproof casserole over a moderate heat. Lightly brown the chicory (endives) 2 or 3 at a time, adding a little more butter and oil if necessary and turning the vegetables so that they colour evenly.

Once all the vegetables have been lightly browned, return them to the casserole, sprinkle them with lemon juice and season them with salt and pepper. Cover the pan and continue to cook gently for 10 minutes. Sprinkle them lightly with a little sugar, turn them carefully in the pan and continue cooking them, covered, over a gentle heat for a few minutes more.

This delicious vegetable makes a perfect accompaniment to all roast meats.

BRAN

see also:
cereal
dietary fibre
flour

The outer husk of cereal grains, bran is usually eliminated to a greater or lesser extent during the refining stage of the flour-making process.

However, as it is mostly cellulose, which the body cannot process, it is very rich source of dietary fibre. It also contains a high concentration of vitamin B and more than half of the grain's mineral content.

Wheat bran, having once been a by-product used as animal feed, is now increasingly used commercially to enrich bread, cereals and some biscuits and crackers. Bran itself is also sold as a dietary aid, principally to add to breakfast cereals and to cakes and pastries.

BRANDADE

see also:
cod
salt cod

A thick and tasty emulsion of puréed salt cod and olive oil in hot milk, brandade is a speciality of the Languedoc and Provence. Some versions are flavoured with garlic, but this is frowned on by purists who, at the most, will allow the saucepan or serving dish to be rubbed with garlic or garlic croutons to be served as an accompaniment.

Other versions of the dish contain puréed potatoes (*brandade de vendredi*) and one version, traditionally served on Christmas Eve, even contains truffles.

Brandade is also available canned, and this can be used to make excellent quick hors d'oeuvres, using it as a stuffing for tartlet or barquette cases, which are then garnished with black olives and warmed briefly in the oven.

Brandade makes a very healthy meal as it is nutritionally balanced and relatively low in calories.

BRANDADE DE MORUE

Salt cod purée

Serves 6
Preparation 10 minutes, 12 hours in advance
Cooking about 20 minutes

METRIC/IMPERIAL	*AMERICAN*
1 kg/2¼ lb salt cod fillets	*2¼ lb salt cod fillets*
2 garlic cloves	*2 garlic cloves*
200 ml/7 fl oz milk	*1 cup milk*
400 ml/14 fl oz olive oil	*1¾ cups olive oil*

Soak the cod fillets in cold water for at least 12 hours to remove the salt, changing the water several times.

Put the drained fillets in a saucepan, cover the fish with cold water and bring it to the boil. Lower the heat and poach the fish gently for 12 minutes.

Drain the fillets, place them in a bowl and flake them with a fork. Pound the flaked fish in a mortar along with the garlic.

Heat the milk. Put the salt cod purée in a large saucepan over a low heat. Add the milk and olive oil alternately, in small amounts, beating each in well with a wooden spoon.

The brandade should be smooth and well mixed, but not liquid. Add just enough oil to reach the desired consistency. If the purée does get too liquid, thicken it by adding some hot boiled potato, roughly mashed.

Serve hot or warm.

To drink: dry white wine, such as Graves.

BRANDIES, EAUX-DE-VIE AND FORTIFIED WINES

see also:
alcohol
deglazing
liqueur
macerating
marinade
spirits
wine

The term BRANDY applies to spirits distilled from wines. The French use the term *eau-de-vie* to denote any distilled alcohol with no added sugar, in contrast to liqueurs. Included are brandies, Calvados and applejack, which are made from cider, and alcohols such as whisky, aquavit and vodka made from fermented grain.

Most of the world's vineyards have their own type of brandy, although the French COGNAC and ARMAGNAC are probably best known. The term brandy is also used of spirits distilled from fruits, such as KIRSCH, distilled from cherries, FRAMBOISE, made from raspberries, or MIRABELLE, from plums.

MARC, or *eau-de-vie-de-marc*, is made by fermenting the waste products of wine-making, that is, the sludge of skin, pulp and seeds left after pressing, with no added sugar. The quality is highly variable and some can be fairly rough, although many French versions, in particular, are quite distinguished.

Brandies and *eaux-de-vie* are very popular flavouring ingredients in cooking and are also much used in dressing and preserving fruit.

A glass of Cognac is traditionally a favourite means of the French chef to deglaze the pan during the making of a complex but delicately flavoured sauce. Many strongly flavoured pâtés and terrines need the presence of brandy for richness and, in contrast, several delicate sauces for fish and shellfish benefit from the judicious addition of a hint of Cognac.

Brandies are also the most popular method of adding flavour – and spectacle – by flaming a dish, such as the traditional English Christmas pudding, which is then served accompanied by brandy-flavoured butter.

FORTIFIED WINES

Wines are fortified by the addition of spirits during their production. This increases their alcohol content, but it also arrests the process of fermentation (conversion of sugars), so fortified wines are generally fairly sweet. The degree of sweetness varies according to when the grape brandy is added during the fermentation process.

The principal fortified wines which find culinary use include:

SHERRY, which is Spanish wine mixed with local brandy. It is usually the sweeter sherries, such as AMONTILLADO and OLOROSO, which are used in the making of sweet dishes, such as English trifle, syllabub and apple sauce; the flavour of MANZANILLA works better in savoury dishes, such as chicken stews and chicken liver, duck and pheasant pâtés.

PORT, a world-renowned dessert wine from Portugal, the flavour of which is often combined with melon or strongly flavoured cheese such as Stilton. In cooking, it marries well with ham, game and poultry, and it is an essential ingredient in some classic English dishes, such as jugged hare and Cumberland sauce.

MADEIRA, made from blended wines from the eponymous Portuguese island, fortified with cane spirit and heated during maturation, has long been a popular flavouring ingredient in soups, particularly consommés, as well as in aspics, poultry and game pâtés and meat and ham dishes. Madeira sauce (*sauce madère*) is a classic *haute cuisine* accompaniment to roast meat and grilled kidneys. A dash of Madeira also adds infinite distinction to carrots.

MARSALA, a dessert wine produced in Sicily from an aromatic white wine base fortified with brandy, may be either white and very dry or sweet and caramel-coloured (in the latter case, grape syrup has been added). In cooking, it is superb as a flavouring for veal, poultry and game, but it finds its most celebrated use in the delicious frothy custard *zabaglione*.

PINEAU DES CHARENTES, a liqueur wine from the Charentais, in the Cognac region, may be white or rosé and makes a delicious macerating liquid for fruit salads.

NOISETTES DE VEAU AU MARSALA

Veal noisettes in Marsala

Serves 4
Preparation 5 minutes
Cooking about 15–20 minutes

METRIC/IMPERIAL	AMERICAN
55 g/2 oz butter	*4 tbsp butter*
4 fresh sage leaves	*4 fresh sage leaves*
600 g/1 lb 6 oz rolled centre leg of veal, cut into 8 noisettes	*1½ lb boneless veal leg roast (rump or sirloin), cut across into 8 noisettes*
15 g/½ oz flour	*1½ tbsp flour*
100 ml/3½ fl oz dry Marsala	*½ cup dry Marsala*
salt and pepper	*salt and pepper*

Melt the butter in a frying pan and add the sage. Season the veal with salt and pepper. When the butter stops foaming, add the veal to the pan.

Cook the noisettes over a high heat for 4–5

minutes, turning them so that they brown evenly. Drain them.

In a cup, mix the flour with 4 tablespoons of water and the Marsala. Pour this mixture into the frying pan and bring it to the boil, stirring well. Lower the heat and cook, stirring, for 10 minutes.

When the sauce is thick and very smooth, reheat the veal noisettes gently in it for 2 minutes.

Put the meat on 4 warmed plates, coat with the sauce and serve immediately.

To drink: a mellow white wine, such as Orvieto.

CHAMPIGNONS AU PORTO

Mushrooms in port

Serves 4
Preparation 10 minutes
Cooking about 20 minutes

METRIC/IMPERIAL	AMERICAN
800 g/1¾ lb small button mushrooms	1¾ lb small button mushrooms
juice of ½ lemon	juice of ½ lemon
45 g/1½ oz butter	3 tbsp butter
75 ml/5 tbsp ruby port	5 tbsp ruby port
3 tbsp crème fraîche or whipping cream	3 tbsp crème fraîche or whipping cream
1 egg yolk	1 egg yolk
salt and pepper	salt and pepper

Preheat the oven to 220C/425F/gas 7.

Trim off the stalks of the mushrooms level with the caps. Rinse them in water to which has been added the lemon juice. Drain them and pat them dry on paper towels. Cut them in half.

Melt the butter in a sauté pan and add the mushrooms. Season with salt and pepper. Cook, uncovered, over a moderate heat for 10–12 minutes, then remove them with a slotted spoon and put them in a baking dish.

Add the port and cream to the cooking juices and boil to reduce the quantity by about half. Remove from the heat and whisk in the egg yolk. Pour the sauce over the mushrooms.

Cook in the oven for 5 minutes and serve very hot with croutons as a first course, or as an accompaniment to fried fish.

FRUITS AU COGNAC

Fruit in Cognac

Serves 4
Preparation 30 minutes, 2 hours ahead

METRIC/IMPERIAL	AMERICAN
4 white peaches, blanched, peeled and stoned	4 white-fleshed peaches, blanched, peeled and pitted
115 g/4 oz white currants, stalks removed	1 cup white currants, stems removed
115 g/4 oz redcurrants, stalks removed	1 cup redcurrants, stems removed
400 g/14 oz tiny strawberries, hulled	1 pt small strawberries, hulled
100 g/3½ oz caster sugar	½ cup superfine sugar
2–3 pinches of ground cinnamon	2–3 pinches of ground cinnamon
100 ml/3½ fl oz Cognac	½ cup Cognac

Cut the peaches in slices. Wash the other fruit and pat it dry.

Combine all the fruit in a deep glass bowl. Sprinkle it with the sugar and cinnamon and pour the Cognac over it. Leave the fruit to macerate in the Cognac for at least 2 hours before serving it in chilled bowls.

Note: this can be done with many different assortments of fruit and different types of alcoholic beverage. Try replacing the red fruit with melon balls and muscat grapes and using white Pineau des Charentes instead of Cognac.

BRAWN OR HEAD CHEESE

Fromage de tête

see also: charcuterie head pork

Also known to the French as *pâté de tête* (head pâté) or *fromage de cochon* (pig cheese), this *charcuterie* product consists of boneless pieces of pig's head, not including the brain, cooked with seasonings and herbs. The meat renders a thick jelly, which sets the brawn firmly when cooled and pressed in a mould.

Brawn is normally served cut in thick slices as a cold first course, accompanied by Dijon mustard and pickles: 100 g/3½ oz of brawn contains 150 calories.

SALADE DE FROMAGE DE TÊTE

Brawn or head cheese salad

Serves 4
Preparation 25 minutes
Cooking 2 minutes

METRIC/IMPERIAL	AMERICAN
225 g/½ lb curly endive (frisée)	½ lb curly endive or chicory
115 g/¼ lb smoked streaky bacon, cut into strips	¼ lb country-style bacon, cut into strips
4 tbsp sunflower oil	4 tbsp sunflower oil
2 tsp Dijon mustard	2 tsp Dijon mustard
2 tbsp white wine vinegar	2 tbsp white wine vinegar
140 g/5 oz brawn, cut into small cubes	5 oz head cheese, cut into small cubes
12 cherry tomatoes	12 cherry tomatoes
bunch of mixed fresh herbs (chervil, parsley, chives), chopped	bunch of mixed fresh herbs (chervil, parsley, chives), chopped
4 shallots, very finely chopped	4 shallots, very finely chopped
salt and pepper	salt and pepper

Rinse the curly endive and separate the leaves into small bunches.

Brown the bacon strips in a frying pan without any additional fat, then drain.

Make a well-seasoned vinaigrette with the oil, mustard, vinegar and salt and pepper. Toss the endive in the vinaigrette and divide it among 4 serving plates.

Arrange the cubes of brawn (head cheese) on top of the endive, along with the warm bacon strips.

Garnish with the cherry tomatoes and sprinkle with the herbs and chopped shallots. Serve at once.

Note: the shallots may also be fried with the bacon, or replaced by a warm poached egg per person.

BREAD

Pain

see also:
breadcrumbs
brioche
canapé
cereal
corn
croque-monsieur
croûte
crouton
dietary fibre
flour
freezing
gratin
pizza
wheat

A basic food made from a baked flour and water dough, bread has been a staple of human nutrition for thousands of years. Bread was unleavened until the Egyptians discovered the process of fermentation. Many different types of cereal were – and still are – used to make bread. The Egyptians used millet which, with wheat and barley, was used throughout Europe, the Middle East and Asia, while pre-Columbian Americans used only maize.

Bread varies enormously in shape, flavour, texture, appearance, colour and thickness of crust. The results depend on the type of flour used and other added ingredients, including liquids such as water or milk, fats such as butter or lard, flavourings such as salt, sugar, honey or molasses, the leavening agent used and the method by which the bread is baked. It may be baked in loaves or the dough used to make rolls, *croissants*, etc.

Until Victorian times, yeast was the normal leavening agent. However, since the advent of baking powders, many different chemical compounds and mixing and aerating techniques have been developed in the commercial manufacture of bread.

In the making of bread at home there are several essential stages. First, if using dried yeast, it must be mixed with a little tepid water and left for a few minutes to ensure that it froths up and is therefore alive. The ingredients are then all mixed together, including the raising agent, and the dough kneaded for some considerable time to distribute the leavening evenly; a good guide is to knead until the dough is no longer sticky. The dough must then be left covered in a warm place to rise to at least twice its volume. This aerates it and stretches the gluten in the flour. The raised dough is then 'knocked back' or 'punched down', ie, kneaded again briefly to remove some of the air before baking. For a lighter loaf the dough can then be left to rise again before baking. Just before it goes into the oven it is usually glazed with salt water, milk, melted butter or beaten egg to give it an attractive crust. It may also be sprinkled with cracked wheat, sesame, pumpkin or poppy seeds, etc.

Initial baking is usually done in a hot oven for about 30 minutes to kill the yeast and set the loaf, otherwise 'oven spring' might push the crust up and away from the body of the loaf. This is followed by longer cooking at a medium heat. A good guide for judging when the bread is cooked is to turn it out of its mould and tap the underside: if it sounds hollow it is done. Bread fresh from the oven is considered extremely indigestible. Good bread should have a thick golden crust, a soft aerated crumb that should not adhere to the fingers and an appealing smell.

Ordinary WHITE BREAD comes in many different forms as varied as the 'plain' loaf and the traditional long, thin French BAGUETTE. It is usually made of refined wheat flour with the bran and germ removed, water, salt and yeast.

WHOLEWHEAT or WHOLEMEAL BREAD is made from unrefined, whole grain flour and thus has a higher proportion of vitamins, minerals, dietary fibre and protein than white bread. It is excellent with cheese or shellfish, lightly toasted to accompany smoked salmon, or eaten at breakfast with honey.

BROWN BREAD is usually made from refined flour with a little wheat bran added to give extra colour and taste. Some caramel is often added to enhance this effect.

In Britain, GRANARY BREAD is made from coarsely ground flour with added malt to give a rough, 'country-baked' appearance, taste and texture. It is delicious with seafood, salads and soft cheeses.

LIGHT RYE BREAD contains a small amount of rye flour mixed with wheat flour and has a characteristic slightly sharp and sour flavour. It goes well with *charcuterie*, *foie gras* or game and is a favourite bread for sandwiches in America. It keeps longer than white bread if stored in a cool, damp place and some say it actually tastes better when slightly stale.

DARK RYE BREAD still contains a little wheat flour, as rye on its own produces too dense a result, which also tends to crack; it has a dense crumb and is very nutritious. It too is best eaten slightly stale, and goes well with oysters and other shellfish.

Specialist WHOLEGRAIN BREADS made of wheat, rye, oats, cornmeal, barley and buckwheat in varying proportions all have distinctive flavours and are excellent with cheese.

Rich VIENNESE BREAD and rolls, made of the finest white flour, also contain milk (and sometimes fat, such as butter) and are more like pastries than bread.

NUT BREADS and breads made with cumin, raisins, figs, onions, olives and the like are usually made from wholewheat or rye flour; they are very rich in protein but have a correspondingly high energy content. Breads like these can turn a simple snack or bowl of soup into a nourishing meal.

A wide variety of international breads are now widely available in supermarkets and food stores. The flat rounds of slightly leavened PITTA BREAD are torn into strips by the Greeks to accompany their classic *hummus* and other *mezze* (mixed hors d'oeuvres), while the Arabs stuff them whole with meat cooked on skewers and salad to make delicious snacks. The Italian PIZZA has become one of the most common convenience foods, either simply spread with garlic butter and served with salad or lightly coated with puréed tomatoes and topped with one of countless combinations of sliced Mozzarella cheese, vegetables and meats. The unleavened Indian *chapatis*, *puris* and *parathas* are also now more widely available.

There are also ready-made mixes for home bread-making on the market. These too can be enriched according to taste with olives, bacon, herbs, etc. Vacuum-packed raw bread dough, which must be kept in the refrigerator, needs about 20 minutes or so in the oven to make into bread. Also increasingly available are partially baked breads which are set in shape, with a lightly coloured crust, and need only a few minutes in the oven to finish them. Both these options provide useful back-ups for feeding unexpected guests, avoiding the necessity of keeping large quantities of fresh bread on hand. However, bread also freezes very well.

Bread finds a wide variety of uses in cooking. Thick slices of bread, or 'trenchers', were used in the Middle Ages as disposable plates and this practice survives in the making of deep fried or baked containers (*croûtes*), shaped from slices of bread, in which to put creamy poultry or seafood mixtures. Slices of bread are also used as the lining for sweet and savoury charlottes and puddings, such as the memorable English soft-fruit treat, summer pudding. Bread sauce is also one of the traditional English accompaniments to roast meats and poultry, especially the Christmas turkey. Breadcrumbs are commonly used to thicken sauces, stuffings, soups and stews and to bind mixtures, such as those for meat loaf and hamburgers. Breadcrumbs provide taste and texture when used as a coating for fried, baked and grilled (broiled) food.

Bread is an indispensable component of most people's daily diet. It slows down the assimilation of other foods, making digestion easier and assuaging hunger. The recommended daily consumption of bread is about 125 g/4½ oz, the equivalent of 4 thick or 5 thin slices or half a baguette. The average energy content of bread, whatever the ingredients, is about 250 calories per 100 g/3½ oz. The more wholewheat flour bread contains, the more dietary fibre it will provide. However, care should be taken in using bread as a source of fibre as many people are allergic to the gluten in bread, particularly in high concentrations.

PÂTE À PAIN

Basic white bread dough

Makes 2 small round loaves
Preparation about 1 hour, resting time 3½ hours
Cooking about ¾–1 hour

METRIC/IMPERIAL	*AMERICAN*
1.5 kg/3½ lb strong plain white or bread flour	*3½ lb (12 cups) white bread flour*
1 tbsp salt	*1 tbsp salt*
30 g/1 oz baker's yeast	*1 oz compressed fresh yeast*

Pour the flour into a large bowl and add the salt.

In a small bowl, mix the yeast to a paste with a little warm water. When the mixture is smooth, add it to the flour along with 800 ml/28 fl oz/3½ cups of warm water (1).

Knead the flour and water mixture into a smooth dough and turn it out on a work surface. If it is too hard and dry, add a little water; if it is too wet, add a little more flour.

1

2

Stretch and fold back the dough several times. Knead it for about 10 minutes until it is firm and does not stick to the work surface (2).

Wash the bowl, dry it and put the dough back into it. Cover with a cloth and put in a warm place to rise for about 2½ hours, until the dough has about doubled in volume (3).

Divide the dough into 2 portions. Leave one under a damp cloth while working with the other. Form it into a ball and then flatten it with the hand, using a twisting motion. Repeat this operation several times, then turn the ball over and work it from the other side. Repeat with the second portion.

Shape the balls of dough into round loaves, dust with flour, cover them and leave them to rise for about 1 more hour.

Meanwhile, preheat the oven to 230C/450F/gas 8 and put a small bowl filled with water into the bottom of the oven.

When the loaves have risen, make a cross-shaped incision on the top of each (4). If preferred, long loaves may be shaped before baking, with diagonal incisions. The deeper the incisions, the thicker the crust will be.

Bake the loaves on a baking sheet in the oven for at least 45 minutes. Check the degree of

doneness by tapping the bottom of each loaf with a finger: it should give off a dull sound. If necessary, return the loaves to the oven for another 10 minutes.

Leave the bread to cool on a wire rack for several hours before slicing.

Note: to make bread rolls, form the basic dough into about 16 rolls, brush with melted butter and sprinkle with cumin, poppy or sesame seeds before baking for 30–35 minutes at 230C/450F/gas 8.

PAIN COMPLET

Wholewheat bread

Makes two 450 g/1 lb loaves
Preparation about 30 minutes, resting 1 hour
Cooking about 15 minutes

METRIC/IMPERIAL	AMERICAN
700 g/1$\frac{2}{3}$ lb wholewheat flour	6 cups whole wheat flour
1 tbsp salt	1 tbsp salt
25 g/$\frac{3}{4}$ oz baker's yeast	1 oz compressed fresh yeast
1 tbsp thick honey	1 tbsp thick honey
2 tbsp soya flour	2 tbsp soybean flour

In a large bowl, mix the wholewheat flour with the salt. In another bowl mix the yeast and honey with 200 ml/7 fl oz/1 cup of warm water. When the mixture is smooth, mix in the soya (soybean) flour and let it stand in a warm place for 5 minutes.

Add this mixture to the wholewheat flour, then add another 300 ml/$\frac{1}{2}$ pt/1$\frac{1}{2}$ cups of water. Knead the dough until smooth and elastic, then put it in a clean bowl, cover it with a cloth and let it rise for 30 minutes.

After this time, knead the dough again for 5 minutes, then separate it into 2 portions and form them into balls. Put each into a deep dish and leave, covered, to rise for a further 30 minutes.

Microwave the loaves one at a time for 7 minutes on High, giving them a half-turn every 3 minutes. Leave the loaves to stand for a minute or two in the microwave oven, then transfer them to wire racks to cool. Do not attempt to slice the bread immediately on removing it from the oven as it will continue to cook until it is cold.

Note: microwave cooking does not give the bread a golden crust, but made with wholewheat flour it has an appetizing brown colour. If desired, the dough may be enriched with pumpkin or sunflower seeds.

PAIN DE SEIGLE AUX NOIX

Rye bread with walnuts

Makes 2 loaves
Preparation 25 minutes, resting 2 hours
Cooking 35 minutes

METRIC/IMPERIAL	AMERICAN
25 g/$\frac{3}{4}$ oz baker's yeast	1 oz compressed fresh yeast
300 g/10 oz wholewheat flour	2$\frac{1}{2}$ cups whole wheat flour
200 g/7 oz rye flour	2 cups rye flour
1 tsp salt	1 tsp salt
2 tbsp walnut oil	2 tbsp walnut oil
200 g/7 oz walnuts, coarsely chopped	1$\frac{1}{2}$ cups coarsely chopped walnuts
butter, for greasing	butter, for greasing

Mix the yeast in a little warm water, adding 3 tablespoons of the wholewheat flour. Sift the remaining wholewheat flour and the rye flour with the salt into a bowl.

Make a well in the middle. Add the yeast mixture and oil and gently pour in 300 ml/$\frac{1}{2}$ pt/ 1$\frac{1}{2}$ cups of water, pulling the flour in from the sides of the bowl to mix well. Knead the dough for 10 minutes.

Add the chopped walnuts and mix in well, then put the dough in a warm place for 2 hours to rise.

Grease 2 cake pans with the butter and dust them with flour. Divide the dough between them and leave to rise for a further 20 minutes.

Preheat the oven to 240C/460F/gas 8–9.

Bake the loaves for 35 minutes. Turn out on wire racks and leave to cool.

BREADCRUMBS

see also:
bread
deep frying
frying
gratin
sauce

Two principal types of breadcrumbs are used in cooking: DRIED BREADCRUMBS, made by toasting the bread in a warm oven and then making it into crumbs, and FRESH BREADCRUMBS, made by rubbing slightly stale bread through a fine sieve.

The former will keep for a long time in an airtight container and are used principally for sprinkling over food to be cooked *au gratin*. The latter will keep for only a day or two and are favoured for coating foods before frying.

Fish fillets, croquettes and escalopes (scallops) of veal are often breaded before being grilled (broiled) or fried. There are several ways of doing it.

The simplest and quickest method is simply to brush the food with clarified butter and then coat it with fresh breadcrumbs. The method known as *à l'anglaise* involves first flouring the food, then dipping it in egg beaten with a little water or oil and seasonings, and then in the breadcrumbs. If grated Parmesan cheese is added to the breadcrumbs for extra flavour, the breading is known as *à la milanaise*.

Any grated dry cheese or a mixture of chopped garlic and herbs may be added to flavour a breadcrumb coating.

Fresh breadcrumbs are also a common means of binding mixtures such as stuffings, hamburgers or meat loaves and are used to thicken some sauces and soups.

Remember that breadcrumbs absorb at least 50 per cent of the butter or oil in which the breaded food is cooked.

COATING FOOD À L'ANGLAISE

Beat one or two eggs in a shallow dish with a little oil and salt and pepper.

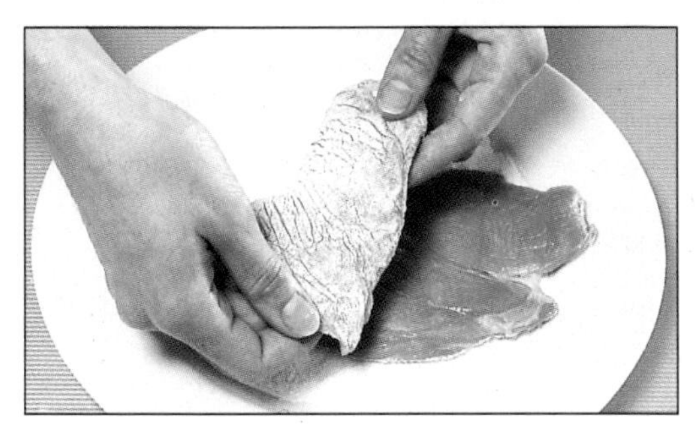

Dredge the food to be breaded in seasoned flour, coating it well.

Dip the floured food in the egg mixture again, then into the breadcrumbs.

BREAM

see Sea bream

BRIE

see also:
canapé
cheese

A large, flat round cows' milk cheese with a creamy coloured, soft interior and a white or pinkish downy crust, it has a fine fruity taste and its aroma can be quite strong when it is fully ripened. Because of the way in which the cheese is drained, it may be of uneven thickness; the thinnest part will ripen first.

Try to buy ripe Brie, as it is difficult to ripen at home, and use within a day or two. Properly ripened Brie should be almost runny, with perhaps the thinnest of chalky white layers in the centre. Never buy an over-ripe Brie which is too runny or has a whiff of ammonia.

Although most Brie is now commercially made in dairies, the best flavoured cheeses are those made on the farm (*Brie fermier*) using unpasteurized milk. There are four main types: BRIE DE MEAUX, which is the best known and most widely available, BRIE DE MELUN, which is smaller and thicker, and is sold either plain or flavoured with pepper or herbs, BRIE DE MONTEREAU, which has the lowest fat content, as little as 40%, and BRIE DE COULOMMIERS, which is at its best in the winter months.

Brie is traditionally served in wedges towards the end of a meal, accompanied by a good red Burgundy or port. It can also be used in canapés and vols-au-vent and savoury pastries.

One 30 g/1 oz portion of Brie (fat content about 45%) contains 83 calories.

GALETTES DE BRIE AU PAPRIKA

Brie rounds with paprika

Serves 4, about 12 rounds
Preparation 25 minutes, plus standing
Cooking about 20 minutes

METRIC/IMPERIAL	AMERICAN
200 g/7 oz Brie cheese (not too ripe)	7 oz Brie cheese (not too ripe)
200 g/7 oz flour	1⅓ cups flour
85 g/3 oz butter, cut into small pieces	6 tbsp butter, cut into small pieces
2 egg yolks	2 egg yolks
pinch of ground nutmeg	pinch of ground nutmeg
½ tsp paprika	½ tsp paprika
pepper	pepper

Remove the crust from the Brie and cut the cheese into small cubes. Lightly grease a baking sheet with a little of the butter.

Sift the flour into a bowl, making a well in the middle. Add the remaining butter and the cheese and mash them into the flour with a fork.

Add the egg yolks and mix well, adding some pepper, nutmeg and a pinch or two of paprika to taste. Leave for 1 hour in a cool place.

Preheat the oven to 180C/350F/gas 4. Roll the dough out to a thickness of about 8 mm/⅓ in and cut it into rounds, with a diameter of about 10 cm/4 in. Place them on the greased baking sheet and bake for 20 minutes.

Serve hot with a salad of bitter leaves such as dandelion or chicory (Belgian endive).

BRILL

Barbue

see also:
fish
turbot

An Atlantic marine flatfish, similar to the turbot only smaller (about 30–60 cm/1–3 ft across), with delicate white flesh which is slightly lacking in flavour compared to the turbot. The best brill are available in the months from April to July.

Brill is fairly expensive as there is a lot of wastage in its preparation, but it is still usually cheaper than turbot. It may be braised or poached whole; brill fillets are often steamed or cooked in butter. Brill is traditionally garnished with seafood and its flavour marries well with champagne and dry (hard) cider.

If the fish is to be cooked whole, it is wise to make a longitudinal incision along the backbone on the dark side, slightly loosen the fillets and then break the backbone in 2 or 3 places so the fish will cook more uniformly and retain its shape.

Like all fish, brill is lean and nutritious; 100 g/3½ oz of brill contains 80 calories.

BARBUE À LA CRÈME ET AUX CREVETTES

Brill in cream sauce with shrimp or prawns

Serves 6
Preparation 10 minutes
Cooking 25 minutes

METRIC/IMPERIAL	AMERICAN
1 whole brill, weighing about 1.2 kg/2½ lb	1 whole brill, weighing about 2½ lb
100 g/3½ oz butter	1 stick butter
25 g/¾ oz flour	3 tbsp flour
400 ml/14 fl oz thick crème fraîche or whipping cream	1¾ cups thick crème fraîche or whipping cream
225 g/½ lb shelled cooked prawns	½ lb peeled cooked shrimp
salt and pepper	salt and pepper

Preheat the oven to 180C/350F/gas 4.

Clean, trim and scale the fish. Prepare it for cooking whole as described on page 87.

Use a little of the butter to grease an ovenproof dish and place the fish on it, white side up. Season with salt and pepper. Dot the fish with 45 g/1½ oz/3 tbsp of the butter and cover the dish with foil.

Bake in the oven for 20 minutes.

Meanwhile, melt the remainder of the butter in a saucepan. Add the flour and stir over a gentle heat for 5 minutes. Gradually add the cream, without allowing the mixture to boil.

Remove the sauce from the heat and add the prawns (shrimp). Season with salt and pepper.

Drain the brill, reserving the cooking juices, and turn it over on a dish so that you can remove the dark skin. Pour the cooking liquid into the sauce and heat for several minutes, stirring constantly. Coat the skinned fish with the sauce and serve at once.

This dish is delicious served with oyster mushrooms which have been cooked slowly in their own juices.

To drink: a good white Burgundy, such as a Meursault.

FILETS DE BARBUE AUX EPINARDS

Brill fillets with spinach

Serves 6
Preparation 30 minutes
Cooking about 40 minutes

METRIC/IMPERIAL	AMERICAN
1 whole brill, weighing about 2 kg/4½ lb	1 whole brill, weighing about 4½ lb
2 onions, sliced	2 onions, sliced
1 carrot, sliced	1 carrot, sliced
bouquet garni	bouquet garni
200 g/7 fl oz crème fraîche or whipping cream	1 cup crème fraîche or whipping cream
1 tbsp tomato purée	1 tbsp tomato paste
450 g/1 lb young spinach leaves, trimmed and cut into very thin strips	1 lb young spinach leaves, trimmed and cut into very thin strips
2 egg yolks	2 egg yolks
salt and pepper	salt and pepper

Fillet the brill, keeping the trimmings including the head. Put the trimmings in a saucepan and add 1 l/1¾ pt/1 qt of water, the onions, carrots, bouquet garni, and salt and pepper. Bring to the boil and cook for 30 minutes only. Strain the stock and leave to cool slightly.

Pour the cooled stock over the fish, return to the heat, cover, bring just to the boil, then remove the pan and poach gently off the heat for 5 minutes. Transfer the brill fillets to a warmed serving dish, cover and keep warm.

Reduce the fish stock over a high heat by about half, then add the cream and tomato purée (paste) and adjust the seasoning. Whisk the egg yolks into the sauce off the heat, then return the pan to the heat but ensure that the sauce does not boil. Add one third of the spinach and mix well.

Pour the sauce over the brill fillets and add the remaining spinach leaves, raw, as garnish. Serve at once.

Note: the spinach leaves should be very tender. If only frozen spinach is available, use it for the sauce with soft lettuce leaves to garnish.

see also:
bread
croûte
French toast

BRIOCHE

A soft French loaf or roll made from a yeast dough enriched with eggs and butter, brioche is traditionally served with tea, coffee or hot chocolate for breakfast, snacks or dessert.

Brioches come in many shapes: the characteristic *brioche parisienne*, or PARISIAN BRIOCHE, which is made up of a small ball of dough placed on top of a larger ball; BRIOCHE LOAVES or *brioches nanterres* with sections marked along them, used sliced for *pain perdu* (French toast) or *croûtes* and eaten with fruit; and the tall, cylindrical cake-like *brioche mousseline*, slices of which are often used as a bed for dishes of cooked sausage and *foie gras*. Brioche dough, sometimes with added raisins, may be baked in a ring mould or as a flat cake. Brioches may be flavoured with cheese, nuts or alcohol.

Hollowed-out brioches are often stuffed with fresh or preserved fruit or used to hold rich savoury *salpicon* mixtures, such as mushroom *duxelles* or seafood. Brioche dough may replace ordinary pastry in baked savoury dishes such as beef *en croûte*: 100 g/3½ oz contains 300 calories.

To reheat a cooked brioche, wrap it in dampened tissue paper and put it in a hot oven for 5 minutes.

BRIOCHE MOUSSELINE

Light brioche

For a 15 cm/6 in diameter brioche
Preparation 30 minutes, resting 6 hours
Cooking 40–45 minutes

METRIC/IMPERIAL	*AMERICAN*
250 g/8½ oz flour	*1⅔ cups flour*
10 g/⅓ oz baker's yeast	*⅓ oz compressed fresh yeast*
3 tbsp warm milk	*3 tbsp warm milk*
210 g/7½ oz unsalted butter	*2 sticks + 1 tbsp unsalted butter*
3 eggs + 1 egg yolk	*3 eggs + 1 egg yolk*
30 g/1 oz caster sugar	*2½ tbsp superfine sugar*
10 g/⅓ oz fine salt	*1 tsp salt*

Plunge a bowl into hot water and then wipe it dry. Sift the flour into the bowl. Mix the yeast with the milk and add a little flour to it to make a soft ball (1).

Soften all but about 25 g/¾ oz/1½ tbsp of the butter with a spatula until it is creamy but not melted. Make a well in the flour and put the softened butter in it, along with the yeast

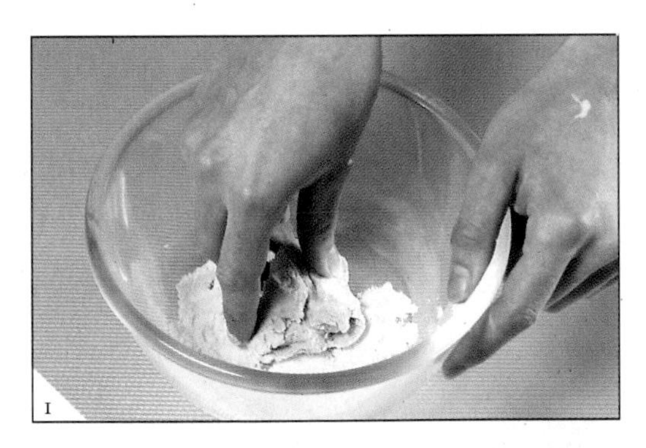
1

2

3

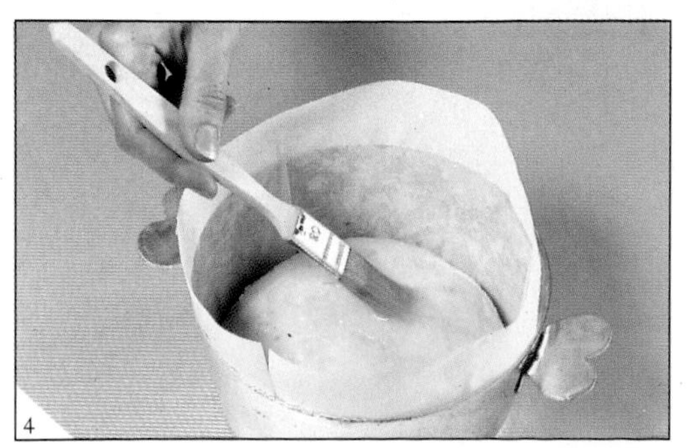
4

mixture, the whole eggs, the sugar and salt (2). Gradually incorporate these ingredients into the flour, then gather the dough into a ball in the middle of the bowl (3). Cover it and put it in a warm place (about 20C/70 F) to rise for about 3 hours.

When the dough has about doubled in volume, knock out the air by pressing it down until it sinks, then leave it in a warm place to rise for a further 1 hour.

Cut out a circle of greaseproof (or parchment) paper to fit in the bottom of a 15cm/6 in diameter round cake pan, and a band of paper to line the sides of the pan. This paper band should be about 6–8 cm/2½–3 in higher than the sides. Grease the two pieces of paper with the remaining butter and line the pan with them.

Knead the dough once more to reduce its volume, then form it into a ball and put the ball into the mould. Leave it to rise again in the pan for at least 2 hours.

Preheat the oven to 210C/415F/gas 6–7. Brush the top of the dough with the egg yolk (4). Bake for 30 minutes (on no account should the oven door be opened during this stage of baking), then reduce the heat to 180C/350F/ gas 4 and cook for a further 10–15 minutes.

Before unmoulding the brioche, check for doneness by inserting a skewer into the centre: it should come out clean. If it does not, return it to the oven for a few minutes' more baking.

Unmould the brioche, remove the paper and leave the brioche on a wire rack to cool.

Note: brioche dough should not be kneaded in the conventional way, but by picking it up and slapping it down forcefully on the work surface and pressing hard with the thumbs. In this way the yeasted dough rises more effectively.

BRIOCHES AUX OEUFS BROUILLÉS

Brioches with scrambled eggs

Serves 4
Preparation 15 minutes
Cooking 15 minutes

METRIC/IMPERIAL	*AMERICAN*
4 small individual Parisian brioches	*4 small individual Parisian brioches*
100 g/3½ oz butter	*1 stick butter*
6 eggs	*6 eggs*
salt and pepper	*salt and pepper*
snipped chives, to garnish	*snipped chives, to garnish*

Preheat the oven to 150C/300F/gas 2.

Slice the tops off the brioches and carefully scoop out the middle of each one, taking care not to pierce the cases. Spread the interiors lightly with a little of the butter and put the brioches to warm in the oven.

Break the eggs into a bowl and whisk them lightly with a fork, then season with salt and pepper. Melt the remaining butter in a saucepan.

Pour the eggs into the pan and cook them over a very low heat, stirring constantly, until they are lightly scrambled.

Remove the scrambled eggs from the heat and divide them among the warmed brioche cases. Season with pepper to taste and sprinkle with snipped chives. Replace the brioche tops.

BROCCOLI

Brocoli

see also: cabbage cauliflower vegetables

A summer brassica, broccoli is a member of the cabbage family, as is cauliflower, with green stalks and small bright green or purple florets.

Popular in Mediterranean countries, particularly Italy, there are several different types. Possibly most familiar is CALABRESE, named after the Italian province of Calabria, which has well-formed, bluish-green buds which keep their colour on cooking. Thinner GREEN and PURPLE SPROUTING BROCCOLI have a fine flavour, particularly when young, but the purple loses its colour on cooking. ROMANESCO has lime-green buds. Never buy any broccoli with open yellow flowers as it is obviously very old.

The flavour of broccoli has been likened to a cross between cauliflower and asparagus and indeed the finer, fresher specimens deserve the same treatment as asparagus. Young fresh broccoli should be cooked in boiling salted water until just tender and then perhaps briefly refreshed under cold running water to retain the colour (they may be reheated in a steamer if necessary). Larger and older specimens may have tougher stalks which need trimming and peeling if fibrous; test by snapping the stalk to see if it breaks cleanly. It is best to break them up into florets to ensure uniform cooking.

Cooked broccoli may be dressed with butter or good olive oil and perhaps a little lemon juice or grated Parmesan, or even a béarnaise or hollandaise sauce.

Broccoli stalks are used for soups or purées and the lightly cooked florets are a popular garnish. Increasingly, florets of young tender broccoli are being offered raw, or briefly blanched, as a crudité or in salads

Broccoli is the most easily digested of the cabbage family, is rich in vitamin A (and thus very good for the skin) and 100 g/3½ oz contains 35 calories.

green broccoli or calabrese

purple broccoli

Romanesco broccoli

BROCOLI AUX HERBES

Broccoli with herbs

Serves 4
Preparation 10 minutes
Cooking 10 minutes

METRIC/IMPERIAL	AMERICAN
1 kg/2¼ lb broccoli, trimmed	*2¼ lb broccoli, trimmed*
1 egg	*1 egg*
juice of 1 lemon	*juice of 1 lemon*
5 tbsp olive oil	*5 tbsp olive oil*
2 tbsp chopped fresh chives	*2 tbsp chopped fresh chives*
1 tbsp chopped fresh parsley	*1 tbsp chopped fresh parsley*
1 tbsp chopped fresh tarragon	*1 tbsp chopped fresh tarragon*
1 tbsp snipped fresh chervil	*1 tbsp snipped fresh chervil*
salt and pepper	*salt and pepper*

Cook the broccoli in rapidly boiling salted water for 8–10 minutes or until just tender. In another pan, hard boil the egg.

Thoroughly drain the broccoli and put it in a warmed serving dish. Leave to cool slightly.

Plunge the cooked egg into cold water, then shell it and remove the yolk. Crush the yolk with a fork and place it in a food processor.

Add the lemon juice and oil and salt and pepper to taste. Blend briefly, add all the herbs and blend again until well mixed.

Pour the herb sauce over the warm broccoli and serve as an hors d'oeuvres or as an accompaniment to poached fish.

*P*URÉE DE BROCOLI

Broccoli purée

Serves 4
Preparation 10 minutes
Cooking 10 minutes

METRIC/IMPERIAL	*AMERICAN*
1.5 kg/3½ lb broccoli	*3½ lb broccoli*
200 ml/7 fl oz crème fraîche or whipping cream	*1 cup crème fraîche or whipping cream*
55 g/2 oz butter	*4 tbsp butter*
salt and pepper	*salt and pepper*
finely grated Parmesan cheese, to serve (optional)	*finely grated Parmesan cheese, to serve (optional)*

Trim the broccoli and peel the stalks. Separate the florets from the stalks and slice the stalks diagonally to ensure even cooking.

Fill a large saucepan with salted water and bring it to the boil. Plunge the broccoli into it and cook for 5 minutes. Drain and put the broccoli immediately into a food processor. Blend to a purée.

Meanwhile, pour the cream into a small pan and reduce it over a high heat until it is thick and smooth.

Heat the butter in another saucepan. When it is very hot, add the broccoli purée and stir vigorously. Add the reduced cream, stir thoroughly and season with salt and pepper. Serve very hot, sprinkled with some grated Parmesan cheese if wished, as an accompaniment to poached fish or any white meat.

BROILING

see Grilling

BROWNING

see also:
frying
roasting
sautéing

The browning or initial rapid cooking of food, usually meat, poultry or vegetables, over a high heat, gives its surface a good colour and forms a crust which seals in its juices.

The cooking is usually carried out in an uncovered frying or sauté pan, or flameproof casserole, and normally in a little oil or oil and butter mixture.

The food should be cooked just long enough to achieve a golden brown colour, but care must be taken not to burn the food.

BRUNOISE

see also:
sauce
vegetables

A term used for a mixture of vegetables, such as carrots, celery, onions or leeks, cut into very fine dice, a *brunoise* is normally sweated briefly in butter before use.

A *brunoise* may be used as a garnish, particularly for soups, to thicken sauces or stuffings, or as a flavouring, especially in fine sauces for fish and shellfish.

Brunoise vegetables should be freshly prepared, otherwise all their vitamins, especially vitamin C, will be lost. However, they will keep for short periods of time if covered with a damp cloth.

Slice the carrots along their length into strips 1 cm/⅜ in thick.

Cut the strips again lengthwise at 1 cm/⅜ in intervals and then slice them crosswise into small cubes.

see also:
cabbage
vegetables

BRUSSELS SPROUTS

Chou de Bruxelles

A green vegetable of the cabbage family, the tiny buds of Brussels sprouts actually resemble miniature cabbages. They are one of the principal sources of winter greens and are generally available fresh from September to March. The purple-tinged variety have a particularly fine nutty flavour.

Choose small, compact buds of uniform size for even cooking. Avoid any which are 'blown' or which have yellow leaves. Remove any loose outer leaves and cut off the stumps not too high up, so that the rest of the leaves still stay attached. For larger sprouts, cut a cross-shaped incision into the stem base to ensure that it cooks as fast as the bud.

Brussels sprouts are best briefly blanched before being cooked in fast boiling salted water, uncovered, for not longer than 10–15 minutes, depending on size, so that they do not become mushy. They should not be left in the cooking water or they will turn yellow.

They are usually simply dressed with a little butter, and possibly some lemon juice, but they may also served in a cream sauce or garnished with bacon or nuts, particularly almonds and chestnuts for special occasions. The French favour them made into a purée and also use them to garnish roast game.

Brussels sprouts freeze very well and 100 g/3½ oz contains 27 calories.

CHOUX DE BRUXELLES AU BEURRE

Brussels sprouts in butter

Serves 4
Preparation 15 minutes
Cooking about 7–15 minutes

METRIC/IMPERIAL	AMERICAN
1 kg/2¼ lb Brussels sprouts, trimmed	2¼ lb Brussels sprouts, trimmed
85 g/3 oz butter	6 tbsp butter
bunch of flat-leaved parsley, freshly chopped	bunch of flat-leaf parsley, freshly chopped
salt and pepper	salt and pepper

Bring a large pan of salted water to the boil, plunge the sprouts into the boiling water and return to the boil. As soon as the water is boiling once more, drain the sprouts.

Fill the pan with water again, this time only lightly salted. Bring it to the boil and add the sprouts. Bring the water back to the boil and then cook the sprouts gently for about 5–12 minutes, or until just tender.

Meanwhile, melt the butter gently in a small saucepan and skim off the foam.

Drain the sprouts very thoroughly and put them in a warmed serving dish. Sprinkle them with the chopped parsley, pour the melted butter over them and serve at once.

GRATIN DE CHOUX DE BRUXELLES AUX AMANDES

Brussels sprouts baked au gratin with almonds

Serves 4
Preparation 25 minutes
Cooking about 25–30 minutes

METRIC/IMPERIAL	AMERICAN
800 g/1¾ lb Brussels sprouts, trimmed	1¾ lb Brussels sprouts, trimmed
25 g/¾ oz butter	1½ tbsp butter
3 tbsp flaked almonds	3 tbsp slivered almonds
2 tomatoes, sliced	2 tomatoes, sliced
2 tbsp chopped chives	2 tbsp chopped chives
200 ml/7 fl oz whipping cream	1 cup whipping cream
4 tbsp freshly grated Parmesan cheese	¼ cup freshly grated Parmesan cheese
pinch of freshly grated nutmeg	pinch of freshly grated nutmeg
salt and pepper	salt and pepper

Preheat the oven to 180C/350F/gas 4.

Cook the sprouts for 5–10 minutes in boiling salted water, until just beginning to become tender, and then drain them.

Use the butter to grease a baking dish. Brown the almonds in the oven for about 3 minutes or quickly under a hot grill (broiler).

Put the Brussels sprouts in the baking dish and cover them with the tomato slices and chopped chives.

In a bowl, mix the cream with the Parmesan, nutmeg and salt and pepper to taste. Pour this mixture over the contents of the baking dish.

Sprinkle with the browned flaked (slivered) almonds and bake in the oven for 20 minutes.

BUFFET

see also:
alcohol
canapé
fruit
salad
wine

Originally the French term for the table in restaurants where cold dishes and pastries were displayed, the word buffet has come to mean a way of serving a wide selection of food to which guests may help themselves at parties.

Buffets are a practical way of entertaining a large number of people, from about 10 upwards, and they work as well outdoors as inside. A successful buffet, however, involves considerable planning.

For a buffet LUNCH OR SUPPER, allow something along the following lines per guest: 2 small kebabs, generally on cocktail sticks, or chicken drumsticks, 4 assorted canapés or small sandwiches, 2–3 devils on horseback or other savouries, 2 small puff pastries or brioches with a savoury filling, 115 g/4 oz smoked salmon or chicken in aspic, 1 portion of cheese, 1 helping of sorbet and 3 petits fours. In addition, offer a selection of easy-to-serve mixed salads and bowls of fresh fruit.

To drink, allow per person: 2–3 glasses of wine or champagne, plus a glass or two of spirits if you wish – or combine the two in a punch – and plenty of fruit juice and mineral water. At a cocktail party you may expect a bit less to be consumed.

For a simple COCKTAIL PARTY, allow the following per guest: 7–10 savouries such as canapés, small open sandwiches, pastries, tiny quiches, choux puffs with cheese, and 3–5 sweet delicacies such as petits fours, macaroons or candied fruits. Food to be eaten with the fingers should be small – 1 or 2 bites at the most.

If you are planning a PICNIC, pack a selection of thinly sliced cold meats, making sure that you provide all the necessary condiments such as pickles, relishes and chutneys, and various types of mustard, along with quantities of raw vegetables and assorted dips, bread, cheese and crackers, fruit tarts and wine or beer, plus fruit juice and mineral water.

BUTTER

Beurre

see also:
brioche
buttercream
cakes and gâteaux
canapé
pastry
sauce

A fatty substance which is obtained from churned cream, butter is a traditional part of our daily diet, usually spread on bread, and is a basic component in most cooking and pastry-making.

Nowadays most butter is manufactured industrially in dairies, using pasteurized or unpasteurized milk. Pasteurized butter, the most commonly available, varies widely in quality according to place of origin, and cheaper varieties tend to be blends.

FARMHOUSE BUTTERS usually have a superior flavour, but they are expensive and do not keep for more than about 3 days. The unmistakably rich, nutty and sweet ivory-coloured butters from *Normandy*, *Isigny* and *Charentes-Poitou* have perhaps the finest flavours, and taste almost like cream itself when spread on bread. There are also other delicious SWEET BUTTERS with a high cream content, and CONCENTRATED BUTTERS (about 96% fat) especially made for pastry.

Good butter should not be brittle, lumpy or sticky and should not sweat droplets of water. It should smell fresh and have a strong nutty flavour. SLIGHTLY SALTED OR SALTED BUTTER (0.5%–2% salt) is usually best for spreading on bread, toast, etc. UNSALTED BUTTER is usually best for cooking, especially in the making of cakes and sauces where the saltiness might upset the balance of the flavour. It is usually worth investing in a better brand of butter as an inferior butter can severely mar the flavour of anything in which it is used.

Butter should always be removed from the refrigerator at least 15 minutes before use, particularly for baking; if it gets too soft, close the packet tightly and put it in a bowl of iced water. Always store butter well away from strong-flavoured items (such as garlic) or soft fruit, as it very readily picks up their taste.

Butter is a good source of vitamin A but contains 82–100% fat. For anyone on a diet, butter intake should be eliminated, or at least limited to a maximum 30 g/1 oz per day.

Low-fat butters (41–65% fat) and 'low-fat dairy spreads' (20–40% fat), where the fat is replaced by water, or in some cases vegetable oils, are now increasingly available in response to dietary concern with the reduction of cholesterol levels; butter contains 250–280 mg of cholesterol per 100 g/3½ oz. However, these preparations tend not to work very well in cooking, as they separate and can easily burn.

Butter is the favoured cooking medium whenever a fine flavour is required, although it usually needs to be clarified or have a little oil added to it to prevent it burning when heated. Butter is also widely used to enrich sauces and other mixtures such as stuffings. Butter is essential ingredient in the making of cakes and gâteaux and many pastries. It is also the choice medium for greasing moulds and pans, where the flavour of oils might be intrusive. In addition, plain or flavoured butter is the simplest and most common means of dressing a wide variety of cooked food.

PREPARED BUTTERS AND BUTTER SAUCES

CREAMED BUTTER is obtained by working the butter with a wooden spatula or spoon until soft, without allowing it to melt, but butter may also be softened in a microwave oven; 30 seconds on High for 100 g/3½ oz/1 stick of butter.

KNEADED BUTTER (*beurre manié*) is a mixture of creamed butter and flour in equal proportions which is used to thicken sauces: it is added in small bits to a very hot, but not boiling, sauce and whisked in thoroughly.

Beurre fondu, which is used to dress poached fish and vegetables, is very simple to prepare. The butter is melted gently in a saucepan over a low heat and skimmed with a spoon or paper towel. The strained juice of a lemon is added, along with seasonings to taste, and the mixture whisked vigorously.

CLARIFIED BUTTER (*beurre clarifié*), or DRAWN BUTTER, which cooks without burning, is prepared by melting butter in a saucepan over a very gentle heat without stirring. The surface is skimmed of foamy impurities using a spoon or paper towel and the melted butter then carefully poured into a clean bowl, leaving behind the whitish sediment at the bottom of the saucepan. It should be kept refrigerated.

For *beurre noisette*, which is used to dress and impart its nutty flavour to sweetbreads, fish, vegetables and egg dishes, the butter is first clarified and then reheated until it turns a golden colour. It is then seasoned and 1 tablespoon of wine vinegar or lemon juice may be added to make *beurre meunière*. Beurre noir, the essential accompaniment to skate, is made by continuing to heat the butter until it is a dark golden brown colour.

Similarly *ghee*, which gives much of Indian cuisine its rich, nutty flavour, is butter clarified as above, but subsequently cooked gently for up to an hour.

FLAVOURED BUTTERS

These are fresh butters to which other flavouring ingredients are added to suit the dish they are to dress. They are usually prepared in advance, formed into a small cylinder, wrapped in foil and hardened in the refrigerator. This allows them to be easily sliced into attractive discs for presentation. Flavoured butters are easy to make in a blender or food processor, and freeze well. The butter should be soft, but not too soft, when the other ingredients are blended in along with generous seasonings. Include more or less salt depending on the other ingredients and whether or not the butter is salted.

For instance, ROQUEFORT BUTTER is excellent with beef, TAPENADE BUTTER goes well with simply grilled (broiled) white fish, THYME BUTTER with cold chicken, SALMON BUTTER on seafood canapés, CHIVE BUTTER with soft-boiled eggs, NUT BUTTERS with fish and vegetables, ANCHOVY and GARLIC BUTTER for canapés, grilled meat or cold chicken, PRAWN, SHRIMP or CRAB BUTTER, seasoned with a little lemon juice and a dash of paprika, for canapés.

Two of the principal dressings in French cuisine are flavoured butters: MAÎTRE D'HÔTEL BUTTER and MONTPELLIER BUTTER. Maître d'hôtel butter is made by mixing the butter with chopped flat-leaved parsley and lemon juice, and is the classic dressing for grilled steaks and fish. Montpellier butter contains chopped parsley, chives and chervil, along with chopped shallots, garlic, anchovy, capers, gherkin (pickled cucumber) and an egg yolk. It is a delicious accompaniment to cold poached fish.

see also:
butter
cakes and gâteaux
Christmas yule log
creams and custards

BUTTERCREAM

Crème au beurre

An egg and butter mixture used for filling or icing pâtisserie items and gâteaux, buttercream is usually flavoured with chocolate, coffee, lemon or orange zest, praline or liquor. As the ingredients are not cooked, buttercream must always be made with top quality butter and the eggs used must be very fresh. A cake or gâteau with buttercream filling will keep for several days in the refrigerator, carefully wrapped.

CRÈME AU BEURRE

Buttercream

For a cake for 6–8 people
Preparation 25 minutes
Cooking 5 minutes

METRIC/IMPERIAL	*AMERICAN*
8 egg yolks	*8 egg yolks*
225 g/½ lb sugar cubes	*½ lb sugar cubes*
225 g/½ lb unsalted butter	*2 sticks + 3 tbsp unsalted butter*
salt	*salt*
flavouring, as wished	*flavoring, as wished*

Put the egg yolks in a bowl, add a pinch of salt and whisk them lightly. Set them aside.

Put the sugar cubes in a small saucepan and add 200 ml/7 fl oz/1 cup of water. Dissolve the sugar over low heat without stirring, tilting the pan from time to time to distribute the heat evenly (1). When the syrup is clear, boil it for 2–3 minutes until it reaches the 'soft ball' or 'short-thread' stage. To test, remove a little syrup on a spoon, cool it slightly, then moisten thumb and forefinger with a little cold water and pull a little of the syrup away from the spoon between your fingers: it should form a tiny thread.

Slowly pour the boiling syrup over the egg yolks, whisking constantly until cool (2). Leave to cool completely.

Meanwhile, cream the butter in another bowl (3). Add the egg yolk and sugar mixture to the creamed butter, stirring continuously (4). When the cream is smooth, firm and very shiny, mix in thoroughly the chosen flavouring: 1 tablespoon of vanilla or coffee essence (extract); 2 tablespoons of unsweetened cocoa or praline, 2 tablespoons of liquor, such as rum, Kirsch or Cointreau.

Use the buttercream at once, or store it in an airtight container in the refrigerator.

C

CABBAGE

Chou

see also:
broccoli
Brussels sprouts
cauliflower
sauerkraut
vegetables

The vegetables of the cabbage family, including such diverse items as Brussels sprouts and cauliflower, are all descended from the wild cabbage which still grows in parts of Britain and Europe.

There are two main types of cabbage: the GREENS OR KALES, which do not have a head and most closely resemble the wild cabbage; and the more culinarily important HEARTED CABBAGES.

There are, in turn, two main groups of hearted cabbage: the dense WHITE, GREEN OR RED CABBAGE, with smooth, tightly closed leaves and the SAVOY CABBAGE, with looser, green crinkly leaves. The former keeps very well for some time, while the latter does not keep well, and should be eaten as soon as possible after being purchased, but has an infinitely finer peppery flavour.

When purchased, cabbage should be heavy in relation to its size, and bright and clear in colour. Crumple one of the leaves between the fingers: it should snap easily and tiny drops of moisture should appear at the breaks. Remember that cabbage shrinks by about half its volume during cooking.

Fortunately, different types of cabbage are in season all year round. Spring cabbage is tender and will cook more quickly than cabbages harvested in summer, autumn or in particular winter, but it tends to cook down more than other cabbages.

When preparing cabbage, remove the large outside leaves and the thick white stalk. Cut the cabbage into quarters and wash it thoroughly under running water or soak it in water with a little salt or vinegar to get rid of any clinging insects; this is particularly necessary in the case of Savoy cabbage.

Good fresh cabbages of all types are delicious – and highly nutritious – shredded raw in salads, marinated or dressed in a vinaigrette or mayonnaise.

White and green cabbage may be simply cooked for 8–10 minutes in boiling salted water until just tender but still crisp, when the pieces start sinking into the cooking water, and then dressed with a little butter and some freshly ground black pepper. A small piece of bread in the cooking water will reduce the pronounced sulphurous odour, particularly of winter cabbage.

For any other treatment, such as poaching or braising, cabbages are generally first blanched for 5–10 minutes in boiling water, salted in the case of green cabbage, to help preserve the colour. Really tender spring cabbage can be finely shredded and simply sweated in butter without being blanched first.

The full flavour of red cabbage is best brought out by long slow braising for 1½ to 2 hours with a little vinegar, wine or stock, and perhaps a little sugar. Apples, raisins and celery are also often added. Red cabbage cooked in this way, or simply pickled, makes an excellent accompaniment to game and rich meat and poultry dishes. Central and Eastern European cooking also favours red cabbage in sweet-and-sour marinades and sauces and, of course, white cabbage soured into *sauerkraut*. Oriental cuisines also pickle cabbage.

Cabbage soup has long been a staple of the rural cuisines of many countries, as have cabbages braised with bacon or sausages or stuffed with meaty mixtures.

All cabbage is rich in fibre, vitamin C and iron; 100 g/3½ oz contains 30–35 calories.

EMBEURRÉE DE CHOU

Buttered cabbage

Serves 4
Preparation 15 minutes
Cooking about 30 minutes

METRIC/IMPERIAL	AMERICAN
1 small green Savoy cabbage, trimmed and cut into quarters	1 small head green Savoy cabbage, trimmed and cut into quarters
100 g/3½ oz slightly salted butter	1 stick lightly salted butter
bunch of chives, chopped	bunch of chives, chopped
salt and pepper	salt and pepper

Bring a large pan of salted water to the boil.

Plunge the cabbage quarters into the boiling water and cook them for 8 minutes. Drain them and immediately refresh them in cold water, then drain them thoroughly once more. Shred them evenly, trimming off the tougher ribs.

Melt two thirds of the butter in a large deep frying pan. Add the shredded cabbage and cook it gently over a low to moderate heat, stirring from time to time. Add a little salt and some pepper.

After about 20 minutes, add the chopped chives and dot with the remaining butter. Stir with a fork to melt the butter and serve at once.

CHOU ROUGE À L'AIGRE-DOUX

Sweet-and-sour red cabbage

Serves 4
Preparation 20 minutes
Cooking about 20 minutes

METRIC/IMPERIAL	AMERICAN
1 tbsp oil	1 tbsp oil
1 onion, chopped	1 onion, chopped
2 shallots, chopped	2 shallots, chopped
100 g/3½ oz celery, trimmed and chopped	1 cup trimmed and chopped celery
1 tbsp ground cumin	1 tbsp ground cumin
450 g/1 lb red cabbage, trimmed and finely shredded	1 lb red cabbage, trimmed and finely shredded
2 tbsp cider vinegar	2 tbsp cider vinegar
1 tbsp honey	1 tbsp honey
salt and pepper	salt and pepper

Put the oil in a dish and microwave it on High for 1 minute. Add the onion and shallots and microwave on High for 2 minutes.

Add the celery, cumin and 1 tablespoon of water. Microwave, covered, for 4 minutes on High, stirring once half-way through cooking.

Add the cabbage, mix well, then add the vinegar and honey. Mix and microwave on High for 10 minutes, stirring 3 times during cooking.

Leave to stand for 3 minutes, then season with salt and pepper and serve while still hot.

CHOU BLANC EN SALADE

White cabbage salad

Serves 6
Preparation 20 minutes, 1 hour ahead

METRIC/IMPERIAL	AMERICAN
200 ml/7 fl oz crème fraîche or sour cream	1 cup crème fraîche or sour cream
juice of 1 lemon	juice of 1 lemon
1 tsp curry powder	1 tsp curry powder
1 apple	1 apple
550 g/1¼ lb white cabbage, finely shredded	1¼ lb white cabbage, finely shredded
2 tbsp raisins	2 tbsp raisins
salt and black pepper	salt and black pepper

Mix together the cream, half the lemon juice and the curry powder and season with salt and pepper.

Peel, quarter and core the apple, then slice the quarters thinly. Sprinkle them with the remaining lemon juice.

Put the cabbage into a salad bowl along with the sliced apple and the raisins.

Pour the cream sauce over the salad and mix well. Chill for at least 1 hour before serving.

CHOU VERT FARCI

Stuffed cabbage

Serves 6
Preparation 25 minutes
Cooking about 2¾ hours

METRIC/IMPERIAL	AMERICAN
1 large green cabbage	1 large head green cabbage
115 g/¼ lb cooked ham, chopped	¼ lb cooked ham, chopped
225g/½ lb sliced streaky bacon, chopped	½ lb bacon slices, chopped
225 g/½ lb pork sausage meat	½ lb pork sausage meat
225 g/½ lb minced veal	½ lb ground veal
3 onions	3 onions
45 g/1½ oz butter	3 tbsp butter
3 shallots, chopped	3 shallots, chopped
1 slice of white bread	1 slice of white bread
5 tbsp milk	5 tbsp milk
1 egg	1 egg
225 g/½ lb pork belly fat, sliced	½ lb pork fatback, sliced
2 carrots, cut into chunks	2 carrots, cut into chunks
1 leek, trimmed and cut into chunks	1 leek, trimmed and cut into chunks
1 clove	1 clove
bouquet garni	bouquet garni
salt and pepper	salt and pepper

Blanch the cabbage for 15 minutes in a large pan of boiling salted water, refresh it immediately in very cold water and drain it thoroughly.

Remove the large leaves one at a time without tearing them. Chop the inner leaves.

Mix the ham and bacon with the sausage meat and the veal.

Chop 2 of the onions. Heat the butter in a flameproof casserole over a moderate heat, add the chopped onions and shallots and brown them for 3–4 minutes.

Add the meats and cook, stirring, for a further 10 minutes. Remove the pan from the heat and leave it to cool. Meanwhile, soak the bread in the milk.

Squeeze excess milk from the soaked bread, then add to the meat mixture with the egg and mix well. Line a bowl with a large cloth.

Line the cloth first with the slices of pork fat, then arrange a layer of the whole cabbage leaves on it. Fill the hollow with alternate layers of the meat stuffing and the chopped cabbage.

Bring the corners of the cloth together to re-form the cabbage, then knot the cloth and tie string around it to keep it in shape during cooking.

Put the carrots and leek in a large pan with the third onion, studded with the clove, and the bouquet garni. Pour in 2 l/3½ pt/2 qt of water and bring it to the boil.

Put the stuffed cabbage into the boiling water, bring back to the boil, then reduce the heat and cook it gently for 2 hours.

At the end of this time, remove the cabbage parcel, unwrap the cloth and discard the barding fat. Place the cabbage in a warmed serving dish.

Boil the cooking liquid rapidly to reduce it by about three-quarters, adjust seasoning and pour a little over the cabbage. Serve very hot accompanied by the remaining reduced stock.
To drink: a medium-bodied red wine, such as a Côtes-du-Rhône.

Chou vert farci (Stuffed cabbage)

CAKES AND GÂTEAUX

see also: baba, baking, brioche, charlotte, chocolate, cookies, etc, tart

The term 'cake' is usually reserved by the French for fruit cake, and 'gâteau' is used for a wide range of pâtisserie items based on most types of pastry, sponge batters and meringue. The British and Americans, on the other hand, use both terms much more generally, and sometimes almost interchangeably.

Cakes and gâteaux are usually defined by their dominant flavouring ingredient, eg, chocolate gâteau, orange fondant cake, etc, but are best differentiated by the means of leavening and the type of fat, if any, used.

The most common type of cake uses baking powder or yeast as a raising agent, although the flavour of yeast is normally too strong for all but the richest and spiciest of cakes, while ANGEL and SPONGE CAKES rely on the air trapped in beaten egg whites in their mixtures.

In most cake-making, however, it is essential that every opportunity is taken to lighten the

cake mixture by incorporating as much air as possible at all stages, from sifting the flour to creaming the sugar and shortening together vigorously to trap air in that mixture. In many cakes this air, and the steam produced during cooking, are the only means of aeration.

Butter is the most usual fat used in the making of cakes, as it has a fine yet unobtrusive flavour. However, margarine and bland vegetable fats may be used to make excellent cakes, which are perhaps healthier and more economical.

Butter is usually creamed with the sugar rather than being rubbed or cut into the flour as in pastry-making. Certain types of cake, such as the GENOESE SPONGE, involve pouring melted butter into a warmed sugar and egg mixture to produce a particularly light and rich effect.

Cakes are flavoured with a wide variety of ingredients: leavened cakes tend to contain heavier items, such as raisins and other dried or candied fruit and whole nuts, while the lighter SPONGE CAKES are usually flavoured with ground nuts, essences (extracts) such as vanilla or almond, or grated citrus zest and liqueurs.

The richer heavier cakes are also traditionally quite highly spiced, usually with mace or allspice, and also often have a fairly high alcohol content from whisky, brandy or rum, or they may be soaked with alcohol after baking. FRUIT CAKES keep well for months in a sealed container in a cool dry place and are actually said to taste better when slightly stale.

SPONGE CAKES are most frequently sliced and filled with fruit, jam or flavoured cream mixtures, and form the basis for numerous elaborate filled and iced gâteaux. Plain sponge cakes will keep for several days in the refrigerator and freeze well, but they should normally be used fairly quickly after filling and decoration. Good quality, ready-made cooked sponge cakes and small sponge fingers (ladyfingers) are now commonly available in shops and supermarkets and greatly simplify the process of making filled and iced cakes at home.

Cakes have traditionally been a means of marking special occasions in most cultures, from elaborate multi-tiered iced cakes at weddings to German *stollen* and jewel-like Italian *pannetone* at Christmas. Birthday cakes can be uniquely personal, perhaps with favourite ingredients and elaborate personalized decoration.

One slice of fruit cake contains about 200 calories; a slice of undecorated Genoese sponge contains only about 135 calories, but fillings and toppings are often more than twice that.

CAKE AUX RAISINS ET AUX FRUITS CONFITS

Fruit cake

Serves 8–12
Preparation 25 minutes
Cooking 45 minutes

METRIC/IMPERIAL	*AMERICAN*
100 g/3½ oz currants	*⅔ cup currants*
100 g/3½ oz mixed candied fruit, cut into small pieces	*⅔ cup chopped mixed candied fruit*
2 tbsp rum	*2 tbsp rum*
200 g/7 oz butter	*2 sticks butter*
125 g/4½ oz caster sugar	*10 tbsp superfine sugar*
pinch of salt	*pinch of salt*
3 eggs	*3 eggs*
250 g/8½ oz flour	*2 cups flour*
1½ tsp baking powder	*1½ tsp baking powder*

Preheat the oven to 210C/415F/gas 6–7. Grease a piece of parchment or greaseproof paper with a little of the butter and use it to line the inside of a 25 cm/10 in loaf pan. Macerate the currants and fruit in the rum.

Put the remaining butter into a bowl and beat it with a wooden spoon until smooth and creamy, then add the sugar a little at a time along with the salt. Beat the mixture until it is light and fluffy.

Beat in the eggs one at a time. Add the flour all at once, then add the currants, candied fruit and rum together with the baking powder and mix all the ingredients thoroughly. Pour the cake batter into the prepared pan; the loaf pan should be three-quarters full.

Bake for 10 minutes – on no account should the oven door be opened during this time – then lower the temperature to 160C/325F/gas 3 and continue baking for about 35 minutes.

Test to see if the cake is done by inserting a skewer or the point of a sharp knife into the centre: it should come out clean. Leave to cool a little while in the pan and then turn the cake out on a wire rack to cool completely before serving or storing.

GÂTEAU AU CHOCOLAT

Chocolate cake

Serves 6
Preparation 30 minutes
Cooking 18 minutes

METRIC/IMPERIAL	*AMERICAN*
300 g/10 oz plain chocolate	*10 oz semisweet chocolate*
100 g/3½ oz butter	*1 stick butter*
3 eggs, separated	*3 eggs, separated*
85 g/3 oz caster sugar	*6½ tbsp superfine sugar*
50 g/1¾ oz flour	*6½ tbsp flour*
3 tbsp rum	*3 tbsp rum*
1 tsp baking powder	*1 tsp baking powder*
salt	*salt*

Preheat the oven to 220C/425F/gas 7.

Break half the chocolate into tiny pieces and put them in a bowl with one-third of the butter. Melt, stirring, in a bain-marie until smooth.

Put the egg yolks in a large bowl. Beat them with the sugar until the mixture falls in a ribbon, then add the flour, the melted chocolate and butter mixture, 1 tablespoon of the rum and the baking powder. Mix well.

Whisk the egg whites with a pinch of salt to stiff peaks and fold carefully into the batter.

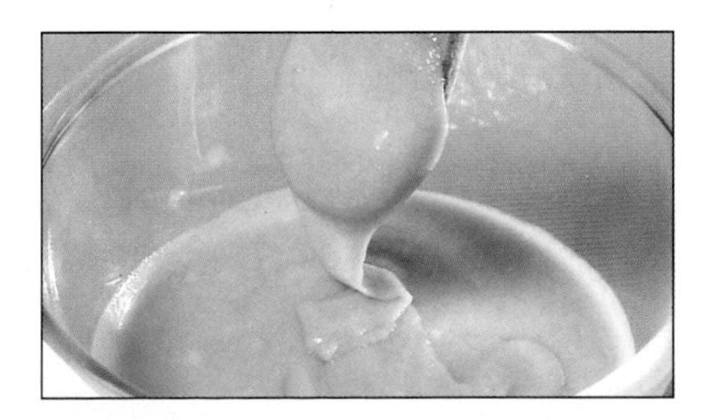

When the egg yolk and sugar mixture has thickened, it falls in a ribbon from a spoon.

Generously grease a 20 cm/8 in round cake pan or 22 cm/8¾ in ring mould with some of the remaining butter and pour the batter into it. Bake for 10 minutes, then reduce the heat to 180C/350F/gas 4 and bake for a further 8 minutes. Remove the cake from the oven and leave to cool.

Turn the cooled cake out on a serving platter. Put the remaining butter and chocolate in a bowl with 2 tablespoons of water and melt in a bain-marie. Stir in the remaining rum.

Pour this mixture evenly over the cake, letting it run down over the edges. Leave until completely cool before serving.

ANGEL CAKE

Makes an 18 cm/7¼ in cake
Preparation 20 minutes
Cooking about 1 hour

METRIC/IMPERIAL	*AMERICAN*
100 g/3½ oz flour	*¾ cup flour*
185 g/6½ oz caster sugar	*15 tbsp superfine sugar*
5–6 (175 ml/5 fl oz) egg whites	*5–6 (¾ cup) egg whites*
½ tsp cream of tartar	*½ tsp cream of tartar*
½ tsp vanilla or almond essence	*½ tsp vanilla or almond extract*

Preheat the oven to 160C/325F/gas 3.

Sift the flour and sugar together 3 or 4 times. Whisk the egg whites until foaming. Add the cream of tartar and whisk again until stiff but not too dry.

Sift the flour and sugar carefully over the whisked egg whites, about 2 tablespoons at a time. Then fold in the flavouring.

Pour the mixture into an ungreased 18 cm/7¼ in diameter deep ring cake pan and bake for 1 hour, or until a skewer inserted into the cake comes out clean. Remove from the oven and leave to cool on a wire rack. When quite cool, turn the cake out of the pan.

This is a sweet cake and it therefore best suits a contrasting, sharp-flavoured icing. Leave the cake whole and ice with chocolate chantilly cream, ie, whipped cream with cocoa powder and icing (confectioners') sugar to taste. Or, slice the cake across in three layers, spread the slices with lemon curd, reassemble the cake and decorate with lemon-flavoured buttercream and candied lemon slices.

BISCUIT DE SAVOIE

Savoy sponge cake

Serves 8
Preparation 20 minutes
Cooking 40–45 minutes

METRIC/IMPERIAL	*AMERICAN*
1 lemon	*1 lemon*
6 medium (size 4) eggs, separated	*6 large eggs, separated*
170 g/6 oz caster sugar	*14 tbsp superfine sugar*
50 g/$1\frac{3}{4}$ oz flour	*$6\frac{1}{2}$ tbsp flour*
50 g/$1\frac{3}{4}$ oz potato flour	*6 tbsp potato starch*
25 g/$\frac{3}{4}$ oz butter	*$1\frac{1}{2}$ tbsp butter*
salt	*salt*

Preheat the oven to 180C/350F/gas 4.

If the lemon is not organically grown and may have been sprayed or coated, scrub it well in warm soapy water, rinse it thoroughly and pat it dry. Finely grate the zest of the lemon.

Put the egg yolks in a bowl with a pinch of salt and 150 g/$5\frac{1}{2}$ oz/$\frac{3}{4}$ cup of the sugar (1). Beat until the mixture is smooth and frothy.

Sift in the flour and potato flour, then add the lemon zest (2).

Whisk the egg whites to stiff peaks (3). Add 2 tablespoons of beaten egg white to the cake batter and whisk in to soften it. Then add the rest of the egg whites all at once and fold them in carefully with a thin wooden spoon so that they remain frothy and full of air (4).

Carefully grease a 26 cm/$10\frac{1}{2}$ in diameter round cake pan with the butter and dust it with the remaining sugar. Pour into it the cake mixture, which should be fluid but not runny.

Bake for 40–45 minutes. To test for doneness, insert a metal skewer into the middle of the cake; it should come out clean. When the cake is cooked, remove it from the oven, let it cool in the pan for 5 minutes and turn it out on a wire rack. Leave it to cool.

Notes: the success of this cake depends entirely on the care taken during cooking. The cake pan should be in the middle of the oven and should stand on the oven rack itself rather than on a baking sheet, so that the heat can circulate freely

1

2

3

4

around it. If the oven is too hot the cake will rise too quickly and brown too fast. If the oven door is opened prematurely, the cake will sink before it is properly cooked.

For a 22 cm/$8\frac{3}{4}$ in cake pan, use 3 eggs and for a 24 cm/$9\frac{1}{2}$ in pan, use 4 eggs. For all practical purposes, other proportions remain the same. The cake pan may be round or square, or even heart-shaped.

PAIN DE GÊNES

Genoa cake

Serves 6
Preparation 20 minutes
Cooking 40 minutes

METRIC/IMPERIAL	*AMERICAN*
150 g/$5\frac{1}{2}$ oz butter, softened	*11 tbsp butter, softened*
150 g/$5\frac{1}{2}$ oz caster sugar	*$\frac{3}{4}$ cup superfine sugar*
100 g/$3\frac{1}{2}$ oz ground almonds	*$1\frac{1}{4}$ cups ground almonds*
3 eggs	*3 eggs*
100 g/$3\frac{1}{2}$ oz flour	*$\frac{3}{4}$ cup flour*
2 tbsp Grand Marnier	*2 tbsp Grand Marnier*
salt	*salt*

Preheat the oven to 180C/350F/gas 4.

Cream 120 g/$4\frac{1}{4}$ oz/$8\frac{1}{2}$ tbsp of the butter with the sugar in a bowl, and then add the ground almonds.

Add the eggs one at a time and beat well. Then add the flour, a pinch of salt and the Grand Marnier. Beat for 3 minutes.

Using the remaining butter, grease a 23 cm/9 in diameter *moule à manqué* or cake pan and a circle of parchment or greaseproof paper cut to the diameter of the pan. Line the pan with the paper, butter side up.

Pour the batter into the prepared cake pan and bake for 40 minutes. Turn out on a wire rack, remove the paper and leave to cool.

PÂTE À GÉNOISE

Genoese sponge cake

For one 22 cm/$8\frac{3}{4}$ in diameter cake
Preparation 30 minutes
Cooking 30–40 minutes

METRIC/IMPERIAL	*AMERICAN*
4 eggs	*4 eggs*
pinch of fine salt	*pinch of fine salt*
125 g/$4\frac{1}{2}$ oz caster sugar	*10 tbsp superfine sugar*
80 g/$2\frac{3}{4}$ oz butter	*$5\frac{1}{2}$ tbsp butter*
$\frac{1}{2}$ sachet (3.75 g/$\frac{3}{4}$ tsp) vanilla sugar or 1 tbsp finely grated lemon or orange zest, for flavouring (optional)	*$\frac{3}{4}$ tsp vanilla-flavored sugar or 1 tbsp finely grated lemon or orange zest, for flavoring (optional)*
140 g/5 oz flour, sifted	*1 cup + 2 tbsp flour, sifted*

Preheat the oven to 200C/400F/gas 6.

Break the eggs into a large, flameproof bowl. Add a pinch of fine salt and the sugar.

Place the bowl containing the eggs and sugar over a saucepan filled with hot water over a very low heat. Whisk the mixture vigorously until it triples in volume (1, pictured overleaf). The water in the saucepan must not be allowed to boil; the batter should be warm but not hot. Remove the bowl from the saucepan.

Melt all but 25 g/$\frac{3}{4}$ oz/$1\frac{1}{2}$ tbsp of the butter in a small saucepan and let it cool.

Mix any flavourings with the sifted flour. Pour 125 g/$4\frac{1}{2}$ oz/1 cup of the flour all at once into the batter and fold it in gently with a thin wooden spatula (2).

When most of the flour has been incorporated, gently pour the melted butter over the mixture, stirring (3). When it is well mixed in, add the rest of the flour. Continue to mix until smooth. It is essential that this operation be carried out quickly with deft, light movements so that the batter keeps the air beaten into it.

Grease a 22 cm/$8\frac{3}{4}$ in round, square or heart-shaped cake pan about 5–6 cm/2–$2\frac{1}{2}$ in deep with the remaining butter and dust it with flour. Pour the batter into it (4). The cake pan should not be more than two-thirds full.

Bake for 30–40 minutes on a rack in the

1

2

3

4

middle of the oven so that the heat is as even as possible. Bake for the first 30 minutes without opening the oven door, and then check for doneness by inserting a metal skewer into the centre of the cake: it should come out completely clean.

When cooked, remove the cake from the oven and turn it out on a wire rack. Cover it with a clean, dry cloth: the cake will lose all its excess moisture as it cools, and will be soft and light and ready to be iced or filled with a pastry cream or jam. Wait until it is completely cold before cutting it in half horizontally for filling.

Note: the requisite oven temperature is governed by the size of the cake: if making small, individual cakes in dariole or tartlet moulds, lower it to 150C/300F/gas 2.

GÂTEAU MOUSSELINE

Chiffon cake

Serves 5–6
Preparation 20 minutes
Cooking 10 minutes

METRIC/IMPERIAL	*AMERICAN*
50 g/1¾ oz butter	*3½ tbsp butter*
4 large (size 1 or 2) eggs, separated	*4 extra large eggs, separated*
125 g/4½ oz caster sugar	*10 tbsp superfine sugar*
100 g/3½ oz flour	*¾ cup flour*

Preheat the oven to 250C/475F/gas 9. Melt 30 g/1 oz/2 tbsp of the butter in a small pan and leave it to cool.

Beat the egg yolks vigorously with the sugar until the mixture has doubled in volume. Whisk the egg whites to stiff peaks. Add one third of the flour to the egg yolk and sugar mixture. Add the cooled, melted butter and mix well. Carefully fold in one third of the beaten egg whites. Continue adding alternate amounts of flour and egg whites until the ingredients are used up.

Grease a 20 cm/8 in diameter cake or springform pan with the remaining butter and pour the batter into it. Bake for 10 minutes.

Turn the cake out on a wire rack and leave it to cool completely. Serve with jam or lemon-flavoured cream.

GÉNOISE À L'ANANAS

Genoese sponge cake with pineapple

Serves 6
Preparation 20 minutes, sponge about 1 hour
Cooking 10 minutes

METRIC/IMPERIAL	AMERICAN
1 round Genoese sponge, about 22 cm/8¾ in diameter	1 round Genoese sponge cake, about 8¾ in diameter
5 tbsp Kirsch	5 tbsp Kirsch
2 eggs	2 eggs
75 g/2½ oz caster sugar	6 tbsp superfine sugar
500 ml/16 fl oz milk	2 cups milk
55 g/2 oz flour	½ cup flour
30 g/1 oz butter, cut in small pieces	2 tbsp butter, cut in small pieces
1 can (425 g/1 lb) crushed pineapple	1 can (1 lb) crushed pineapple
2–3 tbsp pineapple jam, warmed	2–3 tbsp pineapple jam, warmed
24 glacé cherries	24 candied cherries

Cut the Genoese sponge cake in half horizontally and sprinkle the cut surfaces with 3 tablespoons of the Kirsch.

Break the eggs into a bowl and add the sugar. Beat the mixture until it is pale and thick.

Heat the milk in a heavy saucepan. Add the flour to the egg and sugar mixture, then gradually pour the milk into it, stirring constantly. Transfer to the saucepan and cook, stirring, over a low heat until it just comes to the boil. Add the butter and remaining Kirsch. Remove the custard from the heat. Drain the pineapple and add to the custard.

When the custard has cooled and thickened, spread it over one of the sponge cake layers and position the other layer carefully on top.

Spread the pineapple jam over the top of the cake. Decorate with the cherries. Serve chilled.

GÂTEAU AUX ABRICOTS

Apricot refrigerator cake

Serves 8
Preparation 30 minutes, 24 hours ahead

METRIC/IMPERIAL	AMERICAN
300 g/10 oz caster sugar	1½ cups superfine sugar
100 ml/3½ fl oz rum	½ cup rum
100 g/3½ oz raisins	⅔ cup raisins
100 g/3½ oz candied fruit, cut in small pieces	⅔ cup chopped candied fruits
1 can (400 g/14 oz) of apricots	1 can (14 oz) of apricots
juice of 1 lemon	juice of 1 lemon
36 sponge fingers	36 ladyfingers

Prepare a syrup by dissolving 4 tablespoons of sugar in 100 ml/3½ fl oz/½ cup of water and 4 tablespoons of rum in a deep dish. Macerate the raisins and the chopped candied fruit in the remaining rum.

Drain the apricots. Blend them in a food processor to a purée. Add the remaining sugar and the lemon juice.

Dip the sponge fingers (ladyfingers) one at a time into the rum syrup and use one third of them to line the bottom of a 22 cm/8¾ in square cake pan lined with parchment or greaseproof paper. Sprinkle over half of the drained candied fruit and raisins and cover them with a layer of half the apricot purée.

Continue with another layer of sponge fingers (ladyfingers) dipped in syrup, followed by another layer of candied fruit and raisins and

Cut parchment or greaseproof paper to fit. Greasing the pan will help it to stick.

another of apricot purée, reserving at least 3 or 4 tablespoons. Finish with a layer of sponge fingers (ladyfingers).

Chill the cake overnight. Unmould it and serve it with the remaining apricot purée poured over it.

Note: the chilling time is essential to enable the sponge fingers (ladyfingers) to become completely saturated in the fruit purée and rum syrup.

BISCUIT ROULÉ À LA CONFITURE

Jam sponge roll or jelly roll

Serves 6–8
Preparation 30 minutes
Cooking 10 minutes

METRIC/IMPERIAL	*AMERICAN*
60 g/$2\frac{1}{4}$ oz butter	*$4\frac{1}{2}$ tbsp butter*
4 eggs, separated	*4 eggs, separated*
125 g/$4\frac{1}{2}$ oz sugar	*10 tbsp sugar*
50 g/$1\frac{3}{4}$ oz flour	*$6\frac{1}{2}$ tbsp flour*
50 g/$1\frac{3}{4}$ oz potato flour	*6 tbsp potato starch*
$\frac{1}{2}$ tsp baking powder	*$\frac{1}{2}$ tsp baking powder*
1 jar (250 g/8 oz) of any red fruit jam	*1 jar (8 oz) of any red fruit jelly*
2 tbsp rum	*2 tbsp rum*
125 g/$4\frac{1}{2}$ oz flaked almonds, lightly toasted	*1 cup slivered almonds, lightly toasted*

Preheat the oven to 250C/475F/gas 9.

Melt half the butter. Beat the egg yolks with the sugar until very foamy. Whisk the egg whites to stiff peaks.

Mix the flour and the potato flour together.

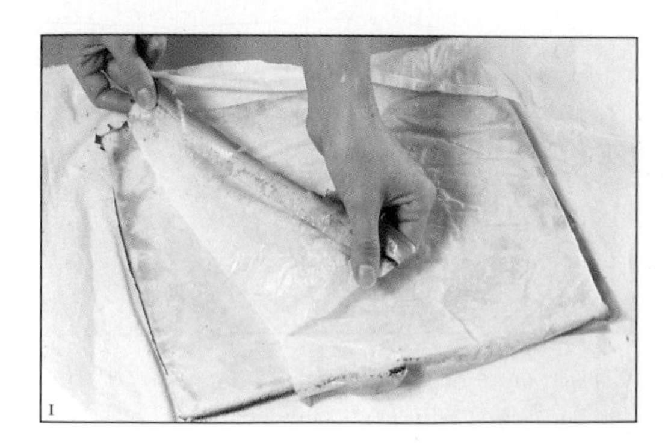
1

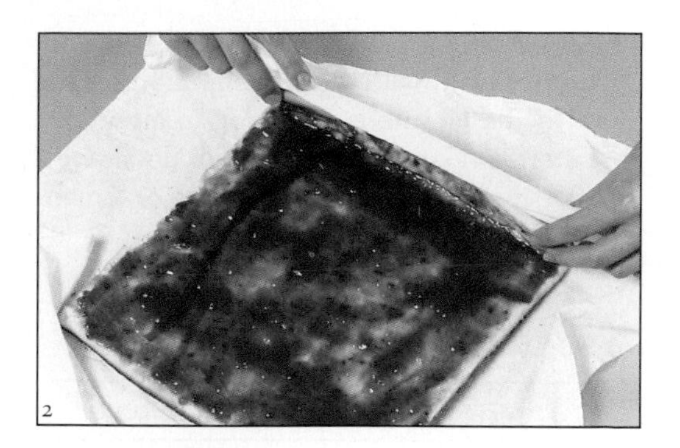
2

Add half to the egg yolk and sugar mixture, then mix in the melted butter and baking powder. In alternating spoonfuls, fold in the egg whites and the remaining flour mixture.

Line a Swiss roll tin (jelly roll pan) or rectangular baking sheet with parchment or greaseproof paper and grease it with the remaining butter. Pour the batter into the centre and spread it smoothly with a spatula until it covers the whole area to a depth of about 1 cm/$\frac{1}{2}$ in. Bake in the hot oven for 10 minutes. The surface should be golden brown and firm to the touch.

Place a clean cloth on top of the cake and turn it over on to a work surface. Remove the baking sheet and the paper (1). Mix the jam with the rum and spread most of this mixture over the surface of the cake to within 2.5 cm/1 in of either short edge.

Lift the cloth at one end to start rolling up the sponge, then little by little roll the cake up on itself, using the cloth to support it (2). When it is rolled up, transfer it carefully to a long dish. Spread the top with the remaining jam and sprinkle with the flaked (slivered) almonds. Trim the two ends of the roll with a sharp knife to neaten its appearance. Serve chilled.

Note: any kind of jam or jelly is suitable for use in this cake, provided it is not too runny.

CALCIUM

see also:
butter
cheese
milk
minerals
phosphorus

Calcium is the mineral present in the highest proportion in the human body, 90% in the bones and teeth. In combination with phosphorus it ensures the rigidity and strength of the skeletal structure. Even in adulthood calcium levels need to be constantly renewed, as it is also essential in the proper working of other bodily functions, such as the clotting of the blood.

Recommended average daily calcium intake in France and America is 700 mg (4–9 years), 900 mg (10–12 years), 1000 mg (for adolescents and pregnant women), 800 mg (adults) and 1200 mg (for nursing mothers), although the evaluation of such needs has recently been substantially reduced after considerable experimentation and observation has shown that the body adjusts satisfactorily to lower calcium levels. In Britain the RDA, or recommended daily intake, for adults is now only 500 mg.

To fulfil these needs it is essential to eat daily at least 30 g/1 oz of cheese along with one or two fat-free dairy products, such as skimmed milk or low-fat yogurt. The cheeses that are highest in calcium are Gruyère, Edam, Gouda, Cantal and Roquefort. Interestingly, full-cream milk is lower in calcium than skimmed milk. Vitamin D is indispensable for the body's absorption of calcium and for its maintenance of correct levels of the mineral.

It is worth noting that certain vegetables, especially sorrel, spinach and rhubarb, along with tea, cocoa, beer, dried beans and peas and wholemeal or whole wheat bread contain a high level of phytates, which inhibit the absorption of calcium into the system. However, recent research would seem to indicate that the body gradually adapts to continued high levels of phytates in the system and the absorption mechanisms adjust.

CALORIE

Energy provided by food and consumed by the human body is expressed in calories. Basically a calorie is the scientific measure of the heat required to raise the temperature of 1 gram of water by 1 degree Centigrade, and 1 Calorie – or kilocalorie – is equal to 1,000 of these calories. It is this larger Calorie which is used in nutrition, although increasingly in ordinary usage it is not differentiated by capitalization.

People's energy requirements are governed by many factors, including sex, age, height, weight, climate and level of physical activity. A sedentary adult uses between 1,200 and 1,400 calories per day. An average active woman requires about 2,200 calories, while an average active man needs about 2,800; the difference is mostly due to the size differential. Strenuous physical activity almost doubles the calorie consumption at any given time, say, from 200 calories per hour to about 400. The intake of excess calories will result in weight increase. A diet of 1,000 calories per day for most people will result in loss of weight, but should be carefully balanced and not undertaken on a prolonged basis without medical supervision.

It is also essential to ensure that calories come from a balanced variety of sources: ideally, 12–15% from proteins, 30–35% from fats and 50–55% from carbohydrates. Generally, it is excess intake of fats and carbohydrates which causes obesity.

CANAPÉ

see also:
buffet
butter
croûte
hors d'oeuvre
sauce

These are a form of open sandwich made from a single slice of bread, often cut into small decorative shapes, usually to be served with drinks.

There is an infinite variety of garnishes for canapés: sliced meats and salamis, smooth pâtés, cheeses, egg, flavoured butters, caviar and smoked salmon and eel for cold canapés; for hot canapés, béchamel with, say, spinach and Parmesan or crab, scrambled eggs, toasted cheese or any of the usual *croûte* fillings.

Cold canapés may be made from sliced white or rye bread, with the crusts removed and often slightly stale to ensure that they do not crumble – and sometimes lightly toasted. They need to be prepared at the last minute so that they do not dry out or allow the bread to become soggy from wet ingredients. Once made, they should be kept in a cold place, covered with a slightly damp cloth.

Hot canapés are usually made with wholemeal, whole wheat or country-style bread. They are generally toasted on one side, turned over, then baked or grilled until the topping bubbles. One of the simplest hot canapés is grated cheese and onion moistened with a little mayonnaise, another is tuna mashed with cream cheese and dill.

The meat of smaller game birds is also traditionally served on canapés, slices of bread fried in butter and spread with a giblet stuffing.

CANAPÉS AU SAUMON FUMÉ

Smoked salmon canapés

Makes 20
Preparation 25 minutes

METRIC/IMPERIAL	AMERICAN
½ cucumber	½ cucumber
10 slices of white bread, 12.5 cm/5 in square and 1.5 cm/¾ in thick, crusts removed	10 slices of white bread, 5 in square and ¾ in thick, crusts removed
55 g/2 oz prawn butter (see Butter)	¼ cup shrimp butter (see Butter)
225 g/½ lb smoked salmon, cut into thin strips	½ lb smoked salmon, cut into thin strips
1 small jar (85 g/3 oz) of salmon caviar	1 small jar (3 oz) of salmon caviar
salt and white pepper	salt and white pepper

Peel the cucumber, chop the flesh finely and sprinkle it with salt. Leave it for 20 minutes in the refrigerator.

Spread the slices of bread with the prawns (shrimp) butter.

Drain the chopped cucumber carefully and arrange it on the slices of bread, pressing it down slightly with a spatula so that it sticks. Season with pepper and decorate with the smoked salmon.

Using a very sharp long knife, cut the bread in half into either triangles or rectangles. Garnish with salmon caviar and serve chilled.

CANNELLONI

see also:
pasta and noodles
sauce

This classic Italian dish consisting of big tubes (*canna*) of pasta, stuffed with cheese, vegetable, seafood or meat mixtures, is baked *au gratin* in a thick tomato sauce. Cannelloni are usually served straight from the baking dish, or more attractively in individual baking dishes.

Ready-made cannelloni tubes are available commercially, but it is quicker and easier to roll large squares of fresh pasta around the appropriate stuffing. Cannelloni are an excellent means of using up leftovers imaginatively.

CANNELLONI AU FROMAGE

Cheese cannelloni

Serves 4
Preparation 15 minutes, sauce 30 minutes
Cooking 20–25 minutes

METRIC/IMPERIAL	AMERICAN
450 g/1 lb ricotta or fromage blanc	1 lb ricotta cheese or fromage blanc
2 whole eggs + 1 egg yolk	2 whole eggs + 1 egg yolk
4 tbsp chopped fresh parsley	¼ cup chopped fresh parsley
5 tbsp grated Parmesan	⅓ cup grated Parmesan cheese
pinch of grated nutmeg	pinch of grated nutmeg
12 pasta squares (about 10 cm/4 in)	12 pasta squares (about 4 in)
25 g/¾ oz butter	1½ tbsp butter
12 slices of raw ham	12 slices of raw ham
300 ml/½ pt fresh tomato sauce	1½ cups fresh tomato sauce
salt and pepper	salt and pepper

Preheat the oven to 250C/475F/gas 9.

Mix the cheese, eggs, egg yolk, parsley and 1 tablespoon of the grated Parmesan together in a bowl. Season with salt and pepper and grated nutmeg to taste.

Cook the pasta squares for 3 minutes in boiling salted water, then drain them flat on a clean cloth. Melt the butter.

On each pasta square place a slice of ham and on top of that a spoonful of the cheese filling. Roll up the cannelloni and arrange them in a deep baking dish; the dish should be just big enough to hold the cannelloni in one layer. Pour the melted butter over them.

Coat them with the tomato sauce and sprinkle with the remainder of the Parmesan. Bake for 15–20 minutes or until the surface is brown and crusty.

To drink: Chianti.

CANNELLONI À LA VIANDE

Meat cannelloni

Serves 4
Preparation 25 minutes
Cooking about 1¾ hours

METRIC/IMPERIAL	AMERICAN
3 tbsp olive oil	3 tbsp olive oil
2 garlic cloves, chopped	2 garlic cloves, chopped
3 onions, chopped	3 onions, chopped
2 stalks of celery, trimmed and chopped	2 sticks of celery, trimmed and chopped
bouquet garni	bouquet garni
450 g/1 lb braising beef, coarsely chopped	1 lb beef chuck, coarsely chopped
6 tomatoes, peeled and coarsely chopped	6 tomatoes, peeled and coarsely chopped
200 ml/7 fl oz beef stock	1 cup beef stock
200 ml/7 fl oz red wine	1 cup red wine
20 pasta squares (about 10 cm/4 in)	20 pasta squares (about 4 in)
5 tbsp tomato purée	5 tbsp tomato paste
3 tbsp grated Parmesan	3 tbsp grated Parmesan cheese
salt and pepper	salt and pepper

Preheat the oven to 250C/475F/gas 9.

Heat the oil in a saucepan over a moderate heat and lightly cook the garlic, onion and celery in it for a minute or two until softened. Then add the bouquet garni along with the meat. Cook, stirring, for 5 minutes and then add the tomatoes. Simmer for 10 minutes, then add the stock and wine. Cover and cook for 1½ hours.

Cook the pasta squares for 3 minutes in salted boiling water, then drain them flat on a clean cloth.

Remove and discard the bouquet garni from the meat mixture, and drain off and reserve the more liquid part of the sauce. Spread the meat and vegetable mixture over the pasta squares and roll them up. Arrange them in a baking dish just big enough to hold them in one layer. Stir the tomato purée (paste) into the reserved sauce and coat the cannelloni with it. Sprinkle with the grated Parmesan and bake for 15–20 minutes, until the top is brown and crusty.

CAPER

Câpre

see also:
flower
mayonnaise
pizza
sauce
skate

The flower bud of the caper shrub, which grows in warmest parts of the world, is usually sold pickled in vinegar or preserved in brine as a condiment. Capers should always be drained, and rinsed in cold water if they are too salty. Their strong, sour sharpness and unique 'goaty' taste are used to heighten the flavour of meatballs, pasta sauces, salad dressings, rice dishes and some fish. They are also a popular garnish on pizzas and hors d'oeuvres.

Their flavour combines well with mustard and horseradish, as well as lemon zest and garlic. Capers have long been one of the classic dressings for skate and cod, and caper sauce is the traditional English accompaniment to boiled mutton. Capers are also an essential element in the French *sauce ravigote*, which is served with calves' head, brains and boiled poultry. Capers can also add interest to the mayonnaise-based *rémoulade* and tartare sauces, which work well with celery, salads and fish and seafood dishes and cold meats.

SAUCE AUX CAPRES

Caper sauce

Makes 500 ml/16 fl oz/2 cups
Preparation 8 minutes
Cooking about 25 minutes

METRIC/IMPERIAL	AMERICAN
55 g/2 oz butter	4 tbsp butter
45 g/1½ oz flour	4 tbsp flour
300 ml/½ pt hot stock	1½ cups hot stock
150 ml/¼ pt crème fraîche or whipping cream	⅔ cup crème fraîche or whipping cream
2 heaped tbsp capers, well drained	2 heaping tbsp capers, well drained
lemon juice	lemon juice
1–2 tbsp chopped parsley (optional)	1–2 tbsp chopped parsley (optional)
salt and pepper	salt and pepper

Make a roux by melting the butter over a gentle heat and stirring in the flour. When the roux begins to foam, gradually pour the very hot stock into it, stirring constantly with a whisk. Cook gently for 15 minutes.

Stir in the cream and continue to cook over a gentle heat for 5 minutes.

Add the capers and lemon juice to taste and stir thoroughly. Taste and adjust the seasoning, adding 1–2 tablespoons of chopped parsley if wished.

This sauce generally accompanies hot poached fish or boiled mutton. Use the appropriate stock from either the fish or the mutton to make the sauce and, if serving with boiled mutton, add a little anchovy essence with the seasonings.

CAPSICUM

see Peppers

CARAMEL

Sugar melted and cooked above a temperature of about 150C/300F becomes different types of caramel, usually identified by the degree of coloration.

It is essential to use a very pure refined sugar or sugar cubes (1). First dissolve the sugar in a little water over a gentle heat in a small, heavy-bottomed stainless steel, aluminium or untinned copper pan (2). The correct proportions for making caramel are 3 tablespoons of water to every 100 g/3½ oz/½ cup of sugar. Once the sugar has all dissolved, increase the heat to moderate and tilt the pan from time to time to mix the contents and ensure even distribution of heat. The contents of the pan must not be stirred, as the caramel will simply clump to any spoon. The change of colour of the mixture is then carefully monitored as it progresses from one stage to the next stage.

VERY PALE CARAMEL: heating stops as soon as the edges of the sugar turn pale yellow. When used to glaze petits fours and sugar-coated fruits, add ½ tsp vinegar or lemon juice per 100 g/3½ oz/½ cup sugar to keep the caramel liquid for longer (3).

PALE OR BLOND CARAMEL: heating stops when the caramel is a uniform pale honey colour. A little cold water is added very slowly to arrest the cooking process (4). This is used to caramelize choux pastry or citrus fruits or to provide the finishing glaze to a confectionery or pâtisserie set piece.

MEDIUM CARAMEL: heating stops when the

see also:
choux pastry
consommé
creams and custards
floating islands
glazing
sauce
sugar

1

2

3

4

caramel has become a deeper golden colour. Again a little cold water is used to arrest the cooking process. This is used to coat moulds or rice gâteaux or to flavour custards or floating islands, etc.

SLAKED CARAMEL: heating stops when the caramel is a good rich mahogany colour. Again a little cold water is added to stop the cooking process. This is used to colour and flavour.

BROWN CARAMEL: heating stops when the caramel is amber-red. By this stage all the sweetness of the sugar has gone and the caramel is too bitter to be used in pâtisserie, but it is used for colouring sauces, stews and consommés.

Ready-made caramel flavourings are also available commercially in liquid form, in either plastic sachets or bottles.

CARAMEL À NAPER

Coating caramel

Makes 200 g/7 oz
Preparation 2 minutes
Cooking 8–12 minutes

METRIC/IMPERIAL
- *200 g/7 oz sugar*
- *4 tbsp water*
- *1 tsp vinegar or lemon juice*

AMERICAN
- *1 cup sugar*
- *$\frac{1}{4}$ cup water*
- *1 tsp vinegar or lemon juice*

In a stainless steel or untinned copper pan, dissolve the sugar in the water over a low heat, keeping a careful watch over it. Add the vinegar or lemon juice and stir to mix well.

When the liquid is boiling, stop stirring the mixture, otherwise all the caramel will simply adhere to the spoon, but tilt the pan from time to time to distribute the heat evenly and obtain a uniform colour.

Clear caramel forms at about 150–160C/300–325F. To test: lift out a little with the tip of a teaspoon and drop it into a white dish – it should be the colour of pale honey. Add 1 tablespoon of hot water and shake the pan to mix it in. Add another tablespoon of hot water and stir.

Use this caramel to coat petits fours or small choux puffs.

CARAWAY

Carvi

see also:
cheese
cumin
gouda
liqueur
sauerkraut
spices

An aromatic plant, related to cumin, caraway is grown mainly for its small spicy seeds which are dried and widely used as a flavouring in the cooking of Central Europe.

German *sauerkraut*, Hungarian *gulash* and many Austrian dishes, especially ragoûts and certain varieties of bread, owe their characteristic taste to the caraway seed. It is also used to flavour cheeses, such as Munster and Gouda, and to make several alcoholic beverages, including schnapps, Kümmel and aquavit.

Although once very popular in English cooking, especially with potatoes and in baking, it is now more or less synonymous with the dry seed cake of Victorian tea-time.

BOEUF AU CARVI

Beef and caraway salad

Serves 2
Preparation 20 minutes
Cooking 20 minutes

METRIC/IMPERIAL
- *2 potatoes*
- *140 g/5 oz red cabbage, shredded*
- *2 mild onions, thinly sliced*
- *225 g/$\frac{1}{2}$ lb boiled beef, cut into small pieces*
- *4 tbsp oil*
- *2 tbsp vinegar*
- *1 tsp caraway seeds*
- *salt and pepper*

AMERICAN
- *2 potatoes*
- *5 oz red cabbage, shredded (about 2 cups)*
- *2 mild onions, thinly sliced*
- *$\frac{1}{2}$ lb boiled beef, cut into small pieces ($1\frac{1}{2}$–2 cups)*
- *4 tbsp oil*
- *2 tbsp vinegar*
- *1 tsp caraway seeds*
- *salt and pepper*

Boil the potatoes and then slice them into rounds. Mix them with the cabbage, onion and meat. Season with salt and pepper, sprinkle with the oil and set aside.

Meanwhile, heat the vinegar and add the caraway seeds to it. Pour it over the meat mixture, stir well and serve.

see also:
beer
ragoût
stewing

CARBONADE

This beef stew in which slices of beef are browned and then simmered for some time with onions in beer is of Flemish origin.

The name carbonade is also given by the French to a particular cut of grilled pork loin, as well as to a dish from the South of France made of beef stewed slowly in red wine.

CARBONADE FLAMANDE

Flemish beef stew

Serves 6
Preparation 25 minutes
Cooking about 2¼ hours

METRIC/IMPERIAL	AMERICAN
30 g/1 oz butter	2 tbsp butter
2 tbsp oil	2 tbsp oil
1.2 kg/2¾ lb braising beef, cut into slices about 1 cm/½ in thick	2¾ lb beef chuck, cut into slices about ½ in thick
5 large onions, thinly sliced	5 large onions, thinly sliced
1 tbsp brown sugar	1 tbsp brown sugar
2 tbsp flour	2 tbsp flour
200 ml/7 fl oz beef stock	1 cup beef stock
200 ml/7 fl oz beer (preferably a pale ale)	1 cup light beer
1 tbsp vinegar	1 tbsp vinegar
bouquet garni	bouquet garni
salt and pepper	salt and pepper

Heat the butter and oil in a frying pan and brown the pieces of meat over a high heat. Remove them from the pan with a slotted spoon and set to one side.

Lower the heat and cook the onions gently, stirring frequently, until softened but not brown. Remove them with a slotted spoon.

Spread a layer of cooked onions on the bottom of a large, flameproof casserole and season with salt and pepper. Add a layer of meat. Repeat in alternating layers until the ingredients are used up.

Put the sugar and flour into the cooking juices in the frying pan and cook, stirring, for 2 minutes. Add a little stock to obtain a thick sauce. Simmer for 2 minutes, then add the remaining stock, the beer and the vinegar. Simmer for 3 minutes.

Pour this sauce over the meat and onion mixture and add the bouquet garni. Cover and simmer for about 2 hours.

Serve piping hot, straight from the casserole.

To drink: beer.

Note: this dish is even better when made a day ahead and reheated.

CARDAMOM OR CARDAMON

see also:
curry powder
spices

The sweet, rich and highly aromatic seeds of this plant, related to ginger, are used as a spice. They are especially popular in the cooking of the Near East and India, where they are used to flavour rice dishes and sweetmeats. In the Scandinavian countries cardamom is used extensively in pâtisserie products. In France it is used mainly for gingerbread. The Arabs commonly drop whole cardamom seeds into cups of coffee to give it an unusual and very pleasant taste.

Cardamom is an expensive spice and its flavouring elements are quite fugitive. For these reasons it should be bought whole and still encased in its pale pods, otherwise it is often both adulterated and stale. Larger blacker cardamom pods contain seeds with much less flavour.

CARDOON

Cardon

see also:
artichoke
vegetables

A winter vegetable related to the globe artichoke, cardoons are mostly grown in their native southern Europe. They are in season from late summer to early winter.

They are usually sold whole, complete with part of the root and a long central stalk from which a number of whitish leafstalks branch. The plump white part of these leafstalks are cooked and eaten. They must first be trimmed of any tough outer fibres and boiled for 20–25 minutes to make them tender and remove their bitterness. The cardoons are then either fried briefly in butter or served with bone marrow, meat gravy or a béchamel or cheese sauce.

Cardoons make an excellent accompani-

ment to roast beef or poached chicken. Like celery, they are sometimes also eaten raw, notably by the Italians to accompany their anchovy and garlic fondue *bagna cauda*.

Cardoons contain 40 calories per 100 g/3½ oz.

CARDONS À LA MOELLE

Cardoons with bone marrow

Serves 6
Preparation 30 minutes
Cooking about 1 hour

METRIC/IMPERIAL	AMERICAN
2 large cardoons, trimmed	2 large cardoons, trimmed
juice of 1 lemon	juice of 1 lemon
2 tbsp flour	2 tbsp flour
55 g/2 oz butter	4 tbsp butter
140 g/5 oz bone marrow, cut into 1 cm/½ in slices	5 oz bone marrow, cut into ½ in slices
chopped fresh chives, to garnish	chopped fresh chives, to garnish
salt and pepper	salt and pepper

Cut the trimmed cardoon stalks into chunks, putting them into water with the lemon juice.

Mix the flour to a smooth paste with a little cold water and pour it into a large pan with 2.5 l/4 pt/2½ qt of water. Bring to the boil, stirring, then add the cardoons, cover the pan and cook them for about 40 minutes over a moderate heat, until tender. Drain them thoroughly.

Melt the butter in a frying pan over a moderate heat and put the drained cardoons into it. Heat them without allowing them to brown for about 10 minutes, stirring from time to time, until almost dry. Season with salt and pepper.

Meanwhile, poach the slices of bone marrow for 2–3 minutes in gently simmering water, then drain them and pat dry on paper towels.

Put the cardoons in a warmed vegetable dish. Arrange the slices of bone marrow on top and sprinkle with chopped chives.

CAROB

see also: chocolate

A leguminous tree grown in the area around the eastern Mediterranean, the carob produces large brown pods which are harvested for the rich sugary pulp and seeds within.

The ground seeds have found a place in the food industry as a texturing and gelling agent. More recently carob has been successfully promoted as a healthy alternative to chocolate. It has none of the caffeine or other stimulants contained in chocolate; unfortunately it also has little of the flavour.

CARP

Carpe

see also: fish trout

There are literally hundreds of species of this freshwater fish which may be found all over the world. The most likely culinary variety is the thick-scaled COMMON CARP, which is very easily farmed and can reach lengths of up to 80 cm/32 in. There are also two artificially bred varieties of interest: MIRROR CARP, which has scales only at the base of its fins and has a very fine flavour; and LEATHER CARP, which is virtually scaleless.

When buying, choose a plump, egg-carrying fish (June to April). Ask the fishmonger to gut it and remove both the gills, which can contribute to the muddy taste, and the gall bladder, which is at the base of the throat and is difficult to extract. As they live on plankton, pond carp may have a slightly muddy taste if raised in stagnant waters; if so, rinse the gutted and scaled fish in a large amount of vinegar water.

Carp may be stuffed whole, or cooked whole or cut into pieces in many ways: poached, cooked like trout *au bleu*, braised with garlic and parsley, baked in the oven or stewed in wine. Small carp may also be fried. Carp is a popular fish in Chinese cuisine, particularly served in sweet-and-sour sauce. The roe is regarded as a great delicacy and is often poached or fried separately and served as an hors d'oeuvre or used to garnish the fish.

Farmed carp, the most commonly available, is high in fat content (9%) and it is therefore wise to grill or broil, bake or poach it plainly with no rich sauces or stuffings; 100 g/3½ oz of steamed carp contains 110 calories.

CARPE À LA CHINOISE

Sweet-and-sour carp

Serves 4
Preparation 20 minutes
Cooking about 30 minutes

METRIC/IMPERIAL	*AMERICAN*
225 g/½ lb cucumber, peeled and cut into strips	*½ lb cucumber, peeled and cut into strips*
150 ml/¼ pt oil	*⅔ cup oil*
2 onions, finely chopped	*2 onions, finely chopped*
2 tbsp white wine vinegar	*2 tbsp white wine vinegar*
1 tbsp caster sugar	*1 tbsp superfine sugar*
1 tsp ground ginger	*1 tsp ground ginger*
2 tbsp sherry	*2 tbsp sherry*
1 whole carp, weighing about 1.5 kg/3½ lb, gutted and cleaned and cut into pieces	*1 whole carp, weighing about 3½ lb, dressed and cut into pieces*
salt and pepper	*salt and pepper*

Sprinkle the cucumber generously with salt and set aside in the refrigerator.

Heat 1 tablespoon of oil in a sauté pan and lightly brown the onions in it. Add the vinegar, sugar, ginger and sherry and mix well. Season with salt and pepper. Add 200 ml/7 fl oz/1 cup of water, cover and simmer for 10 minutes.

Heat the remaining oil in a large frying pan and sauté the pieces of fish, turning them frequently, for 10–12 minutes.

Pour the sauce over the fish, then add the well-drained strips of cucumber. Heat for 2 minutes and serve in a warmed serving dish.

CARPACCIO

see also: beef

An Italian dish of very thinly sliced raw beef with a creamy vinaigrette or oil and onion dressing, usually served as a cold hors d'oeuvre. It is sometimes also dressed with shaved Parmesan cheese. More recent versions of carpaccio using sliced salmon or sea bream (porgy) with a lemon and chopped olive dressing have also become popular.

Raw red meat is highly nutritious and rich in iron, but calorie watchers should be sparing with the dressings.

CARPACCIO DE BOEUF

Raw beef salad

Serves 4
Preparation 30 minutes, 1½ hours ahead

METRIC/IMPERIAL	*AMERICAN*
225 g/½ lb prime fillet of beef	*½ lb beef tenderloin*
4 tbsp extra-virgin olive oil	*¼ cup extra-virgin olive oil*
2 tsp green peppercorns, crushed	*2 tsp green peppercorns, crushed*
2 shallots, finely chopped	*2 shallots, finely chopped*
1 onion, finely chopped	*1 onion, finely chopped*
salt	*salt*

Pat the beef as dry as possible and then wrap it in plastic film. Twist the ends of the plastic film so that the meat is tightly sealed and compact.

Chill it in the freezer for 1 hour.

Unwrap the meat and slice it extremely thinly, using a well-sharpened long knife.

Place each slice between 2 double thicknesses of plastic film and then flatten it with the blade of the knife until it is as thin as possible. Chill again in the refrigerator for about 30 minutes.

Meanwhile, mix the oil and crushed green peppercorns in a bowl and add a little salt.

Lightly brush the surface of 4 plates with some of the oil and arrange the chilled slices of meat on them. Brush the slices of meat with more oil and garnish with the shallots and onion.

To drink: Lambrusco or Chianti, well chilled.

CARROT

Carotte

see also:
brunoise
crudité
macédoine
vegetables

After the potato, the carrot is arguably the most important root vegetable. There are varieties available throughout the year. In the spring there are the delicious crisp baby carrots, which are tender and virtually skinless, usually grown under glass. In summer a number of long, or semi-long, opensoil varieties become available. Large, thick winter carrots are ideal for soups, stocks and stews.

In general, the deeper a shade of orange carrots are the more tender, sweet and vitamin-rich they will be. The skin should be smooth and without blotches, ideally with the green stalks still firmly attached. Carrots are best bought loose or in boxes, as those wrapped in plastic tend to suffer from condensation.

Whether eaten raw or cooked, carrots should be scraped rather than peeled because the outside part contains most of the nutrients. Unfortunately, unless organically grown, even the youngest and most tender specimens should be scraped to remove lingering chemicals, etc. If the carrots are old, split them in half and hollow out the tough yellow core.

Tender young carrots are delicious raw, perhaps dressed with a little lemon juice, either as a crudité or chopped or grated in salads. Carrots are usually boiled until tender, and then lightly coated in butter or a cream sauce; or they may be glazed in a butter and sugar mixture. Their flavour works well with chervil, parsley and fennel. Carrots are a popular flavouring and are used in the making of most stocks, court-bouillons, marinades and stews.

mature carrots *new carrots*

Carrots have a very high sugar content, more than twice that of most other vegetables, but they are rich in minerals and very rich in the materials which the body can turn into Vitamin A; 100 g/3½ oz contains 42 calories.

CAROTTES VICHY

Sugar-glazed carrots

Serves 4
Preparation 15 minutes
Cooking about 1 hour

METRIC/IMPERIAL	AMERICAN
800 g/1¾ lb new carrots, sliced in thin rounds	1¾ lb new carrots, sliced in thin rounds
1 tbsp caster sugar	1 tbsp superfine sugar
30 g/1 oz butter, cut in pieces	2 tbsp butter, cut in pieces
chopped flat-leaved parsley, to garnish	chopped flat-leaf parsley, to garnish
salt	salt

Put the carrots in a large, deep saucepan, season them with salt and sprinkle with the sugar. Add just enough water to cover.

Cook very gently over a low heat, until all the water is absorbed and the carrots are very slightly caramelized.

Transfer the carrots to a warmed vegetable dish, dot with the butter and garnish with the parsley.

COCKTAIL À LA CAROTTE

Carrot cocktail

Serves 4
Preparation 25 minutes

METRIC/IMPERIAL	AMERICAN
2 oranges	2 oranges
550 g/1¼ lb new carrots, cut into chunks	1¼ lb new carrots, cut into chunks
½ red sweet pepper, deseeded and cut into small pieces	½ red sweet pepper, deseeded and cut into small pieces
juice of 1 lemon	juice of 1 lemon
pinch of celery salt	pinch of celery salt
4 celery leaves, to garnish	4 celery leaves, to garnish
salt and white pepper	salt and white pepper

Buy organically grown, unsprayed oranges, or scrub them several times in hot soapy water, rinse well and pat dry. Quarter them without peeling them.

Put the carrots, oranges and sweet pepper in an electric juice-extractor and process.

Add the lemon juice to the vegetable and fruit juice. Add a pinch of celery salt and season lightly with salt and white pepper. Chill in the refrigerator.

Serve in tall glasses garnished with celery leaves.

FLAN DE CAROTTES AU SÉSAME

Carrot and sesame mould

Serves 4
Preparation 15 minutes
Cooking 7½ minutes, standing 2 minutes

METRIC/IMPERIAL	AMERICAN
550 g/1¼ lb carrots, finely diced	1¼ lb carrots, finely diced
100 g/3½ oz well-drained fromage blanc or cottage cheese	½ cup well-drained fromage blanc or cottage cheese
3 tbsp sesame oil	3 tbsp oriental sesame oil
2 tbsp sesame seeds	2 tbsp sesame seeds
salt and pepper	salt and pepper

Put the carrots in a bowl with 2 tablespoons of water. Cover and microwave on High for 5 minutes. Leave to stand for 2 minutes, then drain them.

Blend the carrots in a food processor, adding the cheese and oil. Season with salt and pepper.

Sprinkle the sesame seeds in a round dish and microwave on High for 2 minutes, shaking the dish half-way through cooking.

Pour the carrot purée into the dish on top of the sesame seeds and microwave for 30 seconds. Unmould on a serving dish and serve hot as an accompaniment to grilled meats or poultry.

CASHEW

Cajou

see also: nuts

The fruit of the cashew tree has a smooth, creamy white, kidney-shaped kernel, with a distinctive but delicate flavour.

It plays an important role whole or ground in Indian cooking, especially in lamb curries, prawn or shrimp *pilaus*, poultry stuffings and some cakes and biscuits (cookies). Cashew nuts can also be roasted and salted, to be served with drinks or added to salads.

Cashews are rich in vitamins and minerals, but have a high fat and sugar content. They are thus high in calories, especially when roasted; 100 g/3½ oz contains 610 calories.

SAUTÉ DE LÉGUMES AUX CAJOUS

Sautéed mixed vegetables with cashew nuts

Serves 4
Preparation 20 minutes
Cooking 15 minutes

METRIC/IMPERIAL	AMERICAN
2 thin-skinned courgettes	2 thin-skinned zucchini
1 tbsp olive oil	1 tbsp olive oil
1 onion, finely sliced	1 onion, finely sliced
2 shallots, finely sliced	2 shallots, finely sliced
2 firm tomatoes, peeled, deseeded and cut into cubes	2 firm tomatoes, peeled, deseeded and cut into cubes
pinch of dried thyme	pinch of dried thyme
225 g/½ lb cucumber, peeled, deseeded and cut into sticks	½ lb cucumber, peeled, deseeded and cut into sticks
85 g/3 oz cashew nuts, coarsely chopped	¾ cup coarsely chopped cashew nuts
salt and pepper	salt and pepper

Wash the courgettes (zucchini) and slice them very thinly without peeling them.

Heat the oil in a sauté pan over a moderate heat and add the onions and shallots. Cook them, stirring frequently, until just softened.

Add the tomato cubes and the courgette (zucchini) slices. Season with salt and pepper and add the thyme. Cook very gently, covered, for 8–10 minutes.

Add the cucumber and raise the heat slightly. Cook uncovered for 3–4 minutes. Pour the vegetable mixture into a warmed, deep serving dish. Add the cashew nuts and stir well. Adjust the seasoning, if necessary, and serve as a garnish for pork or turkey.

CASSEROLE

see also:
braising
ragoût
timbale

This term is used both for the indispensable cooking utensil, thick-based and tight-lidded for long slow cooking, usually in the oven, and for the dishes cooked in it.

A good casserole dish should be quite large and sturdy, but not too heavy. It is also essential that it be easy to hold, with built-in handles either side, or with a long handle that is well-insulated and removable. Steel and enamel pans are best for electric ovens, but aluminium is generally too light. Ovenproof porcelain can be decorative and makes it possible to serve a casserole directly from the oven.

In classic French cuisine a casserole was often like a large rice timbale, usually with a rich, meaty filling. In modern usage, however, a casseroled dish usually denotes a slow-cooked stew of meat, poultry or vegetables.

CÔTES DE VEAU EN CASSEROLE

Casseroled veal chops

Serves 2
Preparation 10 minutes
Cooking 30 minutes

METRIC/IMPERIAL	AMERICAN
2 veal chops	2 veal chops
55 g/2 oz butter	4 tbsp butter
3 tbsp oil	3 tbsp oil
12 small new potatoes, peeled	12 small new potatoes, peeled
10 baby onions	10 baby onions
8 slices of lean bacon, cut into strips	8 slices of lean bacon, cut into strips
2 tbsp white wine	2 tbsp white wine
2 tbsp veal or vegetable stock	2 tbsp veal or vegetable stock
salt and pepper	salt and pepper

Pre-heat the oven to 200C/400F/gas 6.

Season the veal chops with salt and pepper. Melt one third of the butter with 2 tablespoons of the oil in a large, flameproof casserole and cook the chops over a moderate heat until golden brown and sealed on both sides.

Meanwhile, sauté the potatoes, onions and bacon over a high heat in the remaining oil and butter in a frying pan. When they are well browned, add them to the chops in the casserole, together with the white wine and stock.

Cover and cook in the oven for about 20 minutes, or until the vegetables are tender.

Note: baby turnips or carrots make a delicious alternative to the new potatoes.

POULET À LA CASSEROLE

Chicken and mushroom casserole

Serves 4
Preparation 25 minutes
Cooking 50 minutes

METRIC/IMPERIAL	AMERICAN
1 chicken, dressed weight about 1.5 kg/3½ lb	*1 chicken, dressed and drawn weight about 3½ lb*
100 ml/3½ fl oz oil	*½ cup oil*
450 g/1 lb white button mushrooms	*1 lb white button mushrooms*
300 g/10 oz chanterelle mushrooms	*10 oz fresh chanterelle mushrooms*
12 baby onions	*12 baby onions*
115 g/¼ lb lean bacon, cut into strips	*¼ lb lean bacon, cut into strips*
2 garlic cloves, chopped	*2 garlic cloves, chopped*
2 tbsp chopped flat-leaved parsley	*2 tbsp chopped flat-leaf parsley*
100 ml/3½ fl oz white wine	*½ cup white wine*
salt and pepper	*salt and pepper*

Cut the chicken into 10 pieces.

Heat the oil in a large, heavy-bottomed pan which has a lid and cook the mushrooms in it for about 10 minutes, then remove them from the pan with a slotted spoon and keep warm.

In the same pan, sauté the baby onions, bacon and chopped garlic for 5–6 minutes. Remove and keep warm with the mushrooms.

Finally, add the chicken pieces to the pan and brown them well on all sides. Return the mushrooms, onions, bacon and garlic to the pan. Season to taste with salt and pepper and add the chopped parsley. Add the wine, cover the pan and simmer very gently for 20 minutes.
To drink: a rich claret, such as Pomerol.

CASSOULET

see also:
bean
confit
ragoût

A tasty and hearty country dish, originally from the Languedoc, it consists of white beans flavoured with pork fat, garnished with fresh and preserved meats (confit) and baked slowly in the oven.

There are three traditional types of cassoulet. That from Castelnaudary contains pork knuckle (fresh hocks), ham, local sausages and fresh pork rinds and is enriched with preserved goose. Carcassonne cassoulet contains leg of lamb and partridge in season. Toulouse cassoulet contains fresh belly of pork, lamb shoulder and local preserved meat and sausage.

Top quality white haricot or navy beans are essential for a good, creamy cassoulet. For best results the dish should be cooked very slowly, preferably well in advance. For an authentic taste, smoked meats or Frankfurter sausages should never be included.

CASSOULET OCCITAN

Old-style cassoulet

Serves 8
Preparation 10 minutes
Cooking about 3 hours

METRIC/IMPERIAL	AMERICAN
1 kg/2¼ lb dried large white haricot beans	*2¼ lb dried large haricot or navy beans (about 5 cups)*
200 g/7 oz fresh pork rinds, coarsely chopped	*7 oz fresh pork skin, coarsely chopped*
300 g/10 oz streaky bacon, coarsely chopped	*10 oz bacon, coarsely chopped*
3 garlic cloves, chopped	*3 garlic cloves, chopped*
bouquet garni	*bouquet garni*
1 onion	*1 onion*
1 clove	*1 clove*
4 pieces of preserved goose or duck (confit)	*4 pieces of preserved goose or duck (confit)*
800 g/1¾ lb pork knuckle or shoulder, cut in pieces	*1¾ lb fresh ham hocks or pork shoulder, cut in pieces*
350 g/¾ lb Toulouse, Cumberland or other fresh pork sausages	*¾ lb fresh pork link sausages*
salt and pepper	*salt and pepper*

Put the beans in a large pan, cover them with cold water and bring them to the boil. Boil for 5 minutes, then drain them and cover them with fresh warm water.

Cassoulet occitan (Old-style cassoulet)

Add the chopped pork rinds (skin), bacon and the garlic to the beans along with the bouquet garni and the onion studded with the clove. Cover and simmer gently for 1 hour, until the beans are tender but not soft.

Meanwhile, put the pieces of preserved meat into a large frying pan over a moderate heat, melt off the fat and brown them lightly in it. Remove them from the pan and set them to one side. Brown the pieces of pork knuckle (hock) or shoulder in the same fat. Remove and drain them. Brown the sausages in the same frying pan.

Preheat the oven to 160C/325F/gas 3.

In a large, ovenproof casserole put a thick layer of the bean mixture with some of the accompanying cooking mixture. Add a layer of meats (pork and preserved goose or duck). Continue with alternating layers until all the ingredients are used up. Season with salt (use sparingly as the meats are usually very salty) and pepper. Arrange the sausages on top and pour over the juices from the frying pan.

Cook in the oven for 1 hour until a golden crust has formed. Break it and allow it to form again. Bake for a further hour, breaking the crust several times. Serve very hot, straight from the casserole dish.

Note: some breadcrumbs sprinkled over the dish before baking help make an even better crust.

To drink: a full-bodied red wine, such as a Cahors.

CAUL OR CAUL FAT

Crépine

see also:
barding
game
pâté
terrine

The thin membrane, veined with fat, which encloses the stomach of the pig is used to wrap, bard and protect delicate items during cooking. After soaking in water for 1 hour, pieces of caul are used to wrap items such as balls of stuffing, pieces of liver and stuffed cabbage leaves. They are also used to wrap pâtés and terrines. Caul is considerably less fatty than barding strips.

CAULIFLOWER

Chou-fleur

see also:
broccoli
charlotte
vegetables

Cauliflower is a member of the cabbage family with a large white flowering head which is eaten rather than the leaves.

Look for cauliflower which is very white, with no blemishes, and very firm with tightly packed florets on short stalks. Avoid cauliflowers which have been trimmed of their surrounding leaves as this has usually been done to hide the fact they are old and stale. The freshness of the leaves is a good indication of the state of the vegetable. Cauliflower is often sold by the piece rather than by weight, but allow about 200 g/7 oz per person, or half that if serving raw.

Cauliflower is usually trimmed of the outer leaves and stalk before cooking. Larger specimens are best divided in even-sized florets. It is useful to soak cauliflower in water with some vinegar to eliminate clinging insects.

Cauliflower may be blanched briefly in boiling salted water prior to further cooking, or simply boiled in lightly salted water until tender; a small piece of bread added to the cooking water will reduce the cabbage-like odour. It is good dressed with a little butter, or *noisette* butter, and lemon juice, which keeps it white. Cauliflower will not retain its colour if cooked in a pressure-cooker.

Cauliflower may be further cooked in a creamy or cheese sauce, braised, sautéed, puréed or made into soufflés. It is also a common ingredient in pickles and relishes. Cauliflower florets are increasingly popular raw as a crudité or in salads.

Cauliflower is very rich in protein and vitamin B compared with other vegetables and 100 g/3½ oz contains 30 calories.

SALADE DE CHOU-FLEUR

Cauliflower salad

Serves 6
Preparation 15 minutes
Cooking 3–4 minutes

METRIC/IMPERIAL	AMERICAN
1 cauliflower, trimmed and separated into even-sized florets	1 cauliflower, trimmed and separated into equal-sized florets
bunch of radishes, trimmed	bunch of radishes, trimmed
6 tbsp olive oil	6 tbsp olive oil

3 tbsp lemon juice	*3 tbsp lemon juice*
bunch of watercress	*bunch of watercress*
chopped fresh chives, to garnish	*chopped fresh chives, to garnish*
salt and black pepper	*salt and black pepper*

Cook the cauliflower florets for 3–4 minutes in lightly salted boiling water and drain them.

Make a cross-shaped cut in the radishes, from the tip almost to the base, so that they open out like flowers.

Make a vinaigrette with the olive oil and lemon juice and season to taste. Put the cauliflower florets in a bowl and toss in the dressing. Transfer them to a deep dish, surround them with the watercress and radishes, and garnish with the chopped chives.

GRATIN DE CHOU-FLEUR

Cauliflower baked au gratin

Serves 6
Preparation 30 minutes
Cooking about 40 minutes

METRIC/IMPERIAL	*AMERICAN*
450 g/1 lb spinach	*1 lb fresh bulk spinach*
3 potatoes	*3 potatoes*
1 cauliflower, trimmed and separated into florets	*1 cauliflower, trimmed and separated into florets*
100 ml/3½ fl oz vinegar	*½ cup vinegar*
85 g/3 oz butter	*6 tbsp butter*
55 g/2 oz flour	*6½ tbsp flour*
pinch of grated nutmeg	*pinch of grated nutmeg*
200 ml/7 fl oz crème fraîche or whipping cream	*1 cup crème fraîche or whipping cream*
100 g/3½ oz grated Beaufort or Gruyère	*½ cup grated Beaufort or Gruyère cheese*
salt and pepper	*salt and pepper*

Preheat the oven to 240C/465F/gas 8–9.

Trim the spinach. Blanch it in boiling water for 5 minutes, then drain. Peel the potatoes and steam them lightly until just tender.

Meanwhile, wash the cauliflower florets in water with the vinegar and rinse them, then cook in lightly salted boiling water for 12 minutes. Drain the cauliflower, reserving 200 ml/7 fl oz/1 cup of the cooking liquid.

Make a roux by melting 55 g/2 oz/4 tbsp of the butter in a pan and stirring in the flour. When the roux is foaming, gradually add the reserved cauliflower cooking liquid, stirring well with a whisk to incorporate. Season with salt and pepper and grated nutmeg to taste. Add the cream and half the grated cheese and mix thoroughly.

Grease a gratin dish with a little of the remaining butter. Slice the cooked potatoes and line the bottom of the gratin dish with them. Add a layer of the spinach, followed by the well-drained cauliflower florets.

Coat them with the sauce and sprinkle the rest of the grated cheese over the top. Melt the rest of the butter and pour it over. Bake for 15 minutes and serve hot.

CAVIAR

see also: fish roe sturgeon

The name for the salt-cured mature eggs of the sturgeon, most caviar comes from the Caspian Sea, and the greatest part of that is processed in Russia. There are three distinct and easily recognizable types of fresh Russian caviar.

BELUGA CAVIAR, the rarest and thus the most expensive, comes from the largest species of sturgeon. The eggs, ranging from light to dark grey in colour, are very fragile but with a wonderful smooth, delicate and mild flavour.

OSIETRA CAVIAR has larger eggs, golden yellow to brown in colour, with a stronger flavour. Some connoisseurs regard this as having the finest flavour.

SEVRUGA CAVIAR comes from the smallest and most prolific species of sturgeon and is thus the most commonly available. The smaller eggs range in colour from pale to dark grey and have a marked nutty taste.

The less expensive PRESSED CAVIAR is processed from immature eggs using hot brine, and is shiny and more compact. It is preferred by people who like a strongly flavoured caviar, but is usually used as a garnish for canapés, etc, rather than being served on its own.

There are also now some quite fine caviars being produced from North American sturgeons and their popularity is gaining ground,

Beluga
Osietra
Sevruga
pressed caviar

even though they are also very expensive.

Caviar is a semi-conserve and thus highly perishable. It should be stored between −2C/28F and +4C/39F. If serving it as an hors d'oeuvre, allow 55 g/2 oz per person. The can should not be opened until just before serving as caviar oxidizes readily. Remove it from the refrigerator 15 minutes before eating and serve it in a small container – the open can or jar is best – set on top of a bed of shaved or crushed ice. Purists advise against the serving of lemon and chopped onion with caviar as they overpower the taste. Spread the caviar, without crushing the eggs, on pieces of white bread or toast spread with unsalted butter. The Russian practice of serving caviar with blinis and sour cream makes a particularly delicious dish, and is an excellent use for the less expensive pressed caviar.

Caviar has a very high fat and protein content and is rich in phosphorus; 100 g/3½ oz contains 280 calories.

To drink: chilled Russian vodka or a high-quality dry champagne.

COQUILLES SAINT-JACQUES CRUES AU CAVIAR

Raw scallops with caviar

Serves 2
Preparation 20 minutes

METRIC/IMPERIAL	AMERICAN
4 scallops	4 sea scallops
2 tbsp olive oil	2 tbsp olive oil
4 tbsp groundnut oil	4 tbsp peanut oil
55–75 g/2–2½ oz caviar	2–2½ oz caviar
4 slices of white toast, to serve	4 slices of white toast, to serve
unsalted butter, to serve	unsalted butter, to serve
salt and pepper	salt and pepper

Open the scallop shells and remove the scallops with their corals. Carefully remove and discard the beards. Wash the scallops thoroughly and quickly, then pat them dry.

Mix the 2 oils together in a bowl. Slice the scallop flesh and corals across into even rounds.

Dip the pieces of scallop in the oil mixture, drain them and remove excess oil. Divide the scallop slices between 2 plates and season them lightly with salt and pepper.

Using a small spoon, arrange the caviar on the scallop slices.

Serve with hot toast and unsalted butter.

To drink: white Graves.

CELERIAC OR CELERY ROOT

Céleri-rave

see also:
acidulation
celery
vegetables

This is a variety of celery grown for its bulbous and flavoursome root which can reach a weight of up to 1 kg/2¼ lb.

The large round root is sold without its stalk and leaves and is at its best in late summer and early autumn. It should be firm, with no cracks in the rough outer skin.

The skin is peeled to reveal the white flesh which oxidizes easily, so it should be sprinkled with lemon juice to prevent discoloration. The celeriac is then usually quartered and blanched in boiling salted water for about 5 minutes prior to further cooking. It is delicious braised in a little stock and makes very good soup. It is also often puréed, and a mixed purée of potato and celeriac is particularly tasty.

To get the best of the celeriac flavour, the root is often first shredded raw, then possibly blanched for 1–2 minutes, and dressed with a vinaigrette or *rémoulade* sauce to serve as a salad or first course.

Dried, crushed celeriac is used to make celery salt, which is a useful seasoning, especially for those on a low-salt diet, and an essential ingredient in a classic Bloody Mary.

Celeriac is very easily digested and is rich in minerals: 100 g/3½ oz contains 40 calories.

CÉLERI-RAVE RÉMOULADE

Celeriac or celery root with rémoulade sauce

Serves 6
Preparation 30 minutes
Cooking 2 minutes

METRIC/IMPERIAL	AMERICAN
200 ml/7 fl oz mayonnaise	*1 cup mayonnaise*
1 tbsp Dijon mustard	*1 tbsp Dijon mustard*
1 tbsp chopped fresh chervil	*1 tbsp chopped fresh chervil*
1 tbsp chopped fresh tarragon	*1 tbsp chopped fresh tarragon*
1 tbsp capers, drained and chopped	*1 tbsp capers, drained and chopped*
4 gherkins, drained and chopped	*4 pickled cucumbers or cornichons, drained and chopped*
1 large celeriac root	*1 large head celeriac (celery root)*
juice of 1 lemon	*juice of 1 lemon*
salt and pepper	*salt and pepper*

Pour the mayonnaise into a bowl and whisk the mustard into it, along with the herbs and chopped capers and gherkins (pickled cucumbers). Taste and adjust the seasoning.

Peel the celeriac and sprinkle it generously with the lemon juice. Cut it into quarters and grate it coarsely.

Blanch the grated celeriac for 2 minutes in a large pan of boiling salted water, then drain and plunge it immediately into a bowl of cold water to refresh it. Drain it again and pat it dry on paper towels.

Put the grated celeriac into a salad bowl, add

CELERY

Céleri

see also:
celeriac
court-bouillon
marinade
vegetables

The stalks, leaves, roots and seeds of this aromatic plant, grown in most temperate parts of the world, are all used in cooking.

The roots of certain varieties are used as a vegetable and known as celeriac. The leaves are

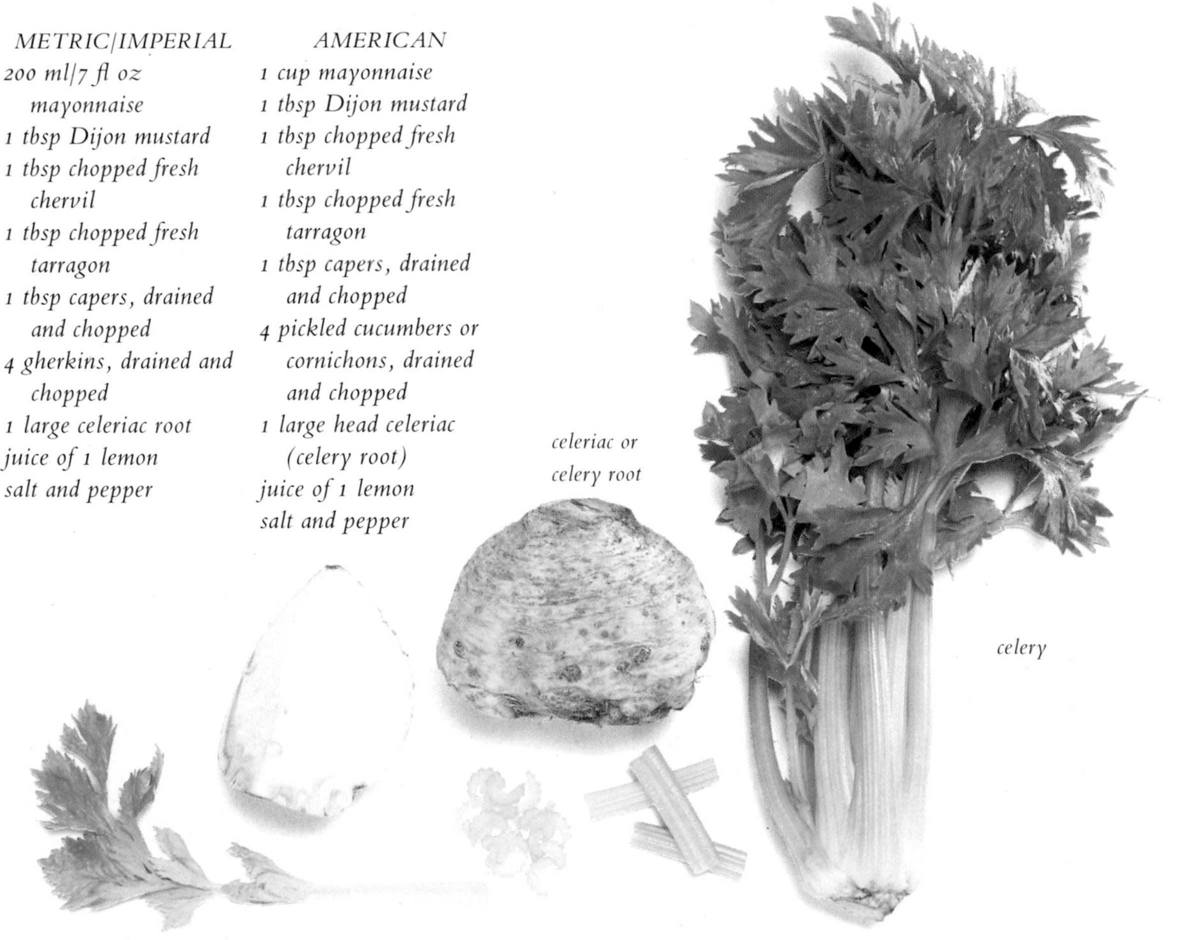

used to flavour court-bouillons, soups and stocks and are popular as a garnish for salads. The seeds, with a taste not unlike fennel, are dried and used as a seasoning. The stalks are eaten raw as a crudité or in salads; boiled, braised or baked *au gratin* as a vegetable; and also find great use as one of the most common flavourings in stocks, stews, soups and marinades.

Leafy stalk celery is available all year round. The stalks should be short, firm, straight and fleshy. They are best kept standing in cold salted water as they may go limp in the refrigerator. Before using, trim the top and bottom and peel off any tough fibres, starting from the bottom.

Leafy stalk celery contains only 20 calories per 100 g/3½ oz.

SALADE DE CÉLERI

Celery salad

Serves 4
Preparation 20 minutes

METRIC/IMPERIAL	AMERICAN
1 heaped tbsp Roquefort	1 heaping tbsp Roquefort cheese
100 ml/3½ fl oz whipping cream	½ cup whipping cream
100 ml/3½ fl oz olive oil	½ cup olive oil
3 tbsp tarragon vinegar	3 tbsp tarragon vinegar
4 lettuce hearts, quartered	4 lettuce hearts, quartered
4 stalks of celery, trimmed and cut into chunks	4 sticks of celery, trimmed and cut into chunks
4 celery leaves, to garnish	4 celery leaves, to garnish
salt and pepper	salt and pepper

Mix the Roquefort with the cream in a bowl. Whisk in the oil a little at a time, then add the vinegar. Season with salt and pepper. The sauce should be very thick.

Combine the lettuce and celery in a salad bowl. Pour the sauce over them and toss thoroughly. Garnish with the celery leaves.

CÉLERI À LA CRÈME

Celery in cream sauce

Serves 6
Preparation 15 minutes
Cooking about 1 hour

METRIC/IMPERIAL	AMERICAN
3 heads of celery	3 bunches of celery
55 g/2 oz butter	4 tbsp butter
200 ml/7 fl oz thick crème fraîche or whipping cream	1 cup thick crème fraîche or whipping cream
chopped fresh parsley, to garnish	chopped fresh parsley, to garnish
salt and pepper	salt and pepper

Preheat the oven to 180C/350F/gas 4.

Trim the base of each head of celery and cut off the tops so each is about 20 cm/8 in long. Wash the celery and trim off any coarse fibres from the outside stalks. Pat dry.

Blanch the celery in a large pan of boiling salted water for 8–10 minutes. Drain them and cut each head in half lengthwise.

Grease a long flameproof casserole with 25 g/¾ oz/1½ tbsp of the butter and arrange the pieces of celery in it. Season with salt and pepper and add 200 ml/7 fl oz/1 cup of water. Cover the casserole and cook in the oven for 1 hour.

Drain the celery and put it in a warmed vegetable dish.

Pour the cream into the casserole dish and boil it over a high heat to reduce the liquid. Add the chopped parsley and whisk in the rest of the butter in small pieces. When the sauce is smooth and creamy, pour it over the celery.

CEREAL

Céréale

see also:
barley
corn
couscous
polenta
rice
rye
wheat

The term cereal refers to any of several types of highly nutritious grains from a range of grasses which have long been cultivated to provide a staple food for humans and livestock.

The principal cereals are wheat, rice, corn (maize), barley, oats, rye, buckwheat and millet. All cereals are approximately equal in food value, but they are more nutritious if they are 'whole', ie, still with the bran and the germ. They have a reasonably high energy content, particularly if combined with small amounts of fat.

Cereals contain slow-absorption sugars which liberate energy throughout the day, and are high in protein (8–13%), fibre, vitamin B complex and a number of mineral salts. To ensure the correct amino acid balance they are best eaten in conjunction with other protein-rich foods. For instance, couscous provides an ideally balanced meal: wheat semolina and chickpeas for slow-absorption sugars and vegetable protein, green vegetables for fibre and vitamin C, meat or fish for animal protein and raisins for rapid-absorption sugars.

To ensure that they have time to swell properly when cooked, cereals should always be cooked over a low heat.

CEVICHE

see Lime

CHAR, ARCTIC CHAR OR CHARR

Omble chevalier

see also:
fish
salmon
trout

This relative of the salmon and the trout is found in the cold waters of the Arctic, and smaller landlocked varieties of char are also to be found in several of the colder lakes of Europe and Canada.

Large and wide-bodied, weighing up to 8 kg/18 lb, with a grey-green, pale spotted back and orange belly, it has possibly the most delicate flesh and one of the finest flavours of any fish, but is becoming increasingly rare.

Char should be cooked like trout or salmon, by the simplest possible method in order to make the most of its unique taste.

OMBLES CHEVALIERS AU FOUR

Baked char

Serves 4
Preparation 15 minutes
Cooking 25 minutes

METRIC/IMPERIAL	*AMERICAN*
2 whole char, each weighing about 400 g/14 oz, gutted	*2 whole char, each weighing about 14 oz, drawn*
55 g/2 oz butter	*4 tbsp butter*
300 g/10 oz mushrooms, wiped and sliced	*10 oz mushrooms, wiped and sliced*
200 ml/7 fl oz dry white wine	*1 cup dry white wine*
juice of 1 lemon	*juice of 1 lemon*
100 ml/3½ fl oz whipping cream	*½ cup whipping cream*
salt and pepper	*salt and pepper*

Preheat the oven to 200C/400F/gas 6.

Rinse the fish, wipe them dry and season them inside and out with salt and pepper. Grease a baking dish with a little of the butter and place the fish in it.

Sauté the mushrooms, uncovered, in the remaining butter for about 5 minutes. Pour the wine over them, add the lemon juice and cream and season with salt and pepper.

Pour this sauce over the fish and bake for 20 minutes. Serve very hot straight from the baking dish.

CHARCUTERIE

see also:
bacon
black pudding
brawn
galantine
ham
offal
pâté
pork
sausage

This term applies to pork and offal (variety meat) products and, in France, the pork-butcher's shops which sell them.

Among the main categories of *charcuterie* are: raw cured pork products, bacon and Bayonne ham, for example, cooked cured pork products, such as *jambon de Paris* and other cooked hams, fresh and smoked sausages, sausage meat and forcemeats, *boudins*, *rillettes*, brawn (head cheese), pâtés, pork cracklings, galantines and preserved meats.

Certain *charcuterie* products, such as hard sausage and raw cured ham, can be stored for a long time in a cool, well-ventilated place; others, such as *boudin* and *rillettes*, should be refrigerated and eaten without delay.

Certain regions of France are renowned for their *charcuterie* specialities, which can be the basis for a buffet meal or an assortment of hors d'oeuvres. Alsace, the Auvergne, the area around Lyon, the Jura and Corsica are particularly renowned for their *charcuterie* products, which are generally served accompanied by a wine from the same region.

Charcuterie products have a very high energy content, in some cases 600–700 calories per 100 g/$3\frac{1}{2}$ oz, and should therefore be avoided by weight watchers. Certain types of ham and *andouille* sausage are relatively harmless if all the fat is removed. If buying so-called 'low-fat' *charcuterie*, check the label with care to determine the actual contents.

CHARD

see Swiss chard

CHARLOTTE

see also:
bain-marie
Bavarian cream
cakes and gâteaux
compote
creams and custards
ices and ice creams

Various moulded desserts, served either hot or cold, are described as charlottes. They are generally characterized by the special mould used, which is deep and round with slanted sides to facilitate unmoulding.

The mould is usually lined with sponge fingers (ladyfingers) or white bread and then filled with fruit purée, mousse, compote, chantilly cream, custard, Bavarian cream, ice cream, etc, or layers of different such ingredients. The charlotte is then either cooked or chilled. The dish is often given added flavour by soaking the lining bread or sponge fingers (ladyfingers) in liqueurs, coffee or other flavouring liquids.

Savoury charlottes are also made along the same lines, with vegetable or fish fillings. They are cooked in the charlotte moulds in a bain-marie, either in the oven or over a low heat.

CHARLOTTE CHAUDE AUX POMMES

Hot apple charlotte

Serves 6
Preparation 30 minutes
Cooking 40–50 minutes

METRIC/IMPERIAL	*AMERICAN*
1 kg/$2\frac{1}{4}$ lb firm-fleshed dessert apples, such as Reinettes or Cox's	*$2\frac{1}{4}$ lb firm-fleshed apples, such as Newtown Pippin*
100 g/$3\frac{1}{2}$ oz caster sugar	*$\frac{1}{2}$ cup superfine sugar*
75 g/$2\frac{1}{2}$ oz butter	*5 tbsp butter*
about 550 g/$1\frac{1}{4}$ lb slightly stale white bread, crusts removed	*about $1\frac{1}{4}$ lb slightly stale white bread, crusts removed*

Preheat the oven to 220C/425F/gas 7.

Peel the apples and remove the core and seeds. Slice them and put them in a saucepan with 2 tablespoons of water.

Bring to the boil, cover and cook over a medium heat for about 10 minutes, without removing the saucepan lid.

Remove the pan from the heat, add the sugar and beat well to make a purée.

Generously grease a 14 cm /$5\frac{1}{2}$ in charlotte mould with some of the butter. Slice the bread and cut one third into triangles and the rest into rectangles. Spread with the remaining butter.

With the buttered sides against the mould, line the bottom of the charlotte mould with some of the bread triangles, overlapping them. Line the sides of the mould with the rectangles.

Pour the apple compote into the middle and then cover with the remaining triangles of bread, butter side up.

Bake in the oven for 30–40 minutes until the bread on top is golden brown. Remove the mould from the oven and let the charlotte cool in the mould. Unmould it just before serving.

This charlotte may be served warm or chilled, plain or with vanilla custard sauce.

Variation: add 2 or 3 tablespoons of Calvados or brandy to the apple compote for an even more delicious charlotte.

Charlotte chaude aux pommes (Hot apple charlotte)

CHARLOTTE AUX POIRES

Pear charlotte

Serves 6
Preparation 1 hour
Cooking about 30 minutes, plus cooling
Chilling 4 hours

METRIC/IMPERIAL	*AMERICAN*
8 gelatine leaves or 2 sachets (30 g/1 oz) powdered gelatine	*8 gelatine leaves or 4 envelopes powdered unflavored gelatine*
500 ml/16 fl oz milk	*2 cups milk*
1 vanilla pod	*1 vanilla bean*
8 egg yolks	*8 egg yolks*
750 g/$1\frac{1}{2}$ lb caster sugar	*$3\frac{3}{4}$ cups superfine sugar*
2 tbsp pear liqueur	*2 tbsp pear liqueur*
500 ml/16 fl oz crème fraîche or whipping cream	*2 cups crème fraîche or whipping cream*
175 g/$6\frac{1}{2}$ oz icing sugar	*$1\frac{1}{2}$ cups confectioners' sugar*
1 kg/$2\frac{1}{4}$ lb pears	*$2\frac{1}{4}$ lb pears*
24 sponge fingers	*24 ladyfingers*
450 g/1 lb fresh raspberries	*2 pt fresh raspberries*
juice of 1 lemon	*juice of 1 lemon*

Soak the gelatine leaves briefly in a bowl of cold water, then squeeze them dry and set aside. (Or soften the powdered gelatine in 5 tablespoons of cold water.)

Put the milk and vanilla in a heavy-based saucepan and bring to the boil. While the milk is heating, beat the egg yolks with 250 g/$8\frac{1}{2}$ oz/ $1\frac{1}{4}$ cups of the caster (superfine) sugar in a bowl. Pour the boiling milk over the mixture, then return to the saucepan and cook over a moderate heat, stirring continuously, without allowing the mixture to boil until the custard has thickened enough to coat the back of the spoon. Remove the pan from the heat and add the gelatine (1). Stir until the gelatine has all dissolved. Leave to cool.

When the custard has cooled to room temperature, add the pear liqueur. Whip the cream with 55 g/2 oz/$\frac{1}{4}$ cup of the icing (confectioners') sugar to soft peaks and mix it into the custard (2).

Peel the pears and poach them in a syrup made with 200 ml/7 fl oz/1 cup of water and the remaining caster (superfine) sugar (3). When they are just tender, drain them and slice them fairly thickly.

Line a 15 cm/6 in charlotte mould with the

1

2

3

4

sponge fingers (ladyfingers). Fill the mould with alternate layers of custard and poached pear slices (4). Cover with more sponge fingers (ladyfingers). Chill for at least 4 hours.

No more than 2 hours before serving, prepare a raspberry coulis by puréeing the fruit in a food mill or processor along with the lemon juice and the remaining icing (confectioners') sugar. Reserve a few whole raspberries to decorate the charlotte. If using a food processor, rub the coulis through a nylon sieve to remove the pips. Cover and chill.

Unmould the charlotte on a round dish. Coat the top of the charlotte with the raspberry coulis and pour the rest of it around the base. Decorate with the reserved whole raspberries.
Notes: the sponge fingers (ladyfingers) should be the variety with curved edges. There is no need to soak them before lining the mould. Trim those used on the top diagonally so that they fit closely.
Variation: strawberries or mangoes may be substituted for the raspberries.

CHARLOTTE DE CHOU-FLEUR

Cauliflower charlotte

Serves 4
Preparation 10 minutes
Cooking about 1 hour

METRIC/IMPERIAL	AMERICAN
1 cauliflower, trimmed and separated into large pieces	1 cauliflower, trimmed and separated into large pieces
4 eggs	4 eggs
55 g/2 oz butter	4 tbsp butter
1 tbsp flour	1 tbsp flour
200 ml/7 fl oz milk	1 cup milk
1 tbsp tomato purée	1 tbsp tomato paste
100 g/3½ oz grated Gruyère	1 cup grated Gruyère cheese
salt and pepper	salt and pepper

Preheat the oven to 180C/350F/gas 4.

Blanch the cauliflower in lightly salted boiling water for 2 minutes. Drain, then cook a second time in fresh, boiling water for 20 minutes. Drain and mash to a purée.

Beat the eggs lightly and season them generously with salt and pepper. Add them to the cauliflower purée.

Use a little of the butter to grease a 14 cm/5½ in charlotte mould and pour the cauliflower mixture into it. Cook in a bain-marie in the oven for 40 minutes.

Make a roux by melting the rest of the butter in a saucepan and stirring in the flour. When the roux is foaming, add the milk, stirring constantly with a whisk. Cook for 10 minutes over low heat, stirring frequently. Add the tomato purée (paste) and the grated Gruyère, mix well and keep hot.

Turn out the cauliflower charlotte and coat it with the sauce just before serving.

CHARLOTTE AU CHOCOLAT

Chocolate charlotte

Serves 6
Preparation 30 minutes
Cooking about 10 minutes, 24 hours ahead

METRIC/IMPERIAL	AMERICAN
140 g/5 oz plain chocolate	5 oz semisweet chocolate
55 g/2 oz butter	4 tbsp butter
30 g/1 oz caster sugar	2½ tbsp superfine sugar
4 eggs, separated	4 eggs, separated
30 sponge fingers	30 ladyfingers
200 ml/7 fl oz very strong black coffee	1 cup very strong black coffee
sweet almond oil, for greasing	sweet almond oil, for greasing
3 tbsp chocolate vermicelli, to decorate	3 tbsp chocolate sprinkles, to decorate

Break the chocolate into small pieces and put them in a pan. Add the butter, sugar and 2 tablespoons of water. Melt the mixture very slowly by putting the pan in a bain-marie set over a low heat.

When the chocolate mixture has melted smoothly, add the beaten egg yolks, still with the pan standing in the bain-marie. When the eggs and chocolate are well blended, remove the pan from the heat.

Whisk the egg whites to stiff peaks. Fold them gently into the chocolate cream mixture and chill.

Lightly grease a 15 cm/6 in charlotte mould with sweet almond oil. Line the bottom and sides with some of the sponge fingers (ladyfingers), curved side against the mould.

One by one, dip the remaining sponge fingers (ladyfingers) into the coffee and fill the mould with alternating layers of the chocolate mousse and the sponge fingers (ladyfingers), reserving 1 large tablespoon of the mousse.

Chill the charlotte overnight. Before serving, unmould it on a round dish and spread the reserved mousse over the top. Decorate with chocolate vermicelli (sprinkles).

CHATEAUBRIAND

see also:
beef
sauce
steak

A thick slice, usually about 3 cm/1¼ in, of very tender beef cut from the large end of the fillet (tenderloin) is known as a chateaubriand, and it is traditionally grilled (broiled) or fried and served with a *béarnaise* sauce.

CHATEAUBRIAND MAÎTRE D'HÔTEL

Chateaubriand with maître d'hôtel butter

Serves 2
Preparation 15 minutes
Cooking about 30 minutes

METRIC/IMPERIAL	AMERICAN
400 g/14 oz very small new potatoes	14 oz very small new potatoes
55 g/2 oz butter	4 tbsp butter
2 chateaubriands, each weighing about 200 g/7 oz	2 chateaubriands, each weighing about 7 oz
55 g/2 oz maître d'hôtel butter (see Butter)	4 tbsp maître d'hôtel butter (see Butter)
salt and pepper	salt and pepper

Scrub the new potatoes and pat them dry.

Heat half the butter in a sauté pan. Add the potatoes and cook them gently, covered, for about 20 minutes. Season with salt and pepper.

Melt the rest of the butter in a frying pan. When it is very hot, fry the chateaubriands over a very high heat for 4 minutes on each side. They should be sealed on the outside and rare inside.

Drain the steaks and put them on warmed plates. Surround them with the new potatoes and garnish with the maître d'hôtel butter.

To drink: a fresh light red wine, such as a Bourgueil.

CHAYOTE

see Squash

CHEDDAR

see also:
cheese

A hard cows' milk cheese with about 45% fat, Cheddar is perhaps the best known and most imitated English cheese. The true farmhouse Cheddars are large or small cylinders which are smooth and firm, either white or creamy yellow and slightly grainy. Good mellow Cheddars have a distinct fruity taste and mature cheeses have a fairly strong, tangy flavour and after-taste.

Good Cheddar makes an excellent snack meal with some pickles or fruit. It may also be served at the end of a meal with a port or a good red Bordeaux. Cheddar, particularly the factory-made blocks, is also much used as a cooking cheese in sauces, on canapés and in salads. It may also be used to make the traditional British savoury dish Welsh rarebit.

One 30 g/1 oz portion of Cheddar cheese contains 115 calories.

WELSH RAREBIT

Serves 4
Preparation 20 minutes
Cooking about 15 minutes

METRIC/IMPERIAL	AMERICAN
55 g/2 oz butter	4 tbsp butter
4 thick slices of white bread	4 thick slices of white bread
225 g/½ lb matured Cheddar cheese, grated	½ lb aged sharp Cheddar cheese, shredded

200 ml/7 fl oz mild beer, preferably a pale ale	*1 cup light beer, preferably English pale ale*
1 tsp English mustard	*1 tsp English mustard*
cayenne pepper	*cayenne pepper*
1 egg yolk	*1 egg yolk*

Preheat the oven to 250C/475F/gas 9.

Melt the butter in a large frying pan and brown the slices of bread in it on both sides. Remove them from the pan and drain on paper towels.

Put the cheese in a saucepan along with the beer, mustard and a pinch of cayenne. Cook, stirring, for 5 or 6 minutes, ensuring that the mixture does not boil, until the cheese has all melted.

Off the heat, add the egg yolk and adjust the seasoning. Mix well and add a little more beer if the mixture is too thick.

Return the pan to a gentle heat and stir until thick and smooth.

Put the slices of bread in 4 warmed, little individual, deep serving dishes. Cover the bread with the cheese mixture and bake for 4 minutes. Serve immediately.

CHEESE

Fromage

see also:
aligot
Brie
Cheddar
croûte
Emmental
feta
fondue
Gorgonzola
Gouda
Gruyère
milk
mozzarella
Parmesan
pasteurization
quiche
Roquefort
sauce
soufflé
tart

A dairy product made from milk curds which are drained, salted, sometimes cooked, and then matured, cheese is one of Europe's most ancient foodstuffs. There are said to be over 1,000 named cheeses. This amazing array of cheese tastes and textures depends on the type of milk used, the means by which the coagulation into curds is induced, by adding acid, rennet or plant extracts, the method of production and the action of various bacteria either occurring naturally within the cheese or introduced by the cheesemaker.

There are 5 basic stages in the making of most cheeses. Firstly the milk is acidified to induce the formation of curds. This will often happen naturally due to yeasts occurring in the milk. However, nowadays a 'starter' is always added just to make sure. A carefully balanced mixture of the correct micro-organisms is added when the milk is still warm.

Rennet or plant extracts are then added to promote the milk protein's coagulation into curds. The amount and type of rennet or plant extract added, and the exact point at which it is added, all vary from cheese to cheese.

When the curds are set, the whey is drained off and the curds are then cut to allow more whey to drain off. The curds may then be either made into fresh cheese or processed further, perhaps cut again, kneaded, salted, bacteria added to them – even cooked – and put into moulds. Curds for most hard cheeses are then weighted or compacted in hydraulic presses.

The most important final stage for all but the fresh cheeses is ripening, which can take anything from a matter of weeks for a Brie to several years for a fine Parmesan.

Most cheeses are now commercially made in large industrial plants. However, those farmhouse (*fermier*) cheeses made locally using the traditional processes, although more expensive, usually have infinitely more flavour and character. Many such cheeses are also made using unpasteurized milk, which gives them much more complex and stronger flavours.

Cheeses are classified into one of several principal groups:

FRESH COWS' MILK CHEESES, such as CURD, COTTAGE OF POT CHEESE, FROMAGE BLANC, FROMAGE FRAIS, RICOTTA, MOZZARELLA, are allowed to coagulate by the action of natural microorganisms within the milk or by the addition of rennet. The curds are simply drained slowly to make a creamy white paste. They usually have a soft texture which may be smooth or lumpy like cottage cheese, depending on the method of production.

Fromage blanc, normal or low-fat, is sold in jars, foil containers or wrapped in cheesecloth in baskets, and is mainly eaten as a dessert with fruit or compotes. In cooking, it is used in much the same way as thick cream or yogurt, to thicken sauces, make dips and to top dishes baked *au gratin*. If unavailable, a passable substitute can be made by mixing yogurt and cottage cheese with a hint of lemon juice.

For those on a diet, *fromage blanc* with 0% fat is the ideal food, supplying good quality protein with the minimum of calories.

Fromage frais has a firmer consistency because it is drained for a longer period. It is also frequently flavoured with garlic, herbs or pepper. For cake recipes, be sure to choose natural-flavoured cheese.

CREAM CHEESES are made from milk or a mixture of milk and a varying amount of cream, and thus fat content. They are used to make the classic French treat *coeurs à la crème*, small cheeses drained in a heart-shaped mould, and to make cheesecake.

Some fresh cows' milk cheeses, such as FONTAINEBLEAU and PETIT-SUISSE are mixtures of curds with cream and make a delicious dessert served with fresh fruit.

Salt is added to some fresh cheeses, such as DEMI-SEL, and these make delicious cheese spreads and dips, and are useful for canapés.

SOFT COWS' MILK CHEESES are shaped and allowed to ripen under the influence of their natural bacteria. There are two types: those with a downy rind which develops naturally, or from being coated with a bacterial culture, eg, *Camembert* and *Brie*; and those with a washed rind, such as *Munster* and *Livarot*, which are usually made with cut curds, and where the rind is washed in brine during ripening to discourage bacterial growth on the surface.

The process of ripening these cheeses is extremely complicated and the supreme exercise of the cheesemaker's skill. When fully ripe, soft cheeses should be just beginning to bulge in the middle and become runny. Make sure that they are at just the right stage of ripeness when they are bought, as it is very difficult to produce domestically the right conditions for a soft cheese to finish ripening. Do not buy any which are too runny or smell of ammonia, as they are past their prime, but an underripe cheese has a chalky texture when cut.

CAMEMBERT is perhaps one of the most celebrated of the soft cheeses, with a downy white skin, pale yellow interior and delicious, subtle sweet flavour. The best come from the Normandy region which, because of its rich, creamy milk, makes the best soft cheeses. Camemberts are normally made in 11 cm/4½ in rounds about 3–4 cm/1½ in thick, although they do come in semi-circles and in wedges.

PONT L'ÉVÊQUE is made in large squares with a smooth golden-yellow or orange washed rind. Its earthy flavour is either adored or disliked. The square should first be cut across in half and then wedges sliced from each cut side.

MUNSTER is made in the Alsace in small, flat rounds. It has a straw-coloured or orange washed rind and a strongly flavoured, smooth interior. The taste goes well with that of onions, cumin and rye bread, and the Alsatians like to serve it with unpeeled boiled potatoes.

BLUE OR VEINED CHEESES, such as ROQUEFORT, GORGONZOLA and STILTON, are cut curd cheeses which have bacteria introduced into them so that they develop green or blue veining during ripening, to give a crumbly texture and intense flavours. The veining should be even and the smell should never be overpowering. Never buy a blue cheese with any hint of brown in the veining. The sharp flavours of blue cheeses are very popular in cooking. They go well with raw vegetables, fruit and nuts and are delicious in salads and salad dressings. They also go well in some meat and game dishes.

ROQUEFORT is one of the best known French cheeses. Made from ewes' milk, it is ripened in limestone caves in the *Aveyron* village from which it takes its name, and contains the same bacterial culture as Stilton.

STILTON is one of England's finest cheeses and is regarded by many as one of the finest cheeses in the world. Made in cylinders with a natural brushed rind, it has a pale cream interior with a very firm but velvety texture. It is delicious served with port, Madeira or a fine old red wine. Some enthusiasts even pour these into holes cut into the top of the cheese to allow it to macerate for a week or two, but this practice can only spoil the flavour of a really good cheese or mask that of an indifferent one.

PIPO CRÈME is a small, cylindrical, Italian blue cheese with a fine smooth texture and subtly piquant taste. Like a mellower version of Gorgonzola without Dolcelatte's blandness, it is a good cheese-board candidate.

PRESSED OR HARD COWS' MILK CHEESES are made by weighting the curds to make a fairly dense cheese. There are two types: those in which the curds are 'cooked' or scalded during the process of cutting the curds, such as GRUYÈRE, COMTÉ, EMMENTAL and PARMESAN, and those which are uncooked and simply pressed, including CANTAL, GOUDA, SAINT-PAULIN, CHEDDAR and CHESHIRE. Their firmness makes them useful in cooking, as they contribute texture as well as taste, and they can be grated for easy incorporation into mixtures or sprinkling over dishes to be gratinéed.

EMMENTAL is a Swiss cheese, similar to *Gruyère* but with more and larger holes. It is used in much the same way as *Gruyère*, in gratins, soufflés, fondues and salads. It is also popular in sandwiches and *croques-monsieur*.

CANTAL is one of the oldest French cheeses; indeed, the French claim that it is the ancestor of English Cheddar, which it resembles. Made in the Auvergne, it is much used in local dishes, such as *aligot*, and in gratins and soufflés.

CHESHIRE is said to be the oldest English cheese and has a crumbly texture and a fine, mild flavour which matures well. Known as 'Chester' in France, it enjoys an international following both after meals and in savoury dishes. There are three types. The red-dyed variety is the most common. The white is favoured by connoisseurs, but the incomparably flavoured blue is unfortunately very rare.

GOATS' MILK CHEESES, like cows' milk cheeses, are produced in fresh, soft, hard and veined varieties. In France, all cheeses made from goats' milk are described as *chèvres*. The package must even specify that it is made from pure goats' milk. Cheeses made from a mixture of cows' and goats' milk (not less than 25%) may only be called *mi-chèvre*.

Goats' milk cheeses are at their best in summer. They may be eaten fresh, half-ripened or dry. Some of them are dusted in wood ash or charcoal; others may be flavoured with herbs, garlic or chives. Goats' milk cheeses sold in winter are made from frozen milk, which removes the strong flavour characteristic of

goats' milk cheeses

blue-veined cheeses

fresh goats' milk cheeses. To find out whether a *chèvre* is dry – and therefore ripe – enough, cut it in half; it should have a velvety texture and slice cleanly. If it is too crumbly, it is made with powdered milk and is therefore not of the best quality. If it is chalky or soapy then it has possibly been frozen or poorly stored. A well-matured *chèvre* is always relatively costly.

Chèvres are delicious in salads, especially with bitter leaves such as chicory (Belgian endive) or dandelion, and in soufflés. Smaller *chèvres* make a tasty hors d'oeuvre when grilled or broiled.

CROTTIN DE CHAVIGNOL is a French goats' milk cheese from the Sancerre region. It comes in the form of a small, flattened ball, with a soft centre and natural crust. It is sold either fresh, when it is mild and almost white, or matured, sometimes to the point when it is very hard and dry. It is at its best when bought from the farm, mature but not over-ripe.

VALENÇAY is possibly the most familiar goats' milk cheese to those outside France, with its characteristic pyramid shape. The natural rind is usually dusted with charcoal. It is firm but soft-textured and has a musty, nutty flavour which works well in salads.

PROCESSED CHEESES are made from a wide variety of cheeses by melting them and adding milk, butter or cream and, possibly, flavourings, such as pepper, herbs or nuts. They are then usually moulded into thin slices or small wedges for easy use as sandwich fillers or spreads. In France, those made from French cheeses are referred to as *Crème de Gruyère*, etc.

Buy cheese from a specialist cheese shop and seek advice about what cheese to buy when. Apart from Vacherin, which is a winter cheese, and the majority of goats' milk cheeses, which are best in summer, there are enough different varieties of cheese throughout the year to create a balanced cheese board. Generally the selection is best in autumn and at the beginning of winter. Always try to include at least one hard cheese, one soft and one blue.

Cheese should never be bought too far in advance. Choose it when it is very nearly ripe, and then eat it within two or three days. Blue cheeses and Roquefort should not be kept very cold, but processed cheeses can be kept in the vegetable compartment of the refrigerator in an airtight wrapper. They should be taken out of the refrigerator one hour before serving. Soft cheeses and goats' milk cheeses are best simply kept in a cool place and not refrigerated.

Cheese is an excellent, protein-rich foodstuff, but is high in fats and salt. Energy content varies depending on the type of cheese: 30 g/1 oz of soft cheese contains 110 calories, blue cheese 160–200 calories, hard cheese 200–250 calories, processed cheese about 90 calories.

The fat content on the label, which is based on the dry extract, can be slightly misleading. The harder a cheese is, the fatter it will be; the more water it contains, the less fat it will contain. For example, if the label says 100 g/3½ oz of Camembert at 45%, it contains in reality only 20% fat; in Gruyère there is 30% fat, in goats' milk cheese 20–25%, and in blue cheese 33%. The calcium content varies from 140 to 1,100 mg per 100 g/3½ oz of cheese; cooked cheeses contain the most, eg, 150 mg in the case of Camembert and 1,090 mg in the case of Gruyère.

GÂTEAU AU FROMAGE BLANC

Cheesecake

Serves 8
Preparation 35 minutes, 2 hours ahead
Cooking 40 minutes, about 2 hours ahead

METRIC/IMPERIAL	AMERICAN
450 g/1 lb fresh soft cheese, such as ricotta	*1 lb fresh soft cheese, such as ricotta*
1 lemon	*1 lemon*
350 g/12 oz flour	*3 cups flour*
200 g/7 oz caster sugar	*1 cup superfine sugar*
1 tbsp baking powder	*1 tbsp baking powder*
175 g/6½ oz butter	*1¾ sticks butter*
5 egg yolks	*5 egg yolks*
100 ml/3½ fl oz white wine	*½ cup white wine*
1 sachet (7.5 g/1¾ tsp) of vanilla sugar	*1¾ tsp vanilla-flavored sugar*
150 g/5½ oz dried apricots, finely chopped	*1 cup finely chopped dried apricots*
salt	*salt*

Put the cheese into a strainer lined with cheesecloth and let it drain for at least 2 hours.

Either buy an organically grown, unsprayed lemon or scrub it several times with hot soapy water, rinse and pat dry. Finely grate the zest.

Preheat the oven to 160C/325F/gas 3.

Put the flour in a heap on a work surface and make a well in the middle of it. Add 150 g/5½ oz/¾ cup of the sugar, a pinch of salt, the baking powder, grated lemon zest, 150 g/5½ oz/11 tbsp of the butter and 2 of the egg yolks.

Rub the ingredients together with the fingertips until all the flour has been mixed in, then add enough of the white wine to bind to a smooth dough.

Cut the dough into 2 pieces, one slightly larger than the other, and roll each piece out to a thickness of about 3 mm/⅛ in. Grease a 20 cm/8 in diameter round cake or springform pan with the remaining butter and dust it with flour, then use the larger piece of dough to line it.

In a bowl, mix the drained cheese with the rest of the sugar, the vanilla sugar, the other 3 egg yolks and the apricots.

Pour this mixture into the pan and spread it out smoothly. Cover with the second piece of dough, trim off the excess round the edges and pinch to seal.

Bake for about 40 minutes. Remove from the oven and leave to cool. When cold, unmould and chill for an hour or two before serving.

Variation: a mixture of candied fruits or raisins can be substituted for the apricots.

SAUCE AU FROMAGE BLANC

Soft cheese sauce

Serves 4
Preparation 10 minutes

METRIC/IMPERIAL	AMERICAN
2 Petits-Suisses cheeses, about 50 g/1¾ oz each	2 Petits-Suisse cheeses, about 1¾ oz each
5 tbsp smooth fresh soft cheese	⅓ cup smooth fresh soft cheese
55 g/2 oz Roquefort	2 oz Roquefort cheese
1 tbsp Cognac	1 tbsp Cognac
several drops of white wine vinegar	several drops of white wine vinegar
cayenne pepper	cayenne pepper
salt and pepper	salt and pepper

In a bowl, mash the Petits-Suisses and mix the soft cheese with them.

In another bowl, crumble the Roquefort and add the Cognac and vinegar to it. Add a little salt, a pinch of cayenne pepper and ground pepper to taste. Blend the two mixtures together in a food processor.

Serve this sauce with potatoes baked in their jackets or as a dip with vegetable crudités.

Variation: instead of the Roquefort, Cognac and cayenne, try adding 3 tablespoons of ketchup, a few drops of Tabasco sauce and 1 teaspoon of Worcestershire sauce to make a good sauce for cold seafood.

FONDUE PIÉMONTAISE

Piedmont cheese fondue

Serves 4
Preparation 20 minutes, 24 hours ahead
Cooking 45 minutes

METRIC/IMPERIAL	AMERICAN
400 g/14 oz mature Fontina cheese	14 oz mature Fontina cheese
200 ml/7 fl oz milk	1 cup milk
75 g/2½ oz butter	5 tbsp butter
2 egg yolks	2 egg yolks
salt and freshly ground black pepper	salt and freshly ground black pepper

Remove and discard the rind from the cheese and cut the cheese into strips. Put them into a bowl, pour the milk over them and chill overnight.

About 45 minutes before serving, put the milk and cheese mixture into a saucepan standing in a bain-marie set over a low heat. Season with salt and pepper.

Add the butter in small pieces, along with the egg yolks. Cook, stirring constantly, until the mixture is smooth and thick. Do not allow the mixture to boil.

Serve hot, in preheated, small, deep, individual bowls, seasoned with freshly ground black pepper and accompanied by toast.

Variation: this dish is particularly delicious if very thin slices of a fresh white truffle are put on top of the cheese mixture in each bowl.

MIMOLETTE AU PORTO

Mimolette cheese in port

Serves 2
Preparation 10 minutes, 1 week ahead

METRIC/IMPERIAL	AMERICAN
170 g/6 oz young or semi-mature Mimolette cheese	6 oz young or semi-mature Mimolette cheese
150 ml/¼ pt sweet port	⅔ cup sweet port wine
crackers, to serve	crackers, to serve
freshly ground black pepper	freshly ground black pepper

Remove and discard the rind from the Mimolette and cut the cheese into small cubes. Put them into a deep dish and season with ground pepper.

Pour the port over them and stir well. Leave to macerate in a cool place, if possible not in the refrigerator, stirring from time to time, for at least 1 week.

To serve, drain the cheese well and accompany with plain crackers.

Note: this dish makes a perfect final course to a meal, offered with a selection of nuts, apples and a bottle of good port or red Bordeaux.

PETITS CHÈVRES MARINÉS À L'HUILE

Small goats' milk cheeses marinated in oil

For a 1 l/1¾ pt/1 qt jar
Preparation 15 minutes, 1 month ahead

METRIC/IMPERIAL	AMERICAN
1 garlic clove	1 garlic clove
3 shallots	3 shallots
8 very dry small chèvres, preferably picodons or pélardons	8 small, very dry goat's milk cheeses (chèvres), preferably picodons or pélardons
sprig of thyme, chopped	sprig of thyme, chopped
1 piece of fresh bulb fennel, chopped	1 piece of fresh bulb fennel, chopped
3 bay leaves	3 bay leaves
1 tbsp juniper berries	1 tbsp juniper berries
1 small red chilli pepper, halved	1 small red chili pepper, halved
about 750 ml/27 fl oz extra-virgin olive oil	about 3¼ cups extra-virgin olive oil

Peel the garlic and shallots. Put them in the bottom of a wide-mouthed preserving jar.

Put the *chèvres* on top, intermingling them with pieces of chopped thyme and fennel. Slide the bay leaves down the sides of the jar. Add the juniper berries and the halves of chilli pepper.

Fill the jar with olive oil and seal it.

Leave to marinate in a cool, dark place for at least 1 month. The marinated cheeses will keep for 7–8 months. Serve them with a herb and curly endive (*frisée*) or lettuce salad and toasted, farmhouse-style bread.

To drink: Sancerre or Anjou rosé.

CHERRY

Cerise

see also:
brandies, etc
cakes and gâteaux
fruit
liqueur
plum

A summer stone fruit related to the plum, cherries are in season from mid-May to the beginning of July, with skin varying from pale yellow to dark red.

There are two types of cherry: the SWEET CHERRIES, such as *bigarreaux*, bings and geans, which make delicious dessert fruit, but produce disappointing results when cooked, and the SOUR CHERRIES, actually slightly tart rather than sour, such as *griottes* or Morellos and English cherries, mainly used for pâtisserie, pies, cakes, jams, tarts and soufflés and for preserving, either as GLACÉ CHERRIES or in *eau-de-vie*. Sweet cherries do not keep well, hence their relatively high price.

Cherries should be purchased when they have a good colour but are not too ripe, as they continue to ripen up to 24 hours after being picked. The stalks should be firmly attached to the fruit and still slightly green, and the skin should be shiny and the flesh firm and never spongy. Fruit with even the smallest bruise or spot should be discarded. The weight of the stone can be quite considerable: 10% of the total weight in the case of *griottes* or English cherries and up to 50% for geans.

If serving raw, wash cherries in plenty of cold water, but do not remove the stalks, and pat dry. Apart from their wide use in sweet dishes, cherries are also common in savoury dishes, notably with game. Sweet-and-sour cherries also make a delicious accompaniment to boiled meats.

A principal use of the sour cherry is in the manufacture of alcoholic beverages such as cherry brandy, Kirsch and maraschino, which are all popular culinary flavourings.

Cherries have a very high sugar content which varies according to type: 100 g/3½ oz of English cherries, for instance, contain 56 calories and the same weight of *bigarreaux*, 77 calories. A notable exception is the CARIBBEAN CHERRY, which is low in calories and rich in vitamin C.

CLAFOUTIS

Cherry batter dessert

Serves 6
Preparation 20 minutes
Cooking 45 minutes

METRIC/IMPERIAL	AMERICAN
450 g/1 lb black cherries	1 lb (about 2 pt) sweet black cherries
4 eggs	4 eggs
125 g/4½ oz caster sugar	10 tbsp superfine sugar
75 g/2½ oz flour	10½ tbsp flour
75 g/2½ oz butter	5 tbsp butter
200 ml/7 fl oz milk	1 cup milk
1 sachet (7.5 g/1¾ tsp) vanilla sugar	1¾ tsp vanilla-flavored sugar
salt	salt

Preheat the oven to 210C/410F/gas 6–7.

Wash the cherries and remove their stalks, but do not take out the stones.

Beat the eggs in a bowl, add a pinch of salt and the caster (superfine) sugar and mix well until foamy.

Sift the flour and pour it into the bowl all at once. Mix again just until the batter is smooth.

Melt 55 g/2 oz/4 tbsp of the butter, let it cool slightly and then add it to the batter. Mix it in with the milk.

Grease a flameproof porcelain flan dish with a little of the remaining butter and arrange the cherries in it. Pour the batter over the fruit and dot the top with the rest of the butter.

Bake for 35–40 minutes, until the top begins to brown. Dust with the vanilla sugar to serve.

Note: versions of this traditional dish from the Limousin region may be made using mirabelle plums, pears or prunes and chopped apples.

TARTE AUX CERISES

Cherry tart

Serves 8–10
Preparation 15 minutes, resting time 30 minutes
Cooking 1 hour

METRIC/IMPERIAL	AMERICAN
200 g/7 oz flour	1¾ cups flour
100 g/3½ oz butter	1 stick butter
100 g/3½ oz caster sugar	½ cup superfine sugar
1 kg/2¼ lb cherries	2¼ lb (about 4½ pt) tart cherries
150 ml/¼ pt crème fraîche or whipping cream	⅔ cup crème fraîche or whipping cream
200 g/7 oz almond macaroons, finely crushed	2 cups finely crushed almond macaroons
1 tbsp Kirsch	1 tbsp Kirsch
salt	salt

Preheat the oven to 240C/465F/gas 8–9.

Make the dough by mixing the flour, butter, a pinch of salt and 1 tablespoon of the sugar together with the fingertips, and binding with 100 ml/3½ fl oz/1 cup of water. Form the dough

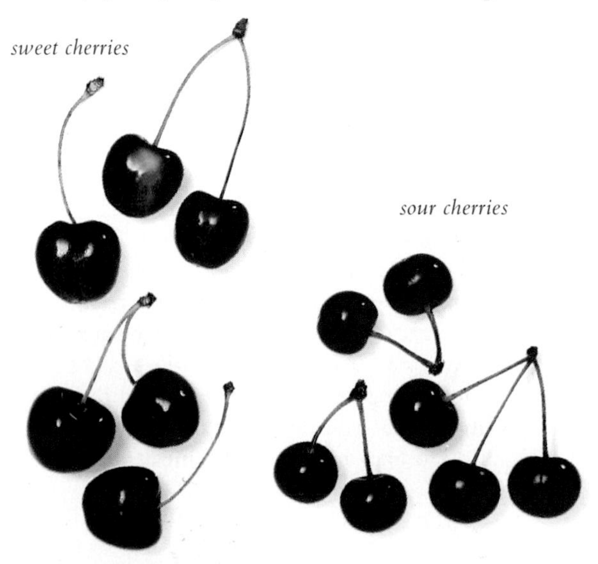

into a smooth ball and chill it for 10 minutes.

Roll the dough out and use it to line a 26 cm/ 10½ in loose-bottomed tart pan. Set aside while washing, drying and stoning the cherries.

Arrange the cherries in the pastry case, making sure they are close together. Sprinkle them with the remaining sugar. Bake for 1 hour in the hot oven.

Leave the tart to cool on a wire rack, then unmould it. Whip the cream and add the powdered macaroons and Kirsch to it. Mix well and spread over the cherry tart to serve.

CÔTELETTES DE CHEVREUIL AUX CERISES

Venison with cherries

Serves 4
Preparation 15 minutes
Cooking about 20 minutes

METRIC/IMPERIAL	AMERICAN
1 small jar or can (425 g/14 oz) of cherries in their own juice	*1 small jar or can (14 oz) of cherries in their own juice*
2 thick slices of slightly stale white bread	*2 thick slices of slightly stale white bread*
100 g/3½ oz butter	*1 stick butter*
8 venison chops	*8 venison rib chops*
100 ml/3½ fl oz crème fraîche or whipping cream	*½ cup crème fraîche or whipping cream*
salt and freshly ground black pepper	*salt and freshly ground black pepper*

Drain the cherries and reserve the juice. Cut the slices of bread into triangles.

Heat half of the butter in a frying pan and sauté the venison chops in it over a high heat for 5 minutes on each side. Drain them and keep them hot on a warmed serving dish.

Heat the cherries in the same frying pan. Meanwhile, melt the rest of the butter in another frying pan and fry the triangles of white bread on both sides until they are golden brown.

Arrange the hot cherries around the chops, then put 2–3 tablespoons of the cherry juice into the pan in which the meat and cherries were cooked to deglaze it. Stir up any sediment and cook over high heat to reduce the liquid by about half, then add the cream, mix well and stir with a wooden spoon until the sauce thickens. Season with salt and pepper.

Pour this sauce over the chops and arrange the triangles of fried bread around the edge of the serving dish.

To drink: a good red Burgundy, such as a Côte-de-Nuits.

CERISES À L'EAU-DE-VIE

Cherries preserved in eau-de-vie

Makes about 4 l/7 pt/4 qt
Preparation 30 minutes, 3 months ahead

METRIC/IMPERIAL	AMERICAN
700 g/1⅔ lb sugar	*3½ cups sugar*
2 l/3½ pt eau-de-vie	*2 qt eau-de-vie*
2 kg/4½ lb sour cherries, preferably griottes or Montmorency	*4½ lb tart cherries, preferably griottes or Montmorency*

Sterilize some preserving jars and set them aside, turned upside-down on a clean cloth. Dissolve the sugar in the *eau-de-vie*, stirring well.

Pick over the cherries and discard any that are not perfect. Wash and dry the cherries and trim off most of the stalk. Prick each cherry with a needle at the end opposite the stalk.

Put the cherries in the jars and cover them completely with the sugared *eau-de-vie*. Seal the jars and keep them in a cool dark place for at least 3 months before eating.

CHERVIL

Cerfeuil

see also: herbs sauce vinaigrette

One of the herbs most commonly used in cooking, chervil has an extremely volatile aroma and should therefore be purchased as fresh as possible and receive as little cooking as possible. Its delicate flavour – like a slightly anise-flavoured parsley – is used to best effect when the raw herb is finely chopped and added at the last minute to salads, soups and omelettes. Chervil freezes well.

POTAGE AU CERFEUIL

Chervil soup

Serves 6
Preparation 20 minutes
Cooking about 40 minutes

METRIC/IMPERIAL	AMERICAN
bunch of chervil	*bunch of chervil*
45 g/1½ oz butter	*3 tbsp butter*
whites of 2 leeks, trimmed and thinly sliced	*whites of 2 leeks, trimmed and thinly sliced*
1.5 l/2½ pt chicken stock	*1½ qt chicken stock*
3 floury potatoes, peeled and diced	*3 floury potatoes, peeled and diced*
2 egg yolks	*2 egg yolks*
100 ml/3½ fl oz whipping cream	*½ cup whipping cream*
salt and white pepper	*salt and white pepper*

Wash the chervil and pat it dry. Snip the leaves finely and chop the stalks.

Melt the butter in a saucepan and add the leeks. Cook them, stirring, until softened without allowing them to brown. Add the chervil stalks and one third of the leaves. Stir for several minutes over a low heat, then pour in the chicken stock and bring it to the boil.

Add the potatoes and season with salt and pepper. Simmer for about 30 minutes. Purée the contents of the saucepan in a food mill or blend very briefly in a food processor. Return the soup to the saucepan placed over a low heat.

Blend the egg yolks with the cream and 3 tablespoons of the hot soup in a bowl. Add this mixture to the soup and cook very gently, stirring constantly, until it is slightly thickened.

Pour the soup into a warmed soup tureen, add the rest of the chervil and serve at once.

CHESTNUT

Châtaigne, marron

The fruit of the sweet chestnut tree, which is edible when cooked, is generally known in France as the *marron*, although the true *marron* is the fruit of a grafted species grown for the size of the nut. Varieties of the nut are grown in most Mediterranean countries and some grow wild in Britain. The USA has several varieties of its own, particularly the Japanese nut, which replaced the American chestnut tree when it was devastated by blight.

The spiky husk contains either one large nut, usually kept for the production of *marrons glacés*, or 2 or 3 smaller chestnuts, known as *châtaignes*, separated by a membrane. Fresh chestnuts are sold in autumn and on into the beginning of winter. Buy shiny nuts, preferably with a smooth surface. They should feel firm, solid and heavy for their size. If buying in quantity, open one or two to check for damage from insect infestation.

To shell chestnuts, make an incision into the husk across the convex side and roast them in the oven for 7–8 minutes. Then peel while warm. If the dark brown inner skins prove difficult to remove at this stage, put the chestnuts into cold water with a little oil and bring to the boil. Simmer gently until the skins start to come away, then take them out a few at a time and rub with a cloth while still hot to remove the skin. Alternatively, lightly sauté the shelled nuts in butter until the skins are crisp. They then rub away easily. Shelled chestnuts are also sold canned in water or in syrup.

Chestnuts are very popular in cooking, especially in pâtisserie, cake making and desserts, usually in the form of *marrons glacés*, whole nuts poached in syrup and glazed, or as CHESTNUT CREAM, a sweetened purée, commonly available commercially. Chestnut cream is used in Bavarian creams, chilled charlottes and *vacherins*, or for filling sponge cake rolls, crêpes or barquettes.

see also:
apple
barquette
Brussels sprouts
cakes and gâteaux
cream
meringue
turkey
vacherin

Chestnuts are also grilled, boiled, braised, puréed or roasted and used as stuffings or accompaniments to poultry, game and vegetables, particularly turkey, pork, venison and Brussels sprouts.

In parts of Europe, chestnuts at one time took the place of potatoes in winter. CHESTNUT FLOUR is also still commonly used, particularly by the Italians. In *castagnaccio* it is baked with sultanas (golden raisins), pine kernels (pine nuts) and fennel seeds to memorable effect.

Chestnuts are very nutritious, with high levels of phosphorus and vitamins B and C; 100 g/3½ oz cooked chestnuts contains 310 calories.

PURÉE DE CHÂTAIGNES

Savoury chestnut purée

Serves 6–8
Preparation 10 minutes
Cooking about 40 minutes

METRIC/IMPERIAL	AMERICAN
500 ml/16 fl oz chicken stock	2 cups chicken stock
1 kg/2¼ lb fresh chestnuts, shelled and peeled	2¼ lb fresh chestnuts, shelled and peeled
3 stalks of young celery, trimmed and chopped	3 sticks of young celery, trimmed and chopped
55 g/2 oz butter	4 tbsp butter
100 ml/3½ fl oz crème fraîche or whipping cream	½ cup crème fraîche or whipping cream
salt and pepper	salt and pepper

Preheat the oven to 200C/400F/gas 6.

Heat the stock in a pan and add the chestnuts. Bring to the boil, then cover, lower the heat and cook for 20 minutes. Drain the chestnuts.

Cook the celery in one third of the butter over a moderate heat for 10 minutes.

Pass the chestnuts through a vegetable mill or purée them very briefly in a food processor and put the resulting purée into another pan with the remaining butter. Heat gently and add the chopped celery. Mix in the cream and season with salt and pepper to taste.

Serve with poultry or game.

GLACE AUX MARRONS

Chestnut ice cream

Serves 6
Preparation 20 minutes
Freezing about 2 hours

METRIC/IMPERIAL	AMERICAN
1 vanilla pod	1 vanilla bean
500 ml/16 fl oz milk	2 cups milk
4 egg yolks	4 egg yolks
55 g/2 oz caster sugar	¼ cup superfine sugar
100 ml/3½ fl oz crème fraîche or whipping cream	½ cup crème fraîche or whipping cream
300 g/10 oz canned chestnut cream (sweetened chestnut purée)	10 oz (about 1¼ cups) canned chestnut cream (crème de marrons)
1 tbsp rum	1 tbsp rum

Add the vanilla to the milk in a heavy-based saucepan and bring slowly to the boil. Meanwhile, beat the eggs with the sugar until thick and smooth.

Remove the vanilla and very slowly pour the milk over the eggs, stirring constantly. Pour back into the saucepan and cook this custard over a low heat, stirring, until it thickens. Do not let it boil. Remove it from the heat and leave it to cool completely.

Add the cream, chestnut cream and rum to the custard. Mix well until smooth.

Put the mixture into an electric ice cream maker and freeze. Or whisk the mixture for 2 minutes until it is frothy, then put into ice-cube trays without dividers and freeze for at least 2 hours.

To serve: scoop the ice cream into individual bowls. If wished, coat it with chocolate sauce or decorate it with chantilly cream and garnish with slivers of marron glacé.

CHÈVRE

see Cheese

see also:
boiling
curry powder
galantine
giblets
gratin
grilling
guinea fowl
kebab
lychee
pie
pigeon
poultry
rice
risotto
roasting
salad
stock
stuffing
turkey
vol-au-vent
wine

CHICKEN

Poulet, poularde

Descended from a species of Far Eastern wild fowl, the chicken is now the world's most popular domestic fowl and has become a mainstay of the Western diet.

To meet today's great demand, most chickens are intensively reared in battery hen houses and sold oven-ready in supermarket packs. Unfortunately, although these offer great value, the birds are usually slaughtered so young and fed on such bland food that they have little flavour. It is also very difficult to gauge their quality. It is wiser to buy chicken from the butcher or poulterer and have them drawn as you buy them: in this way you can better assess quality, and the birds will be that much fresher. Always try to make sure that the giblets come with the chicken as, although they may not be needed for a particular recipe, they can always be used to make stock. A good chicken should have: smooth, delicate skin which feels dry to the touch; firm flesh but with some give; a breast-bone that gives under the touch; pliable beaks and feet; and, on male birds, barely developed spurs.

FREE-RANGE CHICKENS may be more expensive, but the flavour is distinctly better than that of battery hens, mostly due to their rich and varied diet. CORN-FED CHICKEN, with characteristic yellow fat, also has a better taste and none of the fish-meal flavour which is sometimes so prevalent in the dark meat of intensively reared birds.

Chickens for cooking are normally categorized by age, size and gender:

POUSSINS, BABY CHICKENS or SQUAB CHICKENS are usually killed at about 4–6 weeks weighing about 300–550 g/10 oz–1¼ lb and sold ready-prepared. The flesh is very tender but lacking in taste and the birds are usually grilled or broiled, fried or roasted whole or in halves, or prepared like pigeon or other small game birds. The French also sell *coquelets* or young cocks, weighing just a little more and these are prepared in the same ways, but usually dressed in a highly seasoned sauce, such as lemon or green peppercorn sauce, to make up for the lack of flavour. Allow 1 poussin (squab chicken) or *coquelet* for 2 people – or 1 each if small.

The Americans designate birds of either sex about 2–2½ months old, weighing about 1.25 kg/2½ lb, as BROILERS; and those slightly larger, up to 1.5 kg/3½ lb, as FRYERS.

PULLETS, SPRING CHICKENS or *poulets* are slightly older birds, generally weighing 2–3 kg/4½–6½ lb. These birds have very tender, delicate white flesh and a more developed flavour. They are usually poached or roasted whole, or cut into pieces and braised, sautéed or stewed. The vast majority of chickens sold in Britain and the USA are a type of this sort of bird, bred to be slightly fatty and described as YOUNG ROASTING CHICKENS.

CAPONS or *chapons* are young cockerels which have been castrated and fattened up. They are considered a great delicacy by the French, particularly at Christmas and the New Year. They are roasted without stuffing and served whole.

BOILING or STEWING CHICKENS or *poules* are much older birds, upwards from 8 months, weighing over 2 kg/4½ lb. They are generally fairly tough but full of flavour. Younger boiling fowl also roast quite well.

When buying whole birds, allow at least 225–350 g/8–12 oz dressed weight of chicken per person.

Chicken is infinitely variable and marries well with any number of herbs and spices, both delicate and strongly flavoured, but goes especially well with tarragon and with ginger. It also works well with fruit, particularly lemon and apricots, and nuts, especially walnuts and almonds.

Chicken meat, without the skin, is very easily digested and is rich in protein and iron. White chicken meat with the skin removed is an ideal food for those on a weight-reducing diet; 100 g/3½ oz contains only 100 calories.

BONING A CHICKEN

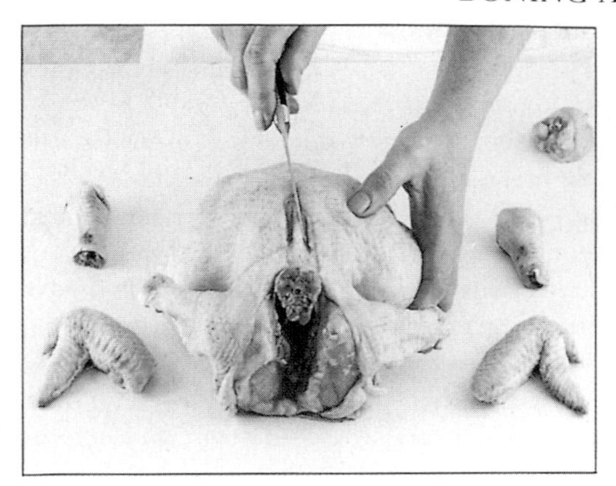

Note: this method of boning can be used for all poultry. A chicken is shown, but turkey and duck have the same general conformation. *Remove the wings at the second joint, the parson's nose (tailpiece) and any bone extending from the first drumstick joint. Place the bird breast side down and, using a short, sharp knife, cut down the centre of the back through skin and flesh to the bone, following the backbone.*

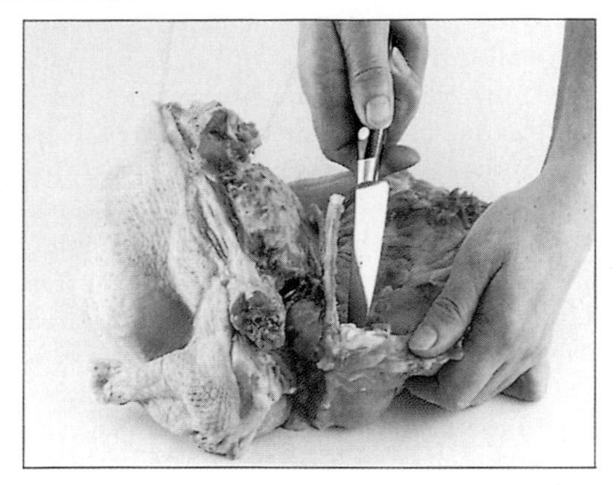

Using the tip of the knife, cut the flesh away from the bone, following the carcass down one side of the rib cage to the breast bone. Keep the knife next to the bone, separating the flesh with short strokes. As you work down the rib cage, the ball and socket joints that connect the legs and the wings to the carcass will become exposed. When you reach them, cut through the joints to separate them from the rib cavity, leaving them in the flesh.

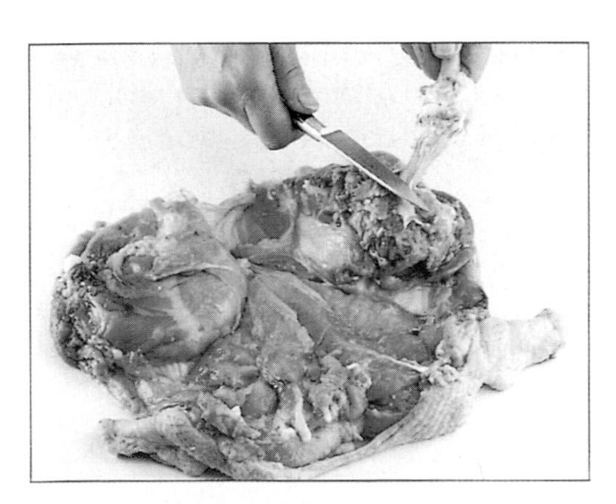

Having removed the flesh from one side of the rib cage, repeat with the other side. Then gently cut along the top edge of the breast bone, being careful not to cut through the skin. Remove the entire rib cage.

Cut around the end of the thigh bone to free it, grasp the end and scrape with the knife, pushing the flesh away from the bone until you can pull it out. Remove the leg and wing bones in this manner. When all the bones are removed, pull out as many of the white sinews as possible by scraping the flesh away from them. Spread out the skin and if you want a more even layer of flesh, pull off the two loose fillets on the breast and position them where needed.

CHAPON RÔTI

Roast capon

Serves 6
Preparation 20 minutes, up to 24 hours ahead
Cooking about $1\frac{1}{4}$ hours

METRIC/IMPERIAL	AMERICAN
1 fresh truffle, trimmed (optional)	1 fresh truffle, trimmed (optional)
1 capon, dressed weight about 2 kg/$4\frac{1}{2}$ lb	1 capon, dressed and drawn weight about $4\frac{1}{2}$ lb
55 g/2 oz butter	4 tbsp butter
salt and pepper	salt and pepper

If using, insert the truffle into the capon and leave it for 24 hours for the bird to absorb the flavour.

When ready to cook the bird, preheat the oven to 230C/450F/gas 8. Remove the truffle if used. Work 25 g/$\frac{3}{4}$ oz/$1\frac{1}{2}$ tbsp of the butter in a bowl with some salt and pepper and put it inside the capon. Sew up all apertures of the bird and truss it or tie it with string. Weigh it to calculate the cooking time, allowing 15 minutes per 450 g/1 lb.

Place the capon on a rack in a roasting pan and roast it until it is lightly browned, turning it several times. Lower the heat to 180C/350F/gas 4 and continue to cook until the calculated period has elapsed. Turn the oven off and leave the bird in it for 5–6 minutes.

Pour the juices from inside the capon into the roasting pan, then carve the bird and keep hot. Add the remaining butter to the roasting pan along with 1 teaspoon of water and the juices from the carved capon. Stir to deglaze the contents of the pan and serve in a sauce boat.

Serve the capon with green beans cooked in butter. If a truffle has been used, slice it and serve it with the bird.

Note: to avoid any risk of burning, add 1–2 tablespoons of water to the pan during roasting.

CARVING A CHICKEN

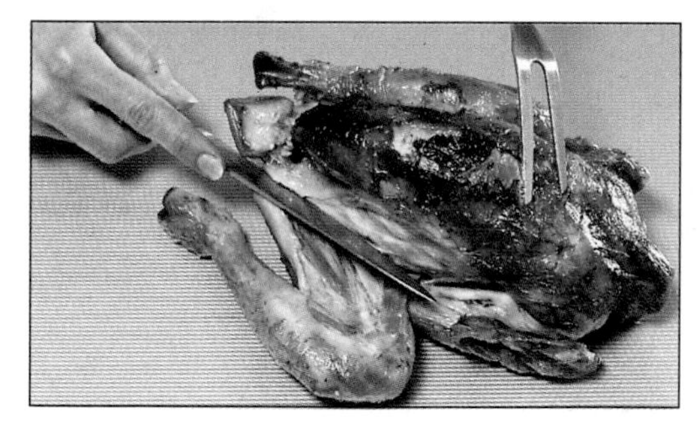

Cut into the depression between the breast and the leg, severing it from the carcass at the joint.

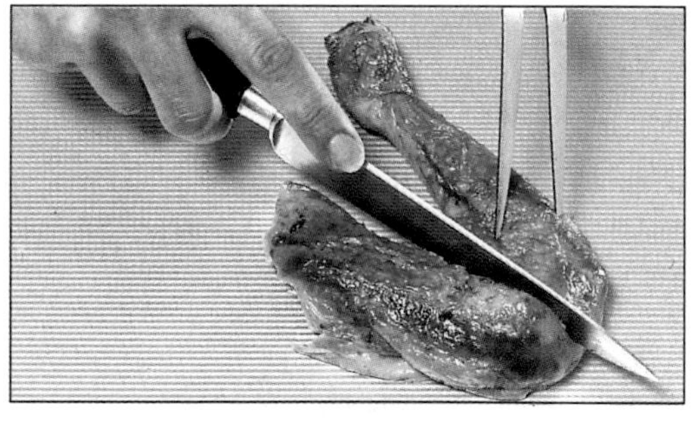

To separate the thigh and drumstick, slice through the centre of the connecting joint.

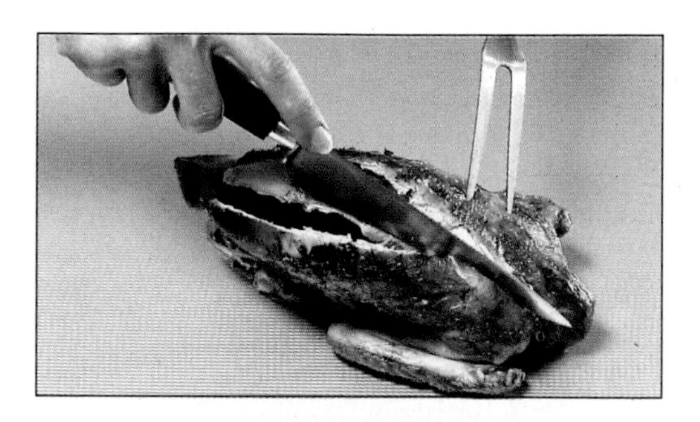

Keeping as close to the ribs as possible, remove the whole breast with the wing attached.

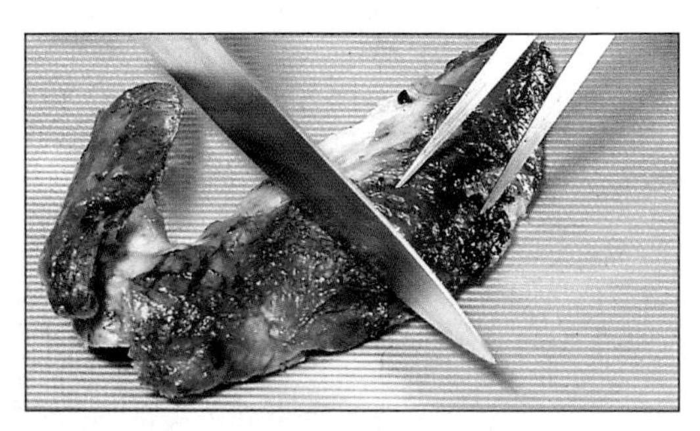

Divide the breast in two. This method of carving will provide 8 pieces of chicken.

POUSSINS FRITS À LA VIENNOISE

Fried breaded poussins

Serves 4
Preparation 15 minutes, 30 minutes ahead
Cooking about 15 minutes

METRIC/IMPERIAL	*AMERICAN*
2 poussins, each weighing about 400 g/14 oz	*2 squab chickens or Cornish game hens, each weighing about 14 oz*
3 tbsp oil	*3 tbsp oil*
2 tbsp lemon juice	*2 tbsp lemon juice*
1 garlic clove, chopped	*1 garlic clove, chopped*
1 tbsp finely chopped parsley	*1 tbsp finely chopped parsley*
3–4 tbsp flour	*3–4 tbsp flour*
2 eggs	*2 eggs*
5 tbsp fine dry breadcrumbs	*⅓ cup fine dry breadcrumbs*
oil, for deep frying	*oil, for deep frying*
salt and pepper	*salt and pepper*
3 lemons, quartered, to garnish	*3 lemons, quartered, to garnish*

Cut the chickens into pieces and put them into a deep dish. Mix the oil, lemon juice, garlic and parsley together and season with salt and pepper. Pour this over the pieces of chicken, stir well and leave to marinate for 30 minutes.

Put the flour in a shallow dish. In a second shallow dish, beat the eggs, adding a little oil. Put the breadcrumbs in a third dish.

Drain the pieces of chicken and pat them dry with paper towels. Then dip each piece first in flour, then in beaten egg and finally in breadcrumbs.

Heat a deep pan of oil to 180C/350F (a small cube of bread will brown in it in 1 minute). Plunge the breaded pieces of chicken into it and fry for 13–15 minutes. When they are golden brown, drain them and serve very hot, garnished with the lemon quarters.

To drink: a fruity white wine, such as Gewürztraminer.

COQUELETS À L'ESTRAGON

Chicken with tarragon

Serves 6
Preparation 30 minutes
Cooking about 40 minutes

METRIC/IMPERIAL	*AMERICAN*
3 very young small chickens, preferably cocks, each weighing about 550–675 g/1¼–1½ lb	*3 squab chickens, preferably cocks, or Cornish game hens, each weighing about 1¼–1½ lb*
4 shallots	*4 shallots*
45 g/1½ oz butter	*3 tbsp butter*
3 tbsp corn oil	*3 tbsp corn oil*
2 carrots, cut into chunks	*2 carrots, cut into chunks*
100 ml/3½ fl oz Cognac	*½ cup Cognac*
600 ml/1 pt white wine	*2½ cups white wine*
bunch of tarragon, finely snipped	*bunch of tarragon, finely snipped*
100 ml/3½ fl oz thick crème fraîche or whipping cream	*½ cup thick crème fraîche or whipping cream*
1 tsp cornflour	*1 tsp cornstarch*
salt and pepper	*salt and pepper*

Cut the birds in half lengthwise. Peel the shallots but leave them whole.

Heat 30 g/1 oz/2 tbsp of the butter and 2 tablespoons of the oil in a flameproof casserole. Gently sauté the pieces of chicken over a moderate heat until lightly browned, turning them several times. Remove them from the casserole and discard the fat.

Put the rest of the oil and butter in the casserole and brown the shallots and carrots. Return the chicken to the casserole and pour the Cognac over. Cover and cook for 3 minutes, then add the white wine. Season with salt and pepper, bring just to the boil and then simmer gently for 10 minutes.

Add the tarragon and continue to cook very gently for a further 10 minutes.

Remove the chicken and keep hot. Skim off excess fat from the juices in the casserole, then add the crème fraîche and the cornflour (cornstarch) mixed with a little cold water. Bring just to boiling point, stirring well to mix and deglaze.

Put the chicken in a warmed, deep serving dish and coat with the sauce. Serve at once, accompanied by *petits pois à la française* and sautéed potatoes.
To drink: white Graves.

POULET CÉLESTINE

Chicken with tomatoes, mushrooms and wine

Serves 4
Preparation 15 minutes
Cooking about 30 minutes

METRIC/IMPERIAL	AMERICAN
1 tender young chicken, dressed weight about 1.2 kg/2¾ lb, cut into pieces	*1 broiler/fryer, dressed and drawn weight about 2¾ lb, cut into pieces*
55 g/2 oz butter	*4 tbsp butter*
140 g/5 oz mushrooms, sliced	*5 oz mushrooms, sliced*
1 tomato, peeled and coarsely chopped	*1 tomato, peeled and coarsely chopped*
200 ml/7 fl oz dry white wine	*1 cup dry white wine*
1 tbsp Cognac	*1 tbsp Cognac*
2 garlic cloves, chopped	*2 garlic cloves, chopped*
4 tbsp finely chopped parsley	*¼ cup finely chopped parsley*
salt and pepper	*salt and pepper*

Brown the chicken pieces in a sauté pan with the butter, turning them frequently.

Add the mushrooms and tomato to the chicken and sauté for 5 minutes. Add the wine and the Cognac. Season with salt and pepper, cover and cook for 20 minutes.

Mix the garlic with the chopped parsley.

Drain the chicken pieces, put them into a warmed, deep serving dish, coat with the sauce and sprinkle with the garlic *persillade*. Serve at once.
To drink: a full-bodied red, such as a Côtes-du-Rhône.

CUISSES DE POULET À LA POLONAISE

Chicken legs with braised red cabbage

Serves 4
Preparation 20 minutes
Cooking about 1½ hours

METRIC/IMPERIAL	AMERICAN
450 g/1 lb red cabbage	*1 lb head red cabbage*
2 tbsp red wine vinegar	*2 tbsp red wine vinegar*
1 tsp cumin seeds	*1 tsp cumin seeds*
55 g/2 oz butter	*4 tbsp butter*
4 chicken legs	*4 chicken leg quarters*
salt and pepper	*salt and pepper*

Quarter the red cabbage, cut out the tough inner ribs and core, then wash it and shred it finely.

Put the shredded cabbage into a sauté pan, sprinkle it with salt, add the vinegar and cumin and mix well. Spread a piece of foil with half the butter and place it on the cabbage mixture, buttered side down, then put on the pan lid and cook for 1 hour.

Heat the remaining butter in a frying pan and gently brown the chicken pieces in it for 10 minutes, turning them several times.

When they are golden brown, drain them and place them on top of the red cabbage in the sauté pan. Continue to cook for 15 minutes.

Serve very hot in a warmed deep serving dish.
To drink: a sharp, light white wine, such as an Alsace Sylvaner.

SAUTÉ DE POULET BASQUAISE

Basque chicken with tomatoes and peppers

Serves 6
Preparation 30 minutes
Cooking about 1 hour

METRIC/IMPERIAL	AMERICAN
1 tender young chicken, dressed weight about 1.5 kg/2¼ lb, cut into pieces	1 broiler/fryer, dressed and drawn weight about 2¼ lb, cut into pieces
½ tsp paprika	½ tsp paprika
4 sweet peppers	4 sweet peppers
100 ml/3½ fl oz olive oil	½ cup olive oil
115 g/¼ lb salted pork belly or streaky bacon, cut into long strips	¼ lb salt pork or bacon, cut into long strips
4 onions, thinly sliced	4 onions, thinly sliced
4 firm tomatoes, peeled and coarsely chopped	4 firm tomatoes, peeled and coarsely chopped
3 garlic cloves, chopped	3 garlic cloves, chopped
bouquet garni	bouquet garni
100 ml/3½ fl oz dry white wine	½ cup dry white wine
salt and pepper	salt and pepper
finely chopped flat-leaved parsley, to garnish	finely chopped flat-leaf parsley, to garnish

Season the chicken pieces with salt and pepper and sprinkle them with a little paprika. Grill (broil) the sweet peppers to char the skin on all sides so that they peel easily, then trim and cut the peeled flesh into strips.

Heat half the olive oil in a flameproof casserole and brown the pork or bacon strips for 2 minutes. Remove them with a slotted spoon and drain.

Brown the chicken pieces in the same casserole, turning them to cook evenly.

Meanwhile, heat 2 tablespoons of oil in another pan. Add the onions and sauté until translucent, then add the tomatoes, garlic and bouquet garni. Simmer gently for 15 minutes. Meanwhile, in another pan, cook the sweet peppers in the remaining oil.

When the chicken pieces are golden brown, add the white wine and return the pork or bacon strips to the casserole along with the tomato and onion mixture and the sweet peppers. Mix well and season with salt and pepper. Add another pinch of paprika and put the lid on the casserole. Cook gently for about 30 minutes. To serve, discard the bouquet garni and sprinkle with chopped parsley.

To drink: a fruity white wine, such as Rioja.

CUISSES DE POULET À L'ORIGAN

Chicken legs baked with oregano

Serves 4
Preparation 20 minutes
Cooking about 35 minutes

METRIC/IMPERIAL	AMERICAN
2 eggs	2 eggs
3 tbsp milk	3 tbsp milk
150 g/5½ oz grated Parmesan	1¼ cups grated Parmesan cheese
100 g/3½ oz fine fresh white breadcrumbs	2 cups fine fresh white breadcrumbs
1 tbsp dried oregano	1 tbsp dried oregano
4 chicken legs	4 chicken leg quarters
olive oil	olive oil
salt and pepper	salt and pepper

Preheat the oven to 220C/425F/gas 7.

Break the eggs into a bowl and beat them with the milk.

Mix the Parmesan, breadcrumbs, oregano and some salt and pepper in another bowl.

Dip each chicken leg in the beaten egg, then into the breadcrumb mixture several times, making sure they are well coated with crumbs.

Oil a baking sheet and arrange the chicken legs on it. Bake for about 35 minutes until golden brown all over. Serve very hot.

To drink: a soft red wine, such as a Chinon.

Sauté de poulet basquaise (Basque chicken with tomatoes and peppers)

POULARDE À L'IVOIRE

Chicken poached in white wine

Serves 8
Preparation 30 minutes
Cooking about 2 hours

METRIC/IMPERIAL	*AMERICAN*
3 tbsp oil	*3 tbsp oil*
1 chicken, weighing 2 kg/$4\frac{1}{2}$ lb (with giblets), cut in pieces	*1 chicken, dressed and drawn weight 4–$4\frac{1}{2}$ lb (with giblets), cut in pieces*
2 carrots, sliced	*2 carrots, sliced*
3 small turnips, sliced	*3 small turnips, sliced*
1 onion, sliced	*1 onion, sliced*
2 garlic cloves	*2 garlic cloves*
150 ml/$\frac{1}{4}$ pt white wine	*$\frac{2}{3}$ cup white wine*
500 ml/16 fl oz chicken stock	*2 cups chicken stock*
45 g/$1\frac{1}{2}$ oz butter	*3 tbsp butter*
45 g/$1\frac{1}{2}$ oz flour	*$\frac{1}{3}$ cup flour*
$\frac{1}{2}$ tsp ground cinnamon	*$\frac{1}{2}$ tsp ground cinnamon*
salt and cayenne pepper	*salt and cayenne pepper*

Heat the oil in a large, flameproof casserole and gently cook the chicken pieces in it for 10–15 minutes without allowing them to brown, turning them occasionally.

Add the vegetables and garlic to the casserole, mixing well. Pour in the wine and stock and season with salt and cayenne. Cover and cook over a moderate heat for $1\frac{1}{4}$ hours.

Clean the chicken's liver, heart and gizzard and add them to the casserole. Cook for a further 20 minutes.

Melt the butter in a saucepan, add the flour and cook for 2 minutes. With a ladle, take out 300 ml/$\frac{1}{2}$ pt/$1\frac{1}{2}$ cups of the cooking liquid and whisk it into the roux. Add the cinnamon and cook, stirring constantly, for 10 minutes, then season with salt and cayenne.

Take the pieces of chicken out of the casserole and put them into a warmed serving dish. Coat with the white sauce and serve at once.

Serve mushrooms or celery cooked slowly in their own juices as accompaniments.

To drink: a fruity white wine, such as Pinot blanc.

Remove the leg quarters, then separate the thigh and drumstick by cutting through the joint.

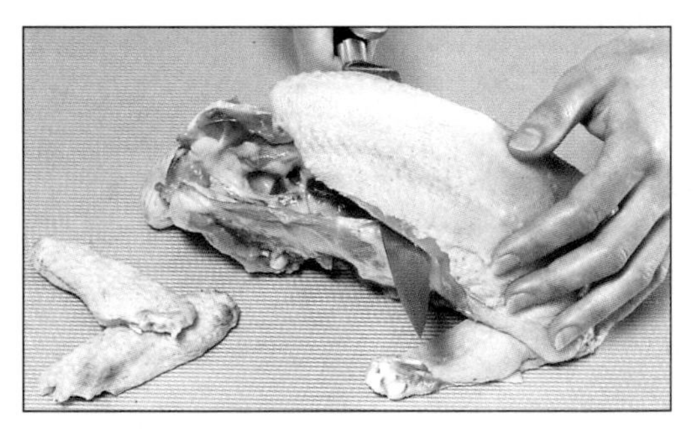

Cut off the wing tips and remove the back by cutting it away from the ribcage.

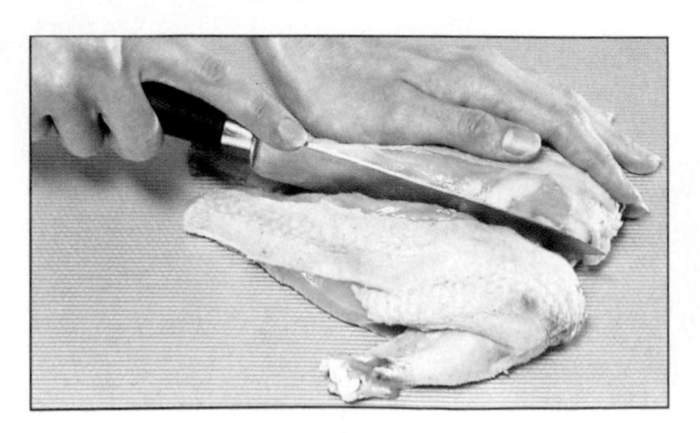

To remove each half of the breast, cut along the cartilage and through the breastbone.

Separate the wing portions from the breasts to make 8 pieces or leave them together for 6 pieces.

WATERZOÏ DE POULET

Flemish chicken stew

Serves 4
Preparation 15 minutes
Cooking about 1¾ hours

METRIC/IMPERIAL	AMERICAN
150 g/5½ oz rice	¾ cup rice
55 g/2 oz butter	4 tbsp butter
1 chicken, dressed weight about 1.5 kg/3½ lb	1 chicken, dressed and drawn weight about 3½ lb
whites of 4 leeks, trimmed and cut into pieces	whites of 4 leeks, trimmed and cut into pieces
3 stalks of celery, trimmed and cut into pieces	3 sticks of celery, trimmed and cut into pieces
2 onions, sliced	2 onions, sliced
2 sprigs of thyme	2 sprigs of thyme
bay leaf	bay leaf
4 tbsp finely chopped parsley	¼ cup finely chopped parsley
2 egg yolks	2 egg yolks
150 ml/¼ pt crème fraîche or whipping cream	⅔ cup crème fraîche or whipping cream
salt and pepper	salt and pepper

Boil the rice in lightly salted water for 10 minutes, drain it and add half the butter to it. Stir well to coat the grains.

Stuff the chicken with the buttered rice and truss it tightly. Brown it lightly in the remaining butter in a flameproof casserole, then remove it.

Add the leeks, celery and onions to the casserole and cook, stirring, for 10 minutes.

Return the chicken to the casserole and add the thyme, bay leaf and chopped parsley. Season with salt and pepper. Add 400 ml/14 fl oz/1¾ cups of water and cover. Cook for 1 hour.

Remove the chicken from the casserole and keep it hot. Boil the cooking liquid rapidly, uncovered, for 5 minutes to reduce it slightly. Carve the chicken and put the pieces into a warmed, deep serving dish with the stuffing.

Mix the egg yolks with the cream and add to the cooking liquid in the casserole. Stir and heat through, without letting the sauce boil. Pour the sauce over the chicken and serve at once.
To drink: lager (light beer).

CHICKEN LIVER

see Giblets

CHICKPEA OR GARBANZO BEAN

Pois chiche

see also:
couscous
pulses
vegetables

The creamy beige-coloured seed of a leguminous plant native to the eastern Mediterranean region, the chickpea or garbanzo bean is one of the most nutritious pulses. Cultivation has now spread to most frost-free climates, including parts of the Americas and Australia. A smaller version of the chickpea, called the *channa*, is grown in the Indian sub-continent.

Although eaten fresh in areas of cultivation, chickpeas are usually sold dried or pre-cooked in cans. Before cooking, dried chickpeas require lengthy soaking, preferably overnight in several changes of water. If still in their skins, they should be soaked for an hour or so in a strong solution of bicarbonate of soda and then boiled in it briefly. The beans are then refreshed in cold water and the skins rub off easily.

To cook chickpeas, boil 450 g/1 lb/2¼ cups in 2 l/3½ pt/2 qt of water for at least 2½ hours, rinse well and drain; it is difficult to overcook them. The cooking water may be flavoured with onions, carrots, celery, leek and bacon.

Chickpeas are a staple of the Arab diet, and have entered the cuisines of other Mediterranean cuisines, such as Greece and Spain. Dishes such as *hummus* (puréed cooked chickpeas mixed with sesame oil and, sometimes, lemon juice, garlic and tahini paste) and the North-African stew *couscous* have become international favourites. Cooked chickpeas are also used in salads, soups and stews and as garnishes. In India, *channa* are used in much the same way as lentils and are also often ground into flour.

Chickpeas are rich in proteins, carbohydrates and many important minerals. 100 g/3½ oz of dried chickpeas contains 361 calories.

SALADE DE POIS CHICHES

Chickpea salad

Serves 6
Preparation 30 minutes

METRIC/IMPERIAL	AMERICAN
1 can (400 g/14 oz) chickpeas	1 1-lb can chickpeas (garbanzo beans)
4 small onions, thinly sliced	4 small onions, thinly sliced
3 stalks of celery, trimmed and cut into chunks	3 sticks of celery, trimmed and cut into chunks
bunch of radishes, trimmed and thinly sliced	bunch of radishes, trimmed and thinly sliced
3 tomatoes, peeled and cut into tiny cubes	3 tomatoes, peeled and cut into tiny cubes
1 can (200 g/7 oz) tuna fish, drained	1 7-oz can tuna fish, drained
12 fresh mint leaves, shredded	12 fresh mint leaves, shredded
6 tbsp olive oil	6 tbsp olive oil
2 tbsp lemon juice	2 tbsp lemon juice
4 hard-boiled eggs, shelled and sliced	4 hard boiled eggs, shelled and sliced
salt and pepper	salt and pepper

Drain the chickpeas, put them in a colander and rinse them well under cold running water, stirring them with the fingers to make sure all the individual peas are rinsed.

In a large salad bowl, mix the chickpeas, onions, celery, radishes and tomatoes. Crumble the tuna fish into the salad bowl, add the mint and mix well.

Make a vinaigrette with the oil, lemon juice and salt and pepper to taste. Pour it over the salad and mix. Garnish the top with slices of hard-boiled egg. Serve at room temperature.

Note: the salad may be dressed with the vinaigrette 30 minutes in advance and left to marinate. However, the eggs should not be added until the last minute.

CHICORY OR BELGIAN ENDIVE

Endive

see also:
braising
chiffonade
endive
radicchio
salad
vegetables

This winter vegetable is forced from roots grown in the dark. Known as Belgian endive in the United States, where most of the crop is still imported from Belgium, there is much confusion between this and the curly-headed salad leaf from a related family which also bears the name endive in England.

Chicory has the advantage of having virtually no wastage. When bought, it should be pale, as any hint of green betrays age, firm, shiny, slightly swollen in the middle and without bruises.

Any damaged leaves should be removed and the head rinsed quickly in water and wiped dry. Avoid prolonged soaking in water, because this brings out any bitterness. To further reduce bitterness, hollow out and discard the small white inner cone at the base of the head. Chicory does not freeze well.

Chicory is equally good raw and cooked and plays an important role in winter salads, especially in alliance with eggs, beetroot, citrus fruits, apples and dried fruit. Whole heads are also often braised, stewed or steamed and served dressed in butter or a béchamel sauce; or the heads are shredded *en chiffonade*, cooked in cream or simply steamed, to make the perfect accompaniment for white meat, game and certain types of fish. Whole heads are also often deep fried or stuffed with meat or cheese mixtures, or baked *au gratin* with ham to make a satisfying main course or light meal.

Chicory is a very healthy vegetable, rich in vitamins and phosphorus. 100 g/3½ oz contains only 15 calories, making it an excellent diet food.

COUPE D'ENDIVES AUX FRUITS

Chicory or Belgian endive and fruit salad

Serves 4
Preparation 15 minutes

METRIC/IMPERIAL	AMERICAN
200 g/7 oz fresh soft cheese (fromage blanc) with 0% fat	1 cup fresh, smooth soft cheese (fromage blanc) with 0% fat
1 tbsp white wine vinegar	1 tbsp white wine vinegar
1 tsp mild mustard	1 tsp mild mustard
4 heads of chicory	4 heads of Belgian endive
juice of 1 lemon	juice of 1 lemon
2 bananas	2 bananas
1 apple	1 apple
walnuts or cashew nuts, to garnish (optional)	walnuts or cashew nuts, to garnish (optional)
salt and pepper	salt and pepper

Whisk the cheese with the vinegar. Season with the mustard, salt and pepper to taste and chill.

Trim the chicory (Belgian endives) and cut them across into thin rounds. Sprinkle them with some of the lemon juice. Peel the bananas and slice them in rounds. Sprinkle them with lemon juice. Peel and core the apple and cut it into thin strips. Sprinkle with lemon juice.

Combine the chicory (Belgian endive), bananas and apple in a serving bowl, add the cheese sauce and stir gently. Serve well chilled. Garnish with walnuts or cashew nuts.

Variation: substitute palm hearts for the bananas and an orange for the apple, and toss the salad in a herbed vinaigrette sauce.

ENDIVES GRATINÉES AU JAMBON

Baked chicory or Belgian endive with ham

Serves 6
Preparation 20 minutes
Cooking about 35 minutes

METRIC/IMPERIAL	AMERICAN
200 ml/7 fl oz dry white wine	1 cup dry white wine
6 firm white heads of chicory (all about the same size), trimmed	6 firm white heads of Belgian endive (all about the same size), trimmed
6 slices of cooked ham	6 slices of cooked ham
30 g/1 oz butter	2 tbsp butter
2 tbsp cornflour	2 tbsp cornstarch
300 ml/½ pt milk	1½ cups milk
pinch of grated nutmeg	pinch of grated nutmeg
pinch of caster sugar	pinch of superfine sugar
1 egg yolk	1 egg yolk
100 g/3½ oz grated Gruyère	1 cup grated Gruyère cheese
salt and white pepper	salt and white pepper

Preheat the oven to 230C/450F/gas 8.

Bring the white wine and 200 ml/7 fl oz/1 cup of water to the boil in a large pan. Add the whole chicory (Belgian endive) heads and some salt. Bring to the boil again, lower the heat, cover and cook for 10 minutes. Drain very carefully and reserve the cooking liquid.

chicory (Belgian endive)

Roll each head in a slice of ham. Grease a baking dish with half the butter and arrange the rolls in it.

Reduce the cooking liquid by half over a high heat. In a cup, mix the cornflour (cornstarch) and the milk until smooth and add gradually to the reduced cooking liquid, stirring, then add more salt if needed, some pepper, and a pinch each of grated nutmeg and sugar.

Stir until the sauce thickens, then remove from the heat and whisk in the egg yolk. Pour the sauce over the chicory (Belgian endive) and ham rolls.

Sprinkle the top with the grated cheese and dot with the remaining butter. Bake for 6–7 minutes, until the top is well browned, and serve at once.

Notes: this dish may also be made with a béchamel sauce flavoured with grated Parmesan or Gruyère, or with Madeira sauce with some added raisins. The ham should be top quality and sliced from the bone.

CHIFFONADE

see also:
hors d'oeuvre
soup

A preparation of lettuce, sorrel, spinach or chicory (Belgian endive) leaves, cut into strips, it is usually used as a garnish for cold hors d'oeuvres, soups or vegetables.

To prepare leaves for a garnish *en chiffonade* they are first trimmed, washed and patted dry, then layered on top of one another, rolled up and these rolls cut across into strips, usually about 1 cm/½ in thick.

CHILI CON CARNE

see also:
bean
peppers

Now an international favourite, rather like pizza, this Mexican-inspired Texan stew is made of cubed or minced (ground) meat simmered with chilli peppers (chilies) or chilli powder and other spices and flavourings. There are many versions, some which include red kidney beans, others using only meat. In North America and Britain, it is often served over rice, with finely chopped raw onions and grated cheese as accompaniments.

Like many such dishes, chili con carne is better made a day ahead. It makes a nutritious meal which is relatively low in calories.

CHILI CON CARNE

Beef or pork with chilli peppers

Serves 8
Preparation 15 minutes
Cooking about 2½ hours

METRIC/IMPERIAL	AMERICAN
4 tbsp corn oil	4 tbsp corn oil
2 large onions, chopped	2 large onions, chopped
3 garlic cloves, chopped	3 garlic cloves, chopped
1.5 kg/3½ lb lean boneless beef or pork, diced or minced	3½ lb lean boneless beef or pork, finely diced or coarsely ground
1 tbsp chilli powder	1 tbsp chili powder
1 tsp cumin seeds	1 tsp cumin seeds
1 tsp dried oregano	1 tsp dried oregano
Tabasco sauce	hot pepper sauce, such as Tabasco
500 ml/16 fl oz beef stock	2 cups beef stock
450 g/1 lb canned tomatoes, drained	1 1-lb can tomatoes, drained
2 cans of red kidney beans (about 800 g/1¾ lb in total), drained	2 14-oz cans red kidney beans, drained
salt and pepper	salt and pepper
chopped raw onion, to serve (optional)	chopped raw onion, to serve (optional)
grated Cheddar, to serve (optional)	grated Cheddar cheese, to serve (optional)

Heat the oil in a large, flameproof casserole and brown the onion and garlic in it for about 10 minutes. Add the meat and cook, stirring constantly, for 5–6 minutes.

Add the chilli powder, cumin, oregano, salt and pepper to taste and several drops of Tabasco sauce. Stir and lower the heat. Add the stock and the tomatoes and simmer, covered, for about 1–1¼ hours.

Add the kidney beans to the casserole and stir to mix. Continue cooking for a further hour.

Serve piping hot with chopped raw onion and grated Cheddar cheese, if wished.

Notes: add 2 or 3 chopped deseeded fresh green chilli peppers (chilies) for a more authentic taste; or add several large pinches of cayenne pepper for a hotter dish.

CHILLI PEPPER

see Peppers

see also:
cabbage
Swiss chard
vegetables

CHINESE OR NAPA CABBAGE OR CHINESE LEAVES

Chou chinois

Of several of the Chinese varieties of the brassica family, two are now commonly available fresh in the West.

The type usually referred to as CHINESE or NAPA CABBAGE is *pe-tsai*, which resembles a large cos (romaine) lettuce with thick white ribs to the outer stalks. With a texture which lies somewhere between that of a cabbage and a lettuce, it is delicious finely chopped or shredded and eaten raw in salads, but it may also be braised or poached. To prepare Chinese cabbage it is only necessary to remove any coarse or damaged outer leaves and trim away the tougher, dense white core at the base.

Pak-choi, or CHINESE MUSTARD GREENS, resembles Swiss chard, but again with the more pronounced white ribs. It is often served like celery, with which it is sometimes confused. The Chinese also pickle it in salt to make a version of *sauerkraut*, which they rinse and steam or add to stir-fried meat and fish dishes.

Of all the cabbage family, Chinese cabbage has the lowest calorie content; 100 g/3½ oz contains only 12 calories.

SALADE DE CHOU CHINOIS AUX MOULES

Chinese cabbage salad with mussels

Serves 4
Preparation 25 minutes
Cooking about 20 minutes

METRIC/IMPERIAL	AMERICAN
4–5 small new potatoes	4–5 small new potatoes
4 tbsp white wine	4 tbsp white wine
450 g/1 lb fresh mussels, trimmed and scrubbed	1 lb fresh mussels, trimmed and scrubbed
1 tbsp sherry vinegar	1 tbsp sherry vinegar
1 tsp mild mustard	1 tsp mild mustard
450 g/1 lb Chinese cabbage, trimmed and finely shredded	1 lb Napa cabbage, trimmed and finely shredded
2 shallots, chopped	2 shallots, chopped
4 tbsp olive oil	4 tbsp olive oil
6 small cherry tomatoes, halved	6 small cherry tomatoes, halved
bunch of basil, chopped	bunch of basil, chopped
salt and pepper	salt and pepper

Boil the new potatoes in their skins for 15 minutes. Peel them, slice them in rounds and immediately pour half the white wine over them. Leave them to cool.

Put the mussels in a large pan with the remaining wine and shake over a high heat until they all open. Remove them from their shells and put them in a bowl. Mix the vinegar with the mustard and pour it over them.

Mix the cabbage with the shallots, season with salt and pepper, pour the olive oil over them and toss well. Put into a deep serving dish.

Add the mussels to the new potatoes and wine, then spread them in a layer over the bed of cabbage. Garnish with the tomato halves and basil. Serve at once.

CHIPOLATA

see Sausage

CHIVE

Ciboulette

This member of the onion family is mainly grown for its thin green leaves which are used as a common culinary herb. One of the classic *fines herbes* of French cuisine, chives are mostly used as an ingredient in salads – and in vinaigrettes and other dressings – and in omelettes and other egg dishes. They are also often used to flavour processed soft cheeses. Chives have a very delicate, fugitive flavour which is quickly lost during cooking. The green leaves should therefore be snipped and added to food at the last minute before serving.

see also:
herbs
salad

SAUCE VERDURETTE

Herb vinaigrette

Serves 6
Preparation 15 minutes

METRIC/IMPERIAL	AMERICAN
4 hard-boiled eggs, shelled and halved	4 hard-boiled eggs, shelled and halved
1 tsp mild mustard	1 tsp mild mustard
200 ml/7 fl oz oil	1 cup olive oil
bunch of chives, finely chopped	bunch of chives, finely chopped
several sorrel leaves, finely chopped	several sorrel leaves, finely chopped
2 tbsp finely chopped parsley	2 tbsp finely chopped parsley
several tarragon and basil leaves, finely chopped	several tarragon and basil leaves, finely chopped
2 tbsp white wine vinegar	2 tbsp white wine vinegar
salt and pepper	salt and pepper

Remove the egg yolks and mash them in a bowl with the mustard and salt and pepper to taste. Whisk the oil in gradually to make a smooth thick sauce.

Mix the chopped herbs with the vinegar and add to the mustard sauce.

Chop 2 of the egg whites very finely. Put the sauce into a serving bowl and scatter the chopped egg whites on top.

Serve with poached cold fish or vegetable crudités.

CHOCOLATE

Chocolat

Made from beans from the pods of the cocoa or *cacao* tree, chocolate is one of the most important flavourings in the manufacture of sweet foods.

The fermented and dried beans are crushed to squeeze out the fat from the beans, or COCOA BUTTER as it is known, leaving a dry chocolate paste. This paste then goes through a sequence of refining procedures, mostly a process called 'conching', in which it is passed repeatedly through sets of rollers to make it finer and smoother. Sugar is usually added at this stage, as well as additional cocoa butter or other fat, to produce what we know as chocolate.

see also:
cakes and gâteaux
charlotte
cocoa
cookies, etc
creams and custards
éclair
fondant
ices and ice creams
meringue
sauce
soufflé

According to sugar content, the chocolate may be designated: UNSWEETENED, BAKING or BITTER CHOCOLATE; PLAIN, SEMISWEET or BITTER-SWEET CHOCOLATE, also called *chocolat pâtissier*; or SWEET or GERMAN CHOCOLATE. FONDANT, COATING or *couverture* chocolate has a high level of added fat. It thus melts at quite low temperatures, making it suitable for moulding and coating in the making of confectionery. Unsweetened or less sweet chocolate is best for cooking as the final sweetness of a dish is then more readily controlled.

MILK CHOCOLATE has up to 40% condensed or dried milk incorporated into it to give a rich, mild and creamy chocolate which has become very popular in confectionery and biscuit (cookie) making, especially with children.

Chocolate is also enhanced with a wide variety of flavourings from fruit and nuts to alcoholic beverages.

UNSWEETENED COCOA POWDER, which is made by removing about half of the cocoa butter from the original chocolate paste, is very convenient for use as a flavouring in recipes. Cocoa powder for hot chocolate drinks is sweetened and enriched with dried milk.

Good-quality chocolate is brown and shiny, breaks cleanly without crumbling, and has no lumps, white spots or tiny burst bubbles. It should melt on the tongue like butter and be neither pasty nor sticky. The less sweet varieties of chocolate should be bitter but not acrid.

Chocolate – even with a high milk content – will keep for several months, if stored in a dry place at a temperature of about 18C/64F. It is best not to refrigerate chocolate, certainly not for extended periods.

Chocolate exposed to sudden heat runs the risk of becoming lumpy and bitter when it melts. In general, in order to retain its flavour and shine, chocolate should be melted at the lowest possible temperature. To flavour a dessert without liquid, such as a mousse, soften the chocolate in a pan over a very low heat, in a bain-marie or in a low oven with the door open. Microwave ovens are particularly good for softening chocolate; cook 3 minutes on High for 55 g/2 oz of chocolate. If adding butter to chocolate, place it on top of the melted chocolate and beat with a spoon until the mixture is smooth. Chocolate used for flavouring a liquid should be cooked in it. The ideal concentration is 125 g/4½ oz per 1 l/1¾ pt/1 qt, or about 1 part chocolate to 8 parts liquid.

Chocolate is a basic ingredient and flavouring for many pâtisserie products and in cakes, biscuits (cookies) and desserts. Most of the world's production, however, goes into the manufacture of confectionery, from chocolate truffles to serve with after-dinner coffee to the bewildering array of chocolate bars so beloved as energy-giving snacks. However, chocolate has long been used in savoury dishes. The Aztecs, who were the first to use chocolate, have bequeathed to the Mexicans their tradition of including bitter chocolate in stews, particularly with poultry. This practice has spread into the cuisines of both Spain and Italy, where the smooth bitterness of chocolate is often added to meat, game and some seafood dishes. One or two pieces of unsweetened or plain chocolate added to a chicken stew or *matelote* gives extra colour and depth of flavour.

Chocolate is a very nutritious food with a high energy content and about 2–9% proteins. It is rich in vitamin D, iron, magnesium and other minerals. It also contains the stimulant caffeine and theobromine, which is held to be a potent enhancer of mental activity and to produce the same pleasurable effects in the brain as those associated with being in love.

CRÈME MEXICAINE

Mexican chocolate cream

Serves 4
Preparation 10 minutes, 1 hour ahead
Cooking about 20 minutes

METRIC/IMPERIAL	AMERICAN
115 g/4 oz plain chocolate, grated	4 oz semisweet chocolate, grated
55 g/2 oz butter, softened	4 tbsp butter, softened
700 ml/1¼ pt milk	3 cups milk
4 tsp instant coffee	4 tsp instant coffee powder
1 cinnamon stick	1 cinnamon stick
1 egg	1 egg
20 g/⅔ oz cornflour	2½ tbsp cornstarch
100 g/3½ oz honey	⅓ cup honey
unsweetened cocoa powder, for sprinkling	unsweetened cocoa powder, for sprinkling

Mix the chocolate with the softened butter.

Heat the milk in a pan. Add the instant coffee and cinnamon stick to the milk. Stir well, then add the chocolate and butter mixture. Cook over a low heat for about 10 minutes, stirring constantly. Remove and discard the cinnamon stick.

Beat the egg, cornflour (cornstarch) and honey in a bowl until the mixture is very smooth. Pour the contents of the pan into the bowl, whisking constantly.

Pour the mixture back into the pan and return it to the heat. Cook, stirring and without letting it boil, until it thickens.

Remove the pan from the heat, pour the contents into 4 bowls and chill. Just before serving, sprinkle a little cocoa powder on the surface of each.

DÉLICE AU CHOCOLAT

Chocolate delight

Serves 6
Preparation 20 minutes
Cooking about 25 minutes

METRIC/IMPERIAL	AMERICAN
150 g/5½ oz butter, softened	11 tbsp butter, softened
4 eggs, separated	4 eggs, separated
150 g/5½ oz caster sugar	¾ cup superfine sugar
200 g/7 oz bitter chocolate, broken into small pieces	7 oz semisweet chocolate, broken into small pieces
1 tbsp very strong black coffee	1 tbsp very strong black coffee
2 tbsp flour	2 tbsp flour
100 g/3½ oz ground almonds	1¼ cups ground almonds

Preheat the oven to 220C/425F/gas 7. Grease a 20 cm/8 in round cake pan lightly with butter.

In a large bowl, beat the egg yolks vigorously with the sugar until foamy.

Place the chocolate and coffee in a bowl set in a bain-marie. When the chocolate has melted, add it to the egg and sugar mixture.

Add the flour, ground almonds and the remaining softened butter and mix to a smooth batter. In another bowl, whisk the egg whites to stiff peaks. Fold the egg whites carefully into the batter.

Pour the batter into the prepared pan and bake for about 20 minutes. Insert a fine skewer into the middle of the cake; in this case, in contrast to the classic test for doneness, the skewer should not come out completely clean.

Leave the cake to cool before turning it out on a wire rack. Serve it cold with a custard sauce or apricot purée.

Note: this dessert will keep very well, in a cool place, for 2 or 3 days.

SAUCE AU CHOCOLAT

Chocolate sauce

Serves 6
Preparation 5 minutes
Cooking 10 minutes

METRIC/IMPERIAL	AMERICAN
55 g/2 oz caster sugar	5 tbsp superfine sugar
140 g/5 oz bitter chocolate, broken into small pieces	5 oz semisweet chocolate, broken into small pieces
15 g/½ oz butter	1 tbsp butter

Put 150 ml/¼ pint/⅔ cup of water into a pan, add the sugar and cook gently until the liquid has reduced by about half. Add the pieces of chocolate to the syrup and melt, stirring until smooth. Add the butter and stir until it has melted.

Use this sauce for profiteroles, ice cream or pears Belle-Hélène.

Variation: simply melt 140 g/5 oz of bitter (semisweet) chocolate, broken into small pieces, in 100 ml/3½ fl oz/½ cup of milk, adding a small piece of butter. Stir until the chocolate has melted and the sauce is smooth.

PAVÉ AU CHOCOLAT ET AU RHUM

Chocolate and rum cake

Serves 6
Preparation 30 minutes
Cooking about 40 minutes

METRIC/IMPERIAL	AMERICAN
4 eggs	4 eggs
200 g/7 oz caster sugar	1 cup superfine sugar
200 g/7 oz plain chocolate, coarsely grated	7 oz semisweet chocolate, coarsely grated
200 ml/7 fl oz crème fraîche or whipping cream	1 cup crème fraîche or whipping cream
200 g/7 oz flour	1⅔ cups flour
2 tbsp rum	2 tbsp rum
15 g/½ oz butter	1 tbsp butter

Preheat the oven to 210C/415F/gas 6–7.

Break the eggs into a large bowl and add the sugar. Set the bowl in a bain-marie containing hot but not boiling water. Whisk for about 10 minutes until the mixture is thick and smooth, then remove the bowl from the bain-marie.

Fold the chocolate in gently then add the cream, followed by the flour, a little at a time, and finally the rum.

Line a 20 cm/8 in square cake pan with parchment or greaseproof paper and grease it with the butter. Pour the batter into it and bake for 30 minutes. Test whether the cake is done by inserting a skewer into the centre. The skewer should come out clean.

Unmould the cake and let it cool before serving.

MOUSSE AU CHOCOLAT

Chocolate mousse

Serves 4–6
Preparation 20 minutes, 5–6 hours ahead

METRIC/IMPERIAL	*AMERICAN*
115 g/4 oz plain chocolate, broken into small pieces	*4 oz semisweet chocolate, broken into small pieces*
30 g/1 oz butter	*2 tbsp butter*
3 eggs, separated	*3 eggs, separated*
2 tbsp icing sugar	*2 tbsp confectioners' sugar*

1

2

3

4

Melt the chocolate in a bowl set in a bain-marie. When it is completely soft, add the butter (1). Then add the egg yolks and mix thoroughly (2). Leave to cool slightly.

Meanwhile, whisk the egg whites to stiff peaks (3). Fold in the sugar.

Fold the egg whites carefully into the chocolate mixture (4). Pour the resulting mousse into a bowl or into individual serving dishes and chill for several hours or overnight.

Serve well chilled, possibly with slices of warm brioche as a delicious contrast. To decorate, the mousse may also be sprinkled with crushed, caramelized hazelnuts, pistachios or almonds just before serving.

Variations: for a richer version of this mousse, melt 250 g/$8\frac{1}{2}$ oz of plain (semisweet) chocolate in a sugar syrup made from 150 g/$5\frac{1}{2}$ oz/$\frac{3}{4}$ cup of sugar and 150 ml/$\frac{1}{4}$ pt/$\frac{2}{3}$ cup of water. Add 200 g/7 oz/2 sticks of butter and 4 egg yolks. Fold in 4 stiffly whisked egg whites. Chill overnight.

For an orange-flavoured chocolate mousse: melt the chocolate in a bain-marie, add the melted butter and egg yolks, and then 2 tablespoons of Cointreau with 55 g/2 oz/$\frac{1}{3}$ cup of chopped candied orange peel, before folding in the whisked egg whites. For a mocha mousse, melt the chocolate with 2 tablespoons of black coffee.

For those not counting calories, try the richest mousse of all: melt 400 g/14 oz of chocolate broken into small pieces with 2 tablespoons of crème fraîche or whipping cream which has been heated just to boiling point. Add 125 g/$4\frac{1}{2}$ oz/9 tbsp butter and 2 egg yolks, followed by 3 egg whites whisked to stiff peaks with 1 tablespoon of icing (confectioners') sugar.

Note: chocolate mousse should always be prepared ahead of time so that it has a chance to firm up in the refrigerator.

CHOCOLAT CHAUD À L'ANCIENNE

Old-fashioned hot drinking chocolate

Serves 4
Preparation 5 minutes
Cooking about 10 minutes

METRIC/IMPERIAL	AMERICAN
225 g/8 oz plain chocolate, broken into small pieces	8 oz semisweet chocolate, broken into small pieces
1 l/1¾ pt milk	1 qt milk
1 sachet (7.5 g/1¾ tsp) of vanilla sugar	1¾ tsp vanilla-flavored sugar
1 or 2 pinches of ground cinnamon	1 or 2 pinches of ground cinnamon
100 ml/3½ fl oz single cream (optional)	½ cup light cream (optional)

Put the chocolate in a heavy-bottomed saucepan and melt it very gently. In another pan, heat the milk until just boiling.

When the chocolate has melted, add the vanilla sugar and cinnamon to taste. Pour a cup of the boiling milk into it.

Whisk the mixture over a low heat, then add the rest of the hot milk, whisking constantly.

Serve the foamy chocolate in a chocolate pot or large mugs. If using, whisk the cream in vigorously just before serving.

CHOLESTEROL

see also:
fats and oils
lipids

An organic substance existing naturally in the bodies of humans and other animals, cholesterol is spread throughout the body but is concentrated in the nerve cells. The system needs it to make such important materials as the sex hormones, vitamin D and bile salts.

High levels of cholesterol combined with high levels of saturated fats in the diet are generally regarded to be responsible for a large percentage of cardiovascular illnesses. The ideal level of blood cholesterol is between 1.8 and 2 g per litre. Foods richest in cholesterol are egg yolk, offal (variety meats), especially brain, meat and crustaceans, where it is concentrated in the head. Lean meat, poultry and fish are low in cholesterol and fruit and vegetables are totally free of it.

However, many nutritionists hold that the level of cholesterol in the blood is relatively unaffected by levels of consumption, and is more governed by the amount and type of fat in the diet: the more saturated fat the higher the blood cholesterol.

CHOPPING

see also:
mousse
pâté
purée
sausage
stuffing
terrine

The division of items of food into small pieces, known as chopping, is normally achieved using kitchen knives or by recourse to machines such as mincers, grinders, choppers and food processors. These can all reduce foods to an extremely smooth, homogenized and, on occasions, virtually liquid state. However, unless a smooth purée is what is required, it is wiser to chop by hand, especially meat, or at least, to be very careful not to over-process, as it is all too easy for ingredients chopped too small to collapse into an unappetizing pulp.

It is generally regarded as preferable to tear salad leaves by hand rather than cutting them, and some herbs may be very speedily cut by snipping them with scissors, although the traditional double-handled rocking herb cutter with the semi-circular blade is held to preserve the flavour better and is certainly very efficient with large quantities. The best means of 'chopping' hard-boiled egg yolk is to force it through a fine sieve. Electric processors and coffee grinders are invaluable for chopping nuts.

CHORIZO

see also:
sausage

This long smoked sausage, of Spanish origin, is seasoned with garlic and either sweet or hot red peppers. Versions are now made in both France and Mexico, where they are very popular, and they vary widely in degree of spiciness and added herbs and other flavourings.

Chorizo may be eaten cold, in salads and cold rice dishes, or served as an appetizer, cut into chunks and threaded on cocktail sticks with olives. The Spanish also grill or fry them in slices, or add them to stews and the classic *paella*.

Chorizo contains about 300 calories per 100 g/3½ oz, depending on the fat content.

RIZ À LA CATALANE

Catalan rice

Serves 4
Preparation 20 minutes
Cooking about 1 hour

METRIC/IMPERIAL	*AMERICAN*
3 large tomatoes, quartered	*3 large tomatoes, quartered*
1 garlic clove, chopped	*1 garlic clove, chopped*
2 tbsp chopped parsley	*2 tbsp chopped parsley*
bay leaf	*bay leaf*
1 sugar cube	*1 sugar cube*
1 tsp dried thyme	*1 tsp dried thyme*
3 tbsp olive oil	*3 tbsp olive oil*
1 onion, chopped	*1 onion, chopped*
1 sweet pepper, deseeded and sliced thinly	*1 sweet pepper, deseeded and thinly sliced*
400 g/14 oz chorizo sausage, sliced into rounds	*14 oz chorizo sausage, sliced into rounds*
250 g/8½ oz long-grain rice	*1⅓ cups long-grain rice*
300 ml/½ pt chicken stock	*1½ cups chicken stock*
salt and pepper	*salt and pepper*

Put the tomatoes and garlic into a saucepan along with the chopped parsley, crumbled bay leaf, sugar cube, thyme and 1 tablespoon of oil. Cover and cook for 25 minutes.

Remove the lid from the pan, raise the heat slightly and continue to cook for 10 minutes. Then pass the contents of the pan through a food mill and keep hot.

Put the remaining oil in another saucepan and add the onion and sweet pepper. Brown them for 5 minutes. Add the chorizo and the puréed tomato mixture to the pan. Stir over a low heat for 4 minutes.

Add the rice, mix well and then add the stock. Season with salt and pepper and cook, covered, for a further 20 minutes.

CHOUX PASTRY OR CHOUX PASTE

Pâte à choux

see also:
croquembouche
éclair

Made with boiling water and whole eggs, well-aerated, rich choux pastry puffs up when cooked to give a very light, fluffy texture, so beloved in French pâtisserie. It may be baked, poached or deep fried, but is normally only cooked in fairly small quantities or in rings, as it is otherwise difficult to cook the interior of the dough. It is made into small buns of various shapes and sizes, which are then either split and filled or stuffed and coated to make items such as éclairs and profiteroles, or built up into large cakes, such as the classic gâteau Saint-Honoré.

CHOUX BUNS, also known as CREAM PUFFS, may be eaten cold on their own or sprinkled with sugar, but are more usually filled: either with a sweet, creamy filling, such as chantilly or pastry cream; or with a light savoury filling, such as cheese or foie gras or salmon mousse, to make hors d'oeuvres and party snacks.

Small CHOUX FRITTERS or *beignets*, flavoured with nuts or cheese, are deep fried and served to accompany drinks.

Because it swells so much, choux is the lightest of pastries and 100 g/3½ oz of unfilled choux pastry contains only 85 calories.

PÂTE À CHOUX

Choux pastry

Makes about 24 choux buns
Preparation 15 minutes
Cooking 30 minutes

METRIC/IMPERIAL	*AMERICAN*
75 g/2½ oz butter	*5 tbsp butter*
1 tbsp caster sugar	*1 tbsp superfine sugar*
150 g/5½ oz flour, sifted	*1¼ cups flour, sifted*
4 (size 4) eggs	*4 large eggs*
½ tsp salt	*½ tsp salt*

Preheat the oven to 210C/410F/gas 6–7.

Into a saucepan put 250 ml/8 fl oz/1 cup of water, 60 g/2 oz/4 tbsp of the butter cut into small pieces, the salt and sugar. Bring to the boil (1, overleaf).

1

2

3

4

When the water comes to the boil, add the flour all at once, mixing vigorously with a wooden spoon (2). The flour will swell and a ball of pastry will begin to form, detaching itself from the sides of the saucepan. If this does not happen spontaneously, stir the pastry over low heat until it starts to pull away from the sides of the pan.

Remove the pan from the heat and add the eggs one at a time (3). Mix thoroughly to make sure the dough is completely smooth before adding the next egg. The dough should be smooth and supple (4). If it seems too dry, add an extra half of a beaten egg. To gauge the correct consistency: if dripped from a spoon the pastry should drop slowly in one large blob.

Lightly grease a baking sheet with the remaining butter. Take a teaspoon of the pastry (about 10 g/$\frac{1}{3}$ oz) and push it out on to the baking sheet with the help of a second spoon. Continue forming balls of pastry, spacing them well apart on the baking sheet. A piping bag may also be used for this operation.

Very lightly spray the choux buns with a little water and bake in the centre of the oven for 15–20 minutes, until the choux buns are puffy and golden brown.

Leave to cool completely in the switched-off oven, with the door open, before filling or icing.

Notes: for successful choux pastry, the flour must be well sifted and the ingredients carefully measured. The choux buns must not be removed from the oven before they are completely cooked or they will sink.

The measures and cooking times given above are for small choux buns, for larger choux they are as follows:

Medium buns: 1 dessertspoon (2 teaspoons) of pastry (15 g/$\frac{1}{2}$ oz), 30–35 minutes cooking.

Large choux: 1 tablespoon of pastry (30 g/1 oz), 40–45 minutes cooking.

CHOUX AUX GROSEILLES

Redcurrant cream puffs

Serves 6
Preparation 15 minutes

METRIC/IMPERIAL	*AMERICAN*
200 ml/7 fl oz crème fraîche or whipping cream	*1 cup crème fraîche or whipping cream*
75 g/2½ oz icing sugar	*⅔ cup confectioners' sugar*
1 sachet (7.5 g/1¾ tsp) of vanilla sugar	*1¾ tsp vanilla-flavored sugar*
300 g/10 oz redcurrants, stalks removed	*3 cups redcurrants, stalks removed*
24 choux buns	*24 choux buns*
icing sugar, to dust	*confectioners' sugar, to dust*

Put the cream into a chilled bowl and dilute it with 2 finely crushed ice cubes. Add half the icing (confectioners') sugar and the vanilla sugar and whip, either with a hand whisk or with an electric beater (if using the latter watch out for splattering), until the cream sticks to the blades.

Fold the redcurrants carefully into the cream. Split the choux buns about two thirds from the top with a pair of scissors and fill with the redcurrant cream, then replace the tops.

Powder with icing (confectioners') sugar and serve at once.

Variations: there are many other possible fillings. Try pastry cream flavoured with rum or Kirsch, or with Calvados and apple compote; coffee-flavoured pastry cream with coffee fondant icing (200 g/7 oz of fondant, 1 tablespoon of coffee and 2 tablespoons of water) or chocolate icing; whipped chestnut cream with crème fraîche or whipping cream.

CHOUX AU FOIE GRAS

Choux buns with foie gras

Makes 20 choux buns
Preparation 15 minutes

METRIC/IMPERIAL	*AMERICAN*
200 ml/7 fl oz thick crème fraîche or whipping cream	*1 cup thick crème fraîche or whipping cream*
140 g/5 oz foie gras mousse (see Foie gras)	*5 oz foie gras mousse (see Foie gras)*
20 choux buns	*20 choux buns*
salt and white pepper	*salt and white pepper*

Whip the cream, adding salt and pepper to taste, until thick. Carefully fold in the foie gras mousse using a metal whisk. Work only until the mixture is smooth and well combined.

Split the choux buns about two thirds from the top using a pair of scissors. Fill a piping bag with the stuffing and fill the choux, then replace the tops.

Pile them on a plate on top of a clean napkin and serve them with aperitifs.

Variations: other possible savoury fillings include whipped crème fraîche or whipping cream with Roquefort cheese and chopped walnuts (no need to add salt), mushroom purée with slivered truffle, chopped smoked salmon with whipped crème fraîche or whipping cream and dill.

CHRISTMAS YULE LOG

Bûche de Noël

see also: buttercream cakes and gâteaux chestnut

A Christmas tradition in France, yule log cakes are usually made of a sponge roll or layers of Genoese sponge filled with buttercream flavoured with chocolate, vanilla or coffee. The cake is cut and shaped to look like a felled log and coated with more buttercream, which is then piped or forked to look like bark. Further decoration often includes marzipan holly leaves and meringue mushrooms.

There are also versions of this cake made from layers of differently flavoured ice creams and parfaits, or chocolate and chestnut cream as in the following recipe.

BÛCHE AUX MARRONS

Chestnut log

Serves 8
Preparation 25 minutes, 24 hours ahead

METRIC/IMPERIAL	AMERICAN
115 g/4 oz bittersweet chocolate, broken into pieces	4 oz semisweet chocolate, broken into pieces
125 g/4½ oz butter	9 tbsp butter
450 g/1 lb canned chestnut cream (sweetened chestnut purée)	1 lb canned chestnut cream (crème de marrons)
125 g/4½ oz icing sugar	1 cup confectioners' sugar

Put the chocolate in a saucepan over a very low heat. Add 2 tablespoons of water and leave it to melt. Meanwhile work the butter with a wooden spoon to soften it.

Put the chestnut cream in a bowl and mash it with a fork to eliminate any lumps. Add the butter and melted chocolate, along with half the sugar. Mix well until smooth.

Put this mixture in spoonfuls on a double thickness of foil. Mould the chestnut mixture into the form of a long thick log and roll it up in the foil. Chill for 24 hours. (If time is short, put the log in the freezer for 2 hours until firm.)

When the roll is quite firm, remove the foil and place the chestnut log on a long dish. Cut the two ends off diagonally. Mark the top of the log with a fork to imitate the bark of a tree and dust it with the rest of the sugar. Keep in the refrigerator until ready to serve.

Variation: the chestnut mixture may be flavoured with a little rum.

CHRISTOPHINE

see Squash

CHUTNEY

see also: condiment pickles

Based on an original Indian condiment which consisted of a paste of raw spices and fruits, today's chutneys – as adapted by the British – are more like sweet pickles or relishes.

Most chutneys now consist of fruit – both fresh and dried – or vegetables cooked in vinegar with dark brown sugar, various spices and sometimes include chilli peppers (chilies). Chutneys vary in spiciness from mild to very very hot indeed. The most common main ingredient in British India was the mango, but domestically this was replaced by apples and raisins or tomatoes.

Chutneys are served to accompany curries and other Indian-inspired dishes, but also find great use in adding interest to plates of cold meat, game and hard cheeses.

CHUTNEY À L'ANANAS

Pineapple chutney

Serves 4
Preparation 10 minutes, 24 hours ahead
Cooking 18 minutes

METRIC/IMPERIAL	AMERICAN
1 apple	1 apple
5 tbsp cider vinegar	⅓ cup cider vinegar
100 g/3½ oz onions, chopped	⅔ cup chopped onions
1 can (200 g/7 oz) pineapple chunks, drained and chopped	7 oz canned pineapple chunks, drained and chopped (about ¾ cup)
100 g/3½ oz raisins	⅔ cup raisins
1 tsp grated fresh root ginger	1 tsp grated fresh ginger root
2 tsp coriander seeds	2 tsp coriander seeds
salt	salt
cayenne pepper	cayenne pepper

Peel and finely dice the apple, put it in a bowl and pour the vinegar over it. Add the onions, pineapple and raisins and cover.

Microwave for 6 minutes on High, stirring once half-way through the cooking time.

Add the ginger, coriander and salt and cayenne pepper to taste. Return to the microwave oven and cook for 12 minutes on High, stirring twice during the cooking time.

Let the chutney stand for at least 24 hours before serving to accompany cold meats, especially ham and pork.

CIDER or HARD CIDER

Cidre

see also: alcohol apple

An alcoholic beverage made from fermented apple juice, cider has been popular in parts of rural France, northern Spain and the English West Country for many centuries. British colonists also quickly established its manufacture in the 'apple states' of North America.

The quality of cider depends on the cider-maker's skill in blending various types of apple (sweet, tart or even sour) and fermenting the juice. The best French ciders are made without the addition of any sugar or yeast.

There are still and sparkling varieties and their quality can vary from a champagne-like, bone-dry brew to the extremely sweet. Alcohol content ranges from 3–5%, less than most beer and wine. In the USA, however, non-alcoholic SWEET APPLE CIDER is more readily available than alcoholic 'hard' cider.

Cider is best serve chilled (10C/50F) and is highly refreshing. In Brittany it frequently accompanies crêpes. The Normans also use it in much of their cooking, notably in *tripes à la mode de Caen* and in some classic goose dishes. Cider goes very well with pork, ham, game, especially rabbit and hare, and with some fish, especially turbot and herrings.

Cider is also made into CIDER VINEGAR which is held to have great health-giving attributes and is also excellent in salad dressings.

JAMBON AU CIDRE

Ham cooked in cider

Serves 2
Preparation 3 minutes
Cooking 5 minutes

METRIC/IMPERIAL	*AMERICAN*
200 ml/7 fl oz dry cider	*1 cup dry hard cider*
2 thick slices of country ham	*2 thick slices of country ham*
55 g/2 oz butter	*4 tbsp butter*
2 tbsp finely snipped parsley	*2 tbsp finely snipped parsley*
2 tbsp finely snipped chervil	*2 tbsp finely snipped chervil*
salt and pepper	*salt and pepper*

Pour the cider into a large sauté pan and bring it to the boil. Put the slices of ham into the pan and cook them over a high heat for 2–3 minutes.

Meanwhile, melt half the butter in a large frying pan over a moderate heat. Drain the ham and put it immediately into the frying pan. Fry for 1 minute on each side.

Place a slice of fried ham on each of 2 warmed plates, sprinkle them with the herbs and top with the remaining cold butter. Season lightly with salt and pepper and serve at once.

CILANTRO

see Coriander

CINNAMON

Cannelle

see also: spices

The dried bark of several trees in the laurel family, cinnamon is one of man's most ancient spices. Grown mostly in Sri Lanka and adjacent parts of India and China, the bark of the tree is peeled and thinly planed so that it curls into rolls, known as 'quills' or sticks. These are often pulverized into the even more familiar ground spice. The ground version does lose its flavour very rapidly, but it is much more convenient to use, especially in sweet dishes, as the sticks are prone to break up into small shards which are difficult to remove.

Cinnamon is widely used to flavour compotes, cakes, biscuits (cookies) and pastries, particularly in association with apples. It is also the principal flavouring in the making of mulled wine. Middle Eastern cooking also frequently uses it in poultry and lamb dishes.

Ground cinnamon is very useful for giving a lift to any stewed fruit dish or desserts made from *fromage blanc*. Spreading a mixture of ground cinnamon, grated nutmeg, sugar, butter and grated lemon zest on toast makes a delicious tea-time treat or snack.

BISCUITS À LA CANNELLE

Cinnamon snaps

Makes 10–12
Preparation 15 minutes
Cooking 2½ minutes

METRIC/IMPERIAL	AMERICAN
1 orange	1 orange
45 g/1½ oz butter, softened	3 tbsp butter, softened
3 tbsp thick sweetened apple purée or apple butter	3 tbsp thick, sweetened applesauce or apple butter
100 g/3½ oz flour	¾ cup flour
2 tbsp ground cinnamon	2 tbsp ground cinnamon

Either buy an organically grown, unsprayed orange or scrub it in soapy water, rinse and pat dry. Grate the zest finely and squeeze the juice.

Beat the butter and apple purée (applesauce) or apple butter together with a wooden spoon until creamy. Add the flour and mix well, then add the orange zest, 1 tablespoon of orange juice and the cinnamon.

Roll this dough out to a thickness of about 3 mm/⅛ in, then cut it into 10–12 rounds using a pastry cutter. Arrange them in the microwave on a piece of greaseproof or parchment paper.

Cover with a piece of paper towel and place an inverted dish on top. Microwave on High for 2½ minutes. Leave to stand for 5 minutes, then turn them out on a wire rack to cool.
Note: do not be tempted to increase the cooking time. The snaps should be soft on removal from the oven; they will harden as they cool.

CITRUS FRUITS

A family of fruits including bergamot, citron, clementines, grapefruit, lemons, limes, mandarin oranges, oranges, Seville (bitter) oranges and tangerines, the term also embraces hybrids, such as satsumas and tangelos, and relatives such as the kumquat. Of Asian origin, citrus fruits have now spread worldwide and are grown mostly in Mediterranean countries and in the United States.

Choose fruit with close-grained, shiny skins; reject any that are moist or slimy. If using the zest, buy organically grown, unsprayed or unwaxed fruit or scrub the peel several times with hot soapy water and rinse well.

The perfect winter fruit, citrus keep well and are rich in vitamin C and minerals such as potassium. Their acid tanginess makes them ideal for marmalades, as well as for use in cakes and pastries. They also work well in sauces for use with fatty meats such as pork and duck.

The candied or crystallized fruit or peel is also a popular ingredient in baking, desserts and confectionery.

see also:
grapefruit
jams, etc
kumquat
lemon
lime
orange
zest

CIVET

This game stew is simmered in red wine, usually with bacon and small onions, and thickened at the end of cooking with the animal's blood or with pig's blood. Certain fish and shellfish are also cooked in this manner, using the roe or coral to thicken the sauce.

see also:
tuna

CIVET DE LIÈVRE

Jugged hare

Serves 6
Preparation 25 minutes, 24 hours ahead
Cooking about 2¼ hours

METRIC/IMPERIAL	AMERICAN
1 hare (with its liver and blood), skinned and gutted and cut into pieces	1 hare (with its liver and blood), skinned, drawn and cut into pieces
1 tbsp vinegar	1 tbsp vinegar
1 bottle (750 ml/27 fl oz) red wine	1 bottle (75 cl) red wine
2 tbsp oil	2 tbsp oil
2 onions	2 onions
2 cloves	2 cloves
1 carrot, coarsely chopped	1 carrot, coarsely chopped
2 garlic cloves, chopped	2 garlic cloves, chopped
1 tsp cracked black pepper	1 tsp cracked black pepper
bouquet garni	bouquet garni
flour	flour
	1½ tbsp lard

25 g/¾ oz lard
140 g/5 oz streaky bacon, cut into strips
100 ml/3½ fl oz crème fraîche or whipping cream
salt and pepper

5 oz bacon, cut into strips
½ cup crème fraîche or whipping cream
salt and pepper

Pour the hare's blood into a bowl, add the vinegar and the hare's liver, cover and set aside in a cool place.

Put the pieces of hare in a large bowl and add the wine and oil. Peel and slice one of the onions; peel the second onion and stud it with the cloves. Add these to the bowl with the carrot, garlic, pepper and bouquet garni. Leave to marinate overnight in a cool place.

The next day, drain the pieces of hare, wipe them dry and dust with flour. Boil the marinade vigorously in a pan for 10 minutes.

Heat the lard in a flameproof casserole over a moderate heat and brown the bacon in it. Add the pieces of hare and cook them until golden brown, turning them frequently. Lower the heat, add the marinade and all its ingredients, cover the casserole and cook gently for 2 hours.

Blend the hare's liver and blood in a food processor and mix in the cream.

When cooking is finished, drain the pieces of hare and arrange them in a warmed, deep serving dish. Pour the blood and cream mixture into the casserole, stirring continuously, and cook for 6–7 minutes without letting the sauce boil. Strain the sauce and pour it over the pieces of hare. Serve very hot.

CLAM

see also:
mussel
oyster
shellfish

A large family of bivalve molluscs, there are thought to be about 50 species of clam all over the world which are commonly eaten.

The CARPET SHELL CLAM or *palourde* and the WARTY VENUS or *praire* are perhaps the most gastronomically important in Europe. The former, also known as *vongola nera* by the Italians, is the classic ingredient in clam sauce for pasta. The latter is prized in France, where it is treated almost as reverently as the oyster. It is common in British waters, but is almost totally overlooked locally as a foodstuff.

The North Americans, on the other hand, make the most of a rich supply of clams and their HARD- OR ROUND-SHELL CLAM was even introduced into French waters early this century. Chowder, a clam soup made either with tomatoes and potatoes (Manhattan) or with hot milk (New England), is now an international favourite.

Fresh clams should be cleaned like mussels, scrubbing the shells and pulling off any beards or clinging matter. Any open clams should be discarded. The clams should then be covered with salt water and left for at least 3 or 4 hours to rinse themselves clean of any grit.

To be eaten raw, they must be opened carefully like oysters, using an appropriate knife to sever the muscles at either end of the shell. Care should be taken to hold the clam curved shell downwards in order to preserve the juices.

If the clams are to be cooked, a few minutes over a high heat will cause the shells to open. They are usually grilled or steamed, and are delicious with garlic or herb butter. Raw, they are best served plain, as even lemon juice will mask their subtle flavour.

Cans of shelled clams are a boon for making chowders or pasta sauces.

PRAIRES FARCIES

Stuffed clams

Serves 6
Preparation 25 minutes
Cooking about 15 minutes

METRIC/IMPERIAL
2 kg/4½ lb large clams, cleaned
125 g/4½ oz butter, cut into small pieces
3 garlic cloves, chopped
bunch of parsley, chopped
1 thick slice of stale white bread, crusts removed
salt and pepper

AMERICAN
4½ lb medium-size hardshell clams, cleaned
9 tbsp butter, cut into small pieces
3 garlic cloves, chopped
bunch of parsley, chopped
1 thick slice of stale white bread, crusts removed
salt and pepper

Preheat the oven to 220C/425F/gas 7.

Put the clams in a large saucepan over a high heat. Remove them after 5 minutes, or as soon as all the shells have opened. Put the butter in a bowl with the garlic and parsley and mash with a fork until smooth. Season with salt and pepper. Crumble the bread into the butter and mix well.

Discard the flat shell from each clam. Spoon the stuffing smoothly over the clams in their curved half shells. Arrange the clams in an ovenproof dish. Bake for 10–12 minutes or until golden brown. Serve immediately.

SOUPE AUX PALOURDES

Manhattan clam chowder

Serves 4
Preparation 25 minutes
Cooking about 25 minutes

METRIC/IMPERIAL	AMERICAN
1 kg/2¼ lb large clams, cleaned	2¼ lb chowder clams, cleaned
45 g/1½ oz butter	3 tbsp butter
2 onions, chopped	2 onions, chopped
bunch of parsley, chopped	bunch of parsley, chopped
sprig of thyme, crumbled	sprig of thyme, crumbled
1 can (400 g/14 oz) of tomatoes	14-oz can tomatoes (about 2 cups)
4 potatoes, peeled and diced	4 potatoes, peeled and diced
salt and pepper	salt and pepper
4 salt crackers, to serve (optional)	4 salt crackers, to serve (optional)

Open the clams, being careful to save the juice. Filter and reserve it and chop the clams.

Melt the butter in a saucepan and lightly brown the onions in it. Add the chopped herbs, the tomatoes with half of the juice from the can and the clam juice. Bring to the boil.

Add the chopped clams and diced potatoes, lower the heat and cook for 20 minutes. Taste and adjust the seasoning. Pour into a hot soup tureen or warmed individual bowls. Crumble the crackers on top, if using, and serve.

CLARIFICATION OR CLEARING

see also:
aspic
butter
consommé
stock

These terms are used to describe the removal of cloudiness or impurities from a liquid – or even some solids, especially fats such as butter.

Most commonly clarification, say of syrups or fruit and vegetables juices, is achieved by filtration through paper, muslin or cheesecloth.

Fats are clarified by melting them, and either straining or skimming off impurities.

Stocks and other cooking liquids are usually clarified to make consommés and aspics by first skimming off all traces of fat and then adding beaten egg whites, which coagulate on being heated and trap the particles which make the liquid cloudy. When the clarified stock is to be used for consommé, the egg white is usually added with some finely chopped lean beef, for beef stock, or chicken giblets, for chicken stock, which both aids the clarification process and strengthens the flavour.

BOUILLON CLARIFIÉ

Clarified chicken stock or consommé

Makes about 1.5 l/2½ pt/1½ qt
Preparation 20 minutes, plus chilling
Cooking 4½ hours

METRIC/IMPERIAL	AMERICAN
1 small chicken, together with the giblets	1 small chicken (with giblets)
1 large onion, finely chopped	1 large onion, finely chopped
1 leek, trimmed and finely chopped	1 leek, trimmed and finely chopped
1 carrot, finely chopped	1 carrot, finely chopped
1 stalk of celery, trimmed and finely chopped	1 stick of celery, trimmed and finely chopped
bouquet garni	bouquet garni
1 calves' foot or veal knuckle (optional)	1 calves' foot or veal shank (optional)
115 g/¼ lb chicken livers, finely chopped	¼ lb chicken livers, finely chopped
1 very fresh egg	1 very fresh egg
salt and pepper	salt and pepper

Combine all the ingredients except the egg and chopped livers in a stockpot. Add water to cover and bring to the boil.

Let the stock simmer very gently for 4 hours, skimming it from time to time. Strain it and chill until it is cold, then remove the congealed fat from the top.

Separate the egg, reserving the shell. Beat the white lightly and mix it with the chopped liver. Add this mixture with the lightly crushed egg shell to the stock and bring it to just below the boil, stirring continuously. Lower the heat and let it simmer very gently, so that the boiling is barely perceptible, for 25 minutes.

Filter the stock very carefully through a piece of muslin or cheesecloth.

Notes: the chicken meat may be used for fricassees, croquettes etc, or to fill vols-au-vent (patty shells).

The calves' foot or veal knuckle (shank) will add extra flavour and natural gelatine to the stock. The egg yolk may be used in thickening sauces or making custards.

To make a beef consommé, replace the chicken and chicken livers with 1.8 kg/4 lb chopped shin of beef (beef shank) on the bone and 170 g/6 oz lean chopped beef respectively.

CLOVE

Clou de girofle

see also:
cinnamon
marinade
pickles
spices

The sun-dried buds of a tall, evergreen tree which grows near the sea in the Far East and in coastal areas in the Indian Ocean, cloves are one of the most common spices. Their warm piquancy is best used subtly as a background flavour, as it can too easily swamp the taste of a dish. The flavour of cloves is often used in tandem with that of cinnamon, especially in mulled wine and apple dishes.

Hams to be glazed and roasted are often studded with cloves, adding decoration as well as flavour. Onions used in the making of sauces and stews may be studded with 1 or 2 cloves. Cloves are also used whole or crushed to flavour marinades and pickles. Whole or crushed cloves are a popular flavouring in preserved fruits and a little ground cloves is common in pastries made with honey.

COCKTAIL

see also:
alcohol
fruit juices

Apart from being the term used to describe various mixed alcoholic beverages, a cocktail in the culinary sense may also be a cold hors d'oeuvre, generally made from shellfish or raw vegetables. These are usually dressed with a flavoured mayonnaise or cream sauce. Such cocktails are normally served in individual bowls or tall glasses, on a bed of shredded lettuce or other salad greens.

Fruit cocktails, made from an assortment of chopped fresh fruit, and frequently dressed with Kirsch or fruit liqueur, are also a popular dessert or first course.

COCKTAIL DE CREVETTES

Shrimp or prawn cocktail

Serves 4
Preparation 20 minutes

METRIC/IMPERIAL	AMERICAN
200 ml/7 fl oz mayonnaise	1 cup mayonnaise
1 garlic clove, finely chopped	1 garlic clove, minced
1 tsp paprika	1 tsp paprika
2 tbsp Dijon mustard	2 tbsp Dijon mustard
2 tbsp chopped flat-leaved parsley	2 tbsp chopped flat-leaf parsley
bunch of watercress	bunch of watercress
24 large shelled cooked prawns	24 large peeled cooked shrimp
4 large lemon slices, to garnish	4 large lemon slices, to garnish

Chill 4 serving dishes.

In a bowl, mix together the mayonnaise, garlic, paprika, mustard and parsley. Chill.

Line the serving bowls with the watercress and put 6 prawns (shrimp) in each bowl. Pour the well-chilled sauce over them.

Cut the lemon slices from the edge to their centre and twist to form butterflies. Place one on the edge of each bowl. Serve well chilled.

Variations: substitute 450 g/1 lb flaked crab meat for the prawns (shrimp). Garnish, if wished, with tomato and/or avocado slices.

see also: chocolate

COCOA

Cacao

Made from the cocoa bean, like chocolate, cocoa is the result of a process which presses out the cocoa butter and treats this residue with alkalis to produce a powder which mixes readily in liquids, such as milk. Cocoa is thus a very convenient means of making a chocolate-flavoured drink and adding this flavour in cooking, especially for cakes and pastries.

Pure cocoa powder, which has no added sugar, should not be confused with the substance used as a beverage and generally called DRINKING OR HOT CHOCOLATE powder, which is a mixture of cocoa, dry milk and sugar.

Unsweetened cocoa powder contains 325 calories per 100 g/3½ oz.

MERINGUES AU CACAO

Cocoa meringues

Makes 10 double meringues
Preparation 35 minutes
Cooking 1 hour

METRIC/IMPERIAL	*AMERICAN*
2 egg whites	*2 egg whites*
100 g/3½ oz caster sugar	*½ cup superfine sugar*
1 tsp cornflour	*1 tsp cornstarch*
2 tbsp unsweetened cocoa powder	*2 tbsp unsweetened cocoa powder*
75 g/2½ oz butter	*5 tbsp butter*
45 g/1½ oz icing sugar	*6½ tbsp confectioners' sugar*

Preheat the oven to 110C/230F/gas ¼.

Place the egg whites and caster (superfine) sugar in a bowl set over a pan of gently boiling water or in a bain-marie. Whisk them until they are firm and shiny.

Remove from the heat and carefully fold in the cornflour (cornstarch) and 1 tablespoon of the cocoa. Put the mixture into a piping bag.

Grease a piece of parchment or greaseproof paper with one third of the butter and pipe 20 little meringues on it.

Bake in the oven for 1 hour. Remove the meringues from the oven, carefully take them off the paper and leave them to cool.

Soften the remaining butter and beat it in a bowl together with the icing (confectioners') sugar and the remaining cocoa. Using the butter and cocoa mixture as a filling, sandwich the meringues together in pairs.

COCONUT

Noix de coco

The fruit of the coconut palm tree, the coconut consists of a hard, fibrous shell enclosing firm, delicately flavoured white meat and delicious, milky-white juice, which remains until the nut dries out.

Nowadays fresh coconuts are less frequently seen outside the hot areas where the trees grow. They are normally opened by cracking the shell with a hammer. The juice is used as a refreshing drink and the white flesh extracted with a knife. Fresh coconuts should feel heavy for their size and it is best to buy only those in which the juices can still be heard when shaken, otherwise they may be very old.

Coconut meat is more usually sold dried and grated and is widely used in confectionery and in the making of biscuits (cookies), creams and

custards, cakes and jams. It also adds an exotic and refreshing note to savoury cooking.

Coconut cream or milk is made by steeping the flesh in boiling water, allowing it to cool and then straining away the liquid. The cream is now quite commonly available in packs in the chilled cabinets of supermarkets and is a popular ingredient in the cooking of India and South-East Asia, where it is used to flavour rice and curries and to marinate meat and poultry.

Coconut flesh is rich in fibre and minerals, but has a high fat content and calorific value: 370 calories per 100 g/3½ oz fresh and 630 calories per 100 g/3½ oz dried.

SALADE TAHITIENNE

Tahitian fish salad

Serves 2
Preparation 15 minutes, 3 hours ahead

METRIC/IMPERIAL	AMERICAN
400 g/14 oz extremely fresh fillets of sea bream, cut into small pieces	14 oz extremely fresh fillets of porgy, cut into small pieces
juice of 2 limes	juice of 2 limes
1 garlic clove, finely chopped	1 garlic clove, finely chopped
1 large onion, finely chopped	1 large onion, finely chopped
2 tomatoes, thinly sliced	2 tomatoes, thinly sliced
2 canned pineapple slices, cut into small cubes	2 canned pineapple slices, cut into small cubes
55 g/2 oz grated fresh coconut	⅔ cup freshly grated coconut meat
salt and freshly ground black pepper	salt and freshly ground black pepper

Put the fish into a bowl. Season with salt and pepper and pour the lime juice over. Add the garlic and onion, stir and marinate for 3 hours in the refrigerator.

Spoon the fish salad into 2 individual bowls, pouring just half the marinade over the fish.

Put the tomatoes and pineapple on top, sprinkle with grated coconut and some freshly ground black pepper. Serve chilled.

COD

Cabillaud

see also:
brandade
filleting
fish

A large fish, up to 1.8 m/6 ft long, cod is relatively abundant in the cold seas of the North Atlantic and was until recently one of the most common fish landed and sold in Britain. Recently, however, cod has become scarcer in the more usual fishing beds and has thus become fairly costly. Younger specimens, weighing up to about 1 kg/2¼ lb are also known as SCROD.

Cod has very fine-flavoured firm, but delicate, flesh which flakes easily when cooked. Apart from young fish up to 2 kg/4½ lb, which are sometimes available whole from September to May, cod is usually sold filleted or in steaks. Those from the part of the fish nearer the head have the better flavour. Avoid any which have any hint of yellow discoloration. Cod fillets are also commonly sold frozen, either ready-prepared in breaded pieces or simply as plain fillets, but the flavour and texture is distinctly inferior to fresh.

Whole cod is delicious plainly grilled (broiled), barbecued, roasted in the oven, or braised in wine or a court-bouillon. Fillets and steaks lend themselves to a wide variety of treatments, from steaming or poaching in milk to braising in a rich cream sauce, frying *à la meunière* or baking with a cheese gratin. The flesh of cod, however, must be cooked gently and with great care, and in the form of fillets and steaks is possibly too delicate to be grilled (broiled). It is delicious deep fried and is a favourite for the traditional British fish and chips and in fish pies and croquettes.

In the days before refrigeration dried SALT COD was a very important foodstuff and became a staple of the cuisines of Mediterranean countries in particular.

COD ROE is also quite commonly available and may be boiled or fried. It is often sold smoked, which makes a delicious appetizer, and may be used to make the Greek hors d'oeuvre *taramasalata*.

Cod is a very healthy food: it is rich in protein and minerals and has the lowest fat content of all fish (only 1%); 100 g/3½ oz contains only 68 calories.

RÔTI DE CABILLAUD

Baked cod

Serves 6
Preparation 25 minutes
Cooking 40 minutes

METRIC/IMPERIAL	AMERICAN
1 whole cod, weighing about 1.2 kg/2¾ lb, trimmed	1 whole cod, drawn weight about 2¾ lb
3 large tomatoes, thickly sliced	3 large tomatoes, thickly sliced
300 g/10 oz white button mushrooms, halved	10 oz white button mushrooms, halved
100 ml/3½ fl oz dry white wine	½ cup dry white wine
100 ml/3½ fl oz oil	½ cup oil
1 onion, finely chopped	1 onion, finely chopped
bunch of parsley, chopped	bunch of parsley, chopped
salt and pepper	salt and pepper

Preheat the oven to 220C/425F/gas 7.

Season the fish with salt and pepper and place it in a baking dish. Arrange the tomato slices and mushrooms on top. Pour over the white wine and oil. Bake for 30 minutes, basting the fish with the liquid from time to time.

Mix the chopped onion with the parsley. Sprinkle this mixture over the fish and cook for a further 10 minutes, then serve.

TRANCHES DE CABILLAUD SAUCE MOUTARDE

Cod steaks in mustard sauce

Serves 4
Preparation 25 minutes
Cooking about 25 minutes

METRIC/IMPERIAL	AMERICAN
25 g/¾ oz butter	1½ tbsp butter
1 tbsp flour	1 tbsp flour
200 ml/7 fl oz milk	1 cup milk
1 onion, coarsely chopped	1 onion, coarsely chopped
sprig of thyme	sprig of thyme
4 tbsp Dijon mustard	¼ cup Dijon mustard
juice of 1 lemon	juice of 1 lemon
4 cod steaks, each weighing about 225–300 g/8–10 oz	4 cod steaks, each weighing about 8–10 oz
salt and pepper	salt and pepper

Melt the butter in a small pan over a moderate heat, sprinkle the flour into it and stir for 2 minutes. Add the milk and bring just to the boil, whisking constantly. Lower the heat and add the onion and the thyme. Season with salt and pepper, cover and simmer for 10 minutes.

Strain the sauce into another pan, add the mustard, adjust seasoning if necessary and keep the sauce hot.

Fill a large pan with water and add the lemon juice. Bring the water to the boil. Lower the cod steaks into the boiling water, reduce the heat and poach very gently for 8 minutes.

Drain the pieces of fish well and serve them coated with the mustard sauce, accompanied by boiled new potatoes.

Note: alternatively the fish may be cooked in the milk with the onion, thyme and seasonings and the strained cooking liquid added to the flour and butter roux to make the sauce. The sauce is then flavoured with the mustard and more lemon juice and seasoning to taste.

COFFEE
Café

Made from the seeds of the coffee tree, which originated in the Middle East but is now grown in many tropical countries, coffee has been a popular beverage since the fifteenth century.

There are two main categories of coffee bean. ARABICA is mild and aromatic and is grown in Brazil, Arabia, Mexico, Costa Rica and Colombia. ROBUSTA coffee contains twice as much caffeine and yields a more full-bodied but bitter drink. It is mostly grown in the Ivory Coast and Angola.

The seed pods or 'cherries' of the tree are first allowed to ferment. The outside pulp is then washed away to reveal the beans. These 'green' beans are then dried and roasted to develop the characteristic flavour.

For the best flavour, buy freshly roasted beans in small quantities, since they tend to lose their flavour within a couple of weeks. Coffee should be kept in a cool place in a hermetically sealed container, as it readily turns rancid if exposed to air. Coffee is also sold ready-ground, but the fugitive natural flavouring oils are lost within a matter of hours after grinding. Many 'instant' coffees are now on the market, and some of the freeze-dried varieties have fairly distinguished aromas and tastes and make excellent culinary flavourings.

Most coffees sold are blends to achieve a good mixture of flavour, strength and acidity. Coffee sold and labelled as arabica must contain only that variety, which may include MOCHA or BOURBON for choice flavour, COLOMBIA for mildness or HAITI for body, for example. If sold without such a label it will either be a robusta or a more expensive mixture of arabica and robusta.

To make perfect coffee it is wisest to use still bottled water, with the minimum of mineral salts as the chlorine in tap water can spoil the flavour of coffee. A porcelain, glass or earthenware coffee pot is preferable to a metallic one, as metal affects the flavour. The water should be just below boiling point when poured over the freshly ground coffee, and the coffee itself should be served hot, not scalding.

The caffeine in coffee is a potent heart stimulant, and can be beneficial in moderation, not more than 25 g/¾ oz of caffeine per day. One average cup of arabica provides about 8 g/¼ oz of caffeine, while a cup of robusta contains about 15 g/½ oz. For many people, drinking coffee later than about 5.00 pm can affect sleep. 'Decaffeinated' coffees are sold in bean form, whole or ground, or as instant granules, and contain not more than 0.1% of caffeine.

After the introduction of coffee to Europe at the end of the 17th century, coffee houses flourished to meet the great demand. Coffee quickly became the favoured beverage for breakfast in many countries, and French high society introduced the custom of serving coffee after meals. The French favour *café au lait* (served with a pot of warmed milk) during the day; the Italians have developed the double-strength *espresso* and the steam-frothed *capuccino*; and the Greeks and Turks take it in the highly concentrated Arab fashion.

As a flavouring in desserts, cakes and confectionery, use coffee essence, very strong, freshly brewed or filtered coffee (6 tablespoons of freshly ground coffee beans to 200 ml/7 fl oz/1 cup of water) or good instant coffee (1 tablespoon with a few drops of water). The flavour of coffee marries well with that of chocolate, nuts, citrus fruit and cream.

BOUCHÉES BRÉSILIENNES

Brazilian candies

Makes 12–15
Preparation 10 minutes
Cooking 5 minutes, 1 hour ahead

METRIC/IMPERIAL	*AMERICAN*
400 g/14 oz caster sugar	*1¾ cups superfine sugar*
1 tbsp honey	*1 tbsp honey*
1 small cup (100 ml/3½ fl oz) of strong coffee, preferably a full-bodied Mocha	*½ cup strong coffee, preferably a full-bodied Mocha*
45 g/1½ oz butter, cut into small pieces	*3 tbsp butter, cut into small pieces*
75 g/2½ oz shelled Brazil nuts, coarsely chopped	*½ cup shelled Brazil nuts, coarsely chopped*
groundnut oil, for greasing	*peanut oil, for greasing*

Lightly oil a 20 cm/8 in square cake pan.

Place the sugar, honey and coffee in a small, heavy-bottomed pan over a low heat. Heat gently, stirring with a wooden spoon.

When the sugar has all dissolved, remove the pan from the heat and add the butter a few pieces at a time. Do not stir it in.

Add the Brazil nuts to the mixture, stirring vigorously.

Pour the mixture into the prepared cake pan, smooth the surface with a palette knife and allow to cool completely.

Cut into small squares and serve with coffee.

COLOURING AGENTS

Various additives are used in the food industry, principally in the areas of confectionery, pastry-making, dairy products and the manufacture of drinks, to give products a more appetizing appearance. For example, pistachio ice cream with no added colouring is white, not green. This practice is by no means new; in the Middle Ages butter was given a richer golden colour using marigold flowers, and saffron, spinach and caramel have also been used for centuries to colour food.

The laws of many nations require the listing of the almost 100 common colouring agents (in Europe, food additives E100 to E199) on food packaging and also limit their concentrations.

About thirty of these colouring agents are from natural sources and include:

CURCUMINE YELLOW (E100), extracted from turmeric root and used in curry powders, mustards, margarines, processed cheeses and certain drinks.

COCHINEAL and CARMINE (E120), made from crushed insects and used in confectionery and cake making.

CHLOROPHYLL GREEN (E140), which is added to canned vegetables, soups, condiments and cooking oils.

BEETROOT RED (E162), which is common in canned and dried packet soups.

VIOLET/PURPLE (E163), extracted from aubergines (eggplant), red cabbage and blackcurrants and used in ice cream, confectionery, syrups and certain charcuterie products.

The artificial colouring agents are mostly coal-tar dyes and include:

TARTRAZINE (E102), which is yellow and is used to colour dried fish and soft drinks. It is being phased out because of its reputed effect on potentially hyperactive children.

CARMOISINE, AMARANTH and PONCEAU (E122, E 123 and E124 respectively), all of them red.

ERYTHROSINE RED (E127), which also carries a risk of allergy.

BRILLIANT BLACK (E151), the use of which is still under review in several nations and which has only temporary authorization in some.

Several colourings may also be used in combination: E151, E122 and E102 to colour black lumpfish roe, for example.

COMPOTE

see also: fruit jams, etc

Like a fresh un-set jam, compotes are preparations of fresh or dried fruit cooked, either whole or in pieces, in sugar syrup. In general, however, they do not have the lengthy keeping qualities of jams. Compotes may be made from most fruits and are frequently made using combinations of various fruits. They are also commonly flavoured with vanilla, cinnamon, orange or lemon zest, ground nuts or crystallized fruit.

Compotes are usually served as a dessert, either slightly warm or chilled, with chantilly cream, grated coconut or vanilla sugar. They may also be used as a tart or pie filling, if of a sufficiently thick consistency.

A microwave oven is extremely useful for making compotes from dried fruit, as there is no need for lengthy soaking of the fruit.

In recent years compotes of vegetables, especially onions, garlic and shallots, have become a popular feature of modern cuisine. Such preparations are often called MARMELADES when the ingredients are reduced to a pulp.

The term compote is also used for savoury dishes, often of game, which are gently cooked for a long time so that the main ingredients are reduced to a pulp-like consistency.

COMPOTE AUX QUATRE FRUITS

Four-fruit compote

Serves 6
Preparation 20 minutes
Cooking about 1 hour, 4 hours ahead

METRIC/IMPERIAL	AMERICAN
3 apples	*3 apples*
3 pears	*3 pears*
juice of 1 lemon	*juice of 1 lemon*
750 ml/27 fl oz apple juice	*3¼ cups apple juice*
55 g/2 oz caster sugar	*5 tbsp superfine sugar*
12 apricots, blanched, peeled, halved and stoned	*12 apricots, blanched, peeled, halved and pitted*
450 g/1 lb mirabelle plums, halved and	*1 lb mirabelles or other small, sweet plums, halved and pitted*

stoned	*1 cinnamon stick*
1 cinnamon stick	*½ cup sweetened apricot purée or jam*
115 g/4 oz sweetened apricot purée or jam	

Peel the apples and pears, then quarter them and remove the cores. Sprinkle with lemon juice.

Pour the apple juice into a large pan with the sugar and bring to the boil. Add the apricots and poach them gently for 10 minutes, then remove them with a slotted spoon and put them in a glass serving bowl. Poach the pears in the same syrup for 10 minutes and transfer them to the bowl. Repeat the operation with the mirabelles.

Poach the apples with the cinnamon stick in the same syrup for 20 minutes. Remove them with a slotted spoon and add to the bowl.

Carefully mix the fruit in the bowl. Remove the cinnamon stick from the syrup and stir in the apricot purée or jam. Reduce the syrup over a slightly lower heat and then pour it over the fruit. Chill until ready to serve.

COMPOTE D'OIGNONS

Onion compote

Serves 4
Preparation 20 minutes
Cooking about 40 minutes

METRIC/IMPERIAL	AMERICAN
450 g/1 lb baby onions	*1 lb small onions*
15 g/½ oz butter	*1 tbsp butter*
1 tbsp oil	*1 tbsp oil*
3 tbsp caster sugar	*3 tbsp superfine sugar*
100 ml/3½ fl oz red wine	*½ cup red wine*
3 tbsp vinegar	*3 tbsp vinegar*
salt and pepper	*salt and pepper*

Bring a pan of water to the boil and plunge the onions into it. Bring the water quickly back to the boil, then immediately drain the onions.

Heat the butter and oil in a heavy-bottomed saucepan over a moderate heat. Put the onions in it to brown. Sprinkle them with the sugar, mix well and let them caramelize for several minutes. Add the wine and the vinegar and season with salt and pepper.

Let the onions cook very gently, covered, for about 30 minutes, then add a little more pepper. The cooking liquid should be thick and syrupy. Remove from the heat and leave to cool.

This onion compote will keep for several days in the refrigerator. It is delicious served with pork chops.

COMPOTE DE LAPEREAU AUX POIVRONS

Compote of young rabbit with sweet peppers

Serves 5
Preparation 10 minutes
Cooking about 50 minutes

METRIC/IMPERIAL	AMERICAN
4 tbsp olive oil	*4 tbsp olive oil*
2 kg/4½ lb green sweet peppers, deseeded and very thinly sliced	*4½ lb green sweet peppers, deseeded and very thinly sliced*
1 young rabbit, dressed weight about 1.2 kg/2¾ lb, cut into pieces	*1 young rabbit, dressed and drawn weight about 2¾ lb, cut into pieces*
150 ml/¼ pt dry white wine	*⅔ cup dry white wine*
salt and pepper	*salt and pepper*

Heat half the oil in a saucepan over a moderate heat and cook the peppers in it gently, stirring frequently, for about 30 minutes until they are soft. Season them with salt and pepper.

Meanwhile, heat the rest of the oil in a flameproof casserole and brown the pieces of rabbit in it over a low heat, turning them frequently. Add the sweet pepper compote to the rabbit pieces, along with the white wine and bring just to boiling point.

Lower the heat, cover and simmer for 15 minutes. Serve straight from the casserole.

CONDIMENT

It is generally held that seasoning is done during cooking, while condiments are those substances served at the table to stimulate the palate and accentuate the flavour of food.

Condiments are usually salty, spicy and piquant and may also serve as a preservative.

see also:
anchovy
chutney
couscous
horseradish
mustard
pepper
peppers
pickles
salt
seasoning
vinegar

The simplest are, of course, salt, pepper, vinegar and mustard. Apart from these, there is a wide variety of raw and cooked preparations, from chopped raw onion, gherkins (pickled cucumbers) and horseradish to the many bottled sauces available commercially. Interestingly, sweet fruit jellies, such as those served with poultry and game, are not regarded strictly as condiments.

Many preparations intended as condiments, such as Tabasco and Worcestershire sauces, have also established themselves as popular flavouring ingredients in the kitchen. Among the most important of these (not dealt with elsewhere in this book) are:

ANCHOVY ESSENCE, a preparation of pounded anchovy fillets in brine or vinegar, is a descendant of the ancient Roman condiment *garum*. Anchovy essence was once used in a wide variety of savoury dishes, but is now more limited to giving strength of flavour to fish sauces and pies. However, used sparingly it can give an indefinable quality to many meat and vegetable dishes.

HARISSA is a North African condiment which has become widely used in France. It is a purée of chilli peppers and garlic in oil, flavoured with various herbs, particularly coriander. It is extremely hot and should therefore be used – and handled – with great care. It is usually diluted before use as a condiment, for instance, with a little stock when served as an accompaniment to couscous, or added to soups in small quantities as a seasoning.

MUSHROOM KETCHUP was once a very common condiment and ingredient in British cooking, especially with meat and fish dishes and in traditional meat pies. After a period of obscurity its dark and earthy flavour is enjoying a revival, particularly in sauces for roasted and grilled meat.

NUOC-NAM is a Vietnamese condiment which has become very popular in France. Made by macerating fish in brine, it is often used to replace salt in cooking and is also set on the table in a small flask and used as an additional seasoning. It has a strong taste, especially when heated. It may be mixed with lemon juice or red chilli pepper or garnished with thinly sliced onion. It works extremely well in salad dressings or in flavouring meat stews. It is perhaps best known and most widely used as a complement to plain boiled rice.

TOMATO KETCHUP is perhaps the most common bottled sauce in Britain and North America. Its sweet piquancy is popular with most meat dishes, especially grills. A good quality tomato ketchup may also be used like tomato purée (paste), to flavour sauces and stews, etc, and gives a good flavour to meat loaves.

WALNUT KETCHUP is made from green (unripe) walnuts and has remained very popular through the years in parts of rural northern England. It works particularly well in cheese, fish and poultry dishes, and can also be used to great effect in salad dressings.

All condiments should be used circumspectly as their strong flavours may easily swamp a dish. They usually have a very high salt content and bottled sauces also often have a very high 'hidden' sugar content and are therefore high in calories.

CONFECTIONER'S CUSTARD

see Creams and custards

CONFIT

see also:
cassoulet
duck
goose

French country cooking, particularly in the regions of the southwest, makes a practice of preserving meat and poultry, especially pork, turkey, goose and duck, by cooking pieces of it in its own fat, and preserving them in jars under a sealing layer of the congealed fat. Such confits will keep for several months and the process gives the meat a fine, rich flavour. It is also regarded as one of the best ways of cooking goose as it tenderizes what is normally very tough meat which does not roast well. Even if the entire contents of a jar are not used after opening, whatever remains will continue to keep well as long as it is well covered in fat.

Confit can be served hot with a vegetable accompaniment or cold with salads. Excess preserving fat should always be removed and the confit cooked in the layer of fat which immediately surrounds it. The remaining fat is very useful in cooking as it can add a great deal of flavour to stews and casseroles. It is usual to split each piece of confit between 2 people.

Confit is used in the preparation of many hearty soups and in the classic bean stew *cassoulet*. It also goes well in most stews and works well with mushrooms, white haricot beans, cabbage or lentils. Finely chopped confit can also be added with good effect to a salad of bitter leaves, such as dandelion, chicory (Belgian endive) or white cabbage.

Obviously, confits have a very high fat content, particularly those made from goose and duck, as both are very fatty meats.

CONFIT SARLADAIS

Preserved duck with potatoes

Serves 6
Preparation 20 minutes
Cooking about 40 minutes

METRIC/IMPERIAL	AMERICAN
3 pieces of preserved duck (confit de canard)	3 pieces of preserved duck (confit de canard)
4 garlic cloves, chopped	4 garlic cloves, chopped
bunch of flat-leaved parsley, chopped	bunch of flat-leaf parsley, chopped
800 g/1¾ lb potatoes, peeled and diced	1¾ lb potatoes, peeled and diced
salt and pepper	salt and pepper

Open the jar of preserved duck and place it in a bain-marie over a low heat. Leave it in the bain-marie until the fat has melted.

Mix the garlic with half of the parsley.

When the duck fat has melted, remove the duck pieces from the jar and put them in a strainer over a bowl to drain.

Put 4 tablespoons of the fat into a flameproof casserole, heat it and add the diced potatoes. Brown them over a high heat for 10 minutes.

Season the potatoes with salt and pepper. Moisten them with 200 ml/7 fl oz/1 cup of water, cover and cook for 10 minutes. Add the garlic and parsley *persillade* and continue cooking, uncovered, for 10 minutes.

Meanwhile, heat a frying pan and put the pieces of duck into it. Cook them gently until golden brown, turning them frequently.

Remove the duck from the pan, drain it and then cut each portion into three. Divide the potatoes between 6 very hot plates, place the duck pieces on top, scatter the rest of the chopped parsley over and serve.

CONGER EEL

Congre

see also:
eel
fish

A sea fish common in the English Channel and along the European Atlantic coast, the conger is a large (0.5–1.5 m/1½–5 ft) relative of the common eel, sometimes known as 'sea eel', with firm but rather tasteless flesh. It is most plentiful in the winter months.

Because it lacks the oiliness and rich, delicate flavour of eel, its main use is in soups, such as *bouillabaisse* and *bourride*, and stews. However, pieces cut between the middle of the body and the head, which contain fewer bones than the tail, which should be avoided, may be roasted or braised with vegetables as you would a piece of meat. Conger is popular in Spanish cooking, where it is prepared with a great deal of garlic.

RAGOÛT DE CONGRE AUX PETITS POIS

Conger eel stew with peas

Serves 4–5
Preparation 15 minutes
Cooking about 50 minutes

METRIC/IMPERIAL	AMERICAN
150 g/5½ oz butter, cut into pieces	11 tbsp butter, cut into pieces
1 kg/2¼ lb conger eel, skinned and boned and cut into chunks	2¼ lb conger eel, skinned, boned and cut into chunks
2 onions, finely chopped	2 onions, finely chopped
1 garlic clove, finely chopped	1 garlic clove, finely chopped
3 shallots, finely chopped	3 shallots, finely chopped
1 tbsp Cognac	1 tbsp Cognac
1 kg/2¼ lb fresh peas, shelled	2¼ lb fresh young peas, shelled
salt and pepper	salt and pepper

Heat the butter in a large, flameproof casserole over a moderate heat and lightly brown the pieces of eel, turning them frequently.

Add the onions, garlic and shallots. Continue to cook, stirring, until all the ingredients are lightly browned.

Moisten with 100 ml/3½ fl oz/½ cup of water and add the Cognac. Cover and simmer for 10 minutes. Add the peas and cook for a further 30 minutes.

Serve very hot accompanied by garlic bread.
To drink: a full-bodied Loire white wine, such as a Gros-Plant.

see also:
clarification
soup
stock

CONSOMMÉ

Clear soups made from meat, poultry, game or fish stock and served hot or cold at the beginning of a meal, true consommés are made from stock which has been clarified and strengthened. They may be garnished with finely chopped meat, croutons, mushroom julienne, poached eggs, shredded sorrel, tapioca or vermicelli. Simple consommés can also be made quickly by just straining stock and garnishing it with flavouring ingredients.

Consommés are highly nutritious and very easily digested, hence their traditional role in the diet of invalids.

CONSOMMÉ MADRILÈNE

Beef consommé with tomatoes and sweet peppers

Serves 6
Preparation 15 minutes
Cooking about 25 minutes

METRIC/IMPERIAL	AMERICAN
1 red sweet pepper	1 red sweet pepper
1 yellow sweet pepper	1 yellow sweet pepper
1.5 l/2½ pt clarified beef stock (see Clarification)	1½ qt clarified beef stock (see Clarification)
3 firm tomatoes, peeled, deseeded and diced	3 firm tomatoes, peeled, deseeded and diced
3 tbsp rice	3 tbsp rice
salt and pepper	salt and pepper

Char the skins of the sweet peppers under a moderate grill (broiler), turning on all sides. Rinse them under cold running water and peel off the skins. Cut them in half, remove the seeds, and chop the flesh into dice.

Pour the clarified stock into a saucepan and heat it. When it is just at boiling point, add the peppers, tomatoes and rice.

Continue to cook at a gentle simmer for 15 minutes. Adjust the seasoning and serve hot.

CONSOMMÉ AU PORTO

Simple chicken consommé with port

Serves 6
Preparation 15 minutes
Cooking 30 minutes

METRIC/IMPERIAL	AMERICAN
2 l/3½ pt chicken stock	2 qt chicken stock
25 g/¾ oz butter	1½ tbsp butter
75 g/2½ oz flaked almonds	⅔ cup slivered almonds
2 egg yolks	2 egg yolks
3 tbsp crème fraîche or whipping cream	3 tbsp crème fraîche or whipping cream
5 tbsp port	⅓ cup port wine
cayenne pepper	cayenne pepper
chopped fresh chervil, to garnish	chopped fresh chervil, to garnish
salt and pepper	salt and pepper

Pour the stock into a large saucepan and cook it gently until the volume is reduced to about 1.5 l/2½ pt/1½ quarts.

Heat the butter in a frying pan over a low heat and gently brown the almonds. Keep them hot.

Mix the egg yolks with the cream and port in a bowl. Whisk for several seconds, adding 3 tablespoons of the stock.

Pour this mixture into the stock and cook for 4 minutes, stirring continuously. Do not let it boil. Remove it from the heat, whisk it again and adjust the seasoning with a little salt and pepper and some cayenne pepper according to taste. Add the almonds and mix well.

Pour immediately into warmed soup cups and sprinkle with the chervil. Serve as hot as possible.

see also:
cakes and gâteaux
macaroon
petit four

COOKIES, CRACKERS AND BISCUITS

The British use the term 'biscuit' very generally to cover small flat baked sweet and savoury items which Americans would refer to as cookies and crackers respectively. However, the British do also use both these terms themselves, and the word 'cookie' has recently become quite current in Britain to describe softer and more chewy sweet 'biscuits'. In North America, however, 'biscuit' usually denotes what the British would call a scone.

COOKIES and SWEET BISCUITS are usually made from one of three different types of dough:

Hard or semi-hard dough, with about 70% flour, a high butter content and no eggs, is used to make *petit beurre*, shortbread and crackers.

Soft dough, made with a high proportion of egg white, is used to make items such as petits fours, *tuiles, langues de chat* and macaroons.

Liquid dough, with a small amount of fat and flour and a large proportion of water or milk, is used to make wafers.

Cookies or sweet biscuits are often flavoured with spices, nuts and dried, candied or crystallized fruit. They may also be filled or sandwiched with a flavoured cream or jam and coated with icing, jam or chocolate. They are usually served with tea or coffee, or after meals (petits fours). Soft, absorbent types are often used in the making or serving of desserts, such as charlottes and ice cream.

SAVOURY BISCUITS, OF CRACKERS, are usually spread with butter before being eaten with cheese or pâté. Some salty items, such as pretzels, are served with drinks before meals.

Cookies and biscuits readily absorb moisture from the air and quickly become soggy, so they should be kept in an airtight container.

They are a common snack in both Britain and the United States, but it should be remembered that they usually have a high sugar and fat content in relation to their weight: for instance, 1 small sweet cookie or biscuit, weighing about 8 g/¼ oz, contains about 64 calories.

COOKIES AU CHOCOLAT

Chocolate chip cookies

Makes about 40
Preparation 30 minutes
Cooking about 10 minutes

METRIC/IMPERIAL	*AMERICAN*
140 g/5 oz butter	*10 tbsp butter*
100 g/3½ oz brown sugar	*⅔ cup light brown sugar*
100 g/3½ oz caster sugar	*½ cup superfine sugar*
few drops of vanilla essence	*few drops of vanilla extract*
1 egg	*1 egg*
225 g/8 oz flour	*2 cups flour*
1 scant tsp baking powder	*1 tsp baking powder*
170 g/6 oz plain chocolate, broken into small pieces	*6 oz (1 cup) semisweet chocolate pieces*
salt	*salt*

Preheat the oven to 180C/350F/gas 4 and reserve 30 g/1 oz/2 tbsp of the butter to grease the baking sheet.

Soften the rest of the butter in a bowl with a wooden spoon and add the brown and white sugars. Beat the mixture until it is smooth and creamy.

Add the vanilla and the egg. Sift the flour with the baking powder and a pinch of salt and add it to the mixture very gradually.

Stir in the chocolate pieces but do not work the dough too much.

Put tablespoons of the dough at regular intervals on the baking sheet. Flatten them slightly with the dampened palm of the hand to form rounds with a diameter of about 4–5 cm/1½–2 in.

Put the baking sheet in the middle of the oven and bake for about 10 minutes. Remove the cookies from the oven and let them cool on the baking sheet for about 5 minutes, then remove them from the baking sheet and put them on a wire rack to cool completely.

Note: large cookies, 10 cm/4 in in diameter, may also be made in this way and baked at 160C/325F/gas 3 for about 15 minutes.

BISCUITS AU CITRON

Lemon curd cookies

Makes about 40
Preparation 25 minutes
Cooking 10 minutes, 1 hour ahead

METRIC/IMPERIAL	AMERICAN
75 g/2½ oz butter	5 tbsp butter
1 lemon	1 lemon
150 g/5½ oz caster sugar	¾ cup superfine sugar
1 egg	1 egg
175 g/6½ oz flour	1⅓ cups flour
1 jar (200 ml/7 fl oz) of lemon curd	1 cup of lemon curd
salt	salt

Preheat the oven to 180C/350F/gas 4 and grease a baking sheet with a little of the butter.

If the lemon is not organically grown and may have been sprayed or coated, scrub it in hot soapy water, rinse and pat dry. Grate the zest.

Beat the remaining butter in a bowl with a wooden spoon until soft, then add the sugar. When the mixture is smooth and white add the egg and 1 tablespoon of the lemon zest.

Sift the flour with a pinch of salt and add it gradually to the butter and sugar mixture, beating constantly. When the dough becomes too stiff to beat, add the remainder of the flour by mixing it in with the fingertips.

Roll the dough out to a thickness of about 8 mm/⅓ in. Using a pastry cutter, cut out about 40 shapes (rounds, hearts, diamonds, etc) and arrange them on the greased baking sheet. Bake them for 10 minutes.

Remove them from the oven and transfer to a wire rack to cool. Sandwich them in pairs with the lemon curd and serve at once.

CORIANDER

Coriandre

see also:
herbs
parsley
spices

An aromatic plant grown widely in warm climates, coriander is used in cooking in several different ways.

The dried seeds, which have a warm, citrus pungency, have been used as a spice in European baking for many centuries. Coriander seeds also have great powers as a preservative and are widely used in marinades and pickles. In French cuisine, anything *à la grecque* has usually been marinated in oil with coriander seeds. They are much used in Indian cooking, particularly with fish, seafood and lamb.

The leaves of the plant, also known as CILANTRO, are widely used outside Europe in the same way as parsley. Their earthy flavour is a distinct part of the background taste in much Indian, Southeast Asian and Latin American cooking, probably because it marries so well with that of the chilli pepper.

The root of the coriander plant is also a key ingredient in Thai cuisine and helps give it a great deal of its distinctive flavour.

POISSON À LA CORIANDRE

Fish with coriander

Serves 4
Preparation 20 minutes, marinating 30 minutes
Cooking about 25 minutes

METRIC/IMPERIAL	AMERICAN
4 coley, whiting, or other white fish steaks	4 pollock or other white fish steaks
2 tbsp lime juice	2 tbsp lime juice
15 black peppercorns	15 black peppercorns
2 tsp coriander seeds	2 tsp coriander seeds
4 tbsp oil	4 tbsp oil
3 small onions, finely chopped	3 small onions, finely chopped
1 tbsp Dijon mustard	1 tbsp Dijon mustard
½ tsp turmeric	½ tsp turmeric
4 tomatoes, peeled, deseeded and diced	4 tomatoes, peeled, deseeded and diced
5 tbsp chopped coriander leaves	⅓ cup chopped fresh coriander leaves (cilantro)
salt and black pepper	salt and black pepper

Put the fish steaks in a dish and sprinkle them with the lime juice and salt and pepper. Leave them to marinate in a cool place for 30 minutes.

Crush the peppercorns and coriander seeds together with a pestle in a mortar.

Heat 2 tablespoons of the oil in a sauté pan and

cook the chopped onion in it for 3–4 minutes, stirring constantly. Add the crushed peppercorns and coriander seeds, the mustard and 2 or 3 pinches of turmeric. Cook, stirring, for 3 minutes. Add the tomatoes and half the fresh coriander leaves. Simmer for 3–4 minutes, then transfer the contents of the pan to a bowl.

Heat the rest of the oil in the same pan and add the fish. Return the tomato and coriander mixture to the pan. Cover and simmer for about 10 minutes.

Arrange on a warmed serving dish and sprinkle with the rest of the coriander leaves.

CORN OR MAIZE

Maïs

see also:
cereals and grains
cornflour or cornstarch
corn syrup
semolina

The term corn was once used to describe any type of grain, but increasingly the American usage of the term to describe maize seems to prevail. Maize is native to the Americas and was introduced to Europe from there. It is now widely grown all over the world.

There are two principal types of maize which are of culinary importance:

GRAIN MAIZE is yellow or white with small cobs and is primarily used as an animal foodstuff, but some varieties are ground into CORNMEAL and used to make soft, cake-like breads, cakes, fritters and CORN FLAKES and other breakfast cereals. Cornmeal, however, does not have the gluten necessary to make leavened bread and lacks some of the amino acids in which other grains are so rich. It has, therefore, not become a dietary staple outside North America, although in the Mediterranean countries it is used to make porridge-like dishes such as the Italian *polenta*.

SWEET CORN, OR CORN ON THE COB, with a larger cob than grain maize and softer pale yellow or white kernels, is widely used as a vegetable. Fresh corn is available from mid to late summer, but the season is expanding. Try to buy ears of corn which still have a full sheath of pale green leaves, indicating freshness. If boiling corn on the cob, do not salt the water or the kernels will become tough; it may also be steamed, grilled (broiled) or cooked in the microwave oven, and then served with butter and salt and pepper or other seasonings. Kernels cut from the cob are available canned or frozen and make a useful vegetable accompaniment and an excellent addition to mixed salads.

Fresh BABY CORN ON THE COB, which may be eaten in its entirety, is increasingly available. It is delicious sautéed, and can give great flavour and crunch to mixed salads.

POPCORN is made from a particular variety of corn kernels, which are removed from the cob and then dried. When heated in a little oil the grains burst, forming soft, white, light puffs which can be salted or caramelized in sugar and butter to make delicious snacks. HOMINY, an American Indian creation, is also made from dried corn kernels, and when ground it becomes grits, so popular in the American South.

CORN OIL, which is polyunsaturated, is widely used in cooking. It supports high temperatures for frying and is a good neutral oil for cold sauces and salad dressings.

Corn is rich in protein and provides 390 calories per 100 g/3½ oz. Corn flakes and popcorn preserve all the goodness of fresh corn because the germ is retained and none of the polyunsaturated fats are lost.

popcorn

ear of corn

ÉPIS DE MAÏS AU NATUREL

Baked corn on the cob

Serves 4
Preparation 15 minutes
Cooking 35 minutes

METRIC/IMPERIAL	AMERICAN
4 fresh corn cobs, still wrapped in their leaves	*4 fresh ears of corn, still wrapped in their husks*
slightly salted butter, to serve	*lightly salted butter, to serve*
freshly ground black pepper, to serve	*freshly ground black pepper, to serve*
sliced white bread, to serve	*sliced white bread, to serve*

Preheat the oven to 180C/350F/gas 4.

Spread the leaves slightly apart in order to remove the silky fibres from each ear of corn cob, then fold the leaves around the corn again and secure the ends with string. Soak them for 10 minutes in cold water and then drain them.

Arrange the corn in a baking dish and cook them for about 35 minutes. Remove the corn from the oven, remove the strings and strip off the leaves. Trim each end and serve very hot with slightly salted butter, freshly ground black pepper and white bread.

Note: a good way to eat corn on the cob is to spread a slice of bread with the butter, sprinkle it with the pepper then place the hot corn on the bread and roll it up. Leave it for a few seconds, then unroll it. Hold the corn at each end and nibble off the buttery kernels.

TARTELETTES AU MAÏS

Corn puddings

Serves 6
Preparation 15 minutes
Cooking about 12 minutes

METRIC/IMPERIAL	AMERICAN
4 tbsp corn oil	*4 tbsp corn oil*
100 g/3½ oz flour	*¾ cup flour*
2 eggs	*2 eggs*
500 ml/16 fl oz milk	*2 cups milk*
1 can (325 g/11 oz) sweetcorn kernels	*1½ cups corn kernels*
cayenne pepper	*cayenne pepper*
salt and pepper	*salt and pepper*

Preheat the oven to 250C/475F/gas 9 and grease 6 deep tartlet pans with half of the corn oil.

In a bowl, mix the flour and eggs. Add the remaining oil and the milk, season with salt and pepper and mix well. Set aside.

Thoroughly drain the corn, add some pepper and a pinch of cayenne but no salt.

Add the corn to the batter and mix well. Spoon this mixture into the tartlet pans, filling them about three quarters full.

Bake for about 12 minutes, then invert the cooked puddings on a warmed serving plate and serve immediately. They make a fine accompaniment to roast meat, grilled chicken, steak and duck breast.

CORNFLOUR OR CORNSTARCH

see also: corn flour sauce

Made from a liquid extracted from grain maize, cornflour or cornstarch is almost pure starch and is much finer and whiter than wheat flour, with very little taste. For this reason it is mainly used for thickening sauces and cream soups, and for making custards and very light sponge cakes. As a sauce thickener, it produces a smoother and more transparent result than wheat flour.

CORN SALAD

see Lamb's lettuce

CORN SYRUP

see also: cornflour maple syrup

The glucose in cornstarch is used to make corn syrup, which is called for in many American recipes for confectionery, frostings, desserts and cookies. Corn syrup is also used as a table syrup in much the same way as maple syrup.

see also:
court-bouillon
pastry
salmon

COULIBIACA OR KULIBIAKA

Coulibiac

True Russian coulibiaca is a pie made of fish (usually salmon) with rice, vegetables and cooked eggs, topped with *vesiga* (the dried spinal marrow of the sturgeon) entirely enclosed in pastry.

Versions of the dish with poultry and meat fillings also exist and it is now usually cooked without the use of a pie dish, although it was once traditional to cook it in fish-shaped earthenware dishes.

COULIBIAC DE SAUMON

Salmon coulibiaca

Serves 10
Preparation about 1 hour
Cooking 40 minutes

METRIC/IMPERIAL	*AMERICAN*
30 g/1 oz butter	*2 tbsp butter*
450 g/1 lb salmon steaks	*1 lb salmon steaks*
1 l/1¾ pt court-bouillon or fish stock	*1 qt court-bouillon or fish stock*
100 g/3½ oz rice	*9 tbsp rice*
300 g/10 oz frozen spinach	*10 oz frozen spinach*
300 g/10 oz mushrooms, thinly sliced	*10 oz mushrooms, thinly sliced*
3 shallots, chopped	*3 shallots, chopped*
juice of ½ lemon	*juice of ½ lemon*
800 g/1¾ lb puff pastry	*1¾ lb puff pastry*
bunch of flat-leaved parsley, chopped	*bunch of flat-leaf parsley, chopped*
bunch of chives, chopped	*bunch of chives, chopped*
4 eggs, hard boiled, shelled and halved + 1 egg yolk	*4 eggs, hard boiled, shelled and halved + 1 egg yolk*
salt and pepper	*salt and pepper*

Preheat the oven to 220C/425F/gas 7 and lightly grease a baking sheet with a little of the butter.

Put the salmon in a pan, add the court-bouillon and bring it to the boil. Poach the salmon very gently for 10 minutes. Remove the fish carefully from the court-bouillon and leave to cool.

Strain 400 ml/14 fl oz/1¾ cups of the court-bouillon into a saucepan and cook the rice in it for 20 minutes. Cook the spinach in boiling salted water as per packet instructions.

Meanwhile, melt the remaining butter in a frying pan over a low heat and sauté the mushrooms and shallots gently for about 12 minutes or until they are just softened but not browned. Season them with salt and pepper and sprinkle them with lemon juice.

Drain the spinach, pressing as much liquid out of it as possible. Drain the rice. Remove and discard the bones and skin from the cooled salmon and flake the flesh roughly with a fork.

On a floured board or work surface roll out two thirds of the puff pastry into a rectangle about 3 mm/⅛ in thick. Spread half the rice over the pastry rectangle, leaving a border about 3.5 cm/1½ in clear all around. Cover the rice with the mushroom and shallot mixture and then sprinkle over the chopped herbs. Place the flaked salmon in a layer over that, then the spinach, finally the eggs and the remaining rice.

Fold the uncovered edges of the pastry up over the filling. Roll out the rest of the pastry into a rectangle big enough to cover the filling. Moisten the edges and pinch the two pieces of pastry together securely all around the edge. Make 2 funnel holes in the top of the pastry.

Brush the top of the coulibiaca with the egg yolk. Bake for 30 minutes, and then lower the heat to 200C/400F/gas 6 and cook for a further 10 minutes. Serve the coulibiaca hot or warm, cut into thick slices.

Note: if serving hot, accompany with melted butter, or pour some into the funnel holes of the coulibiaca when it comes out of the oven.

COULIS

see also:
purée
sauce
tomato

A liquid purée of vegetables, shellfish or fruit, a coulis is either served as a sauce itself or used to enhance the flavour of a sauce or a soup. The ingredients may either be cooked or raw, but they are usually highly seasoned and their consistency can vary from fairly thick to quite fluid, depending on the intended use. A coulis may also be served hot or cold.

The most common example is tomato coulis, which is used to dress dishes of all types, but goes well with poached fish and vegetable terrines.

Fruit coulis, usually made with a red or berry fruit, is served as an accompaniment to ice creams and hot or cold fruit or cream desserts.

COULIS DE TOMATES

Fresh tomato sauce

Serves 4
Preparation 15 minutes
Cooking about 25 minutes

METRIC/IMPERIAL	*AMERICAN*
15 g/$\frac{1}{2}$ oz butter	*1 tbsp butter*
1 tbsp oil	*1 tbsp oil*
1 small onion, finely chopped	*1 small onion, finely chopped*
1 shallot, finely chopped	*1 shallot, finely chopped*
450 g/1 lb tomatoes, peeled and diced	*1 lb tomatoes, peeled and diced*
1 garlic clove, finely chopped	*1 garlic clove, finely chopped*
bouquet garni	*bouquet garni*
salt and pepper	*salt and pepper*

Heat the butter and oil in a saucepan over a low heat and cook the onion and shallot gently until softened but not browned. Add the tomatoes, garlic, bouquet garni and salt and pepper to taste and simmer, uncovered, for 15–20 minutes.

Pass the cooked mixture through a food mill or force it through a sieve, pressing down hard with a wooden spoon to extract as much liquid as possible. Taste the strained coulis and adjust the seasoning. Serve hot or cold.

COURGETTE

see Squash

COURT-BOUILLON

see also:
nage
stock

Seasoned and flavoured liquids, court-bouillons are used for cooking fish, shellfish, offal (variety meats) and sometimes even poultry and veal.

The simplest court-bouillon consists simply of salted boiling water; use 15 g/$\frac{1}{2}$ oz/2 tsp of coarse sea salt per 1 l/1$\frac{3}{4}$ pt/1 qt of water. This is only for shellfish. A flavouring court-bouillon, with vinegar or white wine, aromatic herbs and vegetables, needs about an hour of cooking to develop the flavour fully before use. The court-bouillon is then allowed to cool before the fish or meat is added to it for cooking.

Never discard the court-bouillon once its primary purpose is served; it can always be filtered and stored in the refrigerator for further use, or be a base for soups and sauces.

Sachets of powdered court-bouillon are great time-savers.

COURT-BOUILLON AU VIN BLANC

White wine court-bouillon

Makes about 2 l/3$\frac{1}{2}$ pt/2 qt
Preparation 15 minutes
Cooking about 1 hour

METRIC/IMPERIAL	*AMERICAN*
30 g/1 oz butter	*2 tbsp butter*
140 g/5 oz carrots, thinly sliced	*5 oz carrots, thinly sliced*
6 shallots, thinly sliced	*6 shallots, thinly sliced*
2 onions, thinly sliced	*2 onions, thinly sliced*
115 g/$\frac{1}{4}$ lb mushrooms, chopped	*$\frac{1}{4}$ lb mushrooms, chopped*
1 l/1$\frac{3}{4}$ pt dry white wine	*1 qt dry white wine*
bouquet garni	*bouquet garni*
30 g/1 oz coarse salt	*4 tsp coarse salt*
6 black peppercorns, coarsely crushed	*6 black peppercorns, coarsely crushed*

Melt the butter in a large saucepan over a low heat. Add the vegetables and cook them very gently for 3 minutes.

Add 1 l/1$\frac{3}{4}$ pt/1 qt of boiling water and the white wine along with the bouquet garni and some salt and cook gently for 50–60 minutes. Add the peppercorns towards the end of the cooking time.

Leave the court-bouillon to cool completely before using it to poach fragile fish, such as turbot, John Dory or sole. Strain the liquid after cooking and use to make a sauce.

COURT-BOUILLON AU VINAIGRE

Vinegar court-bouillon

Makes about 1 l/1¾ pt/1 qt
Preparation 10 minutes
Cooking 1 hour

METRIC/IMPERIAL	AMERICAN
100 ml/3½ fl oz white wine vinegar	½ cup white wine vinegar
1 tbsp coarse salt	1 tbsp coarse salt
1 large carrot, thinly sliced	1 large carrot, thinly sliced
2 onions, thinly sliced	2 onions, thinly sliced
bouquet garni	bouquet garni

Pour 1.25 l/2¼ pt/6½ cups of water into a large pan and add the vinegar and coarse salt. Add the carrots and onions to the pan along with the bouquet garni and bring to the boil. Simmer gently for 1 hour, then allow to cool before using.

Use for poaching salmon and shellfish (the vinegar also helps give shellfish a good colour).

COUSCOUS

see also:
condiment
semolina

An ancient Berber dish, couscous has become a dietary staple throughout Northern Africa, France and some other Mediterranean countries. Spicy meat, particularly mutton, or poultry or vegetable stews are cooked in the bottom of special double steamers, known in France as *couscoussiers*, while semolina steams in the upper section of the vessel. Outside North Africa, the semolina itself has become known as couscous.

To make a good couscous the semolina must be made from the finest quality hard wheat and be a mixture of fine and coarse grains. A lengthy process of rubbing the grains between the moistened palms is necessary to prepare the semolina before cooking. However, 'instant' couscous grains are available ready-prepared in packets in quality food stores. The grains must also be soaked in water or stock and cooked correctly so that they develop the right consistency.

Particularly in Sicily, versions of couscous are made with fish (grouper, sea bream, mullet), and there are also Moroccan sweet couscous dishes made with cinnamon and/or dried fruit.

Couscous is an excellent dish for entertaining large numbers of guests. It is usually served with an accompanying hot sauce, usually *harissa* mixed with a little stock. Couscous, with a meat and vegetable accompaniment, provides a perfectly balanced meal on its own.

COUSCOUS AU MOUTON

Mutton couscous

Serves 4–5
Preparation 1 hour
Cooking about 1¼ hours

METRIC/IMPERIAL	AMERICAN
4 tbsp olive oil	4 tbsp olive oil
800 g/1¾ lb mutton collar or shoulder, cut into pieces	1¾ lb boneless mutton or lamb shoulder, cut into pieces
3 onions, thinly sliced	3 onions, thinly sliced
4 tomatoes, peeled and quartered	4 tomatoes, peeled and quartered
3 carrots, coarsely chopped	3 carrots, coarsely chopped
5 turnips, coarsely chopped	5 turnips, coarsely chopped
3 garlic cloves, crushed	3 garlic cloves, minced
1 green sweet pepper, deseeded and cut into thin strips	1 green sweet pepper, deseeded and cut into thin strips
4 courgettes, thinly sliced	4 zucchini, thinly sliced
1 chilli pepper	1 chili pepper
450 g/1 lb couscous (medium-grain hard wheat semolina)	1 lb couscous (about 3 cups)
55 g/2 oz butter	4 tbsp butter
1 tbsp harissa	1 tbsp harissa sauce
cooked chickpeas, to garnish	cooked chickpeas (garbanzo beans), to garnish

Heat 3 tablespoons of the oil in the lower part of a *couscoussier* or heavy-based steamer and gently brown the pieces of meat in it on all sides. Stir the onions into the meat in the pan.

Add the tomatoes, carrots, turnips, garlic and sweet pepper to the meat in the pan, then add lightly salted water to cover. Cook over a moderate heat for 1 hour. After 40 minutes, add the courgette (zucchini) slices and the chilli pepper.

While the meat and vegetables are cooking, prepare the couscous. Rinse the grain quickly under cold running water, then put it in a bowl, cover and leave it for 15 minutes to swell.

Put the couscous in the upper part of the *couscoussier* or steamer, rolling the grain gently between moistened palms to break up any lumps, and cook it for 20 minutes.

Transfer the couscous to a large dish and pour the remaining oil and a little salted water over it. Work again with moistened hands to break up any lumps. Leave it for 10 minutes to swell, then return it to the top of the *couscoussier* or steamer and cook it for a further 15 minutes.

Put the cooked couscous into a warmed, deep serving dish and dot it with the butter. Transfer the meat and vegetables to another warmed, deep serving dish and sprinkle with a little of the cooking liquid. Garnish with the chickpeas.

Mix 1 tablespoon of harissa with some of the remaining hot cooking liquid from the meat and vegetables and serve it as a condiment.
To drink: a robust red, such as an Algerian Côtes de Zaccar or Lebanese Château Musar.

CRAB
Crabe

see also:
cocktail
court-bouillon
lobster
shellfish

Crabs are crustaceans, closely related to lobsters and prawns (shrimp) but with larger flatter bodies under which the tails are tucked.

There are many species of edible crab throughout the waters of the world, from the Tropics to the Arctic. In Britain and France, the type most usually sold and served is the large, pinkish COMMON EDIBLE CRAB or *tourteau*. The SPIDER CRAB or *araignée*, with long claws and pincers, is popular in the Mediterranean region; surprisingly, it is exported there from the English Channel coasts, and is held to be the finest flavoured of all shellfish. The French favour the tiny (5–10 cm/2–4 in across) SWIMMING CRABS or *étrilles*, which are common on the Atlantic coast of France and in the English Channel. They are full of flavour, but as with most small crabs, the meat is so difficult to extract that they are mainly used in soups and bisques.

The most common edible crabs in North America are the BLUE CRAB on the Atlantic seaboard, with very white body meat, and the slightly larger DUNGENESS CRAB of the Pacific, which has a greenish shell and pink-tinged meat. The ALASKAN KING CRAB is like an enormous spider crab and has delicious meat, which is most often available canned.

Fresh crabs should be bought live, with their

common edible crab

male spider crab

female spider crab

claws well secured. Choose crabs which are not too big for their type, but which are heavy for their size and do not make any liquid noise when shaken. It is wise to buy specimens which are quite lively and not too sluggish, and which smell clean. Female crabs, with the broader 'apron' tails, are preferable to male crabs because their tails contain more meat and they also carry the roe. Look for tails which are slightly lifted as this indicates plump generous meat. If crabs are very dirty or slimy, they should be well scrubbed before cooking.

Crabs are usually dropped into a boiling court-bouillon which is then brought back to the boil as quickly as possible. They are then poached gently for a brief period. An alternative method, which is regarded as being slightly more humane, is to put the crabs into a previously boiled and cooled court-bouillon which is then heated. Due to the lack of oxygen in the liquid, the crab apparently becomes insensible long before the water becomes uncomfortably warm.

When cooked, take off the legs and claws, then pull the tail away from the underside and prise open the shell. Remove the creamy substance lying between the inside of the shell and the meat and put it to one side; this is the tomalley, which some connoisseurs consider a delicacy. Remove and discard the stomach (just behind the mouth), intestines (under the tail), feathery gills and any pieces of cartilage. The brown liver (lying next to the gills) is also a delicacy and is often reserved for sauces. The paler meat from the claws is best released using nutcrackers or some other suitable tool.

If the crab meat is to be served in the shells, they should be well scrubbed to remove any algae, etc, and boiled briefly to sterilize them.

Crab meat is delicate and has a wonderful flavour which needs little dressing. It is usually served with little more than a good mayonnaise, perhaps some lemon juice and black pepper, and brown bread and butter.

In season, SOFT-SHELL CRABS – which are caught having just moulted their old hard shell – may be eaten in their entirety and make a wonderful treat. They are very thoroughly washed in several changes of water and then the face is cut out along with the sandbag and gills lying just behind. They are then turned over and the apron pulled away, as for hard-shell crabs, to release the intestinal tract. They are then usually sautéed, fried *à la meunière* or deep fried in an egg-and-crumb coating. They are also sometimes marinated live in beaten egg for a few hours before cooking.

Canned crab meat is very good for making soufflés, crab cocktails, salads and canapés. It must always be kept well refrigerated after the can is opened, and picked over to remove pieces of shell and cartilage before use.

Crab meat is rich in protein and mineral salts and 100 g/3½ oz contains 120 calories.

OPENING A CRAB

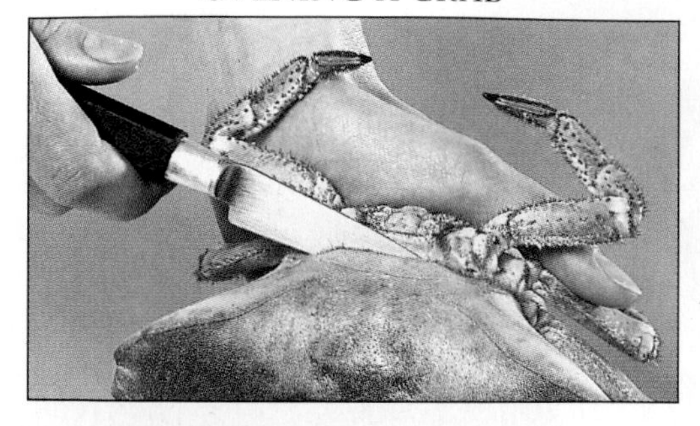

Slide a knife between the shell and the body at the back by the jointed tail and twist firmly to loosen the shell all around.

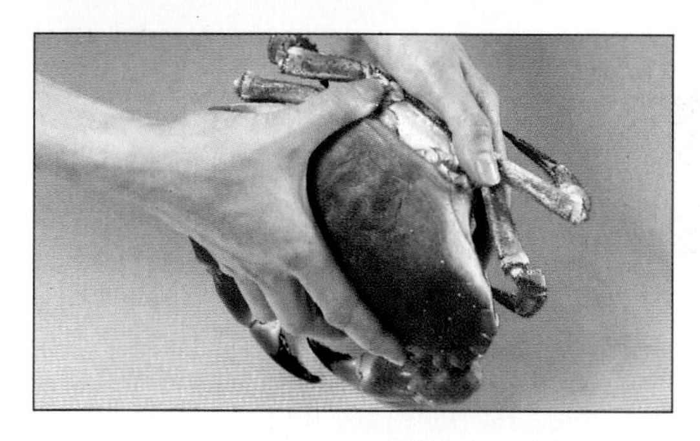

Grasp the shell and pull it off, then wrench off the claws and legs. Carefully crack the claws and legs so as not to damage the flesh.

Use a spoon to remove the flesh from the inside of the shell; extract the meat from the claws, legs and body with a slim fork or pick.

CRABES À LA BRETONNE

Crabs poached in lemon court-bouillon

Serves 4
Preparation 15 minutes
Cooking about 25 minutes

METRIC/IMPERIAL	AMERICAN
225 g/½ lb carrots, thinly sliced	½ lb carrots, thinly sliced
3 onions, coarsely chopped	3 onions, coarsely chopped
sprig of thyme	sprig of thyme
½ bay leaf	½ bay leaf
2 sprigs of parsley	2 sprigs of parsley
30 g/1 oz coarse salt	4 tsp coarse salt
juice of 2 lemons	juice of 2 lemons
2 tsp black peppercorns	2 tsp black peppercorns
4 crabs, each weighing about 450 g/1 lb	4 crabs, each weighing about 1 lb
lettuce leaves, to serve	lettuce leaves, to serve

Make a lemon court-bouillon by combining the carrots, onions, thyme, bay leaf, parsley, coarse salt and lemon juice with 3 1/5 pt/3 qt of water in a large pan. Bring to the boil and simmer for 15 minutes, then add the peppercorns.

Cook for a minute or two more, then increase the heat until the court-bouillon is at a rolling boil. Plunge the crabs into the court-bouillon. Once boiling again, reduce the heat and simmer gently for 8–10 minutes.

Drain the crabs and let them cool. Remove the legs and claws. Carefully scoop out all the meat from the shells as described above and put to one side. Scrub the shells clean and boil them for a minute or two to sterilize them.

Arrange the lettuce leaves on 4 plates. Place 1 upturned crab shell on each plate and fill it with crab meat. Arrange the legs and claws on the lettuce around them. Serve accompanied by mayonnaise.

To drink: Pouilly Fumé, or other good dry white wine.

PAMPLEMOUSSES GARNIES

Crab-stuffed grapefruit

Serves 4
Preparation 25 minutes

METRIC/IMPERIAL	AMERICAN
100 g/3½ oz cooked crab meat, fresh or canned	1 cup cooked crab meat, fresh or canned
juice of ½ lemon	juice of ½ lemon
2 pink grapefruit	2 pink grapefruit
8 large lettuce leaves	8 large lettuce leaves
4 tbsp mayonnaise	¼ cup mayonnaise
paprika	paprika
salt and pepper	salt and pepper

Remove any shell and cartilage from the crab meat. Pour the lemon juice over it and set it aside.

Cut the grapefruit in half, scoop out the pulp and discard the pith. Layer the lettuce leaves on top of each other, roll them up and slice them across into a *chiffonade*.

Mix the grapefruit segments, crab meat, mayonnaise, 2–3 pinches of paprika, salt and pepper and the shredded lettuce.

Fill the grapefruit halves with this mixture and chill until ready to serve.

SOUPE D'ÉTRILLES

Crab soup

Serves 4
Preparation 40 minutes
Cooking about 30 minutes

METRIC/IMPERIAL	AMERICAN
1 carrot, thinly sliced	1 carrot, thinly sliced
2 onions, thinly sliced	2 onions, thinly sliced
200 ml/7 fl oz white wine	1 cup white wine
bouquet garni	bouquet garni
85 g/3 oz long-grain rice	7 tbsp long-grain rice
1.5 kg/3½ lb small swimming crabs	3½ lb small lady or calico crabs
salt and pepper	salt and pepper
croutons, to serve	croutons, to serve

Put the carrots and onions in a pan with the wine, bouquet garni, salt and pepper and 1 l/1¾ pt/1 qt of water. Bring to the boil and simmer for 20 minutes.

Meanwhile, put the rice in boiling salted water and simmer for 15 minutes. Drain.

Wash the crabs in plenty of cold water. Plunge them into the court-bouillon, bring it back to the boil again quickly and then simmer for 5 minutes.

Using a slotted spoon, remove the crabs from the pan and grind them in a food processor. Strain the resulting purée, pressing it well, and return it to the strained court-bouillon.

Add the rice and bring the soup to the boil once more. Adjust the seasoning and serve scalding hot in warmed, deep bowls, garnished with tiny croutons.

CRANBERRY

Airelle

A small red berry with a tart flavour, the cranberry is one of an enormous family of berries in the heather family, including blueberries, bilberries and huckleberries. There are two main species of cranberry: the European and the American. Because of its larger size and better flavour, it is the latter which has become gastronomically important.

Massachusetts is the centre of production in the United States, and about 70% of the total harvest comes from Cape Cod. The berries have extraordinary keeping qualities and used to be shipped to Europe simply stored in barrels filled with water.

Nowadays they are commonly sold fresh, frozen or canned in their own juice. They can be used to make jam, jellies or the traditional sauce for Thanksgiving or Christmas turkey, which is just as good with game birds and venison.

These autumn berries are highly nutritious, containing very little sugar, but having a high pectin and vitamin C content; 100 g/3½ oz of raw cranberries contain 13 calories. Cranberry juice is an increasingly popular refreshment.

COMPOTE D'AIRELLES

Cranberry compote

Serves 6
Preparation 10 minutes
Cooking 25 minutes

METRIC/IMPERIAL	AMERICAN
1 kg/2¼ lb cranberries, defrosted if frozen	2¼ lb (5 pt) cranberries, thawed if frozen
½ lemon	½ lemon
500 g/1 lb 2 oz caster sugar	2½ cups superfine sugar

Wash the berries and remove the stalks. If the lemon is not organically grown and may have been sprayed or coated, scrub it in hot soapy water, rinse and pat dry. Finely grate the zest.

Bring 200 ml/7 fl oz/1 cup of water to the boil along with the sugar and grated lemon zest. Add the cranberries and cook over a high heat for 10 minutes. Drain and place in a bowl.

Reduce the syrup by one third over a high heat and pour it over the berries. Allow the compote to cool completely before serving, accompanied by crème fraîche or whipping cream.

If the compote is to be kept for several days in the refrigerator, reduce the syrup by half.

CRAWFISH

see Spiny lobster

CRAYFISH

Ecrevisses

see also:
court-bouillon
crab
lobster
nage
sauce
shellfish

Freshwater crustaceans about 15–20 cm/6–8 in long resembling small lobsters, crayfish are becoming more and more rare in the mountain streams and rivers where they were formerly plentiful. Their season is from April to October, but they are at their best in the late summer.

The most culinarily important species include: the larger RED-CLAWED CRAYFISH, sought after because of its delicate, sweet flavour; the WHITE-CLAWED CRAYFISH, equally valued and generally found in mountain streams, and the AMERICAN CRAYFISH, recently introduced into numerous European rivers and lakes. The slender-clawed, green TURKISH CRAYFISH, generally of lower quality, is artificially cultured and widely exported.

Like crab and lobster, crayfish must be bought and cooked live. Buy only lively specimens, preferably clean without any trace of slime, which feel heavy for their size. A medium-sized crayfish weighs about 60 g/2 oz: allow about 6–9 per person, if they are to be served whole.

Crayfish need to have the intestinal vein removed: the fishmonger will do this, but you may easily do it yourself by twisting apart the two innermost blades of the tail and then pulling it out in one piece. Alternatively the crayfish may be starved for a day or two to empty the gut, or they may be soaked in a bowl of milk for 2 hours. The crayfish should always be thoroughly washed in plenty of cold water.

Crayfish are generally cooked by plunging them into a boiling court-bouillon which is brought back to the boil as quickly as possible and then gently simmered for about 10 minutes. They may also be cooked in the slightly more humane methods as described for crab and lobster.

They are usually then served whole, possibly without the heads and with their shells partially or completely removed. Most of the meat is to be found in the tails. It is normal to eat crayfish with the hands, so finger-bowls should be

crayfish

provided. The trimmings, including the head, shell, claws and pincers may be pounded and used to flavour bisques or butters.

Crayfish are one of the most important ingredients in French *haute cuisine*. They are used in mousses, soufflés and pies, made into soups, bisques or sauces, such as classic *sauce nantua* to accompany fish quenelles, or used as a garnish. They are best served plain, or with only a little melted butter or mayonnaise, and they have a particular affinity with the flavour of dill.

Served without dressing, crayfish have a very low calorie content; 100 g/3½ oz contains only 72 calories.

ECREVISSES AU BEURRE D'AIL

Crayfish with garlic butter

Serves 4
Preparation 15 minutes, 30 minutes ahead
Cooking about 10 minutes

METRIC/IMPERIAL	AMERICAN
150 ml/¼ pt oil	⅔ cup oil
6–9 crayfish per person (depending on size), cleaned	6–9 crayfish per person (depending on size), deveined
85 g/3 oz butter	6 tbsp butter
juice of 2 lemons	juice of 2 lemons
salt and pepper	salt and pepper
toast, to serve	toast, to serve
FOR THE GARLIC BUTTER:	FOR THE GARLIC BUTTER:
150 g/5½ oz butter	11 tbsp butter
3 garlic cloves, finely chopped	3 garlic cloves, finely chopped
2 shallots, finely chopped	2 shallots, finely chopped
1 tbsp snipped chives	1 tbsp snipped chives

Make the garlic butter by blending the butter, garlic, shallots and chives in a food processor. Put the flavoured butter into a bowl and chill it.

Pour the oil into a large, heavy-bottomed frying pan and set it over a high heat. When the oil is very hot, sauté the crayfish briskly for 2 minutes.

Season with salt and pepper, lower the heat and cook gently for a further 8 minutes.

Add the butter in small pieces along with the lemon juice. Mix well and put the crayfish into a very hot, deep serving dish. Serve, accompanied by the garlic butter and hot toast.

ECREVISSES À LA BORDELAISE

Crayfish in a shallot, wine and herb sauce

Serves 4
Preparation 20 minutes
Cooking about 20 minutes

METRIC/IMPERIAL	AMERICAN
200 g/7 oz butter	2 sticks butter
3 carrots, thinly sliced	3 carrots, thinly sliced
2 onions, finely chopped	2 onions, finely chopped
4 shallots, finely chopped	4 shallots, finely chopped
sprig of thyme	sprig of thyme
bay leaf	bay leaf
pinch of cayenne pepper	pinch of cayenne pepper
24–36 crayfish (depending on size), cleaned	24–36 crayfish (depending on size), deveined
2 tbsp Cognac	2 tbsp Cognac
200 ml/7 fl oz white wine	1 cup white wine
1 tbsp chopped parsley	1 tbsp chopped parsley
1 tbsp chopped tarragon	1 tbsp chopped tarragon
juice of 1 lemon	juice of 1 lemon
salt and pepper	salt and pepper

Melt 55 g/2 oz/4 tbsp of the butter in a flameproof casserole over a low heat and add the carrots. Cook, stirring to avoid browning, until softened. Add the onions and shallots and cook them until translucent. Add the thyme, bay leaf, cayenne and salt and pepper to taste. Mix thoroughly.

Add the crayfish to the casserole and pour the Cognac over. Heat for a few seconds, then flame the Cognac. Sauté the crayfish briefly over a high heat and then cover and cook gently for 3 minutes. Add the white wine and 200 ml/7 fl oz/1 cup of boiling water. Cover once more and cook for a further 5 minutes, stirring frequently.

Remove the crayfish from the casserole and put them in a warmed, deep serving dish. Cover and keep hot.

Discard the thyme and bay leaf from the casserole and add the chopped parsley and tarragon. Stir them in and cook uncovered over a high heat for 2 minutes.

Whisk in the remaining butter in small pieces. Add the lemon juice, and taste to adjust the seasoning; it should be fairly highly seasoned. Pour the sauce over the crayfish and serve at once.

CREAM

Crème

see also:
creams and custards
gratin
milk
sauce
soup
velouté

The fattier part of milk, cream was traditionally obtained by allowing the milk to stand and then skimming off the concentration of larger butterfat globules which had risen to the top. Nowadays, cream is obtained using machines which spin the milk to separate out the butterfat content. Most commercial cream now available has also been pasteurized and therefore lacks the depth of flavour of the farmhouse product. UHT CREAM has a long shelf life, but again correspondingly less flavour.

Different types of cream are identified by their butterfat content:

HALF CREAM or HALF-AND-HALF, which is also called CEREAL CREAM, has a butterfat content of about 12%. It is usually homogenized to prevent it from separating, and is a mixture of cream and milk. It is used mostly in coffee or with breakfast cereals.

SINGLE or COFFEE CREAM, has a butterfat content of 18–20% and is again usually homogenized to discourage separation. It is used in beverages and on breakfast cereals, but its pouring consistency also makes it suitable as a dressing for fruit and desserts. In addition, it is much used in cooking: to enrich soups, sauces and other sweet and savoury dishes.

American LIGHT CREAM or LIGHT WHIPPING CREAM has a butterfat content of 30–32%. It is used in the same ways as single or coffee cream.

CRÈME FRAÎCHE has a butterfat content of about 30%, although it can be as high as 50%, and is made from whole cream by the addition of a harmless bacterial culture which makes it thicken and develop a very pleasant, sharp tang. Traditionally crème fraîche is always slightly thicker than WHIPPING CREAM and is available fresh, pasteurized or UHT. The French regard crème fraîche as an indispensable ingredient in many aspects of cooking, both sweet and savoury, especially in the thickening of sauces. Crème fraîche may be boiled very gently to thicken a sauce to the required consistency. In fact, when cream is called for in French recipes it is usually crème fraîche which is meant, unless otherwise indicated. The distinctive flavour of crème fraîche works particularly well with fish, poultry, game and vegetables, and is delicious on fruit and with fruit pies. If crème fraîche is unobtainable, WHIPPING CREAM may be substituted in any sweet dish or where the cream will be subjected to high temperatures; in uncooked savoury dishes, SOUR CREAM gives a better approximation of the flavour. To make a fairly authentic crème fraîche, add 1½ teaspoons of buttermilk to 300 ml/½ pt/1¼ cups of whipping cream and leave it in a warm place for a few hours.

WHIPPING CREAM, which is also called HEAVY CREAM in the USA, has about 40% butterfat. As a result, it is of the right density and richness to trap air when it is whipped so that it will almost double its volume, and develop a range of consistencies from soft to very stiff without separating. It is thus very useful in cake and dessert fillings and decorations, when it may be piped. It may also be used like crème fraîche to enrich and thicken many sweet and savoury dishes as it has approximately the same texture and fat content.

CHANTILLY CREAM is fresh whipping cream or crème fraîche whipped to the consistency of a mousse. It is then usually sweetened and flavoured (with vanilla, coffee, cocoa, liqueur, etc) and served chilled on its own as a dessert or to dress a wide variety of other desserts, from soufflés to custards. Unsweetened, it also finds use in savoury dishes where it contributes its very characteristic light consistency.

British DOUBLE CREAM has a butterfat content of about 48% and is the ideal luxury pouring cream for fruit and desserts and for floating on top of thick soups and after-dinner coffee. It may also be whipped.

CLOTTED CREAM, traditional to southwest England, has a butterfat content of about 55%. It differs from other types of cream in that it is cooked or 'scalded' to a temperature of about 82C/180F for around 1 hour. This gives it its characteristic rich caramel colour and flavour and also kills off most bacteria to give clotted cream great keeping qualities. It is traditionally served with scones and jam, or as dressing for fruit and fruit pies.

DAIRY SOUR OR SOURED CREAM, or *smetana*, as it is known in Eastern Europe, is 18% butterfat cream to which a harmless bacterial culture has been added to encourage the transformation of all the sugar content into lactic acid. The pleasantly sour and tasty result is very useful in both sweet and savoury dishes, and is a key ingredient in the cooking of Central and Eastern Europe in such dishes as Beef Stroganoff, Hungarian goulash, with blinis and caviar, etc. It makes particularly delicious salad dressings, goes very well with cucumber and pork and with herbs, especially dill and chives, is a popular topping on baked potatoes and also makes very good cheesecakes. If it is difficult to obtain, a passable substitute may be made by simply adding 2 or 3 tablespoons of lemon juice to fresh single (coffee) cream.

When cooking with cream, remember that those with a butterfat content of less than about 30% tend to curdle on being heated, so only gently reheat any preparation to which they have been added. Thicker creams may be cooked successfully, and whipping cream, double cream and crème fraîche are also often boiled to reduce them for sauces.

PARFAIT AU COGNAC

Cognac parfait

Serves 6
Preparation 8 minutes
Freezing at least 2 hours

METRIC/IMPERIAL	*AMERICAN*
1 egg yolk	*1 egg yolk*
3 tbsp Cognac	*3 tbsp Cognac*
55 g/2 oz icing sugar	*½ cup confectioners' sugar*
1 tbsp vanilla essence	*1 tbsp vanilla extract*
200 ml/7 fl oz crème fraîche or whipping cream, whipped to soft peaks	*1 cup crème fraîche or whipping cream, whipped to soft peaks*

In a bowl, mix the egg yolk with the Cognac, sugar and vanilla. Carefully blend in the whipped cream.

Freeze the mixture for at least 2 hours. (An ice cream maker is not necessary for this parfait as it is very simple to make.)

SAUCE MOUSSELINE

Light hollandaise sauce

Serves 4
Preparation 10 minutes
Cooking about 15 minutes

METRIC/IMPERIAL	*AMERICAN*
juice of ½ lemon	*juice of ½ lemon*
2 egg yolks	*2 egg yolks*
100 g/3½ oz butter, cut into tiny pieces	*1 stick butter, cut into tiny pieces*
3 tbsp crème fraîche or whipping cream, whipped to soft peaks	*3 tbsp crème fraîche or whipping cream, whipped to soft peaks*
salt and freshly ground white pepper	*salt and freshly ground white pepper*

Put the lemon juice in a saucepan. Add the egg yolks, a pinch of salt and some freshly ground white pepper. Mix in 1 tablespoon of cold water.

Put the saucepan over a low heat and whisk the mixture until it begins to thicken. Add the butter, piece by piece, whisking constantly.

Remove the saucepan from the heat, add the whipped cream and adjust the seasoning.

This sauce works well with asparagus, steamed vegetables and poached fish.

CRÈME CHANTILLY

Sweetened and flavoured whipped cream

Serves 4–6
Preparation about 10 minutes

METRIC/IMPERIAL	AMERICAN
500 ml/16 fl oz crème fraîche or whipping cream, well chilled	2 cups crème fraîche or whipping cream, well chilled
55 g/2 oz icing sugar	$\frac{1}{2}$ cup confectioners' sugar
1 sachet (7.5 g/1$\frac{3}{4}$ tsp) of vanilla sugar	1$\frac{3}{4}$ tsp vanilla-flavored sugar
1–2 ice cubes, crushed	1–2 ice cubes, crushed

Put the cream in a chilled bowl with a rounded base (1). The cream should be very cold but not straight from the refrigerator; the ideal temperature range is 5–10C/40–50F.

Add both the icing (confectioners') sugar and the vanilla sugar along with the crushed ice cubes (2).

A hand whisk is preferable for making crème chantilly, but if using an electric beater, whip the cream in a tall, steep-sided bowl.

Start whipping the mixture, slowly at first. As the cream begins to thicken, gradually begin to whip more vigorously (3).

Stop whipping when the cream is mousse-like and firm enough to remain in the coils of the whisk and leave trails on the surface of the cream in the bowl when the whisk is removed (4).

Notes: it is important not to over-whip the cream, as globules of fat will start to appear on the surface as the cream starts turning into butter.

Chantilly cream will keep, refrigerated, for only a few hours.

An egg white, stiffly whisked, may be added at the last minute to lighten the cream still further, in which case it should be eaten immediately.

If you have no crème fraîche or whipping cream, try the following as a substitute: whisk vigorously together a 450 g/1 lb can of unsweetened evaporated milk and 150 g/5$\frac{1}{2}$ oz/1$\frac{1}{4}$ cups of icing (confectioners') sugar. Within a few minutes this will turn into a foamy mousse which may be used in place of chantilly cream.

1

2

3

4

see also:
almond paste
Bavarian cream
blancmange
buttercream
cakes and gâteaux
charlotte
choux pastry
cream
egg
floating islands
frangipane
ices and ice creams
milk
mousse

CREAMS AND CUSTARDS

Crèmes d'entremets et de pâtisserie

Made principally from eggs, along with milk and sugar (and sometimes flour and butter), there are a variety of preparations termed creams and custards which have the consistency of thick cream and are used as desserts or in the making of cakes and pastries. They may be set or runny (pouring consistency) and may be served hot or cold. They are usually flavoured with vanilla, chocolate, coffee, caramel, fruit, nuts, spices, liquors, etc. There are 2 basic types: dessert creams and pastry creams.

DESSERT CREAMS include the various set custards and creams, including simple baked egg custard, CARAMEL CREAM (*crème caramel*), *crème brûlée*, etc, as well as the family of pouring custard creams, based on egg custard sauce (*crème anglaise*). Smooth rich custard cream has many uses. It may be served warm on top of puddings, as is traditional in Britain, or chilled as an accompaniment to floating islands, meringue, charlottes, etc. It is also the basis for many types of ice cream.

PASTRY CREAMS are normally used as ingredients in cakes, gâteaux and pastries. They include straightforward whipped cream or flavoured *crème chantilly*, pastry cream or confectioner's custard (*crème patissière*), buttercream and almond cream (*frangipane*).

At its best, *crème patissière* is a smooth thickened custard which melts in the mouth and is extremely popular in all forms of sweet cookery. As well as being used to line pastry cases for tarts and to fill or decorate cakes, it may be flavoured with chocolate, coffee and so on and eaten on its own as a dessert.

OEUFS AU LAIT À LA VANILLE

Baked vanilla egg custard

Serves 6
Preparation 10 minutes
Cooking 35 minutes

METRIC/IMPERIAL	AMERICAN
25 g/¾ oz butter	1½ tbsp butter
1 l/1¾ pt milk	1 qt milk
200 g/7 oz caster sugar	1 cup superfine sugar
1 vanilla pod, split in half	1 vanilla bean, split in half
8 eggs, lightly beaten	8 eggs, lightly beaten

Preheat the oven to 200C/400F/gas 6 and grease a baking dish with the butter.

Pour the milk into a saucepan and add the sugar. Mix well, then add the vanilla and bring to the boil. Remove the vanilla from the milk and pour the boiling milk over the beaten eggs in a large bowl, stirring with a wooden spoon.

Pour the mixture into the baking dish and bake for 15 minutes. Reduce the heat to 180C/350F/gas 4 and bake for a further 20 minutes. The custard is cooked when the blade of a knife inserted into the centre comes out clean.

Variation: brown sugar or 4 tablespoons of honey may be used in place of the white sugar.

CRÈME BRÛLÉE

Burnt cream

Serves 4
Preparation 20 minutes
Cooking about 35 minutes, chilling time 1 hour

METRIC/IMPERIAL	AMERICAN
4 egg yolks	4 egg yolks
125 g/4½ oz caster sugar	10½ tbsp superfine sugar
1 vanilla pod	1 vanilla bean
200 ml/7 fl oz milk	1 cup milk
200 ml/7 fl oz crème fraîche or whipping cream	1 cup crème fraîche or whipping cream
1 tbsp orange liqueur	1 tbsp orange liqueur

Preheat the oven to 150C/300F/gas 2.

Put the egg yolks into a bowl, add 100 g/3½ oz/½ cup of the sugar and whisk until smooth, light in colour and creamy.

Split the vanilla pod (bean) in half and extract the seeds. Add the seeds to the egg and sugar mixture, followed by the milk and whisk until the mixture is smooth. Whisk in the cream and liqueur.

Spoon into ovenproof ramekins and bake for 30 minutes.

Remove from the oven and allow to cool completely. Then chill in the refrigerator for at least 30 minutes.

Preheat a hot grill (broiler).

Sprinkle the top of each cream with the remaining sugar and grill (broil) until the sugar caramelizes. Serve slightly warm or chilled.

CRÈME RENVERSÉE AU CARAMEL

Unmoulded caramel custard

Serves 6
Preparation 30 minutes
Cooking about 50 minutes, 4–5 hours ahead

METRIC/IMPERIAL	AMERICAN
15 sugar cubes	15 sugar cubes
1 vanilla pod, split in half	1 vanilla bean, split in half
500 ml/16 fl oz milk	2 cups milk
75 g/2½ oz caster sugar	6 tbsp superfine sugar
3 eggs	3 eggs

Preheat the oven to 160C/325F/gas 3.

In a small saucepan, moisten the sugar cubes with a little water, then put the pan over a medium heat and melt the sugar to a caramel, shaking the pan gently from time to time to ensure even colouring of the caramel, but on no account stir it.

When the caramel is a clear mahogany colour, pour it into a charlotte or savarin mould or individual ramekin dishes. Tilt the mould or dishes to coat the bottom and sides completely with the caramel.

Put the vanilla and milk in a small pan. Bring the milk to the boil and stir in the sugar. Remove from the heat and leave to infuse for 5 minutes, then remove the vanilla.

Break the eggs into a bowl and whisk them vigorously. Pour the boiling milk over them, beating constantly. Add it slowly at first, so that the eggs do not curdle.

Pour the custard into the caramel-coated mould. Place the mould on a rack in a larger pan and fill the pan with hot water to the level of the top of the custard. Bake in the centre of the oven (making sure the water in the outer pan does not boil) for 35–40 minutes. Check whether the custard is done by pressing the middle with a fingertip: it should resist slightly. When done, remove the custard from the oven and leave it to cool completely.

Slide the blade of a knife around the edges of the cooled custard to loosen, then put a serving dish on top of the mould and quickly turn it upside down. Remove the mould to serve.

Note: the custard will not unmould successfully unless it it completely cold. It should be prepared in advance, preferably the night before.

PETITS POTS DE CRÈME

Little chocolate and coffee custard pots

Serves 6
Preparation 10 minutes
Cooking 25 minutes, 3 hours ahead

METRIC/IMPERIAL	AMERICAN
500 ml/16 fl oz milk	2 cups milk
200 g/7 oz caster sugar	1 cup superfine sugar
2 eggs + 6 egg yolks	2 eggs + 6 egg yolks
500 ml/16 fl oz crème fraîche or whipping cream	2 cups crème fraîche or whipping cream
1 sachet (7.5 g/1¾ tsp) of vanilla sugar	1¾ tsp vanilla-flavored sugar
115 g/4 oz plain chocolate	4 oz semisweet chocolate
1 heaped tbsp instant coffee granules	1 heaping tbsp instant coffee granules

Put the milk into a saucepan and bring it to the boil. Meanwhile, beat the sugar with the whole eggs and yolks in a bowl until the sugar has dissolved.

Add the hot milk to the mixture, then add the cream. Return the mixture to the saucepan and stir it over a very low heat, taking care that it does not boil, until the custard is thick enough to coat the back of a spoon. Then mix in the vanilla sugar and divide the custard between 2 bowls.

Melt the chocolate with 2 tablespoons of water in a bowl set in a bain-marie. Add it to one of the bowls of custard and mix well.

Dissolve the instant coffee in 1 or 2 tablespoons of hot water and add it to the other bowl of custard.

Spoon the 2 custards in alternating layers into 6 small individual custard pots, demi-tasse cups or bowls and chill until ready to serve.

CRÈME PÂTISSIÈRE

Pastry cream or confectioner's custard

Serves 6
Preparation 15 minutes
Cooking 20 minutes, 2 hours ahead

METRIC/IMPERIAL	AMERICAN
1 l/1¾ pt milk	1 qt milk
2 eggs + 4 egg yolks	2 eggs + 4 egg yolks
150 g/5½ oz caster sugar	¾ cup superfine sugar
125 g/4½ oz flour	1 cup flour
55 g/2 oz butter (optional)	4 tbsp butter (optional)
vanilla, coffee, chocolate, caramel, liqueur, etc, to flavour	vanilla, coffee, chocolate, caramel, liqueur, etc, to flavor

Heat the milk in a saucepan, adding a vanilla pod (bean) if the pastry cream is to be vanilla-flavoured.

Break the whole eggs into a bowl, add the egg yolks and beat together. Add the sugar and continue to whisk vigorously until the mixture is thick, white and frothy.

Sift the flour and mix it gradually into the egg and sugar mixture, spoonful by spoonful.

Remove the vanilla from the milk, if used, and add the milk to the mixture very gradually, stirring continuously.

Pour the mixture into the milk pan and slowly bring it to the boil over a very gentle heat, stirring constantly with a wooden spoon. (It is not necessary to cook the pastry cream for any length of time.) Remove the pan from the heat and leave the pastry cream to cool.

If using the butter, add it in tiny pieces, stirring until it melts. Then, if not using vanilla, add the flavouring of your choice: 1 teaspoon of coffee essence (extract), 1 tablespoon of unsweetened cocoa powder, liquid caramel or liqueur, usually Kirsch.

Cold pastry cream is used for filling choux buns, éclairs and *mille-feuilles*, as the base for fruit tart fillings and to make sweet soufflés. It can also be served slightly warm on its own as a dessert, perhaps garnished with fruit.

Notes: to prevent a skin forming on the top of the pastry cream as it cools, sprinkle it with a little fine sugar while still hot or press buttered parchment or greaseproof paper on its surface.

To obtain a lighter pastry cream, beat 2 egg whites with a little sugar to very stiff peaks and add them to the boiling custard. Alternatively, you can use 4 whole eggs rather than 2 whole eggs and 4 yolks, but this will not produce as smooth a result.

CRÈME ANGLAISE

Custard cream or English egg custard sauce

Serves 6
Preparation 10 minutes
Cooking 15 minutes

METRIC/IMPERIAL	AMERICAN
1 l/1¾ pt milk	1 qt milk
1 vanilla pod	1 vanilla bean
6 egg yolks	6 egg yolks
150 g/5½ oz caster sugar	¾ cup superfine sugar

Pour the milk into a heavy-bottomed saucepan. Split open the vanilla pod (bean) without losing any of the seeds and add to the milk. Bring the milk very slowly to the boil and then boil it for 1 minute. Lower the heat and leave to infuse for 3 minutes.

Put the egg yolks and sugar into a bowl and beat until smooth and creamy and the mixture is thick enough to make a ribbon trail on itself when the whisk is lifted out (1, see overleaf).

1

2

3

4

Remove the vanilla from the boiling milk and pour the milk very gradually into the egg and sugar mixture, stirring briskly (2). Take great care at the beginning, to avoid curdling the egg yolks.

Return the mixture to the milk saucepan and cook it over a low heat, stirring constantly with a wooden spoon, until it thickens (3). It should on no account be allowed to boil.

The custard is ready when the froth that formed on the surface disappears and when the mixture coats the back of the spoon (4). Pour the custard immediately into a chilled container.

Notes: if the custard begins to separate just as it reaches boiling point it means that it is beginning to curdle: transfer it immediately to a bowl and allow it to cool down, then whisk it vigorously or mix it rapidly in a food processor.

A small teaspoon of cornflour (cornstarch) added to the egg and sugar mixture will help avoid curdling caused by cooking the custard over too high a heat.

Custard cream can be enriched and thickened by adding even more egg yolks: up to 10–12 per l/$1\frac{3}{4}$ pt/1 qt of milk. On the other hand, it can be diluted by the addition of 150 ml/$\frac{1}{4}$ pt/$\frac{2}{3}$ cup of whipping cream once it has cooled.

Variations: vanilla is the classic flavouring for custard cream and vanilla sugar or vanilla essence (extract) may be substituted for the vanilla pod. Other flavourings include: finely grated lemon or orange zest (or infuse the milk with strips of zest), 1 tablespoon of liqueur, 1 teaspoon of coffee essence (extract), 1–2 tablespoons of liquid caramel added to the boiling milk.

CRÈME FRAÎCHE

see Cream

CRÊPE

see also: galette

Large, thin pancakes made from a flour and milk batter, crêpes may be either sweet or savoury. The flour is usually wheat, although buckwheat is traditional in many parts of rural France. Some recipes also add beer or cider to the batter and this gives a slightly risen crêpe.

Sweet crêpes may be served as a hot dessert, topped with sugar or jam, or filled with fruit, melted chocolate, chestnut cream, etc, or even flamed in alcohol, such as rum or Cointreau.

Crêpes made from an unsweetened batter with a savoury stuffing make a good first course or a quick and easy meal. Popular savoury fillings include: buttered spinach with bacon, tuna fish with tomato coulis, or béchamel sauce with mushrooms, ham or cheese.

To make crêpes, pour just enough batter to coat the bottom of a hot frying pan or special crêpe pan which has been greased with butter or oil. Tilt the pan in all directions to coat the bottom with a thin film and cook the crêpe for a minute or so over a high heat until the edges lift and it comes free of the pan. Turn the crêpe over and cook it for another 2 minutes on the other side, until both sides are a good colour.

To keep crêpes hot while the others are being cooked, stack them on top of each other on a plate placed over a saucepan of simmering water and covered with foil.

Ready-made crêpes may be reheated in a frying pan over a low heat with a little butter. To make unfolding easier, place them briefly on a plate over a saucepan of boiling water.

One plain crêpe without sugar contains 38 calories.

PÂTE À CRÊPES

Crêpe batter

Makes about 24 thin crêpes, 22 cm/8¾ in round
Preparation 20 minutes, 1–2 hours ahead
Cooking 3–5 minutes per crêpe

METRIC/IMPERIAL	AMERICAN
250 g/8½ oz flour	*2 cups flour*
500 ml/16 fl oz milk (for savoury crêpes use half water or beer)	*2 cups milk (for savory crêpes use half water or beer)*
3 eggs, lightly beaten	*3 eggs, lightly beaten*
2 tbsp melted butter or oil	*2 tbsp melted butter or oil*
½ tsp fine salt	*½ tsp salt*
2 tbsp caster sugar (omit for savoury crêpes)	*2 tbsp superfine sugar (omit for savoury crêpes)*
flavouring (for sweet crêpes): 1 tbsp rum or other alcohol, vanilla sugar, citrus zest	*flavoring (for sweet crêpes): 1 tbsp rum or other liquor, vanilla-flavored sugar, citrus zest*
butter or oil, for cooking	*butter or oil, for cooking*

Put the flour into a bowl, make a well in the centre and pour half the liquid into it. Mix in the flour with a wooden spoon, starting from the centre and pulling the flour into the liquid from the sides (1).

Add the eggs to the mixture, still stirring with a circular motion (2). Then incorporate the butter or oil, salt and sugar, if appropriate. A food processor speeds up this operation, but the processor bowl should not be overfilled.

Gradually add the rest of the liquid (3). The batter should be of a good pouring consistency, runny but not too liquid. Add flavourings if desired.

For best results, let the batter stand in a cool place, covered, for 1–2 hours before using as

1

2

3

described on page 199, although it is not strictly necessary if you are pressed for time.

Notes: there are many ways of serving sweet crêpes. Some quick and easy ideas include: sugared and folded in four or sprinkled with lemon juice, spread with jam and rolled up, filled with frangipane cream or pastry cream, sprinkled with rum and flamed.

If making large numbers of crêpes, it may be wise to use 2 pans and make them 2 at a time.

To add a personal touch to commercial crêpe mixtures (made according to the instructions, adding water or milk): add 1–2 tablespoons of sugar to make them crisper, or 1–2 tablespoons of butter to make them softer, and flavour them with 1 tablespoon of grated citrus zest, vanilla sugar or a suitable liqueur.

Crêpes Suzette

Crêpes in orange butter sauce

Serves 6
Preparation 30 minutes, resting 1 hour
Cooking 15 minutes, plus making the crêpes

METRIC/IMPERIAL	AMERICAN
3 mandarin oranges	3 mandarin oranges or tangerines
250 g/8½ oz flour	2 cups flour
3 eggs	3 eggs
400 ml/14 fl oz milk	1¾ cups milk
pinch of salt	pinch of salt
2 tbsp Curaçao	2 tbsp Curaçao
1 tbsp sunflower oil	1 tbsp sunflower oil
85 g/3 oz butter	6 tbsp butter
55 g/2 oz caster sugar	¼ cup superfine sugar
more butter or oil, for frying	more butter or oil, for frying

Scrub 2 of the mandarins thoroughly in warm soapy water, rinse them well and pat dry. Grate the rind of these mandarins and set it aside. Squeeze the juice of all 3 mandarins, and strain it to remove pips and flesh.

Make a crêpe batter with the flour, eggs, milk and pinch of salt.

Whisk in half the mandarin juice, 1 tablespoon of the Curaçao and the oil. Leave to stand for at least 1 hour.

Meanwhile, beat the butter with the rest of the mandarin juice, the zest, the remaining Curaçao and the sugar.

Use the batter to make 24 extremely thin and delicate crêpes. Spread each of them with a little of the mandarin butter and fold it in four. Place on a warmed dish, cover and keep warm.

When all the crêpes are cooked, reheat them together, overlapped in the pan, in the remaining mandarin butter. Arrange them on a warmed serving dish and serve immediately.

Variations: true crêpes Suzette are flavoured and filled with mandarin oranges, but ordinary oranges, or a mixture of oranges and lemons, may be used instead. Cointreau or Grand Marnier may also be used instead of Curaçao. This flavouring alcohol may be reserved until the final reheating of the crêpes in the sauce and used to flame the crêpes spectacularly at the table.

Crêpes Salées au Saumon

Crêpes stuffed with smoked salmon

Serves 4
Preparation 10 minutes
Cooking about 20 minutes, plus making the crêpes

METRIC/IMPERIAL	AMERICAN
140 g/5 oz mushrooms	5 oz mushrooms
juice of ½ lemon	juice of ½ lemon
55 g/2 oz butter	4 tbsp butter
45 g/1½ oz flour	6 tbsp flour
500 ml/16 fl oz milk	2 cups milk
2 large slices of smoked salmon, cut into tiny dice	2 large slices of smoked salmon, cut into tiny dice
8 crêpes	8 crêpes
100 ml/3½ fl oz crème fraîche or sour cream	½ cup crème fraîche or sour cream
55 g/2 oz grated Gruyère	½ cup grated Gruyère cheese
salt and pepper	salt and pepper

Slice the mushrooms thinly and sprinkle them with lemon juice. Melt 25 g/¾ oz/1½ tbsp of the butter in a frying pan over a low heat and cook the mushrooms very gently for a few minutes. Melt the rest of the butter in a small saucepan.

Crêpes Suzette (Crêpes in orange butter sauce)

Add the flour and stir for 2 minutes. Add the milk and cook, stirring continuously, for 10 minutes. Season with pepper.

Drain the mushrooms and mix them into two thirds of the sauce with the salmon. Preheat a hot grill (broiler). Spread the salmon filling on the crêpes and roll them up. Arrange them in a baking dish. Add the cream and grated cheese to the rest of the sauce and season to taste.

Pour this mixture over the crêpes and put the dish under the grill (broiler) for 3 minutes until the surface begins to brown. Serve at once.

CRESS

Cresson

see also: mustard salad

A number of plants belonging to the cabbage family are known as cress and are distinguished by the pungent taste of their leaves.

WATERCRESS is the most common variety and is at its best from spring through summer. Grown in shallow water, it has tender, juicy stalks and the dark green leaves are plump and delicate with a fine, strong, peppery flavour. It is best to keep watercress like parsley, with its stems standing in a bowl of water (do not allow the leaves to soak): it will stay fresh for a day or two this way. Watercress should be carefully picked over, yellowing leaves and thick stems discarded and then washed in several changes of cold water before use. Watercress is at its best used raw in salads, particularly in combination with eggs and fish and preferably dressed with a mustard vinaigrette. Watercress is far richer than lettuce in protein, vitamins and minerals. Watercress butter is a favourite dressing for grilled meats and poultry. Watercress is also often cooked into a soup, blanched and simmered briefly in butter or made into a purée to accompany plainly cooked poultry and fish.

GARDEN CRESS OR PEPPER CRESS has tiny round green leaves on long white stalks. It is available most of the year and is often sold as MUSTARD AND CRESS, growing in small containers interspersed with sprouting mustard. Cress is used in salads and soups and as a garnish for meat and poultry and sandwiches.

Cress is highly nutritious, rich in calcium and iron and low in calories; 100 g/3½ oz contains only 21 calories.

SALADE DE CRESSON

Watercress salad

Serves 4
Preparation 20 minutes

METRIC/IMPERIAL	AMERICAN
1 apple	1 apple
2 tbsp lemon juice	2 tbsp lemon juice
1 tsp Dijon mustard	1 tsp Dijon mustard
3 tbsp oil	3 tbsp oil
1 tbsp vinegar	1 tbsp vinegar
bunch of watercress, thick stalks trimmed	bunch of watercress, thick stems trimmed
115 g/¼ lb Gouda, cut into small dice	¼ lb Gouda cheese, cut into small dice
2 hard-boiled eggs, shelled and sliced	2 hard-boiled eggs, shelled and sliced
salt and pepper	salt and pepper

Peel the apple, cut it in half and remove the core. Sprinkle it with some of the lemon juice and then cut it into small dice about the same size as the cheese.

Make a mustard vinaigrette using the rest of the lemon juice, the mustard, the oil and the vinegar. Season it with salt and pepper.

Put the watercress in a salad bowl along with the diced cheese and apple. Pour the vinaigrette dressing over and toss well.

Garnish with the egg and serve.

VELOUTÉ DE CRESSON

Watercress soup

Serves 6
Preparation 20 minutes
Cooking about 45 minutes

METRIC/IMPERIAL	AMERICAN
3 potatoes, peeled and thinly sliced	3 potatoes, peeled and thinly sliced
1 onion, thinly sliced	1 onion, thinly sliced
bunch of watercress, coarsely chopped	bunch of watercress, coarsely chopped
½ bay leaf	½ bay leaf
45 g/1½ oz butter, cut into small pieces	3 tbsp butter, cut into small pieces

700 ml/1¼ pt chicken stock	*3 cups chicken stock*
100 ml/3½ fl oz crème fraîche or whipping cream	*½ cup crème fraîche or whipping cream*
pinch of grated nutmeg	*pinch of grated nutmeg*
salt and pepper	*salt and pepper*

Combine the potatoes, onion, watercress and bay leaf in a large pan and season with salt and pepper. Add the butter and the stock.

Bring to the boil, then cover the pan, reduce the heat and cook gently for 30 minutes. Remove the bay leaf and blend the soup in a food processor.

Return the soup to the pan and add all but 1–2 tablespoons of the cream. Heat gently, stirring, but do not allow it to boil. Add a little grated nutmeg and adjust the seasoning. Serve as hot as possible, in warmed bowls with a little of the reserved cream swirled into the centre of each. *Note: this soup may also be prepared in advance and served chilled.*

CROISSANT

see also: pastry

A crescent-shaped roll considered typically French, croissants are actually Viennese in origin. They are made using a rich leavened dough with butter layered into it like puff pastry. The dough is rolled flat and cut into triangles which are then rolled up around themselves and shaped into crescents.

Plain butter croissants are usually served with jam for breakfast; sweetened croissants are filled, often with chocolate, or iced and sprinkled with almonds, and served to accompany coffee or tea.

Croissants may also be filled with meat, ham or cheese. Such savoury croissants may be made of shortcrust or rough puff pastry.

One butter croissant contains about 400 calories.

CROISSANTS À LA VIANDE

Beef croissants

Makes about 12 croissants
Preparation 30 minutes, 2 hours ahead
Cooking about 35 minutes

METRIC/IMPERIAL	*AMERICAN*
150 g/5½ oz butter	*11 tbsp butter*
20 g/⅔ oz baker's yeast	*⅔ oz compressed fresh yeast*
400 g/14 oz flour, sifted	*3¼ cups flour, sifted*
5 eggs	*5 eggs*
1 onion, chopped	*1 onion, chopped*
2 tbsp oil	*2 tbsp oil*
300 g/10 oz minced steak	*10 oz ground steak*
100 ml/3½ fl oz beef stock	*½ cup beef stock*
1 tsp Dijon mustard	*1 tsp Dijon mustard*
2 tbsp chopped parsley	*2 tbsp chopped parsley*
1 tbsp crème fraîche or whipping cream	*1 tbsp crème fraîche or whipping cream*
several stoned olives, coarsely chopped	*several pitted olives, coarsely chopped*
salt and pepper	*salt and pepper*

Preheat the oven to 220C/425F/gas 7 and grease a baking sheet with a little of the butter.

Mix the yeast with a little warm water and add it to the flour together with a pinch of salt. Mix well. Beat in the remaining butter and 3 of the eggs. Knead to a smooth dough. Form the dough into a ball and leave it to rise for 2 hours.

Fry the onion in the oil over a moderate heat. Add the beef and brown briefly. Sprinkle over a little flour to absorb the fat and stir well, then add the stock, mustard, parsley, cream and olives. Bind the mixture with one of the remaining eggs. Cook for 10 minutes, stirring frequently, then remove it from the heat.

Divide the ball of dough in half. Roll out each portion into 2 equal rounds. Cut each round into 6 triangles. Spoon some of the beef filling on the base of each triangle. Roll each of them up and form into a crescent.

Place the croissants on the buttered baking sheet. Beat the last egg and brush the croissants with it. Bake for about 20 minutes. Serve hot or cold with a green salad.

GRATIN DE CROISSANTS

Croissants baked au gratin

Serves 6
Preparation 25 minutes
Cooking 10 minutes

METRIC/IMPERIAL	AMERICAN
6 large pure butter croissants	6 large pure butter croissants
3 slices of cooked ham, halved	3 slices of cooked ham, halved
500 ml/16 fl oz milk	2 cups milk
2 eggs	2 eggs
1 tsp paprika	1 tsp paprika
150 g/5½ oz Gruyère, finely grated	1¼ cups finely grated Gruyère cheese
salt and white pepper	salt and white pepper

Preheat the oven to 250C/475F/gas 9.

Split open the croissants. Slide half a slice of ham into each one. Arrange them closely together in a baking dish.

Warm the milk in a saucepan. Break the eggs into a bowl, beat them with a fork and add the milk, which should be very hot, but not boiling. Season with the paprika, salt and white pepper.

Slowly pour the mixture over the croissants and give it some time to soak in (until the croissants have absorbed most of the liquid).

Sprinkle the top evenly with the grated cheese. Bake for a good 10 minutes and serve piping hot.

CROQUETTE

see also:
creams and custards
sauce

Small hot or cold cylinders or balls of sweet or savoury food, croquettes are usually given a coating of flour, breadcrumbs or egg-and-crumbs and then shallow or deep fried.

A useful means of recycling leftovers, savoury croquettes may be served as a garnish, or on their own or with a sauce as hors d'oeuvres, or with vegetables as a main course.

Cooked minced (ground) beef, ham, poultry, fish, rice and mushrooms are the most usual main ingredients, although items such as sweetbreads and seafood also work well. The ingredients are usually bound together with beaten egg or a thick sauce, usually a cheese-flavoured béchamel, and well seasoned and flavoured with herbs and spices.

Sweet croquettes are made using chopped fresh or preserved fruit, chestnuts or rice. The binding medium is normally a thick pastry cream and flavouring is effected with cinnamon, chopped nuts, chocolate, honey or alcohol. A hot, sweet fruit sauce is usually served as an accompaniment.

CROQUETTES DE POISSON

Fish croquettes

Serves 6
Preparation 20 minutes
Cooking about 15 minutes

METRIC/IMPERIAL	AMERICAN
300 g/10 oz cooked salt cod	10 oz cooked salt cod
300 g/10 oz cooked cod	10 oz cooked cod
550 g/1¼ lb boiled potatoes	1¼ lb cooked potatoes
grated nutmeg	grated nutmeg
2 eggs, lightly beaten	2 eggs, lightly beaten
fine breadcrumbs, for coating	fine breadcrumbs, for coating
groundnut oil, for deep frying	peanut oil, for deep frying
pepper	pepper

Flake the salt cod and purée it by passing it through a food mill along with the cod.

Mash the potatoes until smooth and add them to the fish. Season generously with pepper and grated nutmeg. Work the mixture with a wooden spoon for about 10 minutes until it is completely smooth.

Form the mixture into balls about the size of a ping-pong ball. Dip them into the beaten egg, then roll them in the breadcrumbs, making sure the balls are well coated.

Deep fry them in the oil heated to 180C/350F (a small cube of dry bread browns in about 60 seconds) until golden brown. Drain them on paper towels.

Serve with tomato or curry sauce, accompanied by a green salad.

CROQUETTES DE VOLAILLE

Chicken croquettes

Serves 4
Preparation 20 minutes
Cooking about 12 minutes

METRIC/IMPERIAL	AMERICAN
3 slices of white bread, crusts removed	3 slices of white bread, crusts removed
5 tbsp single cream	$\frac{1}{3}$ cup light coffee cream
550 g/1$\frac{1}{4}$ lb cooked white chicken or turkey meat, finely chopped	1$\frac{1}{4}$ lb cooked white chicken or turkey meat, finely chopped
3 tbsp chopped parsley	3 tbsp chopped parsley
45 g/1$\frac{1}{2}$ oz butter	3 tbsp butter
salt and pepper	salt and pepper
flour, for coating	flour, for coating
lemon slices, to garnish	lemon slices, to garnish

Crumble the bread into a dish and pour the cream over it. Stir to mix. When the bread has absorbed all the cream, mash it with a fork.

Mix the bread with the chopped poultry and add the parsley. Season with salt and pepper. The mixture should stick together but not be too wet.

Make 8 balls out of the mixture and flatten them slightly. Roll them in flour. Melt the butter in a large frying pan over a moderate heat and brown the croquettes in it for 2 minutes on each side, then lower the heat and cook for a further 8 minutes, turning the croquettes once or twice.

Arrange the croquettes on a warmed serving dish and garnish them with lemon slices. Serve accompanied by sautéed mushrooms or broccoli purée.

CROSNE OR CHINESE ARTICHOKE

see also:
Jerusalem artichoke
vegetables

Quite unrelated to the artichoke and originally from Japan rather than China, the little known crosne is a root vegetable which is in season in autumn and has a delicious, slightly sweet taste reminiscent of Jerusalem artichokes. It is also known as CHOROGI, KNOTROOT or HEDGE NETTLE.

crosne or Chinese artichoke

Ensure that crosnes are very fresh as they lose their flavour rapidly. They should be very firm, light in colour and the ends should not be dark or crushed in any way. Rub them in a cloth with some coarse salt to remove the delicate skins, then rinse them in cold water.

They are usually blanched briefly in boiling salted water and then simmered in butter until tender, or prepared like Jerusalem artichokes. They go well with game and fish dishes.

Crosnes contain 75 calories per 100 g/3$\frac{1}{2}$ oz.

GRENADINS DE VEAU AUX CROSNES

Veal slices with crosnes

Serves 4
Preparation 5 minutes
Cooking about 15 minutes

METRIC/IMPERIAL	AMERICAN
15 g/$\frac{1}{2}$ oz butter	1 tbsp butter
600 g/1$\frac{1}{2}$ lb crosnes, skinned	1$\frac{1}{2}$ lb crosnes, skinned
2 tbsp oil	2 tbsp oil
4 slices of veal fillet, about 2 cm/$\frac{3}{4}$ in thick	4 slices of veal tenderloin, about $\frac{3}{4}$ in thick
3 tbsp chopped flat-leaved parsley	3 tbsp chopped flat-leaf parsley
300 ml/$\frac{1}{2}$ pt fresh tomato sauce	1$\frac{1}{2}$ cups fresh tomato sauce

Melt the butter in a pan over a moderate heat and cook the crosnes in it for 3–4 minutes, then cover them with lightly salted boiling water and cook for 6 minutes. At the end of cooking, the water should have almost all evaporated.

Meanwhile, lightly oil the veal slices and fry them for 4–5 minutes on each side over a moderate heat. Put the veal on a warmed serving dish, surround with the crosnes, scatter the chopped parsley over the top and serve accompanied by the tomato sauce.

CROUSTADE

see also:
barquette
croûte
sauce
vol-au-vent

A deep container or shell for savoury fillings, *croustades* are popular as garnishes and in the making of first courses. They may be shaped into rectangles, squares, circles or ovals, and made out of baked or fried pastry, hollowed-out, thick slices of slightly stale bread, rice or potato.

To serve as garnishes in *haute cuisine*, they are filled with items such as kidneys, mixed diced vegetables and seafood in rich sauces. To be eaten as hot hors d'oeuvres, popular fillings include chopped ham, mushroom *duxelles*, foie gras, poultry, seafood and vegetable purées, all usually bound in a cream or cheese sauce. Some of this sauce is also often used to coat the *croustade* before being baked or finished *au gratin*.

CROUSTADES AUX CHAMPIGNONS

Mushroom croustades

Serves 6
Preparation 30 minutes
Cooking 25 minutes

METRIC/IMPERIAL	AMERICAN
450 g/1 lb mushrooms, very thinly sliced	1 lb mushrooms, very thinly sliced
100 g/3½ oz butter	1 stick butter
1 loaf of slightly stale white bread, about 30 cm/1 ft long	1 loaf of slightly stale white bread, about 1 ft long
200 m/7 fl oz béchamel sauce (see Sauce)	1 cup béchamel sauce (see Sauce)
1 thick slice of cooked ham, weighing about 140 g/5 oz, cut into small dice	1 thick slice of cooked ham, weighing about 5 oz, cut into small dice
1 tbsp chopped parsley	1 tbsp chopped parsley
3 tbsp crème fraîche or whipping cream	3 tbsp crème fraîche or whipping cream
2 tbsp grated Parmesan	2 tbsp grated Parmesan cheese
1 egg, lightly beaten	1 egg, lightly beaten
salt and pepper	salt and pepper

Filet de boeuf en croûte (Beef in brioche crust)

Preheat the oven to 180C/350F/gas 4.

Cook the mushrooms gently in 30 g/1 oz/2 tbsp of the butter for 10 minutes. Season them with salt and pepper and set aside.

Remove the end crusts from the bread and cut the loaf across into 6 slices, each about 5 cm/2 in thick. Using a very sharp knife, carefully hollow out about 2 cm/¾ in of the centre of each slice to make a container.

Melt the rest of the butter and brush the *croustades* inside and out with it. Bake them in the oven for about 10 minutes, or until they are golden brown.

Meanwhile, prepare the béchamel sauce and mix it with the mushrooms, diced ham, parsley and 2 tablespoons of the cream.

When the *croustades* are browned, remove them from the oven and increase the oven temperature to 220C/425F/gas 7.

Fill the *croustades* with the mushroom mixture. Lightly beat the rest of the cream with the Parmesan and egg, and coat the filling in each *croustade* with it, then brown them for 5 minutes in the hotter oven. Serve at once.

CROÛTE

see also:
brioche
croque-monsieur
croustade
pastry
pâté
roasting
sauce
terrine
timbale

Literally meaning a 'crust', *croûtes* are pastry cases, often baked blind, or slices of bread which are stuffed or coated with hot or cold savoury or sweet mixtures. They may then be grilled (broiled), fried or baked.

Common savoury fillings include ham, cheese, mushrooms, poultry and seafood. These are usually bound in a thick béchamel sauce, and – as with *croustades* – some of this sauce is also often used to coat the *croûte* before being baked or finished *au gratin*.

Certain tender cuts of meat, especially beef fillet (tenderloin), or fish such as salmon, as well as terrines and pâtés, may also be wrapped in pastry and baked *en croûte*.

Sweet *croûtes*, served as hot desserts, are often made of brioche and filled with various types of fresh or preserved fruit in syrup or jam.

CROÛTES AU MUNSTER

Munster cheese toasts

Serves 2
Preparation 15 minutes
Cooking about 5 minutes

METRIC/IMPERIAL	AMERICAN
45 g/1½ oz butter	*3 tbsp butter*
12 sprigs of fresh tarragon, chopped	*12 sprigs of fresh tarragon, chopped*
4 thick slices of wholemeal bread	*4 thick slices of whole wheat bread*
140 g/5 oz Munster cheese, rind removed and cut into strips	*5 oz Munster cheese, rind removed and cut into strips*
115 g/4 oz cooked white chicken meat, cut into strips	*4 oz cooked white chicken meat, cut into strips*

Preheat a hot grill (broiler). Make a flavoured butter by beating the butter with the tarragon.

Toast the slices of bread under the grill (broiler) and spread them with the flavoured butter. Put several strips of cheese on each slice of bread and place some chicken strips on top in a criss-cross pattern.

Return to the grill (broiler) to brown. Serve very hot, accompanied by a creamy coleslaw. *To drink: Riesling.*

FILET DE BOEUF EN CROÛTE

Beef in brioche crust

Serves 8
Preparation 30 minutes, 24 hours ahead
Cooking about 1 hour, 3 hours ahead

METRIC/IMPERIAL	AMERICAN
1 fillet of beef, weighing about 1.5 kg/3½ lb	*1 beef tenderloin roast, weighing about 3½ lb*
15 g/½ oz butter	*1 tbsp butter*
1 egg, beaten	*1 egg, beaten*
salt and pepper	*salt and pepper*
FOR THE BRIOCHE:	FOR THE BRIOCHE:
500 g/1 lb 2 oz flour	*3⅓ cups flour*
450 g/1 lb unsalted butter	*1 lb unsalted butter*
6 tbsp milk	*6 tbsp milk*
25 g/¾ oz baker's yeast	*¾ oz compressed fresh yeast*
6 eggs	*6 eggs*

The day before make the light brioche dough as described on pages 89–90, using all the butter and adding 2 teaspoons of salt.

Three hours before serving, heat a large, heavy-bottomed frying pan over a high heat. Dry fry the beef on all sides to brown and seal. Remove from the pan, season and cool for 2 hours.

Preheat the oven to 200C/400F/gas 6 and grease a baking sheet with the butter. Roll out one third of the dough to a thickness of about 6 mm/¼ in and lay it on the baking sheet. Place the beef on the dough and trim to leave a margin of about 4 cm/1½ in all round. Roll the remaining dough out to the same thickness and wrap round the meat. Brush the edges with beaten egg and pinch them well to make a good seal with the base. Decorate with trimmings and then glaze the dough with egg.

Cook in the oven for about 25 minutes, or until the crust is golden. Cover with foil to prevent it from burning and cook for a further 35 minutes. Switch off the oven and leave it in for a further 10 minutes.

Using a sharp knife, cut into thick slices to serve, accompanied by a Madeira sauce.

CROUTON

Croûton

see also:
aspic
salad
soup

Small pieces of dry bread, often rubbed with garlic and then fried, grilled (broiled) or baked, croutons are a common garnish for soups, salads, omelettes, eggs, leaf vegetables, fish cooked *à la meunière*, *matelotes* or blanquettes.

Croutons are usually small cubes, but they may also be shaped into triangles, hearts or diamonds.

The term crouton is also used to describe similar small, decoratively shaped pieces of aspic used for garnish.

OMELETTE AUX CROÛTONS

Omelette with croutons

Serves 4
Preparation 10 minutes
Cooking about 15 minutes

METRIC/IMPERIAL	*AMERICAN*
1 tbsp olive oil	*1 tbsp olive oil*
1 garlic clove, finely chopped	*1 garlic clove, minced*
2 slices of slightly stale white bread, crusts removed and cut into tiny dice	*2 slices of slightly stale white bread, crusts removed and cut into tiny dice*
6 eggs	*6 eggs*
2 tbsp chopped chives	*2 tbsp chopped chives*
30 g/1 oz butter	*2 tbsp butter*
salt and pepper	*salt and pepper*

Heat the olive oil in a frying pan over a moderate heat. Add the garlic and sauté it without letting it brown. Add the pieces of bread and cook, stirring, until they are golden and well impregnated with the garlic. Remove them from the frying pan and keep them hot.

Break the eggs into a bowl and add salt and pepper to taste. Lightly beat the eggs, then add the chopped chives.

Melt the butter in the frying pan. When it is foamy, add the eggs and stir to mix in the butter. Make the omelette, lifting the edges with a fork and tilting the pan to allow the uncooked egg to run underneath. Stop as soon as it starts to set.

When it is cooked to taste, transfer it to a warmed serving dish, add the garlic croutons and fold the omelette in two over them. Serve at once, accompanied by a thick tomato coulis.

To drink: a fresh lively red, such as a Saumur-Champigny.

CRUDITÉS

see also:
dietary fibre
sauce

The French use this term to describe raw vegetables, and sometimes fruit, served otherwise than in salads.

A plate of crudités is often served with drinks or as an hors d'oeuvre, usually accompanied by a cold sauce in which they may be dipped.

To prepare an attractive crudité platter, choose a varied selection of extremely fresh vegetables in season: tiny baby carrots and pieces of young celery, crisp radishes, very white cauliflower broken into florets, chunks of cucumber, slices of mushroom sprinkled with lemon juice, fresh green beans, strips of fennel, small *poivrade* artichokes, strips of sweet pepper, and so on.

Some crudité selections include cooked beetroot or hard-boiled egg: others feature pieces of fruit, such as chunks of apple, pear, banana, etc.

Arrange the ingredients in attractive groupings in baskets lined with crisp white napkins, accompanied by an assortment of sauces: mayonnaise with *fines herbes*, *tapenade*, tomato coulis with basil, etc. Once prepared, the vegetables should be covered with a damp cloth and kept in the refrigerator until ready to serve.

Baby artichokes, radishes, fresh broad (fava) beans, tomatoes or young fennel are also often eaten *à la croque-au-sel*, that is, raw with nothing but salt and perhaps some butter. Connoisseurs claim that this is the best way to eat fresh truffles.

ASSIETTE DE CRUDITÉS SAUCE AVOCAT

Vegetable platter of crudités with avocado sauce

Serves 6
Preparation 30 minutes

METRIC/IMPERIAL	AMERICAN
4 baby carrots, cut into very fine dice	4 new carrots, cut into very fine dice
1 fennel bulb, trimmed and cut into fine dice	1 fennel bulb, trimmed and cut into fine dice
$\frac{1}{2}$ cucumber, peeled, deseeded and cut into very fine dice	$\frac{1}{2}$ cucumber, peeled, deseeded and cut into very fine dice
225 g/$\frac{1}{2}$ lb cauliflower, cut into florets	$\frac{1}{2}$ lb cauliflower, cut into florets
18 pink radishes, trimmed and cut into thin strips	18 radishes, trimmed and cut into thin strips
3 baby onions, very thinly sliced	3 new onions, very thinly sliced
2 avocados	2 avocados
juice of 1 lemon	juice of 1 lemon
1 garlic clove, chopped	1 garlic clove, minced
1 carton (150 ml/$\frac{1}{4}$ pt) of plain yogurt	$\frac{2}{3}$ cup plain yogurt
125 g/4$\frac{1}{2}$ oz smooth fromage blanc	$\frac{1}{2}$ cup smooth fresh white cheese (fromage blanc)
2 or 3 drops of Tabasco sauce	2 or 3 drops of hot pepper sauce
1 tsp Worcestershire sauce	1 tsp Worcestershire sauce
1 tbsp chopped parsley, to garnish	1 tbsp chopped parsley, to garnish
salt and pepper	salt and pepper

Combine all the vegetables, apart from the avocados, in a salad bowl and mix well.

Peel the avocados, cut them in half and remove the stones, then sprinkle the flesh with lemon juice. Scoop out the flesh and blend it to a smooth purée in a food processor along with the garlic, yogurt, *fromage blanc*, several drops of Tabasco sauce and the Worcestershire sauce. Season with salt and pepper to taste.

Divide the vegetable mixture between 6 individual plates, spoon the avocado sauce over it and scatter the chopped parsley on top. Serve well chilled.

To drink: fresh grapefruit juice or tomato juice.

CUCUMBER

Concombre

see also:
gherkin
squash

The fruit of a member of the squash family, cucumbers originated in the Himalayas but are now grown throughout the world and are available all year round.

There are several different varieties, but all of them are virtually identical in flavour. The JAPANESE CUCUMBER is peculiar in being virtually seedless. A small yellow variety, known as LEMON CUCUMBER, has a very thick skin.

There are two main varieties which are most common: the small, dark green RIDGE CUCUMBER and the long, clear green ENGLISH or HOTHOUSE CUCUMBER. Nowadays cucumbers, particularly the ridge variety, tend to be given protective wax coatings and such specimens have to be peeled before use. They are instantly recognizable from their weight, feel and resistance to the fingernail.

Cucumbers should be bought very fresh and firm, not too large, with tight, shiny green skin

ridge cucumber

English or hothouse cucumber

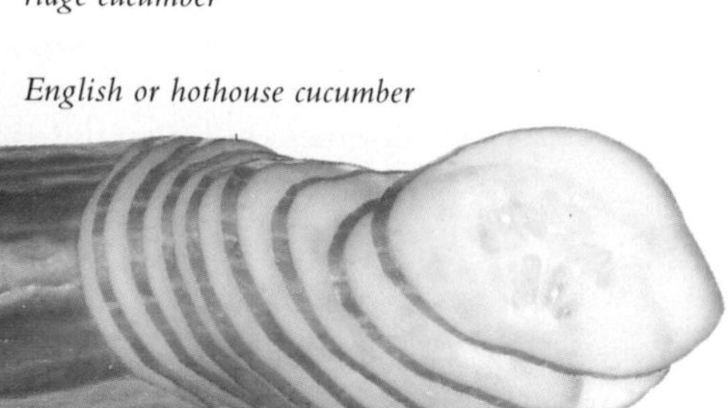

and no trace of wrinkling, bruising or limpness.

They are most commonly eaten raw and sliced in salads, but they may also be lightly steamed, boiled or sautéed. Whatever method is chosen, the cucumber should always be cooked quickly. When served raw, it is often advisable to sprinkle the cucumber with salt and let it drain for 20 minutes to remove excess moisture or any bitter taste. Cucumbers work particularly well in alliance with yogurt. Their shape and texture makes them ideal for stuffing, especially with fish and seafood mixtures.

Because of their very high water content, cucumbers have a very low calorific value: 100 g/3½ oz contains a mere 12 calories. Served in a salad, or even hot with a low-calorie cheese sauce, they are an ideal food for those watching their weight.

SALADE DE CONCOMBRE À LA CRÈME

Cucumber salad in cream

Serves 4
Preparation 15 minutes, resting about 1 hour

METRIC/IMPERIAL	AMERICAN
2 small cucumbers, peeled and very thinly sliced	2 cucumbers, peeled and very thinly sliced
150 ml/¼ pt whipping cream	⅔ cup whipping cream
1 tbsp lemon juice	1 tbsp lemon juice
1 tsp Dijon mustard	1 tsp Dijon mustard
4 sprigs of fresh mint	4 sprigs of fresh mint
white pepper	white pepper

Sprinkle the cucumber slices with salt. Put them in a colander over a bowl and leave them in a cool place for 20 minutes.

Lightly whip the cream, lemon juice and mustard together in a bowl and season with pepper. Finely snip three quarters of the mint with scissors and add it to the cream sauce.

Drain the cucumber and press it between the hands to extract as much liquid as possible. Put it into a deep serving dish.

Add the cream sauce and mix carefully. Chill for 30 minutes.

Snip the rest of the mint over the top before serving as an hors d'oeuvre or as an excellent accompaniment for cold or smoked fish (particularly if horseradish is substituted for the mustard).

Variation: substitute dill or tarragon for the mint and replace half the cream with an equivalent quantity of plain yogurt.

CONCOMBRE FARCI

Stuffed cucumber

Serves 4
Preparation 30 minutes

METRIC/IMPERIAL	AMERICAN
1 large straight cucumber	1 large straight English cucumber
1 can (210 g/7½ oz) of salmon, drained	1 can (7½ oz) salmon, drained
bunch of chives, chopped	bunch of chives, chopped
1 Demi-Sel cheese or other lightly salted fresh cheese weighing 75–100 g/2½–3½ oz	1 Demi-Sel cheese or other lightly salted fresh cheese weighing 2½–3½ oz
paprika	paprika
juice of ½ lemon	juice of ½ lemon
1 lettuce	1 head of lettuce
12 black olives	12 black olives
salt and pepper	salt and pepper

Peel the cucumber and cut off the ends. Cut it across into 4 equal pieces, then cut these in half lengthwise. Remove and discard the seeds; scoop out a little of the pulp with a spoon to make a hollow for the stuffing and chop it.

Put the salmon into a bowl, taking care that all bones and skin have been removed. Mash it with a fork and add the chives. Mix in the cheese, the chopped cucumber, paprika to taste and the lemon juice. Season with salt and pepper.

Fill the hollowed-out pieces of cucumber with the salmon mixture, piling it up and smoothing over the surface.

Line a serving plate with the lettuce leaves, arrange the pieces of stuffed cucumber on top of the lettuce and garnish with the black olives.

DARNES DE SAUMON AU CONCOMBRE

Salmon steaks with cucumber

Serves 4
Preparation 15 minutes
Cooking about 20 minutes

METRIC/IMPERIAL	AMERICAN
1 small cucumber	1 cucumber
4 thick boneless salmon steaks, each weighing about 140 g/5 oz	4 thick boneless salmon steaks, each weighing about 5 oz
100 ml/3½ fl oz white wine	½ cup white wine
300 ml/10 fl oz court-bouillon	1½ cups court-bouillon
200 ml/7 fl oz crème fraîche or whipping cream	1 cup crème fraîche or whipping cream
100 g/3½ oz butter	1 stick butter
salt and pepper	salt and pepper

Peel the cucumber, halve it lengthwise and remove the seeds. Cut the flesh into little sticks.

Place the salmon steaks in a large deep pan and pour over the white wine mixed with the court-bouillon. Bring to the boil, then lower the heat and poach for 8 minutes.

Drain the salmon steaks and arrange them on a warmed serving plate. Cover and keep hot.

Boil the cooking liquid rapidly to reduce it to about 3–4 tablespoons, then stir in the cream. Add the cucumber sticks and season with salt and pepper. Simmer gently for 5 minutes. Add the butter in small pieces. Pour this sauce over the salmon steaks to serve.

AUBERGINES AU CUMIN

Aubergine or eggplant with cumin

Serves 6
Preparation 20 minutes
Cooking 15 minutes, 3–5 hours ahead

METRIC/IMPERIAL	AMERICAN
100 ml/3½ fl oz olive oil	½ cup olive oil
juice of 1 large lemon	juice of 1 large lemon
1 tsp coriander seeds	1 tsp coriander seeds
1 tbsp cumin seeds	1 tbsp cumin seeds
12 black peppercorns	12 black peppercorns
2 tbsp tomato purée	2 tbsp tomato paste
bouquet garni	bouquet garni
4 aubergines	4 eggplants
salt and pepper	salt and pepper

Make a court-bouillon with 500 ml/16 fl oz/2 cups water, the olive oil, lemon juice, coriander, cumin, peppercorns, tomato purée (paste), bouquet garni and a pinch of salt. Bring to the boil.

Peel the aubergines (eggplants) and cut the flesh into small even cubes. Plunge these into the court-bouillon and simmer for 12 minutes.

Remove the aubergine (eggplant) cubes with a slotted spoon and put into a deep dish. Set aside. Strain the court-bouillon through a fine sieve, return to the pan and reduce it by half over a high heat.

Pour the reduced court-bouillon over the aubergine (eggplant) cubes and leave to cool, then chill. Serve well chilled with tuna fish as an hors d'oeuvre, or as a cold variation of ratatouille.

CUMIN

see also:
caraway
curry powder
spices

An aromatic plant related to caraway, the tiny spindle-shaped seeds of cumin have a hot, piquant, slightly bitter taste.

Cumin is a popular flavouring in the cooking of the Middle East and India and is essential in flavouring most curries. In Europe it is used to flavour bread and a number of cheeses, among them Munster and Gouda. The flavour of cumin also works well in vegetable dishes.

CURING

see also:
confit
drying
salt
sauerkraut
smoking

The process of curing or preserving food may be effected in several different ways depending on the nature of the food and the required resulting flavour and intended use.

Raw food, especially sliced meats, whole poultry, whole or filleted fish and whole or shredded vegetables and fruit may be dried, smoked, salted or immersed in brine. Cooked food may be canned or potted in its own fat, like the French *confit*.

CURRANT

see Dried vine fruit

CURRY POWDER

see also: chutney

Various mixtures of ground spices go by this description. They were originated by those Indians working among the British in India, where they were devised to allow the British to recreate Indian dishes for themselves.

The name curry (from the Indian *kari*, a sauce) is now given to a wide variety of spicy dishes based on meat, poultry, vegetables, fish or seafood and usually accompanied by rice.

The classic ingredients for a mild curry powder are as follows: turmeric, ginger, cardamom, fenugreek, cinnamon, cloves, cayenne pepper, mustard, cumin, coriander and nutmeg. The addition of varying amounts of chilli powder dictates how hot the curry is to be.

Better, more authentic, flavours are achieved using CURRY PASTES rather than powders, as these can more successfully incorporate fresh chillis and ginger. A little curry powder or paste is useful for flavouring dried bean dishes.

CURRY DE POULET

Chicken curry

Serves 6
Preparation 25 minutes
Cooking about 50 minutes

METRIC/IMPERIAL	AMERICAN
1 chicken, dressed weight about 1.8 kg/4 lb, cut into 10–12 pieces	1 chicken, dressed and drawn weight about 4 lb, cut into 10–12 pieces
1 apple	1 apple
juice of 1 lemon	juice of 1 lemon
100 ml/3½ fl oz oil	½ cup oil
5 onions, chopped	5 onions, chopped
55 g/2 oz grated fresh coconut	⅔ cup freshly grated coconut meat
2 tbsp curry powder	2 tbsp curry powder
1 carton (150 ml/¼ pt) of plain yogurt	⅔ cup plain yogurt
2 bananas, to serve	2 bananas, to serve
salt and pepper	salt and pepper

Season the pieces of chicken with salt and pepper. Peel and quarter the apple, remove the core and chop the flesh into very tiny dice. Sprinkle with half the lemon juice.

Heat the oil in a flameproof casserole. Add the chopped onions and chicken pieces. Cook over a moderate heat, turning the chicken several times. Remove from the heat. Add the apple and grated coconut, sprinkle with the curry powder and mix thoroughly for 3 minutes. Add 400 ml/14 fl oz/1¾ cups of hot water and return to the heat.

Stir the yogurt into the sauce and cover the pot. Cook over a low heat for 40 minutes.

Slice the bananas and sprinkle with the rest of the lemon juice.

When the curry is ready, the sauce should have become very thick. Transfer it to a warmed serving dish and serve with hot boiled rice and the sliced bananas.

CURRY D'AGNEAU

Lamb curry

Serves 6
Preparation 20 minutes
Cooking about 1½ hours

METRIC/IMPERIAL	AMERICAN
4 tbsp soya oil	4 tbsp soybean oil
2 garlic cloves, chopped	2 garlic cloves, chopped
225 g/½ lb onions, chopped	½ lb onions, chopped
4 tomatoes, quartered	4 tomatoes, quartered
bay leaf, crumbled	bay leaf, crumbled
3 tbsp curry powder	3 tbsp curry powder
1.5 kg/3½ lb lamb shoulder, boned and cut into pieces	3½ lb lamb shoulder, boned and cut into pieces
1 carton (150 ml/¼ pt) of plain yogurt	⅔ cup plain yogurt
400 g/14 oz long-grain rice	2¼ cups long-grain rice
2 strands of saffron	2 strands of saffron
3 tbsp mango chutney	3 tbsp mango chutney
10 canned palm hearts, drained and sliced, to serve	10 canned palm hearts, drained and sliced, to serve
salt and cayenne pepper	salt and cayenne pepper

Heat 2 tablespoons of the oil in a flameproof casserole over a moderate heat and cook the garlic and onion in it until just softened.

Add the tomatoes along with the bay leaf. Cook gently, stirring, for a minute or so, then add the curry powder. Leave to simmer over a very low heat.

Meanwhile brown the meat in a frying pan in the remaining oil over a high heat. Add the browned meat to the curry mixture in the casserole, along with the yogurt and 200 ml/7 fl oz/1 cup of hot water and mix well. Add a little salt, then cover the pot and simmer gently for $1\frac{1}{4}$ hours.

While the curry is cooking, prepare the saffron rice. Place the rice in a saucepan with twice its volume of boiling water. Add the saffron and 1 teaspoon of salt and bring back to the boil. Reduce the heat and simmer gently for about 15 minutes. Five minutes before serving, add the mango chutney and a pinch or two of cayenne to the curry.

Transfer the curry to a warmed serving dish and serve with the rice and palm hearts.

CUSTARD

see Creams and custards

CUSTARD MARROW

see Squash

CUTTLEFISH

Seiche

see also:
shellfish
squid

Related to the squid, the cuttlefish is fished and eaten mainly in the Mediterranean countries and the southwest of France. It is normally about 30 cm/1 ft long and consists of a central body bag enclosing a hard part – the cuttlebone – and 10 limbs, 8 legs and 2 tentacles.

Cuttlefish, which are sold whole or ready cleaned, are cooked like squid, but the flesh is very tough and needs long cooking. The bone, guts and beaky head must all be removed before cooking and the flesh is often beaten vigorously beforehand to tenderize it.

Cuttlefish flesh contains 100 calories per 100 g/$3\frac{1}{2}$ oz.

SEICHES DANS LEUR ENCRE

Cuttlefish in their own ink

Serves 4
Preparation 30 minutes
Cooking about $1\frac{1}{4}$ hours

METRIC/IMPERIAL	*AMERICAN*
1 kg/$2\frac{1}{4}$ lb small cuttlefish	*$2\frac{1}{4}$ lb small cuttlefish*
3 tbsp olive oil	*3 tbsp olive oil*
2 onions, chopped	*2 onions, chopped*
2 tomatoes, peeled and coarsely chopped	*2 tomatoes, peeled and coarsely chopped*
3 garlic cloves, chopped	*3 garlic cloves, chopped*
2 tbsp finely chopped flat-leaved parsley	*2 tbsp finely chopped flat-leaf parsley*
2 slices of white bread, crusts removed and made into crumbs	*2 slices of white bread, crusts removed and made into crumbs*
4 tbsp Cognac	*4 tbsp Cognac*
salt and pepper	*salt and pepper*

Preheat the oven to 180C/350F/gas 4.

Remove and discard the bone, beak and guts from the cuttlefish. Take out the ink sacs and reserve them.

Heat the oil in a sauté pan over a moderate heat and cook the onions and tomatoes until the onions are golden brown. Add the cuttlefish and cook, stirring, until the flesh becomes opaque.

Remove the cuttlefish from the pan and put them into a deep baking dish.

Add the chopped garlic, parsley, breadcrumbs, Cognac and 2 tablespoons of water to the sauté pan. Stir over a high heat, mixing well with the onions and tomatoes, then add the cuttlefish ink and stir well.

Pour this sauce over the cuttlefish, cover the baking dish with foil and bake for at least 1 hour.

Serve straight from the baking dish, accompanied by plain boiled rice. If wished, the rice may be moulded into a ring and the cuttlefish poured into the middle.

To drink: a full-bodied red wine, such as Grozes-Hermitage or Barolo.

D

see also:
brill
fish
lemon sole
sole

DAB
Limande

Several types of flat fish found in the English Channel, the Atlantic and the North Sea are known as dab.

The EUROPEAN DAB is lozenge-shaped with brownish spots, about 20–35 cm/8–14 in long and weighing 175–250 g/6½–8½ oz. The paler YELLOWTAIL DAB or RUSTY FLOUNDER found in American waters is larger and can reach up to 60 cm/2 ft in length.

As with most flat fish, there is a high percentage of waste and it is therefore often best to buy the fillets. Dab may be cooked in the same ways as brill or lemon sole. Smaller fish are excellent skinned and fried whole.

Dab has lean flesh and is ideal for low-calorie diets; 100 g/3½ oz contains only 72 calories.

FILETS DE LIMANDE AUX CREVETTES

Dab fillets with shrimp or prawns

Serves 4
Preparation 5 minutes
Cooking 10 minutes

METRIC/IMPERIAL	AMERICAN
75 g/2½ oz flaked almonds	⅔ cup slivered almonds
150 ml/¼ pt court-bouillon or fish stock	⅔ cup court-bouillon or clam juice
12 peeled cooked prawns, halved	12 peeled cooked shrimp, halved
2 tbsp Sauternes or other good sweet white wine	2 tbsp Sauternes or other good sweet white wine
2 tbsp crème fraîche or whipping cream	2 tbsp crème fraîche or whipping cream
1 dab, weighing about 1 kg/2¼ lb, filleted	1 dab, weighing about 2¼ lb, filleted
15 g/½ oz butter	1 tbsp butter
1 egg yolk	1 egg yolk
salt and pepper	salt and pepper

Spread the almonds on a plate and microwave them on High for 4 minutes until golden, stirring them twice.

Put the court-bouillon into a bowl and

microwave on High for 1 minute. Add the prawns (shrimp) to the court-bouillon along with the wine and cream. Mix well.

Place the dab fillets in a deep dish, season them with salt and pepper and dot with butter. Cover with microwave-safe film and pierce it in several places. Microwave on High for 3 minutes.

Drain the dab fillets and put them in a warmed serving dish. Pour the cooking juices into the bowl containing the prawn sauce.

Microwave the sauce on High for a further 2 minutes, then remove it from the oven and whisk in the egg yolk. Season to taste with salt and pepper. Coat the fish fillets with the sauce, garnish with the almonds and serve at once.
To drink: Sauternes.

LIMANDES AU PLAT

Baked dab fillets

Serves 4
Preparation 20 minutes
Cooking 30 minutes

METRIC/IMPERIAL	AMERICAN
45 g/$1\frac{1}{2}$ oz butter, softened	3 tbsp butter, softened
800 g/$1\frac{3}{4}$ lb dab fillets	$1\frac{3}{4}$ lb dab fillets
juice of 1 lemon	juice of 1 lemon
4 shallots, finely chopped	4 shallots, finely chopped
100 ml/$3\frac{1}{2}$ fl oz dry white wine	$\frac{1}{2}$ cup dry white wine
200 ml/7 fl oz thick crème fraîche or whipping cream	1 cup thick crème fraîche or whipping cream
curry powder	curry powder
salt and pepper	salt and pepper

Preheat the oven to 200C/400F/gas 6 and spread the butter over the bottom of a baking dish.

Sprinkle the dab fillets with a little lemon juice, place them in the baking dish and sprinkle again with lemon juice. Bake for 10 minutes.

Meanwhile, put the shallots in a pan with the wine and bring to the boil. Cook over a high heat until the wine has evaporated and the shallots are very soft. Add the cream and a pinch or two of curry powder and stir over a low heat. Season with salt and pepper.

Remove the baking dish from the oven and coat the dab fillets with the shallot sauce. Reduce the heat to 180C/350F/gas 4, return the dish to the oven and bake for a further 20 minutes. Serve hot from the baking dish.
To drink: Bordeaux blanc or Rosé de Cabernet.

DAIKON

see Mooli

DAMSON

see Plum

DANDELION

Pissenlit

see also:
endive
salad
spinach

A perennial plant, the serrated leaves of dandelion resemble those of the curly endive both in appearance and in their slightly bitter taste. The name dandelion comes from the French *dents-de-lion* (lion's teeth), referring to the shape of the leaves; however, the current French term *pissenlit* refers to the plant's supposed diuretic qualities. Wild dandelion leaves, which should be picked in early spring before flowering, have more flavour than hothouse leaves, which come on the market in autumn. The cultivated variety, however, is usually much more tender.

The thicker parts of the stalk should be removed from dandelion leaves before use. The

wild dandelion

cultivated dandelion

leaves may be cooked like spinach, but are more usually eaten raw and are very useful in winter salads. They suit a highly seasoned vinaigrette dressing and garnish of garlic croutons, bacon, hard-boiled eggs or walnuts.

Dandelion has a relatively high calorie content for a green leaf with 48 calories per 100 g/3½ oz, but it is rich in iron and many vitamins.

SALADE DE PISSENLIT AUX OEUFS DURS

Dandelion salad with hard-boiled eggs

Serves 4
Preparation 15 minutes

METRIC/IMPERIAL	AMERICAN
2 slices of slightly stale white bread, crusts removed	2 slices of slightly stale white bread, crusts removed
1 garlic clove, halved	1 garlic clove, halved
4 tbsp olive oil	4 tbsp olive oil
2 tbsp white wine	2 tbsp white wine
300 g/10 oz dandelion leaves, trimmed	10 oz (6–8 cups) dandelion leaves, trimmed
2 hard-boiled eggs, shelled and sliced	2 hard-boiled eggs, shelled and sliced
salt and pepper	salt and pepper

Rub the bread with the garlic and cut it into tiny cubes. Brown these garlic croutons in the oven, under the grill (broiler) or in a frying pan.

Make a vinaigrette with the oil and white wine, adding salt and pepper to taste.

In a salad bowl, toss the dandelion leaves in the vinaigrette. Add the hot croutons and stir again. Put the slices of egg on top and serve.

DATE

Datte

see also:
fruit
petit four

The fruit of a type of palm tree, dates are cultivated extensively in the eastern Mediterranean and North Africa, and to a lesser extent in Spain, California and Arizona.

Until quite recently, dates usually only reached the shops in the dried or semi-dried state, packed in boxes and almost candied in their own high sugar content. The yellow Smyrna dates, with a delicious honeyed taste, and the delicate Tunisian DEGLET NOUR are among the most highly prized. However, fresh dates, actually fresh-frozen, with a lower sugar content, crisp texture and subtly refreshing flavour are now more readily available.

Dried or semi-dried dates are usually consumed as sweetmeats, often stuffed with nuts and marzipan, and may be used in the making of cakes, breads, pastries and jams. Dried and fresh dates are delicious mixed with sharp fresh fruit in fruit salads. Fresh dates make unusual hors d'oeuvres stuffed with cheese or wrapped in bacon. North African cooking often uses dates to great effect in savoury dishes.

Dates are high in fibre and an excellent energy source because of their high sugar and magnesium levels. Rich in phosphorus and calcium, they are also a useful food for people engaging in strenuous physical activity; 100 g/3½ oz contains 300 calories.

CAKE AUX DATTES

Date cake

Serves 4
Preparation 15 minutes
Cooking 10 minutes, resting 6–8 minutes

METRIC/IMPERIAL	AMERICAN
150 g/5½ oz seedless dates, chopped	1 cup chopped dates
100 g/3½ oz butter	1 stick butter
1 ripe banana, peeled	1 ripe banana, peeled
150 g/5½ oz self-raising flour	1¼ cups self-rising flour
2 tbsp unsweetened cocoa	2 tbsp unsweetened cocoa powder
1 sachet (11 g/2½ tsp) of baking powder	1 tbsp baking powder
2 tbsp orange juice	2 tbsp orange juice
55 g/2 oz flaked almonds	½ cup slivered almonds

Put the dates in a small dish with 200 ml/7 fl oz/1 cup of boiling water. Cover and microwave on High for 3 minutes. Leave to cool, then mash.

Put the date paste into a bowl. Add the butter and beat until the mixture is light and creamy. Mash the banana and add it, along with the flour, cocoa and baking powder.

Stir until the mixture is smooth, then mix in the orange juice and almonds. Line a porcelain gratin dish with parchment or greaseproof paper and put the mixture into it.

Microwave for 7 minutes on High, rotating the dish by a quarter-turn every 2 minutes. Remove the dish from the oven and let it stand for 6 minutes. Unmould the cake and remove the paper to serve.

DAUBE

see also:
beef
braising
marinade

The French use this term to describe food braised in red wine with herbs, usually in a specially designed, tightly sealed cast-iron or earthenware cooking vessel known as a *daubière*. The ingredients are also usually left to marinate for some time even before the lengthy cooking process begins.

The word *daube* used without further qualification usually implies beef as the main ingredient, but the technique may well be applied to pork, lamb, chicken, turkey, duck, goose, rabbit, game birds, some vegetables and even cuttlefish and tuna fish.

DAUBE DE BOEUF

Beef stew

Serves 8–10
Preparation 25 minutes
Cooking 5 hours

METRIC/IMPERIAL	*AMERICAN*
1 orange	*1 orange*
55 g/2 oz butter	*4 tbsp butter*
2 tbsp corn oil	*2 tbsp corn oil*
3 kg/6½ lb beef top rump or chuck, cut into large pieces	*6½ lb beef chuck, cut into large pieces*
450 g/1 lb country ham, finely diced	*1 lb country ham, finely diced*
2 kg/4½ lb onions, thinly sliced	*4½ lb onions, thinly sliced*
2 tbsp Armagnac	*2 tbsp Armagnac*
2 calves' feet, boned and cut into large pieces	*2 calves' feet, boned and cut into large pieces*
2 kg/4½ lb carrots, sliced	*4½ lb carrots, sliced*
4 garlic cloves, crushed	*4 garlic cloves, minced*
bouquet garni	*bouquet garni*
bunch of flat-leaved parsley, chopped	*bunch of flat-leaf parsley, chopped*
12 black peppercorns	*12 black peppercorns*
2 bottles (1.5 l/2½ pt) of red wine (preferably Cahors or Madiran)	*2 bottles (1½ qt) of red wine (preferably Cahors or Madiran)*

If the orange is not organically grown, and may have been sprayed or coated, scrub it in warm soapy water, rinse well and pat dry. Pare the zest from the orange.

Melt the butter and oil in a large, flameproof casserole with a tight-fitting lid and brown the pieces of beef with the ham and sliced onions over a moderate heat. When all are well browned, add the Armagnac, warm through briefly and flame the contents of the casserole.

Add the calves' feet, carrots, garlic, orange zest, bouquet garni, parsley and peppercorns. Pour the wine over and cover tightly to seal the container. Cook over a low heat for 2 hours.

Preheat the oven to 180C/350F/gas 4. At the end of the 2 hours, put the casserole in the oven and continue cooking for a further 3 hours. Adjust the seasoning and serve straight from the casserole.

Note: for more flavour, after adding the wine marinate the ingredients in a cool place for 24 hours.

DEEP FRYING

Friture

see also:
blanching
breadcrumbs
choux pastry
fats and oils
fritter

This technique of cooking food involves totally immersing it in hot oil or fat. As a result, the food cooks very quickly and must therefore be flat, like fish fillets, or cut into quite small pieces, like French-fried potatoes, to enable the insides to cook before the exterior is overdone.

Food to be deep fried must also be as dry as possible to avoid splattering. Thus, foods with a high moisture content are often given a protective coating before being deep fried.

There are three principal methods of sealing food for deep frying: small whole fish or fish fillets are best dipped in milk and then coated with flour; pieces of meat, poultry and croquettes, all of which have a high water content, are sealed by a double or triple coating of flour, beaten egg and dried breadcrumbs; fruit and vegetables, which are mostly water, must be coated in batter and cooked as fritters. These coatings both keep moisture in and protect the exteriors of delicate food from the high temperatures involved. Batter coatings are also useful in cases where the food melts on cooking, say cheese or fruit, as the crisped batter holds the shape.

The temperature of the oil is critical in deep frying. The oil must be properly heated to that temperature before cooking begins and maintained at the correct temperature throughout the cooking to avoid soggy, fat-laden or dried-out food. Gentle frying is done at a temperature of 180C/350F, for initial 'blanching' to ensure food is thoroughly cooked through; moderate frying at 190C/375F is used for most deep frying, especially of coated foods; fast frying at 195C/385F is usually only for a final browning of items already cooked at the lower temperature, or for some small fish like whitebait. Ideally, use a deep fryer with thermostatic control; otherwise a good guide is to drop in a small cube of dry bread that will brown in 60, 40 and 20 seconds respectively.

It is very important never to overheat the cooking oil so that it starts to smoke, as at this stage it begins to break down and will impart an unpleasant flavour to the food. Overheated oil also runs the risk of spontaneously igniting; the process of deep frying must therefore be monitored carefully throughout.

Pans should never be more than one third filled with oil as it froths up so much when the food is first put in. The food must be of a uniform size to ensure even cooking and it should not be cooked in over-large batches. Immerse each batch fairly slowly, to avoid reducing the temperature of the oil too much, and carefully agitate the food to ensure even cooking of larger items. Small items of food are best deep fried in a basket which may easily be lowered into the oil and then lifted clear of it at the end. Deep fried food will normally float to the surface when it is cooked.

The crisp and golden cooked food should be thoroughly drained and then patted dry on paper towels. Deep fried food must be served as soon as possible on being cooked as it quickly loses its appetizing crispness. If it has to be kept warm while another batch is being cooked, leave it on paper towels, but do not cover it, and keep it in a warm oven with the door open.

The best oils for deep frying are vegetable oils, such as groundnut (peanut), sunflower and corn, as they may be heated to the right temperatures without fear of decomposition and do not have intrusive flavours. The oil may be filtered and reused several times provided it is not over-heated. It should be discarded as soon as it discolours and starts to smell stale.

If properly executed, deep frying is not an unhealthy way of cooking as little of the fat is absorbed by the food. It is also an excellent means of preserving the full flavour and texture of some food, especially fish. The process also allows real texture treats, with the contrast of crisp tasty coatings and almost liquid interiors, as with choux *beignets* or fruit fritters.

PÂTE À FRIRE

Batter for deep frying

Serves 4
Preparation 15 minutes, resting 1 hour

METRIC/IMPERIAL	*AMERICAN*
200 g/7 oz flour	*1⅔ cups flour*
¼ sachet (2.75 g/¾ tsp) of baking powder	*¾ tsp baking powder*
3 tbsp groundnut oil	*3 tbsp peanut oil*
2 egg whites	*2 egg whites*
salt	*salt*

Sift the flour into a bowl and add the baking powder. Add the oil, a pinch of salt and about 200 ml/7 fl oz/1 cup of warm water. Mix thoroughly until the batter is smooth, then let it rest for at least 1 hour.

Just before use, whisk the egg whites with a pinch of salt to very stiff peaks and fold them gently into the batter.

Variations: replace some of the water with milk, beer or dry (hard) cider.

DEGLAZING

Déglacer

see also:
brandies, etc
flaming
gravy
roasting
sauce
sautéing
wine

After food has been sautéed or roasted, the pan used is often deglazed by adding a little liquid, such as stock, wine, Cognac, crème fraîche or even water, which is stirred over a moderate heat and the flavorous sediment scraped to dissolve as much of it as possible in the liquid. This liquid can then be used to make a delicious sauce or gravy to accompany the cooked food. It may be cooked further in the pan to drive off any alcohol and caramelize the sugar content to colour it, or boiled to reduce it to a coating consistency and concentrate the flavour. In French cuisine the pan contents are often flamed in Cognac before the deglazing process.

After sautéing, remove the cooked food and add the liquid, scraping to dissolve the brown bits.

Boil gently to reduce the liquid to the desired amount, stirring frequently.

DIETARY FIBRE

see also:
bran
bread
fruit
vegetables

Previously referred to as 'roughage', dietary fibre is the term now used for that part of foodstuffs which is neither digested nor absorbed by the body. Dietary fibre is made up of several different substances, some of which are not fibrous. Most fibre consists of cellulose, which is the basic structural material of plants and from which we make paper; the other principal component is pectin, from some fruits, which makes jam set when it is boiled.

Although it is not digested in any way, fibre plays an important role in the digestive system: as it swells in water and becomes quite bulky it speeds the passage of material through the intestines and prevents constipation. By increasing the speed at which the body eliminates waste, it also reduces the unwanted accumulation of toxic substances. Pectins also slow down the absorption of carbohydrates and thus have a beneficial effect in cases of diabetes, and are also thought to lower levels of cholesterol in the body.

Foods with a natural high fibre content are, obviously, leafy vegetables, fruit and bran. For example, wholemeal and wholewheat bread contain 8% fibre by weight, as against 3% in the case of white bread; raspberries contain 7%; prunes 8%, peas 6%.

If fibre-rich foods are eaten at every meal it is unnecessary to include additional fibre or bran in the diet. Excessive consumption of fibre may cause discomfort and an unwelcome increase in flatulence and bowel movements. There is also evidence that it may inhibit the absorption of minerals, such as iron. Too much bran may have negative effects, possibly causing colitis and distension. The recommended daily intake of fibre is 15–30 g/½–1 oz. This requirement is adequately covered by one vegetable dish, two pieces of fruit and 150 g/5½ oz of wholemeal or wholewheat bread.

DILL

Aneth

see also:
gherkin
herbs
marinade
pickles
salmon

An aromatic plant which is very similar to fennel, sometimes called FALSE ANISE or BASTARD FENNEL. The crushed fresh or dried green leaves of the plant are popular as a culinary herb, particularly in Scandinavia, where it is used in the curing of salmon to make gravlax, and Eastern Europe. The milder-flavoured dill seeds are popular in Middle Eastern cooking and in pickling.

Dill is especially used to enhance the flavour

of cucumber, salmon and shellfish. It works well in marinades for meat and fish, with vegetables such as fennel or courgettes (zucchini) and the seeds are particularly good in fish salads. The seeds and leaves are also used to flavour vinegars and mustards.

SALADE DE CONCOMBRE À L'ANETH

Cucumber salad with dill

Serves 4
Preparation 15 minutes, resting 30 minutes

METRIC/IMPERIAL	AMERICAN
2 cucumbers	2 hothouse cucumbers
300 ml/½ pt natural yogurt	1½ cups unflavored yogurt
1 tbsp thick crème fraîche or sour cream	1 tbsp thick crème fraîche or sour cream
bunch of dill, snipped with scissors	bunch of dill, snipped with scissors
1 tbsp lemon juice	1 tbsp lemon juice
1 large tomato, peeled, deseeded and finely diced	1 large tomato, peeled, deseeded and finely diced
salt and freshly ground black pepper	salt and freshly ground black pepper

Cut one of the cucumbers in half and peel one of those halves and the second cucumber. Slice the peeled cucumber very thinly, sprinkle it with salt and allow to drain for 30 minutes.

Put the yogurt, cream, dill and lemon juice into a bowl, season with black pepper and whisk them together.

Finely slice the unpeeled cucumber half and arrange the slices on a round serving dish.

Mix the drained cucumber in the bowl with the yogurt sauce. Pour it into the middle of the serving dish and put the diced tomato in the centre. Grind more black pepper over the salad and serve well chilled.

This salad is delicious eaten with cold poached fish.

SAUCE AU BEURRE À L'ANETH

Mushroom and butter sauce with dill

Serves 6
Preparation 15 minutes
Cooking about 30 minutes

METRIC/IMPERIAL	AMERICAN
115 g/¼ lb white button mushrooms	¼ lb white button mushrooms
juice of ½ lemon	juice of ½ lemon
150 g/5½ oz butter	11 tbsp butter
5–6 shallots, finely chopped	5–6 shallots, finely chopped
bunch of dill, snipped with scissors	bunch of dill, snipped with scissors
2 tbsp white wine vinegar	2 tbsp white wine vinegar
300 ml/½ pt dry white wine	1½ cups dry white wine
200 ml/7 fl oz crème fraîche or whipping cream	1 cup crème fraîche or whipping cream
salt and pepper	salt and pepper

Wipe and slice the mushrooms and sprinkle them with lemon juice.

Melt 25 g/1 oz/2 tbsp of the butter in a heavy-bottomed, flameproof casserole. Add the shallots and stir over a gentle heat to mix with the butter. Add the mushrooms and half the dill and cook for 2 minutes, stirring, then add the vinegar. Increase the heat and reduce until it has evaporated.

Add the wine and continue to cook, stirring, until this liquid is reduced by half. Add the cream and cook for 5 minutes. Add the remaining butter in small pieces, whisking constantly, then add the rest of the dill and season to taste. The finished sauce should be thick and smooth. It makes an excellent accompaniment for grilled (broiled) or barbecued salmon steaks.

DOLMA OR DOLMADE

see Vine leaf

see also:
baba
cakes and gâteaux
cookies, etc
kugelhopf
stuffing

DRIED VINE FRUIT

Raisin sec

Drying grapes produces several different common types of preserved fruit.

CURRANTS are small, black, sun-dried fruit made from a tiny black grape native to Corinth in Greece, from which they get their name. To this day most of the crop still comes from Greece, although Australia, South Africa and California are increasingly large producers.

SULTANAS OF GOLDEN SEEDLESS RAISINS are golden-brown in colour, very sweet and have a fine, strong flavour. They are made from seedless green grapes dried in the sun, or in the warm shade, immediately after harvest. The best sultanas originally came from Turkey, but now many countries, especially those around the Mediterranean, export sultanas. California and Australia produce a sweeter sultana which has little of the characteristic flavour of the European variety.

RAISINS come in two main varieties: the smaller SEEDLESS RAISIN is made by sun-drying the green Thompson sultana grape. The greater part of the crop comes from the USA, Mexico and South Africa. The more ancient STONED RAISIN is manufactured, mostly in Spain but also in Australia and South Africa, from large red Muscatel grapes which are steamed and pressed to remove the seeds. These raisins have by far the better flavour and are the type usually served as a dessert fruit or sweetmeat.

Dried vine fruit, especially sultanas, are often given protection from mould and bacteria with a light coating of mineral oil. For this reason it is wiser to avoid glossy fruit and always to wash dried fruit in hot water before use. After thorough washing and rinsing, the fruit is usually soaked for an hour or two in fresh warm water, tea, wine, rum, port or other liquor to plump them up before use. This process may be speeded up by using a microwave oven: put each 100 g/$3\frac{1}{2}$ oz/$\frac{2}{3}$ cup of fruit in 150 ml/5 fl oz/$\frac{2}{3}$ cup of boiling water and cook for 3 minutes on High followed by 15 minute's standing time.

Often in alliance with nuts, dried vine fruits are a common ingredient in cooking. They are popular in yeast doughs, such as brioche, babas and *Kugelhopf*, in the making of pastries, desserts, biscuits or cookies and cakes, especially traditional fruit cakes. They also find much use in savoury dishes, particularly in the cooking of Spain, North Africa and the eastern Mediterranean, in dishes such as couscous and *dolmas*. They work well in stuffings and sauces for meat, especially lamb and pork, poultry, game and oily fish, and make a delicious addition to pies, curries, stews, casseroles and meat loaf.

The process of drying the grape concentrates the sugar content and gives the fruit a very high energy level, about 325 calories per 100 g/$3\frac{1}{2}$ oz, but destroys very little of the naturally high vitamin and mineral content. As they are also very high in fibre, but have no fat, no cholesterol and are low in sodium, they are healthy and nutritious.

FLAUGNARDE

Dried fruit pudding

Serves 6
Preparation 20 minutes
Cooking 30 minutes

METRIC/IMPERIAL	*AMERICAN*
45 g/$1\frac{1}{2}$ oz butter	*3 tbsp butter*
8 prunes, stoned	*8 prunes, pitted*
100 g/$3\frac{1}{2}$ oz raisins	*$\frac{2}{3}$ cup raisins*
4 dried apricots, finely chopped	*4 dried apricots, finely chopped*
100 ml/$3\frac{1}{2}$ fl oz rum	*$\frac{1}{2}$ cup rum*
4 eggs	*4 eggs*
100 g/$3\frac{1}{2}$ oz caster sugar	*$\frac{1}{2}$ cup superfine sugar*
100 g/$3\frac{1}{2}$ oz flour	*$\frac{3}{4}$ cup flour*
1.5 l/$2\frac{1}{2}$ pt milk	*$1\frac{1}{2}$ qt milk*
salt	*salt*

Preheat the oven to 220C/425F/gas 7 and grease a large baking dish with some of the butter.

Put the prunes, raisins and apricots into a bowl, pour the rum over and leave to macerate.

Meanwhile, beat the eggs in a bowl with the sugar until pale and thick. Add the flour and a pinch of salt and mix well. Stir in the milk.

Add the fruit and rum. Pour the mixture into the baking dish and dot the surface with the remaining butter.

Bake in the middle of the oven for 30 minutes. Serve warm from the baking dish.

GRATIN DE POMMES AUX FRUITS SECS

Apple and dried fruit bake

Serves 4
Preparation 15 minutes
Cooking 10 minutes

METRIC/IMPERIAL	AMERICAN
25 g/¾ oz butter	1½ tbsp butter
4 dried figs, chopped	4 dried figs, chopped
55 g/2 oz raisins	⅓ cup raisins
1 tbsp shelled pistachio nuts	1 tbsp shelled pistachio nuts
150 ml/¼ pt rum	⅔ cup rum
3 apples	3 apples
juice of 1 lemon	juice of 1 lemon
4 tbsp fresh white breadcrumbs	¼ cup fresh white breadcrumbs
ground cinnamon	ground cinnamon
2 tbsp ground almonds	2 tbsp ground almonds

Preheat the oven to 200C/400F/gas 6 and grease 4 small ovenproof dishes with the butter.

Put the figs in a bowl with the raisins and pistachio nuts. Pour the rum over and set aside.

Meanwhile, peel and coarsely grate the apples into a bowl and sprinkle them with lemon juice. Drain the fruit and nut mixture and add it, along with the breadcrumbs. Mix well.

Spoon the mixture into the buttered dishes, add just a touch of cinnamon to each and sprinkle the ground almonds over the top. Bake for 10 minutes and serve warm or chilled.

PETITS GÂTEAUX AUX RAISINS SECS

Raisin cookies

Makes 24
Preparation 15 minutes
Cooking 15 minutes

METRIC/IMPERIAL	AMERICAN
55 g/2 oz raisins	6 tbsp raisins
1 orange	1 orange
100 g/3½ oz butter, softened	1 stick butter, softened
85 g/3 oz thick sweetened apple purée	4½ tbsp thick sweetened apple purée or apple butter
200 g/7 oz flour	1⅔ cups flour

Rinse the raisins in boiling water and drain well. If the orange is not organically grown and may have been sprayed or coated, scrub it well in warm soapy water, rinse and pat dry. Grate the zest of the orange and squeeze the juice.

In a bowl, beat the softened butter with the apple purée. When the mixture is light and fluffy, add the flour and beat well. Add 2 tablespoons of orange juice along with the zest and the raisins and knead into a smooth dough.

Roll it out to a thickness of about 6 mm/¼ in and cut out 24 rounds using a 5 cm/2 in cutter.

Arrange half the rounds in a circle on a sheet of parchment or greaseproof paper in the microwave oven. Cover them with paper towel.

Microwave on High for 2½ minutes. Let stand for 5 minutes, then transfer them to a wire rack to cool. Cook the second batch in the same way.

Variations: use prune paste instead of the apple purée and 2 mandarins in place of the orange.

Use wholemeal or whole wheat flour to give the cookies a more attractive colour.

SARDINES FARCIES AUX RAISINS SECS

Sardines stuffed with raisins

Serves 6
Preparation 30 minutes
Cooking about 20 minutes

METRIC/IMPERIAL	AMERICAN
4 tbsp olive oil	4 tbsp olive oil
1 kg/2¼ lb large fresh sardines	2¼ lb large fresh sardines
8 tbsp fresh breadcrumbs	½ cup fresh breadcrumbs
100 g/3½ oz raisins	⅔ cup raisins
1 tsp caster sugar	1 tsp superfine sugar
1 tbsp finely chopped parsley	1 tbsp finely chopped parsley
55 g/2 oz pine kernels	⅔ cup pine nuts
2 bay leaves, crumbled	2 bay leaves, crumbled
juice of 1 lemon	juice of 1 lemon
salt and pepper	salt and pepper

Preheat the oven to 200C/400F/gas 6 and grease a baking dish with a little of the oil.

Clean and scale the sardines and remove the heads. Take out the backbone but do not separate the fillets.

In a bowl, mix half the remaining oil with the breadcrumbs, raisins, sugar, chopped parsley and pine kernels (pine nuts), and season with salt and pepper. Stuff each of the sardines with a little of the raisin mixture, arranging them in the oiled baking dish as they are done.

Scatter the crumbled bay leaves over the sardines and then sprinkle the lemon juice and the remaining oil over the top. Bake for 20 minutes and serve straight from the baking dish. *To drink: a fruity white wine, such as a Côtes-de-Provence.*

DRYING

Séchage

see also:
apricot
banana
bean
curing
dried vine fruit
fruit
herbs
mushroom
nuts
prune
pulses
smoking

One of the most ancient means of preserving food is to remove the moisture from it by drying it either in the sun or in wind or warm air currents. This leaves insufficient water to support the life processes of any mould, bacteria or enzyme. However, it does not always kill all micro-organisms, so dried food often spoils very quickly if allowed to get damp. The process may be applied to a wide variety of food, but is most successful with grains, legumes and pulses, fish, fruit, nuts, herbs and some vegetables, meats and meat products.

Drying is often combined with another curing process, particularly salting or smoking in the case of fish and meat. Vegetables are usually first blanched or steamed to kill off insects, discourage enzyme activity and preserve their colour.

Drying used to be done on beaches and in fields immediately after harvest. Nowadays, however, most commercial drying is done by machines which actually dehydrate or draw the moisture out of food, usually by the 'spray-drying' or 'freeze-drying' processes.

The foods most easily dried at home are mushrooms, herbs and fruit. In warm sunny climates outdoor drying can be successful, but other methods are more appropriate in humid areas without sustained periods of sun.

TO DRY MUSHROOMS: clean them, cut them in slices if they are large and spread them in a single layer on a fine rack or netting. Expose them to sunlight in a well-ventilated place, turning them from time to time. When they are completely dry, seal them in jars and store them in a dry place. If there is insufficient sunshine, place them in a very low oven (130C/275F/gas 1) with the door open for periods of 2 hours at a time until completely dry. Eat within a year.

TO DRY HERBS: pick them mid-morning just before flowering for best flavour, wash them and carefully pat dry. If they have small leaves, wrap them in cheesecloth bags and hang them in a warm airy place; if they are large-leaved, dry them hanging in bunches, head downwards. Store them whole or crumbled in small sealed jars. They lose their flavour within 6 months.

TO DRY APPLES: peel them and remove the seeds and core with an apple-corer. Slice them horizontally and plunge them in water acidulated with a little lemon juice. Drain them and arrange them in a single layer, spaced well apart, on a wooden tray in full sunlight. Leave them to dry for 2–3 days; if necessary, complete the drying process in an open cool oven. Apples dried this way should be eaten within 6 months.

In most cases, drying preserves a high percentage of the nutrients in food and keeps a strong flavour. Before use, most dried food needs to be rehydrated by soaking in water, wine, stock or other suitable liquid.

DUBLIN BAY PRAWN

see Langoustine

DUCK

Canard

see also:
confit
foie gras
giblets
goose
salmis

Related to the goose, the duck has been bred for its eggs and tasty, if fatty, meat for many centuries in most of the world, but is used to best advantage in the cuisines of France and China. Several species of domesticated duck are available:

NANTAIS DUCK is probably the most highly regarded in France. It is very fatty, but has a fine, delicate flavour and texture. Usually killed at about 4 months, it weighs about 1.5 kg/3½ lb.

ROUEN DUCK tends to be about twice the size at the same age, and is strangled so that it retains all its blood. This gives the meat a reddish tinge and a very gamy flavour. Rouen duck must be cooked within 24 hours of death and is used to make the classic dish *caneton à la rouennaise* or 'pressed duck' in which the roast breast and legs are served in a sauce made from reduced red wine, Cognac and the pressed juices from the rest of the bird.

The English AYLESBURY DUCK, weighing in the region of 2 kg/4½ lb, is similar to Rouen duck in flavour, but tastes fresher as it is usually bled.

American LONG ISLAND DUCK is said to be descended from the Chinese PEKING DUCK, once reserved only for the Emperor. It has a particularly fine flavour. Grown ducks weigh about 3 kg/6½ lb and ducklings about 2 kg/4½ lb.

The rather ungainly BARBARY or MUSCOVY DUCK, popular in Australia and the USA, is leaner, with firm meat and a distinctly musky flavour which becomes almost unpalatable when the birds are fully grown.

WILD DUCK is leaner and usually has a stronger flavour than domesticated duck, although it tends to have even less meat in proportion to weight. MALLARD is the only type of wild duck which is widely available commercially. A genuinely wild specimen fresh from the fields, such as TEAL or WIDGEON, is generally best consumed fairly promptly as it does not need hanging to develop flavour. Wild duck must be thoroughly plucked, singed and drawn and any shot carefully removed, causing as little damage to the meat and skin as possible.

As with most commercially reared meat, domesticated ducks are killed and sold much younger than was once the case. Most of the birds available nowadays are actually duckling (*canetons*), no more than 8 weeks old. Ducklings are, however, often plumper and more full of flavour than duck, although more expensive by weight. When purchasing duck, test that the wing tips and beak are flexible, the skin supple and the breast plump. Duck is generally at its best during the winter. Allow about 350 g/12 oz on the bone per person. If the duck is not already dressed, always ensure that the two small glands under the tail end are removed before cooking.

Prior to cooking, it is wise to prick domesticated duck all over to allow the fat to run off. The excess fat rendered during or after cooking should be strained and stored: it is very tasty and useful for cooking, especially for frying potatoes. Very tender young duckling is delicious spit-roasted. For ordinary roasting in the oven, place the bird on a rack so that it stands clear of the fat and crisps up well. Allow about 20 minutes per 450 g/1 lb at 230C/450F/gas 8, slightly longer if the bird is stuffed. Duck should never be over-cooked: the full flavour and texture of the meat is best enjoyed while it is still pinkish. Larger, less tender, birds (from 2 kg/4½ lb upwards) are better braised with vegetables or fruit. Very large ducks are best used for pâtés and ballottines.

As WILD DUCKS are generally smaller than domestically reared ducks, allow 1 whole bird for 2 people, particularly if it is to be roasted. Do not prick the skin as the meat may then become too dry. If the bird is very gamy, clean the cavity with a little brandy, rub the skin with a cut lemon and loosely fill the cavity with apples or celery during cooking. Roast a young wild duck for 20–25 minutes per 450 g/1 lb and baste it with port or Madeira to keep the meat moist. Older wild fowl are best fricasséed with potatoes or wild mushrooms.

Duck breasts or *magrets*, breasts from specially fattened ducks, are increasingly available ready-prepared in supermarkets. They are delicious fried or grilled: the skin and fat layer may be removed prior to cooking, or slashed through in several places with a sharp knife to allow the heat to permeate the meat.

Because of its high fat content, duck lends itself to sweet or sharp stuffings and sauces, especially using fruit such as oranges, cherries, apricots, olives and prunes. The crispy duck of Chinese cuisine is first steamed to remove the excess fat and then deep fried.

Domestically reared duck meat contains about 200 calories per 100 g/3½ oz; wild duck, on the other hand, contains only 125 calories per 100 g/3½ oz. The fat, mainly situated just underneath the skin, is easily avoided.

CANARD À L'ORANGE

Duck with orange sauce

Serves 5–6
Preparation 45 minutes
Cooking about 1¼ hours

METRIC/IMPERIAL	*AMERICAN*
5 oranges	*5 oranges*
100 g/3½ oz butter	*1 stick butter*
1 oven-ready duck, weighing at least 2 kg/4½ lb	*1 duck, weighing at least 4½ lb, dressed and drawn weight*
1 carrot, thinly sliced	*1 carrot, thinly sliced*
1 onion, thinly sliced	*1 onion, thinly sliced*
bouquet garni	*bouquet garni*
2 tbsp Cognac	*2 tbsp Cognac*
4 tbsp Cointreau	*4 tbsp Cointreau*
1 tbsp white wine vinegar	*1 tbsp white wine vinegar*
2 tsp cornflour	*2 tsp cornstarch*
salt and pepper	*salt and pepper*

If the oranges are not organically grown, and may have been sprayed or coated, scrub 2 of them in warm soapy water, rinse them well and pat dry. Pare off the zest and cut it into thin strips. Boil these for 5 minutes and then leave them to drain. Squeeze the juice from these 2 oranges plus a third orange, and set the juice aside. Peel the remaining 2 oranges, removing as much of the white pith as possible, slice them and set them on one side.

Melt three quarters of the butter in a flameproof casserole and brown the duck on all sides over a moderate heat, adding the carrot and onion. Add 2 tablespoons of water, the bouquet garni and salt and pepper to taste. Cover, lower the heat and simmer for 45 minutes.

Sprinkle the Cognac and Cointreau over the duck. Cover once more, remove the casserole from the heat and let it stand for 10 minutes. Remove the duck, wrap in foil and keep hot.

Add the vinegar and orange juice to the casserole, stir well and simmer gently for 10 minutes. Strain into a pan and skim off all the fat. Add the cornflour (cornstarch) mixed to a smooth paste with a little water and simmer gently, stirring, until thickened. Set aside.

CARVING A DUCK

Remove the leg quarter from each side of the duck, then cut through the joint to divide the drumstick and thigh pieces.

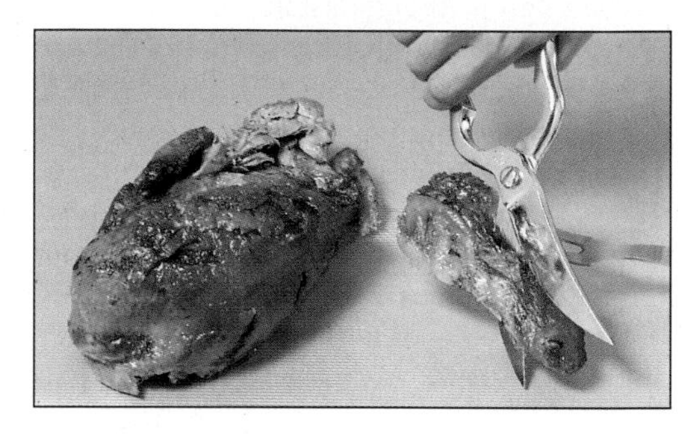

Cut off the wings where they join the breast bone and use a pair of poultry shears to separate the two parts of the wing.

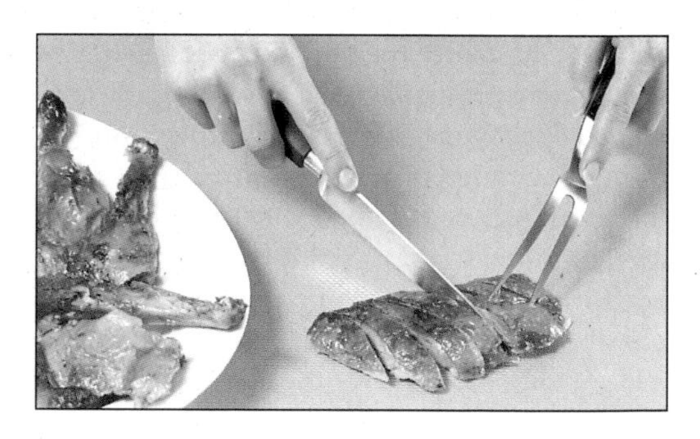

Carve off the breast meat in one piece, then cut it in even slices. Arrange the pieces on a serving platter, saving any juices to add to the sauce.

Melt the remaining butter in a frying pan and heat the orange slices gently in it.

Carve the duck and arrange the pieces on a warmed serving plate. Arrange the warmed orange slices around the duck.

Pour the juices that will have collected in the foil into the sauce and add the strips of orange

Canard à l'orange (Duck with orange sauce)

zest. Heat the sauce and pour some of it over the duck. Pour the rest of the sauce into a sauce boat and serve it with the duck.
To drink: a good, medium-bodied red Burgundy, such as a Côte-de-Beaune.

CANARD AUX POMMES

Wild duck with apples

Serves 2–3
Preparation 25 minutes
Cooking about 50 minutes

METRIC/IMPERIAL	AMERICAN
1 kg/2¼ lb apples	2¼ lb apples
1 wild duck (with giblets), dressed weight about 1.5 kg/3½ lb	1 wild duck (with giblets), weighing about 3½ lb, dressed and drawn weight
45 g/1½ oz butter	3 tbsp butter
2 tbsp Calvados	2 tbsp Calvados
100 ml/3½ fl oz dry white wine	½ cup dry white wine
100 ml/3½ fl oz crème fraîche or whipping cream	½ cup crème fraîche or whipping cream
salt and pepper	salt and pepper

Preheat the oven to 220C/425F/gas 7.

Peel one of the apples and chop it into small pieces. Finely chop the duck liver and gizzard.

Melt one third of the butter in a saucepan and add the chopped apple and giblets, seasoning with salt and pepper. Stir over a high heat, then pour the Calvados over, heat for a moment or two and flame the mixture.

Leave to cool slightly, then stuff the duck with the mixture. Sew up the opening, truss the duck and put it in a roasting pan. Roast it for about 40 minutes.

Meanwhile, peel and quarter the remaining apples. Heat the remaining butter in a frying pan and sauté the apple quarters for 10 minutes.

Remove the duck from the oven, take it out of the pan and keep it hot covered with foil. Remove most of the fat from the cooking juices and deglaze the roasting pan with the white wine. Boil rapidly for 2 minutes, then add the cream and stir for 2 minutes over a gentle heat.

Carve the duck and arrange the pieces on a serving dish. Coat them with the sauce and garnish them with the apples. Serve at once.
To drink: a red Graves.

MAGRETS AU POIVRE VERT

Duck breasts with green peppercorns

Serves 4
Preparation 5 minutes, marinating 1 hour
Cooking about 15 minutes

METRIC/IMPERIAL	AMERICAN
2 large duck breasts or magrets, trimmed	2 large boneless duck breast halves, trimmed
2 tbsp green peppercorns in brine, drained	2 tbsp green peppercorns in brine, drained
150 ml/¼ pt full-bodied red wine	⅔ cup full-bodied red wine
1 tbsp goose fat	1 tbsp goose fat
100 ml/3½ fl oz chicken stock	½ cup chicken stock
2 tbsp crème fraîche or whipping cream	2 tbsp crème fraîche or whipping cream
salt and pepper	salt and pepper

Remove and discard the excess fat from the duck breasts. Put the peppercorns into a bowl with the red wine and leave them to marinate for at least 1 hour.

Heat the goose fat in a sauté pan over a high heat and put the duck breasts in it skin-side down. Cook for 5 minutes, then turn them and cook for a further 3–4 minutes on the other side to seal them.

Reduce the heat to moderate and add the green peppercorns with the wine and chicken stock. Season lightly with salt and add pepper to taste and continue to cook for about 5 minutes. Remove the meat and keep warm.

Reduce the liquid slightly and stir in the cream. Return the meat to the pan and heat through for 1 minute. Serve the duck breasts on a warmed serving dish, coated with the sauce and accompanied by plain boiled rice and grilled wild mushrooms or small sautéed potatoes.
To drink: a hearty red wine, such as a Madiran.

see also:
mushroom
sauce
stuffing

DUXELLES

This term describes a preparation of finely chopped mushrooms and either shallots or onions or both, which are gently sautéed in butter until the liquid they render during cooking has evaporated. Duxelles may be used as a stuffing or garnish or as a basis for a sauce.

A mushroom duxelles makes a delicious stuffing for boned leg of lamb and rolled beef fillet (tenderloin), and for fish, particularly brill or sole. It is also useful for stuffed vegetables, such as tomatoes, artichoke bottoms or aubergine (eggplant). This preparation makes a perfect omelette filling or accompaniment for other egg dishes, for fish and for veal escalopes (scaloppini) or chops.

To make a sauce from duxelles, stir some crème fraîche or whipping cream into the mushroom purée at the end of the cooking time, or add the duxelles to a béchamel or demi-glace sauce or tomato fondue.

Duxelles freezes well, so take advantage of bargain mushrooms. Freeze in several small batches for convenience.

Cut the shallots and onions into very small dice. Slice the mushrooms, then dice them finely.

Cook the vegetables in butter over a low heat, stirring until they are soft and the liquid has evaporated.

DUXELLES DE CHAMPIGNONS

Mushroom duxelles

Makes about 400 g/14 oz
Preparation 15 minutes
Cooking about 20 minutes

METRIC/IMPERIAL	AMERICAN
30 g/1 oz butter	2 tbsp butter
1 onion, finely chopped	1 onion, finely chopped
2 shallots, finely chopped	2 shallots, finely chopped
300 g/10 oz mushrooms, finely chopped	10 oz mushrooms, finely chopped
1 tsp finely chopped flat-leaved parsley	1 tsp finely chopped flat-leaf parsley
salt and pepper	salt and pepper

Heat the butter in a pan over a gentle heat, taking care that it does not brown. Add the chopped onion and shallots and cook them very gently for 3–4 minutes until just softened.

Add the mushrooms and continue to cook over low a heat, stirring from time to time with a wooden spoon, until all the liquid has evaporated. Season with salt and pepper, add the chopped parsley, stir and remove from the heat.

E

see also:
choux pastry
creams and
custards

ÉCLAIR

Traditionally éclairs are small cylindrical choux buns split lengthwise, filled with whipped cream or chocolate- or coffee-flavoured pastry cream and topped with chocolate fondant icing. The filling and icing may also be flavoured variously with rum, fruit or chestnut purée.

One chocolate éclair contains about 300 calories.

CLAIRS

Chocolate and coffee éclairs

Makes 12
Preparation 30 minutes
Cooking 20 minutes, 2 hours ahead

METRIC/IMPERIAL	*AMERICAN*
115 g/4 oz butter	*8 tbsp butter*
15 g/½ oz caster sugar	*4 tsp superfine sugar*
½ tsp salt	*½ tsp salt*
150 g/5½ oz flour	*1¼ cups flour*
5 eggs + 1 egg yolk	*5 eggs + 1 egg yolk*
1 tbsp milk	*1 tbsp milk*
450 g/1 lb fondant icing	*1 lb fondant icing*
1 tbsp instant coffee	*1 tbsp instant coffee powder*
1 tbsp unsweetened cocoa	*1 tbsp unsweetened cocoa powder*
FOR THE PASTRY CREAM:	*FOR THE PASTRY CREAM:*
1 vanilla pod	*1 vanilla bean*
500 ml/16 fl oz milk	*2 cups milk*
150 g/5½ oz caster sugar	*¾ cup superfine sugar*
5 egg yolks	*5 egg yolks*
50 g/1¾ oz flour	*6½ tbsp flour*
1 tbsp instant coffee	*1 tbsp instant coffee powder*
1 tbsp unsweetened cocoa	*1 tbsp unsweetened cocoa powder*

Preheat the oven to 190C/375/gas 5. Grease a baking sheet with a little of the butter.

Make the choux pastry: combine the sugar, the remaining butter, cut into small pieces, and the salt with 200 ml/7 fl oz/1 cup water in a large, heavy-bottomed saucepan. Bring to the boil, stirring to help melt the butter, then add the flour all at once and mix vigorously with a wooden spoon over a low heat until the pastry comes away from the sides of the pan. Remove the pan from the heat. Beat in the whole eggs one at a time, ensuring each is well incorporated before adding the next one.

Put the pastry into a piping bag with a 2 cm/¾ in plain round nozzle and pipe 12 log shapes about 6–7.5 cm/2½–3 in long on the prepared baking sheet, spaced well apart. Beat the egg yolk with the tablespoon of milk and use it to glaze the éclairs. Then bake them for about 20

Éclairs (Chocolate and coffee éclairs)

minutes until pale golden in colour.

Meanwhile, make the pastry cream: put the vanilla and milk in a saucepan and heat to just below the boil. While the milk is heating, beat together the sugar and egg yolks until thick, white and frothy. Add the flour and mix in well. Remove the vanilla from the milk and gradually add the hot milk to the egg mixture, stirring well to incorporate smoothly. Pour the mixture into the milk pan and slowly bring it to the boil over a very gentle heat, stirring constantly with a wooden spoon as it thickens. Remove the pan from the heat. Divide the pastry cream into two portions and add the coffee to one and the cocoa to the other. Leave to cool.

When the éclairs are cooked, allow them to cool completely, then split them lengthwise and, using a piping bag, fill 6 of them with the chocolate cream and 6 of them with the coffee cream.

To finish the éclairs, gently warm the fondant icing. Remove half of it and add the instant coffee mixed with 1 tablespoon of water. Mix the cocoa with 1 tablespoon of water and add it to the rest of the warmed fondant icing. Coat the éclairs with the appropriate icing, spreading it over them smoothly with a spatula. Arrange the éclairs on a serving plate and leave them in a cool place until the icing sets.

EEL
Anguille

see also:
conger eel
fish

Eels are serpentine fish which spawn in the oceans but then travel upstream to develop and feed in fresh water. When young, and beginning their inland journey, they are tiny (6–9 cm/ 2½–3½ in) and transparent: at this stage they are known as GLASS EELS or ELVERS. During their 8–10 year period of growth they are yellow and make poor eating, but prior to returning to the ocean to spawn they turn silver and are about 50 cm–1 m/20–40 in long, and it is at this stage that adult eels are most prized for consumption.

ELVERS are regarded as a great treat by many and are usually just lightly sautéed in butter with lemon juice, or in oil with garlic and chilli in Spain. Small adult eels can be grilled (broiled), barbecued or sautéed; the larger ones may be braised or stewed. It is best to get the fishmonger to skin and clean eels for you, but they must then be cooked fairly promptly. The flesh of the eel is quite fatty.

SMOKED EEL is held to be a great delicacy and is popular for hors d'oeuvres and canapés. In 100 g/ 3½ oz of smoked eel there are 183 calories and 233 in fried eel.

ANGUILLES AU VERT

Eels in green sauce

Serves 6
Preparation 10 minutes
Cooking 25 minutes

METRIC/IMPERIAL	AMERICAN
1.5 kg/3½ lb young eels, skinned and cleaned	*3½ lb small young eels, skinned and cleaned*
115 g/¼ lb fresh spinach	*¼ lb fresh bulk spinach*
115 g/¼ lb fresh sorrel leaves	*¼ lb fresh sorrel leaves*
bunch of flat-leaved parsley	*bunch of flat-leaf parsley*
115 g/4 oz butter	*1 stick butter*
200 ml/7 fl oz dry white wine	*1 cup dry white wine*
bouquet garni	*bouquet garni*
bunch of tarragon	*bunch of tarragon*
2 tbsp snipped fresh sage	*2 tbsp snipped fresh sage*
5 fresh mint leaves	*5 fresh mint leaves*
2 egg yolks	*2 egg yolks*
juice of 1 lemon	*juice of 1 lemon*
salt and pepper	*salt and pepper*

Cut each eel into 4 segments. Trim the spinach, sorrel and parsley, keeping only the leaves. Rinse well and pat dry.

Melt the butter in a flameproof casserole over a moderate heat, add the pieces of eel and sauté them for 5 minutes. Add the spinach and sorrel, lower the heat and cook for a further 5 minutes.

Add the white wine, bouquet garni, parsley and the other herbs. Mix well and season to taste. Simmer for 10–15 minutes.

Mix the egg yolks with the lemon juice in a bowl. Pour this mixture into the casserole and heat without boiling, stirring constantly until it thickens slightly. Serve the eels in the sauce, either hot or cold.

see also:
anchovy
blanquette
creams and custards
floating islands
liaison
mayonnaise
meringue
omelette
quail
sauce
soufflé

EGG
Oeuf

The eggs of many species of bird have been a major food source for man since prehistoric times. A bird's egg consists of a fragile porous shell which encloses the exterior white or albumen and the yellow yolk, which may contain the tiny dark germ. Without further qualification, the term 'egg' applies to the eggs of the domesticated chicken. Tiny quails' eggs are also sold commercially, as are, more rarely, the eggs of guinea hens, geese, ducks and plovers.

The flavour of an egg is infinitely superior when it is relatively fresh. A fresh egg should have a smooth shell, with no hint of a crack, and should feel well filled when shaken. Between the shell and the egg white there is a double layer of protective membrane and as the egg gets older and dries out a pocket of air develops between the membranes. For this reason, a day-old egg placed in a bowl of water will sink to the bottom, while an egg that is a few days old will rise gradually to the surface. If an egg floats immediately, its freshness is in doubt. Another sign of freshness is when the yolk of an egg broken into a plate remains compactly domed and positioned exactly in the middle of the white. The whites of older eggs become runny and do not cohere well to the yolk, which also sits more flatly. Thus only the freshest eggs should be used when poaching and frying. On the other hand, eggs less than 3 days old should not be hard boiled as they may discolour and be difficult to peel, and they may also not whisk well, so should not be used for soufflés and cake-making.

The colour of the yolk and shell have no bearing on the quality of the egg: brown eggs are in no way better or more 'natural' or nutritious than white eggs, only possibly more visually appealing. So-called 'free-range eggs' usually have a better flavour than commercially produced eggs from battery hens, and are commensurately more expensive. The better flavour probably reflects the quality of feed the hens enjoy rather than any illusory freedom.

European eggs are graded according to weight: from a size 1 egg which weighs over 70 g (just under 2½ oz) down through a medium size 4 egg which weighs 55–60 g (about 2 oz) to a size 7 egg weighing less than 45 g (about 1½ oz). In most recipes, medium or size 3 eggs are required unless otherwise stated. In the US, eggs are letter-graded AA, A, B or C, based on how firm or viscous they are and thus give a guide as to the best use. Grade AA eggs have the stiffest whites and yolks, so they are best for frying or poaching; grade A eggs are a little runnier, and so on. Eggs are also graded according to size, based on minimum weights per dozen. Those most useful in recipes are extra large (64 g/2¼ oz), large (57 g/2 oz) and medium (50 g/1¾ oz).

Eggs which have any trace of a bad odour or are even slightly cracked should be discarded as they make a perfect breeding ground for micro-organisms. For the same reason, as the shells are porous, eggs which have been washed must be used promptly. Avoid eggs which are shiny as they may have been washed.

Because of the high levels of salmonella and other bacteria present in poultry, remember that whatever means is used to cook eggs, sufficient heat must be applied to kill all such micro-organisms. Whenever lightly cooked or raw eggs are used, as in soft-boiled eggs or mayonnaise, the risks should always be borne in mind.

Eggs should be stored with the pointed end downwards in a cool place. If they are refrigerated, allow them to come to room temperature before cooking, otherwise they are more difficult to beat and do not coagulate as readily.

quails' eggs *duck egg* *chicken egg*

Because the shells are porous, eggs quickly acquire flavours from foods stored next to them, and should not be placed in direct proximity to melon, pineapple, onions, etc.

Always break each egg separately to avoid the risk of a bad egg contaminating several others. To separate the whites, break the shell cleanly in half and let the yolk settle in one end while allowing the white to pour into a bowl. The yolk may then be passed carefully from one half shell to the other until all the white has gone.

When whisking egg whites, most chefs add a small pinch of salt to make the whites easier to beat to firm peaks, although scientific evidence would contraindicate this. A pinch of cream of tartar will stabilize the beaten foam. For best results, use a wire balloon whisk and a copper bowl, as copper induces a catalytic reaction which encourages the incorporation of air into the egg white and stabilizes the foam.

Preparations containing egg yolk should not be allowed to boil or be heated for too long or they will curdle. If this happens, add the egg a little at a time to a fresh bowl containing a teaspoonful of chilled water or cream and beat the mixture hard; the egg should quickly become smooth again. Egg yolk mixtures may be heated more successfully if they are first stabilized with a little flour or cornflour (cornstarch), or if they have small quantities of hot liquid beaten into them gradually to disperse the proteins.

When poaching eggs, a little vinegar in the water encourages swift coagulation of the egg white. Poached eggs keep well for a day or so in cold water. If preparing them in advance, undercook them slightly, then immerse them briefly in boiling water to reheat for serving.

Both poached and soft-boiled eggs may be served hot or cold. To make soft-boiled eggs for use in salads or further cooking, simmer gently for 6 minutes from when the water returns to the boil after adding the eggs; simmer hard-boiled eggs for 10 minutes. Always refresh them in cold water to prevent overcooking.

Some egg dishes are not suitable for advance preparation. For instance, a soufflé requires that the diners be seated in readiness when it is due out of the oven and scrambled eggs quickly lose their appealing creaminess.

Eggs are an economical food with innumerable applications. As well as making tasty and delicious dishes in themselves in many forms, from the humble boiled egg to the sophisticated soufflé, they also perform indispensable functions in cooking, from leavening cakes and glazing pastries to binding pasta dough and thickening custards and sauces.

An excellent source of high-quality animal protein, eggs are readily assimilated and fully utilized by the body. They contain 90 calories per 100 g/3½ oz and are rich in iron and vitamins A and B12. Until recently eggs were regarded as one of the basic elements of a healthy diet. However, as egg yolks are a significant source of cholesterol, experts currently recommend that weekly intake be restricted to no more than 3 eggs. This dictum does, however, ignore the fact that eggs also contain substances which help clear cholesterol from the blood and that saturated fat levels in the diet are now held to be more significant in blood cholesterol levels than actual cholesterol intake.

OEUFS MOLLETS

Soft-boiled eggs

Serves 2
Preparation 5 minutes
Cooking 2–4 minutes

METRIC/IMPERIAL	*AMERICAN*
4 large eggs	*4 extra large eggs*
4 slices of buttered toast, to serve	*4 slices of buttered toast, to serve*
salt and pepper	*salt and pepper*

Bring a saucepan of water to a rolling boil. Using a spoon, put the eggs into the pan and bring the water back to the boil as quickly as possible, then reduce the heat and simmer gently for the following times from the point that the water returns to the boil: 2 minutes for the white to be milky; 3 minutes for the white to be set but the yolk still runny: 3½ minutes for the white to be very firm and the yolk firm but not hard.

Serve the eggs with salt and pepper and the buttered toast cut into strips to dip into them.

ŒUFS À LA FLORENTINE

Soft-boiled eggs baked on spinach

Serves 6
Preparation 30 minutes
Cooking about 25 minutes

METRIC/IMPERIAL	AMERICAN
75 g/2½ oz butter	5 tbsp butter
25 g/¾ oz flour	3½ tbsp flour
200 ml/7 fl oz milk	1 cup milk
450 g/1 lb spinach, trimmed and chopped	1 lb fresh bulk spinach, trimmed and chopped
100 ml/3½ fl oz crème fraîche or whipping cream	½ cup crème fraîche or whipping cream
6 large eggs	6 extra large eggs
30 g/1 oz grated Parmesan	¼ cup grated Parmesan cheese
freshly grated nutmeg	freshly grated nutmeg
salt and pepper	salt and pepper

Preheat the oven to 220C/425F/gas 7 and grease a baking dish with a little of the butter.

To make a béchamel sauce, melt 25 g/1 oz/2 tbsp of the remaining butter in a heavy-based saucepan, then stir in the flour and mix until smooth. Cook gently for a minute, then slowly add the milk, stirring well to ensure that the sauce is smooth. Season to taste with nutmeg, salt and pepper and cook gently until thick, stirring constantly. Keep the sauce hot.

Melt the remaining butter in a saucepan, add the spinach and stir over a moderate heat for 5 minutes. Add half the cream, season with grated nutmeg to taste and mix. Put the spinach into the baking dish and make 6 hollows in it.

Put the eggs in a saucepan of water at a rolling boil, bring back to the boil as quickly as possible and then reduce the heat and simmer gently for 6 minutes. Remove them immediately from the water, plunge them into cold water and then shell them carefully. Arrange the soft-boiled eggs in the hollows in the spinach.

Add half the grated cheese and the rest of the cream to the béchamel sauce. Coat the eggs with the sauce and sprinkle them with the remainder of the Parmesan. Bake in the hot oven for 7–8 minutes and serve at once.

ŒUFS BROUILLÉS NATURE

Plain scrambled eggs

Serves 4
Preparation 15 minutes
Cooking about 15 minutes

METRIC/IMPERIAL	AMERICAN
75 g/2½ oz butter	5 tbsp butter
8 eggs	8 eggs
salt and freshly ground black pepper	salt and freshly ground black pepper

Grease a 15 cm/6 in diameter enamelled, cast-iron or stainless steel pan with 30 g/1 oz/2 tbsp of the butter. Bring some water to the boil in a large saucepan which will form a bain-marie.

Break the eggs one at a time into a cup and then pour them into the buttered pan. Add 2–3 teaspoons of cold water, 2–3 pinches of salt and 4–5 turns of the pepper mill. Finally, add the rest of the butter, cut into small pieces.

Away from the heat, mix the eggs with a wooden spoon, but do not beat them; the mixture should be smooth but not foamy. Put the pan with the eggs into the bain-marie of boiling water and set that on a gentle heat.

Stir the eggs quickly, scraping the sides and bottom of the pan to prevent them from sticking, until the eggs thicken to a creamy consistency.

If the mixture begins to cook too quickly, remove the pan from the bain-marie and stir vigorously away from the heat for several seconds. The eggs are ready when they are just set but not too firm.

Notes: scrambled eggs may be served in a warmed serving dish, in individual ramekins or, for special occasions, in small, hollowed-out brioches.

If the scrambled eggs are to be served with any kind of accompaniment, prepare it first as the eggs, once cooked, must be served immediately.

Scrambled eggs may be flavoured with smoked salmon, seafood, sautéed chicken livers, chopped tomatoes, mushroom duxelles, *chopped herbs, asparagus tips, grated Cheddar, Gruyère or Parmesan cheese, garlic croutons, chopped ham or cubed chorizo sausage.*

ŒUFS EN GELÉE

Eggs in aspic

Serves 6
Preparation 30 minutes
Cooking 6 minutes, 2 hours ahead

METRIC/IMPERIAL	*AMERICAN*
200 ml/7 fl oz liquid aspic jelly	*1 cup liquid aspic jelly*
2 tbsp Madeira	*2 tbsp Madeira*
6 eggs	*6 eggs*
2 slices of cooked ham	*2 slices of cooked ham*
4 tbsp mixed diced cooked vegetables, drained	*4 tbsp mixed diced cooked vegetables, drained*
1 tbsp chopped parsley	*1 tbsp chopped parsley*
2 gherkins	*2 pickled cucumbers or cornichons*
salt and pepper	*salt and pepper*

Flavour the aspic jelly with the Madeira. Allow it to cool until it is thickened but still liquid.

Meanwhile, put the eggs in boiling water, bring the water back to the boil as quickly as possible and then reduce the heat and simmer them for 6 minutes. Drain the eggs immediately, shell them carefully and chill them.

Cut out 6 circles (or ovals) of ham to fit the bottoms of 6 ramekins or special small moulds for eggs in aspic. Mix the vegetables with the parsley and add the trimmings from the ham, finely chopped. Slice the gherkins (pickled cucumbers) (1). Chill all the ingredients.

Pour the cold but still runny aspic jelly into the bottom of each mould to make a layer about 3 mm/⅛ in thick, then tilt the moulds to coat the sides (2). Put the lined moulds into the coldest part of the refrigerator for 15 minutes.

Dip the circles of ham and several slices of gherkin (pickled cucumber) into the aspic, drain and then place each ham circle and a few slices of gherkin (pickled cucumber) in the bottom of each mould. Put 1 soft-boiled egg into each ramekin and surround it with the vegetables. Pour the remaining aspic carefully into each ramekin until the ingredients are covered (3). If the aspic has set in the meantime, heat it very gently to liquefy it again. Chill the moulds until ready to serve.

1

2

3

To unmould the eggs in aspic, plunge each mould into a saucepan of warm water for about 3 seconds, then slide a knife blade around the edge of the mould between the aspic and the sides of the mould. With a swift movement, invert the mould on a plate and then carefully remove the mould. Serve the eggs in aspic on a bed of shredded lettuce.

Variations: instead of the diced vegetables use more chopped ham to fill the mould.

Fill the moulds with strips of smoked salmon instead of vegetables and ham, and line the bottom of the mould with a criss-cross pattern of tarragon leaves or sprigs of fresh dill.

Two hard-boiled quails' eggs may be used in place of each soft-boiled egg.

ŒUFS POCHÉS SAUCE CREVETTE

Poached eggs with seafood sauce

Serves 6
Preparation 10 minutes
Cooking about 20 minutes

METRIC/IMPERIAL	AMERICAN
30 g/1 oz butter	2 tbsp butter
30 g/1 oz flour	4 tbsp flour
300 ml/$\frac{1}{2}$ pt milk	$1\frac{1}{4}$ cups milk
1 tbsp curry powder	1 tbsp curry powder
2 tbsp crème fraîche or whipping cream	2 tbsp crème fraîche or whipping cream
115 g/4 oz peeled cooked prawns, cut into tiny chunks	4 oz peeled cooked shrimp, cut into tiny chunks
3 tbsp vinegar	3 tbsp vinegar
6 very fresh eggs	6 very fresh eggs (grade AA)
6 slices of white bread	6 slices of white bread
freshly grated nutmeg	freshly grated nutmeg
salt and pepper	salt and pepper

First make a béchamel sauce: melt the butter in a heavy-based saucepan, then stir in the flour and mix until smooth. Cook gently for a minute or so without allowing the mixture to colour and then slowly add the milk, stirring well to ensure that the sauce is smooth. Cook, stirring constantly, until thick.

Add curry powder to taste, the cream and the prawns (shrimp) and stir in well (1). Season with grated nutmeg and pepper. Keep this sauce hot.

Pour 1.5 l/$2\frac{1}{2}$ pt/$1\frac{1}{2}$ qt of water into a large saucepan, add the vinegar and bring to the boil. Then lower the heat so that the water is simmering gently. Break 1 egg into a cup. With a swift movement, carefully tip it into the vinegared water from just above the surface (2). Because it is very fresh, the white will coagulate immediately. Add as many eggs as can fit in the saucepan but still be kept separate.

When the whites are firm, increase the heat slightly and poach very gently for 3–4 minutes, carefully folding any trailing whites around the yolks. When an egg rises to the surface and floats, remove it with a slotted spoon and place it on a folded cloth (3). Cover and keep warm until ready to serve.

1

2

3

Cook all the eggs in the same way and trim them to remove any untidy bits of white.

Meanwhile lightly toast the bread and arrange it on a serving dish. Place a poached egg on top of each piece and coat with the sauce. Serve at once.

Variations: poached eggs can be served hot or cold with a whole range of different sauces. If serving hot, place them on toast or in tartlet cases and serve with Mornay, caper, mushroom, mustard, tomato or tarragon sauce. To serve cold, place them on a bed of shredded lettuce and serve with plain or herb mayonnaise, mustard sauce, Roquefort sauce or sauce gribiche.

EGGPLANT

see Aubergine

EMULSION

see also:
brandade
mayonnaise
milk
sauce
vinaigrette

When one liquid or finely puréed solid is blended with another liquid in such a manner that the tiny droplets or particles of the former are uniformly dispersed throughout the latter, they are described as being held in emulsion. An emulsion will not remain stable unless an emulsifying agent is present and egg protein usually performs this function in cooking. The most usual forms of culinary emulsion consist of a fatty substance such as oil or butter in a liquid, as in vinaigrette or mayonnaise and a number of other sauces. Milk is, in fact, a natural emulsion of fat in a watery solution and its own protein acts as an emulsifier.

Commercial emulsifiers, principally soya lecithin or egg yolk, are among the most common food additives. They are used to maintain the stability of emulsified foodstuffs, such as chocolate and margarine.

ENDIVE

Chicorée

see also:
chicory
lettuce
salad
vegetables

Related to the true chicory or Belgian endive, endives are larger and leafier lettuce-like plants but they do have the same characteristic paler green colour and bitter flavour. There is much confusion over the terms chicory and endive, so for our purposes we will give preference to the British usage.

WILD ENDIVE may be found in the French countryside and is delicious while still in the form of tender young shoots. It is an essential ingredient of *mesclun niçois*, the classic mixed green salad of the French south.

CURLY ENDIVE, or *frisée*, has a yellowish-white heart and thin, serrated, crinkly leaves which become greener towards the edges. When bought, it should always be extremely fresh and compact. It is usually only necessary to trim it of its outermost leaves to ready it for use. It is then usually torn into small bunches or coarsely chopped. It suits a highly seasoned dressing, preferably with mustard and garlic or shallots. *Lardons* or strips of bacon or garlic croutons are the classic garnish for curly endive. It may also be baked *au gratin* with a béchamel sauce, braised or stewed.

BATAVIAN ENDIVE or ESCAROLE looks much more like a variety of lettuce with fleshy, slightly curled leaves. The heart is large, but not as dense as iceberg lettuce. It is at its best in summer and also suits a highly seasoned dressing.

Like all salad leaves, endive is low in energy content (100 g/3½ oz contains 22 calories) but rich in minerals like calcium and potassium.

curly endive

SALADE CROQUANTE AUX POMMES

Crisp apple salad

Serves 6
Preparation 25 minutes

METRIC/IMPERIAL	AMERICAN
2 dessert apples	2 apples
juice of ½ lemon	juice of ½ lemon
100 ml/3½ fl oz whipping cream	½ cup whipping cream
1 tsp mild curry powder	1 tsp mild curry powder
3 tbsp orange juice	3 tbsp orange juice
1 head of Batavian endive, trimmed and torn into small pieces	1 head of escarole, trimmed and torn into small pieces
1 small heart of celery, trimmed and thinly sliced	1 small heart of celery, trimmed and thinly sliced
salt and pepper	salt and pepper

Peel and quarter the apples, then remove the core and seeds. Slice them and sprinkle with all but 2 tablespoons of the lemon juice.

Pour the cream into a bowl. Add the curry powder, then, whisking vigorously, add the reserved lemon juice and the orange juice. Season with salt and pepper to taste.

Combine the salad ingredients in a large bowl. Add the dressing, toss carefully and serve.

Batavian endive or escarole

SALADE DE CHICORÉE AUX ANCHOIS

Curly endive salad with anchovy vinaigrette

Serves 4
Preparation 20 minutes

METRIC/IMPERIAL	AMERICAN
1 small head of curly endive (frisée)	1 small head of curly endive
140 g/5 oz mushrooms	5 oz mushrooms
juice of 1 lemon	juice of 1 lemon
12 anchovy fillets in oil	12 anchovy fillets in oil
4 stalks of celery, trimmed and thinly sliced	4 sticks of celery, trimmed and thinly sliced
1 garlic clove	1 garlic clove
3 tbsp olive oil	3 tbsp olive oil
1 tbsp white wine vinegar	1 tbsp white wine vinegar
55 g/2 oz walnut halves	⅓ cup walnut halves
pepper	pepper

Remove the outer leaves from the endive and snip the rest with scissors, then wash it thoroughly and pat it dry.

Wipe the mushrooms, then slice them thinly and sprinkle them with lemon juice. Drain the anchovies on paper towels.

Divide the endive, celery and mushrooms among 4 individual plates and place 2 anchovy fillets on top of each serving.

Pound the rest of the anchovies in a mortar with a pestle along with the garlic clove and a few drops of oil.

When the paste is smooth, mix it with the rest of the oil and the vinegar and season it with pepper. Pour this sauce over the salad and garnish with the walnuts. Serve at once.

see also:
beef
steak

ENTRECÔTE

A prime quality French cut of beef taken from between two ribs, hence its name. Marbled with fat, tender and full of flavour, entrecôtes are best grilled (broiled), barbecued or fried. Allow 150–200 g/5½–7 oz per person and ensure that the boneless rib steaks are at least 2 cm/¾ in thick. Steaks cut from the lower ribs tend to be firmer. Always take the steaks out of the refrigerator at least 1 hour before cooking, especially if they are to be cooked rare. Trim the fat and make incisions around the edges of the meat before cooking to prevent them from curling up.

ENTRECÔTES AUX ANCHOIS

Entrecôte steaks with anchovies

Serves 4
Preparation 15 minutes
Cooking 5–6 minutes

METRIC/IMPERIAL	AMERICAN
12 green olives, stoned	12 green olives, pitted
12 anchovy fillets in oil	12 anchovy fillets in oil
1 tbsp oil	1 tbsp oil
2 entrecôte steaks, each weighing about 400 g/14 oz, trimmed	2 boneless rib steaks, each weighing about 14 oz, trimmed
12 tarragon leaves	12 tarragon leaves
1 tbsp anchovy butter, chilled (see Butter)	1 tbsp anchovy butter, chilled (see Butter)
salt and pepper	salt and pepper

Blanch the olives for 2 minutes in a pan of boiling water. Drain them and pat them dry.

Drain the anchovies on paper towels and cut them in half lengthwise.

Preheat a grill (broiler), frying pan or barbecue. Lightly oil the steaks and cook them for 2–3 minutes a side, depending on how well done they are to be. Season with salt and pepper.

Cut each steak in half and place on a warmed serving dish. Arrange the anchovies and tarragon leaves in a criss-cross pattern on top of each piece of steak. Cut the anchovy butter into tiny rounds, place one round in each of the central squares made by the anchovies and tarragon leaves and put an olive on top of each of those. Serve immediately with a tomato salad.

ENTRECÔTES À LA BORDELAISE

Entrecôte steaks with shallot and red wine sauce

Serves 4
Preparation 10 minutes, 1 hour ahead
Cooking about 15 minutes

METRIC/IMPERIAL	AMERICAN
125 g/4½ oz butter	9 tbsp butter
1 tbsp oil	1 tbsp oil
2 entrecôte steaks, each weighing about 400 g/14 oz, trimmed	2 boneless rib steaks, each weighing about 14 oz, trimmed
4–5 shallots, finely chopped	4–5 shallots, finely chopped
1 tsp cracked black pepper	1 tsp cracked black pepper
pinch of dried thyme	pinch of dried thyme
2 tbsp chopped flat-leaved parsley	2 tbsp chopped flat-leaf parsley
500 ml/16 fl oz red Bordeaux wine	2 cups red Bordeaux wine
salt	salt

Melt 25 g/¾ oz/1½ tbsp of the butter with the oil in a large frying pan over a moderate heat. Cook the steaks over the same moderate heat for 4–5 minutes, then turn them and cook for 3–4 minutes longer; cooking times vary with how well done the steaks are to be. Drain them, reserving the cooking juices, and put the steaks on a warmed serving dish; keep hot in a warm oven.

Discard the fat from the frying pan and place the pan on the heat with a further 25 g/¾ oz/1½ tbsp of butter. Cook the shallots over a medium heat for 2 minutes, stirring constantly. Add a pinch of salt, the cracked black pepper, the thyme and half the chopped parsley. Stir in the red wine and reduce the sauce over a brisk heat for 5 minutes, then add the meat cooking juices and mix well for a few seconds.

Whisk in the rest of the butter in small pieces. Remove the sauce from the heat and strain it over the steaks. Serve at once, cut in half, garnished with the remaining parsley and accompanied by noisette potatoes.

Entrecôtes à la bordelaise (Entrecôte steaks with shallot and red wine sauce)

ESCABÈCHE

see also:
fumet
marinade
stock

The Spanish make a practice of preserving cooked foods, especially small oily fish (such as sardines, red mullet, mackerel and fresh anchovies), in an *escabèche* or cold marinade. The fish are first fried or lightly browned and then marinated in the aromatic stock for at least 24 hours and served cold. It is also used for poultry; partridge in *escabèche* is traditional. *Escabèche* marinade, or dishes dressed with it, will keep for up to 1 week in the refrigerator.

ESCABÈCHE DE SARDINES

Marinated sardines

Serves 6
Preparation 30 minutes
Cooking 10 minutes, 24 hours ahead

METRIC/IMPERIAL	AMERICAN
1 kg/2¼ lb small fresh sardines, gutted	2¼ lb small fresh sardines, drawn
200 ml/7 fl oz olive oil	1 cup olive oil
3 sweet peppers of different colours, deseeded and cut into strips	3 sweet peppers of different colours, deseeded and cut into strips
115 g/¼ lb baby onions	¼ lb baby onions
200 ml/7 fl oz fish fumet (see Fumet)	1 cup fish fumet (see Fumet)
2 tbsp white wine vinegar	2 tbsp white wine vinegar
10 black peppercorns	10 black peppercorns
salt	salt
flour, for coating	flour, for coating

Pat the sardines dry with paper towels, dredge them in flour and shake them to remove the excess. Heat 3 tablespoons of the oil in a large frying pan over a high heat and sauté the sardines rapidly. Drain them and put them in a large, flameproof glass or porcelain dish.

Heat the remaining oil in a sauté pan over a moderate heat and put the sweet peppers and onions into it. Brown them lightly, stirring, for 2–3 minutes, then pour the mixture over the sardines.

In a small saucepan, bring the fish fumet to the boil with the vinegar, peppercorns and salt to taste. Pour the boiling liquid over the fish and vegetable mixture.

Leave to cool completely, then chill for at least 24 hours. Serve chilled as a first course.

To drink: Rosé de Provence.

ESCAROLE

see Endive

ESSENCE OR EXTRACT

see also:
almond
coffee
vanilla

A concentrated aromatic substance, an essence is used to enhance the flavour of a preparation or simply to endow it with flavour. There are several different types of essence. They are most commonly obtained by extracting the essential oil from items such as citrus fruits, nuts and flowers. They may also be made by cooking highly flavoured foods such as tomatoes, mushrooms, chervil, truffle, fish or meat and reducing an infusion or the cooking liquid. Essence of garlic, onions and herbs may also be obtained by marinating them in olive oil or vinegar.

Commercial essences and extracts for many flavours are commonly available. However, as they are often made with artificial flavourings and colourings and the quality varies enormously, they should be used with caution as they may mar a dish in which they are used rather than enhance it. It is better, say, to invest in a miniature of almond-flavoured liqueur than to use any but the most expensive almond essence or extract.

F

FATS AND OILS

see also:
butter
cheese
cholesterol
cream
deep frying
frying
lard
lipids
low-fat foods
margarine
olive
peanut
sunflower
sesame
walnut

Essentially the same mixtures of fatty acids and glycerol, fats tend to be solid at normal temperatures while oils are liquid. Fats and oils are important in cooking in three principal ways: those used as a medium in the cooking of other foods, such as butter or sunflower oil; those used as an ingredient in their own right, such as olive oil in vinaigrette and cream in desserts; and those which are a constituent part of certain foodstuffs and usually contribute greatly to their flavour, like the fat in beef and lamb.

Fats and oils used as cooking media are normally chosen for their flavour – or lack of it – and their ability to withstand the high temperatures involved in frying, etc. Fats used in this way tend to be saturated and mostly of animal origin, mainly lard, pork fat, beef suet, butter, chicken and goose fat, while the oils are usually monounsaturated or polyunsaturated and derived from vegetables, such as corn, olives, nuts or avocados. Recent health trends have led to a significant move away from cooking with the saturated fats and more use of monounsaturated and polyunsaturated oils.

The finest flavoured oils are those obtained by the first cold pressing of seeds, nuts, olives and suchlike, and these make the best flavouring ingredients in sauces and dressings.

Fats and oils, especially the polyunsaturated varieties, oxidize and go rancid quite rapidly. They should be stored in cool places away from direct sunlight and are best kept closely wrapped or in small bottles to minimize their exposure to air. If being kept for re-use, they should also be carefully filtered as any impurities accelerate decomposition. Try not to mix batches of fresh and re-used fats or oils and never use any batch more than 4 or 5 times.

Whether they are saturated or polyunsaturated, of animal or vegetable origin, fats are an indispensable part of our diet: they contain vitamin A and the essential fatty acids which are important to the correct functioning of the metabolism.

FATTY ACIDS

see also:
cholesterol
fats and oils
lipids

The 40 or so fatty acids are the basic elements of lipids, the chemical term for the family of substances which includes natural fats and oils. They are commonly divided into three principal types according to their complex chemical structure: SATURATED FATS, present at high levels in meat, *charcuterie*, cheese, butter, and other animal fats; MONOUNSATURATED fats, found at high levels in olive oil; and POLYUNSATURATED fats, with concentrations in nuts except coconuts and cashews, in oily fish, corn oil, sunflower oil, soya oil, and grapeseed and rape or canola oils.

High intake of saturated fats is held to be

associated with high cholesterol levels in the blood, increasing the incidence of heart disease. On the other hand, some recent research would seem to indicate that polyunsaturated fats help reduce blood cholesterol. Some of the essential fatty acids, important for growth, cellular structure and the maintenance of good healthy skin, cannot be synthesized by the body. It is therefore considered advisable to maintain a good balance of the different types of fats in the diet.

FENNEL

Fenouil

see also:
herbs
spices
vegetables

Varieties of the fennel plant grow all over Europe and have now also become well established in California. In the coastal regions of Mediterranean countries, wild fennel flourishes by the roadside during winter and spring.

The leaves of the fennel plant have been a common kitchen herb for thousands of years and their subtle aniseed flavour has a widespread tradition of use, especially in fish, chicken and veal dishes.

Dried fennel seeds are also a popular spice and impart a similar flavour. They are used extensively in Italian and Indian cooking and feature in several Italian sausages.

One variety of the plant, known as BULB or FLORENCE FENNEL, until recently mostly cultivated and used in Italy, has a swollen bulbous leaf base with a texture akin to that of celery and a subtle hint of the aniseed flavour. The tough outer leaves are removed and the tender inner heart used raw in salads or braised whole or in portions, or chopped and added to stews, sauces and stuffings.

Fennel is a good source of vitamins A and C, iron and calcium, and 100 g/3½ oz contains only 20 calories.

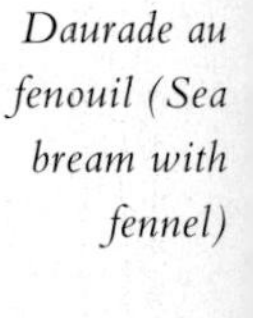

Daurade au fenouil (Sea bream with fennel)

DAURADE AU FENOUIL

Sea bream or porgy with fennel

Serves 6
Preparation 20 minutes
Cooking 20 minutes

METRIC/IMPERIAL	*AMERICAN*
2 sea bream, each weighing about 550 g/1¼ lb, scaled and cleaned	*2 porgy, each weighing about 1¼ lb, scaled and cleaned*
1 tbsp fennel seeds	*1 tbsp fennel seeds*
2 bulbs of fennel, trimmed and thinly sliced	*2 bulbs of fennel, trimmed and thinly sliced*
100 ml/3½ fl oz olive oil	*½ cup olive oil*
1 lemon, sliced	*1 lemon, sliced*
salt and pepper	*salt and pepper*

Preheat the oven to 180C/350F/gas 4.

Season the fish with salt and pepper inside and out and put half the fennel seeds into each fish. Make 2 diagonal incisions deep into the flesh on each side of both fish.

Spread the slices of fennel over the bottom of a baking dish. Place the fish on top and pour the olive oil over. Cover with slices of lemon and season with salt and pepper.

Bake for 20 minutes, turning the fish over once. Serve straight from the baking dish.

To drink: Chardonnay.

FENOUIL AU VIN BLANC

Fennel in white wine

Serves 4
Preparation 10 minutes
Cooking 10 minutes, 1 hour ahead

METRIC/IMPERIAL	AMERICAN
3 bulbs of fennel, trimmed and cut in half	3 bulbs of fennel, trimmed and cut in half
150 ml/¼ pt dry white wine	⅔ cup dry white wine
3 tbsp olive oil	3 tbsp olive oil
2 sprigs of thyme	2 sprigs of thyme
bay leaf	bay leaf
1 tsp coriander seeds	1 tsp coriander seeds
juice of 1 lemon	juice of 1 lemon
salt and pepper	salt and pepper

In a large pan of boiling salted water, blanch the fennel bulbs for 3–4 minutes. Drain them and pat them dry.

Put the wine and olive oil into a very deep microwave dish, adding about 150 ml/5 fl oz/⅔ cup of water, the thyme, bay leaf and coriander seeds. Add the fennel and season with salt and pepper.

Cover and microwave on High for 10 minutes. Leave to cool in the cooking juices.

Sprinkle with lemon juice and serve as an hors d'oeuvre, with mushrooms *à la grecque* or slices of garlic sausage.

FENOUIL EN SALADE

Fennel salad

Serves 4
Preparation 25 minutes
Cooking 20 minutes, 1 hour ahead

METRIC/IMPERIAL	AMERICAN
3 tbsp olive oil	3 tbsp olive oil
1 tbsp tarragon vinegar	1 tbsp tarragon vinegar
100 g/3½ oz long-grain rice, cooked and allowed to cool	½ cup long-grain rice, cooked and allowed to cool
2 hard-boiled eggs, shelled and sliced	2 hard-boiled eggs, shelled and sliced
12 small white onions, thinly sliced	12 small white onions, thinly sliced
1 large bulb of fennel, trimmed and thinly sliced	1 large bulb of fennel, trimmed and thinly sliced
4 small tomatoes, quartered	4 small tomatoes, quartered
12 black olives, stoned	12 black olives, pitted
chopped chives	chopped chives
salt and pepper	salt and pepper

Make a well-seasoned vinaigrette with the olive oil and tarragon vinegar.

In a salad bowl, mix the rice with 2 tablespoons of the vinaigrette, then add the other salad ingredients and the rest of the vinaigrette. Toss gently and garnish with chopped chives. Serve at room temperature.

Variations: substitute green peas for the rice.

FETA

see also: cheese

The best-known Greek cheese, crumbly and salty feta is made from ewes' milk, or sometimes goats' milk, and has a fat content of about 45%. It is a fresh cheese, ripened in brine, which is very white in colour and is sold in slices or cubes, sometimes still immersed in brine. Feta has many uses in cooking, from mixed salads to dishes baked *au gratin*. It works well with pastry and is a popular filling for *feuilletés*. It also marries well with olives and the two are often served together to accompany drinks.

SALADE GRECQUE

Greek salad

Serves 6
Preparation 20 minutes

METRIC/IMPERIAL	AMERICAN
1 small can (115 g/4 oz) of artichoke hearts	1 cup cooked or canned artichoke hearts
juice of 2 lemons	juice of 2 lemons
2 garlic cloves, chopped	2 garlic cloves, chopped
225 g/½ lb mushrooms, wiped and thinly sliced	½ lb mushrooms, wiped and thinly sliced
4 small courgettes, very thinly sliced	4 small zucchini, very thinly sliced
3 tbsp olive oil	3 tbsp olive oil
2 tsp dried thyme	2 tsp dried thyme
2 tsp dried rosemary	2 tsp dried rosemary
2 tsp fennel seeds	2 tsp fennel seeds
225 g/½ lb feta cheese, cut into small cubes	½ lb feta cheese, cut into small cubes
salt and pepper	salt and pepper

Drain the artichoke hearts and sprinkle them with a little of the lemon juice. Add the garlic and stir, then chill.

Sprinkle the mushrooms with a little of the remaining lemon juice. Mix the courgettes (zucchini) and mushrooms together.

Make a vinaigrette with the olive oil, the rest of the lemon juice, the thyme, rosemary, fennel seeds and seasoning to taste.

Combine all the ingredients in a salad bowl, sprinkle over the vinaigrette, stir and serve at room temperature.

Note: if the courgettes (zucchini) look as though they might not be tender enough, peel them and blanch them for 2–3 minutes.

FEUILLETÉ

see also:
croûte
pastry
vol-au-vent

Puff pastry filled or garnished with savoury mixtures, especially cheese, fish, seafood or chicken, *feuilletés* are usually served hot in rectangular, diamond or crescent shapes. Smaller thin sticks of puff pastry sprinkled with cheese, paprika or cumin seeds before being baked are popular hot or cold as party snacks.

Sweet versions may also be filled or topped with fresh fruit, compotes or jams to make an interesting dessert or tea-time treat.

Without any filling 100 g/3½ oz of puff pastry contains 190 calories.

FEUILLETÉS AU CRABE

Crab turnovers

Serves 4
Preparation 40 minutes
Cooking 20 minutes

METRIC/IMPERIAL	AMERICAN
8 mushrooms	8 mushrooms
juice of 1 lemon	juice of 1 lemon
30 g/1 oz butter	2 tbsp butter
1 shallot, chopped	1 shallot, chopped
whites of 2 leeks, finely sliced	whites of 2 leeks, finely sliced
260 g/9 oz crab meat, flaked	9 oz crab meat, flaked
2 tbsp flour	2 tbsp flour
100 ml/3½ fl oz crème fraîche or whipping cream	½ cup crème fraîche or whipping cream
1 tbsp chopped parsley	1 tbsp chopped parsley
1 tbsp dry white wine	1 tbsp dry white wine
300 g/10 oz puff pastry	10 oz puff pastry
2 eggs, beaten	2 eggs, beaten
sprigs of watercress, to garnish	sprigs of watercress, to garnish
salt and pepper	salt and pepper

Preheat the oven to 220C/425F/gas 7.

Wipe the mushrooms, slice them very thinly and sprinkle them with lemon juice.

Melt the butter in a frying pan. Add the shallot and stir for 2 minutes. Add the leeks and stir for a further 3 minutes, then add the mushrooms and crab meat. Stir over a gentle heat for 3 minutes.

Sprinkle with the flour and mix well. Add the cream and chopped parsley, then stir over a low heat for 5 minutes. Stir in the white wine. Season to taste with salt, pepper and lemon juice. Mix and set aside.

Roll out the puff pastry 6 mm/¼ in thick into a

rectangle 20 × 40 cm/8 × 16 in. Cut that into eight 10 cm/4 in squares. Into the centre of each square put 3 or 4 tablespoons of the crab mixture, leaving the edges clear all round for sealing. Brush these edges with beaten egg and fold each square in two, then pinch the edges to seal them. Glaze the *feuilletés* with the rest of the beaten egg.

Make 2 or 3 slits in each of the *feuilletés* to let steam escape and put them on a lightly dampened baking sheet. Bake for 10–12 minutes, until puffy and golden. Serve immediately, garnished with sprigs of watercress.

To drink: a medium-bodied dry white Burgundy, such as a Meursault.

FIBRE

see Dietary fibre

FIG

Figue

see also:
apricot
fruit
prune

The sweet fruit of the fig tree, which originated in Arabia and is now grown extensively in the Mediterranean and regions with similar climates, figs are eaten both fresh as a dessert fruit and are dried as a sweetmeat or for use in cooking.

There are several principal varieties of fresh fig: the large, thick-skinned purple, green and black varieties tend to have coarser flesh and are best used in cooking as an accompaniment to pork, rabbit, duck or guinea fowl, or made into jam. The smaller *petite violette* and the WHITE FIG, as well as the KADOTA, make the best dessert fruit as they are juicy and sweet, but they are also very delicate and perishable.

Many species of fig tree have two crops: one of larger, early fruit in mid-summer; and the other of smaller and sweeter figs in late summer and autumn. When buying ensure that the stalks are still firmly attached to the fruit as an indication of freshness. All but the thickest of fig skins may be eaten, but many people prefer to peel fresh figs. They are often served as an hors d'oeuvre with Parma ham or shaved Parmesan cheese. The delicate flavour of good fresh figs is best enjoyed if the fruit is at room temperature. In cooking they may also be treated in much the same way as apricots.

DRIED FIGS are mainly SMYRNA FIGS from Turkey, called CALIMYRNA when grown in California, which have a strong, nutty flavour. At the beginning of the season in late autumn, they are brown, swollen and full of flavour. As the season progresses they become drier and lighter in colour. Figs sold in blocks are generally the best quality. Italian figs are less delicate, and Greek figs have a tendency to be tough. All recipes for prunes are suitable for dried figs. They make a delicious dessert cooked in wine and served with vanilla custard sauce or rice pudding.

Figs have the highest sugar content of all fruits: 1 small fresh fig contains about 40 calories and as much sugar as a large apple. Dried figs contain about 275 calories per 100 g/3½ oz. Both fresh and dried figs are highly nutritious and are held to be both good for the digestion and excellent natural laxatives.

FIGUES BLANCHES À LA MOUSSE DE FRAISES

White figs with strawberry mousse

Serves 4
Preparation 20 minutes

METRIC/IMPERIAL	AMERICAN
300 g/10 oz strawberries, hulled	*10 oz (about 1 pt) strawberries, hulled*
45 g/1½ oz icing sugar	*6½ tbsp confectioners' sugar*
200 ml/7 fl oz chantilly cream	*1 cup chantilly cream*

450 g/1 lb white figs which are ripe but still firm, peeled and quartered	*1 lb white or other dessert figs which are ripe but still firm, peeled and quartered*

Blend the strawberries with the sugar in a food processor. Pour the purée into a chilled bowl and fold in the chantilly cream. The mixture should be smooth and fluffy.

Divide the fig quarters among 4 individual serving dishes. Cover them completely with the strawberry mousse and chill until ready to serve.

Variations: raspberries may be substituted for the strawberries, and ground hazelnuts sprinkled on the top of the mousse.

PINTADE AUX FIGUES SÈCHES

Guinea fowl with dried figs

Serves 3
Preparation 20 minutes
Cooking 45 minutes

METRIC/IMPERIAL	*AMERICAN*
300 g/10 oz dried figs	*10 oz dried figs*
150 g/5½ oz pine kernels	*1⅔ cups pine nuts*
2 slices of white bread, crumbled	*2 slices of white bread, crumbled*
1 egg	*1 egg*
pinch of ground cinnamon	*pinch of ground cinnamon*
1 guinea fowl, dressed weight about 1.8 kg/4 lb	*1 guinea fowl, drawn and dressed weight about 4 lb*
45 g/1½ oz butter	*3 tbsp butter*
2 tbsp corn oil	*2 tbsp corn oil*
4 shallots, thinly sliced	*4 shallots, thinly sliced*
225 g/½ lb celeriac, peeled and thinly sliced	*½ lb celeriac (celery root), peeled and thinly sliced*
100 ml/3½ fl oz port	*½ cup port wine*
salt and pepper	*salt and pepper*

Coarsely chop half the figs and mix them with 55 g/2 oz/⅔ cup of the pine kernels (pine nuts), the bread, egg and cinnamon. Season with salt and pepper.

Stuff the guinea fowl with this mixture, sew up the aperture and secure with string, taking care not to tie it too tightly.

Heat the butter and oil in a flameproof casserole and brown the guinea fowl on all sides. Add the shallots, celeriac and remaining figs and pine kernels (pine nuts). Season with salt and pepper. Pour the port over and cover the casserole.

Cook gently for 40 minutes, turning the guinea fowl over from time to time. If there is not enough liquid, add some more port mixed with an equal amount of water.

FILBERT

see Hazelnut

FILET MIGNON

see Tournedos

FILLET

Filet

see also: beef, chateaubriand, chicken, duck, fish, lamb, pork, steak, tournedos, turkey, veal

In its most general sense a fillet is a long, narrow strip of meat or fish. The term is today also more usually loosely understood to indicate a piece of meat or fish from which all bones have been removed. For meat, however, the term is used of very specific cuts.

The long, narrow fillet or tenderloin of beef is the undercut of the sirloin. It may be roasted whole, sometimes rolled and tied, and is usually either larded or barded as its delicate meat would dry out during the brief, intense cooking it requires. It may also be braised or baked *en croûte*. More usually beef fillet or tenderloin is cut into steaks, chateaubriands, tournedos or filet mignons, and the trimmings cut into smaller pieces for kebabs or fondues.

Similar tender and tasty cuts from the same parts of the calf, pig and lamb are also referred to as fillet or tenderloin. However, in Britain the term is more usually used in these cases for the best part of the rump.

Fillets of poultry are usually the breasts (half-breasts) and are more commonly referred to as *suprêmes*, or, for fattened ducks, as *magrets*.

Fish fillets are cut lengthwise from the backbone, giving two from a round fish and four from a flat fish.

FILET DE BOEUF À LA MOUTARDE

Fillet or tenderloin of beef with mustard sauce

Serves 6
Preparation 15 minutes
Cooking about 30 minutes

METRIC/IMPERIAL	*AMERICAN*
1 beef fillet roast, weighing about 1.25 kg/2¾ lb	*1 beef tenderloin roast, weighing about 2¾ lb*
2 tbsp oil	*2 tbsp oil*
2 tbsp crushed black pepper	*2 tbsp crushed black pepper*
2 tbsp Armagnac	*2 tbsp Armagnac*
2 tbsp Dijon mustard	*2 tbsp Dijon mustard*
100 ml/3½ fl oz crème fraîche or whipping cream	*½ cup crème fraîche or whipping cream*
salt and pepper	*salt and pepper*

Preheat the oven to 230C/450F/gas 8.

Brush the roast with oil, sprinkle it with salt and roll it in the crushed pepper, pressing down well. Brown it without fat in a frying pan over a high heat for 10 minutes.

Remove the roast to a roasting pan. Roast in the oven for 20 minutes. Remove it from the oven, place it on a warmed serving dish and cover with a sheet of foil.

Pour the Armagnac into the roasting pan and deglaze the meat juices, stirring with a wooden spoon. Add the mustard and cream. Mix well, heat gently and adjust the seasoning.

Carve the roast into slices. Add the carving juices to the gravy, stir well and serve separately. *To drink: a medium-bodied red, such as a Saint-Emilion.*

FILLETING

see Fish

FINES HERBES

see Herbs

FISH

Poisson

see also:
bouillabaisse
bourride
brill
carp
caviar
char
cod
conger eel
court-bouillon
dab
eel
filleting
fumet
grouper
gurnard
haddock
hake
halibut
herring
John Dory
lemon sole
mackerel
monkfish
mullet
perch
pike
plaice
pollack
roe
salmon
salting
salt cod
sea bream
shad
shark
skate
smelt
smoked salmon
smoking
sole
stock
sturgeon
trout
tuna
turbot
whiting

There are over 30,000 known species of fish in the world's waters and most of them are edible. This abundance of fish has long been an important part of man's diet, especially among the poorer nations and those with extensive coastlines. The Japanese island race, for instance, ate only fish and no meat until the fairly recent arrival of Western influence.

Fish are categorized in various ways: sea fish and freshwater fish, surface and deep feeders, bony and cartilaginous (sharks, dogfish, skate), etc. For culinary purposes the most important differentiations are between round fish and flat fish and between white fish and oily fish. The family of eels, long snake-like fish, are also categorized separately for culinary purposes.

Tapered ROUND FISH, adapted to swimming in open waters, are the most common, and include fish like cod, salmon and pike. FLAT FISH, such as plaice, sole and flounder, are bottom feeders, hence their shape, which has adapted to their lying continually on their side. They have both eyes on the side which faces upwards and are usefully divided into sinistral (left-looking) and dextral (right-looking). Some flat fish, like the skate and the ray, have actually adapted to lying on their belly and other so-called flat fish, such as the John Dory, are really very thin round are really very thin round fish.

ROUND FISH lend themselves to a variety of treatments by the cook. They may be baked, roasted, grilled (broiled), or braised whole. They may also be stuffed with a variety of mixtures. Round fish are also commonly cut across into steaks and larger specimens cut into transverse boneless steaks called *darnes*. They are also usually readily filleted into two fillets, one from either side of the backbone. Round fish usually need to be skinned, but the skins are often left on during cooking, especially when whole or in steaks, to retain flavour and keep the flesh intact. In such cases, remove loose scales by dragging the back of a knife or a special fish scaler across the fish against the 'grain'.

FLAT FISH may also be grilled (broiled) or fried whole, but are more usually filleted into four fillets, two from each side. Their soft skins are often left on during cooking, and need no scaling.

FILLETING A ROUND FISH

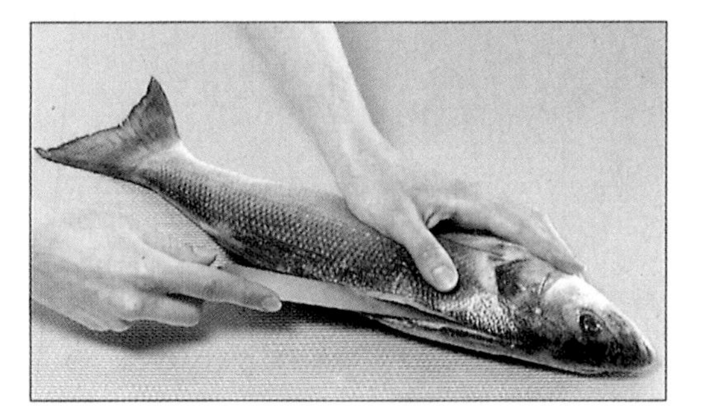

With the tail toward you, cut along the back by the dorsal fin, keeping the knife parallel with the bone.

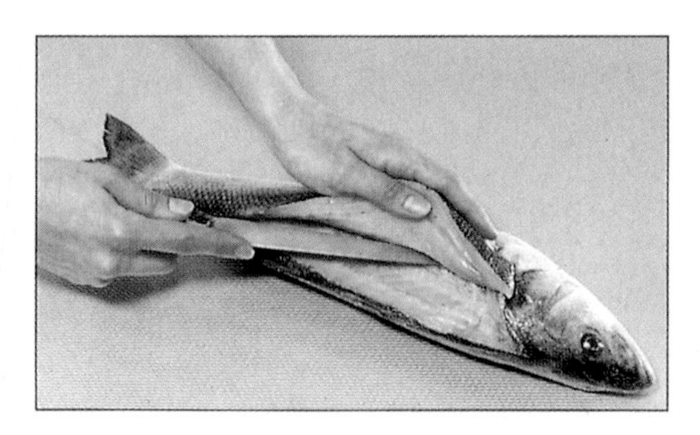

Cut behind the gills, then slide the knife along the backbone to free the top fillet.

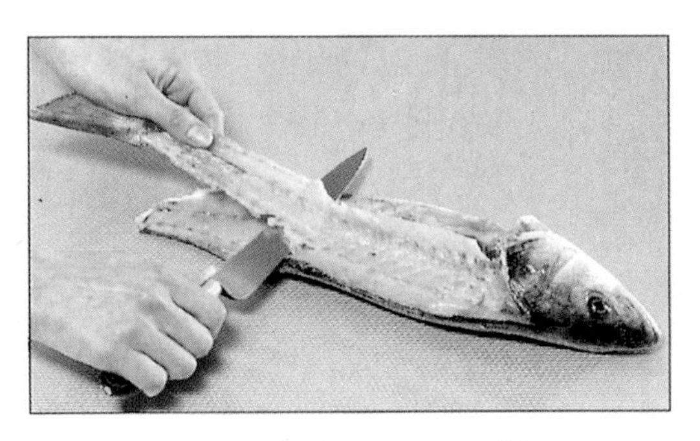

Detach the backbone from the remaining fillet and cut through to free the fillet from the head and skeleton.

FILLETING A FLAT FISH

Cut the skinned fish from the head to the tail along the centre indentation over the backbone.

Holding the knife flat against the bone, cut toward one outer edge, then the other, while lifting the fillets.

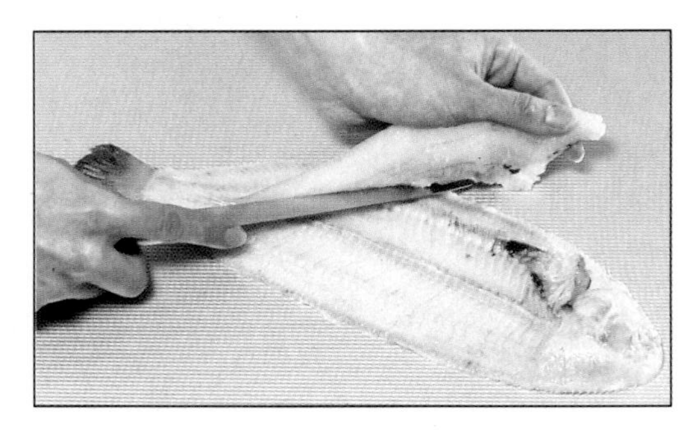

After removing both fillets from one side repeat the procedure on the other side; trim the edges neatly.

EELS are normally skinned before cooking and then they are cut across into pieces, but it is difficult to fillet eel flesh until it has been cooked or smoked.

Fish of all types usually benefit from the lightest possible cooking by techniques which are either very gentle, such as poaching in a court-bouillon or wine, or very fast, such as deep frying, grilling (broiling) or barbecuing. Because of the many variables involved, it is impossible to give or follow formulae for the calculation of cooking times. Observe fish closely during cooking and stop just as soon as the flesh is firm, opaque and readily flaked with a fork. Fish cook extremely well in the microwave oven, retaining their flavour, texture and nutrients.

Once cooked, delicate lean WHITE FISH suits the plainest of treatments, such as melted butter and a little lemon juice or a herb sauce. OILY

scorpion fish
gilt-head bream
blue-mouth
whiting
Pandora sea bream
herrings
lemon sole
whitebait
John Dory
plaice
brill
Dover sole
lisette mackerel
mackerel
turbot
codling
hake

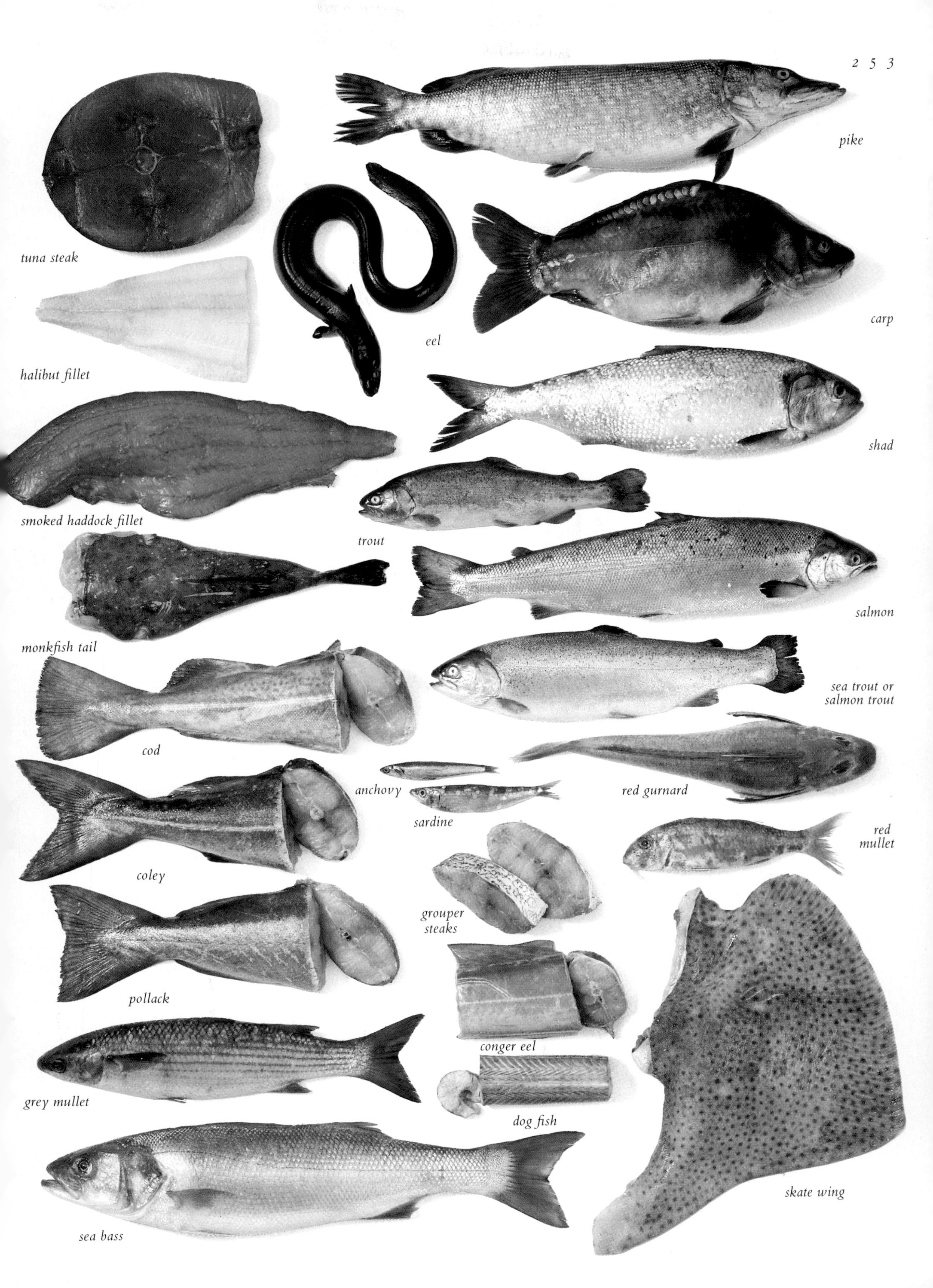
tuna steak
pike
eel
carp
halibut fillet
shad
smoked haddock fillet
trout
monkfish tail
salmon
sea trout or
salmon trout
cod
anchovy
red gurnard
sardine
red
mullet
coley
grouper
steaks
pollack
conger eel
grey mullet
dog fish
skate wing
sea bass

SCALING FISH

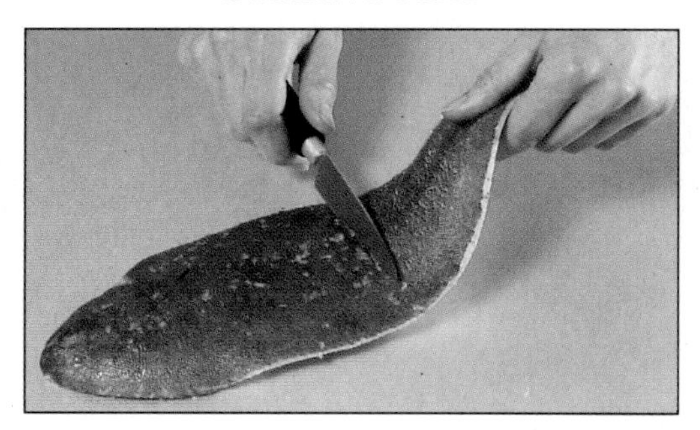

Scrape the fish from the tail toward the head against the direction in which the scales grow.

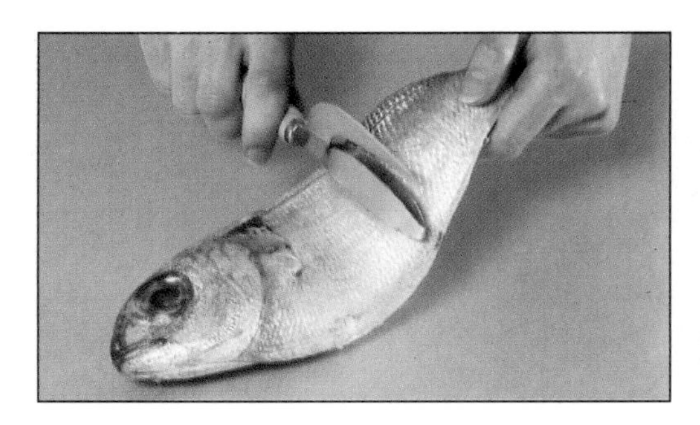

A special fish scaler is handy for this, but a strong knife or even a large flat shell will do.

FISH, like herring, mackerel, trout, sardines, salmon, tuna and eel, may take a richer strong, sweet or sharp dressing like a mayonnaise or fruit sauce.

Fish freezes well, although it loses much of its texture on thawing. However, as most commercially frozen fish is actually processed within hours of being caught, it often has more flavour than fresh fish in the shops. Other traditional methods of preserving fish, such as salting or smoking, are still widely used, and the kipper, salt cod and smoked salmon, for instance, are all common culinary ingredients.

FISH EGGS, or ROE or CAVIAR, are also often highly prized, from those of the humble cod, used for *taramasalata*, to caviar from sturgeons.

Fish is a highly nutritious food. An excellent source of protein, it is also high in many minerals and vitamin B. Fatty fish also has significant vitamin A and D content. Even the fattiest of fish, the eel, has less fat than such meats as lamb or pork.

More importantly, the fat in fish is high in polyunsaturates, meaning that it is held not to be a contributory factor to high blood cholesterol levels. In fact, recent research would seem to indicate that regular consumption of oily fish may produce a significant reduction of blood cholesterol.

FILETS DE POISSON SAUCE PIQUANTE

Fillets of fish in spicy sauce

Serves 4
Preparation 5 minutes
Cooking 7 minutes

METRIC/IMPERIAL	*AMERICAN*
800 g/$1\frac{3}{4}$ lb white fish fillets (cod, whiting, plaice, etc)	*$1\frac{3}{4}$ lb white fish fillets (cod, whiting, flounder, etc)*
45 g/$1\frac{1}{2}$ oz butter	*3 tbsp butter*
2 tbsp flour	*2 tbsp flour*
200 ml/7 fl oz milk	*1 cup milk*
1 tsp mild mustard	*1 tsp mild mustard*
1 tbsp white wine vinegar	*1 tbsp white wine vinegar*
1 small onion, very finely chopped	*1 small onion, very finely chopped*
3 small gherkins, finely chopped	*3 small pickled cucumbers, finely chopped*
salt and pepper	*salt and pepper*

Season the fish fillets with salt and pepper.

Put two thirds of the butter in a bowl. Microwave it on High for 1 minute. Add the flour and mix well. Whisk in the milk. Microwave on High for 3 minutes, whisking 3 times during cooking. Remove from the oven and add the mustard mixed with the vinegar. Stir in the onion and pickle and cover.

Put the fillets of fish into a deep dish. Dot with the remaining butter. Season with salt and pepper. Cover with microwave-safe film, piercing it in several places with a fork. Cook on High for 3 minutes.

Remove the covering. Coat the fish with the sauce. Serve accompanied by steamed courgettes (zucchini).

To drink: Vinho verde or lager (light beer).

GOUJONETTES AU CITRON

Deep-fried strips of sole with lemon

Serves 4
Preparation 10 minutes
Cooking about 10 minutes

METRIC/IMPERIAL	AMERICAN
4 large sole, skinned and filleted	4 large sole or flounder, skinned and filleted
100 ml/3½ fl oz milk	½ cup milk
oil, for deep frying	oil, for deep frying
flour, for coating	flour, for coating
salt	salt
2 lemons, quartered, to serve	2 lemons, quartered, to serve

Cut the sole fillets diagonally into strips about 2 cm/¾ in wide. Pour the milk into a shallow dish and add some salt. Dip the sole *goujonettes* into it then drain them.

Heat the oil to 180C/350F (a small cube of stale bread browns in about 60 seconds).

Dip the *goujonettes* in flour to coat them completely, then plunge them into the hot oil to cook until golden.

Drain the *goujonettes* on paper towels and pile them in a warmed serving dish. Garnish with lemon quarters and serve at once.

FLAN

see also: creams and custards pastry tart

In France, Spain and America this term usually refers to an egg custard cooked in a mould and turned out.

In Britain, open-faced tarts, with or without a pastry crust, are also referred to as flans. These may have a wide variety of sweet or savoury fillings and be served as first or main courses or as desserts. Sweet flans usually contain a flavoured custard, hence the usage, or have a layer of pastry cream or custard topped with fresh or dried fruits. They may consist of a simple batter baked with fruit, as in a *clafouti*. Savoury flan fillings, such as asparagus, seafood or chicken livers, are usually in a creamy sauce or cooked in a custard and served unmoulded.

FLOATING ISLANDS

Iles flottantes

see also: caramel creams and custards

This traditional French dessert usually consists of pieces of liqueur-flavoured sponge cake floating on a bed of custard sauce and dressed with cream. A version, called *oeufs à la neige*, which actually means 'eggs in the snow', substitutes small balls of stiffly beaten egg white and sugar poached in milk for the sponge. The milk and egg yolks are then used to make the custard and the meringue eggs are decorated with caramel.

OEUFS À LA NEIGE

Caramel floating islands

Serves 6–8
Preparation 20 minutes, 30 minutes ahead
Cooking 15 minutes

METRIC/IMPERIAL	AMERICAN
6 eggs, separated	6 eggs, separated
200 g/7 oz caster sugar	1 cup superfine sugar
1 l/1¾ pt milk	1 qt milk
1 vanilla pod, split in half	1 vanilla bean, split in half
10 sugar cubes	10 sugar cubes

Beat the egg whites to very stiff peaks. Sprinkle them with one quarter of the caster (superfine) sugar and whisk that in.

Heat the milk in a large saucepan until it is just simmering. Using 2 large spoons, form some of the egg white mixture into a ball and slide it into the simmering milk. After 15 seconds, turn the meringue ball and poach it on the other side for a scant 10 seconds. Remove and drain on a cloth.

By working quickly, 3 meringue balls can be poached at the same time. Drain them and put them in a single layer on the cloth. Continue until all the egg white has been used.

Strain the milk and return it to the saucepan. Add the vanilla and heat the milk until just boiling. Beat the egg yolks with the remaining sugar until the mixture is foamy. Remove the vanilla from the milk and pour the boiling milk over the egg yolks, stirring vigorously. Pour the mixture back into the saucepan and cook over a low heat, stirring constantly, until the custard is thick enough to coat the back of a spoon.

Pour it into a large serving bowl. Place the meringues on top and set aside.

Make a pale caramel with the sugar cubes and a little water. Dribble it over the egg whites. Serve well chilled.

Oeufs à la neige (Caramel floating islands)

FLOUNDER

see Plaice

FLOUR

Farine

see also:
barley
bread
buckwheat
cereal
choux
cornflour
pasta
pastry
rice
sauce
yeast

Flour is made by finely grinding cereal grains, usually wheat unless otherwise specified, and is mainly used to make breads, cakes and pâtisserie, although it finds countless other culinary uses, from coating foods to thickening sauces.

Flours are categorized in three main ways: by the degree to which they are refined, or stripped of the bran and wheat germ in the exterior of the wheat, by the size of the grain particles, and by the 'strength', or gluten content, of the flour, ie how readily it will stretch and rise during cooking.

WHOLEWHEAT OR WHOLEMEAL FLOURS are made from the whole grain. The best varieties are termed STONE GROUND as they are still processed in this time-honoured way. Because this process involves little heating, very little of the wheat's nutrients are driven off. American wholewheat GRAHAM FLOUR has the bran ground more coarsely than is the case with ordinary wholewheat flour. Wholegrain flours tend to produce dense products which do not rise well, so they are often blended with strong white flours to give lighter results. Sifting whole flours well before use lightens the product. It is also useful to reserve the sifted, large bran particles until the flour has been made into a smooth dough and to add them back at this stage. The other disadvantage of retaining so much of the whole grain is that the oil in the germ goes rancid readily, so the flour does not keep well. Therefore, buy in small quantities and store in cool, dry conditions.

WHEATMEAL OR BROWN FLOURS still contain much of the wheat germ, but little of the bran. They are usually finer, without the bran particles of whole flour, and have properties more like those of plain (all-purpose) flour. They rise well and produce lighter breads, but still keep the fine, strong, nutty taste of the wheat.

WHITE FLOURS have usually had all but minute traces of the bran and wheat germ removed, leaving only the starchy interior or endosperm. They may also be bleached to make them even whiter and also have added to them (a statutory requirement in many countries) many minerals and other nutrients, such as iron, which have been removed by the process of refinement. White flour comes in varying strengths, depending mainly on the gluten content of the wheat from which it was made. STRONG PLAIN OR BREAD FLOUR, high in gluten content, makes the best bread and pastry. British PLAIN FLOUR is a soft, low-gluten flour used for cakes, short pastries, sauces, etc. American ALL-PURPOSE FLOUR is a mixture of hard and soft flours and, as its name suggests, is intended to be suitable for a wide range of baking. American CAKE FLOUR is very soft, refined and finely ground to give the smoothest of batters and produce particularly light cakes.

SELF-RAISING OR SELF-RISING FLOUR is a soft white flour to which has been added its own leavening agent and salt ready for baking. It is used wherever the addition of a baking powder is required, such as in the making of some cakes, tea breads, scones, suet crusts, etc, but is not suitable for yeast bread. Self-raising flours are useful for making low-fat pastries, but do give rather spongy results. The potency of the added chemicals diminishes rapidly, so these flours should be bought in small quantities.

There are many other types of flour formulated for particular purposes, from SUPER-SIFTED FLOURS which mix with liquids more readily and PATENT FLOURS, the most highly refined and expensive, to the wide range of proprietary flours with added wheat germ or bran and rye or malt flour for making speciality breads.

All flours must be kept in cool, dry conditions. They are best kept in their own bag in a well-ventilated place, but if they are likely to be exposed to damp or steam they must be stored in airtight containers. Do not mix old and fresh flours. Unleavened white flours will keep for up to 6 months, but do not store whole or self-raising flours for more than 2 months, and buy them from stores with a rapid turnover.

see also:
caper
clove
salad

FLOWER

Fleur

The flowers of many ornamental plants are used in cooking, either in bud form or in full bloom.

The buds, notably rose and nasturtium, are usually pickled in vinegar like capers, then used as a condiment. Some suitably shaped whole flowers, like acacia, jasmine and squash blossoms, may be stuffed or deep fried as fritters. Others, notably nasturtiums and marigolds, with their peppery bite, are used as a vivid garnish and to add flavour and interest to salads. Petals or crushed flowers, or infusions of the same, are used as flavourings: jasmine and hibiscus in poultry and fish dishes, yellow lilies in sauces and stocks, rose and orange blossom in sweets and jams. Candied violets and orange blossom are also common in confectionery.

Wild specimens of all these flowers may be picked and used, but avoid those that may have been exposed to chemicals. Increasingly, edible fresh flowers, especially those intended as salad ingredients, are available in supermarkets and fine food stores. When making salads incorporating flowers such as nasturtium, marigold, red poppy, borage and honeysuckle, it is wise to dress them at the last minute or dress the salad before adding the flowers, as the dressing may alter their colour dramatically.

SALADE AUX FLEURS DE CAPUCINE

Nasturtium flower salad

Serves 4
Preparation 40 minutes

METRIC/IMPERIAL	AMERICAN
½ cucumber, peeled and thinly sliced	½ hothouse cucumber, peeled and thinly sliced
1 lettuce	1 head of Boston lettuce
2 tbsp white wine vinegar	2 tbsp white wine vinegar
4 tbsp groundnut oil	¼ cup peanut oil
225 g/½ lb small cauliflower florets	½ lb small cauliflower florets (about 2 cups)
20 nasturtium flowers	20 nasturtium flowers
salt and pepper	salt and pepper

Sprinkle the cucumber with salt and leave it to drain for 30 minutes. Separate the outer lettuce leaves and divide the heart into small bunches.

Make a vinaigrette dressing using the wine vinegar, oil and salt and pepper to taste.

Thoroughly dry the cucumber. Combine the cauliflower florets, lettuce heart and cucumber in a bowl. Pour the dressing over and mix well.

Line a shallow salad bowl with the lettuce leaves and put the mixed salad into it. Add the nasturtium flowers and mix gently, then serve.

FLEURS DE COURGETTES FARCIES

Stuffed courgette or zucchini flowers

Serves 4
Preparation 30 minutes

METRIC/IMPERIAL	AMERICAN
1 small cucumber, peeled and thinly sliced	1 small hothouse cucumber, peeled and thinly sliced
1 orange	1 orange
140 g/5 oz peeled cooked prawns, chopped	5 oz peeled cooked shrimp, chopped
200 g/7 oz taramasalata	1 cup taramasalata
8 very fresh, not-too-large courgette flowers, stalks removed	8 very fresh zucchini flowers, stems removed
salt and pepper	salt and pepper

Sprinkle the cucumber slices with salt and chill them. If the orange is not organically grown, and may have been sprayed or coated, scrub it well in warm soapy water, rinse well and pat dry. Grate the zest and squeeze the juice.

Mix the prawns (shrimp) with the taramasalata and season with pepper. Stuff the flowers with this mixture.

Rinse the cucumber slices and wring as much water as possible out of them. Arrange them around the edge of a serving dish and put the stuffed flowers in the middle.

Whisk the orange juice and zest together rapidly with salt and pepper to taste. Pour this over the dish and serve.

see also:
confit
duck
giblets
goose
liver

FOIE GRAS

This celebrated French culinary delicacy is produced by fattening geese and ducks on a rich diet including eggs and milk, confining them closely and then finally force-feeding them with softened maize so that the liver swells to great size (usually 675–900 g/1½–2 lb for goose and 400–550 g/14–20 oz for duck, although they can get much larger) and develops the characteristic rich flavour and creamy texture. The centres of production are mainly in the southwest of France and in Brittany and Alsace.

RAW FOIE GRAS (*foie gras cru*) is available from the end of the autumn until about the beginning of the year and must be bought straight from the place of production, at a local market, or at specialist food stores. It should be beige or pinkish-grey in colour (avoid any with a yellowish tinge), firm and supple in texture, not crumbly, and should not exude fat. It should be eaten or cooked no later than the day after purchase and requires lengthy preparation, so buy only the best livers. More convenient is FRESH FOIE GRAS (*foie gras frais*) which has been cooked and packed in little pots or terrines. It will keep for up to a week in the refrigerator.

SEMI-COOKED FOIE GRAS (*foie gras mi-cuit*) has been cooked very slowly in butter and is ready to eat; it will keep for only 3–4 weeks in the refrigerator. Vacuum-wrapped or canned, it will keep refrigerated for 2–3 months, or 6 months if it has also been pasteurized. Outside France the last form is the one usually available.

PRESERVED FOIE GRAS (*foie gras de conserve*) is cooked and preserved in its own fat in the manner of *confit* and, like wine, improves with keeping. This should be served chilled.

The labelling of all foie gras products is strictly regulated. Anything labelled '100% foie gras' contains the whole liver (*foie gras entier*) or a block of pure foie gras. Cans labelled '*pâté de foie gras*' or '*parfait de foie gras*' contain liver coated in forcemeat, but must have at least 80% foie gras; '*mousse de foie gras*' or '*purée de foie gras*' must contain at least 55% finely pounded foie gras. Relatively inexpensive mousse or purée makes a good garnish and canapé topping, but cannot be used on hot dishes as it melts. Blocks of foie gras labelled '*truffé*' must contain at least 3% truffle.

Foie gras should be served, sliced not too thinly or scooped in curls with a knife, on toasted brioche or country-style bread and accompanied by dry champagne or Sauternes. It is also the traditional garnish on many classics of *haute cuisine*, notably dishes with the appellation *à la périgourdine* or *Rossini*.

Foie gras does not have the nutritional value of ordinary liver and is extraordinarily high in saturated fat and calorie content: about 200 calories for one 30 g/1 oz serving.

SALADE FOLLE

Foie gras salad

Serves 4
Preparation 25 minutes
Cooking 10 minutes

METRIC/IMPERIAL	AMERICAN
225 g/½ lb very thin French green beans, trimmed	*½ lb very thin green beans, trimmed*
115 g/4 oz radicchio	*4 oz radicchio*
3 tbsp olive oil	*3 tbsp olive oil*
1 tbsp sherry vinegar	*1 tbsp sherry vinegar*
2 tomatoes, peeled, deseeded and cut into tiny cubes	*2 tomatoes, peeled, deseeded and cut into tiny cubes*
4 slices of truffled foie gras	*4 slices of truffled foie gras*
salt and freshly ground pepper	*salt and freshly ground pepper*

Cook the beans for 8–10 minutes in a large pan of rapidly boiling salted water. Drain them and plunge them immediately into cold water. They should still be crisp.

Separate the radicchio leaves, wash them and pat them completely dry with paper towels. Dress 4 plates with the radicchio.

Make a vinaigrette with the olive oil, vinegar and some salt and pepper.

In a bowl, mix the beans and tomatoes and toss them gently in the vinaigrette. Spoon on to the plates and place a slice of foie gras on top of each one. Sprinkle with more pepper and serve.

To drink: a spicy, aromatic white, such as a Gewürztraminer.

ESCALOPES DE FOIE GRAS AU RAISIN

Escalopes of foie gras with grapes

Serves 4
Preparation 30 minutes, 24 hours ahead
Cooking about 8 minutes

METRIC/IMPERIAL	*AMERICAN*
225 g/½ lb green grapes, peeled and deseeded	*½ lb green grapes (about 2 cups), peeled and seeded*
200 ml/7 fl oz Frontignan or other rich sweet Muscat wine	*1 cup Frontignan or other rich sweet Muscat wine*
1 raw duck foie gras, weighing 450–550 g/1–1¼ lb, trimmed	*1 raw duck foie gras, weighing 1–1¼ lb, trimmed*
1 tbsp goose fat	*1 tbsp goose fat*
4 slices of white bread	*4 slices of white bread*
flour, for dusting	*flour, for dusting*
salt and pepper	*salt and pepper*

Macerate the grapes overnight in the wine.

The following day, cut the foie gras into 4 thick slices. Season them with salt and pepper and dust them lightly with flour.

Heat the goose fat in a frying pan until very hot, put the slices of foie gras into it and lower the heat to moderate. Cook them for 30 seconds on each side, then drain them. Fry the slices of bread in the same goose fat on both sides.

Discard the fat and pour the macerating liquid from the grapes into the frying pan. Reduce this over a high heat for 3 minutes, then add the grapes and lower the heat.

When the sauce is syrupy, return the slices of foie gras to the pan and reheat for not more than 1 minute at most. Place the liver on top of the fried bread on warmed plates, add the grapes and coat with the sauce.

FONDANT

see also: cakes and gâteaux, glazing, icing, sugar

A malleable, sticky white paste made from a sugar syrup with added glucose cooked to 'soft ball' stage and then kneaded well until smooth and soft, fondant is used for icing cakes, pastries or petits fours and for coating *bouchées*.

Fondant may be bought ready-made and kept in an airtight container. Before using, heat gently in a bain-marie, usually with a little water, light syrup or alcohol, until just runny. It should not be heated above a temperature of 50C/122F because this causes it to lose its shine. It may be coloured and flavoured with a wide variety of essences or extracts, such as chocolate, coffee, lemon, etc. To make it easier to ice gâteaux, Genoese sponge cakes, for example, glaze them first with warmed jam and then pour the fondant over the top.

The name fondant is also given to a particular type of chocolate gâteau, so called because it melts in the mouth.

FONDUE

see also: cheese, stock

The practice of serving fondues originated in Switzerland. The Swiss traditionally melt some of their fine, fruity cheese in white wine and place it on the table in a heated dish set over a spirit lamp. Guests spear cubes of bread on special long forks and dip these into the fondue to coat the bread well with the cheese mixture.

There are countless local variations on this basic CHEESE FONDUE, including the addition of eggs, cream, milk, mushrooms, shallots, truffles or Kirsch. Cheese fondue is classically accompanied by plenty of salad to aid the digestion of the cooked cheese.

The same principles have also been applied to the cooking of other types of ingredients or foods. FONDUE BOURGUIGNONNE has the fondue pot filled with hot oil into which the diners place speared chunks of steak. There is usually a selection of sauces and relishes on the table as accompaniments.

CHINESE FONDUE is based on a traditional Mongolian dish in which a variety of meats, poultry, fish and seafood are cooked in hot beef or chicken stock. The fondue is served with a good selection of vegetables, sauces and condiments and when all the meats have been cooked any remaining vegetables are added to the stock along with noodles and egg threads to make a nourishing and tasty soup.

Pieces of fruit, cake or biscuits (cookies) may also be dipped in a CHOCOLATE FONDUE to make a memorable dessert.

Fondue dishes do tend to be quite high in calories. Guests enjoying a cheese fondue, for instance, can easily consume about 800 calories. Chinese fondue, however, is fairly healthy and constitutes a truly balanced, nutritious meal.

The term fondue is also used of a preparation of finely chopped vegetables which have been cooked gently to a pulp with only a little oil, and perhaps spiced or flavoured with herbs. Fondues of chicory (Belgian endive), tomato, onion, fennel, carrot, leek and suchlike may be used as sauce bases or served as accompaniments or condiments.

FOOD ADDITIVE

see also:
colouring agents
emulsion
preservative

This term is used for any natural or synthetic substance added to processed food in order to improve its nutritional value, flavour, appearance, consistency or keeping qualities, or to facilitate preparation. There are several hundred food additives, which in many countries must be identified on the label of the product in descending order by weight.

The international identification code for additives consists of a letter – E in Europe – plus a number: 100 to 199 for colouring agents; 200 to 299 for preservatives; 300 to 399 for anti-oxidants; 400 to 499 for texturing agents such as emulsifiers, jelling agents and thickeners. Any additives not included in this code, such as water and monosodium glutamate, must be identified by their full names. Certain additives, notably food colourings such as the yellow tartrazine (E102) so common in desserts and soft drinks, can cause allergies and adverse reactions in children and other sensitive people.

The authorities in each country exercise strict controls over additives and the maximum amounts which may be used. Certain substances prohibited in one country may be allowed in others; for example, amaranth (E123) is banned by most nations but its use is permitted in France. Some substances are given only provisional authorization until there is proof of their long-term non-toxicity.

FORCEMEAT

see Stuffing

FRANGIPANE

see also:
almond
creams and custards
macaroon

A pastry cream to which ground almonds or crushed macaroons and possibly a few drops of almond essence are added, frangipane cream is used to fill tarts and classic pâtisserie items, such as *feuilletés*, *pithiviers* and *dartois*. It is also used as a filling for crêpes and cakes and in many desserts.

CRÈME FRANGIPANE

Frangipane cream

Makes about 1.25 l/2¼ pt/6½ cups
Preparation 10 minutes
Cooking about 15 minutes

METRIC/IMPERIAL	AMERICAN
1 l/1¾ pt milk	*1 qt milk*
1 sachet (7.5 g/1¾ tsp) of vanilla sugar	*1¾ tsp vanilla-flavored sugar*
2 eggs + 3 egg yolks	*2 eggs + 3 egg yolks*
150 g/5½ oz caster sugar	*¾ cup superfine sugar*
125 g/4½ oz flour	*1 cup flour*
45 g/1½ oz butter, softened	*3 tbsp butter, softened*
125 g/4½ oz blanched almonds, very finely ground	*1⅓ cups very finely ground blanched almonds*
salt	*salt*

Slowly bring the milk to the boil in a saucepan with the vanilla sugar.

In a bowl, beat the whole eggs with the egg yolks. Add the sugar and a pinch of salt and whisk until the mixture is white and foamy.

Add the flour to the eggs, beating well. Pour the boiling milk over, stirring constantly.

Pour this mixture back into the saucepan and cook over a low heat, stirring continuously, just until it starts to boil and thicken. Then remove from the heat and add the softened butter and ground almonds and mix well. While the custard cream is still hot, sprinkle a little extra sugar over the top so that a skin does not form upon cooling.

Variation: frangipane cream made with ground almonds is extremely rich; for a lighter cream, substitute 75 g/2½ oz of finely crushed almond macaroons (about 4) for the ground almonds and reduce the amount of sugar by a third.

see also: blanching

FREEZING

Food of all sorts may be preserved by maintaining it at very low temperatures (−10 to −18C/14 to 0F). The water in the food solidifies and this inhibits the growth of any micro-organisms and slows the enzyme activity which causes food to spoil. Most foods, including cooked dishes, may be frozen as long as they are properly prepared. For successful freezing the food must be absolutely fresh and the actual freezing operation must take place speedily and at a very low temperature. There is one inviolable rule of freezing: never re-freeze thawed frozen food!

Frozen foods can be stored for periods ranging from 1 month to 1 year. Fatty foods, for instance, do not keep as long as foods with little or no fat; sour fruits can be frozen for a relatively long period of time.

Home freezers should be chosen to suit particular needs. Generally a freezer with a volume of 40–50 l/1½ cu ft will suffice for town living, whereas a 60–80 l/2½ cu ft freezer will be more appropriate in the country. If planning to store mainly small quantities of frozen food, a combined refrigerator-freezer is adequate. If intending to stock larger quantities of frozen foods, a combination model (upright freezer stacked with a refrigerator) will be more practical. However, if planning to freeze foods at home and store them in considerable quantities, a chest freezer has the largest capacity and makes it possible to take full advantage of seasonal availability of produce and the lower costs connected with buying in bulk.

For home freezing to be successful the foods must be cleaned and prepared as appropriate. For instance, meat should have as much of the fat removed as possible and the bones taken out where practicable, vegetables should be blanched, fruit should be rolled in sugar, etc. If freezing cooked dishes, reduce the cooking time by 10–20 minutes. When making casseroles, cakes or pastry, prepare double quantities, use half for your immediate needs and freeze the remainder.

Freeze food in small, meal-size quantities, so that it freezes more quickly and is handier for thawing. Put the food along the sides of the freezer to ensure that it freezes as quickly as possible; many freezers have a quick- or fast-freeze mode which increases its cooling activity during this process. Once it is frozen, arrange it neatly and compactly in rows as close together as possible. Never load the freezer to its maximum capacity or it will not work efficiently.

Use sturdy, light materials for packing: specially made plastic boxes and foil containers and special freezer bags made of plastic or foil ensure that smells do not permeate, to avoid foods tainting each other. Expel any remaining air in the container or bag before sealing it. Items such as hamburgers and pancakes that are cooked singly should be separated with sheets of waxed paper, stacked and overwrapped before freezing. Liquids in rigid containers need room to expand during freezing: allow 1 cm/½ in space at the top of the container. Label each package with a waterproof pen, indicating the date of freezing, contents, quantity and 'use by' date. Reorganize and clear out the freezer regularly.

GUIDELINES FOR FREEZING AND STORAGE TIMES

FOOD	PREPARATION AND HANDLING	MAX TIME (IN MONTHS)
VEGETABLES		
Artichokes	Cut off base and large leaves. Blanch for 8 minutes in water with lemon juice.	10
Asparagus	Scrape the stalks. Blanch for 3 minutes in salted water.	9
Aubergine	Slice but do not peel. Blanch for 4 minutes.	12
Brussels sprouts	Blanch for 3 minutes.	15
Cabbage	Wash leaves, shred and blanch for 2 minutes.	9
Cauliflower	Separate into florets and blanch for 3–4 minutes in water with lemon juice.	9
Carrots	Scrape. Blanch for 3 minutes.	12
Corn on the cob	Shuck. Blanch for 4–8 minutes.	6
Courgettes	Freeze whole and unpeeled if small; or slice and blanch for 2–3 minutes.	10
Eggplant (see Aubergine)		
Green beans	Freshly picked. Top and tail, blanch for 3 minutes.	12
Haricot beans (fresh)	Shell and blanch for 1 minute.	12
Herbs	Wash and pat dry, freeze in bags, or chop and put into ice-cube trays.	12
Leeks	Whites only, cut in chunks. Blanch for 3 minutes.	8
Mushrooms	Clean and blanch for 2–4 minutes.	6
Onions	Baby white onions. Remove outer skin. Blanch for 2 minutes.	4
Peas	Freshly picked. Blanch for 1 minute in water with lemon juice.	12
Potatoes	Small new potatoes. Brush and scald.	12
Sorrel & Spinach	Choose tender leaves and blanch for 2–3 minutes then squeeze moisture out.	10
Sweet peppers	Remove seeds and filaments and slice in 2–3 pieces. Blanch for 2 minutes.	10
Swiss chard	Blanch leaves; trim stalks, cut into small pieces and blanch for 3 minutes in vinegared water.	10
Tomatoes	Unpeeled. Whole or halved. For sauces or stews.	6
Turnips	Baby turnips. Blanch for 2–4 minutes.	10
Zucchini (see Courgette)		
Others	Chicory, cress, lettuce, endive, celery: cooked, then puréed. Do not freeze cucumber, radish, fennel and celeriac (unless cooked and puréed).	
OTHER FOODS		
Cooked dishes	Do not add too much fat or salt. Cool completely before freezing.	
	Vegetable soups.	3
	Dishes in sauce.	8
	Pies and tarts.	4
Bread and pâtisserie	Raw shortcrust or puff pastry: rolled out and put in a tart pan or in a ball wrapped in foil.	2
	Bread, made-up pizzas.	3
	Cooked Genoese sponge, fruit cake, brioche.	3
	Croissants, madeleines, choux puffs (cooked).	2
OTHER FOODS (*cont.*)		
Ice creams & sorbets	Do not allow to melt between preparation and freezing. Soften in the refrigerator.	1
MEAT, POULTRY AND FISH		
Basic method	Wrap small and large pieces separately, depending on intended use. Take care that bones do not pierce wrapping.	
Beef	Remove fat. Cut according to use.	12
Cold cuts	The fattier the product, the shorter the time.	2
Lamb	Remove fat and wrap pieces separately.	9
Offal	Brains: remove skin, wash, wrap in plastic.	4
	Heart: remove tendons and slice.	5
	Liver: slice finely.	6
Pork	Remove fat, cut up, wrap in plastic. Smaller pieces do not keep as long.	5
Variety meats (see Offal)		
Veal	Must be very fresh. Cut in pieces.	9
Poultry	Chicken, guinea fowl, duck: whole, plucked and drawn, not stuffed or trussed.	6
	Turkey: in pieces.	4
Rabbit	Do not freeze raw.	
Game	Skin or pluck, draw and let blood. Freeze game birds whole, cut venison in pieces. Freeze as quickly as possible.	3
Lean fish	Freshly caught only. Bass, cod, flounder, sole, whiting, plaice, trout: whole, scaled, gutted and patted dry.	5
Fatty fish	Freshly caught only. Mackerel, sardine, tuna: same as for lean fish.	3
Shellfish	Remove from shells; cook before freezing.	1
Crustacea	Remove shells and freeze raw.	3
FRUIT		
3 methods for fruits:	1) Raw, in a plastic bag or open freeze, then bag. 2) Rolled in sugar: 140 g/5 oz sugar for each 450 g/1 lb fruit. 3) In syrup: 3 parts sugar/4 parts water. Always thaw at room temperature.	
Apples	Peel, core and quarter.	6
Apricots	Peel and stone. Cut in half or slice.	8
Cherries	Remove stalks and stone.	10
Citrus	Peel down to the flesh, quarter and remove seeds	9
Grapes	Wash and remove seeds.	3
Peaches	Peel and stone. Slice or halve.	8
Pears	Peel, core and quarter.	6
Pineapple	Peel and remove core. Slice or cube.	3
Plums	Remove stones and cut in half.	8
Red berry fruits	Wash, remove any seeds and wipe dry.	10
Rhubarb	Peel and cut in chunks.	10
Strawberries and raspberries	Hull.	12

Many items may be cooked straight from frozen, but some foods, such as large cuts of meat and whole birds, pastry, shellfish and cheeses need to be thawed first, preferably in the refrigerator or in a microwave oven.

Freezing preserves most of the nutritional value of foodstuffs. Protein and sugars undergo no alteration whatsoever; fats, however, may be slightly denatured by the extreme temperature. If the freezing process takes place quickly, the vitamin C and mineral content are unaffected.

FRENCH DRESSING

see Vinaigrette

FRENCH TOAST

Pain perdu

see also:
bread
brioche
fritter

Made from slices of stale bread soaked in milk, dipped in eggs beaten with sugar and lightly fried in butter, French toast was originally conceived as a way of using up leftover bread.

Now a feast-day treat in parts of France and a popular breakfast dish in many other countries, it may also be made with milk bread or brioche and is usually accompanied by custard, jam or maple syrup.

Two slices contain roughly 400 calories.

PAIN PERDU BRIOCHÉ

French brioche toast

Serves 6
Preparation 10 minutes
Cooking about 15 minutes

METRIC/IMPERIAL	AMERICAN
200 ml/7 fl oz milk	1 cup milk
100 g/3½ oz caster sugar	½ cup superfine sugar
1 sachet (7.5 g/1¾ tsp) vanilla sugar	1¾ tsp vanilla-flavored sugar
5 eggs	5 eggs
85 g/3 oz butter	6 tbsp butter
12 slices of slightly stale brioche	12 slices of slightly stale brioche
12 strawberries, to decorate (optional)	12 strawberries, to decorate (optional)

Pour the milk into a saucepan. Add the sugars and heat gently.

Break the eggs into a bowl and beat them lightly. Melt the butter in a small saucepan and clarify it by skimming off the white foam as it appears.

Put 1 tablespoon of this clarified butter in a large frying pan over a moderate heat. One at a time, dip the slices of brioche first into the sugared milk and then into the beaten egg, making sure that both sides are well coated.

Place 3 of the slices in the frying pan and cook for 2 minutes on each side or until golden brown. Remove from the pan, drain briefly on paper towels, put on a warmed serving plate and keep warm. Repeat the operation with the rest of the brioche slices, using more clarified butter as required.

If wished, decorate the top of each slice with a strawberry which has been sliced several times almost through to the stem and then fanned out.

FRICASSEE

Fricassée

see also:
blanquette
ragoût

Light stews, usually containing lamb, veal or chicken, in a creamy white sauce are termed fricassees. They are distinguished from blanquettes in that the meat is usually first lightly sautéed, although not browned, with some aromatic vegetables. The ingredients are then sprinkled with flour and simmered in a white stock. Baby onions and mushrooms are often added late in the cooking as a garnish, and the dish may be thickened with a little cream.

The term fricassee can also refer to any kind of quickly prepared dish in which the main ingredient is pan-fried with herbs and seasonings. Wild mushrooms, small fish, quails and even shellfish and crustacea are often cooked in this way.

Fricassée périgourdine is a name given to a mixture of aromatic vegetables which have been browned in oil ready for use in a *pot-au-feu*, soup or stew.

Pain perdu brioché (French brioche toast)

FRICASSÉE DE VOLAILLE À L'OIGNON

Chicken fricassee with onions

Serves 4
Preparation 15 minutes
Cooking about 35 minutes

METRIC/IMPERIAL	AMERICAN
1 corn-fed chicken, dressed weight about 1.5 kg/3½ lb, cut into pieces	1 chicken, drawn and dressed weight about 3½ lb, cut into pieces
15 g/½ oz butter	1 tbsp butter
1 tbsp oil	1 tbsp oil
4 onions, thinly sliced	4 onions, thinly sliced
1 thick slice of Bayonne ham, weighing about 115 g/4 oz, cut into strips	1 slice of Bayonne ham, weighing about 4 oz, cut into strips
2 tbsp Cognac or Armagnac	2 tbsp Cognac or Armagnac
200 ml/7 fl oz dry white wine	1 cup dry white wine
chopped chives or parsley, to garnish (optional)	chopped chives or parsley, to garnish (optional)
salt and pepper	salt and pepper

Preheat the oven to 190C/375F/gas 5. Season the chicken pieces with salt and pepper.

Heat the butter and oil in a flameproof casserole and brown the chicken pieces over a moderate heat, turning them several times. Push the chicken pieces to the sides of the casserole and add the onions. Cook, stirring, for 2 minutes.

Add the ham and pour the Cognac or Armagnac over. Stir gently for 2 minutes, then add a little salt and some pepper and the white wine. Cover and cook over a moderate heat for 15 minutes.

Put the casserole into the oven and cook for a further 10–12 minutes. Serve straight from the dish. If wished, garnish the fricassee with chopped chives or parsley and accompany with sautéed courgettes (zucchini) or fried mushrooms.

To drink: a light red Burgundy, such as a Givry.

FRICASSÉE DE VEAU AU CITRON

Veal fricassee with lemon

Serves 4
Preparation 5 minutes
Cooking about 1¼ hours

METRIC/IMPERIAL	AMERICAN
1 lemon	1 lemon
45 g/1½ oz butter	3 tbsp butter
300 g/10 oz boned veal breast, cut into 4 cm/1½ in cubes	10 oz boneless veal breast, cut into 1½ in cubes
400 g/14 oz boned veal shoulder, cut into 4 cm/1½ in cubes	14 oz boneless veal shoulder, cut into 1½ in cubes
2 egg yolks	2 egg yolks
3 tbsp crème fraîche or whipping cream	3 tbsp crème fraîche or whipping cream
1 tbsp finely chopped flat-leaved parsley	1 tbsp finely chopped flat-leaf parsley
salt and pepper	salt and pepper

If the lemon is not organically grown and may have been sprayed or coated, scrub it carefully in warm soapy water, rinse well and pat dry. Finely grate the zest and squeeze the juice.

Melt the butter in a heavy-bottomed saucepan over a low heat. Seal the pieces of meat but do not let them get too brown. Sprinkle with 1 tablespoon of lemon zest, add salt and pepper and mix. Add enough hot water to cover the meat and put the lid on the pan. Cook gently for 1 hour. The meat should be very tender. If the cooking liquid seems to be evaporating too fast, add a little more water.

Remove the pieces of meat with a slotted spoon and put them into a hot, deep serving dish. Reduce the cooking juices over a high heat.

In a bowl, beat the egg yolks with the cream, 2 tablespoons of lemon juice, the chopped parsley and salt and pepper to taste. Pour this mixture into the cooking juices and stir for 2 minutes over a very low heat without letting it boil. When the sauce is smooth and thick, pour it over the meat, stir and serve immediately.

Serve this fricassee with boiled rice, carrot purée or braised chicory (Belgian endive).

see also:
choux pastry
deep frying
fats and oils
flower
frying
yeast

FRITTER

Beignet, fritot

Any piece of raw or cooked, sweet or savoury food coated in batter and fried is termed a fritter. Fritters may also be made from flavoured choux pastry or yeast dough or a thick pancake or waffle batter.

Fritter batter for coating is always made in advance to give it time to ferment slightly, which improves the texture, and the fritters are usually deep fried at moderate temperatures. They are served piping hot as soon as they are cooked, either lightly salted or dusted with sugar.

Prawn or shrimp fritters are frequently served as cocktail snacks. Others using ingredients such as mussels, chicken livers, pieces of fish or chicken or chunks of vegetable or cheese are often served as hors d'oeuvres or as a main course with an accompanying sauce. Fritter ingredients may also be marinated beforehand to enhance their flavour.

Sweet fritters made with pieces of fruit such as apple or banana, with flowers or with chunks of cold custard or rice are served as desserts, often with a fruit coulis or custard sauce.

Fritters absorb 40–50% of their weight in cooking oil and are therefore particularly high in calories.

PÂTE À BEIGNETS

Fritter batter

Coats about 20 fritters
Preparation 10 minutes, 1–2 hours ahead

METRIC/IMPERIAL	*AMERICAN*
125 g/4$\frac{1}{2}$ oz flour	*1 cup flour*
1 large egg	*1 extra large egg*
$\frac{1}{2}$ tsp salt	*$\frac{1}{2}$ tsp salt*
1 tbsp oil	*1 tbsp oil*
200 ml/7 fl oz milk (or beer for savoury fritters)	*1 cup milk (or beer for savory fritters)*

Sift the flour into a bowl and make a well in the middle. Put the egg, salt and oil in the well (1). Gradually mix in the flour with a wooden spoon.

1

2

Slowly add the liquid (either milk, equal parts milk and water or beer), beating vigorously, until the batter is smooth and not too runny (2). Let stand for at least 1 or 2 hours before using.

Use to coat a wide range of savoury items, including vegetables such as slices of aubergine (eggplant) or courgette (zucchini), chopped artichoke hearts, asparagus tips and salsify, fish and shellfish such as anchovies, salt cod purée, langoustines, soft roe, and meat or offal such as tongue, brains, ham and even foie gras.

Savoury fritters may also be made by puréeing the selected ingredient and adding it to the fritter batter, then forming it into balls for frying.

For sweet fritters, add 1 tablespoon sugar to the flour and flavour as desired; try a tablespoon of rum, several drops of orange blossom water or vanilla.

Sweet fritters are usually made with whole or sliced fruit: apricots, pineapple chunks, banana slices, small apples.

BEIGNETS DE CREVETTES

Shrimp or prawn fritters

Serves 6
Preparation 20 minutes, 2 hours ahead
Cooking 10 minutes

METRIC/IMPERIAL	AMERICAN
200 g/7 oz flour	1½ cups flour
200 ml/7 fl oz beer	1 cup light beer
1 egg	1 egg
4 tbsp olive oil	¼ cup olive oil
36 king prawns, peeled and deveined	36 large raw shrimp, peeled and deveined
pinch of dried thyme	pinch of dried thyme
juice of 1 lemon	juice of 1 lemon
oil, for deep frying	oil, for deep frying
salt	salt

Make a savoury fritter batter, using the flour, beer, egg, ½ teaspoon of salt and 1 tablespoon of the olive oil, and let it stand for 2 hours.

Meanwhile, put the prawns or shrimp in a deep dish, sprinkle them with thyme and add the rest of the olive oil and the lemon juice. Marinate in a cool place for at least 1 hour.

Heat the oil to 180C/360F, or until a small cube of stale bread browns in 60 seconds. Drain the prawns or shrimp. Dip them one at a time into the fritter batter, then drop them into the hot oil and fry until they are golden and crisp.

Remove them and drain thoroughly on paper towels. Sprinkle lightly with a little more salt and serve at once.

BEIGNETS AUX POMMES

Apple fritters

Serves 4
Preparation 20 minutes, 1 hour ahead
Cooking 15 minutes

METRIC/IMPERIAL	AMERICAN
250 g/8½ oz flour	2 cups flour
2 eggs	2 eggs
2 tbsp corn oil	2 tbsp corn oil
200 ml/7 fl oz milk	1 cup milk
4 apples	4 apples
100 g/3½ oz caster sugar	½ cup superfine sugar
pinch of ground cinnamon	pinch of ground cinnamon
oil, for deep frying	oil, for deep frying
salt	salt

Put the flour in a bowl with ½ teaspoon of salt. Make a well in the flour and break 1 egg into it.

Mix with a wooden spoon, drawing the flour from the sides into the egg. When the first egg is incorporated, add the second and mix as before. Add the corn oil and milk. Mix well to obtain a smooth batter. Let it stand for at least 1 hour.

Peel the apples and remove the core and seeds with an apple corer. Slice them into rings and roll them in the mixed sugar and cinnamon.

Heat the oil to 180C/360F, or until a small cube of stale bread browns in 60 seconds.

Dip the sugared apple rings in the batter, then plunge them into the hot oil. Drain them and serve at once, sprinkled with more sugar.

FROG

Grenouille

There are literally hundreds of different edible types of this web-footed amphibian, but it is the GREEN FROG which the French, in particular, hold in high gastronomic esteem. However, these are now very scarce and the French taste is mostly satisfied by larger species of EUROPEAN EDIBLE FROG imported from Central Europe and Yugoslavia.

Only the hind parts (saddle and legs) are actually eaten. In France they are available fresh on skewers at fishmongers' shops all year round. The feet are cut off with scissors and the frogs' legs soaked in cold water for 1 hour, then wiped dry. Frozen frogs' legs are also available from Indonesia and India. In the United States, BULLFROG legs, sometimes as large as those of guinea fowl but slightly lacking in flavour, are popular and many are also exported to Europe.

It is a good idea to soak fresh frogs' legs and thaw frozen ones in a bowl of equal parts milk and water to make them more succulent. The flavour of frogs' legs, often compared to chicken, is very delicate and is best brought out by simple cooking. Lightly flour them and sauté in butter with garlic and parsley. They may also be grilled or deep fried or used in soups, blanquettes, pies, omelettes and mousselines.

Depending on size, allow 8 pairs of large-sized frogs' legs per person, 10 pairs of medium-sized ones and 12 pairs of the very tasty small ones (usually from male frogs).

Frogs' legs are rich in protein, low in calories (80 calories per 100 g/3½ oz) and easily digested, provided they are not cooked in too much fat.

CUISSES DE GRENOUILLES EN BROCHETTES

Skewered frogs' legs

Serves 4
Preparation 5 minutes, 1 hour ahead
Cooking about 15 minutes

METRIC/IMPERIAL	*AMERICAN*
4 dozen pairs of small frogs' legs	*4 dozen pairs of small frogs' legs*
3 lemons	*3 lemons*
200 ml/7 fl oz olive oil	*1 cup olive oil*
1 garlic clove, chopped	*1 garlic clove, chopped*
2 tbsp finely chopped parsley	*2 tbsp finely chopped parsley*
pinch of cayenne pepper	*pinch of cayenne*
bay leaf, crumbled	*bay leaf, crumbled*
salt and freshly ground pepper	*salt and freshly ground pepper*

Place the frogs' legs in a large, deep dish. Squeeze the juice from 2 of the lemons and cut the third into quarters.

Mix the oil with the lemon juice, garlic, parsley, cayenne, bay leaf and salt and pepper to taste. Pour this mixture over the frogs' legs, mix and leave to marinate for 1 hour.

Drain the frogs' legs, pat them dry, and thread them on skewers through the thickest part of both thighs.

Cook them gently under a preheated moderate grill (broiler) or on a charcoal grill for about 15 minutes, turning them several times. Serve at once with the lemon quarters.

FROSTING

see Icing

FRUIT

see also: *apple*, *apricot*, *banana*, *bilberry*, *blackberry*, *blackcurrant*, *brandies, etc*, *cakes and gâteaux*, *charlotte*, *cherry*, *chutney*, *citrus fruit*, *cranberry*, *date*, *dried vine fruit*, *drying*, *fig*, *freezing*, *fruit juices*, *gooseberry*, *grape*, *grapefruit*, *guava*, *ices and ice creams*, *jams, etc*, *jelly*, *kebab*, *kumquat*, *lemon*, *lime*, *liqueur*, *lychee*, *mango*, *mangosteen*, *melon*, *mulberry*, *nectarine*, *nuts*, *orange*, *papaya*, *passion fruit*, *pear*, *persimmon*, *pie*

Fruits are those parts of plants producing the seed, and many types of fruit are not only edible but delicious, sweet, juicy, highly nutritious and a versatile foodstuff. They are generally distinguished by family, shape, flavour and harvesting season: citrus fruits in winter, soft red fruits in summer, figs and grapes in autumn, etc. However, some of the most commonly known fruits, such as apples, oranges and bananas, are available in the market all year round. Strictly speaking, nuts and vegetable fruits, such as tomatoes and aubergines (eggplant), are also fruits, but they are dealt with elsewhere.

Fruit should be eaten at the peak of its ripeness to obtain the best food value and flavour. Care must be taken when buying fruit, as some varieties continue to ripen after harvesting and others do not. Fruit should be stored in single layers in cool, dark, well-ventilated places, preferably not in the refrigerator. If a fruit is best served chilled, this should be done only briefly before serving. The flesh of most fruits oxidizes readily on contact with air, so it is wise to peel or cut fruit with stainless steel utensils and to coat it with lemon juice after cutting.

Raw fruit is a popular and healthy snack and a common dessert. Salads of chopped mixed fruits, macerated in fruit juice or syrup and flavoured with alcohol, make a simple but luxurious dessert, dressed with cream or custard sauce. Fruit may also be baked, caramelized or made into kebabs. It is also the common filling in sweet pies and tarts, and is made into compotes, charlottes, soufflés, mousses, sauces and ice creams, etc. The sweet sharpness of some fruits also works well in savoury cooking, as in cherries with duck, grapes with chicken and fish, apples with pork, etc. The fruit may be incorporated as a stuffing, an aromatic ingredient during cooking, or as part of a sauce or garnish. Perhaps the most traditional use of seasonal fruit is in the making of preserves, such as jams, jellies and marmalades.

Fruit harvests are also preserved in many other ways, such as in syrup or alcohol, which make luxurious desserts. Most fruits also dry well and make a healthy and energy-giving snack. Dried fruit used in desserts or in cooking in place of fresh fruit is often soaked in water,

pomegranate
prune
quince
rambutan
raspberry
redcurrant
rhubarb
sauce
sorbet
strawberry
tart
watermelon
zest

tea, fruit juice, syrup or alcohol. A large proportion of commercial fruit production is canned in juice or syrup, and this works well for all but the berry fruits. Fruit is also much used in pickles, relishes and chutneys. Most fruits freeze well, although the softer berry fruits lose most of their texture and are best used in cooked dishes.

Fruit is also often candied or crystallized by soaking it in increasingly concentrated sugar syrups, so that the water in the fruit is almost entirely replaced with sugar. Candied citrus peel, apricots, glacé cherries, etc, are popular in confectionery, in the making of cakes, pastries and ice creams and to garnish sweet dishes.

The nutritional value of fruit varies. Not all fruits are rich in vitamin C and some of them have a very high sugar content. For instance, 75 g/$2\frac{1}{2}$ oz of grapes, 1 fig or 1 small banana all contain about 50 calories, the same amount as 300 g/10 oz of melon, watermelon, strawberries or raspberries; 150 g/$5\frac{1}{2}$ oz of undressed mixed fruit salad contains about 75 calories. Dried fruit has a very concentrated sugar content and is often about twice as calorific as equal weights of the fresh fruit. Preserved fruit, especially dried, frozen and bottled or canned in juice or syrup, maintains a high level of the original vitamin and mineral content.

SALADE D'ORANGES AU GRAND MARNIER

Oranges with Grand Marnier

Serves 4
Preparation 20 minutes, macerating 1 hour
Cooking 3 minutes

METRIC/IMPERIAL	AMERICAN
8 juicy oranges	*8 juicy oranges*
3 tbsp caster sugar	*3 tbsp superfine sugar*
4 tbsp Cognac	*4 tbsp Cognac*
1 sachet (7.5 g/$1\frac{3}{4}$ tsp) of vanilla sugar	*$1\frac{3}{4}$ tsp vanilla-flavored sugar*
6 tbsp Grand Marnier	*6 tbsp Grand Marnier*
12 shelled hazelnuts, crushed	*12 shelled hazelnuts, crushed*
freshly ground white pepper	*freshly ground white pepper*

If the oranges are not organically grown and may have been sprayed or coated, scrub them in warm soapy water, rinse well and pat dry. Pare the zest thinly from the oranges or take it off in fine threads using a citrus zester and set it aside, then remove all the white pith and slice the oranges thickly. Remove the seeds.

Arrange the orange slices in layers in a bowl, sprinkling a little sugar on each layer. Pour the Cognac over the oranges. Cover and macerate in the refrigerator for 1 hour.

Cut the orange zest into very thin strips, if not using a citrus zester. Plunge the strips into a saucepan of boiling water, boil for 3 minutes, then drain them. Roll them in the vanilla sugar.

Drain the slices of orange and put them into a serving dish. Add to the macerating liquid the Grand Marnier, crushed hazelnuts, orange zest strips and 2 pinches of white pepper. Mix well and pour over the oranges to serve.

FRUITS EN PAPILLOTES

Fruit kebabs cooked in foil parcels

Serves 4
Preparation 20 minutes, 30 minutes ahead
Cooking 15 minutes

METRIC/IMPERIAL	AMERICAN
3 bananas	*3 bananas*
juice of 1 lemon	*juice of 1 lemon*
2 thin-skinned oranges	*2 thin-skinned oranges*
2 apples	*2 apples*
2 pears	*2 pears*
4 apricots	*4 apricots*
3–4 tbsp caster sugar	*3–4 tbsp superfine sugar*
4 tbsp Curaçao or Grand Marnier	*4 tbsp Curaçao or Grand Marnier*
45 g/$1\frac{1}{2}$ oz butter	*3 tbsp butter*

Peel the bananas, cut them in thick slices, put them in a bowl and sprinkle them with some lemon juice. Peel the oranges, removing all the white pith, segment them and cut into chunks of even size. Add them to the bananas.

Peel the apples and pears, cut them into cubes and sprinkle them with lemon juice. Cut the apricots in half and remove the stones. Add all these to the other fruit in the bowl. Add sugar to

Salade d'oranges au Grand Marnier (Oranges with Grand Marnier)

taste and mix carefully. Pour the alcohol over and leave to macerate for 30 minutes.

Preheat the oven to 250C/475F/gas 9.

Drain the fruits and thread them on 4 skewers. Place each fruit skewer on a sheet of foil and dot with small pieces of butter.

Wrap up the packages and seal them by twisting the foil at each end. Put in a roasting pan and cook for 15 minutes. Serve at once.

see also:
fruit
sorbet

FRUIT JUICES

Jus de fruits

Juices are extracted from fruits by pressing them or processing them in specially designed extractors. Freshly obtained fruit juice contains the most nutrients and gives the best flavour when used in the making of sorbets. Most commercially manufactured fruit juices are made from fruit juice concentrates with added sugar. Look for those labelled 'pure fruit juice' or 'unsweetened', indicating that they are not made from concentrates and contain no sugar or artificial preservatives.

The juice of some fruits, such as lemons and limes, are popular souring ingredients in cooking and serve as useful antioxidants to prevent other cut fruit from discolouring. Fruit juices are also popular in marinades as they add flavour and usually contain enzymes which tenderize ingredients. Fish is also 'cooked' in lime juice in the classic Mexican dish *ceviche*.

Healthy beverages as fruit juices may be, it must not be forgotten that they are usually high in sugar content and thus also in calories.

COCKTAIL SANS ALCOOL

Non-alcoholic cocktail

Serves 4
Preparation 15 minutes

METRIC/IMPERIAL	AMERICAN
1 ripe mango	*1 ripe mango*
1 banana	*1 banana*
juice of 1 lemon	*juice of 1 lemon*
20 raspberries	*20 raspberries*
pineapple or grapefruit juice to taste	*pineapple or grapefruit juice to taste*

Peel the mango, cut it in half and remove the stone. Cut the pulp into cubes. Peel the banana, cut it into chunks and sprinkle with some lemon juice.

Blend the mango, banana and raspberries in a blender or food processor until smooth. Pour this purée over ice cubes in 4 large, chilled glasses and top up with pineapple or grapefruit juice according to taste.

Serve at once.

COCKTAIL VITAMINÉ

Vitamin cocktail

Serves 2
Preparation 15 minutes

METRIC/IMPERIAL	AMERICAN
1 apple	*1 apple*
juice of 1 lemon	*juice of 1 lemon*
1 carrot, cut into chunks	*1 carrot, cut into chunks*
1 stalk of celery, trimmed and cut into chunks	*1 stick of celery, trimmed and cut into chunks*
2 tomatoes, quartered	*2 tomatoes, quartered*
100 g/3½ oz redcurrants, stalks removed	*½ cup fresh redcurrants*

Peel and quarter the apple, remove the core and seeds and sprinkle the quarters with lemon juice.

Pass the fruit and vegetables through a juice extractor. Pour the resulting juice into 2 large glasses and add a little iced water. Mix and serve very cold.

Notes: this cocktail should not be prepared ahead of time, but consumed as soon as it is made. It contains about 70 calories per serving.

If an electric juice extractor is not available, purée the ingredients as finely as possible in a food processor and strain before serving.

see also:
breadcrumbs
deep frying
fats and oils

FRYING

Frire

Cooking foods in a little oil, or butter and oil, usually in a heavy-based pan over a moderate to high heat, is referred to as SHALLOW FRYING or PAN FRYING. This quick method of cooking suits large, relatively thin pieces of food, such as steaks, chops, fish and eggs. The food must usually be turned or moved to ensure even cooking.

Large pieces of meat and poultry may be briefly fried to brown and seal them before further cooking. This procedure can also greatly enhance the flavour of the finished dish.

As with deep frying, delicate food such as fish often needs a protective coating of flour, breadcrumbs or batter before exposure to the hot fat.

A much healthier option is DRY FRYING or SEARING, in which food is fried quickly at very high temperatures without a cooking medium, or fatty food like bacon is cooked over a moderate heat in its own rendered fat only. Both methods produce the leanest possible result.

see also:
court-bouillon
fish
mushroom
sauce
stock

FUMET

A concentrated stock obtained by reducing an ordinary stock or cooking liquid, a *fumet* is used to enhance the flavour of a sauce or give body to another stock. The term is mainly used for strong fish and mushroom stocks.

FUMET DE POISSON

Fish fumet

Makes about 600 ml/1 pt/2½ cups
Preparation 15 minutes
Cooking about 45 minutes

METRIC/IMPERIAL	AMERICAN
1 kg/2¼ lb white fish trimmings, including bones and heads	*2¼ lb white fish trimmings, including bones and heads*
1 onion, finely chopped	*1 onion, finely chopped*
2 shallots, finely chopped	*2 shallots, finely chopped*
bouquet garni	*bouquet garni*
juice of ½ lemon	*juice of ½ lemon*
200 ml/7 fl oz dry white wine	*1 cup dry white wine*
1 tsp coarse salt	*1 tsp coarse salt*
5–6 black peppercorns	*5–6 black peppercorns*

Rinse the fish trimmings under cold running water and drain them.

Put the onion and shallot into a saucepan with the bouquet garni. Put the fish trimmings on top. Sprinkle with the lemon juice, and add the white wine with 1.5 l/2½ pt/1½ qt of water, the salt and peppercorns.

Bring slowly to the boil, then lower the heat and cook gently for 1 hour. Alternatively, cook for only 30 minutes and then strain the stock through a muslin- or cheesecloth-lined sieve into another pan and boil it rapidly, uncovered, to reduce it by about two thirds.

Variations: 115 g/¼ lb chopped mushrooms and some celery leaves may be added to the fumet ingredients.

FUMET DE CHAMPIGNON

Mushroom fumet

Makes about 200 ml/7 fl oz/1 cup
Preparation 10 minutes
Cooking 15 minutes, 30 minutes ahead

METRIC/IMPERIAL	AMERICAN
juice of ½ lemon	*juice of ½ lemon*
45 g/1½ oz butter	*3 tbsp butter*
1 tsp salt	*1 tsp salt*
450 g/1 lb mushrooms, wiped and chopped	*1 lb mushrooms, wiped and chopped*
small bunch of tarragon	*small bunch of tarragon*

Put 500 ml/16 fl oz/2 cups of water into a saucepan and add the lemon juice, butter and salt. Bring to the boil.

Add the mushrooms and tarragon. Boil for 10 minutes then remove from the heat and leave to cool.

Drain the mushrooms (keep them for using in a stuffing or soup or as a garnish) and return the pan to the heat. Boil the liquid rapidly, uncovered, to reduce by about half.

Discard the tarragon, strain the *fumet*, cool and store in the refrigerator until needed.

G

see also:
aspic
ballottine
chicken
stock
terrine

GALANTINE

A cold jellied loaf made of lean poultry, veal, game, pork or foie gras mixed with a forcemeat, cooked in a well-flavoured stock and sometimes pressed in a rectangular terrine, is termed a galantine. Chicken galantines are often made by stuffing a boned bird with the forcemeat. The finished object is then frequently glazed with aspic. Galantines are commonly served in thick slices as a cold first course.

Galantines are extremely rich: an average slice of chicken galantine, weighing about 100 g/3½ oz, contains about 410 calories.

GALANTINE DE POULET BONNE-FEMME

Chicken galantine with onions, mushroom and ham

Serves 6
Preparation 40 minutes
Cooking 1½ hours, 12 hours ahead

METRIC/IMPERIAL	AMERICAN
1 boned chicken, weighing about 1.8 kg/4 lb, with giblets	1 boned chicken, weighing about 4 lb, with giblets
225 g/½ lb minced veal shoulder	½ lb ground veal shoulder
225 g/½ lb pork sausage meat	½ lb pork sausage meat
1 lemon	1 lemon
2 onions, chopped	2 onions, chopped
1 tbsp thyme	1 tbsp thyme
1 tbsp marjoram	1 tbsp marjoram
1 small can (115 g/4 oz) of button mushrooms, chopped	1 4½-oz jar mushrooms, drained and chopped
1 egg	1 egg
1 thick slice of cooked ham, cut into strips	1 thick slice of cooked ham, cut into strips
20 green olives, stoned	20 green olives, pitted
2 l/3½ pt chicken stock	2 qt chicken stock
salt and pepper	salt and pepper

Trim the chicken liver and heart, chop them and put them in a bowl with the veal and sausage meat. Mix well.

If the lemon is not organically grown and may have been sprayed or coated, scrub it in hot soapy water, rinse well and pat dry. Grate the zest and squeeze the juice.

Add the onions, herbs, lemon zest and juice and mushrooms to the meat mixture and mix thoroughly, binding the mixture with the egg. Season with salt and pepper.

Place the boned chicken skin-side down on the work surface. Spread half the stuffing mixture over the chicken, without taking it right up to the edges. Add a layer of all the ham strips and olives and cover with a second layer of stuffing.

Fold the chicken skin up and over to enclose the stuffing and sew it up. Wrap the stuffed chicken in a piece of muslin or cheesecloth folded in two and tie it with string.

Put the galantine into a large saucepan, cover with stock and bring slowly to the boil. Put the lid on the pan and cook very gently for 1½ hours.

Drain the galantine and put it on a plate. Cover with a second inverted plate and place a weight on top to press the galantine slightly while it is cooling. When cool, unwrap it and remove the string, then replace the weighted plate until the galantine is completely cold.

Serve cold with tarragon mayonnaise.

To drink: a fresh lively red, such as a Chinon.

GALETTE

see also:
brioche
cakes and gâteaux
cookies, etc
crêpe
pastry

Various round flat cakes are known as galettes, from the traditional puff pastry Twelfth Night cake or *galette des Rois* to small rich butter pastry biscuits (cookies) common in Brittany. Galettes may be sweet or savoury and are made from a wide variety of cereals, including oats, rye and barley. They may be split and filled, or made in the form of open tarts. There are also versions made from brioche (*galette griaude*) and from potato and onion purée (*galette lyonnaise*).

In Brittany and Normandy, buckwheat crêpes are also called galettes.

GALETTE BRETONNE

Breton butter cake

Serves 6
Preparation 20 minutes
Cooking 50 minutes

METRIC/IMPERIAL	*AMERICAN*
150 g/5½ oz slightly salted butter, cut into pieces	*11 tbsp lightly salted butter, cut into pieces*
250 g/8½ oz flour	*1¾ cups flour*
1 egg, separated + 2 egg yolks	*1 egg, separated + 2 egg yolks*
125 g/4½ oz caster sugar	*10 tbsp superfine sugar*

Preheat the oven to 200C/400F/gas 6 and grease a 22 cm/8¾ in cake pan with a little of the butter.

Put the flour in a mound on a pastry board and make a well in the middle. Put both the egg yolks and the sugar into the well and mix with the tips of the fingers, gradually pulling in the flour from the edges. Add the pieces of butter.

Work the dough for 2–3 minutes until smooth and well combined, then form it into a ball. Press the dough evenly into the greased cake pan.

Smooth the surface and score a decorative pattern on it with a knife. Brush it with a little egg white and bake for 50 minutes. Serve hot.

GAME

Gibier

see also:
civet
daube
duck
grouse
hare
marinade
partridge
pheasant
pigeon
rabbit
salmis
venison
woodcock

Game is the general term for wild creatures killed for sport or as food. In most countries there are laws prohibiting the hunting of many species at those times of the year when they are most vulnerable, and the killing of some endangered species is prohibited all year round.

For culinary purposes, game can be divided into two categories: WINGED OR FEATHERED GAME, which includes quail, wild duck, pheasant, thrush, partridge, pigeon and so on, and GROUND OR FURRED GAME, which again divides into two: small game, such as wild rabbit and hare, etc, and large game, which includes deer, roebuck and wild boar.

Young game has tender, flavourful meat and is usually roasted or sautéed. In older animals the meat is sometimes tough with a stronger aroma; it is used for *daubes*, *civets*, stews, terrines and pâtés. When buying game birds look for a beak that is flexible and feet that are soft to indicate that the bird is young; for young game animals, the ears should be supple and soft to the touch.

Most game benefits from being hung for a period to allow the full flavour to develop and enzyme activity to tenderize the meat, although most game sold commercially has already been allowed to mature. Sometimes game birds are hung without being bled first and this produces a much more gamy flavour. Other birds, such as the thrush and woodcock, are not drawn before being cooked and the innards are spread on *croûtes* to accompany the dish. All game should be carefully inspected and any pieces of shot removed during preparation.

As it tends to be very lean and a little dry, game is often marinated in rich oily mixtures before cooking. Birds are usually barded before being cooked and pieces of meat either barded or larded. It is wise to ensure that all wild creatures are sufficiently cooked as they may harbour *trichinosis* or other micro-organisms.

The rich flavour of game suits fruity stuffings and sauces. Apples, pears, grapes, cherries, cranberries and chestnuts are all popular accompaniments to game. Vegetables which make suitable accompaniments to game include celeriac (celery root), cabbage and chicory (Belgian endive) and mushrooms, especially any of the wild varieties. Noodles, pasta or game chips (potato chips) are also often served with game.

Game is a lean meat, high in iron and protein, but it is considered difficult to digest as it is rich in albumin. Game is also becoming more popular among the health-conscious as it has little of the artificial chemical and hormone content so prevalent in farmed meat.

TERRINE DE GIBIER

Game terrine

Serves 8
Preparation 40 minutes, marinating 24 hours
Cooking 2 hours, 24 hours ahead

METRIC/IMPERIAL	*AMERICAN*
2 kg/$4\frac{1}{2}$ lb boned game (venison or young wild boar), cut into thin strips	*$4\frac{1}{2}$ lb boned game (venison, wild boar or peccary), cut into thin strips*
2 shallots, chopped	*2 shallots, chopped*
1 carrot, sliced	*1 carrot, sliced*
12 juniper berries, crushed	*12 juniper berries, crushed*
1 l/$1\frac{3}{4}$ pt dry white wine	*1 qt dry white wine*
3 tbsp Armagnac	*3 tbsp Armagnac*
bouquet garni	*bouquet garni*
6 slices of streaky bacon	*6 slices of bacon*
350 g/$\frac{3}{4}$ lb pork sausage meat	*$\frac{3}{4}$ lb pork sausage meat*
salt and pepper	*salt and pepper*

Put the meat into a bowl with the shallots, carrot and juniper berries. Add the white wine, Armagnac and bouquet garni, stir and leave to marinate in a cool place for 24 hours.

The following day, preheat the oven to 180C/350F/gas 4. Drain the pieces of meat and pat them dry with paper towels.

Spread half of the bacon over the bottom of an ovenproof porcelain terrine dish. Cover it with a layer of the game strips and then a thin layer of sausage meat. Season with salt and pepper.

Repeat the process of alternating layers of game and sausage meat until the terrine is full, seasoning each layer with salt and pepper. Then press down well and place the remaining bacon on top.

Cover the terrine and place it in a bain-marie. Cook in the oven for 2 hours. At the end of this time, remove the lid from the terrine and leave it to cool. Serve the following day as a cold first course.

Variations: a more delicate terrine may be made with finely minced (ground) pork seasoned with nutmeg and allspice instead of the sausage meat; 100 g/$3\frac{1}{2}$ oz/1 cup of blanched pistachios or hazelnuts may also be added. Cognac or vieux marc may be substituted for the Armagnac.

GARBANZO BEAN

see Chickpea

GARLIC

Ail

see also:
crouton
rouille
tapenade

A bulbous plant of the lily family, related to the leek and onion, garlic has been highly valued as a flavouring agent since Roman times. There are several different varieties: the WHITE or GREY GARLIC is the most common and, in France, usually comes from Provence; PINK GARLIC, which is common in the Auvergne; and TAHITIAN GARLIC, identifiable by its enormous size.

Most of the garlic consumed in Britain is grown in France, Italy or Spain; the USA imports garlic from the same sources but also grows much of its own crop in California, Louisiana and Texas. Most garlic is dried for use, although some prefer the particularly delicate flavour of NEW-SEASON GARLIC, such as the Saint-Clar from the Gers region of France. FRESH GARLIC is available from mid-June to mid-August. Use the green part chopped as a condiment.

DRIED GARLIC should be stored in a cool, dry place and will keep for up to 6 months (12 in the case of the pink variety). The drier the garlic, the easier it becomes to peel the 12–16 individual cloves which form the head. Never buy garlic which is discoloured with patches of brown or which is starting to sprout, as its flavour will have deteriorated considerably.

For use with chopped meats, stuffings or sautéed foods, crush the garlic with a little salt on a board with the flat of a large knife. Otherwise, peel and chop very finely, or use a garlic press, which does save the bother of peeling but is held to produce a very coarse and unsubtle flavour. To make garlic more digestible, remove the green sprout from the centre of each clove. When cooking chopped or crushed garlic it is essential that it is not allowed to brown as this will impart a bitter flavour to the finished dish. To flavour large roasts, such as leg of lamb, cut the peeled cloves in slivers and then push these into deep incisions in the meat before cooking. For the mildest possible garlic flavour, rub the bottom of salad bowls or sauté pans with a halved clove of garlic.

Coarsely chopped and macerated in a bottle of olive oil, garlic makes the oil an excellent seasoning for salads and raw vegetables, used either with or without the garlic pieces. To serve garlic as a deliciously sweet and mild vegetable accompaniment, bake whole cloves in their skins.

Through the centuries, countless medicinal powers have been attributed to this plant and garlic is recognized as having diuretic and aperient qualities. It is also considered to play a role in stimulating the appetite and in the reduction of tension. It is thought, however, in certain cases to promote the formation of body yeasts. If this could be a problem one can merely rub the salad bowl with garlic or use unpeeled cloves in cooking, taking care to remove them before serving.

CRÈME D'AIL

Garlic cream sauce

Serves 4
Preparation 20 minutes
Cooking 20 minutes

METRIC/IMPERIAL	*AMERICAN*
12 garlic cloves	*12 garlic cloves*
200 ml/7 fl oz milk	*1 cup milk*
1 tbsp chopped fresh parsley	*1 tbsp chopped fresh parsley*
1 slice of white bread	*1 slice of white bread*
pinch of ground nutmeg	*pinch of ground nutmeg*
salt and pepper	*salt and pepper*

Peel the garlic cloves. Bring a small saucepan of water to the boil. Plunge the garlic cloves into it for 1 minute, drain them, then repeat the entire operation twice using fresh water each time.

Pour the milk into a saucepan and heat it gently. Add the prepared garlic cloves, parsley and bread. Add nutmeg and salt and pepper to taste. Cook gently for 20 minutes, stirring from

time to time, then blend in a food processor until smooth.

Serve hot to accompany roast, grilled (broiled) or barbecued poultry or game birds, leg of lamb or lamb chops.

TÊTES D'AIL EN PAPILLOTES

Whole garlic cooked in foil parcels

Serves 6
Preparation 5 minutes
Cooking at least 1 hour

METRIC/IMPERIAL	*AMERICAN*
6 whole garlic heads	*6 whole garlic heads*
2 tbsp olive oil	*2 tbsp olive oil*
salt and pepper	*salt and pepper*

Leave the heads of garlic whole, without peeling them or separating the cloves. Spread out a double sheet of foil large enough to wrap around 3 garlic heads. Place the 3 heads in the middle of the sheet, sprinkle with salt, pepper and olive oil, and wrap the foil carefully around them to seal completely. Wrap the other 3 heads in the same way.

Cook the garlic heads around a roast for the same amount of time as the meat or bird.

Take the foil envelopes out of the oven with tongs, open carefully and arrange the garlic heads around the meat or poultry. To eat, gently squeeze the garlic out of its skin.

Note: simply mashing cloves of garlic cooked this way produces a delicious and useful garlic purée which may be stored for later use.

GELATINE OR GELATIN

see also:
aspic
Bavarian cream
blancmange
jelly

A colourless, odourless, flavourless substance extracted from the bones and cartilage of animals and also from certain algae, gelatine is widely used in cooking as a gelling or setting agent. It is available either in the form of a powder or as transparent leaves. It is first dissolved or softened in cold water before being melted or blended with the mixture for which it is intended.

As a rule of thumb, in Britain a sachet of gelatine powder contains 15 g/½ oz which is equivalent to 4 leaves of gelatine and this will set about 600 ml/1 pt of liquid. In the USA an envelope of unflavored gelatin contains 8 g/¼ oz or 1 tbsp and will set 2 cups of liquid. However, different brands of gelatine can vary in their setting properties and different mixtures can require different strengths of setting. Obviously, if a dish has to remain firmly set at room temperature it will require a higher proportion of gelatine. Also, as sugar retards its action, the sweeter a mixture the more gelatine it requires.

CRÈME AUX DEUX FRUITS

Berry cream with pineapple

Serves 4
Preparation 20 minutes
Cooking 3 minutes, chilling 2 hours

METRIC/IMPERIAL	*AMERICAN*
450 g/1 lb fresh or frozen bilberries	*1 lb fresh or frozen bilberries or blueberries (1½–2 pt)*
4 gelatine leaves	*1 envelope powdered unflavored gelatine*
150 g/5½ oz soft fresh cheese containing 0% fat	*⅔ cup fromage blanc or other soft fresh cheese containing 0% fat*
caster sugar or artificial sweetener	*superfine sugar or artificial sweetener*
4 slices of canned pineapple in juice or syrup, drained	*4 slices of canned pineapple in juice or syrup, drained*

Heat the berries in a saucepan over a low heat. Meanwhile, soften the gelatine leaves in cold water and cover for 5 minutes, then drain or dissolve the powdered gelatine in 3 tablespoons of cold water.

Remove the pan from the heat. Add the gelatine and mix it with the berries until completely dissolved. Whip the cheese and fold it in along with sugar or artificial sweetener to taste.

Place a pineapple slice in each of 4 ramekin dishes. Pour the berry mixture over and chill for 2 hours. To unmould, run a knife around the edge of each dish, dip briefly in hot water and invert on 4 small chilled serving plates.

see also:
cucumber
pickles

GHERKIN OR PICKLED CUCUMBER

Cornichon

Miniature cucumbers, pickled in vinegar with herbs and spices, are a very popular condiment in France and are usually served to accompany cold or boiled meats, sandwiches, pâtés and terrines. They are also used as an ingredient in a number of sauces (*ravigote*, *gribiche*, *piquante*) and in some *charcuterie* products. The true gherkin (pickled cucumber), which originated in the Americas, is a very similar, but entirely unrelated, plant which is treated in the same way.

Nowadays, commercially produced gherkins are generally pasteurized during processing. They are crisper than home-pickled ones and will keep longer, though their flavour is not as good. Home preserving of fresh gherkins is time-consuming, but the results are well worth the effort.

In Germany and Eastern Europe larger, softer gherkins or pickling cucumbers are pickled in milder sweet-and-sour or dill-flavoured mixtures and are often served as vegetable accompaniments.

Gherkins (pickled cucumbers) contain only 13 calories per 100 g/$3\frac{1}{2}$ oz. However, because of their acidity, they should be avoided by people suffering from ulcers or other gastric problems.

see also:
brandies, etc
chicken
duck
foie gras
game
goose
kebab
pâté
pie
poultry
terrine
turkey

GIBLETS

Abattis

The edible inner organs, including the gizzard, liver and heart, and the extremities, ie, feet, head, neck and pinions or wing tips, of poultry are known collectively as giblets. They may come from chickens, turkeys, ducks or geese.

Giblets are inexpensive and are a popular ingredient in French home cooking. The external giblets are used to make tasty stews or fricassees. The feet are not usually eaten, but make good stock, while the internal giblets are common ingredients in pies, pâtés, mousses and terrines or may be mixed into stuffing.

Nowadays giblets are usually sold ready prepared and, at most, only need excess fat trimming off. If drawing a bird at home, however, be sure to separate the gall bladder from the liver without bursting it and discard it carefully otherwise the bitter gall will taint the surrounding flesh. The gizzard should be slit down the fleshy side so that the small 'gravel-sac' inside can be removed.

Giblets may be used to make stocks or gravies for roast birds. The liver is not usually included in this case, but may be used in a stuffing or sautéed and served on toast. Livers may also be grilled on skewers, made into fritters, incorporated in risottos or pasta sauces or used sautéed in omelettes and salads. Duck and goose gizzards are minced (ground) for use in stuffings or preserved as *confit* and these are delicious fried and tossed in salads or braised slowly in butter with cabbage.

Chicken livers contain 134 calories per 100 g/$3\frac{1}{2}$ oz.

GÂTEAU BRESSAN

Chicken liver loaf

Serves 4
Preparation 20 minutes
Cooking 1 hour

METRIC/IMPERIAL	AMERICAN
1 garlic clove, finely chopped	*1 garlic clove, minced*
2 tbsp finely chopped parsley	*2 tbsp finely chopped parsley*
6–8 whole chicken livers (preferably from a Bresse chicken), trimmed	*6–8 whole chicken livers (preferably from a Bresse chicken), trimmed*
55 g/2 oz flour	*6 tbsp flour*
4 eggs + 4 egg yolks	*4 eggs + 4 egg yolks*
5 tbsp crème fraîche or whipping cream	*$\frac{1}{3}$ cup crème fraîche or whipping cream*
700 ml/$1\frac{1}{4}$ pt milk	*3 cups milk*
15 g/$\frac{1}{2}$ oz butter	*1 tbsp butter*
300 ml/$\frac{1}{2}$ pt fresh tomato sauce	*$1\frac{1}{2}$ cups fresh tomato sauce*
pinch of grated nutmeg	*pinch of grated nutmeg*
salt and pepper	*salt and pepper*

Preheat the oven to 150C/300F/gas 2.

Mix the garlic with the chopped parsley. Pass

the chicken livers through a food or vegetable mill, using a medium screen, into a large mixing bowl.

Sift the flour into the bowl and mix well. Add the whole eggs, one at a time, mixing well after each one. Add the yolks to the bowl along with the garlic and parsley mixture and mix well.

Stir in 2 tablespoons of the cream and all the milk. Season with grated nutmeg, salt and pepper to taste. Grease a 14 cm/$5\frac{1}{2}$ in charlotte mould with the butter and pour the mixture into it. Bake in a bain-marie in the oven for 1 hour.

Warm the tomato sauce gently for 10 minutes just before serving, mixing in the rest of the cream.

Unmould the loaf on a warmed round serving dish. Coat it with the tomato sauce and serve it in thick slices as a hot first course.

To drink: a good red Rhône wine, such as a Condrieu.

GINGER

Gingembre

see also:
curry powder
spices

Originally from Southeast Asia, the ginger plant is now widely cultivated in most warm climates for its aromatic rhizomes (underground shoots) with their very distinctive spicy flavour.

Widely used in Asian cooking and very popular in medieval Europe, until recently its role in Occidental cuisine had been limited to the use of dried GROUND GINGER or CRYSTALLIZED GINGER in *pâtisserie*, preserves, ice creams and confectionery.

FRESH or GREEN ginger is now again widely available and is peeled and grated or finely chopped and used to flavour a wide variety of savoury dishes, especially with pork, poultry, fish, seafood and vegetables. Fresh ginger can be stored in the refrigerator for up to 3 weeks if kept dry, or it may be marinated in sherry, oil or vinegar. It also freezes well and can be grated while still frozen.

In salt-free diets ginger, along with herbs and other spices, provides a pleasant alternative for the flavouring of fish and poultry.

LÉGUMES CONFITS AU GINGEMBRE

Ginger-glazed vegetables

Serves 4
Preparation 15 minutes
Cooking 30 minutes

METRIC/IMPERIAL	AMERICAN
5 carrots	5 carrots
5 turnips	5 turnips
55 g/2 oz butter	4 tbsp butter
3 tbsp brown sugar	3 tbsp brown sugar
1 tbsp freshly grated ginger	1 tbsp freshly grated ginger
salt and pepper	salt and pepper

Peel the carrots and turnips and cut them into small even-sized chunks. Put them in a saucepan and season them with salt and pepper. Cover with water and cook for about 20 minutes. Drain the vegetables thoroughly.

Melt the butter in a saucepan and add the sugar and ginger, stirring well.

Add the carrots and turnips, stirring until they are well coated, and cook gently for about 10 minutes, stirring from time to time.

Serve very hot, to accompany roast veal or pork chops.

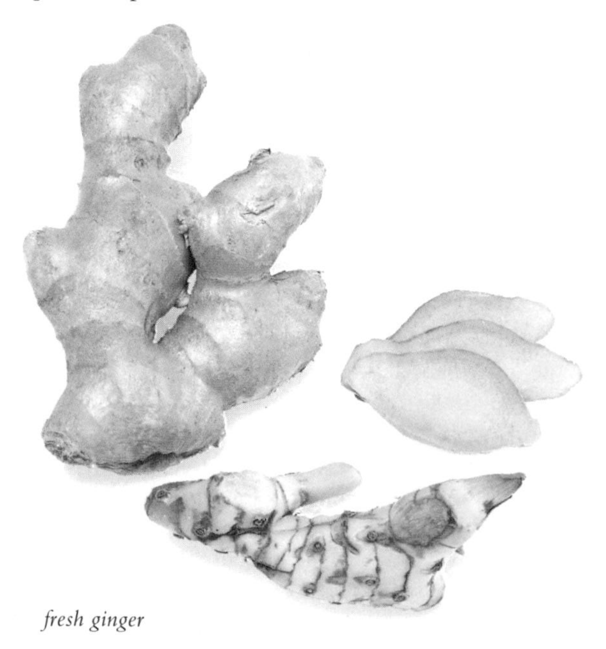

fresh ginger

MOUSSE DE POTIRON AU GINGEMBRE

Pumpkin mousse with ginger

Serves 4
Preparation 20 minutes, 5 hours ahead
Cooking 8 minutes

METRIC/IMPERIAL	AMERICAN
800 g/1¾ lb pumpkin	1¾ lb pumpkin
4 eggs	4 eggs
100 g/3½ oz caster sugar	½ cup superfine sugar
1 tbsp powdered gelatine, dissolved in 3 tbsp water	1 envelope powdered unflavored gelatine, dissolved in 3 tbsp water
1 tbsp grated fresh ginger	1 tbsp grated fresh ginger
pinch of ground cinnamon	pinch of ground cinnamon
pinch of grated nutmeg	pinch of grated nutmeg
200 ml/7 fl oz thick crème fraîche or whipping cream	1 cup thick crème fraîche or whipping cream
45 g/1½ oz thinly sliced crystallized ginger	¼ cup thinly sliced crystallized ginger

Peel the pumpkin and remove the seeds and their surrounding fibres. Cut it into large pieces and put it in a dish. Cover with parchment or greaseproof paper and microwave on High for 6 minutes. Let stand for 2 minutes, then mash the pulp to a smooth purée. Set aside.

Break the eggs into a bowl and beat them, then add the sugar and beat vigorously until the mixture is thick and foamy. Add the gelatine and mix well.

Add the pumpkin purée, grated ginger, cinnamon and nutmeg. Mix well and chill.

Meanwhile, whip the cream to stiff peaks. Take the pumpkin mousse out of the refrigerator and fold in the whipped cream. Spoon it into individual serving bowls and chill until set (at least 5 hours).

Just before serving, decorate the top of each individual mousse with thin slices of crystallized ginger.

GLAZE OR STOCK GLAZE

see also: stock sauce

A syrupy substance obtained by boiling down meat or poultry stock to reduce it. It is used as an essence for flavouring certain soups, sauces and stews or for coating and basting roasts. Good quality commercially made glazes are readily available; usually of French origin they are labelled *glace de viande* (meat glaze), etc.

GLAZING

Glacer

see also: aspic baking canapé cakes and gâteaux caramel carrot grilling pastry tart

This term is used for any process intended to give a shiny surface to food. Cold food like canapés and cold meats may be glazed with aspic or meat glaze. Tarts, cakes and pastries are usually glazed with sieved warmed jam. Food to be baked, especially pastry, is commonly glazed with beaten egg or milk. Vegetables, such as baby onions, carrots or turnips, may be given a final stage of cooking with butter and sugar which caramelizes to give them a shiny coating. Foods coated in a sauce containing egg yolks, fresh whipped butter or reduced cream may also be grilled (broiled) or baked at high temperatures to give them a glossy brown surface.

OIGNONS GLACÉS

Glazed onions

Serves 4
Preparation 5 minutes
Cooking about 15 minutes

METRIC/IMPERIAL	AMERICAN
450 g/1 lb new baby onions	1 lb new baby onions
30 g/1 oz butter	2 tbsp butter
30 g/1 oz caster sugar	2 tbsp superfine sugar
fine salt	fine salt

Peel the onions and put them in a single layer in a large sauté pan. Add just enough water to cover.

Add the butter in small pieces and sprinkle with the sugar. Season with salt.

Cook, uncovered, over moderate heat until all the liquid has evaporated, turning the onions carefully from time to time. When cooked, they should be glossy and golden.

see also:
jams, etc
sugar

GLUCOSE

The simplest of the carbohydrates, glucose is the form of sugar which the body prefers to use. The digestive system breaks down the sugars and starch in food into this form to make best use of their energy content. Forms of glucose occur naturally in many fruits and in honey. Glucose is also made industrially from starch and this is used to prevent sugar solutions becoming grainy, in the making of jams and syrups and in the manufacture of wine and beer.

see also:
choux pastry

GNOCCHI

Small poached sweet or savoury dumplings made from flour, semolina, potato flour or choux pastry are called gnocchi by the Italians. They resemble German *knödeln* and are used in much the same way.

Italian recipes use semolina with grated Parmesan or egg and potato purée as a base, and the gnocchi are then either boiled or deep fried. The French adaptation uses choux paste and the dumplings are then baked *au gratin*.

GNOCCHI À LA PARISIENNE

Choux gnocchi baked in cheese sauce

Serves 6
Preparation 25 minutes
Cooking about 45 minutes

METRIC/IMPERIAL	AMERICAN
100 g/3½ oz butter	*1 stick butter*
150 g/5½ oz flour	*1¼ cups flour*
4 eggs	*4 eggs*
grated nutmeg	*grated nutmeg*
30 g/1 oz grated Beaufort or Gruyère cheese	*¼ cup shredded Beaufort or Gruyère cheese*
salt and pepper	*salt and pepper*
FOR THE SAUCE:	FOR THE SAUCE:
30 g/1 oz butter	*2 tbsp butter*
30 g/1 oz flour	*3 tbsp flour*
500 ml/16 fl oz milk	*2 cups milk*
45 g/1½ oz grated Beaufort or Gruyère cheese	*⅓ cup shredded Beaufort or Gruyère cheese*

Make the choux pastry: put 200 ml/7 fl oz/1 cup water in a pan with 100 g/3½ oz/1 stick of butter cut in small pieces. Add a pinch of salt and bring to the boil, then add the flour all at once, mixing vigorously with a wooden spoon. When a ball of pastry forms and detaches itself from the sides of the pan, remove the pan from the heat and add the eggs one at a time, mixing thoroughly to make sure the dough is completely smooth before adding the next egg.

When the dough is smooth and supple, mix in the nutmeg to taste and then put the dough into a piping bag fitted with a 1 cm/½ in nozzle.

Bring 2 l/3½ pt/2 qt of lightly salted water to the boil. Pipe the choux pastry into the water, cutting it into 3 cm/1¼ in lengths as it comes out. Poach the choux dumplings until they rise to the surface, then drain them on a clean cloth.

Make the sauce: melt the butter in a heavy-based saucepan over a low heat. Add the flour and stir briskly until the mixture is smoothly blended. Gradually add the milk, stirring constantly to make a smooth sauce. Add the cheese and season with grated nutmeg and pepper. Cook for a few minutes more until the sauce is thick and smooth, then add the gnocchi to the sauce and mix well.

Spread the mixture in a lightly buttered gratin dish, dot with the remaining butter and sprinkle with remaining cheese. Bake in the oven for about 30 minutes and serve piping hot as a first course or simple lunch.

GOATS' MILK CHEESE

see Cheese

GOOSE

Oie

see also:
confit
foie gras
giblets

Most of the domestic geese farmed in Europe and North America are descended from the GREYLAG GOOSE. In France geese are primarily bred to provide foie gras, particularly in the Toulouse and Alsace regions. The meat and carcass of such large STRASBOURG GEESE, known as the *paletot*, is cut up in pieces and preserved as *confit d'oie*. The gizzard, heart and stuffed neck are also preserved in the same way.

NORMANDY GOOSE, on the other hand, is bred for its meat and is found on the market mainly around Christmas. In birds up to 3 or 4 months old, the meat is tender and succulent, pale red in colour with yellow fat, and the beaks and feet are brightly coloured. As geese only thrive when permitted to range freely, their meat is usually very tasty.

WILD GEESE are still hunted, although they are considered poor eating compared to other game birds. SNOW, WHITE-FRONTED and CANADA GEESE are popular winter prey in North America, although only young specimens are eaten.

For roast goose allow 25 minutes per 450 g/1 lb, followed by a further 30 minutes in the oven with the heat turned off. Prick the skin all over to allow the fat to run off and set the bird on a rack so that it does not fry in its own grease. Allow 1–1½ hours, depending on the age of the bird, for dishes where the meat is cut in pieces.

In England, geese are traditionally stuffed with sage and onion, although fruity stuffings, such as apples or prunes, are favoured in other cuisines in order to counteract the bird's fattiness.

Goose fat is very useful in cooking and imparts a fine flavour to sautéed potatoes and other vegetables. It is also the preferred cooking medium for foie gras and in much of the cooking of southwest France.

Fillets of smoked goose are also sold in thin slices like smoked ham and make a delicious salad ingredient or appetizer. It goes well with melon, figs or grapes.

Goose is a very fatty meat and 100 g/3½ oz contains about 360 calories. Wild goose, on the other hand, is much leaner.

OIE FARCIE AUX POMMES

Goose with apple stuffing

Serves 8
Preparation 20 minutes, 15 minutes ahead
Cooking 2 hours

METRIC/IMPERIAL	AMERICAN
1 kg/2¼ lb sweet dessert apples, such as reinette or Granny Smith	*2¼ lb apples such as McIntosh or Granny Smith*
2 tbsp Calvados	*2 tbsp Calvados*
45 g/1½ oz butter	*3 tbsp butter*
2 tbsp oil	*2 tbsp oil*
1 onion, finely chopped	*1 onion, finely chopped*
3 shallots, finely chopped	*3 shallots, finely chopped*
2 sage leaves, snipped	*2 sage leaves, snipped*
1 goose, dressed weight about 3 kg/6½ lb	*1 goose, dressed and drawn weight about 6½ lb*
salt and pepper	*salt and pepper*

Peel and quarter the apples. Sprinkle with Calvados and let them macerate for 15 minutes.

Preheat the oven to 180C/350F/gas 4 and grease a roasting pan with the butter and the oil.

In a bowl, mix the onions, shallots, sage and macerated apples with salt and pepper to taste. Stuff the goose with the mixture. Sew up the aperture but do not bard the goose. Place the goose in the roasting pan and put it in the oven.

After 5 minutes of cooking, brush the goose with the melted fat in the pan and continue to baste frequently during the cooking time of about 2 hours. The bird is cooked when it begins to steam slightly and its juices run clear when the meat is pierced with a fork at its thickest part.

Serve with sautéed mushrooms and salsify cooked in butter.

To drink: a good medium-bodied red wine, such as Pomerol.

RAGOÛT D'OIE

Goose stew

Serves 8
Preparation 20 minutes
Cooking about 1¾ hours

METRIC/IMPERIAL	AMERICAN
75 g/2½ oz goose fat	*⅓ cup rendered goose fat*
1 young goose, dressed weight about 3 kg/6½ lb, cut in pieces	*1 young goose, dressed weight about 6½ lb, cut into pieces*
3 onions, sliced	*3 onions, sliced*
2 tbsp flour	*2 tbsp flour*
2 tbsp tomato purée	*2 tbsp tomato paste*
750 ml/27 fl oz chicken stock	*3¼ cups chicken stock*
bouquet garni	*bouquet garni*
salt and pepper	*salt and pepper*

Melt the goose fat in a flameproof casserole. Cook the pieces of goose in the fat over a fairly high heat. When they are sealed and browned, add the onions and brown them for about 5 minutes.

Sprinkle in the flour and stir with a wooden spoon until it browns. Mix the tomato purée (paste) and chicken stock and pour over the pieces of goose. Season with salt and pepper, add the bouquet garni and simmer for 1½ hours.

Remove the casserole from the heat, skim impurities and excess fat from the top of the cooking liquid and discard the bouquet garni.

Arrange the pieces of goose in a warmed, deep serving dish. Reduce the cooking liquid over a high heat until it has a coating consistency and pour it over the goose.

Serve accompanied by steamed turnips or celeriac (celery root).

GOOSEBERRY

Groseille à maquereau

see also: fruit jams, etc redcurrant

Related to the redcurrant, the gooseberry bush produces fruit which are usually green or amber-red, often with a downy skin. Their bitter taste has led to their considerable use as an accompaniment to fatty meat, such as goose, and oily fish, hence the name in both English and in French 'mackerel redcurrant'.

They are most popular in the cooking of Germany and England, where they are used in tarts and fools as well as in jams, jellies and syrups.

Gooseberries are low in calories, with 30 per 100 g/3½ oz, and high in vitamin and mineral content, especially vitamin C and potassium.

SAUCE AUX GROSEILLES À MAQUEREAU

Gooseberry sauce

Serves 4
Preparation 10 minutes
Cooking 15 minutes

METRIC/IMPERIAL	AMERICAN
450 g/1 lb gooseberries	1 lb (1½ pt) gooseberries
75 g/2½ oz caster sugar	6½ tbsp superfine sugar

Put the gooseberries with the sugar into a saucepan and mix well. Add 500 ml/16 fl oz/2 cups of water and cook over a moderate heat, stirring until the fruit is completely soft and the skins begin to come away.

Remove from the heat, force the contents of the pan through a fine sieve and serve hot to accompany goose, duck or oily fish.

Note: if the gooseberries are slightly overripe and have lost their sharpness, a few drops of lemon juice may be added at the last minute.

GORGONZOLA

see also: cheese

This Italian cows' milk cheese is one of the great cheeses of the world. It has a white and creamy textured paste which is streaked with blue. Depending on its degree of maturity it can be mild or sharp. Made in large cylinders, it is good to eat all year round and is excellent on canapés or at the end of a meal with a strongly flavoured red wine. It may be crumbled in salads or used in sauces, gratins, soufflés, savoury pastries and pasta dishes. It can also be used to make delicious desserts, either as a stuffing for pear halves or mixed with mascarpone cheese, cream and Italian sweet mustard pickles. Gorgonzola is high in fat with 400 calories per 100 g/3½ oz.

GOUDA

see also: cheese

A Dutch pressed cows' milk cheese, Gouda can be tender and buttery, firm or very hard, depending on its degree of maturity. After brining it develops a rind which is colourless when young, red if semi-oven-dried, yellow if oven-dried and black on very mature cheeses (*alt gauda*). It is made in flat rounds or rectangular blocks and is served in thin slices by the Dutch at breakfast or grated into sauces or fondues. Some versions are flavoured with caraway or cumin seed. Gouda contains 330 calories per 100 g/3½ oz.

GRANITA

Granité

see also: ices and ice creams sorbet

A type of sorbet made from a lightly sweetened syrup, usually flavoured with liqueur or coffee. The characteristic granular texture of the ice crystals in a granita is very refreshing. It is usually served either at the end of a meal or during the meal as a palate cleanser between courses, known in France as a *trou normand.*

GRANITÉ AU CITRON

Lemon granita

Serves 4
Preparation 10 minutes
Cooking 3 minutes, about 3 hours ahead

METRIC/IMPERIAL	*AMERICAN*
4 tbsp caster sugar	*¼ cup superfine sugar*
450 ml/¾ pt lemon juice with pulp	*2 cups lemon juice with pulp*
150 ml/¼ pt crème fraîche or whipping cream, well chilled	*⅔ cup crème fraîche or whipping cream, well chilled*
1 tbsp icing sugar	*1 tbsp confectioners' sugar*

Turn the freezer or refrigerator to its coldest setting, if necessary. Pour the sugar into a saucepan with 100 ml/3½ fl oz/1½ cup of water and bring to the boil, stirring until the sugar dissolves. Boil for 3 minutes, then leave to cool.

Mix the lemon juice into the cooled syrup. Pour the mixture into 1 or 2 ice cube trays, without dividers, and freeze for 3 hours, stirring from time to time with a fork.

Pour the contents of the ice cube trays into a well chilled bowl and crush the frozen mixture with a pestle. Put it into 4 chilled thick glasses and put them in the refrigerator while finishing the dish.

Whip the cream with the icing (confectioners') sugar to soft peaks. Remove the glasses from the refrigerator and spoon the whipped cream over the top. Serve at once.

Variation: make coffee granita in the same way, using very strong coffee instead of the lemon juice.

GRAPE

Raisin

see also: dried vine fruit wine

Grapes grow in clusters on stalks and ripen between the end of July and mid-November in the northern hemisphere. Varying from blue-

cardinal, *Italia*, *black muscat*, *Alphonse-Lavallée*, *chasselas*

black or purple to red or green in colour, often with a pale surface yeast bloom, they may be very sweet or quite sour.

Most grapes grown are for winemaking. Some are used to make grape juice and others dried to produce currants, raisins and sultanas (golden raisins). Grape seeds are also pressed to extract their clean flavoured oil, which is high in polyunsaturates. Only 5% of the total production is cultivated specifically as table grapes, mostly in southeastern France, other Mediterranean countries and California. South Africa, Australia and South America provide the northern hemisphere with grapes in winter.

The main varieties of BLACK GRAPES include: the large ALPHONSE-LAVALLÉE, with juicy fresh and tender skin; a reddish version of this grape grown in the Americas, known as RED RIVER; the thicker-skinned greenhouse-grown ROYAL, more fragrant and available for all but the summer months; the early bearing seedless American BLACK BEAUTY; the reddish CARDINAL, sweet, slightly musky and grown in many parts of the world.

WHITE GRAPES are generally sweeter and juicier with thinner skins, and include: the yellowish ITALIA, which is crisp, sweet and slightly musky and tends to grow in long clusters; the small and sweet ROSAKI, which is grown in many places and varies widely in shape and colour; the French GOLDEN CHASSELAS is slightly amber in colour with a particularly fine flavour; the SULTANA and THOMPSON SEEDLESS, both small, sweet and juicy, are related.

The family of MUSCAT grapes, which include the black royal, the red cardinal and the white golden chasselas are distinguished by their rich musky perfumed flavour and are among the most prized dessert grapes.

Grapes should be chosen ripe but still firmly attached to their stalks, preferably with their bloom still on them. Some grapes do continue to ripen after being picked and their flavour may be improved by hanging them in the sunshine. One of the best signs of ripeness is the readiness of grapes to fall from the stem. Avoid any with brown patches or wrinkled skin.

Grapes do not keep well, at the most for a day or two in a cool place or a few days more refrigerated, loosely wrapped. Remove from the refrigerator at least one hour before eating as their full flavour develops at room temperature. Always wash grapes carefully before serving.

Grapes are most commonly eaten for dessert or as an accompaniment to the cheese course at the end of a meal. They may be used in both savoury or fruit salads, in pâtisserie or jams and jellies and they are an attractive garnish. They work well in many savoury dishes, particularly with poultry, game birds, foie gras and fish.

To peel grapes, dip briefly in boiling water. Seeds are easily removed using a toothpick or the closed end of a clean hair grip (bobby pin).

The pressed juice of sour grapes is known as VERJUICE and is a traditional souring agent, often used in place of vinegar.

Grapes are among the fruits with the highest sugar content with 80 calories per 100 g/$3\frac{1}{2}$ oz, but they are also rich in vitamins and minerals.

TARTE AU RAISIN

Grape tart

Serves 4
Preparation 30 minutes
Cooking 30 minutes

METRIC/IMPERIAL	AMERICAN
100 g/$3\frac{1}{2}$ oz flour	*$\frac{3}{4}$ cup flour*
45 g/$1\frac{1}{2}$ oz butter, cut in small pieces	*3 tbsp butter, cut in small pieces*
55 g/2 oz caster sugar	*5 tbsp superfine sugar*
450 g/1 lb seedless white grapes	*1 lb seedless white or green grapes*
2 eggs	*2 eggs*
3 tbsp ground almonds	*3 tbsp ground almonds*
100 ml/$3\frac{1}{2}$ fl oz milk	*$\frac{1}{2}$ cup milk*
3 tbsp crème fraîche or whipping cream	*3 tbsp crème fraîche or whipping cream*
1 tbsp Kirsch	*1 tbsp Kirsch*
salt	*salt*

Preheat the oven to 220C/425F/gas 7.

Put the flour in a bowl and add the butter, a pinch of salt, 15 g/$\frac{1}{2}$ oz/1 tbsp of the sugar and 3 tablespoons of water. Combine these ingredients with your fingertips and form into a ball of pastry. Do not knead.

Roll out the pastry and use it to line a 22 cm/8¾ in loose-bottomed tart pan. Arrange the grapes in an even layer in the tart case.

In a bowl, mix the eggs, the rest of the sugar, ground almonds, milk, cream and Kirsch. Pour this mixture carefully over the grapes and bake for 30 minutes.

Remove the tart from the oven, let it cool and unmould it.

FOIES DE VOLAILLE AU RAISIN

Chicken livers with grapes

Serves 4
Preparation 30 minutes
Cooking about 12 minutes

METRIC/IMPERIAL	AMERICAN
550 g/1¼ lb chicken livers, trimmed and cut into bite-sized pieces	1¼ lb chicken livers, trimmed and cut into bite-sized pieces
30 g/1 oz butter	2 tbsp butter
100 ml/3½ fl oz Sauternes	½ cup Sauternes
24 large white grapes, peeled and deseeded	24 large white or green grapes, peeled and deseeded
salt and pepper	salt and pepper

Season the chicken liver pieces with salt and pepper.

Heat the butter in a frying pan. Sauté the chicken livers over a high heat for 7–8 minutes until they are well browned. Drain them on paper towels and put them into a warmed serving dish.

Discard half the melted butter and then deglaze the pan juices over a high heat with the Sauternes.

Add the grapes to the frying pan and stir them gently around in the sauce. Adjust the seasoning. Pour the grapes and sauce over the chicken livers and serve immediately, as a hot first course.

To drink: Sauternes.

SALADE COMPOSÉE AU MUSCAT

Mixed salad with black and white grapes

Serves 4
Preparation 30 minutes

METRIC/IMPERIAL	AMERICAN
225 g/½ lb celeriac	½ lb celeriac (celery root)
juice of 1 lemon	juice of 1 lemon
140 g/5 oz Beaufort or Gruyère cheese, cut into thin sticks	5 oz Beaufort or Gruyère cheese, cut into thin sticks
bunch of black muscat grapes	bunch of black muscat grapes
bunch of white muscat grapes	bunch of white muscat grapes
4 tbsp olive oil	4 tbsp olive oil
2 tbsp white wine vinegar	2 tbsp white wine vinegar
8 walnut halves, coarsely chopped	8 walnut halves, coarsely chopped
salt and pepper	salt and pepper

Peel the celeriac (celery root) and sprinkle it with lemon juice. Grate it coarsely into a salad bowl. Add the cheese sticks and grapes to the bowl and set aside.

Make a vinaigrette with the olive oil and vinegar, adding salt and pepper to taste. Pour it over the salad and mix gently.

Add the chopped walnuts at the last minute and serve at room temperature.

Variations: use cider or raspberry vinegar to give the salad a more unusual flavour.

GRAPEFRUIT

Pamplemousse, pomelo

see also: citrus fruits orange

This large round member of the citrus family has very fibrous flesh which is often quite sharp. The grapefruit is a West Indian cross breed of the larger and drier SHADDOCK OR POMELO from Southeast Asia. Nowadays, however, the centre of the world's grapefruit production is in Florida and other southern states of the USA and in California.

Although it is at its best in the months from

October to June, grapefruit is available all year round. There are three principal types: YELLOW GRAPEFRUIT OR MARSH SEEDLESS, which has very juicy and sharp-tasting white flesh; PINK GRAPEFRUIT OR PINK MARSH, which has pinkish pulp which is also juicy but much sweeter; and the RUBY RED grapefruit which is sweeter still.

Buy grapefruit with thin smooth unshrivelled skins and which feel heavy in relation to their volume. They have very good keeping qualities and will stay fresh in the refrigerator for many weeks.

Grapefruit is served both as an hors d'oeuvre and as a dessert, and is popular for breakfast. The fruit is usually cut in half and then each segment detached from the skin using a special grapefruit knife with a curved serrated blade. It may be served plain or with a little brown sugar, or sprinkled with sugar and briefly glazed under the grill (broiler). Grapefruit is also used to make jams, jellies and marmalades, mousses and sorbets. It can make an interesting accompaniment to chicken or pork, avocados and seafood and works well in savoury and sweet salads, but it must be used with caution as its acid bite can overpower the flavour of other, more subtle ingredients.

Grapefruit juice makes a refreshing drink and is much lower in calories than most other fruit juices. It can also be a useful souring agent in cooking, particularly in sweet and sour dishes, and in mixed drinks.

Rich in vitamin C and potassium, grapefruit contains only 43 calories per 100 g/3½ oz.

PAMPLEMOUSSES COCKTAIL

Grapefruit and seafood cocktail

Serves 4
Preparation 20 minutes

METRIC/IMPERIAL	AMERICAN
2 grapefruit	2 grapefruit
5 tbsp olive oil	5 tbsp olive oil
2 tbsp aged wine vinegar	2 tbsp aged wine vinegar
1 tbsp soy sauce	1 tbsp soy sauce
12 lettuce leaves	12 lettuce leaves
8 cooked langoustines or 16 large prawns, peeled	8 cooked langoustines or 16 jumbo shrimp, peeled
2 stalks of celery, trimmed and chopped	2 sticks of celery, trimmed and chopped
salt and pepper	salt and pepper

Peel the grapefruit and remove the segments by cutting down between the membranes.

Make a highly seasoned vinaigrette with the

ruby red *pink marsh* *marsh seedless*

olive oil, vinegar, soy sauce, salt and pepper.

Line 4 individual serving dishes with lettuce leaves. In a bowl, mix the grapefruit segments, seafood and celery. Pour the dressing over and mix well. Spoon this salad into the lettuce-lined dishes and chill briefly before serving.

Variation: make a salad of segments of grapefruit, chopped apple, grated celeriac (celery root) and julienne strips of ham all tossed in a dressing made with cream and lemon juice.

GRATIN

see also:
baking
breadcrumbs
grilling
sauce

This French culinary term is used to describe the crisp, golden crust which forms on the surface of food when it is baked in the oven or browned under the grill (broiler) and may also be used for the dish in which it is cooked.

By extension, the term has also come to be used to describe dishes cooked in such a way as to produce such a crust. This usually helps keep the rest of the dish beneath the crust moist and locks in its flavour.

To encourage a good and tasty crust to form on such preparations the top is usually covered with grated cheese, breadcrumbs, a white sauce or a cream mixture, and this surface may also be dotted with butter.

Gratin dishes may be cooked in this way from the outset or merely given a finish *au gratin*. Any number of foods can be given a gratin treatment: leftover fish, poultry or meat, pastas and vegetables; or even more sophisticated recipes, such as scallops or sweetbreads or fruit desserts.

A gratin is usually served straight from the dish in which it has been cooked and it must be well greased with butter to prevent ingredients from sticking.

Provided that skimmed milk cheese and low fat cream or milk are used, gratins may form a valuable part of a low-calorie diet.

GRATIN AU CHOU

Baked cabbage with rice

Serves 4
Preparation 30 minutes
Cooking 30 minutes

METRIC/IMPERIAL	*AMERICAN*
55 g/2 oz butter	*4 tbsp butter*
1 small cabbage, finely shredded	*1 small head of cabbage, finely shredded*
2 onions, chopped	*2 onions, chopped*
2 garlic cloves, chopped	*2 garlic cloves, chopped*
2 tbsp olive oil	*2 tbsp olive oil*
250 g/8½ oz rice	*1½ cups long-grain rice*
450 g/1 lb very ripe tomatoes, peeled and chopped	*1 lb very ripe tomatoes, peeled and chopped*
2 tbsp finely chopped parsley	*2 tbsp finely chopped parsley*
45 g/1½ oz flour	*¼ cup flour*
400 ml/14 fl oz milk	*1¾ cups milk*
250 g/8½ oz grated Gruyère	*2 cups grated Gruyère cheese*
salt and pepper	*salt and pepper*

Preheat the oven to 180C/350F/gas 4 and grease a 15 cm/6 in soufflé dish with one third of the butter.

Blanch the cabbage for 5 minutes in boiling water. Drain it and set aside.

Sauté the onions and garlic in the oil until golden brown, then season with salt and pepper. Add the rice and stir for 2–3 minutes. Add the tomatoes to the pan along with the chopped parsley. Cook gently for 10 minutes.

Meanwhile, make a cheese sauce: melt the remaining butter in a small heavy-based saucepan, add the flour and cook the roux, stirring constantly, for a minute or two. Then gradually add the milk, stirring constantly to avoid the formation of lumps. Cook again for a few minutes until smooth and thick, then add half the cheese to the sauce.

Fill the prepared soufflé dish with alternating layers of shredded cabbage and the tomato rice mixture. Coat with the sauce. Sprinkle the top with the rest of the grated cheese and bake for 30 minutes. Serve hot, straight from the dish.

GRATIN DAUPHINOIS

Potatoes baked with cream

Serves 6
Preparation 20 minutes
Cooking 1¼ hours

METRIC/IMPERIAL	AMERICAN
1.5 kg/3½ lb firm waxy potatoes	3½ lb firm-textured potatoes
15 g/½ oz butter	1½ tbsp butter
1 garlic clove, chopped	1 garlic clove, chopped
200 ml/7 fl oz thick crème fraîche or whipping cream	1 cup thick crème fraîche or whipping cream
200 ml/7 fl oz milk	1 cup milk
1 egg	1 egg
salt and freshly ground pepper	salt and freshly ground pepper

Preheat the oven to 200C/400F/gas 6. Peel the potatoes, slice them thinly and pat them dry.

Grease a large baking dish with the butter and sprinkle the chopped garlic over the bottom. Arrange a layer of sliced potatoes in the dish and season with salt and pepper. Sprinkle over 1 tablespoon of cream.

Repeat these layers until the dish is full, reserving 1 tablespoon of cream for later. Pour the milk over the mixture and bake for 1 hour.

Break the egg into a bowl and whisk it with the reserved cream. Season with salt and pepper. Remove the baking dish from the oven and pour the egg mixture evenly over the top.

Return the dish to the oven and bake for a further 15 minutes until well browned. Serve straight from the baking dish.

Variation: to make gratin savoyard, add 125 g/4½ oz/1 cup grated Gruyère, or other strong, nutty cheese, sprinkling a little over each layer and finishing with a layer of cheese.

GRAVY

Jus de viande

see also:
deglazing
sauce
stock

The cooking juices from meat when served as an accompanying sauce are referred to as gravy.

In 'dry' cooking methods, like roasting, a little water, wine, stock or cooking water from accompanying vegetables is usually added to the pan and this liquid is boiled and stirred vigorously to deglaze the meat sediments, incorporating all their goodness and flavour. When roasting poultry, the giblets may be simmered separately to make a good stock which is then reduced to make gravy.

The resulting gravy is seasoned carefully and may also be coloured with caramel and thickened with flour, cornflour (cornstarch), blood, cream or an egg and cream liaison.

GREENGAGE

see Plum

GRILLING OR BROILING

Grillade

see also:
barbecuing
marinade

The cooking of small pieces of food by intense radiant heat is referred to as grilling or broiling. It may be achieved on a barbecue, over an open fire with larger items on a spit, or most commonly, under a domestic grill or broiler.

Most food should be lightly brushed with oil, butter or sauce before, and often during, cooking to protect it from the intense heat and keep it moist. Meat such as steaks may also be marinated before cooking to give added flavour and ensure moist results.

The secret of good grilling or broiling of red meat is to get the fire or grill (broiler) really very hot before cooking, so that the food is immediately seared thus sealing in the juices. In the case of sausages, white meat and poultry, the heat does not need to be quite so high. Meat should not be salted or pricked before or during cooking as this will encourage loss of juices; turn food with tongs rather than forks.

This method of cooking also suits fatty fish, such as sardines, mackerel, herrings, and even salmon steaks and red mullet. Score the flesh of thick whole fish deeply with a knife to allow the heat to penetrate to the interior. Less fatty fish tend to stick to the rack, so they should be lightly dusted with flour after being brushed with oil or butter.

For best results, food to be grilled or broiled should be as uniform as possible. Flatten steaks, etc, with a meat mallet prior to cooking. If the piece of food is of uneven thickness, care should

Gratin dauphinois (Potatoes baked with cream)

be taken not to over-cook the thinner part; if possible, make sure it is placed farthest away from the heat source. Items with a plump centre, like duck breasts, should be deeply scored with a sharp knife, as with whole fish, to allow the heat to reach the inside.

Fatty foods such as duck breasts should be cooked skin side up first to ensure that any melting fat drips through the meat during cooking to flavour it.

Because of the short cooking times involved in grilling and broiling, it is wise to remove the food from the refrigerator several hours before cooking, otherwise it may be difficult to get it properly cooked through without over-cooking the exterior.

After using a charcoal grill clean it thoroughly while still hot, brushing the grill clean with a metal brush. Otherwise the burnt residues will impart a bitter taste to any food subsequently grilled on it.

Gratins and brûlées may be finished under the grill (broiler) for a well-coloured crust.

Grilling and broiling are very healthy means of cooking as they require little or no fat and preserve most of the nutrients in food.

GRILLADES MARINÉES

Grilled marinated steaks

Serves 4
Preparation 20 minutes, marinating 6 hours
Cooking about 12 minutes

METRIC/IMPERIAL	AMERICAN
3 tomatoes, peeled	*3 tomatoes, peeled*
4 tbsp olive oil	*4 tbsp olive oil*
4 tbsp red wine vinegar	*4 tbsp red wine vinegar*
3 tbsp red wine	*3 tbsp red wine*
2 onions, thinly sliced	*2 onions, thinly sliced*
2 garlic cloves, chopped	*2 garlic cloves, chopped*
2 slices of sirloin steak, each weighing about 300 g/10 oz and about 3 cm/1¼ in thick	*2 slices of sirloin steak, each weighing about 10 oz and about 1¼ in thick*
1 tbsp peppercorns	*1 tbsp peppercorns*
1 tsp dried thyme	*1 tsp dried thyme*
salt and pepper	*salt and pepper*

Force the tomato flesh through a sieve to make a purée. Add the oil, vinegar and wine, season with salt and pepper and whisk vigorously.

Spread half the onions over the bottom of a large deep dish along with the garlic. Place the slices of meat on top.

Pour the tomato mixture over, add the peppercorns and thyme and cover with the remaining onions. Marinate for about 6 hours.

Preheat a very hot grill (broiler) or charcoal barbecue. Drain the meat and dry it thoroughly on paper towels. Pour the marinade into a saucepan and heat gently for 10 minutes.

Meanwhile, grill (broil) the steaks or cook over charcoal for 6 minutes on each side.

Cut each steak in two and place each piece on a warmed plate. Blend the contents of the saucepan in a food processor and pour the resulting sauce over the meat.

POULET GRILLÉ

Grilled chicken

Serves 6
Preparation 10 minutes
Cooking about 25 minutes

METRIC/IMPERIAL	AMERICAN
2 chickens, dressed weight of each about 1 kg/2¼ lb, cut into pieces	*2 chickens, dressed and drawn weight of each about 2¼ lb, cut into pieces*
125 g/4½ oz slightly salted butter	*9 tbsp lightly salted butter*
1 garlic clove, chopped	*1 garlic clove, chopped*
3 tbsp chopped parsley	*3 tbsp chopped parsley*
2 tbsp chopped tarragon	*2 tbsp chopped tarragon*
freshly ground black pepper	*freshly ground black pepper*

Preheat the grill (broiler) to as hot as possible.

Season the pieces of chicken with pepper and arrange them in a roasting pan. Place a small piece of butter on top of each piece of chicken.

Grill (broil) for 10–12 minutes. At the end of this time they should be golden brown on one side. Turn them over and cook the other side similarly for 10–12 minutes.

Meanwhile, mix the garlic with the parsley

and tarragon and some more pepper. Beat the remaining butter with a wooden spoon and add it to the herb mixture. Serve the chicken very hot with the flavoured butter on top.
Variation: the pieces of chicken may be marinated for 24 hours in a mixture of mustard, olive oil, white wine, a little garlic and a pinch of cayenne pepper. Keep in the refrigerator.
To drink: a well-chilled rosé wine, such as Tavel.

GROUNDNUT

see Peanut

GROUPER

Mérou

see also:
fish
tuna

A large marine fish related to the sea perch, grouper may be as large as 50 kg/110 lb. At home in warmer waters, several varieties are fished in the Mediterranean and European Atlantic, but only the LINNAEUS may be found farther north than the Bay of Biscay. On the American side of the Atlantic may be found several distinct species, ranging from the small OSBECK and the speckled STRAWBERRY GROUPER to the enormous WARSAW GROUPER.

Grouper have tasty, dense, white flesh and they are particularly good grilled or baked in the form of steaks, although smaller fish may be cooked whole. In cooking, grouper is treated much the same way as tuna.

It also has the same caloric value as tuna: 100 g/3½ oz of grouper contains 225 calories.

FILET DE MÉROU À L'ANIS

Grouper fillets with aniseed

Serves 4
Preparation 10 minutes
Cooking about 15 minutes

METRIC/IMPERIAL	AMERICAN
4 grouper fillets, each weighing about 140 g/5 oz	4 grouper fillets, each weighing about 5 oz
150 ml/¼ pt dry white wine	⅔ cup dry white wine
1 garlic clove, finely chopped	1 garlic clove, finely chopped
4 shallots, finely chopped	4 shallots, finely chopped
15 g/½ oz butter, cut in small pieces	1 tbsp butter, cut in small pieces
sprig of thyme	sprig of thyme
1 tsp aniseed or fennel seeds	1 tsp aniseed or fennel seeds
pinch of saffron	pinch of saffron
150 ml/¼ pt whipping cream	⅔ cup whipping cream
1 tsp cornflour	1 tsp cornstarch
salt and pepper	salt and pepper

Season the grouper fillets with salt and pepper.

Pour the wine into a saucepan and add 100 ml/3½ fl oz/½ cup of water, the garlic, shallots, butter, thyme, aniseed or fennel seeds and salt and pepper to taste. Mix and bring to the boil, then simmer for 3 minutes.

Put the grouper fillets into the saucepan, cover and poach them for 6–7 minutes. Drain them and keep warm. Discard the thyme and reduce the cooking juices over a high heat for 5 minutes. Add the saffron, mix, and set aside.

Heat the cream in a small saucepan, add the cornflour (cornstarch) mixed in a little of the cream and stir over a gentle heat until it thickens. Pour this mixture into the cooking liquid and mix. Adjust the seasoning.

Arrange the grouper fillets on warmed plates, coat them with the sauce and serve at once, accompanied by ratatouille.
To drink: a light red wine, such as Fleurie.

GROUSE

Tétras

see also:
chicken
game
guinea fowl

A family of game birds, very similar to the common fowl and including creatures as diverse as the PTARMIGAN and CAPERCAILLIE, grouse are relatively rare in France but widespread and extremely popular in Britain, Scandinavia and North America.

The RED GROUSE of Scotland has very flavourful meat and is closely related to the French *gélinotte* OR HAZEL GROUSE. The BLACK GROUSE is found on both sides of the Atlantic and the CANADIAN GROUSE is among the game birds most commonly cooked in North America, along with quail or partridge.

In Britain the grouse season begins on the 'glorious 12th' (12 August) and goes on to 10 December. The younger birds are the most tender; look for a flexible breastbone.

Grouse are generally hung for at least a week before being dressed. They are usually simply roasted or braised and the meat is best served still slightly pink. Older, tougher birds are made into pâtés and terrines.

GROUSE AU WHISKY

Grouse flamed in whisky

Serves 2–3
Preparation 15 minutes
Cooking about 50 minutes

METRIC/IMPERIAL	AMERICAN
1 grouse, dressed	1 grouse, dressed
1 slice of pork fat or streaky bacon	1 slice of pork fatback
45 g/1½ oz butter	3 tbsp butter
2 stalks of celery, trimmed and thinly sliced	2 sticks of celery, trimmed and thinly sliced
1 carrot, thinly sliced	1 carrot, thinly sliced
1 turnip, thinly sliced	1 turnip, thinly sliced
1 onion, thinly sliced	1 onion, thinly sliced
150 ml/¼ pt dry white wine	⅔ cup dry white wine
150 ml/¼ pt single malt Scotch whisky	⅔ cup single malt Scotch whisky
salt and pepper	salt and pepper

Preheat the oven to 180C/350F/gas 4. Season the inside of the grouse with salt and pepper. Bard it with the pork fat or bacon and secure this with string.

Melt the butter in a flameproof casserole over a moderate heat. Add the vegetables and stir them in the melted butter. Place the grouse on top, season it with salt and pepper, turn it on all sides to coat it with butter and cook until just golden. Add the white wine and cover. Transfer to the oven and cook for about 40 minutes.

Remove the casserole from the oven and transfer the grouse to a warmed serving dish. Heat the whisky in a small saucepan and pour it over the bird, then flame it.

Arrange the vegetables around the bird, pour the cooking juices over and serve at once, accompanied by turnips or a purée of celeriac (celery root).

To drink: a powerful, mature red, such as a Margaux.

GRUYÈRE

see also: cheese fondue sauce soufflé

A cows' milk cheese made in large rounds from compressed cooked curds, Gruyère contains small holes about the size of hazelnuts and has a fine nutty flavour. It is made both in Switzerland and in the neighbouring parts of France. As the French never saw fit to grant it an *appellation contrôlée*, there are numerous imitations and the French also tend to use the term 'gruyère' to describe the whole family of similar hard cheeses, including Appenzell, Beaufort, Comté, Emmental and Fontina.

Gruyère is enjoyed both fresh and mature and is much used in cooking as it has good melting qualities. Its fine, strong, pungent flavour works well in salads and on gratins, and it is the favoured cheese for cooking all sorts of savoury dishes, including the traditional French snack *croque monsieur*, as well as being classic in fondues and cheese sauces.

Gruyère has one of the highest calcium contents of all cheeses; 100 g/3½ oz contains 390 calories.

SALADE DE GRUYÈRE

Gruyère salad

Serves 4
Preparation 20 minutes

METRIC/IMPERIAL	AMERICAN
400 g/14 oz Swiss Gruyère	14 oz Swiss Gruyère cheese
2 tbsp white wine vinegar	2 tbsp white wine vinegar
1 tsp Dijon mustard	1 tsp Dijon mustard
4 tbsp sunflower oil	4 tbsp sunflower oil
1 onion, very thinly sliced	1 onion, very thinly sliced
1 tomato, peeled, deseeded and diced	1 tomato, peeled, deseeded and diced

115 g/¼ lb saveloy or garlic sausage, skinned and thinly sliced
salt and pepper

¼ lb smoked pork sausage, garlic sausage or salami, skinned and thinly sliced
salt and pepper

Remove and discard the rind from the cheese and cut it into strips about 3 cm/1¼ in long and 5 mm/¼ in thick.

Make a vinaigrette by mixing some salt with the vinegar, adding the mustard (a little more or less according to taste), the oil and some pepper. Whisk it vigorously to emulsify it.

In a bowl, mix the cheese, onion and tomato and spoon the mixture on 4 individual plates. Pour the vinaigrette over and garnish with slices of sausage.

GUAVA

Goyave

see also: fruit

An exotic fruit originally from Central America, the guava is now grown in many parts of the tropics. Those with the best flavour come from Thailand and Brazil. Round, pear-shaped, or even walnut-shaped, guavas are about 5–10 cm/2–4 in across and usually have yellow skin which is often mottled with green. Riper fruit develop black spots on the skin. Among the most prized varieties is the so-called PEAR OF THE INDIES which is about the size and shape of an egg.

The flesh is yellow or pink, depending on the variety, and has a strong exotic taste which is very sweet while retaining an interesting sourness. Guavas may be eaten on their own as refreshing dessert fruit, cut in half, deseeded and perhaps dressed with a little sugar or rum. Their unusual sharp taste also makes them a useful fruit for use in salads and in ice creams, sorbets and preserves. They do not keep well and should be bought on the day they are required for use. Canned guavas are good in tropical fruit salads, but their flavour is not quite as fine as that of the fresh fruit.

Guavas are positively packed with vitamin C (they contain about 10 times more than similarly sized oranges!) and also contain a high level of vitamin A, phosphorus and carotene, a substance that promotes the development of pigment in the skin; 100 g/3½ oz contains 50 calories.

GUINEA FOWL

Pintade

see also: chicken partridge pheasant poultry

A family of fowl, originally from Africa, which was domesticated in Europe in Roman times, guinea fowl have a slightly gamy, reddish meat which is tasty but tends to be dry. Free-range guinea chicks or *pintadeaux* are what is now usually available in the shops. They are particularly succulent and need simply to be barded with pork fat or bacon and roasted for 30 minutes per 1 kg/2¼ lb, or cut in pieces and sautéed like chicken. Older guinea fowl lends itself to recipes for pheasant and partridge, but it does require slightly longer cooking and is best braised or casseroled.

Guinea fowl meat is low in fat and provides a useful element in low-calorie diets; 100 g/$3\frac{1}{2}$ oz contains only 130 calories.

PINTADE AU CHOU

Guinea fowl with cabbage

Serves 4
Preparation 30 minutes
Cooking about $1\frac{3}{4}$ hours

METRIC/IMPERIAL	AMERICAN
1 small green Savoy cabbage	*1 small head of Savoy cabbage*
225 g/$\frac{1}{2}$ lb smoked streaky bacon	*$\frac{1}{2}$ lb smoked bacon*
1 guinea fowl, dressed weight about 1.35 kg/3 lb	*1 guinea fowl, dressed weight about 3 lb*
45 g/$1\frac{1}{2}$ oz butter, softened	*3 tbsp butter, softened*
salt and pepper	*salt and pepper*

Preheat the oven to 220C/425F/gas 7.

Cut the cabbage in quarters and discard the large outside leaves. Blanch the quarters for 5–6 minutes in a large saucepan of salted boiling water, then drain them thoroughly.

Cut the bacon into fairly large pieces and dry fry them over a medium heat in a flameproof casserole until well browned.

Remove the bacon with a slotted spoon, and cook the cabbage quarters in the bacon fat in the casserole for 10 minutes over a low heat. Season with salt and pepper. Return the bacon to the casserole, cover and continue to cook gently.

Meanwhile, rub half the softened butter on the skin of the guinea fowl, place it in a roasting pan and cook it for 15 minutes in the oven, turning it from time to time until it is browned on all sides. Reduce the oven temperature to 180C/350F/gas 4.

Transfer the bird to the casserole, placing it in the middle of the cabbage and bacon. Cover and cook in the oven for about $1\frac{1}{4}$ hours.

Remove the guinea fowl from the casserole, take off the string and carve the bird. Drain the cabbage and bacon and put them into a warmed serving dish with the pieces of guinea fowl on top.

Reduce the cooking juices a little over a high heat, then whisk in the rest of the butter in small pieces and season with salt and pepper. Serve the gravy separately in a sauce boat.

Note: sautéed wild mushrooms and chestnuts make an excellent garnish for this dish. If guinea fowl is not available, a flavourful chicken may be used.
To drink: a medium-bodied red, such as a Saint-Emilion.

PINTADEAU À LA NORMANDE

Young guinea fowl with apples and cream

Serves 2
Preparation 20 minutes
Cooking about 50 minutes

METRIC/IMPERIAL	AMERICAN
3 apples	*3 apples*
juice of $\frac{1}{2}$ lemon	*juice of $\frac{1}{2}$ lemon*
1 young guinea fowl	*1 young guinea fowl*
30 g/1 oz butter	*2 tbsp butter*
2 tbsp Calvados	*2 tbsp Calvados*
3 tbsp crème fraîche or whipping cream	*3 tbsp crème fraîche or whipping cream*
salt and pepper	*salt and pepper*

Peel and quarter the apples and remove the core and seeds. Sprinkle the quarters with lemon juice. Cut the guinea fowl in half.

Melt the butter in a flameproof casserole and brown the guinea fowl halves in it. Season with salt and pepper. Moisten with 200 ml/7 fl oz/1 cup of water, cover and simmer for 20 minutes.

Add the Calvados and apples. Cover and cook for a further 15 minutes.

Drain the guinea fowl halves and place them on a warmed serving dish. Surround them with the apples.

Add the cream to the cooking juices, adjust seasoning and stir over a high heat. Coat the guinea fowl with the sauce and serve at once.

Pintade au chou (Guinea fowl with cabbage)

H

see also:
cod
fish

HADDOCK

Aiglefin, églefin

A fish belonging to the cod family, but smaller than the cod, reaching lengths of up to 1 m/3 ft and weighing about 2–3 kg/4½–6½ lb. The grey-brown fish, easily distinguished from cod by its dark lateral line and a black mark under its first dorsal fin, is normally sold whole and gutted or in fillets. The flesh is firm and lean, containing less than 1% fatty acids, white to slightly pink in colour and with a delicate flavour. There are only 66 calories per 100 g/3½ oz of raw haddock.

Fresh haddock is prepared and cooked in much the same way as cod, and may be poached in a court-bouillon, baked in the oven or fried.

SMOKED HADDOCK is also very popular in Britain and the United States. The freshly caught fish is split, rubbed with salt and hot smoked for 24 hours. The smoked haddock of Finnan, Scotland, is thought to have the finest flavour, and has given its name FINNAN HADDIE to all smoked haddock in the USA. Smoked haddock is a popular breakfast dish in Britain. It is normally poached in milk and served with poached eggs, or the flesh is incorporated in the spiced British-Indian rice dish, kedgeree. It is also served with boiled potatoes or oatcakes as a main meal.

FILETS D'AIGLEFIN À LA MOUTARDE

Haddock fillets in mustard sauce

Serves 4
Preparation 5 minutes
Cooking 11 minutes

METRIC/IMPERIAL	AMERICAN
whites of 4 leeks, thinly sliced	whites of 4 leeks, thinly sliced
800 g/1¾ lb haddock fillets	1¾ lb haddock fillets
juice of 1 lemon	juice of 1 lemon
150 ml/¼ pt crème fraîche or whipping cream	⅔ cup crème fraîche or whipping cream
strong Dijon mustard, to taste	strong Dijon mustard, to taste
salt and pepper	salt and pepper

Put the leeks in a small, deep dish with 2 tablespoons of water. Microwave on High for 3 minutes.

Arrange the fish fillets in a separate dish and sprinkle them with lemon juice. Cover them with microwave-safe film and make 2 or 3 holes in the film with a sharp knife. Microwave on High for 6 minutes, turning the dish once during cooking.

Mix the cream and mustard to taste in a bowl and microwave on Medium for 2 minutes.

Place the fish fillets on individual warmed plates and garnish them with the leeks. Season with salt and pepper, coat with the mustard cream sauce and serve at once.

HADDOCK KEDGEREE

Smoked haddock kedgeree

Serves 4
Preparation 20 minutes
Cooking about 30 minutes, standing 20 minutes

METRIC/IMPERIAL	AMERICAN
4 smoked haddock fillets	4 smoked haddock fillets (finnan haddie)
2 tbsp groundnut oil	2 tbsp peanut oil
1 onion, finely chopped	1 onion, finely chopped
1 heaped tsp curry powder	1 heaping tsp curry powder
150 g/5½ oz long-grain rice	¾ cup long-grain rice
2 hard-boiled eggs, shelled and sliced	2 hard-boiled eggs, shelled and sliced
30 g/1 oz butter	2 tbsp butter
3 tbsp crème fraîche or sour cream	3 tbsp crème fraîche or sour cream
salt and cayenne pepper	salt and cayenne pepper

Put the smoked haddock in a deep dish, cover with 200 ml/7 fl oz/1 cup of boiling water and let stand for 20 minutes.

Drain the haddock fillets and flake them.

Heat the oil in a frying pan over a moderate heat. Add the onion and stir with a wooden spoon for 5 minutes. Add the curry powder, stir, then add the rice. Stir for 2 more minutes, then moisten with 500 ml/16 fl oz/2 cups of water. Cover and simmer for 10 minutes.

Add the flaked haddock and a pinch or two of cayenne pepper, stir carefully and cook, covered, for a further 10 minutes.

Pour the contents of the casserole into a very hot, deep serving dish. Add the hard-boiled egg slices, dot with the butter and add the cream. Mix carefully, adjusting the seasoning if necessary.

Serve this dish for breakfast or as a light supper or brunch.

HAKE

Colin, merlu

see also: cod fish

A member of the cod family, hake is widely available all year round and abundant off the coasts of Ireland and Iberia. The largish fish, 30–75 cm/12–30 in long, is somewhat bland but virtually boneless. The slightly smaller and better flavoured SILVER HAKE or FROSTFISH is common off the Canadian and American coast as far south as Virginia, and varieties of the fish are plentiful in American Pacific waters. Small or medium-sized hake are sold whole, while larger fish are sold as steaks or fillets; bought this way there is less overall wastage. The fish is known as *colin* in France and also as *merlu* in the Mediterranean and the former term is also confusingly used for a wide variety of white fish.

Hake may be poached whole and served either hot or cold, steamed, grilled (broiled) or fried, and is often served with a cheese, herb or caper sauce. It also suits most of the recipes for cod and is popular in Spain and Portugal.

Great care should be taken when cooking hake, especially if poaching, as the flesh is delicate and disintegrates readily. Hake is a lean fish with only 86 calories per 100 g/3½ oz.

COLIN À LA CRÈME DE POIVRONS

Hake in sweet pepper cream sauce

Serves 4
Preparation 10 minutes
Cooking 11 minutes

METRIC/IMPERIAL	AMERICAN
4 hake steaks, each weighing 140 g/5 oz	4 hake steaks, each weighing 5 oz
2 tbsp dry white wine	2 tbsp dry white wine
3 red sweet peppers, halved, deseeded and cut into strips	3 red sweet peppers, halved, deseeded and cut into strips
1 egg	1 egg
1 tbsp crème fraîche or whipping cream	1 tbsp crème fraîche or whipping cream
1 tsp curry powder	1 tsp curry powder
salt and pepper	salt and pepper

Arrange the hake steaks in a circle in a dish and pour the white wine over them. Cover with microwave-safe film and prick several holes in it with a fork. Microwave on High for 4 minutes.

Remove the fish, keeping the juices in the dish, and keep hot. Add the sweet pepper to the juices in the dish, cover and cook on High for 5 minutes.

Blend the contents of the dish in a food processor, adding the egg and cream. Add the curry powder and salt and pepper to taste. Microwave, uncovered, for 2 minutes on High.

Put one hake steak on each of 4 warmed plates and sprinkle with salt and pepper. Coat the fish with the sauce and serve immediately.

To drink: a dry white wine, such as Viré.

HALIBUT

Flétan

see also: brill, fish

One of the largest of the marine flatfish, halibut is found in cold northern waters from the North Sea to New England. The PACIFIC HALIBUT is also closely related, but the so-called CALIFORNIA HALIBUT is actually more closely related to the brill and turbot.

Halibut has firm, white, tasty flesh which tends to be somewhat dry; it can be cooked in the same way as brill. Small specimens, known as CHICKEN HALIBUT, are sold whole, although the larger fish are usually cut in sections.

Halibut is a relatively lean fish with 120 calories per 100 g/3½ oz.

FLÉTAN À LA CRÈME

Halibut in cream sauce

Serves 4
Preparation 5 minutes
Cooking about 20 minutes

METRIC/IMPERIAL	AMERICAN
15 g/½ oz butter	1 tbsp butter
800 g/1¾ lb halibut fillets	1¾ lb halibut fillets
1 lemon	1 lemon
200 ml/8 fl oz thick crème fraîche or whipping cream	1 cup thick crème fraîche or whipping cream
1 onion, finely chopped	1 onion, finely chopped
salt and freshly ground black pepper	salt and freshly ground black pepper
snipped fresh chervil, to garnish	snipped fresh chervil, to garnish

Preheat the oven to 200C/400F/gas 6, and grease an ovenproof dish with the butter.

Season the halibut fillets with salt and pepper and arrange them in the baking dish.

If the lemon is not organically grown and may have been sprayed or coated, scrub it in warm soapy water, rinse well and pat dry. Grate the zest and squeeze the juice.

Mix together the cream, chopped onion, 1 tablespoon of lemon zest and 2 tablespoons of lemon juice. Pour the mixture over the fish and season generously with pepper.

Bake for 15–20 minutes until the fish flakes readily when tested with a fork. Sprinkle with chervil and serve straight from the baking dish.

To drink: a dry but fruity white wine, such as a Vouvray.

HAM

Jambon

see also: bacon, baking, charcuterie, pork

The term used to describe leg of pork, or more specifically, the upper part of the hind leg, hams are usually cured by salting and possible subsequent smoking, although some hams are available fresh and may be braised or roasted like other cuts of pork. The word is also used to describe similar cuts of meat from other animals, such as wild boar and lamb, but is always taken to denote pork unless otherwise specified.

Cured hams have been a mainstay of the rural diet in many parts of Europe since Roman times. The flavour of a ham depends on many factors, from the breed and age of the pig and its diet, to the kind of wood burned to smoke the meat and the length of time it is aged. The interplay of these factors gives ham a diversity almost as rich as that of wine or cheese.

The salting process may involve bathing in brine or rubbing in repeated layers of dry salt. Increasingly nowadays, early stages of curing include injecting brine directly into the meat. Whatever process is used, extra preservative and flavouring ingredients, such as saltpetre (which improves keeping qualities and gives most ham and bacon its distinctive pink colour), herbs and spices, are also added to the cure. Sugar, honey, treacle or molasses are also used at this stage to produce SWEET CURE HAM. The hams are then either air dried or smoked using oak, beech, hickory, sage, juniper berries or even heather. All hams are then matured for anything from a few weeks to two years, either hanging in cool dry places or possibly even buried in wood ash.

There are two main types of cured ham: RAW HAMS, usually dried and intended to be eaten without any cooking, and COOKED HAMS which have usually been boiled in stock and often need to be cooked further before consumption.

Among the best known RAW HAMS are such international favourites as BAYONNE HAM, cured for 4–6 months, sometimes in wine for a distinctive flavour, and now made in many parts of France, and Italian PARMA HAM or *prosciutto crudo* which is matured for 8–9 months. ARDENNES and WESTPHALIAN HAMS are smoked, as are all so-called 'mountain' or 'country' hams (*jambons de campagne*).

RAW HAMS are usually sliced very thinly and are eaten in cold hors d'oeuvres, as in the classic Italian dish of *prosciutto* with figs, melon or shaved Parmesan cheese. They are also a valuable flavouring ingredient in many classic pasta stuffings and sauces and in French country dishes such as *choucroute alsacienne*, and *pipérade*.

COOKED HAMS vary enormously in type and quality. Many are made industrially by steaming ham pressed in moulds to produce the characteristic blocks or cylinders of ham seen in delicatessens and sold sliced in sealed packs. The authorized addition of polyphosphates makes such hams very tender, but moist and with a high water content. Today this type of ham is most readily available and is used in numerous everyday recipes, from mixed salads and sandwiches to omelettes, gratins and soufflés.

More traditional hams are usually left on the bone and most need at least overnight soaking to reduce the high salt content before further cooking. They may or may not have been boiled before sale and it is wise to read labels carefully or check with the shopkeeper to assess what further soaking and boiling, if any, is required. Do not be put off by signs of bloom or light mould on a good ham as this is a natural phenomenon, like the rind on a cheese. Remove all traces, however, before cooking.

CARVING RAW HAM

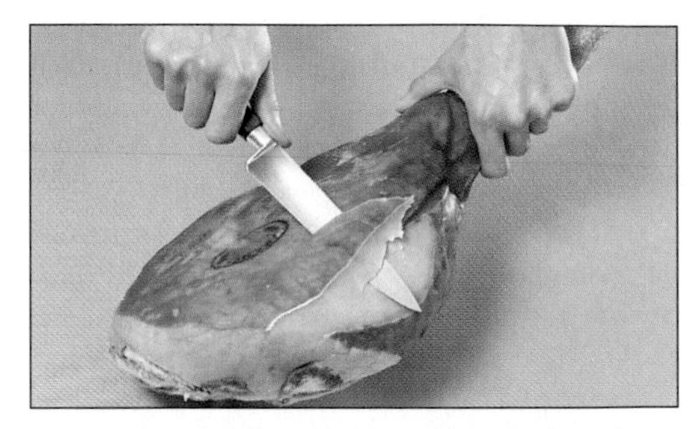

Using a sharp knife, remove most of the fat from the part of the ham to be carved.

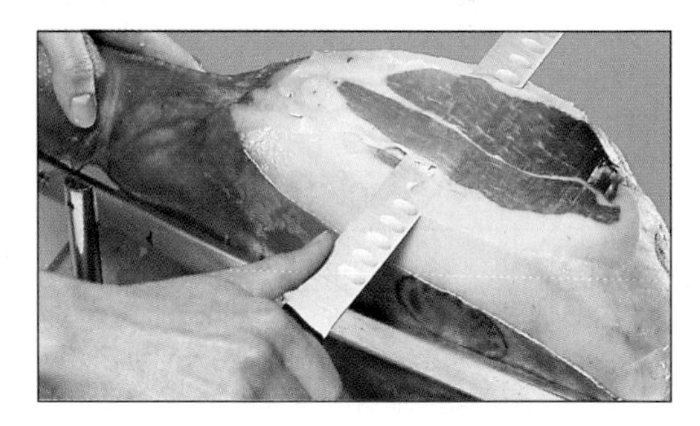

Hold the ham firmly or secure it in a special cradle and carve off long, very thin slices.

Among the best-known cooked hams are: YORK HAM, which is dry-salted, often smoked over oak and matured for 3–4 months; American COUNTRY-CURED HAMS, such as VIRGINIA and KENTUCKY HAM, which have very fine flavours as the pigs have been fed on a rich diet including acorns, clover and corn, and are smoked over very aromatic woods such as hickory or apple and matured for up to a year; and PRAGUE HAM, the most celebrated European ham, which is sweet-cured and smoked over beech, is held to be the best choice when serving ham hot.

Cooked ham may be sliced and served plain or with a fruit, cheese or mustard sauce as a main course or used as a flavouring ingredient in cooking. A festive treatment is to bake a boiled and skinned ham in a brown sugar crust studded with cloves. Ham cooked on the bone usually has a better flavour.

The name 'ham' is also given to a number of regional specialities such as RHEIMS HAM or BURGUNDY HAM, both of which are prepared from pieces of cooked ham and pork shoulder pressed in a mould in parsleyed aspic, as is the delicatessen speciality *jambon persillé*.

Of all *charcuterie* products, ham has the lowest fat content (only 2–5%). Providing all the fat is trimmed off, it has a moderate calorie content: cooked ham has 300 calories per 100 g/3½ oz and raw ham 380. Apart from its high salt content, ham may be considered the nutritional equivalent to other meat, fish or eggs. Commercially produced hams with reduced sodium and fat content are available for people with special dietary requirements.

CAKE AU JAMBON

Ham loaf

Serves 6
Preparation 20 minutes
Cooking about 40 minutes

METRIC/IMPERIAL	AMERICAN
15 g/½ oz butter	1 tbsp butter
3 eggs	3 eggs
100 g/3½ oz flour	¾ cup flour
100 ml/3½ fl oz milk	½ cup milk
3 tbsp corn oil	3 tbsp corn oil
150 g/5½ oz grated Gruyère cheese	1¼ cups grated Gruyère cheese
1 tbsp green peppercorns	1 tbsp green peppercorns
2 tbsp chopped chives	2 tbsp chopped chives
2 thick slices of cooked ham, each weighing about 200 g/7 oz, trimmed of fat and diced	2 thick slices of cooked ham, each weighing about 7 oz, trimmed of fat and diced
1 tbsp baking powder	1 tbsp baking powder
salt and freshly ground black pepper	salt and freshly ground black pepper

Preheat the oven to 180C/350F/gas 4 and grease a 20 cm/8 in loaf pan with the butter.

Break the eggs into a bowl and beat them lightly. Add the flour and mix well. Stir in the milk, oil and a pinch of salt and beat until smooth.

Add the grated cheese, green peppercorns and chives, and finally the diced ham. Mix well, then add the baking powder and some freshly ground black pepper.

Pour the mixture into the prepared pan and smooth the surface. Bake for 40 minutes. Remove from the oven and allow to cool, then turn out on a wire rack.

Cut the loaf in thick slices and serve it warm with a salad of bitter leaves, such as dandelion, or cold as a cocktail snack.

JAMBON POÊLÉ AU CHABLIS

Ham in Chablis

Serves 4
Preparation 15 minutes
Cooking about 35 minutes

METRIC/IMPERIAL	AMERICAN
5 shallots, chopped	5 shallots, chopped
150 ml/¼ pt Chablis or other dry light white wine	⅔ cup Chablis or other dry light white wine
1 tbsp snipped tarragon	1 tbsp snipped tarragon
150 ml/¼ pt beef stock	⅔ cup beef stock
5 tbsp tomato purée	⅓ cup tomato paste
200 ml/7 fl oz crème fraîche or whipping cream	1 cup crème fraîche or whipping cream
25 g/¾ oz butter	1½ tbsp butter
4 slices of cooked ham, each weighing about 200 g/7 oz, rind removed	4 slices of cooked ham, each weighing about 7 oz, any rind removed
salt and freshly ground white pepper	salt and freshly ground white pepper

Put the shallots in a saucepan with the wine. Bring to the boil, then reduce over a low heat for 10 minutes.

Add the tarragon, beef stock and tomato purée (paste). Mix, then cover and simmer for 10 minutes.

Mix in the cream, stirring well, and continue to cook over low heat for 10 minutes.

Melt the butter in a frying pan and heat the slices of ham in it, turning them once.

Roll up the ham slices and place them on a warmed serving plate. Coat them with the sauce and serve at once as a first course or with a salad as a light lunch.

Variations: this treatment works well with a wide variety of sauces: cheese, red wine, Madeira, for example. Try adding some finely chopped smoked bacon, celery, capers, sun-dried tomatoes, walnuts or raisins to the sauce, as appropriate.

see also:
barbecuing
beef

HAMBURGER

A flat, round cake of minced (ground) beef, the hamburger was introduced to the American public by the German immigrants of St Louis during the World's Fair held there in 1904, and has since become one of the world's most favoured convenience foods and a feature of barbecues everywhere.

The beef may be seasoned with onion and herbs and is sometimes bound with egg. It may be grilled (broiled), barbecued or fried and is usually served in a bun. Hamburgers are often accompanied by French fried potatoes and may be garnished with a wide variety of items, especially lettuce and sliced tomato, tomato ketchup, onion, cheese, bacon, dill pickles or chilli sauce and an assortment of relishes.

Hamburgers made from lean meat (about 5% fat) make the best, and most healthy, sandwiches.

see also:
civet
game
rabbit

HARE

Lièvre

A game animal belonging to the same family as the rabbit but with dark rather than white meat and longer, more powerful hind legs. The French tend not to hang hares, but elsewhere they are usually hung for at least 3 or 4 days to allow the flavour to develop and the meat to become more tender. They are usually hung before being drawn and their blood may be used to thicken an accompanying sauce, as in the classic *civet*.

Hare is prepared in different ways depending on the age of the animal. Young hare or LEVERET, up to about 1 year old, makes the best eating and may be recognized by its glossy skin, less pronounced cleft in the lip and soft paws with sharp, fur-covered claws. Such tender specimens are generally roasted or sautéed, while older animals are best made into stews, 'jugged' (made into *civets*), cooked *en daube* or incorporated in pâtés and terrines.

Hares are generally sold already skinned, drawn and cut into portions. The back or 'saddle' of hare has the tastiest meat and is often sold whole, usually larded, for roasting. The hind legs, or haunches, and fillets from the saddle may be roasted or grilled and are usually served with sharp fruit or sweet-and-sour sauces. The meat of wild hare benefits from being marinated for at least a day in red wine or oil mixtures, well seasoned with herbs and juniper berries.

Hare is a lean meat (100 g/3½ oz contains only 150 calories), but can be indigestible, less so if roasted than if cooked in a rich sauce.

SAUTÉ DE LEVRAUT À LA NIÇOISE

Young hare with olive and wild mushroom sauce

Serves 4
Preparation 20 minutes
Cooking about 1¼ hours

METRIC/IMPERIAL	AMERICAN
100 ml/3½ fl oz olive oil	*½ cup olive oil*
1 young hare (2–4 months old), skinned, drawn and cut into pieces	*1 young hare (2–4 months old), skinned, drawn and cut into pieces*
2 tbsp Cognac	*2 tbsp Cognac*
300 ml/½ pt red wine	*1½ cups red wine*
1 garlic clove, cut in half	*1 garlic clove, cut in half*
bouquet garni	*bouquet garni*
10 small onions	*10 small onions*
4 chipolata sausages	*4 small pork link sausages*
55 g/2 oz black olives, stoned	*⅓ cup black olives, pitted*
115 g/¼ lb chanterelles or other wild mushrooms	*¼ lb fresh chanterelles or other wild mushrooms*
salt and pepper	*salt and pepper*

Heat all but 1 tablespoon of the oil in a flameproof casserole and brown the pieces of hare over a moderate heat. Season them with salt and pepper.

Heat the Cognac, pour it into the casserole and flame it. Stir, then add the red wine, garlic and bouquet garni. Cook, covered, for 40 minutes.

Meanwhile, blanch the onions for 2 minutes in boiling water, and brown the sausages in the reserved oil in a frying pan over a moderate heat.

Add the olives and onions to the casserole and cook for a further 10 minutes. Cut the sausages in half and add them, along with the mushrooms. Cook for about 10 more minutes. Serve straight from the casserole.

Variation: this dish also works well with rabbit.

HARICOT

see Bean

HAZELNUT OR FILBERT

Noisette

see also:
almond
nuts
walnut

The fruit of many varieties of hazel tree, hazelnuts are oval, hard-shelled nuts with a very delicate flavour. In Britain smaller nuts are known as COBS and larger types as FILBERTS, although in the United States the term 'filbert' is used for the smaller nuts and GIANT FILBERTS for the larger. Strictly speaking the cob and filbert are different varieties of the nut and terminology really depends on which has become most common in any region. Filberts are distinguished by a husk which completely covers the nut, whereas the cob nut tends to stick out of one end of the husk. To compound the confusion, very tasty and much sought-after KENTISH COBS are actually a type of filbert.

Hazelnuts are mostly produced commercially in Turkey, Italy and Spain. The fresh nuts, sold in their green husks from August to October, are popular as dessert nuts, but are usually kiln-dried for use in cooking. Whole, dried hazelnuts in their shells should be smooth and shiny and free of holes (the holes mean that there may be a grub inside the nut), and should fit tightly inside the shell and not rattle when shaken. Nuts for cooking are often sold ready shelled, or even ground, as the hazelnut keeps well and does not go rancid as readily as most other nuts.

The dried nuts may be served on their own, salted and toasted as cocktail appetizers; or chopped, grated or ground and used in creams and in *pâtisserie* and cake-making. The composition of the nut, with a high fat content, means that it may readily be baked without the benefit of added flour or fat. Although generally eclipsed by the almond in cooking, it also finds considerable use in savoury dishes, especially stuffings and pâtés. It is also used very imaginatively in Spanish cooking, notably with sweet peppers and garlic in their *romesco* sauce for vegetables and fish.

For a high-energy breakfast, crush a handful of hazelnuts into a bowl of a soft cheese, such as *fromage blanc*, or yogurt. Dried hazelnuts contain 655 calories per 100 g/3½ oz.

NOISETTINE

Hazelnut or filbert cake

Serves 6
Preparation 20 minutes
Cooking about 35 minutes

METRIC/IMPERIAL	AMERICAN
115 g/4 oz butter	8 tbsp butter
125 g/4½ oz shelled hazelnuts, coarsely chopped	1 cup shelled hazelnuts (filberts), coarsely chopped
8 egg whites	8 egg whites
150 g/5½ oz caster sugar	¾ cup superfine sugar
45 g/1½ oz flour	⅓ cup flour
icing sugar, for dusting	confectioners' sugar, for dusting

Preheat the oven to 200C/400F/gas 6 and grease a 20 cm/8 in diameter cake pan with 15 g/½ oz/1 tbsp of the butter.

Spread the hazelnuts on a baking sheet and toast them in the oven for 3–4 minutes.

In a bowl mix, but do not whisk, the egg whites with the sugar and add the hazelnuts. Sift the flour into the bowl and mix thoroughly. Melt the remaining butter and add it to the mixture.

Pour the batter into the prepared cake pan and bake for about 30 minutes. Remove the cake from the oven, let it cool, turn it out and dust it with icing (confectioners') sugar.

POULET AUX NOISETTES

Chicken with hazelnuts or filberts

Serves 4
Preparation 20 minutes
Cooking about 40 minutes

METRIC/IMPERIAL	AMERICAN
1 chicken, dressed weight about 1.2 kg/ 2¼ lb, cut into pieces	*1 chicken, dressed and drawn weight about 2¼ lb, cut into pieces*
100 g/3½ oz butter	*1 stick butter*
400 ml/14 fl oz chicken stock	*1¾ cups chicken stock*
150 g/5½ oz shelled hazelnuts	*1¼ cups shelled hazelnuts (filberts)*
3 tbsp crème fraîche or whipping cream	*3 tbsp crème fraîche or whipping cream*
flour, for coating	*flour, for coating*
salt and pepper	*salt and pepper*

Preheat the oven to 230C/450F/gas 8. Season the chicken pieces with salt and pepper. Coat each piece with flour.

Heat 25 g/¾ oz/1½ tbsp of the butter in a flameproof casserole and add the chicken pieces. Brown them for 4–5 minutes, turning them frequently, then add the stock and cook, covered, over a moderate heat for 25–30 minutes.

Meanwhile, spread the hazelnuts on a baking sheet and toast them in the oven for 3–4 minutes. Reserve a dozen whole and pound the rest in a mortar, gradually adding the remaining butter in small pieces.

Remove the chicken pieces from the casserole and place them in a warmed serving dish. Reduce the cooking liquid over a high heat and then whisk in the hazelnut butter, a little at a time. Finally, add the cream and heat through gently for a further 5 minutes.

Coat the chicken pieces with the sauce and garnish with the reserved whole hazelnuts.
To drink: a fruity Chardonnay.

HEAD

Tête

see also: brawn offal veal

A variety of white offal (variety meat) which is rich in gelatine, it is mainly calves' heads that are sold for cooking, although ox and pork heads may be incorporated in pâtés, terrines and brawns (head cheese).

In France, calves' heads are usually sold whole, boned and rolled, and may be stuffed and baked. Look for bright pink meat and clear white gelatinous layers. Alternatively it can be cut in pieces and cooked in a court-bouillon, or fried and served hot or cold with a highly seasoned sauce.

Calves' head contains about 350 calories per 100 g/3½ oz.

HEAD CHEESE

see Brawn

HEART

Coeur

see also: beef lamb offal pork veal

A very lean type of red offal (variety meat), heart makes a highly economical and nourishing dish.

As animals' hearts are largely muscle, they do tend to be tough and thus generally require long slow cooking. CALVES' HEARTS are the most tender, but some consider that they lack flavour compared to full-grown OX and LAMBS' HEARTS.

Buy only the freshest specimens which are bright pink in colour and firm to the touch, and cook them that day. They must be soaked in warm water to blanch out residual blood and then trimmed of any fat, hard fibres, blood vessels or clots of blood .

One OX HEART, braised for 2 hours, will serve 4 people; allow 1 LAMB HEART per person and braise them for 1 hour. One VEAL HEART will make 2 portions and it may be fried for 5–6 minutes, grilled (broiled) or barbecued on skewers or braised for 1½ hours.

The shape of hearts readily lends them to being stuffed with tasty mixtures and they are often barded with fatty bacon during cooking to prevent them from drying out. Tougher hearts, such as PIGS' and LAMBS' HEARTS are cut into pieces and used to give extra flavour to stews and *civets*.

POULTRY HEARTS are also often sold separately and are mostly used in terrines or on kebabs.

Although low in fat, heart is rich in cholesterol (150 mg per 100 g/3½ oz).

COEURS DE VEAU EN BROCHETTES

Veal heart kebabs

Serves 4
Preparation 20 minutes, 30 minutes ahead
Cooking 10 minutes

METRIC/IMPERIAL	*AMERICAN*
2 veal hearts, rinsed, trimmed and cubed	*2 veal hearts, rinsed, trimmed and cubed*
2 cloves, crushed	*2 cloves, crushed*
1 garlic clove, chopped	*1 garlic clove, chopped*
4 tbsp olive oil	*4 tbsp olive oil*
juice of 1 lemon	*juice of 1 lemon*
sprig of thyme	*sprig of thyme*
225 g/½ lb mushrooms	*½ lb mushrooms*
8 cherry tomatoes	*8 cherry tomatoes*
salt and pepper	*salt and pepper*

Put the veal heart pieces, cloves and garlic into a bowl and add the olive oil and half the lemon juice, some salt and pepper and the thyme. Leave to marinate for 30 minutes.

Wipe the mushrooms and sprinkle them with the remaining lemon juice. Cut the larger ones in half. Drain the pieces of heart.

Make up the kebabs as follows: thread on each of 4 skewers first a cherry tomato and then alternating pieces of heart and mushroom, finishing with another cherry tomato.

Preheat a grill (broiler) or barbecue. Brush the kebabs all over with the marinade and cook them for about 10 minutes, turning them several times so that they cook uniformly.

To drink: a fresh, lively red, such as a Chinon.

HERBS

Herbes

In cooking, this term refers to the fresh or dried aromatic leaves of various types of plant which are used as flavourings.

In French cooking, the most commonly used fresh herbs are chervil, chives, dill, parsley, rosemary, tarragon and thyme. The classic *fines herbes* mixture consists of freshly chopped or snipped green aromatic herbs, usually a combination of flat-leaved parsley, chervil, tarragon and chives, and is popular in salads, egg dishes, mayonnaise and sauces.

see also:
basil
bay
chervil
chive
coriander
dill
marjoram
mint
parsley
purslane
rosemary
savory
spices
tarragon
thyme

The ubiquitous *bouquet garni*, mostly just bay, thyme and parsley, is usually made up of dried herbs, as are *herbes de Provence*, which generally consist of a mixture of bay, basil, rosemary, savory and thyme, and are used in flavouring grilled (broiled) or barbecued meats, stews or even small goats' milk cheeses.

Fresh herbs have the best flavour, although dried herbs can be very strong and pungent, and have a quite different flavour from their fresh counterparts. Increasingly, fresh herbs are available in packs and small pots from supermarkets. Many are also easily grown indoors or on window-sills. Bunches of fresh herbs may be kept fresh for several days by storing them in water like cut flowers. They also freeze well. Dried herbs should be bought from large stores with a good turnover of stock and kept in a cool dry place, preferably away from direct light. They lose their powers after a few months, so should be replaced on a regular basis.

Although some combinations are universal favourites, like tarragon with chicken, rosemary with lamb and basil with tomatoes, there are no hard and fast rules about what herbs should be used with different types of food. The cuisines of different countries make use of different repertoires of herbs: the British lean heavily on mint, sage and thyme; north and East Europe favour chervil and dill and the Italians use a great deal of basil, oregano and sage. Much of this is a function of the other ingredients which normally form part of the local diet. When experimenting with the flavours of new and different herbs, use the wisdom of these traditions as a guideline.

OMELETTE AUX FINES HERBES

Herb omelette

Serves 4
Preparation 10 minutes
Cooking 4–5 minutes

METRIC/IMPERIAL	*AMERICAN*
2 tbsp finely chopped flat-leaved parsley	*2 tbsp finely chopped flat-leaf parsley*
2 tbsp finely chopped chervil	*2 tbsp finely chopped chervil*
2 tbsp finely chopped chives	*2 tbsp finely chopped chives*
6 eggs	*6 eggs*
55 g/2 oz butter	*4 tbsp butter*
salt and freshly ground black pepper	*salt and freshly ground black pepper*

Thoroughly mix the chopped herbs.

Break the eggs into a large deep bowl. Add one quarter of the butter in small pieces. Add the herbs. Season with salt and pepper and beat briskly with a fork to mix well.

Melt two thirds of the remaining butter in a heavy-bottomed omelette or frying pan over a moderate heat, tilting it so that the butter covers the bottom completely.

Pour the egg mixture into the pan and pull the edges of the mixture into the centre with the back of the fork 2 or 3 times. When the omelette begins to set, tilt the frying pan from side to side to distribute the mixture evenly .

Roll or fold the omelette in half when it is just set, tilting the frying pan to help. Keep it in the frying pan for a few seconds, then slide it on to a warmed serving plate. Dot the top with the rest of the butter and serve at once.

To drink: a fresh red, such as a Beaujolais.

HERRING

Hareng

see also:
fish
sardine
smoking

A family of marine fish found in colder waters of the North Sea, the Baltic and the North Atlantic including the American Eastern seaboard as far south as Chesapeake Bay. There are several types of herring which are of culinary importance. The COMMON HERRING is no more than 30 cm/12 in long and is silvery in colour. Its tasty flesh has a high fat content. The BALTIC HERRING is slightly smaller and leaner. Fresh herring is best from October to January, when it is carrying the roe and milt. Smaller herring are often confused with the related sardine.

Fresh herring are very easily scaled, gutted and freed from their bones simply by massaging the fish along its length and then pulling the backbone away with the head. They are often sold this way. They are usually coated with flour or oatmeal and fried or grilled (broiled) lightly. They also lend themselves to being stuffed and baked. The Scots and Welsh 'souse' herrings by baking them immersed in a dilution of malt vinegar, sometimes with added herbs and spices.

For many centuries a mainstay of the European diet, herring were once caught in prodigious amounts and were considered 'poor man's food'. Several ways were found of preserving the frequent gluts and many of these have become firm favourites in their own right.

Raw fillets pickled in vinegar with herbs and spices are widely sold as MARINATED HERRING, variously known as ROLLMOPS or BISMARCK or BALTIC HERRING. These are served as cold hors d'oeuvres or in salads.

SMOKED HERRING comes in a wide variety of forms. BLOATERS are very lightly salted, dried and smoked. Because they are not gutted, they have a distinctly gamy taste and do not keep well. They need to be split and boned before being lightly rubbed with butter and grilled (broiled) or barbecued. BUCKLING are smoked whole at a high temperature so that they are almost cooked and resemble smoked trout. They are eaten as they are, or the skinned fillets may be used in salads, etc. The traditional English breakfast KIPPER is slit open, gutted and flattened, so that the head and bones can be removed. They are then briefly salted and cold-smoked for several hours, preferably over oak. They may be lightly grilled (broiled) or simply briefly immersed in hot water.

Varieties of SALTED HERRING include the legendary and now rare RED HERRING, which is heavily salted and then heavily smoked, but which has lost ground to the kipper; and the

German and Dutch speciality MATIE OR MATJES, which are very young first season fish (GREEN HERRINGS) which have been sweet cured. Eaten raw with onions or potatoes, these are a popular street snack and convenience food in these countries.

In spite of the fact that herring contains 10% fat, it is a very healthy food, provided it is eaten on its own or in brine, as the fat is polyunsaturated. Fresh herring contains 120 calories per 100 g/3½ oz; 220 calories if smoked or salted.

HARENGS EN PAPILLOTES

Herrings in foil parcels

Serves 2
Preparation 20 minutes
Cooking 25 minutes

METRIC/IMPERIAL	AMERICAN
4–5 mushrooms, chopped	4–5 mushrooms, chopped
2 shallots, finely chopped	2 shallots, finely chopped
1 hard-boiled egg, chopped	1 hard-boiled egg, chopped
1 tbsp finely chopped flat-leaved parsley	1 tbsp finely chopped flat-leaf parsley
2 fresh herrings, each weighing about 200 g/7 oz, cleaned and gutted	2 fresh herrings, each weighing about 7 oz, drawn
25 g/¾ oz butter	1½ tbsp butter
1 tsp grated horseradish	1 tsp grated horseradish
salt and pepper	salt and pepper

Preheat the oven to 200C/400F/gas 6.

Mix the mushrooms, shallots, hard-boiled egg and chopped parsley, adding salt and pepper to taste. Stuff the herrings with this mixture.

Soften the butter with a wooden spoon and add the horseradish. Spread this mixture on 2 rectangles of foil large enough to wrap the fish and place the stuffed fish on top. Seal the foil parcels securely.

Bake for 25 minutes. Serve the fish in the foil in soup plates so as not to lose any of the delicious cooking juices.

HARENGS POMMES À L'HUILE

Harengs pommes à l'huile (Herrings and potato salad)

Herrings and potato salad

Serves 4
Preparation 20 minutes
Cooking 25 minutes

METRIC/IMPERIAL	AMERICAN
800 g/1¾ lb potatoes	1¾ lb potatoes
1 tbsp white wine	1 tbsp white wine
6 tbsp oil	6 tbsp oil
3 tbsp white wine vinegar	3 tbsp white wine vinegar
8 smoked herring fillets in oil, drained	8 smoked herrings fillets in oil, drained
2 onions, thinly sliced and separated into rings	2 onions, thinly sliced and separated into rings
1 tbsp chopped chives	1 tbsp chopped chives
salt and freshly ground black pepper	salt and freshly ground black pepper

Boil the potatoes in their skins in salted water for 20–25 minutes. Drain them and peel them as soon as they are cool enough to handle. Slice into thick rounds and sprinkle them immediately with the white wine. Season with salt and pepper.

Make a vinaigrette with the oil and vinegar, adding salt and pepper to taste. Pour the vinaigrette over the potatoes and divide them among 4 plates. Add 2 herring fillets to each plate and scatter the onions and chopped chives over them. Serve at once while the potatoes are still warm.

Notes: this typical bistro dish is usually served as a first course before grilled (broiled) or barbecued meat, but can be made into a main course, accompanied by a salad of curly endive. White wine and beer go equally well with it.

HONEY

Miel

see also: nougat sugar

The sweet substance manufactured by bees from flower nectar or tree sap, honey is man's oldest sweetening agent. The honey is extracted from the comb by pressing or, more usually in

today's industrial production, spinning. It is then filtered and sometimes allowed to mature before being put into jars.

The texture, colour and flavour of honey varies widely according to the plant upon which the bees have fed and the season in which the honey is produced. Some honeys can be almost clear while others are a deep amber, almost black, in colour. Younger, fresher honeys tend to be liquid but almost all honeys eventually crystallize to the opaque, more solid form. However, the clear liquid honeys on sale have usually been heat-treated to keep these qualities.

The enormous range of plants and flowers from which bees cull their honey explains the wide variety of honeys available: rapeseed, alfalfa and sunflower honeys, all sweet but muted in flavour and thus good in cooking; pear, apple and orange honeys, very highly flavoured and good for use in confectionery and desserts; acacia honey, exceptionally delicate and excellent for sweetening drinks; lavender, rosemary, thyme and savory, all with their own distinctive flavours; and pine and heather, the strongest honeys of all which are favoured in the baking of strongly spiced cakes such as gingerbread. Creamy clover honey is the variety most highly recommended for everyday use in the kitchen as it is easy to spread and its fine flavour is not too assertive when used in cooking.

If a honey is specified as coming from a particular type of flower, the regulations of most countries insist that it must consist of at least 90% honey made from that flower. Honeys with the label 'product of several different countries' are less reliable in this respect but are usually of a very consistent taste and quality. Spain, Canada, Romania, Australia and California are all major honey exporters.

To get the best out of honey, it should be purchased in glass jars from reliable suppliers, stored in a dark place at room temperature and eaten within 1 year of manufacture. Honey that has become too hard is easily softened by being heated very gently in a bain-marie (never above 40C/104F). The white deposit on the surface of some honey is only residual pollen that has not been eliminated by the filtering process.

Honey can be used like sugar, particularly for sweetening yogurt and drinks. It is also widely used in baking and *pâtisserie*. In savoury cooking it marries well with poultry and ham in sweet-and-sour preparations and sauces, and is often used in sweet curing of hams. It also works well in marinades and glazes for grilled (broiled), roast, baked or barbecued food. By weight, honey is much sweeter than sugar, which must be borne in mind when substituting it in recipes. In baking, honey may also retard the action of the yeast in a recipe and cooking times should be adjusted.

Honey is rich in minerals but is mostly water (about 17%) and natural unrefined sugar (about 75%) broken down by the bees into forms that are more readily assimilated by the body (glucose and fructose); 100 g/3½ oz contains 300 calories. It can be said to produce 'instant' energy and is favoured by athletes. It is also one of man's oldest medicines and can sooth coughs, throat infections and bronchitis.

COTELETTES D'AGNEAU AU MIEL

Lamb chops with honey sauce

Serves 2
Preparation 5 minutes
Cooking about 10 minutes

METRIC/IMPERIAL	AMERICAN
15 g/½ oz butter	*1 tbsp butter*
2 shallots, very finely chopped	*2 shallots, very finely chopped*
2 tbsp acacia honey	*2 tbsp acacia honey*
dash of red wine vinegar	*dash of red wine vinegar*
4 lamb chops	*4 lamb chops*
salt and pepper	*salt and pepper*

Melt the butter in a small saucepan. Add the shallots and cook them over moderate heat, stirring, for 2 minutes.

When the shallots are translucent and golden, add the honey and boil, stirring constantly, for about 2 minutes until it thickens. Add just a dash of vinegar and boil for 1 minute more.

Meanwhile, grill (broil) or barbecue the lamb chops for 3 minutes per side. Turn them with tongs rather than a fork, to avoid the risk of pricking and allowing the juices to escape.

Place the lamb chops on a warmed serving platter, season them, pour the honey sauce over and serve at once, accompanied by grilled (broiled) tomatoes or matchstick potatoes.

To drink: a fruity red wine, such as one from the Côte de Beaune.

JAMBON CRU AU MIEL

Raw ham in honey

Serves 4
Preparation 10 minutes
Cooking about 30 minutes

METRIC/IMPERIAL	AMERICAN
200 g/7 oz brown rice	1 cup brown rice
100 g/3½ oz canned sweetcorn, drained	½ cup canned whole kernel corn, drained
1 tbsp crème fraîche or whipping cream	1 tbsp crème fraîche or whipping cream
4 thick slices of raw ham, such as Bayonne	4 thick slices of raw ham, such as Bayonne
2 tbsp liquid honey	2 tbsp liquid honey
15 g/½ oz butter	1 tbsp butter
salt and freshly ground white pepper	salt and freshly ground white pepper

Cook the rice in boiling salted water for about 20 minutes, then drain it thoroughly. Mix it with the corn, binding the mixture with the cream, and season with salt and pepper.

Brush the slices of ham on both sides with the honey. Preheat a hot grill (broiler), and grease a large flameproof dish with the butter.

Spread the rice and corn mixture over the bottom of the dish and place the slices of ham on top of it. Season with ground pepper.

Grill (broil) for about 10 minutes, and serve piping hot straight from the dish.

HORS D'OEUVRE

see also: canapé

This French term, meaning 'outside the main work', denotes the first course of a meal, particularly selections of cold meats, croquettes or vols-au-vent, served before a formal luncheon.

By extension, in the USA the term has come to be used for finger-food to accompany drinks.

HORSERADISH

Raifort

see also: beef condiment

A southeastern European plant whose roots have white flesh with a strong piquant taste, horseradish is popular in many countries as a condiment and now grows wild in both Britain and North America. Fresh horseradish is simply peeled and sliced or grated. Nowadays it is more generally available dried or ready grated in small jars, often in vinegar or lemon juice, and may be mixed with cream and herbs or breadcrumbs soaked in milk. It is generally eaten with boiled, roast or cold meats, especially beef and pork, pickled or soused herrings or smoked fish. However it also works well in flavoured butters and mayonnaises and other cream sauces to accompany poultry and egg dishes. A little freshly grated horseradish can add interest to any salad or cold vegetable dish, and can be the making of a good Bloody Mary. There are 50 calories in 100 g/3½ oz of horseradish.

SAUCE AU RAIFORT

Horseradish sauce

Serves 4
Preparation 15 minutes

METRIC/IMPERIAL	AMERICAN
1 slice of very fresh white bread	1 slice of very fresh white bread
2 tbsp milk	2 tbsp milk
3 tbsp crème fraîche or sour cream	3 tbsp crème fraîche or sour cream
55 g/2 oz finely grated horseradish	¼ cup finely grated horseradish
pinch of caster sugar	pinch of superfine sugar
salt and freshly ground black pepper	salt and freshly ground black pepper

Remove the crusts from the bread, put it into a saucer, pour the milk over, let it soak and then squeeze out the excess milk.

In a bowl, mix the cream and horseradish. Add the bread and mash with a fork.

When the mixture is well combined, add the sugar, a pinch of salt and some freshly ground black pepper. Serve to accompany cold meats or oily fish.

I

see also:
cakes and gâteaux
charlotte
granita
profiterole
sorbet
soufflé
vacherin

ICES AND ICE CREAMS

Glace et crème glacée

Perhaps the most popular desserts worldwide, ices and ice creams are made by freezing a wide variety of flavoured mixtures.

ICES or WATER ICES are made with flavoured syrups, fruit juices or purées with sugar. Of these, SORBETS are churned continuously as they freeze for a creamy texture and they may also incorporate some egg white or meringue to give them body; GRANITAS are left to freeze naturally so they develop a refreshing texture of frozen shards.

ICE CREAMS are made with milk or cream, sugar and fruit or flavouring. There are several different types: the most usual is the CUSTARD ICE CREAM in which eggs, milk and/or cream and sugar are made into a custard cream and this is then flavoured. This develops a smooth texture in a churn or electric ice cream maker or *sorbetière*, which keeps the mixture moving during the freezing process. The MOUSSE-BASED ICE CREAM or PARFAIT is made with a thickly beaten mixture of egg yolks and sugar or syrup and stiffly whipped cream along with flavouring, and the slightly less rich MERINGUE-BASED ICE CREAM includes egg whites beaten with sugar or syrup to make a meringue which is flavoured and mixed with whipped cream. The latter freezes successfully in the freezer compartment of an ordinary refrigerator.

Ices and ice creams keep very well in the freezer. Always remove them to the refrigerator about 1 hour before serving, to give them a chance to 'ripen' or soften slightly, so that the flavour and texture can be more readily appreciated.

As well as being served as desserts on their own, with a sauce or fruit or as cups or sundaes, ices and ice creams are also incorporated in a wide number of more complex desserts, including moulded *bombes* and the classic *omelette surprise* or baked Alaska, in which the ice cream is insulated by a layer of quickly cooked meringue. They are also used to make a variety of frozen cakes, gâteaux and pastries.

Good quality, ready-made ice creams make excellent quick desserts. Keep on hand one or two cartons or tubs, one vanilla and one chocolate or exotic fruit flavour, and serve with a coulis or sauce, warm compote, slices of fruit rolled in sugar, chopped, crystallized or dried fruit, fresh mint leaves or whipped cream.

Ice cream is an excellent source of calcium, and quality ice creams, without synthetic additives, are recommended as a food for children, although the high sugar content means that they should only be an occasional treat. There are 166 calories in 100 g/3½ oz of vanilla ice cream.

GLACE À LA VANILLE

Vanilla ice cream

Makes 1 l/$1\frac{3}{4}$ pt/1 qt (serves 6)
Preparation 20 minutes
Cooking 15 minutes, freezing 3–4 hours

METRIC/IMPERIAL	*AMERICAN*
1 vanilla pod	*1 vanilla bean*
750 ml/27 fl oz milk	*$3\frac{1}{4}$ cups milk*
6 egg yolks	*6 egg yolks*
185 g/$6\frac{1}{2}$ oz icing sugar	*$1\frac{1}{2}$ cups confectioners' sugar*
100 ml/$3\frac{1}{2}$ fl oz crème fraîche or whipping cream	*$\frac{1}{2}$ cup crème fraîche or whipping cream*

Split the vanilla in half and carefully scrape out the seeds with a knife. Pour the milk into a saucepan and add the split pod (bean) along with the seeds (1). Bring to the boil without stirring, then remove the pan from the heat, cover and leave to infuse for 10 minutes.

Put the egg yolks into a bowl and add the sugar (2). Beat with a spoon until smooth and creamy.

Remove the split vanilla pod (bean) from the milk, and gradually add the milk to the sugar and egg mixture, stirring constantly (3). Pour the mixture back into the saucepan and whisk continuously over a low heat until the mixture thickens. When the custard cream is thick enough to coat the back of a spoon, remove from the heat and leave to cool.

When cool, whisk in the cream until smoothly combined.

Pour the mixture into an electric ice cream maker, filling the compartment only two-thirds full (4). Freeze for 3–4 hours, or according to the manufacturer's instructions.

Variations: the vanilla ice cream may be flavoured with 2 tablespoons of liqueur.

To make glace plombière, macerate 125 g/$4\frac{1}{2}$ oz/$\frac{3}{4}$ cup finely diced glacé or candied fruit in 3 tablespoons of Kirsch. Make a custard as described above, reserving 30 g/1 oz/4 tbsp of the icing (confectioners') sugar. Beat 2 egg whites with the reserved sugar until stiff, then fold into the mixture after the cream. Incorporate the fruit and the macerating liquid just before putting the mixture into the ice cream maker.

Custard-based ice creams do not freeze well by the still-frozen method as they tend to develop slivers of ice.

1

3

2

4

GLACE AU CHOCOLAT

Chocolate ice cream

Serves 4
Preparation 5 minutes
Cooking 15 minutes, freezing 2 hours

METRIC/IMPERIAL	AMERICAN
500 ml/16 fl oz milk	2 cups milk
100 g/3½ oz plain chocolate, broken into small pieces	4 squares semisweet chocolate, broken into small pieces
30 g/1 oz tapioca	3½ tbsp tapioca
2 egg yolks	2 egg yolks
45 g/1½ oz caster sugar	¼ cup superfine sugar
100 ml/3½ fl oz whipping cream	½ cup whipping cream

Turn the refrigerator to its coldest setting, if the freezing compartment does not have a separate control.

Pour the milk into a saucepan and add the chocolate. Bring slowly to the boil, then pour in the tapioca in a steady stream and cook, stirring, for exactly 3 minutes. Remove from the heat.

In a bowl, beat the egg yolks and sugar for 5 minutes, then add the chocolate and tapioca mixture.

Return to the saucepan and cook over a low heat, stirring constantly, until the mixture thickens. Remove from the heat before it comes to the boil.

Immediately strain through a fine sieve to remove the tapioca grains. Leave to cool.

Whip the cream until it stands in stiff peaks, then mix it into the cool chocolate mixture. Pour it into ice-cube trays and freeze for 1 hour.

After this time, pour the ice cream, which will have started to set, into a bowl and whisk for a few moments (or blend in a food processor). Return it to the ice-cube trays and freeze for a further hour.

Note: this is a practical and easy recipe and does not require an electric ice cream maker. To make vanilla ice cream this way, flavour the milk with a split vanilla pod (bean) and use 75 g/2½ oz/7 tbsp of sugar.

GLACE MYSTÈRE

Hazelnut or filbert meringue ice cream

Serves 6
Preparation 30 minutes
Cooking 10 minutes, freezing 2 hours

METRIC/IMPERIAL	AMERICAN
4 eggs, separated	4 eggs, separated
55 g/2 oz caster sugar	5 tbsp superfine sugar
200 ml/7 fl oz crème fraîche or whipping cream	1 cup crème fraîche or whipping cream
1 tsp vanilla essence	1 tsp vanilla extract
45 g/1½ oz icing sugar	⅓ cup confectioners' sugar
2 large plain or caramel meringues	2 large plain or caramel-coated meringues
6 sugar cubes	6 sugar cubes
55 g/2 oz shelled hazelnuts	⅓ cup shelled hazelnuts (filberts)

Turn the refrigerator to its coldest setting, if the freezing compartment does not have a separate control.

Beat the egg yolks with the caster (superfine) sugar until white and foamy. Add the cream and vanilla.

Beat the egg whites to stiff peaks and add the icing (confectioners') sugar. Fold into the egg yolk mixture.

Pour half of the mixture into a deep ice-cube tray or other freezing container. Crumble the meringues over the surface and cover with the rest of the ice cream. Freeze for 2 hours.

Meanwhile make the praline: slightly moisten the sugar cubes with water in a small heavy-bottomed pan and boil to make a pale golden caramel. Add the hazelnuts and continue to caramelize to a deeper brown, then pour out on a baking sheet lined with a doubled sheet of foil.

Leave to cool completely then crack the sheet of hazelnut praline into pieces. Crush these as finely as possible.

To serve the ice cream, unmould it and cut it into equal portions, then coat them with the hazelnut praline.

COUPES GLACÉES AUX GRIOTTES

Ice cream with cherries

Serves 6
Preparation 15 minutes, 1 hour ahead
Chantilly cream 10 minutes

METRIC/IMPERIAL	AMERICAN
24 morello cherries, stoned	24 sweet-sour Duke cherries, pitted
3 tbsp Kirsch	3 tbsp Kirsch
600 ml/1¼ pt cherry sorbet	1¼ pt cherry sorbet
600 ml/1¼ pt glacé fruit ice cream (glace plombière – see Vanilla ice cream)	1¼ pt candied fruit ice cream (glace plombière – see Vanilla ice cream)
100 ml/3½ fl oz chantilly cream	½ cup chantilly cream
chocolate vermicelli, to decorate	chocolate sprinkles, to decorate

Macerate the cherries in the Kirsch for 1 hour.

Put 2 scoops of sorbet and 1 scoop of ice cream into each of 6 small bowls or glasses.

Add the cherries, pipe on a few swirls of Chantilly cream and decorate with chocolate.

ICING OR FROSTING

Glace de sucre

see also: caramel fondant

A number of preparations used to enhance the appearance and taste of cakes, gâteaux, pastries, cookies or biscuits and confectionery are described by these terms. UNCOOKED ICINGS are made simply from icing (confectioners') sugar, flavoured or coloured, and sometimes mixed with egg white. On hardening, the uncooked icing forms a very smooth, glossy coating which is hard enough to support weighty decoration. COOKED ICINGS, which are often called FROSTINGS, OR FONDANT ICINGS are more commonly made with caster or superfine sugar and usually have a much softer consistency and are applied more lavishly than uncooked icings. Cakes to be iced or frosted are often first glazed with apricot (or other fruit) jam so that the icing does not seep into the cake.

GLAÇAGE BLANC

Royal icing

For one 20 cm/8 in diameter cake (serving 6)
Preparation 10 minutes

METRIC/IMPERIAL	AMERICAN
200 g/7 oz icing sugar	1⅔ cups confectioners' sugar
1 egg white	1 egg white
few drops of lemon juice	few drops of lemon juice

Sift the sugar into a bowl and add the egg white and a few drops of lemon juice. Whisk the mixture thoroughly to obtain a smooth white cream.

Using a narrow metal spatula or palette knife, spread this icing over the cake. Let it set at room temperature or in a half-open warm oven.
Notes: to use for piping decorations, make a slightly firmer icing with 300 g/10 oz/2½ cups of sugar to the 1 egg white. The icing may be coloured with a few drops of food colouring.

GLAÇAGE VANILLE

Vanilla water icing

For one 20 cm/8 in diameter cake (serving 6)
Preparation 3 minutes
Cooking 2 minutes

METRIC/IMPERIAL	AMERICAN
150 g/5½ oz icing sugar	1¼ cups confectioners' sugar
½ tsp ground vanilla	½ tsp powdered vanilla

Sift the sugar into a well-chilled bowl. Add the vanilla and mix. Place the bowl in a bain-marie and gradually add 2 tablespoons of water, stirring continuously to obtain a thick but spreadable paste.

Coat the cake with the icing and smooth it over the surface with a narrow metal spatula or palette knife. Chill until ready to serve.

If decorating the cake with crystallized violets or sugared almonds, arrange them on the icing while it is still soft.

Variations: for chocolate icing, melt 30 g/1 oz plain (semisweet) chocolate over a bain-marie and add it to the sugar with the water. For coffee flavoured icing, dissolve 2 tablespoons of instant coffee (powder) in the water. For a citrus flavour, substitute orange or lemon juice for the water, adding grated citrus zest. This icing may also be flavoured with alcohol (Cointreau, rum, Kirsch, etc) using the same procedure, with 4 tablespoons of alcohol and 125 g/4½ oz/1 cup of icing (confectioners') sugar.

ICING A CAKE

Pour the icing on to the centre of the cake allowing it to spread, then smooth the surface with a wooden or metal spatula; for best results work quickly.

INFUSION

see also: creams and custards, essence, tea, vanilla

An infusion is obtained by steeping an aromatic substance in boiling liquid long enough for the liquid to absorb the flavour. Good examples include teas and tisanes, vanilla pods (beans) in milk, and whole spices in mulled wine.

IODINE

see also: mineral salts

A trace element, iodine is essential for the synthesis of thyroid hormones in the human body. Normal daily intake should be in the region of 150 micrograms, depending on how much there is in the water supply. It is present in good quantities in sea salt, marine fish and other seafood, edible seaweed, milk, bread, some vegetables and some bottled mineral waters.

IRON

see also: liver, pulses, spinach

A trace element essential for the formation of red blood cells, the daily requirements of iron for adults are between 10 and 18 mg, more for pregnant women. The principal sources of iron are meat, some offal (variety meats), fish, shellfish, eggs and some vegetables, notably spinach. The richest sources of iron in readily assimilable form are beef, lamb and pig liver and kidneys, which can contain 8–11 mg per 100 g/3½ oz, and red meat, which contains 5–8 mg per 100 g/3½ oz. Iron is added to bread and to some grains, and cereals such as rice and pasta, but research would seem to indicate that most of this passes unused through the body. Oxalic acid, present in many vegetables and fruits, especially spinach and rhubarb, can inhibit the body's absorption of iron. Vitamin C, however, promotes the absorption of iron into the body, hence the nutritional sense in finishing a meal with fruit.

IRRADIATION

A method of preserving food, irradiation bombards it with gamma rays to destroy all micro-organisms. It is mainly used to prevent the sprouting of potatoes, garlic, onions and shallots. The food industry claims that irradiation carries no danger, but opponents are worried about possible abuse by unscrupulous manufacturers selling off very old produce. Any irradiation must be mentioned on the product label.

J

see also:
compote
frangipane
marzipan
pastry

JALOUSIE

Named after the French term for Venetian blinds, *jalousies* are small rectangular puff pastries with characteristic slatted tops revealing the filling underneath. This filling may be frangipane cream, marzipan, apple compote, apricot *marmelade* or any one of a wide range of fruit jams. *Jalousies* are usually eaten warm rather than cold, and may be made in the form of one large pastry which is then sliced to serve.

JALOUSIE AUX POMMES

Apple jalousie tart

Serves 6
Preparation 40 minutes
Cooking 30 minutes

METRIC/IMPERIAL	*AMERICAN*
1 kg/2¼ lb apples	*2¼ lb apples*
juice of 1 lemon	*juice of 1 lemon*
1 sachet (7.5 g/1¾ tsp) of vanilla sugar	*1¾ tsp vanilla-flavored sugar*
1 tsp ground cinnamon	*1 tsp ground cinnamon*
450 g/1 lb puff pastry	*1 lb puff pastry*
1 egg, beaten	*1 egg, beaten*
5–6 tbsp thick apricot purée or jam	*about ⅓ cup thick apricot purée or jam*
45 g/1½ oz caster sugar	*¼ cup superfine sugar*
flour, for dusting	*flour, for dusting*

Preheat the oven to 200C/400F/gas 6.

Peel and quarter the apples and remove the core and seeds. Cut into slices, sprinkle with lemon juice and put them into a saucepan. Add the vanilla sugar, mix and cover. Cook gently over a low heat, without stirring, for about 20 minutes. Remove the saucepan lid and allow the excess liquid to evaporate, stirring over a very low heat for about 2 minutes, until the apples are reduced to a thick purée. Mix in the cinnamon and remove from the heat.

Flour a pastry board or work surface and roll out the puff pastry into a large rectangle about 3 mm/⅛ in thick. Cut it into 2 equal strips about 10 cm/4 in wide. Brush a baking sheet with water and place one of the puff pastry strips on it.

Brush some of the beaten egg all around the edges of the pastry strip. Spread the apple purée in a thick layer on the dry part of the pastry.

Fold the remaining pastry strip in half lengthwise. With a sharp knife, make slanting cuts from the folded side to within 1 cm/½ in of the other edge. Unfold and place it over the first one. Press the edges firmly to seal the pastry. Trim the edges and brush the top with the rest of the beaten egg. Bake for 30 minutes.

Meanwhile, heat the apricot purée with a little water. When the pastry is cooked, brush the top with the hot apricot purée. Sprinkle with sugar and leave to cool. Cut the strip across into 5 cm/2 in slices to serve.

see also:
fruit
glazing
pectin
sauce
sugar

JAMS, JELLIES AND MARMALADES

Confiture

Various preserves of fruit cooked with sugar are termed jams, jellies or marmalades. JAMS use the whole fruit – generally just one kind of fruit, JELLIES just the juice of the fruit, and MARMALADES are made from citrus fruit and often incorporate the peel. There are also BUTTERS made by cooking fruit pulp with sugar for a long time until very thick, and CONSERVES which are made from several fruits, often with spices and/or nuts. The term PRESERVE is also used specifically for whole or large pieces of fruit suspended in a thin or thick syrup.

Most fruit can be used, although only those with a high pectin content, such as redcurrants, white currants, mulberries, bilberries, quinces, apples and citrus fruit, will make a set jelly. Other fruit may be mixed with a pectin-rich fruit, or pectin extracted from apples or citrus fruit may simply be added to the mixture. It is usually best to use perfectly ripe – not overripe – fruit in season; although some fruit, like pears, peaches, apricots, strawberries and raspberries, make better jam if slightly underripe.

Sugar is the other essential element in making jams, jellies and so on because it acts as a preservative; concentrations of sugar in the region of 50–55% inhibit the growth of micro-organisms. Pure, refined sugar should be used. PRESERVING SUGAR, a white coarse sugar with added pectin to promote setting, is sold in Britain specifically for jam making. It reduces the cooking time, thus helping to retain more of the flavour of the fruit, and is particularly recommended for fruit that is very juicy and has a low pectin content, such as strawberries, cherries, melon, pears and peaches. It is a good idea to warm the sugar slightly before use, as it then dissolves more rapidly and speeds up the entire process.

It is worth bearing in mind that too much sugar in the preparation can cause it to crystallize. The ideal proportions when making jams are roughly equal weights of sugar and fruit; evaporation then tilts the balance of concentration. Jellies require slightly higher concentrations: 450 g/1 lb/2¼ cups to each 575 ml/1 pt/2½ cups of fruit juice. The concentration of sugar in the mixture can be gauged by monitoring the temperature at which it is boiling, which varies as the sugar gets more concentrated. A good rule of thumb is that jams should be boiled until they reach 113C/235F.

Lemon juice is also often added to preserves to counter excessive sweetness. Other flavourings are also common, especially spices such as cinnamon or vanilla, and liquors such as whisky, rum or Kirsch. Caramel is another common additive, mostly to give depth of colour to pale jams. This may also be achieved simply by incorporating a more deeply coloured fruit, such as blackberries.

For homemade preserves to be successful, everything used in the preparation must be scrupulously clean: have ready a long-handled wooden spoon, a ladle, a skimmer and a sugar thermometer. Use a clean stainless steel, aluminium or untinned copper preserving pan (preserving kettle), as iron may react with the fruit and tin will melt at the high temperatures. The pan must also have a heavy base, to prevent the fruit at the bottom from scorching, and its capacity should, ideally, be twice that of the total volume of fruit and sugar to be cooked in it. Sterilized jars must be carefully dried in a warm place without being wiped.

The cooking process takes place over high heat because the quicker it is done the more of the flavour of the fruit is captured. It is usually effected in two distinct stages: the first stage simply drives off excess moisture from the fruit and the liquid is skimmed at the end of it. When the steam dies down, the process enters the second stage, in which the fruit actually cooks. At this stage progress must be monitored carefully, either by using a thermometer or taking small samples of the mixture to test its consistency. It is ready when the mixture will coat the back of a spoon, or sets, in the case of a jelly.

Depending on the fruit, the mixture may be bottled hot, warm or cold. It is wise to fill the warmed dry jars as full as possible, allowing a little head space for possible expansion. Do not use over-large jars as, once in use, the contents may go off before the whole jar is finished.

The jars may be sealed with a circle of slightly moistened cellophane drawn tightly in place and held by a rubber band. More traditionally, a circle of parchment or greaseproof paper soaked in alcohol is placed on top of the mixture and this may be further protected by another paper over the top of the jar as above. Jellies, which must be fully set before they are sealed, and cold jams are best sealed with a thin layer of paraffin wax melted in a bain-marie. In the USA it is recommended that all preserves, excluding jellies, be processed in a bath of boiling water to ensure sterile seals on the jars, so all mixtures are hot when bottled, normally in 'canning jars' with screw tops. Immediately label the jars, indicating the fruits used and the bottling date.

As well as their obvious use at breakfast and tea time, fruit preserves are much used in cooking. They are a common filling and topping in cakes and pastries and are used to glaze tarts. They can also give any dessert, such as crêpes, an instant fruit flavour and make quick and easy sweet sauces. They are also very useful in sauces, stuffings and glazes for rich meats and oily fish.

In Europe there are two types of commercially produced jam: so-called 'extra jam', which contains at least 45% fruit, and ordinary jam which contains at least 35%. There are also reduced-sugar jams for diabetics and those on low-calorie diets. Any additives or colourings must be identified on the label by law. Jars of jam, both homemade and bought, should be stored in a cool, dry place, but are best kept refrigerated once opened.

Jam has a high energy value, about 100 calories per tablespoon for the average red fruit jam, and should thus be eaten in moderation.

MARMELADE D'ORANGES

Orange marmalade

Makes 5 jars of 450 g/1 lb each
Preparation 30 minutes
Cooking about 1¾ hours, over a period of 3 days

METRIC/IMPERIAL	AMERICAN
7 large thin-skinned oranges	*7 large thin-skinned oranges*
juice of 1 lemon	*juice of 1 lemon*
1.5 kg/3½ lb sugar	*3½ lb (7 cups) sugar*

If the oranges are not organically grown, and may have been sprayed or coated, scrub in hot soapy water, rinse well and pat dry. Cut the oranges in half and squeeze the juice. Strain out all the seeds and put them into a small muslin or cheesecloth bag.

Chop the orange peel in a food processor. Put the juice, bag of seeds and chopped peel into a bowl. Add 1.2 l/2¼ pt/5½ cups of cold water and leave to stand for 24 hours.

Pour the contents of the bowl into a large pan and boil for 40 minutes. Return the contents to the bowl and leave to stand again for 24 hours.

Add the sugar and lemon juice and leave to stand for 3 hours, then put back into the saucepan and boil for 1 hour. Remove the bag of seeds and ladle the marmalade into warm dry sterile jars. Seal and label.

CONFITURE DE FRAISES

Strawberry jam

Makes 4 jars of 450 g/1 lb each
Preparation 20 minutes, 24 hours ahead
Cooking about 30 minutes, plus cooling

METRIC/IMPERIAL	AMERICAN
1 kg/2¼ lb ripe strawberries	*2¼ lb (about 3½ pt) ripe strawberries*
1 kg/2¼ lb special preserving sugar with added pectin	*2¼ lb (5 cups) sugar*
	1 package (1¾ oz) powdered pectin
juice of 1 lemon	*½ cup water*
	juice of 1 lemon

Wash the strawberries quickly without allowing them to soak, drain and hull them. Put them in a bowl with the sugar and leave to macerate overnight.

Put the fruits and sugar into a preserving pan (preserving kettle). If using powdered pectin, dissolve it in the water and add to the pan. Add the lemon juice. Bring to the boil and boil for 5 minutes. Remove the strawberries with a slotted spoon. Boil the syrup for 5 minutes to reduce it, then return the strawberries to the pan. Repeat this operation twice.

Remove the pan from the heat and pour the jam into warm, dry, sterile jars. Seal and label.

CONFITURE D'ABRICOTS

Apricot jam

Makes 8 jars of 450 g/1 lb each
Preparation 15 minutes
Cooking about 30 minutes, plus cooling

METRIC/IMPERIAL	*AMERICAN*
2.5 kg/$5\frac{1}{2}$ lb apricots	*$5\frac{1}{2}$ lb apricots*
2.5 kg/$5\frac{1}{2}$ lb sugar	*$5\frac{1}{2}$ lb (12 cups) sugar*

Wash the apricots and pat them dry. Cut them in half and remove the stones. Put the fruit into a preserving pan (preserving kettle) or other large pan (1).

With a mallet, break a dozen of the stones open and remove the kernels. Blanch these for several minutes in a saucepan of boiling water. Drain them and remove the hulls, then split them in two and add them to the fruit in the preserving pan.

Pour 500 ml/16 fl oz/2 cups of water over the fruit and cook gently, stirring, until the apricots are very soft. Add the sugar and mix well. Continue to cook, stirring with a wooden spoon, until the sugar is dissolved (2).

Bring to the boil and cook for about 15 minutes. Check to see if the jam has reached the setting stage by putting 1 teaspoon of jam onto a saucer and placing it in the freezer. After a minute or so, when the jam is cold, press it lightly with a fingertip; it should pucker slightly. If it is still runny, cook it for a few minutes longer. Just before removing the jam from the heat, bring it to a full rolling boil and skim it (3).

Using a ladle, pour it immediately into warm dry sterile jars (4). Cover the surface of the jam with circles of parchment or greaseproof paper dipped in brandy or rum, then cover the jar with a piece of slightly moistened cellophane pulled tightly across and secured with a rubber band.

Alternatively, leave the jam to cool in the jars. Pour a 3 mm/$\frac{1}{8}$ in layer of melted paraffin wax over the surface of the jam once it is cold, then cover with cellophane and label the jars.

If the jam is to be stored for a time, it is a good idea to use special preserving (canning) jars with 2-piece screwband lids, and to process the filled jars in a boiling-water bath (100C/212F) for 5 minutes. This will ensure that all harmful micro-organisms are destroyed, and that a good vacuum is created in the sealed jar.

1

3

2

4

CONFITURE DE TOMATES

Tomato preserve

Makes 8–9 jars of 450 g/1 lb each
Preparation 10 minutes
Cooking about 1 hour

METRIC/IMPERIAL	AMERICAN
1 lemon	1 lemon
2 kg/4½ lb firm, not-too-ripe tomatoes	4½ lb firm, not-too-ripe tomatoes
2 kg/4½ lb sugar	4½ lb (10 cups) sugar
450 g/1 lb apples	1 lb apples

If the lemon is not organically grown, and may have been sprayed or coated, scrub it in hot soapy water, rinse well and pat dry.

Wash the tomatoes, pat them dry and quarter them. Put them into a preserving pan (preserving kettle) with the sugar.

Grate the lemon zest and squeeze the juice. Add both to the pan. Bring to a simmer and cook until the mixture begins to thicken (about 30 minutes).

Meanwhile, peel, core and finely slice the apples. Add them to the pan and continue cooking for a further 30 minutes. Put into warm, dry, sterile jars and seal and label as above.

JARDINIÈRE

see also: vegetables

Mixtures of lightly cooked vegetables, jardinières are served to accompany roast or sautéed meat, poultry, etc. They usually include carrots, turnips and green beans along with flageolet beans or small cauliflower florets. The vegetables are cut into uniform chunks and cooked separately. They are then lightly mixed together, often with added fresh garden peas, and dressed with a little butter and/or cream or good concentrated stock.

JARDINIÈRE DE LÉGUMES

Mixed vegetables

Serves 4
Preparation 35 minutes
Cooking about 10 minutes

METRIC/IMPERIAL	AMERICAN
2 carrots	2 carrots
2 turnips	2 turnips
225 g/½ lb French beans, trimmed and cut in half	½ lb green beans, trimmed and cut in half
800 g/1¾ lb fresh green peas, shelled	1¾ lb fresh green peas, shelled
30 g/1 oz butter	2 tbsp butter
100 ml/3½ fl oz whipping cream	½ cup whipping cream
salt and pepper	salt and pepper
chopped chervil, to garnish	chopped chervil, to garnish

Peel the carrots and turnips and cut them across into rounds about 6 mm/¼ in thick, then cut these into small sticks.

Cook the beans and peas in separate saucepans of boiling salted water for 7–8 minutes. Steam the carrots and turnips separately for the same length of time.

Drain all the vegetables and combine them in one saucepan with the butter. Toss and then add the cream. Reheat gently, mixing well. Season with salt and pepper.

Put the vegetables into a warmed serving dish, sprinkle with chervil and serve.

Variations: the peas may be replaced by flageolets or asparagus tips in season.

JELLY OR GELATIN DESSERT

Gelée d'entremets

see also: aspic gelatine jams, etc mousse

This cold dessert is made of fruit juice, wine or liqueur combined with sugar and gelatine or other thickening agents. It is then poured into a decorative mould and chilled until set. Normally turned out of the mould for serving, it may be accompanied by fresh fruit, ice cream or a fruit coulis.

GELÉE AU SAUTERNES

Sauternes jelly

Serves 4
Preparation 2 minutes
Cooking about 12 minutes, standing 5 hours

METRIC/IMPERIAL	AMERICAN
500 ml/16 fl oz Sauternes	2 cups Sauternes
45 g/1½ oz caster sugar	¼ cup superfine sugar
30 g/1 oz arrowroot	¼ cup arrowroot

Pour the Sauternes into a saucepan and dissolve the sugar in it. Mix the arrowroot to a smooth paste with a little water.

Heat the Sauternes and sugar. When it comes to the boil, add the arrowroot paste. Continue to stir over low heat for 10 minutes.

When the mixture becomes clear, remove from the heat. Dip a glass serving bowl in very cold water but do not dry it. Pour the contents of the saucepan into it.

Place in the coldest part of the refrigerator for at least 5 hours. When it is completely set, serve accompanied by macaroons.

Variations: other possible flavourings include 500 ml/16 fl oz/2 cups of very strong coffee mixed with 1 tablespoon of cocoa powder and 1 tablespoon of chocolate or coffee liqueur.

JERUSALEM ARTICHOKE

Topinambour

see also: artichoke vegetables

A vegetable originating in North America, Jerusalem artichokes are cultivated for their firm edible tubers which have a nutty flavour slightly reminiscent of the artichoke itself, although the two are not related. The knobbly tubers are difficult to peel, so may be cooked unpeeled and the skin rubbed off afterwards.

Jerusalem artichokes may be eaten raw, but they are more usually boiled, steamed, roasted or cooked *en papillote*. They are most commonly used in salads and purées, or served in a cream sauce sprinkled with parsley. The French parboil them in seasoned milk before deep frying. The flavour of the Jerusalem artichoke marries particularly well with that of pork.

Jerusalem artichokes are rich in phosphorus and potassium and 100 g/3½ oz contains 80 calories.

SALADE DE TOPINAMBOURS

Jerusalem artichoke salad

Serves 4
Preparation 10 minutes
Cooking 30 minutes, plus cooling

METRIC/IMPERIAL	AMERICAN
800 g/1¾ lb small new Jerusalem artichokes	1¾ lb small young Jerusalem artichokes
5 tbsp sunflower oil	5 tbsp sunflower oil
2 tbsp white wine vinegar	2 tbsp white wine vinegar
3 shallots, finely chopped	3 shallots, finely chopped
3 tbsp finely chopped flat-leaved parsley	3 tbsp finely chopped flat-leaf parsley
salt and pepper	salt and pepper

Boil the Jerusalem artichokes in lightly salted water for 30 minutes. Drain them and allow them to cool.

Make a vinaigrette with the oil and vinegar, adding salt and pepper to taste.

Peel the cooled Jerusalem artichokes and cut them into uniform pieces. Put them into a salad

bowl with the shallots. Pour the vinaigrette dressing over and stir.

Add the chopped parsley. Stir again and serve immediately.

Variations: chopped ham, black olives or anchovy fillets may be added to this salad.

see also:
brill
fish
sole

JOHN DORY

Saint-Pierre

A marine fish found along rocky coasts all year round, mostly in the Mediterranean and around the Bay of Biscay, the John Dory is considered to be one of the tastiest of fish. A related species is found off the Newfoundland coast, but it is not fished in any great quantity so the fish remains a restaurant rarity in North America.

The thin grey or yellowish fish, up to about 65 cm/26 in long, has characteristic dark 'thumb prints' on either side. However, a very large part of the fish is taken up by its enormous and fierce-looking jaw, so the resulting wastage is significant. It is usually cooked as fillets, although the trimmings make excellent stock, and can be prepared like brill or sole. The fillets are best plainly poached, fried or baked, but care should be taken not to over-cook them as the flesh dries out easily. Cream and cheese sauces are also popular accompaniments.

Plainly cooked John Dory is delicious and low in fat; 100 g/3½ oz contains only 70 calories.

FILETS DE SAINT-PIERRE À LA VAPEUR

Steamed John Dory fillets

Serves 4
Preparation 20 minutes, marinating 2 hours
Cooking about 10 minutes

METRIC/IMPERIAL	AMERICAN
2 lemons	2 lemons
2 tbsp olive oil	2 tbsp olive oil
300 g/10 oz mange-tout peas, trimmed	10 oz snow peas, trimmed
800 g/1¾ lb John Dory fillets	1¾ lb John Dory fillets
salt and pepper	salt and pepper
finely chopped chives	finely chopped chives

If the lemons are not organically grown and may have been sprayed or coated, scrub them in warm soapy water, rinse well and pat dry. Peel the zest and cut it into julienne strips. Squeeze the lemon juice.

Arrange the fish fillets in a shallow glass or ceramic dish and season with salt and pepper. Pour over the lemon juice, drizzle with half of the oil and leave to marinate for about 2 hours.

Heat the remaining oil in a small frying pan and add the strips of lemon zest. Cook them for 2 minutes and remove from the heat.

Bring an appropriate amount of water to the boil in a large saucepan or in the bottom compartment of a steamer. Drain the marinade from the fish and add to the water.

Put the fish fillets in one layer in a wide steaming basket and sprinkle the lemon zest over them. Cover tightly and steam. After 10 minutes, add the peas, either directly on top of the fish or in another stacking steaming basket and continue cooking for 5–6 minutes more, or until the fish is opaque and flakes easily.

Place the peas on a warmed serving platter, arrange the fish on top and serve immediately, garnished with chives.

FILETS DE SAINT-PIERRE À LA RHUBARBE

John Dory fillets with rhubarb

Serves 4
Preparation 20 minutes
Cooking about 25 minutes

METRIC/IMPERIAL	AMERICAN
30 g/1 oz butter	2 tbsp butter
1 tbsp oil	1 tbsp oil
1 John Dory, weighing about 1.5 kg/3½ lb, skinned and filleted	1 John Dory, weighing about 3½ lb, skinned and filleted
300 g/10 oz rhubarb, peeled and sliced as thinly as possible	10 oz rhubarb, peeled and sliced as thinly as possible (about 2½ cups)
pinch of caster sugar	pinch of superfine sugar
200 ml/7 fl oz crème fraîche or whipping cream	1 cup crème fraîche or whipping cream
salt and pepper	salt and pepper

Heat the butter in a frying pan with the oil and cook the John Dory fillets over a moderate heat for 4 minutes on each side. Season them with salt and pepper, remove them from the frying pan and keep them hot.

Put the rhubarb into the frying pan and let it cook very gently for 10 minutes in the cooking juices from the fish.

Add the sugar and cream and mix well. Turn the heat up slightly and cook, stirring, for 5 minutes until the sauce thickens.

Reheat the John Dory fillets in the sauce, adjust the seasoning and serve.

Serve with carrot purée or sautéed cucumbers to counteract the acidity of the rhubarb.
To drink: a full-bodied, dry white wine, such as one from the Côtes-de-Provence.

FILETS DE SAINT-PIERRE AUX COURGETTES

John Dory fillets with courgettes or zucchini

Serves 4
Preparation 20 minutes
Cooking about 10 minutes

METRIC/IMPERIAL	*AMERICAN*
1 lemon	*1 lemon*
800 g/1¾ lb John Dory fillets	*1¾ lb John Dory fillets*
125 g/4½ oz butter	*9 tbsp butter*
450 g/1 lb thin-skinned courgettes, sliced	*1 lb thin-skinned zucchini, sliced*
chopped chives, to garnish	*chopped chives, to garnish*
salt and pepper	*salt and pepper*

Preheat the oven to 250C/475F/gas 9. If the lemon is not organically grown and may have been sprayed or coated, scrub it thoroughly in hot soapy water, rinse well and pat dry. Grate the zest and then squeeze the juice.

Halve the fish fillets lengthwise and then cut these across into strips about 2 cm/¾ in wide.

Cut out four large squares of foil big enough to wrap a whole fillet generously and grease them well with some of the butter.

Arrange the courgette (zucchini) slices in a thick layer on one side of each of the foil squares, making sure that there is a border at the edges for sealing.

Arrange the fish fillet in pieces on top of the vegetables. Scatter the lemon zest over the fish and dribble over the lemon juice. Dot with the remaining butter and season well.

Wrap the parcels securely, folding over and pinching the edges to ensure an airtight seal. Bake for 8 or 9 minutes.

Serve in the parcel, opening it up a little, or transfer the contents of each to a warmed serving plate. Garnish with the chives.

JULIENNE

see also: crudités vegetables

Matchstick-thin strips of food, especially vegetables, are known as juliennes. Vegetable juliennes may consist of one vegetable alone or a mixture of, say, carrot, mushroom, sweet pepper and leek. They are cut into slices about 6 mm/¼ in thick, which are then cut into very thin strips from 2.5–10 cm/1–4 in long. Vegetable

To make julienne strips, cut the white part of the leeks in 10 cm/4 in sections, reserving the green for another use, and slice in half along the length.

Flatten out the pieces obtained, then stack them in layers of 4 or 5. Hold them down, keeping the fingers away from the knife blade, and cut into thin slivers.

Filets de Saint-Pierre aux courgettes (John Dory fillets with courgettes or zucchini)

juliennes may be served raw as a crudité or briefly cooked in butter to be used as a garnish for soups.

Pickled tongue, ham, cooked chicken breast and lemon zest are all commonly cut into julienne strips to garnish various dishes.

see also:
court-bouillon
game
marinade
stock

JUNIPER BERRIES

Genièvre

The dried, mature berries of the juniper tree are blackish in colour and have a pungent, resinous flavour often used for seasoning marinades and stocks. Whole or crushed juniper berries are popular in the cooking of northern and Central Europe, especially with sauerkraut and pork and game dishes.

They are also used for flavouring a number of alcoholic beverages, including gin.

Juniper berries aid the digestion and have a diuretic effect.

POMMES DE TERRE AU GENIÈVRE

Potato salad with juniper berries

Serves 4
Preparation 15 minutes
Cooking 25 minutes, plus cooling

METRIC/IMPERIAL	AMERICAN
800 g/1¾ lb potatoes, all roughly the same size	1¾ lb potatoes, all roughly the same size
5 tbsp sunflower oil	5 tbsp sunflower oil
juice of 1 lemon	juice of 1 lemon
1 garlic clove, very finely chopped	1 garlic clove, minced
2 shallots, very finely chopped	2 shallots, very finely chopped
12 juniper berries, crushed	12 juniper berries, crushed
salt and freshly ground black pepper	salt and freshly ground black pepper

Put the potatoes, unpeeled, in a saucepan of salted water. Bring to the boil and cook for about 25 minutes.

In a bowl, combine the oil, lemon juice, garlic, shallots and juniper berries. Whisk for 3 minutes to emulsify. Season with salt and pepper.

Drain the potatoes and peel them as soon as they are cool enough to handle. Slice them in rounds and pour the sauce over them. Mix carefully and season with pepper.

Serve to accompany smoked charcuterie, pickled herrings or cold meat.

JUS DE VIANDE

see Gravy

K

see also:
barbecuing
grilling
lamb
marinade

KEBAB

Brochette

Skewers upon which have been threaded pieces of food cut into uniform pieces are termed kebabs. The original Turkish kebabs were made simply of meat. However, a wide variety of food suits this treatment, from fish to fruit, and many kebabs are mixtures of meats and several different kinds of vegetables.

Kebabs may be grilled (broiled) or barbecued over hot coals. For good results it is wisest to select foods that require more or less the same cooking time and cut them into pieces of equal size. Because of the brief intense cooking, meat and poultry is best marinated beforehand in herb-flavoured oil. The kebabs are often also basted with the marinade during cooking and they must be turned regularly to ensure even cooking. It is wise to use special long skewers which are flattened slightly along their length to ensure that the pieces of food do not swivel around as the kebabs are turned.

Some suggestions for kebab ingredients include: turkey breast meat, strips of thickly cut bacon, slices of banana and mushrooms; chicken livers, lamb kidneys, tomatoes and sweet peppers; cooked ham, pineapple chunks and cubes of cheese; cooked sausage, artichoke hearts, small green tomatoes and large olives; medallions of pork, yellow sweet pepper, lemon slices and button mushrooms; shelled seafood, raw ham, pineapple slices and gherkins (pickled cucumbers).

Kebabs may be served still on the skewers, or slipped off on to a bed of rice. Fresh green or mixed salads with sharp herb dressings make the best accompaniments to most kebabs.

BROCHETTES DE POULET AUX FOIES DE VOLAILLE

Chicken breast and chicken liver kebabs

Serves 6
Preparation 10 minutes, marinating 30 minutes
Cooking 10–12 minutes

METRIC/IMPERIAL	AMERICAN
6 tbsp olive oil	6 tbsp olive oil
2 garlic cloves, chopped	2 garlic cloves, chopped
2 tbsp chopped mixed thyme, rosemary and tarragon	2 tbsp chopped mixed thyme, rosemary and tarragon
400 g/14 oz skinned and boned chicken breasts, cut into 3 cm/$1\frac{1}{4}$ in cubes	14 oz skinned and boned chicken breast, cut into $1\frac{1}{4}$ in cubes
550 g/$1\frac{1}{4}$ lb chicken livers, trimmed and halved	$1\frac{1}{4}$ lb chicken livers, trimmed and halved
24 cherry tomatoes	24 cherry tomatoes

Mix the oil, chopped garlic and herbs together in a deep dish. Add the meats and stir well, then leave them to marinate for 30 minutes.

If you plan to cook the kebabs on a barbecue, light the coals 1 hour beforehand. If cooking indoors, preheat a hot grill (broiler).

Drain the pieces of meat and reserve the marinade. Thread the meat on 12 skewers and place 1 cherry tomato at either end of each skewer.

Cook the kebabs for 10–12 minutes, turning them regularly for even cooking and basting the meat frequently with the marinade.

Note: if using a charcoal barbecue, place a sheet of oiled, heavy-duty foil between the meat and the coals.

CHICHE-KEBAB

Shish kebab

Serves 4
Preparation 25 minutes, marinating 12–24 hours
Cooking 10–12 minutes

METRIC/IMPERIAL	AMERICAN
1 kg/2¼ lb boneless leg or shoulder of lamb, cut into 2.5 cm/1 in cubes	2¼ lb boneless leg or shoulder of lamb, cut into 1 in cubes
2 green sweet peppers, quartered and deseeded	2 green sweet peppers, quartered and deseeded
8 baby onions	8 baby or pearl onions
4 cherry tomatoes	4 cherry tomatoes
8 tiny button mushrooms	8 tiny button mushrooms
1 lemon, quartered, to serve	1 lemon, quartered, to serve
FOR THE MARINADE:	FOR THE MARINADE:
6 tbsp olive oil	6 tbsp olive oil
4 tbsp sherry	4 tbsp sherry
2 garlic cloves, chopped	2 garlic cloves, chopped
2 shallots, chopped	2 shallots, chopped
2 tbsp chopped flat-leaved parsley	2 tbsp chopped flat-leaf parsley
1 tsp dried oregano	1 tsp dried oregano
salt and black pepper	salt and black pepper

First make the marinade: in a bowl mix all the ingredients with salt and pepper to taste.

Put the pieces of meat into the marinade, making sure that they are all well coated. Cover the bowl and store in the refrigerator for at least 12 hours (24 hours if possible), turning the meat several times.

If you plan to cook the kebabs on a barbecue, light the coals 1 hour beforehand. If cooking indoors, preheat a grill (broiler).

Drain the pieces of meat and reserve the marinade. Thread the pieces of lamb along with the various other ingredients on 8 skewers, alternating them to look most effective.

Brush the grill (broiler) rack or the barbecue with oil, then brush the kebabs with the marinade. Cook them for about 10–12 minutes, turning them frequently and basting them with the marinade at regular intervals.

Serve them piping hot, garnished with lemon quarters, accompanied by saffron rice and a green salad with a yogurt dressing.

To drink: a medium-bodied red wine, such as a Corbières.

BROCHETTES DE SCAMPI

Seafood kebabs

Serves 6
Preparation 15 minutes, marinating 30 minutes
Cooking 6–8 minutes

METRIC/IMPERIAL	AMERICAN
18 Dublin Bay prawns or scampi tails	18 Dublin Bay prawns or jumbo shrimp
200 ml/7 fl oz sesame oil	1 cup oriental sesame oil
200 ml/7 fl oz lemon juice	1 cup lemon juice
2 tbsp ground coriander	2 tbsp ground coriander
9 white button mushrooms, halved	9 white button mushrooms, halved
salt and pepper	salt and pepper

Put the seafood in a bowl with the oil, lemon juice, coriander and salt and pepper to taste and stir well. Leave for 10 minutes in a cool place, then drain and reserve the oil.

Preheat a grill (broiler).

Thread 3 prawns, scampi or shrimp lengthwise on each of 6 small wooden skewers. Place a mushroom half at the end of each skewer.

Grill (broil) the kebabs for 3–4 minutes on each side, brushing them during cooking with the herb-flavoured oil. Serve immediately.

KETCHUP, KATCHUP OR CATSUP

see also:
condiment
hamburger
mushroom
tomato
walnut

Sweet-and-sour condiments made with vinegar, sugar and spices are known as ketchups. Although the term almost always refers to TOMATO KETCHUP, made with a thick tomato purée, unless otherwise specified, MUSHROOM and WALNUT KETCHUPS are also common in Britain. The making of ketchups was originally a means of preserving seasonal gluts in order to enjoy those flavours at other times of the year. Ketchups are used to accompany fish, hamburgers and eggs and are particularly good with fried food, especially French fried potatoes. They also make useful flavourings in sauces and stews, and in such dishes as meat loaf and simple pâtés and terrines.

Tomato ketchup is made with varying levels of spice content, and some versions are fiercely flavoured with hot peppers.

Ketchup contains hidden calories, because of its high sugar content, and should therefore be used in moderation.

KIDNEY

Rognon

see also:
beef
lamb
offal
pork
veal

A type of red offal (variety meat) from young animals, VEAL KIDNEYS in particular have the most delicate flavour. LAMB KIDNEYS have a good strong flavour and are those favoured in mixed grills, as well as in the traditional English breakfast and in steak and kidney pie. BEEF KIDNEYS are tougher and require long slow cooking.

The transparent membrane that surrounds the kidneys should be removed, as should the tendons and the central core of fat. VEAL and LAMB KIDNEYS may be fried, sautéed or grilled on skewers and take only a few minutes to cook. Care should be taken when cooking kidneys: they should be still pink inside (a little blood should ooze if they are pierced). Otherwise, if they are over-cooked, they quickly become tough and rubbery.

Kidneys are low in calories (100 g/3½ oz contains only 100), but high in cholesterol content.

ROGNONS DE VEAU EN COCOTTE

Casseroled veal kidneys

Serves 6
Preparation 15 minutes
Cooking about 20 minutes, resting 10 minutes

METRIC/IMPERIAL	AMERICAN
45 g/1½ oz butter	3 tbsp butter
3 veal kidneys, trimmed and halved lengthwise	3 veal kidneys, trimmed and halved lengthwise
100 ml/3½ fl oz Calvados, Cognac, port or Madeira	½ cup Calvados, Cognac, port wine or Madeira
200 ml/7 fl oz crème fraîche or whipping cream	1 cup crème fraîche or whipping cream
1 tsp cornflour	1 tsp cornstarch
1 tsp strong mustard	1 tsp Dijon mustard
salt and pepper	salt and pepper

Melt the butter in a flameproof casserole without allowing it to brown. Add the kidneys and cook them gently for 6–8 minutes until golden, turning them several times.

Add the alcohol and remove the casserole from the heat. Let it stand for 10 minutes.

Remove the kidneys and put them in a warmed dish, covered with foil. Boil the sauce in the casserole to reduce it by half. Season with salt and pepper.

Mix the cream with the cornflour (cornstarch) and add it to the casserole. Stir over a moderate heat for 5 minutes.

Return the kidneys to the casserole and add the mustard. Heat very gently, still stirring, for 5 minutes. Adjust the seasoning, if necessary, and serve at once, accompanied by sautéed mushrooms.

see also:
baking sheet

KITCHEN UTENSILS

Batterie de cuisine

It is difficult to set specific guidelines about the basic utensils required to operate efficiently in the kitchen. Much depends on the sort of cooking done, how often and for how many people.

Different materials also suit different requirements: for example, copper pans look good and conduct heat well, but require a great deal of maintenance, and carbon steel knives can be given a good edge easily at home, but they must be dried thoroughly after washing or they will rust. The pros and cons must be examined before making any expensive investment.

The following are some suggestions for a basic *batterie de cuisine*, for a household starting from scratch. As time goes on it becomes apparent what other items are required. It is also quite possible to make do with less.

POTS AND PANS: 3 or 4 deep saucepans of assorted sizes, with tight-fitting lids and heat-resistant handles; small non-stick milk pan, also good for sauces; 1 cast-iron stewpot and 1 large casserole; 1 heavy-bottomed sauté pan, with lid, and 2 frying pans (one heavy-bottomed with high sides and the other non-stick); 2 or 3 roasting pans (rigid and high-sided); 2 or 3 gratin dishes of assorted sizes; and a soufflé dish.

BAKING EQUIPMENT: several mixing bowls of different sizes, at least one large and sturdy; 2 or 3 large deep-sided cake pans of assorted sizes, charlotte mould, sandwich (layer cake) pans, flan ring, springform pan with removable base; various assorted ramekins; bun or muffin pan; large baking sheet; large pie dish; loaf pan; sturdy long and heavy rolling pin; measuring cups, spoons and scales; wire rack; pastry brush.

CUTTING UTENSILS: small stainless steel paring knife, 2 or 3 general kitchen knives of assorted sizes; good sturdy pair of scissors; long bread knife; long and broad carving knife; large two-pronged carving fork; sharpening steel.

MISCELLANEOUS UTENSILS: large chopping board; several spatulas and wooden spoons; fine metal sieve and colander; grater; ladle and slotted spoon; steel balloon whisk.

KIWI FRUIT OR CHINESE GOOSEBERRY

Kiwi

see also:
fruit

This egg-shaped fruit originated in China but is now grown in New Zealand (hence the names), Israel and North America. It has a grey-green downy skin and bright green, slightly acidic perfumed flesh with edible black seeds. Perfectly ripe fruit are eaten raw for dessert, incorporated in fruit salads and made into tarts, sauces and sorbets. They may also be used as a garnish for savoury dishes, such as pork chops and roast quail.

The decorative speckled appearance of the kiwi fruit when peeled and thinly sliced has recently earned it wide, if perhaps boring, popularity and it has become something of a garnishing cliché.

Kiwis have a high vitamin C content and contain only 53 calories per 100 g/3½ oz.

MÉDAILLONS DE PORC AUX KIWIS

Medallions of pork with kiwi fruit

Serves 4
Preparation 15 minutes
Cooking about 20 minutes

METRIC/IMPERIAL	AMERICAN
4 slices of pork fillet, each weighing about 140 g/5 oz	4 slices of pork tenderloin, each weighing about 5 oz
5 kiwi fruit	5 kiwi fruit
30 g/1 oz butter	2 tbsp butter
3 shallots, chopped	3 shallots, chopped
100 ml/3½ fl oz whipping cream	½ cup whipping cream
salt and freshly ground black pepper	salt and freshly ground black pepper

Season the slices of pork with salt and pepper. Peel the kiwi fruit and slice one of them into thick rounds. Cut the others into dice.

Melt 15 g/½ oz/1 tbsp of the butter in a small saucepan and add the shallots. Cook them gently for 3 minutes, then add the diced kiwi fruit and simmer for 15 minutes.

Melt the rest of the butter in a frying pan and fry the slices of pork over a high heat for 8 minutes on each side.

Add the cream to the kiwi fruit compote, stir for 2 minutes, then blend it until smooth in a food processor.

Drain the medallions of pork, arrange them on a warmed serving dish and coat them with the kiwi fruit sauce. Garnish with the slices of raw kiwi fruit, season with some freshly ground black pepper and serve.

KNEADING

see also:
bread
brioche
pasta
pastry
pizza
yeast

The term used for working a mixture containing flour, usually with the hands, in order to obtain a smooth, soft and more elastic dough by 'stretching' the gluten in the flour. This operation of pressing and stretching is especially necessary when making bread, pizza, yeast or brioche doughs. Air, butter and other ingredients may also be incorporated into the dough by this process.

KOSHER OR KASHER

A word describing the foodstuffs recognized as suitable for human consumption according to the Jewish religion. The Jewish dietary laws (the *kashruth*) prohibit the consumption of blood and state that 'the calf shall not be cooked in the milk of its mother' thus enforcing a strict separation of meat and dairy products; orthodox households have two sets of kitchen equipment to be absolutely rigorous. Animals must be slaughtered according to strict regulations in order to remove all the blood. A wide variety of meats are also forbidden, including pork, game, shellfish and eels.

Kosher butchers may be found in many major cities and certain food departments in supermarkets offer a wide range of products that are guaranteed kosher including jams, drinks, sugar, flour, cookies and biscuits, crackers, bread, condiments, etc.

KUGELHOPF OR KOUGLOF

see also:
brioche
cakes and gâteaux
yeast

A sweet brioche containing raisins or currants and cooked in a special high, round, fluted mould, the *kugelhopf* originated in Austria. It is always better when slightly stale, so is usually prepared the day before it is served. In Alsace, it is traditionally served as a special treat for Sunday breakfast.

KUGELHOPF AUX AMANDES

Kugelhopf with almonds

Serves 8–10
Preparation 50 minutes, standing about 3 hours
Cooking 45 minutes

METRIC/IMPERIAL	AMERICAN
25 g/$\frac{3}{4}$ oz fresh baker's yeast	*$\frac{3}{4}$ oz compressed fresh yeast*
400 ml/14 fl oz milk, warmed	*1$\frac{3}{4}$ cups milk, warmed*
1 kg/2$\frac{1}{4}$ lb flour	*8 cups flour*
2$\frac{1}{2}$ tsp salt	*2$\frac{1}{2}$ tsp salt*
3 eggs, beaten	*3 eggs, beaten*
300 g/10 oz butter, softened	*2$\frac{3}{4}$ sticks butter, softened*
150 g/5$\frac{1}{2}$ oz caster sugar	*$\frac{3}{4}$ cup superfine sugar*
150 g/5$\frac{1}{2}$ oz raisins	*1 cup raisins*
100 ml/3$\frac{1}{2}$ fl oz Kirsch	*$\frac{1}{2}$ cup Kirsch*
75 g/2$\frac{1}{2}$ oz flaked almonds	*$\frac{2}{3}$ cup slivered almonds*
icing sugar, to dust	*confectioners' sugar, to dust*

Crumble the yeast into a bowl, add half the warm milk and enough flour to obtain a smooth paste. Let stand in a warm place until it froths.

Put the rest of the flour into a large mixing bowl and add the salt, eggs and the rest of the warm milk. Mix well. Knead and stretch the dough vigorously for 15 minutes.

Add all but 55 g/2 oz/4 tbsp of the butter along with the sugar and the yeast mixture. Knead and stretch the dough again and put it back in the bowl. Cover the bowl with a damp cloth and let it stand in a warm place for 1 hour.

Meanwhile, put the raisins into a small bowl, pour the Kirsch over them and leave them to swell. When the dough has risen, knead it again, incorporating the raisins and Kirsch.

Grease a large *kugelhopf* mould with the remaining butter and sprinkle with the flaked (slivered) almonds. Shape the dough into a long sausage and then use this to line the mould: it should about half fill it. Let it stand for a further hour: it should by then have reached the top of the mould.

Bake in an oven preheated to 180C/350F/ gas 4 for 45 minutes. If the *kugelhopf* begins to brown too quickly, cover it with parchment or greaseproof paper. When it is cooked, remove it from the oven and let it cool. Turn it out of the mould and sprinkle it with a little icing (confectioners') sugar.

Serve with fresh butter for breakfast, at tea time soaked in Kirsch and decorated with chantilly cream, or as a dessert accompanied by a white Alsace wine.

KUMQUAT

see also:
citrus fruits
orange

Small citrus fruits of Chinese origin, kumquats resemble miniature oranges with very thin skin. They are now grown in Israel, Australia and North America, as well as the Far East. *Narumi* kumquats are round and sweet-tasting; the *nagami* variety are oval and more acidic. Available all year round, except at the height of summer, kumquats will keep for several days in the refrigerator. They are also sold canned in syrup. Crisp and juicy, kumquats may be eaten fresh and unpeeled, or used in fruit salads. They may also be made into jelly or marmalade and are a popular ingredient in cake making. Savoury stuffings for poultry also benefit from their unusual flavour and tartness.

KUMQUATS AU COGNAC

Kumquats in Cognac

Makes 2 jars of 500 ml/16 fl oz/2 cups each
Preparation 25 minutes
Cooking 5 minutes, 3 months ahead

METRIC/IMPERIAL	AMERICAN
225 g/½ lb kumquats	½ lb kumquats
150 g/5½ oz caster sugar	¾ cup superfine sugar
200 ml/7 fl oz Cognac	1 cup Cognac
100 ml/3½ fl oz Cointreau	½ cup Cointreau

Prick the kumquats deeply in several places with a long needle or skewer. Blanch the kumquats in boiling water for 5 minutes. Drain and dry them very carefully one at a time.

Divide them between 2 glass preserving (canning) jars. Sprinkle half the sugar into each jar. Mix the Cognac and Cointreau and pour the alcohol over the fruit. Stir the contents of each jar carefully with a long-handled spoon. Seal.

Allow the fruit to macerate for 3 months before eating, either as a dessert in the same way as cherries preserved in brandy, or added to ice cream sundaes or fruit salads.

Kugelhopf aux amandes (Kugelhopf with almonds)

L

see also:
brain
caper
couscous
curry powder
kebab
mint
noisette
offal
pilaf
ragoût
terrine

LAMB

Agneau

The term lamb is used to describe the meat of sheep under a year old.

MILK-FED BABY LAMB or *agnelet* is killed before being weaned at about 3–5 weeks old, weighing 4–6 kg/9–13 lb. The meat is sold between February and Easter and is very tender and delicate. However, many regard it as lacking in flavour and it does not keep well.

So-called WHITE lamb, *agneau blanc* or *laiton*, aged 2 to 4 months, is fed mainly on cow's milk and has pale, firm meat and white fat which become very tender when cooked. Baby lamb raised indoors during the cold season and slaughtered before it is 10 weeks old is called HOTHOUSE LAMB in the USA.

GREY, GRASS-FED, GRAZING LAMB or *agneau gris*, which can be up to a year old, has grazed on meadow grass, which gives the meat its characteristic flavour and colour. It is also fattier, which contributes greatly to the taste. The ideal combination of flavour and tenderness is said to come from such lambs, aged about 3–4 months and weighing about 10 kg/22 lb. Genuine SPRING LAMB is slaughtered between early March and the end of October. Lambs grazed on salt marshes, such as the *pré-salé* of France's Atlantic coast, are prized for their fine flavour.

The flesh of good quality lamb is a good shade of pink, darkening with age, and is firm to the

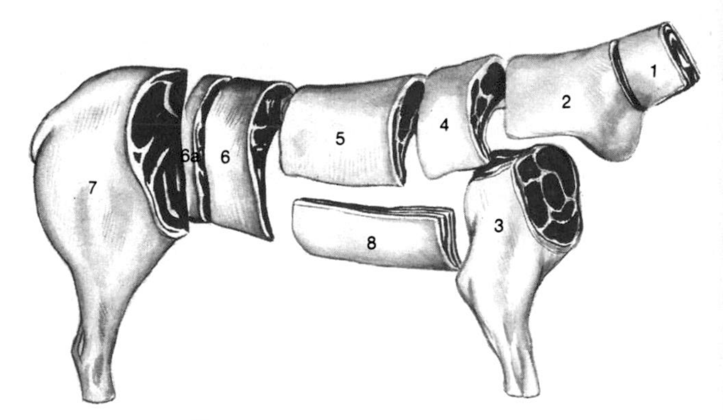

BRITISH CUTS OF LAMB:
1 scrag end of neck, 2 middle neck, 3 shoulder, 4 best end of neck, 5 loin, 6 chump, 6a chump chop, 7 leg, 8 breast

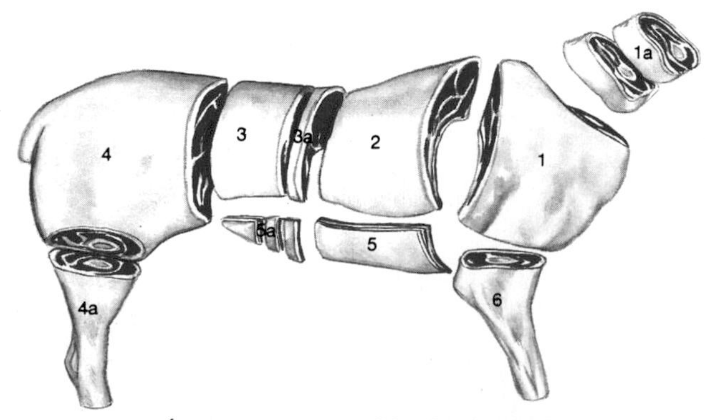

AMERICAN CUTS OF LAMB:
1 shoulder, 1a neck slice, 2 rib, 3 loin, 3a loin chop, 4 leg, 4a hind shank, 5 breast, 5a riblets, 6 fore shank

touch, with a close grain and not too much fat. Avoid meat which looks grey, dry or crumbly.

Leg or *gigot*, best end of neck, which is also known as rack or *carré*, and saddle, which consists of two joined loins, are the most sought-after cuts. Shoulder, breast, chump (sirloin) and middle neck and scrag end (shoulder arm chops and neck) of lamb are tasty and less expensive.

Allow about 300 g/10 oz of lamb on the bone per person or 200 g/7 oz of boneless lamb. Large cuts are normally roasted at 190C/375F/gas 5 for 20 minutes per 450 g/1 lb to give slightly pink lamb, ie cooked to an internal temperature of 54–60C/130–140F, or 25 minutes for well-done meat. Boned loin and breast are often stuffed with kidneys or slightly sweet dried-fruit mixtures. Legs and racks are traditionally cooked plain or flavoured with garlic and rosemary, thyme or savory, either inserted into incisions in the meat or brushed on the surface. Chops and cutlets are best grilled (broiled), barbecued or fried.

Lamb also tastes good flavoured with a little powdered ginger or smeared with mustard. Studding the meat with garlic and coating it with ground cumin gives a rich Middle Eastern flavour, particularly suitable when barbecuing.

A traditional accompaniment for lamb is mint sauce or jelly, but it is equally good served with redcurrant, cranberry or rowan jelly.

SELLE D'AGNEAU BONNE FEMME

Roast saddle of lamb

Serves 6
Preparation 10 minutes
Cooking about 45 minutes

METRIC/IMPERIAL	AMERICAN
1 boneless saddle of lamb, weighing about 1.5 kg/3½ lb	*1 boned saddle of lamb, weighing about 3½ lb*
100 g/3½ oz butter	*1 stick butter*
bunch of parsley, finely chopped	*bunch of parsley, finely chopped*
1 kg/2¼ lb French beans, trimmed	*2¼ lb fine green beans, trimmed*
salt and pepper	*salt and pepper*

Ask the butcher to tie the boneless saddle into a neat shape with string but not to bard it. Preheat the oven to 250C/475F/gas 9.

Place the saddle of lamb on a rack in a roasting pan and put it in the oven. Roast until the saddle is well browned, turning it 3–4 times to ensure even colouring. Season it with salt and pepper.

When the meat is well coloured, lower the heat to 200C/400F/gas 6 and roast for 35–40 minutes longer. The exact cooking time depends on the degree of doneness required and the thickness of the saddle: the thicker it is the longer it will take. Push a skewer into it: if the juices run tinged with a little red then it is still pink, if they are clear it is well done. Or test for doneness using a meat thermometer.

While the meat roasts, soften half the butter and mix it with the parsley. Then chill it.

When the meat is cooked to taste, turn off the oven and let the meat rest for 8–10 minutes to allow the juices inside to be redistributed.

Meanwhile, cook the beans in boiling salted water until just tender. Drain and keep hot.

Deglaze the roasting pan with a little water. Whisk the remaining butter into the juices obtained and pour them into a warmed sauce boat. Carve the saddle of lamb and add the carving juices to the sauce boat.

Serve the lamb accompanied by the sauce and the green beans, tossed in the parsley butter.

To drink: a powerful, mature red wine, such as a Châteauneuf-du-Pape.

CÔTELETTES D'AGNEAU VERT-PRÉ

Lamb chops with parsley butter

Serves 4
Preparation 10 minutes, 1 hour ahead
Cooking about 10 minutes

METRIC/IMPERIAL	AMERICAN
100 g/3½ oz butter	*1 stick butter*
1 tbsp chopped parsley	*1 tbsp chopped parsley*
4 large lamb chops	*4 large lamb chops*
bunch of watercress, trimmed	*bunch of watercress, trimmed*
salt and freshly ground black pepper	*salt and freshly ground black pepper*

Work the butter in a bowl until it is soft, adding a pinch of salt, some pepper and the chopped parsley. Beat well until thoroughly blended, then chill, rolled in a cylinder inside a sheet of foil for easier handling.

Preheat a grill (or broiler), or heat a ridged cast-iron grill pan over a high heat, until very hot. Cook the lamb chops quickly on both sides to seal the meat, then reduce the heat to moderate and continue to cook the meat until done to taste, allowing a total of about 4 minutes per side. Turn the chops with tongs, taking care not to pierce the meat.

Season the chops and place them on a warmed serving dish. Put one quarter of the flavoured butter on top of each chop, surround with small sprigs of the watercress and serve at once, with gratin potatoes and grilled tomatoes.

To drink: a medium-bodied red wine, such as a Saint-Emilion.

Variations: a wide variety of flavoured butters work well with lamb; try garlic, shallot, mustard, fresh mint, thyme or rosemary. Lamb chops or cutlets may also benefit from about 1 hour's marinating in a little seasoned oil, flavoured with mustard or fresh or dried herbs. Brush the lamb with the flavoured oil before and during cooking.

CARRÉ D'AGNEAU À L'AIL

Rack of lamb with garlic

Serves 6
Preparation 5 minutes
Cooking about 30 minutes

METRIC/IMPERIAL	AMERICAN
1 rack of lamb with 12 chops, or 2 best ends of neck with 6 chops each, trimmed and chined	1 rack of lamb with 12 chops, or 2 best ends of neck with 6 chops each, trimmed and chined
10 garlic cloves, halved and green core removed	10 garlic cloves, halved and green core removed
300 ml/½ pt crème fraîche or whipping cream	1¼ cups crème fraîche or whipping cream
salt and pepper	salt and pepper

Preheat the oven to its hottest possible setting. Place the lamb fat side down on a wire rack in a roasting pan and put in the oven.

After about 10 minutes, when the bones begin to brown, turn the meat over and season it with salt and pepper. Continue to cook for about 15–20 minutes, or until the meat is well browned all over. Then switch off the oven and leave the meat in it with the door closed for 5–7 minutes. The meat should be cooked rare: leave in the switched-off oven for longer if well done lamb is required.

While the lamb is cooking, put the garlic in a small pan with the cream, salt and pepper to taste and 150 ml/¼ pt/⅔ cup of water. Bring just to the boil, then reduce the heat and simmer for 15–20 minutes. Purée in a blender.

When the rack is cooked, place it on a warmed serving plate and surround it with the accompanying vegetables or separate the 12 chops and put 2 on each of 6 warmed individual plates. Serve the garlic cream in a sauce boat.

To drink: a mature red wine, such as a Pauillac.

Variation: instead of serving with the garlic cream sauce, before cooking spread the rack with a mixture of 1½ tablespoons Dijon mustard, 3 tablespoons each of olive oil, fine fresh breadcrumbs and chopped parsley, and 3 finely chopped garlic cloves. Pour 30 g/1 oz/2 tbsp of melted butter over the coated rack just before putting it in the oven preheated to 190C/375F/gas 5 and cook for 40 minutes to 1 hour, depending on the degree of doneness required. Add a little wine or meat stock to the cooking juices to make a sauce.

Carré d'agneau à l'ail (Rack of lamb with garlic)

GIGOT D'AGNEAU AUX FLAGEOLETS

Leg of lamb with flageolet beans

Serves 6–8
Preparation 15 minutes, standing 1 hour
Cooking about 1–1½ hours

METRIC/IMPERIAL	AMERICAN
800 g/1¾ lb dried flageolet beans	4 cups dried flageolet or lima beans
4 garlic cloves	4 garlic cloves
1 leg of lamb, weighing about 2 kg/4½ lb	1 leg of lamb, weighing about 4½ lb
2 tbsp groundnut oil	2 tbsp peanut oil
2 onions, thinly sliced	2 onions, thinly sliced
55 g/2 oz butter	4 tbsp butter
sprig of fresh thyme	sprig of fresh thyme
5–6 ripe tomatoes, peeled and coarsely chopped	5–6 ripe tomatoes, peeled and coarsely chopped
salt and pepper	salt and pepper

Put the beans into a bowl, cover them with boiling water and leave to soak for 1 hour.

Drain the beans and put them in a saucepan, cover with fresh cold water, bring slowly to the boil and simmer gently for 1–1½ hours, until just tender. Skim at the beginning of cooking and only add salt halfway through.

While the beans are cooking, roast the lamb: preheat the oven to its highest setting. Cut 2 of the garlic cloves into slivers and chop the others. Make incisions in the meat with a sharp knife and insert a sliver of garlic into each. Lightly brush the meat with the oil, season it and put it on a rack in a roasting pan, fat side up.

Seal the meat for 15 minutes, until well browned all over. Lower the heat to 190C/375F/gas 5 and pour 100 ml/3½ fl oz/½ cup of water into the pan. Turn the meat and roast for 20–25 minutes longer.

Meanwhile, in a flameproof casserole over a moderate heat, cook the onions in half of the butter until translucent, then add the chopped garlic, thyme and tomatoes. Simmer gently for 15 minutes.

Judge when the meat is cooked by putting a skewer into it as far as the bone: it should come out very hot at its tip. Switch off the oven, turn the meat over and let it rest for 10 minutes.

Drain the cooked beans thoroughly and add them to the casserole. Mix well and leave to simmer until ready to serve, then dot with the remaining butter.

Pour the juices from the roasting pan into a sauce boat. Carve the meat and add the carving juices to the sauce boat. Adjust the seasoning and whisk well. Serve the meat on very hot plates.

CARVING A LEG OF LAMB

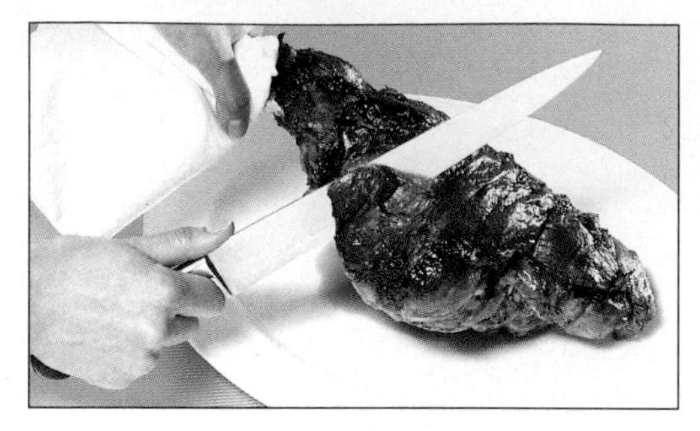

Hold the roast at an angle with the most rounded part up, protecting your hand with a cloth.

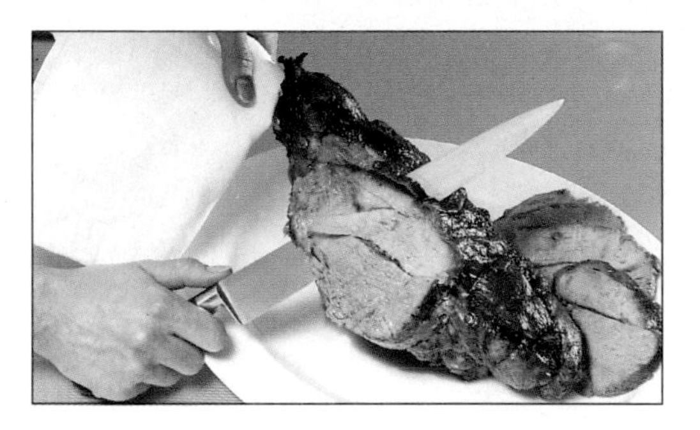

Carve thin slices from this part of the leg until most of the meat is removed.

Turn the roast over and carve off the remainder of the meat.

POITRINE D'AGNEAU BERRICHONNE

Lamb breast stuffed with chestnuts

Serves 6
Preparation 20 minutes
Cooking about 1¼ hours

METRIC/IMPERIAL	AMERICAN
115 g/¼ lb lean bacon, cut into very small strips	¼ lb lean bacon, cut into very small strips
225 g/½ lb minced beef	½ lb ground beef
1 onion, finely chopped	1 onion, finely chopped
3 tbsp finely chopped parsley	3 tbsp finely chopped parsley
55 g/2 oz butter	4 tbsp butter
300 g/10 oz canned unsweetened chestnuts, drained and coarsely crumbled	10 oz canned unsweetened chestnuts, drained and coarsely crumbled
1 kg/2¼ lb boned breast of lamb, cut open for stuffing	2¼ lb boned breast of lamb, cut open for stuffing
2 carrots, sliced	2 carrots, sliced
bouquet garni	bouquet garni
600 ml/1 pt lamb or beef stock	2½ cups lamb or beef stock
salt and pepper	salt and pepper

Heat the bacon in a large frying pan. When the fat starts to run, add the beef and cook over a moderate heat for 5 minutes, stirring occasionally to break up lumps.

Meanwhile, mix the onion with the chopped parsley. Melt one third of the butter in a saucepan and add the onion and parsley mixture. Stir and add the chestnuts. Season with salt and pepper. Cook gently for 3 minutes.

Drain excess fat from the meat mixture, then spread the mixture over the lamb breast. Spread the chestnut and onion mixture on top of that. Roll up the breast and tie it into a neat shape, folding the ends inwards.

Heat the remaining butter in a flameproof casserole and lightly brown the lamb breast all over. Add the carrots and bouquet garni. Pour the stock over, cover the casserole and cook gently for 1¼ hours.

When cooked, remove the string from the lamb and carve it into slices. Serve accompanied by the cooking juices in a sauce boat, and Brussels sprouts.

To drink: a full-bodied red wine, such as Chambertin.

LAMB'S LETTUCE OR CORN SALAD

Mâche

see also: lettuce salad

Small annual plants related to valerian, lamb's lettuce has rounded leaves with a distinctive nutty flavour which is popular in salads, particularly in France and Italy. Native to much of Europe, Britain and the Middle East, the plant is now grown widely in the USA. Wild varieties are harvested in September, but cultivated leaves are available in autumn and winter.

The rounder, more tender, juicy leaves, which the French call *ronde maraîchère*, are from plants forced in hothouses and harvested young. So-called NORTHERN GREEN OR ASSES' EARS are grown under glass to produce larger longer leaves which are less delicate. The ITALIAN variety is distinguished by its slightly yellowish, velvety leaves and milder flavour.

As the plants are often grown in sandy soil, it is usually necessary to separate the leaves before careful washing and drying.

The tender leaves are used in mixed salads and go especially well with sweet ingredients, such as apples, tomatoes and beetroot, as well as walnuts, hard-boiled eggs and potatoes. Tougher leaves may be cooked like spinach and are often used in stuffings for poultry.

Lamb's lettuce is rich in vitamin C, iron and calcium, with 24 calories per 100 g/3½ oz.

SALADE VIGNERONNE

Lamb's lettuce and bacon salad

Serves 4
Preparation 25 minutes
Cooking 2–3 minutes

METRIC/IMPERIAL	AMERICAN
200 g/7 oz lamb's lettuce	7 oz corn salad
140 g/5 oz dandelion leaves	5 oz dandelion leaves
200 g/7 oz cooked beetroot, peeled and cut into thin strips	7 oz cooked beets, peeled and cut into thin strips (1¼ cups)
2 tbsp walnut oil	2 tbsp walnut oil
200 g/7 oz thick-sliced, very lean, smoked streaky bacon, cut into thin strips	7 oz thick-sliced, very lean country-style bacon, cut into thin strips
1 tbsp red wine vinegar	1 tbsp red wine vinegar
pepper	pepper

Put the leaves and beetroot into a salad bowl.

Heat the oil in a frying pan and sauté the bacon until lightly browned. Pour the bacon and oil over the salad and season with pepper.

Put the vinegar into the frying pan and heat it, stirring, for 1 minute, then pour it over the salad. Toss and serve at once.

LANGOUSTE

see Spiny lobster

LANGOUSTINE OR DUBLIN BAY PRAWN

see also:
crayfish
lobster
nage
shrimp

A marine crustacean closely related to the lobster, but only about 10–25 cm/4–10 in long, the langoustine may be recognized by the prismatic shape of its pair of pale-tipped pincers. Langoustines are fished along the European Atlantic coasts and in the Mediterranean. Among the tastiest specimens are those fished in the Adriatic and known to the Italians as *scampi*, a term by which they have become known in Britain, although in the USA this normally applies to an Italian-style preparation of any large shrimp. The langoustine itself is unknown in North American waters, but it is imported from South America, particularly Chile, where it is called *langostino*.

Like most seafood, langoustines cannot live for long out of water as their flesh deteriorates quickly and they are usually sold alive only in fishing ports; look for bright pink shells and bright black eyes. Most of the catch is usually sold pre-cooked and displayed on a bed of crushed ice, or frozen. In Britain a large part of those frozen are sold only for their breaded tails to supply the catering trade's insatiable demand for *scampi*.

Allow 3–6 langoustines per person. They are best gently poached whole *à la nage* and served with a little butter or mayonnaise, but also suit recipes for crayfish and shrimp. Because of their size, they grill (broil) and barbecue well, but should be peeled first. They must never be overcooked as the flesh becomes very tough and the flavour is impaired. Langoustines are a classic ingredient in the traditional Spanish *paella* and substitute well for 'king' prawns or jumbo shrimp in oriental dishes.

Langoustine flesh contains only 90 calories per 100 g/3½ oz.

Langoustine or Dublin Bay prawn

Salade vigneronne (Lamb's lettuce and bacon salad)

LANGOUSTINES GRILLÉES AU BEURRE VERT

Langoustines in herb butter

Serves 4
Preparation 15 minutes, 30 minutes ahead
Cooking about 6 minutes

METRIC/IMPERIAL	*AMERICAN*
200 g/7 oz butter, cut into small pieces and softened at room temperature	*2 sticks butter, cut into small pieces and softened at room temperature*
12 large leaves of fresh basil, chopped	*12 large leaves of fresh basil, chopped*
2 tbsp snipped fresh tarragon	*2 tbsp snipped fresh tarragon*
2 lemons	*2 lemons*
24 langoustines, peeled and deveined	*24 langoustines or large shrimp, peeled and deveined*
corn oil	*corn oil*
salt and pepper	*salt and pepper*

Make a flavoured butter by blending the butter, herbs, juice of half a lemon and some salt and pepper in a food processor. Spoon into a serving dish and chill for at least 30 minutes.

Preheat a grill (broiler) or light a barbecue. Thread the langoustines on skewers, brush with oil and grill them for 3 minutes each side.

Serve the langoustines with the herb butter and the remaining lemons cut into wedges.

To drink: Muscadet or Rosé de Provence.

Variations: a classic way in which the Italians prepare langoustines is to marinate them first in seasoned oil and lemon juice with chopped shallots and garlic. Brushed with a little of the marinade, they are then grilled as above and served with lemon wedges dusted in a mixture of freshly grated Parmesan cheese and finely chopped parsley.

LARD

see also: bacon barding braising deep frying fats and oils frying larding pork

The term lard is given to pork fat used in cooking. The fat, normally from the belly or just under the skin of the back or around the kidneys, is usually rendered at low temperatures to purify it. Its high smoke point makes it a popular medium for deep frying and its creamy texture works well in baking and makes very fine pastry. Lard is the favoured cooking medium in many parts of rural France as well as parts of Britain, Scandinavia, Eastern Europe and the USA, and gives its distinctive flavour to traditional dishes as diverse as pork pies, goulash and sauerkraut.

LARDING

see also: barding lard pork roasting

The process of threading *lardons*, or strips of pork or bacon fat, into a piece of meat keeps it moist during cooking. This operation is best done using a specially designed larding needle, but a very sharp, long-bladed knife will suffice. The fat should be refrigerated until the last minute, as it is easier to handle when firm.

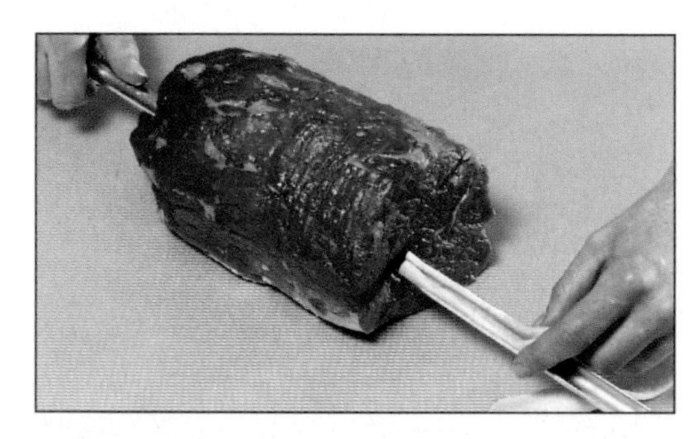

Pierce the roast with a larding needle and put long thin strips of barding fat in the trough.

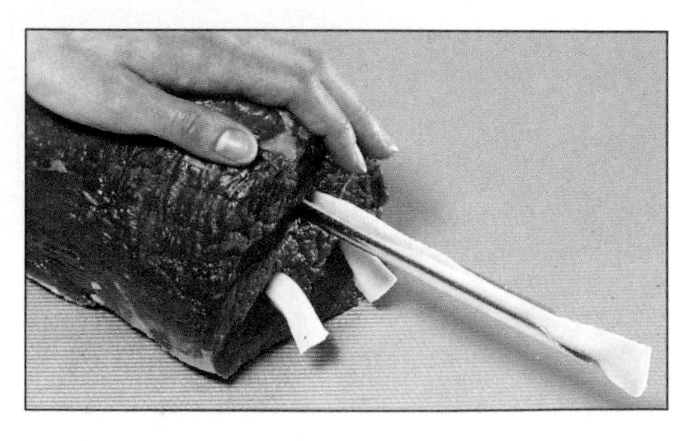

When the needle is pulled out the fat remains in the roast to baste it from the inside.

LASAGNE

see Pasta and noodles

LEAVENING

see also:
baking powder
bread
cakes and gâteaux
pastry
yeast

The process of lightening a dough by filling it with bubbles of gas is referred to as leavening. This gas expands during cooking, causing the bread or cake to rise, giving light results. In most cases, leavening is achieved by encouraging the mixture to ferment, by mixing in a piece of already risen dough or by adding yeast. Where more delicate flavours are involved, as with cakes, leavening may be effected by means of baking powders, beaten egg white or simple creaming techniques which beat air into the mixture just before cooking.

LEEK

Poireau

see also:
brunoise
court-bouillon
onion
quiche
soup

An herbaceous plant of the onion family, the leek consists of a white stem crowned by green leaves. The white and the first few inches of the green are usually consumed. Leeks have a delicate, sweet onion flavour and serve as a vegetable as well as being a popular flavouring and garnish. They are occasionally included in a bouquet garni and are an essential aromatic in most court-bouillons. The green leaf is also used to clarify stocks.

Leeks are sold virtually all year round, but the new baby leeks or *baguettes* in spring are considered to have a better flavour than the large winter leeks, which are primarily used for soups and stews. As the year progresses, the leeks tend to become thicker and have a higher proportion of coarser green leaves. Major centres of production include France, Holland, Belgium, Egypt and Turkey.

Leeks must be bought when very fresh: the white should be smooth and firm, and preferably still with the root attached, with foliage that feels crisp and is not limp or discoloured.

To prepare leeks, the root should be trimmed off and the green trimmed to the level of the tops of the outermost leaves. Larger, tougher specimens may also need to have the tough outer membrane peeled off. They must also be well washed as the leaves tend to harbour dirt and grit. To clean large leeks being kept whole, cut them across with a sharp knife from about one third of the way down the white stem to the tops of the leaves. Give the leek a quarter turn on its axis and then cut this way again. Fan the leek out under cold running water to flush out dirt, holding the leaves downwards so that the dirt washes away rather than being driven deeper in. If the leek is very soiled, lengthy soaking may be necessary.

Sometimes known as 'poor man's asparagus', leeks go well with beef, fish, smoked meats and poultry. Tougher specimens usually need to be blanched before any further cooking. Leeks may be baked *au gratin*, boiled or braised whole and served hot or cold, dressed in just a little butter, oil or vinaigrette as a first course. They are also popular in soups and tarts, and tender young leeks are used raw chopped in salads.

Leeks were popular with the ancient Romans who spread cultivation throughout Europe. For this reason they feature in the traditional dishes of many nations, from Scottish cock-a-leekie soup and French *vichyssoise* to the Belgian *tarte flamiche*, or cheese and leek quiche.

The leek has a low calorific value, only 42 calories per 100 g/3½ oz, but is rich in dietary fibre, vitamin C, calcium and iron. It has diuretic qualities and is thought to help purify the system.

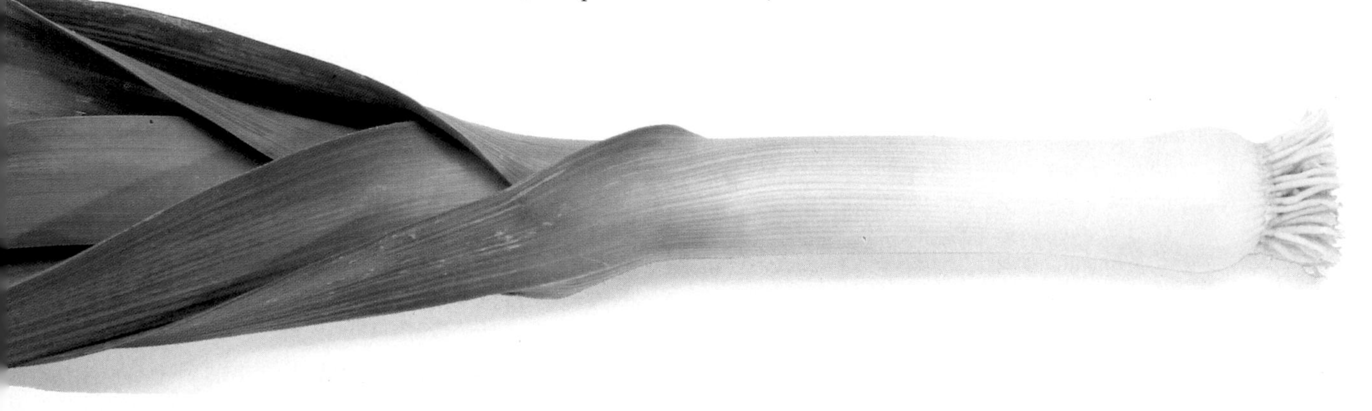

POIREAUX VINAIGRETTE

Leeks vinaigrette

Serves 4
Preparation 10 minutes
Cooking 10 minutes

METRIC/IMPERIAL	AMERICAN
800 g/1¾ lb baby leeks, trimmed	1¾ lb baby leeks, trimmed
8 tbsp corn oil	½ cup corn oil
4 tbsp white wine vinegar	¼ cup white wine vinegar
1 shallot, chopped	1 shallot, chopped
3 tbsp chopped chives	3 tbsp chopped chives
1 tsp strong mustard	1 tsp Dijon mustard
salt and pepper	salt and pepper

Tie the leeks in small bunches and blanch for about 10 minutes in lightly salted boiling water.

Meanwhile, mix the oil and vinegar and season with salt and pepper. Add the shallot, chives and a little mustard to taste.

Drain the leeks, refresh briefly under cold running water and then pat dry on paper towels.

Arrange them in a deep serving dish and pour the vinaigrette over them. Serve warm.

LOTTE AUX POIREAUX

Monkfish with leeks

Serves 4
Preparation 15 minutes
Cooking about 15 minutes

METRIC/IMPERIAL	AMERICAN
800 g/1¾ lb leeks, trimmed	1¾ lb leeks, trimmed
115 g/4 oz butter	8 tbsp butter
150 ml/¼ pt dry white wine	⅔ cup dry white wine
2 shallots, finely chopped	2 shallots, finely chopped
675 g/1½ lb monkfish tails, cut into about 20 small slices	1½ lb boneless monkfish, cut into about 20 small slices
1 tbsp tomato purée	1 tbsp tomato paste
salt and pepper	salt and pepper

Cook the leeks for 8 minutes in a saucepan of boiling salted water. Drain them thoroughly.

Melt 25 g/¾ oz/1½ tbsp of the butter in a sauté pan and add the leeks with 2 tablespoons of the wine. Cook gently for 5 minutes.

Meanwhile, put the shallots into a saucepan with the remaining white wine. Season with salt and pepper. Boil rapidly to reduce until almost all the wine has evaporated. At the same time, melt another 25 g/¾ oz/1½ tbsp of the butter in a frying pan and sauté the monkfish slices for 3–4 minutes on each side, turning them frequently. Set them to one side and keep warm.

Whisk the remaining butter in small pieces into the shallot and wine mixture. Add the tomato purée and adjust the seasoning.

Divide the leeks among 4 warmed plates, place 5 monkfish slices on top of each, and coat with the sauce. Serve at once.

To drink: a dry white wine, such as a Chablis.

LEGUME

see also: bean, carob, lentil, pea, peanut, pulses, soya, split pea, tamarind

Plants which produce seeds in pods are referred to as legumes. Among the most common are peas, beans and lentils. They are an important source of proteins in the diet of most of the developing world and of vegetarians. Many, such as soya beans and peanuts, also produce useful oils. Others, such as carob, fenugreek and tamarind, are very popular flavouring ingredients. The dried seeds of legumes are sometimes known as pulses.

LEMON

Citron

see also: acidulation, cakes and gâteaux, citrus fruit, fruit, jams, etc, lime, orange, zest

A citrus fruit which is thought to have originated in Southeast Asia, the yellow-skinned lemon is now grown all over the world, principally in the Mediterranean and the USA. Lemons, like other citrus fruits, are available all year round and there are several different varieties distinguished only by their size and shape, thickness of the skin and number of seeds. In general, rounder varieties have thinner skins and thus more juice for their weight. Lemons to be exported are picked while still slightly green and allowed to ripen off the tree. Some limes, particularly yellow-skinned varieties, can be confused with lemons, but the smaller green limes are most often available in Europe and North America.

A good lemon should feel heavy for its size, indicating it is full of juice, with close-grained peel and a strong fragrance. Avoid any which are tinged with green as they are not properly ripened. Unfortunately most lemons are nowadays given a chemical-impregnated wax coating to preserve them. If the zest is to be used, therefore, it is better to buy organically grown lemons or, if these are unobtainable, to scrub them thoroughly in hot soapy water and rinse them well. Lemons keep in the refrigerator for several weeks, drying out slowly as they age.

The juice of the lemon finds a great many uses in cooking. Its acidity prevents discoloration of certain fruits and vegetables after they have been peeled or cut; and it is the most common souring agent in Western cooking. A little added lemon juice will help stewing fruit to keep its shape, and rice and poached eggs to keep a good colour. Lemon juice is also used in marinades, court-bouillons and sauces and in place of vinegar in dressings for salads or raw vegetables. It is also used in the preparation of sorbets and various cold drinks, such as classic lemonade.

The grated zest, which is filled with a highly perfumed oil, is a potent flavouring popular in cake making and *pâtisserie* and which also adds greatly to many savoury items, such as stuffings and sauces. When zesting a lemon, take care not to go through to the bitter white pith beneath. Candied lemon peel is also used in baking and cake decorating.

As they are high in pectin, lemons also feature in the making of jams and marmalades, as well as other preserves, such as lemon curd and chutneys. Lemons are also one of the most common garnishes, in halves, quarters, slices or elaborately decorated, in dishes as diverse as fried fish and sweet crêpes.

The riper the lemon, the richer it is in vitamins A and C. It is low in calories, with only 30 per 100 g/$3\frac{1}{2}$ oz, and is held to be a valuable tonic and healthy food: dressing fried food with lemon juice makes it more digestible; using lemon juice in a vinaigrette in place of vinegar allows less oil to be used; and lemon juice is a useful condiment in salt-free diets.

CITRONS FARCIS

Stuffed lemons

Serves 6
Preparation 25 minutes, 1–2 hours ahead

METRIC/IMPERIAL	*AMERICAN*
30 black olives, stoned	*30 black olives, pitted*
6 large round lemons	*6 large round lemons*
1 can (300 g/10 oz) of tuna fish in brine, drained and flaked	*1 10-oz can tuna fish in water, drained and flaked*
4 hard-boiled eggs	*4 hard-boiled eggs*
4 tbsp chopped parsley	*$\frac{1}{4}$ cup chopped parsley*
6 tbsp mayonnaise	*6 tbsp mayonnaise*
1 garlic clove, chopped	*1 garlic clove, chopped*
salt and pepper	*salt and pepper*

Reserve 6 olives and coarsely chop the others.

Cut the stalk ends off the lemons and scoop out all the pulp without piercing the peel. Cut the lemon pulp into tiny dice and add them, plus any juice, to the tuna fish, mixing well.

Cut the hard-boiled eggs in half and remove the yolks. Add them to the tuna fish along with the chopped olives and parsley. The egg whites may be used for garnish or in a salad.

Mix the mayonnaise and garlic and then

blend this with the tuna fish and olive filling.

Adjust the seasoning. Fill the hollowed-out lemons with this mixture, first taking a slice off their bases so they will stand upright. Serve well chilled, garnished with the reserved olives.

LEMON CURD

Lemon curd

Makes three jars of 450 g/1 lb each
Preparation 15 minutes
Cooking about 40 minutes

METRIC/IMPERIAL	AMERICAN
6 large juicy lemons	6 large juicy lemons
8 eggs, beaten	8 eggs, beaten
400 g/14 oz unsalted butter, cut into tiny pieces	4 sticks unsalted butter, cut into tiny pieces
1 kg/2¼ lb caster sugar	5 cups superfine sugar

If the lemons are not organically grown and may have been sprayed or coated, scrub them in hot soapy water, rinse well and pat dry. Finely grate the zest and then squeeze their juice.

Pour the beaten eggs into a large bowl and put the bowl into a bain-marie over a low heat. Add the butter, lemon zest, juice and the sugar and heat, beating gently, until all the butter has melted and the sugar has dissolved.

Continue to cook the mixture in the bain-marie, stirring constantly, until it begins to thicken; this should take about 30 minutes.

Divide between 3 warmed, dry, sterilized jars. Seal the jars, label them and store them in a cool place, but use within 3 months.

Lemon curd makes a good tart, pie and cake filling and is delicious spread on crêpes.

LEMON BALM AND LEMON VERBENA

Citronnelle

see also: herbs

In France both lemon balm and lemon-scented verbena are referred to as *citronnelle*, because of their penetrating lemon aroma, and this has led to the same use of the term citronella in English. However, the flavour of verbena is too coarse to be used in all but the sweetest of dishes, such as fruit cups and salads, and then in moderation.

Whether fresh or dried, lemon balm goes well with fish, shellfish and white meats, and may also be used for flavouring stuffings and sauces and grilled meats. The leaves are also delicious in salads. Lemon balm is used to make the comforting tisane melissa and is the principal flavouring in chartreuse liqueur.

LEMON GRASS

Popular in the cooking of Southeast Asia, the pale green lower leaf stalks of lemon grass are now increasingly available in Western supermarkets, although they have been available dried and ground as SEREH POWDER in specialist shops for many years. The flavour of lemon grass is distinctively spicy, with a hint of ginger. It is usually used in conjunction with garlic, ginger and fresh coriander (cilantro) and goes particularly well with poultry and seafood.

LEMON SOLE

see also: dab fish sole

A dextral flatfish with an oval body and small head, the lemon sole is frequently confused with the dab. In American waters, larger specimens of the thicker and meatier winter flounder are also referred to by this name. Lemon sole has a fine flavour and softer flesh than the true sole. It is best plainly fried or grilled (broiled) with a little butter and lemon juice, although it may be used in most recipes for dab and sole. There are 83 calories in 100 g/3½ oz of lemon sole.

LENTIL

Lentille

see also: bean pulses

The lens-shaped dried seeds which grow in pairs in the flat pod of a plant originating in the Middle East, lentils are an ancient foodstuff and an important part of the diet in some poorer nations. There are two principal varieties, distinguished by size and shape: the smaller, flatter type is more common in the East and the larger, rounder type is usually cultivated in Europe, especially Turkey and Yugoslavia, and the United States.

Of the European lentils, the tiny green French

split red lentils
green Puy lentils
sprouted lentils
yellow lentils

lentille du Puy is generally regarded as having the best flavour. The YELLOW LENTIL or *lentille blonde* is grown in the north of France and is much less tender; the BROWN or GERMAN LENTIL requires lengthier cooking; and the SPLIT RED LENTIL or PERSIAN LENTIL, which comes mostly from India and the Middle East, is very tender and needs no soaking and only very brief cooking.

American lentils include the green to gold-brown CHILEAN LENTIL, which is the most widely grown in the USA, and the red-orange RED CHIEF which turns golden on cooking. Neither require soaking before cooking.

Lentils will keep for a very long time, but harden as they get older. For this reason, purchase them from a shop with a rapid turnover and use them within a year. Pick them over carefully to eliminate any pieces of gravel and then wash them well. Remove any that float as they may be mouldy or harbour parasites.

Conventional wisdom insists on soaking lentils in warm water to soften the skin and make cooking easier. However, this is quite unnecessary with the smaller varieties unless they are old. Treat lentils like dried white beans and cook them in soft or filtered water without added salt, otherwise the skin hardens. Cooking times can vary from as little as 20 minutes to 1½ hours, depending on type and age. Also remember that they absorb as much as 2½ times their own volume of water during cooking.

Lentils are commonly made into soups and purées, although the tastier types are also served as vegetable accompaniments, usually flavoured with garlic and pork fat or bacon. Lentils also work well in combination with many other flavouring ingredients, especially chestnuts, thyme, sage, bay, marjoram and lemon juice. They are a popular garnish for strongly flavoured poultry, such as duck and goose, and for sausages and pork, ham and bacon dishes in many European cuisines, especially in France, Germany, Italy and Spain.

Rich in protein and dietary fibre, lentils also provide iron, phosphorus and vitamin B: 100 g/3½ oz contains 330 calories. They may also be cooked without any added fat.

SALADE TIÈDE DE LENTILLES

Warm lentil salad

Serves 4
Preparation 10 minutes, soaking 1 hour
Cooking about 45 minutes

METRIC/IMPERIAL	AMERICAN
300 g/10 oz green lentils	*1½ cups green lentils*
15 g/½ oz butter	*1 tbsp butter*
2 onions, coarsely chopped	*2 onions, coarsely chopped*
3 garlic cloves, halved	*3 garlic cloves, halved*
sprig of fresh thyme	*sprig of fresh thyme*
bay leaf	*bay leaf*
1 bottle (750 ml/27 fl oz) dry white wine	*1 bottle (75 cl) dry white wine*
FOR THE VINAIGRETTE:	FOR THE VINAIGRETTE:
6 tbsp olive oil	*6 tbsp olive oil*
2 tbsp sherry vinegar	*2 tbsp sherry vinegar*
1 tbsp strong mustard	*1 tbsp Dijon mustard*
2 tbsp finely chopped chives	*2 tbsp finely chopped chives*
salt and pepper	*salt and pepper*

Pick over the lentils, rinse well and soak in warm water to cover for 1 hour, if necessary.

Melt the butter in a flameproof casserole over a moderate heat. Add the onions, garlic, thyme and bay leaf and stir for 2 minutes. Mix in the well-drained lentils, then pour on the wine and bring it to the boil. Lower the heat, cover and simmer for about 40 minutes or until tender.

Make a vinaigrette by whisking together all the ingredients with salt and pepper to taste.

Drain the cooked lentils and put them in a serving bowl, discarding the thyme and bay leaf. Pour over the vinaigrette while the lentils are still hot. Stir, leave to cool slightly, and serve garnished with slices of poached smoked sausage, smoked ham, strips of smoked salmon or fine slices of preserved duck (*confit de canard*).

see also:
chicory
Chinese cabbage
endive
radicchio
salad
spinach
vinaigrette

LETTUCE

Laitue

A member of the daisy family, lettuce has been a popular foodstuff since Roman times, when it was valued for the soothing effect of its milky sap – hence the name. Then, however, the tender green leaves were more commonly cooked, and the practice of dressing them raw in salads was introduced at the court of Louis XVI.

There are several principal types of lettuce. The ROUND OR BUTTERHEAD lettuce has large, soft leaves clustered loosely around a heart. The edges of the leaves are sometimes tinged with deep red. Among the varieties most prized for their delicate buttery taste and texture are BIBB and BOSTON.

The larger, denser, more compact CRISPHEAD lettuce has crisper leaves. Somewhat resembling a cabbage, it may be cut and shredded in the same way. The varieties most usually available are the pale ICEBERG and the larger, greener WEBB'S WONDERFUL.

Those plants where the leaves grow without a central heart are known as LOOSEHEAD OR LEAF LETTUCES and include the peppery OAKLEAF LETTUCE (*feuilles de chêne*), and the Italian LOLLO and red LOLLO ROSSO. Many varieties of loosehead tend to have a reddish tinge to the leaf which makes them very attractive.

COS OR ROMAINE lettuce has firm long leaves with a broad rib in the centre. The heart is elongated and relatively open and the leaves have a refreshing pungency.

Lettuces are cultivated in most parts of the world, often under glass, and different varieties come into season at different times of the year. However, those grown in the open in summer tend to have the best flavour.

Buy only the freshest of specimens with vigorous leaves and, where appropriate, dense hearts. The leaves of round or butterhead lettuces may be floppy, but they will still quickly betray lack of freshness. There should be no hint of brown to the leaves, nor should any cut part be discoloured or slimy.

Fresh lettuces will keep for 2–3 days in the vegetable compartment of the refrigerator,

red oak leaf

Bibb

cos or romaine

lollo rosso

iceberg

sealed in a plastic bag. To revive slightly tired lettuce, plunge in cold water and wrap in a damp cloth.

To prepare lettuce, tear off the tougher outside leaves and then rinse the outermost inner leaves carefully. The leaves of dense hearts and most crisphead lettuces do not really need washing. Raw, dressed leaves need to be completely dry, so pat dry or use a salad spinner. Wherever possible, tear lettuce leaves by hand rather than slicing them with a knife as they lose less sap and will not wilt so readily.

Small lettuces are commonly braised, stewed stuffed or made into purées, but by far their greatest use is raw in salads. The most common dressing is oil and vinegar or lemon juice, either poured over separately as is the practice in Italy, or whisked into a creamy vinaigrette. Richer dressings including eggs, cheese and cream are best suited to the firmer-leaved lettuces.

Lettuces are very low in calories, with only 15 calories per 100 g/3½ oz, and they contain a good deal of calcium, iron and vitamin C.

LAITUES BRAISÉES AUX PETITS OIGNONS

Braised lettuce

Serves 4
Preparation 15 minutes
Cooking about 1 hour

METRIC/IMPERIAL	AMERICAN
100 g/3½ oz butter	*1 stick butter*
24 baby white onions, peeled	*24 baby white onions, peeled*
caster sugar	*superfine sugar*
4 round lettuces, trimmed and halved	*4 heads of butterhead lettuce, trimmed and halved*
bouquet garni	*bouquet garni*
salt and pepper	*salt and pepper*

Melt one quarter of the butter in a saucepan, taking care not to let it brown. Add the baby onions, 1 teaspoon of sugar and a little salt, and cook over gentle heat for 25 minutes until the onions are golden. Drain them.

Tie the lettuce halves with string to keep the leaves together. Melt the rest of the butter in a large frying pan over a low to moderate heat. Put the lettuce halves into it, season them with salt and pepper, sprinkle them lightly with sugar and cook them gently until golden, turning them several times.

Transfer them to a flameproof casserole, put the glazed onions in the middle and add the bouquet garni. Cover and cook gently over a low heat for 20 minutes.

Remove the string and discard the bouquet garni. Serve the lettuces and onions with pork chops or veal escalopes (cutlets).

FEUILLES DE CHÊNE AUX FOIES DE VOLAILLE

Oakleaf lettuce with chicken livers

Serves 4
Preparation 20 minutes
Cooking about 3 minutes

METRIC/IMPERIAL	AMERICAN
400 g/14 oz oakleaf lettuce leaves	*14 oz oakleaf lettuce or other red leaf lettuce leaves*
15 g/½ oz butter	*1 tbsp butter*
few drops of corn oil	*few drops of corn oil*
225 g/½ lb chicken livers, trimmed and cut into bite-size pieces	*½ lb chicken livers, trimmed and cut into bite-size pieces*
salt and pepper	*salt and pepper*
FOR THE VINAIGRETTE:	FOR THE VINAIGRETTE:
2 tbsp sherry vinegar	*2 tbsp sherry vinegar*
4 tbsp olive oil	*4 tbsp olive oil*
1 tbsp finely chopped parsley	*1 tbsp finely chopped parsley*
6–7 chives, snipped	*6–7 chives, snipped*

Make a vinaigrette by mixing the ingredients and seasoning to taste. Tear the lettuce leaves into bite-size pieces.

Heat the butter and corn oil in a frying pan over a moderate heat. Sauté the chicken livers for 2–3 minutes, turning them frequently. Season them with salt and pepper, and remove them with a slotted spoon.

Whisk 1 tablespoon of the cooking juices into the vinaigrette. Divide the lettuce between 4 plates, top with the chicken livers and pour over the vinaigrette. Serve at once.
To drink: a dry rosé wine, such as Tavel.

LIAISON

see also:
blanquette
butter
civet
cornflour
cream
creams and custards
egg
flour
roux
sauce
velouté

In cooking, the term liaison is applied to the various means used to give smoothness or body to a liquid preparation by thickening it with a binding agent. Depending on the mixture, the liaison can be effected by various means.

Flour or cornflour (cornstarch), mixed to a smooth paste with a little water, is added to boiling sauces which are then stirred constantly until thickened.

Flour and butter or other fat, cooked into a roux, is used as a base for many sauces. Boiling liquid, such as milk, court-bouillon, water or stock, is gradually poured over the roux and stirred while it thickens.

Cold butter or *beurre manié*, a paste-like mixture of equal parts butter and flour kneaded together, may be added in small pieces to soups and sauces towards the end of cooking.

Egg yolk mixed with crème fraîche or whipping cream may be whisked into many meat and poultry dishes, such as fricassees or blanquettes.

Eggs are the thickening agent in custard, with the addition of flour in pastry cream.

The blood of the animal being cooked is used to thicken *civets* and classic *coq au vin*.

Liquids thickened using items containing proteins, such as butter, egg, thin cream or blood, should not usually be allowed to boil as they will coagulate or curdle.

In cases where a lighter sauce is desired, fine starches such as cornflour (cornstarch), ground rice, potato flour or starch, or arrowroot are recommended.

LIME

Citron vert

see also:
citrus fruit
fruit
lemon

A citrus fruit, much like a smaller, rounder, more fragrant lemon, with thin, dark green skin and pale green juicy and sharp-tasting pulp, the lime originated in Malaysia but now grows in many tropical countries, as well as in Florida and California.

The principal varieties are distinguished by their relative size and shape. The small, round TAHITIAN LIME is that most commonly encountered in Europe and the USA. Both the yellow INDIAN LIME and the CARIBBEAN LIME find their way to Britain and the large oval and very acid PERSIAN LIME and the small, seedless BEARS LIME are cultivated in Florida and California respectively. Also grown in Florida is the sharp yellow KEY LIME.

Like lemons, varieties of lime are available all year round and keep, refrigerated, for up to about a week. Their thinner skin makes them the citrus fruit with the poorest keeping qualities. Buy those which feel heavy for their size and avoid any green limes tinged with yellow as they are past their best.

Limes are often given the same protective wax coating as lemons. If using the zest, therefore, buy organic unsprayed limes or scrub them thoroughly in hot soapy water and rinse them well. To extract the maximum amount of juice, roll the fruit on a work surface with the heel of the hand or microwave it on High for about 1 minute before squeezing it.

Limes feature prominently in mixed drinks and they are also used in some jams, marmalades and sorbets. In areas of cultivation they have found much wider use: the Peruvians marinate raw fish in lime juice to make *ceviche* and the juice is also widely used in salad dressings. The zest and juice are popular in chicken, pork and liver dishes, as well as in classic desserts, such as Florida's Key lime pie, and in pickles and chutneys. Like lemons, they are a popular garnish, adding a dash of vivid colour. Try using them in place of lemons to dress sweet crêpes and sweet fried food.

The much larger related SWEET LIME, grown principally in India, has little of the lime's acidity. It is a popular ingredient in the cooking of South America, North Africa and India and is used in pickles. Its syrup is used in the making of desserts and in confectionery.

Limes have the same nutritional value as that of lemons.

CEVICHE

Fish 'cooked' in lime juice

Serves 4
Preparation 20 minutes, marinating 4 hours

METRIC/IMPERIAL	AMERICAN
225 g/½ lb very fresh cod or haddock fillets, skinned and cut into bite-size pieces	½ lb very fresh cod or haddock fillets, skinned and cut into bite-size pieces
2 onions, finely chopped	2 onions, finely chopped
1 small green chilli pepper, very finely chopped (deseeded for a milder dish)	1 small green chili pepper, very finely chopped (deseeded for a milder dish)
juice of 2 limes	juice of 2 limes
juice of 1 orange	juice of 1 orange
4 tomatoes, finely chopped	4 tomatoes, finely chopped
1 tbsp finely chopped coriander leaves	1 tbsp finely chopped coriander (cilantro)
5 tbsp corn oil	5 tbsp corn oil
100 g/3½ oz canned sweetcorn, drained	½ cup canned whole kernel corn, drained
2 tbsp tomato purée	2 tbsp tomato paste
dash of Worcestershire sauce	dash of Worcestershire sauce
2 avocados	2 avocados

Put the pieces of fish into a bowl along with the onions and chilli and add the lime and orange juices, reserving 1 tablespoon of the lime juice. Stir and leave to marinate in the refrigerator overnight or for at least 4 hours. The fish will by then have become opaque and firm, as if cooked.

An hour before serving, stir in the tomatoes, coriander, oil, corn, tomato purée (paste) and Worcestershire sauce.

Peel the avocados, cut them in half, remove the stones and cut the flesh into slices. Sprinkle the avocado slices with the reserved lime juice to prevent them from discolouring.

Transfer the mixture to a serving dish or bowl and arrange the avocado on top to serve.

LIPIDS

Lipids are a group of chemical compounds which include the fats and oils contained in certain foodstuffs and those used as cooking media. Lipids are the body's principal source of energy: 1 gram of lipids yields 9 calories. They are also essential to the metabolism's absorption of many vitamins, contain the 'essential fatty acids' which the body cannot make for itself and are the principal means by which the body stores energy. In order to maintain a balanced diet, the daily consumption of lipids should not exceed 30% of the total calorie intake. As a guide: *charcuterie* contains up to 60% of lipids; meats 2%–30%; fish 0.5%–12%, and cheese 15%–30%.

see also:
butter
cheese
cream
fats and oils
fatty acids
fish
low-fat and reduced-calorie foods
margarine
meat
milk

LIQUEUR

Sweet, alcoholic drinks flavoured with herbs, spices, fruit, flowers, nuts, wine, honey, chocolate and coffee etc, liqueurs are about 40–110 degrees proof, but a high sugar content often masks their alcoholic strength.

Liqueurs may be made by infusing the ingredients in an alcoholic base, in which case they are called RATAFIAS or CORDIALS, or they may be distilled after mixing. For the cook, liqueurs are perhaps best distinguished by their main flavouring base.

Among the best-known herb and spice based liqueurs are BENEDICTINE and CHARTREUSE, made from a wide variety of ingredients according to ancient recipes perfected by monks.

Mixtures of herbs are used to flavour a range of liqueurs from many countries, including Italian GALLIANO and STREGA, and Scotch whisky-based DRAMBUIE.

Mint is used to make several liqueurs, including CRÈME DE MENTHE, and they are popular on ice creams and sorbets.

A great many liqueurs are made from caraway seeds. KÜMMEL, in particular, is often used to flavour cabbage and sauerkraut dishes.

Aniseed is also a common base, and drinks such as ANISETTE go well with strong-flavoured fish and fennel dishes.

Orange is perhaps the fruit most often used and produces the liqueurs most popular in the kitchen. GRAND MARNIER is arguably the most

see also:
brandies, etc
creams and custards
fruit
spirits
wine

distinguished, and the French prefer it in soufflés and creams. CURAÇAO, also known as TRIPLE SEC, has a distinctly different flavour and is the preferred liqueur for *crêpes Suzette*. COINTREAU is the most common of the proprietary brands. All find much use in cake- and pastry-making, as well as in chocolate preparations, sweet omelettes and chicken and duck dishes.

Cherry is also a popular base, and liqueurs such as MARASCHINO and so-called CHERRY BRANDY are used to flavour fruit. CRÈME DE CASSIS is made from blackcurrants and is the base for the delicious French aperitif *kir*. It is also good on fruit and ice creams. The apricot flavour in liqueurs such as ABRICOTINE goes well with poultry and sweet desserts.

The almond is by far the most commonly used nut, producing drinks as diverse as French CRÈME D'AMANDES and Italian AMARETTO. These are popular in baking, especially cookies and cakes, and also in icings and frostings.

Among other numerous possible flavourings for liqueurs, of most significance for the cook in the making of cakes, puddings and ice creams are those made from chocolate, such as CRÈME DE CACAO, and coffee, like TIA MARIA.

see also:
beef
foie gras
giblets
lamb
offal
pâté
pork
veal

LIVER

Foie

The most important red offal (variety meat), liver is also the most rewarding and adaptable for the cook. Pale pink CALVES' LIVER is by far the most tender and has the finest flavour. The paler livers from milk-fed calves are the most meltingly textured, but many prefer the fuller flavour of the darker livers from grass-fed animals. Calves' liver is usually lightly and quickly grilled or fried whole or in slices and is best appreciated slightly pink. It is, however, relatively expensive and LAMBS' LIVER makes a more economical substitute. This may also be braised or roasted. PORK LIVER, which has a fairly coarse flavour, is mainly used in pâtés and terrines. It must be cooked until well done, but not over-cooked; all liver becomes very tough if cooked too long. BEEF LIVER has a very strong flavour and needs several hours' slow cooking.

When buying liver, avoid any with the least hint of green or brown discoloration. Most liver is sold ready trimmed, but it may be necessary to remove the outer membrane. Pork liver may also have to have some tough fibres cut out of it. When buying liver already cut in slices, ensure that they are of a uniform thickness so that they cook in the same time.

Liver goes well with bacon and onions and bitter green vegetables, such as watercress. The Italians traditionally flavour it with sage, but it also goes well with thyme and marjoram and suits more adventurous additions, such as lime zest. Many people marinate liver of all types briefly in milk to improve the taste and texture and eliminate any unpleasant flavours.

Nutritionally, liver is the most valuable of all offal products, whatever animal it comes from, as it is very rich in iron. Because of its high cholesterol content it is better not to serve it with a rich creamy sauce. Plainly cooked liver contains 162 calories per 100 g/3½ oz and fried liver 243 per 100 g/3½ oz.

Poultry livers, especially those of chickens and geese, are also important foodstuffs. The livers of some fish, notably turbot, are eaten, and many, like those of the cod, are used to make nourishing oils.

FOIE DE VEAU À LA VÉNITIENNE

Calves' liver with onions and parsley

Serves 4
Preparation 10 minutes
Cooking about 20 minutes

METRIC/IMPERIAL	*AMERICAN*
100 g/3½ oz butter	*1 stick butter*
3 onions, very thinly sliced	*3 onions, very thinly sliced*
2–3 tbsp white wine	*2–3 tbsp white wine*
1 tbsp olive oil	*1 tbsp olive oil*
4 slices of calves' liver, each weighing about 100 g/3½ oz, cut into bite-size pieces	*4 slices of calves' liver, each weighing about 3½ oz, cut into bite-size pieces*
1 tbsp Cognac	*1 tbsp Cognac*
juice of ½ lemon	*juice of ½ lemon*
2 tbsp finely chopped parsley	*2 tbsp finely chopped parsley*
salt and pepper	*salt and pepper*

Foie de veau à la vénitienne (Calves' liver with onions and parsley)

Heat half the butter in a sauté pan over a low heat and cook the onions gently, covered, until soft. When they are translucent and golden, add the white wine and let it reduce for 5 minutes.

Melt the rest of the butter with the oil in a large frying pan over a high heat. When it is really hot, sauté the pieces of liver in it and season them with salt and pepper.

Add the onions in white wine to the frying pan and mix well with the liver. Lower the heat and add the Cognac, several drops of lemon juice and the chopped parsley. Season with salt and pepper and serve at once.

To drink: a fresh red wine, such as Fleurie.

see also:
sauce

LOAF

Pain de cuisine

Preparation made from moulded, highly seasoned forcemeat or minced (ground) fish, meat or vegetables bound with egg and breadcrumbs or a thick sauce. Savoury loaves are an excellent means of using up leftovers. Meat loaves are often simply baked, while more delicate fish and vegetable mixtures are more usually cooked in a bain-marie in the oven. Loaves of all types are often served with a similarly highly seasoned sauce, such as tomato or curry.

PAIN DE VIANDE CAMPAGNARD

Country meat loaf

Serves 6
Preparation 20 minutes
Cooking 1 hour

METRIC/IMPERIAL	AMERICAN
300 g/10 oz minced beef	*10 oz ground beef*
300 g/10 oz lean minced pork	*10 oz lean ground pork*
300 g/10 oz minced veal	*10 oz ground veal*
1 onion, finely chopped	*1 onion, finely chopped*
2 shallots, finely chopped	*2 shallots, finely chopped*
1 slice of white bread, grated into crumbs	*1 slice of white bread, made into crumbs*
1 egg, lightly beaten	*1 egg, lightly beaten*
6 thin slices of smoked streaky bacon	*6 thin slices of country-style bacon*
salt and pepper	*salt and pepper*

Preheat the oven to 180C/350F/gas 4.

Mix the meats in a bowl and knead them together for about 3 minutes. Season with salt and pepper. Add the onion, shallots and breadcrumbs to the meat along with the egg.

With moistened hands, form the mixture into an elongated loaf. Place it in a roasting pan and bake it for 1 hour.

Fry the bacon in a non-stick frying pan until crisp and browned; drain on paper towels.

Remove the loaf from the oven, place it on a warmed serving dish and arrange the bacon diagonally on the top. Serve very hot with a tomato sauce flavoured with basil or tarragon.

To drink: a light red wine, such as Brouilly.

LOBSTER

Homard

see also:
bisque
butter
crab
crayfish
langoustine
shrimp and prawn
spiny lobster

The largest, most delicately flavoured and most sought-after of the crustaceans, the lobster inhabits colder northern waters. These elusive creatures have to be trapped in pots and are thus rarer and more expensive than other seafood. Although lobsters are found in waters as far south as the Mediterranean and the Florida coast, those from colder waters, especially Scotland, Ireland, Brittany, Norway and Maine, are held to be much better fare.

The lobster has 8 legs and 2 large pincers and the articulated shell, covering the torso and long flexible tail, may vary in colour from greeny-brown to blue-black, depending on habitat, but turns bright red on cooking. As with crabs, the shell has to be moulted regularly by the growing lobster. Females, distinguished by their larger size, and sometimes by coral held by fins on the underside of the base of the tail, are reputed to have the tastier meat.

Lobster meat does not keep well, so lobsters must be bought live or ready cooked. A good lobster should always feel very heavy in relation to its size. When buying live lobsters, look for very lively specimens which draw in their tails violently when picked up. Avoid any which have lost a limb or whose shell feels soft, as they

REMOVING MEAT FROM A LOBSTER

Cut the lobster in half with a sharp knife. Remove the grit sac which lies behind the eyes.

Remove and crack the claws and legs and extract the meat, as well as that from the body and tail.

have recently moulted and the flesh is very watery. Make sure the pincers have been taped up to prevent danger when handling and to keep the lobsters from damaging each other in transit. When buying cooked lobsters, check for a fresh smell and a tail which still has some spring in it. If there is any sign of discoloration on the meat at the front of the tail, decomposition has begun. Rinse lobsters well under cold running water just before any other preparation.

There is considerable argument about the most humane way to kill lobsters. The most common method, recommended by animal welfare groups, is simply to plunge them straight into rapidly boiling water and this probably brings about the most rapid and painless extinction. The distressing noise often heard is simply air being expelled from the shell. The practice of dispatching lobsters with a quick knife blow must sever them in half along their length completely as quickly as possible in order to be humane.

If a lobster is split before or after cooking, it is easy to remove the black thread of gut running its length and the grit sac from the head. The creamy green liver, or tomalley, lying either side of the grit sac is regarded as a delicacy and is often used, like the coral under hens' tails, to enrich sauces.

Lobsters are best cooked in boiling sea water, well-salted water or a good, strong, aromatic court-bouillon. Allow about 5 minutes' cooking time for the first 450 g/1 lb and 3 minutes for each thereafter. Refresh in cold water quickly if serving cold. Lobsters may also be split and grilled, sautéed or baked.

To extract all the meat from a lobster pull the tail away from the body and then break off the flippers at its base. The tail meat is then easily pushed out with a fork from that end. Use both hands to pull the body shell apart; the shells may be used in fish soups and bisques. The tasty leg meat is best sucked out.

The best dressing for the meat is lemon juice and melted clarified butter, although many recipes add highly flavoured and creamy sauces.

Lobster meat is lean: 100 g/3½ oz contains 87 calories. It is also rich in proteins and minerals, but sometimes indigestible.

HOMARDS GRILLÉS

Grilled or baked lobsters

Serves 6
Preparation 15 minutes
Cooking about 30 minutes

METRIC/IMPERIAL	AMERICAN
3 lobsters, each weighing about 800 g/1¾ lb	3 lobsters, each weighing about 1¾ lb
200 g/7 oz slightly salted butter	2 sticks lightly salted butter
½ tsp cayenne pepper	½ tsp cayenne
juice of 1 lemon	juice of 1 lemon
salt and pepper	salt and pepper

Ask the fishmonger to tie up each of the lobsters flat. Preheat the grill (broiler), or the oven to 200C/400F/gas 6.

Fill a large stewpot with water, add salt and bring it to the boil.

Plunge the lobsters into the boiling water and continue to boil for 5 minutes. Remove the pot from the heat and leave the lobsters in the water for another 3–4 minutes.

Drain the lobsters and split each of them in half lengthwise. Crack the claws without detaching them from the body.

Melt 85 g/3 oz/6 tbsp of the butter in a small pan. Put the lobster halves shell-side down on a rack in a baking pan. Sprinkle them with the melted butter and season them with salt and pepper and cayenne pepper. Grill (broil) or bake them in the oven for 20 minutes.

Meanwhile, clarify the rest of the butter (see Butter) in a small pan. Add the lemon juice and season with pepper.

Serve the lobsters as soon as they are cooked, with the lemon butter in a warmed sauce boat.

To drink: a dry white wine, such as Riesling.

Variations: the lobsters may be served with hollandaise sauce or maître d'hôtel butter.

SALADE DE HOMARD

Lobster salad

Serves 4
Preparation 40 minutes
Cooking about 10 minutes

METRIC/IMPERIAL	AMERICAN
1 lobster, weighing about 675 g/1½ lb	1 lobster, weighing about 1½ lb
1 can of artichoke bottoms	1 can of artichoke bottoms
juice of 1 lemon	juice of 1 lemon
200 ml/7 fl oz mayonnaise	1 cup mayonnaise
2 lettuce hearts, separated into leaves	2 lettuce hearts, separated into leaves
pinch of paprika	pinch of paprika
1 tbsp Cognac	1 tbsp Cognac
salt and pepper	salt and pepper

Plunge the lobster into a pan of well-salted boiling water, bring back to the boil and simmer gently for 10 minutes; leave it to cool in the cooking liquid.

Meanwhile, drain and slice the artichokes. Sprinkle them with a little of the lemon juice.

Drain the cooled lobster and remove the meat from the shell. Cut the tail meat into even rounds. Crack the claws and extract their meat.

In a bowl, mix the lobster claw meat, half the mayonnaise, 2 tablespoons of lemon juice and some salt and pepper.

Spoon this mixture into individual serving bowls and place the lettuce leaves on top. Add the lobster tail meat and artichoke bottoms.

Whisk the rest of the mayonnaise with a pinch of paprika and the Cognac. Pour some of this sauce over each lobster salad and serve at once as a cold first course.

To drink: a white Sancerre or champagne.

LOGANBERRY

see Raspberry

LONGAN

see Lychee

see also:
butter
cheese
margarine
yogurt

LOW-FAT AND REDUCED-CALORIE FOODS

Not be confused with diet foods, low-fat and reduced-calorie foods should bear no reference to slimming or dieting. In fact, government regulations in most countries stipulate that the description 'low-fat' may only be used to refer to a product that is already on the market, such as cheese or yogurt, and the reduction in calories must not affect the nature of the product. Packaging of such low-fat foods must state precisely the normal calorific value and, in some instances, the percentage by which that is reduced.

Reduced-calorie foods are designed to allow a wider diet with a reduced fat intake, either outside a weight reducing diet or as part of the necessary period of stabilization that follows a reducing diet. Cooked, reduced-calorie foods, usually frozen or canned, are sold ready-to-eat in individual servings of at least 300 calories.

It must be remembered that a regime of processed, low-calorie meals does not constitute a balanced diet and they should each be accompanied by dairy produce and fruit.

see also:
fruit
rambutan

LYCHEE

Litchi

A small oriental fruit which grows in clusters, the lychee has a deep pink to brownish-red rough shell enclosing sweet, whitish, aromatic flesh, with a flavour of rosewater, and a black stone. Originally from China, the lychee is today cultivated in Australia, the USA and many other countries. Lychees are available fresh in winter and spring, and canned in syrup all year round. Unpeeled they will keep for many weeks in the refrigerator. Peeled and stoned, like large grapes, they can be eaten by themselves or used in fruit salads and sorbets.

The LONGAN is smaller and with less flavour. Available fresh in winter, it must be stored away from the light, otherwise its orange-yellow skin will wrinkle. The translucent flesh has a flavour reminiscent of melon. Longans are used in fruit salads, sorbets, drinks and even as a garnish for roast chicken.

Like all exotic fruits, lychees and longans are good sources of vitamin C and 100 g/3½ oz contains about 70 calories.

COUPES DE LITCHIS AU CHAMPAGNE

Lychee champagne cups

Serves 4
Preparation 30 minutes, chilling 1 hour

METRIC/IMPERIAL	AMERICAN
450 g/1 lb fresh lychees or longans	*1 lb fresh lychees or longans*
2 persimmons, peeled, cored and finely diced	*2 persimmons, peeled, cored and finely diced*
3 kiwi fruits, peeled and thinly sliced	*3 kiwi fruits, peeled and thinly sliced*
juice of ½ lemon	*juice of ½ lemon*
3 tbsp caster sugar	*3 tbsp superfine sugar*
3 tbsp plum brandy	*3 tbsp plum brandy*
½ bottle (350 ml/12 fl oz) of dry champagne, well chilled	*½ bottle (1⅔ cups) dry champagne, well chilled*

Peel the lychees by cutting off a little piece of the shell with the point of a knife; the rest will then come away easily. Split them in half and remove the stones.

Put them in a large bowl and add the persimmons and kiwi fruit. Sprinkle with lemon juice and sugar to taste and pour over the brandy. Mix carefully. Chill for 1 hour.

Just before serving, spoon the fruit salad into individual bowls, pour the very cold champagne over it and serve.

M

see also: almond, cakes and gâteaux

MACAROON

Macaron

Small, round cakes made with egg whites, ground almonds and sugar, macaroons should be crunchy outside and soft inside. The basic macaroon mixture may be flavoured with vanilla, coffee, chocolate, nuts or fruit. Pairs of macaroons are often sandwiched with a cream filling. One such filled macaroon contains about 500 calories.

MACARONS MOELLEUX

Soft macaroons

Makes 12
Preparation 30 minutes
Cooking 20 minutes

METRIC/IMPERIAL	AMERICAN
350 g/$\frac{3}{4}$ lb almond paste	*$\frac{3}{4}$ lb almond paste*
3 egg whites	*3 egg whites*
100 g/$3\frac{1}{2}$ oz icing sugar, sifted	*$\frac{3}{4}$ cup + 1 tbsp confectioners' sugar, sifted*
1 sachet (7.5 g/$1\frac{3}{4}$ tsp) of vanilla sugar	*$1\frac{3}{4}$ tsp vanilla-flavored sugar*
1 tbsp thick apricot purée	*1 tbsp thick apricot purée*

Preheat the oven to 190C/375F/gas 5 and spread a sheet of parchment or greaseproof paper on a baking sheet.

In a bowl, mix the almond paste with 2 of the egg whites. When the mixture is smooth, add the sugars. Knead for 7 minutes, then add the third egg white and the apricot purée.

Put the mixture into a piping bag. On the paper, pipe 12 small mounds, about 4 cm/$1\frac{1}{2}$ in across. Using a pastry brush moistened with water, flatten each mound. Bake for 20 minutes in the lower part of the oven.

Remove the baking sheet from the oven and pour a small glass of cold water between the paper and the baking sheet. Lift the macaroons off when they are cold.

see also: nutmeg, sauce, spices

MACE

The outer coating of nutmeg seeds, dried and flaked or ground to a powder, mace is used as a spice and as a condiment. It has a flavour more like a peppery cinnamon than nutmeg, and is used mainly in pork dishes and in spice mixtures. It works well in sauces for meat and may replace nutmeg in many savoury dishes.

MACÉDOINE

Mixtures of vegetables or fruits cut into small dice are termed *macédoines*. Vegetable *macédoines*

see also:
aspic
brandies, etc
fruit
macerating
salad
spirits
vegetables

are usually basically composed of carrots and turnips, sometimes with green beans cut into sections and peas or flageolet beans. Served hot they make good accompaniments to meat or poultry, or they may be served cool bound with mayonnaise and stuffed in tomatoes or rolled ham slices. Fruit *macédoines* are normally macerated in syrup and an alcohol, such as Kirsch or rum, and served chilled.

MACERATING

see also:
alcohol
brandies, etc
fruit
liqueur
marinade
spirits
wine

The process of soaking food in a liquid so that it absorbs flavour, maceration is most usually applied to fresh or dried fruit. The most common liquids used are sugar syrups and alcohol, such as wine, brandy, port, etc. Maceration not only gives the fruit flavour, but softens it and draws out its own juices.

MACKEREL

Maquereau

see also:
fish
gooseberry
herring
smoking

Related to the tuna, the mackerel is an attractive metallic, greeny-blue fish, 30–35 cm/12–14 in long, abundant on both sides of the Atlantic. It is in season all year round, but is at its best in spring and early summer. Very young specimens about the size of sardines, known as *lisettes* in France, are sought after for their delicate consistency and flavour.

The tasty flesh of the mackerel is firm and free of small bones, but very oily. For this reason the fish spoil quickly so must be bought and used as fresh as possible. A fresh mackerel is rigid, with bright eyes and retaining a metallic shimmer to its skin. Mackerel are usually sold whole, already gutted, or drawn, and often with their heads removed, too. Larger fish are best scored deeply 2 or 3 times on each side to facilitate cooking.

The small *lisettes* are usually fried in butter, with perhaps a drop or two of lemon juice or a pinch of cayenne. Larger, whole mackerel may be baked, grilled (broiled) or barbecued, or cooked *en papillote* and fillets are often rolled in oatmeal and fried like herring. The oily flesh suits a sharp sauce or accompaniment. In France and England gooseberries have long been associated with this fish, although other fruits, such as cranberry and rhubarb, and mustard and horseradish sauces also work well.

Because mackerel travel in large shoals, there are occasional gluts, and, as they also perish so quickly, a great part of the catch has traditionally been preserved in some way. They may be sweet-cured with dill in the Scandinavian manner like salmon gravlax, or soused, like herring, in vinegar. The French also pickle them in white wine. They may also be salted or hot-smoked. Smoked mackerel is often used in pâtés and mousses and is an increasingly popular salad ingredient.

Mackerel is a very oily fish and 100 g/3½ oz contains 130 calories, but the oil is high in mono- and polyunsaturates, and the flesh is also rich in vitamins A, B and D.

MAQUEREAUX AU VIN BLANC

Mackerel in white wine

Serves 6
Preparation 20 minutes, 24 hours ahead
Cooking 20 minutes

METRIC/IMPERIAL	AMERICAN
1 kg/2¼ lb small mackerel, gutted and heads removed	2¼ lb small mackerel, drawn and heads removed
1 lemon, sliced	1 lemon, sliced
2 carrots, thinly sliced	2 carrots, thinly sliced
1 onion, thinly sliced	1 onion, thinly sliced
1 l/1¾ pt dry white wine	1 qt dry white wine
2 sprigs of fresh thyme	2 sprigs of fresh thyme
bay leaf	bay leaf
8 peppercorns	8 peppercorns
2 cloves	2 cloves
200 ml/7 fl oz white wine vinegar	1 cup white wine vinegar
salt	salt

Arrange the fish in a deep dish and sprinkle them with salt. Leave for 2 hours.

If the lemon is not organically grown and may have been sprayed or coated, scrub it in hot soapy water, rinse well and pat dry before slicing it.

Put the carrots and onion in a saucepan with the wine, thyme, bay leaf, peppercorns and cloves. Bring to the boil and simmer for 10 minutes.

Add the vinegar and lemon slices. Bring to the boil again and cook for a further 5 minutes. Wipe the salt off the fish with paper towels.

Plunge the fish into the court-bouillon, bring to the boil once more and simmer for 5 minutes. Remove from the heat.

Drain the mackerel and arrange them in an earthenware or flameproof glass bowl. Strain the court-bouillon and return it to the rinsed pan. Bring it to the boil and pour it immediately over the mackerel. Add the slices of onion, carrot and lemon.

Cover the bowl and leave to cool. Once cool, chill overnight before serving. It will keep for up to 1 week in the refrigerator.

Maquereaux au vin blanc (Mackerel in white wine)

MAGNESIUM

see also: minerals

A mineral which plays an important role in maintaining the muscular nervous system, magnesium allows the body to use energy properly and helps avoid anxiety, cramps, fatigue and insomnia. The normal daily requirement of 300–700 mg, depending on degree of physical activity, is easily achieved with most balanced diets. The best sources of magnesium are whole-grain cereals, green vegetables, meat, legumes or pulses, nuts, chocolate, seafood, some mineral waters and dried fruit.

MAIZE

see Corn

MANDARIN

see Orange

MANGO

Mangue

see also: fruit

A large, plump round or oval fruit, the mango originated in India and the Malay Peninsula and is now widely grown in the tropics, especially in Brazil, Mexico, the Philippines and parts of Africa, as well as in Florida and California.

The mango's leathery, inedible skin may be green, yellow tinged with red, deep red or even purple, and the sweet, perfumed, yellow, juicy and fibrous flesh encloses a large, flat stone or pit which is often difficult to remove. Varieties of mango are available all year round. Among the most valued for their fine flavour are the round, reddish MULGOBAS and the related kidney-shaped ALPHONSO, with a spicier taste.

Mangoes should always be bought very ripe. Look for fruit which gives slightly to the touch and with a pronounced aroma. Avoid any with grey patches on the skin, as they may have been kept at too low a temperature; a little brown or black discoloration, on the other hand, is quite normal. Mangoes will keep for several days in the refrigerator.

mango

The fruits are usually cut on either side of the stone and the flesh scooped out or cut in a criss-cross pattern and the skins turned inside out for easy, and less messy, consumption. Alternatively they may be peeled and the flesh sliced.

There can be a distinct turpentine-like flavour to raw mangoes, but this can be eliminated by serving them chilled. Cold mangoes are delicious eaten on their own or in fruit salads with strawberries and raspberries, dressed with lemon or lime juice or rum. Mango flesh is made into delicious tarts, sorbets and preserves. Puréed mango flesh, with a little added lemon or lime juice, can make a refreshing sauce for sweet or savoury dishes. Mangoes work well in many savoury dishes; they go well with meat, poultry and fish and are particularly delicious in curries and with cured hams, like prosciutto. Unripe mangoes are also used for chutneys and pickles.

Mangoes are a particularly rich source of vitamin A, as well as having high levels of vitamins B and C and some minerals, and 100 g/$3\frac{1}{2}$ oz contains 62 calories.

POULET À LA MANGUE

Chicken with mangoes

Serves 4
Preparation 20 minutes
Cooking about 45 minutes

METRIC/IMPERIAL	AMERICAN
1 chicken, dressed weight about 1.5 kg/$3\frac{1}{2}$ lb, cut into pieces	*1 chicken, dressed and drawn weight about $3\frac{1}{2}$ lb, cut into pieces*
2 mangoes, peeled, halved and stoned	*2 mangoes, peeled, halved and pitted*
juice of 1 lemon	*juice of 1 lemon*
15 g/$\frac{1}{2}$ oz butter	*1 tbsp butter*
3 tbsp groundnut oil	*3 tbsp peanut oil*
1 onion, chopped	*1 onion, chopped*
1 tomato, peeled, deseeded and diced	*1 tomato, peeled, deseeded and diced*
8 g/$\frac{1}{4}$ oz fresh ginger, peeled and grated	*2 tsp grated fresh ginger*
150 ml/$\frac{1}{4}$ pt chicken stock	*$\frac{2}{3}$ cup chicken stock*
pinch of cayenne	*pinch of cayenne*
salt and pepper	*salt and pepper*

Season the pieces of chicken with salt and pepper. Mash the mango flesh with a fork, adding the lemon juice. Set it aside.

Melt the butter in a frying pan with 1 tablespoon of the oil over a moderate heat. Add the chicken pieces and brown them on all sides for about 10 minutes.

Heat the remaining oil in a flameproof casserole over a low to moderate heat and soften the onion and tomato, stirring. Add the ginger and then the mango flesh.

Put the chicken pieces into the casserole along with the stock. Season with salt and pepper and add a pinch of cayenne. Cover and simmer for 30 minutes. Serve straight from the casserole or in a warmed deep serving dish.

MANGOSTEEN

Mangoustan

see also: fruit

The distinctive round mangosteen originated in Southeast Asia, but is now also grown in parts of Central and South America. Known as the 'queen of fruits' because of its superlative and unique flavour, the thick purple skin is peeled to reveal segments of creamy and juicy white flesh. As the tree takes many years to bear fruit, mangosteens are relatively rare and thus expensive. Also, as only about one third of the weight of the fruit is edible, they are a very costly item.

They may be eaten on their own, or served with cream or ice cream, added to exotic fruit salads or used to make sorbets or jams. Indonesian cooking uses the flavouring powers of a vinegar made from the fruit and *kokum* powder extracted from the seeds.

MANGOUSTANS AUX FRAMBOISES

Mangosteens with raspberry sauce

Serves 4
Preparation 15 minutes
Cooking 3–4 seconds, 1 hour ahead

METRIC/IMPERIAL	AMERICAN
5 ripe apricots	5 ripe apricots
2 tbsp framboise (raspberry eau-de-vie)	2 tbsp framboise (raspberry eau-de-vie)
200 g/7 oz raspberries	1 pt raspberries
100 g/3½ oz icing sugar	1 cup confectioners' sugar
10 mangosteens, halved and peeled	10 mangosteens, halved and peeled

Plunge the apricots into boiling water for 3–4 seconds, then drain them and refresh in cold water. Peel, halve and stone them.

Cut these halves into quarters and divide them among 4 bowls. Pour over the framboise.

Blend the raspberries quickly in a food processor and stir the sugar into this purée. Mix well and coat the apricots with this sauce.

Put some of the mangosteen into each bowl on top of the other fruit. Serve well chilled.

MAPLE SYRUP

Sirop d'érable

see also: *glazing* *honey* *sugar*

The sap of certain types of maple tree native to North America yields a clear, golden syrup rich in sugar and with a distinctive aromatic flavour. In the USA and Canada it is often used on pancakes and waffles, as a tart filling and to flavour ice creams and sorbets. It may also be used in savoury dishes, such as glazed carrots and other vegetables and on baked hams. However, its strong flavour must be used judiciously.

SORBET AU SIROP D'ÉRABLE

Maple syrup sorbet

Serves 2
Preparation 10 minutes
Freezing 4 hours

METRIC/IMPERIAL	AMERICAN
200 ml/7 fl oz maple syrup	1 cup maple syrup
25 g/¾ oz butter	1½ tbsp butter
3–4 tbsp crème fraîche or whipping cream	3–4 tbsp crème fraîche or whipping cream
3 drops of vanilla essence	3 drops of vanilla extract
1 tbsp chopped pecans	1 tbsp chopped pecans

Pour the maple syrup into a pan and add 2 tablespoons of water. Bring to the boil.

Remove the pan from the heat and add the butter, beating vigorously to mix well.

Add 1 tablespoon of the cream and beat again, then gradually add the remaining cream, beating constantly, to make a thick, smooth mixture.

Add the vanilla and the pecans. Pour into a container and freeze for at least 4 hours.

MARGARINE

see also: *butter* *emulsion* *fats and oils*

Devised as butter substitutes, margarines are nowadays made primarily from vegetable oils. Other ingredients may include low-fat milk solids, animal fats or fish oils, water, emulsifiers, salt and flavouring and colouring agents. British law does not permit the addition of preservatives, but margarines in other countries, including the USA, do contain them. The base oil may be rapeseed, groundnut or peanut, soya, sunflower, safflower, corn, coconut or palm. To produce a harder consistency, manufacturers may add animal fat or hydrogenate some of the vegetable oils.

Margarines marketed as 'high in polyunsaturates' or 'cholesterol-free' contain high proportions of sunflower, safflower, corn or soya oil, and are thus useful for those trying to reduce blood cholesterol levels.

Regular margarine must, by law, have the same 80% minimum fat content as butter. POLYUNSATURATED or PREMIUM margarines contain the same amount of fat; however, low-fat spreads, called DIET OR IMITATION MARGARINES in the USA, contain only 40% fat, with the rest being largely air and water. For this reason, they are not suitable for cooking.

Many margarines may be used in place of butter in most areas of cooking, but produce very different results in baking, as well as giving different flavours. Soft margarines are difficult to rub into flour, so add the flour a little at a time. Hard margarine may also be used as a cooking medium, but not for deep frying; many soft spreading or whipped margarines do not stand up to the temperatures involved in even shallow frying.

Most margarines, excluding low-fat spreads or diet margarines, contain about 750 calories per 100 g/3½ oz, roughly the same as butter.

MARINADE

see also:
escabèche
fish
fritter
frying
game
grilling
herbs
kebab
lemon
pâté
pickles
roasting
sauce
spices
terrine
vinegar
wine

Seasoned liquids in which food is immersed for varying lengths of time are known as marinades. Usually made up of wine, vinegar or lemon juice, oil and aromatic vegetables, herbs and spices, their purpose may be much more than simply flavouring. Acid ingredients tenderize protein, and oils keep dry, lean meat, like game, moist during cooking. Most marinades also act as a preservative for a limited period, in which case they should cover the food well.

In cooked marinades, which are best for longer immersion, all the ingredients are boiled together then cooled and poured over the food to be marinated, usually meat and game. Uncooked marinades may be used immediately without preliminary preparation.

The food being marinated is usually kept chilled and is turned regularly. The larger the piece of meat, the longer the process takes. Chops, chicken drumsticks, kebabs, for instance, need only about 30 minutes, whereas most family roasts need an hour or two. Large pieces of dry meat, such as venison, may require several days, and the cooked marinade should be drained off and re-boiled regularly.

Food which has been marinated must be wiped quite dry before cooking, otherwise the exterior will not seal properly. The marinade is often subsequently used for basting the food during cooking and may be the base for an accompanying sauce. In moist cooking techniques, such as braising, the marinade is often used as the cooking liquid.

'Dry' marinades may be used when flavouring only is required. Herbs, spices, seasonings, finely chopped onion, shallots, citrus zest and suchlike are simply sprinkled over the food.

MARINADE CRUE

Uncooked marinade for meat and game

Preparation 20 minutes
Marinating 4 hours

METRIC/IMPERIAL	*AMERICAN*
1 carrot, thinly sliced	*1 carrot, thinly sliced*
2 onions, thinly sliced	*2 onions, thinly sliced*
2 shallots, thinly sliced	*2 shallots, thinly sliced*
1 garlic clove, thinly sliced	*1 garlic clove, thinly sliced*
4 parsley stalks	*4 parsley stems*
sprig of fresh thyme	*sprig of fresh thyme*
bay leaf	*bay leaf*
about 750 ml/27 fl oz wine (red for meat, white for poultry)	*about 3½ cups wine (red for meat, white for poultry)*
2 tbsp Cognac	*2 tbsp Cognac*
2 or 3 tbsp olive oil	*2 or 3 tbsp olive oil*
salt and cracked black peppercorns	*salt and cracked black pepper*

Season the meat or poultry to be marinated with salt and cracked black peppercorns and put it into a deep bowl. Add the sliced vegetables, parsley, thyme and bay leaf. Mix well.

Pour on enough wine to cover and add the Cognac. Finally, pour the oil over the surface.

Let stand for at least 4 hours to flavour and tenderize a little. For larger or tough cuts of meat marinate for 48 hours or more, turning the meat several times in the marinade.

Note: an effective means of ensuring good overall contact with smaller amounts of marinade is to put the food and marinade in a sturdy plastic bag, expel any air and seal it.

Variation: use a cooked marinade if the process will take more than a day. First gently sauté the carrot, onion, shallots and garlic until translucent. Season with salt and cracked pepper. Add the herbs, spices and seasoning and cook until golden.

Add the Cognac and enough wine to cover the meat to be marinated, taking into account some evaporation during cooking. Add 100 ml/3½ fl oz/ ½ cup of vinegar for each 750 ml/27 fl oz/3½ cups of wine.

Cover, bring to the boil and simmer gently for 30 minutes. Leave to cool completely before use. Strain the marinade and re-boil it every other day.

For more flavour, add 1 or 2 cloves, 5 or 6 juniper berries, particularly with game, a pinch of mustard, some fennel seeds, citrus zest, or a strongly flavoured herb, such as rosemary, mint or tarragon, as appropriate.

MARINADE POUR POISSONS

Marinade for fish

Preparation 10 minutes
Marinating 30–40 minutes

METRIC/IMPERIAL	*AMERICAN*
2 onions, thinly sliced	*2 onions, thinly sliced*
2 shallots. thinly sliced	*2 shallots, thinly sliced*
1 garlic clove, thinly sliced	*1 garlic clove, thinly sliced*
2 tbsp chopped fresh parsley	*2 tbsp chopped fresh parsley*
1 tbsp mixed crushed dried thyme, marjoram and bay leaf	*1 tbsp mixed crushed dried thyme, marjoram and bay leaf*
juice of 1 lemon	*juice of 1 lemon*
200 ml/7 fl oz olive oil	*1 cup olive oil*
salt and cracked pepper	*salt and cracked pepper*

Mix the onions, shallots and garlic with the parsley, the mixed dried herbs and the lemon juice in a deep bowl. Add the oil and season with salt and pepper. Mix well.

Put the fish into the liquid and marinate for at least 30 minutes in the refrigerator.

Note: add 1 tablespoon of grated zest from an organic, or scrubbed, lemon for extra flavour.

MARJORAM

see also: herbs pasta and noodles pizza

An aromatic plant, marjoram is a traditional flavouring herb in the cooking of many countries. The most common variety, SWEET MARJORAM, has a mild flavour which goes well with most types of food, but has a particular affinity with carrots and cucumbers and thus works well in most green and mixed salads. WILD MARJORAM, also known as OREGANO, has a much more pronounced flavour and is more widely used in Mediterranean cuisine, especially by the Italians on pizzas and in pasta sauces, and by the Greeks with lamb. Both herbs dry well, but become much stronger in flavour and should therefore be used with care.

MARMALADE

see Jams, etc

MARRON GLACÉ

see Chestnut

MARROW (VEGETABLE)

see Squash

MARZIPAN

Massepain

see also: almond almond paste petit four

A thick paste of ground almonds, sugar or sugar syrup and egg white cooked together, marzipan is one of the most common flavourings and fillings in cake- and pastry-making and in confectionery. It can be rolled like pastry and is commonly used to top cakes before a layer of thick icing is applied. The French also use the word *massepain* for a small marzipan petit four which may be coated with sugar or praline.

MAYONNAISE

see also: aïoli egg emulsion salad sauce

A creamy cold sauce consisting of an emulsion of oil and egg yolk, mayonnaise is usually thinned and flavoured with a little vinegar or lemon juice. It may be flavoured in many other ways, most usually with a little mustard, and is the base for a family of classic sauces, such as tartare and *rémoulade*. Mayonnaise is most usually served as an accompaniment to cold food, especially egg dishes and poached fish, and may also be mixed with aspic to give a decorative coating to buffet food. Dishes which use mayonnaise as an ingredient or garnish are often themselves termed a mayonnaise.

All the mayonnaise ingredients should be at room temperature, or it may be difficult to get the emulsion to form. As the egg yolks are uncooked, they must come from an impeccable source. For this reason also, mayonnaise and preparations containing it must be well refrigerated and for brief periods only.

One tablespoon of mayonnaise contains about 145 calories.

SAUCE MAYONNAISE

Mayonnaise

Serves 6 (makes about 500 ml/16 fl oz/2 cups)
Preparation 10 minutes

METRIC/IMPERIAL	AMERICAN
2 egg yolks	2 egg yolks
1 tsp strong mustard	1 tsp Dijon mustard
1 tsp white wine vinegar	1 tsp white wine vinegar
500 ml/16 fl oz sunflower oil	2 cups sunflower oil
salt and freshly ground black pepper	salt and freshly ground black pepper

Thirty minutes before starting, make sure that all the ingredients are at room temperature.

Put the egg yolks into a large bowl. Add the mustard, along with a pinch of salt and pepper, and whisk together (1).

Add the vinegar and whisk vigorously. Add a thread of oil and whisk vigorously until the mixture begins to thicken (2). Add the remaining oil a little at a time, whisking constantly until the sauce is pale and firm (3). Keep the mayonnaise in a cool place.

Notes: mayonnaise is made very easily in the food processor, slowly dribbling in the oil as the machine is running.

If the mayonnaise curdles, put 1 tablespoon of very cold water or a fresh egg yolk into a clean bowl. Pour the mayonnaise into it, a little at a time, whisking vigorously until it is smooth and firm again.

1

2

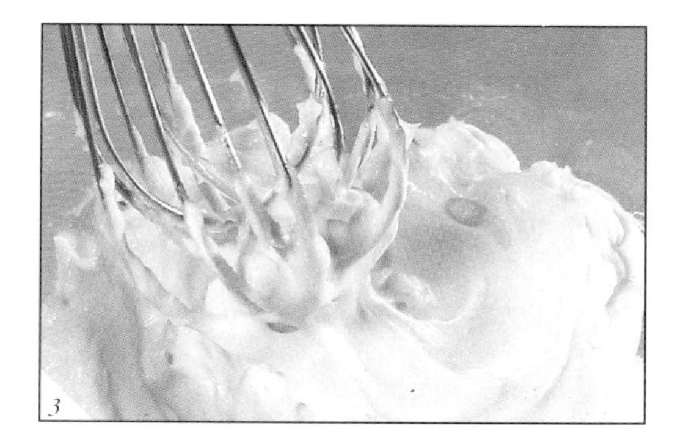

3

Variations: lemon juice may be substituted for the vinegar. Olive, groundnut (peanut) or corn oil may be used, but sunflower oil emulsifies best.

Flavour mayonnaise by adding any of the following: 5 or 6 anchovy fillets, desalted and puréed; 4 tablespoons of finely chopped watercress; 100 g/3½ oz peeled cooked prawns or shrimp, finely chopped, with 1 teaspoon of tomato ketchup; 2 tablespoons of chopped fresh herbs.

Make a low-calorie mayonnaise by beating the yolks of 2 hard-boiled eggs with a little mustard, some lemon juice and 150 g/5½ oz fat-free soft cheese (fromage blanc). This gives 4 portions, with only 50 calories each.

see also:
barding
beef
braising
fats and oils
freezing
frying
game
grilling
lamb
larding
lipids
marinade
offal
pork
protein
steak
stewing
veal

MEAT

Originally a general description for all food, the term meat is now mostly reserved for animal flesh. More particularly, what is usually meant in cooking is RED OR BUTCHER'S MEAT, ie, the flesh of the calf, cow, pig, lamb and sheep. The flesh of poultry, game and seafood is also sometimes referred to as meat, as is the edible part of nuts.

The edible internal organs of farmed animals are known as OFFAL OR VARIETY MEATS, but what is generally meant by RED MEAT is the muscle tissue, made up of long fibres of protein bundled together in parallel. Hence the 'grain' of meat, which is usually best cut across in preparation. These fibres are held together and protected by tougher connective tissue, the proportion of which affects the tenderness of meat. For this reason, also, the centre of each muscle is more tender than the ends.

As the animal ages and as muscles are worked, the fibres become thicker. Therefore tenderness also depends on the age of the animal and how much exercise it has had. Thus younger animals have more tender meat, and the meat of the shoulders or legs is much tougher, for instance, than that of the back. Fat also lies around the muscles and is marbled within them, contributing to tenderness by lubricating the fibres.

Meat must be allowed to mature properly after slaughtering. Enzyme processes make meat more tender and allow a full flavour to develop. The flavour of meat tends to be present in inverse proportion to tenderness, developing with the animal's age and activity, and depends significantly on a good content of marbled fat. The processes of larding and barding help to maintain the fat content of lean meat as it cooks.

When meat is cooked the proteins coagulate and toughen. Tender cuts like the fillet or tenderloin, which are almost purely muscle, need the quickest and lightest possible cooking or they become tough. Steaks are therefore best fried or grilled at the highest possible temperature so that the exterior is seared and the insides merely warmed through. On the other hand, the greater quantity of connective tissue in tougher cuts breaks down during lengthy slow cooking, like stewing or braising, to give very tender results which are also full of flavour.

Connective tissue also breaks down in contact with acids. Marinating is therefore a common means of making tougher meat more tender, and also of giving it greater succulence and flavour. The particular type of connective tissue preponderant in older animals is quite resistant to marinating and cooking and needs to be pounded with a mallet or meat tenderizer.

The fat in butcher's meat, particularly beef, is highly saturated. For this reason, although meat is arguably the best source of quality protein and many vitamins and minerals, nutritionists now advise against a diet too rich in red meat.

MEDALLION

Médaillon

see also:
noisette
tournedos

The French use the term *médaillons* to describe small, round or oval pieces of meat or fish. It may also be used of similar items, such as tournedos, grenadines, mignonettes and noisettes. Medallions may also be cut to shape from chops, poultry suprêmes (boneless half breasts), slices of foie gras, lobster or monkfish, etc. Medallions are always cooked quickly, usually fried or sautéed, and equally suit rich, complex sauces and simple, attractive presentation.

MÉDAILLONS DE VEAU AUX HERBES

Veal medallions with herbs

Serves 4
Preparation 15 minutes
Cooking about 15 minutes

METRIC/IMPERIAL	*AMERICAN*
2 eggs	*2 eggs*
6 tbsp chopped herbs (including thyme, sage and marjoram)	*6 tbsp chopped herbs (including thyme, sage and marjoram)*
150 g/5½ oz fine dry breadcrumbs	*1½ cups fine dry breadcrumbs*
6 prime veal chops, boned and trimmed into medallions	*6 large veal chops, boned and trimmed into medallions*
100 g/3½ oz butter	*1 stick butter*
2 lemons, cut into wedges	*2 lemons, cut into wedges*
salt and pepper	*salt and pepper*

Beat the eggs with a pinch of salt in a shallow dish. Mix the chopped herbs with the breadcrumbs in another shallow dish.

One at a time, dip the veal medallions into the beaten egg so that they are moistened on both sides, then press down well into the breadcrumbs to coat them completely.

Melt the butter in a frying pan over a moderate heat. Put the breaded veal medallions into it and cook them gently for about 15 minutes, turning them half-way during cooking. They should be crisp and golden. Season them with salt and pepper.

Serve the veal medallions on warmed plates surrounded with lemon wedges and accompanied by steamed asparagus tips in butter or courgettes (zucchini) with *fines herbes*.
To drink: a dry white or light red wine, such as those from Saint-Chinian.

MELON

see also: watermelon

The large fruit of a member of the cucumber family, the melon originated in central Asia or Africa and is now widely cultivated in the Mediterranean, South America, the USA and South Africa. The spherical or ovoid fruit is often marked with lines or indentations. The thickish green or yellow skin contains sweet juicy flesh and a core of small seeds.

The slightly flattened CANTALOUPE MELONS are among the most prized by the cook for their good flavour and pleasantly perfumed aroma, a good example being the pale French CHARENTAIS. The small, round OGEN MELON resembles the cantaloupe, of which it is a hybrid, and is said by many to have the finest flavour. NET OR ROCK MELONS are distinguished by the lattice of fibres on the surface of their skins and vary widely in taste and texture. It is the NETTED MUSK MELON, with sweet, pale orange flesh, that Americans call cantaloupe. Other net melons include the yellowish-green-fleshed GALIA and the larger PERSIAN, with beautifully scented orange flesh. WINTER MELONS, so called because they keep well, are usually longer in shape and have thicker skins than other types. They may also be called SMOOTH OR SUGAR MELONS. Examples of winter melons are the pale-fleshed and sometimes insipid HONEYDEW, the sweet and luscious

honeydew
watermelon
Charentais
galia

CRENSHAW, and the CASABA with distinctive thick, deeply ridged skin.

Melons must be eaten when perfectly ripe and do not keep well after this point. They should be bought when a day or so of post-ripening at room temperature will bring them to perfection. A good melon should feel heavy for its size but not liquid when shaken. It should give slightly when gently pressed at the end opposite the stalk and should have no bruises. Any stalk left on smaller melons, like the Ogen, should come away readily, but there should be no sign of rot at this end. Melons should also have a fine developed aroma, but do not go by this alone, as a melon that is overripe can have a very strong smell, and avoid any net melons with patches of bald skin. 'Female' melons of each variety are reputed to have the better flavour: they may be recognized by the large coloured circle around the end opposite the stalk.

Melons should be slightly chilled before serving, preferably in a cool, well-ventilated place. Wrap them tightly in an impermeable plastic bag or film if they are to be stored in the refrigerator, as their aroma tends to infiltrate other foods. Melon freezes well if peeled, sliced and sprinkled with lemon juice and sugar.

Melon is often served cold, but not iced, as an hors d'oeuvre. It may be accompanied by some Parma ham or simply dressed with a little lemon juice and freshly ground black pepper. Larger melons are usually served peeled, deseeded and cut into wedges; smaller specimens are more often simply halved and the seeds are scooped out. It is tempting to fill the resulting cavity with port or some other fortified wine, but this tends to mar the flavour of both the melon and the alcohol. As a dessert, melon is best served plain, sprinkled with lemon juice or garnished with fresh berries. Melon works well in fruit salads, particularly in combination with oranges, grapes and sharp red or black currants. Melon can also contribute flavour and freshness to savoury salads, especially with watercress or curly endive, fresh mint and olives.

In spite of its sweetness, as melon has a very high water content it is very low in calories: 100 g/3½ oz contains only 30. Melon is also rich in carotene and vitamins A and C.

MELON GLACÉ

Melon with ice cream

Serves 6
Preparation 15 minutes, 2 hours ahead
Cooking 5 minutes

METRIC/IMPERIAL	AMERICAN
150 g/5½ oz caster sugar	*¾ cup superfine sugar*
1 vanilla pod, split in half	*1 vanilla bean, split in half*
3 cantaloupe melons	*3 small to medium-size melons*
1 l/1¾ pt vanilla ice cream	*1 qt vanilla ice cream*

Put the sugar and vanilla into a saucepan with 200 ml/7 fl oz/1 cup of water. Bring to the boil and simmer for 5 minutes, then leave to cool.

Cut the melons in half, remove the seeds and scoop out small balls of flesh with a melon baller, leaving the shells intact.

Put the melon balls into a bowl and sprinkle them with the vanilla syrup. Cover the bowl and wrap the melon shells tightly, then chill both in the coldest part of the refrigerator.

Just before serving, fill the melon shells with small cubes of ice cream mixed with melon balls. Serve each melon half in a glass bowl filled with crushed ice.

MERINGUE

A light mixture of egg whites and sugar, meringue has many uses in *pâtisserie* and in a great number of classic dessert dishes. There are three main types of meringue.

SWISS MERINGUE OR ORDINARY MERINGUE is made by simply folding or gradually beating caster (superfine) sugar into beaten egg whites. It may be used uncooked to give a lighter texture to mousses, sorbets, iced soufflés and cake icings, poached in dishes such as floating islands, or cooked as in baked Alaska. It is also baked to make all manner of meringue shells which are usually paired and filled with cream or buttercream or shaped into 'nests' or other containers. For baking, the meringue mixture may be coloured and/or flavoured with vanilla, nuts, chocolate, coffee, alcohol, etc.

see also:
buttercream
cakes and gâteaux
cream
creams and custards
egg
floating islands
tart
vacherin

ITALIAN MERINGUE is made by slowly beating a hot sugar syrup into beaten egg whites. Very white and crisp when baked, and powdery when crushed, it is used mainly for tart bases or for desserts which are put into a hot oven briefly just to brown their tops.

COOKED MERINGUE or *meringue cuite*, a misnomer as it it not actually cooked in the making, uses icing (confectioners') sugar which is added to beaten egg whites and the mixture is beaten until thick and shiny. If beating by hand with a whisk, the bowl should be placed over a pan of hot water as the heat speeds up the thickening process. The meringue is then baked very slowly at a low temperature. As it is hard and stable, it is mainly used by bakers as a cake and dessert topping and for decorative containers.

Meringues should be stored in an airtight container as they readily absorb moisture. For this reason, they should be filled just before serving. Cooked meringues do not freeze well.

PÂTE À MERINGUES

Basic meringue mixture

Makes about 20 meringues
Preparation 20 minutes
Cooking about 3 hours

METRIC/IMPERIAL	*AMERICAN*
whites of 4 eggs	*whites of 4 eggs*
250 g/8½ oz caster sugar	*1¼ cups superfine sugar*
butter, for greasing	*butter, for greasing*
flour, for dusting	*flour, for dusting*

Preheat the oven to 110C/230F/gas ¼. Grease a baking sheet with butter and dust with flour.

Great care should be taken to ensure no trace of yolk remains in the whites, otherwise they will not thicken when beaten. Put them in a large, perfectly clean porcelain, glass or copper bowl and beat them with a figure-of-eight movement, slowly at first. When they become translucent and frothy, beat more quickly, increasing the range of movement of the beaters or whisk to incorporate more air (1).

1

2

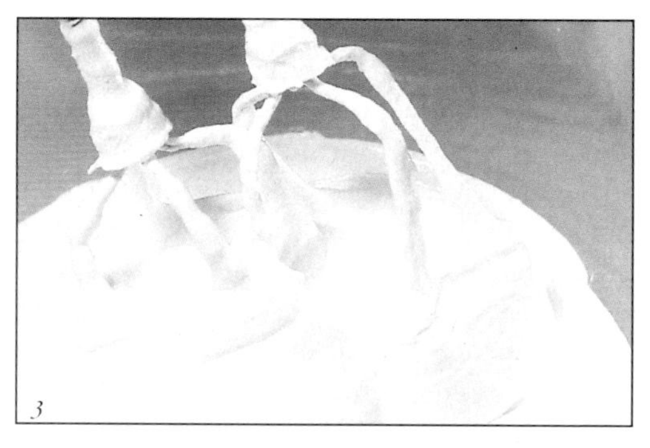

3

4

When the whites begin to thicken, sprinkle on a little sugar, beating constantly (2). Continue to beat, adding the sugar gradually, until the mixture is firm and glossy and holds a stiff peak when the beaters or whisk are lifted out (3).

Put the meringue mixture into a piping bag fitted with a plain or star tube and pipe it in small rounds or ovals on the prepared baking sheet(4).

Alternatively spoon it on the baking sheet.

Bake for 3 hours: it is more a question of drying the mixture out than actually cooking it. At the end of this time let the meringues cool for at least 30 minutes.

Notes: bowls made of copper are by far the best for beating egg white, as the copper induces a catalytic reaction with the egg, producing a very stable structure which holds the air well. Beaten egg white should be used immediately, otherwise it absorbs moisture from the air and liquefies again.

MERINGUE ITALIENNE

Italian meringue

Covers a tart for 6
Preparation 15 minutes
Cooking 7–8 minutes

METRIC/IMPERIAL	AMERICAN
250 g/8½ oz caster sugar	1¼ cups superfine sugar
whites of 4 eggs	whites of 4 eggs

Put the sugar into a heavy-bottomed saucepan with 100 ml/3½ fl oz/½ cup of water. Stir with a wooden spoon over a moderate heat to dissolve the sugar. Once it has all dissolved, skim off the foam on the surface and clean the sides of the saucepan with a brush moistened in water.

Boil until the syrup is at the 'large or soft ball' stage (116C/240F): a drop put in a bowl of cold water forms a ball soft enough to be moulded between the fingers (1). Remove the saucepan from the heat.

Using an electric mixer, beat the egg whites to fairly stiff peaks (2). Add the sugar syrup to the beaten egg whites in a continuous, thin stream, beating constantly (3). This operation is easier with two people: one beating the egg whites, the other boiling and pouring the syrup.

When all the syrup has been incorporated into the egg whites, continue to beat until the mixture is completely cold. The meringue should then be very thick and glossy.

Put it into a piping bag fitted with a plain or decorative tube and use to decorate a fruit or lemon tart (4). Put the tart briefly into a preheated hot oven or under a preheated grill (broiler) to brown the meringue.

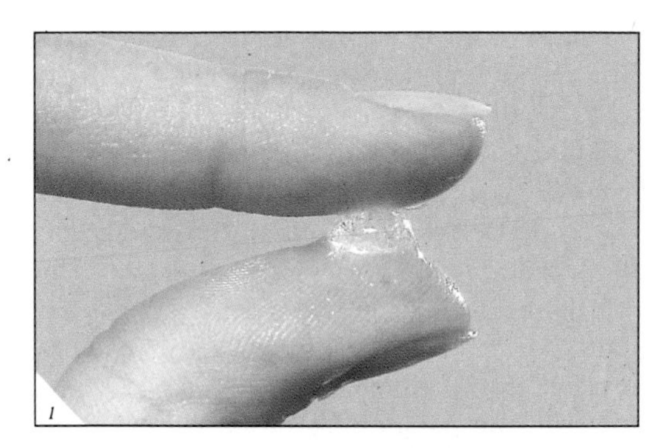

1

2

3

4

Notes: Italian meringue may be kept in the bottom of the refrigerator for several hours in a covered container. It can also be used for making ice cream cakes and petits fours.

see also: freezing

MICROWAVE COOKING

The process of microwave cooking uses high-frequency radio waves which are emitted by a magnetron and fed into the interior of a microwave oven. The waves are absorbed by the water and fat molecules in foodstuffs and heat is produced as these molecules are agitated. The rest of the food is then cooked by the steam produced or by conduction. The better microwave ovens contain devices which 'stir' the waves, or turntables which rotate the food, to ensure even cooking.

Food cooks extremely quickly by this means, and an important element in microwave cooking is 'standing time' which allows the heat generated to spread throughout the food.

Metal containers must not be used in microwave ovens as they cause arcing, or electrical discharge, which may damage the magnetron. Use only glass and special plastic cookware.

Rapid cooking and minimal use of added liquid or fat preserves most of the nutrients in food and keeps a true flavour and texture. The best results are achieved with vegetables, fish, white meat and fruit. Obviously, as the cooking is so rapid, there is no time for tougher types of meat, etc, to become more tender. Therefore only tender cuts may be used, or meat may be marinated beforehand.

Most types of food may be cooked in the microwave oven, with the exception of items such as whole eggs, which may explode as they heat rapidly. Even when cooking shelled eggs, for instance, the membrane covering the yolk should be pricked to allow steam to escape.

Food must be carefully arranged to ensure uniform cooking. The usual way is to distribute items evenly around the compartment, with

Cooking bags are convenient for whole birds.

MICROWAVE COOKING TECHNIQUES

Pierce film covering food to release steam.

Arrange more tender or thinner parts inwards.

MICROWAVE UTENSILS

GUIDELINES AND TIMES FOR MICROWAVE COOKING

FOOD	METHOD	POWER 500	600	700
VEGETABLES		MINUTES		
Artichokes, globe (2)	Cook in bag with 4 tbsp water + 2 tsp lemon juice; turn once. Stand 5 minutes.	10	8	7
Asparagus 250 g/8½ oz	Arrange with tips towards centre. Add 1 tbsp water. Cook covered, turning once. Stand 3 minutes.	8	6	5
Aubergine 450 g/1 lb	Remove stem and pierce skin; turn once. Stand 4 minutes.	8	6	5
Broccoli 450 g/1 lb	Arrange with heads towards centre. Add 3 tbsp water. Cook covered, turning once. Stand 2 minutes.	9	8	6
Brussels sprouts 250 g/8½ oz	Cut cross in base. Add 2 tbsp water. Cook covered, stir twice. Stand 3 minutes.	6	5	4
Cabbage 450 g/1 lb	Slice or shred. Add 2 tbsp water. Cook covered, stirring once. Stand 2–4 minutes.	9	7	6
Carrots 250 g/8½ oz	Slice in rounds. Add 1 tbsp water. Cook covered; stir once. Stand 3 minutes.	6	5	4
Cauliflower 250 g/8½ oz	Separate into florets. Add 2 tbsp water. Cook covered. Stand 3 minutes.	7	6	5
Courgettes 250 g/8½ oz	Slice and cook with herbs, covered, stirring once. Stand 3 minutes.	6	5	4
Eggplant (see Aubergine)				
Green beans 450 g/1 lb	Cook with a little water, covered, stirring once. Stand 3 minutes.	10	8	7
Leeks 250 g/8½ oz	Slice and add 2 tbsp water. Cook covered, stirring once. Stand 5 minutes.	5	4	3
Mushrooms 100 g/3½ oz	Add 2 tbsp lemon juice and a little butter, if wished. Stand 5 minutes.	4	4	3
Onions 250 g/8½ oz	Slice or chop. Add 1 tbsp oil. Cook covered; stir twice. Stand 3 minutes.	5	4	3
Peas 250 g/8½ oz	Add 2 tbsp water. Cook covered, stirring once. Stand 3–5 minutes.	7	6	5
Potatoes 450 g/1 lb	Pierce skin and wrap in paper; turn once. Stand 5 minutes.	12	10	8
Spinach 450 g/1 lb	Do not add water. Cook uncovered, stirring twice. Stand 3 minutes.	6	5	4
Tomatoes 450 g/1 lb	Halve or quarter. Cook with herbs, covered, stirring once. Stand 5 minutes.	7	6	5
Turnips 250 g/8½ oz	Slice and add 1 tbsp water. Cook covered, stirring twice. Stand 3 minutes.	6	5	4
Zucchini (see Courgettes)				
FRUIT				
Apples 450 g/1 lb	Peel and slice. Add lemon juice. Cook covered; stir once. Stand 3 minutes.	8	7	6
Apricots 450 g/1 lb	Stone and add 1 tbsp lemon zest. Cook covered; stir twice. Stand 3 minutes.	9	7	6
Pears 450 g/1 lb	Peel, core and halve. Arrange in a circle with bases outwards. Add 2 tbsp sugar syrup. Cook covered, turning once. Stand 3 minutes.	7	6	5
Plums 450 g/1lb	Stone and add a pinch of cinnamon and 2 tbsp red wine. Cook covered, stirring once. Stand 5 minutes.	6	5	4
Prunes 250 g/8½ oz	Add 500 ml/16 fl oz boiling water. Cook covered; stir twice. Stand 20 minutes.	12	11	10
FISH AND SHELLFISH				
Cod steaks 300 g/10 oz	Dot with 1½ tbsp butter and garlic; turn once. Stand 3 minutes.	6	5	3
Herrings 2 × 140 g/5 oz	Preheat browning plate for 5 minutes with 2 tsp butter; turn once. Stand 3 minutes.	8	7	5
Mackerel 2 × 300 g/10 oz	Cook in buttered dish with 2 tbsp, turning once. Stand 5 minutes.	18	16	14
Monkfish 250 g/8½ oz	Brush with melted butter. Cook covered, turning once. Stand 5 minutes.	5	4	3
Prawns (see Shrimp)				
Salmon steaks 2 × 250 g/8½ oz	Wrap in parchment paper with lemon juice and herbs; turn once. Stand 3 minutes.	6	4	3
Shrimp or prawns 250 g/8½ oz	Cook covered, stirring 2 or 3 times. Stand 3 minutes.	5	3	2
Sole fillets 450 g/1 lb	Cook covered in a buttered dish with herbs, turning once. Stand 3 minutes.	6	5	4
Trout 4 × 250 g/8½ oz	Cook covered in a buttered dish with lemon juice; turn once. Stand 5 minutes.	13	10	7
MEAT AND POULTRY				
Chicken (whole) 1.3 kg/3 lb	Cook in a bag, breast down. Turn over halfway through. Stand 15 minutes.	35	28	22
Chicken breast 250 g/8½ oz	Cook in buttered dish with 3 tbsp stock, covered, turning once. Stand 3 minutes.	6	5	4
Duck 1.8 kg/4 lb	Prick skin and cook breast down on a browning plate in a china dish. Turn halfway through. Stand 15 minutes.	40	30	25
Hamburgers 4 × 100 g/3½ oz	Cook on buttered dish; turn and re-arrange once.	5	4	3
Lamb chops 4 × 85 g/3 oz	Preheat browning plate for 5 minutes with 2 tbsp oil. Arrange with bones towards centre. Cook covered, turning once. Stand 3 minutes.	7	5	4
Pork chops 2 × 125 g/4½ oz	Cook covered with thinner parts towards centre, turning once. Stand 5 minutes.	12	10	8

their thickest ends pointing outwards, eg, broccoli or asparagus stems. Items such as chops or drumsticks, which may cook faster in some parts than others, should have those sensitive parts covered with small pieces of foil during at least part of the cooking, to prevent them from becoming overdone.

As heat does not reach the food from outside, browning the exterior is difficult. This may be achieved by initial browning by conventional means, coating the food with a colouring powder or using specially devised browning plates which heat up in the microwave cooker and brown the food by contact. Some microwave ovens combine both microwave and conventional cooking in sequence or together to overcome such difficulties.

The mirowave oven is invaluable for thawing frozen foods and heating convenience foods. These operations must be carried out according to instructions to avoid the breeding of micro-organisms rather than their elimination. Particularly with re-heated food, all parts of the food must achieve a sufficiently high temperature.

MILK

Lait

see also:
cheese
cream
creams and custards
crêpe
deep frying
sauce
yogurt

Milk is the sweet and nutritious liquid produced by female mammals to feed their young. It is invariably a mixture of sugars, proteins and fats in water. The proteins are partly dissolved and partly held in suspension, as are the tiny droplets of fat. Most milks also contain virtually all necessary minerals and vitamins, except iron and vitamin C. The milk of animals, such as sheep, goats and cows, constitutes an important part of the diet in most parts of the world, as do milk products like cream, yogurt and cheese.

In common usage, the word 'milk' without any further qualification denotes COWS' MILK. It is available commercially in various forms:

RAW, UNTREATED, OR UNPASTEURIZED MILK comes only from dairy herds accredited as free of dangerous bacteria, especially tuberculosis. It must be bottled on the farm, labelled 'raw untreated milk' or 'certified raw milk' and sold within 48 hours of milking. Obviously, it has all the full flavour and nutrient content, and will keep for up to 24 hours in the refrigerator. It is thought wise to boil it for 5 minutes before use.

PASTEURIZED MILK has been heated to a temperature of 71C/160F for 15 seconds and then quickly cooled. This process causes little appreciable change to the milk and its flavour is excellent. It will keep for 3–4 days in the refrigerator once opened. This WHOLE MILK still has a characteristic layer of rich cream on top, especially in summer. The milk may be further treated to distribute the fat particles uniformly. This HOMOGENIZED MILK takes longer to heat through and robs the cook of the chance to skim off and use the creamy top. It also produces thicker results when cooked and is more likely to curdle in the process.

UHT, LONG LIFE OR ULTRAPASTEURIZED MILK is homogenized milk which has been heated to about 132C/270F for only a second or two and then quickly cooled before being vacuum-packed in sterilized containers. The brevity of this process has the minimum effect on the milk, but it will keep unopened for 3 months at room temperature. Once opened, it should be kept in the refrigerator like ordinary milk.

EVAPORATED MILK and CONDENSED MILK are available in cans, tubes and cartons and will keep, unopened, at room temperature for 6 months or longer. To make them, much of the water is removed from whole milk, producing a concentrated product; condensed milk is also usually sweetened. Both evaporated and condensed milk have a distinctly 'cooked' flavour which may be used to advantage in ice cream, many other desserts and confectionery.

POWDERED, DRY OR DEHYDRATED MILK is made either by spray-drying or by passing thickly concentrated milk through heated rollers. However, both processes inevitably destroy much of the milk's nutrients and the milk fat also oxidizes to give reconstituted powdered milk its characteristic, and very inferior, flavour. It is also very prone to scorching when cooked and must be heated even more gently than whole milk. Powdered milk will keep for 4–5 months in a dry place, even if the packet has been opened.

Milks of all types are now available with varying fat contents. SEMI-SKIMMED OR LOW-FAT MILK has had a proportion of the fat taken out by separation. SKIMMED MILK has had virtually all the fat removed. There is a consequential reduction in nutritional content, but much does remain, and many manufacturers also add extra milk solids to restore some of what has been lost. This does allow the goodness of milk to be enjoyed without the associated high intake of saturated fat.

Milk also contains a high level of micro-organisms which find it a perfect breeding ground, converting the sugar or lactose into lactic acid and causing it to sour. Sour milk is also then likely to curdle as the proteins separate out. Store milk in the refrigerator and keep it out of the light, as sunshine destroys some of the vitamin content.

Curdling may also be caused by the milk being exposed to sudden heat or by the addition of acidic agents, natural enzymes or salt. For this reason, care has to be taken when cooking with milk, especially in the making of soups, sauces and creams and custards. Heat milk gently and remove it from the heat just as it begins to bubble, rather than allowing it to boil. This practice of 'scalding' milk avoids a skin of separated proteins forming on top. When heating milk, first rinse out the pan with cold water as this reduces the amount of scorched milk residue left on the pan afterwards.

The natural souring and curdling processes are used to make a wide range of traditional products such as yogurt, buttermilk and cheese. Many traditional desserts, such as curds and whey, are also products of these processes. However, these are best made with raw milk as the different cultures of bacteria in treated milk give a rather bitter flavour.

As well as its wide use in sweet desserts, milk is essential in many doughs and batters, especially for crêpes and pancakes and deep frying. Milk also finds wide use in other aspects of savoury cooking, from basic white sauces, such as béchamel, to court-bouillons for fish. In some countries, milk is also used in the cooking of lamb, pork and poultry.

Milk is a nutritional 'building block' and an irreplaceable natural food which is especially rich in high-quality proteins, easily digested fats and calcium. 100 ml/3½ fl oz/½ cup of whole milk contains 70–90 calories, semi-skimmed or low-fat 50–65 and skimmed 36–40.

RÔTI DE PORC AU LAIT

Pork roasted in milk

Serves 6
Preparation 5 minutes
Cooking about 1¼ hours

METRIC/IMPERIAL	*AMERICAN*
12 garlic cloves, unpeeled	*12 garlic cloves, unpeeled*
1 boned and rolled sparerib of pork, weighing about 1.5 kg/3½ lb	*1 boned and rolled pork butt, weighing about 3½ lb*
1 l/1¾ pt whole milk	*1 qt whole milk*
pinch of nutmeg	*pinch of nutmeg*
salt and pepper	*salt and pepper*

Preheat the oven to 160C/325F/gas 3.

Put the unpeeled garlic cloves in the bottom of a large, flameproof casserole and place the pork on top of them. Pour in the milk, add the nutmeg and season with salt and pepper.

Place the casserole over a gentle heat until the milk is beginning to bubble just below boiling point. Cover and put in the oven.

Roast for 1 hour, turning the meat 3 or 4 times during that time and making sure that the milk does not boil over at any point.

Transfer the cooked pork to a warmed serving plate and cover it with foil to keep it warm.

Strain the cooking liquid and press the garlic cloves to extract all the pulp. Mix this garlic pulp into some of the strained milk and warm it through again, whisking lightly.

Serve the pork cut in thick slices with the milk and garlic sauce poured over them.

To drink: a fruity white wine, like Chardonnay.

MILLE-FEUILLE

see also: creams and custards pastry

From the French for 'a thousand leaves', this term denotes various preparations consisting of several thin layers of puff pastry placed on top of each other and sandwiched with a rich, creamy filling. They are normally made in small rectangles, but may also take the form of large, round cakes. Sweet *mille-feuilles*, which may be called cream slices or Napoleons in English, usually contain cream, jam or pastry cream flavoured with rum or Kirsch, and are liberally dusted with icing (confectioners') sugar or topped with fondant icing. Savoury *mille-feuilles* may be filled with salmon, mushrooms or prawns (shrimp) in a cream sauce, or a mixture of spinach and cheese, etc.

MILLE-FEUILLE AU SUCRE

Iced mille-feuille

Serves 6
Preparation 30 minutes, standing 10 minutes
Cooking 25 minutes

METRIC/IMPERIAL	AMERICAN
15 g/½ oz butter	1 tbsp butter
450 g/1 lb puff pastry	1 lb puff pastry
15 g/½ oz caster sugar	1½ tbsp superfine sugar
icing sugar, for dusting	confectioners' sugar, for dusting
FOR THE PASTRY CREAM:	FOR THE PASTRY CREAM:
300 ml/½ pt milk	1½ cups milk
2 eggs	2 eggs
75 g/2½ oz caster sugar	6½ tbsp superfine sugar
40 g/1¼ oz flour	⅓ cup flour
2 tbsp rum	2 tbsp rum

Preheat the oven to 200C/400F/gas 6 and grease a baking sheet with the butter.

Roll out the pastry into a 40 cm/16 in square about 3 mm/⅛ in thick and place on the baking sheet. Let it stand for about 10 minutes.

At the end of this time, brush the pastry quickly with a little water, then sprinkle lightly with sugar. Prick it all over with a fork and bake for 25 minutes until well risen and browned.

Meanwhile, make the pastry cream: heat the milk in a heavy-bottomed saucepan just to the boil. Beat the eggs lightly with the sugar. Add the flour and then the boiling milk, stirring constantly. Return to the pan and stir over a low heat for 15 minutes until it just comes to the boil. Add the rum and leave it to cool.

Cut and trim the cooked puff pastry sheet into 4 equal strips, each 40 cm/16 in long and 10 cm/4 in wide. Generously spread each of 3 of the strips with one third of the pastry cream and place them one on top of the other. Place the fourth strip on top and sprinkle it generously with icing (confectioners') sugar. Using a very sharp knife, cut this large *mille-feuille* into 6 equal portions. Serve cold with a light custard sauce, if wished.

MILLE-FEUILLE SALÉ

Haddock mille-feuille

Serves 4
Preparation 30 minutes
Cooking 20 minutes

METRIC/IMPERIAL	AMERICAN
55 g/2 oz butter	4 tbsp butter
400 g/14 oz puff pastry	14 oz puff pastry
3 shallots, chopped	3 shallots, chopped
150 ml/¼ pt dry white wine	⅔ cup dry white wine
300 ml/½ pt whipping cream	1¼ cups whipping cream
2 tbsp chopped chives	2 tbsp chopped chives
400 g/14 oz smoked haddock fillets, flaked	14 oz smoked haddock (finnan haddie) fillets, flaked
white pepper	white pepper

Preheat the oven to 200C/400F/gas 6 and grease a baking sheet with a little of the butter.

Roll out the puff pastry into a 40 cm/16 in square about 3 mm/⅛ in thick and place it on the baking sheet. Bake it for about 20 minutes.

Meanwhile cook the shallots in a small saucepan in 25 g/1 oz/2 tbsp of the remaining butter until just soft. Add the wine and reduce over brisk heat until the wine has evaporated. Add the cream and chives and boil for 3–4 minutes. Season and keep hot.

Melt the remaining butter in a frying pan and warm the flaked haddock in it for a few seconds, seasoning with a little white pepper.

Cut and trim the cooked puff pastry sheet into 3 equal strips. Spread the buttered haddock mixture on 2 of the strips and put them one on top of the other. Place the third strip on top and then cut this *mille-feuille* into 4 equal pieces with a very sharp knife. Place a piece on each plate, pour over the sauce and serve at once.

Mille-feuille au sucre (Iced mille-feuille)

MILLET
see Cereal

MINERALS

see also:
calcium
iodine
iron
magnesium
salt

About 25 mineral elements are present in the body, usually as salts, and about 20 of them are essential for correct bodily functioning. For instance: calcium and phosphorus maintain skeletal structure and bony tissue; iron and potassium play a fundamental role in the metabolic process; magnesium is required for nerve and muscle activity; potassium and sodium regulate the amount of water in the body and its acid/alkaline balance.

Daily requirements of each mineral vary widely: 1,000–2,200 mg of sodium, 500–3,750 mg of potassium, 500–1200 mg of calcium, 800–1200 mg of phosphorus and 300–700 mg of magnesium. A balanced diet adequately supplies essential minerals and the body's own systems regulate the amounts of each present by excreting excess. However, this mechanism cannot deal with very high levels, such as the amount of sodium in excessive salt. High levels of sodium are held to cause high blood pressure, a factor in the incidence of strokes.

MINT
Menthe

A very fragrant perennial aromatic plant, mint leaves are among the most common and enduring of culinary herbs. The most prevalent species is GARDEN MINT or SPEARMINT; APPLE MINT is said to make the best mint sauce, the classic accompaniment to lamb and other meat dishes; and the less common WATER MINT and HORSEMINT are used in the same ways. Such mints bring flavour to a wide variety of dishes. They work very well in salads, especially those including cucumber, and with vegetables, particularly potatoes and peas. Mint is also used to flavour jelly, ice creams and other desserts. Tiny mint leaves are also a common garnish on sweet dishes, especially with fresh fruit.

see also:
herbs
lamb
pea
tea

Spicy PEPPERMINT and lemon-scented BERGAMOT or EAU-DE-COLOGNE MINT are very strongly perfumed and are used mainly in confectionery and in the making of liqueurs.

Mint dries particularly well and will keep a good strong flavour for up to 2 years. Dried mint is common in the cooking of the Middle East, notably in tabbouleh. Various types of mint may be infused to make a refreshing tea.

TOMATES À LA MENTHE

Tomato salad with mint

Serves 4
Preparation 15 minutes, standing 15 minutes

METRIC/IMPERIAL	AMERICAN
5 tbsp olive oil	*5 tbsp olive oil*
juice of 1 lemon	*juice of 1 lemon*
800 g/1¾ lb ripe but firm tomatoes, quartered and deseeded	*1¾ lb ripe but firm tomatoes, quartered and deseeded*
10–12 fresh mint leaves, finely chopped	*10–12 fresh mint leaves, finely chopped*
salt and pepper	*salt and pepper*

Mix the oil and lemon juice in a salad bowl and season with salt and pepper.

Put the tomatoes and mint into the salad bowl. Mix and let stand at room temperature (do not refrigerate) for about 15 minutes.

Variations: make salads of cucumber, baby courgettes (zucchini), broad (fava) beans or chickpeas (garbanzo beans) in the same way.

MIRABELLE
see Plum

MIREPOIX

see also:
braising
macédoine
sauce

A mixture of diced vegetables, a mirepoix is used as a base for some sauces and as a bed for cooking braises. Diced carrots, onions and celery are the most usual constituents, usually first gently stewed in butter. A mirepoix may also be used as a flavouring base for many meat, fish, shellfish and vegetable dishes and as an aromatic garnish. Ham or lean bacon may be added to give more flavour.

MIREPOIX DE LÉGUMES

Vegetable mirepoix

Makes about 300 g/10 oz
Preparation 20 minutes
Cooking about 25 minutes

METRIC/IMPERIAL	AMERICAN
25 g/¾ oz butter	1½ tbsp butter
150 g/5½ oz carrots, finely diced	1 cup finely diced carrots
100 g/3½ oz onions, finely diced	½ cup finely diced onions
55 g/2 oz celery, finely diced	⅓ cup finely diced celery
sprig of thyme	sprig of thyme
½ bay leaf	½ bay leaf
salt and pepper	salt and pepper

Melt the butter in a saucepan over a gentle heat. Add the vegetables, thyme and bay leaf. Season with salt and pepper. Stir the mixture well in the butter.

Cover the pan and cook very gently for 20 minutes until the vegetables are very tender. Discard the thyme and bay leaf.

Use as a flavouring base when cooking crayfish and other shellfish and when baking fish.
Variation: add 100 g/3½ oz cured ham, finely diced, and cook with the vegetables.

see also:
blanquette
cod
fish
kebab
medallion
salmon

MONKFISH OR ANGLER FISH

Lotte

A bizarre-looking fish with a huge head, large mouth and a scaleless brownish body, the monkfish catches prey by dangling a piece of fleshy bait at the end of a rod-like protuberance in front of its vicious mouth. Usually about 2 m/6½ ft in length, it is prevalent in cooler Atlantic waters. Because of its appearance, only the skinned tail usually finds its way to the market. A good-size tail will weigh about 1.5 kg/3½ lb and serve 6 people. Although relatively expensive, there is little waste with this fish as it has only one central bone.

The delicately flavoured flesh is reminiscent of lobster, and it is often prepared rather like meat: sautéed in medallions, in blanquettes, in kebabs or roasted. It may also be poached whole, like cod or salmon, but takes about twice as long to cook.

The lean flesh of monkfish is very low in calories: 100 g/3½ oz contains about 77.

MÉDAILLONS DE LOTTE AUX POIVRONS

Monkfish medallions with sweet peppers

Serves 4
Preparation 15 minutes
Cooking about 20 minutes

METRIC/IMPERIAL	AMERICAN
3 green sweet peppers, halved and deseeded	3 green sweet peppers, halved and deseeded
85 g/3 oz butter	6 tbsp butter
dash of Tabasco sauce	dash of Tabasco sauce
800 g/1¾ lb monkfish tail, cut into 8 even-sized medallions	1¾ lb monkfish tail, cut into 8 even-sized medallions
flour, for coating	flour, for coating
1 egg, beaten	1 egg, beaten
55 g/2 oz grated Parmesan	½ cup grated Parmesan cheese
salt and pepper	salt and pepper

Blanch the sweet peppers for 10 minutes in a pan of boiling water. Drain them and peel them. Cut them in small pieces and reduce them to a purée in a food processor.

Put the purée into a saucepan over a gentle heat and add two thirds of the butter, some salt and pepper and a dash of Tabasco. Whisk well to emulsify the mixture and set it aside.

Season the monkfish medallions with salt and pepper. Dip the pieces in flour, then in beaten egg and finally in the grated Parmesan, pressing lightly so that they are well coated.

Heat the rest of the butter in a frying pan over a moderate heat and cook the monkfish pieces in it for 3–4 minutes on each side, turning them carefully.

Arrange 2 medallions on each plate, surround them with the pepper sauce and serve at once.
To drink: an aromatic white wine, such as an Entre-Deux-Mers.

see also:
condiment
salt
soya

MONOSODIUM GLUTAMATE

A white soluble powder, also known as MSG, 'taste powder' or *ve-tsin*, as its name suggests monosodium glutamate is a sodium salt of glutamic acid – the amino acid in the gluten of wheat and other cereals. With only a slight onion flavour, it is nonetheless a very potent flavour enhancer, bringing out the flavours in food to which it is added, especially meat and vegetables. These powers have long been used in Oriental cooking as it occurs naturally in soy sauce, used liberally both in cooking and as a table condiment instead of salt. Since it was first obtained commercially, from wheat and fermented sugar beet molasses, MSG has increasingly been used in processed foods, especially canned goods, bottled sauces and savoury snacks.

Because it is sodium-based, MSG cannot be used in salt-free diets. Use it sparingly: large amounts can produce an allergy known as 'Chinese restaurant syndrome', resulting in vertigo, palpitations and dizziness.

see also:
radish
turnip

MOOLI OR DAIKON

A large variety of radish, resembling a carrot-shaped turnip, the mooli is popular in Japanese cooking. It is widely used grated in fish dishes or shredded into soups. It may also be cooked whole as a vegetable, like the related turnip, or form the basis for pickles.

SALADE DE MAQUEREAU FUMÉ AU DAIKON

Smoked mackerel and mooli or daikon salad

Serves 4
Preparation 20 minutes, plus chilling

Médaillons de lotte aux poivrons (Monkfish medallions with sweet peppers)

METRIC/IMPERIAL	AMERICAN
450 g/1 lb mooli, peeled	1 lb daikon, peeled
675 g/1½ lb smoked mackerel fillets, skinned	1½ lb smoked mackerel fillets, skinned
juice of 1 lemon	juice of 1 lemon
2 tbsp cider vinegar	2 tbsp cider vinegar
5 tbsp sunflower oil	5 tbsp sunflower oil
1 tbsp strong mustard	1 tbsp Dijon mustard
1 cooked beetroot, peeled and diced	1 cooked beet, peeled and diced
salt and pepper	salt and pepper

Coarsely grate three quarters of the mooli (daikon) and thinly slice the remainder.

Flake the mackerel fillets into bite-sized pieces, put them in a bowl and sprinkle the lemon juice over them.

Make a vinaigrette with the cider vinegar, oil, mustard and salt and pepper. Mix it and the grated mooli (daikon) with the mackerel.

Pile this mixture in the centre of 4 plates and arrange the beetroot (beet) and sliced mooli (daikon) around the edges. Serve chilled.

see also:
chocolate
soufflé

MOUSSE

Various smooth, light, sweet or savoury dishes are referred to as mousses. If presented as a first course, a savoury mousse may be hot or cold. Sweet dessert mousses are generally served cold, usually uncooked, and are often lightened with beaten egg whites. Cold mousses may be set in small individual moulds, and turned out and served with a sauce.

MOUSSES DE COURGETTES

Courgette or zucchini mousses with ham

Serves 4
Preparation 25 minutes
Cooking 40 minutes

METRIC/IMPERIAL	AMERICAN
15 g/½ oz butter	1 tbsp butter
450 g/1 lb courgettes, sliced	1 lb zucchini, sliced
1 egg, beaten	1 egg, beaten
2 thick slices of cooked ham	2 thick slices of cooked ham
4 tbsp olive oil	4 tbsp olive oil
1–2 tbsp white wine vinegar	1–2 tbsp white wine vinegar
2 garlic cloves, chopped	2 garlic cloves, chopped
2 tbsp chopped parsley	2 tbsp chopped parsley
salt and pepper	salt and pepper

Preheat the oven to 150C/300F/gas 2 and grease 4 ramekin dishes with the butter.

Steam the courgette (zucchini) slices for 10 minutes, then purée them in a food processor. Add the beaten egg, season with salt and pepper and mix well. Fill the prepared ramekins and bake in a bain-marie in the oven for 30 minutes.

Meanwhile, cut 4 circles of ham slightly larger in diameter than the ramekins. Chop the remaining ham. In a bowl, mix the oil and vinegar and add the chopped ham, garlic, parsley and seasoning to taste. Mix well.

Put a circle of ham on each plate and unmould a mousse on each. Pour over the ham and garlic dressing and serve.

MOUSSES AUX FRAISES

Strawberry mousses

Serves 4
Preparation 15 minutes, standing 1 hour

METRIC/IMPERIAL	*AMERICAN*
550 g/1¼ lb strawberries, hulled	*1¼ lb (1½ pt) strawberries, hulled*
170 g/6 oz caster sugar	*¾ cup + 1 tbsp superfine sugar*
1 tbsp strawberry liqueur	*1 tbsp strawberry liqueur*
4 egg whites	*4 egg whites*
juice of ½ lemon	*juice of ½ lemon*

Blend two thirds of the strawberries in a food processor. Mix the resulting purée with all but 1 tablespoon of the sugar and add the liqueur.

Whisk the egg whites to stiff peaks with the reserved sugar. Fold them into the strawberry purée. Spoon this into serving dishes and chill for at least 1 hour.

Meanwhile, blend the remaining strawberries to a purée and add the lemon juice. Pour this coulis over the mousses just before serving.

MOZZARELLA

see also:
cheese
pizza

A fresh, soft Italian cheese, mozzarella is made in balls of smooth, springy white paste and kept in brine or whey. Mozzarellas from Latium and Campania, where they have their origins, are made from buffaloes' milk and have a subtle flavour distinctly different from those made from cows' milk in the rest of Italy and elsewhere.

Mozzarella is a good cooking cheese and works well in salads, especially with tomatoes, and in gratins. Perhaps its most common appearance is on pizza. The delicate flavour of buffalo mozzarella is best appreciated on its own, or with just a little good olive oil and black pepper.

MULBERRY

see also:
blackberry
raspberry

The sweet-scented fruit of the mulberry tree is used much in the same way as the blackberry or raspberry in jams and jellies and as a filling for tarts. There are three varieties: the BLACK MULBERRY originated in the Middle East, but is now grown widely in parts of Europe, the WHITE MULBERRY comes from the Far East, and the RED MULBERRY is native to the Americas.

Mulberries are watery and, compared to other similar berry fruits, lower in vitamins and higher in calories: 100 g/3½ oz contains 57.

MULLET

Mulet, rouget

see also:
bass
carp
fillet
fish

Two entirely different groups of fish are known as mullet. The GREY or STRIPED MULLET (*mulet*) and the smaller RED MULLET (*rouget*) are both of culinary importance, although the latter is more generally esteemed.

There are up to 100 species of GREY MULLET in warmer waters on both sides of the Atlantic which are difficult to tell apart. The GOLDEN MULLET is said to have the best flavour.

Grey mullet should always be carefully scaled as they bruise easily, and are best gutted through the gills. The flesh of grey mullet, which is lean and white, can be a little soft but has the advantage of containing few bones. As herbivorous fish, their flesh can taste muddy, so, like carp, they are best quickly and thoroughly washed in vinegared water.

Grey mullet are best poached whole in court-bouillon, stuffed and baked in the oven or grilled, and they suit most recipes for bass. They can take a strongly flavoured dressing, such as one containing a dash of Pernod, or a spicy tomato or caper sauce.

The two principal species of RED MULLET, which are better known as GOATFISH in North America, are virtually indistinguishable. The darker of the two, mainly fished in the Mediterranean, is also known as SAND MULLET or *rouget-barbet* in France. It slightly lacks the highly prized, delicate flavour, likened to a cross between sole and prawn or shrimp, of the other bright pink fish found in more northern waters.

Red mullet, at their best from February to June, are very delicate fish, best scaled by the fishmonger as the skin tears readily. Look for fish with a good bright colour which feel stiff and have a tight skin and prominent, clear eyes. Smaller, fresher specimens may be cooked ungutted.

When gutting red mullet, reserve the liver: regarded as a delicacy, it is excellent in stuffings and sauces for the fish. Larger fish may be fried, grilled or baked, often *en papillote*. In Asia, whole fish are also poached or steamed.

Red mullet has protein-rich, lean flesh: 100 g/3½ oz contains 80 calories. It is also rich in minerals, particularly iron, iodine and phosphorus.

ROUGETS EN PAPILLOTES

Red mullet in parcels

Serves 4
Preparation 10 minutes
Cooking 10 minutes

METRIC/IMPERIAL	AMERICAN
4 red mullet, each weighing about 200 g/7 oz	*4 red mullet or goatfish, each weighing about 7 oz*
85 g/3 oz butter, at room temperature	*6 tbsp butter, at room temperature*
2 tbsp anchovy paste	*2 tbsp anchovy paste*
2 tbsp olive oil	*2 tbsp olive oil*
4 tbsp dry white wine	*4 tbsp dry white wine*
2 lemons, sliced	*2 lemons, sliced*
salt and pepper	*salt and pepper*

Preheat the oven to 230C/450F/gas 8.

Gut the red mullet, setting the livers to one side, or get the fishmonger to do it. Do not scale the fish or remove the heads.

Into a bowl, put the fish livers, butter and anchovy paste. Cream the mixture well. Fill the insides of the fish with this mixture.

Cut out 4 large squares of parchment or greaseproof paper and brush them with oil. Place a fish on each square. Sprinkle each with 1 tablespoon of white wine. Season with salt and pepper. Wrap up the parcels carefully, folding the edges to seal them.

Place them on a baking sheet and bake near the top of the oven for 10 minutes. Serve with the lemon slices and with ratatouille.

MULETS AU FOUR

Baked grey mullet

Serves 4
Preparation 15 minutes
Cooking 20 minutes

METRIC/IMPERIAL	AMERICAN
3 lemons	*3 lemons*
4 grey mullet, each weighing about 200 g/7 oz, gutted and scaled	*4 grey mullet, each weighing about 7 oz, drawn and scaled*
4 anchovy fillets in oil	*4 anchovy fillets in oil*
bunch of flat-leaved parsley	*bunch of flat-leaf parsley*
1 garlic clove, finely chopped	*1 garlic clove, finely chopped*
salt and pepper	*salt and pepper*

Preheat the oven to 220C/425F/gas 7. If the lemons are not organically grown and may have been sprayed or waxed, scrub them in hot soapy water, rinse well and pat dry.

Slice 2 of the lemons in rounds. Make 3 or 4 incisions on each side of each fish and slide the lemon slices into them. Drain the anchovies, reserving the oil, and chop them with the parsley. Brush 4 squares of foil with the anchovy oil. Place a fish on each square, wrap up and tightly seal the parcels. Bake for 20 minutes.

Meanwhile, add the garlic to the parsley and anchovy mixture and whisk the juice of the third lemon into it. Mix well.

Remove the parcels from the oven and place the cooked fish on warmed plates. Coat them with the anchovy sauce and serve at once.

see also:
condiment
drying
duxelles
freezing
ketchup
sauce
stuffing
truffle

MUSHROOM

Champignon

A wide range of edible fungi are known as mushrooms and they constitute a useful, tasty and nutritious food. The best-known types consist of an umbrella-shaped cap on a thick round stalk, which may also be eaten.

As mushrooms readily absorb water, even from the atmosphere, they should not be washed. Instead, wipe them clean with a damp cloth or brush and slice off the bottom of the stalk. Those like morels with very irregular surfaces which may trap grit are best cleaned with a soft pastry or paint brush.

Most mushrooms oxidize readily, so use stainless steel knives in their preparation and then sprinkle them lightly with lemon juice.

Mushrooms with a high moisture content, such as fleshy wild types, exude a great deal of liquid in cooking. Dry fry them gently at first until the juices run and drain them off to make a flavouring stock or to return to the dish later. Then brown the mushrooms over a high heat in a little butter or good oil until crisp and golden. Some varieties take appreciably longer to cook, but never overcook mushrooms as they quickly lose their flavour and harden. Add salt only towards the end of cooking.

There are several means of preserving mushrooms. To freeze them, first blanch for 3 minutes and then drain well. Alternatively, sauté them in butter or oil first. They will keep frozen for up to 8 months.

Mushrooms with a drier texture, like the morel or horn of plenty, dry particularly well. Others like ceps are sliced before being dried. Many types of dried mushrooms are also ground and used as condiments. Keep all dried mushrooms in airtight jars.

Reconstitute dried mushrooms by soaking them in water for an hour or so. Microwaved, dried mushrooms rapidly recover their original form without any loss of flavour: put 25 g/$\frac{3}{4}$ oz in a bowl of boiling water, microwave on High for 3 minutes and let stand for 15 minutes. Reserve the flavorous liquid for making sauces and soups.

Mushrooms may also be preserved in vinegar, oil, brine or goose fat, and some types are also canned or made into ketchups.

CULTIVATED MUSHROOMS

The white button mushroom or *champignon de Paris* is now the most common mushroom worldwide and is the species implied by the term used without further qualification.

Available fresh virtually everywhere all year round, they may be either white and smooth or a deeper browny colour, with a scaly skin and generally more flavour. They may be harvested as closed BUTTON MUSHROOMS or allowed to mature to larger CAP MUSHROOMS, which are just opening to reveal the gills under the cap. Very mature specimens become OPEN OR FLAT MUSHROOMS and the gills ripen to a deep brown colour. As the mushroom ages its flavour develops: button mushrooms have little taste, but the large, dark-gilled, open variety have a hint of the potency of their wild relatives.

Cultivated mushrooms should be firm, without spots or bruises and the flesh should be uniformly pale in colour. Store for a few days only in a cool, well-ventilated place.

Small button mushrooms are best used raw in salads or as part of a mixed hors d'oeuvres. Their colour also makes them useful in white sauces and blanquettes, etc. Choose only those which are extremely fresh, white and crisp. Favour the cap variety if the mushrooms are to be cooked. The flavour of open mushrooms is best appreciated when they are lightly grilled, sautéed or stuffed and baked.

Cultivated mushrooms are popular additions to meat and poultry stews and casseroles, but they are best added towards the end of cooking.

cep or porcini mushrooms

More mature mushrooms do also tend to darken dishes and this should be borne in mind when using them with fish and white meats. The flavour of cultivated mushrooms combines well with many other foods, such as cheese, cream, eggs, bacon, poultry, onions and garlic.

Cultivated mushrooms have a very high fibre content, are rich in vitamin B and phosphorus, but low in calories: 100 g/3½ oz contains 44.

morels

WILD MUSHROOMS

The mushrooms of field and forest have long been appreciated for their full, musky flavours. However, the risks attending misidentification are so great that no inexperienced collector should experiment with cooking and eating wild mushrooms unless an expert has checked them. Pharmacists and public health officials in many European countries are trained to advise on mushrooms picked locally. Correct identification of edible species is vital to avoid confusion with poisonous look-alikes. It is also important to choose specimens in prime condition and to prepare them correctly. Some species are toxic raw but edible cooked; others have inedible parts.

Nevertheless, the wild mushrooms on market-stalls, and increasingly in supermarkets, have exciting culinary potential. Nowadays, many wild varieties available commercially are farmed. Most appear in autumn, and the preparation and cooking methods vary according to species.

The CEP (*cèpe de Bordeaux*) or PENNY BUN, also known by the Italians as *porcini*, ranks among the most flavourful of all fungi. It is the tastiest of several members of the important BOLETUS family, characterized by the mass of spore-bearing tubes, rather than gills, on the underside of the cap. If these tubes are pale and firm, they can be eaten, but once they become spongy and soft they should be cut away. Young ceps have dense, firm, white flesh, but mature specimens have more flavour and can grow to a substantial size, with huge swollen stalks which may be eaten if dirty or damaged parts are removed. Ceps cook well and keep their fine texture. They are best sautéed in oil rather than butter, and are usually flavoured with shallots or garlic and chopped parsley. In some parts of France they are simmered in wine. Thinly sliced, they are delicious raw in lightly dressed salads or cooked in omelettes or in meat, poultry or fish dishes.

The CHANTERELLE (*girolle*) is easily identifiable by its orange colour and funnel-shaped cap which has gill-like wrinkles on the underside, extending down the stalk. Its shape harbours dirt, which should be brushed out carefully. The firm, fruity flesh has a slightly peppery flavour, with a hint of apricot, which is delicious raw or sautéed and served in omelettes or with veal or rabbit and even fried fish. Chanterelles usually need long, slow cooking.

The brown or dark grey funnel-shaped HORN OF PLENTY (*craterelle* or *trompette-des-morts*) is cooked in much the same way as the chanterelle, although it is tougher and less fleshy. It is also easily dried and used as a flavouring in pies, terrines and stews.

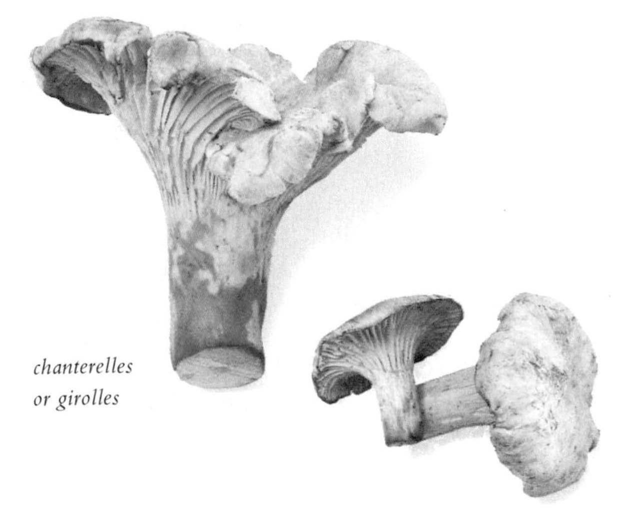

chanterelles or girolles

oyster mushrooms

The pale to dark beige or grey-blue, ear-shaped OYSTER MUSHROOM (*pleurote*) grows in clumps on deciduous trees. One of the most successfully cultivated commercially, it is now generally available all year round. The thick white flesh has a pleasant, mild musky taste. Smaller specimens are best as they contain less water and are less likely to have tough stems.

The MOREL (*morille*) is a spring mushroom recognized by its globular or conical cap. This is hollow, and its surface is honeycombed like a sponge, so the caps need to be carefully cleaned. Raw morels are poisonous: they must be cooked! Their meaty flavour is best brought out by braising in butter or baking, and they go particularly well with red meat, poultry and veal sweetbreads.

Close relatives of the cultivated mushroom, FIELD MUSHROOMS and HORSE MUSHROOMS grow in open pastures and are among the few species commonly gathered and consumed in Britain and the USA. Like their cousins, they expand from buttons to open caps with dark gills. Both have fine, strong flavours and are best grilled, baked, or sliced and sautéed.

EXOTIC MUSHROOMS

Most of the mushrooms used in the cooking of the Far East are only known to us in their dried form. CHINESE BLACK MUSHROOMS, especially the WOOD OR TREE EAR, are the most familiar, and give their meaty taste and texture to a variety of dishes from soups and salads to stews and stir-fries. They need to be reconstituted in warm water and well dried on paper towels before use and may be eaten raw or cooked.

The Japanese have cultivated *take* mushrooms on tree bark for centuries. The *shiitake* and *matsutake*, grown on oak and pine bark respectively, are now often available fresh in the West. Slice and sauté them in oil with finely chopped aromatic vegetables and herbs.

FRICASSÉE DE POISSONS AUX PLEUROTES

Fish fricassee with oyster mushrooms

Serves 4
Preparation 10 minutes
Cooking about 20 minutes

METRIC/IMPERIAL	*AMERICAN*
170 g/6 oz butter	*1¾ sticks butter*
400 g/14 oz turbot fillets, cut into bite-sized pieces	*14 oz turbot fillets, cut into bite-sized pieces*
400 g/14 oz monkfish tail, cut into medallions	*14 oz monkfish tail, cut into medallions*
450 g/1 lb oyster mushrooms, thickly sliced	*1 lb fresh oyster mushrooms, thickly sliced*
juice of 1 lemon	*juice of 1 lemon*
salt and pepper	*salt and pepper*
chopped chives, to garnish	*chopped chives, to garnish*

Season the fish with salt and pepper.

Heat 55 g/2 oz/4 tbsp of the butter in a frying pan over a moderate heat. Add the fish and cook for 7–8 minutes, turning frequently, until well browned all over.

In another frying pan, heat 55 g/2 oz/4 tbsp of the butter over a moderate heat. Add the mushrooms and brown them for 5 minutes, turning them frequently.

Drain the mushrooms and mix carefully with the pieces of fish in a warmed deep serving dish.

Add the lemon juice to the frying pan in which the mushrooms were cooked, along with the remaining butter in small pieces. Boil for 2 minutes, then coat the fish and mushrooms with this sauce. Sprinkle with chives and serve.

Fricassée de poissons aux pleurotes (Fish fricassee with oyster mushrooms)

CHAMPIGNONS FARCIS

Stuffed mushrooms

Serves 4
Preparation 15 minutes
Cooking 11 minutes, standing 2 minutes

METRIC/IMPERIAL	AMERICAN
8 large mushrooms	8 large mushrooms
1 tbsp olive oil	1 tbsp olive oil
3 spring onions, chopped	3 scallions, chopped
2 garlic cloves, chopped	2 garlic cloves, chopped
1 courgette, diced	1 zucchini, diced
1 tbsp dried oregano	1 tbsp dried oregano
3 tbsp tomato purée	3 tbsp tomato paste
salt and pepper	salt and pepper

Remove the stalks of the mushrooms and chop them. Carefully remove any covering over the gills on the inside of each mushroom cap.

Put the oil in a deep dish and microwave on High for 1 minute. Add the onions and garlic. Microwave for a further 2 minutes on High, stirring half-way through.

Add the chopped stalks, courgette (zucchini), oregano and tomato purée (paste). Stir and microwave on High for 4 minutes. Season well.

Fill the caps with this stuffing and put them in a deep dish. Microwave for 4 minutes on High, rotating the dish once half-way through. Allow to stand for 2 minutes and then serve.

POULET AUX MORILLES

Chicken with morels

Serves 6
Preparation 20 minutes
Cooking about 50 minutes

METRIC/IMPERIAL	AMERICAN
1 chicken, dressed weight about 1.5 kg/3½ lb, cut into pieces	1 chicken, dressed and drawn weight about 3½ lb, cut into pieces
flour, for coating	flour, for coating
100 g/3½ oz butter	1 stick butter
300 ml/½ pt fruity white wine	1½ cups fruity white wine
400 g/14 oz morels, stalks removed	14 oz fresh morels, stems removed
500 ml/16 fl oz crème fraîche or whipping cream	2 cups crème fraîche or whipping cream
salt and pepper	salt and pepper

Preheat the oven to 180C/350F/gas 4. Season the pieces of chicken with salt and pepper and dredge them with flour.

Melt the butter in a flameproof casserole over a moderate heat and add the pieces of chicken. Cook on all sides to seal without browning. Cover the casserole and bake in the oven for 20 minutes.

Take the casserole out of the oven and remove as much of the fat as possible, then add the wine and turn the chicken pieces in it, scraping the bottom of the casserole.

Add the morels and cream and mix carefully. Cook over a gentle heat on top of the stove for a further 20 minutes, uncovered.

When the sauce is very thick, adjust the seasoning and serve from the casserole.

Variation: use 150 g/5½ oz dried morels. First soak them in warm water for 20 minutes, then drain and trim off the bases.

FRICASSÉE DE CHAMPIGNONS SAUVAGES

Sautéed wild mushrooms

Serves 4
Preparation 15 minutes
Cooking about 20 minutes

METRIC/IMPERIAL	AMERICAN
1 kg/2¼ lb mixed wild mushrooms (ceps, chanterelles, etc)	2¼ lb mixed fresh wild mushrooms (cèpes, chanterelles, etc)
30 g/1 oz butter	2 tbsp butter
2–3 shallots, finely chopped	2–3 shallots, finely chopped
salt and pepper	salt and pepper
chopped chives, to garnish	chopped chives, to garnish

Slice off the bases of the mushroom stalks. If the caps are large, cut them in half.

Sauté the mushrooms without any fat in a non-stick frying pan over a moderate heat and with the lid on so that their juices collect in the pan. Drain and reserve the juices.

Melt the butter in the frying pan over a moderate heat and return the mushrooms to it. Sauté them for about 10 minutes.

Season with salt and pepper. Add the shallots and continue to cook for 3 minutes over a gentle heat, sprinkling with the reserved juices. Add the chives and serve immediately.

Note: for economy, a proportion of cultivated or field mushrooms can be included.

see also:
oyster
shellfish
snail

MUSSEL

Moule

A bivalve mollusc with an elongated, darkish-blue shell, the mussel is widely found in Atlantic waters, from the Arctic as far south as the Carolinas, and in the Mediterranean. Known as the 'poor man's oyster', mussels have a tendency, like oysters, to be toxic if they have been feeding on certain types of plankton or near polluted effluent. For this reason most mussels for consumption are cultivated in controlled conditions. It is unwise to eat mussels if there is no guarantee of their place of origin.

Cultivation occurs widely on the French and Spanish Atlantic coasts and increasingly in American waters. Among the best are the small *bouchot* type from the Boulogne region, named after the poles on which they are grown, and the larger plumper mussels from Spain's Galician coast, which are grown under rafts.

Mussels are usually sold by volume: 1 litre = 700–800 g; 1 pint = 14–16 oz. Buy a generous ½ litre or 1 pint per person to allow for any which have to be discarded. Live mussels must be bought very fresh and cooked within 3 days of being caught. The shells should be firmly closed or close quickly if tapped. Discard any mussels which do not close, as well as any which are damaged, float or feel heavy for their size, as they may be filled with mud.

Before being cooked the mussels must be washed and scrubbed thoroughly in plenty of running water to remove any clinging parasites and the 'beard' by which they anchored themselves. To be quite safe, soak the mussels in a large pan of salted water for an hour or two to allow them to cleanse themselves of any grit or dirt. A common practice is to add a handful of oats to help the process and plump up the mussels.

Some true enthusiasts prise mussels from their shells, like oysters, and eat them raw with a little lemon juice. However, most mussels are cooked before consumption. Whatever the final dish, live mussels are usually first steamed in a shallow layer in a little boiling water, court-bouillon or wine in a tightly closed pan. They are cooked just long enough for them all to open, as over-cooking makes the flesh shrink and toughen. Any which do not open should be discarded. They may then simply be served in bowls, with the strained cooking liquid as a sauce, as in the classic *moules marinière*, or shelled and used in innumerable dishes.

Mussels are popular in soups and stews, and cream sauces, garlic butter and spicy tomato sauces are common dressings. Mussels in their round shells are often treated like snails or stuffed and grilled (broiled) or baked. Mussels are also delicious deep fried in batter. Cold mussels make delicious hors d'oeuvres, with just a little lemon juice or mayonnaise. Cooked mussels keep for 48 hours in the refrigerator.

Smoked mussels also make delicious salads and hors d'oeuvres. Semi-preserved mussels in

bouchot mussels

Spanish mussels

cans or bottles, either in brine or in a spicy sauce, make useful additions to salads, pasta sauces and rice dishes.

Mussels are rich in calcium, iron and iodine, and 100 g/3½ oz of flesh contains 70 calories.

MOULES MARINIÈRE

Mussels with shallots, white wine and herbs

Serves 4
Preparation 20 minutes
Cooking about 8 minutes

METRIC/IMPERIAL	AMERICAN
30 g/1 oz butter	2 tbsp butter
1 large onion, chopped	1 large onion, chopped
3 l/5 pt (2.3 kg/5 lb) live mussels in their shells, scrubbed	3 qt (5 lb) live mussels in their shells, scrubbed
200 ml/7 fl oz dry white wine	1 cup dry white wine
bunch of parsley, leaves chopped	bunch of parsley, leaves chopped
sprig of thyme	sprig of thyme
bay leaf	bay leaf
salt and pepper	salt and pepper

Melt the butter in a large saucepan over a moderate heat. Cook the onion for 1 minute.

Add the mussels and pour over the wine. Season with salt and pepper and add the chopped parsley, thyme and bay leaf. Stir and cook over a high heat for 6 minutes. Two or three times during the cooking, shake the saucepan and stir the mussels with a wooden spoon.

When all the mussels have opened, remove them from the pan, discarding any empty shells, and put them into a warmed serving bowl. Discard the thyme and bay leaf and strain the cooking liquid over the mussels. Stir and serve.

Variation: the cooking liquid may be strained and then enriched with 3 tablespoons of cream before being poured over the mussels.

SALADE DE MOULES

Mussel salad

Serves 2
Preparation 20 minutes
Cooking 20 minutes

METRIC/IMPERIAL	AMERICAN
3 potatoes	3 potatoes
225 g/½ lb cooked shelled mussels	½ lb cooked shelled mussels
juice of 1 lemon	juice of 1 lemon
1 garlic clove, finely chopped	1 garlic clove, finely chopped
1 shallot, finely chopped	1 shallot, finely chopped
1 stalk of celery, thinly sliced	1 stick of celery, thinly sliced
1 tbsp white wine	1 tbsp white wine
3 tbsp oil	3 tbsp oil
small bunch of chervil, chopped	small bunch of chervil, chopped
salt and pepper	salt and pepper

Cook the unpeeled potatoes for 20 minutes in boiling water. Drain the mussels, if necessary, and sprinkle them with a little lemon juice.

Drain the cooked potatoes and peel them. Slice them in rounds and put them into a salad bowl. Add the garlic, shallot and celery. Pour on the wine and oil and stir carefully.

Add the mussels and remaining lemon juice and season with salt and pepper. Stir carefully, sprinkle with chervil and serve immediately.

MUSTARD

Moutarde

see also: condiment cress mayonnaise sauce vinaigrette

The herbaceous mustard plant is related to the cabbage, and its seeds are widely used as a flavouring ingredient and condiment. The seeds are pressed to extract MUSTARD OIL and the residue ground to a powder. The mustard may be bought in this powdered form, with added colour and thickening agents, as is common in England. More usually the ground seeds are mixed to a paste with vinegar or wine, along with various spices and flavourings, to make the highly seasoned condiments which are also called mustards.

Three principal species of mustard plant are used. The fiercely flavoured NIGRA, TRUE or BLACK MUSTARD is the type most favoured as a condiment in France and Germany, but its resistance to commercial cultivation has led to it becoming rather rare. ALBA, WHITE or YELLOW MUSTARD is native to the Mediterranean and its large, mild seeds are popular in North American and British mustards. It is the type of mustard sprouted in 'mustard and cress' and is frequently used in pickling because of its very strong preservative powers. BROWN or INDIAN MUSTARD is milder than black and coarser in flavour, but has increasingly replaced it in recent years, probably because it is easy to cultivate. Much used in Indian cooking, its oil contributes to the distinctive flavour of Indian cuisine.

Mix MUSTARD POWDER with cold water and leave for at least 15 minutes to develop its full flavour. Sometimes milk is used for a milder flavour, but it is inadvisable to use hot water or vinegar as these make the mustard bitter. Mustard made in this way retains its potency only briefly, so make up just enough for each use. Once opened, jars of liquid mustard should be kept tightly shut in the refrigerator.

The manufacture of mustards in France flourished particularly in the areas of wine manufacture, as the seeds were mixed with the wine and verjuice or grape must. Because the seeds used in DIJON MUSTARDS are stripped of their coarse, dark exteriors, this range of strong but subtly flavoured, pale yellow mustards are the best for use in cooking, in vinaigrettes, and as a condiment for delicately flavoured food such as grilled meat and poultry. BORDEAUX MUSTARD is prepared from whole seeds with grape must and is brown in colour. Milder and more aromatic, but coarser in flavour, it makes a very fine condiment with simple foods like sausage, to bring out flavours. Possibly for this reason, most German mustards are variants of Bordeaux mustard. The distinctive MOUTARDE DE MEAUX is made from whole and coarsely crushed mustard seeds of different colours and lends an interesting, grainy texture to dishes. A recent vogue for this type outside France has led to wider availability.

Mustards are also flavoured, coloured and given texture by many other ingredients, such as peppercorns, tarragon, garlic, lime, paprika, turmeric, curry, horseradish and honey.

Mustard is a classic accompaniment to cold and boiled meat, hard cheese, *charcuterie* and grills. As a flavouring, it is the perfect companion for offal (variety meat), rabbit and pork and for oily fish. It is a useful addition to mayonnaises, vinaigrettes and other sauces, as it stabilizes emulsions as well as adding piquancy.

Mustards free of salt and sugar are available.

SAUCE MOUTARDE

Mustard sauce

Makes 550 ml/18 fl oz/2¼ cups
Preparation 5 minutes
Cooking about 25 minutes

METRIC/IMPERIAL	*AMERICAN*
55 g/2 oz butter	*4 tbsp butter*
55 g/2 oz flour	*4 tbsp flour*
400 ml/14 fl oz milk	*1¾ cups milk*
100 ml/3½ oz crème fraîche or whipping cream	*½ cup crème fraîche or whipping cream*
2 tbsp strong mustard	*2 tbsp Dijon mustard*
salt and pepper	*salt and pepper*

Melt the butter in a saucepan over a gentle heat. Add the flour and stir for 2 minutes to make a roux. Meanwhile, heat the milk.

When the roux begins to foam, pour on the hot milk, whisking. Cook gently for 15 minutes without boiling, stirring occasionally.

Add the cream and stir for 2–3 minutes, then add the mustard. Mix very thoroughly. Taste and adjust the seasoning, if necessary.

Serve this sauce as an accompaniment to poached fish, especially smoked haddock (finnan haddie), or poached poultry.

Variations: the milk may be replaced by fish or chicken stock as appropriate. For a sauce for cold fish, reduce 400 ml/14 fl oz/1¾ cups crème fraîche or whipping cream by one third and then add 4 tablespoons of mustard and the juice of 1 lemon.

MUTTON

see Lamb

N

Navarin d'agneau printanier (Lamb stew with spring vegetables)

NAGE

see also:
court-bouillon
crayfish
fish
lobster
scallop
stock

A white wine court-bouillon flavoured with carrots, onions or shallots and leeks, a nage is used to poach crayfish, lobster or scallops. The finished dish is normally dressed with the seasoned court-bouillon, often mixed with a little cream. Seafood thus served is described as *à la nage*, literally 'swimming'.

COQUILLES SAINT-JACQUES À LA NAGE

Scallops in an aromatic broth

Serves 4
Preparation 30 minutes
Cooking about 15 minutes

METRIC/IMPERIAL	AMERICAN
1 carrot	1 carrot
1 leek	1 leek
1 stalk of celery	1 stick of celery
½ bulb of fennel	½ bulb of fennel
45 g/1½ oz butter	3 tbsp butter
1 garlic clove, chopped	1 garlic clove, chopped
1 shallot, chopped	1 shallot, chopped
bouquet garni	bouquet garni
400 ml/14 fl oz dry white wine	1¾ cups dry white wine
16 shelled scallops	16 shelled sea scallops
salt and pepper	salt and pepper

Trim and thinly slice the carrot, leek, celery and fennel. Melt the butter in a large saucepan over a low to moderate heat. Add the sliced vegetables, along with the garlic and shallot. Season them with salt and pepper and add the bouquet garni. Cook gently for 5 minutes.

Meanwhile, in another pan, bring the wine and an equal volume of water to the boil and boil rapidly for 3–4 minutes to reduce slightly.

Place the scallops on top of the vegetables and gently pour on the wine mixture. Cover and cook over a low heat for 5 minutes. Discard the bouquet garni and adjust the seasoning.

Put the scallops and cooking liquid into a very hot tureen and serve at once.

To drink: a dry white wine, such as Muscadet.

Variation: the sauce may be bound before serving with 3–4 tablespoons of whipping cream.

NAPA CABBAGE

see Chinese cabbage

NAVARIN

see also:
lamb
stewing

Mutton or lamb stews with potatoes and other vegetables are traditionally referred to as *navarins* by the French, probably after the *navet* or turnip which was at one time the most common vegetable ingredient.

NAVARIN D'AGNEAU PRINTANIER

Lamb stew with spring vegetables

Serves 6
Preparation 25 minutes
Cooking about 1½ hours

METRIC/IMPERIAL	AMERICAN
2 tbsp corn oil	2 tbsp corn oil
800 g/1¾ lb boned shoulder of lamb, cut into 6 pieces	1¾ lb boned shoulder of lamb, cut into 6 pieces
800 g/1¾ lb boned lamb collar, cut into 6 slices	6 boned lamb neck slices, weighing 1¾ lb in total
1 tsp caster sugar	1 tsp superfine sugar
1 tbsp flour	1 tbsp flour
200 ml/7 fl oz white wine	1 cup white wine
2 ripe tomatoes, peeled, deseeded and coarsely chopped	2 ripe tomatoes, peeled, deseeded and coarsely chopped
2 garlic cloves, chopped	2 garlic cloves, chopped
bouquet garni	bouquet garni
25 g/¾ oz butter	1½ tbsp butter
300 g/10 oz baby carrots	10 oz baby carrots
200 g/7 oz baby turnips	7 oz baby turnips
100 g/3½ oz baby onions	3½ oz baby onions
300 g/10 oz shelled peas (fresh or frozen)	2 cups shelled peas (fresh or frozen)
300 g/10 oz French beans, trimmed	10 oz fine green beans, trimmed
pinch of freshly grated nutmeg	pinch of freshly grated nutmeg
salt and pepper	salt and pepper

Heat the oil in a large, flameproof casserole over a high heat and seal the pieces of meat in it a few at at time, taking care not to let them burn. When they are all golden brown, pour off two thirds of the fat from the pan.

Return all the meat to the casserole and sprinkle with the sugar. Mix well, then add the flour and cook, stirring, for 3 minutes. Pour the wine over, mix well and season with nutmeg, salt and pepper. Reduce the heat under the casserole to moderate.

Add the tomatoes and garlic to the casserole along with the bouquet garni. Add a little water so that the cooking liquid just covers the meat. Bring to the boil. Cover, reduce the heat and simmer gently for 45 minutes.

After about 30 minutes, melt the butter in a sauté pan over a moderate heat and add the carrots, turnips and onions. Cook, stirring, for 10 minutes, then drain.

Add the carrots, turnips, onions and peas to the casserole. Mix well, cover and cook gently for a further 20–25 minutes.

Meanwhile, steam the green beans for 10–12 minutes, then add to the casserole for the last 5 minutes of cooking. Taste and adjust the seasoning and serve straight from the casserole.

To drink: a light red Burgundy.

NECTARINE

see also:
fruit
peach

A summer fruit related to the peach, the smaller nectarine has smooth red skin, marbled with yellow or orange, and firm yellow or white flesh which does not adhere to the stone. Nectarines should be bought when perfectly ripe, as those which reach the shops still unripe may be neither sweet nor tasty. Ripe nectarines will have a distinct 'give' to the flesh when rolled in the palms and will keep for several days in the refrigerator.

Nectarines may be eaten on their own or incorporated in fruit salads or compotes, and suit all recipes for peaches. Unlike peaches they need not be peeled. Their firmer flesh makes them excellent in tarts and pies.

Nectarines are rich in vitamins A and C and low in calories: 100 g/3½ oz contains 38.

NOISETTE

see also:
beef
lamb
medallion
tournedos
veal
venison

The French for 'hazelnut', the term noisette is also used for various small pieces of tender meat. Lamb noisettes are cut from the rib or loin and have a thin encircling band of fat, like tournedos. Small veal grenadines and 'eyes' of venison or veal chops are similarly described.

Noisettes are usually sautéed in butter and served with a sophisticated garnish and a sauce made from the pan juices deglazed with wine, port or Madeira.

NOISETTES D'AGNEAU À LA MENTHE

Noisettes of lamb with mint

Serves 4
Preparation 20 minutes
Cooking about 15 minutes

METRIC/IMPERIAL	*AMERICAN*
12 small white onions	*12 small white onions*
30 g/1 oz butter, diced	*2 tbsp butter, diced*
5 tsp caster sugar	*5 tsp superfine sugar*
20 fresh mint leaves	*20 fresh mint leaves*
4 tbsp cider vinegar	*4 tbsp cider vinegar*
8 lamb noisettes	*8 lamb noisettes, cut from a rack*
salt and pepper	*salt and pepper*

Put the onions in a saucepan with 2 tablespoons of water, the butter and 2 teaspoons of the sugar. Cover and cook for about 10 minutes over moderate heat, then remove the saucepan lid and allow the liquid to evaporate. Remove from the heat when the onions are caramelized.

Meanwhile, in another pan, bring the remaining sugar and 3 tablespoons of water to the boil. When the sugar has dissolved, remove the pan from the heat and add the mint leaves and vinegar. Mix thoroughly and set aside.

Season the noisettes of lamb with salt and pepper. Cook them for about 3 minutes on each side under a preheated grill (broiler), or over a high heat on a cast-iron grill pan or in a hot non-stick frying pan.

Transfer the noisettes to individual warmed plates, surround them with the glazed onions and serve with the mint sauce. Accompany with fine green beans or steamed beansprouts.

NOODLES

see Pasta and noodles

NOUGAT

see also:
almond
nuts
sugar

A sweetmeat made from sugar, honey, nuts and usually beaten egg white, nougat is a speciality of southeast France. Versions of nougat are, however, manufactured elsewhere.

WHITE NOUGAT is the most common, with at least 15% nuts. MONTÉLIMAR nougat contains at least 30% nuts, in this case toasted sweet almonds and pistachios. PROVENÇAL NOUGAT has an unaerated base of caramelized honey and contains almonds, hazelnuts or filberts, coriander and aniseed, flavoured with orange blossom water. The hard BLACK NOUGAT of Provence is a rare delicacy. ICED NOUGAT is made from almonds, hazelnuts and crystallized fruit mixed with vanilla ice cream.

NOUGATINE

see also:
almond
cakes and gâteaux
caramel

A sweetmeat made from caramel syrup and crushed almonds, nougatine is rolled out and cut into small pieces, or moulded into decorative forms for desserts, cakes and pastries. It is also a popular filling for sweets and chocolates. Nougatine may be bought at confectioners' shops and used to make sweets or items such as little baskets in which to serve sorbet.

The term nougatine is also applied to cakes made from Genoese sponge, which are split and filled with praline cream and then spread with apricot purée and decorated with chopped nuts.

NUTMEG

see also:
creams and custards
gratin
mace
sauce

The seed of a tropical tree, the nutmeg is a wrinkled oval nut, greyish-brown in colour and with a highly spiced flavour and aroma. The outer covering of the seed is stripped off and used as mace, a spice in its own right. Whole nutmegs should be very hard and heavy for their size and are best stored in an airtight container. It is wise to grate as needed, preferably using a special, small, fine grater, as ground nutmeg loses its power rapidly. It is used sparingly, particularly for flavouring custards, potato dishes, spinach, omelettes and soufflés, béchamel sauce and many gratin dishes.

NUTS

Noix

Various trees and shrubs produce fruit encased in hard shells and known as nuts. Rich in nutrients, nuts have been an important part of man's diet since pre-history.

see also:
almond
blancmange
bread
butter
cakes and gâteaux
cashew
chestnut
cookies, etc
dried vine fruit
fats and oils
flour
fruit
hazelnut
macaroon
marzipan
muesli
nougat
nougatine
peanut
pine kernel
praline
tuile
vinaigrette
walnut

Nuts are available dried all year round, but are usually at their best in autumn, when quite fresh and full of their natural juices. It is best to buy them in the shell, as they keep better for longer. Avoid nuts with holes, however tiny, or which rattle or feel light for their size.

Nuts make a popular accompaniment to drinks or may form part of a mixed hors d'oeuvre or dessert course. The most common use of nuts in cooking is probably in breads, cakes and cookies and in desserts, like tarts and ice creams. However, there is also a strong tradition of savoury use for nuts: for example, almonds with trout, chestnuts in stuffings, walnuts in salads, etc. Crushed nuts mixed with butter make delicious dressings for grilled fish and poultry and ground nuts are often used to flavour and thicken soups, sauces and stews.

Many nuts, like chestnuts, are also ground to make flour, which is used to make tasty breads and polentas. The oils in nuts, especially groundnuts or peanuts, walnuts and hazelnuts, are used for cooking and as potent flavourings.

Among the most culinarily important nuts are the ALMOND, CASHEW, CHESTNUT, HAZELNUT OR FILBERT, PEANUT, PINE KERNEL OF PINE NUT and WALNUT, all of which are dealt with in more detail elsewhere. Other nuts of note include:

The long, curved BRAZIL NUT (*noix de Brésil*) or CREAM NUT comes packed together like the segments of an orange inside the woody coconut-like fruit of a giant tree in the Amazonian jungle. These very oily nuts tend to go rancid very quickly so care should be exercised when buying them already shelled. They are normally consumed whole or coated in chocolate. Similar in flavour and texture to almonds, they may be substituted for them in many recipes.

MACADAMIA NUTS (*noix de Macadam*) or QUEENSLAND NUTS are native to Australia but are now widely grown in Hawaii and Florida. They are sweet and buttery and are a delicious dessert nut. They are also used to substitute for the Oriental CANDLE-NUT.

The PECAN (*noix de pacane*) is native to North America and has a smooth, elongated shell about 3.5 cm/1½ in long. The very delicately flavoured kernels are much used in baking, especially pies and cookies, and in savoury cooking. They may be used like walnuts. The HICKORY and BUTTERNUT are also important in North America, but are seldom exported.

pecan *brazil* *cashew*
hazelnuts
walnut

The PISTACHIO (*pistache*) has a pale-green, oval seed enclosed in a light shell. It has a delicate, sweet flavour and has many uses in savoury cooking, especially in stuffings and galantines. Its green colour also makes it a popular decorative addition to sweet dishes.

As well as being rich in protein and many vitamins and minerals, nuts are a good source of energy and are therefore high in calories. For instance, 3 handfuls of pistachios eaten with cocktails will account for about 600 calories.

OATS

see also:
cereal

A cereal which grows well in colder climates, oats have long been a dietary staple in northern Europe, particularly Scotland and Scandinavia. Oats have little gluten so are not used to make leavened products such as bread.

Oats are ground, as with flour, to different grades of oatmeal. COARSE OATMEAL or PINMEAL, called SCOTCH OATS in the USA, is used to make such hearty fare as haggis, while finer grades are preferred for oatcakes, etc. Seasoned, finely ground oatmeal also makes a delicious coating for fried fish. Perhaps the best-known use of oats is breakfast porridge, called oatmeal in the USA, in which rolled oats are cooked with water or milk. According to preference, it may be salted and served with milk or cream or sweetened and topped with jam or marmalade.

Oats are one of the most nutritious cereals, much higher in protein and fat than wheat, and may help reduce blood cholesterol levels.

OCTOPUS

Poulpe

see also:
cuttlefish
squid

A mollusc with eight uniform fleshy tentacles, each having two rows of suckers, the octopus is regarded as a delicacy, especially in France and Portugal. There are many types and at their best, the taste is likened to lobster. To prepare an octopus, remove the insides, possibly retaining any ink sac for a sauce, and cut out the beak and eyes. Larger specimens tend to be tough and the flesh must be beaten before cooking. Octopus may be boiled and simply dressed with lemon juice, oil and parsley. Smaller, tender specimens may also be sliced into pieces and grilled or fried, or simmered in rich, aromatic mixtures. They may also be stuffed like cuttlefish. The calorie content of 100 g/3½ oz of octopus is 75.

POULPES EN COCOTTE AUX OIGNONS

Baked octopus with onions

Serves 4
Preparation 1 hour
Cooking about 2 hours

METRIC/IMPERIAL	AMERICAN
4 octopus, each about 400 g/14 oz, cleaned and skinned	*4 octopus, each about 14 oz, drawn and skinned*
4 large onions, sliced	*4 large onions, sliced*
4 garlic cloves, chopped	*4 garlic cloves, chopped*
3 cloves, ground	*3 cloves, ground*
200 ml/7 fl oz vinegar	*1 cup vinegar*
100 ml/3½ fl oz olive oil	*½ cup olive oil*
2 tbsp flour	*2 tbsp flour*
salt and pepper	*salt and pepper*

Beat the tentacles of the octopus with a wooden mallet for at least 20 minutes, then cut the octopus into chunks.

Put the octopus into a flameproof casserole with the onions, garlic and cloves. Add a very little salt and some pepper along with the vinegar, oil and 400 ml/14 fl oz/1¾ cups of water.

Cover the casserole. Knead the flour with a little water to obtain a sticky paste. Roll the paste into a long sausage shape and use it to seal the casserole lid. If the casserole is not tightly sealed, the octopus will be tough. Once sealed, cook gently for 1 hour 50 minutes.

Serve straight from the casserole, accompanied by saffron rice. The dish may also be served cold as a first course.

To drink: a Côtes-de-Provence rosé.

Poulpes en cocotte aux oignons (Baked octopus with onions)

OFFAL OR VARIETY MEAT

Abats de boucherie

see also:
beef
bone marrow
brain
head
heart
kidney
lamb
liver
oxtail
pork
sweetbread
tongue
tripe
trotters and feet
veal

Offal, or variety meat, is the term for the internal organs and extremities of animals slaughtered for human consumption.

Offal can be RED: such as heart, kidneys, liver, lung, tongue, spleen; or WHITE: *animelles* (testicles), bone marrow, brains, head, mesentery, sweetbreads, feet or trotters, and tripe. Some, such as tripe, is usually sold already cooked, and most white offal is pre-cooked to blanch it clean of residual blood.

Offal is relatively inexpensive and has traditionally been a feature of country cooking, particularly in France and other Mediterranean countries, in dishes such as *boudin noir* (black pudding or blood sausage) and pig's trotters or feet. Black pudding and tripe, for instance, have long been popular in the north of England; chitterlings, sausages stuffed with chopped sheep's intestines, are popular in many parts of Britain and rural North America; and the Scottish haggis consists mainly of offal and coarse oatmeal.

A cardinal rule for all offal is that it must be absolutely fresh. Do not buy any which does not look fresh and clean or is slimy and grey. Most offal, especially liver and kidneys, freezes well. Once bought, or thawed, all offal should be cooked at once; do not keep it in the refrigerator for more than a day.

The most delicately flavoured offal comes from veal calves, particularly liver, kidneys and sweetbreads, and lamb, especially *animelles*, brains, liver, kidneys and sweetbreads.

Offal is very nutritious and rich in mineral content. However, bear in mind that all offal, particularly brains, is high in cholesterol.

OIL

see Fat and oils

OKRA

Gombo

see also:
vegetables

A tropical vegetable related to the cotton plant, okra consists of grooved green pods. There are two main types, one elongated, the other short and squat. Okra is available all year round, but only fresh young pods are good for eating as they become tough and fibrous as they get older.

Inside the pod is a gelatinous mass of seeds. Some recipes insist on soaking the okra in lemon juice or vinegar beforehand to reduce the sliminess. Alternatively, the okra may be deliberately left whole to prevent the contents of the pod seeping out into the rest of the dish, or the pods may be dried.

On the other hand, this vegetable's sliminess is turned to advantage in the classic thick Creole soup known as gumbo. Okra is also used to thicken stews, and much used commercially in canned foods. Unless being kept intact, okra is normally topped and tailed and briefly blanched or fried before further cooking.

Okra is rich in vitamins and iron and 100 g/3½ oz contains 40 calories.

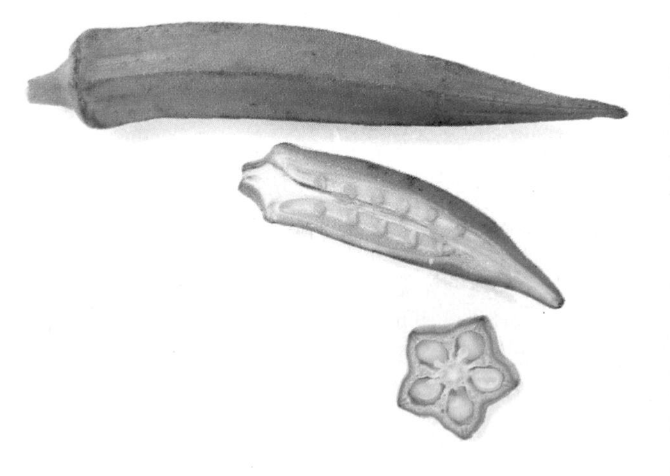

GOMBOS À LA CRÉOLE

Creole-style okra

Serves 6
Preparation 20 minutes
Cooking about 35 minutes

METRIC/IMPERIAL	AMERICAN
450 g/1 lb fresh okra, trimmed	1 lb fresh okra, trimmed
3 tbsp groundnut oil	3 tbsp peanut oil
2 onions, finely chopped	2 onions, finely chopped
3 large tomatoes, peeled and chopped	3 large tomatoes, peeled and chopped
2 garlic cloves, crushed	2 garlic cloves, minced
pinch of cayenne	pinch of cayenne
few strands of saffron	few strands of saffron
salt and pepper	salt and pepper

If the okra are large, cut them in 2 or 3 pieces. Cook for 3 minutes in lightly salted boiling water, then drain them thoroughly.

Heat the oil in a flameproof casserole over a moderate heat. Add the onions and cook, stirring, until translucent. Add the tomatoes and garlic. Season with salt and pepper, then add the cayenne and saffron. Mix well, cover and cook over a low heat for 20 minutes.

At the end of this time, add the okra and reheat it gently. Taste and adjust the seasoning, which should be quite spicy. Serve inside a ring of Creole rice.

Variations: add some peeled prawns or shrimp, or thin strips of smoked ham.

OLIVE

see also:
carpaccio
fats and oils
fatty acids
mayonnaise
salad
tapenade
vinaigrette

The cultivation of the olive tree spread throughout the Mediterranean area with the Romans, and it is now also widely grown in the Americas, South Africa and Australia. Over 90% of today's crop is pressed for olive oil, but some still reaches us, usually pickled, as the delicious small, fleshy, oval fruit.

GREEN OLIVES are the unripe fruit picked in late summer and early autumn. They are first soaked in a caustic soda solution for a few hours to reduce their bitterness. This is then cleaned out by soakings in several changes of water over a period of days, and the olives are then pickled in herb-flavoured brine. They may be 'cracked' or split to allow more bitterness to drain off and permit better penetration of the flavouring pickle ingredients.

BLACK OLIVES are picked at various stages of ripeness and pickled in similar aromatic brines. They may also be dry packed in salt, bottled in oil or simply dried in the sun. Those picked just as they start to turn in colour as known as BITTER OLIVES or *olives d'été*. As a rule, the deeper the colour and the more wrinkled the appearance, the riper the olive and the sweeter and tastier the flesh will be.

An amazing variety of both types of olive is available. Spain is the world's largest producer, especially of green olives, and among the most highly regarded are the large QUEEN OLIVES and small tasty MANZANILLAS. Most of the black olives in Europe come either from the South of France, Italy or Greece.

Pickled olives are a common accompaniment to drinks and are frequently included in mixed hors d'oeuvres. As well as being flavoured with garlic and herbs, they may also be stoned and stuffed, usually with strips of sweet pepper, nuts, citrus zest, anchovies or even foie gras.

Black olives are more usually favoured for use in cooking. They may be puréed and made into tasty pâtés and spreads, like tapenade, added whole or chopped to mixed salads and pizzas, or used as a flavouring ingredient, especially in pasta sauces, stuffings, daubes and poultry dishes. They are also one of the most popular garnishes for a wide variety of savoury dishes.

Olives have a high fat content: 100 g/3½ oz of green olives, or about 12, can contain as much as 130 calories: black olives contain twice as many. However, the lipids contained in olives are an excellent source of so-called 'good' cholesterol and mono-unsaturated fatty acids. Olives are also are rich in vitamins and minerals, such as calcium and potassium.

OLIVE OIL is made from black olives when perfectly ripe. That produced simply by the time-honoured method of cold pressing the olives is known as VIRGIN OLIVE OIL and is usually a rich green in colour with a wonderful aroma and strong flavour. Other, paler and less tasty oils, are expressed by heat or chemical treatment, often from the residue of fruit already pressed. Most of the olive oils sold are actually blends, often with a little added virgin oil to improve the flavour.

The flavour of the oil, like wine, varies from grove to grove and country to country. The best are reputed to be the subtly fruity oils from Italy and Provence, while the Spanish and Greek oils are more assertive.

More commonplace oils are used for cooking, and add flavour to many Mediterranean sautés and stews, particularly in tandem with local vegetables. The virgin oils are better reserved for use in salad dressings or as condiments. The Italians, for instance, pour a little oil over pasta or vegetables, and use it to dress cured meat or carpaccio. A frequent hors d'oeuvre in Italy is simply a plate of fresh bread and a bowl of good oil in which to dip it.

Because of the healthy nature of the lipids in olives, olive oil is enjoying a wide revival in popularity. However, the fact that it is low in saturates means that it goes rancid more readily and cannot be heated to very high temperatures, say for deep frying. Store olive oil in a cool place away from light.

CANARD AUX OLIVES

Duck with olives

Serves 6
Preparation 25 minutes
Cooking about 1 hour

METRIC/IMPERIAL	AMERICAN
300 g/10 oz stoned large green olives	10 oz pitted large green olives (about 60)
2 tbsp olive oil	2 tbsp olive oil
140 g/5 oz streaky bacon, cut into small strips	5 oz bacon, cut into small strips
2 oven-ready ducks, preferably Barbary, each weighing about 1.35 kg/3 lb, with giblets	2 ducks, preferably Barbary, each weighing about 3 lb, dressed, with giblets
4 garlic cloves, finely chopped	4 garlic cloves, finely chopped
225 g/½ lb mushrooms, chopped	½ lb mushrooms, chopped
200 ml/7 fl oz white wine	1 cup white wine
2 onions, finely chopped	2 onions, finely chopped
30 g/1 oz butter, diced	2 tbsp butter, diced
salt and pepper	salt and pepper

Blanch the olives in a saucepan of boiling water for 5 minutes and drain.

Heat 1 tablespoon of the oil in a frying pan. Brown the bacon in it, then add the gizzards cut into small pieces. After 2 minutes, add the duck livers and brown them for 1 minute.

Remove the bacon and giblets with a slotted spoon and put the garlic and mushrooms into the pan. Cook them until well browned and then add one third of the olives. Mix the mushroom and olive mixture with the bacon and giblets, and stuff the ducks with the mixture. Sew up the apertures and truss the birds.

In a flameproof casserole over a high heat, brown the ducks in the remaining oil until golden all over. Discard the fat and add the wine and onions. Cover and simmer gently for 30 minutes, turning once. Add the remaining olives and cook for a further 15 minutes.

Carve the ducks and serve them surrounded by the stuffing and olives. Whisk the butter into the cooking juices and serve in a sauce boat.

To drink: a mellow white wine, such as Castelli di Yesi.

OMELETTE

see also: egg

The classic FRENCH OMELETTE consists of lightly beaten eggs cooked quickly over a high heat in a frying pan or special omelette pan. The eggs are usually stirred with a fork for the first minute or so to expose more of the mixture to the heat. The omelette is then cooked undisturbed until the base is set and golden and the top still slightly creamy. The omelette is rolled or folded and turned out swiftly on a warmed plate.

Almost always served hot as hors d'oeuvres, light meals or desserts, omelettes may be sweet or savoury. They may be flavoured in three main ways: by adding ingredients, such as herbs or grated Parmesan, to the egg mixture before cooking; by putting fillings, such as sautéed kidneys or jam, into the omelette before folding it; or simply by garnishing the cooked omelette with a sweet or savoury mixture.

SOUFFLÉ OMELETTES are made by separating the eggs and whisking the whites to stiff peaks. These are then gently mixed with the yolks and cooked like an ordinary omelette. They may be folded and flavoured or filled in the usual way, and are often finished off briefly under a very hot grill (broiler) to ensure that they rise well and set on top.

The Italians and Spanish prefer flatter, drier omelettes known as FRITTATAS and TORTILLAS respectively, which are made of seasoned egg and vegetable mixtures cooked more slowly for a longer time, until quite solid. They are usually cut in wedges, like cakes, and are often served warm or cold.

For the health-conscious, omelettes may be made using only 2 eggs with a dash of water and dry fried in a non-stick frying pan.

OMELETTE NATURE

Plain omelette

Serves 2
Preparation 10 minutes
Cooking 3–4 minutes

METRIC/IMPERIAL	*AMERICAN*
4 eggs	*4 eggs*
45 g/1½ oz butter	*3 tbsp butter*
salt and freshly ground black pepper	*salt and freshly ground black pepper*

Break the eggs carefully into a bowl. Season with salt and pepper. Using a fork, beat the eggs vigorously just long enough to aerate the mixture. A little cream, milk or water may be added at this stage.

Melt half the butter in a large, perfectly clean frying pan. Some cooks like to mix half of this melted butter into the beaten eggs at this stage. Turn the heat up to high and when the butter begins to foam, pour the beaten eggs into the frying pan all at once (1).

Tilt the frying pan quickly to and fro, stirring the eggs with the back of a fork or wooden spoon using a figure-of-eight movement, until

1

2

3

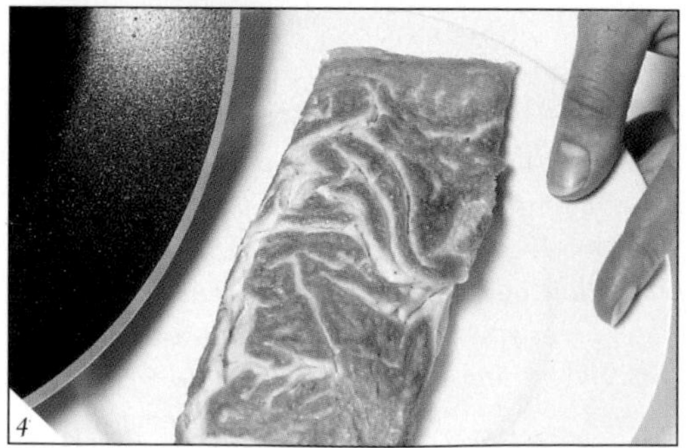

4

they look like creamy scrambled eggs (2). Care should be taken not to overcook them.

Leave the frying pan on the heat without moving it for a few seconds to allow a crisp crust to form on the base. Fold one edge of the omelette inwards to cover the centre, which should remain slightly soft (3).

Grease a serving dish with half the remaining butter. Hold the dish at an angle to the frying pan. Raise the pan and let the omelette slide on to the dish, rolling it as it goes (4). Rub the remaining cold butter over the folded omelette to give it a gloss. Serve at once.

Variations: this type of omelette may be enriched with fines herbes, chopped spinach or sorrel leaves or any other ingredient easily incorporated into the egg mixture.

Alternatively, the omelette may be given any one of a number of delicious fillings before it is folded over: grated cheese, sautéed, chopped sweet peppers, strips of ham, sliced, cooked potatoes with sour cream and chopped chives, sautéed mushrooms, etc.

OMELETTE SOUFFLÉE À LA CONFITURE

Soufflé omelette with jam

Serves 2
Preparation 10 minutes
Cooking 5 minutes

METRIC/IMPERIAL	AMERICAN
4 eggs, separated	4 eggs, separated
30 g/1 oz caster sugar	$2\frac{1}{2}$ tbsp superfine sugar
4 tbsp raspberry jam	$\frac{1}{4}$ cup raspberry jam
25 g/$\frac{3}{4}$ oz butter	$1\frac{1}{2}$ tbsp butter
salt	salt

Beat the egg yolks with a fork, adding a pinch of salt. Whisk the whites to soft peaks with the sugar. Gently fold together the yolks and beaten whites. Warm the jam in a small saucepan and preheat a grill (broiler).

Melt the butter in a frying pan over a fairly high heat until foaming. Pour the egg mixture into the frying pan and cook for about 5 minutes, until the bottom is set.

Slide the omelette on to a warmed flameproof serving dish, spoon the jam over it and fold it over. Place the omelette under the grill for a minute or so, until it rises slightly and browns.

ONION

Oignon

see also:
chive
garlic
leek
sauce
shallot
soup
spring onion

The onion is one of our most ancient vegetables and flavouring ingredients. Originally from the Middle East, varieties of onion are now grown throughout the world and are available all year round. The part of the plant that is eaten is the sweet, pungent and aromatic root bulb, which is covered with a thin, papery layer of skin. The different varieties are distinguished by colour, size and season, usually with a milder flavour early in the season.

YELLOW ONIONS are the most common, and may vary in size from the large, mild SPANISH ONION to the small variety, about the size of shallots, used for pickling and which are roasted for use as garnish.

RED ONIONS are mostly in evidence in summer and autumn and are best used raw and thinly sliced as they lose most of their subtle flavour when cooked. Their colour makes them ideal for use in salads and as a garnish.

red onion

Spanish onion

small yellow onions

WHITE ONIONS are small with silvery skins and appear only in spring and summer, but are now quite difficult to come by. As they do not keep well, they are mostly pickled to make tiny cocktail onions. However, the crisp, mild larger specimens which appear in the later summer, and more resemble pale Spanish onions, are the type preferred by the French for classic dishes such as *coq au vin* and *boeuf bourguignonne*.

Buy only firm onions with crisp skins, a clean, strong odour and no sign of sprouting, mould or wetness. As they do not keep well once peeled or sliced, buy onions of a size appropriate to use. Onions are normally peeled, except perhaps when they are to be roasted or used in soups and stocks, as the skin gives a good colour. To avoid tears when preparing onions, freeze them briefly and keep the knife wet, or peel and slice under running water. To keep excess chopped onions, first sweat them in a little butter.

Onions may be eaten raw, usually chopped or sliced in salads, or as a condiment, as with Indian food and other spicy dishes like *chili con carne*. They may also be boiled, braised or roasted whole as a vegetable. Larger onions are also often stuffed with rich mixtures and baked. Fried sliced onions are a common garnish on everything from sausages to calves' liver, and onion rings deep fried in batter are popular accompaniments to hamburgers.

spring onions (scallions)

It is, however, as a flavouring ingredient that most of our onions find use. There are few savoury dishes which do not begin with the sweating of a chopped onion in some butter, and most stocks, sauces and marinades get much of their basic substance from the humble onion.

Onions are rich in minerals, vitamins and trace elements, but they also have a high sugar content: 100 g/3½ oz contains 90 calories, equivalent to the same weight of potatoes.

PURÉE SOUBISE

Potato and onion purée

Serves 4
Preparation 20 minutes
Cooking about 50 minutes

METRIC/IMPERIAL	*AMERICAN*
300 g/10 oz potatoes, peeled and cut into chunks	*10 oz potatoes, peeled and cut into chunks*
100 g/3½ oz butter	*1 stick butter*
400 g/14 oz onions, chopped	*14 oz onions, chopped*
1 egg, beaten	*1 egg, beaten*
3 tbsp grated Parmesan	*3 tbsp grated Parmesan cheese*
pinch of grated nutmeg	*pinch of grated nutmeg*
salt and pepper	*salt and pepper*

Cook the potatoes in boiling salted water for 20 minutes. Drain them and pass them through a food mill or potato ricer.

Preheat the oven to 200C/400F/gas 6 and grease a baking dish with some of the butter.

Melt all but 25 g/¾ oz/1½ tbsp of the remaining butter in a sauté pan. Add the onions and cook them over a low heat for 10 minutes, stirring frequently.

When the onions are soft and golden, add to the potato purée. Mix well, adding the egg, and season with grated nutmeg, salt and pepper.

Pour the mixture into the baking dish and sprinkle the top with grated Parmesan. Dot with the reserved butter. Bake for 15–20 minutes. Serve straight from the baking dish to accompany roast or braised meat.

GRATINÉE À L'OIGNON

Onion soup with cheese

Serves 6
Preparation 25 minutes
Cooking about 30 minutes

METRIC/IMPERIAL	*AMERICAN*
55 g/2 oz butter	*4 tbsp butter*
1 kg/2¼ lb onions, thinly sliced	*2¼ lb onions, thinly sliced*
2 tbsp flour	*2 tbsp flour*
1.5 l/2½ pt beef or chicken stock	*1½ qt beef or chicken stock*
bouquet garni	*bouquet garni*
1 French baguette, thinly sliced	*1 French baguette, thinly sliced*
3 tbsp port	*3 tbsp port wine*
250 g/8½ oz grated Gruyère	*2 cups grated Gruyère cheese*
pinch of grated nutmeg	*pinch of grated nutmeg*
salt and pepper	*salt and pepper*

Preheat the oven to 150C/300F/gas 2.

Melt the butter in a large saucepan and cook the onions in it over a moderate heat until lightly and evenly browned. Add the flour and stir for 3–4 minutes, then pour two thirds of the cold stock over. Mix well, add the bouquet garni and bring to the boil, stirring constantly. Season with grated nutmeg, salt and pepper. Add the rest of the stock and boil gently for 10 minutes. Meanwhile, lightly toast the slices of French bread in the oven.

Remove the onion soup from the heat, discard the bouquet garni and add the port. Mix and pour into 6 ovenproof porcelain bowls. Arrange the slices of bread on the surface of the soup, gently pushing them into it. Generously sprinkle with grated Gruyère and brown gently in the oven for about 10 minutes. Serve hot.

Variations: the browned onions may be moistened at the beginning of cooking with 200 ml/7 fl oz/1 cup of dry white wine before adding the stock or water. Try making the soup with a blue cheese for an interesting flavour.

ORANGE

see also:
citrus fruit
fruit
jams, etc
lemon
liqueur
zest

A fruit of the citrus family, the orange originated in the Far East but cultivation is now widespread. The USA is the world's largest producer and Spain, Morocco and Israel also export large quantities. Oranges have juicy flesh of varying acidity, arranged in segments under a smooth or grainy aromatic skin.

Of the TIGHT-SKINNED oranges, the BLONDE is the most common and is at its best in the winter months. It has fairly pale skin and flesh, and includes such varieties as the VALENCIA which is probably the most important orange worldwide. BLOOD ORANGES have dark red flesh and FULL-BLOOD ORANGES, like the BLOOD OVAL, also have red skin. The juicy flesh tends to be sweet and full of flavour. In France the MALTESE ORANGE is the most highly regarded blood orange. Thick-skinned NAVEL ORANGES ripen early in the year and have a small characteristic

navel oranges

blood oranges

depression on the flower end of the fruit. They are usually seedless, are very easy to peel and can be quite juicy. The slightly sour WASHINGTON NAVEL is perhaps the most widely known variety. The small SEVILLE, BIGARADE or BITTER ORANGES are a quite distinct species which are too bitter to be eaten, but make delicious marmalades.

LOOSE-SKINNED fruit includes MANDARIN ORANGES, TANGERINES and SATSUMAS, which are all fairly similar and are best distinguished by their origins. The group also includes a host of hybrids, such as the CLEMENTINE, KING, TANGOR, TANGELO or MINNEOLA and the West Indian ORTANIQUE. Partly due to the ease with which they are peeled, loose-skinned oranges are more generally served as dessert fruit. However, the peel of the tangerine, in particular, is a much sought-after flavouring ingredient.

When buying oranges, make sure that they are perfectly ripe, firm to the touch and heavy for their size, with an unbroken and unblemished skin. If the skin and pith are thick, the flesh is generally sweet but lacking in juice.

Like lemons, oranges are nowadays usually given a waxy coating of chemical preservatives. If planning to use the zest or peel, buy organic or uncoated fruit. Otherwise, first scrub the oranges in hot soapy water, rinse them well and pat dry.

As well as being a popular dessert fruit and frequent ingredient in fresh fruit salads, oranges are widely used in *pâtisserie* and confectionery. Orange juice and zest flavour cakes, creams and custards, sorbets and biscuits and cookies. Candied orange peel is popular in cake-making. Oranges also play an important role in savoury cooking. Their bitterness works well with fatty meats, such as duck, and orange-flavoured butters and *sauce maltaise* are commonly served with fish and game. Oranges can be used in place of lemons in many dishes, imparting a fruitier, sweeter flavour.

Orange juice is the most widely consumed fruit juice and has become an essential part of breakfasts in many parts of the world. Oranges are also used to make a variety of fine liqueurs, such as Cointreau, Grand Marnier and Curaçao, which are also valuable flavouring ingredients in their own right.

Oranges are an important source of vitamins, especially vitamin C, and an average orange contains about 45 calories.

minneola

valencia

ORANGES SOUFFLÉES

Soufflé oranges

Serves 6
Preparation 45 minutes
Cooking about 40 minutes

METRIC/IMPERIAL	*AMERICAN*
6 large thick-skinned oranges	*6 large thick-skinned oranges*
3 eggs, separated	*3 eggs, separated*
8 tbsp caster sugar	*½ cup superfine sugar*
2 tbsp cornflour	*2 tbsp cornstarch*
1 tbsp orange liqueur	*1 tbsp orange liqueur*

Using a very sharp knife, cut a cap off the top of each orange and slice a very thin piece off the base so that the fruit will stand upright.

Scoop out the insides of the oranges without damaging the skins. Squeeze the flesh and strain the juice thus obtained.

Preheat the oven to 240C/465F/gas 8–9.

Beat the egg yolks with the sugar and cornflour (cornstarch). Add the orange juice and mix well. Pour into a saucepan and heat gently, stirring constantly. Remove from the heat as soon as it comes to the boil and the mixture has thickened. Add the orange liqueur.

Whisk the egg whites to stiff peaks and fold them gently into the orange cream. Fill the orange shells with the mixture. Place them in an ovenproof dish and bake for 30 minutes. Serve immediately.

SALADE D'ORANGES À L'OIGNON DOUX

Orange and sweet onion salad

Serves 4
Preparation 25 minutes, marinating 20 minutes

METRIC/IMPERIAL	*AMERICAN*
5 blood oranges, preferably Maltese	*5 blood oranges, preferably Maltese*
juice of 1 lemon	*juice of 1 lemon*
1 tsp mild paprika	*1 tsp mild paprika*
3 tbsp olive oil	*3 tbsp olive oil*
1 tsp acacia honey	*1 tsp acacia honey*
1 tbsp dry sherry	*1 tbsp dry sherry*
2 large red onions, sliced	*2 large red onions, sliced*
salt and pepper	*salt and pepper*
fresh chervil, to garnish	*fresh chervil, to garnish*

Squeeze the juice of one of the oranges into a bowl. Add the lemon juice, paprika, olive oil and honey. Season and add the sherry.

Peel the remaining oranges, removing all white pith, and slice the flesh very thinly, trying not to lose any of the juice. Separate the onion slices into rings.

Arrange the orange slices in a deep dish with their juice. Add the onion rings. Coat with the dressing, mix and chill for 20 minutes.

Stir once more and before serving garnish with chervil sprigs.

ORANGE BLOSSOM

see Flower

OREGANO

see Marjoram

ORGANIC FOOD

Agricultural techniques which attempt to maintain natural bacterial levels in the soil produce what is termed 'organic' food. As well as returning to traditional practices such as rotation farming and shallow planting, the organic farmer eschews all chemical fertilizers, insecticides and sprays. For the cook, this may mean tastier fruit and vegetables with a higher nutritional content and less likelihood of chemical residues. Meat reared on such farms using the same principles is also referred to as 'organic'.

ORMER

see Abalone

OXTAIL

see also: beef, offal, soup, stock

The tails of beef cattle, oxtails are used to make delicious soups and stews, especially in Flemish and English cooking. Their flavour and gelatinous quality is best brought out by long, slow cooking. Buy lean pieces with creamy white fat. In stock, oxtails give body as well as flavour.

OYSTER

Huître

see also: mussel, shellfish

A seawater bivalve mollusc, the oyster was once regarded as poor man's fare. However, as heavy consumption and pollution have made them very scarce, they are now a symbol of luxury.

Nowadays most oysters are farmed, like mussels, to ensure that they do not feed on harmful matter. They are usually seeded quite far out to sea and then brought into fattening beds at the mouths of rivers, where the mixture of fresh and salt waters causes them to swell.

They also spend the last day or so before being sent to market on special cleansing beds where they are flushed with continual changes of clean water as they are irradiated with ultra-violet light. Many varieties of oyster become unpleasant to eat during spawning, hence the dictum of not eating them when there is no 'r' in the month, ie, during the summer months.

Oysters are found in all but polar waters and there are literally hundreds of different types. PORTUGUESE OYSTERS or PORTS are farmed in many parts of Europe, including Britain, and are characterized by their irregular shapes. They are considered somewhat inferior and usually cooked, but have the advantage of being edible all year round.

Two main varieties of oyster are farmed in France: the flat FRENCH NATIVE OYSTER and the concave JAPANESE or PACIFIC OYSTER. Different types of both are usually identified by place of origin. Perhaps the best known flat oyster is the pinkish-grey BELON, named after the river in Brittany. More plentiful and less expensive, concave oysters are mainly farmed in Marennes-Oléron, where they are matured in *claires*, or special pits dug from salt marshes and connected by channels to the sea. These pits are also home to a variety of plankton which gives the flesh of these oysters a characteristic green tinge and they are sometimes referred to as *vertes*. *Fines de claires* are matured in this way for two months and larger *spéciales* for six.

British oysters are mostly flat relatives of the French natives and are again identified geographically. Those grown on the Essex and Kent coasts are known as NATIVES, and include the fine sweet ROYALS, WHITSTABLE and COLCHESTER OYSTERS. DUCHY OYSTERS are from the Helford Estuary in Cornwall.

The most famous of the American oysters are the BLUEPOINT from Long Island and the VIRGINIA, but the Atlantic coast is rich in other fine-flavoured species. On the Pacific coast, apart from the tiny OLYMPIA, cultivation is mainly of transplanted East-coast varieties or Japanese varieties.

Huîtres à la diable (Devilled oysters)

Oysters must be bought perfectly fresh and still alive. The shells should be closed or should close when touched. Buy only those which feel heavy for their size, as they should be full of juices. Choose concave oysters if they are to be cooked, as the shell will make a good receptacle. Use oysters as quickly as possible after purchase; they will keep for a day or so wrapped in a damp cloth in the refrigerator. Do not open them until just before they are needed. Oysters sold ready shelled should look fat and creamy and smell sweet. Their liquid should also be clear and not cloudy.

To prepare oyster in their shells, the shells should first be well scrubbed with a brush and any clinging 'beard' removed. To open the oyster, a special stubby oyster knife is needed which is inserted between the shells at the hinge muscle and then slipped along to sever the muscle. A twist of the knife then usually opens the oyster with ease. This can be a fairly hazardous operation, so wrap the hand holding the oyster in a protecting cloth. Always open the oyster with the rounded shell downwards over a bowl to keep the juices. Be sure to remove

butterfly oyster

Japanese or Pacific oysters

Belon oysters

any tiny fragments of shell and strain any juices before returning them to the oysters or using them in cooking.

Devotees insist that oysters are best appreciated raw and dressed with no more than a little lemon juice and black pepper, although the French often dress them with shallot vinegar and the Americans favour a pungent tomato and horseradish sauce. Serve them on a bed of rock salt or crushed ice, with rye bread and iced butter curls. It is a good idea to supply finger bowls as diners will want to lift the shells to drain the juices.

Oysters are also cooked in a variety of ways. They may be stuffed in the shell and grilled (broiled) or baked, or shelled and then poached, sautéed or deep fried. Oysters are also popular in soups and on kebabs and cold poached oysters in creamy sauces are a popular ingredient in buffet canapés. As with most seafood, care must be taken not to overcook oysters as they quickly become very tough.

Oysters have a low fat content, but are rich in proteins, vitamins, minerals and trace elements. They are held by many to be the ideal anti-stress and anti-fatigue food, as well as being an aphrodisiac. A dozen oysters (about 250 g/8½ oz) contains as much protein as 100 g/3½ oz of meat, with approximately 150 calories.

HUÎTRES À LA DIABLE

Devilled oysters

Serves 4
Preparation 40 minutes
Cooking about 20 minutes

METRIC/IMPERIAL	*AMERICAN*
24 concave oysters	*24 fresh oysters in shell*
55 g/2 oz butter	*4 tbsp butter*
30 g/1 oz flour	*¼ cup flour*
100 ml/3½ fl oz crème fraîche or sour cream	*½ cup crème fraîche or sour cream*
stale white breadcrumbs	*stale white breadcrumbs*
pinch of grated nutmeg	*pinch of grated nutmeg*
½ tsp paprika	*½ tsp paprika*
salt and freshly ground white pepper	*salt and freshly ground white pepper*

Preheat the oven to 200C/400F/gas 6 and line a baking sheet with foil.

Open the oysters, remove the flesh and strain the juices into a saucepan set over a moderate heat. Poach the oysters in the juices for 3 minutes. Remove the pan from the heat and drain the oysters, reserving the juices. Boil the deep halves of the oyster shells in water for a minute or two to sterilize them.

Make a béchamel sauce: melt half of the butter in a saucepan over a gentle heat, stir in the flour and cook for a minute or two, stirring constantly. Gradually add 4 tablespoons of the reserved strained oyster juices and the cream. Bring to the boil and cook gently for a minute or two until smooth and thick. Season with grated nutmeg, salt and pepper.

Melt half of the remaining butter in another pan and brown the breadcrumbs in it. In a bowl, mix the oysters with the béchamel sauce.

Fill the boiled oyster shells with the oyster mixture. Sprinkle each with fried breadcrumbs and a touch of paprika, then top each with a bit of the remaining butter.

Arrange the shells on the prepared baking sheet, crinkling the foil to support them as necessary and keep them separate. Cook in the oven for 3–4 minutes and then serve at once.

To drink: a full-bodied, dry, non-fruity white wine, such as a Graves, Pouilly Fumé or Sancerre.

P

see also: artichoke sauce

PALM HEART

Coeur de palmier

The terminal buds of certain palm trees contain a white, firm-textured cylinder which is known as the palm heart. They have a taste somewhat akin to that of the artichoke and the most tender parts may be eaten raw, while the tougher extremities need to be cooked first. In Europe and North America, palm hearts are usually only available canned and are used, thinly sliced, chopped or grated, in mixed salads, as an accompaniment for shellfish or in raw crudité platters. They are also delicious baked *au gratin* with ham in a white sauce.

SALADE DE COEURS DE PALMIER

Palm heart and mussel salad

Serves 4
Preparation 20 minutes
Cooking 3–5 minutes

METRIC/IMPERIAL	*AMERICAN*
4 slices of lean bacon	*4 slices of lean bacon*
5 tbsp oil	*5 tbsp oil*
2 tbsp vinegar	*2 tbsp vinegar*
1 tbsp mild mustard	*1 tbsp mild mustard*
8 canned palm hearts, drained	*8 canned palm hearts, drained*
200 g/7 oz canned mussels in brine, drained	*7 oz canned mussels or clams in brine, drained*
5 gherkins, sliced	*5 pickled cucumbers or cornichons, sliced*
4 tomatoes, thinly sliced	*4 tomatoes, thinly sliced*
salt and pepper	*salt and pepper*

Dry fry the bacon until well browned, drain and allow to cool. Make a vinaigrette with the oil, vinegar, mustard and salt and pepper to taste.

Cut the palm hearts into fairly small chunks and put in a bowl with the mussels, gherkins (pickled cucumbers) and tomatoes. Pour over the vinaigrette dressing and toss the ingredients gently to coat them well with it.

Divide this salad among 4 plates and put a slice of the bacon on top of each. Finish with a sprinkling of freshly ground black pepper.

PANADA

Panade

see also: flour soufflé stuffing

Pastes with a base of flour, potato or white breadcrumbs mixed with milk and butter, panadas are used for thickening stuffings or as bases for croquettes, quenelles and soufflés.

PANCAKE

see Crêpe

see also:
jams, etc
pickles

PAPAYA OR PAWPAW

Papaye

A large, elongated, pear-shaped tropical fruit with a smooth yellow skin, the papaya has soft, perfumed, juicy orange-red flesh. At the core is a mass of small black seeds which are not eaten with the fruit, but are sometimes used as a condiment. The fruit must be picked ripe and does not refrigerate well, and is thus usually quite expensive outside areas of cultivation.

The papaya is a delicious dessert fruit and its musky flavour gives distinction to fruit salads. In the tropics it is served sprinkled with lemon juice for breakfast and used in jams and preserves. Papayas can also make delicious first courses, served with raw ham or smoked mackerel creamed with horseradish. The cavity left after the seeds are removed can be stuffed like the avocado. Papayas also work well in savoury salads, especially with seafood.

Unripe papayas may be cooked as a vegetable, sliced and fried or simmered. They are often added to poultry dishes and are a common ingredient in tropical pickles like *achar*.

Papayas are low in calories, only 67 per 100 g/ 3½ oz of canned papaya or pawpaw, and rich in vitamin C. Like pineapples, they contain an enzyme which tenderizes meat.

SALADE DE CREVETTES À LA PAPAYE

Shrimp or prawn salad with papaya

Serves 4
Preparation 25 minutes, plus chilling

METRIC/IMPERIAL	AMERICAN
1 large papaya	1 large papaya
5 tbsp groundnut oil	5 tbsp peanut oil
2 tbsp sherry vinegar	2 tbsp sherry vinegar
1 tsp Worcestershire sauce	1 tsp Worcestershire sauce
1 small red chilli pepper, deseeded and finely chopped	1 small red chili pepper, deseeded and finely chopped
20 large cooked prawns, shelled and halved	20 large shrimp, cooked, peeled and halved
4 slices of fresh pineapple, cut into chunks	4 slices of fresh pineapple, cut into chunks
2 lemons, closely peeled and sliced	2 lemons, closely peeled and sliced
1 lettuce heart, shredded	1 lettuce heart, shredded
salt and pepper	salt and pepper

Peel the papaya and cut it in half. Scoop out all the seeds and cube the flesh.

Make a vinaigrette with the oil, vinegar, Worcestershire sauce and salt and pepper to taste. Add the chopped chilli pepper.

In a deep bowl, combine the papaya, prawns (shrimp), pineapple, lemon slices and shredded lettuce. Pour over the vinaigrette and stir to coat all the ingredients. Serve well chilled.

PAPER

see also:
baking
cakes and gâteaux
freezing
frying

Various types of paper are invaluable in the kitchen for the preparation, cooking, serving or preserving of food:

Absorbent PAPER TOWELS are very useful for wiping clean food like mushrooms and drying off food after cleaning. They are also perfect for draining excess fat off fried food and may be used to skim fat off the top of stocks.

GREASEPROOF PAPER and BAKING PARCHMENT withstand quite high heat and are good insulators: they are therefore used to line cake pans, wrap foods to be cooked *en papillote* and cover items in the oven which might otherwise brown too quickly. When used in baking, greaseproof paper is usually greased with oil or butter so that it may be removed more easily. Cakes that need very long cooking may require several layers of paper.

ALUMINIUM FOIL is now widely used in place of paper in baking and cooking *en papillote*, as well as for wrapping food to be refrigerated. HEAVY-DUTY OR FREEZER FOIL is favoured for wrapping food to be stored in the freezer, and is also used when barbecuing.

RICE PAPER is edible. It tastes innocuously sweet and is used in the baking of small items like macaroons, and in confectionery.

WAXED PAPER discs are used to cover pots of preserves, although parchment or greaseproof paper may be used if first dipped in egg white. Waxed paper may also be used to wrap food for storage.

Many types of decorative paper are also available, from doilies used for presenting cakes and desserts to paper frills for the ends of the bones on a rack of lamb.

PAPILLOTE

see also:
baking
barbecuing
grilling

Cooking food *en papillote* means wrapping it, along with any flavouring additions, in a sealed parcel of parchment or greaseproof paper or foil. Such packages are then usually baked, grilled (broiled) or barbecued and served still sealed or just opened, for diners to enjoy the aromatic vapour which rises from them.

This simple and useful method of cooking individual portions is also a very convenient way of cooking fish in confined spaces, as it almost entirely eliminates cooking odours. Food cooked in this way also retains more of its natural flavour and nutrients. However, food cooked *en papillote* is effectively steamed, so results are very different from those usually obtained by normal grilling or baking. Fish, seafood, poultry, veal, vegetables and fruit particularly suit this treatment.

As little or no fat need be added, this is also a very healthy cooking method.

TRUITES EN PAPILLOTE

Trout in parcels

Serves 4
Preparation 10 minutes
Cooking 10 minutes

METRIC/IMPERIAL	*AMERICAN*
4 trout, each weighing about 170 g/6 oz, gutted	*4 trout, each weighing about 6 oz, drawn*
4 tsp snipped fresh dill	*4 tsp snipped fresh dill*
2 shallots, finely chopped	*2 shallots, finely chopped*
4 tsp dry vermouth	*4 tsp dry vermouth*
1 tbsp olive oil	*1 tbsp olive oil*
1 lemon, closely peeled and thinly sliced	*1 lemon, closely peeled and thinly sliced*
salt and pepper	*salt and pepper*

Preheat the oven to 240C/465F/gas 8–9.

Season the insides of the fish with salt and pepper and put 1 teaspoon of dill inside each.

Cut out four 35 cm/14 in squares of foil. Place 1 trout in the centre of each. Add a good pinch of chopped shallot, 1 teaspoon of vermouth and a drop or two of olive oil to each. Finally top with 2 lemon slices.

Lift the sides of the foil and wrap up the parcels, sealing them well at the top. Cook in the oven for 10 minutes and then serve at once.

Variation: small, gutted, fresh sardines are delicious cooked plainly this way with only a little salt, pepper and lemon juice.

PAPRIKA

see also:
peppers

A mild sweet or hot spice, paprika is made by drying a particular type of sweet red pepper and then grinding it to a powder. It is a distinctive feature of the cooking of Hungary and Spain, where it is known as *pimenton* and may have a quite different flavour. Paprika is used in generous quantities to season sauces and stews, and also for flavouring and colouring some cheeses. Add paprika to a dish off the heat or mix it into a liquid first, otherwise it may caramelize and give the dish a bitter taste. It is also very useful as a colourful garnish.

PARFAIT

see Ices and ice creams

PARMESAN

see also:
cheese
gratin
pasta and noodles

The hard *grana*, or 'grainy', cheeses of Italy are known as Parmesan in other countries, as the best come from the Parma region and are marked *Parmigiano-Reggiano*.

These large cows' milk cheeses are made of a cooked paste which has a piquant and fruity flavour. Parmesans are normally well aged, for at least three years, so that their flavour develops powerfully and they become very hard. These grate well for use in items baked *au gratin* or for dressing soups or pasta. Fresher cheeses are soft enough to be eaten thinly sliced, either with pears at the end of a meal or with cured meat as a first course.

The flavour of the ready-grated varieties of Parmesan, sold in jars or sachets, bears little resemblance to the true, full flavour of the cheese, and it is well worth buying pieces and grating them freshly as required. Avoid cheeses which look grey or are sweating.

If substituting Parmesan for Gruyère in a dish baked *au gratin*, add very little salt.

A cheese with a very high fat content: 100 g/ 3½ oz of Parmesan contains 390 calories.

PARSLEY

Persil

see also:
bouquet garni
butter
court-bouillon
herbs
snail
stock

An aromatic plant which is available all year round, parsley is the most widely used herb and garnish in Western cooking. The two most common varieties are those known descriptively as MOSS-CURLED or CURLY-LEAVED PARSLEY and FLAT-LEAVED or ITALIAN PARSLEY. There is much debate about which of their different flavours is better; that of the flat-leaved variety is stronger. The latter is especially appropriate for Mediterranean dishes, being the type generally found in French, Spanish and Italian kitchens. Curly-leaved parsley makes a better decorative garnish for hors d'oeuvres and grilled meat and fish, and whole sprigs may be deep-fried.

Parsley is usually finely or coarsely chopped, according to the recipe. It is used raw on salads and in sauces and vinaigrettes or as a final garnish for a dish. The stalks are essential in a bouquet garni and in most court-bouillons and stocks. Parsley freezes well, and new varieties of dried parsley are useful and strong in flavour.

In French cuisine, a mixture of chopped parsley and garlic is known as a *persillade*, and is used in the cooking of snails and roast meats.

SAUCE PERSIL

Parsley sauce

Serves 4
Preparation 10 minutes
Cooking about 10 minutes

METRIC/IMPERIAL	*AMERICAN*
125 g/4½ oz butter	*9 tbsp butter*
30 g/1 oz flour	*¼ cup flour*
4 tbsp finely chopped flat-leaved parsley	*¼ cup finely chopped flat-leaf parsley*
1 tbsp lemon juice	*1 tbsp lemon juice*
salt and pepper	*salt and pepper*

Melt 30 g/1 oz/2 tbsp of the butter in a saucepan. Add the flour and cook for 1 minute.

When the roux is golden, gradually pour in 200 ml/7 fl oz/1 cup of boiling water, whisking until smooth. Cook for a minute or two until thick and then season with salt and pepper.

Add the remaining butter in small pieces, whisking constantly. When the sauce is smooth, incorporate the parsley and lemon juice. Adjust the seasoning and serve at once, to accompany poached fish, potatoes or root vegetables.

see also:
carrot
swede
turnip

PARSNIP

Panais

A fleshy, pale-coloured root vegetable of the carrot family, the parsnip resembles the carrot in shape and is like a very sweet, aromatic turnip in flavour. Parsnips are at their best in winter and spring and are mostly used in soups and stews or par-boiled and baked or roasted as an accompaniment to meat. Small, young roots need simply be scraped, but older, larger ones should be peeled and any woody core removed. Very tender young specimens may even be grated and served as a crudité.

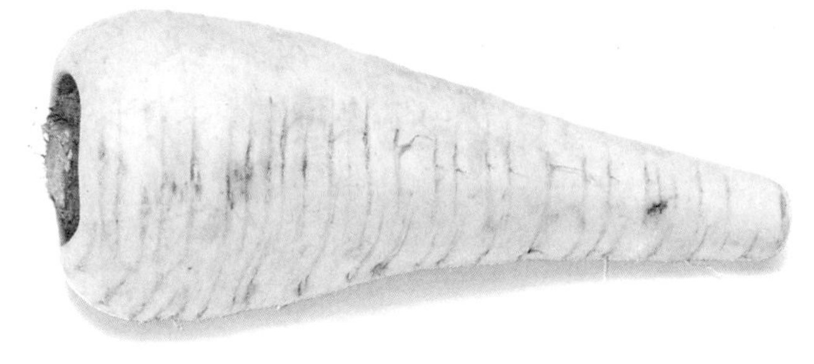

PANAIS AUX FINES HERBES

Parsnips with fines herbes

Serves 4
Preparation 15 minutes
Cooking about 25 minutes

METRIC/IMPERIAL	AMERICAN
45 g/1½ oz butter	3 tbsp butter
800 g/1¾ lb young parsnips, diced	1¾ lb young parsnips, diced
150 ml/¼ pt chicken stock	⅔ cup chicken stock
2 tbsp chopped chervil	2 tbsp chopped chervil
2 tbsp chopped flat-leaved parsley	2 tbsp chopped flat-leaf parsley
salt and freshly ground pepper	salt and freshly ground pepper

Melt the butter in a sauté pan over a moderate heat. Add the parsnips and cook, stirring, until light golden in colour. Add the stock, season and simmer, uncovered, for 15 minutes.

Add the chervil and parsley to the pan and mix well. Cover and cook gently for 2–3 minutes.

Transfer to a warmed serving dish and serve immediately to accompany roast or braised meat.

PARTRIDGE

Perdrix, perdreau

see also:
barding
chicken
duck
game
grouse
pheasant
quail
salmis

A small game bird, the partridge is highly prized for its fine flavour. The principal species found in Britain and Europe is the GREY PARTRIDGE, so called because of its characteristic grey legs. In Spain and in France, particularly in the south, the RED-LEGGED PARTRIDGE is more common, but is regarded as inferior as it has a much duller taste. This latter species has also been successfully introduced into Britain, where it is nicknamed the 'Frenchman'. There are no true native partridges in the USA, but the term is applied to a variety of similar small game birds, especially the quail in southern states and the ruffed grouse in the northeast.

Younger partridges have a fine flavour and much softer and more tender meat. The French differentiate between older birds and birds of either sex up to the age of 1 year, available from the end of August to October, which they term *perdreaux*. As a sign of youth, look for flexible beaks and shorter, pointed feathers with a white tip. The mature partridge or *perdrix* is in season from October to January.

Partridges are hung only briefly, to avoid masking the delicate flavour by letting them become too gamy. Usually sold ready for cooking, they must still be inspected for shot.

Younger birds, or *perdreaux*, should be barded and roasted or spatchcocked, ie split in half and flattened, and then grilled. Tougher old birds respond best to long, slow braising, traditionally with cabbage or sauerkraut. Partridges also suit most recipes for chicken or pheasant and may be cooked as a *salmis* like duck, added to stews or made into pâtés.

Partridge meat is lean and 100 g/3½ oz contains only 115 calories.

ESTOUFFADE DE PERDRIX AUX LENTILLES

Partridge and lentil stew

Serves 4
Preparation 25 minutes, 1 hour ahead
Cooking about 2 hours

METRIC/IMPERIAL	*AMERICAN*
250 g/8½ oz green lentils, preferably lentilles du Puy	*1½ cups green lentils, preferably lentilles du Puy*
2 young dressed partridges	*2 young partridges, dressed and drawn*
55 g/2 oz butter	*4 tbsp butter*
225 g/½ lb lean bacon	*½ lb bacon*
6 small onions, sliced	*6 small onions, sliced*
4 carrots, sliced	*4 carrots, sliced*
150 ml/¼ pt white wine	*⅔ cup white wine*
150 ml/¼ pt chicken stock	*⅔ cup chicken stock*
bouquet garni	*bouquet garni*
225 g/½ lb dried pork sausage, such as Morteau (Jésus) or salami	*½ lb dried pork sausage, such as Morteau (Jésus) or salami*
salt and pepper	*salt and pepper*

Soak the lentils for 1 hour in warm water and then drain them. Meanwhile, roast the partridges for about 20 minutes at 200C/400F/gas 6, basting with the butter.

Cut half the bacon into small pieces. Place the partridges in a flameproof casserole with the chopped bacon and about one quarter of the onions and carrots. Add the wine, stock and the bouquet garni and season with salt and pepper. Simmer, covered, for 1½ hours.

After about 40 minutes, bring a large pan of water to the boil and add the lentils. Cut the remaining bacon into thin slices and add to the lentils with the remaining onions and carrots. Simmer for about 40 minutes, until the lentils are tender. Add only a little salt, if necessary, after about 15 minutes.

Add the sausage or salami to the lentils about half-way through. When ready to serve, drain the lentils and put them with the vegetables into a very hot, deep serving dish. Cut each partridge in half, place them on top of the lentils and surround them with slices of bacon and sausage. Coat with the partridge cooking liquid.

To drink: a full-bodied white wine, such as a Graves, or a mature red wine, such as a Pauillac.

PASSION FRUIT

Fruit de la passion

see also: fruit sorbet

The fruit of the tropical passion flower is also known as the *granadilla*, or 'little pomegranate', and is about the size of an egg. When ripe, the skin is purple and should feel supple, although it wrinkles as the fruit loses moisture. The highly perfumed, pale green flesh is slightly gelatinous and contains a number of small, edible seeds. Its flavour is incomparable, being both sweet and acid at the same time, as well as very fragrant.

The fruit may be cut in half, dressed with a little lemon juice and eaten raw with a small spoon. More usually, the flesh is scooped out and used in fruit salads, tarts and other fruit or cream desserts, such as the classic meringue Pavlova. It may simply be mixed with thick cream to make a delicious syllabub. The strained flesh is also made into sorbets, soufflés and mousses, and can be added to jams.

Passion fruit flesh is rich in vitamins A and C and 100 g/3½ oz contains 75 calories.

Estouffade de perdrix aux lentilles (Partridge and lentil stew)

MOUSSE DE LA PASSION

Passion fruit mousse

Serves 2
Preparation 20 minutes
Cooking 2 or 3 minutes, 2 hours ahead

METRIC/IMPERIAL	AMERICAN
225 g/½ lb passion fruit	½ lb passion fruit
75 g/2½ oz caster sugar	6½ tbsp superfine sugar
1 tsp Kirsch	1 tsp Kirsch
150 ml/¼ pt crème fraîche or whipping cream, well chilled	⅔ cup crème fraîche or whipping cream, well chilled
2 tbsp icing sugar	2 tbsp confectioners' sugar
5 cm/2 in piece of candied angelica, cut into thin strips	2 in piece of candied angelica, cut into thin strips

Cut the fruits in half and remove all the pulp. Pass through a sieve to eliminate the seeds.

Put the pulp into a saucepan with the caster (superfine) sugar and bring slowly to the boil, stirring. Boil for 1 minute.

Remove from the heat and add the Kirsch. Let stand for 5 minutes. Meanwhile, whip the cream with the icing (confectioners') sugar.

Add the fruit syrup to the cream and mix well. Spoon the mixture into 2 dessert glasses and chill for at least 2 hours.

Just before serving, decorate with angelica.

see also:
basil
boiling
cheese
flour
gratin
Parmesan
sauce
soup
stock

PASTA AND NOODLES

Pâtes alimentaires et nouilles

A basic element of Italian cooking since Roman times, pasta is made of a dough with a durum-wheat semolina and water base. The dough may also contain eggs, and is sometimes flavoured and coloured with puréed vegetables, especially spinach (*pasta verde*). Pasta is formed into a wide variety of shapes, from the strings of SPAGHETTI and long, flat strips of TAGLIATELLE OR FETTUCINE to the tiny decorative shells, spirals and stars added to soup (*pasta in brodo*). Irrespective of shape, there are four basic types of pasta:

DRIED PASTA (*pasta secca*) is commercially made using only durum-wheat semolina and water. Good-quality dried pasta is recognized by its smooth, even appearance and it should break evenly without shattering. Unless coloured, it should be a good ivory, verging on yellow, and translucent. It takes a relatively long time to cook, depending on size and shape, and quadruples in volume.

Dried pasta comes in the widest array of sizes and shapes. Perhaps the most important differentiation for the cook is between the solid, plain-surfaced pasta like SPAGHETTI or thinner VERMICELLI and those with a hollow interior, like MACARONI and PENNE, or those with complex shapes, like the spirals of FUSILI or the bow-shaped FARFALLE. The hollow and shaped varieties soak up more sauce, as do ribbed versions of any form of pasta.

FRESH OR EGG PASTA (*pasta all'uovo*) has eggs in the dough and is made daily like bread, either at home or by local concerns. Usually formed simply into spaghetti or tagliatelle, or stuffed, it cooks in a matter of a minute or two and keeps for only a few days.

STUFFED PASTA (*pasta ripiena*), like RAVIOLI and AGNOLOTTI, consists of fresh pasta made into small parcels wrapped around a filling such as ricotta cheese, minced (ground) beef or chicken, chopped ham, mushrooms or vegetables. Stuffed pasta, even if fresh, usually needs quite lengthy boiling to ensure that the fillings are cooked through.

BAKED PASTA (*pasta al forno*) is usually dried pasta in flat sheets or wide cylinders and is made to be incorporated in dishes, like LASAGNE or CANNELLONI, which are baked with their sauce in the oven. As with other pastas, they are first cooked in boiling water.

Certain types of fresh and stuffed pasta are vacuum-packed, frozen or semi-preserved and are sold in the cold cabinets of supermarkets alongside the true, fresh pasta. An increasing number of WHOLEWHEAT PASTAS are available for those wishing to increase the fibre in their diet, but these take longer to cook.

All fresh and dried pasta should be cooked in a large quantity of generously salted boiling water or stock, and the liquid kept boiling rapidly to ensure that the pasta does not become starchy and that all the strands or pieces remain separate. Adding some olive oil also helps keep the pasta from clumping together. For dried pasta allow 115 g/4 oz of pasta per person and cook it in 1 l/2 pt/1 qt of water with 1½ teaspoons of salt added.

Pasta is best cooked until *al dente*, ie tender but still with some resistance when bitten: overcooked pasta is gluey and quite unappealing. It is wise not to take any guiding time too literally, even those given on packets, as cooking times depend on many factors, including how old the pasta is. It is best to test regularly and judge for yourself.

As soon as the pasta is ready, drain well and return it to the warm pan or a warmed serving dish. Some oil or butter mixed in very quickly will keep it from sticking together.

Pasta may be served very simply dressed with good olive oil or butter, some seasoning and a sprinkling of freshly grated Parmesan. There is also a wide range of accompanying sauces, usually with a tomato and herb base, incorporating mushrooms, anchovies, seafood or minced (ground) beef, as in the traditional Bolognese sauce. Cream sauces, often with chopped ham, are also popular, as is the classic *pesto* sauce made with fresh basil and ground pine kernels (pine nuts).

Noodles, usually made with eggs in thin, flat ribbons, feature in the cooking of many countries. They are the classic accompaniment to East European dishes, such as Stroganoff, traditional French *coq au vin* and many game stews and creamy fish dishes.

Oriental cuisine also makes much use of a wide range of noodles produced from wheat, rice or soy flour. Some need only soaking in warm water; others are boiled until tender and then fried in oil along with flavouring ingredients such as spring onions (scallions) and mushrooms.

Pasta is an excellent health food, because it slowly liberates glucose energy into the system. Also contrary to popular belief, it is not fattening: 100 g/3½ oz of plain-cooked, dried pasta contains just over 100 calories. However, sauces and cheese add considerably to the calorie content of most pasta dishes.

Pâte à nouilles

Homemade fresh pasta or noodle dough

Serves 6
Preparation 20 minutes, standing 30 minutes
Drying 2 hours
Cooking 5 minutes

METRIC/IMPERIAL	*AMERICAN*
300 g/10 oz flour	*2½ cups flour*
3 size-2 eggs	*3 extra large eggs*
1 tbsp olive oil	*1 tbsp olive oil*
salt	*salt*

Pile the flour on a work surface and make a well in the middle of it. Break the eggs into the well and add 2 or 3 pinches of salt.

Start to mix the ingredients, slowly bringing in flour from the edges (1). The mixture will be a little soft at the beginning, but firms up very quickly. Add a little water, just enough to make a supple and elastic dough.

Knead the dough with the heel of the hand and form it into a ball. Stretch it out and reform it 2 or 3 times until it is smooth and firm (2). When the dough comes away from the hands of

1

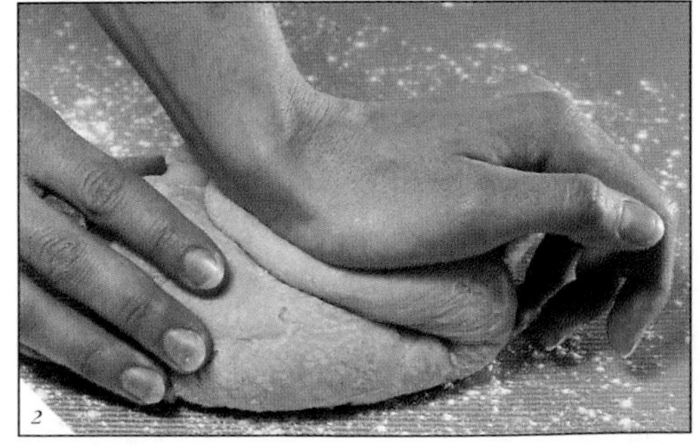
2

3

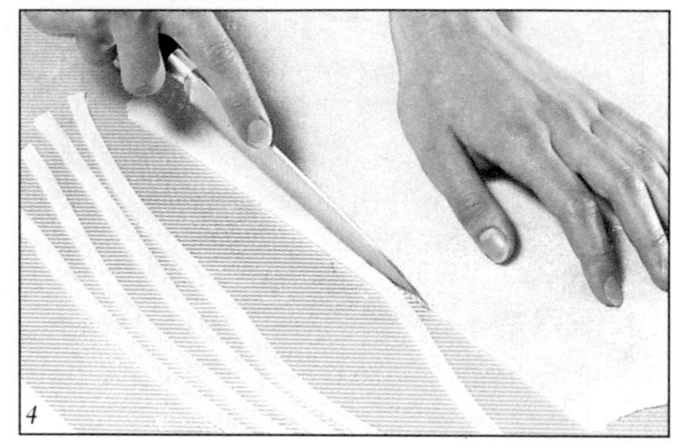
4

its own accord, form it into a ball and let it stand at room temperature for about 30 minutes.

Flour the work surface and rolling pin. Divide the dough into 2 or 3 portions. Roll each out as thinly as possible (3).

Cut strips of the required width with a knife (4). Alternatively use a pasta machine. Leave to dry for 2 or 3 hours at room temperature.

To cook the noodles bring to the boil a large pan of well-salted water with the olive oil. Put the pasta in it, bring back to the boil quickly and then keep at a rolling boil for about 5 minutes, or until cooked *al dente*. Drain well and toss in good olive oil or melted butter to serve.

Notes: durum-wheat semolina may be used to give a more authentic pasta, but the dough will not be easy to knead by hand.

A simple method for cutting noodles is to roll up the sheet of dough into a sort of 'Swiss or jelly roll', then cut this across into strips, and unfold immediately to dry them out.

Do not wait too long before cutting out the noodles once the dough is rolled out as it dries very quickly. A good way of drying noodles is to hang them on a broomstick covered with a cloth and suspended between 2 chairs.

If not cooking the noodles immediately, flour lightly and put them in a clean cloth; they will keep for 3–4 days in the refrigerator.

To freeze, form the noodles into small nests and dry on a tray before putting them into freezer bags. They will keep for 3–4 months.

RAVIOLI FARCIS À LA VIANDE

Meat ravioli

Serves 4
Preparation about 1 hour, resting 30 minutes
Cooking about 10 minutes

METRIC/IMPERIAL	AMERICAN
400 g/14 oz flour	3½ cups flour
4 eggs	4 eggs
450 g/1 lb leftover braised beef with vegetables and sauce	1 lb leftover braised beef with vegetables and sauce (about 2 cups)
2 tbsp olive oil	2 tbsp olive oil
salt	salt
grated Parmesan, to serve	grated Parmesan cheese, to serve

Make the pasta dough: pile the flour on a surface and make a well in it. Break the eggs into the well and add a pinch or two of salt. Mix the ingredients by gradually bringing in the flour from the edges until it forms a smooth elastic dough. Knead until the dough does not stick readily to the hands, then form into a ball and allow to rest at room temperature for about 30 minutes.

Meanwhile, gently reheat the braised meat and vegetables, if necessary, in order to strain off the sauce. Set it to one side. Finely chop the meat and vegetables.

Roll out the pasta dough thinly to make 2 long rectangles, one a little larger than the other. On the smaller rectangle, put little heaps of stuffing at regular intervals about 5 cm/2 in apart, in rows about the same distance apart (1, opposite).

Moisten a brush with water and brush along the rows between the stuffing. Place the second rectangle of dough on top (2, opposite). Press down gently between the heaps of stuffing to seal the dough, then cut out the ravioli squares

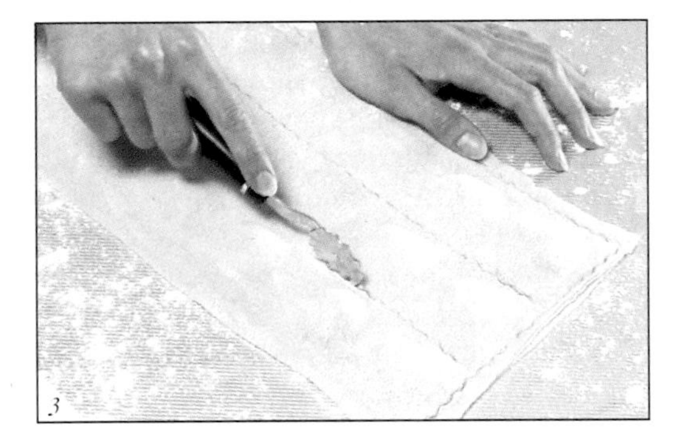

with a pastry wheel (3, above). Pinch the edges of each firmly and leave them to dry for about 10 minutes.

Put the sauce over a gentle heat to warm through. Fill a large saucepan with lightly salted water, add the oil and bring it to the boil. Cook the ravioli in it for about 5 minutes. Drain well and serve very hot, coated in the sauce, with the Parmesan on the side.

Variation: To make a stuffing if you have no leftover meat, mince (grind) 100 g/3½ oz boneless veal, 100 g/3½ oz boneless beef and 100 g/3½ oz raw ham and cook in oil with a chopped onion, some thyme, a bay leaf and a little stock. Mix with 150 g/5½ oz blanched, chopped spinach. Use to stuff the ravioli and serve with tomato sauce.

SPAGHETTI ALLA CARBONARA

Spaghetti with ham and cream sauce

Serves 4
Preparation 5 minutes
Cooking about 15 minutes

METRIC/IMPERIAL	*AMERICAN*
1 tbsp olive oil	*1 tbsp olive oil*
225 g/½ lb thick slices of pancetta or smoked bacon, cut into small dice or strips	*½ lb Italian pancetta or country-style bacon, cut into small dice or strips*
200 ml/7 fl oz whipping cream	*1 cup whipping cream*
30 g/1 oz butter	*2 tbsp butter*
225 g/½ lb spaghetti	*½ lb spaghetti*
2 egg yolks	*2 egg yolks*
100 g/3½ oz grated Parmesan	*1 cup grated Parmesan cheese*
salt and pepper	*salt and pepper*

Bring to the boil a large pan of well-salted water to which the oil has been added.

Meanwhile, dry fry the pancetta or bacon gently in a sauté pan for 3 minutes. Drain well and put the pancetta or bacon into a saucepan. Add the cream and butter and season with salt and pepper. Leave to heat gently.

Add the spaghetti to the rapidly boiling water, pushing it down and around the pan as the bottoms of the strands soften. Bring quickly back to the boil and boil rapidly for about 10 minutes, or until cooked *al dente*.

Just before the pasta is ready, mix the egg yolks with the Parmesan and add to the bacon mixture. Season generously with pepper and stir gently without allowing the mixture to boil.

Drain the spaghetti thoroughly and put it into a very hot serving dish. Add the sauce, mix well and serve immediately.

TAGLIATELLE AUX FRUITS DE MER

Seafood tagliatelle

Serves 6
Preparation 20 minutes
Cooking about 20 minutes

METRIC/IMPERIAL	AMERICAN
1 l/1¾ pt cockles, well scrubbed	1 qt cockles or clams, well scrubbed
1 l/1¾ pt mussels, well scrubbed	1 qt mussels, well scrubbed
1 tbsp olive oil	1 tbsp olive oil
400 g/14 oz green tagliatelle	14 oz green tagliatelle
55 g/2 oz butter, cut into small pieces	4 tbsp butter, cut into small pieces
200 ml/7 fl oz whipping cream	1 cup whipping cream
45 g/1½ oz grated Parmesan	⅓ cup grated Parmesan cheese
18 large cooked prawns, peeled and halved	18 large shrimp, cooked, peeled and halved
salt and pepper	salt and pepper

Steam open the cockles and mussels separately in two saucepans over a brisk heat. Discard any that do not open. Remove the cockles and mussels from their shells. Strain the juices from the cockles into a small pan and boil over a high heat to reduce to about 5 tablespoons.

Bring to the boil a large pan of well-salted water to which the oil has been added. Put the tagliatelle into the rapidly boiling water, bring back to the boil quickly and then keep at a good rolling boil for about 8 minutes, or until cooked *al dente*. Drain well.

Put the drained pasta into a saucepan with the butter. Mix over a gentle heat until the butter has melted. Add the cream and Parmesan, stir, and season with salt and pepper.

Add the cockles, mussels and prawns (shrimp). Mix, adding the reduced cockle juices. Adjust the seasoning, taking care not to over-salt, and serve at once.

To drink: a dry white wine, such as Pouilly-Fuisse.

AGNOLOTTI AU PARMESAN

Agnolotti with Parmesan

Serves 4
Preparation 5 minutes
Cooking 6–8 minutes

METRIC/IMPERIAL	AMERICAN
2 chicken stock cubes	2 chicken bouillon cubes
300 g/10 oz agnolotti	10 oz agnolotti
55 g/2 oz butter	4 tbsp butter
4 fresh basil leaves, snipped	4 fresh basil leaves, snipped
85 g/3 oz grated Parmesan	⅔ cup grated Parmesan cheese

Dissolve the stock (bouillon) cubes in 2 l/3½ pt/2 qt of water and bring to the boil.

Plunge the agnolotti in the stock and cook until they all rise to the surface. Meanwhile, melt the butter gently and add the basil.

Drain the cooked agnolotti thoroughly and place them in a warmed serving dish. Pour the butter and basil mixture over them and sprinkle with Parmesan. Serve at once.

PASTEURIZATION

see also: beer, butter, cheese, cream, milk, wine

The process of pasteurization heat-treats various liquids, especially milk and wine, to destroy most of the bacteria in them. As well as making the liquids safer to drink, it allows them, and foodstuffs like cheese made from them, to be kept for longer. High-temperature pasteurization heats the food very briefly, for no more than 15–20 seconds, up to about 71C/161F and then cools them rapidly. This causes minimal damage to the flavour and kills most potentially dangerous micro-organisms. Low-temperature pasteurization takes about 30 minutes at a lower temperature of about 63C/145F. This latter technique is used for semi-preserved foods, such as beer, cider and occasionally wine, but above all for milk to be made into cheese and other dairy products.

Tagliatelle aux fruits de mer (Seafood tagliatelle)

see also:
baking
baking blind
bread
cakes and gâteaux
choux pastry
cookies, etc
croustade
croûte
pie
pizza
quiche
tart
turnover

PASTRY

Pâte

A number of basic types of pastry dough, enriched with fat, such as butter or margarine or perhaps shortening or lard, and sometimes eggs, have different uses.

SHORTCRUST OR BASIC PIE PASTRY is the most usual for pies, quiches, tarts and tartlets, as well as for turnovers, rissoles, barquettes and pâté *en croûte*.

RICH SWEETENED SHORTCRUST OR PIE PASTRY is used for fine *pâtisserie* and sweet tart bases which are made in advance and filled at the last moment. It is also the pastry used to make rich, sweet biscuits and cookies.

PUFF PASTRY has a wide range of uses in baking and *pâtisserie*. It is good for some pies and tarts, makes a rich case for sweet and savoury fillings, as in a *vol-au-vent*, as well as being essential in items like *palmiers* and *feuilletés*.

For successful pastry be precise with the amount of flour. Measure it or, preferably, weigh it, then sift and add it all at once. In hot weather, or if cursed with 'warm' hands, let pastry stand for at least 1 hour in the refrigerator before rolling it. Ensure that the oven is properly preheated to the required temperature before putting in the pastry.

Shortcrust or basic pie pastry is the lowest in calories, with only about 110 per average unfilled portion. Rich sweetened shortcrust or pie pastry and puff pastry have about 155 and 185 calories respectively.

PÂTE BRISÉE

Shortcrust or basic pie pastry

Makes a tart with a diameter of about 25 cm/10 in
Preparation 15 minutes, chilling 30 minutes
Cooking about 35 minutes

METRIC/IMPERIAL	*AMERICAN*
250 g/8½ oz flour	*2 cups flour*
½ tsp fine salt	*½ tsp fine salt*
1–2 tbsp caster sugar (optional)	*1–2 tbsp superfine sugar (optional)*
100 g/3½ oz butter, cut into tiny pieces	*1 stick butter, cut into tiny pieces*

1

2

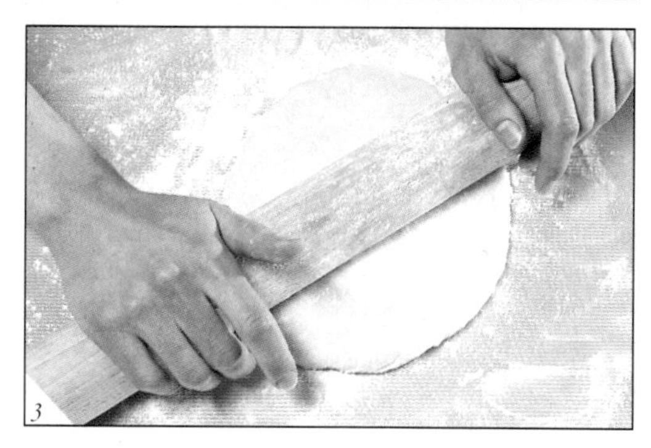
3

Put 200 g/7 oz/1¾ cups of the flour into a bowl and make a well in it. Add the salt along with sugar to taste, if using for a sweet dish.

Add the pieces of butter to the flour, then rub it in with the fingertips (1).

Gradually add about 100 ml/3½ fl oz/½ cup of water, mixing it in rapidly with a spoon or spatula. Form the dough into a ball and work lightly until smooth but not soft or sticky. Try not to handle it more than is necessary. Dust the ball with flour and chill for 30 minutes.

Place the ball of dough on the floured work surface and press the dough with the heel of the hand, until all the remaining visible pieces of butter are mixed in (2).

Flour a rolling pin and roll the dough out to the required thickness (3). Bake in an oven preheated to 250C/475F/gas 9. The average cooking time, if the filling is added right at the beginning, is 30–35 minutes.

Notes: speed up the process using a food processor: put the flour, salt, sugar and butter into the machine and mix briefly. With the machine still running, gradually add the water until the dough readily clumps together. Take it out and form it into a ball as above.

If a pastry case is 'baked blind', ie without the filling, avoid the risk of the pastry puffing up by pricking it all over with a fork or by putting a piece of parchment or greaseproof paper on the bottom and filling with dried beans or special weights. Remove the weighted lining for the last few minutes of cooking to brown and crisp the inside of the pastry case.

When storing the pastry dough in the refrigerator, wrap it tightly or it will dry out and harden. It does freeze very well, whether raw or cooked, filled or unfilled, in a ball or rolled out into a tart case.

PÂTE SABLÉE

Rich sweetened shortcrust or pie pastry

Makes a tart with a diameter of about 25 cm/10 in
Preparation 25 minutes
Cooking about 20 minutes

METRIC/IMPERIAL	*AMERICAN*
1 egg	*1 egg*
$\frac{1}{4}$ tsp salt	*$\frac{1}{4}$ tsp salt*
125 g/4$\frac{1}{2}$ oz caster sugar	*10 tbsp superfine sugar*
250 g/9 oz flour, sifted	*2 cups flour, sifted*
flavouring, such as grated lemon zest, few drops of vanilla essence or rum, etc	*flavoring, such as grated lemon zest, few drops of vanilla extract or rum, etc*
125 g/4$\frac{1}{2}$ oz butter, softened	*9 tbsp butter, softened*

Break the egg into a bowl and beat it, then add the salt and sugar. Beat the mixture until it is pale yellow and foamy (1).

Add the flour all at once along with any flavouring (2). Begin to mix with a wooden spoon, then continue with the fingertips, lifting the mixture and rubbing it until it has the consistency of fine breadcrumbs (3).

Turn out on a floured work surface and knead in the butter to make a dough that does not stick to the fingers. Flour the rolling pin and roll out to the required size and thickness.

Bake in an oven preheated to 180C/350F/gas 4 for about 20 minutes. The tart should be left to cool before being turned out, otherwise the hot pastry will crumble.

Notes: rich sweetened pastry is also easily made by mixing all the ingredients in a food processor.

It is also worth remembering that the weight proportions for this pastry are 2:1:1 flour, sugar and butter.

1

2

3

PÂTE FEUILLETÉE

Puff pastry

Makes a tart with a diameter of about 25 cm/10 in
Preparation 40 minutes, standing 60 minutes
Cooking 20–35 minutes

METRIC/IMPERIAL	*AMERICAN*
200 g/7 oz flour	*1¾ cups flour*
2–3 tbsp caster sugar (optional)	*2–3 tbsp superfine sugar (optional)*
about 150 g/5½ oz butter or margarine	*about 11 tbsp butter or margarine*
salt	*salt*

Pour the flour into a bowl and make a well in the middle. Add the sugar if desired, along with 100 ml/3½ fl oz/½ cup of water and a pinch of salt. Start mixing the flour into the liquid using a wooden spoon, then use the hands, pulling the flour in from the edges and working as quickly as possible (1). Form the dough into a ball and weigh it. Let the dough stand for 20 minutes in the bowl, covered with a cloth.

Flour the work surface and roll the dough into a rectangle slightly thicker in its centre.

Weigh out exactly half the weight of butter or margarine as there is dough and mould it into a square. Put it diagonally in the middle of the dough, fold in the 4 corners to cover and seal the edges (2).

Roll the pastry into a rectangle, about 1 cm/½ in thick and 3 times as long as it is wide (3).

Fold the rectangle into 3, folding the first third inwards, then fold the other third over the top of that (4). Give the pastry one quarter-turn to the right. Roll it out into a rectangle and fold it again as above, then let it stand in a cool place for 20 minutes.

Classic puff pastry should be given a total of 6 'turns', ie 3 sets of 2 turns, with a standing period every 2 turns. If preparing in advance, give it the final 2 turns just before using.

Puff pastry baked blind, ie without a filling, needs 20 minutes in an oven preheated to 250C/475F/gas 9. If the pastry case is filled, the oven should be cooler, 240C/465F/gas 8–9, and the baking will take 30–35 minutes.

Notes: the butter or margarine used should be of the same consistency as the dough. The best solution is to use equal parts of butter and margarine. Flatten the mixture of fats between 2 sheets of parchment or greaseproof paper, then place it in the centre of the dough.

1

2

3

4

LINING A TART PAN WITH PASTRY

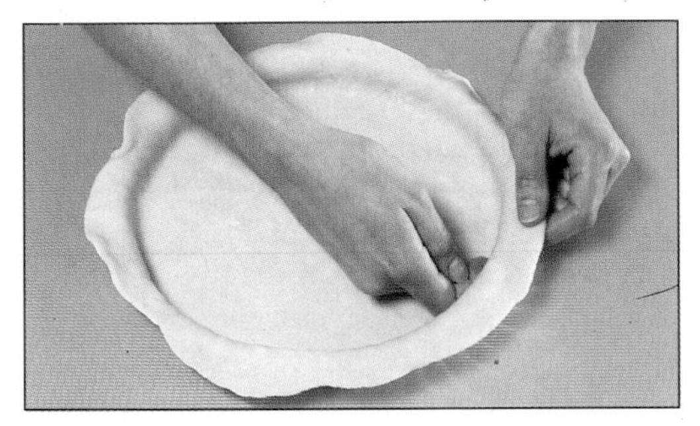

Roll out the pastry into a circle about 3–5 mm/$\frac{1}{8}$–$\frac{1}{4}$ in thick. Lift it into the mould, then gently press the pastry into the corners.

Use the rolling pin to cut off the excess pastry. Chill before baking or freeze for later use.

PASTRY CREAM

see Creams and custards

PÂTÉ

see also:
brawn
giblets
liver
pork
sausage
stuffing
terrine
veal

Rich mixtures of fish and meat, especially pork, veal, poultry, game, offal (variety meats), baked in the oven are known as pâtés. Strictly speaking the term, literally meaning 'pie', should be applied only to such a mixture baked inside a pastry crust (*pâté en croûte*). What is usually referred to as pâté in France is a *pâté en terrine*, in which the mixture is moulded in an earthenware dish lined with barding fat and the finished dish is served cold, cut in slices.

Two basic types of pâté are characterized by their consistency. Coarse pâtés, like *pâté de campagne*, use ingredients chopped not too finely which cook to a crumbly texture. Smooth pâtés incorporate finely minced (ground) ingredients and are spreadable.

The most usual flavourings in pâtés include onion, shallot, garlic, truffle, nutmeg, *quatre-épices* or allspice, wine and brandy. They may be bound with egg, flour or a white sauce, although the high fat content is usually sufficient. The tops of pâtés usually have more barding fat arranged decoratively, or may be sealed with a layer of fat or aspic. Many *pâtés en croûte* have aspic poured through a funnel into the pastry as they cool to fill the spaces between the meat and pastry.

All types of pâté are obviously very high in saturated fat content and 100 g/3½ oz of an average pâté contains about 450 calories.

PÂTÉ DE CAMPAGNE

Country-style pâté

Serves 8
Preparation 40 minutes
Cooking about 1½ hours, 36 hours ahead

METRIC/IMPERIAL
450 g/1 lb fresh pork fat, skin removed
700 g/1⅔ lb boneless pork loin
450 g/1 lb pork liver, trimmed
300 g/10 oz pork belly or green streaky bacon
3 shallots, chopped
2 onions, chopped
½ tsp quatre-épices or ground allspice
1 tbsp chopped fresh sage
2 sprigs of dried thyme, crumbled
1 tbsp finely chopped fresh parsley
bay leaf, finely crumbled
4 tbsp Armagnac
piece of barding fat, beaten flat and cut into strips
salt and pepper

AMERICAN
1 lb fresh pork fatback, skin removed
1⅔ lb boneless pork loin
1 lb pork liver, trimmed
10 oz salt pork or bacon
3 shallots, chopped
2 onions, chopped
½ tsp quatre-épices or ground allspice
1 tbsp chopped fresh sage
2 sprigs of dried thyme, crumbled
1 tbsp finely chopped fresh parsley
bay leaf, finely crumbled
4 tbsp Armagnac
piece of fresh pork fatback for barding, beaten flat and cut into strips
salt and pepper

Preheat the oven to 200C/400F/gas 6.

Chop the pork fat and all the meats into tiny pieces. Do not grind them in a food processor: this pâté needs to be fairly coarse-textured.

Combine the fat and meat in a large bowl with the shallots and onions. Season generously with the spices and salt and pepper and add the sage, thyme, parsley, bay leaf and Armagnac.

Knead the mixture by hand and transfer to an oval earthenware terrine or pâté dish.

Arrange the strips of barding fat in a lattice pattern on the top. Bake for about 1½ hours: the exuded fat should boil gently.

Remove from the oven and let it cool. Place a weighted board on top to compress the pâté and chill it for at least 36 hours.

PÂTÉ DE LAPIN AUX NOISETTES

Rabbit pâté with hazelnuts

Serves 6
Preparation 40 minutes
Cooking 2 hours, plus cooling

METRIC/IMPERIAL	AMERICAN
450 g/1 lb chicken livers, trimmed and cut into bite-sized pieces	*1 lb chicken livers, trimmed and cut into bite-sized pieces*
100 ml/3½ fl oz port	*½ cup port wine*
1 dressed rabbit, weighing about 1.5 kg/3½ lb, boned and cut into small pieces	*1 rabbit, dressed and drawn weight about 3½ lb, boned and cut into small pieces*
450 g/1 lb pork sausage meat	*1 lb pork sausage meat*
1 egg	*1 egg*
2 onions, chopped	*2 onions, chopped*
bunch of chervil, chopped	*bunch of chervil, chopped*
1 tsp thyme, crumbled	*1 tsp thyme leaves, crumbled*
½ bay leaf, finely crumbled	*½ bay leaf, finely crushed*
16 blanched hazelnuts	*16 blanched hazelnuts (filberts)*
piece of barding fat, beaten flat and cut into strips	*piece of pork fatback for barding, beaten flat and cut into strips*
salt and pepper	*salt and pepper*

Preheat the oven to 190C/375F/gas 5. Put the chicken livers into a bowl, pour the port over them and leave them to macerate for 20 minutes.

Meanwhile, put the rabbit pieces into another bowl with the sausage meat. Add the egg and mix well. Season with salt and pepper.

Add to the rabbit mixture the onions, chervil, thyme, bay leaf, whole hazelnuts and half the port used for macerating.

Line a terrine or pâté dish with three quarters of the barding strips. Put half the rabbit mixture into it. Add a layer of the chicken livers and then the rest of the rabbit mixture. Garnish the top with the remaining strips of barding fat.

Bake in a bain-marie in the oven for 2 hours. Remove and allow to cool. Serve cold.

To drink: a medium-bodied red wine, such as a Côtes-du-Rhône.

PÂTÉ PANTIN

Pâté in pastry

Serves 6
Preparation 40 minutes, the day before, plus 2 hours chilling
Cooking 1¼ hours

METRIC/IMPERIAL	AMERICAN
300 g/10 oz pork loin	*10 oz lean boneless pork*
300 g/10 oz noix of veal	*10 oz lean boneless veal*
2 shallots, chopped	*2 shallots, chopped*
3 tbsp finely chopped parsley	*3 tbsp finely chopped parsley*
100 ml/3½ fl oz white wine	*½ cup white wine*
3 tbsp Cognac	*3 tbsp Cognac*
bay leaf	*bay leaf*
sprig of thyme	*sprig of thyme*
250 g/8½ oz flour	*2 cups flour*
140 g/5 oz butter, softened	*10 tbsp butter*
225 g/½ lb pork sausage meat	*½ lb pork sausage meat*
1 egg, beaten	*1 egg, beaten*
salt and freshly ground black pepper	*salt and freshly ground black pepper*

1

3

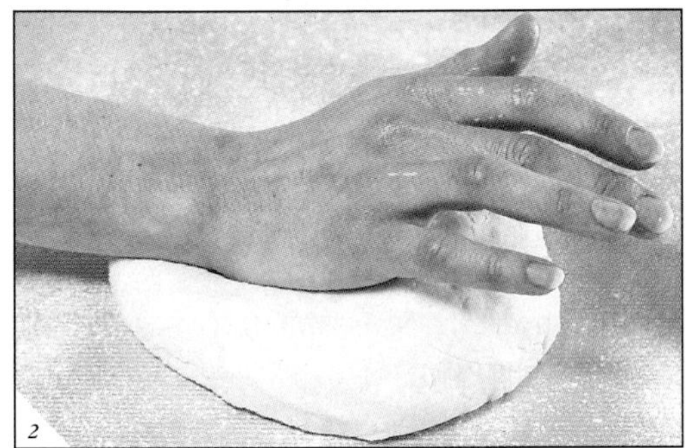
2

4

Cut the meat into thin slices and then cut these into small pieces about 2 cm/¾ in wide. Mix them together in a terrine or bowl and season with salt and pepper. Mix in the shallots along with the parsley (1).

Pour on the wine and Cognac and add the bay leaf and thyme. Cover and chill overnight.

The next day, put the flour and a pinch of salt into a bowl. Add all but 25 g/¾ oz/1½ tbsp of the butter and about 200 ml/7 fl oz/1 cup of water. Rub and mix with the fingertips, then form the dough into a ball and knead it briefly with the heel of the hand on a floured work surface until the dough is smooth (2). Form it into a ball again and chill it for 2 hours.

Preheat the oven to 190C/375F/gas 5 and grease a baking sheet with the reserved butter.

Remove the thyme and bay leaf from the meat and add the sausage meat. Mix together thoroughly with the hands.

Set one third of the pastry dough aside and roll the rest out to an oval shape. Place it on the baking sheet. Arrange the meat filling in the centre of the pastry in an even layer (3).

Moisten the edges of the pastry with a brush dipped in water and fold them up lightly over the meat filling. Roll out the remaining pastry into a rectangle to make a lid for the pâté. Moisten the edges and place it on top of the pâté, pinching to make sure that all edges are sealed. Brush the top with the egg. Score the top in a criss-cross pattern with the tip of a knife without pressing too hard, and place a small funnel in the centre, pressing it down so that it reaches the middle of the meat filling (4). Bake for 1 hour 10 minutes. Serve warm.

Note: the pâté may be kept in the refrigerator before being cooked. In this case the pastry lid should not be put on until just before the pâté is put into the oven.

PATTY PAN SQUASH

see Squash

PAUPIETTE

see also:
cabbage
veal
whiting

A thin slice of meat, usually an escalope (scallop or cutlet) of veal, beef or turkey, spread with a layer of stuffing and then rolled up around itself is termed a paupiette. They may be wrapped in barding fat or bacon and are usually secured in place with string or wooden toothpicks. They may be fried or braised in stock or wine. Fillets of fish, such as sole or whiting, and blanched cabbage leaves are also often given this treatment.

Remember to remove any securing strings or sticks before serving them. Paupiettes are usually served with an accompanying sauce.

PAUPIETTES DE MERLAN

Whiting rolls

Serves 4
Preparation 20 minutes
Cooking 10 minutes

METRIC/IMPERIAL	AMERICAN
5 whiting fillets, each weighing about 140 g/5 oz	*5 whiting fillets, each weighing about 5 oz*
170 g/6 oz fresh crab meat	*6 oz fresh crab meat*
3 tbsp low-fat cream cheese or fromage blanc	*3 tbsp low-fat cream cheese or fromage blanc*
1 egg white	*1 egg white*
200 ml/7 fl oz milk	*1 cup milk*
1 avocado	*1 avocado*
juice of 1 lemon	*juice of 1 lemon*
bunch of chives, chopped	*bunch of chives, chopped*
salt and pepper	*salt and pepper*

Flatten out 4 of the whiting fillets and set them to one side. Drain the crab meat and remove any pieces of cartilage.

Blend the remaining whiting in a food processor with the crab meat, cheese, egg white and half the milk. Season with salt and pepper.

Spread this mousse on the 4 fillets and roll them up. Secure them with wooden toothpicks.

Place the paupiettes in the top half of a steamer, cover and steam them for 10 minutes.

Meanwhile, halve and stone the avocado and then scoop out the flesh. Put it in a food processor bowl along with the lemon juice and chives. Blend to a purée and then heat it in a small saucepan, mixing in enough remaining milk to give a good coating consistency. Season the sauce with salt and pepper.

Serve the paupiettes coated with the avocado sauce and accompanied by steamed green beans.

PAWPAW

see Papaya

PEA

Petit pois, pois gourmand

see also: bean legume pulses

There is evidence that the pea, a leguminous plant which originated in the east Mediterranean, has been eaten by man for over 5,000 years. Nowadays, it is arguably the most widely consumed green vegetable.

The most common type is everyday GREEN OR GARDEN PEAS with fat, smooth, usually green, pods. Only the seeds are eaten: the smooth, round ones are slightly acid and the wrinkled ones sweeter. Of literally hundreds of varieties, perhaps the most important are those dwarf types with tiny, full-flavoured seeds, known as PETITS POIS OR PETITE PEAS, and the large, purple-podded MARROWFAT PEAS, both of which are quite sweet.

The SUGAR PEA has a flat pod and is normally harvested young while the seeds are as yet undeveloped. With such MANGE-TOUT, CHINESE OR SNOW PEAS the pod is cooked and eaten in its entirety. Recently, however, a type known as the STRING PEA, with developed seeds, has been bred in the USA. Referred to as SNAP PEAS, they have large, sweet, juicy green seeds.

DRIED PEAS, whole or split, green or yellow, are made from many varieties of the plant, and are a useful winter staple in many countries.

green and garden peas

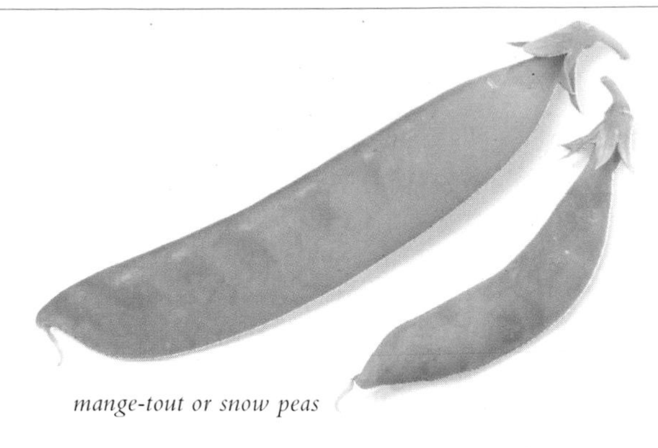
mange-tout or snow peas

Fresh garden peas for shelling should be smooth and shiny and should not have been washed. Insist on opening one pod to sample the seeds: they should be tender, with no hint of flouriness. Push a hand into the middle of the pile of pods: if they feel warm, the peas are old enough to have begun to ferment. Mange-tout or snow pea pods should be unblemished and quite crisp: break one to test for tough strings and to see how moist the flesh is.

Garden peas freeze exceptionally well and many large producers harvest and freeze so quickly and efficiently that their product is superior to all but those just picked from the garden. Canned peas tend to be mushy.

Peas will keep well in their pods for several days, providing they have not been washed. Shell them just before they are needed. Mange-tout or snow peas should be washed, topped and tailed, and any tough strings removed.

Shelled garden peas are normally boiled in lightly salted water for a few minutes until just tender and need only be dressed with a little butter. They may also be flavoured with chopped fresh mint, mixed with onions, shredded lettuce, diced carrots, rice or chopped ham, or even served in a cream or white sauce. Tougher peas may be made into delicious soups and purées or added to stews.

Mange-tout or snow peas can be boiled in the same way, but their crunchy texture is probably best enjoyed by simply sautéing them in a little butter and olive oil and then dressing them with a few drops of lemon juice.

Peas are very rich in nutrients, especially vitamin C, and garden peas are also a good source of iron. Fresh or frozen peas have a higher calorific content than canned, because they are richer in protein and carbohydrates: 100 g/3½ oz of fresh or frozen peas contain 90 calories; canned peas 70. They are also richer in fibre. Mange-tout or snow peas are also rich in carbohydrates and fibre, but as they have a much lower protein content, 100 g/3½ oz contains only 35 calories.

PETITS POIS À LA FRANÇAISE

Peas with lettuce and onions

Serves 4
Preparation 20 minutes
Cooking about 35 minutes

METRIC/IMPERIAL	AMERICAN
1 kg/2¼ lb fresh peas, shelled	*2¼ lb fresh peas, shelled*
1 lettuce, shredded	*1 head lettuce, shredded*
12 baby onions	*12 baby onions*
bouquet garni	*bouquet garni*
75 g/2½ oz butter, cut into small pieces	*5 tbsp butter, cut into small pieces*
2 tsp caster sugar	*2 tsp superfine sugar*
2 tbsp finely chopped fresh chervil	*2 tbsp finely chopped fresh chervil*
salt and freshly ground pepper	*salt and freshly ground pepper*

Combine the peas, lettuce and onions in a flameproof casserole. Add the bouquet garni, two thirds of the butter, the sugar, 1 teaspoon of salt and some freshly ground pepper.

Pour 150 ml/¼ pt/⅔ cup of cold water into the casserole. Stir, cover and bring slowly to the boil. Simmer very gently for 30 minutes.

Discard the bouquet garni; add the rest of the butter and the chervil. Mix and serve.

This dish makes a perfect accompaniment for veal, lamb, pigeon or roast duck.

Variation: for petits pois à la bonne femme, first sauté the onions with 115 g/¼ lb blanched, chopped, lean bacon, then add 15 g/½ oz/2 tbsp of flour and cook for a minute or two longer. Then add 300 ml/½ pt/1¼ cups chicken stock and boil for about 5 minutes. Simmer as above, with the bouquet garni, for 30 minutes. Serve with roast meat, veal escalopes (cutlets) or magrets of duck.

POIS GOURMANDS AU BEURRE D'AMANDE

Mange-tout or snow peas with almond butter

Serves 4
Preparation 10 minutes
Cooking about 10 minutes

METRIC/IMPERIAL	AMERICAN
800 g/1¾ lb mange-tout peas, trimmed	1¾ lb snow peas, trimmed
45 g/1½ oz butter	3 tbsp butter
75 g/2½ oz flaked almonds	⅔ cup slivered almonds
salt and pepper	salt and pepper

Cook the peas for 4–6 minutes in lightly salted boiling water.

Meanwhile, melt the butter in a small frying pan over a moderate heat and add the almonds. Cook them, stirring gently, for 3 minutes until golden, but do not allow them to burn.

Drain the cooked peas, put them into a sauté pan and pour the butter and almonds over them. Heat and stir carefully for a minute or two. Season with salt and pepper and serve at once.

This dish makes a perfect accompaniment to sautéed white meats and to fish, such as trout, medallions of monkfish or baked cod steaks.

see also:
nectarine

PEACH
Pêche

The peach tree originated in China and its fine, delicate, juicy fruit has been a summer treat in Europe since Roman times. The peach is round with an indentation down one side and a creamy white or pale yellow, downy skin which may blush with red as it ripens.

Peaches are of two kinds: FREESTONE in which the stone or pit can be easily removed, and CLINGSTONE. Another way of classifying peaches is by the colour of their flesh. YELLOW PEACHES constitute the greater part of the crop and are sturdier and more plentiful; WHITE PEACHES are smaller but tastier and more highly perfumed, particularly the small VINE PEACHES which mature late in the season. NECTARINES are a smooth-skinned variety of peach and they may have either yellow or white flesh. Yellow peaches are usually peeled before use and are best eaten cooked; they are also available canned or bottled in syrup. White peaches are best appreciated as a dessert fruit.

Look for unblemished peaches which are completely ripe. The stone should rattle when a perfectly ripe peach is shaken. Try to handle the fruit as little as possible as peaches bruise readily. Ripe fruit should peel easily, but brief blanching will help if there is any difficulty. Peaches will

nectarine
yellow peach
white peach
vine peach

keep for a day or two in the refrigerator.

Peaches are eaten either raw or poached in wine or syrup. They are also made into tarts and iced desserts, and used to make jam and chutneys. They are also delicious in some savoury contexts, notably as a garnish for calves' liver or duck.

Peaches are easily digestible and rich in vitamins and minerals, mostly in the skin: 100 g/3½ oz contains only 40 calories.

PÊCHES MELBA

Peaches and ice cream with raspberry purée

Serves 4
Preparation 20 minutes
Cooking about 10 minutes, 1 hour ahead

METRIC/IMPERIAL	AMERICAN
8 peaches	8 peaches
175 g/6½ oz caster sugar	14 tbsp superfine sugar
1 tbsp Kirsch	1 tbsp Kirsch
150 g/5½ oz raspberries	½ pt raspberries
500 ml/16 fl oz vanilla ice cream	1 pt vanilla ice cream
30 g/1 oz flaked almonds	¼ cup slivered almonds

Blanch the peaches in boiling water for 10 seconds and peel them. Cut them in half and remove the stones.

Boil 200 ml/7 fl oz/1 cup of water with 100 g/3½ oz/8 tbsp of the sugar for 2 minutes. Stir in the Kirsch and poach the peach halves gently in this syrup for 5 minutes. Leave to cool in the syrup and then drain.

Meanwhile, blend the raspberries to a purée in a food processor. Add the rest of the sugar and heat the purée gently in a small pan for 5 minutes, stirring. Leave to cool.

Spoon the ice cream into large, chilled glasses or sundae dishes. Add the peach halves, coat with the sieved raspberry purée and sprinkle with flaked (slivered) almonds. Serve chilled, with chantilly cream if wished.

Variation: banana or pear Melba can be made in the same way. Other fruit sauces may be used; try strawberry coulis.

PEANUT OR GROUNDNUT

Arachide, cacahuète

see also: fats and oils nuts

The seeds of an edible leguminous tropical plant, peanuts are unique in that they grow underground.

Originally from South America, peanuts are now an important crop worldwide, Most are used to extract GROUNDNUT OR PEANUT OIL, a cooking medium with a neutral flavour which can safely be heated to high temperatures.

In the West peanuts are generally sold roasted, shelled and salted as a snack or to accompany drinks. Crushed into PEANUT BUTTER, they are a nutritious spread popular with children and a useful flavouring in many sweet dishes, such as sweets (candies) and biscuits (cookies). They also find use, in place of almonds or pistachios, in salads and pastries.

Peanuts are much more imaginatively used in Eastern cooking. They are a common ingredient in Indian and Chinese poultry and seafood dishes; the Egyptians make them into soups and cakes, and they find perhaps their best use in the celebrated Indonesian *saté* sauce, which makes a delicious accompaniment to skewered meat and poultry.

Peanuts have a high energy value and should be avoided by those watching their weight: a mere 30 g/1 oz contains about 200 calories.

CRÈME GLACÉE À LA CACAHUÈTE

Peanut ice cream

Makes 1 l/1¾ pt/1 qt
Preparation 10 minutes
Cooking 15 minutes, 24 hours ahead

METRIC/IMPERIAL	AMERICAN
400 ml/14 fl oz milk	1¾ cups milk
300 ml/½ pt crème fraîche or whipping cream	1½ cups crème fraîche or whipping cream
6 egg yolks	6 egg yolks
100 g/3½ oz brown sugar	½ cup firmly packed brown sugar
200 g/7 oz shelled unsalted peanuts	1⅓ cups shelled unsalted peanuts
6 tbsp peanut butter	⅓ cup peanut butter

Heat the milk and cream gently in a pan.

Whisk the egg yolks with the sugar until thick and creamy. Pour the boiling milk mixture over, whisking vigorously.

Return the mixture to the pan and cook, stirring constantly, until it is thick enough to coat the back of a spoon. Remove it from the heat and leave it to cool.

Pound the peanuts in a mortar. Mix them with the peanut butter and blend this briefly with the cream mixture in a food processor.

Pour into an ice cream maker and freeze until hard. Serve with hot chocolate sauce.

see also:
apple
fruit

PEAR

Poire

The fruit of various types of pear tree are available virtually all year round from different areas of cultivation. Most pears have the characteristic 'tear-drop' shape and their skin, of varying degrees of thickness, is yellow, green, brown or reddish in colour. The soft white or creamy flesh is fine or slightly granular, depending on the variety, and has a fine, aromatic flavour. It may, however, have a slight hint of acetone, known as 'pear drops', and some varieties have woody grains which make them gritty.

The once-common, tougher cooking pears have more or less disappeared as breeding emphasis has eliminated the grittiness and has thus favoured the eating or BUTTERED (*beurré*) varieties with meltingly textured flesh. Among the best known are the WILLIAMS or BARTLETT PEARS, with exceptionally delicate, white, juicy, sweet flesh with a hint of muskiness which stands up well to cooking. They are widely grown in the USA and Australia, where most of the crop is canned. The French favour them in preserves and use them for making brandy. CONFERENCE PEARS originated in England and are long and speckled in appearance, with good, juicy flesh but a rather tough skin. They resemble the American BOSC PEAR, which has a russeted yellow skin and pleasantly tart flesh.

Another popular American pear is the ANJOU, which originated in France and has a distinctive winy taste.

The French are probably the leading cultivators and have produced a wide variety of important specimens, including the large DOYENNÉ-DU-COMICE which is strongly perfumed and a little spicy and is said to be the finest of the dessert pears. The russet-skinned BEURRÉ-HARDY is relatively rare and pleasantly sweet, but does not keep well. The plump PASSE-CRASSANE is a winter pear with a good flavour and interesting after-taste. It keeps well, but some fruit can be quite gritty. The BONNE LOUISE has a very smooth skin and delicious flesh which sometimes has a pink blush. Its keeping qualities have made it an international favourite.

Pears are normally harvested when slightly under-ripe and they continue to ripen off the tree if kept at a good, steady temperature. They do, however, need to be used at their peak as they go off quite quickly after this. Some varieties in particular have a tendency towards 'sleepiness', where they rot from the core outwards. Pears keep well in the refrigerator, but they must be handled and stored with care as they bruise easily. To check pears for ripeness, roll them gently between the palms: there should be a distinct give.

Certain varieties of pear are chemically treated and should be washed and peeled before use. As with apples, the flesh oxidizes rapidly; sprinkle it with lemon juice as soon as it is cut to keep it from going brown. Use firm-fleshed pears for tarts or poaching and eat the more fragile varieties raw.

Pears are normally peeled for cooking and the seedy core removed. They are often poached whole or in portions, usually in a flavoured syrup or wine. They also lend themselves to stuffing and baking like apples, often wrapped in pastry. Pears are used in jams and chutneys and feature widely in compotes and ice cream desserts. They are also delicious in some savoury dishes, notably with poultry and game, and team spectacularly with Roquefort cheese.

Pears are rich in vitamins and phosphorus, magnesium and potassium and 100 g/$3\frac{1}{2}$ oz contain about 65 calories.

GRATIN DE POIRES AUX AMANDES

Baked pears with almonds

Serves 4
Preparation 10 minutes
Cooking 25 minutes

METRIC/IMPERIAL	*AMERICAN*
55 g/2 oz butter	*4 tbsp butter*
12 plump pears, preferably Passe-Crassane	*12 plump pears, preferably Passe-Crassane*
juice of 1 lemon	*juice of 1 lemon*
55 g/2 oz brown sugar	*$\frac{1}{3}$ cup brown sugar*
100 ml/$3\frac{1}{2}$ fl oz white wine	*$\frac{1}{2}$ cup white wine*
3 tbsp strawberry liqueur	*3 tbsp strawberry liqueur*
75 g/$2\frac{1}{2}$ oz flaked almonds, coarsely crumbled	*$\frac{2}{3}$ cup slivered almonds, coarsely crumbled*

Preheat the oven to 220C/425F/gas 7 and grease a baking dish with one third of the butter.

Peel the pears, cut them in half lengthwise and remove the cores. Sprinkle the pear halves lightly with lemon juice to keep them white.

Arrange them in the baking dish, flat side down. Sprinkle with the remaining lemon juice.

In a bowl, mix the sugar, wine and strawberry liqueur. Pour this mixture over the pears. Place a small piece of butter on each pear half and sprinkle them with flaked (slivered) almonds.

Bake for 25 minutes and serve hot or cold.

Poires belle-Hélène

Cold poached pears with ice cream and hot chocolate sauce

Serves 6
Preparation 20 minutes
Cooking 20 minutes

METRIC/IMPERIAL	AMERICAN
6 Williams or Bartlett pears	6 Bartlett pears
55 g/2 oz caster sugar	¼ cup superfine sugar
125 g/4½ oz plain chocolate, broken into small pieces	4 oz semisweet chocolate, broken into small pieces
30 g/1 oz butter	2 tbsp butter
1 l/1¾ pt vanilla ice cream	1 qt vanilla ice cream

Peel the pears, but leave them whole and do not remove the stalks. Dissolve the sugar in 250 ml/8 fl oz/1 cup of water in a saucepan and poach the pears gently in this syrup for about 20 minutes or until quite tender, turning them about halfway through. Drain them and put them to chill.

Meanwhile, boil the syrup rapidly to reduce it by half. Melt the chocolate in it, followed by the butter, and stir until the sauce is smooth and creamy. Immediately remove from the heat.

Divide the ice cream between 6 very cold ice cream coupes or glasses. Add 1 chilled, poached pear per coupe and immediately coat with the hot chocolate sauce. Serve immediately, accompanied by almond biscuits (cookies).

Note: this dish may be made with peaches or apricots and is easily made with canned pears, peaches or apricots in syrup. Put the block of ice cream on a serving dish, surround with drained fruit and serve the sauce separately.

Variation: for a simpler, but still classic dessert, poach the pears in sweetened red wine with a little cinnamon and nutmeg and serve with cream instead of sauce.

PECTIN

see also: dietary fibre fruit jams, etc

One of the constituent substances of natural dietary fibre, pectin is particularly abundant in certain fruits such as apples, quinces, redcurrants and citrus fruits. Pectin is the agent which helps jams and jellies set.

Special preserving sugar has pectin added to it and is invaluable for making jam with fruits such as strawberries, pears and cherries that contain very little natural pectin. An alternative is to put a small muslin or cheesecloth bag containing the skins and seeds of apples, oranges or quinces into the preserving pan and boil it along with the fruit. Commercially made pectin, available as powder or syrup, may also be added.

For pectin to be most effective the acid and sugar balance must be correct, hence the addition of lemon juice to some jams.

Pectin forms a gel-like screen in the intestines which helps slow down the absorption of carbohydrates and lipids.

PEPPER

Poivre

see also: condiment paprika peppers sauce seasoning

The berries from the Oriental pepper vine, peppercorns are the most universal condiment and seasoning. The appearance and properties of varieties of pepper depend on the degree of maturity when harvested.

GREEN PEPPERCORNS (*poivre vert*) are picked before fully ripe and are dried or pickled in vinegar or brine. The fruity rather than piquant flavour is used to season fish, lamb, duck, cream sauces, terrines and mixed salads.

BLACK PEPPERCORNS (*poivre noir*) are picked when just ripe and then dried in the sun. This most common form of whole pepper is very pungent and full of flavour.

WHITE PEPPER (*poivre blanc*) is made from pepper picked when very ripe. The dark outer shell is allowed to ferment and is then removed to give a purer and more pungent flavour. White pepper is often relatively expensive and is considered by many to have the finest flavour. It is very useful for seasoning white sauces and other pale dishes where a black-speckled appearance would be inappropriate.

Poires belle-Hélène (Cold poached pears with ice cream and hot chocolate sauce)

GREY PEPPER (*poivre gris*) is a mixture of white

and black pepper. SHOT PEPPER or *mignonette* is a mixture of the two peppers coarsely crushed. It is used in terrines and pâtés and on steaks and other grilled meats.

PINK PEPPER (*baies roses*) is a totally different species. The little, aromatic and decorative coral-coloured berries from a small South American shrub have a mild flavour and are used in the same ways as green peppercorns.

The term pepper is used of several other unrelated species, particularly CAYENNE PEPPER (*poivre de Cayenne*), which is actually a preparation made from ground, dried chilli peppers, and PAPRIKA which is made from a variety of sweet pepper or capsicum.

Buy whole peppercorns which are compact and seem heavy for their size and which show no tendency to crumble. Keep them in an airtight container away from the light. Have one peppermill for use in the kitchen and another for the table. Ready-ground pepper loses its flavour and power very readily.

Whole or crushed peppercorns are used to flavour marinades, court-bouillons, stocks and vinaigrettes. Ground pepper is used to flavour almost every savoury dish and freshly ground black pepper may even be used to give piquancy to a dish of fresh summer fruit. Some dishes, such as steak *au poivre*, are based on the power of the peppercorn.

SAUCE POIVRADE

Black peppercorn sauce

Makes 500 ml/16 fl oz/2 cups
Preparation 10 minutes
Cooking about 50 minutes

METRIC/IMPERIAL	AMERICAN
55 g/2 oz butter	*4 tbsp butter*
1 carrot, chopped into tiny dice	*1 carrot, chopped into tiny dice*
2 onions, finely chopped	*2 onions, finely chopped*
85 g/3 oz streaky bacon, cut into thin strips	*3 oz bacon, cut into thin strips*
½ tsp thyme	*½ tsp thyme*
½ bay leaf, crumbled	*½ bay leaf, crumbled*
55 g/2 oz flour	*6½ tbsp flour*
500 ml/16 fl oz beef stock	*2 cups beef stock*
4 shallots, chopped	*4 shallots, chopped*
1 tsp crushed black peppercorns	*1 tsp crushed black peppercorns*
150 ml/¼ pt white wine	*⅔ cup white wine*
salt	*salt*

Melt the butter in a saucepan over a moderate heat and add the carrot and onions. Cook, stirring, for 3 minutes. Add the bacon and cook for a further 2 minutes.

Sprinkle with the thyme and the bay leaf followed by the flour and cook for 3 minutes.

Pour on the hot stock and stir vigorously until well mixed. Lower the heat and simmer gently for 20–25 minutes.

Meanwhile, put the shallots into a saucepan with the peppercorns and the wine. Reduce the liquid by half, then pour it into the sauce and cook for a further 10–15 minutes.

This sauce goes well with red meat and game.

SAUCE AU POIVRE VERT

Green peppercorn sauce

Serves 4
Preparation 5 minutes, 30 minutes ahead
Cooking about 10 minutes

METRIC/IMPERIAL	AMERICAN
55 g/2 oz dried green peppercorns	*⅓ cup dried green peppercorns*
2 tbsp very cold cider vinegar	*2 tbsp very cold cider vinegar*
3 egg yolks	*3 egg yolks*
200 g/7 oz butter, cut into small pieces	*2 sticks butter, cut into small pieces*
salt and white pepper	*salt and white pepper*

Put the green peppercorns into a small bowl. Crush them coarsely, add the vinegar and mix. Leave to macerate for 30 minutes.

Transfer the mixture to a larger bowl or the top of a double boiler, add the egg yolks, season with salt and pepper and whisk vigorously for 1 minute. Place the bowl in a bain-marie, or the double boiler over a bottom pan of barely simmering water. The water should not boil. Stir the mixture with a wooden spoon.

Incorporate the butter a little at a time, stirring constantly. When the sauce has the consistency of mayonnaise, add 1 tablespoon of hot water and whisk vigorously.

This sauce makes a good accompaniment for seafood kebabs and poached fish fillets.

see also:
chili con carne
paprika
pepper
vegetables

PEPPERS OR CAPSICUMS

Poivrons et piments

The fruits of several members of a family of plants related to the potato and tomato are known as peppers or capsicums. Originally from South America and the West Indies, they have become indispensable to the cooking of many nations from Hungary to China. There are two principal types:

CHILLI PEPPERS OR CHILIES

Normally long and thin or short and stubby, these small peppers are characterized by their fieriness. Most chillies start off green and turn yellow and then red as they ripen. In areas of cultivation, notably Mexico, there are literally hundreds of varieties, each of different appearance, flavour and potency. The short, fat green *jalapeño* is one of the most popular and is also quite widely available in the USA. The rich, mild *poblano* is often skinned and stuffed; dried it becomes a dark brown *ancho*, which is probably the most commonly used form of chilli flavouring in Mexican cuisine.

Until recently, the most usual form in which chillies were encountered in Europe and the USA was dried and ground as CAYENNE PEPPER and CHILLI POWDER. Nowadays, however, an increasing number of chillies are available fresh, dried, frozen or pickled.

Although red peppers tend to be hotter than green, and the smaller the chilli the more potent it is likely to be, it is unwise to put too much store by appearances. Many innocuous-looking green peppers can have twice the power of the seemingly most potent tiny red chilli.

Chilli peppers should be handled with great care as the compound responsible for their fiery bite is also quite corrosive. Wear rubber gloves when preparing them or wash your hands immediately afterwards. This blistering effect may also affect the internal organs, so seeds in particular should not be incorporated in food for those with delicate constitutions.

For use in cooking, chillies are usually chopped or sliced and the seeds are removed unless a really hot result is required. For optimum flavour and minimum fire, use the chillies whole and remove them from the dish before serving.

Remember that the concept of making a chilli dish to an 'authentic' degree of hotness will only taste that way to someone who eats such food regularly. To anyone else, all flavour will be drowned out by the burning sensation.

Chillies may also be skinned or charred, as described for sweet peppers, to make them more digestible and give them a wonderful smoky flavour. The larger, fatter ones may also be stuffed. The flavour and power of chillies are best utilized in meat, vegetable and bean dishes

chilli peppers or chilies

dried hot peppers

involving long slow cooking, such as *chili con carne*. They are much used in pickles, and feature strongly in the cooking of North Africa, India, China and Southeast Asia.

Chillies are used in a wide range of condiments, from North African *harissa*, the chilli and garlic paste for couscous, to the wide range of HOT PEPPER SAUCES, which includes American TABASCO, so popular with seafood. A useful way of having chilli flavour on tap is to macerate some whole, blanched red chillies in good olive oil for a month or two. This oil may be used in vinaigrettes for summer vegetables and salads, for brushing fish to be grilled (broiled) and when browning beef or lamb before stewing.

SWEET PEPPERS

Generally large and round, or occasionally somewhat square, these are also known as BELL PEPPERS or CAPSICUMS. Available year round, they may be green, red or yellow or a mixture of these colours. In general, the redder they are, the milder and sweeter the flavour.

Sweet peppers should always be firm, glossy and smooth, without any blemishes or soft spots. For easy removal of the skin, spear the pepper on a long fork and hold it for several seconds over a gas flame or under the grill (broiler), turning it until evenly charred: the skin can then be detached easily using a small pointed knife. The seeds and white filaments inside are always removed before use.

Sweet peppers are eaten raw in salads where their bright colours and crunchy texture are invaluable. They are also added to sautés and stews, and are a characteristic feature of many Mediterranean dishes. They go well with other vegetable fruits, especially tomatoes, and with chicken, lamb, rice and oily fish. Their shape lends them to being stuffed, either halved or whole, and they may be briefly blanched beforehand or baked with their stuffing.

Varieties of sweet pepper are dried and ground to produce the Hungarian spice PAPRIKA and its Spanish equivalent *pimentón*, so characteristic of these cuisines.

Sweet peppers are rich in vitamins A and C and have a low calorific value: 100 g/3½ oz contains only 22 calories. They can be slightly indigestible unless skinned.

sweet or bell peppers

ROUGAIL DE TOMATES

Spicy pepper and tomato sauce

Serves 4
Preparation 10 minutes, plus chilling

METRIC/IMPERIAL	AMERICAN
1 large onion, chopped	1 large onion, chopped
25 g/¾ oz grated fresh ginger	2 tbsp grated fresh ginger
4 tomatoes, peeled, deseeded and coarsely chopped	4 tomatoes, peeled, deseeded and coarsely chopped
juice of ½ lemon	juice of ½ lemon
1 red chilli pepper, deseeded and cut into tiny pieces	1 small red chili pepper, deseeded and cut into tiny pieces
1 small green chilli pepper, deseeded and cut into tiny pieces	1 small green chili pepper, deseeded and cut into tiny pieces
salt and pepper	salt and pepper

Combine the onion, ginger, tomatoes, lemon juice and chillies in a food processor and add ½ teaspoon of salt and several pinches of pepper. Blend to a purée, put it into a bowl and chill.

Serve this West Indian condiment with rice dishes, grilled fish or savoury fritters.

POIVRONADE À L'ORIGAN

Sweet peppers with oregano

Serves 4
Preparation 15 minutes
Cooking 10 minutes

METRIC/IMPERIAL	AMERICAN
140 g/5 oz smoked streaky bacon, cut into tiny cubes	5 oz country-style bacon, cut into tiny cubes
2 onions, thinly sliced	2 onions, thinly sliced
4 sweet peppers (varied colours), deseeded and cut in strips	4 sweet peppers (varied colours), deseeded and cut in strips
1 heaped tsp oregano	1 heaping tsp oregano
3 tomatoes, peeled and cubed	3 tomatoes, peeled and cubed
salt and pepper	salt and pepper

Put the bacon and onions into a deep dish. Microwave, covered, on High for 2 minutes.

Add the sweet pepper strips and oregano, and season with salt and pepper. Stir and cook on High for a further 5 minutes.

Add the tomatoes to the dish, stir, and microwave on High for a further 3 minutes. Adjust the seasoning, if necessary, and serve with pork steaks or lamb kebabs.

Variations: for Basque pipérade eggs, add 4 lightly beaten eggs and cook for 3 to 4 minutes, until scrambled, stirring once.

Alternatively, omit the bacon and cook the onions in 3 tablespoons of olive oil. Serve at room temperature as a salad, with black olives, anchovy fillets, plenty of lemon juice and a little parsley.

POIVRONS FARCIS À L'ITALIENNE

Sweet peppers stuffed with meat, rice and tomatoes

Serves 6
Preparation 15 minutes
Cooking about 1 hour

METRIC/IMPERIAL	AMERICAN
100 ml/3½ fl oz olive oil	½ cup olive oil
6 large red sweet peppers	6 large red sweet peppers
2 onions, chopped	2 onions, chopped
225 g/½ lb sausage meat	½ lb pork sausage meat
200 g/7 oz leftover cooked meat, chopped	1 cup chopped leftover cooked meat
100 g/3½ oz cooked rice	⅔ cup cooked rice
2 slices of cooked ham, finely chopped	2 slices of cooked ham, finely chopped
3 tbsp finely chopped parsley	3 tbsp finely chopped parsley
3 garlic cloves, chopped	3 garlic cloves, chopped
1 egg, beaten	1 egg, beaten
450 g/1 lb tomatoes, peeled and coarsely chopped	1 lb tomatoes, peeled and coarsely chopped
bouquet garni	bouquet garni
juice of 1 lemon	juice of 1 lemon
salt and pepper	salt and pepper

Preheat the oven to 180C/350F/gas 4 and grease an ovenproof dish with a little of the oil.

Cut the stalk ends off the sweet peppers and reserve them. Remove the seeds and white filaments from the insides. Season the insides lightly with salt. Turn them upside-down on a clean cloth and set aside.

In a sauté pan, cook the onions gently in 2 tablespoons of the oil until soft. Add the sausage meat and cooked meat. Cook for a further 5 minutes. Remove from the heat and add the rice, ham, parsley, garlic and beaten egg. Season with salt and pepper and mix thoroughly.

Stuff the peppers with the mixture and replace the reserved caps. Put the tomatoes into the greased dish, add the bouquet garni, and place the peppers on top, standing them upright. Sprinkle with the remaining olive oil and the lemon juice.

Bake for 50 minutes. Serve piping hot, straight from the baking dish.

To drink: a fresh, lively Italian red wine, such as a Valpolicella.

PERCH AND PIKE-PERCH

Perche et sandre

see also:
carp
fish
pike

The PERCH is a small, greenish-gold freshwater fish with delicately flavoured, firm flesh. It is prepared and cooked like carp: fried if small, and made into fish stew or cooked in white wine if larger. Other fish often called perch include the BLACK BASS, GUDGEON and the American SUNFISH.

The PIKE-PERCH, ZANDER OF YELLOW PERCH is a larger, freshwater fish resembling a cross between the perch and the pike. Commonly farmed like trout, it has a much superior flavour and delicate but firm white flesh with few bones. It is best prepared and cooked like pike, and goes well with mushrooms and onions.

Like most river fish, pike-perch is quite high in fat: 100 g/3½ oz contains 120 calories.

SANDRE À LA BIERE

Pike-perch fillets in beer

Serves 4
Preparation 15 minutes
Cooking about 35 minutes

METRIC/IMPERIAL	AMERICAN
4 pike-perch steaks, each weighing about 200 g/7 oz	4 pike-perch steaks, each weighing about 7 oz
55 g/2 oz butter	4 tbsp butter
225 g/½ lb onions, thinly sliced	½ lb onions, thinly sliced
1 heaped tsp paprika	1 heaping tsp paprika
100 ml/3½ fl oz lager	½ cup light beer
200 ml/7 fl oz crème fraîche or whipping cream	1 cup crème fraîche or whipping cream
salt and pepper	salt and pepper

Preheat the oven to 180C/350F/gas 4 and season the fish steaks with salt and pepper.

Melt half the butter in a frying pan over a moderate heat, cook the fish steaks in it for 3 minutes on each side and then remove.

Discard the melted butter and set the frying pan back over a low heat. Add the rest of the butter and the sliced onions. Cook them gently for 8 minutes, stirring constantly.

Sprinkle with most of the paprika, mix and add the lager (light beer). Simmer gently for 10 minutes, then mix in the cream.

Pour half of the mixture into an ovenproof dish. Place the fish steaks on top and cover with the rest of the cream mixture. Sprinkle over the remaining paprika, cover with a sheet of foil and cook in the oven for 10 minutes.

PERSIMMON

Kaki

see also:
fruit

Looking a little like a coral-coloured tomato with a four-leaved calyx at the stem end, the persimmon originated in Japan but is now widely grown in the Mediterranean area as well as in California and Florida. Its sweet, perfumed flesh is eaten raw or used in fruit salads or tarts. The unripe flesh has a very high tannin content

which tastes overwhelmingly bitter, so the fruit must be eaten when perfectly ripe or even slightly over-ripe. The Israeli variety known as the SHARON FRUIT lacks this bitterness, and may be eaten while still firm and crisp.

Persimmons have a very high vitamin A content and 100 g/3½ oz contains 65 calories.

KAKIS GLACÉS

Persimmon ice cream with chantilly cream

Serves 4
Preparation 20 minutes
Macerating 1 hour
Freezing 1 hour

METRIC/IMPERIAL	*AMERICAN*
4 very ripe persimmons	*4 very ripe persimmons*
2 tbsp rum	*2 tbsp rum*
2 large scoops of vanilla ice cream	*2 large scoops of vanilla ice cream*
100 ml/3½ fl oz crème fraîche or whipping cream	*½ cup crème fraîche or whipping cream*
15 g/½ oz icing sugar	*2½ tbsp confectioners' sugar*
4 glacé cherries	*4 candied cherries*

Cut off the top of each persimmon at the stalk end. Remove the flesh with a small spoon, taking care not to damage the skin.

Pour several drops of rum into each fruit shell and macerate, chilled, for 1 hour.

Mix the persimmon flesh with the vanilla ice cream. Fill the fruit shells with this mixture and freeze for at least 1 hour.

A few minutes before serving, whip the cream with the sugar to make a very stiff chantilly cream. Decorate the iced persimmons with the cream and top each with a cherry.

PETIT FOUR

see also:
baba
buffet
cakes and gâteaux
cookies, etc
éclair
fruit
macaroon
meringue
pizza
quiche
tart
vol-au-vent

Little bite-size pastry or confectionery items are termed petits fours. They are served either as part of a buffet, with tea or drinks, or with coffee after dinner.

PLAIN OR DRY PETITS FOURS are small, dry biscuits or cookies, such as *tuiles*, *cigarettes*, macaroons, *sablés*, *langues-de-chat* and meringues. These are also often served as accompaniments to creamy and iced desserts and to sweet dessert wines.

FRESH PETITS FOURS include small versions of larger cakes and pastries, such as éclairs, tarts, babas and filled and iced pieces of Genoese sponge cake, or even sugar-coated fruits.

SAVOURY PETITS FOURS again may be miniature versions of larger pastries, such as tarts, quiches, turnovers, pizzas or vols-au-vent (patty shells), or matchstick pieces of pastry flavoured with cheese, paprika or anchovy.

The essence of serving petits fours is to provide an interesting assortment.

PHEASANT

Faisan

see also:
game
salmis

A long-tailed game bird of Asiatic origins closely related to the chicken, the pheasant was introduced into Europe in the Middle Ages and from there into North America. The season for shooting pheasant runs from October to February in Britain, but begins only in November in the USA. Birds reared for slaughter and released just before shooting starts are less flavourful than truly wild pheasants.

The female makes better eating than the male and has much moister and more delicate flesh. Choose plump, young pheasants: look for pliable beaks and claws. If buying still in feather, rub the fingers under the feathers: if the skin feels slightly damp the bird has been frozen.

Pheasants are generally hung for anything from 2 or 3 days to a week or two, to allow their flavour to develop fully. Many pheasant aficionados prefer them really gamy, to the point of smelling very high. Pheasants bought dressed have usually already had the requisite hanging, and feathered birds are judged ready when the tail feathers come away easily.

Young pheasants can be barded and simply roasted and are then traditionally served with fried breadcrumbs, a sharp fruit sauce, such as cranberry or rowan, and a clear gravy made from the pan juices. Older birds are better braised and flavoured with Cognac and cream, celery, bacon and onions, mushrooms or sauerkraut and also make fine pâtés and terrines.

Pheasant meat is lean if plainly roasted; 100 g/3½ oz contains 110 calories.

FAISAN À L'ALSACIENNE

Pheasant in Riesling with chanterelles

Serves 4
Preparation 20 minutes
Cooking about 1¼ hours

METRIC/IMPERIAL	*AMERICAN*
3 Petit-Suisse cheeses	*3 Petit-Suisse cheeses*
bunch of chives, chopped	*bunch of chives, chopped*
1 dressed hen pheasant	*1 dressed hen pheasant*
55 g/2 oz butter	*4 tbsp butter*
200 ml/7 fl oz Riesling	*1 cup Riesling wine*
300 g/10 oz fresh chanterelles	*10 oz fresh chanterelles*
1 tbsp beef extract	*1 tbsp beef extract*
15 g/½ oz flour	*2 tbsp flour*
salt and cracked black pepper	*salt and cracked black pepper*

Beat the cheese and chopped chives together with a little salt and pepper. Stuff the pheasant with this mixture and truss it.

Melt half the butter in a flameproof casserole over a moderate heat and brown the pheasant in it on all sides. Moisten with 100 ml/3½ fl oz/½ cup of the wine, cover and cook gently for 1 hour.

About 10 minutes before the end of cooking time, sauté the mushrooms in half the remaining butter. Season with salt and pepper. Transfer the pheasant from the casserole to a warmed serving platter. Arrange the mushrooms around it, cover with foil and keep warm.

Deglaze the casserole over a high heat with the rest of the wine and the beef extract, stirring well to pick up any sediment. Mix the remaining butter with the flour and whisk it into the reduction to make a smooth sauce.

Carve the pheasant and serve with the sauce.
To drink: Riesling.

PHOSPHORUS

see also: calcium, minerals

The adult human body normally contains about 600 mg of phosphorus, an essential element which, together with calcium, assures the replacement of bone tissue. As most foodstuffs, with the exception of sweets and other sugar items, contain some phosphorus, daily requirements are easily met by an average varied diet. Foods with the highest phosphorus content include: dairy products, particularly cheese and eggs; fish, especially canned sardines; liver; dried fruit, nuts, legumes and pulses; cocoa; rice and soya.

PICKLES

see also: chutney, condiment, fruit, gherkin, onion, preserving, sauerkraut, vegetables, vinegar

Pickling is the time-honoured practice of preserving food in brine or vinegar. Although meat, especially pork and tongue, can be cured in this way, the term pickles most commonly refers to condiments made of preserved vegetables or fruits in flavoured vinegar.

Baby onions, gherkins (pickled cucumbers), green walnuts and beetroots (beets) are often pickled on their own, and cabbage is used to make sauerkraut. Most pickles are composed of mixtures of chopped vegetables, especially onions, pumpkins, green beans, cabbages, cauliflowers, mushrooms, tomatoes and capers. Fruit pickles are normally based on peaches, plums, cherries or apples. More exotic pickles, like West Indian *achar* or those of the Middle East and India, can contain bamboo shoots, dates, limes, mangoes, palm hearts and even rose petals.

Usually flavoured with at least pepper and mustard, the pickling liquid may also contain garlic, shallots, cayenne or whole chilli peppers, horseradish, bay leaves, dill, fennel, sage, cinnamon, cloves, coriander, cumin, ginger, fenugreek, tamarind seeds, turmeric and citrus rind. Ready-mixed pickling spices are usually a little too strong on mustard seed. The mixture can be of varying degrees of sweetness and piquancy depending on the ingredients, but the secret of a good pickle is the right balance of sweet and sour.

Pickles usually accompany cold meats and poultry, cheeses and curries, and may form part of a mixed hors d'oeuvre or enliven sandwiches. Items like pickled onions and gherkins (pickled cucumbers) are traditional garnishes to hamburgers and cured meats like pastrami. The thick, brown, syrupy pickle served with cheese as part of the so-called British 'ploughman's lunch' is actually more of a chutney or relish.

Pickles should be avoided by those on salt-free diets and by anyone suffering from stomach ulcers. Like many condiments, they are often high in hidden sugar content.

PIE

see also:
pastry
tart

Strictly speaking a pie is any mixture enclosed or covered in pastry and then baked. However, the term is also used of dishes topped with mashed potato, like shepherd's pie and fish pie, while North American pies often have no pastry top and are more like tarts.

Pies may have sweet or savoury fillings and may be made with shortcrust (basic pie pastry) or puff pastry. Savoury pies, such as steak and kidney, chicken or game, are usually served hot as main courses. Sweet pies may be served hot, warm or cold, often with cream or ice cream.

Traditional English pie dishes are deep and round or oval, with wide, flat rims to support the pastry lid. The usual American pie pans or plates are shallow and round with gently sloping sides. Pie toppings are often adorned with pastry trimmings cut into decorative shapes, and then glazed with water, milk or beaten egg. The pastry must be pierced to allow steam to escape or it will become soggy and collapse during cooking. The tops of large pies are often supported by pie funnels, which also act as vents.

TOURTE AUX POMMES

Apple pie

Serves 6
Preparation 30 minutes
Cooking 40 minutes

METRIC/IMPERIAL	*AMERICAN*
1 orange	*1 orange*
700 g/1⅔ lb apples	*1⅔ lb apples*
juice of 1 lemon	*juice of 1 lemon*
100 g/3½ oz caster sugar	*½ cup superfine sugar*
15 g/½ oz flour	*2½ tbsp flour*
½ tsp grated nutmeg	*½ tsp grated nutmeg*
½ tsp ground cinnamon	*½ tsp ground cinnamon*
400 g/14 oz shortcrust pastry	*14 oz basic pie pastry*
55 g/2 oz raisins	*⅓ cup raisins*
25 g/¾ oz butter	*1½ tbsp butter*

Preheat the oven to 200C/400F/gas 6.

If the orange is not organically grown and may have been sprayed or coated, scrub it in hot soapy water, rinse well and pat dry. Grate the orange zest and squeeze the juice.

Peel and quarter the apples, remove the core and seeds and sprinkle the quarters with lemon juice. Mix the sugar with the flour, orange zest, nutmeg and cinnamon.

Roll out about two thirds of the pastry to a thickness of about 3 mm/⅛ in and use it to line a round pie dish or pan, slightly overhanging the edge. Sprinkle the pastry case with 1 tablespoon of the sugar mixture.

Fill the pastry case with the apples, adding some of the sugar mixture and some raisins at regular intervals. Sprinkle with the orange juice and dot with butter.

Roll out the remaining pastry to a thickness of about 5 mm/¼ in. Cut out a lid slightly larger than the pie dish. Moisten the rim of the bottom pastry with a brush and place the pastry lid on top. Press down well to seal.

Brush the top with a little water or milk to glaze and score it with a fork. Make 2 or 3 incisions in it to allow the steam to escape.

Bake for 40 minutes and serve hot.

see also:
game
woodcock

PIGEON AND SQUAB

Literally hundreds of species of small birds are referred to as pigeons. Most commonly encountered in the wild in Europe are the WOOD PIGEON OF RING DOVE and the ROCK DOVE, from which both the pigeons found roosting in big cities and the bird reared as food are descended. In the USA MOURNING DOVES and WHITE-WINGED DOVES are found in various states.

Young birds no more than a few weeks old, known as SQUAB or *pigeonneaux*, have delicate, tender flesh and make the best eating. Look for soft and supple feet as a sign of youth. Both domestic and wild pigeons have dark flesh which is almost entirely concentrated in the breast. Wild birds should be bled and hung for a day or two to mature. Pigeons should be plucked and dressed while still warm; the liver is often left in the cavity as it has great flavour and no bile.

Squab are usually barded and roasted, spatch-cocked, brushed with oil and grilled (broiled) or barbecued, or cooked *en papillote*. Older birds may be marinated to tenderize them, but are best braised or made into compotes, pâtés or stews. Pigeons may also be substituted in many recipes for woodcock. Peas, braised onions and mushrooms are traditional accompaniments.

Pigeon is lean, with about 2% fat, although when roasted, 100 g/3½ oz contains 217 calories.

PIGEONS À LA NIÇOISE

Pigeons with onions and olives

Serves 6
Preparation 25 minutes
Cooking about 45 minutes

METRIC/IMPERIAL	AMERICAN
55 g/2 oz butter	4 tbsp butter
18 white pickling onions	18 small white onions
6 dressed squab pigeons	6 dressed squab pigeons
bay leaf	bay leaf
½ tsp dried savory	½ tsp dried savory
100 ml/3½ fl oz white wine	½ cup white wine
200 g/7 oz small black olives	1 cup small black olives
900 g/2 lb mange-tout peas	2 lb snow peas

Melt one third of the butter in a saucepan over a moderate heat. Add the onions along with some salt and pepper. Add 3 tablespoons of water, cover tightly and cook for about 20 minutes.

Meanwhile, melt the remaining butter in a large flameproof casserole over a moderate to high heat and brown the pigeons on all sides.

Add the bay leaf and savory, followed by the wine and the drained onions. Mix and leave to simmer for 15 minutes. Add the olives and cook for a further 5–10 minutes.

While the pigeons are cooking, steam the peas until they are just tender.

Arrange the peas on a warmed serving platter and place the pigeons on top. Garnish with the onions and olives. Remove and discard the bay leaf from the cooking juices, boil to reduce them a little and serve separately as a sauce.

To drink: Rosé de Cabernet.

PIGEONNEAUX À LA CRAPAUDINE

Spatchcocked squab

Serves 4
Preparation 30 minutes, standing 30 minutes
Cooking about 30 minutes

METRIC/IMPERIAL	AMERICAN
2 large squab pigeons	2 large squab pigeons
2 garlic cloves, chopped	2 garlic cloves, chopped
4 tbsp finely chopped parsley	¼ cup finely chopped parsley
4 tbsp olive oil	4 tbsp olive oil
salt and pepper	salt and pepper

Split the squab down the backbone without separating them completely. Flatten them with a meat pounder. Season with salt and pepper.

In a bowl, mix the garlic, parsley and oil. Put the flattened squab in a dish, pour the sauce over them, turn to coat well and leave for 30 minutes.

Preheat the grill (broiler) or light a charcoal barbecue. Grill the squab, not too close to the heat, for 25–30 minutes, turning them several times, until crisp and golden. Serve very hot, garnished with sprigs of watercress.

To drink: a medium-bodied red wine, such as a Saint-Emilion.

Pigeons à la niçoise (Pigeons with onions and olives)

see also:
court-bouillon
fish
quenelle
trout

PIKE

Brochet

A handsome, green-backed freshwater fish with silvery fins, the pike has a mouth full of ferocious teeth and is a vicious predator. This reputation, combined with the slime it gives off when landed, a rather unpleasant smell and an abundance of small bones make it an unpopular catch in most countries. However, the French particularly prize its firm white flesh.

River pike is generally preferred to darker still-water or pond pike which may taste muddy. Like carp, these should be washed in a lot of well-vinegared water. Pike roe is slightly toxic during spawning, but is regarded as a delicacy in parts of Eastern Europe.

Baby pike, weighing 1–2 kg/2–4½ lb, are very tender and are best simply poached in a court-bouillon, while very small fish may be cooked *au bleu* like trout. Larger, older fish, with tougher flesh, may be marinated but are best suited for fish terrines or *quenelles*.

Pike flesh is particularly low in fat.

BROCHET AU BEURRE D'HERBES

Pike in herb butter

Serves 4
Preparation 25 minutes
Cooking 30 minutes

METRIC/IMPERIAL	AMERICAN
1 whole pike, weighing about 1.35 kg/3 lb	1 whole pike, weighing about 3 lb
juice of 1 lemon	juice of 1 lemon
75 g/2½ oz butter	5 tbsp butter
2 shallots, chopped	2 shallots, chopped
3 tbsp chopped parsley	3 tbsp chopped parsley
10 tarragon leaves, chopped	10 tarragon leaves, chopped
salt and pepper	salt and pepper

Preheat the oven to 200C/400F/gas 6.

Remove the head from the pike, then clean, scale and wash the fish. Slit it lengthwise and remove the backbone. Sprinkle the insides of the pike with lemon juice, salt and pepper.

Grease a deep, ovenproof dish with some of the butter and spread the shallots over the bottom. Put the opened-out pike on top of the shallots, flesh side downwards, and make 6–7 diagonal incisions in the skin with a sharp knife.

Work the remaining butter in a bowl until it is soft, then mix in the chopped parsley and tarragon. Force small quantities of this mixture into each incision in the fish skin.

Bake the fish for 30 minutes, basting from time to time with the cooking juices. Serve straight from the baking dish.

PILAF OR PILAU

see also:
rice

A pilaf is a rice dish of Middle Eastern origin in which the grain is browned with onions in oil or butter and then cooked in stock. It usually incorporates a garnish which may be added during the cooking or as it is served.

The rice may be highly spiced and is often coloured with saffron. Garnishes such as finely chopped lamb or beef, kidneys, thinly sliced chicken or chicken livers, prawns or shrimp and fish in sauce are often served in the centre of the rice moulded into a ring.

PINEAPPLE

Ananas

see also:
fruit

The most popular tropical fruit, pineapples originated in Brazil where they still grow wild. Today, however, the main producer is Hawaii. Most of the crop is canned in syrup or its own juice, sliced or in chunks.

The most common type is the smooth-skinned and dark-fleshed SMOOTH CAYENNE, grown in Hawaii and in equatorial and southern Africa. QUEEN pineapples are round, bumpy and dry-fleshed and come mainly from Africa, Malaysia and Australia. The squat, flat PERNAMBUCO, descended from the first pineapples brought to Europe from South America, is held to have the best flavour but has poor keeping qualities and is therefore very expensive.

Full ripening of pineapples can only occur on the plant and therefore the best pineapples are air-freighted and will carry a label attesting to this. Never buy unripe fruit as they will not ripen under any conditions. Ripe fruit will continue to ripen after picking so avoid any that are discoloured, soft or damaged. Colour varies according to type. The leaves should be dark green and firmly attached to the fruit, but come away easily and cleanly, and none should be shrivelled or brown. The fruit should feel heavy for its size and have a pronounced, clean, sweet smell.

Pineapples will keep for several days at room temperature or longer in the refrigerator, but wrap them carefully in an airtight bag to avoid interaction with other foods.

Pineapple is popular in the cooking of poultry and ham and in salads, but comes into its own in cakes, pastries and desserts. Served on its own, it may be dressed with Kirsch or vodka.

It contains the enzyme bromelin which breaks down proteins but has no effect on lipids, so pineapple juice is a useful addition to marinades for tough meat. Pineapples are also rich in fibre and contain relatively little sugar by weight compared to other fruit; 100 g/3½ oz of canned pineapple contains 77 calories, including the syrup.

ANANAS SURPRISE

Pineapple surprise

Serves 4
Preparation 20 minutes, 3 hours in advance

METRIC/IMPERIAL	AMERICAN
1 large, or 2 small, pineapples	*1 large, or 2 small, pineapples*
2 bananas	*2 bananas*
1 orange	*1 orange*
½ grapefruit	*½ grapefruit*
3 mandarin oranges	*3 mandarin oranges or tangerines*
juice of 1 lemon	*juice of 1 lemon*
125 g/4½ oz caster sugar	*⅔ cup superfine sugar*
500 ml/16 fl oz vanilla ice cream	*1 pt vanilla ice cream*

Slice the pineapple in half lengthwise. Carefully cut out the flesh from each half; chill the shells.

Peel the other fruit; slice the bananas, segment the citrus fruits and dice the pineapple.

Place all the fruit in a bowl. Sprinkle with the lemon juice and sugar to taste. Mix well and macerate in the refrigerator for 2–3 hours.

To serve: line each pineapple shell with a layer of ice cream. Put some fruit mixture on top and cover with another layer of ice cream.

see also:
nuts

PINE KERNEL OR PINE NUT

Pignon

The small, elongated, pale seed extracted from the cones of certain species of pine tree, the pine kernel or nut has a fine taste a little reminiscent of almond with a resinous undertone. Pine kernels are used whole or crushed, usually first lightly browned, in *pâtisserie* and in cakes and biscuits or cookies. They also find innumerable uses in savoury cooking, notably as an omelette filling, in stuffings for fish, seafood and poultry, and as a garnish for spinach, cauliflower, mixed salads and rice. They are an essential element in the cuisines of many Mediterranean nations, notably Spain, where they are added to salt cod, and Italy, where they are ground with basil, garlic and cheese to make the sauce for pasta *pesto alla genovese*. Pine kernels are highly calorific: 100 g/3½ oz contains 600 calories.

CROISSANTS AUX PIGNONS

Pine kernel macaroons

Makes about 30
Preparation 20 minutes
Cooking about 10 minutes, plus cooling

METRIC/IMPERIAL	AMERICAN
250 g/8½ oz caster sugar	1¼ cups superfine sugar
55 g/2 oz flour	6½ tbsp flour
150 g/5½ oz ground almonds	2 cups ground almonds
2 eggs, lightly beaten + 3 egg whites	2 eggs, lightly beaten + 3 egg whites
200 g/7 oz pine kernels	2¼ cups pine nuts
oil, for greasing	oil, for greasing

Preheat the oven to 200C/400F/gas 6. Line a baking sheet with a sheet of parchment or greaseproof paper and grease lightly with oil.

Put 55 g/2 oz/¼ cup of the sugar into a saucepan, add 4 tablespoons of water and mix until the sugar has all dissolved. Boil for 2 minutes, then remove from the heat.

In a bowl, mix the flour, almonds and the rest of the sugar. Add the 3 egg whites to the bowl. Mix to a smooth dough, divide it into 3 portions and then divide each of those into 10.

Flatten each portion into a square and then roll up from one corner and shape into a crescent. One at a time, dip them in the beaten whole eggs, then roll them in the pine kernels (pine nuts) and arrange them on the baking sheet. Bake them for 8–10 minutes.

Remove from the oven, brush them with the sugar syrup and leave them to cool. Detach them from the paper by pouring a few drops of cold water between it and the sheet.

Store in an airtight container in a dry place.

PIZZA

see also:
bread
coulis
pastry

An Italian speciality, the pizza has now become one of the most popular forms of convenience food in many parts of the world. At its most basic it consists of a round of olive oil bread dough covered with a seasoned thick tomato coulis or sauce, sprinkled with grated Parmesan and baked in the oven. Pizza doughs differ from region to region and vary from thin and crisp to fat and doughy. As well as bread doughs, shortcrust (basic pie pastry) and puff pastry may be used, and small pizzas can even be made on scone or muffin bases.

The traditional pizza topping usually consists of thinly sliced mozzarella on the tomato sauce, garnished with black olives and anchovy fillets. Other toppings include strips of ham or prosciutto, pepperoni or salami, mushrooms, eggs, artichoke hearts, or seafood.

Small pizzas make an excellent first course and tiny, bite-sized ones are useful in buffets or as snacks to serve with drinks. Traditional pizza dough is also delicious on its own or with salads, smeared with garlic butter or good olive oil and cut into strips or wedges. 100 g/3½ oz of cheese and tomato pizza contains 217 calories.

PIZZA À LA TOMATE

Basic pizza

Makes 4 individual pizzas
Preparation 20 minutes, rising 1½ hours
Cooking 10 minutes

METRIC/IMPERIAL	AMERICAN
15 g/½ oz fresh baker's yeast	½ oz fresh compressed yeast
pinch of sugar	pinch of sugar
400 g/14 oz flour	3⅓ cups flour
1 tsp salt	1 tsp salt
3 tbsp olive oil	3 tbsp olive oil

Preheat the oven to 180C/350F/gas 4. Put the yeast in a cup with the sugar, add 3 tablespoons of warm water and mix until well blended. Turn off the oven and put the yeast in it for 5 minutes. By the end of this time it should be frothy and about doubled in volume.

Pour 350 g/12 oz/3 cups of the flour into a bowl. Make a well in the centre of it and add the yeast mixture, the salt, 2 tablespoons of water and the oil. Mix with the fingers until a large, smooth ball of dough is formed.

Flour the work surface and knead the dough for 10 minutes until it is smooth and elastic.

Roll the dough into a ball, dust it with flour, put into a clean bowl and cover it with a dish. Leave it to rise in a warm place away from draughts for about 1½ hours. The dough should double in volume. Knock out the air with the fist, then divide the dough into quarters.

Knead one quarter of the dough on a floured board for 1 minute, adding a little flour if it sticks. Flatten it with the palm of the hand to make a fairly thick round. Stretch the dough out by holding it up in front of you and passing it between the hands like a wheel while stretching the hands wider apart: the dough will be elastic enough to stretch quite far.

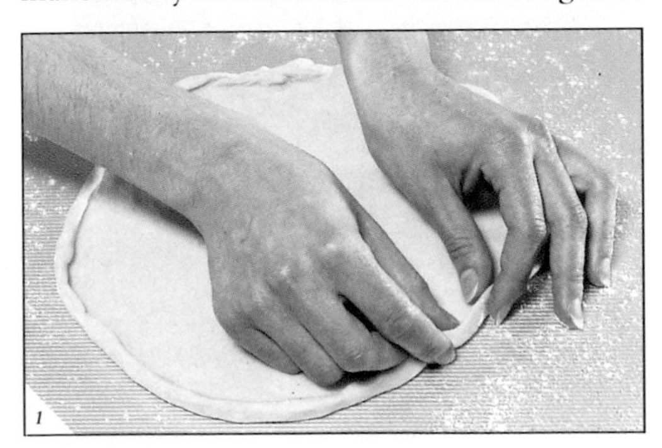
1

Spread it out once more on the floured work surface to make it smooth: it should have a diameter of about 25 cm/10 in and be about 3 mm/⅛ in thick. Pinch up the edge slightly to form a rim (1). Put it on a floured cloth, then repeat with the other pieces of dough.

The simplest garnish for pizza is several spoonfuls of thick tomato sauce, highly seasoned with garlic and oregano. Cover generously with grated Parmesan and add thin slices of mozzarella cheese. Sprinkle with a few drops of olive oil and cook for 10 minutes in an oven preheated to 250C/475F/gas 9.

To drink: a medium-bodied Italian red wine, such as a Chianti.

PLAICE

Plie, carrelet

see also:
brill
fish
sole

A diamond-shaped flatfish abundant in European Atlantic waters and the North Sea, plaice is characterized by the orange spots on its brown upper side. The AMERICAN or CANADIAN PLAICE, also known as SAND DAB, is a separate species, closer to the flounder.

Plaice is available all year round, but of better quality in winter. Its very delicate flesh lends it to being cooked like sole or brill, and it is considerably less expensive. Allow at least 200 g/7 oz of fish per person as there is significant wastage, or buy fillets. Small plaice are particularly good grilled, and deep fried fillets are a popular treat in British fish and chip shops.

Plaice is a lean fish: 100 g/3½ oz contains only 65 calories.

PLIE AU FOUR

Plaice fillets in a tomato and white wine sauce

Serves 4
Preparation 10 minutes
Cooking 8 minutes

METRIC/IMPERIAL	AMERICAN
55 g/2 oz butter	4 tbsp butter
45 g/1½ oz flour	⅓ cup flour
200 ml/7 fl oz milk	1 cup milk
100 ml/3½ fl oz dry white wine	½ cup dry white wine
1 tbsp tomato purée	1 tbsp tomato paste
3 tbsp finely chopped parsley	3 tbsp finely chopped parsley
4 plaice fillets	4 plaice or flounder fillets
juice of ½ lemon	juice of ½ lemon
salt and pepper	salt and pepper

Put two thirds of the butter in a bowl and heat for 1 minute on High. Add the flour and mix, then gradually stir in the milk and the wine.

Microwave the sauce for 3 minutes on High, whisking after each minute. Add the tomato purée (paste) and parsley, mix and season with salt and pepper. Cover and set aside.

Arrange the plaice fillets in a dish and dot with the rest of the butter. Sprinkle with lemon juice and season with salt and pepper. Cover with microwave-safe film, pierce it in several places and microwave on High for 3 minutes, turning the dish around half-way through if not using a turntable.

Transfer the fillets to a warmed serving dish suitable for microwaving. Incorporate the fish cooking juices into the sauce, whisk vigorously and coat the fish with it. Microwave for 1 minute on High and serve at once.

To drink: a dry white wine, such as Soave.

PLUM

Prune

see also:
fruit
jams, etc
prune
tart

A summer stone fruit related to the peach, apricot and cherry, the plum is small and round or slightly elongated. The thin skin varies widely in colour, from green or yellow to red, purple or bluish-black. The moist, soft, fragrant flesh may be sweet or slightly sour, depending on variety. Plums lend themselves well to cross-breeding, and there are literally thousands of varieties. Most of those now cultivated are either descended from the JAPANESE PLUM or are a cross between the SLOE and the Asiatic CHERRY PLUM.

The sweeter types more suited to being eaten raw as a dessert fruit include:

The GREENGAGE (*Reine Claude*) which may actually be yellow or pale purple as well as green. Its firm, perfumed flesh has a wonderful honeyed taste, and it is also often made into compotes and jams. Greengages are mostly grown in Western Europe and are generally available in late summer. The fruit which is grown farther south in warmer years makes the best eating.

Long, purple VICTORIA PLUMS have good keeping qualities and have thus become a popular commercial plum in Britain. They have a good flavour, but can have a rather gummy texture.

Sweet purple SANTA ROSA and BURBANK

PLUMS were first cultivated in California but are now grown in Chile and South Africa, ensuring winter supplies of the fruit.

Varieties more suited to cooking include:

DAMSONS, which are cultivated forms of the wild plum and are large, elongated fruit with purple skins and sweet yellow pulp. They are made into tarts, compotes, pies, puddings, jam and thick damson cheese. The late damsons from Alsace are also delicious preserved in brandy.

The deep-purple, small and heavy QUETSCHE has dry, spicy flesh which makes delicious cakes and jams. It is also used to make alcoholic drinks, such as *quetsch* and *slivovitz*.

The MIRABELLE, MYROBALAN or CHERRY PLUM is a small, juicy, yellow late-summer plum which grows wild in Asia but is mainly cultivated in eastern France, Belgium and Holland. Vosges mirabelles, sweet, juicy, round and almost orange in colour, are particularly fragrant and regarded by many as the best eating fruit. Mirabelles are preserved in syrup and make delicious jams and tarts. They are also used for making *eau-de-vie*.

SLOES are small, blue-black and very bitter fruits. They are inedible raw but are used in jellies with other sweeter fruit. Perhaps their most familiar use is in the flavouring of gin.

Plums should be bought ripe or just under-ripe but should still be firm and unwrinkled. A slight whitish bloom is a sign that they have not been handled too much. If perfectly ripe, they should be used within a day: if just under-ripe, they will ripen in a day or so in a warm place or keep 2 or 3 days in a cool place.

Fresh plums in season make delicious dessert fruit and are excellent in fruit salads, tarts, compotes or jam. The Germans and Austrians also use them, like apricots, in dumplings and in strudel pastries, and favour them in bean and smoked sausage stews. Plums have a wide range of use in savoury cooking. They go particularly well with beef, pork, fatty poultry and game. The Chinese make a memorable sauce from them, with chillies and garlic, which is best-known as an accompaniment to Peking duck. Commercially, a large part of the plum crop is canned in syrup, bottled in alcohol, made into jam and brandy or dried to make prunes.

Plums are rich in minerals, fibre and vitamin A. Their calorie content varies according to variety: 100 g/3½ oz contains 30–80 calories.

BOEUF AUX PRUNES

Braised beef with plums

Serves 4
Preparation 15 minutes
Cooking about 1¾ hours

METRIC/IMPERIAL	AMERICAN
800 g/1¾ lb large plums	1¾ lb large plums
200 ml/7 fl oz red wine	1 cup red wine
25 g/¾ oz butter	1½ tbsp butter
2 tbsp oil	2 tbsp oil
800 g/1¾ lb boneless shoulder of beef, cut into pieces	1¾ lb beef chuck, cut into pieces
4 onions, thinly sliced	4 onions, thinly sliced
2 tbsp vinegar	2 tbsp vinegar
1 tsp ground cinnamon	1 tsp ground cinnamon
150 ml/¼ pt whipping cream	⅔ cup whipping cream
juice of ½ lemon	juice of ½ lemon
salt and pepper	salt and pepper

Poach the plums in the wine for 8 minutes. Drain, reserving the wine, and remove the stoness from the fruit.

Melt the butter with half the oil in a frying pan over a moderate heat. Brown the pieces of meat on all sides for about 5 minutes, then drain them and put in a flameproof casserole.

Add the remaining oil to the frying pan and cook the onions until soft. Drain and add to the meat. Deglaze the frying pan with the vinegar. Pour the pan juices into the casserole and add the wine and cinnamon. Season, cover and cook gently for about 1¼ hours.

Mix the cream with the lemon juice and stir into the casserole. Add the plums, cover and cook for a further 15 minutes. Adjust the seasoning and serve from the casserole.

TARTE AUX QUETSCHES

Quetsch or damson tart

Serves 6
Preparation 30 minutes
Cooking about 25 minutes

METRIC/IMPERIAL	AMERICAN
200 g/7 oz flour	1⅔ cups flour
100 g/3½ oz butter, cut into small pieces	1 stick butter, cut into small pieces
200 g/7 oz caster sugar	1 cup superfine sugar
800 g/1¾ lb quetsches or damsons, halved and stoned	1¾ lb quetsches or damsons, halved and pitted
pinch of salt	pinch of salt

Make the pastry: place the flour in a heap on a work surface, make a well in the middle and add all but 1 tablespoon of butter, 1 tablespoon of sugar and the salt. Gradually add 100 ml/3½ fl oz/½ cup of water, mixing to a smooth dough. Knead to a smooth ball and let rest for 20 minutes.

Preheat the oven to 250C/475F/gas 9 and grease a 25 cm/10 in tart pan with the reserved butter.

Roll out the pastry and use it to line the tart pan. Sprinkle 55 g/2 oz/¼ cup of the remaining sugar over the bottom of the pastry case. Arrange the plum halves over the bottom, cut side up. The juice will then not run out as they cook and the pastry will remain crisp.

Sprinkle the surface generously with the rest of the sugar and bake for 20–25 minutes. The plums will caramelize slightly. Serve warm.

POACHING

see also:
court-bouillon
egg
fish
floating islands
fruit
pear
quenelle

Various foodstuffs are poached by immersing them in boiling liquid and then simmering them gently. The liquid may be water, stock, court-bouillon, wine, milk or syrup. Poaching differs from boiling in that the liquid is kept just barely moving. The method thus suits fragile foods, like fish, eggs, fruit or dumplings, or foods which may over-cook easily, like seafood. The gentle nature of the cooking leaves most of the nutrients and flavour in the food.

POLLACK AND SAITHE

Lieu jaune et lieu noir

see also:
cod
fish
haddock
whiting

Large seawater fish of the cod family, pollack and saithe are very similar to the whiting. The pollack is fished mainly in cold Atlantic waters between Europe and Iceland. The darker-coloured saithe, also known as COLEY, COALFISH or POLLOCK is found on both sides of the Atlantic and in the North Sea. The former has whiter and more delicate flesh than the latter. Young fish of both species make fine eating, usually plainly poached or fried with a fine oatmeal coating, but are rarely encountered. Steaks and fillets may be prepared like cod or haddock. Both fish are excellent in pies, pâtés and fish cakes.

Very nutritious fish, they are a good source of phosphorus. They are also quite lean and 100 g/3½ oz contains only 100 calories.

LIEU À LA MOUTARDE

Pollack in mustard sauce

Serves 4
Preparation 10 minutes
Cooking about 15 minutes

METRIC/IMPERIAL	AMERICAN
115 g/¼ lb celeriac	¼ lb celeriac (celery root)
juice of 1 lemon	juice of 1 lemon
45 g/1½ oz butter	3 tbsp butter
3 tbsp flour	3 tbsp flour
300 ml/½ pt milk	1½ cups milk
1 tbsp strong mustard	1 tbsp Dijon mustard
4 pollack steaks, each weighing about 140 g/5 oz	4 pollock steaks, each weighing about 5 oz
salt and pepper	salt and pepper

Peel the celeriac and chop it finely. Put it into a dish with 2 tablespoons of lemon juice. Cover it with microwave-safe film and prick the film in several places with the point of a sharp knife. Microwave on High for 8 minutes.

Put the butter in a bowl. Melt it on High for 1 minute. Add the flour and mix, then pour on the milk and stir in the mustard. Microwave on High for 3 minutes, whisking after each minute.

Remove the sauce from the oven and season with salt and pepper. Mix in the celeriac.

Arrange the fish steaks in a shallow dish, with the thinnest sides inwards. Add the rest of the lemon juice and season with salt and pepper. Cover with film and pierce in several places. Microwave on High for 4 minutes.

Arrange the fish steaks on individual warmed plates, coat with the sauce and serve.

see also:
condiment
fruit

POMEGRANATE

Grenade

An autumn fruit, the pomegranate came originally from Persia but is now grown in most sub-tropical climates. Its tough, shiny skin encloses a multitude of edible seeds in a pale-red pulp held in compartments separated by inedible white pith. The leathery skin ensures that the fruit will keep well and stay juicy for a long time, hence its early popularity with travellers. Pomegranates are ripe when the skin is a dull pinkish colour. Avoid buying fruit with brown spots or bruises. The juice and flesh of the fruit stain readily, so handle them with care.

The refreshing, slightly acid pulp can be eaten on its own or used in fruit salads. The juice can be used for making *coulis*, sorbets or cold drinks. The seeds of sour fruit are also commonly used as a condiment and both seeds and juice have a long tradition of use in savoury cooking in the Middle East and India, especially with meat, poultry and fish dishes, couscous and salads.

Much of the crop is used to make grenadine syrup, refreshing in cocktails and mixed drinks.

Pomegranates are rich in vitamin C, but also sugar: 100 g/3½ oz contains 65 calories.

SALADE CALIFORNIENNE

Californian salad

Serves 2
Preparation 25 minutes, plus chilling

METRIC/IMPERIAL	AMERICAN
2 pomegranates	2 pomegranates
200 g/7 oz cooked sweetcorn kernels	1 cup cooked whole kernel corn
juice of 1 lemon	juice of 1 lemon
1 small can (200 g/7 oz) of tuna fish in brine, drained and flaked	1 7-oz can tuna fish in water, drained and flaked
2 tomatoes, peeled and sliced	2 tomatoes, peeled and sliced
100 g/3½ oz low-fat fromage blanc or cottage cheese	½ cup low-fat fromage blanc or cottage cheese
1 tsp paprika	1 tsp paprika
dash of Tabasco	dash of Tabasco
salt and pepper	salt and pepper

Carefully cut open the pomegranates and remove the pulp. Put it into a bowl and chill it.

Put the corn in another bowl and sprinkle with lemon juice. Add the tuna, tomatoes, cheese, paprika, Tabasco and seasoning to taste. Mix well.

Spoon the salad into 2 individual bowls and serve well chilled. At the last minute, top with the reserved pomegranate flesh.

POPPY

Pavot

see also:
bread
cheese
creams and custards
fats and oils

The poppy plant has traditionally found many uses in the kitchen. The bright red petals are employed in confectionery and the leaves cooked, like sorrel, as a vegetable.

However, the tiny blue-grey seeds of the opium poppy are the plant's most common contribution to today's cooking. They are used mainly in baking, sprinkled over bread, rolls and pastries, and to flavour fresh cheese and creams and custards. They can also be used on salads and fresh pasta, but are best first lightly roasted or pan fried to bring out their flavour.

Indian cooks use them to season and thicken meat and vegetable dishes. They are also a classic ingredient in chutneys and in *garam masala*, the basic flavouring mix for most curries.

The oil expressed from the seeds is also an important cooking oil, having a fine flavour akin to that of a nutty olive oil.

SALADE AU PAVOT

Poppy seed salad

Serves 4
Preparation 20 minutes
Cooking 10 minutes

METRIC/IMPERIAL	*AMERICAN*
3 stalks of celery, trimmed and chopped into small pieces	*3 sticks of celery, trimmed and cut into small pieces*
1 cooked beetroot, finely diced	*1 cooked beet, finely diced*
2 carrots, coarsely grated	*2 carrots, coarsely grated*
juice of 1 lemon	*juice of 1 lemon*
3 tbsp sunflower oil	*3 tbsp sunflower oil*
2 squares of Demi-Sel cheese, cubed	*2 square Demi-Sel cheeses, cubed*
1 tsp poppy seeds	*1 tsp poppy seeds*
2 hard-boiled eggs, shelled and sliced	*2 hard-boiled eggs, shelled and sliced*
salt and pepper	*salt and pepper*

Mix the celery, beetroot (beet) and carrots in a salad bowl. Sprinkle with lemon juice and add the oil. Season and mix well.

Roll the cubes of cheese in poppy seeds, and garnish the salad with them and the egg slices.

PORGY

see Sea bream

PORK

Porc

see also:
bacon
barding
charcuterie
fats and oils
ham
kidney
lard
larding
liver
meat
offal
pâté
sausage
smoking
trotters and feet

The uncured flesh of the domesticated pig, pork is probably the most reasonably priced and versatile of meats. The pig has always been an abundant source of food, and through the centuries great resourcefulness has been applied to making the best use of every part of the animal in an extensive range of bacons, hams, sausages and other *charcuterie*. Even pigs' feet, intestines and ears are used in peasant cooking. The pig is also the only mammal whose skin is also eaten, pork crackling being regarded by many as the tastiest part of a roast.

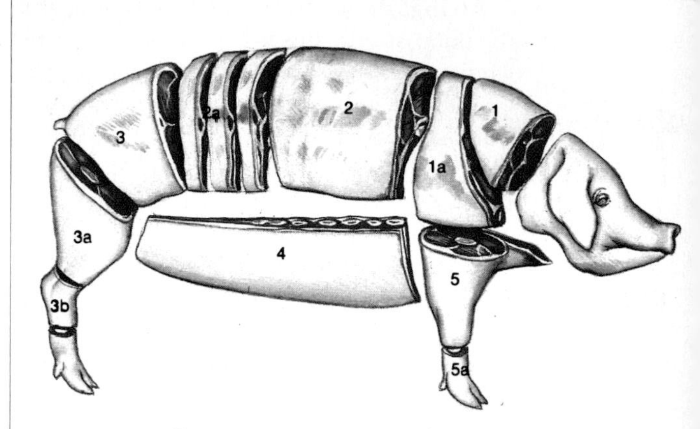

BRITISH CUTS OF PORK:
1 spare rib, 1a blade, 2 loin, 2a loin chops, 3 leg fillet end, 3a leg knuckle end, 3b hock, 4 belly, 5 hand, 5a trotter

Today's pigs have been carefully bred to be longer and larger, with a much lower percentage of fat than their ancestors. Very young animals, between 3 and 8 weeks old, are sold as SUCKLING PIGS. Usually spit-roasted whole, their pale, succulent meat is tender, sweet and rich in flavour. Pigs up to 4 months old are known as YOUNG PIGS OR PIGLETS, becoming MATURE HOGS at 6 months. Animals slaughtered between the ages of 6 months and 1 year are termed PORKERS and these provide most of our meat.

Mature pork meat should be delicately pink and smell fresh. The fat should be firm and white and the skin dry and light in colour. Any deep colour in the meat, dry flesh or dark and discoloured flesh probably indicates meat from a fairly old animal. Pieces of meat which look slimy have been stored badly.

Fillet (butt) end of leg and loin of pork are suitable for roasting. The loin also provides the enduringly popular pork chops, as does the chump (sirloin). Chops may be fried, grilled (broiled) or baked. The rather dry and bland meat of the fillet (tenderloin) may be roasted whole, but is also often cut into *filets mignons*,

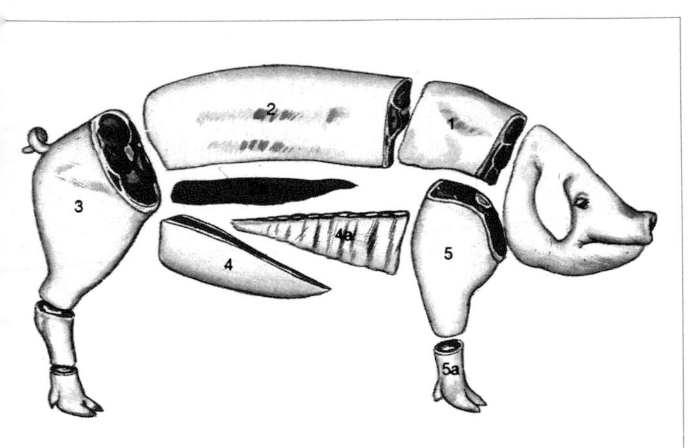

AMERICAN CUTS OF PORK:
1 blade shoulder, 2 loin, 2a tenderloin, 3 leg, 4 side, 4a sparerib, 5 arm shoulder, 5a hock

medallions or escalopes (cutlets) for grilling or frying. Other less tender cuts, such as the sparerib, blade and hand (Boston and picnic shoulder), are best braised, casseroled or stewed.

The belly of the pig is normally cured or made into salt pork, but fresh bellies also provide spare ribs for grilling or barbecuing and fat for larding and barding. Pieces of pork belly fat are also potent flavouring ingredients.

Fresh pork must be well cooked as even the best meat may harbour the parasite which causes trichinosis: all parts of the meat should reach a sufficiently high temperature to leave not a trace of pink. Also resist any temptation to sample small pieces of meat before full cooking, and thoroughly clean utensils and work surfaces after preparing the meat.

Large cuts of pork should be given at least 40 minutes per 450 g/1 lb at 180C/350F/gas 4. Cuts with crackling should be well scored and roasted at about 220C/425F/gas 7 for 25 minutes per 450 g/1 lb plus 25 minutes over. Sprinkling the skin with a little oil and salt gives it a fine crumbly texture. Stand the roast on a trivet or rack and do not baste the skin as this makes the crackling inedibly hard.

Flavour pork roasts by studding them with garlic slivers, sprinkling with fresh or dried thyme, sage, rosemary or basil or smearing with mustard. Boned, rolled roasts may be stuffed with chestnuts, sage and onion or fruit, such as prunes, apricots or apples. Cider or Calvados is also often used in pork dishes and apple sauce is a traditional accompaniment.

Pork is an excellent source of vitamin B1, but it is a fatty meat: 100 g/3½ oz contains 290 calories. However, the exterior fat of prime-quality cuts is easily removed.

CARRÉ DE PORC AU THYM

Pork loin with thyme

Serves 6
Preparation 15 minutes, marinating 2 hours
Cooking 1½ hours

METRIC/IMPERIAL	*AMERICAN*
1 garlic clove, cut into slivers	*1 garlic clove, cut into slivers*
1 pork loin, weighing about 1.5 kg/3½ lb	*1 pork loin roast, weighing about 3½ lb*
350 ml/12 fl oz white wine	*1⅔ cups white wine*
4 or 5 sprigs of dried thyme, crumbled	*4 or 5 sprigs of dried thyme, crumbled*
2 tbsp fine breadcrumbs	*2 tbsp fine breadcrumbs*
1 tbsp chopped parsley	*1 tbsp chopped parsley*
salt and ground pepper	*salt and pepper*

Using a pointed knife, slide the garlic slivers into the meat close to the bone at several places along its length. Season the meat.

Put the meat into a deep roasting pan, sprinkle with two thirds of the wine and the crumbled thyme and leave to marinate for 2 hours, turning it over 2 or 3 times.

Preheat the oven to 220C/425F/gas 7. Cover the meat in the pan with foil and roast for 1 hour.

Mix the breadcrumbs and parsley together. Take the meat out of the oven and spread this mixture over the fatty part of the meat, pressing down well to make it stick.

Return to the oven, uncovered, and cook for a further 30 minutes at 160C/325F/gas 3, basting from time to time with the cooking juices.

When the fat is crusty and golden, serve very hot. Skim the fat off the cooking juices and deglaze the pan with the remaining wine. Serve as a gravy, reduced a little if necessary.

To drink: a lively red wine, such as Beaujolais.

Travers de porc marinés et grillés

Grilled marinated pork spare ribs

Serves 6
Preparation 10 minutes, marinating 4 hours
Cooking about 15 minutes

METRIC/IMPERIAL	AMERICAN
4 tbsp tomato purée	¼ cup tomato paste
juice of 1 lemon	juice of 1 lemon
3 tbsp oil	3 tbsp oil
2 tsp sugar	2 tsp sugar
1 tsp chilli powder	1 tsp chili powder
½ tbsp dried oregano	½ tbsp dried oregano
2 garlic cloves, chopped	2 garlic cloves, chopped
2 kg/4½ lb pork spare ribs, cut into 6 sections, each weighing about 350 g/12 oz	4½ lb pork spare ribs, cut into 6 sections, each weighing about 12 oz
salt and pepper	salt and pepper

In a large bowl, mix the tomato purée (paste), lemon juice, oil, sugar, chilli powder and oregano. Season with salt and pepper, add the garlic and stir. Put the pieces of spare rib into the mixture and turn them several times to coat them completely. Marinate them in the refrigerator for 4 hours.

Preheat a grill (broiler) or barbecue. Drain the pieces of spare rib and grill them for 8 minutes on each side, basting with a little of the marinade as they cook.

Variation: try marinating the pork spare ribs in a Chinese 'lacquer' sauce, consisting of 5 tablespoons of soy sauce, 1 tablespoon of five-spice powder, 1 tablespoon of honey, 2 cloves of chopped garlic, 1 tablespoon of chopped fresh ginger, 1 tablespoon of Cognac, 1 teaspoon of oil and 1 teaspoon of vinegar.

Côtes de porc au vin blanc

Pork chops with white wine sauce

Serves 4
Preparation 20 minutes
Cooking about 25 minutes

METRIC/IMPERIAL	AMERICAN
4 pork chops	4 pork chops
2 or 3 pinches of dried thyme	2 or 3 pinches of dried thyme
45 g/1½ oz butter	3 tbsp butter
1 tbsp oil	1 tbsp oil
300 g/10 oz mushrooms, stalks removed and thinly sliced	10 oz mushrooms, stems removed and thinly sliced
1 tsp tomato purée	1 tsp tomato paste
100 ml/3½ fl oz dry white wine	½ cup dry white wine
100 ml/3½ fl oz chicken stock	½ cup chicken stock
1 tsp cornflour	1 tsp cornstarch
5 tbsp port	⅓ cup port wine
salt and pepper	salt and pepper
chopped flat-leaved parsley, to garnish	chopped flat-leaf parsley, to garnish

Season the pork chops with salt and pepper and sprinkle with the thyme. Melt half the butter with the oil in a frying pan over a moderate heat and cook the chops in it for 8 minutes on each side, turning them several times.

Meanwhile, in another pan, melt the remaining butter over a moderate to high heat and sauté the mushrooms.

Drain the pork chops. Mix the tomato purée (paste) with the wine and stock and use this to deglaze the frying pan used for the chops, scraping up the sediment with a wooden spoon. Boil this sauce rapidly to reduce it by half.

Mix the cornflour (cornstarch) with the port and add to the sauce. Simmer, stirring constantly, for 5 minutes. Adjust the seasoning.

Arrange the chops on a warmed serving dish and surround with the mushrooms. Coat with the sauce, sprinkle with parsley and serve at once.

To drink: a medium-bodied red wine, such as Fleurie.

Côtes de porc au vin blanc (Pork chops with white wine sauce)

PORRIDGE

see Oats

POTASSIUM

see also:
minerals
salt

A mineral which, along with sodium, regulates the diffusion of liquids between body cells, it is also responsible for the correct functioning of the autonomic muscular system and the body's utilization of sugars. Potassium is so widely available in a well-balanced diet, especially in fruit and vegetables, and so readily absorbed and excreted by the healthy body that daily requirement levels are easily met.

POTATO

Pomme de terre

see also:
baking
boiling
croquette
deep frying
gnocchi
gratin
pie
purée
vegetables

The potato plant is one of the nightshade family and related to peppers and tomatoes. Native to South and Central America, the plant is now the most widely grown vegetable in the world with a greater area of cultivation than that for wheat. Only the tubers which grow extensively in the roots are eaten.

There are at least 100 different varieties. In the spring and first weeks of summer, early varieties such as the CYPRUS are sold as NEW POTATOES. Later in the summer MATURE or MAIN CROP POTATOES become available; these are stored to provide supplies through the winter.

According to variety, the flesh may be either white or yellow, but this does not correspond directly to either taste or texture. The most important characteristic for the cook is whether the flesh is floury or waxy. Floury potatoes cook to a crumbly texture and thus bake and mash well, but tend to fall apart when cooked in any other way, including boiling. Waxy potatoes have a more substantial texture and keep their shape better when boiled and deep fried, and make the best potato salads, but are too sticky to mash or purée.

Among the most important floury potatoes are IDAHO or RUSSET potatoes, which are very long and large and are by far the best potatoes for baking, and the PENTLAND CROWN potato, which is thin-skinned and white-fleshed and at its best in the weeks before Christmas.

Popular waxy potatoes include BELLE DE FONTENAY, with firm, yellow, fine-grained flesh, which are ideal for sautéing, frying, steaming and for use in potato salads. DÉSIRÉES are quite large and oval in shape, with red skins

new potato *Idaho*

Bintje *red waxy potato*

Ratte potatoes *BF 15*

Belle de Fontenay

small new potatoes

and firm yellow flesh. CALIFORNIAS are a relatively new breed with a smooth thin skin and an even shape, making them very economical. The RATTE is the potato held in the highest esteem by French cooks. Its firm, waxy yellow flesh is also full of taste, and plainly boiled in their skins and dressed with a little butter they make a fine dish on their own. They are also excellent in warm potato salads.

Medium-firm, ALL-PURPOSE varieties suit most forms of cooking and are the types most commonly sold in supermarkets, etc. Some of the most familiar are:

KING EDWARDS or KERR'S PINKS, both with red skins, are probably the most popular potatoes in Britain. The BINTJE, which is the most common potato in France, has slightly floury, yellow flesh and is held to make the best French fries. It is also excellent for soups and stews and mashes well. MARIS PEER potatoes are large and white-fleshed and are probably the variety most suited for boiling as they do not blacken readily.

Buy potatoes which are firm, smooth and even in shape. Avoid any with bruised, dark or green patches or which are beginning to sprout. Potatoes should be kept in a cool dark place which is neither too damp nor too dry. Exposure to light causes them to turn green and this renders them slightly toxic. Do not keep them in the refrigerator: lengthy exposure to low temperatures causes them to become sweet. Ready-cleaned potatoes do not keep as well as those with a healthy patina of soil.

Potatoes are peeled as appropriate, although most of the nutrients and a good deal of the flavour lie in the skin or just under it, and the potato holds together better with it intact. A good scrub with a stiff brush is preferable, but do remove any 'eyes'. Wash off excess starch after peeling and slicing, but do not soak peeled potatoes as they will lose more nutrients, harden and take longer to cook.

As well as their universal role as the principal accompanying vegetable, a large potato baked and dressed with a little butter or sour cream makes an ideal and nutritious snack or light meal. They may also be stuffed with rich meat or cheese mixtures to make very substantial main courses.

Potato purée is also a classic garnish. It may be enriched with egg or choux pastry and is often piped or moulded into decorative shapes. It may also be used as a topping for pies and other baked dishes.

An enormous part of the potato crop is used by the food industry to make that most ubiquitous of snacks, the potato crisp or chip, as well as convenience foods such as frozen, oven-ready French fries and freeze-dried, instant mashed potato. POTATO FLOUR is popular in the manufacture of crackers, biscuits and scones. Its fine grains and neutral flavour also make it a useful thickening agent.

Potatoes are nutritious and, contrary to popular wisdom, they are very low in calories provided they are plainly boiled or steamed: 100 g/3½ oz of boiled potatoes contain only 90 calories, while the same weight of French fries contains a staggering 420 calories.

SALADE DE POMMES DE TERRE

Potato salad

Serves 4
Preparation 20 minutes
Cooking 25 minutes

METRIC/IMPERIAL	AMERICAN
800 g/1¾ lb small new potatoes	*1¾ lb small new potatoes*
4 tbsp chopped chervil	*¼ cup chopped chervil*
3 tbsp whipping cream	*3 tbsp whipping cream*
1 tbsp sherry vinegar	*1 tbsp sherry vinegar*
2 small jars of salmon or trout roe	*2 small jars salmon roe*
salt and pepper	*salt and pepper*

Scrub the potatoes and cook them in a large pan of boiling salted water for 20–25 minutes.

Meanwhile, mix the chervil, cream and vinegar in a bowl. Season with salt and pepper.

Drain the potatoes, allow them to cool a little, then peel and slice them into rounds. Place the slices of potato in a bowl, coat them with the sauce and stir carefully.

Spoon the potato salad on 4 individual plates. Garnish with the roe and serve at once.

POMMES DUCHESSE

Baked mashed potato

Serves 4
Preparation 30 minutes
Cooking about 30 minutes

METRIC/IMPERIAL	AMERICAN
55 g/2 oz butter	*4 tbsp butter*
800 g/1¾ lb floury potatoes, peeled and quartered	*1¾ lb floury potatoes, peeled and quartered*
pinch of grated nutmeg	*pinch of grated nutmeg*
1 egg + 2 yolks	*1 egg + 2 yolks*
salt and pepper	*salt and pepper*

Preheat the oven to 200C/400F/gas 6 and lightly grease a baking sheet with a little butter.

Cook the potatoes for 15 minutes in a large pan of boiling salted water. Drain them and put them in another baking dish.

Dry them in the oven with the door ajar. When they have whitened, press them through a fine sieve or potato ricer.

Put the potato purée into a saucepan and add nutmeg, salt and pepper to taste. Incorporate the remaining butter and stir for 3 minutes with a wooden spoon. Add the whole egg and the yolks. Mix thoroughly.

Fit a piping bag with a fluted nozzle and fill it with the mixture. Pipe crowns, nests, shells or other decorative shapes on the baking sheet and bake for about 10 minutes.

Serve as a garnish for roasts, pieces of sautéed meat or baked fish.

Variations: the mixture may also be deep fried in oil heated to 180C/360F. Fit the piping bag with a plain nozzle with a diameter of about 2 cm/¾ in. Pipe the mixture into the hot oil, cutting it off into sections about 4 cm/1½ in long. Cook until golden brown, then drain the croquettes on paper towels. Serve piping hot.

POMMES DAUPHINE (potato croquettes) are made by mixing the seasoned potato purée with an equal weight of choux pastry and deep frying spoonfuls of the mixture. The purée may also be flavoured with grated Parmesan cheese or finely chopped parsley or ham.

POMMES PONT-NEUF

French fried potatoes

Serves 2
Preparation 15 minutes
Cooking about 10 minutes per batch

METRIC/IMPERIAL	AMERICAN
450 g/1 lb waxy potatoes	*1 lb waxy potatoes*
groundnut oil, for deep frying	*peanut oil, for deep frying*
salt	*salt*

Peel the potatoes and cut them lengthwise into slices about 1 cm/½ in thick, then cut each slice into uniform sticks. Rinse them well, rubbing them with the hands, then drain well and dry them thoroughly in a clean cloth. This will help to avoid spattering.

Put enough oil in a large heavy-bottomed pan to cook about 20 potato sticks at a time. Heat to a temperature of about 180C/360F: drop a piece of raw potato into the pan – if it rises to the surface, bubbling, after about 20 seconds, the oil is ready. Try to keep the heat adjusted throughout the cooking process so that the temperature remains steady at this level, particularly after each batch of potatoes is immersed for the first time.

Plunge a deep-frying basket into the oil for a few seconds to heat it, then remove it and put a handful of potato sticks into it. Cook small batches at a time so that the oil temperature does not drop too drastically when the potatoes are lowered into it.

Return the basket to the hot oil. Let the potatoes sizzle for 6–7 minutes to seal them and cook them through. Remove them from the basket and keep warm in an uncovered dish in a warm oven with the door ajar. Continue in this way until all the potatoes are cooked.

Repeat the whole operation, putting the potato sticks back into the basket in small quantities and cooking them a second time for 3–4 minutes until brown and crisp. Drain them well on paper towels and sprinkle them with fine salt. Keep them warm and serve as soon as all are cooked.

Variations: to make POTATO NESTS *as a garnish for roast game birds or as novel 'serving dishes' for vegetables, cut the potatoes into fine matchsticks, rinse and dry them very well, then sprinkle generously with potato flour. Arrange them in nest shapes between two metal sieves or in a special basket and deep fry until golden brown.*

To make SOUFFLÉ POTATOES*: cut them into 3 mm/⅛ in slices. Rinse them briefly and pat dry again. Heat the oil to 150C/300F and cook the potato slices in it for 8 minutes, then drain them on paper towels and let them cool. Heat the oil to 180C/360F and put the potatoes back in it. Cook for 3 or 4 minutes, until puffy and brown, then drain them on paper towels and serve sprinkled with salt as an accompaniment to roasts, chicken and game.*

POMMES SAUTÉES SARLADAISES

Potatoes sautéed in goose fat

Serves 4
Preparation 20 minutes
Cooking about 20 minutes

METRIC/IMPERIAL	AMERICAN
800 g/1¾ lb waxy potatoes	1¾ lb waxy potatoes
55 g/2 oz goose fat	2 oz (¼ cup) goose fat
4 or 5 garlic cloves, chopped	4 or 5 garlic cloves, chopped
bunch of parsley, stalks removed and chopped	bunch of parsley, stems removed and chopped
salt and pepper	salt and pepper

Peel the potatoes and slice in rounds about 5 mm/¼ in thick. Rinse and drain well and pat thoroughly dry with a cloth or paper towels.

Melt the goose fat in a large, heavy-bottomed frying pan over a moderate heat. Put the potatoes into it along with ½ tablespoon of chopped garlic. Sauté the potatoes over a moderate to high heat for 15 minutes, until well browned on all sides.

Mix the rest of the garlic with the parsley. Add it to the frying pan with salt and pepper to taste and mix well. Lower the heat and cover the pan. Cook gently for a further 4–5 minutes.

Serve at once, as an accompaniment for roast or grilled meats, poultry or game.

Variations: a fresh truffle, peeled and thinly sliced, along with 1 more tablespoon of goose fat added to the potatoes with the garlic and parsley gives a delicious, authentic flavour.

To make the tiny POMMES NOISETTES *which make such an elegant garnish for grilled meats, scoop balls from the peeled potatoes using a melon baller or parisienne cutter. Rinse them well and wipe them dry, then brown them in a mixture of butter and oil in a large, cast-iron frying pan. They are also delicious flavoured with garlic or a little thyme.*

POT-ROASTING

see also: braising larding marinade roasting

Large and fairly tender cuts of meat are often pot-roasted. As in simple braising, the food is initially browned in the cooking pot, often without any added fat, to give the look of meat roasted in the oven. The pot is then tightly covered and the meat cooked gently, effectively baking it. The meat may be set on a bed of chopped vegetables or some pork rind to prevent the bottom from over-cooking.

Meat to be pot-roasted benefits from being marinated or larded prior to cooking.

POULTRY

see also: barding boiling braising chicken duck fats and oils game giblets goose guinea fowl meat stock stuffing turkey

The generic term for farmyard birds, poultry includes chicken, turkey, duck, goose and even guinea fowl. However, unless otherwise specified, it usually means chicken.

Poultry usually reaches the customer ready to cook, ie plucked and drawn. Try to retain the giblets for making stocks and sauces. As an indication of freshness look for skin which is soft and smooth to the touch and which has a pleasant, clean, fresh smell.

A large proportion of modern poultry has, of course, been frozen. Although there is a tendency for the meat of frozen birds to be dry and for them not to have been hung long enough for their flavour to develop fully, the quality of poultry depends much more on the breed of the birds, what they were fed, and how they were reared. Free-range and corn-fed birds have a much better flavour.

Look for birds with plump meat which has some give in it. Signs of youth, and thus tenderness, are difficult to find on oven-ready dressed birds; however, the breastbone should still be pliable if firmly pressed.

Tender, whole, young birds are usually roasted, often with a stuffing. Older birds are generally boiled or braised or cut into portions and used in stews or casseroles. Poultry portions also lend themselves to frying or grilling. Poultry goes well with fresh or dried fruit, mushrooms and nuts, especially almonds, chestnuts and cashews. The flavours of tarragon, marjoram, sage and paprika also complement poultry particularly well. Leftover roast or poached poultry can be used for salads, stuffings, croquettes and sandwiches.

Poultry is as rich in protein as red meat and is full of other nutrients, especially vitamin B complex. Apart from duck and goose, it is also much less fatty, and as most of the fat is in the skin it may easily be avoided.

PRALINE

see also:
almond
cakes and gâteaux
caramel
creams and custards
hazelnut
ices and ice creams
nuts

A preparation made with almonds or hazelnuts (filberts) which are roasted and caramelized with sugar and then crushed, praline is a common flavouring for creams, custards, ice creams, cream fillings for cakes and gâteaux and in *pâtisserie* and confectionery. It is easily made at home using equal proportions of nuts and sugar, but does not keep well. Quality ready-made versions are available in good supermarkets and speciality food shops.

In French cooking, the term *praliné* is used to indicate anything almond-flavoured.

PRAWN

see Shrimp and prawn

PRESERVATIVE

see also:
food additive
salt
vinegar

Any additive which prevents or slows down the natural deterioration of food is known as a preservative. Many natural substances are used for their powers in this area, especially alcoholic beverages, vinegar, salt and saltpetre. Increasingly, however, synthetic additives are used.

Most of the chemical preservatives used are antiseptics which simply inhibit the growth of micro-organisms. Anti-fungal agents are also used to treat the exteriors of some foods, especially fruit such as bananas, pineapples, oranges and lemons. Any such fruit should be well washed if the skin or zest is to be consumed or used in cooking.

Like all permitted food additives, synthetic preservatives are obviously tested to ensure that they are harmless, and many are already present in the human metabolism. However, some can have adverse effects, such as destroying the vitamins in food, or they may even inhibit the body's metabolization of nutrients or cause allergic reactions. For these reasons, be aware of the synthetic preservatives in food and try to avoid making any item with a high content of such additives a regular part of the diet.

PRESERVES

see also:
fruit
jams, etc
pickles
vegetables

Bottled and canned foods are known by the general term of preserves. Foods bottled and canned commercially include meats, poultry, fish and seafood, as well as an increasing array of cooked dishes. Home preserving is generally of fruit and vegetables, either whole or as jams, jellies and marmalades or pickles.

Foods are usually preserved in their own juices or with added sugar, alcohol, salt or vinegar as a preservative. They are generally briefly cooked to a certain temperature to kill off micro-organisms and then put in warmed, dry, sterilized containers and hermetically sealed.

Acid foodstuffs, such as those containing tomatoes or white wine and fruit, should generally be eaten within a year of being canned or bottled. On the other hand, foodstuffs rich in oil or fat, such as sardines or tuna fish, may easily be kept for up to 5 years. Some foods, such as sardines, are even thought to improve on lengthy keeping. Canned and bottled foods should be kept in a cool, dry place. Buy cans which are undamaged and show no signs of rust or of bulging: this may indicate that the contents are fermenting.

Always wash cans before opening them, and do not necessarily discard the liquid which contains nutrients and flavour from the food and may be used in cooking. Preserved foodstuffs, once opened, should be treated like fresh food and eaten without delay. Once a can is opened do not leave the food inside it.

In general, commercially bottled foods should be avoided. They are usually more expensive and in any case foodstuffs preserved in jars are exposed to light, which encourages oxidization and can adversely affect flavour.

SEMI-PRESERVED foods are not given quite the same heat treatment as other preserves and thus have a shorter storage life than foodstuffs which have been sterilized. They should display a 'use-by' date and need to be stored in the refrigerator. They are most often seafood, cooked dishes, pasta and cold meats.

Technological advances have made it possible to augment the number of classic preserved foods with a whole range of new foodstuffs. In addition to semi-preserved foods, which have by now become almost traditional in themselves, the most common innovations are vacuum-packed food and cooked-chilled, ready-made dishes.

PRESSURE COOKER

see also:
steaming

A hermetically sealed saucepan, the pressure cooker permits food to be cooked in superheated steam at a temperature of 112–125C/230–250F instead of the 100C/212F achieved by boiling in ordinary pans. At this high temperature, cooking may take only one third of the time of conventional cooking and require less than half the cooking liquid, added fat and salt. Above all, this method has the advantage of retaining a higher percentage of the food's vitamins and minerals. It is therefore a very healthy form of cooking.

However, the flavours of different items cooked together do have a tendency to mix indiscriminately and the texture of meat cooked this way is a little soft.

Length of cooking is calculated from the point when the valve begins to hiss. Before opening a pressure cooker after cooking, be sure to lower the pressure by releasing steam through the valve or by lowering the internal temperature.

Pressure cookers are also useful for sterilizing items such as bottles for preserving, and for the initial cooking at high temperatures of the preserves themselves.

PROFITEROLE

see also:
choux pastry
cream
creams and custards
sauce

Small choux pastry buns filled with a stuffing, profiteroles may be either sweet or savoury.

Savoury profiteroles, containing cheese, foie gras or salmon mousse, are served as part of a buffet or as a first course.

Sweet versions are filled with pastry cream, jam, cream or ice cream. They may be served for dessert, coated with more cream, ice cream or chocolate sauce, and are also used as the building blocks in the construction of more elaborate sweet dishes, such as croquembouche and gâteau Saint-Honoré.

One profiterole coated with chocolate contains about 100 calories.

PROTEINS

see also:
amino acid
bread
cheese
cream
egg
fish
legume
meat
milk
nuts
poultry
pulses
vegetables
vegetarianism

Chains of amino acids linked together, proteins are the most complex substances known to man and are essential components of living matter.

They are present in most foods, but in order to get the necessary range of essential amino acids the proteins in the diet must come from a wide variety of sources.

Continual debate rages about the minimum daily requirement of proteins: a good guide is 1 gram of protein per kilo of body weight, or about 1 ounce for every 60 pounds. Traditional wisdom dictates that, for proper nutritional balance, half the protein consumed should be of animal origin. However, the protein mix in soya beans, for example, is of a much higher quality than that in many meat products. As with most nutrition, variety and balance in the diet seem to be the key elements.

Many people are allergic to some forms of protein and, as some proteins can go straight into the bloodstream virtually unaltered by the body, foods such as milk and seafood can have an adverse effect on such metabolisms.

see also:
drying
fruit
plum

PRUNE

Pruneau

Red or purple plums are dried to make prunes. Major centres of production include California and the region of south-western France around Agen. At one time they were mostly dried in the sun, but nowadays most are dehydrated in ovens. Increasingly they are also treated with chemicals to soften their skins, and sometimes even coated with glycerine or liquid paraffin to preserve them and make them look glossy.

There many varieties of prune, depending on the type of plum used and the method used to process them. Some, such as the *pistole*, are peeled, stoned and flattened; others may be blanched or pricked to facilitate drying. Speciality fruit, such as the large plump and juicy CARLSBAD PLUM are actually preserved in syrup and are usually served as dessert fruit.

Good quality prunes should be black and shiny, with amber pulp which is not excessively sweet. They should seem soft but not sticky. Store them in a place that is neither too damp nor too dry or they will 'bloom', with sugar crystals forming on their surface.

Before use, most prunes need to be rehydrated by soaking them in warm water, tea or wine for 2 or 3 hours, or a matter of minutes in a microwave oven. Some varieties need no soaking and the process is unnecessary if they are to be puréed or made into compotes, etc. However, they should always be washed in case they are dusty or have been coated with chemicals.

Stoned prunes are used widely in *pâtisserie* and cake-making and are common in fruit compotes, puddings, turnovers and ice creams. In savoury cooking they go very well with rabbit, pork, game, goose and turkey. The east Europeans stuff fish, such as carp, with them, and the Arabs team them with lamb. Stuffed with Roquefort cheese or nuts, or wrapped in thin strips of bacon and grilled, they make good hors d'oeuvres and savouries.

Like most dried fruit, prunes have a very high sugar content: 100 g/3½ oz contains 290 calories. They have a deserved reputation as an effective laxative, but the skin of unpeeled varieties of prune can irritate the alimentary tract and excessive consumption can result in serious digestive disorders.

LAPIN AUX PRUNEAUX

Rabbit with prunes

Serves 4
Preparation 20 minutes, 2 hours ahead
Cooking about 1 hour

METRIC/IMPERIAL	AMERICAN
350 g/12 oz prunes, stoned	12 oz prunes, pitted
2 cups of very strong tea	2 teacups of very strong tea
1 dressed rabbit, liver reserved, cut into pieces	1 dressed rabbit, liver reserved, cut into pieces
15 g/½ oz butter	1 tbsp butter
2 tbsp oil	2 tbsp oil
2 shallots, chopped	2 shallots, chopped
1 tsp dried thyme	1 tsp dried thyme
200 ml/7 fl oz dry white wine	1 cup dry white wine
1 tbsp vinegar	1 tbsp vinegar
salt and pepper	salt and pepper

Soak the prunes in the tea for 2 hours.

Season the rabbit pieces with salt and pepper. Melt the butter with the oil in a flameproof casserole. Cook the rabbit pieces in it over a high heat until they are browned on all sides.

Lower the heat and add the shallots, thyme and wine. Cover and simmer for 40 minutes.

In a food processor, purée the rabbit liver with the vinegar. Add this mixture to the casserole along with the drained prunes. Continue to cook gently for 15 minutes.

Serve very hot, straight from the casserole, accompanied by rice and sautéed mushrooms.
To drink: a dry white wine, such as Riesling.

PUFF PASTRY

see Pastry

PULSES

see also:
bean
chickpea
legume
lentil
pea

The dried, ripe seeds of legumes, pulses have long been a major part of the diet in poorer countries. Recently, however, the high nutritional value of items such as dried white haricot and navy beans, peas, broad or fava beans, soya beans, lentils, chickpeas and split peas, has earned them a well-deserved revival in Western kitchens. They are rich in vitamin B and minerals such as zinc, iron and magnesium and are an important source of vegetable proteins. Combined with cereals they provide all the essential amino acids.

Their keeping qualities are so exceptional that many people think of them as having an indefinite storage life. However, the older they are the drier they become and the more difficult they are to cook properly. So buy from shops with a rapid turnover.

Pulses do have a reputation of being indigestible and of causing flatulence. To minimize these effects, pre-cook them briefly and then rinse them well and cook in fresh water. Lengthy soaking may encourage harmful enzyme activity. Pulses are best given long, slow cooking in unsalted water to which has been added a little bicarbonate of soda to soften the skins. Do not add salt until about half-way through cooking or they will harden.

As well as making simple, humble stews, pulses are excellent in salads and also feature in a wide variety of classic dishes from French cassoulet and lamb with flageolets to *chili con carne* and Middle Eastern hummus.

Pulses have a high energy value: on average 100 g/3½ oz contains about 330 calories.

PUMPKIN

see Squash

PURÉE

see also:
coulis
gratin
mousse
pâté
quenelle
sauce
soufflé
soup
stuffing

Cooked foods which have been finely chopped, mashed, blended in a food processor or sieved to a smooth creamy consistency are said to have been puréed. The term is most commonly used of fruit and vegetable preparations, although soft-fleshed meats like livers or fish are also given this treatment to make stuffings, quenelles, mousses or smooth pâtés, sometimes bound with a white or brown sauce.

Plain vegetable purées are often served as accompaniments to meat, poultry and fish. They may also be highly seasoned or even enriched with eggs, cheese or cream and baked *au gratin*. Purées of watery vegetables, such as the tomato, may be thickened by reduction or bound with a thickening agent like cornflour (cornstarch) or a béchamel sauce. Diluted with stock, vegetable purées also make fine soups, which the French also call purées.

Fruit purées are used to make sauces, soufflés, mousses and ice creams.

The nutritional value of a plain fruit or vegetable purée is the same as the food itself.

PURÉE DE CÉLERI-RAVE

Celeriac or celery root purée

Serves 6
Preparation 20 minutes
Cooking about 1 hour

METRIC/IMPERIAL	*AMERICAN*
2 celeriac roots	*2 heads of celeriac (celery root)*
juice of 2 lemons	*juice of 2 lemons*
about 450 g/1 lb floury potatoes, peeled	*about 1 lb floury potatoes, peeled*
2 tbsp flour	*2 tbsp flour*
100 ml/3½ fl oz milk	*½ cup milk*
pinch of grated nutmeg	*pinch of grated nutmeg*
55 g/2 oz butter, cut into small pieces	*4 tbsp butter, cut into small pieces*
salt and pepper	*salt and pepper*

Peel the celeriac, sprinkle with half the lemon juice and cut into thick slices. Weigh the vegetables: the weight of peeled potatoes should be one quarter of that of the celeriac.

Bring 3 1/5 pt/3 qt of water to the boil in a large pot along with the flour and remaining lemon juice. Add the potatoes and celeriac.

Simmer for 30–40 minutes until the vegetables begin to crumble. Drain well and return to the warm pan for a minute or two to dry them, then put through a food mill or potato ricer.

Put the resulting purée into a saucepan and stir over a low heat, adding the milk. Season with salt and pepper and grated nutmeg to taste. Add the cold butter a few pieces at a time, stirring well to incorporate.

Serve to accompany roasts and game.

PURÉE DE POIS CASSÉS

Split pea purée

Serves 6
Preparation 10 minutes, soaking 2 hours
Cooking about $1\frac{1}{4}$ hours

METRIC/IMPERIAL	AMERICAN
1 kg/$2\frac{1}{4}$ lb split peas	$2\frac{1}{4}$ lb (5 cups) split peas
2 onions	2 onions
2 cloves	2 cloves
bouquet garni	bouquet garni
1 pig's trotter	1 pig's foot
15 g/$\frac{1}{2}$ oz butter	1 tbsp butter
2 tbsp thick crème fraîche or sour cream	2 tbsp thick crème fraîche or sour cream
salt and pepper	salt and pepper

Soak the split peas in cold water for 2 hours. Drain them and put them into a large stewpot.

Stud each of the onions with a clove. Add them to the stewpot along with the bouquet garni and the pig's trotter (foot).

Bring slowly to the boil and cook for 1 hour over a moderate heat, stirring occasionally.

Remove the pig's trotter (foot), bouquet garni and onions. Drain the split peas. Reserve the cooking juices to make soup, to which can be added the meat from the pig's trotter (foot).

Pass the split peas through a vegetable mill. Put the purée in a saucepan over a low heat, add the butter and stir until it melts. Add the cream and season with salt and pepper. The purée should be very smooth.

Serve with sausages, pork or braised ham.

PURSLANE

Pourpier

A green vegetable with fleshy leaves, purslane grows wild in many parts of the world but the French cultivate it widely in the north. The bottoms of the stalks are removed and the peppery leaves eaten raw in salads, rather like watercress, or cooked like spinach and are particularly favoured in omelettes.

The WATERLEAF or SURINAME PURSLANE is a slightly different species which originated in South America and is characterized by its bitterness, due to a high oxalic acid content, and its slightly mucilaginous quality, rather like okra. It can be treated like the cardoon.

Purslane is very nutritious and high in calcium, iron and vitamin A and C content and 100 g/$3\frac{1}{2}$ oz contains only about 10 calories.

see also:
cardoon
salad
spinach
vegetables

SALADE DE POURPIER

Purslane salad

Serves 4
Preparation 20 minutes

METRIC/IMPERIAL	AMERICAN
200 g/7 oz large black radishes	7 oz large black radishes or daikon
5 tbsp sunflower oil	5 tbsp sunflower oil
2 tbsp white wine vinegar	2 tbsp white wine vinegar
1 tsp mild mustard	1 tsp mild mustard
300 g/10 oz young purslane leaves, trimmed	10 oz young purslane leaves, trimmed
100 g/$3\frac{1}{2}$ oz diced cooked beetroot	$\frac{2}{3}$ cup diced cooked beets
4 soft-boiled eggs, shelled	4 soft-boiled eggs, shelled
salt and pepper	salt and pepper

Peel the black radish. Slice half of it into fine rounds and grate the rest.

Prepare a vinaigrette with the oil, vinegar, mustard, salt and pepper.

In a bowl, combine the purslane, grated radish and beetroot (beets), pour the vinaigrette over them and stir to coat well.

Line 4 plates with the radish slices. Put one quarter of the seasoned salad on each plate and place a soft-boiled egg in the middle of each.

Just before serving, split the egg white just a little to allow the yolk to seep out and sprinkle with pepper.

see also:
egg
game

QUAIL

Caille

A small, migratory game bird, the wild quail is now very rare and a protected species in many countries. Most quail eaten today are reared in captivity and the farmed birds have firm, white flesh which is sometimes slightly flavourless.

Allow at least 1 quail per person, 2 if they are very small. Quails are easy to prepare, and may be used in a large variety of recipes. They may be simply sautéed in butter, barded or wrapped in vine (grape) leaves and roasted, spatchcocked and grilled (broiled), or braised with grapes. The tiny dressed birds can be presented on croûtes or in potato nests. They also work well barbecued on skewers, alternating them with small sausages and bacon.

QUAILS' EGGS are tiny and very decorative. Hard-boiled quails' eggs with a watercress mayonnaise make an unusual first course and they are also increasingly used as a garnish. Quails' eggs in aspic, or preserved in brine, are a common buffet item or cocktail snack.

Quail meat is lean and low in calories; 100 g/ 3½ oz of grilled or roasted quail contains 67 calories.

CAILLES EN FEUILLES DE VIGNE

Quails in vine or grape leaves

Serves 4
Preparation 15 minutes
Cooking about 20 minutes

METRIC/IMPERIAL	AMERICAN
4 dressed quails	4 dressed quails
55 g/2 oz butter	4 tbsp butter
4 large fresh vine leaves	4 large fresh grape leaves
8 thin slices of streaky bacon	8 thin slices of bacon
salt and pepper	salt and pepper

Preheat the oven to 180C/350F/gas 4.

Season the quails and grease the breasts and thighs generously with the butter.

Wrap a leaf round the breast of each bird and fold the ends underneath, then wrap 2 bacon slices side by side around the breasts. Secure each quail with string.

Wrap each bird in a piece of foil and fold the edges carefully to seal them. Cook the parcels in the oven for about 20 minutes.

Remove the foil, string and bacon and cut the cooked birds in half lengthwise. Serve accompanied by game chips (deep-fried potato slices) and watercress or grilled (broiled) mushrooms.

To drink: a light fruity Bordeaux.
Notes: the quails may be cooked on a wood fire for 20 minutes or spit-roasted for 15 minutes.

If using preserved vine (grape) leaves, rinse them thoroughly, pat dry and remove the stalks.

QUATRE-ÉPICES

see Spices

QUENELLE

see also:
mousse
pike
poaching
purée
stuffing
veal

Small dumplings made from spiced, finely minced (ground) forcemeat bound with eggs or cream, quenelles are usually poached and served in a cream sauce or baked *au gratin*. They may be made with a number of different types of meat, chicken or fish, but veal and pike are the most usual ingredients. They are served as first or main courses, and tiny quenelles are also used to garnish soups and stews and to fill buffet items like vols-au-vent and bouchées.

All quenelles contain at least 12% fat.

QUENELLES DE BROCHET

Pike quenelles

Serves 6
Preparation 30 minutes, 20 minutes chilling
Cooking about 45 minutes

METRIC/IMPERIAL	AMERICAN
450 g/1 lb pike flesh	1 lb pike flesh
½ tsp grated nutmeg	½ tsp grated nutmeg
1 tsp salt	1 tsp salt
3 egg whites	3 egg whites
600 ml/1 pt crème fraîche or whipping cream	2½ cups crème fraîche or whipping cream
75 g/2½ oz butter	5 tbsp butter
55 g/2 oz flour	6½ tbsp flour
500 ml/16 fl oz milk	2 cups milk
pepper	pepper

Purée the pike in a food processor, adding the nutmeg, salt and about 6 pinches of pepper.

Incorporate the egg whites one at a time. When the mixture is very smooth, chill for at least 20 minutes along with the cream: both ingredients should be well chilled.

Add one third of the cream to the chilled pike purée and blend it for several seconds in the food processor. Reserve 3 tablespoons of the cream and then add the rest of it in two parts in the same way. The pike and cream mixture should be uniform and very smooth.

Preheat the oven to 180C/350F/gas 4 and grease a baking dish with one third of the butter.

Bring a large saucepan of water to the boil. Using 2 tablespoons, shape the quenelles and slide them gently into the water. Let them poach gently for 15 minutes.

Meanwhile, prepare a béchamel sauce: melt the remaining butter in a saucepan, add the flour and cook for a minute or two, then gradually add the milk. Cook until smooth and thick, then incorporate the reserved cream.

Pour half of the sauce into the prepared baking dish, place the well-drained quenelles on top and coat with the rest of the béchamel. Bake for 12–15 minutes, until the top is well coloured, and serve very hot.

To drink: a mellow white wine, such as Alsace Tokay.

QUICHE

see also:
egg
pastry
tart

Any number of flat tarts filled with custard are known as quiches. Outside France, however, the term has now more or less been reserved for such tarts with savoury fillings.

Mostly made with a shortcrust (basic pie) pastry base, quiches are filled with a mixture of eggs and cream which is classically flavoured with bacon or cheese, or they may contain mushrooms, chopped vegetables, nuts and beans, smoked salmon, or seafood.

Quiches are cooked until the filling is just set and then they are usually served hot as a first course. They also make good, light meals on their own or with a salad.

An average portion of quiche lorraine contains about 340 calories.

Cailles en feuilles de vigne (Quails in vine (grape) leaves)

QUICHE LORRAINE

Bacon and egg tart

Serves 6
Preparation 30 minutes, 2 hours ahead
Cooking about 1 hour

METRIC/IMPERIAL	*AMERICAN*
140 g/5 oz butter, cut into small pieces	*10 tbsp butter, cut into small pieces*
250 g/8½ oz flour	*2 cups flour*
5 eggs	*5 eggs*
225 g/½ lb streaky bacon, cut into small strips	*½ lb bacon, cut into small strips*
300 ml/½ pt thick crème fraîche or whipping cream	*1½ cups thick crème fraîche or whipping cream*
pinch of grated nutmeg	*pinch of grated nutmeg*
salt and pepper	*salt and pepper*

Prepare the pastry: rub or cut 125 g/4½ oz/9 tbsp of the butter into the flour. Make a well in the centre and put a pinch of salt into it with 1 of the eggs, lightly beaten, and 3 tablespoons of cold water. Mix the ingredients together to make a dough, shape into a ball and chill for 2 hours.

Preheat the oven to 200C/400F/gas 6 and grease a 25 cm/10 in high-sided tart or quiche mould with some of the remaining butter. Flour it lightly.

Roll the chilled pastry out to a thickness of about 3 mm/⅛ in and use it to line the prepared tart mould. Prick the pastry case all over and bake it blind for 12–15 minutes, until lightly browned. Take it out of the oven and let it cool slightly while making the filling, but keep the oven hot.

Blanch the bacon in boiling water for 5 minutes, refresh in cold water and pat dry. Melt the remaining butter in a frying pan over a moderate heat and lightly brown the bacon.

Spread the bacon out over the bottom of the pastry case. In a bowl, lightly beat the remaining eggs and mix in the cream. Add a little salt and season with nutmeg and pepper.

Pour this mixture over the bacon and bake the quiche for 30 minutes. Serve very hot.

Variations: add any good, sharp grating cheese, such as Gruyère, to the mixture.

Make a seafood quiche by adding 450 g/1 pt cooked, shelled mussels and 250 g/8½ oz large peeled, cooked prawns or shrimp to the egg and cream mixture. Season with a little lemon juice and a few drops of Tabasco rather than nutmeg.

Mushroom or spinach quiches can be made in the same way substituting 450 g/1 lb sautéed, sliced mushrooms or coarsely chopped leaf spinach.

FLAMICHE AUX POIREAUX

Leek quiche

Serves 4
Preparation 40 minutes
Cooking 30 minutes

METRIC/IMPERIAL	*AMERICAN*
75 g/2½ oz butter	*5 tbsp butter*
225 g/½ lb shortcrust pastry	*½ lb basic pie pastry*
whites of 12 leeks, cut into small chunks	*white parts of 12 leeks, cut into small chunks*
4 eggs, beaten	*4 eggs, beaten*
150 ml/¼ pt thick crème fraîche or whipping cream	*⅔ cup thick crème fraîche or whipping cream*
grated nutmeg	*grated nutmeg*
salt and pepper	*salt and pepper*

Preheat the oven to 180C/350F/gas 4. Grease a tart pan with a little of the butter.

Roll out the pastry to a thickness of about 3 mm/⅛ in and use it to line the prepared pan. Prick the base with a fork and chill it while making the filling.

Cook the leeks for 5 minutes in boiling salted water. Drain and refresh them in cold water, then pat them dry.

Melt the remaining butter in a sauté pan over a low heat. Cook the leeks gently, stirring occasionally, for 10 minutes until they are soft but not coloured.

Meanwhile, mix the beaten eggs and cream in a bowl and season with grated nutmeg and salt and pepper. Remove the leeks from the heat, add the egg mixture and mix well.

Pour the mixture into the pastry case, making

sure that it spreads out to the edges. Bake in the middle of the oven for 30 minutes. Serve hot, cut into wedges.
To drink: a dry white wine, such as a Gros-Plant.

see also:
fruit
jams, etc
pectin

QUINCE
Coing

The fruit of a tree related to the apple and pear, the quince came originally from the Caspian region but is now widely grown in warmer, temperate climates. The downy skin is greenish-yellow in colour and the fruit may resemble the apple or be more pear-like in shape. Its raw flesh is hard, bitter and inedible, but has a strong aroma and flavour and makes tasty compotes, jams and jellies.

If the fruit is not being peeled, the skin should be well washed to remove the down. As with pears, the seedy core is always removed and whole cored fruit may be stuffed and baked.

Quince flesh is also widely boiled to a paste with sugar and used in confectionery. The hardened paste may also simply be eaten on its own or with cheese, as in Spain. Middle Eastern cooking makes considerable savoury use of quince, combined with beef, lamb, veal, chicken, onions and game birds.

Quince is rich in pectin and thus in dietary fibre. It is low in calories, but is generally cooked with sugar to make it palatable; 100 g/3½ oz of raw quince contains 17 calories.

GELÉE DE COING

Quince jelly

Makes 1 kg/2¼ lb
Preparation 20 minutes
Cooking about 1 hour, 12 hours ahead

METRIC/IMPERIAL	*AMERICAN*
1.5 kg/3½ lb ripe quinces, peeled and sliced	*3½ lb ripe quinces, peeled and sliced*
5 black peppercorns	*5 black peppercorns*
sugar	*sugar*
juice of 1 lemon	*juice of 1 lemon*

Put the quince in a large pan with 500 ml/16 fl/2 cups of water and the peppercorns. Bring to the boil and simmer gently for 45 minutes, until the fruit is very soft and tender.

Put the fruit pulp into a cloth or jelly bag which has been boiled and then wrung dry. Tie up the corners and suspend over a large bowl.

Leave the juice to drain out for at least 12 hours. Discard the pulp and measure the juice.

Pour the juice into a preserving pan and add 350 g/12 oz/1¾ cups of sugar and 1 tablespoon of lemon juice for every 500 ml/16 fl oz/2 cups of quince juice. Heat gently, stirring until the sugar has completely dissolved.

Bring to the boil and boil for 10 minutes without stirring, then skim. With a spoon, fill warm, dry, sterile jelly jars to within 2 cm/¾ in of the top. Seal, label and store in a cool place.
Note: this jelly has a slightly tart flavour which goes very well with roast pork or game.

R

see also:
civet
game
hare

RABBIT

Lapin

A small burrowing mammal, closely related to the hare, the rabbit was once very prolific in the wild in Britain and Europe and was an inexpensive foodstuff favoured by country folk. However, numbers were devastated by disease in the 1950s, and most rabbit now consumed is commercially reared and thus more expensive.

A good rabbit weighs between 1.5–1.8 kg/ 3½–4 lb and should be rather short with a rounded back. If buying rabbits still in fur, look for plump specimens with shiny eyes and flexible paws, as signs of youth and freshness. Rabbits are almost always paunched immediately after they are killed and nowadays usually reach the buyer already skinned. Unlike hare, rabbits are not hung, so avoid any which have very dark flesh smelling high. The flesh should be bright pink, indicating that it has been properly bled, and covered with a transparent whitish membrane.

The flavour of reared rabbit can be bland, depending on their diet, but farmhouse rabbit, reared on grain and grass, can be almost as tasty as wild specimens. The French *Angevin* rabbit, for instance, lives on a diet of herbs and other flavourful and aromatic substances to produce memorable meat. An average-sized rabbit is usually cut into 6–8 pieces. Raw or cooked, rabbit meat freezes very well.

Rabbit is regarded as a white meat and is delicate and close-textured, a little like chicken only less succulent. Very young specimens may be roasted, but they best suit braising and stewing. Rabbits which are either old and tough or young and bland benefit from being marinated or cooked with a rich stuffing. Whatever cooking method is used, the aim is to avoid drying out the meat, which should be barded for roasting, or wrapped in caul and braised with tomatoes and chopped fatty bacon. Older rabbits make delicious pâtés or terrines.

Rabbit meat is lean; 100 g/3½ oz contains only 150 calories, as long as it it is roasted rather than simmered in creamy or fatty stews.

Lapin à la moutarde (Rabbit in mustard sauce)

CUTTING UP A RABBIT

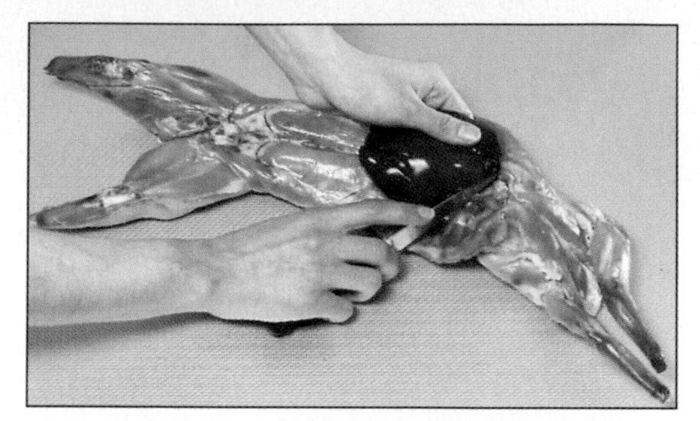

Remove the liver from the stomach cavity. If not required in recipe, reserve it for another dish.

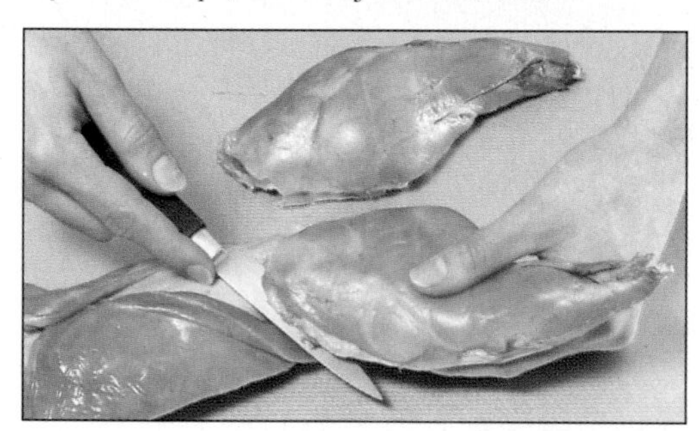

Cut off the rear legs at the top of the thigh. Divide the breast in half.

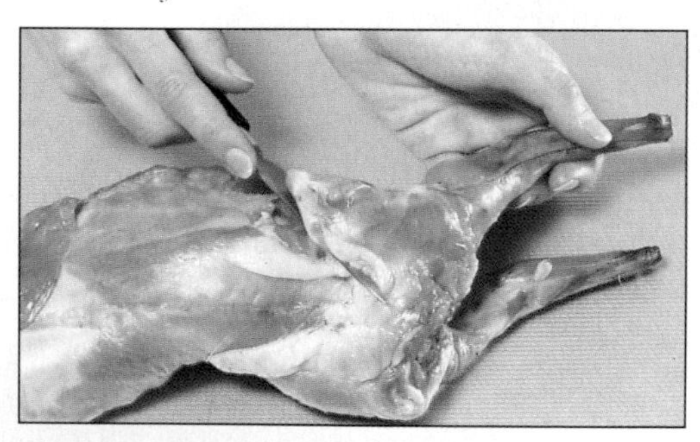

To remove the front legs, separate them from the body at the shoulder joint.

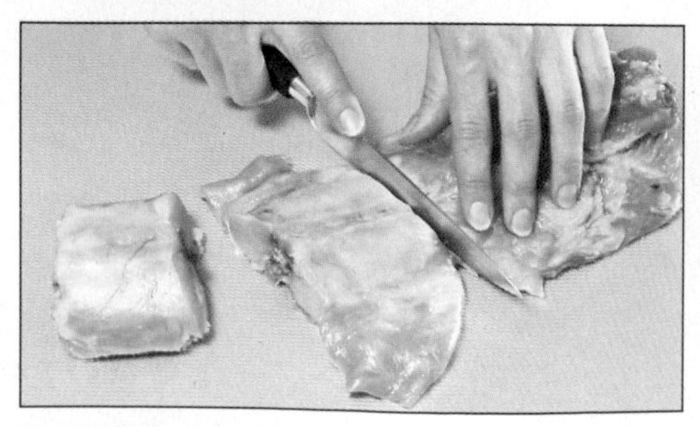

Cut the body crossways into 2 or 3 pieces.

LAPIN À LA MOUTARDE

Rabbit in mustard sauce

Serves 6
Preparation 10 minutes
Cooking about 1 hour

METRIC/IMPERIAL	AMERICAN
1 dressed rabbit, weighing about 1.5 kg/3½ lb, cut into pieces	1 rabbit, dressed and drawn weight about 3½ lb, cut into pieces
pinch of dried thyme	pinch of dried thyme
3 tbsp olive oil	3 tbsp olive oil
5 tbsp strong mustard	5 tbsp Dijon mustard
200 ml/7 fl oz crème fraîche or whipping cream	1 cup crème fraîche or whipping cream
salt and pepper	salt and pepper
chopped fresh chervil, to garnish	chopped fresh chervil, to garnish

Season the pieces of rabbit with salt and pepper and the dried thyme.

Heat the oil in a flameproof casserole over a moderate heat and brown the rabbit pieces in it, turning them frequently.

Discard as much of the fat as possible. Put the mustard into the casserole and stir to coat the rabbit pieces with it. Lower the heat, cover and simmer for 10 minutes.

Add the cream with a spoonful or two of water. Cover and cook gently for a further 45 minutes.

Taste and adjust the seasoning. Sprinkle with the fresh chervil and serve accompanied by courgettes (zucchini) baked *au gratin*, fine green beans or fresh pasta.

To drink: a fresh lively red wine, such as a Chinon.

LAPIN EN GELÉE

Jellied rabbit terrine

Serves 6
Preparation 30 minutes, plus 2 hours marinating
Cooking 2 hours, setting 3 hours

METRIC/IMPERIAL	AMERICAN
1 dressed rabbit, weighing about 1 kg/ 2¼ lb, cut into pieces	1 rabbit, dressed and drawn weight about 2¼ lb, cut into pieces
1 bottle (750 ml/27 fl oz) of Riesling	1 bottle (75 cl) of Riesling
2 onions, sliced	2 onions, sliced
2 carrots, sliced	2 carrots, sliced
2 garlic cloves, chopped	2 garlic cloves, chopped
bunch of chives, finely chopped	bunch of chives, finely chopped
bunch of flat-leaved parsley, finely chopped	bunch of flat-leaf parsley, finely chopped
bunch of chervil, finely chopped	bunch of chervil, finely chopped
salt and pepper	salt and pepper

Put the rabbit into a large bowl, season with salt and pepper and pour over the wine. Let stand in a cold place for at least 2 hours.

Put the marinated rabbit into a flameproof casserole along with the wine, add the vegetables and garlic and simmer gently for 2 hours. Remove the rabbit pieces, strain the liquid and season it generously to taste.

Bone the cooked rabbit. Fill a terrine mould or loaf pan with the meat, sprinkling the layers with mixed chopped herbs.

Carefully pour the cooled cooking liquid into the mould, making sure it penetrates right to the bottom. Place a weighted board on the mould and chill until the jelly has set. Serve in thick slices as a cold first course.

To drink: Riesling.

RADICCHIO

Trévise

see also: chicory salad

A variety of chicory mostly grown in Italy, radicchio resembles a small head of lettuce and has crisp, red leaves, usually veined with white. Their acid, peppery flavour and strong colour makes them useful in salads of mixed leaves, and they particularly suit a walnut-oil vinaigrette dressing.

Radicchio heads may also be cooked like chicory (Belgian endive), either by baking or braising them in a little stock, or coating them in good oil and grilling (broiling) or barbecuing them briefly. These make a delicious accompaniment to roast pork or grilled fish.

Radicchio is very nutritious, with a high content of calcium, iron and vitamins A and C, and low in calories: 100 g/3½ oz contains only 15.

TRÉVISE AUX LARDONS

Radicchio and bacon salad

Serves 4
Preparation 10 minutes
Cooking about 5 minutes

METRIC/IMPERIAL	AMERICAN
350 g/¾ lb radicchio, separated into leaves	¾ lb radicchio, separated into leaves
bunch of chives, snipped	bunch of chives, snipped
2 shallots, thinly sliced	2 shallots, thinly sliced
115 g/¼ lb streaky smoked bacon, cut into small strips	¼ lb country-style bacon, cut into small strips
2 tbsp red wine vinegar	2 tbsp red wine vinegar
3 tbsp corn oil	3 tbsp corn oil
salt and pepper	salt and pepper

Put the radicchio leaves into a salad bowl and add the chives and shallots.

Dry fry the bacon in a non-stick frying pan. Drain it and add to the salad.

Deglaze the frying pan with the vinegar. Pour the liquid over the salad, add the oil and season with salt and pepper. Toss well to coat all the ingredients and serve at once.

Serve with game terrines or pâtés.

RADISH

Radis

see also: mooli salad

A member of the cabbage family, radishes have been grown for centuries for their tasty peppery root. They are generally eaten raw, whole with salt and butter or goats' cheese as an hors d'oeuvre, or sliced in salads.

There are two related roots known as radishes. The COMMON RADISH is most usually round with an edible red skin and pale white flesh like the classic CHERRY BELLE. However, there are varieties, such as the ICICLE RADISH, which are elongated and have white skins. The skin of the other type of root, the BLACK RADISH, is usually peeled. Although once usually black, many varieties are now being bred with white skins. These radishes are normally much larger, more like carrots or turnips in shape, and with a great deal more pungency.

Varieties of both types of radish are available all year round, although hothouse radishes tend to have considerably less flavour and most types are at their best in the summer. Those grown at the height of summer, however, do have a tendency to be woolly or brittle and hollow.

There are good winter varieties of the black radish, such as the CHINA ROSE which closely resembles the Japanese daikon or mooli and may be used in the same way as a condiment.

In summer, buy bunches of radishes with green, undamaged leaves which indicate freshness. The leaves may be also be added to soups.

Rich in vitamins and minerals, radishes are low in calories: 100 g/3½ oz contains only 20.

pink radishes

common red radishes

decorative radish rose

SALADE AUX RADIS ROSES

Radish salad

Serves 4
Preparation 15 minutes

METRIC/IMPERIAL	AMERICAN
bunch of round red radishes, trimmed and sliced	*bunch of round red radishes, trimmed and sliced*
2 firm-fleshed dessert apples, such as Reinettes	*2 firm-fleshed apples, such as Reinettes or McIntosh*
juice of 1 lemon	*juice of 1 lemon*
4 tbsp olive oil	*4 tbsp olive oil*
2 tbsp tarragon vinegar	*2 tbsp tarragon vinegar*
1 mild onion, thinly sliced and separated into rings	*1 mild onion, thinly sliced and separated into rings*
salt and pepper	*salt and pepper*

Put the radish slices in a salad bowl.

Peel and core the apples, slice them thinly and sprinkle them with lemon juice. Add them to the radishes and mix well.

Prepare a vinaigrette with the oil and vinegar and season it with salt and pepper.

Pour the dressing over the salad, mix and garnish with the onion rings.

CANAPÉS DE RADIS NOIR

Black radish appetizer

Serves 4
Preparation 15 minutes

METRIC/IMPERIAL	AMERICAN
2 squares of Demi-Sel cheese	2 square Demi-Sel cheeses
bunch of chives, snipped	bunch of chives, snipped
1 black radish, peeled and sliced	1 black radish or daikon, peeled and sliced
140 g/5 oz peeled cooked prawns	5 oz small peeled cooked shrimp
parsley, to garnish	parsley, to garnish

In a bowl, mash the Demi-Sel cheese with a fork and mix in the chives. Spread the slices of radish with this mixture.

Garnish the top of each slice with 1 or 2 prawns (shrimp). Serve as an hors d'oeuvre, surrounded by sprigs of parsley or sprinkled with some reserved chives.

Variations: replace the Demi-Sel cheese with avocado purée and the prawns or shrimp with sliced, hard-boiled egg sprinkled with paprika.

Make more substantial open sandwiches by spreading the cheese mixture on rye bread and arranging sliced black or pink radish on top.

RAGOÛT

see also: casserole stewing

The French use the term ragoût to denote any dish made by the long, slow stewing of cubed meat, chicken, vegetables, or even firm fish, in a thickened and flavoured liquid. In so-called 'brown' ragoûts, meat is usually first browned in some fat, then sprinkled with a little flour to thicken the sauce. 'White' ragoûts are like fricassees and the meat is only cooked briefly to seal it without any browning, but flour is still the thickening agent. In ragoûts *à l'anglaise*, there is again no browning, but potatoes are cooked with the meat to thicken the sauce.

RAISIN

see Dried vine fruit

RAMBUTAN

Ramboutan

see also: fruit lychee sorbet

Nicknamed the 'long-haired lychee', the rambutan is an exotic fruit imported from South-east Asia in winter and spring, but generally available canned all year round. The same colour as the lychee, it is slightly longer with almost the same flavour, if a little less pronounced. It may be eaten on its own or peeled and stoned and used in fruit salads or to make sorbets. It also goes well with poultry and pork.

COMPOTE DE RAMBOUTANS À LA MENTHE

Rambutan compote with mint

Serves 4
Preparation 20 minutes, 24 hours ahead
Cooking 5 minutes, plus cooling and chilling

METRIC/IMPERIAL	AMERICAN
450 g/1 lb rambutans, peeled, halved and stoned	1 lb rambutans, peeled, halved and pitted
2 peaches, peeled, quartered and stoned	2 peaches, peeled, quartered and pitted
55 g/2 oz caster sugar	$\frac{1}{4}$ cup superfine sugar
300 ml/$\frac{1}{2}$ pt Muscatel wine	$1\frac{1}{2}$ cups Muscatel wine
8 ripe strawberries, hulled and sliced	8 ripe strawberries, hulled and sliced
8 fresh mint leaves	8 fresh mint leaves

Mix the rambutans and peaches in a bowl. Sprinkle with the sugar and Muscatel and let stand overnight.

About 1 hour before serving, put the fruit and its liquid into a saucepan. Bring slowly to the boil. Remove from the heat and allow to cool.

Spoon the fruit and wine compote into 4 serving bowls, add the slices of strawberry and decorate with the mint. Serve chilled.

see also:
blackberry
fruit
strawberry

RASPBERRY

Framboise

The soft fruit of the raspberry bush, related to the strawberry and blackberry, is one of the most eagerly awaited of the summer fruits. The small, tear-shaped compound fruits are mostly red in colour and have sweet, juicy, aromatic flesh containing small hard, edible, seeds. The fruit grows best in slightly damp woodland areas which are not too warm, for instance the best raspberries in Britain come from Perthshire in Scotland.

There are many varieties, some of which, like the YELLOW RASPBERRY, are distinguished by their colour. Some fruits may be black, orange, brown or even, very rarely, white, as well as a wide range of pinks to dark reds. The large, juicy, wine-red WILLIAMETTE is the type most widely grown in the USA and the MALLING PROMISE is a tasty early variety popular in Britain. Other early hothouse raspberries tend to be pale and bland compared to the deep-coloured main crop of summer.

Raspberries are extremely delicate and do not keep well. They are usually sold ready-hulled in small containers or punnets. Examine the punnet base for red stains as a sign that fruit on the bottom is damaged or rotten. Use a toothpick to take any rotten or mouldy fruit out of the container. If possible, it is best not to wash raspberries before use. Raspberries freeze well, but it is better to purée them first as they tend to be mushy when thawed.

Raspberries are an incomparable dessert fruit served on their own or with a little sugar and cream, and they are also popular in fruit salads, tarts, jams, ice creams and sorbets, and may be puréed into a *coulis* to make a delicious sauce for fruit desserts. Raspberry juice is also a popular refreshing drink in many parts of Europe, and the French make liqueurs and brandy from the fruit. There is also some savoury use of the berries, notably with game birds, and they are a popular garnish for sweet and savoury dishes.

The LOGANBERRY is a cross between the raspberry and blackberry which originated in California. The long, red fruit has a fine, full flavour with a hint of tartness, which some people prefer to the raspberry. Another American hybrid, created by crossing raspberry, loganberry and blackberry, is the BOYSENBERRY. It has fewer and larger seeds than the raspberry. Both loganberries and boysenberries make good jams and preserves.

Raspberries, loganberries and boysenberries are rich in fibre, iron, calcium, phosphorus and vitamins, and low in calories: 100 g/3½ oz contains only 40.

PARFAIT AUX FRAMBOISES

Raspberry parfait

Serves 6
Preparation 20 minutes, 2 hours ahead

METRIC/IMPERIAL	*AMERICAN*
800 g/1¾ lb raspberries	*1¾ lb raspberries (about 3½ pt)*
100 ml/3½ fl oz crème fraîche or whipping cream	*½ cup crème fraîche or whipping cream*
115 g/4 oz thick fromage blanc or fresh soft cream cheese	*½ cup thick fromage blanc or fresh soft cream cheese*
250 g/8½ oz icing sugar	*2 cups confectioners' sugar*

In a bowl, mash three quarters of the raspberries to a purée. Add the cream and cheese. Mix well, then add the sugar. Whisk the mixture for 2 minutes until it is fluffy.

Pour into 2 ice-cube trays, without dividers, and freeze for about 2 hours, without opening the freezer door unless absolutely necessary.

To unmould, dip the bases of the trays into cold water for 20 seconds and invert them one at a time on a long, chilled serving dish.

Decorate with the reserved raspberries and serve with a selection of biscuits (cookies).

RATATOUILLE

see also: ragoût vegetables

A Provençal vegetable ragoût, ratatouille combines onions, courgettes (zucchini), tomatoes, sweet peppers and aubergines (eggplants). The vegetables are chopped or sliced, lightly cooked in olive oil and simmered gently with herbs until they have the soft consistency of a compote. Ratatouille is traditionally served as an accompaniment to meat, chicken and fish, and is also good in omelettes. It may also be served cold, sprinkled with lemon juice, as a first course.

RATATOUILLE NIÇOISE

Mediterranean vegetable stew

Serves 4
Preparation 30 minutes
Cooking about 1¼ hours

METRIC/IMPERIAL	AMERICAN
5 tbsp olive oil	5 tbsp olive oil
450 g/1 lb aubergines, sliced into rounds	1 lb eggplants, sliced into rounds
450 g/1 lb courgettes, sliced into rounds	1 lb zucchini, sliced into rounds
450 g/1 lb sweet peppers, halved, deseeded and cut into strips	1 lb sweet peppers, halved, deseeded and cut into strips
3 onions, thinly sliced	3 onions, thinly sliced
450 g/1 lb tomatoes, peeled and quartered	1 lb tomatoes, peeled and quartered
bay leaf	bay leaf
sprig of thyme	sprig of thyme
2 garlic cloves, chopped	2 garlic cloves, chopped
salt and pepper	salt and pepper

Heat 2 tablespoons of oil in a frying pan and cook the aubergines (eggplants) for 5 minutes to brown both sides. Season them with salt and pepper and remove them.

Add 1 more tablespoon of oil to the frying pan and sauté the courgettes (zucchini) for 5 minutes, then season them with salt and pepper and remove them. Proceed in the same manner with the sweet peppers.

Heat the remaining oil in a flameproof casserole and lightly brown the onions, stirring, for 5 minutes. Mix in the tomatoes.

Add the other vegetables to the casserole. Stir over a high heat for 5 minutes. Add the bay leaf and thyme and season with salt and pepper. Cover, lower the heat and simmer gently for 30 minutes. Stir in the garlic, adjust the seasoning and cook for a further 10–15 minutes.

Serve hot to accompany grilled (broiled) chicken or cold as a first course.

Note: ratatouille will keep for 2 days in the refrigerator and 2 months frozen.

Variation: for a low-fat ratatouille, simmer all the ingredients without oil in 100 ml/3½ fl oz/½ cup of vegetable stock with a bouquet garni and 2 or 3 tablespoons of tomato purée (paste).

REDCURRANT

Groseille

see also: blackcurrant fruit jams, etc

Small red berries which grow in straggly clusters, redcurrants are closely related to the blackcurrant and gooseberry. Their flesh has a high acid and pectin content, making them particularly useful in the making of jams and jellies. They are becoming increasingly rare and are now usually quite expensive. The closely related WHITE CURRANT, now extremely rare, is similar in every way apart from colour, although it is distinctly sweeter and lower in pectin content. A new variety, known as the REDCURRANT-GRAPE, has larger berries much in demand for use in tarts.

Redcurrants are eaten and cooked with their skins, and simply need to be stripped from their stalks. This may be done quickly by pulling clusters through the prongs of a fork. Redcurrants freeze very well.

Redcurrants may be eaten raw with lots of sugar or custard sauce, added to fruit salads and compotes or baked in tarts. They are a useful souring agent and an essential ingredient in the traditional English summer pudding. However, most of the crop is used in the making of preserves. Redcurrant jelly, either plain or made into Cumberland sauce with added port and citrus zest, is the classic garnish for many sweet and savoury dishes from red cabbage to game.

Redcurrants are rich in vitamin C and fibre: 100 g/3½ oz contains only 28 calories.

GROSEILLES PANACHÉES AUX FRAMBOISES

Redcurrants with raspberry purée

Serves 4
Preparation 15 minutes, 2 hours ahead
Cooking 6–7 minutes

METRIC/IMPERIAL	AMERICAN
450 g/1 lb mixed redcurrants and white currants, removed from their stalks	2 pt fresh currants, preferably mixed red and white, removed from their stems
250 g/8½ oz raspberries	1 pt raspberries
150 g/5½ oz caster sugar	¾ cup superfine sugar
200 ml/7 fl oz crème fraîche or whipping cream, well chilled	1 cup crème fraîche or whipping cream, well chilled

Put the currants in a bowl. Put the raspberries into a saucepan and heat them gently.

Mash the raspberries with the back of a spoon. When they come to the boil, remove from the heat. Force the pulp through a very fine sieve.

Add the sugar to the raspberry purée and coat the currants with it while it is still warm. Chill until ready to serve.

Just before serving, whip the cream to soft peaks. Spoon the currants in raspberry syrup into parfait glasses, decorate with whipped cream and serve at once.

Note: if using frozen redcurrants, allow 1 hour for them to thaw at room temperature.

REDUCTION

see also:
deglazing
sauce
stock

The concentration or thickening of a liquid, especially a stock or sauce, by boiling off some of the liquid content is referred to as reduction. It is usually intended both to make the liquid thicker and to concentrate the flavour.

REFRESHING

see also:
blanching
boiling
pasta and noodles
rice
vegetables

The practice of running cold water over food which has just been cooked or immersing it in iced water, refreshing is intended to arrest the cooking process and cool the food rapidly. The technique is used especially when boiling items such as green vegetables, so that they keep their colour and texture. It is particularly important when they are being blanched briefly prior to any other form of treatment. Pasta and rice can also benefit from refreshing to help stop them clumping together.

REFRIGERATION

see also:
freezing
preserves

The storing of foodstuffs in a refrigerator at low temperatures, −1 to 8C/30–46F, can dramatically increase the length of time that food may be kept fresh. There are several guidelines to efficient refrigeration.

Food should never be put straight into the refrigerator while still hot. Allow it to cool at least to room temperature first, otherwise it will raise the temperature in the refrigerator to dangerous levels.

The refrigerator should not be over-filled, as the air inside must be free to circulate.

Pre-wrapped foods should be removed from their packaging and re-wrapped in foil or plastic food bags.

Fresh foods and leftover dishes should be carefully wrapped or placed in covered containers to avoid them tainting each other.

Extremely perishable items, such as minced (ground) meat, offal (variety meats) and seafood should not be stored in the refrigerator for more than a day or so.

Canned foods should not be refrigerated, without first being removed from the can.

The vegetable compartment of the refrigerator is the least cold and most humid part of the refrigerator. It should be used for keeping fruit and cheese, as well as vegetables. Uncooked fish and meat should be placed in the coldest area – at the top, nearest the freezing compartment if there is one.

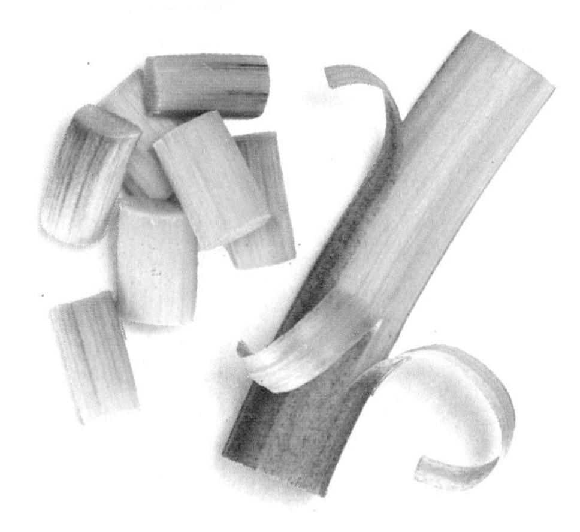

REHEATING

see also: bain-marie freezing microwave cooking

The reheating of cooked foods to the correct temperature for eating is a delicate operation. The process needs to be very carefully watched to prevent the food from drying out, disintegrating, burning or boiling. Slow heating in a bain-marie in the oven is often the best solution. For reheating a dish on top of the stove, use a heat diffuser. Certain dishes, such as gratins, roasts and grills, cannot be successfully reheated, but others, such as stews, often taste better the second time. Microwave ovens are invaluable for reheating foods without drying or burning, especially those which have been frozen.

RHUBARB

Rhubarbe

see also: sorrel

A hardy perennial plant related to buckwheat and sorrel, rhubarb has large, ornamental leaves which are poisonous. However, it is the crisp fleshy stalks which are eaten. Although quite acidic, rhubarb is widely grown in northern Europe as a fruit substitute early in the year.

There are several varieties, and the stalks range from green to various shades of mauve. Some are forced in darkened hothouses in the winter months and these tend to be pale in colour and less acidic than the varieties available in summer. Rhubarb grown outdoors usually has fibrous skins which must be peeled.

Rhubarb is mostly used in compotes, pies and tarts and jams. Its strong flavour goes well with citrus zest, spices such as cinnamon and ginger, and pungent herbs like angelica. Rhubarb compote complements fish and fatty meats like pork.

Rhubarb is highly nutritious, with an abundance of iron and calcium and vitamin C. It contains only 16 calories per 100 g/3½ oz, but a great deal of sugar has to be added to make it palatable.

COMPOTE DE RHUBARBE

Rhubarb compote

Serves 4
Preparation 20 minutes
Cooking 35 minutes

METRIC/IMPERIAL	AMERICAN
1 orange	1 orange
1 kg/2¼ lb rhubarb, trimmed and cut into 3 cm/1¼ in pieces	2¼ lb rhubarb, trimmed and cut into 1¼ in pieces
400 g/14 oz caster sugar	2 cups superfine sugar

Preheat the oven to 180C/350F/gas 4.

If the orange is not organically grown and may have been sprayed or coated, scrub it in hot soapy water, rinse well and pat dry. Grate the orange zest and squeeze the juice.

Put a layer of rhubarb into a baking dish. Sprinkle with sugar. Fill the dish with alternating layers of rhubarb and sugar. Scatter the orange zest on top and pour the juice over.

Cover the dish and cook in the oven for 35 minutes. Take it out, uncover and allow to cool.

Serve the compote accompanied by custard sauce, crème fraîche or whipped cream.

Variations: flavour the rhubarb with chopped, crystallized ginger or candied orange peel.

see also:
cereal
croquette
curry powder
flour
milk
paper
pilaf
risotto
salad
stuffing

RICE

Riz

A cereal widely cultivated throughout the tropical and temperate regions of the world, rice is the staple of over half the world's population. The grains are always eaten cooked, hot or cold, as a sweet or savoury dish. Most of the rice imported into cooler climes comes from Asia or the USA, although the Camargue in France and the Po valley in Italy have both become important regions of rice cultivation.

There are literally hundreds of varieties of rice and the average Asian market stall might display at least two dozen. However, in Europe and the USA, rice is usually characterized in one of two ways: LONG-GRAIN, which keeps its shape better on cooking and the grains remain separate; and SHORT-GRAIN or ROUND-GRAIN which cooks to a softer and more sticky result. The latter is usually reserved for sweet dishes, and is usually cooked in milk.

Before being sold, rice is treated in various ways which alter its appearance and taste. In its raw state, when it is known as 'paddy', it is inedible. Cleaned and husked, it is known as CARGO, WHOLEGRAIN or BROWN RICE and retains most of the original nutrients, although it takes considerably longer to cook. WHITE RICE has had the germ and all the outer layers of the grain removed to produce a softer item which is much easier to cook, but is a significantly inferior food and is actually more difficult to digest. POLISHED or PEARL RICE has also had all the residual grain particles washed away. Some types of rice have also been CONVERTED, ie pre-treated with steam or pre-cooked briefly, before or after being milled, to produce grains which do not stick together and which cook very quickly indeed.

Other varieties are now more common in Western supermarkets, such as Indian PATNA and BASMATI rice with long, very thin grains and distinctive flavours, or Italian *arborio* or risotto rice which has large fat grains which are very absorbent. All-purpose, long-grain American CAROLINA RICE is favoured for puddings as it absorbs a great deal of liquid without breaking up and is rather bland in flavour. WILD RICE is actually the seeds of a distantly related aquatic grass native to Canada, and its long, thin, black grains have an extremely fine flavour. It is, however, very expensive and is often sold mixed with brown rice to make a little go further.

In addition to grains, rice is made into a number of other products including flour, thickening agents and breakfast cereals, such as popped rice and rice flakes. The flour is also used to make rice pancakes and oriental noodles as well as edible paper. Rice is also fermented to make various alcoholic beverages, principally Japanese saké and rice wine.

Rice is usually sold ready-to-cook, but those types imported directly from the East should be picked over for small stones and pieces of husk.

white glutinous rice *long-grain Carolina rice* *round rice*

wild rice *basmati rice* *brown rice*

It is also wise to rinse all rice well under cold running water. Pre-soaking of rice is not strictly necessary and is inadvisable if the subsequent recipe involves the rice absorbing a flavouring liquid during cooking as it will have become less absorbent. Allow about 75 g/2½ oz/scant ½ cup of uncooked rice per person for a main dish, and about half that for an hors d'oeuvre or dessert.

Raw white rice can be stored in a cool, dry place for 7–8 months and brown rice keeps a little longer. It is best not to keep cooked rice for longer than 24 hours.

Rice is best cooked by steaming for 25–30 minutes, or by the absorption method to produce what the French term Creole rice: measure the volume of the rice and then bring twice that volume of lightly salted water or stock to the boil, add the rice, stir well, cover and simmer gently until all the liquid has been absorbed. When well cooked, rice grains should become soft, while still retaining a little firmness. It is also common first to gently cook the rice in a little hot fat or oil before the water or stock is added. This adds flavour and helps ensure that the grains do not stick together. For sweet rice desserts and for rice to be used in croquettes and stuffings, round-grain rice is used and is cooked to a melting sticky mass.

As well as the classic accompaniment to curries and most Asian dishes, rice is also a good foil to cream sauces, fish dishes and kebabs. It is also useful in soups, salads and in stuffings for fish and poultry. Dishes like pilafs, paellas and risottos are based on rice, flavoured and garnished in a multitude of ways.

Boiled white rice contains only 90 calories per 100 g/3½ oz and is a good source of carbohydrates. Brown rice has a higher calorie content, but is much richer in nutrients, especially vitamin B1.

RIZ CANTONNAIS

Cantonese rice

Serves 6
Preparation 30 minutes
Cooking about 45 minutes

METRIC/IMPERIAL	*AMERICAN*
300 g/10 oz long-grain rice	*1⅔ cups long-grain rice*
55 g/2 oz butter	*4 tbsp butter*
1 slice of pork fillet	*1 slice of pork tenderloin*
1 turkey escalope	*1 turkey cutlet from the breast*
225 g/½ lb mushrooms, thinly sliced	*½ lb mushrooms, thinly sliced*
3 carrots, thinly sliced	*3 carrots, thinly sliced*
3 onions, thinly sliced	*3 onions, thinly sliced*
1 can (200 g/7 oz) of peas	*1 7-oz can of peas*
1 thick slice of ham, finely diced	*1 thick slice of ham, finely diced*
225 g/½ lb peeled cooked prawns	*½ lb small peeled cooked shrimp*
salt and pepper	*salt and pepper*

Put the rice in a large pan of salted boiling water, bring back to the boil and then simmer gently for 15 minutes. Drain and keep warm.

While the rice is cooking, start preparing the other ingredients. Melt half the butter in a frying pan over a moderate heat and cook the slice of pork for 6 minutes on each side. Then cook the turkey for 4 minutes on each side. Season them both with salt and pepper. Drain each as they are cooked, and keep warm.

Cook the mushrooms in the pan for 5 minutes in half the remaining butter. Drain and keep warm.

Cook the carrot and onion in the remaining butter for 10 minutes. Drain and keep warm.

Drain the peas, reserving 100 ml/3½ fl oz/½ cup of the liquid. Cut the meats into thin strips.

In a large pan, combine the rice with the meat strips, vegetables, ham and prawns (shrimp). Mix and add the pea liquid; season to taste. Heat gently, covered, for 6–7 minutes and serve in individual warmed bowls.

Variation: the rice may be garnished with thin strips of omelette and finely chopped chives.

SALADE DE RIZ AU POULET

Rice salad with chicken

Serves 6
Preparation 20 minutes
Cooking about 40 minutes, 1 hour ahead

METRIC/IMPERIAL	AMERICAN
300 g/10 oz long-grain white rice	1⅔ cups long-grain white rice
2 chicken breasts	2 chicken breast halves
2 chicken thighs	2 chicken thighs
bouquet garni	bouquet garni
2 red sweet peppers	2 red sweet peppers
6 tbsp olive oil	6 tbsp olive oil
3 tbsp tarragon vinegar	3 tbsp tarragon vinegar
1 tsp strong mustard	1 tsp Dijon mustard
1 can (200 g/7 oz) of peas, drained	1 7-oz can of peas, drained
1 tbsp chopped fresh tarragon	1 tbsp chopped fresh tarragon
salt and pepper	salt and pepper

Bring a large pan of salted water to the boil, put in the rice and bring back to the boil. Simmer gently for 15 minutes. Drain and reserve the liquid.

Poach the chicken pieces with the bouquet garni gently in the liquid for 20 minutes.

Preheat the oven to 250C/475F/gas 9.

Drain the chicken pieces and allow them to cool a little. Remove and discard the bones and skin and cut the meat into tiny dice.

Put the sweet peppers into the very hot oven for 5–6 minutes. Remove and refresh under cold running water and then peel them. Cut them in half, remove the seeds and dice the flesh.

Make a tarragon vinaigrette with the oil, vinegar, mustard and seasoning to taste.

In a salad bowl, combine the rice, chicken, sweet pepper and peas. Add the vinaigrette and stir thoroughly. Chill until ready to serve.

Serve well chilled, sprinkled with tarragon.

Variations: slices of hard-boiled egg, black olives or capers may be added for a more substantial salad.

RIZ AU LAIT

Rice pudding

Serves 4
Preparation 2 minutes
Cooking about 40 minutes

METRIC/IMPERIAL	AMERICAN
250 g/8½ oz round-grain rice	1¼ cups round-grain rice
1 vanilla pod	1 vanilla bean
1 l/1¾ pt milk	1 qt milk
55 g/2 oz butter	4 tbsp butter
pinch of salt	pinch of salt
100 g/3½ oz caster sugar	½ cup superfine sugar

Bring a large pan of water to the boil and cook the rice in it for 3 minutes. Meanwhile, add the vanilla to the milk and heat it until just below boiling point.

Drain the rice. Remove the vanilla from the milk. Put the rice into the milk and add the butter and salt. Cook over a very gentle heat for 15 minutes.

Stir in the sugar and cook for a further 20 minutes. Serve warm or cold, with poached fruit or fruit compote.

Variations: the pudding may be thickened with 2 egg yolks and flavoured with a bay leaf or cinnamon or nutmeg rather than vanilla.

Rice pudding may also be cooked in an oven preheated to 150C/300F/gas 2: after adding the sugar, pour the mixture into a dish greased with butter or coated with caramel, sprinkle with nutmeg or cinnamon and bake for 2 hours.

RISOTTO

see also: rice

A classic Italian rice dish, risotto is made using local *arborio* rice with large, fat grains which absorb a lot of liquid. The rice is first fried in fat with chopped onion until translucent, and then stock is added, a little at a time, and cooked until it is all absorbed.

Risottos may simply be flavoured with a good stock, onion and garlic or Parmesan and served to accompany poultry and fish dishes. They may also be enhanced with a wide range of other ingredients, from chopped vegetables,

Salade de riz au poulet (Rice salad with chicken)

poultry, ham and seafood to crumbled blue cheese, to make flavourful, nutritious and complete meals. The sticky texture makes them suitable to serve in decorative, moulded shapes.

RISOTTO AU SAFRAN

Saffron risotto

Serves 4
Preparation 10 minutes
Cooking about 20 minutes

METRIC/IMPERIAL	*AMERICAN*
250 g/$8\frac{1}{2}$ oz risotto rice	*1 cup risotto rice*
600 ml/1 pt chicken stock	*$2\frac{1}{2}$ cups chicken stock*
30 g/1 oz butter	*2 tbsp butter*
2 tbsp olive oil	*2 tbsp olive oil*
2 onions, chopped	*2 onions, chopped*
pinch of saffron	*pinch of saffron*
75 g/$2\frac{1}{2}$ oz grated Parmesan	*$\frac{2}{3}$ cup grated Parmesan cheese*
salt and pepper	*salt and pepper*

Measure the volume of the rice, then pour $2\frac{1}{2}$ times that volume of chicken stock into a pan and place over the heat.

Heat half the butter with the oil in a large heavy-bottomed saucepan. Add the chopped onion and cook, stirring, until golden.

Add the rice and stir until all the grains are well coated with fat. When they are translucent, pour a large ladleful of hot stock into the pan. Cover and cook very gently.

When all the liquid has been absorbed, pour on another ladleful of stock and repeat until the liquid is all used up, stirring well after each addition. Add the saffron along with the final ladleful of stock. Season with salt and pepper.

Incorporate the remaining butter and the Parmesan into the cooked rice. Mix until they are melted and serve immediately as an accompaniment to roast veal or braised fish.

Variations: replace the first ladle of stock by the same volume of white wine. Add other ingredients such as mushrooms, crumbled Gorgonzola cheese or seafood. Add extra colour and flavour with chopped sweet peppers or peas.

ROASTING

Rôtir

see also:
baking
barding
basting
gravy
grilling
larding
sealing
stuffing

The term roasting at one time was only used to describe the cooking of food on a revolving spit over an open fire, a method more akin to grilling (broiling). Nowadays, however, it nearly always refers to the cooking of large pieces of meat, whole birds or large fish by dry heat at fairly high temperatures in the oven.

As with grilling (broiling) and barbecuing, roasting attempts to cook the food as quickly as possible to maintain its natural flavour, tenderness and succulence. For this reason, only prime cuts of meat and fairly young and tender birds suit this means of cooking.

It is usually advisable to seal red meats first, either by browning them in a pan over a high heat or by putting them in the hottest possible oven for the first 10 minutes or so of cooking. A crust then forms on the surface of the meat to seal in the flavour and juices. Also the meat should not be pierced during cooking or its juices will run out. Poultry and white meats are cooked more gently so that the outside and inside cook at the same pace.

Small game birds and meat and poultry that might otherwise dry out during roasting are often barded with sheets of caul or pork fat. Some cuts of meat, particularly veal, are even larded through with strips of fat. Marinating also helps keep meat and game succulent.

It is wise to set pieces of food to be roasted on a trivet or rack or on a bed of diced vegetables to prevent the bottom from frying. Roasts should be cooked with the fat uppermost so that it drips down through the meat. For the same reason, start poultry cooking breast side down, turning half-way through cooking.

Food being roasted is usually regularly basted with the pan juices as the cooking proceeds. This helps build up the seal around the food, keeps it moist and adds flavour.

After they come out of the oven, large pieces of meat and poultry are best left in a warm place before being carved. This allows the juices to seep back out to the edges of the food so it will be uniformly moist and easier to slice. Remove any string securing the meat and any bards prior to presenting the roast at the table.

The sediment in the roasting pan, after pouring off excess fat, may be deglazed with a little water, stock or wine and the resulting gravy served in a sauce boat.

A great advantage of roasting is that accompanying vegetables, such as potatoes, onions and parsnips, may be roasted in the same pan.

RÔTI DE PORC À LA DIJONNAISE

Roast pork with mustard sauce

Serves 6
Preparation 10 minutes
Cooking about 1½ hours

METRIC/IMPERIAL	AMERICAN
1.5 kg/3½ lb boned and rolled pork loin	3½ lb boned and rolled pork loin roast
5 tbsp Dijon mustard	5 tbsp Dijon mustard
1 sheet of caul fat	1 sheet of pork caul
200 ml/7 fl oz dry white wine	1 cup dry white wine

Preheat the oven to 220C/425F/gas 7. Cover the meat with mustard as evenly as possible, then wrap it in the caul.

Put the roast into the oven in a deep dish. After 20 minutes, baste it with 3 tablespoons of the wine. Baste three more times during cooking, allowing 20–25 minutes per 450 g/1 lb.

At the end of the cooking time, turn off the oven and leave the roast in it for a further 5 minutes. Transfer the meat to a carving dish, pour off most of the excess fat from the roasting pan and deglaze it with 1 or 2 tablespoons of boiling water.

Serve the pork carved into slices, accompanied by the gravy in a sauce boat and a potato and celeriac (celery root) purée.

ROASTING PAN

see Baking pan

ROCKET OR ARUGULA

see also: salad

A member of the cabbage family, rocket grows wild in Europe and has pungent green leaves which make an interesting addition to salads. It is particularly popular in Italy and in France, where it forms part of the traditional Provençal *mesclun* salad mix, and tender milder varieties are widely cultivated in this part of the world.

ROE

Oeufs de poisson, laitance

see also: caviar fish

The eggs of female fish are referred to as roes. The roes of many types of fish are eaten and are often regarded as a delicacy, particularly caviar from sturgeons.

COD ROES are available in the natural state, but may also be salted and smoked. The latter are popular on canapés or served on toast as a snack, and are the basic ingredient of the classic

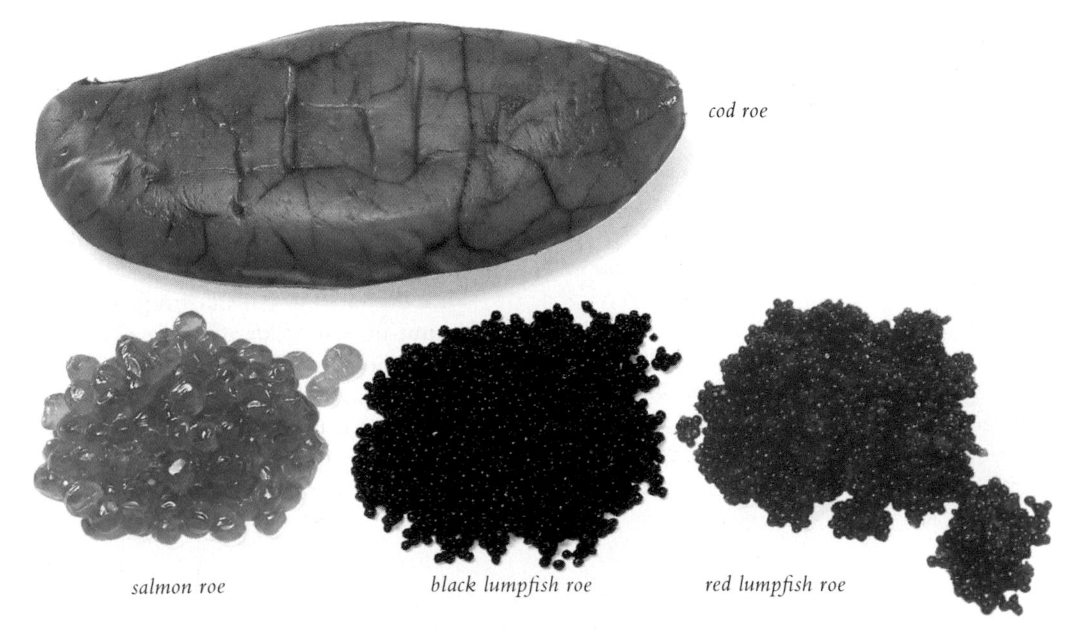

cod roe

salmon roe *black lumpfish roe* *red lumpfish roe*

Greek taramasalata. In Britain, uncured cod roes are usually boiled in salted water and sliced. They may subsequently be fried to make a delicious light meal or first course. The same treatment is given to the roes of haddock, coley and other white fish.

GREY MULLET and TUNA ROES are often salted and pressed to make *boutargue*, a Provençal speciality served with a lemon vinaigrette.

Sold in jars as semi-preserved foods, SALMON EGGS or SALMON CAVIAR, TROUT CAVIAR and LUMPFISH ROE or LUMPFISH CAVIAR make useful substitutes for real sturgeon caviar and play an important role in the garnishing of cold hors d'oeuvres, appetizers, mixed salads and canapés. It is wise to add red and black lumpfish roes at the last moment as their colours may easily bleed. Other unusual roes available include those from CRAB, FLYING FISH and WHITEFISH.

SOFT ROE or MILT is the sperm of a male fish and is very rich in phosphorus. During the spawning season, the soft roe is eaten at the same time as the fish itself. When cooked on their own, soft roes are generally pan fried.

All roe is very rich in proteins and lipids: 100 g/3½ oz contains about 280 calories.

TOMATES FARCIES

Stuffed tomatoes

Serves 4
Preparation 15 minutes

METRIC/IMPERIAL	AMERICAN
8 small round firm tomatoes	8 small round firm tomatoes
4 canned artichoke bottoms, drained	4 canned artichoke bottoms, drained
bunch of chives	bunch of chives
juice of ½ lemon	juice of ½ lemon
2 tbsp crème fraîche or sour cream	2 tbsp crème fraîche or sour cream
1 jar of black lumpfish roe	1 jar of black lumpfish caviar
1 jar of red lumpfish roe	1 jar of red lumpfish caviar
salt and pepper	salt and pepper
bunch of watercress, to garnish	bunch of watercress, to garnish

Cut the tops off the tomatoes and scoop out the seeds without piercing the skins. Sprinkle the interior with salt, turn the tomatoes upside down on a cloth and leave them to drain.

Purée the artichoke bottoms in a food processor. Chop the chives and add to the artichoke purée, along with the lemon juice, cream and pepper to taste.

Drain the tomato shells. Fill them with the artichoke mixture, then pile a dome of lumpfish roe (caviar) on top, alternating the colours.

Line a serving plate with watercress. Place the stuffed tomatoes on it and serve.

LAITANCES AU BEURRE NOISETTE

Soft roe in brown butter

Serves 2
Preparation 5 minutes, 10 minutes ahead
Cooking 8 minutes

METRIC/IMPERIAL	AMERICAN
4 soft roes	4 soft roes (milt)
juice of 1 lemon	juice of 1 lemon
court-bouillon or fish stock	court-bouillon or fish stock
45 g/1½ oz butter	3 tbsp butter
1 tsp white wine vinegar	1 tsp white wine vinegar
salt and freshly ground black pepper	salt and freshly ground black pepper
chopped chervil, to garnish	chopped chervil, to garnish

Put the roes into a bowl of cold water, add the lemon juice and leave to soak for 10 minutes.

Half fill a large saucepan with court-bouillon. Add the roes and bring to the boil. Poach them gently for 5 minutes, then drain them and wipe them dry.

Heat the butter in a small saucepan until it just turns nut-brown. Skim off the foam and season with salt and pepper.

Put the roes in a very hot, deep serving dish. Pour on the butter, trickle over a thread of vinegar and garnish with the chervil.

To drink: a dry white wine, such as a Gros-Plant.

see also: cheese

ROQUEFORT

One of the most ancient of French cheeses, roquefort is a blue-veined cheese made from ewes' milk. Produced in 20 cm/8 in cylinders, it is matured in caves for at least three months for the full veining and flavour to develop, and the cheeses are at their best in the latter part of the year.

Roquefort's fine, distinctive taste and unique texture, which is at once firm, crumbly and buttery, has made it a favoured cheese both after dinner and in cooking.

Popular in salads, soufflés and pastries, it is much used in sauces and flavoured butters to accompany grilled meat and poultry. It also goes well with firm fruit, especially pears. Roquefort is high in calories: 333 per 100 g/3½ oz.

FEUILLETÉS AU ROQUEFORT

Roquefort in a puff pastry tart

Serves 6
Preparation 20 minutes
Cooking 35 minutes

METRIC/IMPERIAL	AMERICAN
450 g/1 lb puff pastry	1 lb puff pastry
200 g/7 oz Roquefort	7 oz Roquefort cheese
150 g/5½ oz fromage frais	⅔ cup fromage frais
100 ml/3½ fl oz crème fraîche or whipping cream	½ cup crème fraîche or whipping cream
3 tbsp chopped chives	3 tbsp chopped chives
3 eggs, lightly beaten	3 eggs, lightly beaten
pepper	pepper

Preheat the oven to 230C/450F/gas 8.

Roll half the pastry out to a thickness of about 3 mm/⅛ in and use to line a 25 cm/10 in tart pan. Prick the bottom. Roll the remaining pastry into a round just big enough to cover the tart.

Crumble the Roquefort into a bowl and add the fromage frais and cream. Mix well, adding the chives and eggs along with pepper to taste.

Spread the mixture in the case and then cover with the pastry round. Pinch the edges to seal.

Bake the tart for 20 minutes, then cover with foil to prevent the pastry from browning too much and cook for a further 15 minutes.

Serve cut into wedges.

see also: herbs

ROSEMARY

Romarin

An aromatic, evergreen shrub with a very pungent and pervasive flavour and smell, rosemary grows wild in many parts of Mediterranean Europe. The tiny, needle-shaped leaves are as highly perfumed dried as fresh: it is wise to use rosemary sparingly, as its flavour can be quite overpowering. Rosemary is particularly popular in Italian cooking, and their practice of using it to flavour roast meat, particularly veal, suckling pig and lamb, has been widely adopted in other countries. It is also used to flavour grilled (broiled) meat and game, baked fish, potatoes and some stews and marinades. Rosemary also finds some use in sweet dishes, notably in infusing milk for creams and custards, and it is used to flavour honey.

SAUTÉ DE VEAU AU ROMARIN

Sautéed veal with rosemary

Serves 4
Preparation 10 minutes
Cooking about 1¼ hours

METRIC/IMPERIAL	AMERICAN
4 tbsp olive oil	4 tbsp olive oil
1 tbsp dried rosemary	1 tbsp dried rosemary
3 onions, thinly sliced	3 onions, thinly sliced
1 kg/2¼ lb boneless veal shoulder, cut into pieces	2¼ lb boneless veal shoulder, cut into pieces
2 green sweet peppers, deseeded and cut into strips	2 green sweet peppers, deseeded and cut into strips
3 large tomatoes, peeled and quartered	3 large tomatoes, peeled and quartered
100 ml/3½ fl oz dry white wine	½ cup dry white wine
½ bay leaf	½ bay leaf
salt and pepper	salt and pepper

Heat half the oil in a flameproof casserole over a moderate heat. Add half the rosemary and then the onions. Stir for 10 minutes.

Meanwhile, heat the rest of the oil in a frying pan over a moderate to high heat and brown the meat in it, turning 2 or 3 times. Drain the meat and add to the casserole.

Cook the strips of sweet pepper in the frying pan quickly and add them to the casserole along with the tomatoes and the rest of the rosemary. Mix well and then add the white wine and bay leaf and season with salt and pepper. Cover and simmer gently for 1 hour.

At the end of cooking, the sauce should have reduced considerably and the vegetables should have the consistency of a compote.

Discard the bay leaf and serve the sautéed veal along with the sauce in a warmed, deep dish, accompanied by plain boiled rice.

To drink: a powerful, mature red wine, such as a Châteauneuf-du-Pape.

ROUILLE

see also:
bouillabaisse
fish
mayonnaise
sauce

A typically Provençal sauce, rouille is served to accompany fish soups, notably bouillabaisse, boiled fish and octopus. It is made with breadcrumbs or cooked potatoes pounded with garlic and red chilli peppers, blended with a little fish stock and then emulsified with oil, like a mayonnaise. One tablespoon of rouille contains about 90 calories.

ROUX

see also:
flour
sauce
stock
thickening

A mixture of equal weights of butter and flour, a roux is used to thicken stocks and sauces. The mixture must be cooked, stirring constantly, for varying lengths of time to eliminate the flouriness. A WHITE OR BLOND roux is cooked for only a few minutes, until the mixture just starts to colour, and is used in white sauces, such as *béchamel*. A BROWN ROUX is cooked until it is a good light brown in colour and is used for most brown sauces, such as *espagnole* and *demi-glace*. The roux is subsequently mixed with water, milk, stock or a court-bouillon, as appropriate.

RUTABAGA

see Swede

RYE

Seigle

see also:
beer
bread
cereal
flour
spirits

A cereal grain cultivated originally on poor soil in the mountains of western Asia, rye became popular in northern Europe and with the North American settlers due to its sturdiness and ability to thrive in cold climates.

RYE BREAD, which is usually made from a mixture of wheat and rye, has a dense brown texture and keeps well. In fact, many prefer its flavour when slightly stale. The gently sour taste goes particularly well with seafood and smoked *charcuterie* products and it is the classic bread for Scandinavian open sandwiches. Black and pumpernickel bread are also based on rye flour. Rye flour is also traditional in many Russian and Scandinavian cakes, pastries and crispbreads and rye flakes are usually included in most muesli and granola mixtures.

Rye is also used for making grain alcohols such as beer, whisky, gin and vodka.

Rye is not as rich in protein as the other cereals, but it is rich in minerals: 100 g/3½ oz of rye contains 335 calories.

S

SAFFLOWER

see also:
fats and oils
fatty acids
lipids
sunflower

The safflower plant originated in India and its petals are still widely used there as a dye, saffron substitute and spice. Most of the cultivated crop, however, is used to express oil from the seeds. SAFFLOWER OIL is low in saturates and cholesterol and is increasingly favoured as a cooking medium, especially as it also has a mild flavour.

SAFFRON

Safran

see also:
bouillabaisse
curry
safflower
spices

The bulbous saffron crocus originated in the East where its stigmas were dried to make an orange-yellow spice prized for its culinary value and its medicinal and reputed magical powers. Cultivation was brought to Europe by the Arabs and spread from there to North America.

As it takes over 150 saffron stigmas to make a mere 1 gram of spice, it is very expensive, although little is usually required. Many cheaper spices are used to mimic its colouring and flavouring powers, notably safflower, turmeric and marigold.

Try to buy saffron in the form of dried strands as the powder does not have the same potency. Soak the strands briefly in warm water or milk before adding them to any dish.

The unique flavour and colour of saffron is essential to guarantee authenticity in many Mediterranean and eastern fish and rice dishes.

MOULES AU SAFRAN

Mussels with saffron

Serves 6
Preparation 30 minutes
Cooking about 40 minutes

METRIC/IMPERIAL	*AMERICAN*
3 onions	*3 onions*
2 fish heads	*2 fish heads*
bouquet garni	*bouquet garni*
1 tbsp olive oil	*1 tbsp olive oil*
3 shallots, chopped	*3 shallots, chopped*
1 carrot, thinly sliced	*1 carrot, thinly sliced*
350 ml/12 fl oz dry white wine	*1⅔ cups dry white wine*
2 tomatoes, peeled and quartered	*2 tomatoes, peeled and quartered*
pinch of saffron	*pinch of saffron*
3 l/5 pt mussels	*3 qt mussels*
200 ml/7 fl oz crème fraîche or whipping cream	*1 cup crème fraîche or whipping cream*
salt and pepper	*salt and pepper*

Slice one of the onions and finely dice the others. Put the sliced onion in a pan with the fish heads, bouquet garni, salt and pepper and 1 l/1¾ pt/1 qt of water. Simmer for 20 minutes. Strain this stock and reserve 500 ml/16 fl oz/2 cups.

Heat the oil in a sauté pan over a moderate heat. Add the diced onions, shallots and carrot. Cook gently for 5 minutes.

Add one third of the white wine, the tomatoes, saffron and the reserved fish stock. Cover and cook gently for 15 minutes more.

Meanwhile, put the mussels in a large pan with the remaining wine and place over a high heat until they all open. Discard any that remain stubbornly closed. Remove them from their shells and strain the cooking liquid.

Add the mussels to the sauté pan along with the strained cooking liquid and the cream. Heat for 1–2 minutes, adjust the seasoning and serve in warmed deep plates as a hot first course.

To drink: a medium-bodied white wine, such as a Meursault.

see also:
herbs
stuffing

SAGE

Sauge

A perennial aromatic herb with large, thick, sometimes velvety leaves, sage has a penetrating, almost pungent, camphor-like smell and flavour. It is used fresh or dried for flavouring soups, vegetables and fatty meats such as pork. Sage is particularly favoured in Italian cuisine as it goes well with veal. It is also enduringly popular in Britain and North America, usually in combination with onions, to make stuffings for poultry.

FOIE DE VEAU À LA SAUGE

Calves' liver with sage

Serves 4
Preparation 10 minutes
Cooking about 35 minutes

METRIC/IMPERIAL	AMERICAN
4 slices of calves' liver, each weighing about 125 g/4½ oz	*4 slices of calves' liver, each weighing about 4½ oz*
15 g/½ oz butter	*1 tbsp butter*
225 g/½ lb mushrooms, sliced	*½ lb mushrooms, sliced*
115 g/¼ lb smoked streaky bacon, cut into strips	*¼ lb country-style bacon, cut into strips*
3 onions, thinly sliced	*3 onions, thinly sliced*
200 ml/7 fl oz dry white wine	*1 cup dry white wine*
16 fresh sage leaves	*16 fresh sage leaves*
150 ml/¼ pt whipping cream	*⅔ cup whipping cream*
flour, for coating	*flour, for coating*
salt and pepper	*salt and pepper*

Season the slices of liver with salt and pepper and dust them with flour. Set them aside.

Melt the butter in a sauté pan over a moderate heat and sauté the mushrooms for 5 minutes. Season to taste and remove from the heat.

Dry fry the bacon gently in a large non-stick frying pan until the fat is rendered. Cook the onions for 10 minutes in the bacon fat.

Push the bacon and onions to the sides of the pan and increase the heat to high. Place the slices of liver in it and cook them for 4 minutes on each side. Remove and keep hot on a warmed serving plate with the onions and bacon.

Deglaze the frying pan with the white wine.

Snip 12 of the sage leaves into the pan and cook rapidly to reduce the liquid by half.

Add the mushrooms and cream and whisk over a high heat until well combined. Coat the liver slices with the sauce and place a whole sage leaf on top of each.

To drink: a dry white wine, such as a Viré.

SALAD

Salade

The term 'salad' used without any qualification generally denotes a green salad, ie a mixture of leaves, or more usually just lettuce, dressed with a vinaigrette. By extension, the term has come to be used of mixed salads which usually include green leaves and any number of other raw or cooked ingredients, and plain salads in which an item of cold, raw or cooked food is dressed with a sauce.

GREEN SALADS may be served before, with or following the main course. A wide variety of leaves are commonly used apart from the lettuce family, including the many types of chicory and endive, lamb's lettuce, rocket (arugula), watercress, spinach, sorrel, dandelion and purslane. Inclusion of items such as radicchio and lollo

see also:
chicory
Chinese cabbage
cress
dandelion
endive
flowers
herbs
lamb's lettuce
lettuce
mayonnaise
potato
radicchio
radish
rice
rocket
sorrel
tomato
vinaigrette

rosso can also add great colour to such salads, making them far from just 'green'.

Good green salads usually also contain chopped fresh herbs, such as parsley, chives, tarragon, basil, chervil, coriander (cilantro) and mint. Dressings can be as simple as a light sprinkling of salt or plain olive oil in the Italian manner, or complex vinaigrettes flavoured with herbs, mustard, shallots, etc, or mayonnaise-based mixtures.

Salad leaves should be well dried before dressing at the last minute to keep the ingredients crisp. Green salads are also frequently garnished with croutons, nuts, chopped, cooked bacon or edible flowers.

MIXED SALADS are usually served as a first or main course and can combine a great variety of ingredients, both raw and cooked, including meat, poultry and seafood as well as vegetables. Such salads incorporate a variety of complementary tastes and contrasting textures, such as celery and grapes with chicken or fish with cucumber, and usually have an appealing combination of colours. Dressings for mixed salads are usually simple vinaigrettes which will bring out rather than overpower the flavour of the ingredients and will also enhance their appearance.

PLAIN SALADS are popular for buffets and consist of one cold, raw or cooked item in a dressing. Salads of poultry and seafood are often dressed with a thick, creamy mayonnaise, as are some salads of root vegetables, like potato and celeriac (celery root). Other vegetables, such as tomatoes and green beans, are usually coated with a vinaigrette.

Salads are valuable and important elements of a healthy diet, providing a great deal of fibre and encouraging the consumption of raw food. Eaten plain, or dressed with just a dash of lemon juice, green salad is very low in calories: 100 g/3½ oz contains only 15. However, all dressings add considerably to the energy content of salads, for instance in 100 g/3½ oz of tomato salad dressed with a vinaigrette, the tomatoes contain only 22 calories and the dressing more than 100.

SALADE DE FRUITS DE MER

Seafood salad

Serves 4
Preparation 25 minutes
Cooking 10 minutes, 1 hour ahead

METRIC/IMPERIAL	*AMERICAN*
1.5 l/2½ pt cockles	*1½ qt clams*
1.5 l/2½ pt mussels	*1½ qt mussels*
½ tsp curry powder	*½ tsp curry powder*
140 g/5 oz mushrooms	*5 oz mushrooms*
juice of 2 lemons	*juice of 2 lemons*
6 tbsp olive oil	*6 tbsp olive oil*
1 tsp strong mustard	*1 tsp Dijon mustard*
1 shallot, chopped	*1 shallot, chopped*
2 tbsp finely chopped parsley	*2 tbsp finely chopped parsley*
1 tbsp capers, drained	*1 tbsp capers, drained*
1 lettuce, separated into leaves	*1 head lettuce, separated into leaves*
115 g/¼ lb peeled cooked prawns, roughly chopped	*¼ lb peeled cooked shrimp, roughly chopped*
salt and pepper	*salt and pepper*

In separate pans, open the cockles or clams and the mussels over a high heat. Remove from their shells and strain the liquid from the shells.

Put the shelled cockles or clams and mussels in a bowl and pour the liquid over them, adding the curry powder. Leave to stand for 1 hour.

Wipe the mushrooms, slice them thinly and sprinkle them with some of the lemon juice.

In a bowl mix the olive oil, remaining lemon juice and mustard. Season with salt and pepper. Add the shallot, parsley and capers.

Line a deep salad bowl with the larger lettuce leaves. Shred the heart. Drain the cockles or clams and mussels and put them in a bowl with 2 tablespoons of the liquid, the prawns (shrimp), mushrooms and shredded lettuce.

Pour over the shallot vinaigrette and toss. Put the salad on top of the lettuce leaves in the salad bowl and serve.

To drink: a light, dry white wine, such as a Muscadet.

SALADE NIÇOISE

Tomato, olive and anchovy salad

Serves 4
Preparation 20 minutes

METRIC/IMPERIAL	AMERICAN
1 small cucumber, peeled and sliced	1 small cucumber, peeled and sliced
6 tomatoes, sliced	6 tomatoes, sliced
5 tbsp olive oil	5 tbsp olive oil
2 tbsp white wine vinegar	2 tbsp white wine vinegar
1 garlic clove	1 garlic clove
3 small new onions, thinly sliced	3 small new onions, thinly sliced
115 g/¼ lb fresh broad beans, shelled, blanched and skinned	¼ lb fresh fava or lima beans, shelled, blanched and skinned
1 green sweet pepper, halved, deseeded and cut into strips	1 green sweet pepper, halved, deseeded and cut into strips
5 fresh basil leaves, snipped	5 fresh basil leaves, snipped
2 hard-boiled eggs, shelled and sliced	2 hard-boiled eggs, shelled and sliced
24 tiny black olives	24 tiny black olives
10 rolled anchovy fillets in oil, drained and patted dry	10 rolled anchovy fillets in oil, drained and patted dry
salt and freshly ground black pepper	salt and freshly ground black pepper

Sprinkle the cucumber and tomato slices with salt and set aside to drain in a cool place.

Prepare a vinaigrette with the oil, vinegar and salt and pepper to taste.

Rub the sides of a wooden salad bowl with the garlic. Put in the well-drained cucumber and tomatoes with the onions, broad (fava or lima) beans and sweet pepper. Toss them in the vinaigrette, adding the basil.

Garnish with the hard-boiled egg slices, the olives and rolled anchovy fillets.

Variations: add 150 g/5½ oz fine green beans cooked briefly in boiling water, quartered artichoke hearts or half a sliced fennel bulb.

Salade niçoise (Tomato, olive and anchovy salad)

SALADE ÉNERGÉTIQUE

Energizing salad

Serves 4
Preparation 25 minutes

METRIC/IMPERIAL	AMERICAN
140 g/5 oz lamb's lettuce	5 oz lamb's lettuce
8 mushrooms	8 mushrooms
juice of 2 lemons	juice of 2 lemons
2 tomatoes, quartered	2 tomatoes, quartered
10 radishes, sliced	10 radishes, sliced
3 carrots, grated	3 carrots, grated
8 fresh lychees	8 fresh lychees
1 mango	1 mango
1 avocado	1 avocado
30 g/1 oz pine kernels	⅓ cup pine nuts
salt and pepper	salt and pepper

Arrange the leaves of lamb's lettuce on 4 individual plates.

Thinly slice the mushrooms and sprinkle with some of the lemon juice. Combine the mushrooms, tomatoes, radishes and carrots in a salad bowl.

Peel the lychees. Peel the mango; halve it, remove the stone and dice the pulp. Add the fruit to the bowl. Stir to mix, then spoon on top of the lamb's lettuce on each plate.

Cut the avocado in half, remove the stone, scoop out the pulp and put it into a food processor with the remaining lemon juice. Blend until smooth. Pour this sauce over the plates of mixed salad. Season, garnish with pine kernels (pine nuts) and serve at once.

To drink: fresh grapefruit juice.

SALMIS

A type of game dish, usually made with duck, pheasant, pigeon or woodcock, a salmis involves partially roasting the bird, which is then carved and the cooking finished in a wine sauce. The sauce is also often enriched by the addition of the chopped giblets.

see also:
duck
game
pheasant
stewing
woodcock

SALMIS DE CANARD

Salmis de canard

Serves 4
Preparation 20 minutes
Cooking about 1½ hours

METRIC/IMPERIAL	*AMERICAN*
1 oven-ready duck, weighing 1.5 kg/ 3½ lb, giblets retained	*1 duck, dressed and drawn weight 3½ lb, giblets retained*
15 g/½ oz butter	*1 tbsp butter*
1 tbsp oil	*1 tbsp oil*
4 shallots, finely chopped	*4 shallots, finely chopped*
10 baby onions	*10 small onions*
bouquet garni	*bouquet garni*
1 garlic clove, finely chopped	*1 garlic clove, finely chopped*
500 ml/16 fl oz full-bodied mature red wine, such as a Chambertin	*2 cups full-bodied mature red wine, such as a Chambertin*
salt and pepper	*salt and pepper*

Preheat the oven to 250C/475F/gas 9.

Season the duck inside and out with salt and pepper then roast it for 30 minutes.

Carve the duck and chop the heart and liver.

Heat the butter with the oil in a sauté pan over a moderate heat. Cook the shallots and onions in the sauté pan for 5 minutes, stirring. Add the bouquet garni, garlic, wine and seasonings.

Put the pieces of duck in the sauce. Cover and simmer very gently for 40 minutes. Add the heart and liver and cook for 5 more minutes.

Serve hot, with celeriac (celery root) purée. *To drink: Chambertin.*

SALMON

Saumon

see also:
barbecuing
court-bouillon
fish
mayonnaise
roe
sauce
smoking

Often called the 'king of fish', the salmon is born in fresh water, migrates to the sea to live, and returns annually to its native river to spawn. Those on their first return are known as GRILSE and are only about 50 cm/20 in long, while fish on their second and subsequent trips up-river are considered adult salmon and it is at this stage they are generally fished, weighing anything from 4–12 kg/9–27 lb. Fish up to 3 years old are thought the best eating.

There are several principal species, of which the ATLANTIC SALMON is held in the highest regard. BALTIC SALMON tend to be smaller with paler and less tasty flesh. PACIFIC SALMON are mostly canned as SOCK-EYE or RED SALMON or the even more abundant PINK SALMON.

Once common in many European and New England rivers, pollution and the construction of dams have meant that salmon fishing is almost entirely limited to northern Europe, especially Scotland and Scandinavia, and Canada. However, salmon farming has recently flourished greatly, bringing down prices, but farmed salmon have a significantly less fine flavour and are difficult to differentiate visually.

Salmon have silvery blue skins and pink, oily flesh which is tasty and very nourishing. When buying whole fish look for bright eyes and red gills. It is also advisable to buy rigid fish with broad centres and short, stubby heads as otherwise the head can account for a large part of the weight. Get the fishmonger to scale and gut the fish if it is to be cooked whole. Salmon is also commonly sold as steaks, fillets or escalopes (cutlets) and these should have a good bright colour but not look too moist.

Whole fish are usually cooked very gently in a court-bouillon and served either hot or cold. Cooking times depend on size, variety and age but an unerring way of poaching salmon to be served cold is to immerse it in the cold court-bouillon and then bring this gently to the boil. If the heat is turned off as soon as the liquid begins to bubble, and the fish allowed to cool in the liquid, it will be moist, succulent and cooked to perfection. Cold poached salmon is often skinned and coated with aspic or mayonnaise.

Steaks and escalopes (cutlets) may also be poached, but they are probably better grilled (broiled), barbecued or pan-fried, usually first protected with a light coating of butter or oil and cooked at a fairly high heat to sear them and keep in their juices. Cold salmon is best served with mayonnaise flavoured with herbs, while hot salmon suits rich butter sauces, such as hollandaise or *beurre blanc*. New potatoes and cucumber are traditional accompaniments.

SMOKED SALMON

When subjected to the traditional process of salting and cold-smoking, salmon acquires an unrivalled flavour and succulence. It may be dry-salted or brined and smoking is effected over smouldering hardwoods, such as beech, or even peat, often with flavourings like juniper, heather or whisky.

Smoked salmon is usually served in almost transparently thin slices as a cold hors d'oeuvre. It is best dressed with lemon juice and freshly ground black pepper, accompanied by brown bread and butter. The French prefer it with crème fraîche seasoned with horseradish or chopped onion, toast or blinis and lemon quarters. Jewish-Americans traditionally serve *lox* with bagels and cream cheese. Smoked salmon is also used, both hot and cold, in recipes.

Plain cooked salmon contains about 200 calories per 100 g/3½ oz; the same amount of smoked salmon has 270 calories.

SAUMON À L'OSEILLE

Salmon with sorrel

Serves 4
Preparation 15 minutes
Cooking about 40 minutes

METRIC/IMPERIAL	AMERICAN
4 fresh skinless salmon fillets, each weighing about 200 g/7 oz	4 pieces of fresh skinless salmon fillet, each weighing about 7 oz
100 ml/3½ fl oz white wine	½ cup white wine
100 ml/3½ fl oz fish fumet or concentrated fish stock	½ cup fish fumet or concentrated fish stock
3 shallots, chopped	3 shallots, chopped
400 ml/14 fl oz crème fraîche or whipping cream	1¾ cups crème fraîche or whipping cream
400 g/14 oz sorrel, trimmed and shredded	14 oz sorrel, trimmed and shredded
30 g/1 oz butter	2 tbsp butter
1 tbsp sunflower oil	1 tbsp sunflower oil
salt and pepper	salt and pepper
½ lemon, sliced, to garnish	½ lemon, sliced, to garnish

Season the salmon pieces and set aside.

Put the white wine and fish fumet or stock into a saucepan. Add the shallots and cook for 15 minutes over a high heat, stirring. Add the cream and continue to cook, stirring, for 5 minutes, then add the sorrel and mix. Season to taste and keep hot.

Melt the butter with the oil in a frying pan over a low heat. Add the salmon pieces and cook gently for 7–8 minutes on each side. The salmon should still be pink and juicy.

Put the sorrel mixture on very hot individual plates and place the salmon on top. Garnish with some quartered lemon slices.

To drink: an aromatic white wine, such as a Sancerre or dry Graves.

MOUSSE DE SAUMON FUMÉ

Smoked salmon mousse

Serves 4
Preparation 15 minutes

METRIC/IMPERIAL	AMERICAN
450 g/1 lb smoked salmon	1 lb smoked salmon
100 ml/3½ fl oz crème fraîche or sour cream	½ cup crème fraîche or sour cream
1 tsp lemon juice	1 tsp lemon juice
1 tbsp strong mustard	1 tbsp Dijon mustard
bunch of watercress	bunch of watercress
pepper	pepper

Slice about one fifth of the smoked salmon into strips. Blend the rest in a food processor.

Add the cream, lemon juice and mustard into the purée, whisking vigorously. Season lightly with pepper and chill.

Line a serving plate with the watercress. Put the well-chilled mousse on the watercress and garnish it with the strips of smoked salmon.

The ideal accompaniment to this dish is thin slices of rye bread.

Variation: dissolve 4 leaves of gelatine or 1 tablespoon powdered gelatine in a little water and add it to the mousse. Spoon the mousse into ramekins. Garnish with slices of avocado sprinkled with lemon juice.

see also:
vegetables

SALSIFY

Salsifis

The elongated roots of several vegetables in the lettuce family are known as salsify. TRUE or WHITE SALSIFY has long white roots looking a little like bunches of slender parsnips and BLACK SALSIFY or SCORZONERA has even longer single-stemmed roots with a black skin which is slightly easier to peel than the hairier white varieties. Both have pale, white, milky flesh which bleeds its juices very readily on peeling and has a distinctive, strong, bitter flavour.

WILD SALSIFY, also known as GOAT'S BEARD or SPANISH OYSTER PLANT is like a white-skinned version of scorzonera. Its young shoots are also used like baby spinach in salads.

Buy only firm and unwrinkled salsify which feels heavy for its size. To make peeling easier, either soak them in cold water for at least 2 hours or partly cook them and rub the skins off before finishing the cooking. After the roots have been peeled they should be rinsed in acidulated water to prevent them turning brown.

Salsify is popular sautéed in butter and lemon juice, deep-fried, baked or stewed. It makes a good accompaniment to chicken, veal and lamb. It is available canned in brine.

Salsify contains 76 calories per 100 g/3½ oz and it is rich in fibre, minerals and vitamin C.

BEIGNETS DE SALSIFIS

Salsify fritters

Serves 4
Preparation 30 minutes, 1 hour ahead
Cooking about 20 minutes

METRIC/IMPERIAL	AMERICAN
800 g/1¾ lb salsify	1¾ lb salsify
juice of 1 lemon	juice of 1 lemon
100 g/3½ oz flour	¾ cup flour
1 l/1¾ pt groundnut oil	1 qt peanut oil
1 tbsp finely chopped parsley	1 tbsp finely chopped parsley
1 egg, separated + 1 egg white	1 egg, separated + 1 egg white
2 tbsp beer	2 tbsp beer
salt and pepper	salt and pepper

Peel the salsify and cut it into chunks about 5–6 cm/2–2½ in long. Rinse them in water to which half the lemon juice has been added.

Half fill a large saucepan with water and add 1 tablespoon of the flour, 1 tablespoon of the lemon juice and a pinch of salt. Bring to the boil, then add the salsify. Lower the heat and cook it gently for 10 minutes, then drain.

In a deep dish, mix 1 tablespoon of the oil, 1 tablespoon of lemon juice and the parsley. Season with salt and pepper. Put the salsify into this mixture and leave it to marinate for 1 hour, turning it frequently.

About 30 minutes before making the fritters, mix together in a bowl the egg yolk, the rest of the flour and the beer. Whisk the egg whites to firm peaks and fold them into the batter.

Heat the remaining oil to a temperature of about 180C/360F or until a small cube of stale bread will brown in it in 60 seconds.

Drain the chunks of salsify, dip them in the fritter batter and deep fry them in 4 or 5 batches for 3–4 minutes each. When the fritters in each batch are golden brown, drain them and sprinkle them with fine salt. Keep them warm, uncovered, in a warm oven with the door open while the remaining fritters are being fried.

SALT

Sel

see also:
cheese
curing
ham
preserving
seasoning
smoking

In cooking, the term salt is used almost exclusively to denote sodium chloride. An abundant and almost pure source of two minerals essential to life, this crystalline, sharp-tasting, odourless substance has long been used as a condiment, cooking aid and preserving agent. So significant is it to our diet that it is one of the few substances for which we have specialized sensors in our palate, hence the importance attached to using exactly the right amount in food.

Salt comes in various forms. SEA SALT is extracted from the sea by evaporation in bays or on salt marshes. In its unrefined state it can be fairly grey and is known as *sel gris*. In this state it is full of traces of other important minerals and is thus a rich dietary source. The refined white crystals are held by many to be the best and tastiest form of salt for use as a condiment.

ROCK SALT is extracted from the earth, but with some notable exceptions is generally inferior in flavour. Ordinary COMMON SALT is mined from the residues of ancient dried seas and sold in the form of COOKING SALT, which is fairly coarse, and TABLE SALT. The latter consists of very fine crystals which have usually been coated with other chemicals to improve their pouring qualities and keep them from absorbing atmospheric moisture. Because of its fineness, this form of salt is by far the most common form used as a seasoning and is essential in some forms of cooking, particularly baking. Forms of table salt are sold as IODIZED SALT, with added iodine for those in areas without an adequate supply of this essential mineral. KOSHER SALT contains no additives and is coarsely crushed.

PICKLING OR BLOCK SALT is a refined form of rock salt which is particularly suited to the process of pickling, having the right consistency and little added flavouring.

Several types of SEASONED SALTS, in which the grains are mixed with aromatic items such as celery, onion, garlic or herbs and spices, are used as condiments and flavouring ingredients.

Salt very readily absorbs moisture from the air and from food with which it comes into contact. For this reason it should always be kept in an airtight container in a dry place. However, this also makes it very useful for drawing out fluids and bitter juices from foods such as cucumbers, aubergines (eggplant) and courgettes (zucchini). Also for this reason meat should not be salted prior to cooking as salt draws moisture to the surface and prevents a sealing crust forming on the food.

This property is also what gives salt its preservative powers as it takes away all the fluid which might otherwise allow micro-organisms to flourish in food. Meat, fish and vegetables have been preserved in salt or brine since the dawn of time and food may also be salted prior to another form of curing, such as pickling or smoking.

Another important property of salt is that it can cause food to harden, hence its use with foods to be pickled. On the other hand, items such as dried beans should be salted only halfway through cooking as the salt will otherwise harden their exteriors. Salt is also held to help maintain the colour of green vegetables during cooking.

Salt also has the effect of lowering the freezing point of liquids in which it is dissolved. Hence its use on roads in winter and in the kitchen when making ice cream, etc.

The human body needs about 5 g of salt per day for correct functioning. Nowadays, however, we ingest enormous amounts of salt as so much is added to our food in the course of preservation, preparation and cooking. Many people are so inured to its presence in high quantities that they still also season food with salt without even tasting it first, and there are great quantities hidden in canned and other convenience foods. Excess salt is known to contribute to high blood pressure, arteriosclerosis and heart disease, so it is wise to use as little as possible and to limit consumption of heavily salted foods such as bacon, hams, smoked foods and cheeses. Various forms of salt substitutes are available for those on salt-free diets.

POULET EN CROÛTE DE SEL

Chicken baked in salt

Serves 6
Preparation 10 minutes
Cooking 1½ hours

METRIC/IMPERIAL	*AMERICAN*
7 kg/15 lb unrefined coarse sea salt	*15 lb unrefined coarse sea salt*
1 oven-ready chicken, weighing about 1.8 kg/4 lb, trussed	*1 chicken, dressed and drawn weight about 4 lb, trussed*

Preheat the oven to 250C/475F/gas 9.

Line a large, deep casserole with foil. Pour a layer of salt into it to a depth of about 4 cm/1½ in. Place the bird on top of it, breast down. Fill the casserole with salt, pressing it down all round the bird. Place another layer of salt about 3–4 cm/1¼–1½ in thick on top so that the chicken is completely covered. Do not cover the casserole with a lid.

Bake in the oven for 1½ hours.

Tip the contents of the casserole out on a board. Break the salt crust with a mallet. Carve the well-browned chicken to serve.

Variation: try this with whole fish, such as trout. Serve with a herb vinaigrette.

SARDINE

see also:
fish
escabèche
papillote
pilchard

Young pilchards are known as sardines. These members of the herring family are abundant in the European Atlantic and the Mediterranean, particularly during spring and summer. They were the first type of fish to be preserved by canning, and in Europe and North America many kinds of small fish in cans are now known as sardines. There are no true sardines in North American waters, but small herring are often treated in a similar fashion.

When bought fresh, sardines should still be rigid, with brilliant eyes and no blood on the gills. Smaller specimens, which tend to be a little dry, are best fried or made into *escabèche*. Larger, fattier fish, available in summer, are delicious grilled (broiled), barbecued or cooked en papillote, but need to be scaled and gutted prior to cooking.

Most of the sardine catch is still canned and it is in this form that they are most familiar. The best quality canned sardines carry the label 'extra', and the place of origin is specified, as is the type of oil or flavouring herbs used. Sardines canned in oil improve in flavour with age: they are sold six months after canning but can easily keep for 10 years. Certain brands even have a vintage. Turn the cans once or twice a year, but never store them in the refrigerator. Sardines are often eaten as hors d'oeuvres, but can also be made into rillettes, used for filling feuilletés, or as an accompaniment for baked potatoes or baked eggs.

Fresh sardines are semi-oily fish: 100 g/3½ oz contains 175 calories. Even canned in oil the calorie content is not really much higher: 100 g/3½ oz contains 190 calories. The lipids in the fish oils are also healthy ones.

SARDINES AU VIN BLANC

Sardines in white wine

Serves 4
Preparation 20 minutes
Cooking 12 minutes

METRIC/IMPERIAL	*AMERICAN*
55 g/2 oz butter	*4 tbsp butter*
3 shallots, thinly sliced	*3 shallots, thinly sliced*
12 large fresh sardines, scaled, gutted and heads removed	*12 large fresh sardines, dressed and heads removed*
juice of ½ lemon	*juice of ½ lemon*
4 tbsp white wine	*¼ cup white wine*
2 tbsp chopped chives	*2 tbsp chopped chives*
salt and pepper	*salt and pepper*

Preheat the oven to 250C/475F/gas 9.

Grease a baking dish with one third of the butter. Spread the chopped shallots over the bottom and place the sardines on top.

Sprinkle the lemon juice over the sardines and pour on the white wine. Dot with the rest of the butter, season and bake for 12 minutes.

Remove from the oven, add the chopped chives and serve straight from the baking dish.

To drink: an aromatic white wine, such as an Entre-Deux-Mers.

SAUCE

see also:
aïoli
aspic
bain-marie
butter
chaud-froid
condiments
cornflour
court-bouillon
cream
creams and custards

Highly flavoured liquids served with food to enhance or complement its flavour are known as sauces. They may be integral to the dish, as with braised or stewed food or the gravy made from roasting pan juices. They may also be prepared separately and poured over the dish at the last minute or served apart in a bowl or sauce boat. Such sauces may be hot or cold, thick or thin, sweet or savoury.

There are several types of hot savoury sauces: WHITE SAUCES are based on a pale, slightly

deglazing
duxelles
egg
emulsion
essence
fumet
gravy
ketchup
liaison
mayonnaise
mirepoix
purée
reduction
roux
stock
velouté
vinaigrette

cooked roux. The classic 'mother' white sauce is béchamel in which warmed milk, possibly infused with bay leaves or bouquet garni, is added to the roux along with seasoning and other flavourings, such as nutmeg. Variations include cheese-flavoured *mornay*, and *soubise* with chopped onion. White sauces are normally served to accompany vegetables and egg, fish, poultry and white meat dishes. They are also often used in gratins and to thicken mixtures for soufflés and croquettes.

BLOND SAUCES or *veloutés* are types of white sauce based on a pale roux to which a white stock is added. It is cooked for longer to develop a fuller flavour and a fine, glossy texture. *Velouté* sauces may have various additions, including mushrooms and tomato purée (paste) for *chasseur* or lobster coral for *cardinale*. Such sauces suit richer fish and poultry dishes and sweetbreads. They may also be used as a base for soups.

BROWN SAUCES are based on a reduced, rich meat stock and normally thickened with a well-browned roux. The mother sauce of the group is *espagnole*, in which chopped flavouring vegetables and bacon are gently browned in butter before the flour is added to make the roux. Brown sauces most usually accompany red meats, offal (variety meats), poultry and game dishes. Variations include *bordelaise* which has a base of chopped shallots and includes red wine, and *périgueux* with truffles.

EMULSION SAUCES fall into two main groups: the HOLLANDAISE family, which also includes BÉARNAISE, in which egg yolk and butter is emulsified over a gentle heat. These versatile sauces go equally well with grilled (broiled), barbecued or roast meat and poached fish. In a WHITE BUTTER SAUCE or *beurre blanc*, butter is incorporated into a reduction of white wine and vinegar flavoured with chopped shallots. Slightly less robust, they are best reserved for fish and vegetables.

Cold sauces are usually cold emulsions like MAYONNAISE, plain mixtures of cold ingredients like VINAIGRETTES and FLAVOURED BUTTERS or simple purées and coulis.

Sweet sauces are generally either sweetened fruit purée, custard, caramel or melted chocolate. Sometimes a hot sauce on a cold dessert gives a pleasing contrast.

The making of a successful sauce depends on the skilful use of several techniques, including reduction to concentrate flavours, sieving or puréeing to ensure smoothness, and whisking to aerate and ensure complete incorporation of added ingredients. Sauces should also be very carefully seasoned, ideally at a late stage for maximum control. Unsalted butter should always be used for the same reason. Most sauces should be made in small pans with heavy bottoms which will conduct heat well without scorching the ingredients. Others, particularly emulsion sauces, are best prepared in a bain-marie set over a gentle heat.

Various binding agents used to thicken sauces not based on a roux include flour, often kneaded with butter to a paste, cream, egg yolk, or blood and chopped giblets in the case of some meat, poultry and game. Cornflour (cornstarch) and arrowroot are also favoured, as their fine grains help give a smooth texture and, as so little is required, results are much lighter and less calorific. Many sauces without a butter base have some cold, diced butter whisked into them at the last minute to give extra smoothness, flavour and sheen.

There are many traditionally unbeatable sauce associations, such as kidneys in Madeira sauce, leeks vinaigrette, hard-boiled eggs *à l'aurore*, salt cod with aïoli, turbot with hollandaise sauce, pike with *beurre blanc*, chicken mayonnaise and chateaubriand with *béarnaise*. Such classic combinations give an indication of what works best. However, unlikely pairings, such as poached cod with vinaigrette, can be surprisingly effective.

A wide variety of commercial ready-made sauces are sold, from mayonnaise to tomato ketchup. Many are widely used as condiments and some, like Worcestershire sauce, have become valued flavouring ingredients in their own right.

Long held to be heavy, indigestible and fattening, sauces nowadays tend to be lighter and fresher. They can form an integral part of healthy cooking, especially if they are thickened with cornflour (cornstarch), low-fat cream cheese or other soft cheese, plain yogurt or puréed vegetables.

SAUCE BÉCHAMEL

Basic white sauce

Makes about 500 ml/16 fl oz/2 cups
Preparation 5 minutes
Cooking about 20 minutes

METRIC/IMPERIAL	*AMERICAN*
55 g/2 oz butter	*4 tbsp butter*
55 g/2 oz flour	*¼ cup flour*
500 ml/16 fl oz milk	*2 cups milk*
pinch of freshly grated nutmeg	*pinch of freshly grated nutmeg*
salt and pepper	*salt and pepper*

Melt the butter in a saucepan over a gentle heat. Pour in all the flour at once and whisk vigorously (1). Cook over a gentle heat for 2 minutes, stirring constantly. Remove it from the heat and gradually add the milk to it, whisking vigorously until smooth (2).

Return it to a low heat and cook gently for 12 minutes, stirring constantly (3).

Season with salt, pepper and grated nutmeg.

Notes: the sauce should be smooth but not too thick. Avoid rapid boiling as this will give the sauce a gluey taste.

The milk may be brought to the boil and then added to the roux. However, in this case the roux should first be allowed to cool slightly or the mixture will become lumpy.

The milk used in making the sauce may be flavoured by infusing it with bay or celery leaves, parsley or thyme.

Depending on what the sauce is to be used for, milk or an equal parts mixture of milk and stock or vegetable cooking liquid may be used.

For mornay sauce, add grated Gruyère and an egg yolk; for nantua sauce, to accompany fillets of brill or monkfish, add prawn or shrimp butter.

1

2

3

SAUCE ESPAGNOLE

Spanish or basic brown sauce

Makes about 500 ml/16 fl oz/2 cups
Preparation 20 minutes
Cooking about 45 minutes

METRIC/IMPERIAL	*AMERICAN*
500 ml/16 fl oz beef stock	*2 cups beef stock*
55 g/2 oz butter	*4 tbsp butter*
75 g/2½ oz salt pork or streaky bacon, finely diced	*½ cup finely diced salt pork or country-style bacon*
1 carrot, finely diced	*1 carrot, finely diced*
2 onions, finely chopped	*2 onions, finely chopped*
4 shallots, finely chopped	*4 shallots, finely chopped*
1 celery stalk, trimmed and finely chopped	*1 celery stick, trimmed and finely chopped*
55 g/2 oz flour	*¼ cup flour*
bouquet garni	*bouquet garni*
salt and pepper	*salt and pepper*

Put the stock to heat in a small pan.

Melt the butter in a heavy-bottomed saucepan over a moderate heat and add the pork or bacon, carrot, onions, shallots and celery. Cook, stirring, until the mixture is well browned.

Sprinkle in the flour and cook for 2 or 3 minutes, stirring continuously, until browned.

Add the bouquet garni and pour the stock over, mixing well. Cook very gently for 30 minutes, preferably with a heat-diffusing mat.

Discard the bouquet garni and strain the sauce, pressing it hard with the back of a spoon to get as much liquid out of it as possible. Taste and adjust the seasoning.

Variation: for bordelaise sauce, boil 500 ml/16 fl oz/2 cups red Bordeaux with 2 more chopped shallots, a bay leaf, and some thyme, parsley stalks and peppercorns until reduced by half. Strain and add to the sauce along with 1 tablespoon of meat extract and some lemon juice. Finish by whisking in 75 g/2½ oz/5 tbsp diced, chilled butter. Serve with pan-fried or grilled (broiled) meats.

SAUCE CHASSEUR

Mushroom and tomato white wine sauce

Makes about 500 ml/16 fl oz/2 cups
Preparation 15 minutes
Cooking 30 minutes

METRIC/IMPERIAL	AMERICAN
350 ml/12 fl oz chicken stock	1⅔ cups chicken stock
75 g/2½ oz butter	5 tbsp butter
140 g/5 oz mushrooms, thinly sliced	5 oz mushrooms, thinly sliced
5 shallots, finely chopped	5 shallots, finely chopped
sprig of thyme	sprig of thyme
1 heaped tbsp flour	1 heaping tbsp flour
150 ml/¼ pt white wine	⅔ cup white wine
2 tbsp tomato purée	2 tbsp tomato paste
1 tbsp chopped parsley	1 tbsp chopped parsley
salt and pepper	salt and pepper

Put the stock to heat in a small pan.

Melt one third of the butter in a saucepan over a moderate heat and brown the mushrooms for 5 minutes, stirring frequently. Remove.

Add the remaining butter to the pan, increase the heat and add the shallots and thyme. Stir for 2 minutes, then sprinkle in the flour. Cook this roux for 2–3 minutes over a gentle heat.

Add the hot stock, stirring vigorously, then add the wine mixed with the tomato purée (paste). Simmer for about 20 minutes.

Remove the thyme. Add the mushrooms to the sauce and continue to cook for 2–3 minutes. Taste and adjust the seasoning.

Stir in the parsley and serve to accompany sautéed chicken or rabbit, veal escalopes (scallops) or braised vegetables.

SAUCE ALLEMANDE

German or enriched white sauce

Makes about 500 ml/16 fl oz/2 cups
Preparation 10 minutes
Cooking about 1 hour

METRIC/IMPERIAL	AMERICAN
500 ml/16 fl oz chicken stock	2 cups chicken stock
75 g/2½ oz butter	5 tbsp butter
55 g/2 oz flour	¼ cup flour
3 egg yolks	3 egg yolks
salt and pepper	salt and pepper

Heat the stock in a pan over a moderate heat.

Put 50 g/2 oz/4 tbsp of the butter in another pan and melt over low heat. Add the flour and stir with a wooden spoon to mix. Do not let the roux brown. When it begins to foam, pour in the chicken stock, stirring constantly.

Place a flameproof mat or other heat diffuser under the pan and cook gently for 50 minutes.

Mix the egg yolks in a bowl with a little of the sauce, then pour this mixture into the saucepan. Stir over a low heat, adding the remaining butter and seasoning to taste. Ensure that the sauce does not boil. Keep the sauce warm in a bain-marie until ready to use.

Notes: use white pepper to avoid a speckled appearance.

Add 2 tablespoons of mushroom cooking juices and use fish stock instead of chicken stock to make a sauce for fish.

1

2

3

Notes: if the sauce starts getting lumpy, plunge the base of the pan into cold water and whisk vigorously until smooth again.

Melted butter may be used, but it must first be clarified. In either case, however, the butter must be added a little at a time over a very low heat, otherwise the sauce will curdle.

SAUCE HOLLANDAISE

Egg and lemon butter sauce

Serves 6
Preparation 2 minutes
Cooking about 12 minutes

METRIC/IMPERIAL	*AMERICAN*
225 g/8 oz best-quality butter, well chilled	*2 sticks + 2 tbsp best-quality butter, well chilled*
1 lemon	*1 lemon*
3 very fresh egg yolks	*3 very fresh egg yolks*
salt and white pepper	*salt and white pepper*

Dice the butter. Squeeze the juice from the lemon and strain out the seeds.

Put the egg yolks into a heavy-bottomed saucepan or the top of a double boiler. Add 1 or 2 tablespoons of water, a pinch of salt and pepper. Mix the yolks without whisking (1).

Heat some water in a large saucepan or the bottom of the double boiler. When the water is on the point of boiling, put the pan containing the egg yolks into it and lower the heat so the water is just gently simmering.

Whisk the egg mixture until it thickens, then add the butter one piece at a time, whisking constantly. Wait until each piece of butter is incorporated before adding the next and whisk the mixture until all the butter is absorbed and it is thick and smooth (2).

Remove from the heat and whisk in the lemon juice (3). Adjust the seasoning. Serve with poached or grilled (broiled) fish or steamed vegetables.

Variations: add 1 tablespoon of Dijon mustard for a classic sauce moutarde to accompany oily fish such as mackerel, or stir in some whipped cream to make a light sauce mousseline for sole.

For a sauce maltaise to serve with asparagus, replace the lemon with an uncoated or scrubbed blood orange and add the grated zest as well as the juice.

BEURRE BLANC

White butter sauce

Serves 4
Preparation 10 minutes
Cooking about 15 minutes

METRIC/IMPERIAL	*AMERICAN*
8 shallots, finely chopped	*8 shallots, finely chopped*
2 tbsp white wine vinegar	*2 tbsp white wine vinegar*
4 tbsp dry white wine	*$\frac{1}{4}$ cup dry white wine*
250 g/8$\frac{1}{2}$ oz butter, cut into pieces and chilled	*2 sticks + 3 tbsp butter, cut into pieces and chilled*
salt and white pepper	*salt and white pepper*

Place the shallots in a heavy-bottomed saucepan and add the vinegar and wine (1). Cook over a moderate heat, stirring, until the shallots are reduced to a purée. Strain to obtain about 1 tablespoon of liquid and return it to the pan.

Lower the heat and add the butter one piece at a time, whisking constantly (2). The butter should melt to make a thick and creamy sauce.

Season the sauce, still whisking, and increase the heat slightly until the sauce is very hot (3).

Serve immediately in a sauce boat which has been warmed but is not too hot or the sauce will curdle. If unable to serve at once, keep the sauce warm in a bain-marie over a gentle heat and whisk it from time to time.

Variations: malt vinegar may be used instead of wine vinegar; its acidity will impart an interesting flavour to the sauce.

A tablespoon of cream may be stirred into the sauce just before the butter is added.

Tarragon is a popular flavouring, but other herbs are often used, especially fresh mint, basil, parsley, young sorrel leaves or dill. Several pinches of grated zest from an uncoated or scrubbed lemon or orange provide an interesting flavour in a sauce for fish, as do puréed anchovy fillets. Red wine may be used in place of white for a sauce to accompany grilled (broiled) meat. Use champagne if the sauce is to be served as an accompaniment to veal sweetbreads.

1

2

3

Notes: the shallots should be chopped by hand and not in a food processor.

For a frothier sauce add 3 tablespoons of warm water at the end, whisking constantly.

It is easier to control the temperature if the sauce is cooked in a bain-marie.

Some chefs recommend whisking this sauce vigorously over a brisk heat rather than cooking it slowly over a low heat, in which case the butter should be very cold.

SAUCE BÉARNAISE

Egg, shallot and tarragon butter sauce

Serves 6
Preparation 10 minutes
Cooking about 12 minutes

METRIC/IMPERIAL	*AMERICAN*
4 shallots, finely chopped	*4 shallots, finely chopped*
2 tbsp chopped tarragon	*2 tbsp chopped tarragon*
2 tbsp snipped chervil	*2 tbsp snipped chervil*
sprig of thyme	*sprig of thyme*
bay leaf	*bay leaf*
4 tbsp white wine vinegar	*$\frac{1}{4}$ cup white wine vinegar*
4 tbsp white wine	*$\frac{1}{4}$ cup white wine*
2 egg yolks	*2 egg yolks*
125 g/4$\frac{1}{2}$ oz butter, finely diced	*9 tbsp butter, finely diced*
3–4 drops of lemon juice	*3–4 drops of lemon juice*
salt and coarsely ground black pepper	*salt and coarsely ground black pepper*

Put the shallots in a small saucepan with 3 pinches of ground black pepper, half the tarragon, half the chervil, the thyme and the bay leaf (1). Add the vinegar and white wine with a pinch of salt and boil to reduce until 1 tablespoon of liquid remains.

Remove from the heat and leave to cool, then strain and return the liquid to the saucepan or put into the top of a double boiler.

Add the egg yolks and whisk well, then add 1 tablespoon of cold water. Put the pan in a larger saucepan of hot but not boiling water, or over the bottom of the double boiler.

Add the butter a few pieces at a time, whisking constantly; the mixture should be very smooth after each addition of butter (2).

When the sauce is thick and smooth like mayonnaise, add the remainder of the tarragon and chervil. Add several drops of lemon juice, taste and adjust the seasoning (3). Serve with grilled (broiled) meat or fish.

Variations: Add 1 tablespoon onion purée, 2 tablespoons snipped fresh mint or some spinach purée to the basic sauce.

1

2

3

Notes: it is important to measure the ingredients accurately and to whisk constantly.

If the sauce begins to curdle, remove it from the bain-marie or hot water and plunge the base of the pan in cold water. Alternatively put several drops of cold water in a fresh bowl and beat the curdled sauce into it. When it is smooth again, return it to the bain-marie. To avoid any risk of curdling, add no more than $\frac{1}{2}$ teaspoon of flour along with the egg yolks.

SAUCE VIERGE

Uncooked tomato sauce

Makes 500 ml/16 fl oz/2 cups
Preparation 15 minutes, 2 hours ahead

METRIC/IMPERIAL	AMERICAN
4 tomatoes, peeled, deseeded and cut into tiny dice	4 tomatoes, peeled, deseeded and cut into tiny dice
2 garlic cloves, chopped	2 garlic cloves, chopped
small bunch of chives, finely chopped	small bunch of chives, finely chopped
12 fresh tarragon leaves, finely chopped	12 fresh tarragon leaves, finely chopped
8 fresh basil leaves, finely chopped	8 fresh basil leaves, finely chopped
juice of 1 lemon	juice of 1 lemon
200 ml/7 fl oz olive oil	1 cup olive oil
salt and pepper	salt and pepper

In a bowl, combine the tomatoes, garlic, chopped herbs, lemon juice and oil. Season with salt and pepper. Mix and leave to marinate for 2 hours. Stir again just before serving.

This sauce goes well with cold cooked vegetables and steamed or poached fish.

SAUCE PIZZAIOLA

Spicy tomato sauce

Makes about 500 ml/16 fl oz/2 cups
Preparation 15 minutes
Cooking 40 minutes

METRIC/IMPERIAL	AMERICAN
3 tbsp olive oil	3 tbsp olive oil
2 onions, chopped	2 onions, chopped
1 green sweet pepper, halved, deseeded and cut into strips	1 green sweet pepper, halved, deseeded and cut into strips
3 garlic cloves, chopped	3 garlic cloves, chopped
4 large tomatoes, chopped	4 large tomatoes, chopped
2 tbsp tomato purée	2 tbsp tomato paste
bay leaf	bay leaf
1 tbsp dried marjoram	1 tbsp dried marjoram
7 basil leaves, chopped	7 basil leaves, chopped
caster sugar	superfine sugar
Tabasco sauce	Tabasco sauce
salt and pepper	salt and pepper

Heat the oil in a saucepan and add the onions and sweet pepper strips. Cook them, stirring, over a low heat for 8 minutes. When they are completely soft, add the garlic and season with salt and pepper. Cook, stirring, for 2 minutes.

Add the tomatoes with all their juice to the pan along with the tomato purée (paste), bay leaf, marjoram and basil. Cover and simmer very gently for 30 minutes, stirring occasionally.

Discard the bay leaf. Add a pinch of sugar, and season to taste with salt, pepper and Tabasco sauce. Use for pasta or to accompany grilled (broiled) meats and meat croquettes.

SAUCE AUX FRUITS

Mixed fruit sauce

Serves 4
Preparation 10 minutes

METRIC/IMPERIAL	AMERICAN
250 g/8½ oz canned apricot halves in syrup, drained	1 cup canned apricot halves in syrup, drained
200 g/7 oz strawberries	1 cup strawberries
½ mango, diced	½ mango, diced
1 tbsp caster sugar	1 tbsp superfine sugar
1 tsp framboise or other raspberry liqueur	1 tsp framboise or other raspberry liqueur

Blend the apricots to a purée in a food processor and set aside in a bowl. Blend the strawberries and mango together in the food processor.

Mix the 2 purées together, adding the sugar and liqueur. Whisk for 2 minutes and chill.

Use to coat a rice pudding or ice cream.

SAUERKRAUT

Choucroute

see also: *cabbage* *curing* *salting*

White cabbage which has been preserved by finely shredding and salting it so that it ferments is known as sauerkraut. This ancient means of preserving the goodness of vegetables for the winter is prevalent throughout Central and northern Europe. According to local recipes, it may be flavoured with juniper berries, caraway, fennel or even quince or beetroot.

Better delicatessens sell raw sauerkraut and it is readily available in cans. It is usually rinsed before use, unless a really sour flavour is required, and usually needs to be teased with a fork to separate the strands. It may be lightly steamed and served as a vegetable accompaniment or braised with flavouring items such as onions, potatoes, apples, white wine, bacon or other cured meats.

Sauerkraut is more digestible cooked than raw. Plain sauerkraut eaten as a vegetable accompaniment is low in calories: 100 g/$3\frac{1}{2}$ oz contains only 27. However, it should be avoided by anyone on a low-salt diet.

CHOUCROUTE ALSACIENNE

Sauerkraut with assorted meats and sausages

Serves 8–10
Preparation 20 minutes, 12 hours ahead
Cooking about 4 hours

METRIC/IMPERIAL	*AMERICAN*
2 kg/$4\frac{1}{2}$ lb raw sauerkraut	*$4\frac{1}{2}$ lb ($8\frac{1}{2}$ cups) raw sauerkraut*
3 tbsp lard	*3 tbsp lard*
2 onions, chopped	*2 onions, chopped*
2 tbsp juniper berries	*2 tbsp juniper berries*
1 bottle (750 ml/27 fl oz) of Riesling	*1 bottle (75 cl) Riesling*
700 g/$1\frac{2}{3}$ lb smoked streaky bacon, in one piece	*$1\frac{2}{3}$ lb country-style bacon, in one piece*
1 smoked pork chop	*1 smoked pork chop*
1 lightly salted ham knuckle	*1 lightly salted ham hock*
1 knackwurst sausage	*1 knackwurst or other large garlic sausage*
8 frankfurters	*8 frankfurters*
pepper	*pepper*

Rinse the sauerkraut in cold water, then plunge it into a large pan of boiling water. Drain it immediately and disentangle it with a fork.

Heat the lard in a very large, flameproof casserole and cook the onions, stirring, until they are soft and translucent. Add the sauerkraut along with the juniper berries. Heat gently, lifting the sauerkraut from time to time with a fork. Pour half the wine over it and season with pepper.

Add the bacon, smoked pork chop and ham knuckle (hock), pushing them well down so that they are buried in the sauerkraut. Cover the casserole and simmer gently for 3 hours, adding the rest of the wine a little at a time.

After this time, add the knackwurst and cook for a further 15 minutes. Add the frankfurters and cook for 15 minutes longer.

To serve, remove the meats and slice them. Arrange the sauerkraut on a large, warmed serving plate and garnish with sliced meats, along with boiled potatoes if wished.
To drink: Riesling.

SAUSAGE

Saucisse, saucisson, cervelas

see also:
black pudding
brioche
charcuterie
chorizo
pâté
paupiette
pork
stuffing
terrine

Originally a method of preserving the scraps of meat which had not been cured in other ways, sausages basically consist of chopped or ground meat mixed with flavourings and, sometimes, preservatives, stuffed into a tube of animal intestine. Most of the sausages consumed in Britain and North America are eaten while still fresh, whereas those preferred in many European countries are cured by a wide range of traditional methods which cause the sausages to mature to full and complex flavours.

FRESH SAUSAGES

Most fresh sausages are made of coarsely ground pork or beef and may sometimes include a cereal filler and preservatives. They are usually stuffed into a length of intestine which is tied off at regular intervals to produce the familiar 'links'. Inferior brands may use synthetic skins, recognizable by the bulkier knots between the links, but these are usually fairly indigestible. Better sausages, on the other hand, are made from pure quality meat and may be flavoured with herbs .

The traditional CUMBERLAND SAUSAGE from the north of England is studded with cracked peppercorns and made in a continuous spiral, while the long, coarse-textured French SAUCISSE DE TOULOUSE is subtly seasoned with garlic and spices. Other varieties of French *saucisse* may be flavoured with anything from nuts to champagne and this habit is now spreading into gourmet sausages made in Britain and the USA. German varieties include the pale WEISSWURST and BRATWURST made from veal. So-called ITALIAN SAUSAGE in the USA is a coarse-textured and highly seasoned pork link sausage that may be spiced with chillies or sweetly flavoured with fennel and garlic. Tiny COCKTAIL SAUSAGES or CHIPOLATAS make ideal party food and are often also served as a garnish for roast or braised poultry.

Fresh SAUSAGE MEAT is sold loose by weight for use in stuffings, pies and other baked items. It is very easy to mix in flavourings such as chopped parsley, shallots, pistachio nuts or even truffles.

Fresh sausages and sausage meat must be used within a day or two as ground meat does not keep well. They should have a good clean colour, be fairly stiff and not too moist.

Before cooking sausages, prick the skin all over so that they do not burst as the contents expand. Pork sausages, in particular, must be well cooked through and they are usually fried, grilled (broiled), barbecued or braised whole. However, some, like the German veal sausages, may first be poached.

Sausages are a traditional breakfast item in Britain and North America; they may also be served with sautéed or mashed potatoes and fried onions, with seasoned, cooked cabbage or as part of a mixed grill or 'fry-up'. They may even be baked in batter to make the British dish, 'toad-in-the-hole'. The French like their *saucisses* with fried apples, or baked in a brioche dough crust.

COOKED SAUSAGES

Those sausages which have already been cooked in some way may be ready to eat or may require some further cooking.

Among the most familiar cooked sausage worldwide is the long, thin German FRANKFURTER; traditionally, it is made of a highly spiced mixture of pork and beef and is lightly smoked. The mild-flavoured American frankfurter or HOT DOG may be made from beef only and is often not smoked at all. Both traditional German and American frankfurters are generally heated gently in water prior to serving. The thicker knackwurst, flavoured with garlic and sometimes cumin, is very similar and, like the frankfurter, is traditionally sold in linked pairs.

The large French *saucisson cuit*, like the garlic-flavoured *saucisse de Paris*, is generally either cooked in dishes such as *choucroute alsacienne*, baked in brioche dough, or sliced and served as hors d'oeuvres or snacks. The short, thick garlic-flavoured *cervelas* is usually fairly mature and dry and may be lightly smoked. It has a full, rich flavour which works well in dishes like pot-au-feu. Its British equivalent, the SAVELOY, is fresher and a great deal less distinguished.

The French also make a speciality of sausages based on offal (variety meats), such as *andouillettes* and the larger, darker-skinned *andouilles*. Blood is also used to make sausages, like the famed French *boudin noir*, German BLUTWURST, Spanish MORCILLA, and the BLACK PUDDINGS which are still a feature of daily fare in the north of England and Scotland. Blood sausages are generally sliced and grilled (broiled) or fried. WHITE PUDDINGS contain oatmeal and fat, or they may be made with white meat such as poultry, rabbit or pale pork.

The Scottish national dish is the HAGGIS which is made from a mixture of sheep's offal (variety meats), oatmeal and herbs boiled in the sheep's stomach. Because of its size and density it needs lengthy steaming to reheat it before serving with its traditional accompaniments of 'tatties and neeps', mashed potatoes and swede (rutabaga).

Among the cooked sausages are a whole range of large slicing sausages, such as the Italian MORTADELLA and North American BOLOGNA or BALONEY. Studded with cubes of pork fat, they make delicious additions to plates of mixed hors d'oeuvres or antipasto and are excellent in sandwiches. They may also be flavoured with wine, coriander or pistachio nuts. German variants include JAGDWURST and larger BIERWURST which is flavoured with garlic and studded with pieces of ham.

Many sausages made with very smooth mixtures, like LIVER SAUSAGE, liverwurst and German *leberkase*, are more like pâtés and may be sliced and fried or used as spreads.

CURED SAUSAGES

Paradoxically, those sausages made of raw ingredients and dried, but never cooked, are those which are most likely to be eaten without further cooking.

The most important of the cured sausages are the SALAMI family. The Italians have literally thousands of regional types of salami which vary widely in texture, flavour and degree of dryness. Some may also be lightly smoked. They are usually based on pork but can sometimes contain beef, veal or even wild boar. GENOA SALAMI contains a high proportion of veal and a great deal of pork fat to compensate, while the salami of the Parma region is made using the same fine meat as the local hams, with little added fat and seasoning, and matured only for a matter of a few months. The salamis of southern Italy tend to be highly spiced with chillies. Other flavourings include wine and fennel and many are studded with peppercorns or pistachios.

Danish and Hungarian salami is also widely exported, the former characterized by its mild flavour and bright pink colour and the latter by its paprika content. The French *saucisse de Lyons* is also more or less a salami, as is the long, thin, spicy Spanish *chorizo*. The North American CERVELAT or SUMMER SAUSAGE is made from pork or beef, or a mixture of both, with herbs and spices. Air-dried and then smoked, it is finer-textured and less heavily seasoned than salami but is otherwise very similar.

Salamis are almost always sliced for use, and the casing is usually inedible and must be peeled off before the salami is sliced. The drier the sausage, the more thinly it should be sliced. Cutting at an oblique angle produces larger slices and more attractive shapes.

Sausages of all sorts have a high fat and cholesterol content and the cured types also usually contain a great deal of salt. The average energy content of fresh sausages is 200–500 calories per 100 g/3½ oz and 2 average slices of salami contain 150 calories.

SALADE DE LENTILLES AU CERVELAS

Saveloy and lentil salad

Serves 4
Preparation 10 minutes
Cooking about 1 hour

METRIC/IMPERIAL	*AMERICAN*
250 g/8½ oz lentils	*1½ cups lentils*
1 carrot	*1 carrot*
1 onion	*1 onion*
1 clove	*1 clove*
bouquet garni	*bouquet garni*
2 cervelas or saveloys	*2 cervelas or other cooked garlic-flavored sausages*
4–5 tbsp corn oil	*4–5 tbsp corn oil*
2 tbsp white wine vinegar	*2 tbsp white wine vinegar*
2 shallots, finely chopped	*2 shallots, finely chopped*
4 tbsp chopped parsley	*¼ cup chopped parsley*
salt and pepper	*salt and pepper*

Put the lentils in a large pan of water, bring to the boil and simmer for 15 minutes. Drain.

Return the lentils to the rinsed-out saucepan with the carrot, the onion stuck with the clove and the bouquet garni. Add water to cover, season well and cook over a moderate heat for 40 minutes. Drain the cooked lentils.

Meanwhile, poach the sausages gently for 10 minutes. Make a shallot vinaigrette by whisking the oil and vinegar with seasoning to taste and stirring in the shallots.

Put the drained lentils into a deep dish. Drain the sausages, slice them and add them to the lentils. Pour the vinaigrette over and stir well. Sprinkle with parsley and serve warm.

To drink: a light, dry white wine, such as a Riesling.

SAUCISSON CHAUD EN BRIOCHE

Hot saucisson in brioche dough

Serves 4
Preparation 5 minutes, about 1½ hours ahead
Cooking about 55 minutes

METRIC/IMPERIAL	AMERICAN
1 cooked saucisson, preferably from Lyons, with truffles	1 cooked sausage, preferably from Lyons, with truffles
225 g/½ lb brioche dough	½ lb brioche dough
flour, for dusting	flour, for dusting
1 egg yolk, lightly beaten	1 egg yolk, lightly beaten

Bring a large pan of salted water to the boil. Put the sausage into it and cook at a gentle simmer for 30 minutes. Drain and leave to cool.

On a floured work surface, roll out the brioche dough to make a rectangle that is slightly longer than the sausage.

Using a small, pointed knife, skin the sausage. Sprinkle it lightly with flour and place it on the dough. Roll it up in the dough and fold up the ends, pinching to seal the edges. Leave to rise for 30 minutes.

Preheat the oven to 210C/415F/gas 6–7. Brush the dough with egg and bake for 25 minutes.

Serve hot with a curly endive salad dressed with a mustard vinaigrette.

SAUTÉING

see also:
frying
stewing

From the French for 'to jump', the process of sautéing involves cooking food uncovered over a high heat until browned, stirring vigorously and possibly shaking the pan so that the food is rapidly and uniformly cooked. Food to be sautéed is usually fairly small or chopped into uniform pieces. A sauce may be made by deglazing the pan with a suitable liquid.

The name *sauté* is also given to a dish in which larger items of food are first browned over a high heat and then gently simmered in added liquid with flavouring ingredients.

Successful sautéing can be effected in any large frying pan or heavy-bottomed saucepan. However, specially designed sauté pans with high sides to accommodate the vigorous movement of the ingredients as well as any subsequent simmering, together with tight-fitting lids, make sautéing very easy. Non-stick sauté pans brown food with little or no added fat.

SAUTÉ DE DINDE À L'AIL

Sauté of turkey with garlic

Serves 4
Preparation 10 minutes
Cooking about 15 minutes

METRIC/IMPERIAL	AMERICAN
2 tbsp oil	2 tbsp oil
1 large onion, sliced	1 large onion, sliced
2 chipolatas, cut into chunks	2 small pork link sausages, cut into chunks
550 g/1¼ lb boneless turkey breast, cut into small pieces	1¼ lb boneless turkey breast, cut into small pieces
4 garlic cloves, chopped	4 garlic cloves, chopped
3 tomatoes, sliced	3 tomatoes, sliced
8 basil leaves, snipped	8 basil leaves, snipped
salt and pepper	salt and pepper

Heat the oil in a sauté pan over a moderate heat. Add the onion and cook it until golden, stirring often. Add the sausages and brown them, then add the turkey pieces and garlic and cook until all the ingredients are brown, stirring frequently. Add the tomatoes, mix and simmer for 5 minutes. Transfer to a deep, warmed dish and sprinkle over the basil. Serve with rice.

SAVORY

Sarriette

see also:
bean
cheese
herbs
marinating

A highly perfumed herb which originated in southern Europe, savory has a flavour akin to both thyme and mint. There are two main types: milder summer savory is normally used in cooking, especially with legumes and pulses; the coarser winter variety, with narrow leaves, is mainly used to wrap goats' cheese.

FÈVES À LA SARRIETTE

Broad or fava beans with savory

Serves 4
Preparation 20 minutes
Cooking about 35 minutes

METRIC/IMPERIAL	AMERICAN
450 g/1 lb fresh broad beans	1 lb fresh fava or lima beans
small bunch of summer savory	small bunch of summer savory
30 g/1 oz butter	2 tbsp butter
100 ml/3½ fl oz crème fraîche or sour cream	½ cup crème fraîche or sour cream
salt	salt

Shell and skin the beans and put them in a large saucepan. Add the savory, ½ teaspoon of salt and water to cover. Bring to the boil and then simmer gently for about 30 minutes or until the beans are tender but still firm.

Drain the beans, discarding the savory, and put them into a sauté pan. Set it over a low heat and let the beans dry out for 2 minutes.

Dot with the butter and stir until it melts, then add the cream. Mix carefully so as not to crush the beans.

Serve to accompany roast lamb or veal.

SCALLION

see Spring onion

SCALLOP

Coquille Saint-Jacques

see also:
nage
oyster
roe
seaweed

Varieties of the scallop, a large bivalve mollusc, are found in many of the world's waters. Characterized by their fan-shaped shell and the fact that they uniquely move around by opening and closing their shells, they usually measure about 10–15 cm/4–6 in and contain about 85 g/3 oz of fine, white, delicately flavoured, but firm-textured, meat. The pale pink roe, known as the coral, turns orange-red close to breeding time.

There are several principal varieties: the GREAT SCALLOP and the smaller, paler and even firmer-fleshed ICELAND SCALLOP are the types most familiar in Britain, while the smaller MEDITERRANEAN OR PILGRIM SCALLOP is popular in France. The Atlantic waters of North America produce the large SEA SCALLOP, as well as the tiny, rich and sweet QUEEN SCALLOP and BAY or CAPE SCALLOP which may be eaten raw. From the Gulf of Mexico and the south Atlantic comes the CALICO SCALLOP, which is slightly larger than the Bay scallop but not as sweet.

Scallops are available fresh or frozen all year round, but are at their best fresh from September to May. If bought in the shell, thoroughly clean the shell with a stiff brush under running water. Open it with a knife as you would an oyster, or place it curved side down in a heavy-based frying pan over a high heat. Reserve the curved shells for cooking and serving the scallops or other seafood and fish dishes.

Scallops may be eaten raw in salads or marinated in olive oil with lemon juice and chervil. They are, however, most often served cooked, but care must be taken not to overcook scallops as they toughen very readily. Because of their firm texture, they deep fry well and are excellent skewered on kebabs. They may also be baked *en papillote*, grilled (broiled) or barbecued, steamed or poached gently in an aromatic *nage*. Cooked scallops are then often served in a cream or *beurre blanc* sauce in the curved shell.

Scallops are rich in iodine and in vitamins A and B and 100 g/3½ oz contains 80 calories.

COQUILLES SAINT-JACQUES À LA VAPEUR D'ALGUES

Scallops steamed with seaweed

Serves 6
Preparation 20 minutes
Cooking 10 minutes

METRIC/IMPERIAL	AMERICAN
2–3 handfuls of fresh edible seaweed	2–3 handfuls of fresh edible seaweed
18 shelled scallops, preferably with coral roe	18 shucked sea scallops, preferably with coral roe
200 g/7 oz butter	2 sticks butter
ground white pepper	ground white pepper

Coquilles Saint-Jacques à la vapeur d'algues (Scallops steamed with seaweed)

Preheat the oven to 220C/425F/gas 7 and cut out 6 large squares of foil.

Wash the seaweed very carefully in running water. Divide the seaweed among the 6 pieces of foil and put 3 scallops on top of each. Season lightly with pepper and dot with butter.

Wrap up the foil envelopes loosely, sealing the edges carefully, and bake for 10 minutes.

Remove the foil envelopes from the oven. Open them and put the scallops and seaweed on 6 warmed plates. Pour the cooking juices over them, add a little pepper if needed and serve.

To drink: a well-chilled, full-bodied white wine such as a Graves.

SALADE DE SAINT-JACQUES

Scallop salad

Serves 4
Preparation 20 minutes
Cooking 3 minutes

METRIC/IMPERIAL	AMERICAN
200 g/7 oz courgettes, thinly sliced	7 oz zucchini, thinly sliced
12 shelled scallops, sliced	12 shucked sea scallops, sliced
2 tbsp lemon juice	2 tbsp lemon juice
3 tbsp olive oil	3 tbsp olive oil
1 tbsp chopped parsley	1 tbsp chopped parsley
1 tbsp vinegar	1 tbsp vinegar
2 lettuce hearts, separated into leaves	2 lettuce hearts, separated into leaves
salt and pepper	salt and pepper

Combine the courgette (zucchini) and scallop slices in a deep dish and season with salt and pepper. Sprinkle with the lemon juice and stir well to mix. Leave to marinate for 10 minutes.

At the end of this time, microwave on High for 3 minutes, stirring half-way through.

Strain off the cooking juices into a bowl and add the oil, parsley and vinegar. Season well and whisk to emulsify the vinaigrette.

Spread out the lettuce leaves in the bottom of a serving dish and arrange the cooled scallops and courgettes (zucchini) on top, then pour the vinaigrette over them, turning them gently so they are well coated.

SCAMPI

see Langoustine

SEA BREAM OR PORGY

Daurade, dorade, pagre

see also: fish

A marine fish found in many warm and cooler waters and characterized by its oval body and blunt head, the sea bream has long been considered one of the tastiest of fish.

There are several principal species. The true SEA BREAM OR RED PORGY (*pagre*) is found on both sides of the Atlantic as well as in Oriental waters, while the fish considered to have the finest flavour, the silvery-scaled GILT HEAD BREAM (*daurade royale*) with a golden crescent between its eyes, is native to the waters of the Mediterranean and Bay of Biscay. The slightly smaller RED SEA BREAM (*dorade commune*), which is dark pink in colour with drier flesh but a good flavour, and the slightly less distinguished, dark-coloured BLACK SEA BREAM (*dorade grise*) are the most common members of the family in European Atlantic waters. The dark-striped SHEEPSHEAD and the much larger NORTHERN PORGY are common on the American side of the Atlantic and have tasty, firm flesh which may be bony.

When buying sea bream look for bright, shiny scales and eyes and fresh-coloured gills. The firm flesh lends itself to all manner of cooking methods. It may be pan-fried, poached, baked or grilled (broiled) with herbs, such as thyme, and responds well to barbecuing. The Japanese favour it raw in *sashimi*.

Sea bream is one of the leanest of fish: 100 g/ 3½ oz contains only 77 calories.

DAURADE AU VIN BLANC

Sea bream in white wine

Serves 6
Preparation 40 minutes
Cooking about 40 minutes

METRIC/IMPERIAL	AMERICAN
1 sea bream, weighing about 1.35 kg/3 lb, cleaned and scaled	1 sea bream or porgy, weighing about 3 lb, dressed
55 g/2 oz butter	4 tbsp butter

2 carrots, chopped	*2 carrots, chopped*
2 onions, chopped	*2 onions, chopped*
1 garlic clove, chopped	*1 garlic clove, chopped*
2 shallots, chopped	*2 shallots, chopped*
2 stalks of celery, trimmed and chopped	*2 sticks of celery, trimmed and chopped*
140 g/5 oz mushrooms, chopped	*5 oz mushrooms, chopped*
sprig of thyme	*sprig of thyme*
bay leaf	*bay leaf*
400 ml/14 fl oz aromatic white wine, such as Muscadet	*1¾ cups aromatic white wine, such as Muscadet*
1 lemon, sliced	*1 lemon, sliced*
salt and pepper	*salt and pepper*

Preheat the oven to 230C/450F/gas 8. Season the fish inside and out with salt and pepper.

Melt the butter in a saucepan. Add all the chopped vegetables with the thyme and bay leaf and cook over a moderate heat for about 15 minutes, stirring from time to time.

Spread this mixture over the bottom of a baking dish and place the fish on top. Add the white wine and enough water to make the liquid reach halfway up the sides of the fish. Place the lemon slices on top of the fish.

Bake for 15 minutes. When it begins to brown, baste frequently with the cooking juices. Turn the oven off, cover the dish with foil and leave in the oven for about 10 minutes. Serve very hot, straight from the dish.

SEALING

see also:
frying
grilling
meat
roasting
sautéing

In cooking, this term is mostly applied to the rapid cooking of meat over a high heat to form an impermeable crust which will keep in the juices. This is usually done by grilling (broiling), barbecuing, frying or sautéing, but roasts are also frequently sealed by initial roasting at the highest possible temperature.

SEASONING

see also:
condiment
pepper
salt
sauce
spices

The practice of adding various ingredients, such as salt, pepper, oil, vinegar, lemon juice, aromatics, spices or condiments, seasoning is meant to bring out, augment or lift the flavour of a dish. Often the term simply refers to the addition of salt and pepper during preparation, cooking or at the table.

It is wise to season with caution, tasting regularly and adding a pinch at a time as required. To bring out the best in a dish or a sauce, different quantities of the various spices and condiments are obviously required. As a rule, however, they should never mask the flavour of the basic ingredients and no one seasoning addition should stand out.

Green salads and raw vegetables should be seasoned at the last moment, but salads containing rice, potatoes or pasta benefit from being seasoned in advance as the starchy ingredients readily absorb any added flavour.

Steamed or boiled vegetables, fish cooked in broth, and white meats always need to be seasoned a little more heavily, as do dishes to be served cold or chilled.

SEAWEED

Algues

see also:
fish
food additive
iodine

Many types of seaweed are edible and form part of the culinary tradition of several cultures. They are an excellent source of proteins, minerals and vitamins. The French serve some types of seaweed as vegetable accompaniments or steam fish on a bed of seaweed so that it acquires a very pleasant flavour of the sea. However, the Scots, Welsh and Irish and the Japanese have made the most of seaweed.

The Scots and Irish use reddish-purple LAVER, coarser DULSE, nutritious KELP and delicate CARRAGHEEN or IRISH MOSS in soups and sauces, served as vegetables with boiled potatoes, or mixed with finely ground oats and baked into oatcakes and savoury biscuits or crackers. The traditional Welsh 'laver bread' is in fact not a bread but just puréed, cooked seaweed.

About 10% of Japanese food production comprises seaweed: laver or *nori* is dried and compressed into wafer-thin sheets and, after toasting, is used to wrap balls of vinegared rice or fish to make *sushi*, or it is ground into a salt-like condiment; kelp or *kombu* is used to flavour stocks, sauces and rice and vegetable dishes.

In Europe and North America seaweed is mainly used by the food industry in gelling agents, emulsifiers and food colourings. However, fresh seaweed is becoming increasingly available from good fishmongers and speciality food stores. Crisp and tasty MARSH SAMPHIRE or SALICORNIA is one European variety of seaweed considered to be a delicacy. After careful washing young plants may be served raw with a vinaigrette, or cooked to be eaten as a vegetable, dressed with melted butter and seasoning.

Many health food shops stock dried seaweed which can be used in mixed or green salads, sauces, rice or vegetable soups and pastries. The seaweed is easily rehydrated by the addition of a little water. Japanese dried, chopped *kombu* makes an excellent sauce for pasta or raw vegetables, and *wakame* gives an unusual depth of flavour to meat broths.

BAR À LA VAPEUR D'ALGUES

Steamed sea bass with seaweed

Serves 2 or 3
Preparation 15 minutes
Cooking 20 minutes

METRIC/IMPERIAL	AMERICAN
1 whole sea bass, weighing about 800 g/$1\frac{3}{4}$ lb	1 whole sea bass, weighing about $1\frac{3}{4}$ lb
2 generous handfuls of fresh edible seaweed	2 generous handfuls of fresh edible seaweed
salt and pepper	salt and pepper

Clean the fish and remove the dorsal fins, but do not scale it. Season the fish inside and out with salt and pepper. Wash the seaweed carefully in several changes of water.

Spread half the wet seaweed over the bottom of an oval casserole. Place the fish on the bed of seaweed, then cover it with the remaining seaweed. Cover the casserole and cook it over a moderate to high heat for 20 minutes.

To serve, place the fish on a platter and remove the skin: leaving the scales intact should allow the skin to come away easily. Lift off the fillets and season them to taste. Serve a fresh tomato coulis or mayonnaise to accompany.
Note: this method of cooking enhances the flavour of any delicately flavoured fish.

SEMOLINA

Semoule

see also: cereal, corn, couscous, pasta and noodles, rice, wheat

Various types of semolina are made by grinding different cereal grains. The most familiar YELLOW SEMOLINA is made from durum wheat and is the basis of all commercially produced pasta. WHITE SEMOLINA is ground from rice, and other types come from corn and buckwheat.

The best quality and finest wheat semolina is made using just the kernels and it is this that is used for pasta. The semolina that is used in cooking is made from wheat from which the bran and most of the germ have been removed.

Fine semolina, called FARINA in the USA, can be used to thicken soups and is an excellent binding agent in mixtures for croquettes and rissoles. It is also used for making puddings, soufflés, cakes and custards and is a feature of sweet dishes and confectionery in the Middle East and India. More coarsely ground semolina is the basis for dishes such as couscous in which the grains are steamed to make them swell.

As fine semolina is easily digested as well as being highly nutritious, it is a popular baby and invalid food and a breakfast cereal; 100 g/$3\frac{1}{2}$ oz cooked semolina contains 380 calories.

SESAME

see also: condiments, fats and oils

An annual plant grown widely in the Orient, sesame produces small seeds which have many uses in cooking. In the Middle East they are ground with sugar and almonds to make the sweetmeat known as *halva*, and are mixed into a paste with lemon juice and seasonings to produce the condiment *tahini*. This is used in salads, on grilled meat, and with crudités, but is probably best known blended with chickpeas in the traditional dip *hummus*. The seeds are also used in baking as a topping for bread, etc.

Pressed sesame seeds yield a sweet, delicately flavoured oil which is mainly used as a seasoning, but is also a popular cooking medium.

SHAD

Alose

A member of the herring family which is born in river water, grows to adulthood in sea water but returns to fresh water to spawn, shad is

see also:
court-bouillon
fish
roe
sorrel

generally available between March and June.

There are several types: the GREAT or ALLIS SHAD is reared on fish farms in the Garonne and can be up to 60 cm/2 ft in length; the smaller TWAITE SHAD (*alose finte*) is generally caught at sea or in estuaries; LAKE SHAD is popular in the north of Italy. The AMERICAN SHAD is more highly prized than its European counterparts.

Although it has a great many fine bones, the flesh is delicate and slightly oily. If cooked quickly and gently, by grilling (broiling) or barbecuing, or by braising or poaching in white wine or a court-bouillon, the bones will remain attached to the backbone, but care must be taken as the flesh disintegrates readily. Sorrel, as a stuffing or in a cream sauce, is the classic accompaniment for shad.

Shad roe is considered a great delicacy and held by many to be an aphrodisiac. It is best served freshly sautéed on brown toast.

ALOSE À L'OSEILLE

Shad with sorrel

Serves 4
Preparation 20 minutes
Cooking about 30 minutes

METRIC/IMPERIAL	AMERICAN
4–5 shallots, finely chopped	4–5 shallots, finely chopped
150 ml/¼ pt dry white wine	⅔ cup dry white wine
200 ml/7 fl oz crème fraîche or whipping cream	1 cup crème fraîche or whipping cream
100 g/3½ oz butter	1 stick butter
court-bouillon or fish stock	court-bouillon, fish stock or clam juice
1 whole shad, weighing about 800 g–1 kg/ 1¾–2¼ lb, gutted and scaled	1 whole shad, weighing about 1¾–2¼ lb, dressed
450 g/1 lb fresh sorrel leaves, trimmed and shredded	1 lb fresh sorrel leaves, trimmed and shredded
salt and pepper	salt and pepper
sprigs of parsley, to garnish	sprigs of parsley, to garnish

Cook the shallots in a pan with the wine over a moderate heat for 8–10 minutes, stirring frequently. Stir in the cream and cook gently for another 10 minutes. Whisk in half the butter in small pieces. Season and set aside.

In a fish kettle or large, oval casserole, heat enough court-bouillon or stock to cover the fish. When it comes to the boil, put the shad in it and allow to return to the boil. Reduce the heat and poach gently for 10 minutes.

Meanwhile, melt the remainder of the butter in a saucepan, add the sorrel and cover. Cook gently for 10 minutes, then add the shallot mixture and stir well.

Drain the cooked shad, place it on a warmed serving dish and garnish it with the parsley. Serve the sorrel sauce separately.

SHALLOT

Echalote

see also:
butter
garlic
onion
sauce
wine

A vegetable from the same family as onion and garlic, the flavour of the shallot is more subtle and piquant than the former and less assertive than the latter. There are two main types: the smaller and finer-flavoured GREY SHALLOT and the slightly larger, rounder and milder RED or JERSEY SHALLOT.

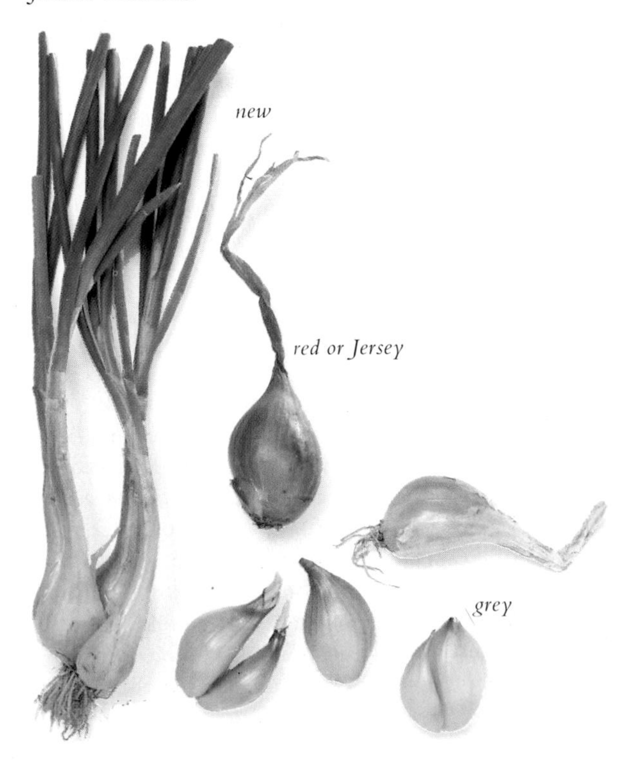

Shallots should feel very firm, the skins should be intact and they should show no signs of sprouting. Once cut, use them fairly quickly and do not keep shallots in the refrigerator as their odour readily taints other foods.

As well as being used raw and chopped in salads, fresh shallots are widely used as a flavouring ingredient, especially in the cooking of northern France. They are the basis for a host of classic sauces, particularly the *beurre blanc* family, *béarnaise* and *sauce bercy* for fish, and are used in many stocks and marinades. Cooked in butter or lightly sautéed in a little wine and vinegar, they add a wonderful flavour to poached fish, grilled (broiled) and roast meats and wine sauces. They bake well whole to make a tasty vegetable accompaniment.

SAUCE BERCY

Shallot and white wine sauce

Makes about 500 ml/16 fl oz/2 cups
Preparation 15 minutes
Cooking about 45 minutes

METRIC/IMPERIAL	AMERICAN
400 ml/14 fl oz strained court-bouillon or fish fumet	*1¾ cups strained court-bouillon or fish stock*
125 g/4½ oz butter	*9 tbsp butter*
45 g/1½ oz flour	*⅓ cup flour*
5 shallots, finely chopped	*5 shallots, finely chopped*
300 ml/½ pt dry white wine	*1½ cups dry white wine*
1 tbsp chopped flat-leaved parsley	*1 tbsp chopped flat-leaf parsley*
salt and pepper	*salt and pepper*

Heat the court-bouillon or fumet (stock).

Melt 55 g/2 oz/4 tbsp of the butter in a large saucepan over a low heat. Add the flour and stir to mix with a wooden spoon. Cook for 2 or 3 minutes, then gradually add the hot court-bouillon or fumet, whisking well.

Lower the heat to its lowest possible setting and simmer very gently for 30 minutes.

Meanwhile, melt one third of the remaining butter in a small saucepan and cook the shallots gently until softened without being browned. Pour in the white wine and add pepper to taste. Boil to reduce the liquid by half. Whisk the reduced shallot mixture into it. Cook gently for 5 minutes, then remove from the heat.

Add the rest of the butter in small pieces, whisking constantly. Adjust the seasoning, mix in the chopped parsley and serve.

SHARK

Requin

see also:
fish
skate
tuna

The largest marine fish, the shark is found in most warm oceans but is not very common in Europe where the smaller related dogfish and skate are more prevalent. Lean shark meat lends itself to the same sort of treatment as tuna and swordfish, and is used in Caribbean soups and stews. Slices of smoked shark meat are also frequently available and these may be used as an interesting alternative to smoked salmon.

SALADE DE BOEUF AU REQUIN FUMÉ

Smoked shark salad

Serves 4
Preparation 15 minutes

METRIC/IMPERIAL	AMERICAN
4 slices of smoked shark meat, cut into strips	*4 slices of smoked shark meat, cut into strips*
5 tbsp olive oil	*5 tbsp olive oil*
2 tbsp cider vinegar	*2 tbsp cider vinegar*
2–3 tbsp chopped chives	*2–3 tbsp chopped chives*
450 g/1 lb boiled or roast beef, trimmed of fat and cartilage and cut into cubes	*1 lb boiled or roast beef, trimmed of fat and cartilage and cut into cubes*
1 onion, chopped	*1 onion, chopped*
salt and pepper	*salt and pepper*
sprigs of flat-leaved parsley, to garnish	*sprigs of flat-leaf parsley, to garnish*

Sprinkle the shark meat with 1 tablespoon of the oil and season with pepper. Set aside.

Prepare a highly seasoned vinaigrette with the vinegar, the remaining oil, and salt and pepper to taste. Add the chopped chives.

In a salad bowl, combine the beef, onion and vinaigrette and stir. Add the strips of shark meat and stir again. Serve at room temperature, garnished with the parsley.
Variations: add mango or tomato slices.

SHELLFISH

see also:
abalone
clam
crab
crayfish
cuttlefish
lobster
mussel
octopus
oyster
scallop
shrimp and prawn
squid

Invertebrate aquatic creatures with shells are known collectively as shellfish. There are two types, MOLLUSCS and CRUSTACEANS.

The molluscs include BIVALVES, such as oysters, scallops, mussels, clams and cockles, GASTROPODS like winkles (periwinkles), whelks, abalone and ormers, and CEPHALOPODS, such as octopus, squid and cuttlefish. Bivalves and gastropods must be bought live and their shells should be firmly closed or should snap shut when lightly tapped. Plunge them into rapidly boiling water to open the shells and discard any that remain closed after cooking. Judge the freshness of gastropods and cephalopods by a strong, fresh smell.

The crustaceans, like lobsters, crab, crayfish, prawns and shrimp, are ARTHROPODS with articulated shells. These are also best bought live in their shells although a great deal are now available shelled and frozen. Buy those which feel heavy for their size, which move vigorously and have no missing limbs.

Shellfish are a very nutritious food as they are rich in vitamins and minerals, a source of high-quality protein and contain virtually no fat. Crustacean meat is digested very slowly by the system, so can seem very filling.

SHERBET

see Sorbet

SHRIMP AND PRAWN

Crevette

see also:
lobster
shellfish

A wide variety of small crustaceans, tiny relatives of the lobster, are known as shrimps or prawns. In Britain, the word shrimp is generally reserved for really small specimens, whereas in most of North America the term is used more generally and the word prawn refers to large specimens such as Dublin Bay prawns.

The most important varieties for the cook are: the COMMON OR PINK PRAWN which is now actually quite rare but very tasty and a feature of the cuisine of northern France. The DEEP-WATER, NORWEGIAN OR NORTHERN SHRIMP OR PRAWN is actually the creature most commonly fished and sold both in Europe and on both coasts of the USA. Cooked frozen shrimps or prawns are almost certainly this variety. The large and strongly flavoured RED PRAWN or GAMBA is native to the Mediterranean and is popular in the restaurants of Italy and Spain as well as France. The NORTH PACIFIC PRAWN and the WHITE OR GRAY SHRIMP found in warmer waters south of Florida are popular in the USA.

The tiny COMMON OR BROWN SHRIMP is becoming an expensive rarity because of the labour-intensive task of prising the meat out the shells. They are found on both sides of the northern Atlantic, although the term BROWN SHRIMP is used in the USA for a larger variety, like the white shrimp native to warmer waters.

Generally most shrimps and prawns are translucent when raw but go their distinctive pink or red colours only on being cooked. A large proportion of the commercial catch is cooked immediately for a few minutes in sea water, then peeled and sold fresh or frozen in an ice glaze. Buy only those which have a good colour and which look and smell fresh and clean. Avoid any which look dry. If buying them unpeeled, again smell for freshness and look for bright, shiny shells which have some spring left in them and tails well tucked in.

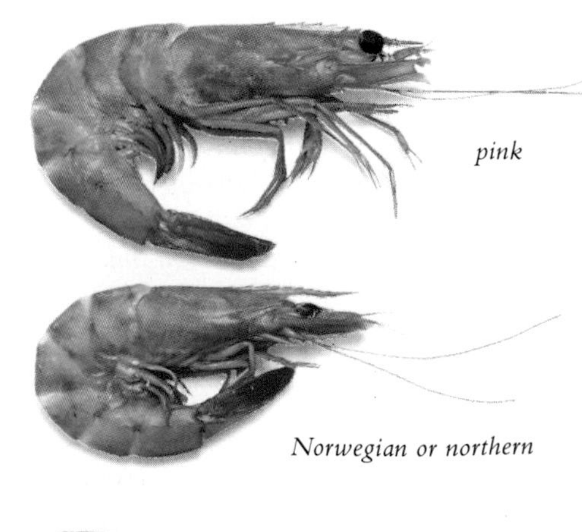

pink

Norwegian or northern

grey

Larger, fresh specimens will need to be peeled and deveined before or after cooking, and the heads are not normally eaten. The shells and heads, however, are full of flavour and are useful for soups, stocks and sauces.

Small whole shrimps and prawns are delicious served plainly with lemon wedges, accompanied by bread and butter. They are popular in canapés, in cocktails with tomato-mayonnaise dressings as hors d'oeuvres, and are used to make delicious bisques. Larger ones in their shells are often used in salads and as garnishes for fish and shellfish dishes. They may also be deep fried, or 'butterflied' and grilled (broiled) or barbecued. Take care when cooking shrimps or prawns which have already been cooked as they quickly become hard. In Britain, tiny brown shrimps are traditionally potted in butter flavoured with a little mace.

In Japan, where the local varieties of prawn form a very large part of the diet, they are commonly consumed raw like oysters, and dried, rotten shrimps are used to make the flavouring *trasi* which is such a feature of the cooking of Indonesia and Southeast Asia.

Shrimps and prawns are a very healthy food: 100 g/3½ oz contain only 95 calories and they are rich in minerals.

GAMBAS EN SALADE

Shrimp or prawn salad

Serves 4
Preparation 25 minutes
Cooking 5 minutes

METRIC/IMPERIAL	AMERICAN
12 fresh, raw and unpeeled large prawns or gambas	*12 fresh, raw jumbo shrimp in shell*
5 tbsp olive oil	*5 tbsp olive oil*
2 courgettes, thinly sliced	*2 zucchini, thinly sliced*
3 tbsp lemon juice	*3 tbsp lemon juice*
200 g/7 oz radicchio, separated into leaves	*7 oz radicchio, separated into leaves*
20 black olives, stoned	*20 black olives, pitted*
salt and pepper	*salt and pepper*
chervil, to garnish	*chervil, to garnish*

Bring a large pan of salted water to the boil. Cook the prawns (shrimp) in it for 2 minutes. Drain, peel and devein them.

Heat 1 tablespoon of oil in a frying pan over a high heat and sauté the courgettes (zucchini) for 3 minutes. Drain on paper towels.

Whisk the remaining olive oil with the lemon juice and season with salt and pepper.

Divide the courgettes (zucchini) among 4 warmed plates. In separate bowls, toss the radicchio and prawns (shrimp) in the dressing, then add them to the plates with the olives. Garnish with finely snipped chervil.

To drink: a good rosé, such as Tavel.

CREVETTES GRISES SAUTÉES À L'HUILE

Shrimps sautéed in oil

Serves 6
Preparation 10 minutes
Cooking 5 minutes

METRIC/IMPERIAL	AMERICAN
500 ml/16 fl oz oil	*2 cups oil*
550 g/1¼ lb raw, unpeeled brown shrimps	*1¼ lb small raw shrimp in shell*
salt	*salt*

Heat the oil in a large sauté pan over a moderate to high heat. When the oil is hot but not smoking, plunge the shrimps into it. Stir and cover at once. Remove the cover once the oil stops splashing. Cook for 2 or 3 minutes.

With a slotted spoon, transfer the shrimps to paper towels to drain and then into a deep warmed dish. Sprinkle them with salt.

Serve at once, with bread and butter.

Variation: sauté the shrimps in a mixture of butter and oil and sprinkle with some lemon juice and a little mace.

SIMMERING

see also: boiling braising poaching stewing

The process of cooking food in a liquid, especially water, stock or sauce, at a temperature just below boiling point is known as simmering. The liquid should be just barely bubbling and it is usually important that the heating remains gentle at all times, especially when poaching, braising and stewing. Where dishes are not stirred, care should be taken to ensure that the ingredients do not stick to the bottom of the cooking container. Heat-diffusing mats help control the simmering process.

SKATE

Raie

see also:
fish
shark

A large cartilaginous fish, the skate or ray is a flat relative of the shark and numerous varieties may be found in most seas. The THORNBACK RAY and the SPOTTED RAY are the most sought-after for their flavour, while the COMMON OR BARNDOOR SKATE is a rarer catch and not much valued in comparison.

Skate is available all year round and is rarely seen whole unless very small, usually being sold in chunks or in 'wings'. These are sometimes sold already skinned, but if the viscous skin is still present it can be a good indication of freshness: if rubbed away it should regenerate quickly.

Skate is one of the few fish which actually improves with a day or two of hanging as this allows the urea in its system to break down. This process gives it a strong smell of ammonia which is best eliminated by washing the fish in cold water and then rinsing several times in vinegared water. The skin may be removed before or after cooking and the cartilaginous skeleton is easily removed from the very delicate, but meaty, pinkish-white cooked flesh.

Skate wings may be poached, baked or fried. However cooked, they are usually served with black butter or *beurre noisette*. The flavour of skate also works well with a strong herb hollandaise or a mustard vinaigrette, especially when served cold.

Skate liver is rarely sold, but is considered a true delicacy. It is first poached, then pan fried, and often served with a cider vinegar sauce.

A lean-fleshed fish, 100 g/3½ oz of skate contains only 90 calories.

RAIE AU FROMAGE

Skate wings with cheese

Serves 4
Preparation 20 minutes
Cooking about 15 minutes

METRIC/IMPERIAL	*AMERICAN*
55 g/2 oz butter	*4 tbsp butter*
3 shallots, chopped	*3 shallots, chopped*
2 tbsp finely chopped flat-leaved parsley	*2 tbsp finely chopped flat-leaf parsley*
140 g/5 oz mushrooms, thinly sliced	*5 oz mushrooms, thinly sliced*
800 g/1¾ lb skate wings, skinned	*1¾ lb skate wings, skinned*
100 ml/3½ fl oz dry white wine	*½ cup dry white wine*
2 tbsp crème fraîche or whipping cream	*2 tbsp crème fraîche or whipping cream*
55 g/2 oz grated Gruyère	*½ cup grated Gruyère cheese*
salt and pepper	*salt and pepper*

Preheat the oven to 230C/450F/gas 8 and grease a baking dish with a little of the butter.

Mix together the shallots, parsley and mushrooms and spread over the bottom of the baking dish. Place the skate wings on top. Pour over the wine and dot with half of the remaining butter. Bake for about 10 minutes.

Preheat a grill (broiler).

Remove the skate from the baking dish. Stir the cream into the cooking juices, then return the fish to the baking dish and turn to coat it in the sauce. Sprinkle with the grated Gruyère and dot with the remaining butter.

Grill (broil) for 5 minutes, until the top has browned lightly.

SKIMMING

see also:
aspic
clarification
sauce
stock

Fats and impurities which rise to the top of cooking liquids are skimmed off to clarify the liquid. The process may be carried out with a spoon or a specially designed fine mesh skimming ladle. Paper towel is also a very efficient skimming tool.

see also:
fish

SMELT

Eperlan

A small, silvery marine fish with delicate flesh, the smelt is related to the salmon. It spawns in the spring, but is best near the end of summer.

When buying smelt look out for a second dorsal fin which distinguishes it from similar but inferior fish. Smelt has an unusual flavour and is quite delicious when really fresh. They need to be gutted before cooking and are generally fried, grilled (broiled) or barbecued.

FRITURE D'ÉPERLANS

Fried smelt

Serves 6–8
Preparation 10 minutes
Cooking 2–3 minutes

METRIC/IMPERIAL	AMERICAN
1 kg/2¼ lb gutted smelt	2¼ lb gutted smelts
200 ml/7 fl oz milk	1 cup milk
flour, for coating	flour, for coating
oil, for frying	oil, for frying
salt and pepper	salt and pepper
4 lemons, quartered, to garnish	4 lemons, quartered, to garnish
parsley, to garnish	parsley, to garnish

Heat the oil to 190C/375F, or until a small cube of dry bread browns in it in 40 seconds.

Season the smelt with salt and pepper. Dip them in the milk, shake off the excess, and then dredge them in flour.

Skewer the smelt through the eyes, about 10 to a skewer, and plunge into the oil. When crisp and golden, remove and drain on paper towels.

Serve them immediately, garnished with the lemon quarters and sprigs of parsley.

SMOKING

see also:
bacon
cheese
curing
drying
mackerel
salmon
salt
sausage
trout

Prolonged exposure to smoke is one of the most ancient methods of preserving food, and is usually effected in combination with initial salt-curing or drying. Nowadays, with the advent of modern methods of refrigeration, freezing and canning, smoking is more usually a means of adding a distinctive flavour.

There are two principal methods of smoking:

COLD-SMOKING is carried out over smouldering embers at a temperature of 20–30C/67–85F and is most suited to fish, particularly salmon.

HOT-SMOKING is done in a current of very hot air over a rapidly burning fire at temperatures in the region of 60–80C/140–175F and is preferred for most meats, poultry and game.

The process can take anything from 20 minutes to several days and usually takes place over wood fires, but in Scotland and Ireland peat is often preferred. Hardwoods such as beech and oak are most commonly used, although this depends on locale: hickory is favoured in the USA. Juniper, sage, fennel, etc, may be added to the fires for flavouring.

The most usual candidates for smoking are meat and *charcuterie*, such as ham, pork belly or sides, bacon, various kinds of sausage, cooked chicken, roast turkey and goose. Apart from salmon the fish most often smoked include sturgeon, mackerel, herring, trout and eel.

Because of initial curing, smoked foods are always extremely salty; this should be considered when seasoning dishes containing them. It is also unwise to include smoked foods in the diet on too regular a basis.

SNAIL

Escargot

see also:
butter
shellfish

A land gastropod mollusc, the snail was a much revered delicacy to the Romans and has thus become a particular feature of French gastronomy, although the Spanish and Italians still also retain a little of this tradition. There are two common species cooked in France: the most highly prized is the large BURGUNDY or ROMAN SNAIL, which the Romans are said to have introduced to many parts of Europe, including Britain, but which resists commercial rearing and is mainly gathered in eastern France. The smaller PETIT-GRIS, which comes mostly from the south, has a fruity flavour and is relatively easy to farm.

Live snails are available from butchers' shops in France all year round but are at their best in winter when their shells are sealed for hibernation. It takes time and patience to prepare snails, involving weeks of fasting or special cleansing diets, repeated washing, boiling, shelling, gutting and lengthy simmering in an aromatic stock for several hours until tender, before they are ready to be used in various recipes.

Even in France, therefore, most snails are bought already cooked, canned or frozen. Canned snails simply require draining and refreshing in cold water before use. Frozen snails should be plunged in a mixture of boiling water and white wine to prepare them for cooking.

The simplest and most usual method of cooking snails is to put them back in their shells and stuff them with butter flavoured with chopped shallots, garlic and parsley. They are then briefly grilled (broiled) or baked. They may also be served shelled with mayonnaise, lightly fried or simmered in a wine sauce. Some *haute cuisine* dishes traditionally stuff the snail with chicken or sweetbread forcemeat and serve them with rich cream sauces.

Plain boiled snails contain only 77 calories per 100 g/3½ oz and provide the daily requirement of protein. Unfortunately, rich sauces add greatly to the calorie content.

CASSOLETTES D'ESCARGOTS

Snails in mushroom, shallot and wine sauce

Serves 6
Preparation 15 minutes
Cooking about 25 minutes

METRIC/IMPERIAL	AMERICAN
1 garlic clove, finely chopped	*1 garlic clove, minced*
2 shallots, finely chopped	*2 shallots, minced*
3 tbsp chopped flat-leaved parsley	*3 tbsp chopped flat-leaf parsley*
100 g/3½ oz butter, softened	*1 stick butter, softened*
450 g/1 lb button mushrooms, thinly sliced	*1 lb button mushrooms, thinly sliced*
6 dozen canned Burgundy snails, drained	*6 dozen canned Burgundy snails, drained*
200 ml/7 fl oz dry white wine	*1 cup dry white wine*
200 ml/7 fl oz crème fraîche or whipping cream	*1 cup crème fraîche or whipping cream*
6 round slices of white bread	*6 round slices of white bread*
pinch of grated nutmeg	*pinch of grated nutmeg*
salt and pepper	*salt and pepper*

Mix the garlic, shallots and parsley. Add 75 g/2½ oz/5 tbsp of the butter and season with grated nutmeg, salt and pepper.

Melt this herbed butter in a sauté pan over a gentle heat, add the mushrooms and cook them for 4–5 minutes.

Add the snails and mix well. Pour in the wine, stir and simmer for 8–10 minutes. Add the cream and reduce over a high heat for 8 minutes.

Meanwhile, fry the slices of bread in the rest of the butter. Drain them and place one on each of 6 warmed plates. Spoon the snail mixture on top and serve very hot.

To drink: Riesling.

SOLE

see also:
fish
lemon sole

A dextral flat sea fish, the sole is oval in shape, with a creamy-white underside and a dark brown or grey upper side. Whole fish can weigh from 170 g/6 oz to over 800 g/1¾ lb and the firm-textured flesh has a very fine flavour.

The tastiest and best-known variety is DOVER SOLE which is found in the Atlantic and the North Sea from Spain as far north as Norway. The smaller SAND OR PARTRIDGE SOLE and the THICKBACK SOLE are not as delicate in flavour. No true soles are found in American waters.

Sole is at its best about 24 hours after being caught. The most flavour is obtained from sole left whole on the bone. However, as there is a great deal of waste it is possibly more economic to buy fillets, although the trimmings are excellent for making stock. The fin which runs around the edge of the sole should be removed as it contains many fine bones and the fillets are best skinned before cooking.

Smaller sole are best deep fried, medium-sized ones pan fried or grilled (broiled), and the largest are poached or braised. Fillets are delicious plainly grilled (broiled) or steamed, but

SKINNING A SOLE

Make an incision on the dark side of the fish just through the skin at the tail and peel back a little flap.

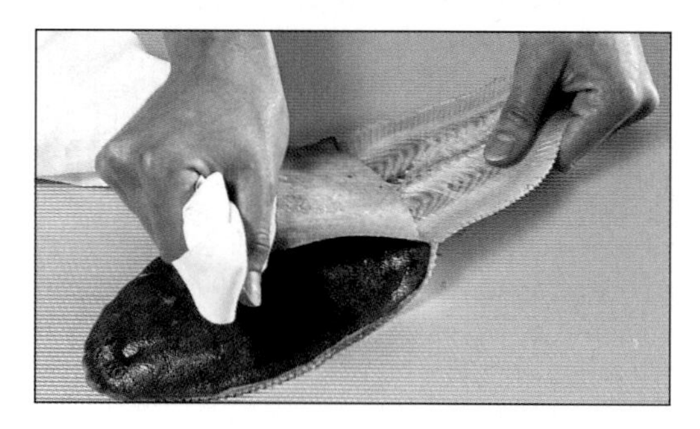

Grasp the skin firmly with a cloth and rip it off in one motion. Repeat on the lighter side if wished.

are also often rolled into paupiettes around stuffings and served with a creamy sauce. However, the flavour of sole requires little more than some butter and lemon juice.

Sole is a lean fish, rich in vitamins B1 and B2: 100 g/3½ oz contains only 75 calories.

PAUPIETTES DE SOLES FARCIES

Stuffed rolled fillets of sole

Serves 4
Preparation 20 minutes
Cooking about 20 minutes

METRIC/IMPERIAL	AMERICAN
8 skinned sole fillets	8 skinned sole fillets
200 g/7 oz skinned whiting fillets, chilled	7 oz skinned whiting or other white fish fillets, chilled
1 egg	1 egg
12 tarragon leaves, snipped	12 tarragon leaves, snipped
200 ml/7 fl oz crème fraîche or whipping cream	1 cup crème fraîche or whipping cream
55 g/2 oz butter	4 tbsp butter
1 tbsp Cognac	1 tbsp Cognac
400 ml/14 fl oz canned or frozen lobster bisque	1¾ cups canned or frozen lobster bisque
115 g/¼ lb peeled cooked prawns	¼ lb small cooked shrimp, shelled
pinch of grated nutmeg	pinch of grated nutmeg
cayenne pepper	cayenne pepper
salt and pepper	salt and pepper

Paupiettes de soles farcies (Stuffed rolled fillets of sole)

Flatten the sole fillets.

Purée the whiting in a food processor, adding the egg and tarragon. Add the cream with the machine still running. Season with nutmeg, salt, pepper and a small pinch of cayenne.

Spread this stuffing on the sole fillets, roll them into paupiettes and tie them with string.

Melt the butter in a sauté pan over a moderate heat. Brown the paupiettes lightly on all sides.

Heat the Cognac in a little pan or ladle, pour it over the paupiettes and set alight. Cover and cook very gently for 15 minutes.

Remove the paupiettes and place them in a deep, warmed serving dish. Remove the string. Add the lobster bisque to the sauté pan along with the prawns (shrimp). Heat without boiling, then coat the paupiettes with the sauce.

SORBET

see also:
fruit
ices and ice creams
meringue

Usually made from fruit juice or purée, wine or other alcohol sweetened with a sugar syrup, sorbets were the earliest form of iced desserts. During freezing, they may be gently churned in a *sorbetière* or other ice cream machine, or they can be 'still-frozen' and whisked just once or twice during freezing to prevent the formation of large ice crystals. Stiffly beaten egg whites or Italian meringue may be added to the frozen mixture to give it volume. Milk or cream may also be added, when the dessert is usually called a SHERBET, although that term is also used interchangeably with sorbet in North America.

Sorbet is the ideal refreshing, light dessert to finish off a heavy meal, and is traditionally served between courses to refresh the palate during elaborate, rich meals. A common practice is to pour alcohol, such as a fruit brandy, over sorbet just before serving.

SORBET AU CITRON

Lemon sorbet

Serves 6
Preparation 45 minutes, 5 hours ahead
Freezing at least $3\frac{1}{2}$ hours

METRIC/IMPERIAL	*AMERICAN*
10 lemons, preferably organic	*10 lemons, preferably organic (uncoated)*
300 g/10 oz caster sugar	*$1\frac{1}{2}$ cups superfine sugar*
550 ml/18 fl oz still mineral water	*$2\frac{1}{4}$ cups still mineral water*
1 egg white	*1 egg white*
55 g/2 oz icing sugar	*$6\frac{1}{2}$ tbsp confectioners' sugar*

If the lemons are not organically grown and may have been sprayed or coated, scrub them in hot soapy water, rinse well and pat dry. Peel the zest with a very sharp knife. Squeeze the juice and strain it to eliminate the seeds. Measure the juice obtained: there should be 200 ml/7 fl oz/1 cup. If there is not enough, add the juice of another lemon; do not add water.

Put the caster (superfine) sugar into a bowl, add one quarter of the mineral water with the lemon juice and mix until the sugar has dissolved (1). Add the remaining mineral water and the lemon zest. Leave the mixture to macerate for 5 hours in the refrigerator.

Strain through a fine sieve (2). Pour into a *sorbetière* or other ice cream machine. Freeze according to manufacturer's instructions.

Meanwhile, whisk the egg white to very stiff peaks. Put it into a small saucepan in a bain-marie over a gentle heat and stir in the icing (confectioners') sugar (3). Let it cool.

When the sorbet is half frozen, remove it and incorporate the meringue mixture into the sorbet (4). Return it to the *sorbetière* to complete the freezing.

Remove the sorbet about 30 minutes before serving so that it is soft enough to scoop. Serve it in chilled coupes or parfait glasses.

Variation: about 12 limes may be used for this recipe instead of the lemons. Serve sprinkled with iced vodka or tequila, if wished.

SORBET EXOTIQUE

Mixed fruit sorbet

Serves 6
Preparation 10 minutes
Cooking about 5 minutes
Freezing $2\frac{1}{2}$ hours

METRIC/IMPERIAL	AMERICAN
450 g/1 lb passion fruit	1 lb passion fruit
1 ripe mango, peeled and halved	1 ripe mango, peeled and halved
1 pear, peeled, cored and quartered	1 pear, peeled, cored and quartered
200 g/7 oz preserving sugar	1 cup preserving sugar

Halve the passion fruit and scoop out the pulp. Strain through a sieve to eliminate the seeds.

Cut the mango flesh into cubes. Blend the pear and mango in a food processor and mix in the strained passion fruit pulp.

Mix the sugar with 120 ml/4 fl oz/generous $\frac{1}{2}$ cup of water. Boil for 2 minutes, then leave to cool.

Mix the sugar syrup with the fruit purée. Freeze for $2\frac{1}{2}$ hours until set, stirring once or twice to break up large ice crystals.

Serve the sorbet in parfait glasses and coat it with a fruit coulis, if wished.

Variations: this sorbet can be made with any kind of fresh fruit, including strawberries, raspberries, apricots, peaches, melon with a dash of port, or ready-made fruit purée.

SORREL

Oseille

see also:
lettuce
salmon
shad
spinach
vegetables

This plant, related to dock and sourgrass, is prized for its pleasantly bitter, green, trowel-shaped leaves. Sorrel leaves should be very fresh, shiny and firm. The larger and darker they are, the more acidic and bitter sorrel usually is. For soups or purées, it is often mixed with lettuce to tone down this acidity.

Sorrel is prepared and cooked in the same ways as spinach and is usually served as an accompaniment to veal, eggs and freshwater fish, such as shad and pike. It is also used in soups and sauces and to add flavour to other green vegetables being boiled. Fresh, tender young leaves may be used raw in salads.

Sorrel is very acidic, but is rich in minerals and vitamin C and very low in calories: 100 g/$3\frac{1}{2}$ oz contains only 25.

CONSERVE D'OSEILLE

Preserved sorrel

Makes 2 jars, each containing about 250 g/$8\frac{1}{2}$ oz
Preparation 20 minutes
Cooking 5 minutes

METRIC/IMPERIAL	AMERICAN
100 g/$3\frac{1}{2}$ oz butter, cut into pieces	1 stick butter, cut into pieces
1.5 kg/$2\frac{1}{4}$ lb sorrel, trimmed and shredded	$2\frac{1}{4}$ lb sorrel, trimmed and shredded
salt and pepper	salt and pepper

Melt half the butter gently in a saucepan but do not let it brown. Add half the sorrel and stir it with a wooden spoon. Season it with salt and

pepper. When the leaves have wilted, remove the saucepan from the heat.

Put the sorrel into a bowl and press down well with the back of a spoon. Pour off the juices. Spoon the sorrel into a warmed sterilized wide-mouthed preserving jar. Seal and label.

Repeat the operation with the remaining sorrel and butter and put it into the second jar. Alternatively, the sorrel may be frozen in trays.

Preserved sorrel may be used plain as a garnish, or made into a sauce with a little crème fraîche or whipping cream.

POTAGE À L'OSEILLE

Sorrel soup

Serves 4
Preparation 15 minutes
Cooking about 5 minutes

METRIC/IMPERIAL	*AMERICAN*
15 g/½ oz butter	*1 tbsp butter*
300 g/10 oz sorrel, trimmed	*10 oz sorrel, trimmed*
700 ml/1¼ pt vegetable or chicken stock	*3 cups vegetable or chicken stock*
200 ml/7 fl oz thick crème fraîche or whipping cream	*1 cup thick crème fraîche or whipping cream*
salt and pepper	*salt and pepper*
sprigs of chervil, to garnish	*sprigs of chervil, to garnish*

Melt the butter in a saucepan over a moderate heat. Add the sorrel and stir for 2 minutes or until it has wilted, then stir in the stock.

Bring slowly to the boil, then remove from the heat and cover.

Season the cream with salt and pepper, whisk vigorously and pour into a warmed soup tureen.

Pour the sorrel soup on top, whisking constantly. Adjust the seasoning, add the chervil sprigs and serve at once.

Variation: this soup may be served chilled, supplemented with strips of smoked salmon, sardines or chunks of tuna fish in olive oil.

SOUFFLÉ

see also: baking; creams and custards; egg; ices and ice creams; mousse; sauce; sugar

A sweet or savoury preparation incorporating stiffly beaten egg whites, a successful soufflé is considered a great culinary achievement. Hot soufflés are served straight from the oven, while they are still fully puffed up.

Most savoury soufflés are based on a béchamel sauce into which is incorporated the chosen flavouring, such as chopped or puréed ham, cheese, crab meat, chicken or vegetables. This is enriched and bound with the egg yolks and the stiffly beaten egg whites are then carefully folded in at the last moment.

Dessert soufflés are usually based on a flavoured pastry cream or fruit purée enriched and lightened in the same way.

Soufflé moulds are cylindrical to allow even rising and made of porcelain or flameproof glass. Small soufflé dishes or ramekins may be used to make individual soufflés.

Soufflés have an unjustified reputation for being difficult to cook. They are really very easy as long as the following tips are observed:

Use fresh eggs and only beat the whites just before they are needed.

Fold a little of the beaten egg white into the base mixture and mix thoroughly to slacken it before gently folding in the rest of the egg white. It is important not to stir out any of the air patiently beaten into the egg whites.

Make sure that the mould, including the rim, is thoroughly greased so that the mixture does not stick to anything as it rises.

Do not fill the mould more than three quarters full.

Make sure the oven is properly preheated before putting the soufflé into it.

Never open the oven door during cooking.

ICED SOUFFLÉS are chilled desserts which resemble true soufflés, in that the preparation rises above the level of the mould in which it is presented. However, they are actually made of ice cream or iced mousse, decorated with fruit or chantilly cream, sometimes interspersed with layers of sponge cake soaked in liqueur or alcohol.

Savoury soufflés make an excellent main course, accompanied by a salad and followed by fresh fruit. One portion of cheese soufflé contains about 350 calories.

SOUFFLÉ AU FROMAGE

Cheese soufflé

Serves 4
Preparation 15 minutes
Cooking about 40 minutes

METRIC/IMPERIAL	*AMERICAN*
55 g/2 oz butter	*4 tbsp butter*
45 g/$1\frac{1}{2}$ oz flour	*$\frac{1}{4}$ cup flour*
400 ml/14 fl oz milk	*$1\frac{3}{4}$ cups milk*
140 g/5 oz Comté or Beaufort cheese, finely grated	*5 oz ($1\frac{1}{4}$ cups) Comté or Beaufort cheese, finely grated*
4 eggs, separated	*4 eggs, separated*
pinch of grated nutmeg	*pinch of grated nutmeg*
salt and pepper	*salt and pepper*

Melt two thirds of the butter in a saucepan. Add the flour and mix. Cook gently, stirring continuously, for 2 minutes to a blond roux.

Pour on the milk a little at a time, stirring constantly. Cook for 6–7 minutes until the mixture is fairly thick. Taste and season lightly with salt, pepper and grated nutmeg.

Add the grated cheese to this béchamel, mixing thoroughly (1). Remove the saucepan from the heat.

Grease a 22 cm/9 in soufflé mould with the remaining butter, and preheat the oven to 200C/400F/gas 6. Once the béchamel has cooled, incorporate the egg yolks (2).

Whisk the egg whites to stiff peaks with a pinch of salt. Fold gently into the mixture (3).

Pour the soufflé mixture into the greased mould. Put in the middle of the oven and bake for about 30 minutes. Serve straight from the oven when golden brown and well risen (4).

Variation: any type of hard cheese is suitable for this recipe. Choose strongly flavoured cheeses like Fribourg, Appenzell or even a fairly ripe Edam. Crumbled blue cheese, such as Roquefort or Stilton, may also be used but take care not to over-salt the mixture.

This soufflé may be cooked in individual dishes or ramekins, in which case reduce the cooking time to 15–20 minutes. Ovenproof porcelain gives better results than ovenproof glass, which takes a little longer to heat up.

1

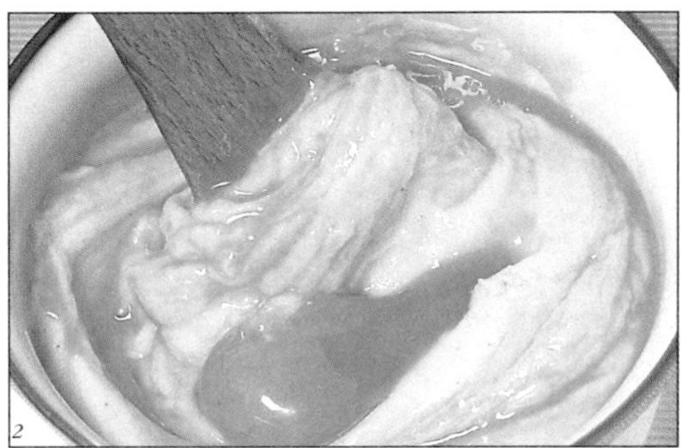
2

3

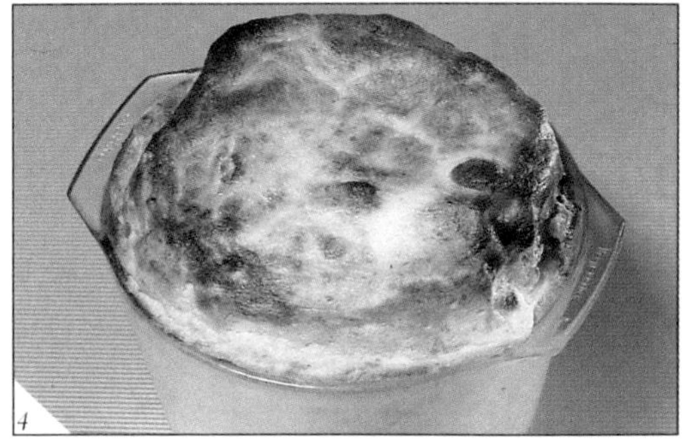
4

SOUFFLÉ AU CHOCOLAT

Chocolate soufflé

Serves 6
Preparation 30 minutes
Cooking about 35 minutes

METRIC/IMPERIAL	AMERICAN
15 g/$\frac{1}{2}$ oz butter	1 tbsp butter
125 g/4$\frac{1}{2}$ oz caster sugar	10 tbsp superfine sugar
200 g/7 oz cooking chocolate, broken into pieces	7 oz semisweet chocolate, broken into pieces
45 g/1$\frac{1}{2}$ oz cornflour, sifted	$\frac{1}{3}$ cup cornstarch, sifted
6 eggs, separated	6 eggs, separated
1 sachet (7.5 g/1$\frac{3}{4}$ tsp) of vanilla sugar	1$\frac{3}{4}$ tsp vanilla-flavored sugar

Preheat the oven to 220C/425F/gas 7. Grease a 15 cm/6 in soufflé mould right up to the top, and around the rim, with the butter. Dust it with a little of the caster (superfine) sugar.

Put the chocolate into a heavy-bottomed pan along with 1 tablespoon of water. Place the pan in a bain-marie over a gentle heat.

Mix the cornflour (cornstarch) with half the remaining caster (superfine) sugar.

Add the egg yolks 2 at a time to the melted chocolate, followed by the vanilla sugar and the cornflour (cornstarch) and sugar mixture.

Whisk the egg whites to very stiff peaks and fold in the remaining caster (superfine) sugar. Fold the beaten egg whites gently into the chocolate mixture. Pour into the mould and bake the soufflé for 25–30 minutes.

SOUFFLÉ GLACÉ AUX FRAISES

Strawberry iced soufflé

Serves 6
Preparation 30 minutes
Freezing 3 hours

METRIC/IMPERIAL	AMERICAN
250 g/8$\frac{1}{2}$ oz caster sugar	1$\frac{1}{4}$ cups superfine sugar
550 g/1$\frac{1}{4}$ lb strawberries	1$\frac{1}{2}$ pt strawberries
5 egg whites	5 egg whites
2 tbsp raspberry liqueur	2 tbsp raspberry liqueur
250 ml/8 fl oz whipping cream, well chilled	1 cup whipping cream, well chilled
salt	salt

1

2

3

4

Make a sugar syrup by melting 200 g/7 oz/1 cup of the sugar with 4 tablespoons of water. Bring to the boil and cook it to the large thread or gloss stage (110C/230F), when bubbles form on a skimmer dipped in the syrup when it is blown on (1, opposite). Cool the syrup.

Meanwhile, cut out 6 strips of parchment or greaseproof paper 3 cm/1¼ in wide and a little longer than the circumference of an individual soufflé dish or ramekin. Fix a strip around each of 6 dishes to extend its height.

Purée 350 g/12 oz/1¾ cups of the strawberries in a food processor. Add the strawberry purée to the syrup with half the raspberry liqueur.

Whisk the egg whites with a pinch of salt to very stiff peaks (2, opposite). Whip the cream to soft peaks and add to the mixture. Finally, fold in the strawberry mixture (3, opposite).

Spoon the mousse into the prepared ramekins: it should almost reach the top of the paper (4, opposite). Freeze for 3 hours.

Set the 6 best-looking strawberries to one side. Reduce the rest to a smooth purée with the remaining sugar and liqueur.

Just before serving, remove the paper strips. Coat each soufflé with the strawberry coulis and decorate with a whole strawberry.

see also:
bisque
bouillabaisse
brunoise
consommé
court-bouillon
pasta and noodles
purée
sauce
stock

SOUP

Soupe, potage

It is a common practice in many cultures to begin a meal with a liquid dish made from a flavoured stock. Such soups are usually served hot but may also be chilled.

There are basically two kinds of soup: CLEAR SOUPS such as consommé, and THICK SOUPS which contain a wide variety of especially chopped vegetables, legumes and pulses, fish and seafood. In CREAM SOUPS the ingredients are puréed until smooth and the soup possibly thickened with potato or rice flour, tapioca or a white sauce. Soups made from puréed shellfish and cream are known as *bisques*, while those enriched with an egg and cream liaison are termed *veloutés*.

In Italy small pasta shapes are commonly added to soups, while the Germans prefer dumplings and the French favour rich garlic sauces, such as *pistou* and *rouille*, as well as slices of bread and cheese, as with classic onion soup.

FRUIT SOUPS consist of poached fruit served in the cooking liquid or a fruit coulis.

The flavour of a soup usually depends on that of the basic stock. Soups are highly nutritious and can make a satisfying light meal.

SOUPE AU PISTOU

Vegetable soup with basil and garlic sauce

Serves 8
Preparation 30 minutes, soaking 12 hours
Cooking about 2¼ hours

METRIC/IMPERIAL	AMERICAN
450 g/1 lb dried haricot beans	2½ cups dried navy beans
bouquet garni	bouquet garni
2 carrots, finely diced	2 carrots, finely diced
2 turnips, finely diced	2 turnips, finely diced
225 g/½ lb French beans, trimmed	½ lb green beans, trimmed
2 courgettes, very thinly sliced	2 zucchini, very thinly sliced
2 tomatoes, peeled	2 tomatoes, peeled
200 g/7 oz vermicelli	7 oz vermicelli
55 g/2 oz grated Parmesan	½ cup grated Parmesan cheese
salt and pepper	salt and pepper
FOR THE PISTOU:	FOR THE PISTOU:
4 tbsp snipped fresh basil	¼ cup snipped fresh basil
5 garlic cloves	5 garlic cloves
4 tbsp olive oil	¼ cup olive oil

Soak the beans for 12 hours. Drain them and put them in a pot with 2.5 l/4 pt/2½ qt of cold water. Add the bouquet garni and salt to taste, and bring to the boil. Simmer for 1½ hours.

Add the carrots and turnips to the stewpot. Cook for 20 minutes. Add the green beans and courgettes (zucchini) and cook for a further 10 minutes. Add the tomatoes along with the vermicelli. Cook for a further 10 minutes.

Make the *pistou*: in a mortar, pound the basil and garlic cloves. Mix in the olive oil. Pour this mixture into the soup and season with pepper. Stir, sprinkle over the Parmesan and serve.

CRÈME DE LAITUE

Cream of lettuce soup

Serves 4
Preparation 15 minutes
Cooking about 15 minutes

METRIC/IMPERIAL	*AMERICAN*
500 ml/16 fl oz milk	*2 cups milk*
2 bay leaves	*2 bay leaves*
6–7 black peppercorns	*6–7 black peppercorns*
1 mild onion	*1 mild onion*
1 tbsp oil	*1 tbsp oil*
3 small white onions, finely chopped	*3 small new onions, finely chopped*
1 garlic clove, finely chopped	*1 garlic clove, minced*
1 tsp grated nutmeg	*1 tsp grated nutmeg*
1 lettuce, shredded	*1 head lettuce, shredded*
salt	*salt*

Pour the milk into a large bowl. Crumble in the bay leaves and add the peppercorns and mild onion. Microwave on High for 4 minutes, let stand for 3 minutes then strain. Chop the onion.

Pour the oil into a bowl and heat it on High for 1 minute. Add all the chopped onions and the garlic. Sprinkle with the nutmeg. Mix well, cover and microwave on High for 2 minutes.

Add the lettuce, cover again and cook on High for 3 minutes. Pour the contents of the bowl into the strained milk, add salt to taste and blend it in the food processor.

Return the soup to the bowl, cover and cook on High for 1 minute to reheat. Serve at once.

SOYA OR SOY

Soja

see also:
beansprout
condiment
fats and oils
flour
legume

A legume which originated in China, soya is still a basic foodstuff in many parts of the Orient. The pods enclose yellow, green or black seeds the size of peas which are used fresh or dried, or made into a number of widely different substances, including oil, flour and 'milk'.

FRESH OR DRIED SOYA BEANS are cooked in the same way as white beans such as haricots and navy beans, and are very nutritious with an unusually high protein content.

SOYA BEANSPROUTS are also eaten, but have a coarser flavour and texture than the mung and alfalfa sprouts more usually eaten in the West. For this reason, soya beansprouts are usually first cooked rather than being used raw.

SOYA FLOUR is unique in that it is low in carbohydrates and high in protein. It is often used as a filler cereal in poorer quality sausages, etc, and many bakers use it to improve bread doughs. In the Far East it is used to thicken sauces and to make sticky cakes and pancakes.

SOYA OIL is one of the cheapest and most bountiful vegetable oils, much used by the canning industry and in margarines. However, it has a somewhat intrusive flavour.

SOYA MILK is used as a beverage and to make bean curd or *tofu* which is becoming a popular and nutritious alternative to meat and dairy products in foods from soups to ice creams.

SOY SAUCE, or *shoyu*, is a condiment made from cooked soya beans, anchovies, ginger and sugar. It is a traditional flavouring in innumerable Far Eastern dishes and a common table condiment instead of salt.

Soya beans are very rich in vegetable protein and contain 422 calories per 100 g/3½ oz.

SPICES

Epices

see also:
allspice
aniseed
caraway
cardamom
cinnamon
clove
condiment
coriander
cumin
curry powder
ginger
juniper
mace
mustard
nutmeg
paprika
pepper
saffron
tamarind
vanilla

The term spice in cooking was originally applied only to plant-derived aromatic substances imported from the Orient. Nowadays, however, the term also embraces dried berries, seeds and some fruits like sweet and hot peppers. Spices are always strongly flavoured, whether they be piquant, hot or bitter.

Spices are widely used in Oriental, Indian, Chinese, Caribbean and Latin American cooking. Until quite recently they were used somewhat indiscriminately in Europe, but modern usage is more moderate and effective. Pepper and nutmeg are universal ingredients. The French spice blend *quatre-épices* unites them with clove and cinnamon to flavour terrines and stews. In Spain and Hungary paprika is an indispensable part of the cuisine. The use of spices is traditional in many dishes, from vanilla in custard to juniper berries with game and the saffron in bouillabaisse and paella.

Spices are often sold ready-ground to a powder but this diminishes their flavour. Buy spices in small quantities from shops with a rapid turnover and keep them in a cool, dry place in airtight containers large enough to allow some internal movement of air.

see also:
salad
sorrel
vegetables

SPINACH
Epinard

A green vegetable with shiny, bright-coloured leaves, spinach is a member of the beet family and originated in the region around Iran. Now widely grown in warmer parts of Europe and the USA, varieties are available all year round. However, spinach does not stand the heat well and is best avoided at the height of summer.

Spinach tends to be gritty and should be soaked in water for some time and then rinsed in several changes of water. It is at its best when very young and fresh and may be eaten raw in salads. Older leaves need to have the tough stems trimmed off and are best cooked simply in the residual water from rinsing. Spinach should always be cooked briefly or the leaves become mushy. Allow 100 g/3½ oz per person if using spinach raw, but about 450 g/1 lb when serving it cooked, as the leaves lose a lot of water during cooking with consequent shrinkage.

Spinach does not keep well: raw, it should be eaten the same day; cooked, it quickly becomes toxic and should not be kept longer than 24 hours. Spinach freezes well but canned spinach tends to be bland and uninteresting.

Cooked spinach is usually dressed with butter, and perhaps a little nutmeg, and it may be chopped or puréed. Spinach makes the ideal accompaniment for roast meat served in its own gravy, for veal escalopes (cutlets) and for ham. It also goes well with white fish, especially as a stuffing. It is traditionally teamed with eggs, as in the classic *oeufs florentine*, and is popular in soufflés, quiches and gratins.

Spinach is rich in vitamins and minerals, especially iron, but it also contains a high level of oxalic acid which inhibits the body's absorption of nutrients. For this reason spinach should not be eaten too frequently or used regularly as a slimming food, even if it does contain only 25 calories per 100 g/3½ oz.

FLANS À L'ÉPINARD

Spinach creams

Serves 4
Preparation 15 minutes
Cooking 30 minutes

METRIC/IMPERIAL	AMERICAN
55 g/2 oz butter	*4 tbsp butter*
1 kg/2¼ lb fresh young spinach, trimmed	*2¼ lb fresh bulk young spinach, trimmed*
200 ml/7 fl oz thick crème fraîche or whipping cream	*1 cup thick crème fraîche or whipping cream*
1 whole egg + 2 egg yolks	*1 whole egg + 2 egg yolks*
salt and white pepper	*salt and white pepper*

Preheat the oven to 180C/350F/gas 4. Grease 8 dariole (timbale or baba) moulds with half the butter.

Cook the spinach for 3 minutes in salted boiling water. Refresh in cold water and then squeeze to extract all the water.

Melt the remaining butter in a pan over a high heat and cook the spinach in it, stirring, for 4–5 minutes. Meanwhile, put the cream in a small pan and reduce slightly over a moderate heat.

Pass the spinach through a food mill and then add the cream. Season with salt and pepper. Stir in the whole egg and the 2 egg yolks.

Spoon this mixture into the prepared moulds. Bake in a *bain-marie* in the oven for 20 minutes, then unmould and serve, allowing 2 per person, to accompany chicken supremes, fish fillets or grenadines of veal.

Salade d'épinards au poisson fumé

Spinach salad with warm smoked fish

Serves 4
Preparation 15 minutes
Cooking about 5 minutes

METRIC/IMPERIAL	AMERICAN
450 g/1 lb fresh spinach, trimmed	1 lb fresh bulk spinach, trimmed
4 tbsp groundnut oil	¼ cup peanut oil
225 g/½ lb smoked fish, such as salmon, halibut or trout, cut into bite-size pieces	½ lb smoked fish, such as salmon, finnan haddie or trout, cut into bite-size pieces
1 tbsp hazelnut oil	1 tbsp hazelnut oil
1 tbsp white wine vinegar	1 tbsp white wine vinegar
1 tbsp sherry vinegar	1 tbsp sherry vinegar
1 tsp strong mustard	1 tsp Dijon mustard
salt and pepper	salt and pepper

Blanch the spinach for 3 minutes in salted boiling water. Refresh in cold water and squeeze out excess liquid. Pat dry.

Heat 1 tablespoon of the groundnut (peanut) oil in a frying pan and brown the fish in it.

Make a vinaigrette with the remaining groundnut (peanut) oil, the hazelnut oil, vinegars, mustard and salt and pepper to taste.

In a salad bowl, toss the spinach in the vinaigrette and put it on 4 serving plates. Add the pieces of hot fish and serve at once.

Note: if the spinach leaves are very young and tender, there is no need to blanch them.

Variation: the vinaigrette may be flavoured with a little chopped shallot.

Spiny lobster

Langouste

see also:
crayfish
langoustine
lobster
shellfish

The spiny lobster is a marine crustacean also known as the ROCK LOBSTER or CRAWFISH, which causes great confusion with the crayfish. It differs from the lobster in that it lacks the large front claws and prefers slightly warmer waters. It is found in European waters from southwest England to the Mediterranean, in North American waters from North Carolina to Mexico, in the Caribbean and off the coasts of Central and South America. It may also be found in the Pacific, off the coasts of California and Mexico.

It is prepared and cooked in much the same way as lobster, although the milder flavour of its flesh suits richer and more highly flavoured dishes. The French favour it grilled or poached in salads or with spicy mayonnaise, and a classic Spanish dish teams the *langosto* with bitter chocolate and nuts.

Spiny lobster is quite low in calories: 100 g/3½ oz of flesh has only 90.

Langouste à la Parisienne

Spiny lobster with mustard mayonnaise

Serves 2–4
Preparation 20 minutes
Cooking about 35 minutes, 2 hours ahead

METRIC/IMPERIAL	AMERICAN
1 lemon	1 lemon
1 onion, sliced	1 onion, sliced
1 carrot, sliced	1 carrot, sliced
1 garlic clove	1 garlic clove
2 or 3 parsley stalks	2 or 3 parsley stems
sprig of thyme	sprig of thyme
bay leaf	bay leaf
6 black peppercorns	6 black peppercorns
½ tsp salt	½ tsp salt
100 ml/3½ fl oz vinegar	½ cup vinegar
1 live spiny lobster, weighing about 1 kg/2¼ lb	1 live spiny lobster, weighing about 2¼ lb
8 large lettuce leaves	8 large lettuce leaves
300 ml/½ pt mayonnaise, to serve	1½ cups mayonnaise, to serve

Salade d'épinards au poisson fumé (Spinach salad with warm smoked fish)

If the lemon is not organically grown and may have been sprayed or coated, scrub it in hot soapy water, rinse well and pat dry. Slice it.

Put the onion, carrot and garlic in a large saucepan with 2 l/3½ pt/2 qt of water. Add the parsley stalks, thyme, bay leaf, peppercorns, the salt, vinegar and the lemon slices. Bring to the boil and simmer gently for 20 minutes.

At the end of this time, increase the heat and plunge the spiny lobster into the boiling court-bouillon. Bring back to just below the boil and simmer very gently, with the water just bubbling, for 15 minutes. Remove from the heat and allow to cool in the liquid.

When cool, take out the spiny lobster and split it lengthwise in half. Chill the pieces.

Arrange the lettuce on a serving plate and then place the lobster halves on it. Serve well chilled as a first course, with the mayonnaise.

SPIRITS

see also:
alcohol
brandies, etc
creams and custards
flaming
fruit
maceration
marinating

Distilled alcoholic beverages, spirits have a high alcohol content and strong flavours. Those most commonly used in cooking include:

GIN, which is made from grains mainly in England and Holland, is usually flavoured with juniper. Because of this strong flavour its culinary use is fairly limited to some lamb dishes, game marinades and offal (variety meat), especially kidneys, and on orange salads.

RUM is made from sugar cane, mostly in the West Indies, and is a widely used flavouring in *pâtisserie*, from crêpe batters to sponge cakes, and in creams and custards. It is often used to flame sweet omelettes and crêpes and to flavour fruit salads and macerate dried fruit. Rum's affinity with tropical fruit is also used in savoury cooking, in dishes marrying bananas or pineapple with chicken, pork or fish.

VODKA is distilled from grain, potatoes or beets. It is widely made in Eastern Europe and may be flavoured with herbs, berries or spices, such as cinnamon or ginger. Vodka is the classic accompaniment for caviar and for smoked fish hors d'oeuvres. Again vodka is favoured to dress fresh fruit and may be used to flavour sorbets. Its savoury uses are rare, but it can be used for flaming fish dishes and for deglazing pans for fish and poultry sauces.

WHISKY originated in Scotland and is made from malted barley, wheat, rye or oats, dried over peat fires to give it its particular flavour. Whisky is also made in Ireland, Canada and the USA, where it is spelled 'whiskey'. The North Americans make fine RYE WHISKEY and BOURBON WHISKEY from a mixture of grains, with corn predominating. Whisky works well in creamy dishes, both sweet and savoury. It is mixed with honey, cream and oats to make the traditional Scots dessert Atholl Brose, and is used in Irish coffee and to flavour fruit. In savoury cooking it adds an original touch to certain chicken and seafood dishes, and it is preferred by many to brandy for flaming.

When cooking with spirits, there is no need to use expensive, matured varieties. The plainest spirits will do, especially if they are heated.

POULET AU RHUM

Chicken with rum

Serves 4
Preparation 30 minutes, macerating 24 hours
Cooking 35 minutes

METRIC/IMPERIAL	*AMERICAN*
1 ripe pineapple, weighing about 1 kg/2¼ lb, peeled, cored and diced	*1 ripe pineapple, weighing about 2¼ lb, peeled, cored and diced*
½ tsp cayenne pepper	*½ tsp cayenne pepper*
200 ml/7 fl oz rum	*1 cup rum*
1 oven-ready chicken, weighing about 1.35 kg/3 lb, jointed	*1 chicken, dressed and drawn weight about 3 lb, cut into pieces*
30 g/1 oz butter	*2 tbsp butter*
2 tbsp groundnut oil	*2 tbsp peanut oil*
bunch of parsley, finely chopped	*bunch of parsley, finely chopped*
2 garlic cloves, chopped	*2 garlic cloves, chopped*
salt and pepper	*salt and pepper*

Put the pieces of pineapple into a bowl and add several pinches of cayenne pepper and the rum. Stir and macerate overnight.

Season the chicken with salt and pepper.

Melt the butter with the oil in a flameproof casserole over a moderate heat. Brown the chicken pieces, turning them several times. Add the parsley and garlic and stir for 5 minutes.

Add 4 tablespoons of the pineapple marinade to the casserole. Lower the heat, cover and simmer for 20 minutes, adding the rest of the marinade in spoonfuls at regular intervals.

Add the pineapple to the casserole and cook very gently for a further 5 minutes. Adjust the seasoning and serve in a warmed, deep dish accompanied by a purée of sweet potatoes.

SPONGE

see Cakes and gâteaux

SPRING ONION OR SCALLION

Ciboule

see also: chives, herb, onion, salad, shallot, vegetables

Seed onions harvested when young are known as spring onions, scallions or GREEN ONIONS and the white bulb and stem and the long green leaves are used. The size and shape of the bulb varies according to the variety of onion. The flavour of spring onions is more delicate than onion but stronger than chives and may be used both raw and cooked in the same way as shallots. Chopped spring onions are a popular salad ingredient and in Oriental stir-fried dishes.

ÉMINCÉ DE BOEUF AUX CIBOULES

Beef with spring onions or scallions

Serves 4
Preparation 20 minutes, 15 minutes ahead
Cooking about 15 minutes

METRIC/IMPERIAL	AMERICAN
450 g/1 lb rump steak, cut into very thin strips	1 lb boneless sirloin steak, cut into very thin strips
6 tbsp oil	6 tbsp oil
1 tbsp cornflour	1 tbsp cornstarch
300 g/10 oz spring onions, thinly sliced	10 oz (3 cups) scallions, thinly sliced
1 stalk of celery, trimmed and chopped	1 stick of celery, trimmed and chopped
1 garlic clove, chopped	1 garlic clove, chopped
2 tbsp soy sauce	2 tbsp soy sauce
1 tbsp white wine	1 tbsp white wine
1 tsp caster sugar	1 tsp superfine sugar
1 tsp vinegar	1 tsp vinegar
3 pinches of chilli powder	3 pinches of chili powder
salt and pepper	salt and pepper

Put the meat in a bowl and add 1 tablespoon of the oil mixed with the cornflour (cornstarch). Stir, then let it stand for 15 minutes.

In another bowl, mix together the vegetables, soy sauce, wine, sugar, vinegar, chilli powder, salt and pepper.

Heat the remaining oil in a large frying pan over a high heat. When it is very hot, add the strips of meat and stir fry until they are golden brown. Remove the strips and drain them.

Pour most of the oil out of the pan, leaving only about 2 tablespoons. Drain the vegetables, reserving the liquid, and sauté for 2–3 minutes over a high heat. Add the reserved liquid and stir for 1 further minute. Return the meat to the pan for a few seconds, then serve immediately.

SQUAB

see Pigeon

SQUASH

Courge

see also: cucumber, flower, vegetables

The squash or gourd family of moist-fleshed vegetable fruits is related to the cucumber and melon and embraces several species.

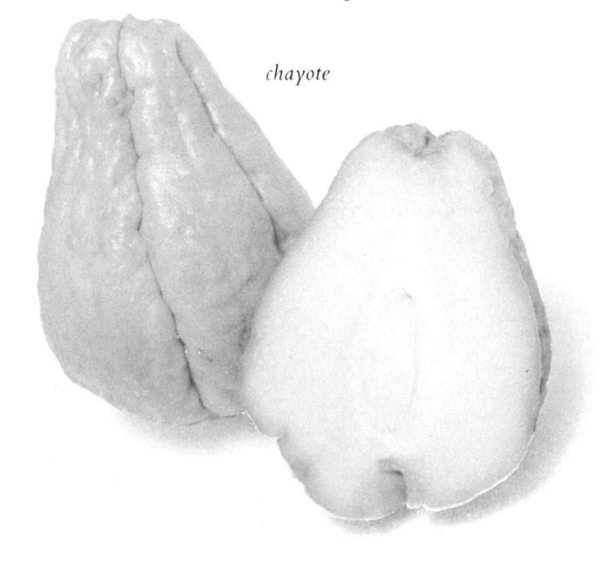

chayote

SOFT-SKINNED OR SUMMER SQUASHES are completely edible, skin and all, and are often eaten raw. They include the large, green-striped VEGETABLE MARROW which epitomizes the worst aspects of these vegetables with its watery flesh and insipid flavour. It is best served stuffed with a rich and tasty mixture.

Dwarf versions of the marrow harvested young are the green or yellow COURGETTES or ZUCCHINI which have much more flavour. They are best sliced or shredded and quickly sautéed in oil with a little garlic or lemon juice. The Italians deep fry them in batter and the FLOWERS attached to very young specimens are also often given the same treatment.

YELLOW SQUASH, straight or crook-necked, is best when very small. The pale green CHAYOTE, also called CHRISTOPHINE OR CHOW CHOW, resembles a flattened pear with deep longitudinal ribs and delicate creamy flesh. When small and tender, the delicious CUSTARD MARROW OR PATTY PAN SQUASH can be eaten whole or prepared in the same ways as courgettes or zucchini; older specimens are best peeled before cooking, or they can be slightly hollowed out, stuffed and baked.

When buying any of the soft-skinned squashes test one with a finger nail. If the skin is not pierced with ease, the vegetable is not in good condition. They should also be quite rigid with no sign of wrinkling near the stalk end.

WINTER SQUASHES are generally larger and have a thick or tough skin and firm flesh surrounding fairly hard seeds which are normally removed before cooking. Both the smaller winter squashes, such as the green-skinned ACORN SQUASH and the superb BUTTERNUT SQUASH with its sweet orange flesh, and large winter squashes such as the PUMPKIN and HUBBARD, can be made into soups and purées. They may also be baked *au gratin* and used in pies, pickles or jams.

The cooked flesh of smooth, oval SPAGHETTI SQUASH looks like a mass of string. It may be served with a savoury sauce or made into jam.

Winter squashes keep well and can survive until spring in good condition if carefully stored.

PUMPKIN SEEDS are dried and sold as snacks.

Squashes are very low in calories: 100 g/3½ oz of pumpkin contains only 23.

COURGETTES FARCIES

Stuffed courgettes or zucchini

Serves 4
Preparation 25 minutes
Cooking about 40 minutes

METRIC/IMPERIAL	*AMERICAN*
2 large thick courgettes	*2 large thick zucchini*
100 g/3½ oz lentils	*½ cup lentils*
1 tbsp sunflower oil	*1 tbsp sunflower oil*
1 onion, chopped	*1 onion, chopped*
2 stalks of celery, trimmed and chopped	*2 sticks of celery, trimmed and chopped*
115 g/¼ lb mushrooms, chopped	*¼ lb mushrooms, chopped*
1 tbsp mild curry powder	*1 tbsp mild curry powder*
1 tbsp chopped parsley	*1 tbsp chopped parsley*
salt and pepper	*salt and pepper*

Cut the courgettes (zucchini) in half lengthwise. Using a teaspoon or melon ball cutter, remove the seeds along with a little of the flesh to make a cavity. Discard the seeds, but chop the removed flesh and reserve it.

Bring 1 l/1¾ pt/1 qt of water to the boil. Put the lentils in a deep dish, pour the boiling water over them, cover and microwave on High for 15 minutes, stirring twice during cooking. Leave to stand for 5 minutes then drain the lentils.

courgette (zucchini)

Put the oil in a dish and microwave it on High for 1 minute. Add the onion, stir and microwave again on High for 1 minute. Add the celery, mushrooms, reserved courgette (zucchini) flesh and cooked lentils. Mix and cook for 2 minutes on High. Stir, cover and microwave for a further 6 minutes on High, stirring once.

Add the curry powder to the stuffing and season with salt and pepper. Fill the courgette (zucchini) halves with this stuffing, scatter the parsley over them and put them in a large dish. Cover and microwave on High for 8 minutes, rotating the dish half-way through.

Serve very hot with a tomato coulis.

To drink: any fruity rosé wine, such as Tavel.

SOUPE AU POTIRON

Pumpkin soup

Serves 6
Preparation 30 minutes
Cooking about 1¼ hours

METRIC/IMPERIAL	AMERICAN
55 g/2 oz butter	4 tbsp butter
2 onions, thinly sliced	2 onions, thinly sliced
2 leeks, trimmed and sliced	2 leeks, trimmed and sliced
1 kg/2¼ lb pumpkin flesh, diced	2¼ lb pumpkin flesh, diced
500 ml/16 fl oz milk	2 cups milk
500 ml/16 fl oz chicken stock	2 cups chicken stock
2 floury potatoes, peeled and diced	2 floury potatoes, peeled and diced
3 tbsp crème fraîche or whipping cream	3 tbsp crème fraîche or whipping cream
salt and pepper	salt and pepper

Melt the butter in a flameproof casserole over a moderate heat and cook the onions and leeks for 5 minutes.

Add the pumpkin and cook it for 5 minutes, stirring over a low heat. Season with salt and pepper. Cook gently, covered, for 5 minutes.

Meanwhile, in separate pans, heat the milk and the stock. Pour the milk and then the stock into the casserole, stirring constantly, then add the potatoes and cook, covered, for 1 hour.

Pass the contents of the casserole through a vegetable mill, return the soup to the casserole and reheat it gently. Add the cream and season with salt and pepper. Serve hot.

GRATIN DE CHAYOTTES AUX FOIES DE VOLAILLE

Baked chayote with chicken livers

Serves 4
Preparation 10 minutes
Cooking about 50 minutes

METRIC/IMPERIAL	AMERICAN
4 firm chayotes	4 firm chayotes
45 g/1½ oz butter	3 tbsp butter
1 tbsp oil	1 tbsp oil
1 shallot, chopped	1 shallot, chopped
115 g/¼ lb chicken livers, trimmed and cut into equal pieces	¼ lb chicken livers, trimmed and cut into equal pieces
½ tsp grated nutmeg	½ tsp grated nutmeg
2 tbsp crème fraîche or whipping cream	2 tbsp crème fraîche or whipping cream
100 g/3½ oz grated Gruyère	1 cup grated Gruyère cheese
salt and pepper	salt and pepper

Steam the chayotes for 20 minutes, then leave them to cool.

Preheat the oven to 180C/350F/gas 4 and grease a baking dish with half the butter.

Melt the remaining butter with the oil in a frying pan over a moderate heat and lightly brown the shallot in it. Add the chicken livers and sauté them briskly for 8 minutes.

Season with salt, pepper and nutmeg and add the cream. Reduce the sauce for 3–4 minutes, stirring. Remove the pan from the heat.

Peel the chayotes, cut in quarters and then thinly slice them, discarding the kernel.

Arrange a layer of chayote slices in the dish and spread over the chicken livers in cream sauce. Cover with the rest of the chayote slices. Add a little more salt and grated nutmeg and sprinkle with the grated Gruyère.

Bake for 20 minutes in the oven. Serve straight from the baking dish.

To drink: a Rosé de Provence.

see also:
cuttlefish
octopus
shellfish

SQUID OR CALAMARI

Calmar

The most common of cephalopod molluscs, the spindle-shaped squid can vary from finger nail size to some 20 m/65 ft in length, but those eaten are seldom longer than 50 cm/20 in. Like cuttlefish, they are 'ten-footed' with 8 shorter 'arms' and 2 long tentacles, normally retracted, and they have characteristic triangular fins at their tail end.

When buying squid, look for vestiges of their natural iridescence as an indication of freshness. Only the tentacles and fleshy pouch, or body, of squid are edible. The head must first be removed from the mantle, and most of the rest of the innards come away with it. The ink sacs are often retained for use in cooking. The clear cartilaginous 'pen' and the beak must also be cut out and the dark skin rubbed off.

Larger squid are generally stuffed. The tentacles are chopped and added to the stuffing. The bodies may also be sliced across into rings and deep fried, sautéed, simmered in white wine or used in seafood salads. The Spanish and Portuguese cook squid in a black sauce made from the ink.

Squid contains only 90 calories per 100 g/ 3½ oz when plainly cooked.

CALMARS FARCIS À LA PROVENÇALE

Stuffed squid

Serves 4
Preparation 20 minutes
Cooking about 50 minutes

METRIC/IMPERIAL	AMERICAN
4 tbsp olive oil	4 tbsp olive oil
8 small squid, cleaned, with their tentacles	8 small squid, cleaned, with their tentacles
100 g/3½ oz stale bread	4 slices stale bread
5 tbsp milk	⅓ cup milk
3 large onions, finely chopped	3 large onions, finely chopped
4 garlic cloves, finely chopped	4 garlic cloves, finely chopped
bunch of parsley, finely chopped	bunch of parsley, finely chopped
2 tomatoes, peeled and coarsely chopped	2 tomatoes, peeled and coarsely chopped
2 egg yolks	2 egg yolks
150 ml/¼ pt dry white wine	⅔ cup dry white wine
2–3 tbsp breadcrumbs	2–3 tbsp breadcrumbs
salt and pepper	salt and pepper

Preheat the oven to 180C/350F/gas 4. Use one quarter of the oil to grease a large, flameproof dish and a sheet of foil to cover it.

Chop the squid tentacles. Soak the bread in a little milk, then squeeze it out and mix with the chopped tentacles and two of the onions.

Heat 2 tablespoons of the olive oil in a sauté pan and brown the mixture in it. Add three quarters of the garlic and half the chopped parsley along with the tomatoes. Remove from the heat and stir in the egg yolks. Fill the squid with this stuffing and sew them up.

Pack the squid tightly together in the baking dish. Sprinkle the remaining garlic, parsley and onion over the squid. Season with salt and pepper. Moisten with the white wine and 150 ml/¼ pt/⅔ cup of water.

Cover the dish with the foil. Start the cooking on top of the stove over a high heat until the liquid is bubbling, then transfer to the oven to cook for a further 30 minutes.

Uncover the dish and cook for 5 minutes over a high heat on top of the stove to reduce the liquid. Sprinkle the squid with the remaining oil and the breadcrumbs and brown under a preheated grill (broiler) for 3 minutes.

see also:
beef
chateaubriand
entrecôte
fillet
fish
tournedos

STEAK

Bifteck

Slices of prime meat for grilling (broiling) or frying are steaks. The most tender beef steaks come from the fillet (tenderloin) but those from the rump and the sirloin, including the T-bone and entrecote, tend to have more flavour.

Steaks are best cooked quickly at the highest possible temperature to seal the exterior and keep in all their natural juices. For this reason it is important to ensure that steaks are allowed some time at room temperature before cooking or the inside may stay cool in the short times involved.

As they cook without exuding much of their juices to make a gravy, they are often served with a flavoured butter. Nowadays more economical steaks are also taken from traditional braising cuts, such as the topside (top round) or flank, and these are delicious cooked more slowly, perhaps in a wine sauce, or marinated first to tenderize them.

The term steak is also used of thick slices of whole fish cut across the backbone.

STEAK TARTARE is a dish of best quality, raw minced (ground) steak mixed with seasonings, onions and capers and bound with an egg.

STEAK AU POIVRE

Pepper steaks

Serves 4
Preparation 10 minutes, 15 minutes ahead
Cooking about 10 minutes

METRIC/IMPERIAL	*AMERICAN*
4 slices of beef fillet, each 3 cm/1¼ in thick and weighing about 170 g/6 oz	*4 filet mignons, each 1¼ in thick and weighing about 6 oz*
3 tbsp Cognac	*3 tbsp Cognac*
4 tbsp cracked black pepper	*¼ cup cracked black pepper*
30 g/1 oz butter	*2 tbsp butter*
150 ml/¼ pt crème fraîche or whipping cream	*⅔ cup crème fraîche or whipping cream*
salt	*salt*

Take the steaks out of the refrigerator 30 minutes before cooking.

Pour the Cognac into a dish and dip both sides of the steaks in it. Put the cracked pepper into a shallow soup plate and press the steaks into it on both sides firmly so that the pepper adheres to the meat. Let stand for 15 minutes.

Melt the butter in a frying pan over a high heat and brown the steaks for 2–3 minutes on each side. Add 1 tablespoon of the Cognac to the pan and flame it. Remove the steaks from the pan and keep hot on a warmed dish.

Pour off the butter used for cooking the steaks and pour the cream into the pan. Bring to the boil, stirring up the sediments in the pan with a wooden spoon. Remove from the heat and stir in the juices from the steaks. Put the steaks on warmed plates and coat with the sauce.

STEAMING

see also:
boiling
pressure cooker

Cooking food very gently in the vapour from a little liquid in a tightly closed utensil is termed steaming. The food is normally set in a basket over a seasoned liquid which gives rise to aromatic steam. Alternatively, as in the cooking of spinach, the food may simply steam in the vapour from any residual water.

Steaming is effected in a wide range of utensils. The Chinese use bamboo baskets placed one on top of another so that an entire meal may be cooked at the same time. There are purpose-built double saucepans or pans with built-in baskets, but a simple metal strainer with legs in a large stewpot will suffice.

The liquid must usually be sufficient in quantity not to dry out during cooking, but must not touch the food. Salted water flavoured with with herbs and spices is the most common steaming medium, but beef or chicken stock or fish court-bouillon or stock may also be used.

Only the best and freshest of ingredients should be steamed as the process brings out any unpleasant odours.

Steaming is the perfect cooking method for fish; they cook more quickly than in the oven or in court-bouillon, and the flesh does not disintegrate. Whole fish should not be scaled, simply placed on a bed of fennel, dill or edible seaweed. The same method can be applied to shellfish.

It is also particularly effective with vegetables, as it preserves more flavour, texture and colour, as well as a much higher level of vitamins and minerals.

Steaming for a minute or so also makes items such as tomatoes and peaches easier to peel. Shellfish open in a matter of about 3 minutes and dried fruit rehydrates in 4–5 minutes.

Traditional English suet puddings are also described as steamed, although they are really immersed in the water and boiled.

Steaming is a very healthy means of cooking, as a much higher level of nutrients is retained and there is no need for added fat.

FILETS DE SOLE AU BASILIC

Steamed sole fillets with basil

Serves 4
Preparation 20 minutes
Cooking about 15 minutes

METRIC/IMPERIAL	AMERICAN
8 sprigs of fresh basil	8 sprigs of fresh basil
8 sole fillets	8 sole fillets
2 eggs	2 eggs
4 tbsp olive oil	4 tbsp olive oil
2 shallots, chopped	2 shallots, chopped
1 tsp strong mustard	1 tsp Dijon mustard
juice of 1 lemon	juice of 1 lemon
3 tomatoes, peeled and chopped	3 tomatoes, peeled and chopped
1 tbsp finely snipped chervil	1 tbsp finely snipped chervil
salt and pepper	salt and pepper

Spread out 7 of the basil sprigs in the bottom of a steamer basket. Fold the sole fillets in half, place them on the basil and season.

Pour 400 ml/14 fl oz/1¾ cups water into the steamer and bring to the boil. Set the steamer basket over the water. Cover and cook for 10 minutes.

Meanwhile, soft boil the eggs, refresh in cold water and shell. Finely chop the remaining basil.

Steak au poivre (Peppered steaks)

Heat 1 tablespoon of the oil in a saucepan. Add the shallots and stir for 2 minutes. Add the mustard and lemon juice. Whisk in the remaining oil. Add the tomatoes and chervil.

Put the fillets on individual plates and coat them with sauce. Add half a soft-boiled egg to each and garnish with the chopped basil.

To drink: a white wine or dry rosé, such as those from Saint-Chinian.

STERILIZATION

see also: jams, etc pasteurization preserving

One of the surest methods of preservation, sterilization eliminates all micro-organisms plus their spores so that they will not regenerate. Whereas other methods of killing micro-organisms, such as pasteurization, are usually not rigorous enough also to kill the spores, sterilization does this effectively by boiling a raw foodstuff or a cooked preparation in a hermetically sealed container, or autoclave, at a temperature of at least 100C/212F for about 30 minutes.

In the food industry, sterilization is widely used for milk, canned goods and jam. Domestically, usually jams, jellies and bottled fruit and some vegetables are sterilized.

To sterilize jars before filling them with preserves they should be put in the oven preheated to 180C/350F/gas 4 for at least 1½ hours. Once sealed, jars of preserves should be sterilized in boiling water at a temperature of 110–115C/230–240F for 15–20 minutes, depending on jar size. Foods preserved in this way will keep for 10–12 months at cool room temperature.

STEWING

see also: braising ragoût sautéing steaming

Slow, gentle cooking in a liquid is termed stewing. It differs from poaching in that the liquid, usually a stock, only partly covers the stewing food and the cooking is done in a covered pan so that the method also has the beneficial effects of both steaming and braising. Food to be stewed is usually cut into small pieces before cooking and there may be some initial browning. Some gentle stewing often follows sautéing to cook food through.

Tougher cuts of meat benefit greatly from stewing, which tenderizes and develops flavour. Dishes of stewed mixed vegetables and meat are termed 'stews' and many classic dishes, such as ragoûts, carbonnade, *boeuf à la bourguignonne* and most curries are effectively stews.

Hard fruit is often stewed in a sugar syrup.

see also:
aspic
braising
clarification
consommé
court-bouillon
essence
fumet
roux
sauce
seasoning
soup
stewing

STOCK

Bouillon, fond

A flavoured liquid used as the base for soups, sauces, stews and braised dishes is known as a stock. It is made by simmering flavouring items, like beef, chicken or fish, together with aromatics, such as onions and peppercorns. For richer sauces and soups, whole chickens and meat or fish on the bone are used, but good stocks can also be made using bones and trimmings alone. It is important when making fish stock not to cook for more than about 30 minutes as the bones will start to break down and make the stock bitter. However, meat and poultry stocks benefit from lengthy cooking.

Home-made stock is time-consuming but not difficult, and can greatly improve the flavour of a dish. Stocks are only very lightly salted initially, as they may be reduced to concentrate the flavour and thicken them. Commercial concentrated stock cubes and canned bouillons tend to have coarser flavours and may be salty.

Stock may be kept in the refrigerator for up to a week, but can always be boiled up to keep it fresh, although the flavour and nutrients will suffer. Concentrated stock freezes well.

Strain the stock, allow to cool, then chill.

Remove the hardened fat from the surface.

FOND DE BOEUF

Beef stock

Makes about 1 l/1¾ pt/1 qt
Preparation 30 minutes
Cooking about 2 hours, 24 hours ahead

METRIC/IMPERIAL	AMERICAN
1 kg/2¼ lb oxtail, cut into small pieces	2¼ lb oxtail, cut into small pieces
3 carrots, sliced	3 carrots, sliced
1 onion, sliced	1 onion, sliced
2 garlic cloves, sliced	2 garlic cloves, sliced
bouquet garni	bouquet garni
small bunch of parsley	small bunch of parsley

Preheat the oven to 250C/475F/gas 9.

Cook the oxtail pieces in a roasting pan in the oven for 10 minutes, or until well browned.

Transfer the pieces to a large stewpot and cover with 1.5 l/2½ pt/1½ qt of water. Add the vegetables, garlic and bouquet garni. Bring to the boil and simmer gently for about 1½ hours. Skim several times during cooking.

Strain the stock and return it to the pot with the parsley. Simmer for a further 20 minutes and strain again. Allow to cool and then chill.

Once the fat has congealed on the surface, remove it and discard it. Bring the stock to the boil again and allow to cool. Keep it in the refrigerator until needed. Before using, remove any fat that forms on the surface.

Variation: for veal stock, use veal knuckle bones and add 115 g/¼ lb of sliced mushrooms.

FOND DE VOLAILLE

Chicken stock

Makes about 1 l/1¾ pt/1 qt
Preparation 20 minutes
Cooking about 50 minutes

METRIC/IMPERIAL	AMERICAN
1 onion	1 onion
1 clove	1 clove
1 chicken carcass, broken into pieces, with giblets	1 chicken carcass, broken into pieces, with giblets

2 carrots, cut into chunks	*2 carrots, cut into chunks*
2 stalks of celery, sliced	*2 sticks of celery, sliced*
white of 1 leek, sliced	*white of 1 leek, sliced*
cracked black pepper	*cracked black pepper*
bouquet garni	*bouquet garni*
salt and pepper	*salt and pepper*

Stud the onion with the clove.

Bring 1.5 l/$2\frac{1}{2}$ pt/$1\frac{1}{2}$ qt of water to the boil in a stewpot. Add the chicken carcass and giblets and all the vegetables, plus some salt, several pinches of cracked pepper and the bouquet garni. Cook gently for 45 minutes.

Strain the stock and leave it to cool, then chill it. Before using, carefully skim off any fat that has formed on the surface.

Variation: for a vegetable stock, omit the chicken, add another onion, sliced, and use 2 whole leeks coarsely chopped. Simmer for only 30 minutes, then strain. There will be no fat, but impurities must still be skimmed off.

STOCK GLAZE

see Glaze

STRAWBERRY

Fraise

see also:
fruit
jams, etc
mousse

Small, red berry fruit, strawberries are unique in that they are so-called 'false fruit', carrying their seeds on their outsides instead of within them.

Strawberries have been widely grown in temperate climates in Europe, Asia and North America for centuries, but most of the varieties cultivated worldwide today are descended from species native to North America.

The best-known and most widely grown is the small and fragrant WOOD STRAWBERRY. The conical, often deep-coloured RED GAUNTLET is also popular with growers as it has good keeping qualities, but it is quite acidic and can be fairly flavourless. The large GORELLA is available early in the summer and can be quite juicy and sweet. Very large American HOLIDAY strawberries have firm flesh and are one of the few varieties which freeze well.

Tiny, deeply coloured WILD STRAWBERRIES (*fraises de bois*) grow wild in many parts of the world and are incomparable in flavour. Some species are white and make an unusual garnish; others have a distinctly musky flavour which is delicious in fruit salads.

Unfortunately, commercial growers have gone mainly for size and appearance: larger strawberries may look appealing, but they are often insipid. Also, as strawberries do not keep well, they are usually harvested slightly underripe when the flavour has not developed properly. For good flavour, buy medium-sized berries with a good colour and strong smell. Forced hothouse strawberries sold out of season are generally woody in texture and flavourless.

Strawberries should be clear and unbruised, firm, and not too shiny red in colour. As good indicators of ripeness, the tip of the strawberry should be red rather than pale white and the stalk should be bright green.

Strawberries can moulder within a few hours, particularly in thundery weather, and will last for only two days in the refrigerator. They do not freeze well, as they lose their texture, so frozen berries are best used for purées. Strawberries should be rinsed quickly just before being hulled, and never soaked, or they will absorb water and lose their flavour.

Like most summer fruit, strawberries are best enjoyed on their own or with cream. They are very good in fruit salads and their flavour is brought out by a light dusting of black pepper, a little chopped fresh mint or a sprinkling of eau-de-vie. Strawberries are also used to make mousses, creams, cakes, tarts, sorbets and ice creams, as well as jams and jellies.

Strawberries are rich in minerals and vitamin C and are very low in calories: 100 g/$3\frac{1}{2}$ oz contains only 20.

FRAISES GINETTE

Champagne strawberries with lemon sorbet

Serves 4
Preparation 20 minutes, macerating 30 minutes

METRIC/IMPERIAL	AMERICAN
450 g/1 lb strawberries, hulled	1¼ pt strawberries, hulled
100 g/3½ oz caster sugar	½ cup superfine sugar
100 ml/3½ fl oz Curaçao	½ cup Curaçao
150 ml/¼ pt champagne	⅔ cup champagne
200 ml/7 fl oz whipping cream	1 cup whipping cream
1 sachet (7.5 g/1¾ tsp) of vanilla sugar	1¾ tsp vanilla-flavored sugar
500 ml/16 fl oz lemon sorbet (see Sorbet)	1 pt lemon sorbet (see Sorbet)
75 g/2½ oz crystallized violets, coarsely chopped	2½ oz crystallized violets, coarsely chopped
115 g/¼ lb candied orange peel, cut into very thin strips	¼ lb candied orange peel, cut into very thin strips

Put the strawberries into a bowl with half the sugar. Pour the Curaçao and champagne over them, stir and macerate for 30 minutes.

Whip the cream with the rest of the sugar and the vanilla sugar. Drain the strawberries and strain the syrup through muslin or cheesecloth.

Spoon the sorbet into 4 chilled bowls. Arrange the strawberries on top of the sorbet. Pour the syrup over and coat with the whipped cream. Sprinkle over the chopped violets and strips of orange peel to decorate.

STUFFING OR FORCEMEAT

Farce

see also:
ballottine
pasta
paupiette
quenelle
sausage

The ingredients of any seasoned mixture used as a stuffing vary according to the type of meat, poultry, vegetable or pasta, etc, to be stuffed. They most usually consist of chopped, raw or cooked meat or poultry, flavoured with onion and herbs or spices. They are often bulked out with breadcrumbs and possibly bound with eggs or a sauce.

A stuffing for meat or poultry that is to be boiled needs to be more highly seasoned than one destined for a roast and the latter needs to have a fairly high fat content. Never use a very highly flavoured stuffing to stuff a delicately flavoured food. Some stuffings, such as chopped lemons or herbs in poultry, are intended simply to add flavour and are not themselves eaten.

Stuffings usually swell during cooking and should therefore never be too tightly pushed into a cavity. It is important to secure edges or sew up all apertures of the meat or bird firmly, so that the stuffing does not burst out. As a general rule, the average chicken needs about 450 g/1 lb of stuffing and a large, whole fish about 225 g/8 oz. Remember that roasts which contain stuffings, particularly those made of raw ingredients, take a great deal longer to cook.

Some stuffing mixtures are rolled into balls and baked separately. This is a good method when the food being cooked is quite dry, as stuffing tends to absorb its juices.

FARCE AUX CHAMPIGNONS

Mushroom forcemeat

Makes about 450 g/1 lb stuffing
Preparation 10 minutes
Cooking 15 minutes

METRIC/IMPERIAL	AMERICAN
45 g/1½ oz butter	3 tbsp butter
225 g/½ lb cultivated or wild mushrooms, wiped and finely chopped	½ lb cultivated or wild mushrooms, wiped and finely chopped
2 shallots, chopped	2 shallots, chopped
1 slice of white bread	1 slice of white bread
3 tbsp milk	3 tbsp milk
2 tbsp chopped parsley	2 tbsp chopped parsley
3 egg yolks	3 egg yolks
grated nutmeg	grated nutmeg
salt and pepper	salt and pepper

Melt the butter in a saucepan over a high heat. Add the mushrooms and shallots and sauté them, then lower the heat and cook, uncovered, until the mushroom juices have evaporated.

Season with nutmeg, salt and pepper. Remove from the heat and cool. Meanwhile, moisten the bread in the milk and mash it.

Add the bread and parsley to the mushrooms, then mix in the egg yolks. The stuffing may be blended in a food processor or left as it is.

Use to stuff vegetables, poultry or fish.

FARCE AUX FRUITS

Dried fruit stuffing

To stuff 1 small bird
Preparation 10 minutes

METRIC/IMPERIAL	AMERICAN
150 g/5½ oz raisins	1 cup raisins
3 dried apricots, coarsely chopped	3 dried apricots, coarsely chopped
100 g/3½ oz pine kernels	1 cup pine nuts
3 tbsp soft cooked rice	3 tbsp soft cooked rice
2 eggs	2 eggs
ground cinnamon	ground cinnamon
cayenne pepper	cayenne pepper
salt	salt

Put the raisins into a bowl. Add the apricots, pine kernels (pine nuts) and the rice. Season with salt and cayenne and mix well.

Add the eggs one at a time, mixing well after each addition. Add a pinch of cinnamon.

This stuffing may be used for a small chicken, guinea fowl or pheasant, and also for firm-fleshed fish such as sea bream or cod.

STURGEON

Esturgeon

see also: caviar, coulibiaca, fish, salmon, tuna

A large, migratory marine fish which travels back up river to spawn, the sturgeon is fished mainly in the Black Sea and the Caspian. It is mainly valued for its eggs, the great delicacy caviar, rather than for its flesh.

Fresh sturgeon may be poached whole like salmon. Whole fish or steaks may also be braised like tuna or veal in a wine sauce with onions and herbs, and steaks can be grilled or pan fried. Sturgeon suits rich seafood sauces and prawn (shrimp), crab or crayfish butters.

A great deal of sturgeon is smoked and sold thinly sliced, like smoked salmon, and may be served and used in the same ways. The dried spinal marrow of the fish is known as *vesiga* and is traditionally used to flavour *coulibiaca.*

SUGAR

Sucre

see also: cakes and gâteaux, caramel, cream, creams and custards, fondant, fruit, honey, icing, jams, etc, maple syrup, milk, nutrition, preserves

In general terms, sugars are carbohydrates of vegetable origin. There are the simple sugars or monosaccharides, such as glucose and the fructose found in fruit juice, and the disaccharides which include lactose in milk and sucrose. In cooking it is almost always sucrose that is implied when the term sugar is used.

Ordinary sugar is extracted from sugar cane or sugar beet and is sold in various forms. Less processed varieties of cane sugar tend to be brown, while beet sugar and more highly refined types are white. Sugar readily absorbs atmospheric moisture, so store well sealed.

BARBADOS or MOLASSES SUGAR possibly has the most natural 'rummy' flavour of the cane and is favoured in fruit cakes and steamed puddings. Its dark colour and moist texture also make it popular in confectionery.

DEMERARA SUGAR is paler and has a sandy, dry texture. Its large crystals and good, strong flavour make it very useful in cooking and baking, although like honey it does have the effect of retarding yeast action.

Highly refined white sugar is available in GRANULATED form or ground into smaller crystals, when is it called CASTER or CASTOR sugar in Britain and SUPERFINE sugar in the USA. British granulated sugar has larger crystals than American granulated sugar and for this reason caster sugar is recommended for British cooks when making cakes, pastries and creams, for general sweetening in cooking and for sprinkling on crêpes and fritters. American granulated sugar is suitable for all dessert-making, except meringues, where the quicker-dissolving superfine sugar is used.

White sugar pulverized to a fine powder is called ICING sugar in the UK and CONFECTIONERS' or POWDERED sugar in the USA. It is used for making icings and frostings and for decorating desserts. It is also favoured for sweetening whipped cream, mousses and certain kinds of confectionery.

CUBE OF LUMP SUGAR is crystalline sugar pressed into small cubes. It was first devised for the restaurant trade, but it is very useful in cooking as the lumps may be used to soak up flavourings, such as alcohol, or they may even be rubbed on uncoated citrus fruit to pick up the zest. Highly refined, it is the sugar of choice for making caramel.

PRESERVING SUGAR contains added pectin and citric acid to help jams and jellies set. The jam also cooks more quickly and keeps longer. Preserving sugar can also give a pleasant texture to homemade fruit sorbets.

VANILLA SUGAR is used to impart the flavour of vanilla to cake batters, creams and custards etc. It is sold ready-made but can also be prepared at home by simply leaving a vanilla pod (bean) in a jar of sugar for a week or so. Alternatively, very finely chop 30 g/1 oz of vanilla pods (beans) and mix them with 250 g/8½ oz/1¼ cups of sugar, then pound it in a mortar and force it through a fine sieve.

Sugars flavoured with items such as bergamot, lemon, mint, cinnamon, etc, may be bought in specialist shops and are used in baking, *pâtisserie* and confectionery.

As well as its obvious sweetening action, sugar is a very potent preservative and is widely used to preserve fruit and in the curing of some meats, especially hams and bacon.

To cook sugar successfully it must be done in a completely grease-free, heavy, untinned pan over a gentle heat to begin with until the sugar has dissolved. It is best to use a highly refined sugar and to moisten it with just a little water. The sugar should not be stirred, but the pan can be shaken, and a brush should be used to reincorporate any crystals which adhere to the side of the pan. The cooking can be stopped at any stage by removing it from the heat and adding a few drops of cold water, or by immersing the base of the pan in cold water.

It is wise to use a special sugar thermometer to monitor the process. However, the stages in the cooking of sugar may also be judged by assessing the consistency of tiny amounts removed with a spoon or skimmer and dipped in ice water. They are as follows:

SMALL THREAD, SHORT THREAD or GLOSS at 103C/217F forming threads of 1 cm/½ in, used for fruit pastes.

LARGE THREAD, LONG THREAD or LARGE GLOSS at 110C/230F forming threads of 2.5–3 cm/1–1½ in, used for sweets.

SMALL BALL or SOFT BALL at 116C/240F forming rounded squashy bubbles, for fondant, butter cream and fudge.

LARGE BALL or HARD BALL at 123C/250F forming harder balls, for Italian meringue and almond paste.

SMALL CRACK or SOFT CRACK at 132C/270F cracks when cool but still pliable and sticky, used for soft nougat, some caramels and taffy.

HARD CRACK or LARGE CRACK at 150C/300F cracks like glass but is dry to the touch and is colourless, used for pulled and spun sugar, glazed fruits and sweets.

PALE CARAMEL at 154C/310F changes colour to a pale gold.

Sugar has a very high calorie content as it is pure carbohydrate, so it gives a quick boost to the system: 100 g/3½ oz contains 400 calories and 1 lump or teaspoonful of sugar contains 25–30. Reasonable daily intake is about 85 g/3 oz or about 12 teaspoonfuls. The control of sugar consumption is made more difficult by the high hidden sugar content in things like alcohol, processed foods and soft drinks.

SULTANA

see Dried vine fruit

SUNFLOWER

Tournesol

see also:
fats and oils
frying
margarine
mayonnaise

An oleaginous annual plant originally from South America, the sunflower is now widely cultivated for both its large decorative flowers and its seeds.

Dried and salted sunflower seeds are a popular snack and are good in salads. However, most of the crop is pressed to yield oil. Sunflower oil is light, easily digestible and high in polyunsaturates, making it a very popular cooking oil in today's health-conscious climate. For this reason, it has also become a common base for modern margarines. The first cold pressing of oil has a very fine flavour which merits being used on salads, but most of the oil on sale has little of this distinction. As it emulsifies well sunflower oil is very suitable for mayonnaise.

Sunflower seeds contain 500 calories per 100 g/3½ oz. The oil is low in saturates and rich in polyunsaturates, particularly linoleic acid, which is essential for health and is thought to counteract the injurious effects of cholesterol.

SWEDE OR RUTABAGA

see also:
turnip
vegetables

A root vegetable of the cabbage family, swedes are cooked in much the same way as turnips. In many parts of the world, especially Scotland, they are actually known as turnips. They tend to be larger and have a characteristic ribbed skin near the base of the stalk. The skin may be white or purple, according to variety. The flesh is usually yellow and tends to be drier and sweeter than that of the turnip.

Swedes bake well, are popular in stews and are often mashed or puréed, like the traditional 'mashed neeps' served with Scots haggis.

Swede is very nutritious, rich in protein, minerals and low in calories: 26 per 100 g/3½ oz.

GRATIN DE RUTABAGAS

Baked swede or rutabaga with parsley

Serves 4
Preparation 15 minutes
Cooking about 35 minutes

METRIC/IMPERIAL	*AMERICAN*
100 g/3½ oz butter	*1 stick butter*
800 g/1¾ lb swede, cut into pieces	*1¾ lb rutabaga, cut into pieces*
225 g/½ lb turnips, cut into pieces	*½ lb turnips, cut into pieces*
55 g/2 oz flour	*6½ tbsp flour*
200 ml/7 fl oz chicken stock	*1 cup chicken stock*
200 ml/7 fl oz whipping cream	*1 cup whipping cream*
55 g/2 oz grated cheese	*½ cup grated cheese*
5 tbsp finely chopped flat-leaved parsley	*⅓ cup finely chopped flat-leaf parsley*
salt and pepper	*salt and pepper*

Preheat the oven to 220C/425F/gas 7 and grease a baking dish with a little of the butter.

Blanch the vegetables in salted boiling water for 5 minutes. Drain them.

Melt one third of the remaining butter in a saucepan and add the vegetables. Cook very gently, covered, for 10 minutes.

Meanwhile, make a white sauce by melting the rest of the butter in a saucepan over a moderate heat. Add the flour and cook for 3 or 4 minutes, stirring all the time. Gradually add the stock and cream and simmer gently for a few minutes until thick and smooth. Add the cheese and 2 tablespoons of the chopped parsley.

Put the drained vegetables into the baking dish, coat with sauce and bake for 20 minutes.

Sprinkle the top with the rest of the parsley and serve at once to accompany roast meats.

SWEETBREAD

Ris

see also:
blanching
heart
offal
veal

A type of white offal (variety meat), sweetbreads may be the thymus gland or pancreas of a calf or, less often, a lamb or pig. The round part of a calf's thymus gland or *noix* is regarded as a particular delicacy.

Sweetbreads require careful preparation. To eliminate all impurities and traces of blood, they should be soaked for at least 3 hours in several changes of cold water, briefly blanched in a flavouring stock or court-bouillon and then pressed under a weighted cloth. Any skin and covering membrane must then be rubbed off.

Sweetbreads may be braised, baked or poached whole, or fried, grilled or deep fried in slices. Their fine texture and very delicate flavour suit rich, creamy sauces and they are often married with bacon, ham, tongue and truffles. Sweetbreads are also popular in forcemeats for pâtés and savoury pastries.

Sweetbreads are high in cholesterol but low in calories; 100 g/3½ oz contains 115 calories.

RIS DE VEAU AUX MORILLES

Veal sweetbreads with wild mushrooms

Serves 4
Preparation 20 minutes, 3 hours ahead
Cooking about 40 minutes

METRIC/IMPERIAL	AMERICAN
200 g/7 oz butter	2 sticks butter
2 onions, sliced	2 onions, sliced
2 carrots, sliced	2 carrots, sliced
4 noix of veal sweetbreads, trimmed, soaked and blanched	2 pairs veal sweetbreads, preferably round heart sweetbreads, trimmed, soaked and blanched
450 g/1 lb fresh morels, stalks removed	1 lb fresh morels, stems removed
200 ml/7 fl oz crème fraîche or whipping cream	1 cup crème fraîche or whipping cream
salt and pepper	salt and pepper

Melt three quarters of the butter in a flameproof casserole just large enough to hold the sweetbreads. Add the onions and carrots and stir over a moderate heat for 5 minutes, then add the sweetbreads.

Cook over a low heat for 25 minutes, half covering the casserole and turning them frequently so they cook lightly on all sides.

Meanwhile, sauté the morels gently in a pan with the rest of the butter. Add the cream and cook very gently, stirring occasionally so the mushrooms are well coated. Season well.

When the sweetbreads are cooked, remove them and strain the cooking juices. Add the sweetbreads and cooking juices to the morels and cream. Stir carefully and cook very gently, covered, for 5 minutes. Adjust the seasoning and transfer to a warmed serving dish to serve.

To drink: a Châteauneuf-du-Pape.

SWEET PEPPER

see Peppers

SWEET POTATO

Patate douce

see also: potato vegetables

A large, fleshy, oval-shaped edible tuber of the convolvulus family, the sweet potato is thought to be native to South America but is now widely grown in the Tropics, Mediterranean countries and the southern states of the USA. Its sweet, tasty and nutritious flesh is a staple of many of the world's poorer nations.

According to variety, it has beige, yellow or deep pink skin and flesh that is yellow, orange or purple. As a rule, the deeper the colour of the flesh the sweeter the potato, and the paler-fleshed varieties tend to be more floury.

Sweet potatoes are prepared and cooked in much the same ways as ordinary potatoes for savoury dishes. They also find a lot of use in sweet recipes, notably in pies, cakes and jams.

Sweet potatoes are rich in protein, vitamins and minerals and higher in carbohydrates than potatoes: 100 g/3½ oz contains 110 calories.

GRATIN DE PATATES DOUCES AUX ÉPICES

Spiced sweet potato

Serves 4
Preparation 15 minutes
Cooking about 45 minutes

METRIC/IMPERIAL	AMERICAN
800 g/1¾ lb sweet potatoes	1¾ lb sweet potatoes
45 g/1½ oz butter	3 tbsp butter
4 eggs, lightly beaten	4 eggs, lightly beaten
½ tsp cayenne pepper	½ tsp cayenne pepper
½ tsp chilli powder	½ tsp chili powder
1 tsp ground cumin	1 tsp ground cumin
grated nutmeg	grated nutmeg
salt and pepper	salt and pepper

Ris de veau aux morilles (Veal sweetbreads with wild mushrooms)

Steam the sweet potatoes in their skins for 20 minutes or until tender. Allow them to cool.

Preheat the oven to 180C/350F/gas 4 and grease a baking dish with a little of the butter.

Peel the cooled sweet potatoes and mash them with a fork. Add the eggs with 2 pinches of cayenne, the chilli powder and cumin. Season with grated nutmeg, salt and pepper.

Put the mixture into the baking dish, dot with the rest of the butter and bake for 20 minutes.

Serve straight from the dish as a garnish for roast pork or chicken.

SWISS CHARD

Bette

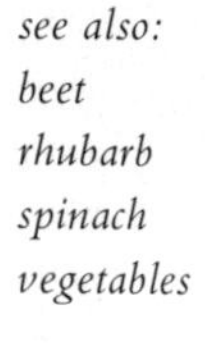

see also:
beet
rhubarb
spinach
vegetables

A member of the beet family grown for its edible stalks and leaves, Swiss chard is also often known as SPINACH BEET.

The large leaves vary from light to dark green in colour, and may be smooth or curly. They are prepared and cooked much like spinach and have a similar, but milder, flavour.

The long, fleshy white stalks may need to have any fibrous strings removed, as with celery, and are boiled, stewed or braised. The red stalks are like rhubarb and are treated similarly.

Swiss chard is rich in vitamins A and C, protein, fibre and calcium; the leaves also contain a lot of iron: 100 g/3½ oz contains only 28 calories. However, like spinach, the leaves contain oxalic acid which inhibits the body's absorption of nutrients, though at much lower levels than spinach, probably making them effectively more nutritious.

BETTES À LA SAVOYARDE

Swiss chard with eggs and cheese

Serves 4
Preparation 10 minutes
Cooking about 40 minutes

METRIC/IMPERIAL	*AMERICAN*
1 kg/2¼ lb Swiss chard stalks, trimmed and cut into 5 cm/2 in pieces	*2¼ lb Swiss chard stems, trimmed and cut into 2 in pieces*
juice of 1 lemon	*juice of 1 lemon*
55 g/2 oz butter	*4 tbsp butter*
85 g/3 oz grated Gruyère	*¾ cup grated Gruyère cheese*
2 eggs	*2 eggs*
salt and pepper	*salt and pepper*

Fill a pan with water and add the lemon juice along with salt to taste. Bring to the boil and cook the pieces of Swiss chard, uncovered, for 30 minutes. Drain them thoroughly.

Melt the butter in a sauté pan over a moderate heat. Brown the chard, stirring frequently, for 5 minutes. Sprinkle with the cheese and stir for 3 minutes. Remove from the heat.

Lightly beat the eggs in a bowl with some salt and pepper. Return the pan to the heat and add the eggs. Stir with a wooden spoon until the eggs are just cooked. Serve at once, very hot.

If this dish is served as an accompaniment to a roast, add 2 tablespoons of meat juices to the eggs when seasoning them.

To drink: a medium-bodied red wine, such as a Côtes-du-Rhone.

Note: the leaves may be served separately, cooked like spinach.

T

see also:
condiment
spices

TAMARIND

The tamarind tree originated in East Africa but is now widely cultivated in India, Africa and Asia for its elongated pods. These contain a thick, brown, bitter-sweet pulp widely used in the cooking of these regions as a condiment and in curries, stews and sweet-and-sour dishes, and to make thirst-quenching drinks. In the West, tamarind is usually sold dried in blocks and these need to be soaked in water before use. Tamarind is also commonly available as a sticky concentrate which must be diluted before use. Tamarind is possibly most familiar as an ingredient of Worcestershire sauce.

TANGELO, TANGERINE

see Orange

see also:
anchovy
caper
condiment
olive

TAPENADE

A condiment from Provence, tapenade is made with capers, black olives and anchovies, pounded in a mortar with olive oil, herbs and lemon juice to make a black paste. It goes well with crudités and with grilled fish or meat. It can also be spread on toast or mixed with egg yolks and used to stuff hard boiled eggs. Tapenade may be enriched with garlic and flaked tuna.

Tapenade contains about 480 calories per 100 g/3½ oz.

TAPENADE

Tapenade with tuna, garlic and thyme

Makes 2 jars of 300 g/10½ oz each
Preparation 10 minutes

METRIC/IMPERIAL	*AMERICAN*
225 g/8 oz black olives, stoned	*8 oz (about 1½ cups) black olives, pitted*
1 garlic clove, chopped	*1 garlic clove, chopped*
100 g/3½ oz canned anchovies in oil, well drained	*3½ oz canned anchovies in oil, well drained*
100 g/3½ oz canned tuna, drained	*3½ oz (about ⅔ cup) canned tuna, drained*
100 g/3½ oz capers, drained	*½ cup capers, drained*
pinch of dried thyme	*pinch of dried thyme*
100 ml/3½ fl oz olive oil	*½ cup olive oil*
pepper	*pepper*

Combine the olives, garlic, anchovies, tuna and capers in the bowl of the food processor and purée them finely. Add the thyme and then the oil in a thin stream, processing until thoroughly mixed. Season with pepper but no salt.

Put the tapenade into jars, seal, label and store in the refrigerator for up to 3 or 4 weeks.

Variation: add 1 tablespoon of marc or brandy.

see also:
creams and custards
jelly etc
milk
soup

TAPIOCA

A starchy food extracted from the tropical cassava plant and ground to varying degrees of fineness, tapioca is used mainly for thickening soups, making milk puddings and helping other desserts and moulded savoury items to set.

The addition of 1 teaspoon of tapioca to egg yolks helps to set creams and custards, and fruit gelatine desserts. It is also useful sprinkled in pastry cases when using juicy fruit.

Tapioca is very digestible, but it is low in nutrients and very rich in carbohydrates: 100 g/3½ oz contains 340 calories.

TIMBALE DE POIVRONS

Sweet pepper and tapioca timbale

Serves 4
Preparation 30 minutes
Cooking about 1 hour 20 minutes

METRIC/IMPERIAL	*AMERICAN*
6 red sweet peppers, halved and deseeded	*6 red sweet peppers, halved and deseeded*
30 g/1 oz butter	*2 tbsp butter*
200 ml/7 fl oz milk	*1 cup milk*
45 g/1½ oz tapioca	*¼ cup tapioca*
4 eggs, separated	*4 eggs, separated*
150 ml/¼ pt whipping cream	*⅔ cup whipping cream*
salt and cayenne pepper	*salt and cayenne pepper*

Finely dice one of the sweet peppers. Cook the others for 20 minutes in boiling salted water. Drain and purée them in a food processor.

Preheat the oven to 180C/350F/gas 4 and lightly grease a 14 cm/5½ in charlotte mould with a little of the butter.

Pour the milk into a saucepan and season with salt and cayenne pepper. Bring it to the boil. Gradually sprinkle in the tapioca, stirring, and cook for 10 minutes, stirring continuously.

Remove the tapioca from the heat and add the remaining butter in small pieces, along with the egg yolks, three quarters of the sweet pepper purée and the diced pepper. Whisk the egg whites to stiff peaks and fold into the mixture.

Fill the charlotte mould with the pepper mixture and bake in a bain-marie in the oven for about 45 minutes. Let it stand in the oven with the heat turned off for 5 minutes.

Meanwhile, heat the remaining purée with the cream and season with salt and cayenne. Pour into a deep serving dish, unmould the timbale on top and serve as a hot first course.

TARRAGON

Estragon

see also:
chicken
herbs
sauce
vinegar

An aromatic perennial plant with thin green leaves, tarragon originated in Asia but has been widely cultivated and used as a flavouring herb in Europe for centuries. There are two main varieties: the finer-flavoured FRENCH TARRAGON and the paler-coloured RUSSIAN TARRAGON which is sharper and less delicate. The flavour of tarragon is subtle but distinctive and strong, and it stands up well to cooking. It goes best with chicken and eggs and it is used to flavour numerous hot and cold sauces. Tarragon is also used to infuse white wine vinegar for salads.

POULET À L'ESTRAGON

Chicken with tarragon

Serves 6
Preparation 30 minutes
Cooking about 1¼ hours

METRIC/IMPERIAL	*AMERICAN*
45 g/1½ oz butter	*3 tbsp butter*
1 oven-ready chicken, weighing about 1.8 kg/4 lb, cut into 10–12 pieces	*1 chicken, dressed and drawn weight about 4 lb, cut into 10–12 pieces*
bunch of tarragon	*bunch of tarragon*
200 ml/7 fl oz white wine	*1 cup white wine*
½ tsp cracked black pepper	*½ tsp cracked black pepper*
2 tbsp flour	*2 tbsp flour*
150 ml/¼ pt chicken stock	*⅔ cup chicken stock*
150 ml/¼ pt crème fraîche or whipping cream	*⅔ cup crème fraîche or whipping cream*
1 tbsp lemon juice	*1 tbsp lemon juice*
salt and pepper	*salt and pepper*

Melt the butter in a flameproof casserole over a moderate heat and brown the pieces of chicken in it. Season them with salt and pepper.

Remove the leaves from the tarragon and put 2 tablespoons of them in a small pan with the white wine and the cracked black pepper. Boil rapidly to reduce by half.

Sprinkle the chicken with the flour and stir for 2 minutes. Add the tarragon mixture and the stock. Cover and cook gently for 1 hour.

Snip the rest of the tarragon and mix half with the cream and lemon juice. Pour over the chicken and simmer for 7 or 8 minutes more.

Put the chicken and sauce in a deep, warmed dish and sprinkle with the remaining tarragon.

To drink: a fruity white wine, such as a Chardonnay.

TART

Tarte

see also:
baking blind
flan
pastry
pie
quiche

A shallow, round pastry case made with a short or puff pastry and filled with savoury or sweet ingredients is termed a tart. In North America it may also be called a single-crust pie. A French *tourte*, usually with a savoury filling, has a covering layer of pastry making it more like a pie. Savoury tarts are normally served as a hot first course or as a light meal with salad, while sweet tarts are served warm or cold as desserts or with tea and coffee.

Savoury tarts, often called quiches – or flans in Britain – may contain various ingredients such as onions, tomatoes, ham and cheese, mushrooms, potatoes and other vegetables.

Sweet tarts are usually filled with fruit or creams, or a combination of the two, and are among the most common form of *pâtisserie*. They are often finished with a fruit or jam glaze to improve their flavour and appearance.

Tarts to receive little or no cooking after filling are first baked unfilled or 'blind'.

Small, round or boat-shaped tartlets with savoury or sweet fillings make perfect buffet and party food.

One portion of apple tart contains about 230 calories.

TARTE TATIN

Upside-down apple tart

Serves 6
Preparation 30 minutes, 1 hour ahead
Cooking about 30 minutes

METRIC/IMPERIAL	*AMERICAN*
200 g/7 oz flour	*1¾ cups flour*
125 g/4½ oz butter	*9 tbsp butter*
2 tbsp caster sugar	*2 tbsp superfine sugar*
100 g/3½ oz sugar lumps (about 40)	*3½ oz sugar cubes (about 40)*
1 kg/2¼ lb firm dessert apples, such as Granny Smiths	*2¼ lb firm apples, such as Granny Smiths*
salt	*salt*

Make the pastry: sift the flour with ½ teaspoon of salt. Make a well in the centre and add all but 2 tablespoons of the butter, 1 tablespoon of the sugar and 100 ml/3½ fl oz/½ cup of very cold water. Mix with the fingertips very quickly to a smooth dough (1). Roll it into a ball and chill for about 1 hour.

Meanwhile, prepare a light caramel syrup by dissolving the sugar lumps (cubes) in 3 table-

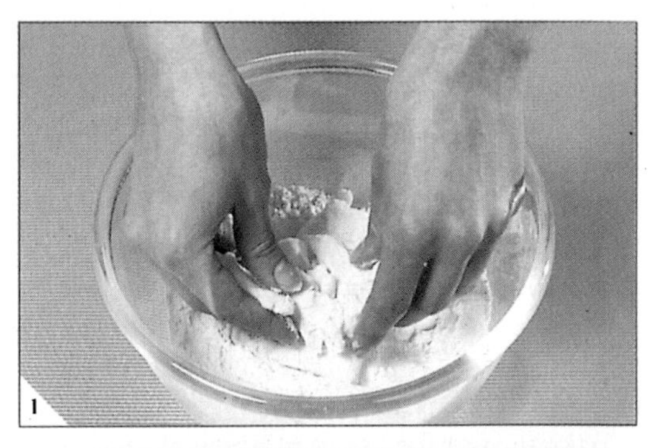
1

2

spoons of water in a small pan and cooking over a high heat until golden brown. Pour the caramel into a fairly deep tart pan with a diameter of about 20 cm/8 in (2, previous page). The caramel may be prepared directly in the pan if it is heavy-based. Leave to cool.

Preheat the oven to 230C/450F/gas 8.

Peel, quarter and core the apples. Cut the apple quarters into chunky slices. Arrange the apple slices in the tart pan in concentric circles. Sprinkle them with the remaining sugar (3). Dot with the remaining butter.

Roll out the pastry dough to a round about 3 mm/$\frac{1}{8}$ in thick and big enough to cover the pan generously. Place the pastry over the apples and tuck it inside the edges of the pan so that the fruit is completely enclosed.

Bake the tart for 25–30 minutes. Watch over it carefully: the pastry should be deep golden but not dark brown. While the tart is still hot, place a serving dish on top of the pan and invert the tart on it (4). Serve warm, with well-chilled whipped cream.

Note: an alternative method of making this tart dispenses with making caramel separately. Simply butter the pan very generously, then line it with apple slices, sprinkling them abundantly with sugar and dotting them with more butter.

TARTE FINE MERINGUÉE

Meringue fruit tart

Serves 6
Preparation 20 minutes, 1 hour ahead
Cooking about $1\frac{1}{2}$ hours

METRIC/IMPERIAL	*AMERICAN*
250 g/$8\frac{1}{2}$ oz flour	*2 cups flour*
140 g/5 oz butter	*10 tbsp butter*
1 egg yolk	*1 egg yolk*
255 g/9 oz caster sugar	*$1\frac{1}{4}$ cups + 1 tbsp superfine sugar*
150 g/$5\frac{1}{2}$ oz fresh redcurrants, stalks removed	*1 cup fresh redcurrants, stems removed*
150 g/$5\frac{1}{2}$ oz bilberries	*1 cup bilberries or blueberries*
6 egg whites	*6 egg whites*
100 g/$3\frac{1}{2}$ oz hazelnuts, chopped	*1 cup chopped hazelnuts (filberts)*
3 tbsp icing sugar	*3 tbsp confectioners' sugar*
salt	*salt*

Make the pastry: sift the flour with a pinch of salt. Make a well in the centre and add all but 1 tablespoon of the butter, the egg yolk, 1 tablespoon of the caster (superfine) sugar and 2 tablespoons of very cold water. Mix quickly to a smooth dough. Wrap and chill for 1 hour.

Roll out the pastry and use to line a 25 cm/10 in tart pan lightly greased with the remaining butter. Chill the pastry case for 10 minutes.

Preheat the oven to 200C/400F/gas 6.

Mix the redcurrants with the bilberries. If using frozen fruit, drain it well.

Line the pastry case with a circle of foil, parchment or greaseproof paper, prick the pastry through this with the tip of a sharp knife and cover with dried beans or rice.

Bake the pastry case blind for 15 minutes. Remove the lining and bake for a further 5–10 minutes without allowing it to brown. Reduce the oven temperature to 110C/230F/gas $\frac{1}{4}$.

Whisk the egg whites to stiff peaks. Add the remaining caster (superfine) sugar a spoonful at a time, whisking constantly.

Set 6 generous tablespoons of egg white to one side. Mix the rest with the fruit. Spread the

Tarte fine meringuée (Meringue fruit tart)

chopped hazelnuts over the bottom of the cooked pastry case. Cover them with the fruit mixture.

Cover with the remaining egg white mixture or pipe it on in a lattice. Sprinkle with icing (confectioners') sugar and bake for 1 hour.

TARTELETTES AUX CHAMPIGNONS

Mushroom tartlets

Makes 15 tartlets
Preparation 20 minutes, 1 hour ahead
Cooking about 25 minutes

METRIC/IMPERIAL	*AMERICAN*
450 g/1 lb mushrooms, wiped and sliced	*1 lb mushrooms, wiped and sliced*
55 g/2 oz butter	*4 tbsp butter*
300 g/10 oz shortcrust pastry	*10 oz basic pie pastry*
30 g/1 oz flour	*¼ cup flour*
100 ml/3½ fl oz milk	*½ cup milk*
100 ml/3½ fl oz crème fraîche or whipping cream	*½ cup crème fraîche or whipping cream*
45 g/1½ oz grated Parmesan	*⅓ cup grated Parmesan cheese*
grated nutmeg	*grated nutmeg*
salt and pepper	*salt and pepper*

Preheat the oven to 250C/475F/gas 9.

Sauté the mushrooms in half the butter in a sauté pan over a moderate heat for 10 minutes.

Roll out the pastry to a thickness of about 3 mm/⅛ in and line 15 tartlet moulds with it. them blind for 10 minutes.

Meanwhile, prepare a béchamel sauce by melting the remaining butter in a small pan over a low heat. Add the flour and cook, stirring, for 2 or 3 minutes. Gradually stir in the milk until the mixture is smooth and cook for 3 or 4 minutes until it has thickened. Add the cream and season with grated nutmeg, salt and pepper. Mix the sauce with the mushrooms and Parmesan.

Unmould the tartlet cases. Fill the cases with the mushroom mixture and put them back in the oven for 5 minutes.

TARTARE

see also: mayonnaise steak sauce

A term denoting a preparation of seasoned, finely minced (ground) steak, served with herbs and condiments. By analogy, tartares may also be made with raw fish, most frequently salmon, tuna or sea bream.

Mayonnaise-based tartare sauce is flavoured with herbs, onion, mustard and capers and is served with fried food, especially fish.

TEA

Thé

see also: coffee infusion

The young leaves of an Oriental shrub, tea is used to make one of the world's most popular beverages. The word 'tea' also refers to the beverage itself, and to the light meal in the afternoon at which it is served, accompanied by sandwiches, scones and pastries.

Originally from China, tea is now also grown in India, Sri Lanka (Ceylon), Japan and Indonesia. There are 3 main types of tea, varying according to the way in which the freshly harvested leaves are processed. BLACK TEA, the most commonly encountered, is wilted and rolled, allowed to ferment and then dried. GREEN TEA, a speciality of China and Japan, is roasted fresh. It is also very popular among Muslims as fermented products are prohibited by their religion. OOLONG TEA, which falls between black and green, is semi-fermented. It has a very delicate and velvety flavour, but is increasingly difficult to come by. Some teas, like Chinese LAPSANG SOUCHONG, are dried over wood fires to give them an added smoky taste.

Teas are categorized according to their leaf type and size and their place of origin. But most of the teas on sale are blends adjusted to the local tastes, water type and price.

CEYLON TEA has a strong, simple flavour: SUPERIOR ORANGE PEKOE, delicate and amber-coloured, and FLOWERY PEKOE, more robust, are among the best. INDIAN TEAS are particularly fragrant, the most prestigious of them being DARJEELING, the flavour of which varies according to the particular plantation in the Himalayan foothills in which it was grown. CHINA TEAS are generally more robust.

There is also a wide variety of teas flavoured with aromatics, such as jasmine, rose, lemon, lotus and mint. Perhaps the best known is EARL GREY which is flavoured with bergamot.

Tea is best bought loose by weight in specialist shops and should be stored in an airtight container away from the light. All but the best quality tea-bags are made with tea dust or tea leaf fragments, and their quality is distinctly inferior to leaf tea. Alternatives include freeze-dried and instant teas in powder form.

Good tea is made according to a few simple rules: bring some fresh filtered water to the boil; warm the teapot, which should preferably be unglazed earthenware, usually with a little of the water; put into the dried pot 1 teaspoon of tea per person and 'one for the pot'; taking the pot to the kettle, pour the boiling water over the tea and allow to infuse for 3–5 minutes, stirring half-way through. Do not allow tea to brew for more than about 5 minutes or it will become excessively tannic: strain out the leaves and keep it warm or serve it cold.

In Britain, tea is served hot with milk, perhaps sweetened with sugar or honey. Whether the milk should be added to the cup before or after the tea is purely a matter of taste: if the hot tea is poured into the milk it tends to caramelize the milk's lactose to give a quite different flavour. Tea is also often served with lemon slices, particularly when cold, but connoisseurs hold that this masks the flavour.

Particularly in Eastern cooking, there is a strong tradition of using tea as a flavouring ingredient. The north Africans use it with lamb, the Chinese with eggs, duck and rice and the Southeast Asians with fish. Tea also makes a deliciously refreshing sorbet.

Tea has a high tannin and caffeine content, so its consumption should be carefully monitored as excess can cause severe indigestion and overstimulation. Ceylon teas have the highest caffeine content. There are now on the market brands of decaffeinated tea, but remember that they still contain just as much tannin.

TENDERIZING

Attendrir

Several processes are used to make food more tender. The simplest method is to cook food, having first cut it into small pieces. Brief cooking by boiling or steaming is generally sufficient to tenderize fruit and vegetables, while more prolonged cooking will tenderize tougher foods such as meat.

With meat, poultry and game, the practice of hanging for several days allows natural enzyme activity to break down the tissues. This promotes tenderness as well as allowing a full, strong flavour to develop.

Skilful butchery and the cutting of meat along its grain are also very important factors.

The process of marinating meats in acidic mixtures also tenderizes as well as adding flavour and is used with a wide variety of foods.

Larding meat and poultry with fat contributes to tenderness as well as succulence.

The high percentage of a certain type of connective tissue in older animals makes them immune to most such ploys. The meat needs to be beaten with a mallet to break down the tough fibres.

So-called chemical 'meat tenderizers' are to be avoided, as any effect they have is normally limited to the exterior of the meat, which becomes unappetizingly mushy.

see also:
blanching
game
larding
marinating
meat
poultry
vegetables

TERRINE

A long, narrow, deep container made of glazed earthenware, porcelain or ovenproof glass with a tight-fitting lid, the terrine is used for moulding or cooking a preparation which the French term a *pâté en terrine*. In Britain and North America such preparations, especially if made with meat, tend to be known as pâtés and the two terms are used somewhat interchangeably. Increasingly, however, the term terrine denotes those made using fish, seafood or vegetables, or meat in aspic.

Fish or vegetable terrines are often layered with differently coloured mixtures or studded with colourful ingredients so that they are particularly attractive when sliced. They may be served warm or cold and are often accompanied by a light sauce or coulis.

One 100 g/3½ oz serving of a fish or vegetable terrine contains about 225 calories, only half that of an equivalent piece of meat pâté.

see also:
fish
loaf
pâté
stuffing
vegetables

TERRINE D'AGNEAU EN GELÉE

Terrine of lamb in aspic

Serves 6
Preparation 30 minutes
Cooking 2½ hours, 24 hours ahead

METRIC/IMPERIAL	*AMERICAN*
5 garlic cloves, crushed	*5 garlic cloves, minced*
bunch of flat-leaved parsley, finely chopped	*bunch of flat-leaf parsley, finely chopped*
bunch of chives, finely chopped	*bunch of chives, finely chopped*
1 bay leaf, crumbled	*1 bay leaf, crumbled*
1 tsp dried thyme	*1 tsp dried thyme*
1.5–2 kg/3½–4½ lb boned lamb shoulder or middle neck, trimmed and cut into pieces	*3½–4½ lb boned lamb shoulder, trimmed and cut into pieces*
500 ml/16 fl oz dry white wine	*2 cups dry white wine*
1 l/1¾ pt beef consommé	*1 qt beef consommé*
1 sachet (15 g/½ oz) powdered gelatine	*2 envelopes powdered unflavored gelatine*
salt and pepper	*salt and pepper*

Preheat the oven to 180C/350F/gas 4. Mix together the garlic and fresh and dried herbs.

Arrange the pieces of lamb in layers in a terrine or deep rectangular pâté or baking dish, sprinkling each layer generously with the herb and garlic mixture and season to taste. Pour the white wine and half the consommé into the dish. Cook in the oven for 2½ hours.

Remove the terrine from the oven, add a little more consommé and allow to cool.

When cold, remove any congealed fat from the surface of the terrine. Heat the remaining consommé and mix it with the gelatine until dissolved. Pour carefully all over the terrine. Cover with a suitably shaped plate or board, or another dish of the same shape and size, and place a weight on top. Chill overnight to allow the aspic to set. Serve very cold cut in thick slices as an hors d'oeuvre, or in chunks and accompanied by pickles.

TERRINE DE COURGETTES

Courgette or zucchini terrine

Serves 6
Preparation 30 minutes
Cooking 1¾ hours, 24 hours ahead

METRIC/IMPERIAL	*AMERICAN*
2 tbsp olive oil	*2 tbsp olive oil*
150 g/5½ oz onions, chopped	*1 cup chopped onions*
1 kg/2¼ lb courgettes, thinly sliced	*2¼ lb zucchini, thinly sliced*
100 g/3½ oz white bread	*4 slices white bread*
100 ml/3½ fl oz milk	*½ cup milk*
3 eggs, lightly beaten	*3 eggs, lightly beaten*
45 g/1½ oz butter	*3 tbsp butter*
225 g/½ lb spinach, trimmed and shredded	*½ lb bulk spinach, trimmed and shredded*
sprig of fresh tarragon	*sprig of fresh tarragon*
grated nutmeg	*grated nutmeg*
salt and pepper	*salt and pepper*

Preheat the oven to 160C/325F/gas 3.

Heat the oil in a frying pan over a moderate heat. Add the onions and cook for 5 minutes. Mix in the courgettes (zucchini) and cook the vegetables gently for a further 5 minutes. Remove from the heat and mash with a fork.

Soak the bread in the milk and mash it. Add to the vegetables. Add the beaten eggs. Season with grated nutmeg, salt and pepper.

Melt one third of the butter and cook the spinach in it for 5 minutes, then drain it.

Grease an ovenproof porcelain terrine with the remaining butter and put half the courgette (zucchini) mixture in it. Add the spinach and the tarragon and finish with the remaining courgette (zucchini) mixture. Bake the terrine in a bain-marie in the oven for 1¼ hours. Turn off the oven and leave the terrine in it for 15 minutes, then take it out. Let it cool, then chill it.

THYME

Thym

see also:
bouquet garni
herbs

A perennial plant native to southern Europe and the Mediterranean area, thyme is now widely cultivated for its small, aromatic, grey-green

aromatic leaves and is one of the most commonly used herbs, both fresh and dried.

There are several varieties, of which the most prevalent is GARDEN THYME. The tiny leaves of the wild thyme from Provence, known as *farigoule*, are held to have the finest flavour and WINTER THYME is slightly bitter. Various commercial hybrids are available, such as LEMON THYME with its yellow-tinged leaves.

Thyme, with its subtle hint of cloves, has a very wide range of uses and responds best to long, slow cooking. For this reason it is one of the classic constituents of a bouquet garni and is much used in stews, daubes and marinades. Thyme is particularly good with tomatoes, meat, poultry and pulses.

CANARD AU THYM

Duck with thyme

Serves 4
Preparation 20 minutes
Cooking about 1½ hours

METRIC/IMPERIAL	AMERICAN
55 g/2 oz butter	4 tbsp butter
1 oven-ready duck, weighing about 1.5 kg/3½ lb	1 duck, dressed and drawn weight about 3½ lb
4 sprigs of fresh thyme	4 sprigs of fresh thyme
800 g/1¾ lb new potatoes, unpeeled	1¾ lb new potatoes, unpeeled
1 tbsp oil	1 tbsp oil
2 tbsp dried thyme	2 tbsp dried thyme
100 ml/3½ fl oz chicken stock	½ cup chicken stock
2 onions, quartered	2 onions, quartered
salt and pepper	salt and pepper

Preheat the oven to 220C/425F/gas 7. Grease a large baking dish with some of the butter.

Season the duck and insert the fresh thyme into the cavity with the remaining butter.

Cook the potatoes for 15 minutes in boiling salted water. Drain and peel them. Cut them into even-sized pieces.

Brush the duck with oil and sprinkle with half the dried thyme. Pour the stock in the dish, put in the duck and surround with the potatoes and onions. Sprinkle with the remaining thyme.

Roast for about 1 hour 10 minutes, less if you prefer the flesh pink, basting from time to time with the cooking juices. Serve very hot.

To drink: white wine, such as a medium Hungarian Tokay.

TIMBALE

see also:
mousse
pie
rice
vol-au-vent

From the French for a drinking goblet, the term timbale denotes either a pie made in a deep, round dish like a large vol-au-vent, or more commonly a preparation cooked in individual deep, round moulds, such as those for darioles or babas.

Such moulded timbales are most commonly made with vegetables, or sometimes rice or pasta exteriors surrounding a meat or fish forcemeat filling. They are usually served unmoulded and are often coated with a sauce. Larger versions of these dishes, cooked in charlotte moulds, are now also called timbales.

TIMBALE DE RIZ FARCIE

Rice timbale

Serves 6
Preparation 20 minutes
Cooking about 2 hours

METRIC/IMPERIAL	AMERICAN
300 g/10 oz rice	1⅔ cups rice
125 g/4½ oz butter	9 tbsp butter
3 tbsp grated Parmesan	3 tbsp grated Parmesan cheese
3 egg yolks	3 egg yolks
3 tbsp breadcrumbs	3 tbsp breadcrumbs
2 onions, chopped	2 onions, chopped
1 garlic clove, chopped	1 garlic clove, chopped
225 g/½ lb lean minced veal	½ lb lean ground veal
225 g/½ lb minced ham	½ lb ground ham
225 g/½ lb minced chicken livers	½ lb ground chicken livers
125 g/4½ oz shelled peas	1 cup shelled peas
2 ripe tomatoes, peeled and chopped	2 ripe tomatoes, peeled and chopped
2 tbsp white wine	2 tbsp white wine
½ tsp oregano	½ tsp oregano
salt and pepper	salt and pepper

Cook the rice in salted boiling water for 15 minutes. Drain and put into a bowl. Add one third of the butter with the Parmesan and egg yolks. Season with salt and pepper and mix.

Preheat the oven to 180C/350F/gas 4. Generously grease a large charlotte mould with half the remaining butter and coat the bottom and sides with an even layer of breadcrumbs.

Pour in two thirds of the rice mixture and press it against the sides and bottom. Make a large well in the middle of the rice.

Melt the rest of the butter in a sauté pan over a moderate heat. Add the onions and garlic and stir for 2 minutes. Add all the meats and cook, stirring, for 10 minutes. Add the peas, tomatoes, wine, oregano and seasoning. Cook gently, stirring, for 15 minutes or until fairly thick.

Pour it into the rice well, press down firmly and cover with the remaining rice.

Bake in the oven for about 1¼ hours. Turn the timbale out on a round dish and serve it hot, coated with tomato or mushroom cream sauce.

TOMATO

Tomate

see also:
coulis
ketchup
jams, etc
salad
sauce

A vegetable fruit from the same family as the potato and sweet pepper, tomatoes originated in South America but are now widely cultivated throughout the world, much under glass.

Unripe tomatoes are green and, like green potatoes, are slightly toxic if eaten raw. When fully ripe they are most usually red in colour, although there are pink, yellow, orange and white fruits. Size and shape varies widely according to variety.

The most common are the round, red SALAD TOMATOES which are juicy and not too acidic. Tiny, sweet and tasty CHERRY TOMATOES closely resemble the original tomato, which stills grows wild in Mexico. PLUM TOMATOES are best for concentrates and sauces as they have little seeds or juice. Large BEEFSTEAK or DUTCH TOMATOES are also meaty, but their size and shape suits them to sandwiches and some salads.

When bought, tomatoes should be ripe, smooth and without bruises. They will keep for several days stored in a single layer in a cool, dry place. Their texture does not benefit from refrigeration. Slightly under-ripe tomatoes will continue to ripen if kept in a warm place.

Tomato skin may irritate the alimentary tract, so they are peeled for use in many dishes. This is made easier by immersing them in boiling water. The seeds are also often removed.

Tomato salads, perhaps with herbs, sliced onions or Mozzarella cheese, make good, cold first courses, and cherry tomatoes are increasingly popular crudités. Larger tomatoes are also often stuffed to make substantial dishes. Halved or sliced tomatoes and diced tomato pulp are almost universal garnishes in savoury cooking.

Tomatoes are probably one of the most common ingredients in Western cooking. Despite their relatively recent appearance on the international scene, they are now an integral part of many cuisines. Sauces made from tomatoes are a traditional accompaniment to many foods. They are popular in soups and stews for their flavour and colour, and are used to make pickles, jams and sorbets. Tomatoes go well with onion, shallots, garlic and herbs such as mint, basil and tarragon, and their flavour suits dishes with eggs, olives, oily fish, chicken, beef and veal. In the cooking of tomatoes, it is common to add a pinch or two of sugar if they are too acidic.

Tomatoes are rich in vitamins and low in calories: 100 g/$3\frac{1}{2}$ oz contains only 22.

TOMATES FARCIES CHARCUTIÈRE

Meat-stuffed tomatoes

Serves 6
Preparation 20 minutes
Cooking about 30 minutes

METRIC/IMPERIAL	AMERICAN
2 tbsp olive oil	2 tbsp olive oil
6 large firm round beefsteak tomatoes	6 large firm round beefsteak tomatoes
45 g/$1\frac{1}{2}$ oz butter	3 tbsp butter
1 garlic clove, finely chopped	1 garlic clove, minced
85 g/3 oz onions, finely chopped	$\frac{1}{3}$ cup finely chopped onions
350 g/$\frac{3}{4}$ lb sausage meat	$\frac{3}{4}$ lb sausage meat
4 tbsp finely chopped flat-leaved parsley	$\frac{1}{4}$ cup finely chopped flat-leaf parsley
1 tsp crumbled thyme	1 tsp crumbled thyme
3 tbsp breadcrumbs	3 tbsp breadcrumbs
1 egg	1 egg
salt and pepper	salt and pepper

Preheat the oven to 220C/425F/gas 7. Grease a baking dish lightly with some of the oil.

Cut the tops off each tomato at the stalk end. Scoop out the seeds and flesh with a small spoon without piercing the skin. Season the interiors with salt and pepper. Leave the tomatoes upside down on a clean cloth to drain.

Melt the butter in a sauté pan over a moderate heat and add the garlic and onion. Stir for 3 minutes, then add the sausage meat. Cook for 10 minutes, stirring from time to time.

Add the parsley along with the thyme and two thirds of the breadcrumbs. Season with salt and pepper and remove from the heat.

Add the egg and mix well. Stuff the tomatoes with the mixture. Arrange them in the dish and replace the caps. Sprinkle over the remaining oil and breadcrumbs.

Bake for 20 minutes and then serve hot.

Variations: any amount of leftover cooked meat may be finely minced (ground) and added to the stuffing; reduce the quantity of sausage meat proportionately. Fresh basil or thyme also flavour the stuffing well.

GRANITÉ À LA TOMATE

Tomato granita

Serves 4
Preparation 20 minutes
Freezing about 3 hours

METRIC/IMPERIAL	AMERICAN
1 kg/$2\frac{1}{4}$ lb very ripe tomatoes, peeled	$2\frac{1}{4}$ lb very ripe tomatoes, peeled
300 g/10 oz preserving sugar	$1\frac{1}{2}$ cups preserving or granulated sugar
$1\frac{1}{2}$ tbsp vodka	$1\frac{1}{2}$ tbsp vodka
1 egg white	1 egg white
55 g/2 oz icing sugar	$\frac{1}{2}$ cup confectioners' sugar

Press the tomatoes through a sieve. There should be about 200 ml/7 fl oz/1 cup of juice.

Dissolve the preserving sugar completely in 150 ml/$\frac{1}{4}$ pt/$\frac{2}{3}$ cup of cold water. Mix in the tomato juice and vodka. Pour into an ice-cube tray without dividers and freeze for 1 hour.

In a bowl in a warm bain-marie, whisk the egg white with the icing (confectioners') sugar.

Take the tomato preparation out of the freezer, stir it with a fork and incorporate the beaten egg white. Return it to the freezer and leave it for another 2 hours to set.

see also:
offal

TONGUE

Langue

The tongues of various livestock animals may be eaten and they are classified as white offal (variety meat).

BEEF OR OX TONGUES have the best flavour and can weigh up to 2 kg/4½ lb, although any larger than 1.35 kg/3 lb are unpalatably tough. They require lengthy cooking, usually by boiling or braising in an aromatic stock, and are often sold already cooked like ham – salted, rolled and pressed. They may even be smoked.

CALVES' TONGUES are tender and suit being braised in a sharp Madeira or tomato sauce.

LAMBS' TONGUES are small and delicate with a more subtle flavour. They are usually grilled on skewers, baked au gratin or served in a salad with a highly seasoned vinaigrette.

If preparing tongue at home, scrub it well. Cured tongues will also require soaking or blanching before any further cooking. For ease, tongues are normally skinned after cooking.

Tongue goes well with sauerkraut and suits piquant, fruity sauces, especially with raisins. It may also be glazed with aspic and served with pickles, mustard and horseradish sauce.

Tongue is very fatty: lambs' and ox tongues contain about 200–250 calories per 100 g/3½ oz; while calves' tongues have only about 150.

LANGUE DE BOEUF BRAISÉE

Braised ox tongue

Serves 6
Preparation 30 minutes, 1 hour ahead
Cooking about 3¾ hours

METRIC/IMPERIAL	AMERICAN
1 fresh ox tongue, weighing about 2 kg/4½ lb	*1 fresh beef tongue, weighing about 4½ lb*
large piece of pork rind, trimmed of fat	*large piece of pork rind, trimmed of fat*
4 onions, thinly sliced	*4 onions, thinly sliced*
3 carrots, thinly sliced	*3 carrots, thinly sliced*
bouquet garni	*bouquet garni*
200 ml/7 fl oz dry white wine	*1 cup dry white wine*
1 l/1¾ pt beef stock	*1 qt beef stock*
25 g/¾ oz butter	*1½ tbsp butter*
1 tbsp flour	*1 tbsp flour*
5–6 gherkins, chopped	*5–6 pickled cucumbers or cornichons, chopped*
2 tbsp capers, drained	*2 tbsp capers, drained*
1 tsp tarragon mustard	*1 tsp tarragon mustard*
salt and pepper	*salt and pepper*

Boil the tongue for 25 minutes in a large pan of water, skimming several times. Then soak it in a bowl of cold water for about 1 hour, changing the water several times. Drain and remove the white skin that covers it. If using salted tongue, soak it overnight in cold water.

Preheat the oven to 180C/350F/gas 4.

Put the pork rind on the bottom of a flameproof casserole, skin side down. Add the onions and carrots to the casserole along with the bouquet garni. Place the tongue on top, cover and set over a moderate heat.

After about 20 minutes, pour in the wine and boil uncovered for about 5 minutes in order to reduce to a syrupy consistency. Then pour in the stock and bring to the boil again. Season with salt and pepper and cover.

Cook in the oven for 3 hours, turning the tongue several times. Prick with a skewer to see if it is cooked: it should go in easily.

Drain the tongue and carve it across at an angle in even slices. Arrange some of the slices on a warmed serving dish and keep hot. Strain the cooking juices.

Make a roux by melting the butter in a saucepan over a gentle heat and then adding the flour. Cook gently, stirring continuously, until the roux just begins to colour, then add the strained cooking juices to it. Bring to the boil, stirring, and simmer for a few minutes until thick and smooth, then incorporate the gherkins (pickled cucumbers), capers and mustard. Adjust the seasoning and serve in a sauce boat.
To drink: a medium-bodied red, such as a Cahors.

Tournedos chasseur (Tournedos with mushroom wine sauce)

TOURNEDOS OR FILET MIGNON

see also:
beef
meat
sauce
steak

Round slices of beef fillet (tenderloin), measuring about 8 cm/3¼ in across and 2 cm/¾ in thick, tournedos (filet mignon) are usually barded around the edge with a layer of fat.

Tournedos are best grilled (broiled), barbecued or pan fried and served with their juices deglazed with port and cream, or any one of a wide variety of sauces and garnishes: tomato or *béarnaise* sauce, anchovy butter, asparagus tips or perhaps, as in the famous *tournedos Rossini*, with truffles, foie gras and a Madeira sauce.

Due to their size and shape these steaks are often served on *croûtes*, potato cakes, slices of aubergine (eggplant) or artichoke bottoms.

Other prime quality cuts of beef are also sometimes prepared in the style of tournedos.

TOURNEDOS CHASSEUR

Tournedos with mushroom wine sauce

Serves 6
Preparation 10 minutes
Cooking about 35 minutes

METRIC/IMPERIAL	AMERICAN
6 tournedos, weighing 200 g/7 oz each	*6 filet mignon steaks, weighing 7 oz each*
100 g/3½ oz butter	*1 stick butter*
115 g/¼ lb mushrooms, wiped and thinly sliced	*¼ lb mushrooms, wiped and thinly sliced*
5 shallots, chopped	*5 shallots, chopped*
350 ml/12 fl oz beef stock	*1⅔ cups beef stock*
45 g/1½ oz flour	*⅓ cup flour*
1 tbsp tomato purée	*1 tbsp tomato paste*
150 ml/¼ pt dry white wine	*⅔ cup dry white wine*
sprig of thyme	*sprig of thyme*
salt and pepper	*salt and pepper*
parsley, to garnish	*parsley, to garnish*

Make sure the steaks are at room temperature before cooking.

Melt 15 g/½ oz/1 tbsp of the butter in a sauté pan over a moderate heat and sauté the mushrooms until just soft. Remove the mushrooms with a slotted spoon and set aside.

Melt 55 g/2 oz/4 tbsp of butter in the pan and sauté the shallots, stirring all the time. Heat the stock in a small saucepan.

Sprinkle the shallots with the flour and cook, stirring, until just beginning to brown. Blend the tomato purée (paste) into the hot stock and add to the pan. Mix thoroughly, then add the wine and thyme. Cook gently for 20 minutes.

Remove the thyme and add the mushrooms. Melt the rest of the butter in a large frying pan over a high heat and put the steaks into it. Seal them for 2–3 minutes on each side. Drain and put on a warmed serving dish. Coat with the sauce, garnish with parsley and serve.

TRIPE

Tripes, gras-double

see also: offal

The stomach of ruminant animals, usually cows or calves, tripe is sold as white offal (variety meat). It requires such lengthy preparation and cooking that it is mostly sold dressed, needing only a little more cooking.

VEAL TRIPE has by far the best flavour, especially the thick, white honeycombed type. Avoid darker tripes as these are tougher with a very strong, coarse smell and taste.

Tripe is usually braised gently in an aromatic stock with onions, or it may be cut into strips and browned or stewed in a rich, creamy sauce.

Among the numerous French regional recipes for tripe, probably the best known is *tripes à la mode de Caen*, in which it is simmered for many hours in cider with a calves' foot, onions, leeks and carrots. The Spanish cook it with garlic, chorizo and chilli peppers to make their classic *callos a la madrileña*; the Italians cook it with beans, and the north Africans flavour it with cumin and caraway and incorporate it in couscous.

Tripe is comparatively low in calories for offal (variety meats): 95–100 per 100 g/3½ oz.

GRAS-DOUBLE À LA LYONNAISE

Tripe with onions

Serves 4
Preparation 10 minutes
Cooking about 15 minutes

METRIC/IMPERIAL	AMERICAN
30 g/1 oz butter	*2 tbsp butter*
4 tbsp sunflower oil	*4 tbsp sunflower oil*

4 onions, thinly sliced	4 onions, thinly sliced
800 g/1¾ lb cooked tripe, cut into thin strips	1¾ lb cooked tripe, cut into thin strips
2 tbsp white wine vinegar	2 tbsp white wine vinegar
3 tbsp finely chopped parsley	3 tbsp finely chopped parsley

Melt half the butter with half the oil in a frying pan over a moderate heat and brown the onions in it for about 5 minutes.

Melt the rest of the butter and oil in another frying pan over a high heat. Put the strips of tripe into it and brown them, stirring frequently and ensuring that they do not burn.

Add the onions to the tripe and mix, then cook over a moderate heat for a further 3–4 minutes. Everything should be well browned. Pour into a warmed, deep serving dish.

Deglaze the frying pan with the vinegar, stirring with a wooden spoon to pick up the sediment. Pour this over the tripe and onions and sprinkle with the parsley.

Serve at once, accompanied by a green salad with hard-boiled eggs and a shallot dressing. *To drink: Beaujolais.*

TROTTERS OR FEET

Pieds

see also: aspic, daube, offal, sauce

The trotters, or feet, of livestock are classified as white offal (variety meat) and generally sold ready prepared and cooked.

CALVES' FEET are rich in gelatine and are used mainly for making aspic or for enriching daubes, stews and braises, such as *boeuf à la mode*. They may also be boned and cooked in a white stock and then fried or grilled (broiled) and served with tartare sauce.

PIGS' FEET OR TROTTERS are usually grilled (broiled) or fried and served with mustard or piquant sauce. They may also be boned and stuffed or added to stews and daubes.

SHEEP'S FEET OR TROTTERS are generally simmered in an aromatic stock until tender. They may then be grilled (broiled) or fried, used in fricassees or served cold in salads.

Feet are the fattiest of all offal (variety meats): 100 g/3½ oz contains 350 calories.

PIEDS DE COCHON À LA SAINTE-MENEHOULD

Grilled breaded pigs' trotters or feet

Serves 4
Preparation 15 minutes
Cooking about 20 minutes

METRIC/IMPERIAL	AMERICAN
2 cooked pigs' trotters	2 cooked pig's feet
55 g/2 oz butter	4 tbsp butter
2 eggs	2 eggs
150 g/5½ oz browned breadcrumbs	1½ cups browned breadcrumbs
salt and pepper	salt and pepper

Preheat a grill (broiler). Cut each trotter (foot) in half lengthwise. Melt the butter in a pan and skim the froth to clarify it.

Break the eggs into a deep plate, season them with salt and pepper and beat them lightly. Put the breadcrumbs in another plate.

Dip each piece of pig's trotter (foot) first into the beaten egg and then into the breadcrumbs, pressing down well so that they are coated with a thick layer of crumbs.

Arrange on a baking sheet and brush them with the clarified butter. Grill (broil) gently for 15–20 minutes, turning and basting several times. Serve very hot, with mustard.

TROUT

Truite

see also: char, fish, roe, salmon

A small, freshwater member of the salmon family, the trout is a highly prized catch for anglers and is also extensively farmed.

There are several varieties of importance to the cook. The COMMON TROUT is the type most often found wild in Europe. Those beautiful speckled specimens found in rivers and streams are termed BROWN TROUT, while those fished after a spell at sea are known as SEA TROUT. Perhaps because they have fed on small crustaceans, the latter develop a fine-flavoured pink flesh which earns them their alternative name of SALMON TROUT. The RAINBOW TROUT is native to the western USA, but due to its extraordinary hardiness it has been introduced into waters all over the world, to the detriment of native species, and is the type most often farmed. It is fairly large, weighing 170–300 g/6–10 oz, but can have an undistinguished taste.

Trout is a delicate fish with firm, succulent flesh of varying degrees of pink depending on type and diet. Wild specimens are generally available from spring to autumn. The cooking method is determined by the size of the fish. The smallest are best fried *à la meunière* or baked *en papillote*, possibly with a stuffing. Larger fish are best poached in court-bouillon or braised in red wine, and suit most recipes for salmon. Trout is commonly garnished with nuts.

There is a long tradition of smoking trout and the product is sold whole or in fillets. Smoked trout makes delicious hors d'oeuvres, served with horseradish sauce, and is good in salads. Smoked sea trout is also sold thinly sliced like smoked salmon. Many actually prefer its flavour to that of smoked salmon.

Rainbow trout contains 140 calories per 100 g/3½ oz. Wild trout has a lower fat content.

TRUITES À L'ÉPINARD

Trout with spinach

Serves 4
Preparation 10 minutes
Cooking about 10 minutes

METRIC/IMPERIAL	*AMERICAN*
55 g/2 oz butter	*4 tbsp butter*
2 garlic cloves, chopped	*2 garlic cloves, chopped*
800 g/1¾ lb fresh spinach, trimmed and chopped	*1¾ lb fresh bulk spinach, trimmed and chopped*
4 rusks, crumbled	*4 rusks, crumbled*
1 egg, beaten	*1 egg, beaten*
4 ready-to-cook trout, each weighing about 200 g/7 oz	*4 dressed trout, each weighing about 7 oz*
2 tbsp lemon juice	*2 tbsp lemon juice*
salt and pepper	*salt and pepper*

Put one third of the butter in a bowl and microwave it on High for 30 seconds. Add the garlic and microwave on High for 1 minute.

Mix the spinach, crumbs and egg. Add the garlic butter and season with salt and pepper.

Stuff the trout with the mixture, securing the opening of each with a wooden toothpick. Place the trout in a dish, cover with microwave-safe film and pierce it in 3 or 4 places.

Microwave on High for 7–8 minutes, rotating the dish half-way through the cooking time.

Put the remaining butter in a bowl and microwave it on High for 30 seconds. Season it with salt and pepper and add the lemon juice. Pour this mixture over the trout.

TRUFFLE

Truffe

see also:
chocolate
mushroom

Subterranean mushrooms which form tubers of varying sizes near the roots of certain types of tree, particularly the oak and to some extent beech, hazel and chestnut, truffles may be black, dark brown or off-white, depending on variety. They are gathered on a small scale in a number of select areas, often using pigs or dogs to sniff them out, and elude all attempts at artificial cultivation, so it is therefore no surprise that they are very costly.

For the cook, the most sought-after truffle is the BLACK OR PÉRIGORD TRUFFLE, found also in Provence, which weighs 15–55 g/½–2 oz. It is gathered between mid-November and February and has very compact flesh with a pronounced aroma. The summer truffle (*truffe d'été*), which is gathered from June to November but is also occasionally found in winter, is deep brown and white-veined. The WHITE OR ITALIAN TRUFFLE, which resembles a smooth-skinned, slightly lumpy potato, is very

fragile and is in season from the end of September to January. It is even rarer and thus more expensive. It has less flavour than the black truffle, but a much more powerful aroma and they are best enjoyed raw.

Fresh, black truffles will keep for up to 4–5 days in the refrigerator. White truffles are very delicate and will keep for only 3 or 4 days at most. Truffles must be kept in an airtight container as they very readily give off their moisture – and aroma – and can lose up to 10% of their weight overnight. If very fresh eggs are stored in the same container, they will absorb some of the truffle flavour. The Italians also store their truffles in rice or oil which is then imbued with a strong truffle flavour.

A good fresh truffle should be heavy, firm and dry. Check that it has no cracks or holes which may be filled with earth. Do not wash it, simply brush it gently or carefully peel it, if necessary. The peelings may be used in sauces.

Canned black truffles are widely sold, graded by quality: *surchoix* which are firm and uniform; *extra*, which are firm but may be irregular; and *premier choix* which are irregular and may have abrasions. They are not cooked before canning, simply scrubbed and lightly salted. They are also sold in pieces, or as trimmings and peelings, which are all very good for cooking, particularly in sauces. However, canned truffles cannot match the flavour and aroma of fresh truffles.

A large part of the black truffle crop goes into the making of *pâté de foie gras* and truffles are widely used to flavour sauces and garnish meat and poultry dishes. However, the best way to enjoy a fresh truffle, black or white, is to slice it thinly over a plate of risotto, fresh pasta or potato salad, stir it into scrambled eggs or brandade of salt cod, or to garnish fresh foie gras or roast partridge.

Truffles have twice the calorie content of cultivated mushrooms and three times that of wild mushrooms: 100 g/3½ oz contains about 90.

CHOCOLATE TRUFFLES are small balls of chocolate mixed with sugar, butter or cream and sometimes eggs. They are often flavoured with items such as rum, champagne, brandy, whisky, vanilla, cinnamon or coffee and are finished with a light dusting of cocoa powder, giving them the look of black truffles.

TAGLIATELLE À LA TRUFFE

Tagliatelle with truffles

Serves 4
Preparation 10 minutes
Cooking about 6 minutes

METRIC/IMPERIAL	AMERICAN
2 tbsp olive oil	*2 tbsp olive oil*
450 g/1 lb fresh tagliatelle	*1 lb fresh tagliatelle*
1 fresh black or white truffle, weighing about 30 g/1 oz	*1 fresh black or white truffle, weighing about 1 oz*
75 g/2½ oz cold butter, diced	*5 tbsp cold butter, diced*
salt	*salt*

Fill a large pan with water and add a generous pinch of salt and the oil. Bring to the boil. Add the pasta and cook at a rolling boil for about 6 minutes, until the pasta is just tender but still firm to the bite.

While the pasta is cooking, cut the truffle into tiny cubes or strips.

Drain the pasta well and put it into a warmed serving dish. Mix in the butter. When it has melted, stir in the truffle pieces and serve.

To drink: Pomerol.

TRUSSING

see also: game poultry roasting

Before cooking, most birds are trussed with string so that their legs and wings remain closely tucked in to their sides. This makes them sit and look better and facilitates basting and turning.

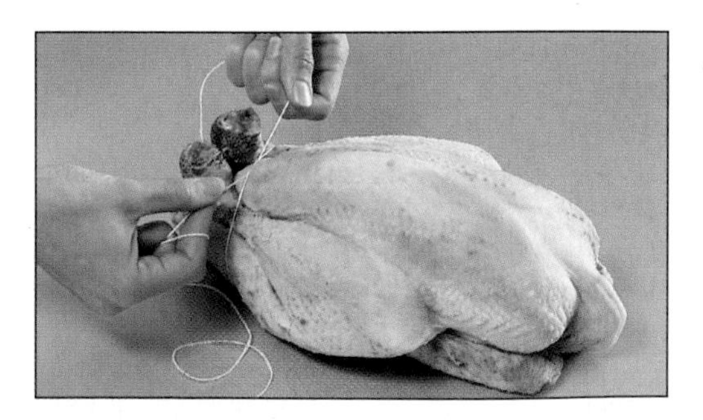

Bring the knobby ends of the legs together, loop the string around the back and tie securely.

It is often enough just to tie the bird at the top of the wings and thighs. More complex procedures, involving piercing the bird's flesh, are usually effected with a long, specially designed trussing needle. However, these increase the loss of juices during cooking. The trussing thread is always removed before carving, partly to check that the sections of the bird that have been pressed against each other are properly cooked.

see also:
fish
veal

TUNA
Thon

A name given to several large marine fish related to the mackerel, tuna have long been valued for their firm, tasty flesh. They are found in the Mediterranean, Black Sea and both sides of the Atlantic, as far south as Africa and the Caribbean. As they usually congregate in large shoals, when they migrate towards the shore they are caught in very great numbers, usually between May and October. The resulting gluts have produced a strong tradition of preserving tuna.

The BLUE-FIN TUNA (*thon rouge*) is almost always sold fresh, sliced or in pieces; it has compact flesh which should be glossy and bright red. However the flavour is quite mild and is better if the fish is allowed to mature for several days. The LONG-FIN TUNA OR ALBACORE (*thon blanc* or *germon*) has arguably the best flavour and is the type of tuna most commonly canned. Its flesh is paler and less dense. The much larger YELLOW-FIN tuna is confusingly called *albacore* in France. It is mostly fished in warmer waters, has pinkish flesh and is often canned. The closely related PACIFIC BONITO OR SKIPJACK is widely sold canned.

Fresh tuna is surprisingly meaty and is, in fact, one of the few fish with identifiable 'cuts'. The *ventresca* or lower belly is regarded as the prime cut. Fish are usually hung to allow the blood to drain out to help make the flesh as pale as possible, especially before canning. Fresh tuna suits the same sort of treatment as veal and similarly needs to be protected from drying out during cooking. It may be grilled (broiled), barbecued, baked or braised, usually in highly seasoned sauces.

Tuna is a fatty fish, but is very rich in vitamins and minerals: 100 g/3½ oz fresh plainly cooked tuna contains 230 calories; 100 g/3½ oz canned tuna in oil contains 280.

DARNES DE THON BASQUAISE

Tuna steaks with Mediterranean vegetables

Serves 6
Preparation 30 minutes
Cooking about 1 hour

METRIC/IMPERIAL	*AMERICAN*
1 fresh tuna steak, preferably mature blue-fin, weighing about 800 g/1¾ lb	*1 fresh tuna steak, preferably mature blue-fin or albacore, weighing about 1¾ lb*
3 tbsp olive oil	*3 tbsp olive oil*
2 red sweet peppers, halved, deseeded and cut into strips	*2 red sweet peppers, halved, deseeded and cut into strips*
1 aubergine, finely diced	*1 eggplant, finely diced*
1 garlic clove, chopped	*1 garlic clove, chopped*
2 onions, chopped	*2 onions, chopped*
4 tomatoes, peeled and chopped	*4 tomatoes, peeled and chopped*
sprig of thyme	*sprig of thyme*
bay leaf	*bay leaf*
flour, for dusting	*flour, for dusting*
salt and cayenne pepper	*salt and cayenne pepper*

Dust the tuna with the flour. Heat 2 tablespoons of the oil in a flameproof casserole over a moderate heat. Add the tuna and let it brown on both sides, then remove it.

Add the remaining oil to the casserole and sauté the peppers for 3 minutes, then add the aubergine (eggplant), garlic, onions, tomatoes, thyme, bay leaf and a pinch each of salt and cayenne. Mix well and bring to the boil.

Return the tuna to the casserole, cover tightly and simmer gently for 45 minutes. Serve hot with steamed courgettes (zucchini).

TURBOT

A large, marine sinistral flatfish found in the European Atlantic and Mediterranean, turbot is generally regarded as one of the finest of fish.

Turbot poché hollandaise (Poached turbot with hollandaise sauce)

see also:
brill
fish
John Dory
sole

More readily available in winter than in summer, it is lozenge-shaped with a brown top and light under-side, and has delicate, firm white flesh. Related species are found off the Canadian Atlantic coast and in the Pacific.

Turbot normally weigh 2–4 kg/4½–9 lb, but can reach up to 20 kg/45 lb. Depending on size, it is sold whole and cleaned, in fillets or in sections. Because there is significant wastage, it is a relatively expensive fish. Generally speaking, the lighter the skin, the better the fish. Small chicken turbot (*turbotin*), weighing 1–1.5 kg/2¼–3½ lb, are also delicate, cheaper and more easily managed.

Whole turbot is cooked like brill or John Dory, ideally in a container shaped especially to take its unusual shape and known as a *turbotière*; turbot fillets are prepared in the same ways as sole. Turbot should always be cooked very carefully, as the flesh dries out readily and loses its flavour. Although it features greatly in *haute cuisine*, with sauces of lobster, champagne, saffron or capers, turbot best suits simple cooking and presentation. It is often poached in milk, like haddock, to keep the flesh white, and served with hollandaise sauce, or grilled and served with *béarnaise* sauce.

Turbot is a fairly fatty fish: 100 g/3½ oz contains 120 calories.

TURBOT POCHÉ HOLLANDAISE

Poached turbot with hollandaise sauce

Serves 8
Preparation 30 minutes
Cooking about 20 minutes

METRIC/IMPERIAL	*AMERICAN*
1 turbot, weighing about 2 kg/4½ lb, skinned and cut into about 24 equal-sized pieces	*1 turbot, dressed weight about 4½ lb, skinned and cut into about 24 equal pieces*
court-bouillon or fish stock	*court-bouillon or fish stock*
3 egg yolks	*3 egg yolks*
2 tbsp white wine vinegar	*2 tbsp white wine vinegar*
250 g/8½ oz butter, diced	*2 sticks + 3 tbsp butter, diced*
juice of 1 lemon	*juice of 1 lemon*
salt and pepper	*salt and pepper*
sprigs of parsley, to garnish	*sprigs of parsley, to garnish*

Place the turbot in a single layer in 1 or 2 large saucepans; the pieces of fish must not overlap each other. Add enough court-bouillon to cover the fish completely.

Bring to the boil, then turn down the heat as low as possible and cover. Cook for 15 minutes.

Meanwhile, make the sauce: put the egg yolks into a saucepan or the top of a double boiler and mix in the vinegar and some pepper. Put the pan in a bain-marie, or set it over the bottom of the double boiler, and heat gently.

Incorporate the butter in tiny pieces, stirring continuously. When the sauce is thick and smooth, add the lemon juice a little at a time. Adjust the seasoning.

Drain the fish and put it on a large, warmed dish. Surround it with sprigs of parsley. Serve the sauce in a sauce boat.

TURKEY

Dinde, dindon, dindonneau

see also:
ballottine
casserole
chicken fricassee
giblets
poultry
stuffing

The turkey is a large bird native to the Americas. It was first introduced into Europe in the mid-sixteenth century and is now widely farmed, although attempts to induce it to breed wild in many parts of Europe have failed.

Traditionally, turkeys were bred to weigh 6–9 kg/13–20 lb, but medium-size and small birds are now being bred and reared to conform to today's smaller households and ovens. Turkey farmers also breed an even larger type of turkey, with much blander meat, to produce escalopes (cutlets) from the breast, legs and thighs, plus roasts and ballottines.

A good roasting turkey should be young and plump with a high ratio of breast meat. It should have been hung for at least 4 or 5 days to allow the flavour to develop. Try to buy a hen, as the meat of the female is tastier and moister than that of the male. Look for dry pale skin, with no hint of blue. If the skin feels moist the bird may have been frozen.

CARVING A TURKEY

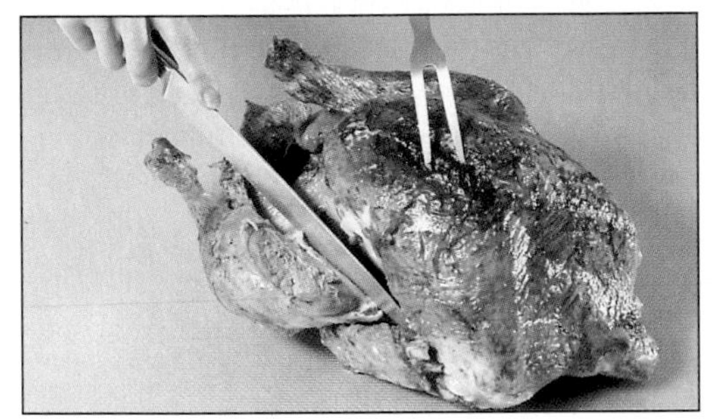

Remove the leg quarters, cut off the drumsticks and slice the meat from the thighs

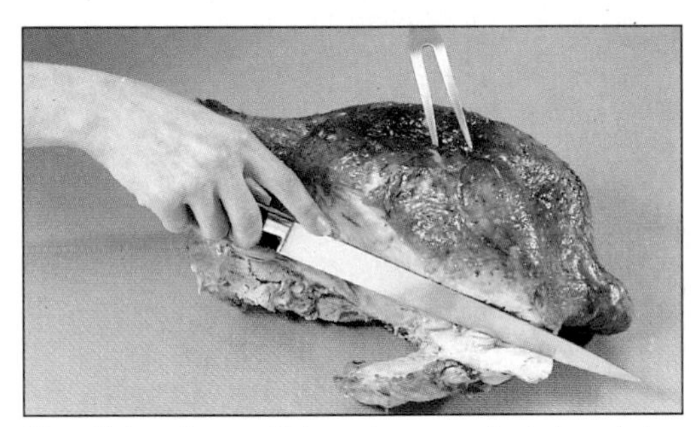

Cut off the wings, which are best served whole as it is difficult to slice them neatly.

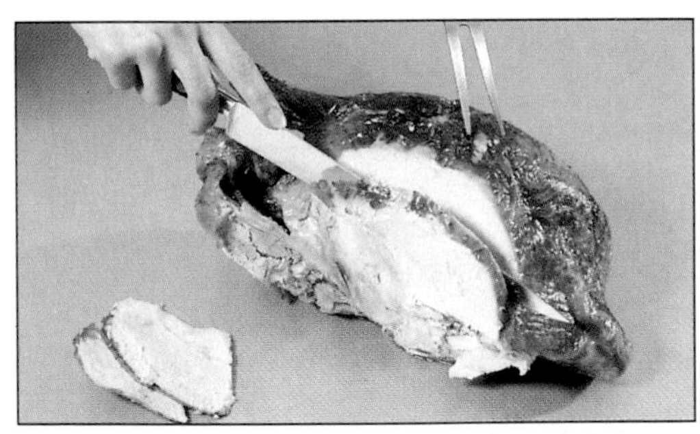

Carve the breast meat into thin, even slices. It is best to carve one side at a time.

Many oven-ready turkeys are now sold frozen and these are good value, but do remember that larger birds can take about 4 days to thaw completely in the refrigerator. Unfortunately, many birds are frozen without proper hanging and their flavour suffers accordingly.

As a guide, buy 450 g/1 lb fresh turkey per person; 350 g/12 oz if the bird is oven-ready (dressed) or frozen. Try to get the giblets with the bird as they make a delicious gravy, and the chopped liver and heart are good in stuffings.

Turkey meat can be rather dry, so the birds are best barded, especially males. They may also be cooked first breast-side down in some melted butter. The French often add a little water, stock or wine to the pan during cooking. Continual basting is also essential. Small birds may be cooked quite quickly, like chickens, at 200C/400F/gas 6, allowing 10 minutes per 450 g/1 lb of total stuffed weight. Larger birds are best cooked more slowly as below. If the breasts are not barded, they should be protected with foil for the early part of cooking. Both foil and bards need to be removed for the last 40 minutes of cooking to make sure the breasts brown properly.

Rich, fatty stuffings also keep the meat moist, and highly seasoned mixtures help combat the blandness of many turkeys. Popular stuffing ingredients include chestnuts, finely chopped chicken, veal or sausage meat, mushrooms, onions, celery, apples, prunes, apricots and even oysters. Larger birds can take two stuffings, usually a mild one in the chest and a more highly seasoned mixture in the vent.

Roast turkey has become a fairly universal festive dish. The early American settlers began the habit of serving turkey with giblet gravy and cranberry sauce at Thanksgiving in recognition of the wild turkey's role in their survival. In Britain, turkey supplanted the traditional goose at Christmas festivities in Victorian times, usually accompanied by roast potatoes, Brussels sprouts and bread sauce. Feast days in Mexico are celebrated with the rich turkey stew *mole poblano de guajalote*, flavoured with chocolate.

In addition to stuffed roast turkey, there are numerous ways of cooking the birds. They may be braised or stewed, or boiled and served warm or cold with a vinaigrette. Tender, younger turkeys (*dindonneaux*) are also commonly made into fricassees or casseroles. Turkey escalopes (cutlets), taken from the breast, need to be highly seasoned, because their flavour is always slightly bland. The giblets also make nutritious and economical dishes.

Compared to other poultry, turkey has a low fat content: 100 g/$3\frac{1}{2}$ oz contains 110 calories.

DINDE FARCIE AUX MARRONS

Roast turkey stuffed with chestnuts

Serves about 10
Preparation 30 minutes
Cooking about 2½ hours

METRIC/IMPERIAL	AMERICAN
45 g/1½ oz butter	3 tbsp butter
140 g/5 oz slices of lean bacon, cut into strips	5 oz slices of lean bacon, cut into strips
2 onions, chopped	2 onions, chopped
225 g/½ lb lean pork, finely chopped	½ lb lean boneless pork, finely chopped
115 g/¼ lb pork fat, finely chopped	¼ lb pork fatback, finely chopped
1 apple, peeled, cored and coarsely chopped	1 apple, peeled, cored and coarsely chopped
allspice	allspice
24 canned chestnuts, well drained	24 canned chestnuts, well drained
1 oven-ready turkey, weighing about 4 kg/9 lb	1 turkey, dressed weight about 9 lb
1 thin slice of barding fat	1 thin slice of barding fat
1 tbsp oil	1 tbsp oil
salt and pepper	salt and pepper

Preheat the oven to 180C/350F/gas 4.

Heat the butter in a saucepan and brown the bacon strips and onions, stirring all the time. Add the pork and pork fat to the pan, stirring well. Continue to cook for a few minutes, stirring. Add the apple to the pan. Season lightly with salt and pepper and a little allspice.

Remove the pan from the heat and add the chestnuts. Mix gently and adjust the seasoning, if necessary.

Stuff the turkey through the neck, pressing the stuffing well down. Sew up the opening. Place the barding fat on the breast and tie it in place with string. Lightly grease the turkey with oil and put it in a large roasting pan.

Roast in the oven for 15 minutes per 450 g/1 lb stuffed weight, about 2½ hours in total. Turn the bird several times to ensure that it browns evenly and baste it frequently. Allow the bird to rest for at least 15 minutes after it has come out of the oven.

Serve the turkey carved, with the stuffing piled in the middle. Accompany with potatoes sautéed in butter. Skim all fat from the cooking juices and serve them in a sauce boat.

To drink: Margaux or Chambolle-Musigny.

Dinde farcie aux marrons (Roast turkey stuffed with chestnuts)

BLANCS DE DINDE À LA CRÈME

Turkey breast with cream sauce

Serves 4
Preparation 15 minutes
Cooking about 30 minutes

METRIC/IMPERIAL	AMERICAN
115 g/¼ lb mushrooms	¼ lb mushrooms
juice of ½ lemon	juice of ½ lemon
30 g/1 oz butter	2 tbsp butter
4 turkey escalopes	4 turkey cutlets cut from the breast
150 ml/¼ pt dry white wine	⅔ cup dry white wine
1 tsp tarragon mustard	1 tsp tarragon mustard
150 ml/¼ pt thick crème fraîche or whipping cream	⅔ cup thick crème fraîche or whipping cream
1 egg	1 egg
salt	salt

Slice the mushrooms very thinly and sprinkle them with the lemon juice.

Melt the butter in a frying pan over a moderate heat and seal the turkey escalopes (cutlets) for 7–10 minutes on each side. Drain and keep them hot.

Deglaze the pan with the wine and bring to the boil. Mix in the mustard. Return the turkey to the pan and season with salt and pepper.

Add the mushrooms with three quarters of the cream and cook gently for 10 minutes.

Put the escalopes (cutlets) on a warmed serving dish. Beat a little of the hot sauce into the egg, then stir this back into the frying pan. Add the rest of the cream and a few drops of lemon juice and stir gently to obtain a smooth sauce, but do not allow it to boil.

Coat the escalopes (cutlets) with the sauce and serve immediately.

see also:
carrot
swede
vegetables

TURNIP
Navet

A vegetable of the cabbage family, the turnip is grown for its roots and its young leaves.

The roots of GARDEN TURNIPS are either round or elongated and usually have a pale yellow or white skin, often tinged with violet. Look for firm turnips, with compact flesh under a clear, smooth, unblemished skin. Turnips are usually peeled and chopped prior to cooking.

Turnips have a great capacity for absorbing fat and flavour, and are one of the traditional vegetables for soups and hearty stews like *pot-au-feu*. They may also be boiled and served as an accompaniment to fatty meats, such as duck or mutton, cubed and sautéed like potatoes, stuffed, puréed or baked *au gratin*.

Baby new turnips (*petits navets*) may be grated raw as a crudité or added to coleslaw. They are also braised or glazed whole and unpeeled to make a delightful garnish.

The leaves, known as TURNIP GREENS OR TOPS may be used raw and finely chopped in salads or are more usually cooked like cabbage, spinach or broccoli. Finely shredded, dusted with five-spice powder and deep fried they may become the 'seaweed' served in many Chinese restaurants.

Turnip roots contain a little sulphur, which can make them difficult to digest, but they are also rich in protein, iron, calcium and vitamin C: 100 g/3½ oz contains 35 calories. The leaves are even more nutritious, containing a good deal of iodine and vitamin A, and lower in calories: 100 g/3½ oz contains only 11.

VELOUTÉ AUX NAVETS

Cream of turnip soup

Serves 4
Preparation 20 minutes
Cooking about 40 minutes

METRIC/IMPERIAL	AMERICAN
1 tbsp sunflower oil	1 tbsp sunflower oil
1 garlic clove, chopped	1 garlic clove, chopped
1 onion, chopped	1 onion, chopped
450 g/1 lb turnips, peeled and diced	1 lb turnips, peeled and diced

spring turnips

winter turnip

2 tbsp finely chopped parsley	*2 tbsp finely chopped parsley*
2 stalks of celery, trimmed and cut into chunks	*2 sticks of celery, trimmed and cut into chunks*
500 ml/16 fl oz chicken stock	*2 cups chicken stock*
100 g/3½ oz split peas	*½ cup split peas*
salt and pepper	*salt and pepper*

Put the oil into a deep dish. Microwave it on High for 1 minute. Add the garlic and onion and mix. Microwave on High for 1 further minute.

Add the turnips, parsley and celery, cover and microwave on High for 3 minutes. Meanwhile, heat the stock in a saucepan.

Add the very hot stock and the split peas to the dish, cover and microwave on High for 30 minutes, stirring 3–4 times during cooking.

Remove the dish from the oven. Let the mixture cool slightly, then blend it in a food processor. When the soup is smooth and velvety, taste it and adjust the seasoning.

Return it to the microwave oven and cook for 1 minute on High to serve piping hot.

Variation: small garlic croutons or toast spread with tapenade may accompany the soup.

TURNOVER

Chausson

see also: pastry

Normally made with puff pastry, turnovers are formed from thinly rolled rounds of pastry folded over a filling to make a semi-circle. They are usually made as individual servings, but larger, pie-size turnovers can be made. The most usual sweet fillings include apples or other fruit. Smaller turnovers with savoury fillings, such as meat, mushrooms, ham, chicken or fish, may be served as hot hors d'oeuvres.

CHAUSSONS AUX POMMES

Apple turnovers

For 10–12 small turnovers
Preparation 30 minutes, pastry 1 hour
Cooking 45 minutes

METRIC/IMPERIAL	*AMERICAN*
5 firm dessert apples, such as Reinettes or Granny Smiths	*5 firm apples, such as Granny Smiths*
juice of 1 lemon	*juice of 1 lemon*
450 g/1 lb puff pastry	*1 lb puff pastry*
150 g/5½ oz caster sugar	*¾ cup superfine sugar*
1 tbsp very thick crème fraîche or whipping cream	*1 tbsp very thick crème fraîche or whipping cream*
1 egg, beaten	*1 egg, beaten*
30 g/1 oz butter	*2 tbsp butter*

Preheat the oven to 250C/475F/gas 9.

Peel and core the apples. Dice them very finely and sprinkle them with lemon juice.

Roll out the pastry to a thickness of about 3 mm/⅛ in and cut it into rounds with a diameter of about 12 cm/4¾ in.

Drain the diced apples and mix them in a bowl with the sugar and cream.

Brush around the edge of each pastry round with egg. Pile the apple mixture on half of each round and dot with butter.

Fold the pastry over the filling and press the edges together, moistened with a little water if necessary. Brush the top of each with beaten egg and allow to dry for a few minutes.

Lightly score crosses on the top of each turnover and put them on a baking sheet. Bake in the oven for 45 minutes. Serve warm or cold.

Variation: make one large turnover, adding several stoned (pitted) prunes to the apple filling.

U

UGLI

see also:
fruit
grapefruit
orange

A tropical fruit of the citrus family, the ugli is thought to be a cross between the grapefruit, tangerine and Seville orange. It has thick, knobbly green, yellow or brown skin surrounding sweet, perfumed flesh and is usually eaten fresh or made into jams.

UHT

see Cream, Milk

UNMOULDING

see also:
aspic
cakes and gâteaux
creams and custards
ices and ice creams
jelly or gelatin dessert
mousse
terrine

Many dishes made in moulds need to be turned out of the mould to serve them. There are various unmoulding techniques to facilitate this difficult operation. Aspic and gelatine preparations and chilled and frozen items, such as ice creams, need only be plunged into hot water for a few seconds and then given a gentle shake from side to side. It is also helpful to run a knife around the top edge to loosen it. The most straightforward way of effecting the unmoulding itself is to place a plate over the top of the mould and then carefully and quickly to turn them over together.

The successful unmoulding of cakes usually depends on the proper preparation of the pan, greasing it with butter and also sometimes lining it with parchment or greaseproof paper or dusting it with flour. If a cake resists being being unmoulded, turn the pan over and place a damp cloth over the base for a few minutes, then rap sharply.

TURNING OUT A MOULDED DISH

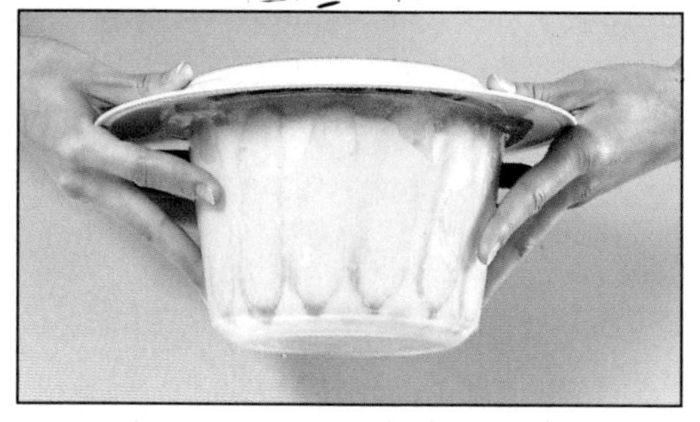

Invert the serving dish on top of the mould, hold securely and turn them over together.

Settle the contents, moving the position gently if necessary, and lift the mould away.

see also:
ices and ice creams
meringue

VACHERIN

Named after the pancake-shaped Alpine cheese which it closely resembles, the vacherin is a dessert made from discs of meringue filled with ice cream or fruit and topped with chantilly cream. Classic vacherins are built on a pastry base, but nowadays this is often omitted. Depending on the filling, vacherins may be decorated with crystallized fruit, marrons glacés or toasted almonds.

VACHERIN AUX MARRONS

Chestnut vacherin

Serves 8
Preparation 30 minutes
Cooking 3 hours, 24 hours ahead

METRIC/IMPERIAL	AMERICAN
225 g/8 oz caster sugar	1 cup + 2 tbsp superfine sugar
225 g/8 oz ground almonds	2⅔ cups ground almonds
25 g/¾ oz flour	3 tbsp flour
5 egg whites	5 egg whites
140 g/5 oz icing sugar	1 cup + 2½ tbsp confectioners' sugar
15 g/½ oz butter	1 tbsp butter
1 l/1¾ pt chestnut ice cream	1 qt chestnut ice cream
4 large marrons glacés	4 large candied chestnuts (marrons glacés)

Preheat the oven to 160C/325F/gas 3.

In a bowl, mix the caster (superfine) sugar, ground almonds and flour.

Whisk the egg whites to very stiff peaks with 125 g/4½ oz/1 cup of the icing (confectioners') sugar. Fold them into the mixture in the bowl, making sure they are well blended in.

Draw 2 circles with a diameter of 22 cm/8¾ in on two large pieces of parchment or greaseproof paper. Grease each with half the butter and place on 1 or 2 baking sheets.

Pipe a flat spiral of meringue inside the circle drawn on each of the pieces of paper, starting from the centre.

Bake the meringues for 30 minutes, then lower the heat to 130C/275F/gas 1 and cook for 1 hour more.

Let the meringues cool completely on a cold, damp surface to help get them off the paper.

The following day, 1 hour before serving, remove the ice cream from the freezer to soften it. Using a spatula, spread a single thick layer of ice cream over the first disc of meringue. Cover with the second disc, dust with the remaining icing (confectioners') sugar and decorate with the marrons glacés (candied chestnuts).

see also:
cakes and gâteaux
creams and custards
ices and ice creams
sugar

VANILLA

Vanille

The dried bean or pod of the vanilla plant, a climbing orchid native to Mexico and other parts of Central America, was used by the Aztecs to flavour chocolate drinks. The Spanish introduced it to Europe and since then it has become possibly the most common flavouring for sweet dishes. The Mexicans monopolized its production for several hundred years, until the nineteenth century, when the French successfully introduced it to several of their tropical colonies, notably Madagascar and Réunion.

The pods are harvested while they are still unripe, yellow and tasteless. A lengthy maturing process, which involves stacking them together until they blacken, encourages the formation of a crystalline coating of vanillin which is the flavouring element. If buying whole pods, or beans, look for a good coating of this crust. Vanilla is also sold as a powder and as concentrated essence or extract, both of which are very powerful and should be used judiciously. One of the most common ways in which vanilla is used domestically is as vanilla sugar, the better varieties of which contain about 10% vanillin.

Whole pods or beans, although expensive, are a good buy in that they may be used intact to flavour milks or custards, for instance, and then cleaned, dried and stored for reuse. They are also often kept in jars of sugar to which they impart a good flavour. The pods may also be split and the tiny seeds used as a flavouring.

A great deal of commercial vanilla flavour is produced by synthetic means and synthetic vanilla essence or extract is also widely sold in shops. However, the flavour of the synthetic version is quite inferior to the real thing and is liable to ruin any dish in which it is used.

The warm, penetrating flavour of vanilla is mainly used in desserts, such as milk puddings, custards and ice creams, in baking, particularly sponge cakes and *pâtisserie*, and confectionery. It does also find some savoury use, added in sparing quantities to dishes such as fish or mussel soup, roast white meats, shellfish *à la nage* and creamed vegetables.

Vacherin aux marrons (Chestnut vacherin)

BEURRE BLANC À LA VANILLE

Savoury vanilla butter sauce

Serves 4
Preparation 10 minutes
Cooking about 15 minutes

METRIC/IMPERIAL	AMERICAN
6 shallots, very finely chopped	6 shallots, very finely chopped
2 tbsp white wine vinegar	2 tbsp white wine vinegar
4 tbsp dry white wine	¼ cup dry white wine
250 g/8½ oz cold butter, cut in small pieces	2 sticks + 3 tbsp cold butter, cut in small pieces
seeds from 2 vanilla pods	seeds from 2 vanilla beans
salt and white pepper	salt and white pepper

Put the shallots in a saucepan with the vinegar and white wine and place over a moderate heat. Cook, stirring, until very soft and reduced.

Add the butter in small pieces to the shallot mixture, whisking constantly. Season with salt and pepper. Add the vanilla seeds and mix.

This is an unusual sauce for shellfish.

VARIETY MEAT

see Offal

VEAL

Veau

see also:
aspic
barding
beef
blanquette
fricassee
grenadine
larding
meat
offal
paupiette

The meat of the calf, veal is classified as a white meat and is very delicate and tender. In the UK, meat from milk-fed calves slaughtered between the ages of 3 and 4 months and grass-fed calves between 4 and 5 months is termed veal. In the USA, BOB VEAL is meat from a calf slaughtered before it is 1 month old, VEAL comes from calves between 1 and 3 months old, and BABY BEEF from animals between 3 and 12 months old. The quality of veal depends entirely on the breed of cattle and the method of feeding the animal. The best quality veal, sometimes known as FARMHOUSE VEAL, is fed purely on the milk of its mother, but it is rare and very expensive.

The widespread method of battery-raising calves is a practice of debatable ethics. Public demand has led to improved rearing conditions and better quality veal in recent years, and it still remains one of the most highly valued meats, particularly in France and Italy.

Good quality, milk-fed veal is firm, smooth and satiny, neither too dry nor too damp, with the finest possible grain. It should be pearly white in colour with a slight pinkish tinge and have some firm, white fat. Greyness, softness or dampness indicate that the calf has been fed on poor quality reconstituted milk or that it has had a diet with a high chemical content. The meat of those slightly older calves which have been fed on grass should be slightly darker in colour, but never actually red as this indicates that the animal was too old when slaughtered.

As the animal has not had a chance to build up much marbled fat in its tissues, veal is quite dry and needs to be larded or barded before being cooked. For this reason also, large cuts need constant basting during roasting and are probably better braised or pot-roasted; small pieces, such as chops, fillet (tenderloin) slices or escalopes (scaloppini), are fried rather than grilled (broiled).

Although some consider veal a little tasteless, it responds well to highly seasoned sauces or garnishes. Onion, lemon, smoked bacon or ham and anchovies are classic flavouring accompaniments. Other items, such as olives, sorrel and cheese are also popular and the Italians make particular use of veal in strong-flavoured combinations, such as *vitello tonnato* with tuna fish and *saltimbocca* with sage. The pale colour of the meat also makes it a common ingredient in white-sauced dishes such as blanquettes.

Veal offal (variety meat) is particularly sought-after: calves' liver, kidneys, sweetbreads and brains are generally the most tender and have the finest flavour, as do heads and feet.

Veal bones are particularly rich in gelatine and are thus very useful in the making of stocks, aspics and sauces.

Veal freezes quite well, but once it has been frozen its texture tends to be softer.

Veal meat is rich in minerals, especially iron and phosphorus, and is comparatively lean: 100 g/3½ oz contains 170 calories.

VEAU ORLOFF

Roast veal with mushrooms

Serves 6
Preparation 30 minutes
Cooking about 1 hour

METRIC/IMPERIAL	AMERICAN
1 boned veal roast, weighing about 1.35 kg/3 lb	*1 boned veal roast, weighing about 3 lb*
450 g/1 lb mushrooms	*1 lb mushrooms*
juice of ½ lemon	*juice of ½ lemon*
55 g/2 oz butter	*4 tbsp butter*
25 g/¾ oz flour	*3 tbsp flour*
200 ml/7 fl oz milk	*1 cup milk*
1 onion, chopped	*1 onion, chopped*
2 eggs, separated	*2 eggs, separated*
grated nutmeg	*grated nutmeg*
salt and pepper	*salt and pepper*

Ask the butcher to lard the meat or bard it with fat or several slices of bacon.

Preheat the oven to 220C/425F/gas 7. Roast the veal for about 50 minutes, basting frequently.

After about 30 minutes, start making the sauce. Clean and slice the mushrooms and sprinkle them with lemon juice.

Melt one third of the butter in a saucepan over a moderate to high heat and add the mushrooms. Cook uncovered, stirring frequently, for 10 minutes, then drain them.

Melt half the remaining butter in another saucepan over a moderate heat and stir in the flour. Cook for a minute or two, stirring, to make a blond roux. Gradually add the milk and cook for a few minutes until thick and smooth.

Stir in the onion and season with grated nutmeg, salt and pepper.

Set 2 tablespoons of the sauce aside, and mix the rest with the mushrooms and egg yolks.

Take the veal out of the oven and increase the temperature to 230C/450F/gas 8.

Remove the string and any barding fat or bacon from the roast veal and carve it into fairly thick slices, carefully reserving any carving juices. Spread each slice with the mushroom sauce. Re-shape the slices of meat into a 'roast' and secure it with 1 or 2 loops of string tied around it lengthwise.

Whisk the egg whites to stiff peaks. Fold in the reserved sauce and carving juices.

Grease a fresh baking dish with the remaining butter and put the veal in it. Spread it with the egg white and sauce mixture and put it in the hot oven for 7–8 minutes.

To drink: a fruity white wine, such as Frascati.

ESCALOPES VIENNOISES

Breaded veal escalopes with anchovies and capers

Serves 4
Preparation 15 minutes
Cooking about 12 minutes

METRIC/IMPERIAL	AMERICAN
4 veal escalopes, each weighing about 140 g/5 oz	4 veal cutlets, each weighing about 5 oz
2 eggs	2 eggs
100 g/3½ oz dry white breadcrumbs	1 cup dry white breadcrumbs
45 g/1½ oz butter	3 tbsp butter
2 tbsp oil	2 tbsp oil
4 canned rolled anchovy fillets in oil, drained	4 canned rolled anchovy fillets in oil, drained
1 lemon, sliced	1 lemon, sliced
1 tbsp capers, drained	1 tbsp capers, drained
flour, for coating	flour, for coating
salt and pepper	salt and pepper

Pound the escalopes (cutlets) to flatten them, season them and then dredge them in flour.

Break the eggs into a deep plate and beat lightly. Put the breadcrumbs on a second plate.

Dip both sides of each slice of veal into the egg and then into the breadcrumbs, pressing so that they are well coated.

Melt the butter with the oil in a frying pan over a moderate heat. Cook the slices of veal for 5–6 minutes on each side.

Put the veal on a warmed serving dish. On each escalope (cutlet), put an anchovy fillet and 1 or 2 lemon slices. Sprinkle with capers.

Note: chill the veal for 15 minutes after breading to dry out a little for a crisper coating.

CÔTES DE VEAU À LA NORMANDE

Veal chops with apples

Serves 4
Preparation 25 minutes
Cooking about 30 minutes

METRIC/IMPERIAL	AMERICAN
4 veal chops	4 veal chops
85 g/3 oz butter	6 tbsp butter
3 tbsp Calvados	3 tbsp Calvados
150 ml/¼ pt crème fraîche or whipping cream	⅔ cup crème fraîche or whipping cream
2 apples, sliced	2 apples, sliced
salt and white pepper	salt and white pepper

Season the veal chops with salt and pepper.

Melt half the butter in a large frying pan. Brown the chops on both sides over a fairly high heat. Lower the heat and continue to cook gently for 10 minutes.

Heat the Calvados and pour it into the frying pan, then flame it. When the flames have gone out, remove the chops and keep them hot.

Put the cream into the pan and stir until the sauce begins to thicken. Keep it hot.

Melt the remaining butter in a sauté pan over a fairly high heat and sauté the apples in it.

Reheat the chops in the cream sauce. Put them into a warm serving dish and coat with the sauce. Surround with apple slices to serve.

VEGETABLES

Légumes

see individual entries; see also: acidulation blanching boiling braising brunoise chutney crudités curing dietary fibre freezing fruit

Edible herbaceous plants are referred to as vegetables. They are usually categorized by the part of the plant which is eaten: LEGUMES OR SEED VEGETABLES are grown for their peas or beans or the pods in which they grow; VEGETABLE FRUITS include tomatoes, sweet peppers, squashes and aubergine (eggplant); LEAF VEGETABLES embrace the cabbage family and spinach, as well as lettuce and the wide variety of salad leaves; STALKS AND SHOOTS incorporate celery, leeks, asparagus, bamboo and bean sprouts; BULBS include fennel and onion; and TUBERS OR ROOT

fumet
herbs
jardinière
julienne
mirepoix
nutrition
pickles
preserves
purée
ratatouille
refreshing
salad
salt
sauce
soup
steaming
stock
stuffing
vitamins

VEGETABLES are things like potatoes, carrots, turnips and radishes. Many vegetables, like beet and turnips, fall into several categories and are harvested at varying stages of growth for different parts to be used. For culinary purposes, mushrooms are also considered vegetables.

To enjoy the full flavour and nutritional goodness of vegetables they should be eaten as fresh as possible, preferably in season and at the peak of ripeness. Look for firmness and crispness, and avoid any which are either soft or too hard. Try to buy them as whole as possible as this helps in judging freshness, for example carrots with their green tops.

Many vegetables are best enjoyed raw. Any cooking should be as brief as possible in the minimum of water, preferably by steaming or in the microwave oven. A little salt is usually added to the cooking water, especially with green vegetables, to help keep a good colour. Wherever possible vegetables with skins should be left unpeeled, as the skin has the highest concentration of nutrients.

All but the vegetable fruits freeze well. As commercially frozen vegetables are usually processed within hours of harvesting, they are often as flavourful and nutritious as when fresh.

Vegetables are also traditionally preserved in a variety of ways to save their goodness for the winter months. Root vegetables, such as potatoes and onions, are simply stored in a cool, dark place covered in soil. Others, like cabbages and green beans, may be salted. Legumes are also dried to produce pulses, and a great many vegetables are pickled or made into chutneys.

Most fresh vegetables are rich in fibre, minerals such as potassium, iron and copper, and vitamins, especially B and C. Any healthy, balanced diet should include at least one large portion of fresh vegetables each day.

VELOUTÉ

see also:
sauce
soup

From the French for 'velvety', the term velouté is used both to describe a family of flour-based sauces made with stock, and smooth, creamy soups, usually made with puréed vegetables, fish or seafood and thickened with cream, egg yolk and butter. Velouté soups are thus often extremely rich.

VELOUTÉ À LA TOMATE

Tomato cream soup

Serves 6
Preparation 15 minutes
Cooking about 30 minutes

METRIC/IMPERIAL	*AMERICAN*
30 g/1 oz butter	*2 tbsp butter*
2 onions, chopped	*2 onions, chopped*
1 garlic clove, chopped	*1 garlic clove, chopped*
1 kg/$2\frac{1}{4}$ lb ripe tomatoes, quartered	*$2\frac{1}{4}$ lb ripe tomatoes, quartered*
4 tbsp cornflour	*$\frac{1}{4}$ cup cornstarch*
1 tsp caster sugar	*1 tsp superfine sugar*
100 ml/$3\frac{1}{2}$ fl oz thick crème fraîche or whipping cream	*$\frac{1}{2}$ cup thick crème fraîche or whipping cream*
salt and pepper	*salt and pepper*
sprigs of fresh chervil, to garnish	*sprigs of fresh chervil, to garnish*

Melt half the butter in a saucepan over a low heat and put the onions into it. Cook, stirring, until they are translucent.

Add the garlic and tomatoes along with the rest of the butter. Stir over a low heat for 5 minutes, then pour in 1.5 l/$2\frac{1}{2}$ pt/$1\frac{1}{2}$ qt of water. Simmer for 20 minutes.

Strain the contents of the pan, pressing down well to extract all the pulp, and return the resulting soup to the saucepan. Blend the cornflour (cornstarch) with a little cold water and add to the soup with the sugar. Bring to the boil, stirring. Season.

At the last minute, add the cream and whisk over a very low heat until smooth and creamy. Pour into a warmed soup tureen and sprinkle with the fresh chervil. Serve immediately.

Velouté à la tomate (Tomato cream soup)

VELOUTÉ AUX CHAMPIGNONS

Mushroom cream soup

Serves 4
Preparation 10 minutes
Cooking about 15 minutes

METRIC/IMPERIAL	AMERICAN
25 g/¾ oz dried ceps	¾ oz dried cèpes
1 tbsp olive oil	1 tbsp olive oil
500 ml/16 fl oz chicken stock	2 cups chicken stock
4 garlic cloves, crushed	4 garlic cloves, minced
450 g/1 lb mushrooms, thinly sliced	1 lb mushrooms, thinly sliced
100 ml/3½ fl oz thick crème fraîche or whipping cream	½ cup thick crème fraîche or whipping cream
2 tbsp finely chopped flat-leaved parsley	2 tbsp finely chopped flat-leaf parsley
salt and pepper	salt and pepper

Put the dried ceps (cèpes) in a bowl, cover with boiling water and cook on High for 3 minutes to reconstitute. Let stand 10 minutes.

Meanwhile, put the oil in a deep dish and the stock into a bowl, adding 2 tablespoons of liquid from the ceps. Heat both for 1 minute on High. Add the garlic to the oil and cook on Medium for 2 minutes. Add the sliced mushrooms and transfer the hot stock to the dish. Cover and cook for 6 minutes on Medium.

Whip the cream with the parsley and season it with salt and pepper. Add this mixture to the soup and cook for 1 minute on Medium.

Drain the ceps (cèpes), chop and add them. Heat the soup for 1–2 minutes on Medium.

VENISON

Chevreuil

see also:
game
meat

The meat of all types of deer is known as venison and its flavour varies widely depending on the variety of animal and its feeding habits. The tiny ROE DEER has dark red and very tender meat which has probably the best flavour. The less flavoursome FALLOW DEER, commonly reared in parks, and the coarser and tougher RED DEER of the Scottish Highlands are also found on sale. REINDEER is bred for the table in Scandinavia, but its very strong flavour enjoys little popularity elsewhere. In North America, the term venison is also used for the meat of other related antlered species such as the elk, moose, caribou and antelope.

Venison needs at least 4 or 5 days hanging to develop its flavour. Until recently it was often hung for much longer periods, but nowadays fresher, less gamy meat is preferred. Look for dark flesh with a close grain. Any fat should be a clear white, but should be well trimmed as it does not have a good flavour. Meat from bucks is thought to have the best flavour.

All but the meat of the youngest animals tends to be tough and dry, so venison is generally given lengthy marinating to help make the meat more tender and succulent and to boost flavour. The whole leg, or haunch, the loin and the saddle are usually also larded and then roasted. In young animals the shoulder can often be tastier than the haunch but does not carve as easily. Loin chops and *noisettes* are generally grilled and are preferred pink or rare, like beef steaks. Tougher cuts are made into stews or civets or incorporated in pies and pâtés.

Venison suits highly flavoured marinades and sauces, particularly with juniper berries, bitter and spices, such as cloves.

Venison has the lowest fat content of all game at only 96 calories per 100 g/3½ oz, but it can be indigestible, especially with a rich sauce.

SELLE DE CHEVREUIL RÔTIE

Roast saddle of venison

Serves 6
Preparation 15 minutes
Cooking about 1 hour

METRIC/IMPERIAL	AMERICAN
1 saddle of venison, weighing about 1.35 kg/3 lb	1 saddle of venison, weighing about 3 lb
115 g/¼ lb fatty bacon, cut into long thin strips	¼ lb bacon, cut into long thin strips
	½ cup oil
	2 onions, thinly sliced

100 ml/$3\frac{1}{2}$ fl oz oil
2 onions, thinly sliced
2 stalks of celery, trimmed and chopped
150 ml/$\frac{1}{4}$ pt red wine
100 ml/$3\frac{1}{2}$ fl oz crème fraîche or whipping cream
1 tbsp Kirsch
2–3 pinches of paprika
salt and pepper

2 sticks of celery, trimmed and chopped
$\frac{2}{3}$ cup red wine
$\frac{1}{2}$ cup crème fraîche or whipping cream
1 tbsp Kirsch
2–3 pinches of paprika
salt and pepper

Preheat the oven to 220C/425F/gas 7.

Make a number of deep incisions in the meat going with the grain, and push the strips of bacon into them using a knife. Brush the meat all over liberally with the oil.

Place the saddle in a roasting pan and put the onions and celery around it. Season with salt and pepper and roast in the oven, allowing 15 minutes per 450 g/1 lb.

When the meat is done, remove it and keep hot. Deglaze the pan with the red wine and a little hot water. Boil to reduce the liquid by half, then blend the contents of the pan in a food processor to purée the vegetables.

Add the cream, Kirsch and paprika. Stir over a low heat for 10 minutes. Adjust the seasoning.

Carve the meat into slices, coat them with the hot sauce and serve immediately, accompanied by apples sautéed in butter, small *noisette* potatoes or celeriac (celery root) purée.

To drink: Châteauneuf-du-Pape.

VINAIGRETTE

see also: fats and oils, olive, salad, sauce, vinegar

A type of cold sauce, vinaigrette is made by mixing oil and vinegar with seasoning. It is also often flavoured with additional ingredients, such as mustard, garlic, crumbled blue cheese, shallots, herbs, chopped hard-boiled egg or anchovies, and lemon juice may be used in place of vinegar.

Vinaigrettes are most commonly used as salad dressings. They are also served with a variety of cold vegetables, such as asparagus and leeks, and poached fish, cold meats and offal (variety meats).

One tablespoon of vinaigrette contains about 105 calories.

SAUCE VINAIGRETTE

Vinaigrette dressing

Serves 4
Preparation 5 minutes

METRIC/IMPERIAL	*AMERICAN*
2 tbsp vinegar	*2 tbsp vinegar*
6 tbsp olive oil	*6 tbsp olive oil*
salt and freshly ground black pepper	*salt and freshly ground black pepper*

Put 2 pinches of salt into a bowl. Add the vinegar and stir until the salt is dissolved.

Add some freshly ground black pepper, then slowly pour in the oil, whisking to emulsify.

Variations: the vinegar may be replaced by lemon juice and the salt by celery salt. Also try adding 1 heaped teaspoon of mustard; mix it with the vinegar before adding the oil. As with salt, it will only dissolve in the vinegar; it should not be added at the end.

The classic vinaigrette may be supplemented as follows: for chicory (Belgian endive) salad, add 55 g/2 oz of crumbled Roquefort; for tomato salad, add 1 teaspoon of anchovy paste and some chopped fresh basil; for chicken salad, add 1 tablespoon of toasted pine kernels (pine nuts).

To make a low-calorie vinaigrette, use 2 tablespoons of oil and 2 tablespoons of water, or replace the oil with low-fat plain yogurt.

VINEGAR

Vinaigre

see also: acidulation, chutney, gherkin (pickling cucumber), marinade, mustard, pickles, sauce, shallot

From the French for 'sour wine', vinegars are made by allowing wine or other alcohol to ferment to produce dilute solutions of acetic acid. Acetification takes place on contact with air and gives rise to a velvety grey film on the surface known as 'the vinegar plant' or 'mother of vinegar' which thickens and drifts down through the liquid. This may also be cultured and introduced as a 'starter' to help keep the process pure. Made from the local alcoholic beverage, be it beer, wine, cider or rice wine, vinegar has been used in many parts of the world for thousands of years as a souring agent, preservative, condiment and seasoning.

The quality of a vinegar depends on the quality of the base and the manufacturing process. Cheaper vinegars are made by a rapid process in which a great deal of heat is generated, driving off finer flavouring elements. Better vinegars are made using a longer, cooler process which preserves much more of the original qualities of the base. Some vinegars, like Italian BALSAMIC VINEGAR, are also then aged in wooden casks to allow them to mature and develop a full aroma and flavour.

Vinegars are made from both white and red wines, as well as champagne and sherry. Wine vinegars are often infused with flavouring ingredients, especially herbs such as tarragon or mint and aromatics like garlic, shallots and chilli peppers. Vinegars flavoured with fruit, like raspberries and blackcurrants, were once popular in France as the basis of refreshing summer drinks and they are currently enjoying a revival as culinary flavourings both in salad dressings and on fruit.

Mild-flavoured but penetratingly sharp vinegars made from a beer base are known as MALT VINEGARS and are popular in Britain, particularly as a condiment on traditional fish and chips and in the 'sousing' of herring and mackerel. Strong, clear SPIRIT VINEGARS are made specifically for pickling vegetables or other items which might otherwise dilute ordinary vinegars below critical concentration.

Apart from the making of pickles and chutneys, perhaps the most common use for vinegar is in sauces and dressings, especially vinaigrettes and *beurre blanc* sauces. It is also often used in the process of deglazing. White wine vinegars are usually preferred for such purposes, while red wine vinegars are reserved for dressing mild-flavoured leaves and meat dishes. A dash of vinegar may be added when poaching eggs to help keep the egg intact, and to red cabbage to keep its colour in cooking. Vinegar is also used in marinades, to both flavour and tenderize, and is the preferred souring agent in sweet-and-sour dishes.

Vinegars, especially those made from cider, are attributed with many beneficial properties and should be included in a healthy diet.

POULET AU VINAIGRE

Chicken with vinegar sauce

Serves 4
Preparation 15 minutes
Cooking about 30 minutes

METRIC/IMPERIAL	*AMERICAN*
1 oven-ready chicken, weighing 1.5 kg/3½ lb, cut in pieces	*1 chicken, dressed and drawn weight 3½ lb, cut in pieces*
15 g/½ oz butter	*1 tbsp butter*
3 tbsp oil	*3 tbsp oil*
4 shallots, thinly sliced	*4 shallots, thinly sliced*
200 ml/7 fl oz aged red wine vinegar	*1 cup aged red wine vinegar*
200 ml/7 fl oz crème fraîche or whipping cream	*1 cup crème fraîche or whipping cream*
salt and pepper	*salt and pepper*

Season the chicken pieces with salt and pepper.

Melt the butter with the oil in a large flameproof casserole over a moderate heat. Put in the pieces of chicken and brown them well all over, for about 20 minutes altogether.

Remove the pieces of chicken from the casserole and put them in a warmed deep serving dish. Cover with a sheet of foil.

Put the shallots into the casserole and stir over a moderate heat for 2 minutes. Pour on the vinegar, bring to the boil and reduce slightly.

Add the cream, stir and cook for a further 5 minutes. Adjust the seasoning. Coat the pieces of chicken with the sauce and serve.

To drink: a fresh, lively red wine, such as a Fleurie.

VINE LEAF OR GRAPE LEAF

Feuille de vigne

see also: roasting stuffing

The young leaves from the vine of any edible grape have a subtle and distinctive lemony flavour which finds a variety of culinary uses. They are usually first well washed and the stalks removed, then simmered for about an hour to make them tender.

The most common use for vine or grape leaves is rolled around a savoury stuffing to make the eastern Mediterranean speciality *dolmas* or *dolmades*, from the Greek for leaf. The stuffing traditionally consists of a mixture of meat, usually lamb, with rice and vegetables, flavoured with pine kernels (pine nuts) or mint. The stuffed rolls are braised in olive oil with lemon juice and herbs and served hot or cold as an hors d'oeuvre.

Vine or grape leaves are also wrapped around small birds under their bards before roasting, used to line dishes in which vegetables, especially mushrooms, are being braised or baked, and the freshest and most tender of specimens may be shredded into salads.

Look for flat leaves without deep indentations as these are more easily manipulated. Leaves are also sold canned in brine.

FEUILLES DE VIGNE FARCIES

Stuffed vine or grape leaves

Serves 6
Preparation 30 minutes
Cooking about 1¼ hours, 2 hours ahead

METRIC/IMPERIAL	*AMERICAN*
24 cooked or canned vine leaves, drained	*24 cooked or canned grape leaves, drained*
4 tbsp olive oil	*4 tbsp olive oil*
3 large onions, chopped	*3 large onions, chopped*
3 garlic cloves, chopped	*3 garlic cloves, chopped*
1 tbsp finely chopped parsley	*1 tbsp finely chopped parsley*
1 tbsp finely chopped fresh mint + 6 whole leaves	*1 tbsp finely chopped fresh mint + 6 whole leaves*
125 g/4½ oz rice	*⅔ cup rice, cooked*
85 g/3 oz raisins	*½ cup raisins*
2 lemons	*2 lemons*
salt and pepper	*salt and pepper*

Rinse the leaves in boiling water, drain and spread them out on a clean cloth.

Heat 1 tablespoon of the olive oil in a frying pan over a moderate heat and brown the onions and garlic for 5 minutes. Add the chopped herbs and season with salt and pepper. Stir for 1 minute and remove from the heat.

Mix the rice and raisins into the mixture. Spoon it on the leaves and roll them into cylinders, folding under the tips and bases.

Heat the remaining olive oil in a sauté pan. Add the stuffed leaves. Squeeze the juice from 1 of the lemons over the rolled leaves and add 150 ml/¼ pt/⅔ cup of water. Cook gently, covered, for 1 hour. Leave to cool.

Snip the whole mint leaves and finely slice the other lemon into rounds.

Serve the stuffed leaves as a cold first course garnished with lemon and mint.

VITAMINS

see also:
freezing
fruits
meat
vegetables

Vitamins are those few organic substances found in food which the body is unable to make for itself, but which are essential for its proper growth and functioning.

Vitamins are classified either as water soluble, like vitamins B and C, which are mostly found in fruit and vegetables, and fat soluble, such as vitamins A, D, E and K, which are mostly obtained from meat and dairy products.

Vitamins are fragile: the storage, preparation and cooking of foodstuffs all destroy vitamins to some degree. It is therefore wise to buy the freshest of foods in season and not to keep them for too long before use. Wherever possible wash vegetables but do not soak them or peel them, and do this at the last possible moment. Some foods, like milk, keep their vitamin content better if not exposed to light. Steaming maintains a higher level of vitamins than boiling, and roast and grilled (broiled) meat preserves more than meat which is boiled or braised. Always try to incorporate any cooking liquid in a sauce or stock to benefit from the vitamins which have been transferred to it.

A balanced diet, especially one rich in raw fruit and vegetables, provides all necessary vitamins.

VOL-AU-VENT

From the French for 'fly away in the wind', a vol-au-vent is a large, baked puff pastry case filled with a savoury mixture bound with sauce. These pastry cases are also called patty shells in North America. Chicken, seafood and fish are

see also:
canapé
croûte
pastry
sauce

popular fillings and the sauces are usually variations of béchamel. Vols-au-vent should be piping hot and assembled at the last minute so that the filling does not soak into the pastry. Small, individual vols-au-vent, known in France as *bouchées*, are popular party food.

The combination of puff pastry and sauce makes vols-au-vent extremely rich, providing about 100 calories at a single bite.

VOL-AU-VENT FINANCIÈRE

Ham and chicken vol-au-vent with truffle sauce

Serves 6
Preparation 40 minutes
Cooking about 15 minutes

METRIC/IMPERIAL	AMERICAN
1 kg/2¼ lb puff pastry	2¼ lb puff pastry
1 egg, beaten	1 egg, beaten
45 g/1½ oz butter	3 tbsp butter
45 g/1½ oz flour	¼ cup flour
200 ml/7 fl oz chicken stock	1 cup chicken stock
3 tbsp Madeira	3 tbsp Madeira wine
1 small can of truffle peelings	1 small can of truffle peelings
300 g/10 oz cooked white chicken meat, cut into tiny dice	10 oz cooked white chicken meat, cut into tiny dice (2½ cups)
200 g/7 oz cooked ham, cubed	7 oz cooked ham, cubed (1½ cups)
140 g/5 oz mushrooms, thinly sliced	5 oz mushrooms, thinly sliced
salt and pepper	salt and pepper

Preheat the oven to 230C/450F/gas 8.

Divide the pastry in half and roll out each piece to a thickness of about 6 mm/¼ in. Cut from each an 18 cm/7 in disc.

Place one of the discs on a slightly dampened baking sheet. Remove the centre of the second disc, leaving a 5 cm/2 in wide ring. Moisten the first disc lightly with water and place the ring of pastry on top of it.

Roll the inner circle of pastry to obtain a disc the same size as the larger disc. Dampen the ring of pastry and place the new disc on top of it. Using a knife, trace the circumference of the inner circle to facilitate removal of the 'lid' after cooking. Glaze with the beaten egg and bake in the oven for about 15 minutes.

While the pastry is cooking, make a white sauce by melting the butter in a small saucepan over a gentle heat and stirring in the flour. Cook for a few minutes, stirring constantly, to make a blond roux. Gradually add the chicken stock and cook for a few minutes until thick and smooth. Season to taste.

Add the Madeira to the sauce along with the truffle peelings. Turn into a large saucepan and stir in the chicken, ham and mushrooms. Heat gently, stirring occasionally.

Take the pastry case out of the oven and remove the lid. Fill with the chicken mixture, replace the lid and serve immediately.

To drink: a medium-bodied, dry white wine, such as a Meursault.

see also:
condiment
fats and oils
hazelnut
ketchup
nuts
pickles

WALNUT
Noix

The fruit of the walnut tree consists of a hard shell which contains two wrinkled kernels covered by a fine, bitter skin. Walnuts originated in the Caspian region but were spread throughout the Mediterranean area by the Romans.

Fresh walnuts, with delicate, white and tasty flesh, are sold from the end of September to November. The best-looking and largest walnuts are not necessarily the finest flavoured, and beware of completely clean walnuts which have usually been treated with chemicals. Look for nuts with tightly sealed shells which do not readily prise apart, and be wary of those which feel a little heavy for their size as they may have been soaked in water to plump them up. The shelled and skinned nuts, either whole or in chunks, are also sold in vacuum packs or cans.

Fresh walnuts do not keep well; 15 days at the most. Walnuts should never be refrigerated because the oil they contain hardens and this impairs their flavour. The flesh of dried walnuts becomes greyer as it gets older. If soaked overnight in milk, kernels of dried walnuts regain much of the flavour of fresh specimens. The skin around the kernels of both fresh and dried nuts is usually quite bitter and is best removed. This is easily effected by blanching them in boiling water and refreshing them in iced water; the skins will then rub off easily.

Apart from simply being enjoyed as a dessert nut, walnuts are mainly used in cakes and pastries, often ground or chopped as an ingredient. The intact half kernels are good for decoration. They are also common in ice cream desserts and in confectionery. The savoury use of walnuts is also extensive. They are popular in salads and in stuffings, and go well in fish and chicken dishes and with pasta.

GREEN WALNUTS in which the shells have not yet completely formed are pickled or made into WALNUT KETCHUP. Ripe walnuts are also pickled or preserved in syrup, and various alcoholic beverages are also made from the nut.

Richly flavoured WALNUT OIL was once as common and valued as olive oil in many places, but its cost now limits its use to salad dressings.

Dried walnuts have a very high calorific content: 100 g/3½ oz contains 660 calories. They are, however, very rich in protein, phosphorus and vitamins B and D.

GRENOBLOIS

Walnut cake

Serves 8
Preparation 25 minutes
Cooking 1 hour, plus cooling

METRIC/IMPERIAL	AMERICAN
45 g/1½ oz butter	3 tbsp butter
5 eggs, separated	5 eggs, separated
275 g/9½ oz caster sugar	1¼ cups + 1½ tbsp superfine sugar
2 tbsp rum	2 tbsp rum
225 g/½ lb shelled and skinned walnuts, very finely chopped	½ lb/2 cups shelled and skinned walnuts, very finely chopped
100 g/3½ oz cornflour	1 cup cornstarch
10 walnut halves	10 walnut halves

Preheat the oven to 190C/375F/gas 5. Generously grease a 25 cm/10 in cake pan and a disc of parchment or greaseproof paper with some of the butter and line the pan with the paper.

Put the egg yolks into a bowl, add 250 g/8½ oz/1¼ cups of the sugar and beat until thick and pale. Add the rum.

Whisk the whites to very stiff peaks, then fold them into the egg yolk mixture. As quickly and gently as possible, fold in the walnuts and then the cornflour (cornstarch), making sure they are evenly mixed in.

Pour the batter into the cake pan and bake for 50 minutes. Take it out of the oven and, once it has cooled slightly, turn it out on a rack.

Dissolve the remaining sugar in a minimum of water in a saucepan. Dip the walnut halves into this syrup and decorate the top of the cake with them. Serve chilled.

Variation: this cake may also be coated with coffee icing, made with 150 g/5½ oz/1¼ cups icing (confectioners') sugar blended with 1 tablespoon of water and 2 tablespoons of coffee essence. Put the walnuts in place while the icing is still soft.

SALADE DE POMMES AUX NOIX

Apple and walnut salad

Serves 4
Preparation 25 minutes

METRIC/IMPERIAL	AMERICAN
55 g/2 oz raisins	⅓ cup raisins
100 ml/3½ fl oz crème fraîche or sour cream	½ cup crème fraîche or sour cream
juice of ½ lemon	juice of ½ lemon
3 crisp apples	3 crisp apples
100 g/3½ oz walnut kernels	1 cup shelled walnuts
2 chicory heads	2 heads of Belgian endive
2 stalks of celery, trimmed and cut into small chunks	2 sticks of celery, trimmed and cut into small chunks
salt and pepper	salt and pepper

Soak the raisins in a bowl of very hot water. Meanwhile, mix the cream with 1 tablespoon of lemon juice and season. Set aside.

Peel and slice the apples. Sprinkle them with some lemon juice. Chop most of the walnuts and add them to the apples.

Cut the bitter core from the chicory (Belgian endive) heads and slice them very thinly. Sprinkle them with the remaining lemon juice.

In a bowl, combine the apples and walnuts, chicory (Belgian endive) and celery. Add the drained raisins with the cream. Mix thoroughly. Adjust the seasoning, garnish with the reserved walnuts and serve at room temperature.

Grenoblois (Walnut cake)

WATER

see also:
coffee
infusion
minerals
tea

Drinking water must be clear, odourless and above all free of dangerous bacteria. It must also be sufficiently 'soft', ie containing a balanced proportion of minerals. In addition, it must be aerated and contain dissolved oxygen, otherwise it is termed 'heavy'. If it contains too much calcium it is termed 'hard'.

Domestic drinking water, nowadays treated and safe to drink, often has a slight taste of chlorine. This may be minimized by putting it in the refrigerator for a few hours in a stone or

ceramic container. However, for reasons of flavour and safety, many people now also filter their tap water and quickly become unable to tolerate the taste of it unfiltered.

Several varieties of bottled waters are sold: TABLE WATER is simply purified tap water; SPRING WATER comes from an authorized spring, which is not treated but is regularly analysed; and MINERAL WATER usually bears the analysis of mineral content on the label. Be cautious with mineral waters as they may be very high in salt content and can also have laxative qualities if rich in magnesium sulphate. Bottled waters may also be designated 'sparkling', which means that they are naturally fizzy, or 'carbonated', in which case they have been aerated artificially or their natural carbonation has been increased.

Water plays an essential role in cooking, especially for boiling vegetables, rice and pasta, and making soups, stocks and stews. In general, soft water is better for cooking, especially when it is boiled, as the minerals in hard water separate out as a discolouring cloud of alkaloids which neutralize some of the food's flavour. The flavour of water is also critical to many dishes, particularly where the water is absorbed by the food, like rice, dried beans and peas, and in the making of pastry, pasta, coffee and tea. Bottled water can be used in such instances.

Water is indispensable for proper functioning of the human body: drink at least 1 l/1¾ pt/4 cups each day. Good water is also the perfect health drink, cleansing the system and supplying valuable minerals.

WATER CHESTNUT

see also: chestnut

The tuber of an oriental plant, the CHINESE WATER CHESTNUT has a prickly skin surrounding sweet, tasty flesh. This is eaten fresh as a dessert fruit or candied in syrup. More often water chestnuts are used to provide texture to stir-fried dishes and stuffings, and in salads with bamboo shoots. In the West they are most commonly available canned in water.

The COMMON WATER CHESTNUT of Europe is an aquatic plant which produces chestnut-like nuts with floury and tasty meat used in the cooking of many parts of rural France.

WATERCRESS

see Cress

WATERMELON

Pastèque

see also: fruit melon

A large spherical or oval summer fruit, generally with a green rind which is often mottled or striped, the watermelon has pink, watery flesh which has a crunchy texture and is sweet.

Originally from India, they are now grown in many warm climates and hundreds of varieties have been bred, some even without seeds or with yellow skin and pale, creamy flesh. The most common varieties include the pale-striped CRIMSON which has deep-coloured flesh with few seeds and the popular, sweet SUGAR BABY.

The ripeness of watermelons is very difficult to judge. They should feel heavy for their size and make a dull noise when they are tapped. As they are so large, watermelons are often sold cut into pieces. They are usually cut in slices and the black seeds removed before being eaten or mixed into fruit salads.

The white pith under the skin is often pickled and in some places, the dried seeds are also eaten or ground as a condiment.

Watermelons have a particularly low calorie content, but they are full of vitamins and can be eaten in unlimited quantities.

PASTÈQUE À LA PROVENÇALE

Watermelon with rosé wine

Serves 6
Preparation 20 minutes
Standing 2 hours

METRIC/IMPERIAL	AMERICAN
1 very ripe watermelon	*1 very ripe watermelon*
1 bottle (750 ml/27 fl oz) of Provençal rosé wine	*1 bottle (75 cl) of Provençal rosé wine*

Make a large, circular incision around the stalk end of the watermelon. Remove the end and as many of the seeds as possible. Scoop out a little of the flesh.

Pour the wine into the watermelon, replace the cut-off end, and chill for at least 2 hours, standing it upright in a bowl.

Remove the end and strain out the wine. Cut the remaining watermelon flesh into even-sized cubes and put them into 6 serving bowls. Pour over the chilled wine and serve.

WHEAT

Blé

see also:
bran
bread
cereal
couscous
dietary fibre
flour
pasta
pastry
semolina

One of the most versatile of cereal grains, wheat is a staple of diets all over the world.

There are two main varieties of wheat. COMMON OR BREAD WHEAT is ground to make flour, the harder varieties giving strong flours which make good breads, and softer varieties producing the weaker flours used to make cakes and pastries. DURUM WHEAT, high in gluten, is used in the manufacture of pasta and semolina.

The embryo or WHEAT GERM, a by-product of the refining of flour, is tasty and rich in proteins, vitamins and minerals. It is popular as a health food and is often served with honey and yogurt for breakfast. It is also used in salads and to thicken soups and stews. Rich in oil, it quickly goes rancid, so should be refrigerated.

Hulled whole wheat or WHEAT BERRIES may be germinated and used in salads or boiled to make types of porridge. CRACKED WHEAT is made by crushing the whole wheat grains (berries) into pieces and may be cooked like rice. BURGHUL OR BULGUR is produced by partially cooking whole wheat grains and then cracking the kernels. This is flavoured with parsley and mint in the eastern Mediterranean dish *tabbouleh*.

SALADE DE BLÉ GERMÉ

Germinated wheat salad

Serves 6
Preparation 1 hour, 48 hours ahead

METRIC/IMPERIAL	*AMERICAN*
200 g/7 oz whole wheat grains	*1 cup wheat berries*
2 thin-skinned courgettes, thinly sliced	*2 thin-skinned zucchini, thinly sliced*
3 tbsp olive oil	*3 tbsp olive oil*
3 tbsp lemon juice	*3 tbsp lemon juice*
4 tbsp raisins	*¼ cup raisins*
1 canned pimiento, preferably yellow, drained and sliced	*1 canned pimiento, preferably yellow, drained and sliced*
salt and pepper	*salt and pepper*

Place the wheat in a bowl, cover with water and leave to soak for 24 hours. Rinse the wheat and return to the bowl, without water, for a further 24 hours. Add a little water from time to time to keep the wheat slightly moist. Rinse again the next day.

Sprinkle the courgette (zucchini) slices with oil and lemon juice. Leave them to marinate for 30 minutes. Soak the raisins in warm water.

Combine the germinated wheat with the courgettes (zucchini) in their marinade in a salad bowl and add the pimiento and drained raisins. Season with salt and pepper to taste. Mix thoroughly and serve at room temperature.

Note: once wheat grains have germinated they must be used the same day.

WHITING

Merlan

see also:
cod
fish
haddock

Small sea fish related to the cod and haddock, whiting are found in the North Atlantic from as far north as Iceland and Norway to the Mediterranean, but are mainly fished in the shallow coastal waters of the North Sea. Usually about 25 cm/10 in long, they have dark backs and white bellies and are readily differentiated from haddock by the lack of a barbel.

Whiting have very delicate, flaky flesh which is rather dry and falls apart easily. They require careful cooking and one of the best methods is to cook them *en papillote*. The fillets are also good fried, grilled (broiled) or poached, or rolled into paupiettes around a stuffing. As whiting tends to be lacking in flavour, it is best served with a well-seasoned sauce. Its melting texture makes it excellent in soups, fish loaves and terrines. In France it is traditionally served *en colère*, deep fried with its tail tucked into its mouth.

A lean fish, 100 g/3½ oz of whiting contains only 70 calories; it is very easy to digest and traditionally it is steamed as an invalid food.

PÂTÉS DE MERLAN À L'ESTRAGON

Individual whiting mousses with herbs

Serves 6
Preparation 40 minutes
Cooking 20 minutes

METRIC/IMPERIAL	*AMERICAN*
800 g/1¾ lb whiting fillets, chilled	*1¾ lb whiting fillets, chilled*
2 egg whites	*2 egg whites*
200 ml/7 fl oz crème fraîche or whipping cream	*1 cup crème fraîche or whipping cream*
1 tbsp tomato purée	*1 tbsp tomato paste*
small bunch of tarragon, chopped	*small bunch of tarragon, chopped*
small bunch of chervil, coarsely chopped	*small bunch of chervil, coarsely chopped*
55 g/2 oz butter	*4 tbsp butter*
salt and pepper	*salt and pepper*

Preheat the oven to 160C/325F/gas 3.

Blend the chilled raw whiting in a food processor and season it with salt and pepper. Add the egg whites and process again for several seconds. Add the cream and tomato purée (paste). Blend for a further 10 seconds. Add the herbs and mix in with a wooden spoon.

Melt the butter and use half to grease 6 ramekins. Chill them, then repeat the process.

Fill the ramekins with the mixture. Bake in a bain-marie in the oven for 20 minutes.

Unmould the ramekins on individual plates and serve at once coated with tomato sauce or *beurre blanc* with tarragon. They may also be chilled and served with tomato salad or a green salad with hard-boiled eggs.

WINE

Vin

see also:
alcohol
deglaze
marinade
sauce

An alcoholic drink made from fermented grape juice, wine can be red, white or rosé, sparkling or still, depending on the grape and method of production.

The rich, complex flavours of wines have been employed in cooking for as long as wines have been made. In particular, French and Italian cuisine would be inconceivable without them.

White wines, generally dry, are used in fish, seafood and poultry stews and sauces. They are also favoured for deglazing pans when making sauces for grilled (broiled) and fried meats and used in sorbets and other desserts. Red wines, ideally full-bodied, are preferred in meat and game stews and braises, although they also work well with some poultry, as in *coq au vin*, and strong-flavoured fish dishes such as bouillabaisse. The French also simmer some vegetables, notably red kidney beans, in red wine, and it may also be used to poach pears and macerate strawberries. Champagnes are used in the cooking of some fish and poultry dishes and in luxurious sauces for shellfish. They are also used to macerate berry fruits and in sorbets.

Wines used in cooking are often first boiled rapidly uncovered for a few minutes to reduce them. As well as concentrating the flavour this also has the effect of reducing their acidity and driving off the alcohol.

Use the best wine you can afford in cooking, as cheap, rough wines, so-called 'cooking wines' or accumulated dregs, may well ruin a dish and mar the flavour of more costly ingredients.

Perhaps the greatest skill the cook needs to learn is that of matching wines to food. There are no hard and fast rules, but there are several reliable relationships, including: aromatic, dry whites with oily and smoked fish, fish soups, ham and pâté; light, dry white wines with mild-flavoured fish and shellfish; medium-bodied white wines with cold fish, veal and rice dishes and fresh cheeses; full-bodied, dry white wines with shellfish, meaty fish such as turbot, and creamy chicken dishes; medium and sweet white wines with fruit, desserts and cakes; honeyed sweet wines with foie gras, nuts and salty cheeses; fresh, lively red wines with salmon, liver and blue cheeses; medium-bodied red wines with red meat, roast game and meat pies; full-bodied red wines with rich stews and casseroles; powerful, mature reds with game, roast turkey and mature hard cheeses; rosés with cold meats and hors d'oeuvres.

Champagne seems to have the capacity to go

with almost any dish or course. It is perhaps most favoured with smoked salmon and caviar, although many would say that they are best accompanied by vodka.

Spicy foods are difficult to match with wines and Oriental dishes are probably best served with local rice wines or lager (light beer).

Each type of wine has an ideal serving temperature, but red wines should generally be served *chambré*, at cool room temperature, and white and rosé wines well chilled. It is probably wiser to risk over-chilling these than serving them too warm, as the wine quickly reaches its optimum temperature at the table or certainly in the glass. However, do not leave wine chilling for more than a few hours as this can mar its flavour and make it flat.

SAUMON AU CHAMPAGNE

Salmon in champagne

Serves 6–8
Preparation 30 minutes
Cooking about 45 minutes

METRIC/IMPERIAL	*AMERICAN*
30 g/1 oz butter	*2 tbsp butter*
1 whole salmon, weighing about 2 kg/ 4½ lb, gutted	*1 whole salmon, weighing about 4½ lb, drawn*
6 shallots, chopped	*6 shallots, chopped*
500 ml/16 fl oz dry champagne	*2 cups dry champagne*
350 ml/12 fl oz whipping cream	*1⅔ cups whipping cream*
salt and pepper	*salt and pepper*

Preheat the oven to 220C/425F/gas 7. Grease a large, ovenproof dish or pan with the butter.

Season the salmon inside and out. Wrap the head and tail in 2 pieces of foil.

Put the salmon in the oven dish and place the chopped shallots around it. Pour all but 2 or 3 tablespoons of the champagne over it and then coat it with the cream.

Cook in the oven for 20 minutes, then lower the heat to 180C/350F/gas 4 and bake for a further 20 minutes. To test whether it is cooked, slide a pointed knife along the plumpest section of the backbone: the flesh should come away easily from the bone.

Remove the salmon from the oven dish and put it on a long, warmed dish. Discard the foil. Carefully remove the skin from the top side, then put a second long, warmed serving dish on top of the fish and turn them upside down together to remove the skin from the bottom side. Keep the fish hot between the two dishes.

Strain the cooking juices into a small saucepan. Whisk them over a high heat for a few minutes, then add the reserved champagne. Whisk again and pour into a sauce boat.
To drink: dry champagne.

COQ AU VIN

Chicken in red wine

Serves 6
Preparation 20 minutes
Cooking about 1¾ hours

METRIC/IMPERIAL	*AMERICAN*
1 oven-ready chicken, weighing about 2 kg/ 4½ lb, cut into pieces	*1 chicken, drawn and dressed weight about 4½ lb, cut into pieces*
115 g/¼ lb lean bacon, cut into strips	*¼ lb lean bacon, cut into strips*
1 tbsp oil	*1 tbsp oil*
100 g/3½ oz butter	*1 stick butter*
12 small white onions	*12 small white onions*
1 tbsp Cognac	*1 tbsp Cognac*
1 bottle (750 ml/27 fl oz) of red wine	*1 bottle (75 cl) of red wine*
bouquet garni	*bouquet garni*
2 garlic cloves, crushed	*2 garlic cloves, minced*
225 g/½ lb white button mushrooms, thinly sliced	*½ lb white button mushrooms, thinly sliced*
1 tbsp flour	*1 tbsp flour*
3 tbsp chicken or pig's blood	*3 tbsp chicken or pig's blood*
salt and pepper	*salt and pepper*

Season the pieces of chicken with salt and pepper. If the bacon is very salty, blanch it briefly in boiling water. Drain and pat dry.

Heat the oil and 55 g/2 oz/4 tbsp of the butter in a flameproof casserole and brown the bacon and onions in it evenly. Remove them with a slotted spoon.

Brown the chicken pieces in the casserole, turning them several times. Return the onions and bacon to the pan and stir well.

Heat the Cognac in a ladle, pour it over the contents of the pan and flame it. When the flames have died down, pour the wine into the pan and add the bouquet garni and garlic.

Bring slowly to the boil, then cover, lower the heat and simmer for at least 1 hour, stirring from time to time so that the pieces of meat do not stick to the bottom of the pot.

Meanwhile, sauté the mushrooms in 25 g/¾ oz/1½ tbsp of the butter until lightly browned. When the chicken has cooked for 1 hour, add the mushrooms to the casserole. Continue cooking for 20–25 minutes.

About 10 minutes before serving, soften the remaining butter in a bowl and mix in the flour, along with a little of the hot sauce from the chicken. Add the butter and flour mixture very gradually to the chicken, stirring, then cook uncovered for 5 minutes, stirring constantly. Add the blood and cook very gently for a further 4–5 minutes so that the sauce thickens. Adjust the seasonings.

Serve hot with steamed potatoes or fresh pasta.

Notes: this dish may be prepared ahead, say in the morning, for dinner. If the blood is difficult to obtain, add another ½ tablespoon of flour to thicken the sauce.

Coq au vin (Chicken in red wine)

WOODCOCK

Bécasse

see also: barding croûte game salmis

A small, migratory game bird with dark brown plumage, woodcock is relatively rare in Europe and is regarded as something of a delicacy. In the USA, however, woodcock is one of the most popular game birds for hunting as it is found in giant flocks during the autumn migration.

Woodcocks may be hung for several days, until their bellies are shiny and the tail feathers come away easily.

They may be cooked *au salmis* and are made into pâtés and mousses, but in modern practice they are usually briefly roasted or grilled (broiled), barded and undrawn. They are served slightly pink, on a *croûte* to mop up the juices and entrails. Allow 1 bird per person, or 1 between 2 people if it is large.

Many gourmets make feasts of the entrails alone, mixed with lemon juice, bacon or foie gras and brandy.

BÉCASSES RÔTIES SUR CANAPÉS

Roast woodcock on a fried bread croûte

Serves 4
Preparation 10 minutes
Cooking about 20 minutes

METRIC/IMPERIAL	AMERICAN
2–4 woodcocks, according to size	2–4 woodcocks, according to size
2–4 thin slices of bacon	2–4 thin slices of bacon
100 ml/3½ fl oz champagne	½ cup champagne
4 slices of bread	4 slices of bread
55 g/2 oz butter	4 tbsp butter
55 g/2 oz foie gras	2 oz foie gras
salt and pepper	salt and pepper

Preheat the oven to 200C/400F/gas 6.

Do not draw the woodcocks. Wrap each in a slice of bacon and season with salt and pepper. Roast in the hot oven for 10 minutes, turning them so that they brown evenly.

Pour half the champagne into the roasting pan and cook for a further 5 minutes. Meanwhile, fry the bread in half the butter until lightly browned on both sides.

Remove the birds from the oven. Scrape out their insides with a small spoon.

Melt the remaining butter in a small pan and add the foie gras, entrails and cooking juices. Heat gently, adding the remaining champagne.

Strain the liquid into a sauce boat. Spread the fried bread with the foie gras. Cut the woodcocks in half (if using larger birds) and serve on the slices of fried bread, with the sauce served separately in a sauce boat.

To drink: a medium-bodied red wine, such as a Pomerol or Côte-de-Nuits.

Y-Z

see also:
potato
sweet potato
vegetables

YAM

Igname

The large, edible, starchy tubers from a family of tropical climbing plants, yams can be round or elongated, with skin that is rough, white, brown or pink and sometimes hairy. The white, yellow or pink flesh has a sweetish taste and they are a staple in many parts of the tropics.

Smaller, younger specimens may be baked in their skins, but larger yams are peeled and boiled and then treated like potatoes or sweet potatoes. They may be incorporated in soups and stews, made into purées and gratins or deep fried. They can also be used in sweet pies and tarts.

GUIANA ARROWROOT is a starchy extract from yams which is widely used in confectionery.

Yams have a higher calorific content than potatoes: 100 g/3½ oz contains 100 calories.

RAGOÛT D'IGNAMES

Tomato and yam stew

Serves 4
Preparation 20 minutes
Cooking about 40 minutes

METRIC/IMPERIAL	AMERICAN
2 tbsp oil	2 tbsp oil
1 kg/2¼ lb yams, cut into thin slices	2¼ lb yams, cut into thin slices
4 tomatoes, peeled and sliced	4 tomatoes, peeled and sliced
1 tsp dried thyme, crumbled	1 tsp dried thyme, crumbled
1 bay leaf, crumbled	1 bay leaf, crumbled
1 tbsp rum	1 tbsp rum
150 ml/¼ pt white wine	⅔ cup white wine
salt and cayenne pepper	salt and cayenne pepper

Put the oil into a flameproof casserole. Spread half of the yams out over the bottom, followed by all of the tomatoes.

Add the thyme and bay leaf. Add some salt and 1 or 2 pinches of cayenne pepper.

Finish with the remaining yams. Sprinkle with the rum, pour on the white wine and cover. Simmer for 40 minutes.

Serve with roast pork or veal.

YEAST

see also:
baking
baking powder
bread
pastry

A microscopic fungus, yeast is widely used as a leavening agent. In the right warm, moist conditions, it multiplies very quickly and causes fermentation in dough, converting sugar and starch into bubbles of carbon dioxide which make it rise and almost double in volume.

There are two main types of yeast: BAKER'S YEAST and BREWER'S YEAST. The latter is used only in brewing and is of little culinary importance. Baker's yeast is used in the making of breads and some cakes. It may be bought fresh in compressed form and this should be kept in the refrigerator. Dried yeast is also available and this must first be soaked in a warm liquid for a few minutes until it starts to reactivate and become spongy. As it is concentrated, only half the weight of dried yeast is required when substituting it for fresh yeast in recipes.

A yeast dough must be allowed to stand for several hours in a warm place, covered and sheltered from draughts, to allow fermentation to take place. If a small indentation made in the top of the dough does not quickly come back up then it has finished rising. It is then knocked back, or punched down, by folding it over on itself a few times to strengthen the dough and improve results.

Yeast doughs have a very strong and distinctive flavour which works well in bread but is not suitable for all baking. It does, however, give much of the character to items such as brioche, croissants and savarins.

Dried brewer's yeast, sold in slabs or tablets, is rich in vitamin B and is often taken as a dietary supplement to promote a healthy complexion.

PÂTE LEVÉE

Yeast dough

Makes 350 g/12 oz dough
Preparation 20 minutes
Standing 2 hours 20 minutes
Cooking about 45 minutes

METRIC/IMPERIAL	*AMERICAN*
150 g/5½ oz flour	*1¼ cups flour*
½ tsp salt	*½ tsp salt*
1 tbsp caster sugar	*1 tbsp superfine sugar*
2 large eggs	*2 large eggs*
15 g/½ oz fresh baker's yeast	*½ oz compressed fresh yeast*
100 ml/3½ fl oz milk	*½ cup milk*
75 g/2½ oz melted butter	*5 tbsp melted butter*

Pour the flour into a bowl and make a well in the centre. Add the salt, sugar and eggs (1).

Crumble the yeast into the milk which has been warmed to a temperature of about 30–35C/86–95F. Mix and then put into the well. Stir with a wooden spoon, then incorporate the melted butter and mix well (2). With the hands, gradually draw the flour from the sides into the liquids in the well, and mix to a smooth dough.

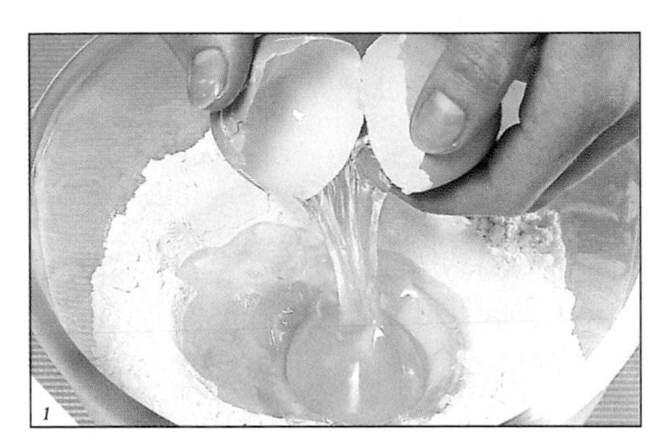
1

2

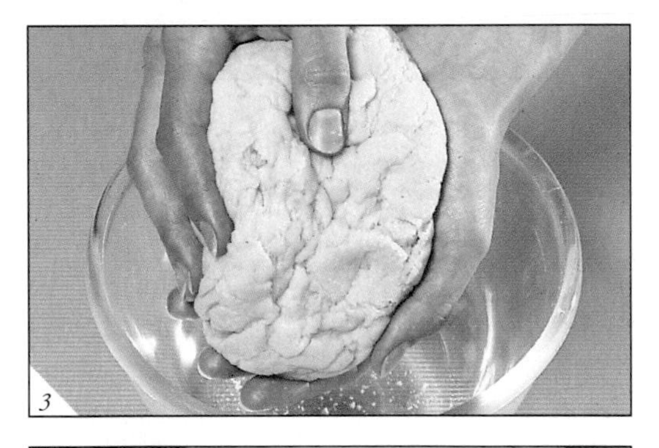
3

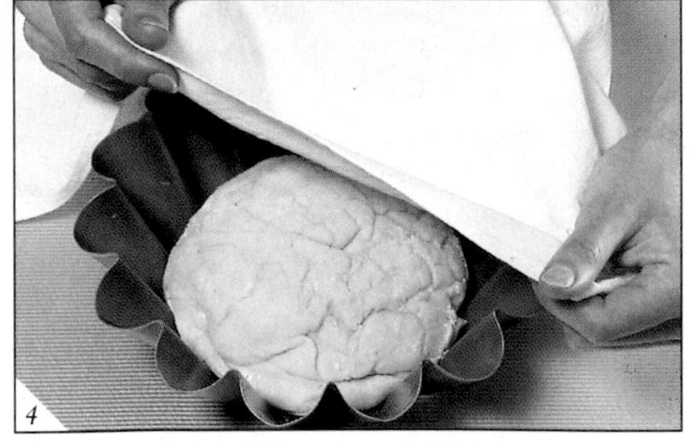
4

Cover the bowl with a cloth and let it stand in a warm place away from any draughts for 2 hours. The exact time needed for the dough to rise will vary with the room temperature. In cool weather, the dough will take longer to rise.

The dough is ready when doubled in volume. Knead gently without beating it, preferably by hand. It should be smooth and elastic (3, previous page).

Generously grease a pan or brioche mould with some butter and put in the dough, which should half fill the pan, and cover (4, previous page). Let rise for 20 minutes so that it reaches its maximum volume, before baking in an oven preheated to 210C/415F/gas 6–7 for 45 minutes.
Notes: this dough is used for babas, savarins, brioches and kugelhopfs. It may be enriched with raisins or crystallized fruit. After baking, it may be soaked in syrup or fruit juice.

SAVARIN À LA CRÈME

Cream-filled savarin

Serves 6
Preparation 20 minutes
Cooking 35 minutes, 1 hour ahead

METRIC/IMPERIAL	*AMERICAN*
15 g/½ oz butter	*1 tbsp butter*
350 g/12 oz rich yeast dough, (see p. 603)	*12 oz rich yeast dough, (see p. 603)*
250 g/8½ oz caster sugar	*1¼ cups superfine sugar*
6 tbsp rum	*6 tbsp rum*
12 glacé cherries	*12 candied cherries*
100 ml/3½ fl oz crème fraîche or whipping cream	*½ cup crème fraîche or whipping cream*
15 g/½ oz icing sugar	*2 tbsp confectioners' sugar*
45 g/1½ oz candied angelica	*1½ oz candied angelica*
salt	*salt*

Grease a 25 cm/10 in ring or savarin mould with the butter.

Make the rich yeast dough as described above. After the first rising, punch it down and shape it into a long cylinder. Wind this into the mould and pinch the ends together where they meet to form a continuous ring.

Cover the mould and allow the dough to rise again for about 20 minutes, or until doubled in volume. Preheat the oven to 210C/415F/gas 6–7 and bake the savarin for 30–35 minutes.

Meanwhile, in a pan, mix the caster (superfine) sugar, 500 ml/16 fl oz/2 cups water and the rum. Heat, stirring constantly to dissolve the sugar. Remove from the heat as soon as the syrup comes to the boil.

Unmould the savarin on a round dish and immediately pour the hot rum syrup over it. All the syrup should be absorbed. Leave to cool, then put the cherries round the edge.

Prepare a chantilly cream by whipping the cream with the icing (confectioners') sugar until it stands in soft peaks. Spoon it into the centre of the savarin and decorate with small pieces of candied angelica.

YOGURT

Yaourt

see also:
milk
liaison
marinade
sauce

A fermented milk product first made in the Balkans, Turkey and Central Asia, yogurt uses the action of various lactic bacteria to develop its creamy consistency and characteristic, pleasantly sour taste.

Within the last generation yogurt has become a very familiar item on Western supermarket shelves, often sweetened and flavoured with fruit or nuts, and it can also be made quite easily at home. Differences in taste and consistency among the different brands depend on the type of milk used and the balance between the various fermenting agents.

Yogurt is made from sheep's, goats' or cows' milk or even thin cream. Commercial brands are usually made from skimmed milk enriched with milk solids and sometimes set with gelatine. Low-fat yogurts are made from fat-free milk.

Yogurt is traditionally served with honey, jam or fruit, as a dessert or for breakfast, and is also an ingredient in refreshing drinks. It is important in cooking, particularly used in place of fresh cream in light sauces, and also in Turkish and Middle Eastern dishes, where it is even employed to marinate meat.

Yogurt has a tendency to curdle when heated, so allow it to come to room temperature before

Savarin à la crème (Cream-filled savarin)

adding it to hot food. A pinch of cornflour (cornstarch) dissolved in a little water and added to yogurt will help stabilize it, but it still should not be boiled. Make sure you do not buy set yogurt for use in cooking.

A small carton of plain, whole-milk yogurt contains 80 calories, low-fat yogurt 50, and fruit yogurt 120. Yogurt is an extremely healthy food. It is very readily digested, aids and cleanses the digestive system, facilitates the metabolization of some minerals, and so-called 'live' yogurt, especially that containing acidophilous bacteria, is recommended to replenish the intestinal flora, particularly during and after taking antibiotics.

SAUCE AU YAOURT

Yogurt sauce

Serves 4
Preparation 5 minutes, 20 minutes ahead

METRIC/IMPERIAL	*AMERICAN*
300 g/10 oz cucumber, peeled and finely diced	*10 oz hothouse cucumber, peeled and finely diced (2 cups)*
250 ml/7 fl oz plain un-set yogurt	*1 cup plain un-set yogurt*
1 onion, finely chopped	*1 onion, finely chopped*
$\frac{1}{2}$ tsp paprika	*$\frac{1}{2}$ tsp paprika*
1 tbsp chopped chives	*1 tbsp chopped chives*
salt and pepper	*salt and pepper*

Sprinkle the cucumber with salt and marinate in the refrigerator for 20 minutes.

Pour the yogurt into a bowl. Add the well-drained cucumber and the onion. Whisk in the paprika and chives. Season with pepper.

Serve the sauce with a selection of *crudités*, on leek salad or cold fish, or as an accompaniment to highly seasoned dishes.

Variations: the cucumber may be replaced by chopped, peeled sweet pepper, chopped tomatoes or chopped watercress. Try fresh mint or basil in place of the chives.

GLACE AU YAOURT

Yogurt sorbet

Serves 4
Preparation 10 minutes
Freezing at least 2 hours

METRIC/IMPERIAL	*AMERICAN*
1 lemon	*1 lemon*
1 orange	*1 orange*
600 ml/1 pt plain whole-milk yogurt	*$2\frac{1}{2}$ cups plain whole-milk yogurt*
1 sachet (7.5 g/$1\frac{3}{4}$ tsp) of vanilla sugar	*$1\frac{3}{4}$ tsp vanilla-flavored sugar*
sugar or powdered artificial sweetener	*sugar or powdered artificial sweetener*

If the lemon and orange are not organically grown and may have been sprayed or coated, scrub them in hot soapy water, rinse well and pat dry. Finely grate the zest and squeeze and mix the juices.

Put the yogurt into a bowl. Add the vanilla sugar and beat the mixture for 2 minutes. Add the citrus zest and 3 tablespoons of juice, then 1 tablespoon or more of sugar or sweetener, according to taste. Whisk for 5 minutes.

Put the preparation into a *sorbetière* or other ice cream machine and freeze according to the manufacturer's instructions.

Serve the sorbet, spooning it out with a tablespoon. Accompany it with a fruit coulis or decorate it with chopped, dried fruit.

Variations: for grapefruit yogurt sorbet, replace the lemon and orange with 2 pink grapefruit and serve garnished with mint.

For peach yogurt sorbet, use the puréed flesh of 4 fresh peaches in place of the citrus zest and juice, adding a few drops of almond essence (extract) to complete.

ZEST

see also:
citrus fruit
grapefruit
lemon
lime
orange
preservative

The coloured outer rind of citrus fruit is known as the zest and contains most of the essential flavouring oils. It is best to pare off the zest with a potato peeler or a specially designed zester to make sure that none of the bitter white pith underneath comes with it. A potent flavouring

CHANNELLING LEMON ZEST

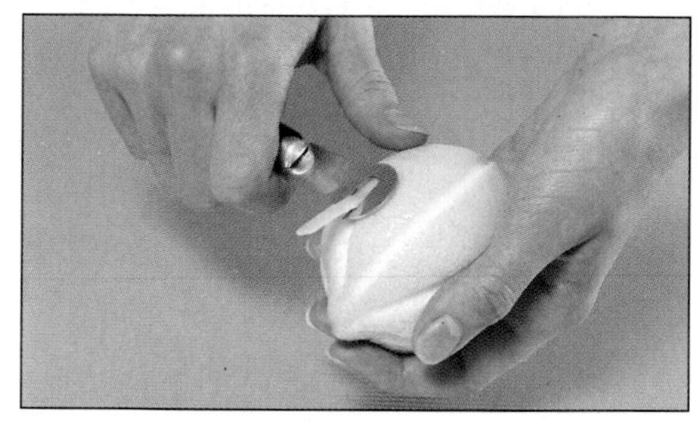

Cut grooves from stem to base at even intervals around the fruit using a special cannelle knife.

When the lemon zest has been channelled in this way, the slices make an attractive garnish.

ingredient, the zest is usually cut into julienne strips or chopped to use in *pâtisserie* or desserts. It may also be grated or rubbed into lump sugar for use in sauces, cake batters, creams and infusions.

Zest cut into julienne strips is often softened by being blanched before use and may also be crystallized in sugar syrup. Orange and lemon zest crystallized and then coated with chocolate makes a delicious confection.

Citrus fruit is a useful and readily available granish. If the zest is channelled before slices are cut, it is more decorative.

As most citrus fruit is nowadays given a waxy coating of preservative chemicals, if the zest is to be eaten, buy only organically grown, uncoated fruit. If uncertain or forced to use coated fruit, scrub the skin well in hot soapy water with a stiff brush and then rinse well.

SOUPE D'ORANGES AUX KIWIS

Orange and red wine soup with kiwi fruit

Serves 4
Preparation 25 minutes
Cooking 10 minutes, 6 hours ahead

METRIC/IMPERIAL	AMERICAN
4 thin-skinned oranges	4 thin-skinned oranges
500 ml/16 fl oz red wine	2 cups red wine
juice of 1 lemon	juice of 1 lemon
2 cloves	2 cloves
1 cinnamon stick	1 cinnamon stick
5 tbsp sugar or powdered artificial sweetener	5 tbsp sugar or powdered artificial sweetener
450 g/1 lb kiwi fruit, peeled and thinly sliced	1 lb kiwi fruit, peeled and thinly sliced

If the oranges are not organically grown and may have been sprayed or coated, scrub them in hot soapy water, rinse well and pat dry.

Pare the zest from 2 of the oranges and cut into julienne strips. Plunge them into a saucepan of boiling water, blanch for 5 minutes, drain them and set to one side.

Peel all 4 oranges and separate the segments. Remove and discard the membrane surrounding the segments and put them into a salad bowl with the strips of zest.

Pour the wine into a pan and add the lemon juice, cloves and cinnamon. Boil for 5 minutes.

Pour the wine through a strainer over the oranges. Add the sugar or sweetener and mix. Allow to cool and then chill for 5–6 hours.

Put the soup into individual soup plates and garnish with the slices of kiwi fruit to serve.

ZUCCHINI

see Squash

GLOSSARY

ABAISSE Sheet of rolled pastry or, by extension, biscuit (cookie) or plain sponge cake.

AFFINÉ(E) Literally 'refined', used of cheeses ripened to perfection.

AIGUILLETTE Long, narrow piece of meat, usually poultry or game, cut from the breast.

AÏLLADE Garlic sauce, similar to *aïoli*, versions of which feature in the cooking of many parts of southern France.

AL DENTE Italian term, literally 'to the tooth', used to describe food, mostly vegetables and pasta, cooked until just tender but still firm to the bite.

ALLEMANDE (À L') German-style; with potatoes or noodles, or with a *sauce allemande*. Also used of marinated game roasted with vegetables.

ALLUMETTE Literally 'matchstick', used of thinly cut potatoes or pieces of pastry.

ALSACIENNE (À L') In the style of the Alsace; with sauerkraut, ham, bacon, sausages and foie gras. Also used of fish or poultry cooked in Riesling.

AMÉRICAINE (À L') American-style; with bacon and tomatoes. Lobster served *à l'américaine*, or incorrectly '*à l'armoricaine*' (actually Breton-style), is chopped lobster meat sautéed in oil, white wine and brandy with garlic, shallots and tomatoes.

AMUSE-GUEULE Small snacks, usually served with drinks before meals.

ANCIENNE (À L') In the style of the old school; used of many braised dishes and blanquettes or fricassees garnished with onions and small mushrooms.

ANDOUILLE Large, coarse sausage native to Normandy and Brittany made from the long intestine of the pig. Usually cooked and smoked, it is generally served cold and thinly sliced as an hors d'oeuvre or snack.

ANDOUILLETTE Small sausage made from the short intestine of the pig. Usually cooked, and often smoked, it is generally grilled or fried and served with mustard, mashed potato, fried onions, apples or sauerkraut.

ANGLAISE (À L') English-style; used by the French to indicate a number of plainly cooked dishes, especially boiled or poached meat, poultry and vegetables and breaded and fried fish.

ANTIPASTO From the Italian for 'before the meal', a variety of assorted cold hors d'oeuvres.

APPELLATION D'ORIGINE (CONTRÔLÉE) Strictly regulated designation for a region which is the place of origin for a quality French product. Applied to cheese and other foods, such as lentils from Puy and butter from Charentes-Poitou, but above all to fine brandies and wines.

AROMATIC Any plant used for its strong aroma, especially herbs and vegetables such as onions, garlic and leeks.

ASSIETTE Plate or serving platter; this term is often used to indicate an assortment of foods.

BARON A saddle of beef or lamb with both legs still attached.

BASQUAISE (À LA) Basque-style; with tomatoes, sweet peppers, garlic and Bayonne ham.

BERCY Dishes which originated in the Quai de Bercy, Paris's wine warehouse region, usually with wine and shallots.

BLANC (À) Food cooked gently so that it does not colour, especially onions and pastry.

BLANC (AU) Food cooked in a white stock or white wine.

BLEU(E) Term denoting meat cooked very rare. Trout cooked *au bleu* is plunged in a vinegared court-bouillon within hours after being caught so that the slime on the skin turns blue.

BONNE-FEMME Simple rustic-style; usually casseroles and stews with potatoes and leeks or onions, mushrooms and bacon.

BOUCHÉE Literally 'mouthful', a small, round pastry case filled with creamy savoury mixtures, or a petit four made from hollowed-out sponge cake filled with creams or custards.

BOULANGÈRE (À LA) Meaning 'from the baker's oven'; casseroles were at one time taken to the baker to be cooked with the bread; the term is used of many dishes baked or braised with onions and potatoes.

BOUQUETIÈRE (À LA) In the style of the flower-seller; garnished with mixed vegetables arranged in differently coloured bunches.

BRETONNE (À LA) In the style of Brittany; particularly lamb with white beans, or poultry, eggs and fish with a rich cream sauce.

BUGNE A sweet fritter made of knotted strips of dough, characteristic of the Lyon area.

BUTTERFLYING Cutting pieces of meat, especially chops, poultry breasts, thick fish fillets or large prawns (shrimp), almost all the way across, then opening them out like butterfly wings for more efficient cooking.

CARDINAL (À LA) Usually anything red in colour, especially red fruit desserts and cooked lobster. By extension the term is also used of many dishes garnished with lobster or which use lobster stock.

CASSOLETTE Small, ovenproof container with handles, used in the preparation of hors d'oeuvres and desserts, in individual portions, and the dishes cooked in it.

CHARCUTIÈRE (À LA) In the style of the pork butcher; with a wine, onion, mustard and gherkin or pickled cucumber sauce.

CHASSEUR Literally 'huntsman', once applied to dishes using a game purée; now mainly to sautéed dishes with a sauce of wine, mushrooms, shallots and tomato.

CHEMISER To line a mould or pan with something, such as parchment or greaseproof paper, which prevents the contents sticking or burning or which forms part of the finished dish, such as aspic, caramel or sponge fingers (ladyfingers).

CHINING The technique of removing the backbone from a rib roast or rack of lamb before cooking to make carving easier.

CHINOIS Conical metal sieve traditionally used to strain sauces, creams and jellies.

CHOP Small cut of meat attached to an individual rib bone, sometimes termed 'cutlet' in veal and lamb and simply 'rib' for beef.

COCOTTE Traditional, large oval casserole used for braising; also small, open dish used for baking fragile food, like eggs, usually in a *bain-marie*.

CONCASSÉ(E) Term used to describe ingredients which have been finely chopped, especially tomatoes and herbs, or crushed, particularly ice.

CROQUEMBOUCHE Elaborate pâtisserie in the shape of a tall cone built of small items, usually choux buns, stuck together with caramel; traditional at weddings.

CUISSE The French for 'thigh', this term is mostly used of poultry and generally also includes the drumstick.

DARIOLE Small cylindrical mould used to make pastries, babas, creams and custards; also the dish made in it.

DARTOIS Hot pâtisserie made of two strips of puff pastry sandwiching a sweet or savoury filling. Large meat roasts served *à la d'Artois* are garnished with glazed carrots and turnips, celery hearts and fried potatoes.

DEGORGING Cleansing food, especially white offal (variety meats) and fish from muddy waters, of impurities or blood by soaking in water. Also the practice of removing excess water from vegetables, especially cucumber and aubergine (eggplant), by sprinkling them with salt.

DEVILLING Serving food, often leftovers, with a pungent sauce usually containing mustard, cayenne and Worcestershire sauce.

DIANE (À LA) In the style of Diana, the Huntress; venison or beef garnished with a highly peppered cream sauce.

DIEPPOISE (À LA) Dieppe-style; fish, especially sole, whiting and brill, and some vegetables, notably artichokes, cooked in white wine and garnished with mushrooms, prawns (shrimp) and mussels in a white sauce.

DIJONNAISE (À LA) Dijon-style; with mustard sauce if savoury and blackcurrants if sweet.

DU BARRY (À LA) Various dishes containing cauliflower, usually with a Mornay (cheese and egg) sauce, dedicated to Madame du Barry, mistress to Louis XV.

ENTRÉE Literally the 'way in' to a meal, this term once signified the course which preceded the roast, but is now mostly used of the main course.

ENTREMETS Once used of anything served between courses, this term signified vegetable side dishes as well as sweet dishes, but current usage is now mostly limited to the latter.

ESPAGNOLE (À L') Spanish-style; with sweet peppers, tomatoes, onions and garlic, or with an *espagnole* sauce.

FERMIÈRE (À LA) In the style of the farmer's wife; braises or pot-roasts with vegetables.

FLAMANDE (À LA) Flemish-style; generally with cabbage, carrots, turnips, potatoes and chopped pork or sliced sausage.

FLORENTINE (À LA) In the style of Florence; generally anything served on a bed of spinach, usually with a Mornay sauce.

FORESTIÈRE (À LA) In the style of the forest; with sautéed mushrooms, usually wild, and sometimes potatoes and bacon.

FRANÇAISE (À LA) French-style; garnished with asparagus tips, cauliflower florets in hollandaise sauce, braised lettuce and potato nests filled with chopped, mixed vegetables.

GLUTEN Proteins in cereal grains, especially wheat, form gluten when water is added to them. Its long molecules, stretched and aligned by kneading, give dough its elastic properties and allow bread to rise successfully in baking.

GOUJON The French term for gudgeon is also applied to many other small, freshwater fish and to fish fillets cut into strips.

GRAND'MÈRE (À LA) Grandmother's-style; a traditional, homely dish or one with a garnish of onions, mushrooms, potatoes and bacon.

HANGING The technique of allowing meat, poultry and game to hang in a cool, airy place for anything from a few days to several weeks to mature after slaughter, allowing enzyme activity to tenderize the flesh and develop the flavour fully.

IVOIRE (À L') Like ivory; in an enriched white sauce with mushrooms and quenelles.

JARDINIÈRE (À LA) Gardener's-style; garnished with mixed vegetables, especially carrots, turnips, peas and green beans.

LANGUEDOCIENNE (À LA) In the style of the Languedoc region; dishes including vegetables such as tomatoes, aubergines (eggplants) and ceps.

LIÉGEOISE (À LA) Liége-style; with juniper berries and sometimes flamed with gin.

LIMOUSINE (À LA) In the style of the Limoges area; with red cabbage and chestnuts or an omelette with ham and potato.

LORRAINE (À LA) In the style of the Lorraine; garnished with red cabbage braised in red wine and apples. Also used of a variety of egg dishes with Gruyère and smoked bacon, notably quiche.

LYONNAISE (À LA) In the style of the Lyon area; sautéed dishes garnished with glazed onions.

MADRILÈNE (À LA) Madrid-style; with tomato pulp.

MALTAISE (À LA) From the Maltese blood orange, any sweet or savoury dish incorporating orange flesh, juice or zest.

MARAÎCHÈRE (À LA) In the style of the market gardener; garnished with mixed glazed vegetables.

MARÉCHALE (À LA) Small cuts of meat or fish fillets breaded and sautéed, then garnished with asparagus tips and truffles, *maître d'hôtel* butter or mushrooms and tomatoes.

MARINIÈRE (À LA) Seafood, notably mussels, prepared in white wine with onions and shallots. By extension also a garnish of mussels.

MÉNAGÈRE (À LA) Housewife-style; plain-cooked food, often using leftovers, especially with onions and potatoes.

MESCLUN Provençal term for mixed young salad leaves and herbs, usually including curly endive, dandelion and lamb's lettuce.

MILANAISE (À LA) Milan-style; food dipped in an egg, crumb and grated Parmesan coating and fried or browned *au gratin*.

MOULE À MANQUÉ The classic, round French sponge cake pan, about 20 cm/8 in across. Sloping sides facilitate unmoulding and give an attractive shape which is easier to decorate.

NANTAISE (À LA) In the style of the Nantes area; with a white wine and butter sauce, or roast and braised dishes garnished with glazed turnips, peas and creamed potatoes.

NEIGE From the French for 'snow', a term used of stiffly beaten egg whites, especially when incorporated in dishes such as soufflés and meringues; also used of red fruit sorbets.

NIÇOISE (À LA) In the style of Nice; dishes using produce abundant in the Mediterranean port, principally tomatoes, garlic, green beans, courgettes (zucchini), olives and anchovies.

NORMANDE (À LA) Normandy-style; dishes using produce typical of the region, principally cream, butter, apples, cider, Calvados and seafood, or with a *normande* sauce of fish velouté with cream and mushrooms. In *haute cuisine*, an elaborate garnish of mixed seafood.

NOUVELLE CUISINE In France in the 1970s a movement of 'new cooking' arose which eschewed the excesses of *haute cuisine* to favour simpler food with more emphasis on bringing out natural flavours, lighter and healthier sauces and dressings and less elaborate presentation.

PARBOILING Boiling or simmering food in water or stock until it is partially cooked, as with potatoes to be sautéed.

PARISIENNE (À LA) In the style of metropolitan restaurants; mostly dishes served with *parisienne* potatoes, ie sautéed with herbs, and artichoke hearts and braised lettuce, or chicken dishes with mushrooms.

PAYSANNE (À LA) Peasant-style; dishes braised with chopped vegetables, especially potatoes, carrots, turnips and cabbage.

PÉRIGOURDINE (À LA) Périgord-style; usually with a *Périgueux* sauce, ie with truffles and sometimes foie gras.

PIÉMONTAISE (À LA) In the style of Piedmont; usually with risotto and sometimes white truffles, or pastries with hazelnuts or filberts.

PISTOU Provençal condiment, akin to pesto, using garlic and basil ground with olive oil and sometimes Parmesan and tomato, used to dress thick vegetable soups and vegetable dishes.

PITHIVIERS Large puff pastry filled with almond cream, traditionally served on Twelfth Night in the Orleans region.

POINT (À) Any dish cooked to the correct stage, particularly medium steaks, or produce like cheese and fruit ripened to the right degree.

POIVRADE (À LA) Any dish featuring peppercorns, especially when lightly crushed.

POLONAISE (À LA) Polish-style; garnished with chopped, hard-boiled egg, parsley and breadcrumbs fried in butter.

PORTUGAISE (À LA) Portuguese-style; dishes containing tomatoes or with a tomato sauce or garnish.

PRIMEUR Early fruit or vegetable of the season.

PRINTANIÈRE (À LA) Spring-like; garnished with spring vegetables.

PROVENÇALE (À LA) In the style of Provence; generally a dish using olive oil, tomatoes, garlic and often olives and aubergines (eggplants).

RAMEKIN Small, round, individual soufflé dish, about 7.5 cm/3 in across, mostly used to mould mousses, custards and aspics.

RÉCHAUFFÉ(E) Literally 're-heated', any dish made with cooked meat.

REINE (À LA) A dish with chicken, usually in a rich white sauce.

ROMAINE (À LA) Roman-style; usually dishes featuring spinach, eggs and anchovies or garnished with gnocchi; also small birds casseroled with peas and ham and a sweet-and-sour dried fruit and pine kernel (pine nut) sauce for game.

ROUENNAISE (À LA) Rouen-style; a variety of duck dishes or a dish with a duck and red wine or duck liver sauce; also used of fish in red wine sauce.

ROYALE (À LA) Clear soups garnished with a *royale*, a chicken-flavoured custard cut into small decorative shapes, or a poached chicken or fish dish coated with a cream sauce and garnished with quenelles and mushrooms and often truffles.

RUSSE (À LA) Russian-style; fish or seafood coated in aspic, *chaud-froid* sauce or thick mayonnaise and served with a *salade russe*, ie mixed, diced vegetables bound in mayonnaise.

ST-HONORÉ Classic Parisian gâteau made up of a short or puff pastry base topped with a crown of caramelized choux puffs; the centre is filled with pastry cream and lightly browned under the grill (broiler).

SCALDING Rinsing in boiling water, as with preserving jars, some vegetables and offal (variety meats); or bringing milk to just below the boil.

SLAKING Dissolving a thickening agent in a little liquid before mixing it into a dish.

SUPRÊME The breast of a chicken, or other bird, with the wing fillet still attached.

SWEATING Cooking food, especially onions, very gently until softened but not coloured.

TOSCANE (À LA) Tuscan-style; with Parmesan cheese and ham, or macaroni with foie gras and truffles.

VÉRONIQUE Term for poultry or fish poached in a white wine and cream sauce with grapes.

VERT-PRÉ Meaning 'green-meadow', a term for green garnishes, such as peas or asparagus, but more usually used of grilled meats garnished with watercress, *maître d'hôtel* butter and straw potatoes or cold dishes in a green mayonnaise.

VIENNOISE (À LA) Viennese-style, mostly used of veal escalopes (scaloppini) dipped in egg and breadcrumbs, fried and served with a garnish of chopped, hard-boiled egg, fried parsley, lemon and capers.

VIGNERONNE (À LA) In the style of the wine-grower; usually incorporating grapes, vine leaves, wine or autumn produce.

INDEX